VOLUME II – ASIA, AUSTRALIA, OCEANIA

CONSTITUTIONS OF NATIONS

VOLUME II –
ASIA, AUSTRALIA and OCEANIA

by

AMOS J. PEASLEE

★ ★

REVISED FOURTH EDITION

Prepared by Dorothy Peaslee Xydis

SPRINGER-SCIENCE+BUSINESS MEDIA, B.V. 1985

(Revised for volume 2)

Peaslee, Amos Jenkins, 1887-
Constitutions of nations.

Includes bibliographies.
Contents: v. 1. Africa -- v. 2. Asia, Australia, and Oceania.
1. Constitutions. I. Xydis, Dorothy Peaslee.
II. Title.
K3157.E5P4 1974 342'.023 75-305264
342.223

ISBN 978-90-247-2905-0 ISBN 978-94-017-1147-0 (eBook)
DOI 10.1007/978-94-017-1147-0

Copyright

NEW ZEALAND

SUMMARY

INTERNATIONAL STATUS

New Zealand is a member of the United Nations (October 24, 1945).[1] It is a constituent member of the Commonwealth of Nations and a member of other international organizations. It ratified in 1978 the International Conventions on Social, Economic and Cultural Rights and on Civil and Political Rights. It was a member of the League of Nations.

New Zealand was first accorded international status at the Versailles Peace Conference in 1919, pursuant to a request by the United Kingdom for separate representation in the Assembly of the League of Nations for Australia, Canada, New Zealand and the Union of South Africa. The Statute of Westminster, which acknowledged the established fact that the Imperial Parliament could not legislate for the Dominions except at their request, and freed the Dominion legislatures from any territorial limits, was passed in 1931. Specific adoption legislature of the Statute was taken by New Zealand in 1947.

New Zealand was inhabited by the Maoris, a Polynesian race, when it was discovered by Tasman in 1642. Captain Cook explored the coastline in 1769, and in 1792 occurred the first attempt at colonization. The town of Wellington was founded by the first immigrants in January 1840. By the Treaty of Waitangi of February 6, 1840, following the declaration of British sovereignty on January 29, all sovereignty was ceded to the Queen of England and all territorial rights were secured to the chiefs and their tribes. This applied to the North Island. Sovereignty

[1] New Zealand has accepted the compulsory jurisdiction of the International Court of Justice under Article 36 of its Statute.

over the South Island and Stewart Island was claimed by right of discovery. For a year it was dependent on New South Wales until, on May 3, 1841, it was created a separate colony. An Act granting representative institutions was passed by the Imperial Parliament on June 30, 1852. On September 26, 1907, it received the title of 'Dominion' in lieu of colony.

FORM OF NATIONAL GOVERNMENT

New Zealand is a monarchical state with a parliamentary form of government. The constitutional documents are as follows:

1. New Zealand Constitution Act 1852 (UK) of June 30, 1852, amended 1947 and 1973.
2. Demise of the Crown Act of August 4, 1908.
3. Judicature Act of August 4, 1908, as amended to 1981.
4. Commissions of Inquiry Act of August 4, 1908, amended and consolidated to 1975.
5. Deputy Governor Powers Act of September 12, 1912.
6. Letters Patent relating to the Office of Governor General of April 17, 1919.
7. Statute of Westminster Adoption Act of November 25, 1947.
8. Civil List Act of October 26, 1979.
9. Royal Titles Act of February 6, 1974.
10. Royal Powers Act of September 17, 1953.
11. Electoral Act of October 26, 1956, amended to 1981.
12. Western Samoa Act of November 24, 1961.
13. Cook Islands Constitution Act of November 17, 1964, amended to 1981.
14. Nieue Constitution Act of August 29, 1974.

The source of sovereign power is not stated, except insofar as there are references to the Crown in some of the Acts. By the Statute of Westminster Adoption Act, it is provided that, in accordance with the established constitutional position of all members of the Commonwealth in relation to one another, alterations in the laws concerning the Crown require the assent of the Parliaments of the 'Dominions', and that only the New Zealand Parliament can legislate for New Zealand. The Western Samoa Act of 1961, provides for the independence of the former trust territory of Western Samoa (see Samoa). The Cook Islands Constitution Act of 1964, and the Nieue Constitution Act of 1974, provide for the self government of those places, The Cook Islands have a sovereign Parliament of 24 elected members, a cabinet of ministers, a High Commissioner appointed by the Governor General of New Zealand who represents the Queen and the government of New Zealand. Nieue has an Assembly of 20 elected members and a Speaker, a cabinet of Ministers; the Governor General of New Zealand represents the Queen in relation to Nieue. There is a High Court and Court of Appeal of the Cook Islands, and a High Court and Land Court of Nieue. The other associated territories are the Arctic Ross Dependency and the atolls of Tokelau.

RIGHTS OF THE PEOPLE

British laws and customs in respect of human rights prevail. There is no statement of rights in the constitutional documents except in the Constitution of the Cook Islands, Part IVA of which, entitled Fundamental Human Rights and Freedoms, states that in the Cook Islands there exist and shall continue to exist the rights, without discrimination, to life, liberty and security of the person, equality before and protection of the law, the right to own property, freedom of thought, conscience and religion, speech and expression, peaceful assembly and association. Specifically forbidden are arbitrary detention, imprisonment or exile, cruel and unusual treatment or punishment, or to deprive anyone of the right to a fair hearing, legal counsel, presumption of innocence until proved guilty, reasonable bail, or conviction for offenses other than those legally prescribed when an offence is committed. It is also declared that every person has duties to others and is accordingly subject to such limits in the exercise of his rights as the law imposes for the protection of others and the general welfare and security.

LEGISLATIVE DEPARTMENT

Legislative authority is exercised by a unicameral Parliament or General Assembly, composed of the House of Representatives and the Governor General.[1] The House of Representatives is composed of one member per electoral district; the number of these is determined by a system relating the number in the North Island to the 25 districts in the South Island in relation to the population as shown after each census (in 1981 92).[2] There are also four Maori electoral districts and Maori voters may choose to be registered either as an elector of a Maori electoral district or of a General electoral district.[3] There is universal adult suffrage for residents regardless of nationality, and compulsory registration as an elector.[4] The term of Parliament is three years subject to dissolution.[5] Qualifications and incompatibilities for membership are provided.[6] There are provisions relating to financial matters.[7] The maintenance of Maori laws, customs and usages is prescribed.[8] It is specifically provided that the New Zealand legislature has the right to change in any way the New Zealand Constitution Act.[9]

[1] Const. Act, Art. 32.
[2] Electoral Act, Art. 11, 16, 39.
[3] Id., Art. 41.
[4] Id., Art. 43.
[5] Id., Art. 12.
[6] Id., Art. 25–31.
[7] Civil List Act. Const. Act, 61, 64–66.
[8] Const. Act, Art. 71.
[9] Const. Amdt. Acts.

EXECUTIVE DEPARTMENT

The Monarch is represented in New Zealand by a Governor General, Commander-in-Chief, with customary powers to summon and dissolve Parliament, make appointments, grant honors, grant pardons.[10] He acts on the advice of Ministers and Parliamentary Under-Secretaries who must be members of Parliaments.[11] The powers conferred on the Governor General are royal powers and exercisable either by him or by the sovereign.[12] There is provision for a Deputy Governor to exercise the powers of the Governor General during the latter's temporary absence.[13] The Executive Council consists of all Ministers and is presided over by the Governor General. It is one of the instruments for giving the imprint of legal form to policy determined by the Cabinet, which may or may not comprise all Ministers and of which the Governor General is not a member.

JUDICIAL DEPARTMENT

The Judicature Act 1908, as frequently amended, makes provision for a High Court which is a Court of Record, composed of a Chief Justice and 26 other judges appointed by the Governor General.[14] It contains detailed provisions regarding its jurisdiction, officers and their powers, and procedure.[15] The Act provides for a Court of Appeal composed of the Chief Justice, a Judge of the High Court appointed by the Governor General as President of the Court of Appeal and four other Judges of the High Court.[16] Proceedings in the High Court may be removed to the Court of Appeal whose decisions are final, provided that leave may be given by the Court of Appeal to appeal to the Privy Council (of the United Kingdom).[17]

There is provision for Commissions of Inquiry to examine the administration of the government and the conduct of officials, the working of or necessity for legislation, and to inquire into disasters and accidents; its members are appointed by the Governor General and have the power and status of magistrates.[18]

The Supreme Court has authority to try petitions concerning contested elections.[19]

[10] Const. Act, Art. 32; Letters Patent re Governor General.
[11] Civil List Atc, Art. 9–12.
[12] R. Powers Act.
[13] Dep. Gov. Powers Act.
[14] Juidc. Act., Art. 3, 4.
[15] Id., Art. 15–560.
[16] Id., Art. 57.
[17] Id., Art. 64, 65.
[18] Comm. of Inquiry Act.
[19] Electoral Act, Art. 161.

AREA, POPULATION, ETC.

The area of New Zealand is 269,057 square kilometres, its population (1982 estimate) 3,190,100. The Cook Islands have an area of 234 square kilometres and a population (1981 census) of 17,695; Nieue's area is 259 square kilometres, its population (1981 census), 3.298; the Ross Dependency's area is 730,000 square kilometres (400,000 land and 330,000 ice shelf) with no population; Tokelau's area is 12 square kilometres, its population 1,615. The languages are English and Maori. The Cook Islands Constitution Act and the Nieue Constitution Act stipulate that debates in the Parliament and Assembly, respectively shall be in Maori and also in English for the Cook Islands, in the Nieuean language or the English language for Nieue. The capital is Wellington.

CONSTITUTIONAL DOCUMENTS

OF

NEW ZEALAND

I. New Zealand Constitution Act 1852 (U.K.)[1]

June, 30 1852, amended 1973

Preamble–Repealed.

Short Title–The New Zealand Constitution Act 1852.

1–31. Repealed.

32. Establishment of a General Assembly. There shall be within the Colony of New Zealand a General Assembly, to consist of the Governor and House of Representatives.

The title of the Dominion of New Zealand was substituted for the title of the Colony of New Zealand as from 26 September 1907 by Royal Proclamation dated 9 September 1907; see *New Zealand Gazette*, 1907, Vol. II, pp. 2837 and 2901. In view of its present position as a member of the British Commonwealth of Nations as set out in the Statute of Westminster 1931 (U.K.), the country is now generally referred to by the title of New Zealand.

33–43. Repealed.

44. Time and place of holding the General Assembly. The General Assembly of New Zealand shall be holden at any place and time within New Zealand which the Governor shall from time to time by Proclamation for that purpose appoint; and the Governor may at his pleasure prorogue or dissolve the General Assembly.

45. Repealed.

46. Oath of Allegiance. No member of the said House of Representatives shall be permitted to sit or vote therein until he shall have taken and subscribed the following oath before the Governor, or before some person or person authorized by him to administer such oath:

I, A. B., do sincerely promise and swear that I will be faithful and bear true allegiance to Her Majesty Queen Victoria. So help me God.

47–51. Repealed.

53. (1) The General Assembly shall have full power to make laws having effect in, or in respect of, New Zealand or any part thereof and laws having effect outside New Zealand.

(2) Without limiting the validity of any Act of the General Assembly passed before the 25th day of November 1947 (being the date of the passing of the

[1] 15 and 16 Vict., Ch. 72. *An Act to grant a Representative Constitution to the Colony of New Zealand.* Reprint as amended by Government Printer, Wellington, 1960 and containing amendments of 1973. All documents supplied by Department of External Affairs in March 1965 and reproduced by permission of Government Printer and brought to date with amendments supplied by New Zealand Embassy in Athens in February 1982. Ed.

Statute of Westminster Adoption Act 1947), every Act of the General Assembly duly passed on or after that date, and every provision of every such Act, are hereby declared to be and always to have been valid and within the powers of the General Assembly.

54. Approriation and issue of money. It shall not be lawful for the House of Representatives to pass, or for the Governor to assent to, any Bill appropriating to the public service any sum of money from or out of Her Majesty's revenue within New Zealand, unless the Governor on Her Majesty's behalf shall first have recommended to the House of Representatives to make provision for the specific public service towards which such money is to be appropriated; and (save as herein otherwise provided) no part of Her Majesty's revenue within New Zealand shall be issued except in pursuance of Warrants under the hand of the Governor directed to the Public Treasurer thereof.

55. Governor may transmit drafts of laws to House of Representatives. It shall and may be lawful for the Governor to transmit by message to the said House of Representatives for its consideration the drafts of any laws which it may appear to him desirable to introduce; and all such drafts shall be taken into consideration in such convenient manner as shall in and by the rules and orders aforesaid be in that behalf provided.

56. Governor may assent to, refuse assent to, or reserve or amend Bills. Whenever any Bill which has been passed by the said House of Representatives shall be presented for Her Majesty's assent to the Governor, he shall declare according to his discretion, but subject nevertheless to the provisions contained in this Act, that he assents to such Bill in Her Majesty's name, or that he refuses his assent to such Bill.

Provided always, that it shall and may be lawful for the Governor, before declaring his pleasure in regard to any Bill so presented to him, to make such amendments in such Bill as he thinks needful or expedient, and by message to return such Bill with such amendments to the House of Representatives; and the consideration of such amendments by the said House shall take place in such convenient manner as shall in and by the rules and orders aforesaid be in that behalf provided.

57–63. Repealed.

64. Grant of sums mentioned in Schedule for civil and judicial services. There shall be payable to Her Majesty, every year, out of the revenue arising from such taxes, duties, rates, and imposts, and from the disposal of such waste lands of the Crown in New Zealand, the several sums mentioned in the Schedule to this Act; such several sums to be paid for defraying the expenses of the services and purposes mentioned in such Schedule, and to be issued by the Treasurer of New Zealand in discharge of such warrants as shall be from time to time directed to him under the hand and seal of the Governor.

65. Alteration of sums mentioned in Schedule. It shall be lawful for the General Assembly of New Zealand, by any Act or Acts, to alter all or any of the sums mentioned in the said Schedule, and the appropriation of such sums to the services and purposes therein mentioned; but every Bill which shall be passed by the said House of Representatives altering the salary of the Governor or altering the sum described as for Maori purposes, shall be reserved for the signification of Her Majesty's pleasure thereon; and until and subject to such alteration by Act or Acts as aforesaid the salaries of the Governor and Judges shall be those respectively set against their several offices in the said Schedule; and accounts in detail of the expenditure of the several sums for the time being appropriated under this Act, or such Act or Acts as aforesaid of the General Assembly, to the several services and purposes mentioned in the said Schedule, shall be laid before the said House of Representatives within thirty days next after the beginning of the session after such expenditure shall have been made:

Provided always, that it shall not be lawful for the said General Assembly, by any such Act as aforesaid, to make any diminution in salary of any Judge to take effect during the continuance in office of any person being such Judge at the time of the passing of such Act.

66. Appropriation of revenue. After and subject to the payments to be made under the provisions hereinbefore contained, all the revenue arising from taxes, duties, rates, and imposts levied in virtue of any Act of the General Assembly shall be subject to be appropriated to such specific purposes as by any Act of the said General Assembly shall be prescribed in that behalf.

67–70. Repealed.

71. Provision as to Maori laws and customs. And whereas it may be expedient that the laws, customs, and usages of the aboriginal or Maori inhabitants of New Zealand, so far as they are not repugnant to the general principles of humanity, should for the present be maintained for the government of themselves, in all their relations to and dealings with each other, and that particular districts should be set apart within which such laws, customs, or usages should be so observed:

It shall be lawful for Her Majesty, by any letters patent to be issued under the Great Seal of the United Kingdom, from time to time to make provision for the purposes aforesaid, any repugnancy of any such Maori laws, customs, or usages to the law of England, or to any law, statute, or usage in force in New Zealand, or in any part thereof, in anywise notwithstanding.

72. General Assembly may regulate sales, etc., of waste lands. Subject to the provisions herein contained, it shall be lawful for the said General Assembly to make laws for regulating the sale, letting, disposal, and occupation of the waste lands of the Crown in New Zealand; and all lands wherein the title of Maoris shall be extinguished as hereinafter mentioned, and all such other lands as are described in an Act of the session holden in the tenth and eleventh years of Her Majesty, chapter one hundred and twelve, to promote colonisation in New Zealand, and to authorize a loan to the New Zealand Company, as demesne lands of the Crown, shall be deemed and taken to be waste lands of the Crown within the meaning of this Act.

73–79. Repealed.

80. Interpretation of 'Governor'. In the construction of this Act the term 'Governor' shall mean the person for the time being lawfully administering the Government of New Zealand.

81. Repealed.

82. Proclamations to be published. The Proclamation of this Act, and all Proclamations to be made under the provisions thereof, shall be published in the New Zealand Government Gazette.

SCHEDULE

Repealed.

THE NEW ZEALAND CONSTITUTION AMENDMENT (REQUEST AND CONSENT) ACT 1947 (N.Z.)[1]

November 25, 1947

1. Short Title. This Act may be cited as the New Zealand Constitution Amendment (Request and Consent) Act 1947.

2. Request and consent to enactment of Act of Parliament of United Kingdom. For the purposes of section four of the Statute of Westminster 1931, as adopted by teh Statute of Westminster Adoption Act 1947, the enactment by the Parliament of the United Kingdom of an Act in the form or to the effect of the draft Bill set out in the Schedule to this Act is hereby requested and consented to.

SCHEDULE

Draft of a Bill

To provide for the Amendment of the Constitution of New Zealand.

Whereas provision for the Constitution of New Zealand was made by the New Zealand Constitution Act 1852, and the power to amend that Act conferred on the Parliament of New Zealand by the New Zealand Constitution (Amendment) Act 1857 was subject to certain restrictions therein specified: *And whereas* on the twenty-fifth day of November, nineteen hundred and forty-seven, the Parliament of New Zealand, by an Act intituled the Statute of Westminster Adoption Act 1947, adopted sections two, three, four, five, and six of the Statute of Westminster 1931: *And whereas* it is provided by section eight of the said Statute of Westminster 1931 that nothing in that Act shall be deemed to confer any power to repeal or alter the Constitution Act of New Zealand otherwise than in accordance with the law existing before the commencement of the said Statute: And whereas New Zealand has requested and consented to the enactment of this Act:

Now therefore be it enacted, etc.:

1. Power of New Zealand Parliament to amend, suspend, or repeal the New Zealand Constitution Act 1852 (U.K.). It shall be lawful for the Parliament of New

[1] 1947, No 44. *An Act to request and consent to the enactment by the Parliament of the United Kingdom of an Act to provide for the amendment of the Constitution of New Zealand.*

Zealand by any Act or Acts of that Parliament to alter, suspend, or repeal, at any time, all or any of the provisions of the New Zealand Constitution Act 1852; and the New Zealand Constitution (Amendment) Act 1857 is hereby repealed.

2. Short Title. This Act may be cited as the New Zealand Constitution (Amendment) Act 1947.

THE NEW ZEALAND CONSTITUTION (AMENDMENT) ACT 1947 (U.K.)[1]

December 10, 1947

Whereas provision for the Constitution of New Zealand was made by the New Zealand Constitution Act 1852, and the power to amend that Act conferred on the Parliament of New Zealand by the New Zealand Constitution (Amendment) Act 1857 was subject to certain restrictions therein specified: *And whereas* on the twenty-fifth day of November, nineteen hundred and forty-seven, the Parliament of New Zealand, by an Act intituled the Statute of Westminster Adoption Act 1947, adopted sections two, three four, five and six of the Statute of Westminster 1931: *And whereas* it is provided by section eight of the said Statute of Westminster 1931 that nothing in that Act shall be deemed to confer any power to repeal or alter the Constitution Act of New Zealand otherwise than in accordance with the law existing before the commencement of the said Statute: *And whereas* New Zealand has requested and consented to the enactment of this Act:

1. Power of New Zealand Parliament to alter, suspend, or repeal the New Zealand Constitution Act 1852. It shall be lawful for the Parliament of New Zealand by any Act or Acts of that Parliament to alter, suspend, or repeal, at any time, all or any of the provisions of the New Zealand Constitution Act 1852; and the New Zealand Constitution (Amendment) Act 1857 is hereby repealed.

2. Short Title. This Act may be cited as the New Zealand Constitution (Amendment) Act 1947.

II. The Demise of the Crown Act, 1908[2]

August 4, 1908

1. Short Title, & c. (1) The Short Title of this Act is the Demise of the Crown Act, 1908.

(2) This Act is a consolidation of the enactments mentioned in the Schedule hereto.

2. Parliament not dissolved by demise of the Crown. The General Assembly in being at any demise of the Crown shall not be determined or dissolved by such

[1] 11 Geo, VI, Ch. 4. *An Act to provide for the amendment of the Constitution of New Zealand.*
[2] 1908, No. 42. *An Act to consolidate certain Enactments of the General Assembly relating to the Necessary Provision for certain Matters in case of any Demise of the Crown.* This Act was extended to the Cook Islands by the Cook Islands Act, 1915, s. 629, title Dependencies.

demise, but shall continue as long as it would have continued but for such demise, unless it is sooner prorogued or dissolved by the Governor General.

3. *Members of General Assembly to take fresh oaths.* At the first meeting of the General Assembly after any demise of the Crown the members of the General Assembly shall take fresh oaths of allegiance to the sovereign for the time being, and section forty-six of the Constitution Act shall be read and apply accordingly:

Provided that nothing herein shall be construed to require the General Assembly to meet on account of the demise of the Crown.

4. *Demise of the Crown not to affect things done before Proclamation thereof.* Any demise of the Crown shall not affect anything done in New Zealand before the day whereon the Governor General by Proclamation notifies such demise; and all things done in New Zealand at any time after such demise, but before the day of the publication of the *Gazette* containing the aforesaid Proclamation, and which but for this Act might be affected by any such demise, shall have the same effect and be of the same force as if no demise had happened.

5. *All appointments, & c., by the Governor General to continue in force.* Every Commission, warrant, or other authority for the exercise of any office or employment of any kind or nature issued or exercised by the Governor General in Council or the Governor General, or by any other person in the name and on behalf of His Majesty, in virtue of his office, or under the authority of any Act, of the Imperial Parlaiment or of the General Assembly, or of any rules or regulations made thereunder respectively, shall continue in full force, notwithstanding any demise of the Crown, until duly revoked or cancelled, and shall be of the same effect as if no such demise had happened, anything in an Act of the Imperial Parliament passed in the first year of His late Majesty King William the Fourth, chapter four, to the contrary notwithstanding.

6. *All civil or criminal process, on behalf of His Majesty to continue.* No action or other process or proceedings, civil or criminal, in or to which His Majesty is a party, or which has been commenced or carried on in his name or by his authority shall by reason of his demise abate, discontinue, or be in any manner affected; but every such action, process, or proceeding shall and may be carried on, enforced, or otherwise completed or acted on in the name of his successor and as if such demise had not happened.

7. *Contracts not affected by demise.* All contracts of every kind lawfully entered into by or on behalf of His Majesty with any person, body, or authority, and all benefit and advantage thereof, and all liability in respect thereof, shall respectively attach and belong to the heirs and successors of His Majesty, although they are not expressly named in any such contract.

III. The Judicature Act 1908[1]

August 4, 1908, as amended to 1981

1. Short Title, etc.

(1) The Short Title of this Act is the Judicature Act 1908.

(2) This Act is a consolidation of the enactments mentioned in the First Schedule hereto.[2]

(3) Without affecting the specific saving provisions of this Act, it is hereby declared as follows:

(*a*) All Proclamations, Orders in Council, districts, offices, appointments, commissions, patents, scales of fees, rules, regulations, orders, registers, records, instruments, and generally all acts of authority which originated under any of the enactments mentioned in the First Schedule hereto or any enactment thereby repealed, and are subsisting or in force on the coming into operation of this Act, shall ensure for the purposes of this Act as fully and effectually as if they had originated under the corresponding provisions of this Act, and according shall, where necessary, be deemed to have so originated.

(*b*) All actions, matters, and proceedings commenced under any such enactment, and pending or in progress on the coming into operation of this Act, may be continued, completed, and enforced under this Act.

(4) This Act is divided into Parts, as follows:

Part I. The Supreme Court. (Sections 3 to 56).

Part II. The Court of Appeal. (Sections 57 to 75).

Part III. Rules and Provisions of Law in Judicial Matters Generally. (Sections 76 to 101).

2. Interpretation. In this Act, if not inconsistent with the context,

'Action' means a civil proceeding commenced by writ or in such other manner as may be prescribed by rules of Court, and does not include a criminal proceeding by the Crown:

'Cause' includes any action or other original proceeding between a plaintiff and a defendant, and any criminal proceeding by the Crown:

'Defendant' includes every person served with any writ of summons or process, or served with notice of or entitled to attend any proceedings:

'Existing' means existing on the coming into operation of this Act:

'Inferior Court' means and includes all Courts of judicature within New Zealand of inferior jurisdiction to the Supreme Court:

'Judge' means a Judge of the Supreme Court:

'Judgment' includes decree:

[1] 1908, No. 89. *An Act to consolidate certain enactments of the General Assembly relating to the Supreme Court and the Court of Appeal, and to certain rules and provisions of laws in judicial matters generally, as amended by various Judicature Amendment Acts to 1981. Ed.*

[2] Not reproduced.

'Matter' includes every proceeding in the Court not in a cause:

'Party' includes every person served with notice of or attending any proceeding, although not named on the record:

'Petitioner' includes every person making any application to the Court, either by petition, motion, or summons, otherwise than as against any defendant:

'Plaintiff' includes every person asking any relief (otherwise than by way of counterclaim as a defendant) against any other person by any form of proceeding, whether the same is taken by action, petition, motion, summons, or otherwise.

PART I

THE SUPREME COURT

3. Constitution of the Court.

(1) There shall continue to be in and for New Zealand a Court of record, for the administration of justice throughout New Zealand, henceforth to be called the High Court of New Zealand.

(2) The High Court is hereby declared to be the same Court as that established by this Act, and called, before the commencement of section 2 of the Judicature Amendment Act 1979, the Supreme Court.

4. The Judges of the High Court.

(1) Subject to the provisions of this Act, the High Court shall consist of one Judge, who shall be called the Chief Justice of New Zealand, and 26 other Judges:

Provided that an additional Judge or additional Judges may be appointed whenever the Governor General deems it necessary by reason of the absence or anticipated absence of any of the Judges on leave preliminary to retirement; and every such appointment shall be a permanent appointment from the time when it is made, and shall fill the vacancy next occurring in the office of Judge, not being a vacancy filled by an earlier appointment under this proviso.

(2) The Judges of the High Court shall be appointed by the Governor General in the name and on behalf of Her Majesty.

(3) Subject to the provisions of this Act, the Judges of the High Court other than the Chief Justice shall have seniority among themselves according to the dates of their appointments as Judges of the High Court. If two or more of them are so appointed on the same day, they shall have seniority according the the precedence assigned to them by the Governor General on their appointment as such Judges or, failing any such assignment, according the the order in which they take the Judicial Oath:

Provided that every permanent Judge shall have seniority over every temporary Judge.

(4) The jurisdiction of the High Court shall not be affected by any vacancy in the number of the Judges of that Court.

5. Senior Judge to act as Chief Justice in certain circumstances.

(1) While any vacancy exists in the office of Chief Justice, or during any

absence from New Zealand of the Chief Justice, the senior Judge in New Zealand, not being a Judge of the Court of Appeal, shall be deemed to be the principal judicial officer of New Zealand, and shall have authority to act as Chief Justice and to execute the duties of that office and to exercise all powers that may be lawfully exercised by the Chief Justice.

(2) Whenever by reason of illness or any cause other than absence from New Zealand the Chief Justice is prevented from exercising the duties of his office, the Governor General may authorize the senior Judge in New Zealand not being a Judge of the Court of Appeal, to act as Chief Justice until the Chief Justice resumes his duties, and during that period to execute the duties of that office and to exercise all powers that may be lawfully be exercised by the Chief Justice.

(3) The authority conferred on the acting Chief Justice by or by virtue of this section shall not include power to preside as Chief Justice at any sitting of the Court of Appeal.

6. *Judges to be barristers or solicitors.* No person shall be appointed a Judge unless he has held a practising certificate as a barrister or solicitor for a least 7 years.

7. *Commissions of Judges to continue during good behavior.* The commissions of the said Chief Justice and other Judges shall continue in full force during good behavior, notwithstanding the demise of His Majesty.

8. *Judges may be removed or suspended on address of the House of Representatives.* It shall be lawful for His Majesty, upon the address of the House of Representatives, to remove any Judge from his office and to revoke his commission, and for the Governor General in Council to suspend any such Judge upon a like address.

9. *Governor General may suspend Judge when Parliament not sitting.* It shall be lawful for the Governor General in Council at any time when Parliament is not in session to suspend any Judge from his office, and such suspension, unless previously revoked, shall continue in force until the end of the next ensuing session and no longer.

10. *Salaries of Judges.*

(1) There shall be paid to the Chief Justice and to the President of the Court of Appeal and to the other Judges,

(*a*) Salaries at such rates as the Governor General, by Order in Council from time to time determines; and

(*b*) Such allowances as are from time to time prescribed by the Governor General by Order in Council; and

(*c*) Such additional allowances, being traveling allowances or other incidental or minor allowances, as may be fixed from time to time by the Governor General.

(2) No Order in Council shall be made under this section except on the recommendation of the Minister of Justice made after consultation by him with the Chief Justice.

(3) Any Order in Council made under paragraph (*a*) or paragraph (*b*) of sub-section (1) of this section, and any determination made under paragraph (*c*) of that sub-section and any provision of any such order or determination, may be made so as to come into force on a date to be specified in that behalf in the order

or determination, being the date of the making of the order or determination or any other date, whether before or after the date of the making of the order or determination or the date of the commencement of this section.

(4) Every such Order in Council or determination, and every provision of any such order or determination, in respect of which no date is specified as aforesaid shall come into force on the date of the making of the order or determination.

(5) Every Order in Council made under sub-section (1) of this section shall be deemed to be a regulation for the purposes of the Regulations Act 1936.

(6) The salary of a Judge shall not be diminished during the continuance of his commission.

11. Temporary Judges.

(1) Subject to section 11B of this Act, at any time during the illness or absence of any Judge, or for any other temporary purpose, the Governor General may, in the name and on behalf of Her Majesty, appoint any person (including a former Judge) to be a Judge for such term, not exceeding 12 months, as the Governor General may specify.

(2) Any person appointed a Judge under this section may be re-appointed, but no Judge shall hold office under this section for more than 2 years in the aggregate.

(3) Every person appointed a Judge under this section shall, during the term of his appointment, be paid the salary and allowances payable by law to a Judge other than the Chief Justice.

11A. Former Judges.

(1) Subject to section 11B of this Act, the Governor General may, in the name and on behalf of Her Majesty, appoint any former Judge to be an acting Judge for such term not exceeding 2 years or, if the former Judge has attained the age of 72 years, not exceeding 1 year, as the Governor General may specify.

(2) During the term of his appointment, the former Judge may act as a Judge during such period or periods only and in such places only as the Chief Justice may deremine.

(3) Every former Judge appointed under this section shall, during each period when he acts as a Judge, but not otherwise, be paid a salary at the rate for the time being payable by law to a Judge other than the Chief Justice, and shall also be paid such travelling allowances or other incidental or minor allowances as may be fixed from time to time by the Governor General.

(4) Every former Judge appointed under this section shall, during each period when he acts as a judge, have all the jurisdiction, powers, protections, privileges, and immunities of a Judge.

11B. Certificate by Chief Justice and 3 other Judges prerequisite. No appointment may be made under section 11 or section 11A of this Act otherwise than on a certificate signed by the Chief Justice and not less than 3 other permanent Judges to the effect that, in their opinion, it is necessary for the due conduct of the business of the Court that 1 or more temporary Judges, or (as the case may require) 1 or more acting Judges, be appointed.

12. Repealed.

13. Age of retirement. Every Judge, other than a former Judge appointed under section 11 or section 11A of this Act or a person who is deemed by section 58(10) of this Act to be a Judge, shall retire from office on attaining the age of 68 years.

14. If the Chief Justice or the President of the Court of Appeal resigns from office before attaining the age of sixty-eight years and is, at the time of his resignation and but for the fact of his resignation, entitled to a period of leave of absence, he shall continue to receive the salary, privileges, and allowances of his former office until the expiration of that period or until he attains the age of sixty-eight years or until he dies, whichever is the sooner, and his rights and obligations under the Superannuation Act 1956 and all the rights which his widow may have under that Act shall be the same as they would have been if he had been in office while his salary, privileges, and allowances so continued.

15. Repealed.

Jurisdiction of the Court

16. General jurisdiction. The Court shall continue to have all the jurisdiction which it had on the coming into operation of this Act and all judicial jurisdiction which may be necessary to administer the laws of New Zealand.

17. Jurisdiction as to infants, mentally defective persons, etc. The Court shall also have within New Zealand all the jurisdiction and control over the persons and estates of infants, idiots, mentally defective persons, and persons of unsound mind, and over the guardians and committees of such persons and estates respectively, as the Lord Chancellor of England, or any Judge or Judges of His Majesty's High Court of Justice or of His Majesty's Court of Appeal, so far as the same may be applicable to the circumstances of New Zealand, has or have in England under the Sign Manual of His Majesty or otherwise.

18. No jurisdiction in cases of felonies or misdemeanors committed before 14 January 1840. The Court shall not have jurisdiction to try any felony or misdemeanor committed before the fourteenth day of January on thousand eight hundred and forty.

19. Powers of the Court may be exercised by one or more Judges. Each Judge or any two or more Judges may in any part of New Zealand exercise all the powers of the Court, except such powers as may by any statute be required to be exercised by the full Court or by any specified number of Judges.

19A. Certain actions may be tried by jury.

(1) This section applies to actions in which the ony relief claimed is payment of a debt or pecuniary damages or the recovery of chattels.

(2) If the debt or damages or the value of the chattels claimed in any action to which this section applies exceeds $3,000 either party may have the action tried before a Judge and a jury on giving notice to the Court and to the other party, within the time and in the manner prescribed by the rules of the Supreme Court, that he requires the action to be tried before a jury.

(3) Notwithstanding anything in sub-section (2) of this section, in any case where, after notice has been given pursuant to that sub-section but before the trial has commenced, the debt or damages or the value of the chattels claimed is reduced to $3,000 or less, the action shall be tried before a Judge without a jury.

(4) If, in any action to which this section applies, the defendant sets up a counterclaim, then, unless pursuant to this section the action and the counterclaim are both to be tried before a Judge without a jury, the following provisions shall apply:

(*a*) On the application of either party made with the consent in writing of the other party, both the action and counterclaim shall be tried before a Judge without a jury, or before a Judge with a jury, whichever is specified in the application:

(*b*) If no such application is made, the action and the counterclaim shall, subject to any direction of the Court or a Judge under section *19B* of this Act, be tried in accordance with the foregoing provisions of this section:

Provided that if the Court or a Judge order that the action and the counterclaim be tried together, they shall be tried before a Judge with a jury.

(5) Notwithstanding anything to the contrary in the foregoing provisions of this section, in any case where notice is given as aforesaid requiring any action to be tried before a jury, if it appears to a Judge before the trial

(*a*) That the trial of the action or any issue therein will involve mainly the consideration of difficult questions of law; or

(*b*) That the trial of the action or any issue therein will require any prolonged examination of documents or accounts, or any investigation in which difficult questions in relation to scientific, technical, business, or professional matters are likely to arise, being an examination or investigation which cannot conveniently be made with a jury,

the Judge may, on the application of either party, order that the action or issue be tried before a Judge without a jury.

(6) Nothing in this section shall apply in respect of any action to be heard by the Court in its admiralty jurisdiction.

19B. All other actions to be tried before a Judge alone, unless Court otherwise orders.

(1) Except as provided in section *19A* of this Act, every Action shall be tried before a Judge alone.

(2) Notwithstanding sub-section (1) of this section, if it appears to the Court at the trial, or to a Judge before the trial, that the action or any issue therein can be tried more conveniently before a Judge with a jury the Court or Judge may order that the action or issue be so tried.

20–22. Repealed.

23. Governor General may appoint special sittings. The Governor General in

Council may from time to time appoint special sittings of the Court for the despatch of civil and criminal business, to be held at such time and place or places, and before such Judge or Judges, as he thinks fit.

23A. Offices of the High Court.

(1) The Governor General may form time to time, by notice in the *Gazette*, declare an office or offices of the Court to be estabiished at such place or places as may be specified in the notice, as from such date, in the case of each office, as may be so specified.

(1A) Notwithstanding anything in the Chattels Transfer Act 1934 the Governor General may direct in any notice under sub-section (1) of this section that any office of the Court to which the notice relates is not to be an office in which instruments within the meaning of that Act may be filed.

(2) The Governor General may ai any time in like manner abolish any office of the Court or revoke any direction given pursuant to sub-section (1A) of this section.

(3) Where any office of the Court is abolished, the Minister of Justice may direct that all documents, books and records in that office shall be delivered to some other office of the Court (in this section referred to as the substituted office). From the time of their delivery to the Registrar of the substituted office, those documents, books, and records shall be deemed to be in the lawful custody of that Registrar.

(4) Where any office of the Court is abolished, the following provisions shall apply:

(*a*) Any act or thing that could have been done under any enactment or rule by the Registrar of that office may be done by the Registrar of the substituted offfice:

(*b*) Any step in any proceedings that would, but for the abolition of office, have been taken there under any enactment or rule may be taken at the substituted office:

(*c*) Any act or thing required or authorized by any enactment or rule to be done by any person at that office, whether in respect of any proceedings or in respect of any transaction recorded or document filed there, may be done at the substituted office:

(*d*) Any address for service, being an address conforming to the requirements of the rules .of Court, that has been given by any party to any proceedings in respect of which the records are delivered to the substituted office shall continue to be the address for that party for the purposes of those proceedings, notwithstanding that because of its distance from the substituted office it may cease to conform to those requirements:

Provided that where, because of its distance from the substituted office, the address does not conform to the requirements of of the rules, the party shall give a new address for service conforming to those requirements when he first files in the substituted office any document in the proceedings:

(*e*) If in respect of any proceedings, or of any transaction, document, record, or other matter, any question arises as to the application of any provision of this section or as to the proper procedure to be followed, the Court or a Judge may determine the question and make such order thereon as the Court or Judge thinks fit.

24. Repealed.

25. Administrative Division of the Supreme Court.

(1) There shall be in the Supreme Court an Administrative Division.

(2) The Division shall consist of not more than six Judges of the Supreme Court, being Judges assigned to the Division from time to time by the Chief Justice.

(3) Nothing in this section shall prevent any Judge of the Administrative Division from exercising any of the powers of a Judge of the Supreme Court, whether or not in his capacity as a Judge of the Division.

26. Jurisdiction of Administrative Division.

(1) Notwithstanding anything in section *19* of this Act, the Administrative Division shall hear and determine

(*a*) Such appeals as are, under or by virtue of any enactment for the time being in force, to be heard and determined by the Division:

(*b*) Such proceedings, other than appeals, as are, under or by virtue of any enactment for the time being in force, to be heard and determined by the Division:

(*c*) Such applications or classes of applications to the Supreme Court for writs of *certiorari*, prohibition, or *mandamus*, and such applications or classes of applications to the Court for declaratory judgments or orders or injunctions and such applications or classes of applications to the Court for review under Part I of the Judicature Amendment Act 1972, as may from time to time be referred to the Division by the Chief Justice.

(2) Any one or more of the Judges of the Division may exercise all the powers of the Division, except such powers as may by any enactment be required to be exercised by any specified number of Judges of the Division.

(3) Notwithstanding anything in paragraphs (*a*) and (*b*) of sub-section (1) of this section, the Chief Justice may in his discretion direct that any particular appeal or proceedings, not being one that is required by any enactment to be heard by a specified number of Judges of the Division, be heard and determined by a Judge who is not a member of the Administrative Division if in the Chief Justice's opinion, having regard to the special nature of the subject-matter of the appeal or proceedings and the circumstances of the case, it is one that would more appropriately be dealt with by that Judge.

(4) Except as othewise expressly provided in any enactment, nothing in section *64* to *66* of this Act shall apply in respect of ay proceedings required by paragraphs (*a*) and (*b*) of sub-section (1) of this section to be heard by the Administrative Division, whether or not they are heard by the Division.

26A. Lay member or assessors in certain cases. Sections *25* and *26* of this Act shall be read subject to the provisions of any enactment that provides for the appointment of persons other than Judges to sit as members of or assessors with the Administrative Division in respect of any specified proceedings or class of proceedings.

26B. Rules relating to Administrative Division.

(1) Rules may from time to time be made, in the manner prescribed by this Act,

(*a*) Regulating the pratice and procedure of the Administrative Division:

(*b*) Prescribing the form and manner in which appeals, applications, and other proceedings shall be made to or brought before the Division:

(*c*) Fixing scales of costs in respect of matter within the jurisdiction of the Division.

(2) Any such rules may modify the provisions of any enactment relating to any matters to which sub-section (1) of this section applies; and so far as any such enactment is inconsistent with or repugnant to the rules it shall be read subject to the rules.

Officers

27. Governor General may appoint officers. The Governor General may from time to time appoint such Registrars, Deputy Registrars, Clerks, criers, and other officers as may be required for the conduct of the business of the Court throughout New Zealand, and all such officers shall severally hold office under and subject to the provisions of the Acts for the time being in force relating to the Civil Service.

REGISTRARS

28. Powers of Registrars. In order that the Court may be enabled to exercise the jurisdiction conferred upon it by this Act, every Registrar and Deputy Registrar shall have all the powers and perform all the duties in respect of the Court (except such powers and duties as any other officer may be specially appointed to exercise and perform) which Registrars and Deputy Registrars have hitherto performed or which by any rule or statute they may be required to perform.

SHERIFFS

29. (1) Every Registrar of the Supreme Court for the time being shall be a Sheriff for New Zealand.

(2) There may be appointed under the State Services Act 1962 in respect of any office of the Court one or more Deputy Sheriffs.

(3) Every Deputy Sheriff shall, in the absence of the Sheriff or when acting for the Sheriff, have the powers and privileges, duties and responsibilities of the Sheriff under this Act or any other enactment.

30, 31. Repealed.

32. Duties, etc., of Sheriffs. Every Sheriff shall have such powers and privileges, duties and responsibilities, as a Sheriff by law has or is liable to in England as a ministerial officer of one of His Majesty's Courts at Westminster.

33. Sheriff to act as King's bailiff. In addition to his powers and privileges, duties and responsibilites, as a ministerial officer, each Sheriff shall also have and exercise the powers and duties of the Kings's bailiff.

34. Sheriff not to act as barrister or solicitor. No Sheriff shall be in any way concerned in any action in any Court in New Zealand either as a barrister, solicitor, or agent.

35. Service of process when Sheriff disqualified. Where any process issues which the Sheriff ought not by law to execute, the Supreme Court shall authorize some fit person to execute the same; and in every such case the cause of such special proceedings shall be entered upon the records of the Court.

36. Person arrested by Sheriffs may be committed to prison at once. Where any Sheriff, Sheriff's officer, bailiff, or other person employed under the Sheriff, has arrested any person under or by virtue of any writ or process whatsoever, he may forthwith thereafter convey such person, or cause him to be conveyed, to such prison as he ought to be sent to by virtue of the writ or process against him.

37–41. Repealed.

42. Fees and poundage to be paid into Public Account. All fees taken by any Sheriff under this Act shall be forthwith paid into the Public Account and shall form part of the Consolidated Fund.

43–46. Repealed.

COMMISSIONERS TO ADMINISTER OATHS

47. Commissioners to take affidavits, etc., out of New Zealand.

(1) Any Judge of the High Court, by a commission to be issued under the seal of the Court, may from time to time appoint any person to be and act as a Commissioner of the Court in any country or place beyond the jurisdiction of the Court, for the purpose of administering and taking any oath, affidavit, or affirmation, whether in any action, cause, proceeding, matter, or thing commenced or pending in the said Court or in any Court of concurrent or inferior jurisdiction in New Zealand, or in any proceeding, matter or thing whatsoever within the cognisance or jurisdiction of any such Court.

(2) Every such appointment shall be gazetted.

48. Affidavits, etc., so taken to be of like effect as if taken in New Zealand. Every oath, affidavit, or affirmation taken or made before any such Commissioner as aforesaid shall within New Zealand be of the like effect in all respects as if the same had been administered, made, or taken by or before any Court or persons having authority to administer or take the same in New Zealand.

49. Commission may be revoked.

(1) Any commission issued as aforesaid may be revoked by any Judge of the Court for any cause which such Judge deems sufficient; but no such revocation

shall affect or prejudice any act, matter, or thing done by any Commissioner by virtue of his commission prior to a notification of such revocation having been given or sent to him.

(2) Every revocation of any such appointment shall be gazetted, and the notice published in the *Gazette* shall state the date when notice of revocation was given or sent to the Commissioner affected thereby.

Practice and Procedure of the Court

50. Seal of the Court and Registrar's seal.

(1) The Court shall have in the custody of each Registrar a seal of the Court, for the sealing of all writs and other instruments or documents issued by such Registrar and requiring to be sealed.

(2) *Repealed.*

51. Code of Civil Procedure.

(1) Subject to the power of revocation and alteration hereinafter contained, the practice and procedure of the Court in all causes and matter within the jurisdiction of the Court shall be regulated by the rules contained in the Code of Civil Procedure set forth in the Second Schedule hereto, except only in those matters as to which the practice or procedure of any of the Superior Courts of England is by the said code expressly retained.

(2) *Repealed.*

52. District rules. Any three or more of the Judges, of whom the Chief Justice shall be one, may from time to time appoint sittings of the Court for the despatch of civil and criminal business, and may from time to time make for each place where an office of the High Court is established rules respecting the places and times for holding sittings of the Court, sittings in Chambers, the order of disposing of business, the attendance at the office or offices of the officers thereof, and other such matters;

Provided that such rules shall not be inconsistent with the Code of Civil Procedure or the laws of New Zealand:

Provided also that any Judge may from time to time adjourn a sitting of the Court to any time and place he may think fit; and in the event of a Judge not being present at the time appointed for a sitting of the Court, the Registrar may adjourn the sitting to such time as may be convenient.

Note: *Constitution of Rules Committee.* Section 2 of the Judicature Amendment Act 1930, amended 1968 and 1970 provides as follows:

(1) For the purposes of the principal Act there shall be a Rules Committee, to consist of
- (*a*) The Chief Justice and two other Judges of the Supreme Court:
- (*b*) The Attorney General:
- (*c*) The Solicitor General:
- (*d*) The Secretary for Justice:
- (*e*) Two persons, being barristers or solicitors of the Supreme Court, nominated by the Council of the New Zealand Law Society and approved by the Chief Justice.

(2) The members of the Rules Committee, other than the Chief Justice and those mentioned

53. Application of fees. All fees of the Court prescribed to be paid by the Code of Civil Procedure or by regulations made under this Act shall be paid into the Public Account and shall form part of the Consolidated Fund.

54. Service of process on Sundays void.

(1) Subject to any Rule of Court, no person shall serve or execute, or cause to be served or executed, on Sunday any writ, process, warrant, order, judgment, or decree of the High Court or Court of Appeal (except in cases of crime or of breach of the peace), and such service or execution shall be void to all intents and purposes whatsoever.

Provided that nothing in this sub-section shall apply to the service of any writ in rem or warrant of arrest in respect of any action heard or to be heard by the Supreme Court in its admiralty jurisdiction.

(2) *Repealed.*

(3) Nothing in this section shall be construed to annul, repeal, or in any way affect the common law, or the provisions of any statute or rule of practice or procedure, now or hereafter in force, authorizing the service of any writ, process, or warrant, in cases other than those hereinbefore excepted.

54A. Verdict of three fourths. If three fourths at least of any jury trying any civil case shall, after the jury has retired to consider its verdict for a period of at least 4 hours, intimate to the Judge presiding that the jury has considered its verdict, and that there is no probability of such jury being unanimous, the verdict of three fourths shall have the same effect as the verdict of the whole number.

---

in paragraphs (*b*) to (*d*) of sub-section (1) of this section, shall be appointed by the Chief Justice for a term not exceeding three years. Any such member may be reappointed, or may at any time resign his office by writing addressed to the Chief Justice.

(3) In addition to the members of the Rules Committed specified in sub-section (1) of this section, the Chief Justice may from time to time appoint any other person to be a member of the Committee for any special purpose. Every person so appointed shall hold office during the pleasure of the Chief Justice.

4. Power to make rules. (1) The Judicature Amendment Act 1930 is hereby amended (1974) by repealing section 3, and substituting the following section:

(1) The Governor General in Council, with the Concurrence of the Chief Justice and any 2 or more members of the Rules Committee, of whom at least 1 shall be a Judge, may for the purposes of facilitating the expeditious, inexpensive, and just dispatch of the business of the Court, or otherwise assisting in the due administration of justice, from time to time

(*a*) Repeal the Code of Civil Procedure set forth in the Second Schedule to the principal Act, and substitute a new code:

(*b*) Alter or revoke any of the rules contained in the said Code or in any substituted code:

(*c*) Add to the said Code or any substituted code any further rules touching the practice and procedure of the Supreme Court in all or any of the causes and matters within its jurisdiction:

(*d*) Alter or revoke any of the rules contained in the Court of Appeal Rules 1955:

(*e*) Make any additional rules touching the practice and procedure of the Court of Appeal:

(*f*) Alter or revoke any other rules of the Supreme Court or the Court of Appeal that are now or may hereafter be in force.

(2) In this Act the power to make rules of procedure includes the power to fix scales of costs.

54B. Discharge of jury.

(1) Subject to the provisions of this section, the Court may in its discretion, in the case of any emergency or casualty rendering it, in the opinion of the Court, highly expedient for the ends of justice to do so, discharge the jury without their giving a verdict.

(2) Without limiting sub-section (1) of this section, where a jury has remained in deliberation for such period as the Judge thinks reasonable, being not less than 4 hours, and does not agree on the verdict to be given, the Judge may discharge the jury without their giving a verdict.

(3) If, at any time before the verdict of the jury is taken, any juror becomes in the opinion of the Court incapable of continuing to perform his or her duty, or it becomes known to the Court that the juror is disqualified or that the juror's spouse or a member of the juror's family or a member of the family of the juror's spouse is ill or has died, the Court may in its discretion

(*a*) Discharge the jury without their giving a verdict; or

(*b*) Proceed with the remaining jurors and take their verdict.

(4) Notwithstanding sub-section (3)(*b*) of this section, the Court shall not proceed with less than 11 jurors unless all the parties consent.

(5) Where under sub-section (3)(*b*) of this section the Court proceeds with less than 12 jurors, their verdict shall have the same effect as the verdict of the whole number.

(6) Where the Court discharges a jury under this section, it shall either direct that a new jury be empanelled during the sitting of the Court, or postpone the trial on such terms as justice requires.

(7) If the presiding Judge becomes incapable of trying the case or directing that the jury be discharged, the Registrar shall discharge the jury.

(8) No Court may review the exercise of any discretion under this section.

Miscellaneous Rules of Law and of Practice

ABSCONDING DEBTORS

55. Power under certain circumstances to arrest defendant about to quit New Zealand.

(1) A person shall not be arrested upon mesne process in any action in the High Court.

(2) Where in any action the High Court in which, if brought before the first day of October, one thousand eight hundred and seventy-four (being the date of the coming into operation of the Imprisonment for Debt Abolition Act 1974), the defendant would have been liable to arrest, the plaintiff proves at any time before final judgment, by evidence on oath to the satisfaction of a Judge of the Court, that the plaintiff has good cause of action against the defendant to the amount of fifty pounds or upwards, and that there is a probable cause for believing that the defendant is about to quit New Zealand unless he is apprehended, and that the absence

of the defendant from New Zealand will materially prejudice the plaintiff in the prosecution of his action, such Judge may, in the prescribed manner, order such defendant to be arrested and imprisoned for a period not exceeding six months, unless and until he has sooner given the prescribed security, not exceeding the amount claimed in the action, that he will not go out of New Zealand without the leave of the High Court.

(3) Where the action is for a penalty, or sum in the nature of a penalty, other than a penalty in respect of any contract, it shall not be necessary to prove that the absence of the defendant from New Zealand will materially prejudice the plaintiff in the prosecution of his action; and the security given (instead of being that the defendant will not go out of New Zealand) shall be to the effect that any sum recovered against the defendant in the action will be paid or that the defendant shall be rendered to prison.

(4) All the powers conferred by this action upon a Judge may be exercised by the Registrar of the Court;

Provided that such powers shall be exercised by the said Registrar only in the absence of the Judge from the place where the office of the Court is situate at which the application for such order as aforesaid is made.

FOREIGN CREDITORS

56. Memorials of judgments obtained out of New Zealand may be registered.

(1) Any person in whose favor any judgment, decree, rule, or order, whereby any sum of money is made payable, has been obtained in any Court of any of His Majesty's dominions may cause a memorial of the same containing the particulars hereinafter mentioned, and authenticated by the seal of the Court wherein such judgment, decree, rule, or order was obtained, to be filed in the office of the High Court; and such memorial being so filed shall thenceforth be a record of such judgment, decree, rule, or order, and execution may issue thereon as hereinafter provided.

(2) Every seal purporting to be the seal of any such Court shall be deemed and taken to be the seal of such Court until the contrary is proved, and the proof that any such seal is not the seal of such Court shall lie upon the party denying or objecting to the same.

(3) Every such memorial shall be signed by the party in whose favor such judgment, decree, rule, or order was obtained, or his attorney or solicitor, and shall contain the following particulars, that is to say: The names and additions of the parties, the form or nature of the action or other proceeding, and, when commenced, the date of the signing or entering-up of the judgment, or of passing the decree, or of making the rule or order, and the amount recovered, or the decree pronounced, or rule or order made, and, if there was a trial, the date of such trial and amount of verdict given.

(4) The Court or any Judge thereof, on the application of the person in whose favor such judgment, decree, rule, or order was obtained, or his solicitor,

may grant a rule or issue a summons calling upon the person against whom such judgment, decree, rule, or order was obtained to show cause, within such time after personal or such other service of the rule or summons as such Court or Judge directs, why execution should not issue upon such judgment, decree, rule, or order, and such rule or summons shall give notice that in default of appearance execution may issue accordingly; and if the person served with such rule or summons does not appear, or does not show sufficient cause against such rule or summons, such Court or Judge, on due proof of such service as aforesaid, may make the rule absolute, or make an order for issuing execution as upon a judgment, decree, rule, or order of the Court, subject to such terms and conditions (if any) as such Court or Judge thinks fit.

(5) All such proceedings may be had or taken for the revival of such judgment, decree, rule, or order, or the enforcement thereof by and against persons not parties to such judgment, decree, rule, or order as may be had for the like purposes upon any judgment, decree, rule, or order of the Court.

WITNESSES

56A. Failure of witness to attend.

(1) If any witness who is compellable to attend to give evidence at the hearing of any civil proceedings in the High Court and who has been duly summoned fails to attend at the time and place appointed, the Court may issue a warrant to arrest him and bring him before the Court, and may adjourn the hearing.

(2) The Court may impose on any such witness who fails without just excuse (the proof of which excuse shall be on him) to attend as aforesaid a fine not exceeding five hundred dollars.

(3) No witness shall be compellable to attend at the hearing of any civil proceedings in the High Court unless at the time of the service of the order of subpoena, or at some other reasonable time before the hearing, a sum in respect of his allowances and travelling expenses in accordance with the scale prescribed for the time being by regulations made under the Summary Proceedings Act 1957 is tendered or paid to him.

56B. Refusal of witness to given evidence.

(1) If any witness in any civil proceeding in the High Court, without offering any just excuse, refuses to give evidence when required, or refuses to produce any document which he has been required to produce, or refuses to be sworn, or having been sworn refuses to answer such questions concerning that proceeding as are put to him, the Court may order that, unless he sooner consents to give evidence or to produce the document or to be sworn or to answer the questions put to him, as the case may be, he be detained in custody for any period not exceeding seven days, and may issue a warrant for his arrest and detention in accordance with the order.

(2) If the person so detained, on being brought up again at the hearing, again refuses to give evidence or to produce the document or to be sworn or, having

been sworn, to answer the questions put to him, the Court if it thinks fit, may again direct that the witness be detained in custody for the like period, and so again from time to time until he consents to give evidence or to produce the document or to be sworn or to answer as aforesaid.

(3) Nothing in this section shall limit or affect any power or authority of the Court to punish any witness for contempt of Court in any case to which this section does not apply.

CONTEMPT OF COURT

56C. (1) If any person:

(*a*) Assaults, threatens, intimidates, or wilfully insults a Judge, or any Registrar, or any officer of the Court, or any juror, or any witness, during his sitting or attendance in Court, or in going to or returning from the Court; or

(*b*) Wilfully interrupts or obstructs the proceedings of the Court or otherwise misbehaves in Court; or

(*c*) Wilfully and without lawful excuse disobeys any order or direction of the Court in the course of the hearing of any proceedings;

any constable or officer of the Court, with or without the assistance of any other person, may, by order of the Judge, take the offender into custody and detain him until the rising of the Court.

(2) In any such case as aforesaid, the Judge, if he thinks fit, may sentence the offender to imprisonment for any period not exceedings three months, or sentence him to pay a fine not exceeding one hundred pounds for every such offence; and in de default of payment of any such fine may direct that the offender be imprisoned for any period not exceeding three months, unless the fine is sooner paid.

(3) Nothing in this section shall limit or affect any power or authority of the Court to punish any person for contempt of Court in any case to which this section does not apply.

PART II

THE COURT OF APPEAL

Constitution of the Court

57. Constitution of the Court.

(1) There shall continue to be in and for New Zealand a Court of record called, as heretofore, the Court of Appeal of New Zealand:

Provided and it is hereby declared that the Court of Appeal heretofore and now held and henceforth to be held is and shall be deemed and taken to be the same Court.

(2) Subject to the provisions of this Part of this Act, the Court of Appeal shall consist of:

(*a*) The Chief Justice of New Zealand, who shall be a member of the Court by virtue of his office as the head of the Judiciary;

(*b*) A Judge of the High Court, to be appointed by the Governor General as a Judge of the Court of Appeal and as President of that Court;

(*c*) Four other Judges of the High Court, to be appointed by the Governor General as Judges of the Court of Appeal.

(3) Any Judge may be appointed to be a Judge of the Court of Appeal either at the time of his appointment as a Judge of the High Court or at any time thereafter.

(4) Every Judge of the Court of Appeal shall continue to be a Judge of the High Court, and may from time to time sit as or exercise any of the powers of a Judge of the High Court.

(5) Every Judge of the Court of Appeal shall hold office as a Judge of that Court so long as he holds office as a Judge of the High Court;

Provided that, with the prior approval of the Governor General, any Judge of the Court of Appeal may resign his office as a Judge of that Court without resigning his office as a Judge of the High Court.

(6) The Judges of the Court of Appeal shall have seniority over all the Judges of the High Court (including any Judge who is for the time being an additional Judge of the Court of Appeal), except the Chief Justice or the acting Chief Justice. The President of the Court of Appeal shall have seniority over the four Judges of that Court referred to in paragraph (*c*) of sub-section two of this section; and those four Judges shall have seniority between themselves according to the dates of their appointments as Judges of the Court of Appeal or, if they are so appointed on the same day, according to their seniority as Judges of the High Court. If any Judge of the Court of Appeal resigns his office as a Judge of that Court without resigning his office as a Judge of the High Court, he shall then have, as a Judge of the High Court, the seniority that he would have had if he had not been appointed as a Judge of the Court of Appeal.

(7) While any vacancy exists in the office of President of the Court of Appeal, or during any absence from New Zealand of the President, or while by reason of illness or any other cause he is prevented from exercising the duties of his office, the senior Judge of the Court of Appeal, not being the Chief Justice, shall have authority to act as President of the Court of Appeal and execute the duties of that office and to exercise all powers that may be lawfully exercised by the President.

(8) The jurisdiction of the Court of Appeal shall not be affected by any vacancy in the number of the Judges of that Court.

58. Additional Judges of Court of Appeal in certain circumstances.

(1) At any time during the illness or absence of any Judge of the Court of Appeal, the Governor General may appoint some other Judge to hold office as an additional Judge of the Court of Appeal during the pleasure of the Governor General.

(2) At any time while there is a vacancy in the office of any Judge of the

Court of Appeal, or while any Judge of that Court is on leave preliminary to retirement, the Governor General may appoint some other Judge to hold office as an additional Judge of the Court of Appeal. Subject to sub-section (5) of section *57* of this Act, every Judge so appointed shall hold that office for such period, not exceeding 6 months, as is specified in the appointment or until the vacancy is filled by an appointment under the said section *57*, whichever period is the shorter.

(3) The power conferred by sub-section (2) of this section shall be exercised only on a certificate signed by the Chief Justice and the President of the Court of Appeal to the effect that, in their opinion, it is necessary for the due conduct of the business of the Court that one or more additional Judges should be temporarily appointed.

(4) Whenever the Chief Justice and the President of the Court of Appeal certify that it is necessary for the due conduct of the business of the Court of Appeal that the Court be enabled to sit in divisions in accordance with section *60A* of this Act, and that, for that reason, it is expedient that any Judge or Judges who is or are or has or have been nominated by the Chief Justice should act as an additional Judge, or, as the case may be, additional Judges of the Court of Appeal for such period, not exceeding 3 months, as may be specifed in the certificate, the Judge or Judges so nominated may act as a Judge or Judges of the Court of Appeal during the period so specified.

(5) Whenever the Chief Justice and the President of the Court of Appeal certify that in any appeal or proceeding before that Court it is expedient that any Judge or Judges nominated by the Chief Justice should act as an additional Judge or, as the case may be, as additional Judges of the Court of Appeal, the Judges so nominated may act as a Judge or Judges of the Court of Appeal for the purposes of that appeal or proceeding.

(6) Every additional Judge acting pursuant to this section shall be deemed while so acting to be a Judge of the Court of Appeal.

(7) The fact that any Judge acts as an additional Judge of the Court of Appeal shall be conclusive evidence of his authority to do so; and no judgment or determination given or made by that Court while he so acts shall be questioned on the ground that the occasion for his so acting had not arisen or had ceased to exist.

(8) Every Judge who pursuant to this section has acted as an additional Judge of the Court of Appeal may attend the sittings of that Court for the purpose of giving judgment or passing sentence in or otherwise completing any proceedings in relation to any case that has been heard by that Court while he so acted, notwithstanding that he is no longer an additional Judge of that Court.

(9) Without limiting sub-section (4) or sub-section (5) or this section, whenever the Chief Justice and the President of the Court of Appeal give a certificate under either of those sub-sections, the Governor General in Council may, with the concurrence of the Chief Justice and the President of the Court of Appeal, appoint any former member of the Court of Appeal (with that former member's consent) to act as an additional Judge of that Court in accordance with and for the purposes of that sub-section.

(10) Every person appointed under sub-section (9) of this section shall, while he is acting as an additional Judge of the Court of Appeal in accordance with that appointment, be deemed to be, and to have all the powers of, a Judge of the High Court.

(11) Every person appointed under sub-section (9) of this section shall, during each period when he acts as an additional Judge of the Court of Appeal, but not otherwise, be paid a salary at the rate for the time being payable by law to a Judge (other than the President) of that Court, and shall also be paid such travelling allowances or other incidental or minor allowances as may be fixed from time to time by the Governor General.

58A. (1) For the purposes of any appeal to the Court of Appeal against conviction or sentence entered or imposed under the Crimes Act 1961 (except section *406* of that Act), or of any application for leave to appeal to the Court of Appeal against any such conviction or sentence, the Court of Appeal shall comprise

(*a*) At least 2 Judges of the Court of Appeal; and

(*b*) One of the following, namely:

(i) The Chief Justice; or

(ii) A Judge of the High Court who is for the time being acting as a Judge of the Court of Appeal pursuant to section *58* of this Act; or

(iii) One of the Judges of the High Court nominated by the Chief Justice pursuant to sub-section (6) of this section.

(2) For the purpose of any other proceeding, the court of Appeal shall comprise at least 3 Judges of the Court of Appeal.

(3) Notwithstanding anything in sub-section (1) of this section, the President of the Court of Appeal may at any time, at his discretion, if he considers that, for whatever reason, it is appropriate to depart from the normal rule prescribed by that sub-section, direct that any appeal or application for leave to appeal to which that sub-section would otherwise apply shall be heard without any of the Judges referred to in paragraph (*b*) of that sub-section; and, where the President gives such a direction, the Court shall comprise at least 3 Judges of the Court of Appeal.

(4) No direction given by the President of the Court of Apeal under sub-section (3) of this section shall be called in question on any ground in any Court; and no judgment or determination of the Court of Appeal in relation to any appeal or application for leave to appeal in respect of which the President has given such a direction shall be called in question in any Court on the ground that none of the Judges referred to in sub-section (1)(*b*) of this section sat in the Court of Appeal for the purposes of that appeal or application.

(5) The provisions of section *58*(7) of this Act, with any necessary modifications, shall apply to every case where a Judge of the High Court sits in the Court of Appeal for the purposes of any appeal or application referred to in sub-section (1) of this section.

(6) Except where the work of the High Court renders it impracticable for him to do so, the Chief Justice shall from time to time, after consulting the Presi-

dent of the Court of Appeal, nominate sufficient Judges of the High Court to sit in the Court of Appeal to enable that Court to exercise its criminal jurisdiction in accordance with this section. Every such nomination shall be made either in respect of a specified case or specified cases, or in respect of every case to be heard by the Court of Appeal during a specified period not exceeding 3 months.

59. Judgment of Court of Appeal.

(1) Subject to section *58A* of this Act any three or more Judges of the Court of Appeal may exercise all the powers of the Court.

Provided that any two Judges of the Court shall have power to act as the Court of Appeal for the purpose of delivering any judgment of the Court or of hearing any application for leave to the Privy Council.

(2) The judgment of the Court shall be in accordance with the opinion of the majority of the Judges present.

(3) If the Judges present are equally divided in opinion, the judgment, decree, or order appealed from or under review shall be deemed to be affirmed.

60. Sittings of Court of Appeal.

(1) The Court of Appeal may from time to time appoint ordinary or special sittings of the Court, and may from time to time make rules, not inconsistent with the rules of practice and procedure of the Court of Appeal for the time being in force under this Act or with the laws of New Zealand, in respect of the places and times for holding sittings of the Court, the order of disposing of business, and any other necessary matters.

(2) At every sitting of the Court at which the President of the Court of Appeal is present he shall preside unless the Chief Justice is also present, in which case the Chief Justice shall preside.

(3) In the absence of the Chief Justice and of the President from any sitting of the Court the senior Judge of the Court of Appeal present shall preside.

(4) The Court shall have power from time to time to adjourn any sitting till such time and to such place as it thinks fit.

60A. Court may sit in divisions.

(1) The Court of Appeal may from time to time, as the President directs, sit in divisions, and all the powers of the Court may be exercised by any such division.

(2) Each Division shall consist of such Judges of the Court (of whom at least 1 shall be a member of the Court pursuant to section *57*(2) of this Act) as are for the time being assigned to that Division by the President.

(3) A Division of the Court may exercise any powers of the Court notwithstanding that another Division of the Court is exercising any powers of the Court at the same time.

(4) The provisions of this section shall be read subject to the provisions of section *58A* and *59*(1) of this Act.

61. Adjournment in cases of absence of some of the Judges. Where, by reason of the absence of all or any one or more of the Judges of the Court of Appeal at the time appointed for the sitting of the Court or any adjournment thereof, it is necessary to adjourn the sitting of the Court to a future day, any one or more of the Judges at the time appointed for such sitting, or at the time of any adjournment thereof, or the Registrar of the said Court in case none of the Judges thereof are present, may adjourn or further adjourn such sitting to such future day and hour as such Judge or Judges or such Registrar think fit.

61A. (1) In any civil appeal or in any civil cause or matter pending before the Court of Appeal, any Judge of that Court, sitting in Chambers, may make such incidental orders and give such incidental directions as he thinks fit, not being an order or a direction that determines the appeal or disposes of any question or issue that is before the Court in such appeal, cause, or matter.

(2) Every order or direction made or given by a Judge of the Court of Appeal under sub-section (1) of this section may be discharged or varied by any Judges of that Court who together have jurisdiction, in accordance with section *59* of this Act, to hear and determine the proceeding.

(3) Any Judge of the Court of Appeal may review a decision of the Registrar made within the civil jurisdiction of the Court under a power conferred on the Registrar by any rule of Court, and may confirm, modify, or revoke that decision as he thinks fit.

(4) The provisions of this section shall apply notwithstanding anything in section *59* of this Act.

(5) This section shall have effect from a date to be appointed by the Governor General by Order in Council.

62. Power to remit proceedings to the High Court. The Court of Appeal shall have power to remit any proceedings in any cause pending before it to the High Court or a single Judge thereof.

63. Judgments of Court of Appeal may be enforced by the High Court. All judgments, decrees, and orders of the Court of Appeal may be enforced by the High Court as if they had been given or made by that Court.

Civil Jurisdiction

REMOVAL OF PROCEEDINGS FROM THE HIGH COURT

64. Proceedings in High Court may be removed into Court of Appeal. The High Court may order the removal into the Court of Appeal of the following proceedings, that is to say:

(*a*) Any rule *nisi* granted;
(*b*) Any notice of motion made;
(*c*) Any petition presented;
(*d*) Any special case stated;
(*e*) Any question of law ordered to be argued;
(*f*) Facts stated by a jury that has not found for either party;

and on removal the Court of Appeal shall have the same power to adjudicate on the proceedings as the High Court had.

65. Decisions of Court of Appeal final as regards tribunals of New Zealand. On the removal of any case from the High Court to the Court of Appeal under the last preceding section, the decision of the Court of Appeal shall be final as regards the tribunals of New Zealand; and the same judgment shall be entered up in the High Court, and the same execution and other consequences and proceedings shall follow thereon, as if the decision has been given in the High Court;

Provided that the Court of Appeal may give leave to either party to appeal to the Privy Council.

APPEALS FROM DECISIONS OF THE HIGH COURT

66. Court may hear appeals from judgments and orders of the High Court. The Court of Appeal shall have jurisdiction and power to hear and determine appeals from any judgment, decree, or order save as hereinafter mentioned, of the High Court, subject to the provisions of this Act and to such rules and orders for regulating the terms and conditions on which such appeals shall be allowed as may be made pursuant to this Act.

APPEALS FROM INFERIOR COURTS

67. No appeal on appeals from inferior Courts without leave. The determination of the High Court on appeals from inferior Courts shall be final unless leave to appeal from the same to the Court of Appeal is given by the High Court or, where such leave is refused by that Court, then by the Court of Appeal.

68. Direct appeal from decision of inferior Courts.

(1) If either party in any cause in any inferior Court having extended jurisdiction is dissatisfied with the determination or direction of that Court in point of law or upon the admission or rejection of any evidence, and intimates the same and states the grounds of dissatisfaction to the Judge of that Court either at the hearing of the cause or within six days after such determination or direction, and the Judge certifies under his hand such grounds of dissatisfaction, and that they seem in his opinion to involve some question of law of considerable difficulty or great importance, the party so dissatisfied may appeal directly to the Court of Appeal.

(2) On notice of such appeal and of such certificate and grounds being given to the other party or his solicitor, and also on security being given, such proceedings shall be had, such case stated and settled, and such judgment or order shall be made by the Court of Appeal as if the appeal had been made to the High Court; and the judgment of the Court of Appeal on the said appeal shall be final.

Criminal Jurisdiction

TRIAL AT BAR

69. Trial at bar.

(1) Where a bill of indictment has been found in the High Court, or any inquisition has been found, or any criminal information been granted against any person for any crime, if it appears to the High Court on affidavit on the part of the accused or of the prosecutor that the case is one of extraordinary importance or difficulty, and that it is desirable that it should be tried before the Judges at bar, the High Court may grant a rule *nisi*, and, if no sufficient cause is shown, may make the same absolute for the removal of such indictment, inquisition, or information, and the proceedings thereon, into the Court of Appeal, and for the trial of the same at bar at the next or other sitting of such Court of Appeal, and may direct that a special or common jury, as the High Court thinks fit, be summoned from such jury district as the Court directs, to serve upon such trial; and such proceedings, as nearly as may be, shall thereupon be had as upon a trial at bar in England.

(2) The Court of Appeal shall have the same jurisdiction, authority, and power in respect thereof as the King's Bench Division of the High Court of Justice has in England in respect of a trial at bar.

APPEALS FROM CONVICTIONS

70. Repealed.

Miscellaneous

71. Rules of practice.

(1) Subject to the power of revocation and alteration hereinafter contained, the practice and procedure of the Court of Appeal shall be regulated by the rules contained in the Third Schedule hereto, except only in those matters as to which any other practice and procedure is provided by this Act.

(2), (3) *Repealed.*

72. Governor General may appoint officers.

(1) The Governor General may from time to time appoint such Registrars, Deputy Registrars, ushers, Clerks, criers, and other officers as may be required for the conduct of the business of the Court of Appeal, and all such officers shall severally hold office under and subject to the provisions of the Acts for the time being in force relating to the Civil Service.

(2) Until such appointment by the Governor General, it shall be competent for any Registrar, Deputy Registrar, usher, Clerk, crier, or other officer for the time being of the High Court to act in the like capacity in the Court of Appeal.

73. Powers and duties of offficers. All such Registrars and other officers shall have in respect of the Court of Appeal such powers and duties as are prescribed by rules made under this Act.

74. Court seal. The Court of Appeal shall have in the custody of the Registrar a seal for the sealing of writs, orders, decrees, office copies, certificates, reports, and other instruments issued by such Registrar and requiring to be sealed.

75. Repealed.

PART III

RULES AND PROVISIONS OF LAW IN JUDICIAL MATTERS GENERALLY

76–83. Repealed.

84. A surety who discharges the liability to be entitled to assignment of all securities held by the creditor. Every person who, being surety for the debt or duty of another, or being liable with another for any debt or duty, pays or satisfies such debt or performs such duty shall be entitled to have assigned to him, or a trustee for him, every judgment, specialty, or other security held by the creditor in respect of such debt or duty, whether such judgment, specialty, or other security is or is not deemed at law to be satisfied by the payment of the debt or performance of the duty.

85. Rights of surety in such cases.

(1) Every such person shall be entitled to stand in the place of the creditor, and to use all the remedies, and if need be, and upon a proper indemnity, to use the name of the creditor in any action or other proceeding in order to obtain from the principal debtor or any co-surety, co-contractor, or co-debtor, as the case may be, indemnification for the advances made and loss sustained by the persons paying or satisfying such debt or performing such duty.

(2) Such payment, satisfaction, or performance made by such surety shall not be pleadable in bar of any such action or other proceedings by him.

86. Rights of co-sureties, etc., as between themselves. A co-surety, co-contractor, or co-debtor shall not be entitled to recover from any other co-surety, co-contractor, or co-debtor by the means aforesaid more than the just proportion to which, as between those parties themselves, such last-mentioned person is justly liable.

INTEREST ON MONEY

87. Power of Courts to award interest on debts and damages.

(1) In any proceedings in any Court for the recovery of any debt or damages, the Court may, if it thinks fit, order that there shall be included in the sum for which judgment is given interest at such rate, not exceeding the prescribed rate, as it thinks fit on the whole or any part of the debt or damages for the whole or any part of the period between the date when the cause of action arose and the date of the judgment;

Provided that nothing in this sub-section shall:

(*a*) Authorize the giving of interest upon interest; or

(*b*) Apply in relation to any debt upon which interest is payable as of right, whether by virtue of any agreement, enactment, or rule of law, or otherwise; or

(*c*) Affect the damages recoverable for the dishonor of a bill of exchange.

(2) In any proceedings in any Court for the recovery of any debt upon which interest is payable as of right, and in respect of which the rate of interest is not agreed upon, prescribed, or ascertained under any agreement, enactment, or rule of law or otherwise, there shall be included in the sum for which judgment is given interest at such rate, not exceedings the prescribed rate, as the Court thinks fit for the period between the date as from which the interest became payable and the date of the judgment.

(3) In this section the term ' the prescribed rate' means the rate of 7½ percent per annum, or such other rate as may from time to time be prescribed for the purposes of this section by the Governor General by Order in Council.

LOST INSTRUMENTS

88. Actions on lost instruments. In case of any action founded on any negotiable instrument, the Court may order that the loss of such instrument shall not be taken advantage of, provided an indemnity is given to the satisfaction of the Court or a Registrar thereof against the claims of any other person upon such negotiable instrument.

MISCELLANEOUS PROVISIONS AND RULES OF LAW

88A. (1) If, on an application made by the Attorney General under this section, the Supreme Court is satisfied that any person has persistently and without any reasonable ground instituted vexations legal proceedings, whether in the Supreme Court or in any inferior Court, and whether against the same person or against different persons, the Court may, after hearing that person or giving him an opportunity of being heard, order that no civil proceeding or no civil proceeding against any particular person or persons shall without the leave of the Supreme Court or a Judge thereof be instituted by him in any court and that any civil proceeding institued by him in any court before the making of the order shall not be continued by him without such leave.

(2) Leave may be granted subject to such conditions (if any) as the Court or Judge thinks fit and shall not be granted unless the Court or Judge is satisfied that the proceeding is not an abuse of the process of the court and that there is prima facie ground for the proceeding.

(3) No appeal shall lie from an order granting or refusing such leave.

89. Repealed.

90. Stipulations not of the essence of contracts. Stipulations in contracts as to time or otherwise which would not, before the date mentioned in the last preceding section, have been deemed to be or to have become the essence of such contracts in a Court of equity shall receive in all Courts the same construction and effect as they would have theretofore received in equity.

91. Repealed.

92. Discharge of debt by acceptance of part in satisfaction. An acknowledgment in writing by a creditor, or by any person authorized by him in writing in that behalf, of the receipt of a part of his debt in satisfaction of the whole debt shall operate as a discharge of the debt, any rule of law notwithstanding.

93. Repealed.

94. Judgment against one of several persons jointly liable not a bar to action against others. A judgment against one or more of several persons jointly liable shall not operate as a bar or defence to an action or other proceeding against any of such persons against whom judgment has not been recovered, except to the extent to which the judgment has been satisfied, any rule of law notwithstanding.

94A. Recovery of payments made under mistake of law.

(1) Subject to the provisions of this section, where relief in respect of any payment that has been made under mistake is sought in any Court, whether in an action or other proceeding or by way of defence, set off, counterclaim, or otherwise, and that relief could be granted if the mistake was wholly one of fact, that relief shall not be denied by reason only that the mistake is one of law, whether or not it is in any degree also one of fact.

(2) Nothing in this section shall enable relief to be given in respect of any payment made at a time when the law requires or allows, or is commonly understood to require or allow, the payment to be made or enforced, by reason only that the law is subsequently changed or shown not to have been as it was commonly understood to be at the time of the payment.

94B. Payments made under mistake of law or fact not always recoverable.
Relief, whether under section ninety-four A of this Act or in equity or othewise, in respect of any payment made under mistake, whether of law or of fact, shall be denied wholly or in part if the person from whom relief is sought received the payment in good faith and has so altered his position in reliance on the validity of the payment that in the opinion of the Court, having regard to all possible implications in respect of other persons, it is inequitable to grant relief, or to grant relief in full, as the case may be.

95–97. Repealed.

98. Custody and education of infants. In questions relating to the custody and education of infants the rules of equity shall prevail.

99. In cases of conflict rules of equity to prevail. Generally in all matters in which there is any conflict or variance between the rules of equity and the rules of the common law with reference to the same matter the rules of equity shall prevail.

99A. (1) Where the Attorney General or Solicitor General or any other person appears in any action or in any proceedings on any appeal and argues any question of law or of fact arising in the action or proceedings the Court may, subject to the provisions of any other Act, make such order as it thinks just, (*a*) As to the payment by any party to the action or proceedings of the costs incurred by the Attorney General or the Solicitor General in so doing; or

(*b*) As to the payment by any party to the action or proceedings or out of public funds of the costs incurred by any other person in so doing; or

(*c*) As to the payment by the Attorney General or the Solicitor General or that other person of any costs incurred by any of those parties by reason of his so doing.

(2) Where the Court makes an order pursuant to paragraph (*b*) of subsection (1) of this section the Registrar of the Court shall forward a copy of the order to the Secretary for Justice who shall make the payment out of money appropriated by Parliament for the purpose.

100. Independend medical examination of person injured by accident.

(1) Where any person injured or alleged to have been injured by an accident, throught the wrongful act, neglect, or default of any other person, claims compensation or damages on account of the injury, any Judge of the Court in which proceedings to recover such compensation or damages are taken may order that the person injured be examined by one or more duly qualified medical practitioners named in the order, and not being witnesses on either side, and may make such order with respect to the costs of such examination as he thinks fit.

(2) If the person injured refuses to submit himself to such examination, or in any way obstructs the same, his right to compensation or damages under any Act or law shall be suspended, and all proceedings brought by him in respect of such compensation or damages shall be stayed, while such refusal continues.

(3) This section applies to the Crown and to every Department of the public service.

(4) Nothing in this section shall affect the provisions of the Workers' Compensation Act 1956.

100A. Notwithstanding anything in section 3 of the Judicature Amendment Act 1930, the Governor General may from time to time, by Order in Council, make regulations for all or any of the following purposes:

(*a*) Prescribing the matters in respect of which fees are payable under this Act:

(*b*) Prescribing scales of fees for the purposes of this Act and for the purposes of any proceeding before the Supreme Court or the Court of Appeal, whether under this Act or any other enactment:

(*ba*) Prescribing the fees, travelling allowances, and expenses payable to interpreters and to persons giving evidence in proceedings to which this Act applies:

(*c*) Prescribing the poundage payable under section *37* and section *38* of this Act:

(*d*) Conferring on a Registrar, a Deputy Registrar, or any other person the power to determine the amount of the fee or poundage payable in a particular case and whether any fees or poundage should be refunded, remitted, or reduced:

(*e*) Altering or revoking the Sheriffs' Fees Notice 1952 and any rules relating to fees contained in the Code of Civil Procedure set forth in the Second Schedule to this Act or in the Rules of the Court of Appeal set forth in the Third Schedule to this Act or any other rules of the Supreme Court of Court of Appeal relating to fees made before the commencement of this section.

AN ACT TO AMEND THE JUDICATURE ACT 1908[1]

October 20, 1972 amended 1977, 1978

BE IT ENACTED by the General Assemnly of New Zealand in Parliament assembled, and by the authority of the same, as follows:

1. Short Title. This Act may be cited as the Judicature Amendment Act 1972, and shall be read together with and deemed part of the Judicature Act 1908 (hereinafter referred to as the principal Act).

PART I

SINGLE PROCEDURE FOR THE JUDICIAL REVIEW OF THE EXERCISE OF OR FAILURE TO EXERCISE A STATUTORY POWER

2. Relation to Part I of principal Act and commencement of this Part.

(1) This Part of this Act shall be deemed part of Part I of the principal Act.

(2) This Part of this Act shall come into force on the 1st day of January 1973.

3. Interpretation. In this Part of this Act, unless the context otherwise requires,

'Application for review' means an application under sub-section (1) of section *4* of this Act:

'Decision' includes a determination or order:

'Licence' includes any permit, warrant, authorization, registration, certificate, approval, or similar form of authority required by law:

'Person' includes a corporation sole, and also a body of persons whether incorporated or not ; and, in relation to the exercise, refusal to exercise, or proposed or purported exercise by any person of a statutory power of decision, includes a Magistrate's Court, the Court of Arbitration, the Compensation Court, the Maori Land Court, and the Maori Appellate Court:

'Statutory power' means a power or right conferred by or under any Act – or by or under the constitution or other instrument of incorporation, rules, or byelaws of any body corporate;

[1] *Judicature Amendment* 1972, No. 130.

(*a*) To make any regulation, rule, byelaw, or order or to give any notice or direction having force as subordinate legislation; or

(*b*) To exercise a statutory power of decision; or

(*c*) To require any person to do or refrain from doing any act or thing that, but for such requirement, he would not be required by law to do or refrain from doing; or

(*d*) To do any act or thing that would, but for such power or right, be a breach of the legal rights of any person; or

(*e*) To make any investigation or inquiry into the rights, powers, privileges, immunities, duties, or liabilities of any person.

'Statutory power of decision' means a power or right conferred by or under any Act or by or under the constitution or other instrument of incorporation, rules or bylaws of any body corporate, to make a decision deciding or prescribing or affecting

(*a*) The rights, powers, privileges, immunites, duties, or liabilities of any person; or

(*b*) The eligibility of any person to receive, or to continue to receive, a benefit or licence, whether he is entitled to it or not.

4. Application for review.

(1) On an application which may be called an application for review, the High Court may, notwithstanding any right of appeal possessed by the applicant in relation to the subject-matter of the application, by order grant, in relation to the exercise, refusal to exercise, or proposed or purported exercise by any person of a statutory power, any relief that the applicant would be entitled to, in any one or more of the proceedings for a writ or order of or in the nature of mandamus, prohibition, or certiorari or for a declaration or injunction, against that person in any such proceedings.

(2) Where on an application for review the applicant is entitled to an order declaring that a decision made in the exercise of a statutory power of decision is unauthorized or otherwise invalid, the Court may, instead of making such a declaration, set aside the decision.

(2A) Notwithstanding any rule of law to the contrary, it shall not be a bar to the grant of relief in proceedings for a writ or an order of or in the nature of certiorari or prohibition, or to the grant of relief on an application for review, that the person who has exercised, or is proposing to exercise, a statutory power was not under a duty to act judicially; but this sub-section shall not be construed to enlarge or modify the grounds on which the Court may treat an applicant as being entitled to an order of or in the nature of certiorari or prohibition under the foregoing provisions of this section.

(3) Where in any of the proceedings referred to in sub-section (1) of this section the Court had, before the commencement of this Part of this Act, a discretion to refuse to grant relief on any grounds, it shall have the like discretion, on like grounds, to refuse to grant any relief on an application for review.

(4) Sub-section (3) of this section shall not apply to the discretion of the Court, before the commencement of this Part of this Act, to refuse to grant relief

in any of the said proceedings on the ground that the relief should have been sought in any other of the said proceedings.

(5) Without limiting the generality of the foregoing provisions of this section, on an application for review in relation to the exercise, refusal to exercise, or purported exercise of a statutory power of decision the Court if it is satisfied that the applicant is entitled to relief under sub-section (1) of this section, may, in addition to or instead of granting any other relief under the foregoing provisions of this section, direct any person whose act or omission is the subject-matter of the application to reconsider and determine, either generally or in respect of any specified matter, the whole or any part of any matter to which the application relates: In giving any such direction the Court shall

(*a*) Advise the person of its reasons for so doing; and

(*b*) Give to him such directions as it thinks just as to the reconsideration or otherwise of the whole or any part of the matter that is referred back for reconsideration.

(5A) If the Court gives a direction under sub-section (5) of this section it may make any order that it could make by way of interim order under section *8* of this Act, and that section shall apply accordingly, so far as it is applicable and with all necessary modifications.

(5B) Where any matter is referred back to any person under sub-section (5) of this section, that person shall have jurisdiction to reconsider and determine the matter in accordance with the Court's direction notwithstanding anything in any other enactment.

(5C) Where any matter is referred back to any person under sub-section (5) of this section, the act or omission that is to be reconsidered shall, subject to any interim order made by the Court under sub-section (5A) of this section, continue to have effect according to its tenor unless and until it is revoked or amended by that person.

(6) In reconsidering any matter referred back to him under sub-section (5) of this section the person to whom it is so referred shall have regard to the Court's reasons for giving the direction and to the Court's direction.

5. Defects in form, or technical irregularites. On an application for review in relation to a statutory power of decision, where the sole ground of relief established is a defect in form or a technical irregularity, if the Court finds that no substantial wrong or miscarriage of justice has occurred, it may refuse relief and, where the decision has already been made, may make an order validating the decision, notwithstanding the effect or irregularity, to have effect from such time and on such terms as the Court thinks fit.

6. Disposal of proceedings for mandamus, prohibition, or certiorari. Where proceedings are commenced for a writ or order of or in the nature of mandamus, prohibition, or certoirari, in relation to the exercise, refusal to exercise, or proposed or purported exercise of a statutory power, the proceedings shall be treated and disposed of as if they were an application for review.

7. Disposal of proceedings for declaration or injunction. Where proceedings are commenced for a declaration or injunction, or both, whether with or without a claim for other relief, and the exercise, refusal to exercise, or proposed or purported exercise of a statutory power is an issue in the proceedings, the Court on the application of any party to the proceedings may, if it considers it appropriate, direct that the proceedings be treated and disposed of, so far as they relate to that issue, as if they were an application for review.

8. (1) Subject to sub-section (2) of this section, at any time before the final determination of an application for review, and on the application of any party, the Court may, if in its opinion it is necessary to do so for the purpose of preserving the position of the applicant, make an interim order for all or any of the following purposes:

(*a*) Prohibition or staying any proceedings, civil or criminal, in connection with any matter to which the application for review relates: Declaring any licence that has been revoked or suspended in the

(*b*) Prohibition or staying any proceedings, civil or criminal, in connection with any matter to which the application for review relates:

(*c*) Declaring any licence that has been revoked or suspended in the exercise of the statutory power, or that will expire by effluxion of time before the final determination of the application for review, to continue and, where necessary, to be deemed to have continued in force.

(2) Where the Crown is the respondent (or one of the respondents) to the application for review the Court shall not have power to make any order against the Crown under paragraph (*a*) or paragraph (*b*) of this section; but, instead, in any such case the Court may, by interim order

(*a*) Declare that the Crown ought not to take any further action that is or would be consequential on the exercise of the statutory power:

(*b*) Declare that the Crown ought not to institute or continue with any proceedings, civil or criminal, in connection with any matter to which the application for review relates.

(3) Any order under sub-section (1) of sub-section (2) of this section may be made subject to such terms and conditions as the Court thinks fit, and may be expressed to continue in force until the application for review is finally determined or until such other date, or the happening of such other event, as the Court may specify.

9. (1) An application for review shall be made by motion accompanied by a statement of claim.

(2) The statement of claim shall

(*a*) State the facts on which the applicant bases his claim to relief:

(*b*) State the grounds on which the applicant seeks relief:

(*c*) State the relief sought.

(3) It shall not be necessary for the statement of claim to specify the proceedings referred to in section *4*(1) of this Act in which the claim would have been made before the commencement of this Part of this Act.

(4) The person whose act or omission is the subject-matter of the application for review, and, subject to any direction given by a Judge under section *10* of this Act, every party to the proceedings (if any) in which any decision to which the application relates was made, shall be cited as a respondent.

(5) For the purposes of sub-section (4) of this section where the act or omission is that of any 2 or more persons acting together under a collective title, they shall be cited by their collective title.

(6) Subject to any direction given by a Judge under section *10* of this Act, every respondent to the application for review shall file a statement of his defence to the statement of claim.

(7) Subject to this Part of this Act, the procedure in respect of any application for review shall be in accordance with the rules of Court.

10. (1) For the purpose of ensuring that any application or intended application for review may be determined in a convenient and expeditious manner, and that all matters in dispute may be effectively and completely determined, a Judge may at any time, either on the application of any party or intended party or without any such application, and on such terms as he thinks fit, direct the holding of a conference of parties or intended parties or their counsel presided over by a Judge.

(2) At any such conference the Judge presiding may

(*a*) Settle the issues to be determined:

(*b*) Direct what persons shall be cited, or need not be cited, as respondents to the application for review, or direct that the name of any party be added or struck out:

(*c*) Direct what parties shall be served:

(*d*) Direct by whom and within what time any statement of defence shall be filed:

(*e*) Require any party to make admissions in respect of questions of fact; and, if that party refuses to make an admission in respect of any such question, that party shall be liable to bear the costs of proving that question, unless the Judge by whom the application for review is finally determined is satisfied that the party's refusal was reasonable in all the circumstances, and accordingly orders otherwise in respect of those costs:

(*f*) Fix a time by which any affidavits or othe documents shall be filed:

(*g*) Fix a time and place for the hearing of the application for review:

(*h*) Require further or better particulars of any facts, or of the grounds for relief, or of the relief sought, or of the grounds of defence, or of any other circumstances connected with the application for review:

(*i*) Require any party to make discovery of documents, or permit any party to administer interrogatories:

(*j*) In the case of an application for review of a decision made in the exercise of a statutory power of decision, determine whether the whole or any part of the record of the proceedings in which the decision was made should be filed in Court, and give such directions as he thinks fit as to its filing:

(*k*) Exercise any powers of discretion or appointment vested in the Court or a Judge by the rules of Court in respect of originating applications:

(*l*) Give such consequential directions as may be necessary.

(3) Notwithstanding any of the foregoing provisions of this section, a Judge may, at any time before the hearing of an application for review had been commenced, exercise any of the powers specified in sub-section (2) of this section without holding a conference under sub-section (1) of this section.

IV. The Commissions of Inquiry Act 1908[1]

August 4. 1908. as amended and consolidated to 1975

1. Short Title and savings.

(1) The Short Title of this Act is the Commissions of Inquiry Act 1908.

(2) This Act is a consolidation of the enactments mentioned in the Schedule hereto, and with respect to those enactments the following provisions shall apply:

(*a*) All Commissions, appointments, rules, Orders in Council, orders, instruments, and generally all acts of authority which originated under any of the said enactments or any enactment thereby repealed, and are subsisting or in force on the coming into operation of this Act, shall enure for the purposes of this Act as fully and effectually as if they had originated under the corresponding provisions of this Act, and accordingly shall, where necessary, be deemed to have so originated:

(*b*) All matters and proceedings commenced under any such enactment, and pending or in progress on the coming into operation of this Act, may be continued, completed, and enforced under this Act.

2. Appointment of Commissions of Inquiry. The Governor General may, by Order in Council, appoint any person or persons to be a Commission to inquire into and report upon any question arising out of or concerning

(*a*) The administration of the Government; or

(*b*) The working of any existing law; or

(*c*) The necessity or expediency of any legislation; or

(*d*) The conduct of any officer in the service of the Crown; or

(*e*) Any disaster or accident (whether due to natural causes or otherwise) in which members of the public were killed or injured or were or might have been exposed to risk of death or injury:

(*f*) Any other matter of public importance.

[1] The Commissions of Inquiry Act 1908, No. 25. An Act to consolidate certain enactments of the General Assembly relating to commissions of inquiry appointed by the Governor General in Council or by the Governor General. *4, August 1908.*

3. Members of Commissions protected. So long as any member of any such Commission acts ***bona fide*** in the discharge of his duties, no action shall lie against him for anything he may report or say in the course of the inquiry.

4. Commissioners' powers.

(1) For the purposes of the inquiry, every such Commission shall have the powers of a Magistrate's Court, in the exercise of its civil jurisdiction, in respect of citing parties, summoning witnesses, administering oaths, hearing evidence, and conducting and maintaining order at the inquiry.

(2) For the purposes of this section, the power to issue summonses requiring the attendance of witnesses or the production of documents, or to do any other act preliminary or incidental to the hearing of any matter by the Commission, including any such power vested in a Registrar of any Court by any Act or rules, may be exercised by the Commission or its Chairman, or by an officer of the Commission purporting to act by direction or with the authority of the Commission or its Chairman.

4. Persons interested entitled to be heard at inquiry. Any person interested in the inquiry shall, if he satisfies the Commission that he has an interest in the inquiry apart from any interest in common with the public, be entitled to appear and be heard at the inquiry as if he had been cited as a party to the inquiry.

5. Service of summons. Every summons to a witness shall be served either by delivering the same to the person summoned or by leaving the same at his usual place of abode at least 24 hours before his attendance is required.

6. Protection of witnesses and counsel. Every witness attending and giving evidence in pursuance of any such summons, and every counsel appearing before any Commission, shall have the same privileges and immunities as witnesses and counsel in Courts of law.

7. Witnesses' allowances. Every witness attending in pursuance of any such summons shall be entitled to expenses for travelling and maintenance during his absence from his usual place of abode according to the scale allowed to witnesses in civil cases by the rules of the Supreme Court:

Provided that persons prosecuting any claim before a Commission shall not be entitled to be paid any money under this section.

8. Payment of witnesses' allowances.

(1) Where the Commission had obtained the authority in writing of the Minister of Internal Affairs for summoning any witness, the expenses of what witness shall, if certified by the Chairman of the Commission, be paid by the Minister of Finance out of the Consolidated Revenue Account.

(2) In every other case the person requiring the evidence of any witness shall, before the summons is issued, deposit with the Commission such sum of money as the Commission deems sufficient, and the expenses of the witness shall be paid out of the sum so deposited.

9. Non-attendance, etc., of witness. Every person who, after being duly summoned to attend before the Commission, or to produce thereto any books, papers, writings, or documents, (*a*) Fails to appear according to the exigency of such summons; or

(*b*) Refuses to be sworn or to give evidence, or to make answer to such questions as may be put to him by the Commission or any member thereof touching the subject of the inquiry; or

(*c*) Fails to produce any such books, papers, writings, or documents,

is liable for every such default to a fine not exceedings $40:

Provided that no person so summoned shall be liable to any such fine unless at the time of the service of the summons there was made to him a payment or a tender of his travelling expenses, according to the scale allowed to witnesses in civil cases by the rules of the Supreme Court.

10. References of point of law to Supreme Court.

(1) The Commission may refer any disputed point of law arising in the course of an inquiry to the Supreme Court for decision, and for this purpose may either conclude the inquiry subject to such decision or may at any stage of the inquiry adjourn it until after such decision has been given.

(2) The question shall be in the form of a special case to be drawn up by the parties (if any) to the inquiry, and, if the parties do not agree, or if there are no parties, to be settled by the Commission.

(3) The decision of he Supreme Court shall be final and binding upon all parties to the inquiry and upon the Commission.

11. Power to award costs. The Commission, upon the hearing of an inquiry, may order that the whole or any portion of the costs of the inquiry or of any party thereto shall be paid by any of the parties to the inquiry, or by all or any of the persons who have procured the inquiry to be held:

Provided that no such order shall be made against any person who has not been cited as a party or authorized by the Commission, pursuant to section *4A* of this Act, to appear and be heard at the inquiry or summoned to attend and give evidence at the inquiry.

12. Enforcing orders for costs.

(1) For the purpose of enforcing any order of the Commission for the payment of costs. a duplicate of such order may be filed by the person to whom the costs are payable in the office of the Court named in the order, and shall thereupon be enforceable in all respects as a final judgment of that Court in its civil jurisdiction.

(1) In every case where an order for costs is made, the order shall name the Court in which the order may, of necessary, be enforced.

(3) The Court so named shall, where the amount recoverable under the order

(*a*) Exceeds $200, be the Supreme Court; and

(*b*) Does not exceed $200, be the Magistrate's Court.

13. Powers of Judges when Commissioner.

(1) In every case where under this Act, or any other Act or the Letters Patent constituting the office of Governor General, the Governor General or the Governor General in Council appoints one or more Judges of the Supreme Court to

be members of a Commission for the purpose of holding any inquiry, every such Judge, and the Commission of which he is a member, shall for all the purposes of such inquiry, have the same powers, privileges, and immunities as are possessed by a Judge of the Supreme Court in the exercise of his civil jurisdiction under the Judicature Act 1908.

(2) For the purpose of enforcing any order made by such Commission the order shall, as soon as conveniently may be after the making thereof, be drawn up and signed by the Chairman (whose signature and status shall be judicially noticed), and may be filed in any office of the Supreme Court, whereupon the order shall be enforceable in the same manner as a final judgment of that Court in civil proceedings.

(3) In the case of every such member the provisions of this section shall be deemed to supersede those of section *3* hereof; and, in the case of every Commission of which he is a member sub-section (1) of section *4* hereof shall be read as if the words 'Judge of the Supreme Court' were substituted for the words 'Magistrate's Court', and section *10* substituted for the words 'Supreme Court'.

14. Power to make scale of costs. Any 3 or more Judges of the Supreme Court, of whom the Chief Justice shall be one, may from time to time make rules prescribing a scale of costs payable in respect of any inquiry under this Act:

Provided that all such rules shall be subject to the approval of the Governor General in Council.

15. Extent of Act. This Act shall extend and apply to all inquiries held by Commissioners appointed by the Governor General or the Governor General in Council under any Act or such Letters Patent as aforesaid.

V. The Deputy Governor 's Powers Act, 1912[1]

September 12, 1912

Whereas by certain Letters Patent passed under the Great Seal of the United Kingdom of Great Brtiain and Ireland, bearing date the eighteenth day of November, nineteen hundred and seven, permanent provision was made for the office of Governor in and over the Dominion of New Zealand: *And whereas* by the said Letters Patent it is provided that in certain circumstances all the powers and authorities therein granted to the Governor shall be vested in the Lieutenant Governor, or , if there be no such officer in the Dominion, then in such person or persons as may be appointed by Royal Sign Manual and Signet to administer the Government of the Dominion: *And whereas* by the said Letters Patent it is further provided that in certain circumstances the Governor may, by an instrument under the Public Seal of the Dominion, constitute and appoint a Deputy to exercise, perform, and execute for and on behalf of the Governor, during his temporary absence from the seat of Government or from the Dominion, all such powers and authoritties vested in the

[1] 1912, No. 4. *An act to provide for the Exercise by Deputy of certain Powers and Authorities vested in the Governor General.*

Governor by the said Letters Patent as shall in and by such instrument be specified and limited, but no others: *And whereas* by the law in force in New Zealand certain powers and authorities have been from time to time and may hereafter be conferred on the Governor General of New Zealand: And whereas it is expedient to extend the powers and authorities which any such Deputy if and when appointed may exercise, and to validate the acts of any person previously appointed as such Deputy;

1. Short Title. This Act may be cited as the Deputy Governor's Powers Act, 1912.

2. Interpretation. In this Act the expression ' the said Letters Patent' means the Letters Patent mentioned in the preamble of this Act, or any Letters Patent at any time passed in lieu therof or in addition thereto.

3. Governor General's statutory as well as other powers exercisable by Deputy. During the temporary absence of the Governor General from the seat of Government or from New Zealand all the powers and authorities conferred on or vested in the Governor General by any Act or law in force in New Zealand, as well as the powers and authorities conferred upon or vested in the Governor General by the said Letters Patent, shall and may be exercised by the person appointed by the Governor General to be his Deputy during such absence, subject, nevertheless, to anything expressed in the instrument appointing such Deputy.

4. Same provision as to Deputy of Lieutenant Governor or Administrator. During such time as the powers and authorities in the said Letters Patent granted to the Governor General are vested in the said Lieutenant Governor, or such other persons as is appointed as aforesaid to administer the Government of New Zealand, the provisions of section three hereof shall apply to the person appointed to be the Deputy of the Lieutenant Governor, or of such other person appointed to administer the Government as aforesaid, during his temporary absence from the seat of Government or from New Zealand, subject, nevertheless, to anything expressed in the instrument appointing such Deputy.

5. Act to be retrospective. The exercise, before the passing of this Act by a Deputy of the Governor General, or of any other person for the time being appointed to administer the Government of New Zealand, of any of the powers or authorities conferred on or vested in the Governor General by any Act or law then in force in New Zealand shall be and be deemed to have been of the same validity, and shall have and be deemed to have had the same force and effect, as if the same had been authorized by any Letters Patent then in force.

VI. Letters Patent Relating to the Office of Governor General

April 17, 1919

His Excellency the Governor General has it in command from His Majesty the King to publish the following Letters Patent constituting the office of Governor General of New Zealand, further Letters Patent amending the same, and Instructions relating to the execution of that office, and the Commission appointing the Governor General.

Liverpool, Governor General.

Government House,
Wellington 17th April, 1919.

LETTERS PATENT, DATED 11TH MAY, 1917,[1] AMENDED 1918

George the Fifth, by the Grace of God of the United Kingdom of Great Britain and Ireland and of the British Dominions beyond the Seas King, Defender of the Faith, Emperor of India: To all to whom these Presents shall come, Greeting.

Recites Imperial Act 26 & 27 Vict., c. 23

Whereas by an Act passed in the Session holden in the Twenth-sixth and Twenty-seventh years of the reign of Her Majesty Queen Victoria, entitled 'An Act to alter the Boundaries of New Zealand.' the Colony of New Zealand was defined as comprising all Territories, Islands, and Countries lying between the one hundred and sixty-second degree of East Longitude and the one hundred and seventy-third degree of West Longitude and between the thirty-third and fifty-third parallels of South Latitude:

Recites Governor's Proclamation of 21st July, 1887

And Whereas by a Proclamation bearing date the twenty-first day of July 1887, issued by the Governor of New Zealand under authority of Letters Patent passed under the Great Seal of Our United Kingdom, bearing date the eighteenth day of January 1887, the Islands situate in the South Pacific Ocean between the parallels of 29 degrees and 32 degrees South Latitude and the meridians of 177 degrees and 180 degrees West Longitude, known as the Kermadec Group, were, from and after the first day of August, 1887, annexed to and become part of the Colony of New Zealand:

Recites Governor's Proclamation of 10th June, 1901

And whereas by a Proclamation bearing date the tenth day of June 1901, issued by the Governor of New Zealand by authority of an Order by His late Majesty King Edward the Seventh in His Privy Council dated the thirteenth day of May 1901, made by virtue and in exercise of the powers vested in Him by the Colonial Boundaries Act 1895, the Boundaries of the Colony of New Zealand were on and after the eleventh day of June 1901 extended so as to include the islands of the Cook Group,

[1] *Letters Patent passed under the Great Seal of the United Kingdom, constituting the Office of Governor General and Commander-in-Chief of the Dominion of New Zealand.* The New Zealand Gazette, April 24, 1919, amended by Letters Patent of December 18, 1918.

and all other the Islands and Territories which were then or might hereafter form part of Our Dominions situate within the following boundary line, viz.: A line commencing at a point at the intersection of the 23rd degree of South Latitude and the 156th degree of Longitude West of Greenwich, and proceeding due North to the point of intersection of the 8th degree of South Latitude and the 156th degree of Longitude West of Greenwich, thence due West to the point of intersection of the 8th degree of Sough Latitude and the 167th degree of Longitude West of Greenwich, thence due South to the point of intersection of the 17th degree of South Latitude and the 167th degree of Longitude West of Greenwich, thence due West to the point of intersection of the 17th Degree of South Latitude and the 170th degree of Longitude West of Greenwich, thence due South to the point of intersection of the 23rd degree of South Latitude and the 170th degree of Longitude West of Greenwich, and thence due East to the point of intersection of the 23rd degree of South Latitude and the 156th degree of Longitude West of Greenwich:

Recites Royal Proclamation of 9th September, 1907

And whereas by Royal Proclamation, bearing date the ninth day of September, 1907, His said Majesty did ordain, declare, and command that on and after the Twenty-sixth day of Sepember 1907 the Colony of New Zealand and the territory belonging thereto should be called and known by the title of the Dominion of New Zealand:

Recites Letters Patent of 18th November, 1907

And whereas, by certain Letters Patent, under the Great Seal of Our United Kingdom of Great Britain and Ireland, bearing date at Westminister the Eighteenth day of November 1907, His said Majesty did constitute, order, and declare that there should be a Governor and Commander-in-Chief in and over the Dominion of New Zealand (therein called the Dominion) and that appointments to the said Office when vacant should be made by Commission under the Royal Sign Manual and Signet:

And whereas it has been represented to Us that it is expedient that the designation of the Officer administering the Government of Our Dominion of New Zealand should be changed from Governor and Commander-in-Chief to Governor General and Commander-in-Chief and it has accordingly become necessary to make provision for the office of Governor General and Commander-in-Chief in and over Our Dominion of New Zealand:

Revokes Letters Patent of 18th November, 1907, Constitutes the Office of Governor General and Commander-in-Chief of the Dominion, Boundaries

1. Now therefore We do by these presents revoke and determine the above-recited Letters Patent of the Eighteenth day of November 1907 but without prejudice to anything lawfully done thereunder. And We do by these presents constitute, order, and declare that there shall be a Governor General and Commander-in-Chief in and over Our Dominion of New Zealand (herein-after called the Dominion), comprising the Territories, Islands, and Countries forming the Colony of New Zealand as defined in the above recited Act, passed in the Session holden in the Twenty-sixth and Twenty-seventh Years of the Reign of Her Majesty Queen Victoria, entitled "An Act to alter the Boundaries of New Zealand," together with the further Islands and Territories included within the Boundaries of the Colony of New Zealand by the above-recited Proclamations of the Governor thereof, dated respectively the Twenty-first day of July, 1887, and the Tenth day of June 1901; and that appointments to the said office when vacant shall be made by Commission under Our Sign Manual and Signet.

Governor General's powers and authorities

II. We do hereby authorize, empower, and command Our said Governor General and Commander-in-Chief (herein-after called the Governor General) to do and execute all things that belong to his said Office, according to the tenor of these Our Letters Patent and of such Commission as may be issued to him under Our Sign Manual and Signet, and according to such Instructions as may from time to time be given to him under Our Sign Manual and Signet, or by Our Order in Our Privy Council, or by Us, through one of Our Principal Secretaries of State, and to such Laws as are now or shall hereafter be in force in the Dominion.

Publication of Governor General's Commission. Oaths to be taken by Governor General. Imperial Act 31 & 32 Vict., c. 72

III. Every person appointed to fill the Office of Governor General shall, with all due solemnity, before entering on any of the duties of his Office, cause the Commission appointing him to be Governor General to be read and published at the seat of Government, in the presence of the Chief Justice, or some other Judge of the Supreme Court of the Dominion, and of the Members of the Executive Council thereof, which being done, he shall then and there take before them the Oath of Allegiance, in the form provided by an Act passed in the Session holden in the Thirty-first and Thirty-second years of the Reign of Her Majesty Queen Victoria intituled an Act to amend the Law relating to Promissory Oaths; and likewise the usual Oath for the due execution of the Office of Governor General and for the due and impartial administration of justice; which Oaths the said Chief Justice or Judge is hereby required to administer.

Public Seal

IV. The Governor General shall keep and use the Public Seal of the Dominion for sealing all things whatsoever that shall pass the said Public Seal.

Executive Council: Constitution of

V. There shall be an Executive Council for the Dominion, and the said Council shall consist of such persons as were immediately before the coming into force of these Our Letters Patent Members of the Executive Council of New Zealand, or as may at any time be Members of the Executive Council of the Dominion in accordance with any Law enacted by the Legislature of the Dominion, and of such other persons as the Governor General shall, from time to time, in Our name and on Our behalf, but subject to any Law as aforesaid, appoint under the Public Seal of the Dominion to be Members of the Executive Council of the Dominion.

Grant of lands

VI. The Governor General, in Our name and on Our behalf, may make and execute, under the said Public Seal, grants and dispositions of any lands which may be lawfully granted and disposed of by Us within the Dominion.

Appointment of Judges, Justices, &c.

VII. The Governor General may constitute and appoint, in Our name and on Our behalf, all such Judges, Commissioners, Justices of the Peace, and other necessary Officers and Ministers of the Dominion as may be lawfully constituted or appointed by Us.

Grant of pardons. Remission of fines. Proviso. Banishment

VIII. When any crime has been committed within the Dominion, or for which the offender may be tried therein, the Governor General may as he shall see occasion, in Our name and on Our behalf, grant a pardon to any accomplice in such crime who shall give such information as shall lead to the conviction of the principal offender, or of any one of such offenders if more than one; and further, may grant to any offender convicted in any Court, or before any Judge, or other Magistrate, within the Dominion, a pardon, either free or subject to lawful conditions, or any remission of the sentence passed on such offender, or any respite of the execution of such sentence for such period as the Governor General thinks fit; and further may remit any fines, penalties, or forfeitures, due or accrued to Us. Provided always that the Governor General shall in no case, except where the offence has been of a political nature unaccompanied by any other grave crime, make it a condition of any pardon or remission of sentence that the offender shall absent himself or be removed from the Dominion.

Suspension or removal from office

IX. The Governor General may, so far as We Ourselves lawfully may, upon sufficient cause to him appearing, remove from his office, or suspend from the exercise of the same, any person exercising any office or place within the Dominion under or by virtue of any Commission or Warrant granted, or which may be granted, by Us, in Our name, or under Our authority.

Summoning, proroguing or dissolving any Legislative Body
Appointment of Members

X. The Governor General may exercise all powers lawfully belonging to Us in respect of the summoning, proroguing, or dissolving any Legislative Body, which now is or hereafter may be established within the Dominion, and in respect of the appointment of Members thereto.

Succession to the Government. Lieutenant-Governor Administrator.
Proviso. Lieutenant-Governor, &c., to take Oaths of office before administering the Government Duties and authorities under Letters Patent

XI. In the event of the death, incapacity, or removal of the Governor General, or of his departure from the Dominion, Our Lieutenant Governor, or, if there be no such Officer in the Dominion, then such person or persons as We may appoint under Our Sign Manual and Signet, shall, during Our pleasure, administer the Government of the Dominion, first taking the Oaths herein-before directed to be taken by the Governor General, and in the manner herein prescribed; which being done, We do hereby authorize, empower, and command Our Lieutenant Governor, and every other such Administrator as aforesaid, to do and execute during Our pleasure all things that belong to the Office of Governor General and Commander in Chief according to the tenor of these Our Letters Patent, and accorfing to Our Instructions as aforesaid, and the Laws of the Dominion.

Governor General may appoint a Deputy during his temporary absence

XII. In the event of the Governor General having occasion to be temporarily absent for a short period from the seat of Government or from the Dominion, he may in every such case, by an Instrument under the Public Seal of the Dominion, constitute and appoint Our Lieutenant Governor, or if there be no such Officer, then any other person to be his Deputy during such temporary absence, and in that capacity to exercise, perform, and execute for and on behalf of the Governor-General during such absence, but no longer, all such powers and authorities vested in the Governor General by these Our Letters Patent, as shall in and by such Instrument be specified and limited, but no others. Provided, nevertheless, that, by the appointment of a Deputy as aforesaid, the power and authority of the Governor General shall not be abridged, altered, or in any way affected, otherwise than We may at any time hereafter think proper to direct.

Officers and others to obey and assist the Governor General

XIII. And We do hereby require and command all Our Officers and Ministers, Civil and Military, and all other inhabitants of the Dominion, to be obedient, aiding, and assisting unto the Governor-General, or such person or persons as may from time to time, under the provisions of these Out Letters Patent, administer the Government of the Dominion.

Power reserved to His Majesty to revoke alter,
or amend the present Letters Patent

XIV. And We do hereby reserve to Ourselves, Our heirs and successors, full power and authority from time to time to revoke, alter, or amend these Our Letters Patent as to Us or them shall seem meet.

Publication of Letters Patent

XV. And We do direct and enjoin that these Our Letters Patent shall be published within Our Dominion at such time and in such manner as the Officer administering the Government thereof shall think fit. They shall commence and come into operation as from the twenty-eighth day of June 1917, and that date shall be and shall be deemed for all purpose to be the date of their commencement.

In Witness whereof We have caused these Our Letters to be made Patent. Witness Ourself at Westminster, the Eleventh day of May in the Eighth year of Our Reign.

By Warrant under the King's Sign Manual.

Schuster

INSTRUCTIONS TO OUR GOVERNOR GENERAL AND COMMANDER-IN-CHIEF IN AND OVER OUR DOMINION OF NEW ZEALAND, OR IN HIS ABSENCE TO OUR LIEUTENANT GOVERNOR OR OTHER OFFICER FOR THE TIME BEING ADMINISTERING THE GOVERNMENT OF OUR SAID DOMINION[1]

Dated 11th May, 1917

PREAMBLE

Recites Letters Patent, constituting the Office of Governor General

Whereas by certain Letters Patent bearing even date herewith We have constituted, ordered and declared that there shall be a Governor General and Commander-in-Chief (therein and herein-after called the Governor General) in and over Our Dominion of New Zealand (therein and herein-after called the Dominion):

[1] Instructions passed under the Royal Sign Manual and Signet to the Governor General and Commander-in-Chief of the Dominion of New Zealand.

And whereas We have thereby authorized and commanded the Governor General to do and execute all things that belong to his said office, according to the tenor of of Our said Letters Patent, and of such Commission as may be issued to him under Our Sign Manual and Signet, and according to such Instructions as may from time to time be given him under Our Sign Manual and Signet or by Our Order in Our Privy Council or by Us through one of Our Principal Secretaries of State, and to such Laws as are now or shall hereafter be in force in the Dominion:

Now Know you that We do by these Our Instructions under Our Sign Manual and Signet direct and enjoin and declare Our will and pleasure as follows:

Interpretation

I. In these Our Instructions, unless inconsistent with the context, the term "the Governor-General" shall include every person for the time being administering the Government of the Dominion, and the term "the Executive Council" shall mean the members of the Executive Council for the Dominion who are for the time being the responsible advisers of the Governor General.

Oaths to be administered by Governor General

II. The Governor General may, whenever he thinks fit, require any person in the public service to take the Oath of Allegiance, together with such other Oath or Oaths as may from time to time be prescribed by any Law in force in the Dominion. The Governor-General is to administer such Oaths or cause them to be administered by some Public Officer of the Dominion.

Governor General to communicate Instructions to Executive Council

III. The Governor General shall forthwith communicate these Our Instructions to the Executive Council, and likewise all such others, from time to time, as he shall find convenient for Our service to impart to them.

Quorum, Executive Council

IV. The Executive Council shall not proceed to the despatch of business unless two members at the least (exclusive of the Governor General or of the member presiding) be present and assisting throughout the whole of the meetings at which any such business shall be despatched.

Governor-General to take advice of Executive Council

V. In the execution of the powers and authorities vested in him, the Governor General shall be guided by the advice of the Executive Council, but if in any case he shall see sufficient cause to dissent from the opinion of the said Council, he may act in the exercise of his said powers and authorities in opposition to the opinion of the Council, reporting the matter to Us without delay, with the reasons for his so acting.

In any such case it shall be competent to any Member of the said Council to require that there be recorded upon the Minutes of the Council the grounds of any advice or opinion that he may give upon the question.

Laws sent home to have marginal abstracts
Journals and Minutes of Parliament

VI. The Governor General is to take care that all laws assented to by him in Our name, or reserved for the signification of Our pleasure thereon, shall, when transmitted by him, be fairly abstracted in the margins, and be accompanied, in such cases as may seem to him necessary, with such explanatory observations as may be required to exhibit the reasons and occasions for proposing such laws; and he shall also transmit fair copies of the Journals and Minutes of the proceedings of the Parliament of the Dominion which he is to require from the clerks, or other proper officers in that behalf, of the said Parliament.

Regulation of power of pardon

VII. The Governor General shall not pardon or reprieve any offender without first receiving in capital cases the advice of the Executive Council and in other cases the advice of one, at least, of his Ministers; and in any cases in which such pardon or reprieve might directly affect the interests of Our Empire, or of any country or place beyond the jurisdiction of the Government of the Dominion, the Governor-General shall, before deciding as to either pardon or reprieve, take those interests specially into his own personal consideration in conjunction with such advice as aforesaid.

Judges, &c., to be appointed during pleasure

VIII. All Commissions granted by the Governor-General to any persons to be Judges, Justices of the Peace, or other officers, shall, unless otherwise provided by law, be granted during pleasure only.

Governor General's absence. Temporary absence

IX. The Governor General shall not quit the Dominion without first having obtained leave from Us for so doing under Our Sign Manual and Signet, or through one of Our Principal Secretaries of State, except for the purpose of visiting the Governor General of the Commonwealth of Australia, or the Governor of any neighbouring Colony or State for periods not exceeding one month at any one time, nor exceeding in the aggregate one month for every year's service in the Dominion.

Governor General's absence and departure from the Dominion
Interpretation clause

X. The temporary absence of the Governor General for any period not exceeding one month shall not, if he have previously informed the Executive Council, in writing, of his intended absence, and if he have duly appointed a Deputy in accordance with Our said Letters Patent, nor shall any extension of such period sanctioned by one of Our Principal Secretaries of State and not exceeding fourteen days, be deemed a departure from the Dominion within the meaning of Our said Letters Patent.

Revokes Instructions of 18th November, 1907

XI. From and after the date of the coming into operation of Our above-recited Letters Patent of even date, the Instructions issued to the Governor of the Dominion of New Zealand under the Sign Manual and Signet of His late Majesty King Edward the Seventh, bearing date the Eighteenth day of November 1907 shall, without prejudice to anything lawfully done thereunder, be revoked.

Given at Our Court at Saint James's this Eleventh day of May 1917, in the Eighth year of Our Reign.

VII. Statute of Westminster Adoption Act 1947[1]

November 25, 1947

Be it enacted by the General Assembly of New Zealand in Parliament assembled, and by the authority of the same, as follows:

1. This Act may be cited as the Statute of Westminster Adoption Act, 1947.

2. Sections two, three, four, five, and six of the Act of of the Parliament of the United Kingdom cited as the Statute of Westminster, 1931 (which Act is set out in the Schedule to this Act), are hereby adopted, and the adoption of the said sections shall have effect from the commencement of this Act.

3. (1) For the purposes of section four the said Statute of Westminster, 1931, the request and consent of New Zealand to the enactment of any Act of the Parliament of the United Kingdom shall be made and given by the Parliament of New Zealand, and not otherwise.

[1] 1947, No. 38. An Act to adopt certain Sections of the Statute of Westminster, 1931.

(2) Every Act of the Parliament of the United Kingdom passed after the commencement of the Statute of Westminster, 1931, and before the commencement of this Act, that purports to apply to New Zealand, or to extend to New Zealand as part of the law of New Zealand, shall be deemed so to apply and extend and to have always so applied and extended according to its tenor, notwithstanding that it may not be expressly declared in any such Act that New Zealand has requested, and consented to, the enactment thereof.

SCHEDULE

STATUTE OF WESTMINSTER, 1931 (22 GEO. V, C. 4)

An act to give Effect to certain Resolutions passed by Imperial Conferences held in the years 1926 and 1930.

11th December, 1931

Whereas the delegates of His Majesty's Governments in the United Kingdom, the Dominion of Canada, the Commonwealth of Australia, the Dominion of New Zealand, the Union of South Africa, the Irish Free State and Newfoundland, at Imperial Conferences holden at Westminster in the years of our Lord nineteen hundred and twenty-six and nineteen hundred and thirty did concur in making the declarations and resolutions set forth in the Reports of the said Conferences;

And whereas it is meet and proper to set out by way of preamble to this Act that, inasmuch as the Crown is the symbol of the free association of the members of the British Commonwealth of Nations, and as they are united by a common allegiance to the Crown, it would be in accord with the established constitutional position of all the members of the Commonwealth in relation to one another that any alteration in the law touching the Succession to the Throne or the Royal Style and Titles shall hereafter require the assent as well of the parliaments of all the Dominions as of the Parliament of the United Kingdom;

And whereas it is in accord with the established constitutional position that no law hereafter made by the Parliament of the United Kingdom shall extend to any of the said Dominions as part of the law of that Dominion otherwise than at the request and with the consent of that Dominion;

And whereas it is necessary for the ratifying, confirming and establishing of certain of the said declarations and resolutions of the said Conferences that a law be made and enacted in due form by authority of the Parliament of the United Kingdom;

And whereas the Dominion of Canada, the Commonwealth of Australia and the Dominion of New Zealand, the Union of South Africa, the Irish Free State, and Newfoundland have severally requested and consented to the submission of a measure to the Parliament of the United Kingdom for making such provision with regard to the matters aforesaid as is hereafter in this Act contained;

Now, therefore, be it enacted by the King's most Excellent Majesty by and with the advice and consent of the Lords Spiritual and Temporal, and Commons, in this present Parliament assembled, and by the authority of the same, as follows:

1. In this Act the expression "Dominion" means any of the following Dominions, that is to say, the Dominion of Canada, the Commonwealth of Australia, the Dominion of New Zealand, the Union of South Africa, the Irish Free State and Newfoundland.

2. (1) The Colonial Laws Validity Act, 1865, shall not apply to any law made after the commencement of this Act by the Parliament of a Dominion.

(2) No law and no provision of any law made after the commencement of this Act by the Parliament of a Dominion shall be void or inoperative on the ground that it is repugnant to the law of England, or to the provisions of any existing or future Act of Parliament of the United Kingdom or to any order, rule or regulation made under any such Act, and the powers of the Parliament of a Dominion shall include the power to repeal or amend any such Act, order, rule or regulation in so far as the same is part of the law of the Dominion.

3. It is hereby declared and enacted that the Parliament of a Dominion has full power to make laws having extraterritorial operation.

4. No Act of Parliament of the United Kingdom passed after the Commencement of this Act shall extend, or be deemed to extend, to a Dominion as part of the law of that Dominion, unless it is expressly declared in that Act that that Dominion has requested, and consented, to the enactment thereof.

5. Without prejudice to the generality of the foregoing provisions of this Act, sections seven hundred and thirty-five and seven hundred and thirty-six of the Merchant Shipping Act, 1894, shall be construed as though reference therein to the Legislature of a British possession did not include reference to the Parliament of a Dominion.

6. Without prejudice to the generality of the foregoing provisions of this Act, section four of the Colonial Courts of Admiralty Act, 1890 (which requires certain laws to be reserved for the signification of His Majesty's pleasure or to contain a suspending clause), and so much of section seven of the Act as requires the approval of His Majesty in Council to any rules of Court for regulating the practice and procedure of a Colonial Court of Admiralty, shall cease to have effect in any Dominions as from the Commencement of this Act.

7. (1) Nothing in this Act shall be deemed to apply to the repeal, amendment or alteration of the British North America Acts, 1867 to 1930, or any order, rule or regulation made thereunder.

(2) The provisions of section two of this Act shall extend to laws made by any of the Provinces of Canada and to the powers of the legislatures of such Provinces.

(3) The powers conferred by this Act upon the Parliament of Canada or upon the legislatures of the Provinces shall be restricted to the enactment of laws in relation to matters within the competence of the Parliament of Canada or of any of the legislatures of the Provinces, respectively.

8. Nothing in this Act shall be deemed to confer any power to repeal or alter the Constitution or the Constitution Act of the Commonwealth of Australia or the Constitution Act of the Dominion of New Zealand otherwise than in accordance with the law existing before the commencement of this Act.

9. (1) Nothing in this Act shall be deemed to authorize the Parliament of the Commonwealth of Australia to make laws on any matter within the authority of the States of Australia, nor being a matter within the authority of the Parliament or Government of the Commonwealth of Australia.

(2) Nothing in this Act shall be deemed to require the concurrence of the Parliament or Government of the Commonwealth of Australia in any law made by the Parliament of the United Kingdom with respect to any matter within the authority of the States of Australia, not being a matter within the authority of the Parliament or Government of the Commonwealth of Australia, in any case where it would have been in accordance with the constitutional practice existing before the commencement of this Act that the Parliament of the United Kingdom should make that law without such concurrence.

(3) In the application of this Act to the Commonwealth of Australia the request and consent referred to in section four shall mean the request and consent of the Parliament and Government of the Commonwealth.

10. (1) None of the following sections of this Act, that is to say, sections two, three, four, five and six, shall extend to a Dominion to which this section applies as part of the law of that Dominion unless that section is adopted by the Parliament of the Dominion, and any Act of that Parliament adopting any section of this Act may provide that the adoption shall have effect either from the commencement of this Act or from such later date as is specified in the adopting Act.

(2) The Parliament of any such Dominion as aforesaid may at any time revoke the adoption of any section referred to in subsection (1) of this section.

(3) The Dominions to which this section applies are the Commonwealth of Australia, the Dominion of New Zealand and Newfoundland.

11. Notwithstanding anything in the Interpretation Act, 1889, the expression "Colony" shall not, in any Act of Parliament of the United Kingdom passed after the commencement of this Act, include a Dominion of any Province or State forming part of a Dominion.

12. This Act may be cited as the Statute of Westminster, 1931.

VIII. The Civil List Act 1979[1]

October 26, 1979

1. Short Title and commencement.

(1) This Act may be cited as the Civil List Act 1979.

(2) Except as provided in section 19 (4) of this Act, this Act shall come into force on the day on which it receives the Governor General's assent.

[1] 1979, No. 33. An Act to consolidate and amend the law relating to the civil list.

2. *Grants for civil purposes.* The several sums specified in this Act shall be payable in every year out of the Consolidated Account and (except as by this Act expressly provided) without further appropriation than this section.

PART I

THE GOVERNOR GENERAL

3. *Salary and allowance of Governor General.*

(1) There shall be paid to the Governor General

(*a*) A salary, which shall be paid

(i) In respect of the period beginning with the commencement of this Act and ending with the close of the 31st day of March 1980, at the rate of $26,000 a year; and

(ii) On and after the 1st day of April 1980, at the rate of $45,000 a a year; and

(b) An allowance, at a rate fixed from time to time by Order in Council, for expenses.

(2) Any Order in Council made under sub-section (1)(*b*) of this section shall come into force on a date to be specified therein, whether on or before or after the date of the making of the order.

(3) The salary and allowance of the Governor General shall

(*a*) Commence to be payable on the earliest of the following dates:

(i) The date on which he assumes the duties of his office:

(ii) The date on which he embarks or emplanes for New Zealand to assume the duties of this office:

(iii) The date on which, in the case of a person domiciled in New Zealand immediately before his appointment, he, as a preliminary to his appointment, embarks or emplanes for a destination outside New Zealand to be received in audience by the Sovereign; and

(*b*) Continue to be payable until the date on which he ceases to hold office as Governor General or on which he leaves New Zealand with the intention of vacating his office, whichever date is the earlier.

(4) Where the office of Governor General becomes vacant (otherwise than by the death of the person holding that office), there shall, in respect of the period of 3 months beginning with the date on which the vacancy occurs or on which the Governor General leaves New Zealand with the intention of vacating his office, whichever is the earlier, be paid to him a sum equal to the salary and allowance of the Governor General for that period of 3 months.

4. *Annuity for former Governor General and spouse of former Governor General.*

(1) Where a person who has held office as Governor General (whether before or after the commencement of this Act) was, at the time of that person's appointment domiciled in New Zealand, there shall (as from the end of the period of 3

months specified in section *3*(4) of this Act, but subject of sub-sections (3) to (5) of this section) be paid to that person, until the person dies.

(*a*) If that person held office as Governor General for a total period of less than 2 complete years, an annuity at the yearly rate of $3,000:

(*b*) If that person held office as Governor General for a total period of 2 complete years of more, an annuity at the yearly rate of $3,000 for each complete year (not exceeding 5) of that total period.

(2) Where a person who has held office as Governor General (whether before or after the commencement of this Act) dies, being a person who was, at the time of that person's appointment, domiciled in New Zealand, there shall, subject to sub-sections (3) to (5) of this section, be paid to the widow or widower of that person, until that widow or widower dies or remarries

(*a*) If that person held office as Governor General for a total period of less than 2 complete years, an annuity at the yearly rate of $1,500:

(*b*) If that person held office as Governor General for a total period of 2 complete years or more, an annuity at the yearly rate of $1,500 for each complete year (not exceeding 5) of that total period.

(3) No annuity shall be paid to any person under sub-section (1) or sub-section (2) of this section in respect of any period during which that person

(*a*) Is not resident or is not domiciled in New Zealand; or

(*b*) Holds an office for which a salary is payable under this Act.

(4) For the purposes of sub-section (3)(*a*) of this section, a person entitled to an annuity under sub-section (1) or sub-section (2) of this section shall be deemed not to have ceases to reside in New Zealand by reason only of his temporary absence for New Zealand occasioned by holiday or other temporary purpose.

(5) Where any person would be entitled, but for this sub-section, to be paid both an annuity under sub-section (1) or sub-section (2) of this section and an annuity under section *22* of this Act, that person,

(*a*) If the annuity payable to that person under section *22* of this Act is equal to or greater than the annuity payable to that person under sub-section (2) of this section, shall be entitled to be paid, of the applicable annuities, only an annuity under section *22* of this Act; or

(*b*) If the annuity payable to that person under section *22* of this Act is less than the annuity payable to that person under sub-section (1) or sub-section (2) of this section, shall be entitled to be paid, of the applicable annuities, only an annuity under sub-section (1) or sub-section (2) of this section.

5. Compensation for lost or adversely affected superannuation rights.

(1) Where tha superannuation rights of a person who has been appointed to the office of Governor General, or the superannuation rights of the spouse or any child of any such person, have been lost or otherwise adversely affected by that person's acceptance of the office of Governor General, there shall, from the date on which that person ceases to hold the office of Governor General, be paid to that person or to the widow or widower or child of that person, by way of compensation,

such sum or annuity or both, as may be provided for in a written agreement made between that person and the Minister of Finance before that person assumed office as Governor General.

(2) An agreement made pursuant of sub-section (1) of this section may provide for the payment of contributions by the Governor General.

(3) Every agreement made pursuant to sub-section (1) of this section shall have effect according to its tenor and, where it provides for the payment of an annuity, may provide for any annuity payable pursuant to section *4* of this Act to be payable at a rate less than that prescribed by that section.

6. Travelling expenses. There shall be paid to the Governor General all expenditure incurred in respect of the transport to and from New Zealand, and the travelling within or outside New Zealand during the Governor General's term of office, of the Governor General and the family and staff of the Governor General.

7. Power to grant exemptions from taxation.

(1) Notwithstanding anything to the contrary in any Act, but without limiting any exemption under any other Act, the Minister of Finance may from time to time wholly or partly exempt from any public or local tax, duty, rate, levy, or fee, any of the following persons:

( ) The Governor General:

(*b*) A member of the personal staff of the Governor General, if that person is resident in New Zealand solely for the purpose of performing his duties as such a member:

(*c*) The wife and any dependent child or children of the Governor General or of any person to whom paragraph (*b*) of this sub-section applies.

(2) The powers conferred on the Minister of Finance by sub-section (1) of this section shall be deemed to include

(*a*) Power to exempt from stamp duty under the Stamp and Cheque Duties Act 1971 and from any fee or duty under any other Act any instrument or class of instruments to which any of the persons referred to in that sub-section is a party:

(*b*) Power, on the death of any person referred to in that sub-section,

(i) To exempt wholly or partly from estate duty under the Estate and Gift Duties Act 1968 the estate of any such person who was not domiciled in New Zealand at the time of the appointment of the Governor General; and

(ii) To exempt any instrument or document or class of instruments or documents made for or relating to the appointment of an executor or administrator in the estate of that person, or to the administration or distribution of the estate, from stamp duty under the Stamp and Cheque Duties Act 1971 and from any fee or duty under any other Act.

(3) Any exemption granted under sub-section (1) of this section may be granted either unconditionally or subject to such conditions as the Minister of

Finance thinks fit, and the Minister may at any time revoke any such exemption or revoke, vary, or add to any such conditions.

(4) Every such exemption shall come into force on such date as may be specified in that behalf by the Minister of Finance. The date so specified may be before or after the date of the granting of the exemption or before or after the commencement of this Act.

(5) If any question arises as to the persons entitled to any such exemption or as to the extent of any such exemption, it shall be determined by the Minister of Finance, and his decision shall be final.

(6) The Minister of Finance may direct that such refunds or payments be made from any public fund or account or from the money of any local authority, public body, or person as may in the opinion of the Minister be necessary to give effect to any such exemption.

(7) Where any loss is suffered by any public fund or account other than the Consolidated Account by the granting of any such exemption or by the making of any refund or payment directed under this section, the Minister of Finance may direct that such payments be made from the Consolidated Account to that other fund or account as may be necessary in the opinion of the Minister to reimburse that loss.

(8) Where any loss is suffered by any local authority, public body, or person by the granting of any such exemption or by the making of any refund or payment directed under this section, the Minister of Finance shall direct that such payments be made from the Consolidated Account to that local authority, public body, or person as may be necessary in the opinion of the Minister to reimburse that loss.

(9) All refunds or payments directed under this section to be made from any public fund or account shall be made without further appropriation than this section.

8. Salary of Administrator of the Government.

(1) Where any person is sworn to administer the Government during the absence or incapacity of the Governor General or during a vacancy in the office, that person shall, for the period of that person's administration, be paid

- (*a*) A salary at half the rate of the Governor General's salary; or
- (*b*) Where that person is the holder of any other office, either
  - (i) A salary at half the rate of the Governor General's salary and a salary at half the rate of the salary of the other office; or
  - (ii) A salary at the rate of the salary of the other office,

  whichever is the greater.

(2) Where any person to whom sub-section (1) of this section applies is also the holder of any other office, the salary paid under sub-section (1)(*b*) of this section shall, for the period of that person's administration, be in substitution for the salary payable in respect of the other office.

(3) This section shall have effect notwithstanding anything in section *10* of the Judicature Act 1908.

(4) Notwithstanding sub-sections (1) and (2) of this section, if a person to

whom those sub-sections apply is also, during the period of that person's administration both the holder of any other office and a contributor to the Government Superannuation Fund, that person's rate of salary shall, for the purposes of the Government Superannuation Fund Act 1956, be deemed to remain, during that person's period of administration, that of the other office.

PART II

MINISTERS OF THE CROWN AND PARLIAMENTARY UNDER-SECRETARIES

Ministers of the Crown

9. Ministers to be members of Parliament.

(1) No person shall be appointed as a Minister of the Crown or as a member of the Executive Council unless that person is at the time of appointment a member of Parliament.

(2) Every member appointed as a Minister of the Crown or as a member of the Executive Council shall vacate that office within 21 days if that person ceases to be a member of Parliament:

Provided that no person who is in office as a Minister of the Crown or as a member of the Executive Council immediately before the dissolution of any Parliament shall, by the operation of this section, vacate office on that dissolution.

10. Order of precedence of Ministers. The Governor General may from time to time fix the order of precedence of Ministers.

Parliamentary Under-Secretaries

11. Appointment of Parliamentary Under-Secretaries.

(1) The Governor General may from time to time, by warrant under the hand of the Governor General, appoint any member of Parliament to be a Parliamentary Under-Secretary.

(2) The office of Parliamentary Under-Secretary shall be held in relation to one or more Ministerial offices, to be specified in that behalf in the warrant of appointment.

12. Term of office.

(1) Every person appointed as a Parliamentary Under-Secretary shall vacate that office if that person ceases to be a member of Parliament:

Provided that no person who is in office as a Parliamentary Under-Secretary immediately before the dissolution of any Parliament shall, by the operation of this section, vacate office on that dissolution.

(2) Subject to the foregoing provisions of this section, every person appointed as a Parliamentary Under-Secretary shall hold office as such during the pleasure of the Governor General.

13. Notice of appointment and vacation of office. Notice of the appointment of any person as a Parliamentary Under-Secretary, and of the vacation by any person, by resignation or otherwise, of the office of Parliamentary Under-Secretary, shall be published in the *Gazette* forthwith after the appointment or vacation of office, as the case may be.

14. Functions of Parliamentary Under-Secretaries.

(1) A Parliamentary Under-Secretary holding office as such in respect of any Ministerial office shall have and may exercise under the direction of the Minister concerned

(*a*) Such of the powers, duties, and functions of the Minister of the Crown for the time being holding that office as may from time to time be assigned to the Parliamentary Under-Secretary by that Minister; and

(*b*) Such of the powers, duties, and functions of the Minister of the Crown for the time being holding any other Ministerial office as may from time to time be assigned to the Parliamentary Under-Secretary by the Prime Minister.

(2) No Minister shall be debarred from personally exercising any power, duty, or function by reason of the fact that any power, duty, or function has been assigned to a Parliamentary Under-Secretary.

(3) The fact that any person holding office as a Parliamentary Under-Secretary purports to exercise any power, duty, or function of a Minister of the Crown shall be conclusive evidence of that person's authority to do so.

15. Execution of instruments by Parliamentary Under-Secretary.

(1) Every instrument that is executed by a Parliamentary Under-Secretary on behalf of a Minister of the Crown shall be signed by the Parliamentary Under-Secretary with the personal signature of the Parliamentary Under-Secretary, to which shall be added the words 'Parliamentary Under-Secretary, for the Minister of ', or words to the like effect.

(2) Every instrument that is executed by a Parliamentary Under-Secretary on behalf of a Minister of the Crown shall be as valid and effective as if it had been executed by that Minister.

PART III

REMUNERATION OF MINISTERS OF THE CROWN, PARLIAMENTARY UNDER-SECRETARIES, AND MEMBERS OF PARLIAMENT

16. Salaries and allowances to be fixed by Higher Salaries Commission.

(1) The Higher Salaries Commission shall from time to time, in accordance with the Higher Salaries Commission Act 1977, fix the salaries and allowances to be paid to the Prime Minister and other Ministers of the Crown or members of the Executive Council, to Parliamentary Under-Secretaries, to the Speaker of the House of Representatives, to the Chairman of Committees of the House of Representatives, to the Leader of the Opposition, and to other members of Parliament.

(2) Such salaries and allowances may differ in accordance with the office that the member of Parliament holds (whether or not that office is specified in sub-section (1) of this section) or with the electorate that the member represents or in accordance with such other considerations as may be determined by the Higher Salaries Commission.

(3) The salaries and allowances fixed pursuant to sub-section (1) of this section shall be payable in every year out of the Consolidated Account without further appropriation than this section.

17. Speaker of House of Representatives and Chairman of Committees. The person holding the office of Speaker of the House of Representatives at the time of the dissolution of any Parliament and the person holding the office of Chairman of Committees of the House of Representatives at that time shall, for the purposes of this Act, each be deemed to hold his office until the first meeting of the next Parliament or, if he sooner dies, until the date of his death.

18. Salaries and allowances of members of Parliament.

(1) The salary and allowance of each member of Parliament shall be payable in respect of the period commencing on the day after polling day for the election at which the member is elected and ending with the earlier of the following days:

(*a*) Polling day for the next general election of members of Parliament:

(*b*) The day on which the members's seat becomes vacant, by death or otherwise.

(2) Notwithstanding sub-section (1) of this section, where a member is returned unopposed at a by-election that is not contested, the period in respect of which the salary and allowance of that member shall be payable shall commence on the day on which the Returning Officer publicly declares that member to be elected.

(3) Notwithstanding sub-section (1) of this section, where any person who was a member immediately before the dissolution of any Parliament is an unsuccessful candidate at the next election of members of Parliament, a salary at the rate payable, as at polling day for that election, to a member of Parliament, shall be payable.

(*a*) In the case of a person who was a Minister of the Crown or a member of the Executive Council or the Speaker or Chairman of Committees of the House of Representatives, in respect of the period commencing on the day after the day on which that person ceases to hold that office and ending with the day 3 months after polling day or, if that person sooner dies, with the date of that person's death:

(*b*) In the case of any other person, in respect of the period commencing on the day after polling day and ending with the day 3 months after polling day or, if that person sooner dies, with the date of that person's death.

(4) The payment of the salary and allowance of a member of Parliament shall not be made to any member of Parliament for any period during which that member is in receipt of any other salary payable under this Act.

(5) In this section the expression 'polling day', in relation to any election, means the day appointed in the writ for that election for the polling to take place if a poll is required.

19. Questioned elections of members of Parliament.

(1) Where, at the conclusion of the trial of an election petition, the Supreme Court determines that the person whose election or return was complained of was not duly elected or returned or that the election at which that person was elected or returned was void, the salary and allowance to which that person would have been entitled if that person had been duly elected and returned as a member of Parliament shall be paid to that person, in respect of the period commencing on the day after polling day and ending with the earlier of the following days:

(*a*) The day on which the House of Representatives, pursuant to section *172*(2) of the Electoral Act 1956, gives directions for the altering of the return:

(*b*) The day on which the seat becomes vacant, by death or otherwise.

(2) Where, at the conclusion of the trial of an election petition, the Supreme Court determines that a person, other than the person whose election or return was complained of, was duly elected and the return, in accordance with directions given under section *172*(2) of the Electoral Act 1956, is altered to carry out that determination, the salary and allowance to which the person declared elected pursuant to the altered writ would have been entitled if that person's name had been endorsed on the writ when it was first returned shall, notwithstanding anything in sub-section (1) of this section, be paid to that person.

(3) In this section the expression 'polling day' has the meaning assigned to that term by section *18*(5) of this Act.

(4) This section shall be deemed to have come into force on the 28th day of November 1978.

20. Deductions from members' salaries and allowances. The payment under this Act of salaries and allowances to persons who are members of Parliament shall be subject to the following provisions:

(*a*) If during any session a member is absent for any number of sitting days exceeding 14, there shall be deducted from the payment to be made to the member the sum of $10 for every sitting day (exclusive of those 14 sitting days) during which the member was absent:

(*b*) The exemption from deduction for absence for 14 sitting days during any session shall be reckoned from the commencement of the session and allowed accordingly, after which the prescribed deduction for absence shall be made from the instalment or instalments accruing due next after the occurrence of any such absence:

(*c*) No deduction for absence shall be made where the absence is certified by the Speaker of the House ot be caused

(i) By illness; or

(ii) By any other cause certified by the Speaker of the House to be unavoidable:

(*d*) No deduction for the absence of the member shall be made where the absence is caused by the member's attendance at any conference, meeting, or ceremony, or the member's travelling on any mission or business, as a representative of Parliament or with the authority of the House of Representatives:

(*e*) In this section the expression ' sitting day' means a day on which the House of Representatives is appointed to sit for the transaction of business during any session.

21. Limits on allowance payable to members travelling within New Zealand on public business. Where the Higher Salaries Commission determines that travelling allowances and expenses are payable to any member of Parliament who travels within New Zealand on public service at the request of any Minister of the Crown,

(*a*) The rate of any travelling allowance so determined shall not exceed the rate of travelling allowance for the time being payable to members of the Executive Council; and

(*b*) The travelling allowances and travelling expenses so determined shall not be payable in respect of travelling undertaken by a member wholly within the member's own electorate.

PART IV

MISCELLANEOUS PROVISIONS

22. Annuity for former Prime Minister and spouse of former Prime Minister.

(1) Where a person has held the office of Prime Minister for a period or periods amounting in all to not less than 2 years, whether before or after the commencement of this section, there shall, subject to sub-section (2) of this section and to section *4*(5) of this Act, be paid

(*a*) To that person, until he dies, an annuity at a rate to be fixed from time to time be the Higher Salaries Commission:

(*b*) To the widow or widower of that person (including the widow of any such person who has died before the commencement of this Act), until that widow or widower dies or remarries, an annuity at a rate to be fixed from time to time by the Higher Salaries Commission.

(2) No annuity shall be paid to any person under sub-section (1) of this section in respect of any period during which that person holds an office for which a salary (other than the salary of a member of Parliament) is payable under this Act.

(3) Every determination under this section shall come into force on a day to be specified in the determination, whether on or before or after the date of the determination.

(4) Every determination under this section shall be deemed to be a regulation for the purposes of the Regulations Act 1936.

23. Payments to spouse or dependent children of member of Parliament dying in office.

(1) Where a member of Parliament dies, the following provisions shall apply

(*a*) If the member leaves a wife or husband, these shall be paid to the surviving wife or husband as income a sum of money equivalent to that which would have been paid to the member if a salary, at the rate payable as at the date of death to a member of Parliament, had been payable to the member in respect of the period of 3 months commencing on the day after the date of death:

(*b*) If the member does not leave a wife or husband but leaves one or more dependent children, there shall be payable to that child or those children (and if more than one in equal shares) as income a sum of money equal to the sum mentioned in paragraph (*a*) of this sub-section.

(2) Any sum of money payable pursuant to paragraph (*a*) or paragraph (*b*) of sub-section (1) of this section shall be paid out of the Consolidated Account without further appropriation than this section.

(3) In any case where a sum of money is payable under this section to any person who is a minor, that sum may by direction of the Prime Minister be paid to

(*a*) That person; or

(*b*) Any guardian of, or any person caring for, that person to be applied for the maintenance, education, advancement, or benefit of that person.

(4) The receipt of any person or guardian to whom payment is so made shall be a sufficient discharge therefor.

(5) For the purposes of this section the dependent children of a deceased member comprise such of the children of the member as the member had a legal duty to support in whole or in part at the time of the death of the member.

24. Payment of salaries, annuities, and allowances.

(1) Every salary, annuity, or allowance payable pursuant to any provision of this Act shall, subject to sub-sections (2) to (4) of this section, be paid by equal monthly instalments on the last day of each month.

(2) The Governor General may from time to time by Order in Council, direct that any salary, annuity, or allowance payable pursuant to any provision of this Act shall be paid by equal periodic instalments at the end of such other period (being a period of less than 1 months) as may be specified in the order; and every such order shall have effect according to its tenor.

(3) A proportionate payment is to be made for any fraction of

(*a*) A month; or

(*b*) Any other period prescribed pursuant to sub-section (2) of this section.

(4) Nothing in sub-sections (1) to (3) of this section shall apply in respect of

(*a*) Any payment made pursuant to section *3*(4) or section *23* of this Act; or

(*b*) Any allowance (such as a setting-up allowance) which is of such a nature as to require it to be paid in a lump sum.

25. Appropriation of money for benefits and privileges.

(1) The appropriation by Parliament of money for the purpose of providing benefits or privileges of a specified kind for

(*a*) The Governor General or a former Governor General; or
(*b*) The Prime Minister or a former Prime Minister; or
(*d*) Parliamentary Under-Secretaries; or
(*e*) Members or former members of Palriament; or
(*f*) Members of the families (including a wife, husband, widow, widower, or issue) of any of the persons specified in paragraphs (*a*), (*b*), (*c*), (*e*) of this sub-section,

shall be sufficient authority for the grant of such benefits or privileges, and where money is so appropriated it shall not be necessary as a condition for the lawful expenditure of any money so appropriated that the appropriation be implemented by any statutory authority other than this section.

(2) Nothing in this section shall authorize the payment of any money to any member of Parliament or to any member of the family of any member of Parliament.

(3) The operation of this section shall not be limited in its application to any benefits or priviliges by reason merely of the fact that, with respect to any specified benefits or privileges, there may, in addition to the authority conferred by this section, be an express statutory authority:

Provided that nothing in this sub-section shall be construed to authorize the expenditure of any money contrary to the express provisions of any Act.

26. Repeals, revocations, and savings.

(1) The enactments specified in the First Schedule to this Act are hereby repealed.

(2) The Orders in Council specified in the Second Schedule to this Act are hereby revoked.

(3) Notwithstanding the revocations effected by sub-section (2) of this section, the annuities in respect of which the Higher Salaries Commission may make determinations under section *22* of this Act shall, until the rates at which those annuities are payable are superseded by a determination of the Commission, continue to be payable at the rates applicable at the commencement of this Act under clause *18B* of the Parliamentary Par and Allowances Order 1970 (as inserted by clause *5* of the Parliamentary Pay and Allowances Order 1970, Amendment No. 3).

SCHEDULES
(*Not reproduced*)

IX. The Royal Titles Act 1974[1]

February 6, 1974

Whereas, in accordance with the Royal Titles Act 1953, Her Majesty, by Proclamation dated the 28 the day of May 1953, adopted as the royal style and titles to be used in relation to New Zealand and to all other territories for whose foreign relations Her Government in New Zealand is responsible the style and titles set forth in that Act: And whereas it is desirable that the form of the royal style and titles to be used in relation to New Zealand and to those other territories be altered so as to reflect more clearly Her Majesty's position in relation to New Zealand and all those other territories; And whereas the proposed new style and titles, being the style and titles set forth in section *2* of this Act, retain the common element referred to in the Preamble to the Royal Titles Act 1953:

Be it therefore enacted by the General Assembly of New Zealand in Parliament assembled, and by the authority of the same, as follows:

1. Short Title. This Act may be cited as the Royal Titles Act 1974.

2. Royal style and titles. The royal style and titles of Her Majesty, for use in relation to New Zealand and all other territories for whose foreign relations Her Government in New Zealand is responsible, shall be

Elizabeth the Second, by the Grace of God Queen of New Zealand and Her Other Realms and Territories, Head of the Commonwealth, Defender of the Faith

instead of the style and titles at present appertaining to the Crown.

3. Application of Act to Nuie, the Tokelau Islands, and the Cook Island.

(1) This Act shall be in force in Nuie and in the Tokelau Islands.

(2) Whereas in accordance with Article *46* of the Constitution of the Cook Islands (as set out in the Second Schedule to the Cook Islands Constitution Amendment Act 1965) the Government of the Cook Islands has requested and consented to the enactment of a provision extending the provisions of this Act to the Cook Islands as part of the law of the Cook Islands: Be it therefore enacted as follows:

This Act shall extend to the Cook Islands as part of the law of the Cook Islands.

4. Repeal. The Royal Titles Act 1953 is hereby consequentially repealed.

X. The Royal Powers Act 1953[2]

September 17, 1953

1. Short Title. This Act may be cited as the Royal Powers Act 1953.

2. Exercise of royal powers by Her Majesty the Queen or the Governor General.

(1) It is hereby declared that every power conferred on the Governor General by any enactment is a royal power which is exercisable by him on behalf of Her

[1] 1974, No. 1. *An Act to define Her Majesty's royal style and titles in relation to New Zealand.*
[2] 1953, No 19. *An Act relating to the royal powers exercisable by Her Majesty the Queen or the Governor General.*

Majesty the Queen, and may accordingly be exercised either by Her Majesty in person or by the Governor General.

(2) It is hereby further declared that every reference in any Act to the Governor General in Council or any other like expression includes a reference to Her Majesty the Queen acting by and with the advice and consent of the Executive Council of New Zealand.

XI. The Electoral Act 1956[1]

October 26, 1956, amended to 1981

1. Short Title, commencement, and division into Parts.

(1) This Act may be cited as the Electoral Act 1956.

(2) This Act shall come into force on the 1st day of January 1957:

Provided that sections *15* to *24* of this Act shall come into force on the passing of this Act.

(3) This Act is divided into Parts, as follows:

Part I. Preliminary. (Sections 2 to 10).
Part II. The House of Representatives. (Sections 11 to 36).
Part III. Registration of Electors. (Sections 37 to 69).
Part IV. Elections. (Sections 70 to 139).
Part V. Corrupt and Illegal Practices. (Sections 140 to 154).
Part VI. Election Petitions. (Sections 155 to 183).
Part VII. Miscellaneous Provisions. (Sections 184 to 190).

PART I

PRELIMINARY

2. Interpretation.

(1) In this Act, unless the context otherwise requires,

'Adult' means of or over the age of [18 years]:

'Bribery' has the meaning assigned to that term by section 141 of this Act:

'By-election' means any election other than a general election:

'Candidate' means any person who has been nominated as a candidate for a seat in the House of Representatives; and in Parts V and VI of this Act includes any person who has declared his intention of becoming a candidate:

'Chief Electoral Officer' means the Chief Electoral Officer appointed under this Act; and includes any person authorized to exercise the powers, duties, and functions of the Chief Electoral Officer:

'Chief Registrar' means the Chief Registrar of Electors holding office under section 7A of this Act; and includes his deputy:

[1] 1956, No. 107, *An Act to consolidate and amend the enactments relating to the election of members of the House of Representatives.* Reprinted as on 1st March 1981.

'Clerk of Writs' means the Clerk of the Writs appointed under this Act; and includes any person authorized to exercise the powers, duties, and functions of the Clerk of the Writs:

'Corrupt Practices List', in relation to any district, means the Corrupt Practices List made out for that district under section *59* of this Act:

'Corrupt practice' means any act declared by this Act to be a corrupt practice:

'Costs' includes charges and expenses:

'Crown' means Her Majesty in respect of the Government of New Zealand:

'Deputy Returning Officer' means a Deputy Returning Officer appointed under this Act; and includes any person authorized to exercise the powers, duties, and functions of a Deputy Returning Officer:

'District' or 'electoral district' or 'electorate' means a General electoral district or Maori electoral district constituted under this Act:

'Election: means an election of a member of the House of Representatives:

'Election expenses', in relation to a candidate at an election in any district, means expenses incurred by or on behalf of the candidate within the 3 months immediately preceding polling day, and relating exclusively to the campaign for the return of the candidate:

'Electoral roll', in relation to any district, means, subject to sections *60* to *60B* of this Act, the forms of application for registration kept by the Registrar of persons registered as electors of that district (including the forms deemed by section of this Act, the forms of application for registration kept by the Registrar of persons registered as electors of that district (including the forms deemed by *41B*(5) or section *43A*(4)(*a*) of this Act to be applications for registration for the purposes of this deifinition):

'General election' means an election which takes place after the dissolution or expiration of Parliament:

'General electoral district' means an electoral district other than a Maori electoral district:

'General electoral population' means total population with the following exceptions:

(*a*) Maori electoral population:

(*b*) Persons residing on board any ship, whether as passengers or members of the crew or otherwise:

(*c*) Persons residing temporarily as guests in any guest house, hotel, or motel, whether licensed or not:

(*d*) Persons residing temporarily in any defence area as defined in the Defence Act 1971:

(*e*) Persons residing as patients or inmates in any hospital or private hospital or institution under the Mental Health Act 1969 or the Hospitals Act 1957 or the Alcoholism and Drug Addiction Act 1966:

(*f*) Persons (not being persons detained in a police station pursuant to section *12*(2) of the Penal Institutions Act 1954) detained in any penal institution as defined in the Penal Institutions Act 1954:

'Government' means the Government of New Zealand:

'Hospital' means an institution or separate institution under the Hospital Act 1957:

'Illegal practice' means any act declared by this Act to be an illegal practice:

'Main roll', in relation to any district, means, subject to section *63A* of this Act, the main roll printed for the district and for the time being in force:

'Maori' means a person of the Maori race of New Zealand; and includes any descendant of such a person:

'Maori electoral district' means an electoral district named in section *23*(1) of this Act:

'Maori electoral population' means the sum of

(*a*) The total number of persons registered as electors of the Maori electoral districts as at the close of the last day of the period last specified under section *41A*(2) or (3) of this Act; and

(*b*) A figure representing, in relation to the persons so registered as electors of Maori electoral districts, the number of their Maori children under the age of 18 years, which figure shall be fixed

(i) By ascertaining the proportion which the number in paragraph (*a*) of this definition bears to the total Maori adult population as determined by the last periodical census; and

(ii) Subject to sub-paragraph (iii) of this paragraph, by applying that proportion to the number of Maori children under the age of 18 years as determined by the last periodical census; and

(iii) By treating as Maori children under the age of 18 years all of the children under that age who at the last periodical census had at least one parent whose particulars showed that that parent was a Maori:

Provided that where particulars were obtained from both parents and only one of those parents was shown by those particulars to be a Maori, only half ot the children under the age of 18 years of those parents shall be treated as Maori children:

'Mental institution' means a hospital under the Mental Health Act 1969:

'Minister' means the Minister of Justice:

'Nomination day', in relation to any election as the latest day for the nomination of candidates:

'Ordinarily resident in New Zealand' has the meaning assigned thereto by section *38* of this Act:

'Penal institution' means a penal institution under the Penal Institutions Act 1954:

'Personation' has the meaning assigned to that term by section *140* of this Act:

'Polling day', in relation to any election, means the day appointed in the writ for that election for the polling to take place if a poll is required:

'Prescribed' means prescribed by this Act or by regulations made thereunder or (for the purposes of Part VI of this Act) by rules of Court:

'Prohibited immigrant' has the meaning given to it by section *2*(1) of the Immigration Act 1964:

'Public money' has the same meaning as in the Public Finance Act 1977:

'Public notice' or 'public notification' means a notice printed in some newspaper circulating in the district intended to be affected by the notice:

'Public place' has the same meaning as in Part II of the Police Offences Act 1927:

'Public servant' means a person employed in the service of the Crown, not being honorary service; and includes a person employed in the Education service as defined in the Government Superannuation Fund Act 1956 or in the Cook Islands Public Service or in the Western Samoan Public Service; but does not include any person to whom sub-section (2) of this section applies; and does not include

(*a*) Any person by reason of his holding an office for which a salary is payable under the Civil List Act 1979; or

(*b*) Any person by reason of his being employed in any of Her Majesty's forces except the Royal New Zealand Navy, the Regular Force of the New Zealand Army, or the Regular Air Force of the Royal New Zealand Air Force; or

(*c*) Any person remunerated by fees or commission and not by wages or salary:

'Registrar', in relation to any district, means the Registrar of Electors appointed for that district under section *7B* of this Act; and includes his deputy:

'Residence' and 'to reside' have the meanings assigned thereto by section *37* of this Act:

'Returning Officer' means a Returning Officer appointed under this Act; and includes any person authorized to exercise the powers, duties, and functions of a Returning Officer:

'Roll' means an electoral roll, a main roll, or a supplementary roll, as the case may be; and includes a composite roll printed under section *63A* of this Act:

'Serviceman' means any person resident in New Zealand within the meaning of this Act who is for the time being a member of the naval , military, or air forces of New Zealand; and includes any person so resident who is attached to, or employed by, or carries out duties which necessitate his accompanying, any such force when outside New Zealand:

'Speaker' means the Speaker of the House of Representatives:

'Special voter', in relation to any election, means a person qualified under this Act to vote as a special voter at that election:

'Statement' includes not only words but also pictures, visual images, gestures, and other methods of signifying meaning:

'Supplementary roll', in relation to any district, means a supplementary roll printed for the district and for the time being in force:

'Treating' has the meaning assigned to that term by section *142* of this Act:

'Undue influence' has the meaning assigned to that term by section *143* of this Act:

'Writ' means a writ for an election issued under this Act:

'Writ day', in relation to any election, means the day of the issue of the writ for that election:

A reference to a numbered form is a reference to the form so numbered in the First Schedule to this Act.

(2) Where any person

(*a*) Is appointed by the Crown, or the Government, or any Department or agency of the Government to be a member of any Commission, Council, Board, Committee, or other body; or

(*b*) Is a member of any Commission, Council, Board, Committee, or other body of which any members receive any payment out of public money,

he shall not by reason of that membership be deemed to be a public servant, whether or not he receives any travelling allowances or travelling expenses.

Officers

3. *Clerk of the Writs.*

(1) The Governor General shall from time to time, by Warrant under his hand, appoint some fit person to be Clerk of the Writs, by whom writs for the election of members of Parliament shall in all cases be issued, and to whom all such writs shall be returnable.

(2) Nothing in the State Services Act 1962 shall apply to the Clerk of the Writs.

4. *Deputy Clerk of the Writs.*

(1) The Governor General shall also from time to time, by Warrant under his hand, appoint some fit person to be Deputy Clerk of the Writs.

(2) On the occurrence from any cause of a vacancy in the office of Clerk of the Writs (whether by reason of death, resignation, or otherwise), and in case of the absence from duty of the Clerk of the Writs (from whatever cause arising), and so long as any such vacancy or absence continues, the Deputy Clerk of the Writs shall have and may exercise all the powers, duties, and functions of the Clerk of the Writs.

(3) The fact that the Deputy Clerk of the Writs exercises any power, duty, or function of the Clerk of the Writs shall be conclusive evidence of his authority to do so.

(4) Nothing in the State Services Act 1962 shall apply to the Deputy Clerk of the Writs.

5. *Chief Electoral Officer.* There shall from time to time be appointed under the State Services Act 1962 some fit person to be Chief Electoral Officer, who shall be an employee of the Department of Justice and, under the direction of the Minister and of the Secretary for Justice, shall be charged with the duty of carrying the provisions of this Act (except those of Part III) into effect.

6. *Deputy Chief Electoral Officer.* There may also from time to time be appointed

under the State Services Act 1962 some fit person to be Deputy Chief Electoral Officer, who, subject to the control of the Chief Electoral Officer, shall have and may exercise all the powers, duties, and functions of the Chief Electoral Officer.

7. *Returning Officers and other employees.* There may from time to time be appointed under the State Services Act 1962 as many Returning Officers, clerks, and other officials as are required to be appointed under that Act for the purposes of this Act.

7A. *Chief Registrar of Electors.*

(1) There shall be a Chief Registrar of Electors who shall be the person exercising the powers, duties, and functions for the time being of the Director General of the Post Office.

(2) The Chief Registrar shall, under the direction of the Minister of Justice, be charged with the duty of carrying Part III of this Act into effect and to that end the Chief Registrar may, both in that capacity and in his capacity as the Director General of the Post Office, provide such computer and other services and such facilities as he thinks necessary.

(3) The Chief Registrar may from time to time appoint an officer of the Post Office to be the Deputy Chief Registrar of Electors, who, subject to the control of the Chief Registrar, shall have and may exercise all the powers, functions, and duties of the Chief Registrar.

7B. *Registrar of Electors.*

(1) There shall be for each electoral district a Registrar of Electors to be appointed by the Chief Registrar.

(2) Every Registrar shall be an officer of the Post Office appointed by name or as the holder for the time being of any specified office and shall, subject to sub-section (3) of this section, be stationed at a post office within the electoral district of which he is Registrar.

(3) Where, in the opinion of the Chief Registrar,

(*a*) There is no suitable major post office in an electoral district; or

(*b*) An officer more suitable for appointment is stationed at a post office in an adjoining district; or

(*c*) It appears to be in the public interest to do so,

he may appoint as the Registrar for the district an officer of the Post Office stationed at a post office in an adjoining electoral district.

(4) The Registrar shall, under the direction of the Chief Registrar,

(*a*) Compile and keep, as required by this Act, the electoral roll for the Registrar's electoral district; and

(*b*) Carry out such other functions and duties as are specified in this Act.

(5) The Chief Registrar may from time to time appoint an officer of the Post Office to be the Deputy Registrar for any electoral district, who, subject to the control of the Registrar, shall have and may exercise all the powers, functions, and duties of the Registrar.

(6) Neither the Registrar nor his deputy shall hold any official position in any political organization.

(7) The powers conferred on the Chief Registrar by sub-sections (1) and (5) of this section include the power to appoint a Registrar or a Deputy Registrar for a named electoral district that is not yet in being or in respect of which a roll has not been compiled.

7C. Appropriation of expenses of Post Office. The expenses incurred by the Post Office in the administration of Part III of this Act shall be paid from the Consolidated Account out of money appropriated by Parliament.

8. Employees appointed by Chief Electoral Officer.

(1) The Chief Electoral Officer, with the approval of the Director General of the Post Office, may from time to time appoint any employee of that Department to be a Returning Officer, or a substitute for a returning Officer.

(2) Every substitute while acting for any Returning Officer shall have all the powers, duties, and functions of that Returning Officer.

(3) Nothing in the State Services Act 1962, shall apply to any person appointed under this section.

9. General provisions as to Returning Officers.

(1), (2) *Repealed.*

(3) No Returning Officer shall hold any official position in any political organization.

10. Returning Officers to make declaration. Every Returning Officer and every Deputy Returning Officer, shall, before entering on the duties of his office, make a declaration in form 1.

PART II

THE HOUSE OF REPRESENTATIVES

11. Constitution of the House of Representatives. The House of Representatives constituted as part of the General Assembly by section *32* of the New Zealand Constitution Act 1852 shall consist of

(*a*) The members elected for the General electoral districts constituted under this Part of this Act, being one member for each such district; and

(*b*) The members elected for the Maori electoral districts, being one member for each such district.

12. Duration of House of Representatives. The House of Representatives, as existing on the date of the commencement of this Act, and every House of Representatives elected after that date, shall, unless Parliament is sooner dissolved, continue for a period of 3 years, computed from the day fixed for the return of the writs issued for the general election of members of that House of Representatives, and no longer.

13. Members of Parliament. Members of the House of Representatives shall be known and designated by the title of 'members of Parliament', and in this Act and all other Acts the term 'member of Parliament' shall be construed accordingly.

14. Election of Speaker. The House of Representatives shall, immediately on its first meeting after the general election of its members, and immediately on its first meeting after any vacancy occurs in the office of Speaker (whether by death, resignation, or otherwise), choose one of its members as its Speaker during the continuance of the said House, and every such choice, on being confirmed by the Governor General, shall be valid and effectual.

The Representation Commission

15. Representation Commission.

(1) In order to provide for the periodical readjustment of the representation of the people of New Zealand in the House of Representatives there shall be a Commission to be known as the Representation Commission.

(2) The Commission shall consist of 8 members of whom

(*a*) The Surveyor General, the Government Statistician, the Chief Electoral Officer, the Director General of the Post Office, and the Chairman of the Local Government Commission shall be the official members:

Provided that the Chairman of the Local Government Commission shall not be entitled to vote on any matter before the Commission, and shall not be regarded as a member of theCommission for the purpose of forming part of a quorum pursuant to section *21*(1) of this Act:

(*b*) Two persons (not being public servants directly concerned with the administration of this Act or members of the General Assembly) shall be appointed by the Governor General by Order in Council on the nomination of the House of Representatives as the unofficial members of the Commission, one of those being nominated to represent the Government and one to represent the Opposition:

(*c*) One person (not being a public servant directly concerned with the administration of this Act or a member of the General Assembly) shall be appointed by the Governor General by Order in Council on the nomination of the official and unofficial members of the Commission, or a majority of them, to be the Chairman of the Commission.

(3) The Chairman and every unofficial member of the Commission, unless he sooner ceases to be a member as provided in sub-section (4) of this section, shall cease to be a member on the date on which the first periodical census of population is taken after the date of his appointment.

(4) The Chairman or any unofficial member of the Commission may resign his appointment by writing addressed to the Governor General, in which case, or in case of any such member being convicted of any indictable offence, or of his refusing to act, or of his death or mental or physical incapacity, or of his absence from New Zealand when his services are required, the Governor General may, by Order in Council, appoint another person in his stead on the same nomination as in the case of the original appointment:

Provided that, if the House of Representatives is not in session at the time, an appointment of an unofficial member to represent the Government or the Opposition may be made on the nomination of the Prime Minister or of the Leader of the Opposition, as the case may be.

(5) There shall be paid out of money appropriated by Parliament for the purpose to the Chairman and each unofficial member of the Commission remuneration by way of fees, salary, or allowances and expenses in accordance with the Fees and Travelling Allowances Act 1951, and the provisions of that Act shall apply accordingly, and the Commission shall be a statutory Board for the purposes of that Act.

16. Division of New Zealand into General electoral districts after each census.

(1) After the census taken in the year 1966, and after each periodical census thereafter, it shall be the duty of the Commission to divide New Zealand into General electoral districts according to the following basis, that is to say:

(*a*) The South Island shall be divided into 25 General electoral districts:

(*b*) The General electoral population of the South Island shall be divided by 25, and the quotient so obtained shall be the quota for the South Island:

(*c*) The General electoral population of the North Island shall be divided by the quota for the South Island, and the quotient so obtained shall be the number of General electoral districts in the North Island. Where that quotient includes a fraction the fraction shall be disregarded unless it exceeds a half, in which case the number of such districts shall be the whole number next above that quotient:

(*d*) The quota for the North Island shall be ascertained by dividing the General electoral population of that Island by the number of General electoral districts in that Island, as ascertained under paragraph (*c*) of this sub-section:

(*e*) The extent of each district in each Island shall be such that at the time of making the division the General electoral population thereof shall, subject to the provisions of section *17* of this Act as to the allowance, be equal to the quota for that Island:

(*f*) In forming the several districts due consideration shall be given to the existing boundaries of electoral districts, to community of interest, to facilities of communications, and to topographical features.

(2) As soon as possible after each periodical census the Government Statistician shall for the purposes of this section report the results of the census to the Surveyor General.

(3) Upon receipt of the report of the Government Statistician the Surveyor General shall prepare maps showing the distribution of the population and provisional boundaries for the electoral districts, and shall then call a meeting of the official and unofficial members of the Commission for the purpose of nominating a person for appointment as Chairman of the Commission.

(4) The report of the Government Statistician of the results of the census last taken before the making of any such division, and the maps so prepared by the Surveyor General, shall be sufficient evidence as to the General electoral population of New Zealand or of the North Island or of the South Island or of any district.

17. Allowance for adjustment of quota. Where in the opinion of the Commission districts cannot be formed consistently with the considerations hereinbefore provided for so as to contain exactly the quota, the Commission may for any district make an allowance by way of addition or subtraction of General electoral population to an extent not exceeding 5 percent.

18. Notice of proposed boundaries. Where the Commission proposes to make any such division due notice of the boundaries of the proposed districts shall be given in the *Gazette*, and objections in writing to the proposed boundaries may be lodged with the Commission within one month thereafter, and the Commission shall duly consider any objections so lodged before coming to a final determination.

19. Report of Commission to be proclaimed by Governor General.

(1) The Commission shall in every case within 6 months after the appointment of the Chairman report the names and boundaries of the electoral districts fixed by it to the Governor General, who shall proclaim them in the *Gazette*.

(2) From the date of the Proclamation the electoral districts fixed by the report shall be the electoral districts of New Zealand for the purpose of the election of members of Parliament after the dissolution or expiration of the then existing Parliament, and shall so continue until the next report of the Commission is proclaimed and similarly takes effect.

20. Report and maps to be laid before Parliament.

(1) A copy of every report of the Commission, together with properly authenticated maps of the electoral districts fixed by the report, shall be presented by the Governor General to the House of Representatives within 28 days after the date of the receipt thereof if Parliament is then in session, and, if not, then within 28 days after the date of the commencement of the next ensuing session.

(2) The Minister shall forthwith after every report of the Commission is proclaimed cause to be deposited in the office of the Clerk of the House of Representatives properly authenticated maps of the electoral districts fixed by the report.

20A. Index of streets and places.

(1) The Surveyor General shall from time to time, at the request of the Chief Electoral Officer, compile an index of the streets and places within each electoral district.

(2) Copies of the latest index compiled under this section shall be kept for inspection by the public at the office of each Registrar and at such other convenient places within each district as the Minister from time to time directs.

(3) Every index compiled under this section shall be forwarded to the Government Printer and shall be printed and sold by him.

21. Proceedings of Commission.

(1) Any 4 members of the Commission of whom 2 are the unofficial members shall be a quorum, and may exercise all functions vested in the Commission.

(2) The Commission may make such rules for the conduct of its business, not inconsistent with the provisions of this Act, as it thinks fit.

22. Commissioner not eligible as member of House of Representatives. No member of the Commission shall within 2 years after he ceases to be a member, be capable of being elected to be a member of the House of Representatives.

Maori Representation

23. Maori representation.

(1) For the purpose of the representation of the Maori people in the House of Representatives, New Zealand shall be divided into 4 Maori electoral districts, to be known as

The Northern Maori Electoral District:

The Eastern Maori Electoral District:

The Western Maori Electoral District:

The Southern Maori Electoral District:

(2) The Governor General may at any time, by Proclamation, redefine and declare, and from time to time alter, the boundaries of the several Maori electoral districts.

(3) From the date of every Proclamation issued under this section, the boundaries of the Maori electoral districts as declared or altered by the Proclamation shall be the boundaries thereof for the purpose of the election of Maori members of Parliament after the dissolution or expiration of the then existing Parliament, and shall so continue until the next Proclamation under this section is issued and similarly takes effect.

Chatham Islands

24. Electoral districts for and polling in Chatham Islands.

(1) The area comprised in the Chatham Islands shall be included within the Lyttelton Electoral District.

(1A) For the purposes of the election of Maori members of Parliament, the Chatham Islands shall be deemed to form part of the Western Maori Electoral District.

(2) *Repealed.*

(3)–(5) *Repealed.*

Qualifications of Members

25. Registered electors may be members, unless disqualified.

(1) Subject to the provisions of this Act, every person registered as an elector of any electoral district, but no other person, is qualified to be a candidate and to be elected a member of Parliament for that or any other electoral district:

Provided that a person shall not be so elected

(*a*) If he is disqualified for registration as an elector under any of the provisions of this Act; or

(*aa*) Unless he is a New Zealand citizen; or

(*ab*) Unless he was registered as an elector on the date of the commencement of this paragraph.

(*b*) *Repealed.*

(*c*) *Repealed.*

(2), (3) *Repealed.*

26. *Offence for public servant to sit.* Every member of Parliament who sits or votes therein after his seat has become vacant by reason of his becoming a public servant, knowing that his seat is so vacant, shall be liable on summary conviction to a fine not exceeding $100 for every day on which he so sits or votes.

27. *Removal of name from roll without cause.* Any person duly qualified as an elector who has been registered in any electoral roll but whose name has become removed from that roll through no fault of his own shall not, by reason only of not being registered as an elector, be disqualified from becoming a candidate and being elected for any electoral district; but in every such case he shall forward to the Returning Officer, at the time when he sends his consent to be nominated, a statutory declaration to the effect that he is not disqualified as an elector for the district in respect of which he was previously registered under the provisions of this Act or any other Act, that he still retains that qualification, and that his name has been removed from the roll of that district through no fault of his own.

28. *Effect of registration on wrong roll.* The nomination of any person as a candidate for election, or his election as a member of Parliament, shall not be questioned on the ground that, though entitled to be registered as an elector of any district, he was not in fact registered as an elector of that district but was registered as an elector of some other district.

29. *Member ceasing to be an elector.* A member of Parliament ceasing to be registered as an elector shall not from that cause only be disqualified from sitting as a member.

30. *Public servants may become candidates or be elected.*

(1) Any public servant who desires to become a candidate for election as a member of Parliament shall be placed on leave of absence for the purposes of his candidature.

(2) That leave shall commence on such date as his controlling authority determines, being not later than nomination day, and, in the event of his nomination as a candidate, shall continue until the 7th day after polling day, unless he withdraws his nomination.

(3) During the period of his leave he shall not be required or permitted to carry out any of his official duties, nor shall he be entitled to receive any salary or other remunerations as a public servant in respect of that period or any part thereof, except to the extent to which he takes during that period any leave with pay to which he is entitled:

Provided that a candidate who at the time of his nomination is a member of the staff of a university or a university college may continue to teach or supervise the studies of students at that university or university college who are preparing for an examination and may engage in marking the examination papers of such students, and may receive remuneration in respect of such teaching, supervision, and marking.

(4) Except as provided in the foregoing provisions of this section, his rights as a public servant shall not be affected by his candidature.

31. Members disqualified from being public servants.

(1) If any public servant is elected as a member of Parliament he shall forthwith, on being declared so elected, be deemed to have vacated his office as a public servant.

(2), (3) *Repealed*

Vacancies

32. How vacancies created. The seat of any member of Parliament shall become vacant

(*a*) If for one whole session of Parliament he fails, without permission of the House of Representatives, to give his attendance in the House; or

(*b*) If he takes any oath or makes any declaration or acknowledgment of allegiance or adherence to any foreign Prince or Power; or

(*c*) If he does or concurs in or adopts any act whereby he may become a subject or citizen of any foreign State or power, or entitled to the rights, privileges, or immunities of a subject or citizen of any foreign State or Power; or

(*d*) *Repealed*

(*e*) If he is convicted of a crime punishable by death or by imprisonment for a term of 2 years or upwards, or is convicted of a corrupt practice, or is reported by the High Court in its report on the trial of an election petition to have been proved guilty of a corrupt practice; or

(*f*) If he becomes a public servant; or

(*g*) If he resigns his seat by writing under his hand addressed and delivered to the Speaker of the House, or to the Governor General if there is no Speaker or the Speaker is absent from New Zealand, or if the resigning member is the Speaker; or

(*h*) If on an election petition the Court declares his election void; or

(*i*) If he dies; or

(*j*) If he becomes mentally disordered as provided in section *33* of this Act; or

(*k*) If he is proved to the satisfaction of a Committee of the House to have acted, for commission or other reward, as agent on behalf of the owner or of any other person having an interest in any land for the purpose of securing the purchase or acquisition of that land by the Crown.

33. Member becoming mentally disordered.

(1) Where a member of Parliament is received or detained in any mental

hospital otherwise than as an informal patient, the Court or person upon whose order, and every medical practitioner upon whose certificate, that member was so received or detained, and the Medical Superintendent or other person having charge of the hospital shall, as soon as may be, certify the reception or detention to the Speaker.

(2) The Speaker shall forthwith transmit those certificates to the Director of the Division of Mental Health of the Department of Health, who, together with some registered medical practitioner named by the Speaker, shall without delay visit and examine the member to whom the certificates relate, and shall report to the Speaker whether he is of unsound mind.

(3) If the report is to the effect that he is of unsound mind the Speaker shall, at the expiration of 6 months from the date of the report if Parliament is then in session, and, if not, then as soon as may be after the date of the commencement of the next ensuing session, require the said Director, together with the said medical practitioner or some other registered medical practitioner named by the Speaker, again to visit and examine the member; and if they report that he is still of unsound mind the Speaker shall forthwith lay both reports on the table of the House of Representatives, and thereupon the seat of the member shall be vacant.

(4) Every registered medical practitioner, or Medical Superintendent or other person having charge of any mental hospital in which any such member is received or detained, who wilfully commits a breach of this section shall be liable on summary convictions to a fine not exceeding $200.

34. Registrar of Court to notify cause of vacancy in certain cases.

(1) The Registrar of the Court in which any member of Parliament has been convicted of a crime punishable by death or by imprisonment for a term of 2 years or upwards, or has been convicted of a corrupt practice, shall, within 48 hours after the conviction, notify the fact to the Speaker, or to the Governor General if there is no Speaker or if the Speaker is absent from New Zealand.

(2) Every Registrar who fails to send any notice required by this section commits an offence, and shall be liable on summary conviction to a fine not exceeding $10 for every day during which he fails to send the notice.

35. Registrar of Births and Deaths to notify Speaker of death of member.

(1) The Registrar of Births and Deaths by whom the death of any member of Parliament is registered shall, within 12 hours of making the registration, notify the fact by telegram to the Speaker, or to the Governor General if there is no Speaker or if the Speaker is absent from New Zealand.

(2) Every Registrar who fails to send any notice required by this section commits an offence and shall be liable on summary conviction to a fine not exceeding $10 for every day during which he fails to send the notice.

36. No person to be candidate for more than one district.

(1) No person shall be a candidate for more than one district at any general election.

(2) If 2 or more by-elections are held on the same polling day, no person shall be a candidate at more than one of those by-elections.

(3) If any person is a candidate for more than one district or at more than one by-election in breach of this section, all nominations of that person as a candidate for those districts or, as the case may be, for those by-elections, shall be void, and the deposits made by him shall be forfeited and be paid into the Consolidated Account.

PART III

REGISTRATION OF ELECTORS

37. Rules for determining place of residence within New Zealand.

(1) Subject to the provisions of this section, the place of a person's residence within New Zealand at any material time during any material period shall be determined for the purposes of this Act by reference to the facts of the case.

(2) For the purposes of this Act a person can reside in one place only.

(3) A person shall be deemed to reside where he has his usual place of abode notwithstanding

(*a*) That he is occasionally or temporarily absent from that place; or

(*b*) That he is absent from that place for any period because of his service or that of his spouse under the Crown or as a member of Parliament:

(*c*) That he is absent from that place for any period because of his occupation or employment or that of his spouse, whether as a seaman, an actor, or a commercial traveller, or otherwise.

(4) A person who has permanently left his former place of abode shall be deemed not to reside at that place notwithstanding that his place of abode for the time being is temporary only:

Provided that a New Zealand citizen who is outside New Zealand shall be deemed, subject to section *42*(1)(*a*) of this Act, to reside where he had his last usual place of abode in New Zealand.

(5) If a person has 2 or more usual places of abode he shall be deemed to reside on the place in which he spends the greatest part of time.

(6) In the case of a person who is appointed to be a member of the Executive Council, or who is the spouse of any person so appointed, the following provisions shall apply notwithstanding anything to the contrary in this section, namely:

(*a*) So long as he holds that office he shall be deemed to continue to reside at the place of residence in respect of which he was registered as an elector of an electoral district (in this sub-section referred to as the original district), notwithstanding his absence therefrom at the seat of Government or elsewhere, unless and until he duly applies for registration as an elector of another electoral district of which he is, apart from the provisions of this paragraph, qualified to be an elector:

(*b*) Upon being registered as an elector of the other district pursuant to an application as aforesaid the applicant shall cease to be entitled to continue to be registered under this sub-section as an elector of the original district.

(7) A person whose place of abode is in any ship, boat, or vessel permanently located in any harbour shall be deemed to reside in the electoral district in which the wharf or landing place or the main wharf or landing place in the harbour is situated. If any question arises under this sub-section as to the district in which the wharf or landing place or the main wharf or landing place in any harbour is situated, it shall be determined by the Representation Commission.

38. Meaning of 'permanent resident of New Zealand'. For the purposes of this Act a person is a permanent resident of New Zealand if, and only if, that person

(*a*) Resides in New Zealand; and

(*b*) Is not

(i) A prohibited immigrant; or

(ii) A person obliged, by or pursuant to any Act, to leave New Zealand immediately or within a specified time.

Qualifications of Electors

39. Qualification of electors. Subject to the provisions of this Act, every adult person is qualified to be registered as an elector of an electoral district if

(*a*) That person is

(i) A New Zealand citizen; or

(ii) A permanent resident of New Zealand; and

(*b*) That person has at some period resided continuously in New Zealand for not less than one year; and

(*c*) That person

(i) Has resided in that electoral district for not less than 3 months immediately before the date of that person's application for registration; or

(ii) Has resided continuously in that electoral district for not less than 3 months and has not subsequently resided continuously for 3 months or more in any one electoral district; or

(iii) Resides in that electoral district, or has resided in that district and has not subsequently resided in any other electoral district, and, because of that person's occupation or employment or that of that person's spouse, whether as a seaman, an actor, or a commercial traveller, or otherwise, that person has not resided continuously for 3 months or more on any one electoral district.

40. No person to be registered in more than one district. A person shall not be entitled to be registered as an elector of more than one electoral district.

41. Maori option.

(1) Subject to this section and to sections *41A* to *41C* of this Act, a Maori who possesses the qualifications prescribed in that behalf by this Act shall have the

option of being registered either as an elector of a Maori electoral district or as an elector of a General electoral district.

(2) Every such option shall be exercised

(*a*) At the time the Maori first qualifies and applies to be registered as an elector of any electoral district; or

(*b*) In the case of a Maori who was not registered as an elector of any electoral district on the first day of the period last specified under section *41A*(2) or (3) of this Act, on any subsequent application for application for registration as an elector; or

(*c*) In any other case, in accordance with section *41A* or section *41B* of this Act.

41A. Periodic exercise of Maori option and determination of Maori population.

(1) Every elector who is a Maori may exercise periodically, in accordance with this section, the option given by section *41*(1) of this Act.

(2) In the year 1982 and thereafter in every year that a quinquennial census of population is taken, the Minister of Justice shall specify, by notice in the *Gazette*, a period of 3 months during which any Maori may exercise the option given by section *41*(1) of this Act.

(3) Notwithstanding sub-section (2) of this section, where a Parliament is due to expire in a year in which a quinquennial census of population is to be taken, the Minister of Justice shall not, in that year, exercise the power conferred on him by that sub-section, but shall instead, in the year following the year in which the quinquennial census of population is taken, specify, by notice in the *Gazette*, a period of 3 months during which any Maori may exercise the option given by section *41*(1) of this Act.

(4) For the purpose of enabling the Government Statistician to calculate the Maori electoral population, the Chief Registrar shall, as soon as practicable after the last day of each period specified under sub-section (2) or sub-section (3) of this section, supply to the Government Statistician the total number of persons registered as electors of the Maori electoral district as at the close of that last day.

41B. Exercise of Maori option.

(1) Notwithstanding section *43A*(4)(*b*) of this Act, every Maori who is an elector on the first day of any period specifed under section *41A*(2) or (3) of this Act may exercise once during the period beginning with that day and ending with the day immediately preceding the first day of the next succeding period specified under section *41*(2) or (3) of this Act the option given by section *41*(1) of this Act.

(2) In each period specified under section *41A*(2) or (3) of this Act, the Registrar shall sent to every person registered as an elector of the electoral district on the first day of that period a notice in the form prescribed for the purposes of this section.

(3) Every Maori

(*a*) Who is registered as an elector on the first day of the period during which notice is sent under sub-section (2) of this section; and (*b*) Who

(i) Being registered as an elector of a Maori electoral district wishes to be registered as an elector of a General ele^toral district; or

(ii) Being registered as an elector of a General electoral district wishes to be registered as an elector of a Maori electoral district,

shall indicate his choice on the prescribed form, sign it, and return it to the Registrar.

(4) The Registrar, on receipt of any duly completed form, shall send the form to the Registrar in whose district the elector resides.

(5) Every duly completed form received by a Registrar pursuant to sub-section (4) of this section shall be deemed, for the purposes of the definition of the term 'electoral roll' in section *2*(1) of this Act and for the purposes of sections *56* and *60B* of this Act, to be an application for registration as an elector and shall be treated accordingly.

(6) No elector shall, by reason only of a failure to return a form sent to him under sub-section (2) of this section, have his name removed from the electoral roll.

41C. Restrictions on transfer between General and Maori electoral rolls. Except as provided in sections *41* to *41B* of this Act, no Maori may transfer from a General electoral roll to a Maori electoral roll or vice versa.

42. Disqualifications for registration.

(1) The following persons are disqualified for registration as electors:

(*a*) A New Zealand citizen who (subject to sub-section (3) of this section) is outside New Zealand and has not been in New Zealand within the last 3 years:

(*b*) A permanent resident of New Zealand (not being a New Zealand citizen) who (subject ot sub-section (3) of this section) is outside New Zealand and has not been in New Zealand within the last 12 months:

(*c*) A person who is detained in a hospital under the Mental Health Act 1969, being

(i) A person who, having been found by a Court or a Judge to be under disability, or having been acquitted on account of insanity, within the meaning of Part VA of the Criminal Justice Act 1954, is detained as a special patient or a committed patient pursuant to an order or direction under section *39G*(1) or section *39H* or section *39I* of the Criminal Justice Act 1954:

(ii) A person who, having been found by a Court, on conviction of of any offence, to be mentally disordered, is detained as a committed patient pursuant to an order under section *39I* of the Criminal Justice Act 1954:

(iii) A person who is subject to a reception order made on an application under section *42* of the Mental Health Act 1969:

(iv) A person detained under section *43* of the Mental Health Act 1969:

(*d*) A person detained in any penal institution pursuant to a conviction:

(*e*) A person whose name is on the Corrupt Practices List made out for any district.

(2) The Registrar of the Court in which any reception order or any order under section *39G*(1) or section *39J* of the Criminal Justice Act 1954 is made or any person is convicted of a corrupt practice shall, not later than the fifth day of the month next succeeding the date of the order or conviction, forward to the Registrar of Electors of the electoral district in which the patient or offender was residing a certificate showing the name, place of abode, and description of the patient or offender and particulars of the order or conviction.

(3) Nothing in sub-section (1)(*a*) or (*b*) of this section applies to

(*a*) A public servant who is outside New Zealand in the course of his duties; or

(*b*) A person who

(i) Is accompanying a public servant who is outside New Zealand in the course of the public servant's duties; and

(ii) Is the spouse or the child or the child of the spouse of any such public servant.

Registration

43. Compulsory registration of electors.

(1) Every person qualified to be registered as an elector of any electoral district shall if he is in New Zealand make application in the prescribed form to a Registrar of Electors for registration as an elector within one month after the date on which he first becomes qualified to be registered as an elector.

(2) Every person qualified to be registered as an elector of any electoral district may if he is outside New Zealand make application in the prescribed form to a Registrar of Electors for registration as an elector of that district an any time.

(3) Where a Maori is qualified to be registered as an elector of both a Maori electoral district and of a General electoral district, this section shall apply with respect to one only of those districts, being the district in respect of which he has exercised his option under section *41* of this Act.

(4) Where it appears to the Registrar that an applicant is qualified to be registered as an elector of another electoral district, the Registrar shall forthwith send the application to the Registrar of that district.

(5) Every person commits an offence against this section who, being required by this section to apply for registration as an elector during any period, fails to become so registered during that period, unless he proves that he duly applied for registration or that his failure to apply for registration was not due to wilful default.

(6) Every such offence shall be a continuing offence until application for registration is duly made.

(7) Every person who commits an offence against this section shall liable on summary conviction to a fine not exceeding $20 on a first conviction, and to a fine not exceeding $10 on any subsequent conviction.

43A. Revision of electoral rolls.

(1) Subject to sub-section (2) of this section, in every year that a Parliament is due to expire, every Registrar shall direct an inquiry to be made concerning the particulars of all persons whose names are on the roll for that district.

Provided that where a roll that is not yet in force has been compiled under section *60*(1) of this Act the inquiry directed to be made under sub-section (1) of this section shall be in respect of that poll.

(2) Where a Parliament is dissolved while an inquiry under sub-section (1) of this section is in progress, the Registrar shall not be obliged to complete that inquiry.

(3) Every inquiry shall be in the prescribed form and shall require the person to whom it is addressed to sign and return the form together with any corrections to the information contained in it.

(4) Every completed form accepted by the Registrar as being in order

(*a*) Shall be deemed, for the purposes of the definition of the term 'electoral roll' in section *2*(1) of this Act and for the purposes of section *60B* of this Act, to be an application for registration as an elector; and

(*b*) In the case of an elector who is a Maori, shall constitute a sufficent record of the manner in which the elector last exercised his option to register as an elector of a Maori electoral district or as an elector of a General electoral district.

(5) Where any person fails to respond to an inquiry under sub-section (3) of this section the Registrar shall, after making such further inquiry as he thinks fit, or the Chief Registrar directs, remove the name of that person from the roll.

(6) Notwithstanding sub-section (1) of this section, the inquiries that would be required, but for this sub-section, to be directed and undertaken under subsection (1) of this section in the year 1981 shall be directed and undertaken instead in the period of 6 months beginning on the 13th day of October 1980.

44. Changes of address to be notified.

(1) Every registered elector who while remaining resident within an electoral district changes his place of residence within that district, and who failed for 2 months to notify the Registrar of his new address, commits an offence, which shall be a continuing offence while the default continues.

(2) Every person who commits an offence against this section shall be liable on summary conviction to a fine not exceeding $2 of a first conviction, and to a fine not exceeding $4 on any subsequent conviction.

45. Effect of failure to notify change of address. A registered elector who has changed his place of residence within an electoral district as aforesaid shall not be disqualified from voting at an election in that district by reason only that he has not given notice of that change of address as herein before required.

46. Notification of death of registered elector. Every Registrar of Births and Deaths shall forthwith after the registration of the death of an adult person notify the Registrar of Electors for the district in which the deceased person resided of the fact of the death, together with such particulars known to the Registrar of Births and Deaths as may be required to enable the appropriate Registrar of Electors to amend to the roll if necessary.

47. Notification of marriages of women electors.

(1) Where the woman to whom a notice of intended marriage under the Marriage Act 1955 relates is registered as an elector of any district, she or the other party to the intended marriage shall complete the form prescribed for the purposes of this section and give it to the Registrar of Marriages for transmission to the Registrar of Electors for that district.

(2) The Registrar of Electors who receives the notice shall, after the date of the intended marriage, send to the elector by post a notice inquiring whether any change in the name, address, and description under which she is registered on the roll is required as a result of the marriage.

(3) If the elector states that a change is required the Registrar of Electors shall amend his roll in accordance with the particulars supplied.

(4) Where an amendment to the roll is necessary under sub-section (3) of this section and the amendment is not made before the issue of the writ for any election, the elector shall, if otherwise qualified, be entitled to vote at that election in respect of her former name as appearing on the roll.

48. Application for registration.

(1) Every person making any application or declaration in respect of registration as an elector shall either sign or place his mark on the application or declaration.

(2) The place of residence in respect of which registration is claimed must be specified in such manner as to enable it to be clearly identified.

49. Procedure following application for registration.

(1) If the Registrar is satisfied that any applicant for registration as an elector (whether by transfer from another district, or otherwise) is qualified to be registered, he shall forthwith enter the name of the applicant on the roll.

(2) Where it appears to the Registrar that an applicant who is a Maori is prevented, by the manner in which he has exercised the option given by section *41* of this Act, from being registered as an elector of the district to which his application relates, the Registrar shall forthwith sent the application to the Registrar of the district in respect of which the applicant is entitled to be registered and shall notify the elector of his reasons for refusing the application and of the Registrar to whom the application has been sent.

(3) The Registrar to whom the application is sent under sub-section (2) of this section may register the applicant as an elector of the Registrar's district (irrespective of the indication on the application of the manner in which the applicant last exercised the option conferred by section *41* of this Act).

49A. Questioning of applicant for registration.

(1) If the Registrar, after making such inquiries as he thinks fit, has reason to believe that any application for registration as an elector is not qualified to be registered, he shall forthwith give notice in writing to the applicant setting forth the particulars of which proof is required.

(2) The Registrar shall within 3 days after the day of the issue of a writ deal under sub-section (1) of this section with all applications received before 6 o'clock in the afternoon of writ day.

(3) If the applicant fails to furnish proof of his qualifications satisfactorily to the Registrar within 10 days after the giving of notice to him under sub-section (1) of this section, the Registrar shall refuse the application and forthwith notify the applicant accordingly.

(4) Within 14 days after the giving to the applicant of a notice of refusal under sub-section (3) of this section, the applicant may require the Registrar to refer the application to a District Court.

(5) The Registrar shall notify the applicant of the time and place appointed for the hearing of the application by the District Court.

50. Applicants received after issue of writ. Where a writ has been issued for an election in any district, then, subject to sub-section (3) of section *2* of this Act, no person whose application is received after 6 o'clock in the afternoon of writ day shall be registered as an elector of the district before the expiration of 7 clear days after polling day:

Provided that this section shall not apply to any applicant who satisfies the Registrar that he has become qualified for registration as an elector of the district not earlier than one month before writ day.

51. Assistance to be given to Registrar.

(1) All members of the Police shall at the request of the Registrar assist him by informing him of the name of any person who they have reason to believe is qualified to be registered as an elector but is not registered, or is registered but is not qualified to be registered, and shall give the Registrar any information he requests relating to the qualifications of any person for registration as an elector.

(2) All members of the Police shall also assist the Registrar by making such inquiries and obtaining such information as he requests.

52. Elector's objection.

(1) Subject to section *54* of this Act, any elector may at any time object to the name of any person being on the roll for any district on the ground that that person is not qualified to be registered as an elector of that district.

(2) Every such objection shall be made in writing to the Registrar for the district, and shall specify particulars of the objection.

(3) On receipt of any such objection the Registrar shall forthwith give notice in writing to the person objected to of the objection and of the particulars specified.

(4) Unless within 7 days after the giving of notice to him of the objection the person objected to notifies the Registrar that he consents to the removal of his

name from the roll, or the objection is withdrawn, the Registrar shall refer the objection to a District Court and shall notify the parties of the time and place appointed for the hearing.

53. Registrar's objection.

(1) Subject to section *54* of this Act, the Registrar for any district may at any time object to the name of any person being on the roll for the district on the ground that that person is not qualified to be registered as an elector of that district.

(2) The Registrar shall forthwith give notice in writing to the person objected to of the objection and of the particulars thereof.

(3) Unless within 7 days after the giving of notice to him of the objection the person objected to notifies the Registrar that he consents to the removal of his name from the roll, or satisfies the Registrar that he is qualified to be registered as an elector of the district, or the objection is withdrawn, the Registrar shall refer the objection to a District Court and shall notify the person objected to of the time and place appointed for the hearing.

(4) Nothing in this section shall affect the provisions of this Act as to the removal of names from the roll by the Registrar.

54. Time limit for objections and hearings by District Court after issue of writ. Where a writ has been issued for an election in any district

(*a*) No objection shall be made under section *52* or section *53* of this Act in respect of that district after the expiration of 3 clear days from writ day and before polling day:

(*b*) No application or objection referred to a District Court under section *49A* or section *52* or section *53* of this Act shall be determined by the Court after the expiration of 14 clear days from writ day and before polling day.

55. Procedure on reference of application or objection to District Court.

(1) The following provisions of this section shall apply with respect to proceedings on the reference to a District Court of an application under section *49A* of this Act or of an objection under section *52* or section *53* of this Act.

(2) The Registrar of Electors, any objector, and the person objected to may appear before the Court either in person or by some person appointed by him in writing or by a barrister or solictor.

(3) In the case of an objection the person objected to may forward to the Registrar of the Court a statement signed by him giving reasons why his name should be retained on the roll, and the Court shall take any such statement into account in determining the objection.

(4) If any person objected to does not either appear or forward a statement as aforesaid the Court shall make an order that his name be removed from the roll.

(5) Except as otherwise provided in this section, the name of any person objected to shall not be removed from the roll until the objection has been determined.

(6) At the hearing of an objection no grounds of objection shall be taken into account except those specified in the particulars of the objection.

(7) In any proceedings to which this section applies the Court may make such order as to costs as it thinks fit.

(8) Subject to the provisions of this section, the ordinary rules of procedure of the Court shall apply.

(9) The Registrar of Electors shall make any additions, deletions, and alterations to the roll that may be necessary to give effect to the order of the Court.

56. Notice of registration.

(1) Subject to subsection (2) of this section, the Registrar shall, not later than 14 days after the registration of a person, deliver to that person personally, or send to him by post, notice in writing of his having been so registered.

(2) Subsection (1) of this section shall not apply where

(*a*) An inquiry in the form prescribed for the purposes of section *43A* of this Act is to be sent to the elector within one month after the date of his registration; or

(*b*) The registration is effected on the basis of a form to which section *43A*(4)(*a*) of this Act applies.

57. Removal of names from roll by Registrar.

(1) The Registrar shall, at any time except between the issue of a writ for an election in the district and the return of the writ, remove from the roll

(*a*) The name of every person not qualified to be registered as an elector of the district who requests in writing that his name be removed from the roll for the purpose of transferring it to another roll

(*aa*) The name of every person who, consequent on a change in his place of residence,

(i) Is not qualified to be registered as an elector of the district; and

(ii) Resides in, and is registered as an elector of, another district:

(*b*) The name of every person of whose identity the Registrar is satisfied and whose death has been notified to him by any Registrar of Births and Deaths:

(*c*) The name of every person who, on an inquiry made at that person's address on the roll cannot be found, or who, as a result of any such inquiry, the Registrar of Electors has reason to believe has ceased for 3 months or upwards to reside in the district:

(*d*) The name of every person whose name is entered on the Corrupt Practices List made out for any district:

(*e*) The name of every person whose disqualification under section *42* of this Act is duly certified to him.

(2) The Registrar shall at any time except between the expiration of 6 days from the day of issue of a writ for an election in the district and the return of the writ, remove from the roll the name of every person whose subsequent registration for any other district is notified to him by the Registrar for that other district.

(3) Notwithstanding anything in this Act the Registrar on being satisfied

that the name of any person has been omitted or removed from the roll by mistake or clerical error, or through false information, may restore the name of that person to the roll at any time.

57A. Correction of errors.

(1) In addition to other powers of alteration conferred by this Act, the Registrar may at any time, subject to subsection (3) of this section, alter the roll

(*a*) By correcting any mistake or omission in the particulars of the enrolment of an elector:

(*b*) By striking out the superfluous entry when the name of an elector appears more than once on the roll.

(2) Where an error made by or on behalf of the Chief Registrar or a Registrar, or, before the commencement of this section, by the Chief Electoral Officer or an Electorate Officer, has resulted in an elector being registered as an elector of a district other than the district in respect of which the elector should have been registered

(*a*) The Registrar of the district in respect of which the elector has been incorrectly registered may, subject to subsection (4) of this section, remove the elector's name from the roll for that district; and

(*b*) The Registrar of the district in respect of which the elector should have been registered may, subject to subsection (4) of this section, place the elector's name on the roll for that district.

(3) Where, under subsection (1)(*a*) or subsection (2) of this section, the particulars of any elector have been altered or the name of any elector has been removed from or placed on a roll, the Registrar shall, not later than 14 days after the date on which the roll is altered, deliver to the elector personally or send to him by post, notice in writing of the alteration to the roll.

(4) No alteration pursuant to this section shall be made to the roll for a district between the issue of a writ for an election in that district and the return of the writ.

58. Repealed.

59. Corrupt Practices List.

(1) Where it is proved before the Registrar for any district that any person who is registered or who applies for registration as an elector of the district has within the immediately preceding period of 3 years

(*a*) Been convicted of a corrupt practice; or

(*b*) Been reported by the High Court in its report on the trial of an election petition to have been proved guilty of a corrupt practice,

the Registrar shall enter the name, residence, and description of that person and particulars of the conviction or report on a list to be called the Corrupt Practices List.

(2) The Registrar shall remove the name of every person from the Corrupt Practices List at the expiration of 3 years from the data of the conviction or report in respect of which his name is entered on the list, or sooner if so ordered by the High Court.

(3) Whenever a main roll is printed for the district a copy of the Corrupt Practices List for the district shall be appended to it and printed with it.

(4) Whenever a supplementary roll is printed for the district a copy of so much of the Corrupt Practices List as has not been printed with the main roll or any existing supplementary roll for the district shall be appended to the supplementary roll and printed and published with it.

Electoral Rolls

60. New rolls on change of boundaries.

(1) Where the gazetting of a Proclamation pursuant to section *19*(1) of this Act defines the boundaries of the electoral districts fixed by the Representation Commission, the Chief Registrar shall, immediately before the next succeeding revision of the rolls under section *43A* of this Act,

(*a*) Decide, on the basis of the then existing rolls, which of the electors are entitled to be registered as electors of each electoral district to which that Proclamation relates; and

(*b*) Compile for each electoral district to which that Proclamation relates a list of persons appearing to be entitled to be registered as electors of that electoral district.

(2) For the purposes of the revision of the rolls mentioned in subsection (1) of this section, each list compiled under paragraph (*b*) of that subsection shall be the electoral roll for the district to which it relates.

(3) Every roll compiled under section *43A* of this Act pursuant to subsection (1) of this section shall come into force as the electoral roll for the district on the dissolution or expiry of the then existing Parliament.

(4) Every roll to which subsection (3) of this section applies shall, subject to any revision of that roll, continue in force until a new roll for the district is compiled and comes into force.

(5) The Registrar shall keep every roll to which subsection (3) of this section applies up to date by making all such additions, alterations, and deletions as become necessary.

60A. Maintenance of rolls being replaced.

(1) Where a revision of rolls has been begun pursuant to section *60*(1) of this Act, the respective Registrars of Electors shall not be obliged to keep up to date the rolls for the districts that were in existence immediately before the gazetting of the Proclamation that immediately preceded the revision of the rolls.

(2) Notwithstanding subsection (1) of this section, the Chief Registrar shall ensure that each Registrar of a district to which that subsection applies has available to him until the roll for that district ceases to be in force all information necessary to enable him to bring his roll up to date in the event of a by-election in that district (which information may include or consist of photo-copies of original documents).

(3) Where a by-election is to take place in a district to which subsection

(1) of this section applies, the Registrar of that district shall cause an up to date composite roll for the district to be closed and printed as at writ day for the by-election.

(4) Where a by-election has taken place in a district to which subsection (1) of this section applies, the Registrar of that district shall, after the time allowed for the filing of an election petition in respect of the by-election has expired or, where an election petition is filed in respect of that by-election, after that election petition has been finally disposed of, send to other Registrars of Electors such of the original applications for registration as electors held by him as the Chief Registrar specifies.

60B. Rolls where Parliament dissolved after change of boundaries and before new rolls completed.

(1) Where Parliament is dissolved in the period between the gazetting of a Proclamation pursuant to section *19*(1) of this Act and the completion of the revision of the rolls under section *43A* of this Act which next succeeds the gazetting, the Chief Registrar shall

(*a*) Comply with paragraphs (*a*) and (*b*) of section *60*(1) of this Act; and

(*b*) Direct which of the applications for registration as electors which constituted the rolls of the electoral districts that were defined immediately before that Proclamation took effect shall be sent to the respective Registrars of the electoral districts to which that Proclamation relates.

(2) Subject to subsection (3) of this section, each list compiled under section *60*(1)(*b*) of this Act (as applied by subsection (1)(*a*) of this section) shall be the electoral roll for the district to which it relates and shall come into force as soon as it is compiled.

(3) The applications for registration sent, pursuant to a direction under subsection (1)(*b*) of this section, to the Registrar of an electoral district shall, on being received by that Registrar, constitute the electoral roll for the district and the electoral roll specified in subsection (2) of this section shall (without its status as a main roll being affected) then cease to have effect as the electoral roll for the district.

(4) Every electoral roll to which subsection (3) of this section applies shall, subject to any revision of that electoral roll, continue in force until a new electoral roll for the district is compiled and comes into force.

(5) The Registrar shall keep every electoral roll to which subsection (2) or subsection (3) of this section applies up to date by making all such additions, alterations, and deletions as become necessary and any additions, alterations, and deletions made to an electoral roll to which subsection (2) of this section applies shall be incorporated, where necessary, in the electoral roll which supersedes it by virtue of subsection (3) of this section.

60C. Habitation indexes.

(1) The Chief Registrar

(*a*) May from time to time compile in respect of any electoral district a habitation index listing, in accordance with their residential addresses, the electors who reside in that electoral district; and

(*b*) Shall, as soon as practicable after the printing of a main roll for an electoral district, compile a habitation index under paragraph (*a*) of this subsection in respect of that district.

(2) Copies of the latest index compiled under this section in respect of any electoral district shall be kept for inspection by the public at the office of the Registrar and at such other convenient places within the district as the Chief Registrar from time to time directs.

(3) Any person may on paying the prescribed fee obtain a copy of an index compiled under this section.

(4) Regulations made under section *188* of this Act may provide for any fee payable under subsection (3) of this section to be reduced where the copy of the index is required for any purpose related to an election or poll.

61. Main roll to be printed.

(1) The Registrar for every district shall, at least once in each year, cause to be printed a main roll for the district, which shall contain a list of all persons whose names are lawfully on the electoral roll for the district on a date to be fixed for the closing of the main rolls.

(2) The date to be fixed for the purposes of subsection (1) of this section shall

(*a*) In the case of a year in which Parliament is due to expire, be fixed by the Governor General by Order in Council; and

(*b*) In the case of any other year, be fixed by the Chief Registrar by notice in the *Gazette.*

(3) Every main roll printed for any district under this section shall be the main roll for the district until a new main roll is printed for the district.

62. Supplementary rolls to be printed.

(1) The Registrar for every district shall from time to time cause to be prnted a supplementary roll for the district, which shall contain a list of all persons whose names do not appear on the main roll or any existing supplementary roll for the district but are lawfully on the electoral roll for the district on a date to be fixed for the closing of that supplementary roll by the Chief Registrar of Electors:

Provided that a supplementary roll shall be printed as soon as may be after the issue of a writ for an election in the district, and the date for the closing of that roll shall be writ day.

(2) Every supplementary roll printed for any district under this section shall be a supplementary roll for the district until a new main roll is printed for the district.

62A. Unpublished names.

(1) Notwithstanding sections *60, 60C, 61, 62, 63A,* and *64*(2) (*c*) and (*d*) of this Act, where the Chief Registrar is satisfied on the application of any person,

that the publication of that person's name would be prejudicial to the personal safety of that person or his family, the Chief Registrar may direct that

(*a*) The name, residence, and occupation of that person shall not be published in any main or supplementary roll or in any list or index that may be available for inspection by the public; and

(*b*) The name and particulars of that person shall not be available for inspection under section *64*(2)(*c*) of this Act; and

(*c*) The application for registration of that person shall not be available for inspection under section *64*(2)(*d*) of this Act.

(2) Without limiting the discretion conferred on the Chief Registrar by subsection (1) of this section, he may on the production of

(*a*) A non-molestation order that is in force in respect of any person; or

(*b*) A statutory declaration from a member of the Police to the effect that he believes that the personal safety of a person or of a person's family could be prejudiced by the publication of that person's name,

exercise in respect of that person's name, and without further evidence or inquiry, the power conferred on the Chief Registrar by that subsection.

63. Form of main roll and supplementary rolls.

(1) Every main roll or supplementary roll printed for any district shall show the names, residences, and occupations (if any) of the persons included therein, arranged alphabetically in order of surnames .

(2) The names on each page of the main roll and of every supplementary roll printed for any district shall be numbered consecutively, beginning with the number one in the case of the first name on each page.

(3) The pages of every main roll or supplementary roll printed for any district shall be numbered consecutively, beginning with the number one in the case of the first page of the main roll and, in the case of a supplementary roll, with the number immediately following the number of the last page of the last printed roll of the district, whether main or supplementary.

(4) The number appearing on the main roll or, as the case may be, on any supplementary roll printed for any district against the name of any elector, preceded by the number of the page on which his name appears, shall be deemed to be his number on the roll.

(5) With the consent of the Government Statistician, the Registrar may divide the main electoral roll and every supplementary roll into such statistical subdivisions as the Government Statistician approves.

(6) The main roll and supplementary rolls so subdivided shall be available for public inspection at the office of the Registrar, without payment, at any time when the office is open for the transaction of business, and any person may obtain copies of or extracts from the rolls so subdivided on payment of the prescribed fee.

63A. Composite rolls.

(1) The Registrar of Electors for any district may from time to time cause to be printed a composite roll for the district, which roll

(*a*) Shall, subject to any additions, alterations, and deletions made to the electoral roll for the district, contain a list of

(i) All persons whose names appear on the main roll for the district; and

(ii) All persons whose names appear on any existing supplementary roll for the district; and

(iii) All persons whose names do not appear on the main roll for the district or any existing or supplementary roll for the district but are lawfully on the electoral roll for the district on the date to be fixed for the closing of that composite roll by the Chief Registrar of Electors; and

(*b*) Shall, subject to paragraph (*a*) of this subsection, be printed in the manner prescribed by section *63* of the Act in respect of a main roll.

(2) Where the date for the closing of a composite roll for a district is writ day in relation to an election in that district, the Registrar of Electors

(*a*) Shall cause the composite roll to be printed as soon as may be after the issue of the writ for the election; and

(*b*) Shall not be obliged to issue a supplementary roll for the district under the proviso to section *62*(1) of this Act in relation to that election.

(3) Where a composite roll for a district is printed under this section,

(*a*) The composite roll shall, notwithstanding section *61*(2) of this Act, be the main roll for the district until a new main roll is printed for the district under section *61*(1) of this Act or a new composite roll is printed for the district under this section; and

(*b*) The main roll and any supplementary rolls that were in force for the district immediately before the date of the closing of the composite roll shall cease to be in force.

(4) Nothing in this section

(*a*) Limits the provisions of section *61*(1) of this Act; or

(*b*) Prevents any main roll or supplementary roll that is no longer in force from being examined for the purpose of determining

(i) Whether any person's name should appear on the main roll or any supplementary roll for the time being in force for any district; or

(ii) Whether any person is qualified to vote in a district as a special voter.

63B. Composite rolls required for by-elections. Notwithstanding anything in section *63A*(1) of this Act, in the case of a by-election in any district, the Registrar of Electors for that district shall cause a composite roll for that district to be closed and printed under section *63A* of this Act as at writ day for the by-election.

64. Inspection and purchase of main and supplementary rolls.

(1) Copies of the main roll and of the supplementary rolls for any district

shall be kept for inspection by the public at the office of the Registrar, and at each post office within the district that is controlled by a departmental officer of the Post Office, and at such other convenient places within the district as the Minister from time to time directs.

(2) Any person may inspect at the Registrar's office without payment at any time between 9 a.m. and 4 p.m. on any day on which the office is open for the transaction of business

(*a*) The main roll and supplementary rolls so kept:

(*b*) The most recent computer compiled list which is held by the Registrar and which shows the names and particulars of the persons who are on the roll for the district:

(*c*) The names and particulars of any person whose name is on the electoral roll but not on the main roll or any supplementary roll or the most recent computer compiled list to which paragraph (*b*) of this subsection applies:

(*d*) The application of any person who has applied to be registered as an elector of the district but who is prevented, by section 50 of this Act, from being registered as an elector of the district:

(*e*) His own application for registration as an elector:

(*f*) The application for registration of any person whose name is on the electoral roll if

(i) That person consents to his application being inspected; or

(ii) The Registrar is satisfied that the inspection of the application is justified by a genuine and proper interest.

(3) The power of inspection conferred by subsection (2) of this section does not, in the case of a computer compiled list, include the power to copy that list.

(4) Where any person is entitled to inspect any application, the Registrar shall produce it for inspection not later than 2 working days after a request has been made.

(5) Any person may on paying the prescribed fee obtain copies of or extracts from the main roll and the supplementary rolls.

(6) Where any candidate or any person acting on behalf of a political party wishes to obtain for the purposes of the candidate or the political party (and not for resale or commercial purposes) a computer tape containing the names, residences, and occupations (if any) of electors of an electoral district, the Chief Registrar may, in accordance with regulations made under this Act and on being supplied with a computer tape by that candidate or person and on payment of the prescribed fee, record those names, residences, and occupations on that tape and return it to that candidate or person.

(7) Regulations made under section *188* of this Act

(*a*) May prescribe a scale of fees for the purposes of subsection (5) or subsection (6) of this section; and

(*b*) May provide for any fee payable under subsection (5) of this section to be reduced where the copy of the roll is required for any purpose related to an election or poll.

65. Copies of rolls for Returning Officer. The Registrar shall supply to the Returning Officer for the district as many copies as he may require of the main roll and the supplementary rolls, showing all deletions from the electoral roll and certified correct by the Registrar.

65A. Dormant file.

(1) The Registrar shall keep a dormant file showing the particulars of those persons whose names have been removed from the roll for the district in the course of the latest revision of the roll under section *43A* of this Act.

(2) The file kept under subsection (1) of this section may be used for the purpose of determining whether any person is qualified, under section *99*(*c*) or (*d*) of this Act, to vote at any election in the district.

(3) Notwithstanding section *64* of this Act, any file kept under subsection (1) of this section shall not be available for public inspection.

Offences

66. False statements and declarations. Every person who knowingly and wilfully makes a false statement in any application, certificate, or declaration for the purposes of this Part of this Act shall be liable to summary conviction to a fine not exceeding $500 or to imprisonment for a term not exceeding 3 months.

67. Wilfully misleading Registrar.

(1) Every person shall for each offence be liable on summary conviction to a fine not exceeding $500 who

(*a*) Wilfully misleads any Registrar in the compilation of any roll or list, or wilfully enters or causes to be entered thereon any false or fictitious name or qualification or the name of any person whom he knows to be dead:

(*b*) Signs the name of any other person, whether requested to do so or not, or any false or fictitious name to any form of application or objection for the purposes of this Part of this Act either as applicant, objector, or witness:

(*c*) Signs his name as witness to any signature upon any such form of application or objection without either seeing the signature written or hearing the person signing declare that the signature is in his own handwriting and that the name so signed is his own proper name.

(2) It shall be the duty of the Registrar to institute a prosecution against any person whom he believes to have committed any offence against this section, or of aiding, abetting, counselling, or procuring the commission of any such offence by any person in the district.

68. Failure to deliver application. Every person shall be liable on summary conviction to a fine not exceeding $500 or to imprisonment for a term not exceeding

3 months who, having obtained possession of an application for registration signed by any other person for the purpose of being delivered to the Registrar or registration, wilfully or negligently fails so to deliver it so that the applicant's name is not entered on the roll.

69. Misfeasance of Registrar. Every Registrar who knowingly and wilfully does anything contrary to the provisions of this Part of this Act, or who knowingly and wilfully omits to do anything required by this Part of this Act to be done by him, shall be liable to summary conviction, if no other penalty is elsewhere in this Act provided, to a fine not exceeding $500.

PART IV

ELECTIONS

General Elections

70. Governor General's warrant for issue of writs. For every general election the Governor General shall, not later than 7 days after the day of the dissolution or expiration of the then last Parliament, as the case may be, by warrant under his hand in form 2, direct the Clerk of the Writs to proceed forthwith to issue writs for the election of members of Parliament for all electoral districts within New Zealand.

71. Writs for general election. On the receipt of the Governor General's warrant the Clerk of the Writs shall within 3 days issue a writ in form 3 to the Returning Officer for each electoral district.

By-elections

72. Speaker's warrant for issue of writ.

(1) Where during a recess of the House of Representatives, whether by prorogation or adjournment, it appears to the Speaker that the seat of any member has become vacant, he shall forthwith cause a notice of the vacancy and of the cause thereof to be published in the *Gazette.*

(2) Where the vacancy arises from death or resignation the Speaker shall, forthwith upon the publication of the notice in the *Gazette,* by warrant under his hand in form 4, direct the Clerk of the Writs to proceed forthwith to issue a writ to supply the vacancy.

(3) Where the vacancy arises from any cause other than death or resignation, then, as soon as conveniently may be after the expiration of 10 days from the date of the publication of the notice in the *Gazette*, the Speaker on its being established to his satisfaction that a vacancy does exist, shall, by warrant under his hand in form 4, direct the Clerk of the Writs to proceed forthwith to issue a writ to supply the vacancy.

(4) Where a vacancy exists at the commencement of any session and no

writ has been issued to supply the vacancy, or where a vacancy occurs during a session, the Speaker shall forthwith upon being ordered to do so by the House, by warrant under his hand in form 4, direct the Clerk of the Writs to proceed forthwith to issue a writ to supply the vacancy.

73. When Governor General to act for Speaker. Where a vacancy occurs at a time when there is no Speaker or the Speaker is absent from New Zealand, the Governor General shall cause a like notice to be inserted in the *Gazette*, and the like proceedings to be taken as are provided for in section *72* of this Act.

74. Writ for by-election. The Clerk of the Writs shall as soon as reasonably practicable after receiving a warrant, but in any case not later than 21 days after the date of the receipt of the warrant, issue a writ in form 3 to the Returning Officer for the district in which the vacancy has occurred:

Provided that, in any case in which it appears to the Governor General to be necessary for special reasons, the Governor General may, by Order in Council, authorize the Clerk of Writs to postpone the issue of a writ until such day as may be specified in the Order in Council, not being later than 42 days after the date of the receipt of the warrant.

75. No writ to issue pending election petition. If after a petition has been presented against the return of any member his seat becomes vacant on any of the grounds mentioned in section *32* of this Act, no writ to fill the vacancy shall be issued until after the petition has been disposed of, and not then if the Court determines that that member was not duly elected or returned and that some other person was duly elected or returned.

Issue of Writs

76. Contents of writ.

(1) In every writ for the election of a member of Parliament there shall be appointed:

(*a*) The latest day for the nomination of candidates; and

(*b*) A day for the polling to take place if a poll is required, being a Saturday; and

(*c*) The latest day for the return of the writ.

(2) The nomination day shall be not less than 20 or more than 27 days before the polling day.

(3) In the case of a general election the same polling day shall be appointed in each writ.

(4) The latest day for return of the writ shall be the 50th day after its issue:

Provided that in the case of a writ issued pursuant ot section *89*(8) of this Act (relating to the death of a candidate after the close of nominations) the latest day for the return of the writ shall be the 78th day after its issue.

77. Clerk of Writs to notify Registrar. The Clerk of the Writs shall forthwith on signing a writ for an election to be held in any district cause a notice of the issue of the writ to be sent by letter or telegram to the Registrar for the district.

78. Notice to Returning Officer by telegram.

(1) The Clerk of the Writs may, on signing a writ for an election to be held in any district, cause a notice to be sent by telegram to the Returning Officer for the district informing him of the issue of the writ and of the nomination day and the polling day.

(2) The receipt by the Returning Officer of such a notice shall be deemed to be the receipt by him of the writ, and the date of that receipt shall be endorsed on the writ.

79. Returning Officer to give public notice of nomination day and polling day. Every Returning Officer shall forthwith on the receipt of a writ give public notice of the nomination day and of the polling day in form 5.

80. Nomination of candidates.

(1) Any person qualified under Part II of this Act may, with his consent, be nominated as a candidate for election for any district, by not less than 2 registered electors of that district, by a nomination paper in form 6.

(2) Consent to the nomination of any person shall be given by that person in writing or by telegram, but need not be given at the time when the nomination paper is lodged:

Provided that the consent of any person who is for the time being outside New Zealand may be signified to the Returning Officer in any manner approved by the Chief Electoral Officer.

(3) Every nomination paper and every consent shall be lodged with or given to the Returning Officer for the district not later than noon on nomination day. The Returning Officer shall give a receipt in writing for every nomination accepted by him.

(4) Each candidate shall be nominated by a separate nomination paper in such manner as, in the opinion of the Returning Officer, is sufficient to identify the candidate.

(5) No elector may nominate more than one candidate.

(6) Any registered elector of the district may inspect any nomination paper or consent at the Returning Officer's office without payment at any time when the office is open for the transaction of business.

81. Deposit by candidate.

(1) Every candidate, or some person on his behalf, shall deposit with the Returning Officer the sum of $100 not later than noon on nomination day.

(2) The deposit shall be paid in the form of money, a money order, a money order telegram, a bank draft, or a bank cheque.

(3) If the total number of votes received by any unsuccessful candidate is less than one-fourth of the total number of votes received by the successful candidate the deposit of the unsuccessful candidate shall be forfeited and paid into the Consolidated Account, but in every other case the deposit shall be returned to the person who paid it.

82. Acceptance or rejection of nomination.

(1) The Returning Officer shall reject the nomination of any candidate

(*a*) If the nomination paper and the consent of the candidate are not lodged with him not later than noon on nomination day; or

(*b*) If the nomination paper does not state that the candidate is a registered elector of a specified electoral district, or, where section *27* of this Act applies, is a qualified elector of a specified electoral district; or

(*c*) If the nomination paper is not signed by at least 2 registered electors of the district for which the nomination is made; or

(*d*) If the required deposit is not paid as required by this Act.

(1A) Subject to the concurrence of the Chief Electoral Officer, the Returning Officer shall not accept the nomination of any candidate if the Returning Officer is not satisfied, by such evidence (if any) as he requires, that the name under which the candidate is nominated is

(*a*) The name under which his birth was registered, with any alteration or addition made thereto under section *17* of the Births and Deaths Registration Act 1951; or

(*b*) In the case of a person who has been adopted, the name conferred on him by the adoption order; or

(*c*) The name by which he was commonly known on the date 6 months immediately preceding nomination day; or

(*d*) The name which he had adopted by deed poll registered under section *17A* of the Births and Deaths Registration Act 1951 (as inserted by section 2 of the Births and Deaths Registration Amendment Act 1953) at least 6 months before nomination day:

Provided that in the case of any female candidate who is or has been married, her husband's surname may be substituted for her surname in any of the cases specified in paragraphs (*a*) to (*d*) of this subsection, unless, if her husband were nominated as a candidate under that surname, the Returning Officer would be required to reject his nomination under the provisions of this subsection:

Provided also that the Returning Officer may, with the concurrence of the Chief Electoral Officer, accept the nomination of any candidate under a name that does not comply with the foregoing provisions of this subsection, if the Returning Officer is satisfied that the candidate has publicly announced before the commencement of this subsection his intention to become a candidate under that name, and that the name has been adopted by the candidate in good faith and for good reason and is not indecent or offensive or likely to deceive or cause confusion.

(2) In every other case the Returning Officer shall accept the nomination:

Provided that nothing in this subsection shall limit the jurisdiction of the Court hearing an election petition.

83. Withdrawal of nomination.

(1) Any candidate may withdraw his nomination by a notice in form 7, signed by him and witnessed by a Justice of the Peace or a solicitor.

(2) No withdrawal of nomination shall have any effect unless it is lodged with the Returning Officer not later than noon on nomination day.

(3) Where a candidate has duly withdrawn his nomination his deposit shall be returned to the person who paid it.

84. Advertisement of nominations and polling places.

(1) After the close of nominations in any district the Returning Officer shall forthwith forward to the Chief Electoral Officer at Wellington the names of the candidates nominated who have not withdrawn their nominations.

(2) In each district in which a poll is required to be taken the Returning Officer shall advertise the names of the several candidates in at least one newspaper circulating in the district in such manner as he deems most likely to give full publicity thereto, and shall similarly advertise the polling places for the district not later than 2 days before polling day.

(3) The Chief Electoral Officer shall forthwith notify to every Returning Officer the names of the candidates nominated who have not withdrawn their nomination in each district in which a poll is required to be taken.

85. Procedure where election not contested.

(1) If only one candidate is nominated, or if any candidate who has been nominated duly withdraws his nomination and there remains only one candidate, the Returning Officer shall, by public notice on or before polling day, declare that candidate to be duly elected.

(2) The name of the person so elected shall be endorsed on the writ by the Returning Officer, and the writ shall be returned by him to the Clerk of the Writs forthwith.

Contested Elections

86. If necessary, poll to be taken. If more than one candidate is nominated, and a sufficient number do not withdraw their nominations so as to leave only one candidate, a poll for deciding between the candidates shall be taken by secret ballot at the several polling places of the district on polling day.

87. Form of ballot papers.

(1) Forthwith after nomination day the Returning Officer shall cause ballot papers to be printed in form 8 in sufficient number for the election.

(2) The ballot papers shall contain a list of all the persons nominated as candidates who have not withdrawn their nominations (each name being inserted once only, whether nominated in one or more nomination papers), and of no other persons, arranged alphabetically in order of their surnames in large characters; and where 2 or more candidates have the same surname, or for any other reason the Returning Officer considers that confusion may arise, the candidates shall be distinguished on the ballot papers by the addition in smaller characters of their Christain names or other given names and such other matter as may be necessary to distinguish them.

(3) Every ballot paper shall have a counterfoil in form 9.

(4) If the Returning Officer so decides, there may also be printed on the top right-hand corner of every ballot paper and in the space provided in the counterfoil attached thereto a number (called a consecutive number) beginning with the number one in the case of the first ballot paper printed, and on all succeeding ballot

papers printed the numbers shall be consecutive, so that no 2 ballot papers for the district shall bear the same number.

Death of Candidate

88. Death before close of nominations.

(1) Where a candidate who has been nominated and has not withdrawn his nomination dies before the close of nominations his nomination shall be treated in all respects as if it had not been made, and his deposit shall be returned to his personal representatives or, as the case may be, to the person who paid it.

(2) Where in any such case the candidate dies on nomination day or on the day before nomination day the time for the close of nominations in that district shall be deemed to be postponed by 4 days.

89. Death after close of nominations.

(1) If any candidate dies after the close of nominations and before the close of the poll or if the successful candidate dies after the close of the poll and before the declaration of the result of the poll, the provisions of this section shall apply.

(2) The election shall be deemed to have failed and the writ shall be deemed to be vacated.

(3) Where the candidate dies before polling day the Returning Officer shall, upon being satisfied of the fact of the death,

(*a*) Countermand the notice of the poll;

(*b*) Report the death to the Chief Electoral Officer;

(*c*) Endorse on the writ the fact of the death, the date of the proof thereof, and the date of the countermand of the notice of the poll; and

(*d*) Return the writ so endorsed to the Clerk of the Writs.

(4) Where the candidate dies on polling day before the close of the poll the Returning Officer shall, upon being satisfied of the fact of death,

(*a*) Immediately close the poll and declare it to be null and of no effect;

(*b*) Report the death to the Chief Electoral Officer;

(*c*) Endorse on the writ the fact of death and the time of the close of the poll; and

(*d*) Return the writ so endorsed to the Clerk of the Writs.

(5) Where the candidate dies after the close of the poll and before the declaration of the result of the poll, and it is found on the completion of the count of votes or on a recount that the candidate, if still living, would have been elected, the Returning Officer shall, upon being satisfied of the fact of the death,

(*a*) Report the death to the Chief Electoral Officer;

(*b*) Endorse on the writ the fact of the death and that the candidate, if still living, would have been elected; and

(*c*) Return the writ so endorsed to the Clerk of the Writs.

(6) The provisions of this Act as to an equality of votes between candidates shall apply notwithstanding the death of one of those candidates after the close of the poll.

(7) Where the poll is interrupted in consequence of the death of a candidate all ballot papers placed in the several ballot boxes shall be taken out by the several Deputy Returning Officers and, being made up into secured packages, shall be sent unopened to the Returning Officer, who shall forthwith destroy them in the presence of a District Court Judge or a Justice of the Peace.

(8) Upon the return to the Clerk of the Writs of a writ which has been vacated as aforesaid a fresh writ shall be issued forthwith for a new election and, except as otherwise provided, all proceedings in connection with the new election shall be had and taken anew.

(9) The main roll and supplementary rolls which were to be used at the election which has failed shall be used at the new election without any amendment or addition.

(10) It shall not be necessary to nominate afresh any candidate who at the time of the countermand or close of the poll was a duly nominated candidate:

Provided that any such candidate may withdraw his nomination before the time appointed for the close of nominations for the new election.

(11) All appointments of polling places made in respect of the election which has failed shall continue in respect of the new election.

Candidates' Meetings

90. Use of public schoolrooms for election meetings.

(1) Any candidate at an election may, for the purpose of holding public meetings of electors for electoral purposes during the period of an election, use free of charge, other than the cost of lighting, and of cleaning after use, and of repairing any damage done, any suitable room in any public primary school or intermediate school or secondary school after the ordinary school hours, subject to the following provisions:

(*a*) Three days' notice of the proposed public meeting shall be given to the School Committee of the school in the case of a primary school, to the committee of the school in the case of an intermediate school, or to the governing body in the case of a secondary school.

(*b*) The use of the school shall be granted on the order of receipt of applications by or on behalf of the candidates:

(*c*) No candidate shall have the use of the same room on a second occasion if any other candidate who has not before used it desires to make use of it at the same time under this section.

(2) If it is proved that any such meeting was not a public meeting within the meaning of this section, the person by whom and the candidate on whose behalf the meeting was convened shall each be liable on summary conviction to a fine not exceeding $100.

(3) For the purposes of this section thie term 'candidate' means any person who has declared his intention of becoming a candidate either by advertisement in a newspaper, or by a circular, or by announcement at a public meeting, or by duly consenting to nomination, but does not include a candidate who has withdrawn his nomination.

Polling at Elections

91. Governor General may appoint polling places.

(1) In respect of each election, the Governor General may from time to time appoint polling places for any district within the limits of that district, and revoke, alter, or add to any such appointment:

Provided that where a building suitable for use as a polling place is situated within the limits of any district and within half a mile of the boundary of an adjoining district, the Governor General may appoint that building to be a polling place for both districts.

(1A) In respect of each election, the Governor General may also from time to time appoint any suitable building to be a group polling place for any 2 or more specified districts (whether or not it is within the limits of any of those dstricts) for the purpose of enabling electors of those districts to vote there on polling day; and may from time to time revoke, alter or add to any such appointment.

(2) No polling place shall be appointed in any licensed premises under the Sale of Liquor Act 1962.

(3) Any public primary school or intermediate school or secondary school may be appointed to be a polling place under this section, and in every such case it shall be the duty of the Education Board having jurisdiction over the school or, as the case may be, of the governing body of the school, and, in the case of a primary school or intermediate school, of the School Committee or the committee of the school, to place it at the free disposal of the Returning Officer from 4 o'clock in the afternoon of the day before polling day and for the whole of polling day.

(4) The cost of cleaning any school after use as a polling place, and of repairing any damage, shall be defrayed by the Returning Officer out of money to be appropriated by Parliament.

(5) Public notice of every appointment, revocation, alteration, or addition under this section shall be given in the *Gazette* and in at least one newspaper circulating in the district.

92. Polling booths, ballot boxes, ballot papers, etc.

(1) The Returning Officer shall provide the following things for taking the poll:

(*a*) One or more rooms for polling booths at each polling place, and in each booth one or more inner compartments, separated from but opening into the booth and having no other opening:

(*b*) In each inner compartment pencils for the use of the voters or other suitable facilities for the marking of ballot papers:

(*c*) In each booth one or more ballot boxes having a lock and key and a slit in the upper side by which the ballot papers may be put into box:

(*d*) In each booth one or more copies of the main roll and supplementary rolls for the district, and a sufficient number of voting papers:

(*e*) In each inner compartment, in a prominent position, a card showing in large print the names of all the candidates in alphabetical order with their party designations.

(2) At every group polling place appointed under sub-section (1A) of section *91* of this Act, the polling booths, ballot boxes, rolls, voting papers, and cards required by sub-section (1) of this section shall be provided in respect of each district for which the group polling place has been so appointed, and each such ballot box, roll, and card shall be marked with the name of the district to which it relates.

93. Deputy Returning Officers, poll clerks, and interpreters.

(1) The Returning Officer shall appoint for each polling booth a Deputy Returning Officer to conduct the poll at that booth and one or more poll clerks to assist the Deputy Returning Officer, and may appoint such additional Deputy Returning Officers and poll clerks and such interpreters as he considers necessary.

(2) The Returning Officer may himself exercise all the powers, duties, and functions of a Deputy Returning Officer in respect of any one polling booth.

(3) Any Returning Officer or Deputy Returning Officer may at any time on polling day appoint in writing a substitute to act for him in respect of that election in case of his absence from duty.

(4) If the Deputy Returning Officer fails to open the polling at any booth, or if he is absent from duty and has not appointed a substitute, the poll clerk at the booth may act for him and in that event shall be deemed to be his substitute.

(5) Every substitute while acting for any Returning Officer or Deputy Returning Officer shall have all the powers, duties, and functions of that Returning Officer or Deputy Returning Officer.

(6) Nothing in the State Services Act 1962 shall apply to any person appointed under this section, or to any substitute acting under this section.

94. Deputy Returning Officers, poll clerks, and interpreters to make declaration. Every Deputy Returning Officer and poll clerk and interpreter shall before the poll, and every substitute for a Deputy Returning Officer shall before acting, make a declaration in form 1 before the Returning Officer, or a Justice of the Peace, or a solicitor, or a postmaster, or another Deputy Returning Officer.

95. Scrutineers.

(1) Each candidate may, by writing under his hand, appoint one or more scrutineers for each polling booth at any election.

(2) Every scrutineer shall, before being allowed to act, make a declaration in form 1 before the Returning Officer or the Deputy Returning Officer or a Justice of the Peace or a solicitor or a post master.

(3) Where a candidate appoints more than one scrutineer for any polling booth, not more than one scrutineer for that candidate shall be present in the polling booth at any time.

(4) Any scrutineer may at any time during the hours of polling leave and re-enter the polling booth for which he is appointed.

(5) Nothing in this Act shall render it unlawful for a scrutineer to communicate to any person information as to the names of persons who have voted.

96. Hours of polling.

(1) The poll at every election shall commence at 9 o'clock in the morning of polling day, and, except as otherwise provided in this Act, shall finally close at 7 o'clock in the evening of the same day.

(2) Every elector who at the close of the poll is present in a booth for the purpose of voting shall be entitled to receive a ballot paper and to mark and deposit in the same manner as if he had voted before the close of the poll.

97. Repealed.

98. Employees to have time off to vote.

(1) Subject to the provisions of this section, on the polling day at any election every employer shall allow every worker in his employment who is an elector of any electoral district in which the election is being held, and who has not had a reasonable opportunity of voting before commencing work, to leave his work for the purpose of voting not later than 3 o'clock in the afternoon for the remainder of the day, and it shall not be lawful for any employer to make any deduction from any remuneration payable to any such worker in respect of any time after the time of his leaving his work as aforesaid.

(2) Where any such worker is required to work after 3 o'clock in the afternoon of polling day for the purpose of carrying on any essential work or service, his employer shall on that day allow the worker to leave his work for a reasonable time for the purpose of voting, and it shall not be lawful for the employer to make any deduction from any remuneration payable to the worker in respect of any time, not exceeding 2 hours, occupied in voting as aforesaid.

(3) Every person who commits any offence against the foregoing provisions of this section shall be liable on summary conviction to a fine not exceeding $40.

(4) Every master of a ship that happens to be in any port in New Zealand at the time of any general election or by-election in any district, at the request of any of the crew being registered or qualified to be registered as electors of that district, shall allow them to go ashore at a proper time to admit of their voting at the election; and every master who without reasonable cause commits any breach of this sub-section shall be liable on summary conviction to a fine not exceeding $100.

(5) For the purposes of this section

'Employer' and 'worker' have the same meaning as in the Annual Holidays Act 1944:

'Master', in relation to any ship, includes any person (except a pilot) having command or charge of the ship.

(6) This section shall bind the Crown.

Persons Qualified to Vote

99. Who may vote. Subject ot the provisions of this Act, the following persons, and no others, shall be qualified to vote at any election in any district, namely:

(*a*) Any person whose name lawfully appears on the main roll or any supplementary roll for the district:

(*b*) Any person who has applied for registration as an elector of the district between writ day and polling day and has satisfied the Registrar before or within 7 days after polling day that he became qualified for registration as an elector of the district not earlier than one month before writ day and not later than the day before polling day:

(*c*) Any person who is qualified to be registered as an elector of the district, and was at the time of the last preceding election duly registered as an elector of the district or, where a change of boundaries has intervened, of some other district in which his then place of residence within the first-mentioned district was then situated:

(*d*) Any person who is qualified to be registered as an elector of the district, and has since the last preceding election and before 6 o'clock in the afternoon of writ day applied for registration as an elector of the district or, where a change of boundaries has intervened, or some other district in which his then place of residence within the first-mentioned district was then situated:

(*e*) Any serviceman who is outside New Zealand, if he is or will be of or over the age of 18 years before polling day, and his place of residence immediately before he last left New Zealand is within the district.

100., Special voters. Any person who is qualified to vote at any election in any district may vote as a special voter if

(*a*) His name does not appear on the main roll or any supplementary roll for the district or has been wrongly deleted from any such roll:

(*b*) He will on polling day be outside New Zealand:

(*c*) He is or will be absent from the district on polling day:

(*d*) He will not throughout the hours of polling on polling day be within 2 miles by the nearest practicable route of any polling place in the district:

(*e*) He will throughout the hours of polling on polling day be travelling under conditions which will preclude him from attending to vote at any polling place in the district:

(*f*) He is ill or infirm, and by reason of that illness or infirmity will be precluded from attending to vote at any polling place in the district:

(*g*) In the case of a woman, she will by reason of approaching or recent maternity be precluded from attending to vote at any polling place in district:

(*h*) He is a lighthouse keeper or member of a lighthouse keeper's staff, or is the wife of a lighthouse keeper or the wife of a member of a lighthouse keeper's staff, and will be precluded from attending to vote at any polling place in the district:

(*i*) He has a religious objection to voting at a polling place on the day of the week on which polling day falls:

(*j*) He satisfies the Returning Officer or Deputy Returning Officer that on any other ground it will not be possible for him to vote as a polling place in the district without incurring hardship or undue inconvenience.

The Ballot

101. Ballot box to be kept locked during poll. The Deputy Returning Officer shall, before the opening of the poll, and in the sight of any of the scrutineers present, see that the ballot box is empty, and shall close and lock it, and retain the key in his possession; and the ballot box shall not again be opened until after the close of the poll:

Provided that, if the lock of a ballot box is damaged or defective so that the box cannot be locked, the Deputy Returning Officer shall securely seal the box instead locking it.

102. Persons to to remain in polling places. No person not actually engaged in voting shall be allowed to remain in a polling place except the Deputy Returning Officers and poll clerks, any of the scrutineers, an interpreter, and as many constables as the Deputy Returning Officer in charge of the polling place thinks necessary to keep the peace.

103. Voters not to be spoken to in booth.

(1) No scrutineer or other official or unofficial person shall speak to any voter in a polling booth either before or after the voter has given his vote, except only the Deputy Returning Officer or poll clerk (with an interpreter if necessary), who may ask the questions he is authorized to put, and give such general directions as may assist any voter to give his vote, and in particular may on request inform a voter orally of the names of all the candidates in alphabetical order with their party designations.

(2) Every person who offends against this section shall be liable on summary conviction to a fine not exceeding $40 and may be at once removed from the booth by order of the Deputy Returning Officer.

104. Questions may be put to voter.

(1) The Deputy Returning Officer may, and if so required by any scrutineer shall, before allowing any person to vote, put to him the following questions:

(*a*) Are you the person whose name appears as A. B. in the electoral roll now in force for the [*Name of district*] Electoral District?

(*b*) Have your already voted at this election in this or any other electoral district?

(2) In every such case the Deputy Returning Officer shall require the questions to be answered in writing signed by the person to whom they are put.

(3) Every person to whom those questions are put who does not answer them, or does not answer the first in the affirmative and the second in the negative, shall be liable on summary conviction to a fine not exceeding $100, and shall be prohibited from voting then or afterwards at that election.

(4) Every person who wilfully and knowingly makes a false answer to either of the questions that the Deputy Returning Officer may put to him under this section shall be liable on summary conviction to a fine not exceeding $100.

105. Issue of ballot papers.

(1) Every Deputy Returning Officer shall, in accordance with the provisions of this section, issue ballot papers to all electors who apply to vote at the booth in respect of which he is appointed.

(2) The elector shall state his name to the Deputy Returning Officer and shall give such particulars as may be necessary to identify the entry in the printed rolls relating to the elector.

(3) If the name of the elector appears in the rolls a line shall be drawn through his name and number.

(4) If the name of the elector appears in the rolls the Deputy Returning Officer shall then issue to the elector a ballot paper after he has prepared it in the following manner:

(*a*) Unless a consecutive number has been printed on the ballot paper and on the counterfoil, he shall enter on both the counterfoil and the ballot paper in the spaces provided a number (called a consecutive number), beginning with the number one in the case of the first ballot paper issued by him, and on all succeeding ballot papers issued by him the numbers shall be consecutive, so that no 2 ballot papers issued in the same booth shall bear the same number:

(*b*) He shall firmly fix a piece of gummed paper over the consecutive number on the ballot paper so as the conceal it effectively:

(*c*) On the counterfoil of the ballot paper he shall writ his initials, and the number appearing in the roll against the name of the elector preceded by the number of the page on which that name appears:

(*d*) He shall place his official mark on the ballot paper so that the booth in which the ballot paper was issued may be identified.

(5) Every Deputy Returning Officer who fails faithfully to perform the duty imposed on him by this section, by reason whereof any of the requirements of this section are not effectively fulfilled, shall be liable on summary conviction to a fine not exceeding $100.

Provided that, in so far as the failure relates to the duty of fixing a piece of gummed paper over the consecutive numbers so as to conceal it effectively, it shall be a sufficient defence if he satisfies the Court that he took all reasonable precautions to secure the same.

106. Method of voting.

(1) The voter having received a ballot paper, shall immediately retire into one of the inner compartments provided for the purpose, and shall there alone and secretly exercise his vote by marking his ballot paper by striking out the name of every candidate except the one for whom he wishes to vote.

(2) Every voter shall, before leaving the inner compartment, fold his ballot paper so that the contents cannot be seen, and shall then deposit it so folded in the ballot box.

107. Spoilt ballot papers.

(1) Any voter who, not having deposited his ballot paper in the ballot box, satisfies the Deputy Returning Officer that he has spoilt it by inadvertence may be supplied with a fresh ballot paper, but only after the spoilt one has been returned to the Deputy Returning Officer.

(2) The Deputy Returning Officer shall

(*a*) Cancel every such spoilt ballot paper by writing across the face thereof the words 'Spoilt by voter, and a fresh ballot paper issued' and writing his initials thereon:

(*b*) If any ballot paper is inadvertently spoilt by the Deputy Returning Officer or any other official, cancel it by writing across the face thereof the words 'Spoilt by official' and also the words 'and a fresh ballot paper issued' if that is the case, and writing his initials thereon:

(*c*) Retain all spoilt ballot papers in his possession until the close of poll.

108. Blind, disabled, or illiterate voters.

(1) Any elector who is wholly or partially blind, or is unable to read or write (whether because of physical handicap or otherwise), or is not sufficiently familiar with the English language to vote without assistance, may vote in accordance with the provisions of this section.

(1A) At the request of any such voter who has received a ballot paper and is wholly or partially blind, and person nominated by the voter, or, if no person is so nominated, the Deputy Returning Officer, shall accompany him into one of the inner compartments provided for the marking of ballot papers, and the ballot paper may there be marked by the voter with the assistance of the person nominated or, as the case may be, of the Deputy Returning Officer, or may be marked by the person nominated or, as the case may be, by the Deputy Returning Officer in accordance with the instructions of the voter.

(2) At the request of any such voter who has received a ballot paper (not being a voter to whom sub-section (1A) of this section applies) the Deputy Returning Officer shall accompany him into one of the inner compartments provided for the marking of ballot papers, and the ballot paper may there be marked by the voter with the assistance of the Deputy Returning Officer or may be marked by the Deputy Returning Officer in accordance with the instructions of the voter.

(3) *Repealed.*

(4) A poll clerk or some othe person nominated by the voter (not being a

voter to whom sub-section (1A) of this section applies) shall also accompany him into the inner compartment and may, if so desired by the voter, inspect the ballot paper before it is deposited in the ballot box.

(5) Any elector voting as a special voter may vote in the manner prescribed by this section, with any necessary modifications, or in any manner prescribed by regulations made under this Act.

(6) Every person who is present in accordance with this section or with any regulations when an elector votes and who communicates at any time to any person any information obtained as to the candidate for whom the voter is about to voter or has voted, or as to the number on the ballot paper given to the voter, commits an offence, and shall be liable on summary conviction to imprisonment for a term not exceeding 3 months.

109. Procedure when second vote given in same name. If any person proposing to vote an any election gives as his name the name of any person to whom a ballot paper has already been given at the same election, he shall be dealt with in all respects in like manner as any other voter:

Provided that the ballot paper of any such person shall not deposited in the ballot box or allowed by the Deputy Returning Officer, but shall be set aside for separate custody.

Special Voting

110. Voting by special voters.

(1) Notwithstanding anything to the contrary in this Act, a special voter may vote at such place (whether at a polling place or not and whether in or outside New Zealand), at such time, in such manner, and upon or subject to such conditions as may be prescribed in that behalf by regulations made under this Act.

(2) Different methods of voting may be prescribed for different classes of special voters.

(3) The ballot papers for use by special voters or by any class of special voters may be in such form as is prescribed by regulations, and the consecutive numbers of the special ballot papers for any district may be in a different series from that used for the ordinary ballot papers.

(4) Subject to the provisions of this section and section *100* of this Act, and to the provisions of any regulations made for the purposes of this section, all the provisions of any regulations made for the purposes of this section, all the provisions of this Act shall, as far as applicable and with the necessary modifications, apply with respect to voting by special voters and to their votes.

Preliminary Count of Votes

111. Procedure after close of poll.

(1) At each polling booth the Deputy Returning Officer shall, as soon as practicable after the close of the poll, in the presence of such of the scrutineers

(including those lawfully in the polling booth under any other Act) as choose to be present, and the poll clerks, but of no other person, perform the following duties:

(*a*) He shall make up into separate parcels

(i) The certified copies of the main roll and supplementary rolls on which the fact of any person having received a ballot paper has been noted; and

(ii) All the counterfoils of ballot papers that have been issued to voters; and

(iii) All the spoilt ballot papers; and

(iv) All the unused ballot papers:

(*b*) He shall then open the ballot boxes and, taking therefrom all the ballot papers therein, proceed to ascertain the number of votes received by each candidate:

(*c*) He shall set aside as informal all ballot papers which do not clearly indicate the candidate for whom the voter desired to vote:

(*d*) He shall arrange for the result of the voting to be transmitted as soon as possible to the Returning Officer:

(*e*) He shall make up into separate parcels

(i) The used ballot papers, together with (but in separate enclosures) the ballot papers set aside as informal, and the ballot papers set aside under section *109* of this Act; and

(ii) A certificate signed by himself and by such of the scrutineers as are present and consent to sign it of the number of votes received by each candidate, the number of ballot papers set aside as informal, the number of ballot papers set aside under section *109* of this Act, the number of spoilt papers, the number of ballot papers delivered to special voters, the number of unused ballot papers, and the number of ballot papers originally delivered to him.

(2) Each parcel made up under this section shall be endorsed by the Deputy Returning Officer with a description of its contents, the name of the district, the name of the polling place, the number of the booth and the date of the polling; and the endorsement shall be signed by the Deputy Returning Officer and by such of the scrutineers as are present and desire to sign it; and the parcel shall be enclosed in paper or similar material and shall be properly secured.

(3) The Deputy Returning Officer shall forthwith forward all the parcels mentioned in this section to the Returning Officer.

Scrutiny of the Rolls

112. Scrutiny of the rolls

(1) The Returning Officer shall make arrangements for a scrutiny of the rolls as soon as practicable after the close of the poll, and shall give notice in writing to each of the candidates or their scrutineers of the time and place at which he will commence the scrutiny.

(2) No person other than the Returning Officer and his assistants, and one person appointed as scrutineer by each candidate for the purpose, shall be present at the scrutiny.

(3) No candidate shall act as scrutineer under this section.

(4) A scrutineer appointed under this section may be appointed by telegram.

113. Marked copies of rolls to be compared.

(1) The Returning Officer shall, in the presence and hearing of his assistants (if any) and such scrutineers as are entitled to be present under this Act or any other Act, but of no other person, compare one with another all the certified copies of the main roll and supplementary rolls on which the fact of any person having received a ballot paper has been noted, and all records of special votes exercised in respect of his district, and shall on an unmarked copy of the main roll and every supplementary roll (called the master roll) draw a line through the number and name of any elector who is shown on any of the certified copies of the rolls or in any record of the special votes issued as having received a ballot paper.

(2) If on that comparison, or from the checking of declarations in respect of special votes, or from the report of a Deputy Returning Officer on the Ballot papers set aside under section *109* of this Act, and after such inquiry as the Returning Officer deems necessary, it appears that the same voter has received more than one ballot paper, the Returning Officer shall, in the presence of his assistants (if any) and such scrutineers as choose to be present, but of no other person, open the parcel or parcels of ballot papers used at the polling booth or polling booths at which that voter appears to have received a ballot paper, and shall select therefrom the ballot papers which appear from their consecutive numbers and counterfoils to have been issued to that voter, and shall disallow every vote appearing to have been given by means of the ballot papers so selected:

Provided that, if the Returning Officer is satisfied that one and only one of the ballot papers was lawfully received by the voter entitled thereto and that he was not in any way concerned in the issue of the other ballot paper or ballot papers, the Returning Officer shall allow the vote of that voter and shall disallow the other vote or votes.

(3) For the purposes of sub-section (2) of this section, every ballot paper issued to a special voter shall be deemed to have been issued at a polling booth.

(4) Ecxept in the case of the ballot papers so selected therefrom, the Returning Officer shall inspect only the consecutive numbers on the ballot papers in the several parcels so opened, and shall so cover the ballot papers that no person present shall have the opportunity of determining the candidate for whom any particular voter has voted.

114. Parcels to be secured after scrutiny.

(1) When the Returning Officer has selected from any parcel all the ballot papers he is required to select therefrom, he shall forthwith, in the presence of his assistants (if any) and such scrutineers as are present, but on no other person, close and secure the parcel, and shall endorse thereon a memorandum of the fact of the

ballot papers having been selected from that parcel, specifying the same by the name of the person to whom the same appear to have been delivered, and shall sign the endorsement with his name.

(2) The Returning Officer shall set aside all ballot papers selected by him from any parcel as herein provided, and shall in the presence of his assistants (if any) and such scrutineers as are present, but of no other person, secure those ballot papers in a separate parcel, and shall endorse the parcel with a description of the contents thereof, and shall sign the endorsement with his name.

Official Count and Declaration of Poll

115. Counting the votes.

(1) On completion of the scrutiny hereinbefore directed the Returning Officer, with such assistants as he deems necessary, and in the presence of such of the scrutineers appointed under section *112* of this Act as are present, and also in the presence of some Justice (who shall attend at the request of the Returning Officer), but of no other person, shall select and open one of the parcels of used ballot papers referred to in paragraph (*e*) of sub-section (1) of section *111* of this Act and shall mark each ballot paper therein with a number in consecutive order, beginning with the number one, so that no 2 ballot papers in that parcel shall bear the same number:

Provided that the procedure set out in this sub-section need not be delayed until the inquiries under sub-section (2) of section *113* of this Act have been completed, but the ballot papers from any particular polling booth shall not be counted until any inquiries in respect of ballot papers from that booth have been completed.

(1A) No special vote shall be disallowed by reason only of some error or omission on the part of an official, if the Returning Officer is satisfied that the voter was qualified to vote at the election.

(2) When the ballot papers from the parcel so selected have been marked as aforesaid the Returning Officer shall make a record of the last number marked, and shall then, in the presence of his assistants (if any) and the scrutineers and Justice as aforesaid, but of no other person, deal with the ballot papers as follows:

(*a*) He shall reject as informal

(i) Any ballot paper that does not bear the official mark if there is reasonable cause to believe that it was not issued to a voter by any Deputy Returning Officer; and

(ii) Any ballot paper that does not clearly indicate the candidate for whom the voter desired to vote:

Provided that no ballot paper shall be rejected as informal by reason only of some informality in the manner in which it has been dealt with by the voter if it is otherwise regular, and if in the opinion of the Returning Officer the intention of the voter in voting is clearly indicated:

Provided also that no ballot paper shall be rejected as informal by reason only of some error or ommission on the part of an official, if the Returning Officer is satisfied that the voter was qualified to vote at the election:

(*b*) The Returning Officer shall then count the number of votes received by each candidate, and the number of votes rejected as informal, and compare the result of that count with the certificate of the Deputy Returning Officer in respect of the preliminary count, and shall, where necessary, amend that certificate; and every such certificate shall be initialled by the Returning Officer and the Justice attending:

(*c*) The Returning Officer shall then make up and secure the parcel anew, and endorse thereon a memorandum specifying the number of ballot papers contained in the parcel, the number of votes received by each candidate, the number of informal ballot papers, and the number of the booth at which the votes were recorded; and the endorsement shall be signed by the Returning Officer and Justice attending.

(3) After the ballot papers from one parcel have been dealt with in the manner aforesaid, those from the remaining parcels shall be successively dealt with in the like manner, the marking of the ballot papers to commence with the number one in the case of each parcel.

(4) The ballot papers of special voters shall be dealt with in like manner, after which they shall be made up together into a parcel which shall be properly secured and shall be endorsed in the manner hereinbefore described.

(5) When all the ballot papers have been dealt with in the prescribed manner the Justice attending shall sign a certificate stating the total number of ballot papers used at the election, the number of votes received by each candidate, and the number of informal votes, and that certificate shall be preserved by the Returning Officer for production when required.

(6) Where at any count of the ballot papers under this section the numbering of the ballot papers extends beyond one day, the Justice attending shall give his certificate day by day showing the progress of that numbering and describing the parcels counted in his presence.

116. Declaration of result of poll.

(1) When all the ballot papers have been dealt with as aforesaid the Returning Officer, having ascertained the total number of votes received by each candidate, shall declare the result of the poll by giving notice thereof in form 10.

(2) Where there is an equality of voters between candidates and the addition of a vote would entitle one of those candidates to be declared elected, the Returning Officer shall forthwith apply to a District Court Judge for a recount under section *117* of this Act, and all the provisions of that section shall apply accordingly, except that no deposit shall be necessary.

(3) In any case where on any recount under section *117* of this Act there is an equality of votes between candidates and the addition of a vote would entitle

one of those candidate to be declared elected, the Returning Officer shall determine by lot which candidate shall be elected.

Recount

117. Application to District Court Judge for recount.

(1) Where any candidate has reason to believe that the public declaration by the Returning Officer of the number of votes received by each candidate is incorrect, and that on a recount thereof the first-mentioned candidate might be found to be elected, he may within 3 days after the public declaration apply to a District Court Judge for a recount of the votes.

(2) Every such application shall be accompanied by a deposit of $40.

(3) The District Court Judge shall cause a recount of the votes to be commenced within 3 days after receiving the application, and shall give notice in writing to the Returning Officer and to each of the candidates or their scrutineers of the time and place at which the recount will be made.

(4) The recount shall be made in the presence of the District Court Judge or of an officer appointed by him for the purpose, and shall as far as practicable be made in the manner provided in the case of the original count:

Provided that no person shall be present at the recount except the District Court Judge or the officer appointed by him, his assistants (if any), the Returning Officer and his assistants (if any), and the scrutineers appointed under section *112* of this Act.

(5) The District Court Judge shall have all the powers that the Returning Officer had on the original count, and may reverse any decision made by the Returning Officer in the exercise of those powers.

(6) If on the recount the District Court Judge finds that the public declaration was incorrect he shall order the Returning Officer to give an amended declaration or the result of the poll.

(7) The District Court Judge may make such order as to the costs of and incidental to the recount as he deems just, and, subject to any such order, shall direct the deposit made under this section to be returned to the person who paid it.

118. Ballot papers and certificate to be compared on recount.

(1) At any recount made as aforesaid the Returning Officer shall produce to the District Court Judge all the used ballot papers, together with the Justice's certificate stating the total number of ballot papers used at the election.

(2) If on comparing the number of ballot papers stated in the certificate with the ballot papers used at the election the District Court Judge finds that any of the ballot papers have been lost, stolen, or in any way interfered with during the interval between the official count and the recount, the offical count made by the Returning Officer shall be deemed to be correct, and the result of the poll declared accordingly. Where in any such case there is an equality of votes between candidates and the addition of a vote would entitle one of those candidates to be declared elected, the Returning Officer shall determine by lot which candidate shall be elected.

Return of Writ

119. Endorsement and return of writ.

(1) The Returning Officer shall endorse on the writ

(*a*) The name of the person declared to be elected; and

(*b*) The date of the endorsement,

and having signed the endorsement, shall forthwith transmit the writ to the Clerk of the Writs.

(2) The date of the endorsement of the writ shall be deemed to be the day for the return of the writ.

(3) The writ shall be returned within the time specified in the writ for its return:

Provided that where it appears to the Returning Officer that an application for a recount of the votes may be made as hereinbefore provided, he may postpone the return of the writ until the time for making the application has expired, and, if within that time application is made, he shall further postpone the return of the writ until the recount has been completed.

120. Copy of writ to be forwarded to Speaker. As soon as conveniently may be after the return of the writs the Clerk of the Writs shall forward to the Speaker of the House of Representatives a list of the names of the members elected, together with a copy of the writs endorsed as aforesaid.

Disposal of Ballot Papers

121. Disposal of ballot papers, rolls, ets.

(1) As soon as practicable after polling day the Returning Officer shall enclose in separate packets in the following manner all the parcels transmitted to him by the several Deputy Returning Officers or made up and secured by himself, that is to say:

(*a*) He shall enclose in one or more separate packets all the parcels of used ballot papers, including the special voters' ballot papers, and all counterfoils corresponding to those ballot papers; in one or more other separate packets all parcels of unused and spoilt ballot papers; in another all parcels of ballot papers set aside under sections *109* and *114* of this Act; and in one or more other separate packets all parcels containing ballot paper accounts, copies of rolls (except the master roll), books, or other papers, as in this Act provided, and all telgrams, letters, and other papers received from any Deputy Returning Officer in respect of the votes of special voters:

(*b*) He shall properly secure the said several packets, and endorse them with a description of the contents thereof respectively; and the name of the district and the date of the polling, and shall sign the endorsement; and shall forthwith forward the said packets to the Clerk of the House of Representatives:

(*c*) He shall also at the same time properly secure and transmit to the Clerk of the House of Representatives a parcel containing all ballot papers printed for the election and not used by the Returning Officer or distributed for use to his Deputies.

(2) The Clerk of the House of Representatives shall forthwith give or send to the Returning Officer a receipt under his hand for the said packets and parcel.

(3) The Returning Officer shall send the master roll to the Registrar of Electors for the district, and the Registrar of Electors shall keep it until the next general election. Any registered elector of the district may inspect any master roll at the Registrar's office without payment of any fee at any time when the office is open for the transaction of business.

122. Disposal of packets.

(1) The packets and parcel shall be safely kept for one year unopened, unless a Court of competent jurisdiction or the House of Representatives orders them, or any of them to be opened.

(2) At the end of one year the packets and parcel shall be destroyed unopened in the presence of the Clerk of the House of Representatives and the Clerk of the Writs.

123. Papers taken from parcels as evidence in certain cases.

(1) Any ballot paper, and any copy of a roll, and any book purporting to be taken from any such parcel as aforesaid, and having written thereon respectively, under the hand of the Clerk of the House of Representatives, a certificate of the several particulars by this Act required to be endorsed on the parcel, shall be conclusive evidence in any Court or before any Committee of the House of Representatives that it was so taken and that it, if a ballot paper, was deposited and, if a roll or book, was kept or used at the election and booth to which the endorsement and writing relate.

(2) Every ballot paper so certified shall be evidence of a vote given at the poll, and of the correspondence of the number appearing on the ballot paper with the number appearing on any roll so certified as of the same election and booth, according to the tenor of the said ballot paper.

(3) But in the case of the ballot paper set aside or selected by a Deputy Returning Officer or by the Returning Officer the correspondence shall be evidence only of some person having voted in the name appearing on the roll.

Maintenance of Order at Elections

124. Deputy Returning Officers to maintain order.

(1) Every Deputy Returning Officer shall maintain order and keep peace at the polling place where he is conducting the poll, and may, without any other warrant than this Act.

(*a*) Cause to be arrested and taken before a Justice any person reasonably suspected of committing or attempting ot commit at the polling place any of the offences mentioned in section *130* of this Act; or (*b*) Cause to be removed any person who obstructs the approaches to a polling booth, or wilfully and unnecessarily obstructs the proceedings at the polling, or conducts himself in a disorderly manner, or causes a disturbance, or wilfully acts in any manner in defiance of the lawful directions of the Deputy Returning Officer.

(2) All constables shall aid and assist the Deputy Returning Officer in the performance of his duty.

Adjournment of poll

125. Adjournment of poll.

(1) Where the polling at any polling place cannot start or has to be suspended whether by reason of riot or open violence, natural disaster, or any other cause, the Deputy Returning Officer shall adjourn the taking of the poll at that polling place to the following day, and if necessary from day to day until the poll can be taken, and shall forthwith give public notice of the adjournment in such manner as he thinks fit:

Provided that the poll shall not be kept open for more the 10 hours in all at any polling place.

(2) Where the close of the poll at any polling place is adjourned under this section for any number of days, the day on or before which the writ is made returnable shall be postponed by the same number of days.

Custody of Ballot Papers

126. Prevention of irregularities as to ballot papers. In order to prevent the commission at any election of irregularities in respect of the improper possession of ballot papers the following provisions shall apply:

(*a*) The Returning Officer shall give to the person printing the ballot papers a receipt specifying the total number of ballot papers received by him, and it shall be the duty of the printer to see that all copies of the ballot paper other than those delivered to the Returning Officer are immediately destroyed:

(*b*) Every Deputy Returning Officer shall give to the Returning Officer a receipt specifying the total number of ballot papers received by him, and shall be personally responsible for the safe custody of all such ballot papers from the time they are received by him until they are issued or otherwise disposed of in accordance with this Act:

(*c*) Every Deputy Returning Officer shall be personally responsible for the safe custody of all ballot papers used at the polling booth at which he presides from the time each ballot paper was placed in the ballot box by the voter until the parcel of used ballot papers has been delivered to the Returning Officer as in this Act provided and the Deputy Returning Officer has obtained from the Returning Officer a receipt in writing for the parcel, which receipt the Returning Officer is in all cases required to give on such delivery:

(*d*) In like manner every Returning Officer shall be personally responsible for the safe custody of all ballot papers used at the polling booth at which he presides until they have been sent to the Clerk of the House of Representatives as hereinbefore provided, and also for the safe custody of all parcels of used ballot papers for which he has given a receipt to a Deputy Returning Officer, until they have been sent by him to the Clerk of the House of Representatives as aforesaid:

(*e*) Every Returning Officer or Deputy Returning Officer who fails to take reasonable steps to secure the safe custody of all ballot papers for which he is responsible, with the result that any such ballot paper is removed from his custody, shall be liable on summary conviction to a fine not exceeding $200 or to imprisonment for a term not exceeding one year:

(*f*) Every person shall be liable on summary conviction to a fine not exceeding $200 who wilfully or negligently allows any copy of a ballot paper printed by him to come into the possession of any person other than the Returning Officer:

(*g*) Every person shall be liable on summary conviction to a fine not exceeding $200 who, except in accordance with any regulations made under this Act in relation to special voters, obtains possession of or has in his possession any ballot paper other than the one given to him by the Returning Officer or Deputy Returning Officer for the purpose of recording his vote, or retains any ballot paper in his possession after leaving the polling booth.

Offences at Elections

127. Interfering with or influencing voters.

(1) Every person commits an offence and shall be liable on summary conviction to a fine not exceeding $200 who at an election

(*a*) In any way interferes with any elector, either in the polling booth or while on his way thereto, with the intention of influencing him or advising him as to his vote:

(*b*) At any time on polling day before the close of the poll in or in view or hearing of any public place holds or takes part in any demonstration or procession having direct or indirect reference to the poll by any means whatsoever:

(*c*) At any time on polling day before the close of the poll makes any statement having direct or indirect reference to the poll by means or any loudspeaker or public address apparatus or cinematograph or television apparatus:

(*d*) At any time on polling day before the close of the poll, or at any time on any of the 3 days immediately preceding polling day, prints or distributes or delivers to any person anything being or purporting to be in imitation of any ballot paper to be used at the poll and having thereon the names of the candidates or any of them, together with any direction or indication as to the candidate for whom any person should vote, or in any way containing any such direction or indication, or having thereon any matter likely to influence any vote:

(*e*) At any time on polling day before the close of the poll exhibits in or in view of any public place, or publishes, or distributes, or broadcasts,

(i) Any statement advising or intended or likely to influence any elector as to the candidate or party for whom he should vote; or

(ii) Any party name, emblem, slogan, or logo:

Provided that this paragraph shall not apply to any statement, name, emblem, slogan, or logo in a newspaper published before 6 o'clock in the afternoon of the day before polling day:

Provided also that where any statement, name, emblem, slogan, or logo is so exhibited before polling day in a fixed position not in view of a polling place, it shall not be an offence to leave the statement, name, emblem, slogan, or logo so exhibited on polling day:

Provided further that this paragraph shall not restrict the publication of any party name in any news which relates to an election and which is published in a newspaper or other periodical or in a radio or television broadcast made by the Broadcasting Corporation of New Zealand or other holder of a warrant under the Broadcasting Act 1976:

(*f*) At any time on polling day before the close of the poll prints or distributes or delivers to any person any card or paper (whether or not it is an imitation ballot paper) having thereon the names of the candidates or any of them:

(*g*) Exhibits or leaves in any polling booth any card or paper having thereon any direction or indication as to how any person should vote or as to the method of voting:

(*h*) At any time on polling day before the close of the poll, within, or at the entrance to, or in the vicinity of, any polling place,

(i) Gives or offers to give any person any written or oral information as to any name or number on the main roll or any supplementary roll being used at the election:

(ii) Permits or offers any person to examine any copy of the main roll or any supplementary roll being used at the election.

(2) It shall not be an offence against this section for any person to wear or display (whether on his person or on any vehicle), in the form of ribbons, streamers, or rosettes, his party's colors or to wear a party lapel badge.

(3) Nothing in this section shall apply to any official statement or announcement made or exhibited under the authority of this Act.

127A. Power to remove statements, names, emblems, slogans, or logos.

(1) The Returning Officer may at any time on polling day before the close of the poll cause to be removed or obliterated

(*a*) Any statement advising or intended or likely to influence any elector as to the candidate or party for whom he should vote; or

(*b*) Any party name, emblem, slogan, or logo,

which is exhibited in or in or in view or any public place and which is so exhibited within 800 metres of a polling place.

(2) Nothing in sub-section (1)(*b*) of this section shall apply to ribbons, streamers, or rosettes which are worn or displayed by any person (whether on his person or on any vehicle) in his party's colours or to a party lapel badge worn by any person.

(3) All expenses incurred by the Returning Officer in carrying out the power conferred by sub-section (1) of this section may be recovered by him from the persons by whom or by whose direction the statement, name, emblem, slogan, or logo was exhibited, as a debt due by them jointly or severally to the Crown.

128. Publishing defamatory matter at election time. Every person shall be liable on summary conviction to a fine not exceeding $ 500 or to imprisonment for a term not exceeding 3 mnoths who at any time between writ day and the close of the poll publishes or exposes, or causes to be published or exposed, to public view any document or writing or printed matter containing any untrue statement defamatory of any candiate and calculated to influence the vote of any elector.

129. Erasing and altering official mark on ballot paper. Every person shall be liable on summary conviction to a fine not exceeding $500 who erases, obliterates, or alters any official mark, stamp, or writing on any ballot paper, or places thereon any writing, print, or other matter which might lead persons to believe that it was put thereon by any official or person duly authorized in that behalf.

130. Offences in respect of ballot papers and ballot boxes.

(1) Every person commits an offence against this section who

(*a*) Forges, or counterfeits, or fraudulently defaces or fraudulently destroys any ballot paper, or the official mark on any ballot paper:

(*b*) Without due authority supplies any ballot paper to any person:

(*c*) Fraudulently puts into any ballot box any paper other than the ballot paper that he is authorized by law to put therein:

(*d*) Fraudulently takes out of a polling booth any ballot paper:

(*e*) Without due authority destroys, takes, opens, or otherwise interferes with any ballot box, or box or packet or parcel of ballot papers, then in use for the purposes of any election, or in course of transmission by post or otherwise, or thereafter whenever the same may be kept as a record of the election.

(2) Every person who commits an offence against this section shall be liable on conviction on indictment

(*a*) If a Returning Officer or Deputy Returning Officer, or an official or a clerk in attendance at a polling booth, to imprisonment for a term not exceeding 2 years:

(*b*) If any other person, to imprisonment for a term not exceeding 6 months.

(3) Every person who attempts to commit any offence against this section shall be liable on conviction on indictment to imprisonment for a term not exceeding one-half of the longest term to which a person committing the offence may be sentenced.

(4) *Repealed.*

131. Property to be stated as being in Returning Officer. In any prosecution for an offence in relation to any ballot boxes, ballot papers or marking instruments at an election the property in the boxes, papers, and instruments may be stated as being in the Returning Officer.

132. Infringement of secrecy.

(1) Every official, clerk, scrutineer, interpreter, and constable in attendance at a polling booth shall maintain and aid in maintaining the secrecy of the voting in the booth, and shall not communicate to any person, except for some purpose authorized by law, any information likely to defeat the secrecy of the ballot.

(2) No person, except for some purpose authorized by law, shall

(*a*) Interfere with or attempt to interfere with a voter when marking his vote:

(*b*) Attempt to obtain in a polling booth information as to the candidate for whom any voter in a booth is about to vote or has voted:

(*c*) Communicate at any time to any person any information obtained in a polling booth as to the candidate for whom any voter at the booth is about to vote or has voted, or as to the consecutive number on the ballot paper given to any voter at the booth.

(3) Every person in attendance at the counting of the votes shall maintain and aid in maintaining the secrecy of the voting, and shall not communicate any information obtained at the counting as to the candidate for whom any vote is given in any particular ballot paper.

(4) No person shall directly or indirectly induce any voter to display his ballot paper after he has marked it, so as to make known to any person the name of any candidate for or against whom he has voted.

(5) Every person who offends against this section shall be liable on summary conviction to imprisonment for a term not exceeding 3 months.

Candidates' Election Expenses

133. Periods for claiming and paying expenses. Subject to such exceptions as are permitted by this Act, it is hereby declared as follows:

(*a*) No claim against a candidate, or against any agent of a candidate, in respect of any election expenses shall be recoverable unless it is sent in to the candidate within 30 days after the day on which the candidate returned is declared to be elected:

(*b*) All election expenses incurred by or on behalf of a candidate shall be paid within 60 days after the day on which the candidate returned is declared to be elected, and not otherwise:

(*c*) Every person who makes any payment in breach of any of the provisions of this section is guilty of an illegal practice.

134. Procedure where claim disputed.

(1) If a candidate in the case of a claim for election expenses sent in to him within the time limited by this Act disputes it, or fails to pay it within the said period of 60 days, the claim shall be deemed to be a disputed claim, and the claimant may, if he thinks fit, within 30 days after the expiration of the said 60 days, bring an action for the disputed claim in any Court of competent jurisdiction.

(2) Any sum paid by the candidate in pursuance of the judgment or order of the Court in any such action shall be deemed to be paid within the time limited by this Act.

135. Leave to pay claim after time limited.

(1) On cause shown to the satisfaction of a District Court the Court may, on application by the claimant or by the candidate, grant leave to the candidate to pay a disputed claim, or to pay a claim for any election expenses, although sent in after the time limited by this Act.

(2) Any sum specified in the order granting that leave may be paid by the candidate, and when so paid shall be deemed to be paid within the time limited by this Act.

136. Payments to be vouched by bill. Every payment made in respect of any election expenses shall, except when less than $4, be vouched be a bill stating the particulars, and by a receipt.

137. Return of election expenses.

(1) Within 70 days after the day on which the candidate returned at any election is declared elected, every candidate at the election shall transmit to the Returning Officer a return of the candidate's election expenses in form 11 or to the like effect.

(2) Where the candidate is outside New Zealand on the day on which the candidate returned is declared elected, the return shall be transmitted by him to the Returning Officer within 21 says after the date of his return to New Zealand.

(3) Every candidate who fails to transmit the return to the Returning Officer within the time prescribed by this section shall be liable on summary conviction to a fine not exceeding $100, and, if he has been elected, to a further fine not exceeding $40 for every day on which he sits or votes in the House of Prepresentatives until the return is transmitted.

(4) Every candidate who transmits a return that is false in any material particular commits a corrupt practice, unless he satisfies the Court that he had no intention to mis-state or conceal the facts.

(5) It shall be the duty of the Returning Officer to see that the provisions of this section are faithfully complied with, or, if not faithfully complied with, to institute a prosecution for an offence against this section.

138. Return to be open for public inspection. The Returning Officer shall keep every such return in his office, or at some other convenient place to be appointed by the Minister, for a period of one year after it has been received by the Returning Officer, and during that period the return shall be open to inspection by any person on payment of a fee of 20 cents or such other fee as may be prescribed by regulations under this Act; and at the expiration of that period the Returning Officer shall cause the return to be destroyed.

139. Maximum amount of election expenses.

(1) The total election expenses of a candidate shall in no case exceed $4,000.

(2) Every candidate or other person is guilty of a corrupt practice who directly or indirectly pays or knowingly aids or abets any person in paying for or on account of any election expenses any sum in excess of the maximum amount prescribed by this section.

PART V

CORRUPT AND ILLEGAL PRACTICES

Corrupt Practices

140. Personation.

(1) Every person is guilty of a corrupt practice who commits, or aids or abets, counsels, or procures the commission of, the offence of personation.

(2) Every person commits the offence of personation who

(*a*) Votes as some other person, whether that other person is living or dead or is a fictitious person; or

(*b*) Having voted at any election, votes again at the same election; or

(*c*) Having voted at an election in any district at a general election. votes at an election in another district at the same general election.

(3) For the purposes of this section a person shall be deemed to have voted if he has applied for a ballot paper for himself, or has applied to vote as a special voter, or has marked a ballot paper for himself, whether validly or not.

(4) It shall be the duty of the Returning Officer to institute a prosecution against any person whom he believes to have committed the offence of personation, or to have aided, abetted, counselled, or procured the commission of that offence by any person, at the election for which he is Returning Officer.

141. Bribery.

(1) Every person is guilty of a corrupt practice who commits the offence of bribery.

(2) Every person commits the offence of bribery who, directly or indirectly, by himself or by any other person on his behalf.

(*a*) Gives any money or procures any office to or for any voter, or to or for any other person, on order to induce any voter to vote or refrain from voting; or

(*b*) Corruptly does any such act as aforesaid on account of any voter having voted or refrained from voting; or

(*c*) Makes any such gift or procurement as aforesaid to or for any person in order to induce that person to procure, or endeavour to procure, the return of any person at an election or the vote of any voter,

or who, upon or in consequence of any such gift or procurement as aforesaid, procures, or engages, promises, or endeavours to procure, the return of any person at any election or the vote of any voter.

(3) For the purposes of this section

(*a*) References to giving money shall include references to giving, lending, agreeing to give or lend, offering, promising, or promising to procure or endeavour to procure, any money or valuable consideration:

(*b*) References to procuring any office shall include references to giving, procuring, agreeing to give or procure, offering, promising, or promising to procure or to endeavour to procure, any office, place, or employment.

(4) Every person commits the offence of bribery who

(*a*) Advances or pays or causes to be paid any money to or to the use of any other person with the intent that that money or any part thereof shall be expended in bribery at any election; or

(*b*) Knowingly pays or causes to be paid any money to any person in discharge or repayment of any money wholly or in part expended in bribery at any election.

(5) The foregoing provisions of this section shall not extend or be construed to extend to any money paid or agreed to be paid for or on account of any legal expenses incurred in good faith at or concerning an election.

(6) A voter commits the offence of bribery if before or during an election he directly or indirectly, by himself or by any other person on his behalf, receives, or agrees or contracts for, and money, gift, loan, or valuable consideration, office, place, or employment for himself or for any other person for voting or agreeing to vote or for refraining or agreeing to refrain from voting.

(7) Every person commits the offence of bribery if after an election he directly or indirectly, by himself or by any other person on his behalf, receives any money or valuable consideration on account of any person having voted or refrained from voting or having induced any other person to vote or refrain from voting.

(8) In this section the term 'voter' includes any person who has or claims to have a right to vote.

142. Treating.

(1) Every person is guilty of a corrupt practice who commits the offence of treating.

(2) Every person commits the offence of treating who corruptly, by himself or by any other person on his behalf, either before, during, or after an election, directly or indirectly gives or provides, or pays wholly or in part the expense of giving or providing, any food, drink, entertainment, or provision to or for any person

(*a*) For the purpose of corruptly influencing that person or any other person to vote or refrain from voting; or

(*b*) For the purpose of procuring himself to be elected; or

(*c*) On account of that person or any other person having voted or refrained from voting, or being about to vote or refrain from voting.

(3) Every person commits the offence of treating who, being the holder of a licence for the sale by retail of intoxicating liquor, knowingly supplies any food, drink, entertainment, or provision

(*a*) To any person where the supply thereof is demanded for the purpose of treating, or for any corrupt or illegal practice; or

(*b*) To any persons, whether electors or not, for the purpose of procuring the return of a candidate at an election. and without receiving payment for it at the time when it is supplied.

(4) Every elector who corruptly accepts or takes any such food, drink, entertainment, or provision also commits the offence of treating.

(5) Notwithstanding anything in this section, the provision of a light supper after any election meeting shall be deemed not to constitute the offence of treating.

143. Undue influence.

(1) Every person is guilty of a corrupt practice who commits the offence of undue influence.

(2) Every person commits the offence of undue unfluence who

(*a*) Directly or indirectly, by himself or by any other person on his behalf, makes use of or threatens to make use of any force, violence, or restraint, or inflicts or threatens to inflict, by himself or by any other person, any temporal or spiritual injury, damage, harm, or loss upon or against any person, in order to induce or compel that person to vote for or against a particular candidate or to vote or refrain from voting, or on account of that person having voted for or against a particular candidate or having voted or refrained from voting; or

(*b*) By abduction, duress, or any fraudulent device or contrivance, impedes or prevents the free exercise of the franchise of an elector, or thereby compels, induces, or prevails upon an elector either to vote or to refrain from voting.

Illegal Practices

144. Payments for exhibition of election notices.

(1) No payment or contract for payment shall for the purpose of promoting or procuring the election of a candidate at an election be made to an elector on account of the exhibition of, or the use of any house, land, building, or premises for the exhibition of, any address, poster, notice, unless it is the ordinary business of the elector to exhibit for payment posters and advertisements and the payment or contract is made in the ordinary course of that business.

(2) If any payment or contract for payment is knowingly made in contravention of this section before, during, or after an election, the person making the payment or contract and, if he knew it to be in contravention of this Act, any person receiving the payment or being a party to the contract is guilty of an illegal practice.

145, 146. Repealed.

147. Providing money for illegal purposes. Where any person knowingly provides money for any purpose which is contrary to the provisions of this Act, or for any election expenses incurred in excess of the maximum amount allowed by this Act, or for repaying any money expended in any such payment or expenses, that person is guilty of an illegal practice.

147A. Advertisements for candidates.

(1) No person shall publish or cause or permit to be published in any newspaper, periodical, poster, or handbill, or broadcast or cause or permit to be broadcast over any radio or television station, any advertisement used or appearing to be used to promote or procure the election of any candidate at an election unless

(*a*) The publication of that advertisement is authorized in writing by the candidate or, in the case of an advertisement relating to more than one candidate, the candidates or the party to which they belong; and

(*b*) The advertisement contains a statement setting out the true name of the person for whom or at whose direction it is published and the address of his place of residence or business.

(2) The cost of every advertisement used or appearing to be used to promote or procure the election of a candidate forms part of the election expenses of that candidate, if, and only if,

(*a*) It relates solely to that candidate as a candidate for a particular electoral district; and

(*b*) It is published or broadcast

(i) By him; or

(ii) With his authority.

(3) Every person is guilty of an illegal practice who wilfully contravenes any provision of sub-section (1) of this section.

(4) A candidate shall not be liable for an illegal practice under this section committed by an agent without the consent or connivance of the candidate.

(5) Nothing in this section shall restrict the publication of any news or comments relating to an election in a newspaper or other periodical or in a radio or television broadcast made by the Broadcasting Corporation of New Zealand or other holder of a warrant under the Broadcasting Act 1976.

148. Procurement of voting by unqualified voters. Every person is guilty of an illegal practice who induces or procures to vote at any election any person whom he knows at the time to be disqualified or prohibited, whether under this Act or otherwise, from voting at that election.

General Provisions

149. Cinematograph films.

(1) For the purposes of this Act, the exhibition of any cinematograph film shall not be deemed to constitute bribery or treating or an illegal practice, and any payment or contract for payment in respect of any such exhibition shall not be deemed to constitute an illegal practice notwithstanding that the film may be wholly or mainly an advertisement.

(2) For the purposes of this section the expression 'cinematograph film' or 'film' includes any screen advertisement of any description.

150. Punishment for corrupt or illegal practice.

(1) Every person who is guilty of any corrupt practice or any illegal practice shall be liable on conviction on indictment

(*a*) In the case of a corrupt practice, to imprisonment for a term not exeeding one year or to a fine not exceeding $500 or to both:

(*b*) In the case of an illegal practice, to a fine not exceeding $300.

(2) *Repealed.*

151. Persons charged with corrupt practice may be found guilty of illegal practice. Any person charged with a corrupt practice may, if the circumstances warrant that finding, be found guilty of an illegal practice; and any person charged with an illegal practice may be found guilty of that offence notwithstanding that the act constituting the offence amounted to a corrupt practice.

152. Time limit for prosecutions. A prosecution against any person for a corrupt practice or an illegal practice shall be commenced within 6 months after the offence was committed:

Provided that where the person charged has been reported by the High Court in its report on the trial of an election petition to have been proved guilty of the offence a prosecution shall be commenced within 6 months after the offence was committed or within 3 months after the date of the report, whichever period is the later to expire.

153. Punishment for disqualified person voting. If any person, while his name is on the Corrupt Practices List for any district, votes or applies for a ballot paper or applies to vote as a special voter at any election in that or any other district, he shall, notwithstanding that his name may be on the main roll or any supplementary roll, be liable on summary conviction to a fine not exceeding $200 and his vote shall be void.

154. Reversal of disqualification procured through perjury. Where the name of any person is entered on the Corrupt Practices List for any district by reason of any conviction or any report by the High Court and any witness who gave evidence against that person in the proceedings resulting in that conviction or report is convicted of perjury in respect of that evidence, that person may apply to the High Court and that Court, if satisfied that the conviction or report so far as it relates to that person was based on perjury, may order that the name of that person be removed from the Corrupt Practices List.

PART VI

ELECTION PETITIONS

155. Method of questioning election.

(1) No election and no return to Parliament shall be questioned except by a petition complaining of an unlawful election or unlawful return (in this Act referred to as election petition) presented in accordance with this Part of this Act.

(2) A petition complaining of no return shall be deemed to be an election petition, and the High Court may make such order thereon as the Court thinks expedient for compelling a return to be made or may allow the petition to be heard as provided with respect to ordinary election petitions.

156. Election Petitions.

(1) An election petition may be presented to the High Court by one or more of the following persons.

(*a*) A person who voted or had a right to vote at the election:

(*b*) A person claiming to have had a right to be elected or returned at the election:

(*c*) A person alleging himself to have been a candidate at the election:

(2) The member whose election or return is complained of shall be the respondent to the petition, and if the petition complains of the conduct of a Returning Officer or Registrar of Electors he shall be a respondent.

(3) The petition shall be in such form and state such matters as are prescribed by rules of Court, and be signed by the petitioner or all the petitioners if more than one.

(4) The petition shall be presented by filing in the registry of the High Court nearest to the place where the election was held, The Registrar of the Court shall forthwith send a copy of the petition to the Returning Officer.

(5) The petition shall be served as nearly as may be in the manner in which a writ of summons is served, or in such other manner as may be prescribed by rules of Court.

157. Time for presentation of election petition.

(1) Subject to the provisions of this section, an election petition shall be presented within 49 days after the day on which the Returning Officer had publicly notified the result of the poll.

(2) If the petition questions the election or return upon an allegation of a corrupt practice and specifically alleges a payment of money or other reward to have been made by the member or on his account or with his knowledge and consent since the day of the said declaration in pursuance or furtherance of the alleged corrupt practice, it may be presented within 49 days after the date of the payment.

(3) For the purposes of this section an allegation that an election is avoided under section *164* of this Act shall be deemed to be an allegation of corrupt practices, notwithstanding that the offences alleged are or include offences other than corrupt practices.

158. Security for costs.

(1) At the time of presenting an electon petition or within 3 days after the expiration of the time limited for the presentation of the petition the petitioner shall give security to the satisfaction of the Registrar of the Court for all costs which may become payable by him to any witness summoned on his behalf or to any respondent.

(2) The security shall be an amount of $1,000 and shall be given by recognisance to the Crown entered into by any number of sureties not exceeding 5 or by a deposit of money, or partly in one way and partly in the other.

(3) If no security is given as required by this section no further proceedings shall be taken on the petition.

159. More than one petition relating to same election. Where more petitions than one are presented relating to the same election or return, all those petitions shall be dealt with as one petition.

160. Rules of Court.

(1) Rules of Court may be made n the manner prescribed by the Judicature Act 1908 for the purposes of this Part of this Act.

(2) All rules made under this section shall be laid before Parliament within 28 days after the date of the making thereof, if Parliament is then in session, and, if not, shall be laid before Parliament with 28 days after the date of the commencement of the next ensuing session.

Trial of Election Petition

161. Court and place of trial.

(1) Every election petition shall be tried by the High Court, and the trial shall take place before 3 Judges of the Court to be named by the Chief Justice.

(2) If any Judge before the conclusion of the trial, becomes unable to act, the Chief Justice shall name another Judge to act in his place.

(3) The place of trial shall be at the registry of the Court where the petition is filed:

Provided that the High Court, on being satisfied that special circumstances exist rendering it desirable that the petition should be tried elsewhere, may appoint such other place for the trial as appears most convenient.

162. Trial of petition.

(1) An election petition shall be tried in open Court without a jury, and notice of the time and place of trial shall be given not less than 14 days before the day of trial.

(2) The Court may in its discretion adjourn the trial from time to time, but the trial shall, so far as is practicable consistently with the interests of justice in respect of the trial, be continued from day to day on every lawful day until its conclusion.

(3) The trial of an election petition shall be proceeded with notwithstanding that the respondent may have become disqualified as a member of Parliament, or that Parliament may have been prorogued.

(4) Subject to this Act the Court shall have jurisdiction to inquire into and adjudicate on any matter relating to the petition in such manner as it thinks fit, and in particular may at any time during the trial direct a recount or scrutiny of the votes given at the election, and shall disallow the vote of every person proved to have been guilty of any corrupt practice, or whose name has been wrongly placed or retained on the poll:

Provided that the vote of any person who on polling day was entitled to be registered as an elector of the district shall not be disallowed on the ground that his name has beeen wrongly placed or retained on the roll.

(5) On the trial of an election petition, unless the Court otherwise directs, any charge of a corrupt or illegal practice may be gone into, and evidence in relation thereto received before any proof had been given that any candidate was aware of or consenting to the corrupt or illegal practice.

(6) On the trial of an election petition complaining of an unlawful election or return and claiming the seat for some person. the respondent may give evidence to prove that that person was not duly elected, in the same manner as if he had presented a petition against the election of that person.

163. Avoidance of election of candidate guilty of corrupt practice. Where a candidate who had been elected at any election is proved at the trial of an election petition to have been guilty of any corrupt practice at the election, his election shall be void.

164. Avoidance of election for general corruption.

(1) Where it is reported by the High Court on the trial of an election petition that corrupt or illegal practices committed in relation to the election for the purpose of promoting or procuring the election of any candidate thereat have so extensively prevailed that they may be reasonably supposed to have affected the result, his eclection, if he has been elected, shall be void.

(2) Except under this section, an election shall not be liable to be avoided by reason of the general prevalence of corrupt or illegal practices.

165. Votes to be struck off for corrupt practices. Where, on the trial of an election petition claiming the seat for any person, a candidate is reported by the High Court to have been proved guilty of bribery, treating, or undue influence in respect of any person who voted at the election, there shall, on a scrutiny, be struck off from the number of votes appearing to have been received by the candidate one vote for every person who voted at the election and is reported to have been proved to have been so bribed, treated, or unduly influenced.

166. Real justice to be observed. On the trial of any election petition

(*a*) The Court shall be guided by the substantial merits and justice of the case without regard to legal forms or technicalities:

(*b*) The Court may admit such evidence as in its opinion may assist it to deal effectively with the case, notwithstanding that the evidence may not otherwise be admissible in the High Court.

167. Irregulatities not to invalidate election. No election shall be declared invalid by reason of

(*a*) Any failure to comply with the times prescribed for doing any act; or

(*b*) Any omission or irregularity in filling up any form prescribed by this Act or by regulations made thereunder; or

(*c*) Any want or defect in the appointment of any official or scrutineer; or

(*d*) Any absence of, or mistake or omission or breach of duty by, any official, whether before, during, or after the polling.

if the Court is satisfied that the election was so conducted as to be substantially in compliance with the law as to elections, and that the failure, omission, irregularity, want, defect, absence, mistake, or breach did not affect the result of the election.

168. Decisions of Court to be final. All decisions of the High Court under this Part of this Act shall be final and conclusive and without appeal, and shall not be questioned in any way.

169. Certificate of Court as to result of election. At the conclusion of the trial of an election petition the Court shall determine whether the member whose election or return is complained of, or any and what other person, was duly elected or returned, or whether the election was void, and shall forthwith certify in writing the determination to the Speaker, and the determination so certified shall be final to all intents and purposes.

170. Report of Court as to corrupt or illegal practices.

(1) Where in an election petition any charge is made of any corrupt or illegal practice having been committed at the election, the Court shall, in addition to giving a certificate and at the same time, report in writing to the Speaker as follows:

(*a*) Whether any corrupt or illegal practice has or has not been proved to have been committed by or with the knowledge and consent of any candidate at the election, and the nature of the corrupt or illegal practice:

(*b*) Whether any of the candidates has been guilty by his agents of any corrupt or illegal practice in reference to the election:

(*c*) The names of all persons proved at the trial to have been guilty of any corrupt or illegal practice and whether they have received certificates of indemnity:

(*d*) Whether there is reason to believe that corrupt or illegal practices have extensively prevailed at the election.

(2) In the case of someone who is not a party to the petition nor a candidate on behalf of whom the seat is claimed by the petition, the Court, before reporting him to have been proved guilty of any corrupt or illegal practice, shall first cause notice to be given to him, and if he appear in pursuance of the notice, shall give him an opportunity of being heard and of calling evidence in his defence to show why he should not be so reported.

(3) For the purposes of this Act, if it is reported by the Court that a corrupt or illegal practice was committed with the knowledge and consent of a candidate, he shall be treated as having been reported to have been proved guilty of that corrupt or illegal practice.

(4) If a candidate is reported to have been guilty by his agents of treating, undue influence, or any illegal practice, and the Court further reports

(*a*) That no corrupt or illegal practice was committed at the election by the candidate with his knowledge or consent, and that the offences mentioned in the report were committed without the sanction or connivance of the candidate; and

(*b*) That all reasonable means for preventing the commission of corrupt and illegal practices at the election were taken by and on behalf of the candidate; and

(*c*) That the offences mentioned in the report were of a trivial, unimportant, and limited character; and

(*d*) That in all other respect the election was free from any corrupt or illegal practice on the part of the candidate and of his agents,

the candidate shall not be treated for the purposes of this Act as having been reported to have been proved guilty of the offences mentioned in the report.

171. Special report. At the same time as it give its certificate at the conclusion of the trial of an election petition, the Court may make a special report to the Speaker as to any matters arising in the course of the trial an account of which, in the judgment of the Court, ought to be submitted to the House of Representatives.

172. Signature and effect of certificate and report.

(1) The certificate and any report of the Court at the conclusion of the trial of an election petition shall be signed by at least 2 of the Judges presiding at the trial.

(2) On being informed by the Speaker of the certificate and any report of the Court, the House of Representatives shall order the same to be entered in the Journals of the House, and shall give the necessary directions for confirming or altering the return, or for issuing a writ for a new election, or for carrying out the determination, as the circumstances may require.

(3) Where the Court makes a special report the House may make such order in respect of that report as it thinks proper.

Witnesses

173. Summons and examination of witnesses.

(1) Witnesses may be summoned and sworn on the trial of an election petition in the same manner, as nearly as circumstances admit, as in the trial of an ordinary action.

(2) The High Court may by order require any person who appears to the Court to have been concerned in the election to attend as a witness, and every person who refuses to obey any such order shall be guilty of contempt of Court.

(3) The Court may examine any person so required to attend or any person in Court, although he is not called or examined by any party to the petition.

(4) After the examination of a witness as aforesaid by the Court he may be cross-examined by or on behalf of the petitioner and respondent, or either of them.

174. Certificate of indemnity to witness.

(1) A person called as a witness on the trial of an election petition shall not be excused from answering any question relating to any offence at or connected with the election on the ground that the answer thereto may incriminate or tend to incriminate himself, or on the ground of privilege:

Provided that

(*a*) An answer by a person to a question put by or before the Court shall not, except in the case of any criminal proceeding for perjury in respect of the evidence, be admissible in evidence against him in any proceeding, civil or criminal:

(*b*) A witness who answers truly all questions which he is required by the Court to answer shall be entitled to receive a certificate of indemnity, stating that he has so answered.

(2) Where a person has received a certificate of indemnity in relation to an election, and any legal proceeding is at any time instituted against him for any offence committed by him at or in connection with the election previously to the date of the certificate, the Court having cognisance of the case shall on production of the certificate stay the proceeding, and may in its discretion award to the said person such costs as he has been put to in the proceeding.

(3) Nothing in this section shall be deemed to relieve a person receiving a certificate of indemnity from any incapacity under this Act or from any proceeding to enforce any such incapacity (other than a criminal prosecution).

175. Expenses of witnesses.

(1) The reasonable expenses incurred by any person in appearing to give evidence at the trial of an election petition, according to the scale allowed to witnesses on the trial of civil actions, may be allowed to him by the Court.

(2) Any such expenses, if the witness was called and examined by the Court, shall be deemed to be part of the expenses of the Court, and in other cases shall be deemed to be costs of the petition.

Costs

176. Costs of petition.

(1) All costs of and incidental to the presentation of an election petition, and to the proceedings consequent thereon, except such as are by this Act otherwise provided for shall be defrayed by the parties to the petition in such manner and in such proportions as the High Court may determine; and in particular any costs which in the opinion of the Court have been caused by vexatious conduct, unfounded allegations, or unfounded objections on the part either of the petitioner or of the respondent, and any needless expenses incurred or caused on the part of the petitioner or respondent, may be ordered to be defrayed by the parties by whom they were caused or incurred, whether those parties are or are not on the whole successful.

(2) If a petitioner fails for 6 months after demand to pay to any person summoned as a witness on his behalf, or to the respondent, any sum certified to be due to him for costs, and the failure is within one year after the demand proved to the satisfaction of the High Court, every person who has under this Act entered into a recognisance relating to the petition shall be held to have made default in the recognisance, and it shall be dealt with in manner provided by section *21* of the Crown Proceedings Act 1950.

177. Costs payable by persons proved guilty of corrupt or illegal practices.

(1) Where on the trial of an election petition it appears to the Court that any person has been guilty of any corrupt or illegal practice, the Court may, after giving that person an opportunity of making a statement to show why the order should not be made, order the whole or any part of the costs of or incidental to any proceedings before the Court in relation to that offence or to that person to be paid by that person to such other person or person as the Court thinks fit.

(2) All costs so ordered to be paid may be recovered as a debt due by the person by whom they are ordered to be paid to the person or persons to whom they are ordered to be paid.

Withdrawal and Abatement of Petitions.

178. Withdrawal of petition.

(1) A petitioner shall not withdraw an election petition without the leave of the High Court upon special application to be made in the prescribed manner.

(2) No such application shall be made until the prescribed notice of the intention to make it has been given in the district to which the petition relates.

(3) Where there are more petitioners than one, an application to withdraw the petition shall not be made except with the consent of all the petitioners.

(4) If a petition is withdrawn, the petitioner shall be liable to pay the costs of the respondent.

179. Substitution of new petitioner.

(1) On the hearing of an application for the leave to withdraw a petition,

any person who might in the first instance have presented the petition may apply to the Court to be substituted as a petitioner.

(2) The Court may, if it thinks fit, substitute any such applicant as petitioner, and may, if the proposed withdrawal is in the opinion of the Court the result of any corrupt bargain or consideration, by order direct that the security given on behalf of the original petitioner shall remain as security for any costs incurred by the substituted petitioner, and that to the extent of the sum named in the security the original petitioner shall be liable to pay the costs of the substituted petitioner.

(3) If the Court does not so direct, security to the same amount as would be required in the case of a new petition, and subject to the like conditions, shall be given on behalf of the substituted petitioner within 3 days after the order of substitution.

(4) Subject as aforesaid, a substituted petitioner shall as nearly as may be stand in the same position and be subject to the same liabilities as the original petitioner.

180. Report on withdrawal. In every case of the withdrawal of an election petition the High Court shall make a report to the Speaker stating whether in its opinion the withdrawal of the petition was the result of any corrupt arrangement or in consideration of the withdrawal of any other election petition and, if so, the circumstances attending the withdrawal.

181. Abatement of petition.

(1) An election petition shall be abated by the death of a sole petitioner or of the survivor of several petitioners.

(2) The abatement of a petitioner shall not affect the liability of the petitioner or any other person to the payment of costs previously incurred.

(3) On the abatement of a petition notice of the abatement shall be given in the prescribed manner; and within 28 days after the notice is given any person who might have been a petitioner in respect of the election may apply to the High Court in the prescribed manner to be substituted as a petitioner. On any such application the Court may, if it thinks fit, substitute the applicant accordingly.

(4) Security shall be given on behalf of a petitioner so substituted, as in the case of a new petition.

General Provisions

182. Withdrawal and substitution of respondents before trial.

(1) If before the trial of an election petition a respondent other than the Returning Officer

(*a*) Dies; or

(*b*) Gives the prescribed notice that he does not intend to oppose the petition; or

(*c*) Loses his seat by reason of the House of Representatives resolving that the seat is vacant, notice thereof shall be given in the prescribed manner; and, within 28 days after the notice is given, any person who might have been a petitioner in respect of the election may apply to the High Court to be admitted as a respondent to oppose the petition, and shall be admitted accordingly, except that the number of persons so admitted shall not exceed 3.

(2) A respondent who has given the prescribed notice that he does not intend to oppose the petition shall not be allowed to appear or act as a party against the petition in any proccedings thereon, and shall not sit or vote in the House of Representatives until that House has been informed of the report on the petition.

(3) Where a respondent has given the prescribed notice as aforesaid, the Court shall report that fact to the Speaker.

183. Submission of report to Attorney General. Where the High Court reports that certain persons named have been proved at the trial of an election petition to have been guilty of any corrupt or illegal practice the report shall be laid before the Attorney General.

PART VII

MISCELLANEOUS PROVISIONS

184. Service of notices.

(1) Any notice under this Act may be served on any person by delivering it to that person, and may be delivered to him either personally or by leaving it at his place of residence as stated on the roll or by posting it by registered letter addressed to him at that place of residence.

(2) A notice so posted shall be deemed to have been served at the time when the registered letter would in the ordinary course of post be delivered.

(3) Where any notice is sent by registered letter addressed to any person at his place of residence as stated on the roll, with a special request that the letter be returned to the sender a the expiration of 15 days if the person to whom the letter is addressed cannot be found, the return of the letter by the Post Office shall be deemed sufficient proof that the person has quitted that place of residence.

185. Voting machines.

(1) The Governor General may from time to time, by Order in Council, direct that at any election a voting maching specified in the Order shall be used by way of experiment, and every such Order shall be complied with by the Returning Officer at that election.

(2) By every such Order the Governor General shall prescribe the mode in which the machine shall be used.

(3) On the making of any such Order the Chief Electoral Officer shall provide the Returning Officer with a sufficient number of voting machines.

186. Registrars of Electors exempt from Court fees. Registrars of Electors shall be exempt from the payment of any Court fees in respect of any proceedings under this Act.

187. Validation of irregularities. Where anything is omitted to be done or cannot be done at the time required by or under this Act, or is done before or after that time, or is otherwise irregularly done in matter of form, or sufficient provision is not made by or under this Act, the Governor General may, by Order in Council gazetted, at any time before or after the time within which the thing is required to be done, extend that time, or validate anything so done before or after the time required or so irregularly done in matter of form, or make other provision for the case as he thinks fit:

Provided that this section shall not apply with respect to the presentation of an election petition or to the giving of security for costs in relation to an election petition.

188. Regulations.

(1) The Governor General may from time to time, by Order in Council, make all such regulations as may be deemed necessary or expedient for the purpose of giving full effect to the provisions of this Act and for the due administration thereof.

(2) Regulations made under this section may prescribe penalties for offences against the regulations, not exceeding imprisonment for a term of 3 months or a fine of $100, or both.

(3) All regulations made under this section shall be laid before Parliament within 28 days after the date of the making thereof if Parliament is then in session, and, if not, shall be laid before Parliament within 28 days after the date of the commencement of the next ensuing session.

189. Restriction on amendment or repeal of certain provisions.

(1) This section applies to the following provisions of this Act (hereinafter referred to as reserved provisions), namely:

- (*a*) Section *12*, relating to the duration of the House of Representatives:
- (*b*) Section *15*, relating to the Representation Commission:
- (*c*) Section *16*, and the definition of the term 'General electoral population' in sub-section (1) of section *2*, relating to the division of New Zealand into General electoral districts after each census:
- (*d*) Section *17*, relating to the allowance for adjustment of the quota:
- (*e*) Section *39*, and the definition of the term 'adult' in sub-section (1) of section *2*, and paragraph (*e*) of section *99*, so far as those provisions prescribe 18 years as the minimum age for persons qualified to be registered as electors or to vote:
- (*f*) Section *106*, relating to the method of voting.

(2) No reserved provision shall be repealed or amended unless the proposal for the amendment or repeal

- (*a*) Is passed by a majority of 75 percent of all the members of the House of Representatives; or
- (*b*) Has been carried by a majority of the valid votes cast at a poll of the electors of the General and Maori electoral districts:

Provided that this section shall not apply to the repeal of any reserved provision by a consolidating Act in which that provision is re-enacted without amendment and this section is re-enacted without amendment so as to apply to that provision as re-enacted.

(3) Subject to the provisions of any regulations made under this Act for the purposes of this section, and subject to any necessary modifications, the provisions of the Licensing Act 1908 and of this Act shall, so far as they are applicable, apply to every poll under this section as if it were a general licensing poll taken simultaneously with a general election.

190. Repeals and savings.

(1) The enactments specified in the Second Schedule to this Act are hereby repealed.

(2) Without limiting the provisions of the Acts Interpretation Act 1924, it is hereby declared that the repeal of any provision by this Act shall not affect any document made or anything whatsoever done under the provision so repealed or under any corresponding former provision, and every such document or thing, so far as it is subsisting or in force at the time of the repeal and could have been made or done under this Act, shall continue and have effect as if it had been made or done under the corresponding provision of this Act and as if that provision had been in force when the document was made or the thing was done.

XII. Western Samoa Act 1961[1]

November 24, 1961

Whereas at the date of the passing of this Act the Government of New Zealand is the administering authority for the Territory of Western Samoa under the Trusteeship Agreement for that Territory approved by the General Assembly of the United Nations on the thirteenth day of December nineteen hundred and forty-six: *And whereas* the Trusteeship Agreement will terminate on the first day of January, nineteen hundred and sixty-two, and Western Samoa will thereupon become a fully independent sovereign State under the name of the Independent State of Western Samoa having a constitution which has been adopted by the people of Western Samoa: *And whereas* it is expedient that provision be made declaring that Her Majesty shall have not jurisdiction over the Independent State of Western Samoa on and after the date on which the termination of the Trusteeship Agreement takes effect and for the repeal or amendment of such of the laws of New Zealand as would be incompatible with the status of Western Samoa as a fully independent sovereign State:

Be it therefore enacted by the General Assembly of New Zealand in Parliament assembled, and by the authority of the same, as follows:

1. Short Title. This Act may be cited as the Western Samoa Act 1961.

[1] 1261, No. 68. *An Act to make provisions in connection with the attainment of independence by the people of Western Samoa.* See 'Samoa,' page 1259 *et seq.*

2. Commencement.

(1) Except where this Act otherwise provides, this Act shall come into force at the hour of eleven o'clock in the evening on the first day of January, nineteen hundred and sixty-two, being the time in New Zealand corresponding to the commencement of the first day of January, nineteen hundred and sixty-two, in Western Samoa (that date being the date appointed by the General Assembly of the United Nations for the termination of the Trusteeship Agreement for the Territory of Western Samoa).

(2) The period of twenty-four hours following the commencement of this Act is hereinafter referred to as Independence Day.

3. Independence of Western Samoa. It is hereby declared that on and after Independence Day Her Majesty in right of New Zealand shall have no jurisdiction over the Independent State of Western Samoa.

4. Future New Zealand Acts not to be in force in Western Samoa. No Act of the Parliament of New Zealand passed on or after Independence Day or passed before Independence Day and coming into force on or after Independence Day shall be in force in Western Samoa.

5. New Zealand law to apply as if Western Samoa a member of the Commonwealth. On and after Independence Day all law for the time being in force in New Zealand – that is to say, all law whether it is a rule of law or a provision of an Act of any Parliament or a provision of any other enactment or instrument whatsoever – shall, subject to any express provision to the contrary in that law, and unless express provision to the contrary is subsequently made by the authority having power to alter that law, have the same operation in relation to the Independent State of Western Samoa as it would have if the Independent State of Western Samoa were part of Her Majesty's dominions and a member of the Commonwealth.

6. Citizens of Western Samoa not required to register as aliens. The Aliens Act 1948 is hereby amended by inserting, before section *6* and under the heading 'Registration,' the following section:

'5A. In sections *6* to *13* of this Act the term 'alien' does not include a citizen of the Independent State of Western Samoa.

7. Abolition of appeals and cases stated to Supreme Court.

(1) On and after Independence Day the Supreme Court of New Zealand shall have no jurisdiction to hear or determine any appeal from any Court in Western Samoa or any case stated by any Court in Western Samoa.

(2) Every appeal to the Supreme Court of New Zealand from the High Court of Western Samoa for determination by the Supreme Court of New Zealand which is pending on Independence Day shall abate on that day.

8. Ordinances not invalid on ground of repugnancy with certain New Zealand Acts and regulations.

(1) Notwithstanding anything in paragraph (*a*) of sub-section (1) of section *32* of the Samoa Amendment Act 1957, no Ordinance of the Legislative Assembly of Western Samoa and no provision of any such Ordinance shall be void or inoperative on the ground that it is repugnant to any provision of any enactment

specified in the First Schedule of this Act, and for the purposes of that section the enactments so specified shall be deemed not to be reserved enactments.

(2) Every Ordinance of the Legislative Assembly of Western Samoa passed before the date of the passing of this Act which would have been valid if this section had been in force when the Ordinance was passed is hereby declared to be valid.

(3) This section shall come into force on the date of the passing of this Act.

9. Enactments amended. The enactments specified in the Second Schedule to this Act are hereby amended in the manner indicated in that Schedule.

10. Repeals, revocations, and savings.

(1) The enactments specified in the Third Schedule to this Act are hereby repealed.

(2) The regulations, rules, orders, and notices specified in the Fourth Schedule ot this Act are hereby revoked.

(3) On and after Independence Day the Western Samoa Order in Council 1920 made by His late Majesty with the advice of the Privy Council on the eleventh dya of March, nineteen hundred and twenty, shall cease to have effect.

(4) Notwithstanding the repeal or amendment or revocation of any enactment by this Act.

(*a*) The provisions of sub-sections (4) to (7) of section *75* of the Samoa Act 1921 shall continue to apply, as if the Act had not been passed, with respect to any memorial under that section filed in the Supreme Court of New Zealand before Independence Day;

(*b*) Every reception order made pursuant to section *328* of the Samoa Act 1921 with respect to any person who is subject to such an order immediately before Independence Day shall continue in full force and effect;

(*c*) The Controller and Auditor General may continue to exercise and perform all powers and functions conferred on him under any such enactment until the duties imposed on him by that enactment have been completed in respect of any period before Independence Day, and for that purpose every such enactment shall be deemed to continue in force as if this Act had not been passed;

(*d*) The provisions of the British Nationality and New Zealand Citizenship Act 1948 shall apply with respect to every application received under that Act before Independence Day for registration as a New Zealand citizen or for a certificate of naturalization as if this Act had not been passed.

SCHEDULES

(not reproduced)

XIII. Constitution of the Cook Islands[1]

November 17, 1964, amended to 1981

1. Interpretation,

(1) In this Constitution, unless the context otherwise requires,

'Act' means an Act of the Parliament of the Cook Islands;

'Cabinet' means the Cabinet of Ministers of the Cook Islands;

'Constitution' means this Constitution; and includes any amendment thereof;

'Constitution Day' means the date appointed for the commencement of this Constitution;

'The Cook Islands' means all islands in the South Pacific Ocean lying between the 8th and 23rd degrees of south latitude and the 156th and 167th degrees of longitude west of Greenwich; and each island of the Cook Islands shall be deemed to include all smaller islands lying within ten miles of the coasts thereof;

'Court of Appeal' means the Court of Appeal of the Cook Islands established under this Constitution;

'Enactment' means any Act of the Parliament of the Cook Islands, any Ordinance, any Act of Parliament of New Zealand in force in the Cook Islands, and any Proclamation, order, regulation, or rule, or any Island Council Ordinance or bylaw;

'Executive Council' means the Executive Council of the Cook Islands established under this Constitution;

'Existing law' means any law in force in the Cook Islands immediately before Constitution Day; and includes any enactment passed or made before Constitution Day and coming into force on or after Constitution Day;

'High Court' means the High Court of the Cook Islands established under this Constitution;

[1] An Act to amend the Cook Islands Constitution Act 1964 (June 7, 1965), N. Z. Statutes 1965.

'Law' means any law for the time being in force in the Cook Islands; and includes this Constitution and any enactment;

'Legislative Assembly' or 'Assembly' where it appears in this Constitution or any other enactment means the Parliament of the Cook Islands established under this Constitution;

'New Zealand' means New Zealand exclusive of the Cook Islands;

'Ordinance' means an Ordinance of the Legislative Assembly of the Cook Islands made before Constitution Day and continuing in force on and after Constitution Day;

'Queen's Representative' means the representative of Her Majesty the Queen in the Cook Islands appointed under Article *3* hereof;

'Parliament' means the Parliament of the Cook Islands established under this Constitution, and the term 'Legislative Assembly' or 'Assembly' where it appears in this constitution or in any other enactment shall have the same meaning;

'Prime Minister' means the Prime Minister of the Cook Islands;

'To reside', in relation to the Cook Islands or to any constituency in the Cook Islands, means to have a usual place of abode in the Cook Islands, or, as the case may be, in that constituency, notwithstanding any temporary absence for the purpose of undergoing a course of education or of technical training or instruction, and notwithstanding any occasional for any other purpose and 'resident' and 'residing' have corresponding meanings;

(2) Where under the provisions of this Constitution any person is required to subscribe an oath, he shall be permitted, if he so desires, to comply with that requirement by taking and subscribing an affirmation.

(3) Where in this Constitution reference is made to the functions of any office, that reference shall, unless the context otherwise requires, be construed as a reference to the functions of that office and to any powers and authorities that may lawfully be exercised by, and any duties that may be required to be performed by, the holder of that office.

PART I

THE GOVERNMENT OF THE COOK ISLANDS

2. The Head of State. Her Majesty the Queen in right of New Zealand shall be the Head of State of the Cook Islands.

Queen's Representative

3. The Queen's Representative in the Cook Islands.

(1) There shall be a representative of Her Majesty the Queen in the Cook Islands, to be known as the Queen's Representative.

(2) The Queen Representative shall be appointed by Her Majesty the Queen, and shall hold office for a period of three years, and may from time to time be reappointed.

4. *Oath of office.* The Queen's representative shall, before assuming the functions of his office, take and subscribe before the Chief Justice of the High Court the following oath:

I, ..., swear by Almighty God that I will be faithful and bear true allegiance to Her [*or* His] Majesty [*Specify the name of the reigning Sovereign, as thus:* Queen Elizabeth the Second] as the Head of State of the Cook Islands, Her [*or* His] heirs and successors, according to law, and that I will uphold the dignity of the office of Queen's Representative of the Cook Islands, and will justly and faithfully carry out my duties in the administration of the Cook Islands in accordance with the Constitution and the law. So help me God.

5. *Queen's Representative to act on advice.*

(1) Except as otherwise provided in this Constitution, the Queen's Representative in the performance of his functions as the representative of Her Majesty the Queen shall act on the advice of Cabinet, the Prime Minister, or the appropriate Minister, as the case may be.

(2) If the Cabinet, the Prime Minister, or an appropriate Minister tenders advice to the Queen's Representative as to the performance of any function as the representative of Her Majesty the Queen and if the Queen's Representative does not, within fourteen days after the date on which the tendering of that advice comes to his notice, accept that advice or take some other action in relation thereto which he is entitled to take under the provisions of this Constitution or of any other law, the Queen's Representative shall be deemed to have accepted that advice; and an instrument under the hand of the Secretary to the Cabinet, acting on the instruction of the Prime Minister, to that effect shall operate as to the performance of the function concerned in accordance with that advice.

6. *Information to Queen's Representative.* It shall be the duty of the Prime Minister

(*a*) To arrange for the circulation to the Queen's Representative of copies of the agenda and minutes of Cabinet and of all other papers laid before Cabinet at the time when they are circulated to Ministers. and

(*b*) To furnish such information relating to the affairs of the Cook Islands and proposals for legislation as the Queen's Representative may call for.

7. (1) Whenever the office of Queen's Representative is vacant or the holder of that office is absent from the Cook Islands or is for any reason unable to perform any functions conferred on him by law, those functions shall be performed by the Chief Justice of the Cook Islands, or, if the Chief Justice is also for any reasons unable to act, those functions shall be performed by the Judge of the High Court authorized by Article *50* hereof to exercise the functions of the Chief Justice.

(2) Nothing in this Article shall preclude the Queen's Representative from performing at any time when he is absent from the Cook Islands any of the functions conferred on him by law.

(3) No act done by the Chief Justice of the Cook Islands, or by the Judge of the High Court exercising the functions of the Chief Justice, in the performance of any function of the Queen's Representative shall be questioned or invalidated on the ground that the occasion therefor had not arisen or had ceased.

The House of Arikis of the Cook Islands

8. *The House of Arikis of the Cook Islands.*

(1) There shall be a House of Arikis of the Cook Islands (hereinafter referred to as the House of Arikis).

(2) The House of Arikis shall comprise the following members:

(*a*) One Ariki representing the Island of Aitutaki and the Island of Manuae:

(*b*) One Ariki representing the Island of Atiu:

(*c*) On Ariki representing the Island of Mangaia:

(*d*) One Ariki representing the Island of Manihiki and the Island of Rakahanga:

(*e*) One Ariki representing the Island of Mauke:

(*f*) One Ariki representing the Island of Mitiaro:

(*g*) One Ariki representing the Island of Penrhyn:

(*h*) One Ariki representing the Island of Pukapuka and the Island of Nassau:

(*i*) Such number of Arikis representing the Island of Rarotonga and the Island of Palmerston, being not more than six, as is prescribed by law.

(3) Subject to the provisions of this Article, the members of the House of Arikis shall be appointed by the Queen's Representative.

(4) If there is for the time being only one Ariki for any of the islands or groups of islands specified in paragraphs (*a*) to (*h*) of sub-clause (2) of this Article, that Ariki shall be appointed to be a member of the House of Arikis as representing that island or group; but, if there are two or more Arikis as representing that island or group, the High Commissioner shall appoint the Ariki for that island or group who is nominated for appointment in the manner prescribed by law.

(5) If there are for the time being not more than the number of Arikis prescribed by law to be appointed as representing the group of islands comprising the Islands of Rarotonga and Palmerston, those Arikis shall be appointed to be members of the House of Arikis as representing that group; but, if there are more than the number so prescribed, the Queen's Representative shall appoint the Arikis for that group who are nominated for appointments in the manner prescribed by law.

(6) Subject to the provisions of this Article, the qualifications of Arikis, the qualifications and disqualifications of members of the House of Arikis, and the terms and conditions of their membership shall be as prescribed by law.

(7) If any vacancy occurs in the office of a member of the House of Arikis, the vacancy shall be filled in the same manner as an appointment to that office, and the appointee shall hold office for the unexpired portion of the term of office of his predecessor.

9. *Functions of House of Arikis.* The House of Arikis shall have the following functions:

(*a*) It shall consider such matters relative to the welfare of the people of the

Cook Islands as may be submitted to it by the Queen's Representative for its consideration, and it shall express its opinion and make recommendations thereon to the Queen's Representative; and

(*b*) It shall have such other functions as may be prescribed by law.

10. Members to take Oath of Allegiance. Except for the purposes of enabling this Article to be complied with, no member of the House of Arikis shall be permitted to sit or vote therein until he has taken and subscribed the following oath before the Queen's Representative namely:

I, ..., swear by Almighty God that I will be faithful and bear true allegiance to Her [*or* His] Majesty [*Specify the name of the reigning Sovereign, as thus:* Queen Elizabeth the Second] as the Head of State of the Cook Islands, Her [*or* His] heirs and successors, according to law, and that I will justly and faithfully carry out my duties as a member of the House of Arikis of the Cook Islands. So help me God.

11. Attendance of Prime Minister and other persons at House of Arikis.

(1) The Prime Minister may, at any time, attend and address the House of Arikis.

(2) A Minister or a person appointed in that behalf by a Minister may attend the proceedings of the House of Arikis when any matter for which the Minister is responsible is under consideration by the House.

(3) The presiding member of the House of Arikis, when in his opinion any matter before the House makes it desirable, may invite any member of the Parliament to attend meetings of the House relating to that matter.

(4) A person attending the proceedings of the House of Arikis by virtue of the Provisions of sub-clause (2) or sub-clause (3) of this Article shall be entitled to take part in the proceedings of the House relating to the matter for which the Minister has responsibility or in respect of which he was invited to attend, as the case may be, as if he were a member of the House.

11A. Procedure.

(1) The House of Arikis shall be presided over by one of its members, who shall be elected by the members of the House in the manner prescribed by law and shall hold office for such period and subject to such conditions as may be prescribed by law.

(2) The House of Arikis shall meet in Rarotonga at such times as may be prescribed by law:

Provided that the House of Arikis shall meet at least once in every period of twelve months.

(3) Meetings of the House of Arikis shall be summoned by the Queen's Representative, acting on the advice of the Prime Minister.

(4) No business shall be transacted at any meeting of the House of Arikis if the number of members present is less than eight.

(5) Subject to the provisions of this Constitution and to the provisions of any law, the House of Arikis may from time to time make, amend, and repeal Standing Orders for the regulation and orderly conduct of its proceedings and the despatch of business.

(6) Subject to the provisions of this Article and to the provisions of any law, the House of Arikis shall determine its own procedure.

(7) The House of Arikis shall not be disqualified for the transaction of business by reason of any vacancy among its members, and any proceedings therein shall be valid notwithstanding that some person who was not entitled to do so sat or voted in the House or otherwise took part in the proceedings.

11B. Privileges of House of Arikis and its members. Provision may be made by law for the application to the House of Arikis, its members and officers, persons entitled to speak therein, and person publishing by or under the authority of the House any report, paper, vote, or proceeding of any of the provisions of any law for the time being in force relating to the privileges and immunities of the Parliament, its members and officers, persons entitled to speak therein, and persons publishing by or under the authority of the Parliament any report, paper, vote, or proceeding.

PART II

THE EXECUTIVE GOVERNMENT OF THE COOK ISLANDS

12. Executive authority.

(1) The executive authority of the Cook Islands shall be vested in Her Majesty the Queen in right of New Zealand.

(2) Subject to the provisions of this Constitution, the executive authority of the Cook Islands may be exercised on behalf of Her Majesty by the Queen s Representative, either directly or through officers subordinate to him.

(3) Nothing in this Article shall prevent the Parliament from conferring functions on persons or authorities other than the Queen's Representative.

Cabinet

13. Cabinet.

(1) There shall be a Cabinet of Ministers, comprising the Prime Minister of the Cook Islands (who shall preside over Cabinet) and not fewer than three nor more than six other Ministers, which shall have the general direction and control of the executive government of the Cook Islands, and shall be collectively responsible therefor to the Parliament.

(2) The Prime Minister shall be appointed as follows:

(*a*) If the appointment is to be made while the Parliament is in session the Queen's Representative shall appoint as Prime Minister a member of the Parliament who commands the confidence of a majority of the members of the Parliament.

(*b*) If the appointment is to be made while the Parliament is not in session, the Queen's Representative shall appoint as Prime Minister a member of the Parliament who in the opinion of the Queen's Representative, acting in his discretion, is likely to command the confidence of a majority of the members of the Parliament:

(*c*) If the appointment is to be made after a dissolution of the Parliament and before the holding of the general election of the Parliament following that dissolution, the Queen's Representative shall appoint as Prime Minister a person who was a member of the Parliament immediately before that dissolution and who in the opinion of the Queens's Representative, acting in his discretion, is likely to command the confidence of a majority of the persons who were members of the Parliament immediately before that dissolution:

Provided that where the Parliament has been dissolved pursuant to sub-clause (2) of Article *37* hereof, the Queen's Representative shall appoint as Prime Minister a person who was a member of the Parliament immediately before that dissolution and who in the opinion of the Queen's Representative, acting in his discretion, is capable of performing the functions of the Prime Minister.

(3) The Ministers other than the Prime Minister shall be appointed by the Queen's Representative on the advice of the Prime Minister. No person shall be so appointed unless

(*a*) He is a member of the Parliament; or

(*b*) If the appointment is to be made after a dissolution of the Parliament and before the holding of the general election of the Parliament following that dissolution, he was a member of the Parliament immediately before that dissolution; or

(*c*) If the appointment is to be made after the holding of a general election of the Parliament and before the commencement of the first session of the Parliament following that election, he was elected as a member of the Parliament at that election.

(4) Appointments under the provisions of this Article shall be made by instrument under the Seal of the Cook Islands.

(5) If any employee of the Cook Islands Public Service is appointed to be a Minister, he shall forthwith be deemed to have vacated his office as an employee of that Service.

14. Duration of office of members of Cabinet.

(1) The appointment of the Prime Minister who is in office immediately before the date of the holding of a general election of the Parliament may be terminated by the Queen's Representative, acting in his discretion, after the date of the holding of that election and before the date of the commencement of the first session of the Parliament following that election.

(2) The appointment of the Prime Minister who is in office at the commencement of the first session of the Parliament following a general election thereof shall be terminated by the Queen's Representative on the seventh day of that session if the Prime Minister has not sooner resigned.

(3) The appointment of the Prime Minister shall also be terminated by the Queen's Representative.

(*a*) If the Prime Minister ceases to be a member of the Parliament for any reason other than the dissolution of the Parliament; or (*b*) If the Parliament passes a motion in express words of no confidence in Cabinet or if Cabinet is defeated on any question or issue which the Prime Minister has declared to be a question or issue of confidence:

Provided that, if after the passing of such a motion or after that defeat the Prime Minister so requests, the Queen's Representative, acting in his discretion, may dissolve the Parliament instead of terminating the appointment of the Prime Minister; or

(*c*) If the Prime Minister resigns his office by writing under his hand delivered to the Queen's Representative; or

(*d*) If the Prime Minister is absent from the Cook Islands, otherwise than on official business, for a period of more than three months without written authority given by the Queen's Representative acting in his discretion.

(4) The office of any other Minister shall become vacant

(*a*) If the appointment of the Prime Minister has been terminated under the provisions of sub-clause (1) or sub-clause (2) or sub-clause (3) of this Article; or

(*b*) If the appointment of the Minister to that office is revoked by the Queen's Representative, acting on the advice of the Prime Minister, by instrument under the Seal of the Cook Islands; or

(*c*) If the Minister ceases to be a member of the Parliament for any reason other than the dissolution of the Assembly; or

(*d*) If the Minister resigns his office by writing under his hand delivered to the Queen's Representative.

(5) Whenever, by reason of illness or of absence from the Cook Islands, the Prime Minister is temporarily prevented from performing, in the Cook Islands, the functions of this office, the Queen's Representative may, by instrument under the Seal of the Cook Islands, appoint another Minister to perform those functions until such time as the Prime Minister is capable of again performing them or has vacated his office.

(6) The power conferred on the Queen's Representative under the provisions of sub-clause (5) of this Article shall be exercised by the Queen's Representative, acting in his discretion, if in his opinion it is impracticable to obtain the advvice of the Prime Minister by reason of the illness or absence of the Prime Minister and, in any other case, shall be exercised by the Queen's Representative, acting on the advice of the Prime Minister.

(7) The Queen's Representative, acting on the advice of the Prime Minister, may, by instrument under the Seal of the Cook Islands,

(*a*) Declare a Minister to be by reason of illness temporarily incapable of performing his functions as a Minister; or

(*b*) Suspend a Minister during the period of any investigation or inquiry into the conduct of that Minister.

(8) Any Minister in respect of whom action has been taken under the pro-

visions of sub-clause (7) of this Article shalll not perform any of the functions of his office or sit in or otherwise take part in the proceedings of Cabinet or of the Executive Council until the Queen's Representative, acting on the advice of the Prime Minister, has revoked the aforesaid instrument under the Seal of the Cook Islands.

15. Official oath. Every Minister shall, before assuming the functions of his office, take and subscribe before the Queen's Representative the following oath:

I, ..., being chosen and accepted as Prime Minister (*or* a Minister) and member of Cabinet, swear by Almighty God that I will to the best of my judgment, at all time when thereto required, freely give my counsel and advice to the Queen's Representative of the Cook Islands for the good management of the affairs of the Cook Islands, and that I will not directly or indirectly reveal such matters as shall be debated in Cabinet and committee and in Executive Council and committed to my secrecy, but that I will in all such things be a true and faithful Prime Minister (*or* Minister). So help me God.

16. Assignment of responsibilities to Ministers.

(1) The Prime Minister may, be direction in writing under his hand,

(*a*) Charge any Minister with the responsibility for any Department or subject; and

(*b*) Revoke or vary and direction given under the provisions of this sub-clause.

(2) The Prime Minister may retain in his charge any Department or subject.

17. Summoning of Cabinet. Cabinet shall be summoned only by the Prime Minister or, in his absence, by such Minister as the Prime Minister appoints in that behalf.

18. Cabinet procedure.

(1) Subject to the provisions of this Constitution, Cabinet may regulate its procedure (including the fixing of a quorum) in such manner as it thinks fit.

(2) Cabinet shall not be disqualified for the transaction of business by reason of any vacancy in the number of its members, and any proceedings of Cabinet shall be valid notwithstanding that some person who was not entitled to do so sat or voted in Cabinet or otherwise took part in the proceedings.

(3) It shall be the duty of the Prime Minister, if the Queen's Representative, acting in his discretion, so requires, to submit for the consideration of Cabinet any matter on which a decision has been taken by a Minister (including the Prime Minister) but which has not been considered by Cabinet.

(4) A decision of Cabinet shall be recorded in minutes, which shall, under the hand of the Secretary to the Cabinet, be communicated to the Queen's Representative within forty-eight hours of the making of the decision or, if the decision is one to which paragraph (*c*) of sub-clause (1) of Article *19* hereof applies, within twenty-four hours of the making of the decision.

(5) A decision of Cabinet shall not take effect except under the provisions of Article *19* hereof.

19. When decision of Cabinet takes effect.

(1) A decision of Cabinet shall take effect

(a) On its approval by the Queen's Representative, acting in his discretion;

(*b*) On the expiry of four days after the date of the decision, unless a meeting of the Executive Council is sooner held under the provisions of Article 25 hereof; or

(*c*) If the issue involved in the decision is, in the opinion of the Cabinet, of extreme urgency, on the expiry of two days after the date of the decision, unless a meeting of the Executive Council is sooner held under the provisions of Article 25 hereof; or

(*d*) Under the provisions of Article 25 hereof.

(2) For the purposes of paragraphs (*b*) and (*c*) of sub-clause (1) of this Article, the date of a decision of Cabinet shall be the date on which the minutes in which the decision is recorded are communicated to the Queen's Representative under the provisions of sub-clause (4) of Article 18 hereof.

(3) An instrument under the hand of the Secretary to the Cabinet certifying that a decision of Cabinet has taken effect shall be conclusive evidence that that decision has taken effect.

20. Secretary to the Cabinet. There shall also be a Secretary to the Cabinet, who shall be appointed under Article 74BB hereof.

21. One minister may act for another. In this Constitution and in every enactment, unless, the context otherwise requires, words directing or empowering any Minister to do any act or thing, or otherwise applying to him by his title of office, include any other Minister acting for, or, if the office is vacant, in the place of that first-mentioned Minister, and also his successors in that office.

The Executive Council

22. Executive Council.

(1) There shall be an Executive Council of the Cook Islands, which shall consist of

(*a*) The Queen's Representative; and

(*b*) The members of Cabinet.

(2) No business shall be transacted at any meeting of the Executive Council unless there are present the Queen's Representative and at least three members of Cabinet or, if there are for the time being only four members of Cabinet, unless there are present the Queen's Representative and at least two members of Cabinet.

(3) Subject to the provisions of this Constitution, the Executive Council may regulate its procedure in such manner as it thinks fit.

23. Clerk of the Executive Council. The Secretary to the Cabinet shall also be the Clerk of the Executive Council.

24. Meetings of Executive Council. The Executive Council shall be summoned only by the Queen's Representative, acting in his discretion, or by the Premier.

25. Consideration of Cabinet decisions by Executive Council.

(1) A meeting of the Executive Council may be summoned to consider any decision recorded in the minutes of a Cabinet meeting.

(2) If at a meeting of the Executive Council thus summoned the Queen's Representative, acting in his discretion, concurs in the decision concerned, that decision shall take effect as a decision of the Cabinet.

(3) If at a meeting of the Executive Council thus summoned the Queen's Representative, acting in his discretion, does not concur in the decision concerned or requests any amendment thereto, Cabinet shall thereupon be summoned under the provisions of Article 17 hereof and requested to reconsider that decision.

(4) If Cabinet after that reconsideration reaffirms its original decision or accepts the amendment requested by the Queen's Representative the original decision or the decision as so amended, as the case may be, shall forthwith take effect as a decision of Cabinet.

(5) If Cabinet after that reconsideration adopts a decision which incorporates an amendment to its original decision, other than an amendment requested by the Queen's Representative, the decision as so amended shall operate as a new decision of Cabinet to which the provisions of subclauses (4) and (5) of Article 18 hereof shall apply.

The Seal of the Cook Islands

26. Seal of the Cook Islands.

(1) There shall be a Public Seal of the Cook Islands (in this Constitution referred to as the Seal of the Cook Islands), to be in such form or forms as the Executive Council from time to time approves.

(2) The Seal shall be in the custody of the Queen's Representative.

(3) The Seal may be used by the Queen's Representative for the authentication of any public document in relation to the government of the Cook Islands or for the execution of any document required by law to be executed under the Seal of the Cook Islands.

(4) Judicial notice shall be taken of the Seal in all Courts in the Cook Islands and in New Zealand (including Niue and the Tokelau Islands).

PART III

THE PARLIAMENT OF THE COOK ISLANDS

27. The parliament of the Cook Islands.

(1) There shall be a sovereign Parliament for the Cook Islands, to be called the Parliament of the Cook Islands.

(2) Parliament shall consist of 24 members, to be elected by secret ballot under a system of universal suffrage by the electors of the following islands or groups of islands or areas and in the following numbers:

(*a*) The Island of Aitutaki and the Islands of Manuae and Te-Au-O-Tu,

3 members being 1 member for each of the 3 constituencies together comprising those islands, having the names and boundaries set out in Part I of the First Schedule to this Constitution:

(*b*) The Islands of Atiu, 2 members, being 1 member for each of the 2 constituencies having the names and boundaries set out in Part IV of the First Schedule to this Constitution:

(*c*) The Island of Mangaia, 3 members, being 1 member for each of the 3 constituencies having the names and boundaries set out in Part III of the First Schedule to this Constitution:

(*d*) The Island of Manihiki, 1 member:

(*e*) The Island of Mauke, 1 member:

(*f*) The Island of Mitiaro, 1 member:

(*g*) The Island of Penrhyn, 1 member:

(*h*) The Island of Pukapuka and the Island of Nassau, 1 member:

(*i*) The Island of Rakahanga, 1 member:

(*j*) The Island of Rarotonga and the Island of Palmerston, 9 members, being 1 member for each of the 9 constituencies together comprising those islands, having the names and boundaries set out in Part II of the First Schedule to this Constitution:

(*k*) The islands comprising New Zealand and all other areas outside the Cook Islands, 1 member (that constituency being hereinafter referred to as the Overseas Constituency).

(3) Subject to this Article and to Articles *28, 28A, 28B, 28C* and *28D* hereof, the qualifications and disqualification of electors and candidates, the mode of electing members of Parliament, and the terms and conditions of their membership shall be as prescribed by Act.

28. Qualification of electors.

(1) Without limiting the provisions of any law prescribing any additional qualifications not inconsistent with any provision of this Constitution, a person shall be qualified to be an elector for the election of a Member of Parliament for any constituency other than the Overseas Constituency, if, and only if,

(*a*) He is a Commonwealth citizen, or he has the status of a permanent resident of the Cook Islands as defined by Act; and

(*b*) He has been resident in the Cook Islands throughout the period of three months immediately preceding his application for enrolment as an elector and has not subsequently qualified as an elector under sub-clause (2) of this Article; and

(*c*) He has at some period actually resided continuously in the Cook Islands for not less than 12 months.

(2) Without limiting the provisions of any law prescribing any additional qualifications not inconsistent with any provision of this Constitution, a person shall be qualified to be an elector for the election of a Member of Parliament for the Overseas Constituency, if, and only if,

(*a*) He is a Commonwealth citizen, or he has the status of a permanent resident of the Cook Islands as defined by Act; and (*b*) He has resided outside the Cook Islands throughout the period of 3 months immediately preceding his application for enrolment as an elector; and

(*c*) At the date of his application for enrolment as an elector he has been absent from the Cook Islands for a continuous period of not more than 3 years, and has had ever since he left the Cook Islands, an intention to return and reside therein indefinitely; and

(*d*) He has at some period actually resided continuously in the Cook Islands for not less than 12 months.

(3) Where any person has ceased to be qualified to be enrolled as an elector for any constituency by reason of his residence outside the Cook Islands for a period of more than 3 years, he shall not be entitled to apply for enrolment as an elector of any constituency unless he has returned to the Cook Islands and has actually resided in the Cook Islands throughout the continuous period of not less than 3 months.

(4) In calculating for the purposes of paragraph (*c*) of sub-clause (2) or of sub-clause (3) of this Article the period for which any person has been outside the Cook Islands

(*a*) Any period for which he has been outside the Cook Islands for the purpose of undergoing a course of education or of technical training or instruction shall be disregarded; and

(*b*) His absence from the Cook Islands during any period shall be deemed to be continuous, notwithstanding any visit to the Cook Islands in that period, unless during that visit he remained in the Cook Islands for a continuous period of not less than 3 months.

28A. Special voting.

(1) Any person who is enrolled as an elector of any constituency may vote as a special voter at an election of Members of Parliament, if, on polling day, he is absent from the constituency for which he is enrolled.

(2) Any person who is enrolled as an elector of a constituency other than the Overseas Constituency and who is outside the Cook Islands on polling day but has not qualified for enrolment as an elector of the Overseas Constituency may vote outside the Cook Islands, as a special voter, for the constituency for which he is enrolled.

(3) Any person who is enrolled as an elector of the Overseas Constituency and who is in the Cook Islands on polling day may vote for that Constituency as a special voter, at any polling place in the Cook Islands.

(4) A special voter may vote at such place (whether a polling place or not), at such time, in such manner, and upon and subject to such conditions as may be prescribed by Act.

(5) Nothing in this Article shall affect the right of an elector of any constituency to vote by postal vote at an election of a member representing that constituency conducted by postal vote pursuant to Article 28C hereof in the case of the Overseas Constituency and Article 28D hereof in the case of any other constituency.

28B. Qualification of candidates.

(1) Notwithstanding anything in sub-clause (2) of this Article, a person shall not be qualified to be a candidate at an election of members of Parliament, if

(*a*) He is not an elector duly enrolled pursuant to the provisions of an Act of Parliament, or

(*b*) He has been adjudicated bankrupt within the meaning of the bankruptcy laws in force in the Cook Islands (whether before or after the commencement of this Article)[1], unless he has obtained an order of discharge; or

(*c*) He has been convicted (whether before or after the commencement of this Article)[1] of any of the offences specified in Part I of the Second Schedule to this Constitution; or

(*d*) He has been convicted (whether before or after the commencement of this Article)[1] of any of the offences specified in Part II of the Second Schedule to this Constitution, unless a period of 5 years has elapsed from the date of his conviction.

(2) Subject to sub-clause (1) of this Article,

(*a*) Every person enrolled as an elector of any constituency shall be capable of being elected as a member for that constituency or for any other constituency:

(*b*) In the case of any by-election for any constituency, a person shall be capable of being elected as a member for that constituency if he was enrolled as an elector on the roll of any constituency at the preceding general election, and at the time of nomination still possesses the qualifications to be enrolled as an elector.

28C. Election of Member for Overseas Constituency. The following provisions shall apply with respect to the member representing the Overseas Constituency:

(*a*) He shall be elected by persons who are for the time being residing in New Zealand or elsewhere outside the Cook Islands who are qualified as electors under sub-clause (2) of Article *28* and are enrolled as electors of that constituency; and

(*b*) His election shall be by postal vote, special vote, or by vote cast at one or more polling places outside the Cook Islands shall be prescribed by Act.

28D. Postal voting for electors of Cook Islands Constituencies. Provision may be made by Act for any elector of a constituency other than the Overseas Constituency who is outside the Cook Islands on polling day to vote by postal vote at any election of a member representing the constituency for which the elector is enrolled.

29. Meetings of Parliament.

(1) Parliament shall meet at such places and at such times as the High Commissioner from time to time appoints in that behalf:

Providing that Parliament shall meet not later than 90 days after the holding of a general election and at least once in every year thereafter, so that a period of 12

---

[1] 1980

months shall not intervene between the last sitting of Parliament in one session and the first sitting thereof in the next session.

(2) Notwithstanding anything contained in sub-clause (1) of this Article, Parliament shall not meet after the holding of a general election until all election petitions filed in the High Court in respect of that election have been finally determined.

30. Members to take Oath of Allegiance. Except for the purpose of enabling this Article to be complied with and for the election of a Speaker, no member of Parliament shall be permitted to sit or vote therein until he has taken and subscribed the following oath before the Speaker of Parliament, namely:

'I, ..., swear by Almighty God that I will be faithful and bear true allegiance to Her (or His) Majesty (specify the name of the reigning Sovereign, as thus: Queen Elizabeth the Second) as the Head of State of the Cook Islands, Her (or His) heirs and successors, according to law and that I will justly and faithfully carry out my duties as a member of Parliament of the Cook Islands. So help me God.'

31. The Speaker of Parliament.

(1) Parliament shall, immediately when it first meets after a general election and as soon as possible after any vacancy occurs in the office of Speaker otherwise than by reason of a dissolution of Parliament, and before it proceeds to the dispatch of any other business, elect a person (not being a Minister) to be Speaker of Parliament.

(2) The Speaker may be elected in such manner as Parliament decides from time to time, either from among the members of Parliament who are not Ministers or from among persons who are not members of Parliament:

Provided that a person who is not a member of Parliament shall not be elected Speaker unless he is qualified for election as a member of Parliament.

(3) Before a person who has been elected Speaker enters upon the duties of his office, he shall, unless he has already done so in accordance with Article 30 hereof, take and subscribe before the High Commissioner the Oath of Allegiance prescribed in that Article, substituting the word 'Speaker' for the words 'a member' where they appear in that oath.

(4) The salary of the Speaker shall be determined by enactment, and shall be charged on the Cook Islands Government Account.

32. Tenure of office of Speaker. The Speaker may at any time resign his office by writing under his hand addressed to the Clerk of Parliament, and shall vacate his office

(*a*) On the dissolution of Parliament next following his election; or
(*b*) If he becomes a Minister; or
(*c*) If, being a member of Parliament at the time of his election, he ceases to be a member; or
(*d*) If, not being a member of Parliament at the time of his election, he ceases to be qualified for election as a member; or
(*e*) If Parliament passes a resolution supported by the votes of not less than

two thirds of all the members thereof (including vacancies) requiring his removal from office.

33. Deputy Speaker.

(1) Parliament may elect a member of Parliament, not being the Speaker or a Minister, to be Deputy Speaker.

(2) The Deputy Speaker may at any time resign his office by writing under his hand addressed to the Clerk of Parliament, and shall vacate his office

(*a*) On the dissolution of Parliament next following his election; or

(*b*) If he ceases to be a member of Parliament; or

(*c*) If he becomes a Minister; or

(*d*) If he is elected Speaker; or

(*e*) If Parliament passes a resolution supported by the votes of not less than two thirds of all the members thereof (including vacancies) requiring his removal from office.

(3) Subject to the provisions of this Constitution and of the Standing Orders of Parliament, the functions conferred by this Constitution or those Standing Orders upon the Speaker shall, if there is no person holding the office of Speaker or if the Speaker is absent from the Cook Islands or is otherwise unable to perform those functions, be performed by the Deputy Speaker.

34. Procedure.

(1) The Speaker, or in his absence the Deputy Speaker, shall preside over sittings of Parliament. In the absence from any sitting of both the Speaker and the Deputy Speaker, the members present shall choose one of their number (not being a Minister) to preside over that sitting.

(2) Subject to the provisions of Article *41* hereof and of sub-clause (3) of this Article, every question before Parliament shall be decided by a majority of the votes of the members present.

(3) The person presiding over any sitting of Parliament shall not have a deliberative vote, but in case of an equality of votes, he shall have a casting vote.

(4) No business shall be transacted at any sitting of Parliament if the number of members present (excluding the Speaker if he is a member) is less than 12.

(5) Subject to the provisions of the Constitution, Parliament may from time to time make, amend, and repeal Standing Orders for the regulation and orderly conduct of its proceedings and the dispatch of business.

(6) Parliament shall not be disqualified for the transaction of business by reason of any vacancy among its members including any vacancy not filled at a general election, and any proceedings therein shall be valid notwithstanding that some person who was not entitled to do so sat or voted in Parliament or otherwise took part in the proceedings.

35. Languages.

(1) All debates and discussion in Parliament shall be conducted in the Maori language as spoken in Rarotonga and also in the English language.

(2) Every Bill introduced into Parliament and every Act shall be in the Maori language as spoken in Rarotonga and also in the English language:

Provided that Parliament may, by resolution, determine that any Bill or Act shall be in the English language only.

(3) The records of proceedings in Parliament, or in committees thereof shall be in the English language, and such of those records as are specified in the Standing Orders of Parliament shall also be in the Maori language as spoken in Rarotonga.

(4) Where there is any conflict between the Maori version and the English version of any Bill or Act or of any such record, the English version shall prevail.

36. Privileges of Parliament and its members.

(1) The validity of any proceedings in Parliament or in any committee thereof shall not be questioned in any Court.

(2) No officer or member or Speaker of Parliament in whom powers are vested for the regulation of procedure or the conduct of business of the maintenance of order shall in relation to the exercise by him of any of those powers be subject to the jurisdiction of any Court.

(3) No member or Speaker of Parliament and no person entitled to speak therein shall be liable to any proceedings in any Court in respect of anything said or any vote given by him in Parliament or in any committee thereof.

(4) No person shall be liable to any proceedings in any Court in respect of the publication by or under the authority of Parliament of any report, paper, vote or proceeding.

(5) Subject to the provisions of this Article, the privileges of Parliament and of the committees thereof, and the privileges of members and the Speaker of Parliament and of the persons entitled to speak therein may be determined by Act:

Provided that no such privilege of Parliament or of any committee thereof may extend to the imposition of a fine or to committal to prison for contempt or otherwise, unless provision is made by enactment for the trial and punishment of the person concerned by the High Court.

37. Prorogation and dissolution of Parliament.

(1) The High Commissioner may at any time, by notice published in the *Cook Islands Gazette,* prorogue Parliament.

(2) If at any time the office of Prime Minister is vacant, the High Commissioner shall, by notice published in the *Cook Islands Gazette,* dissolve Parliament as soon as he is satisfied, acting in his discretion, that a reasonable period has elapsed since that office was last vacated and that there is no member of Parliament who commands the confidence of a majority of the members.

(3) The High Commissioner may at any time, by notice published in the *Cook Islands Gazette,* dissolve Parliament if he is advised by the Prime Minister to do so, but shall not be obliged to act in this respect in accordance with the advice of the Prime Minister unless the High Commissioner is satisfied, acting in his discretion, that in tendering that advice the Prime Minister commands the confidence of a majority of the members of Parliament.

(4) Notwithstanding anything in the foregoing provisions of this Article, Parliament shall not be prorogued or dissolved before all electoral petitions filed

in the High Court in respect of the last preceding general election of members have been finally determined.

(5) The Queen's Representative shall dissolve Parliament at the expiration of 5 years from the date of the last preceding general election, if it has not been sooner dissolved.

(6) There shall be a general election of the members of Parliament at such time within 3 months after every dissolution of Parliament as the High Commissioner appoints by notice published in the *Cook Islands Gazette.*

38. Clerk of Parliament.

(1) There shall be a Clerk of Parliament.

(2) The Clerk shall keep a record of the proceedings of Parliament and shall transmit a copy of these records to the Queen's Representative as soon as practicable.

39. Power to make laws.

(1) Subject to the provisions of this Constitution, Parliament may make laws (to be known as Acts) for the peace, order, and good government of the Cook Islands.

(2) The powers of Parliament shall extend to the making of laws having extra-territorial operation.

(3) Without limiting the generality of the power conferred by sub-clause (1) of this Article to make laws for the peace, order, and good government of the Cook Islands, that power shall, subject to the provisions of this Constitution, include the repeal or revocation or amendment or modification or extension, in relation to the Cook Islands, of any law in force in the Cook Islands.

(4) Except to the extent to which it is inconsistent with this Constitution, no Act and no provision of any Act shall be deemed to be invalid solely on the ground that it is inconsistent with any law in force in the Cook Islands.

(5) For the avoidance of doubt, it is hereby declared that the power conferred on the Legislative Assembly of the Cook Islands by Article *39* of this Constitution (as originally enacted) to make laws for the peace, order, and good government of the Cook Islands always conferred on that Assembly power to make laws, notwithstanding anything in Article *46* of this Constitution (as originally enacted), declaring that any specified Act of the Parliament of New Zealand or any regulations, rules, or order under any Act of that Parliament should extend to the Cook Islands as part of the law of the Cook Islands.

40. No property to be taken compulsorily without compensation.

(1) No property shall be taken possession of compulsorily, and no right over or interest in any property shall be acquired compulsorily, except under the law, which of itself or when read with any other law,

- (*a*) Requires the payment within a reasonable time of adequate compensation therefor; and
- (*b*) Gives to any person claiming that compensation a right to access, for the determination of his interest in the property and the amount of compensation, to the High Court; and

(*c*) Gives to any party to proceedings in the High Court relating to such a claim the same rights of appeal as are accorded generally to parties to civil proceedings in that Court sitting as a Court of original jurisdiction.

(2) Nothing in this Article shall be construed as affecting the general law

(*a*) For the imposition or enforcement of any tax, rate, or duty; or

(*b*) For the imposition of penalties or forfeitures for breach of the law, whether under civil process or after conviction of an offence; or

(*c*) Relating to leases, tenancies, mortgages, charges, bills of sale, or any other rights or obligations arising out of contracts; or

(*d*) Relating to the vesting and administration of the property of persons adjudged bankrupt or otherwise declared insolvent, of infants or persons suffering under some physical or mental disability, of deceased persons, and of companies, other corporate bodies and unincorporated societies, in the course of being wound up; or

(*e*) Relating to the execution of judgments or orders of Courts; or

(*f*) Providing for the taking of possession of property which is in a dangerous state or is injurious to the health of human beings, plants, or animals; or

(*g*) Relating to trusts and trustees; or

(*h*) Relating to the limitation of actions; or

(*i*) Relating to property vested in statutory corporations; or

(*j*) Relating to the temporary taking of possession of property for the purposes of any examination, investigation, or inquiry; or

(*k*) Providing for the carrying out of work on land for the purpose of soil conservation or for the protection of water catchment areas.

41. Power of Parliament to repeal or amend this Constitution.

(1) Subject to the provisions of subclause (2) of this Article, no Bill repealing or amending or modifying or extending this Constitution or any provisions thereof or making any provision inconsistent with any provision of this Constitution shall be deemed to have been passed by the Parliament unless

(*a*) At both the final vote thereon and the vote preceding that final vote it receives the affirmative votes of not less than two thirds of the total membership (including vacancies) of the Parliament; and;

(*b*) There is an interval of not less than ninety days between the date on which that final vote was taken and the date on which the preceding vote was taken;

and no such Bill shall be presented to the Queen's Representative for assent unless it is accompanied by a certificate under the hand of the Speaker to that effect.

(2) No Bill repealing or amending or modifying or extending any of the provisions of sections 2 to 6 cf the Cook Islands Constitution Act 1964 or Article 2 of this Constitution or this Article or making any provision inconsistent with any

of those provisions shall be submitted to the Queen's Representative for his assent, unless

(*a*) It has been passed by the Parliament in accordance with the provisions of sub-clause (1) of this Article; and
(*b*) It has been submitted to a poll, conducted in a manner prescribed by law, of the persons who are entitled to vote as electors at a general election of members of the Parliament; and
(*c*) It has been supported by not less than two thirds of the valid votes cast in such a poll; and
(*d*) It is accompanied by a certificate under the hand of the Speaker to that effect.

42. Introduction of Bills, etc., into Parliament. Subject to the provisions of this Constitution and of the Standing Orders of Parliament, any member of Parliament may introduce any Bill or propose any motion for debate in or present any petition to Parliament, and the same shall be considered and disposed of in accordance with the Standing Orders.

43. Restrictions with regard to financial measures. Except upon the recommendation of the Queen's Representative, Parliament shall not

(*a*) Proceed upon any Bill (including an amendment to a Bill) that, in the opinion of the person presiding, makes provision for any of the following purposes:
   (i) For the imposition or alteration of taxation; or
   (ii) For the imposition of any charge upon the Cook Islands Government Account or any other public fund or account or for the alteration of any such charge otherwise than by way of reduction; or
   (iii) For the payment, issue, or withdrawal from the Cook Islands Government Account or from any other public fund or account of any money not charged thereon or any increase in the amount of such a payment, issue, or withdrawal; or
   (iv) For the composition or remission of any debt due to the Crown:
(*b*) Proceed upon any motion (including any amendment to a motion) the effect of which, in the opinion of the person presiding, would be to make provision for any of those purposes:
(*c*) Receive any petition that, in the opinion of the person presiding, requests that provision be made for any of those purposes.

44. Assent to Bills by Queen's Representative.

(1) No Bill shall become law until it has been passed by Parliament and has been assented to by the Queen's Representative.

(2) Whenever any Bill which has been passed by Parliament is presented to the Queen's Representative for his assent, the Queen's Representative shall, acting on the advice of the Prime Minister, declare that he assents to the Bill or that he refuses his assent to the Bill:

Provided that the Queen's Representative, acting in his discretion may summon a meeting of the Executive Council, to be held within 14 days after the Bill is presented to him for his assent to consider amendments to the Bill proposed by him or to consider whether he should refuse his assent to the Bill.

(3) If at a meeting of the Executive Council thus summoned the Executive Council decides that the Bill should be returned to Parliament for consideration of the amendments proposed or, as the case may be, that the Queen's Representative should refuse his assent to the Bill, the Queen's Representative shall by Message,

(*a*) Return the Bill with the amendments proposed to Parliament for consideration by Parliament; or, as the case may be,

(*b*) Return the Bill to Parliament for reconsideration by Parliament.

(4) If at a meeting of the Executive Council thus summoned the Executive Council decides that the Bill should not be returned to Parliament for consideration of the amendments proposed or, as the case may be, that the Queen's Representative should not refuse his assent to the Bill, he shall declare that he assents to the Bill.

(5) Where any Bill is returned to Parliament under the provisions of paragraph (*a*) of sub-clause (3) of this Article, and the Bill is again passed by Parliament with the amendments proposed, but with no other amendments, or in the form in which it was originally presented to the Queen's Representative for his assent, then, when the Bill is again presented to the Queen's Representative for his assent, he shall declare that he assents to the Bill.

(6) Where any Bill is returned to Parliament under the provisions of paragraph (*b*) of sub-clause (3) of this Article, and the Bill is again passed by Parliament in the form in which it was originally presented to the Queen's Representative for his assent, he shall declare that he assents to the Bill.

(7) Where any Bill is returned to Parliament under the provisions of this Article and the Bill is again passed by Parliament with any amendments other than amendments proposed under the provisions of this Article, then, when the Bill is again presented to the Queen's Representative for his assent, the foregoing provisions of this Article shall apply with respect to the Bill as if it had not previously been presented to the Queen's Representative for his assent.

(8) A Bill assented to by the Queen's Representative as herein provided shall be known as an Act of Parliament.

45. Commencement of Acts. Every Act shall come into operation either on the day on which the Bill is assented to, or on any date (whether earlier or later than the date on which it is assented to) specified in that behalf in the Act, and different dates may be so specified in respect of different provisions of the Act.

46. New Zealand Parliament not to legislate for the Cook Islands. Except as provided by Act of the Parliament of the Cook Islands, no Act, and no provision of any Act, of the Parliament of New Zealand passed after the commencement of this Article shall extend or be deemed to extend to the Cook Islands as part of the law of the Cook Islands.

PART IV

THE JUDICIARY

The High Court of the Cook Islands

47. High Court established.

(1) There shall be a Court of record, to be called the High Court of the Cook Islands, for the administration of justice throughout those islands.

(2) Except as provided in this Constitution or by law, the High Court shall have all such jurisdiction (both civil jurisdiction, including jurisdiction relating to land, and criminal juridisction) as may be necessary to administer the law in force in the Cook Islands.

(3) There shall be 3 Divisions of the High Court, namely

(*a*) A Civil Division:

(*b*) A Criminal Division:

(*c*) A Land Division.

(4) A Judge of the High Court may exercise any of the jurisdiction and powers of a Judge of any Division.

(5) Nothing in this Article shall prevent a Judge of any Division from exercising any of the powers of a Judge of the High Court, whether or not in his capacity as a Judge of that Division.

(6) Subject to the foregoing provisions of this Article and to Article *48* hereof, each Judge of the High Court, or any 2 or more Judges, may, in any part of the Cook Islands and at any time or place, exercise all the powers of the High Court.

48. Jurisdiction of Divisions of the High Court.

(1) Each Division of the High Court shall hear and determine

(*a*) Such proceedings as are, under or by virtue of any enactment, to be heard and determined by that Division:

(*b*) Such other proceedings as may from time to time be determined by the Chief Justice, either generally or in any particular proceedings or classes of proceedings.

(2) Subject to sub-clause (3) of this Article, the Land Division shall have all the jurisdiction and powers in relation to land that immediately before the commencement of this Article were conferred on the Land Court of the Cook Islands, and shall have such other jurisdiction as may be conferred on it by enactment.

(3) Notwithstanding anything in this Article, the Land Division shall not exercise any jurisdiction or power in relation to land in any of the Islands of Mangaia, Mitiaro, and Pukapuka that was not, according to local custom, being exercised by the Land Court before the commencement of this Article unless

(*a*) In the case of land in the Island of Mangaia, the exercise of such jurisdiction or power is requested by the Aronga Mana of Mangaia:

(*b*) In the case of land in the Island of Mitiaro, the exercise of such jurisdiction or power is requested by the Aronga Mana of Mitiaro:

(*c*) In the case of land in the Island of Pukapuka, the exercise of such jurisdiction or power is requested by the Aronga Mana of Pukapuka.

49. Judges of the High Court.

(1) The High Court shall consist of 1 or more Judges, each of whom shall be appointed under the provisions of this Constitution.

(2) If only 1 Judge is so appointed, he shall be the Chief Justice of the Cook Islands, but if more than 1 Judge is appointed, one of them shall be appointed as the Chief Justice of the Cook Islands.

(3) A person shall not be qualified for appointment as a Judge of the High Court under this Article, unless

(*a*) He holds or has held office as a Judge of the High Court of New Zealand or of the Supreme Court of New Zealand or of the Court of Appeal of New Zealand or an equivalent office in any other part of the Commonwealth or in a designated country; or

(*b*) He has been in practice as a barrister in New Zealand or in any other part of the Commonwealth or in a designated country, or partly in New Zealand and partly in any other part of the Commonwealth or in a designated country, for a period of, or periods amounting in the aggregate to, not less than 7 years.

(4) The High Commissioner, acting in his discretion, may declare to be a designated country for the purposes of this Article any country which in his opinion has a legal system similar to that existing in New Zealand.

50. Acting Chief Justice of the High Court.

(1) Where any vacancy exists in the office of the Chief Justice of the High Court or the Chief Justice of the High Court is absent from the Cook Islands or is, by reason of illness or any cause other than absence from the Cook Islands, unable to perform the office or exercise any function of Chief Justice of the High Court, the senior other Judge of the High Court for the time being in the Cook Islands may perform that office or exercise that function until a Chief Justice of the High Court is appointed or, as the case may be, the Chief Justice of the High Court resumes that office or exercises that function.

51. Acting Judge of the High Court.

(1) The High Commissioner, acting on the advice of the Chief Justice and the Minister of Justice, may appoint any person who is qualified for appointment as a Judge of the High Court to act as a Judge of the High Court, if there is no Judge of the High Court for the time being in the Cook Islands or, by reason of illness or other cause, there is no Judge of the High Court available to act.

(2) Any appointment made under this Article may be revoked at any time by the High Commissioner, acting on the advice of the Chief Justice.

Appointment, Tenure of Office, and Salaries of Judges

52. Appointment of Judges. The Chief Justice and other Judges of the High Court shall be appointed as follows:

(*a*) The Chief Justice of the High Court shall be appointed by the Queen's Representative, acting on the advice of the Executive Council tendered by the Prime Minister:

(*b*) The other Judges of the High Court shall be appointed by the Queen's Representative, acting on the advice of the Executive Council tendered by the Chief Justice of the High Court and the Minister of Justice.

53. Tenure of office of Judges.

(1) Except in the case of an appointment made under sub-clause (2) of this Article, no person who has attained the age of 70 years shall be appointed to or continue to hold office as the Chief Justice or other Judge of the High Court.

(2) Any person of any age who does not reside in the Cook Islands and who is qualified for appointment may be appointed to hold office as the Chief Justice or other Judge of the High Court for a term of not more than 3 years, but may be re-appointed for one or more further terms, being in each case a term of not more than 3 years.

(3) Nothing done by the Chief Justice or other Judge of the High Court in the performance of his functions shall be deemed to be invalid by reason only that he has reached the age at which he is required by this Article to retire or that his term has expired, as the case may be.

(4) The Chief Justice or any other Judge of the High Court may resign his office by writing under his hand addressed to the Queen's Representative.

54. Removal of Judge from office.

(1) The Chief Justice or any other Judge of the High Court, other than a Judge appointed under the provisions of Article *51* hereof, may be removed from office by the Queen's Representative only for inability to discharge the functions of his office (whether arising from infirmity of body or mind or from any other cause) or for misbehavior, and shall not be so removed unless the question of the removal of the Chief Justice or other Judge from office has been referred to a tribunal appointed under sub-clause (2) of this Article and that tribunal has recommended that the Chief Justice or other Judge be removed from office for inability as aforesaid or misbehavior.

(2) If the Prime Minister advises the Queen's Representative that the question of removing from office the Chief Justice or any other Judges of the High Court for inability as aforesaid or misbehavior ought to be investigated, then

(*a*) The Queen's Representative shall appoint a tribunal consisting of a chairman and 2 other members; and

(*b*) The tribunal shall inquire into the matter and report on the facts thereof to the Queen's Representative and recommend to the Queen's Representative whether or not the Chief Justice or other Judge should be removed from office; and

(*c*) If the tribunal recommends that the Chief Justice or other Judge be so removed, the Queen's Representative shall, by warrant, revoke the appointment of the Chief Justice or other Judge, as the case may be.

(3) No person shall be qualified for appointment as a member of a tribunal under this Article unless he is qualified for appointment as a Judge of the High Court under Article *49* hereof.

(4) No business shall be transacted by a tribunal appointed under this Article unless all 3 members are present, and all questions proposed for decision by the tribunal shall be decided by the votes of a majority of those members.

(5) Subject to this Article, the tribunal shall determine its own procedure.

(6) If the question of removing from office the Chief Justice or any other Judge of the High Court has been referred to a tribunal under sub-clause (2) of this Article

(*a*) The Queen's Representative, acting on the advice of the Prime Minister, may suspend the Chief Justice or other Judge from performing the functions of his office for a period of 1 month:

(*b*) If the decision of the tribunal has not been given before the expiration of that period, the Queen's Representative, acting on the advice of the Executive Council tendered to him by the Prime Minister, may suspend the Chief Justice or other Judge from performing the functions of his office for a further period of 1 month.

(7) Any such suspension may be at any time revoked by the Queen's Representative, acting on the advice of the Prime Minister in the case of a suspension under paragraph (*a*) of sub-clause (6) of this Article and on the advice of the Executive Council in the case of a suspension under paragraph (*b*) of that sub-clause, and shall in any case cease to have effect if the tribunal

(*a*) Before the expiration of the total period of suspension, recommends to the High Commissioner that the Chief Justice or other Judge be not removed from office; or

(*b*) Does not, before the expiration of the total period of suspension, recommend to the High Commissioner that the Chief Justice or other Judge be removed from office.

55. Salaries of Judges.

(1) The salaries of the Chief Justice and other Judges of the High Court shall be determined by Act, and shall be charged on the Cook Islands Government account.

(2) The salaries of those Judges shall not be diminished during their period of office, unless as part of a general reduction of salaries applied proportionately to all persons whose salaries are determined by enactment.

56. Court of Appeal established.

(1) There shall be a Court of Appeal of the Cook Islands, which shall be a superior Court of record.

(2) Subject to Articles *57* and *58* hereof, the Judges of the Court of Appeal shall be

(*a*) A Judge of the Court of Appeal of New Zealand, or a person who has held office as a Judge of that Court, or a Judge of the High Court of New Zealand, to be appointed by the Queen's Representative acting on the advice of the Executive Council tendered to him by the Prime Minister; and

(*b*) The Chief Justice and other Judges of the High Court; and

(*c*) Such other persons, possessing the qualfications prescribed by sub-clause (3) of this Article, as may from time to time be appointed by the Queen's Representative acting on the advice of the Executive Council tendered to him by the Prime Minister.

(3) No person shall be qualified for appointment as a Judge of the Court of Appeal under paragraph (*c*) of sub-clause (2) of this Article, unless he is qualified under Article *49* hereof to be appointed as a Judge of the High Court.

(4) The Judge of the Court of Appeal of New Zealand, or, as the case may be, the person who has held office as a Judge of that Court or the Judge of the High Court of New Zealand who is a member of the Court of Appeal of the Cook Islands, shall be the President of the Court of Appeal of the Cook Islands, but in his absence the Chief Justice of the High Court, if present, shall preside, but if the Chief Justice is also absent, the Judge present who is highest in seniority shall preside.

(5) Judges of the Court of Appeal shall take seniority according to the respective dates of their first appointment as Judges, whether of the High Court or of the Court of Appeal or of any Court in any place outside the Cook Islands.

(6) An appointment under paragraph (*c*) of sub-clause (2) of this Article shall be for a period of time or for the trial or hearing of one or more particular causes or matters, as may be specified in the instrument of appointment.

57. Number of Judges.

(1) Any 3 Judges of the Court of Appeal may exercise all the powers of the Court:

Provided that the Court may have its judgment delivered by any one of its members who is also a Judge of the High Court, and, if there is no such member, then through the Registrar of the Court of Appeal.

(2) The judgment of the Court of Appeal shall be in accordance with the opinion of the majority of the Judges present.

58. Judges not to sit on appeals from own decision. A Judge of the Court of Appeal shall not sit on the hearing of an appeal from any decision made by him or by a Court on which he sat as a member.

59. Determination of Court of Appeals.

(1) Except as provided in sub-clause (2) of this Article, the determination of the Court of Appeal shall be final, and there shall be no appeal to the High Court of New Zealand or to the Court of Appeal of New Zealand from any judgment of the Court of Appeal of the Cook Islands.

(2) There shall be a right of appeal to Her Majesty the Queen in Council, with the leave of the Court of Appeal, or, if such leave is refused, with the leave of Her Majesty the Queen in Council, from judgments of the Court of Appeal in such cases and subject to such conditions as are prescribed by Act.

60. Jurisdiction of Court of Appeal.

(1) Subject to the provisions of this Constitution, the Court of Appeal shall have jurisdiction to hear and determine any appeal from a judgment of the High Court.

(2) Subject to the provisions of this Constitution, and except where under any Act a judgment of the High Court is declared to be final, an appeal shall lie to the Court of Appeal from a judgment of the High Court.

(*a*) As of right, if the High Court certifies that the case involves a substantial question of law at to the interpretation or effect of any provision of this Constitution:

(*b*) As of right, from any conviction by the High Court in the exercise of its criminal jurisdiction whereby the appellant has been sentence to death or to imprisonment for life or for a term exceeding 6 months or to a fine of not less than $200 and from any such sentence (not being a sentence fixed by law):

(*c*) As right, when the matter in dispute on the appeal amounts to or is of the value of $400 or upwards:

(*d*) As of right, from any judgment of the High Court involving any question as to the interpretation or application or effect of any provision of Part IVA of this Constitution:

(*e*) With the leave of he High Court in any other case, if in the opinion of that Court the question involved in the appeal is one which by reason of its general or public importance, or of the magnitude of the interest affected, or for any other reason, ought to be submitted to the Court of Appeal for decision.

(3) Notwithstanding anything in sub-clause (2) of this Article, the Court of Appeal may, in any case in which it thinks fit and at any time, grant special leave to appeal to that Court from any judgment of the High Court, subject to such conditions as to security for costs and otherwise as the Court of Appeal thinks fit.

(4) In this Article, the term 'judgment' includes any judgment, decree, order, writ, declaration, conviction, sentence, or other determination.

61. Transmission of order of Court of Appeal. The determination of the Court of Appeal on any appeal from the High Court shall be transmitted to the Registrar of the High Court by the Registrar of the Court of Appeal under the seal of the Court of Appeal, and judgment shall thereupon be entered by the High Court in conformity with that determination, or such other proceedings by way of a new trial or otherwise shall be taken in the High Court as are required by that determination.

Justices of the Peace

62. Justices of the Peace.

(1) The Queen's Representative, acting on the advice of the Executive Council tendered to him by the Minister of Justice, any appoint Justices of the Peace for the Cook Islands, who shall hold office for such time as may be prescribed in their warrants of appointment and may be paid such remuneration as may be prescribed by enactment.

(2) No person who has attained the age of 72 years shall be appointed to or continue to hold office as a Justice of the Peace for the Cook Islands.

(3) An Act shall prescribe the jurisdiction and powers of Justices of the Peace appointed under this Article and for an appeal to lie to the High Court from a final judgment of a Justice of the Peace.

(4) A Justice of the Peace for the Cook Islands shall not be removed from office as such, except by the Queen's Representative, acting on the advice of the Chief Justice.

(5) In sub-clause (3) of this Article the term 'judgment' includes any judgment, decree, order, writ, declaration, conviction. sentence, or other determination.

Oath of Allegiance and Judicial Oath

63. Oath of Allegiance and Judicial Oath.

(1) Every Judge of the Court of Appeal who is not a Judge of the Court of Appeal of New Zealand or of the High Court of New Zealand or a Judge of the High Court of the Cook Islands and every Justice of the Peace for the Cook Islands, shall, as soon as may be after his acceptance of office, take and subscribe before the Queen's Representative the following oaths:

(*a*) An Oath of Allegiance in the following form

I, ..., swear by Almighty God that I will be faithful and bear true allegaince to Her [*or* His] Majesty [*Specify the name of the reigning Sovereign, as thus:* Queen Elizabeth the Second] as the Head of State of the Cook Islands, Her [*or* His] heirs, and successors, in accordance with the Constitution and the law. So help me God:

(*b*) The Judicial Oath in the following form

I, ..., swear by Almighty God that I will well and truly serve Her [*or* His] Majesty [*Specify as above*] as the Head of State of the Cook Islands, Her [*or* His] heirs, and successors, in accordance with the Constitution and the law, in the office of ; and I, will do right to all manner of people, without fear or favour, affection or ill will. So help me God.

(2) If any person mentioned in this Article declines or neglects when the oaths required to be taken by him under this Article are duly tendered, to take those oaths, he shall if he has already entered on his office vacate the same, and if he has not entered on the same be disqualified from entering on the same; but no person shall be compelled in respect of the same appointment to the same office to take any oath more than once:

Provided that no proceedings before any such person may be questioned in any Court solely on the ground that that person has failed to take the oaths prescribed by this Article.

PART IVA

FUNDAMENTAL HUMAN RIGHTS AND FREEDOMS

64. Fundamental human rights and freedoms.

(1) It is hereby recognised and declared that in the Cook Islands there exists and shall continue to exist, without discrimination by reason of race, national origin, color, religion, opinion, belief, or sex, the following fundamental human rights and freedoms:

(*a*) The right of the individual to life, liberty, and security of the person, and the right not to be deprived thereof except in accordance with law:

(*b*) The right of the individual to equality before the law and to the protection of the law:

(*c*) The right of the individual to own property, and the right not to be deprived thereof except in accordance with law:

Provided that nothing in this paragraph or in Article *40* of this Constitution shall be construed as limiting the power of Parliament to prohibit or restrict by Act the alienation of Native land (as defined in section *2*(1) of the Cook Islands Act 1915 of the Parliament of New Zealand):

(*d*) Freedom of thought, conscience, and religion:

(*e*) Freedom of speech and expression:

(*f*) Freedom of peaceful assembly and association.

(2) It is hereby recognised and declared that every person has duties to others, and accordingly is subject in the exercise of his rights and freedoms to such limitations as are imposed, by any enactment or rule of law for the time being in force, for protecting the rights and freedoms of others or in the interests of public safety, order, or morals, the general welfare, or the security of the Cook Islands.

65. Construction of law.

(1) Subject to sub-clause (2) of this Article and to sub-clause (2) of Article *64* hereof, every enactment shall be so construed and applied as not to abrogate, abridge, or infringe or to authorize the abrogation. abridgement, or infringement of any of the rights or freedoms recognised and declared by sub-clause (1) of Article *64* hereof, and in particular no enactment shall be construed or applied so as to

(*a*) Authorize or effect the arbitrary detention. imprisonment, or exile of any person; or

(*b*) Impose or authorize the imposition on any person of cruel and unusual treatment or punishment; or

(*c*) Deprive any person who is arrested or detained

(i) Of the right to be informed promptly of the act or omission for which he is arrested or detained, unless it is impracticable to do so or unless the reason for the arrest or detention is obvious in the circumstances; or

(ii) Of the right, wherever practicable, to retain and instruct a barrister or solicitor without delay; or

(iii) Of the right to apply, by himself or by any other person on his behalf, for a writ of *habeas corpus* for the determination of the validity of his detention, and to be released if his detention is not lawful; or

(*d*) Deprive any person of the right to a fair hearing, in accordance with the principles of fundamental justice, for the determination of his rights and obligations before any tribunal or authority having a duty to act judicially; or

(*e*) Deprive any person charged with an offence of the right to be presumed innocent until he is proved guilty according to law in a fair and public hearing by an independent and impartial tribunal; or

(*f*) Deprive any person charged with an offence of the right to reasonable bail, except for just cause; or

(*g*) Authorize the conviction of any person of any offence except for the breach of a law in force at the time of the act or omission; or

(*h*) Authorize the imposition on any person convicted of any offence of a penalty heavier than that which might have been imposed under the law in force at the time of the commission of the offence.

(2) Every enactment, and every provision thereof shall be deemed remedial, whether its immediate purpose is to direct the doing of anything that the enacting authority deems to be for the public good, or to prevent or punish the doing of anything it deems contrary to the public good, and shall accordingly receive such fair, large, and liberal construction and interpretation as will best ensure the attainment of the object of the enactment or provision thereof according to its true intent, meaning, and spirit.

(3) In this Article the term 'enactment' includes any Act of the Parliament of England or of the Parliament of Great Britain or of the Parliament of the United Kingdom, being an Act in force in the Cook Islands, and any regulation, rule, order, or other instrument made thereunder.

66. Saving. Nothing in this Part of this Constitution shall limit or affect any right or freedom, not specified in this Part, that may exist in the Cook Islands at the commencement of this Part.

PART V

THE PUBLIC REVENUES OF THE COOK ISLANDS

67. Public Funds. There shall be a Cook Islands Government Account and such other public funds or accounts as may be provided by law.

68. Restriction on taxation. No taxation shall be imposed except by law.

69. Public revenue. All taxes and other revenues and money raised or received by the Government of the Cook Islands shall be paid into the Cook Islands Government Account unless required or permitted by law to be paid into any other public fund or account.

70. Revenue and expenditure of Cook Islands Government Account.

(1) Except as provided in sub-clause (3) of this Article, or by any specific appropriation contained in any enactment, all expenditure in any financial year from the Cook Islands Government Account or from any other public fund or account shall be charged to votes specified in an Appropriation Act and in accordance with the statement of proposed expenditure for that financial year as approved by the Parliament.

(2) Every Appropriation Act shall lapse at the end of the financial year to which it relates.

(3) Subject to such limits and restrictions as may from time to time be prescribed by any enactment, the Minister responsible for finance, or, where any enactment so provides, the Executive Council, may approve the expenditure of such sums as he or it considers necessary

(*a*) In anticipation of provision to be made in an Appropriation Act for any financial year:

Provided that the total amount issued and paid under this paragraph (*a*) in any financial year shall not exceed the unexpended balance of the vote in an Appropriation Act or Acts for the preceding financial year together with an amount equal to five-twelfths of that vote; or

(*b*) Where during the period between the passing of the last Appropriation Act for any financial year and the end of that year it is desirable that money should be expended in excess of or without the appropriation of the Parliament:

Provided that the total amount of all sums issued and paid under this paragraph (*b*) in any financial year shall not exceed one and a half per cent of the total amount of all sums appropriated by the Appropriation Act or Acts for that year.

(3A) The Audit Office shall, in the last Session of Parliament before the date on which a general election of Parliament is required to be held, forward to the Speaker for presentation to Parliament a separate report specifying any expenditure made in any financial year that is in excess of the limits prescribed by sub-clause (3) of this Article or by any other enactment and has not been reported in any report previously presented pursuant to this sub-clause, and Parliament may be Act validate the whole or any part of the expenditure.

(4) A statement of the unauthorized expenditure for any financial year shall be included in the accounts for that year laid before the Parliament.

(5) Subject to the foregoing provisions of this Article, the collection, receipt, custody, banking, issue, expenditure, care, and management of money credited or to be credited to the Cook Islands Government Account or to any other public fund or account shall be as prescribed by enactment.

71. Audit.

(1) The Audit Office of New Zealand shall be the auditor of the Cook Islands Government Account and of all other public funds or accounts, and of the accounts of all Departments and offices of executive government and of such other public, statutory, or local authorities or bodies as may be provided by law.

(2) The Audit Office shall, at least once annually, forward to the Speaker of the Parliament for presentation to the Parliament a report containing such information as is required to be submitted by any enactment, together with such other information relating to the Cook Islands Government Account or other funds or accounts which under this Constitution or under any other enactment are required to be audited by the Audit Office as that Officer considers desirable.

PART VI

THE COOK ISLANDS PUBLIC SERVICE

72. The Cook Islands Public Service. There shall be a Cook Islands Public Service, which shall comprise such persons in the service of the Government of the Cook Islands as may from time to time be prescribed by law.

73. Public Service Commissioner.

(1) There shall be a Public Service Commissioner appointed by the High Commissioner acting on the advice of the Prime Minister.

(2) No person shall be appointed to be or shall remain the Public Service Commissioner

(*a*) If he is not or ceases to be a citizen of the Commonwealth; or a permanent resident of the Cook Islands; or

(*b*) If he is or becomes a member of Parliament.

(3) The Public Service Commissioner shall not hold concurrently any other office in the Cook Islands Public Service.

(4) The actions of the Public Service Commissioner shall not be invalidated in consequence of the subsequent discovery of some defect with regard to his appointment.

(5) The Public Service Commissioner shall be paid such remuneration by way of salary and allowances as may from time to time be appropriated by the Parliament.

74. Term of Office of the Public Service Commissioner.

(1) The Public Service Commissioner shall be appointed for a term of not more than four years but shall be elegible for re-appointment.

(2) The Public Service Commissioner may at any time resign his office by writing under his hand addressed to the Prime Minister.

74A. Removal from office of Public Service Commissioner.

(1) The Public Service Commissioner may be suspended or removed from office in accordance the following provisions of this Article and not otherwise.

(2) The Queen's Representative, acting on the advice of the Prime Minister,

may suspend the Public Service Commissioner from office for misbahavior or incompetence, but the Public Service Commissioner shall not be removed from office except as provided in this Article.

(3) The Queen's Representative shall cause to be laid before the Parliament a full statement of the grounds of any suspension within seven days after the date of that suspension if the Parliament is then in session, or if the Parliament is not in session then within seven days after the date of the commencement of the next ensuing session.

(4) Unless the Parliament, within twenty-one days from the date on which the statement in respect of the suspension of the Public Service Commissioner under this Article has been laid before it, declares by resolution that he ought to be removed from office, the Public Service Commissioner shall be deemed to be restored to office as from the date of his suspension; and if the Parliament within the said time does so declare, the Public Service Commissioner shall be removed by the Queen's Representative from the date of his suspension.

74B. Functions of the Public Service Commissioner.

(1) Subject to the provisions of Article *74BB* hereof and of sub-clauses (2), (3), and (4) of this Article, the Public Service Commissioner shall be responsible for the appointment, promotion, transfer, termination of appointment, dismissal, and disciplinary control of employees of the Cook Islands Public Service, and shall have such other functions as may be prescribed by law.

(2) Any promotion or appointment to the position of head of a department of the Cook Islands Public Service, other than those specified in sub-clause (2) of Article *74BB* hereof, shall be made by the Public Service Commissioner in accordance with a decision of the Public Service Appointments Board, which shall consist of

(*a*) The Public Service Commissioner, who shall be Chairman:

(*b*) One person, to be appointed by and hold office at the pleasure of the Queen's Representative acting on the advice of the Minister responsible for the Public Service:

(*c*) One person, nominated by the Cook Islands Public Service Association Incorporated, to be appointed by and hold office at the pleasure of the Queen's Representative.

(3) An Act shall make provision for the grading of positions in the Cook Islands Public Service and, except as provided in Article 74BB hereof and in sub-clause (2) and (4) of this Article, any promotion or appointment to such graded positions shall be made by the Public Service Commissioner and 2 heads of departments of the Cook Islands Public Service. The appointment of those heads of departments for the purposes of this sub-clause shall be as prescribed by Act.

(4) Subject to sub-clause (2) of this Article, an Act may provide for the appointment of persons from outside the Cook Islands to positions in the Cook Islands Public Service and the conditions on which such appointments are to be made; and the appointment of any such person shall be made with the concurrence of Cabinet.

(5) A decision of Cabinet under sub-clause (4) of this Article shall be deemed to be a decision to which Article *25* hereof (which relates to reconsideration of Cabinet decisions by the Executive Council) applies.

(6) In the performance of their functions under this Article

(*a*) The Public Service Commissioner when acting alone; and

(*b*) The Public Service Appointments Board; and

(*c*) The Public Service Commissioner and the heads of departments when acting together

shall have regard to the general policy of Cabinet relating to the Cook Islands Public Service, and shall give effect to any decision of Cabinet defining that policy conveyed to him or them, as the case may be, in writing signed by the Prime Minister.

74BB. (1) The positions specified in sub-clause (2) of this Article are hereby designated as exempted positions.

(2) The exempted positions shall be

(*a*) The Secretary to the Cabinet;

(*b*) The Secretary to the Prime Minister's Department:

(*c*) The Chief Administration Officer in each of the islands of the Cook Islands other than Rarotonga.

(3) Appointments to the exempted positions and the removal of any person from an exempted position shall be made by the Public Service Commissioner in accordance with a decision of Cabinet.

(4) The positions designated as special posts pursuant to sub-clause (3) of Article *74B* hereof (as enacted by section *2* of the Constitution Amendment (No. 6) Act 1973) shall cease to be designated as such and are hereby declared to have been vacated at the commencement of this Article[1].

(5) Where

(*a*) Any person who before his appointment to an exempted position was an employee of the Cook Islands Public Service is removed from that position by the Public Service Commissioner in accordance with a decision of Cabinet; or

(*b*) A person whose appointment to a position designated as a special post has terminated under sub-clause (4) of this Article is not appointed to an exempted position, and before his appointment to that special post he was an employee of the Cook Islands Public Service,

he shall be re-appointed to that Service with the grading held by him immediately before his appointment to the exempted position or to that special post as the case may be.

(6) Every decision of Cabinet under sub-clause (3) or sub-clause (5)(*a*) of this Article or to remove any person from an exempted position shall be deemed to be a decision to which Article *25* hereof (which relates to the reconsideration of Cabinet decisions by the Executive Council) applies.

---

[1] 1973

74C. Procedure of Public Service Commissioner.

(1) Subject to the provisions of this Constitution and of any law, the Public Service Commissioner may

(*a*) Exercise his functions in such manner as he sees fit; and

(*b*) Delegate any of his functions to any person or persons.

(2) When acting with the heads of departments for the purposes of making promotions or appointments or in graded positions pursuant to sub-clause (3) of Article *74B* of the Constitution the Public Service Commissioner and the heads of departments shall regulate their own procedure and exercise their functions in such manner as they see fit.

75. Staff of Queen's Representative.

(1) Except as provided in subclause (2) of this Article, the appointment, terms of service, disciplinary control, termination of appointment, and dismissal of the staff of the Queen's Representative shall be matters for the Queen's Representative, acting in his discretion.

(2) The Queen's Representative, if he so decides, may appoint to his staff such employees of the Cook Islands Public Service as he may select, acting in his discretion but after consultation with the Premier, from a list submitted to the Public Service Commission; and the provisions of sub-clause (1) of this Article (except so far as they relate to the appointment) shall apply in relation to a person so appointed in respect of his service on the staff of the Queen's Representative but not in respect of his service as an employee of the Cook Islands Public Service.

76. Board of Appeal.

(1) There shall be a Cook Islands Public Service Board of Appeal, which shall consist of

(*a*) The Chief Judge of the High Court:

(*b*) One person, being an employee or former employee of the Cook Islands Public Service to be appointed by, and hold office at the pleasure of, the Queen's Representative, acting on the advice of the Prime Minister:

(*c*) One person, being an employee or former employee of the Cook Islands Public Service to be elected by the employees of that Service or nominated by an organisation of those employees, and to hold office for a period of three years.

(2) The Chief Justice shall be Chairman of the Board of Appeal.

(2A) In the absence of the Chief Justice from any sitting of the Board of Appeal, any other judge of the High Court nominated by him, either generally or in any particular case, may attend the sitting in his stead, and while so attending shall be the Chairman of the Board of Appeal.

(3) An Act

(*a*) Shall prescribe whether or not the person to be appointed under the provisions of paragraph (*c*) of sub-clause (1) of this Article is to be elected or nominated and the manner of that election or nomination:

(*b*) May provide for the appointment of deputies to act for members of the Board of Appeal appointed under the provisions of paragraph (*b*) or paragraph (*c*) of subclause (1) of this Article:

(*c*) Shall prescribe the jurisdiction of the Board of Appeal to hear and determine appeals from the decisions of the Public Service Commissioner in relation to the Cook Islands Public Service:

(*d*) Shall prescribe the procedure of the Board of Appeal.

(4) Subject to the provisions of any Act, the Board of Appeal shall determine its own procedure.

(5) In this Article the term *employee* does not include a temporary or probationary employee.

PART VIA

MISCELLANEOUS PROVISIONS

76A. Persons entitled to permanent residence.

(1) A person shall have the status of a permanent resident of the Cook Islands if he was born in the Cook Islands, and

(*a*) Either or both of his parents had the status of a permanent resident of the Cook Islands at the date of his birth; or

(*b*) In the case of a child who was born after the death of his father to a mother who did not have that status at the date of birth of the child, his father had that status at the date of his death; or

(*c*) He was adopted by a person who at the date of adoption had that status.

(2) Any person may apply, pursuant to the provisions of an Act of Parliament, for a certificate granting to him the status of a permanent resident of the Cook Islands.

(3) An Act may

(*a*) Prescribe the qualifications to be held by a person to whom sub-clause (2) of this Article applies who is an applicant for such a certificate, and the circumstances in which such an applicant is disqualified from being granted such a certificate; and

(*b*) Prescribe the conditions subject to which such a certificate may be granted to a person whom sub-clause (2) of this Article applies; and

(*c*) Confer on a Minister a discretion to grant or refuse such a certificate to a person to whom sub-clause (2) of this Article applies; and

(*d*) Prescribe the circumstance in which such a certificate granted may be revoked;

Provided that any certificate granted may only be revoked by a Judge of the High Court.

(4) Notwithstanding any of the provisions of this Article, the Minister Responsible for Immigration may cancel any certificate granted if the person to whom the certificate relates is absent from the Cook Islands continuously for a

period exceeding three years in circumstances indicating that the person has ceased to make his home in the Cook Islands.

(5) Nothing in this Article shall affect the status of a permanent resident of the Cook Islands of any person holding that status pursuant to the Entry, Residence, and Departure Act 1971–72, immediately before the commencement of this Article[1].

76B. The Prerogative of Mercy and Pardon. The Prerogative of Mercy and Pardon shall be exercised by the Queen's Representative acting pursuant to a resolution of Parliament, provided that any such resolution must receive the support of not less than two thirds of the total membership (including vacancies) of Parliament.

76C. The Cook Islands Ensign.

(1) The Cook Islands Ensign shall be the flag described in the Third Schedule to this Constitution.

(2) The Cook Islands Ensign is hereby declared to be the recognized flag of the Cook Islands.

(3) Provision may be made by enactment prescribing the circumstances in which and the conditions subject to which the Cook Islands Ensign may be flown, and prohibiting the defacing of the ensign by placing any sign, representation, or letter thereon.

76D. National anthem of the Cook Islands.

(1) The anthem entitled 'Te Atua Mou E' shall be the national anthem of the Cook Islands.

(2) The words of the national anthem shall be as set out in the Fourth Schedule to this Constitution.

PART VII

TRANSITIONAL PROVISIONS

77. Existing law to continue. Subject to the provisions of this Constitution,

(*a*) The existing law shall, until repealed, and subject to any amendment thereof, continue in force on and after Constitution Day:

(*b*) All rights, obligations, and liabilities arising under the existing law shall continue to exist on and after Constitution Day, and shall be recognized, exercised, and enforced accordingly.

78. Repealed.

79. Parliament. (1), (2), (3), *Repealed.*

(4) Subject to the provisions of this Constitution, the Standing Orders of the Legislative Assembly in force immediately before Constitution Day shall continue to be the Standing Orders of the Assembly, and they may be amended, repealed, or added to under the provisions of Article 34 hereof.

81. Ordinances of former Legislative Council or Legislative Assembly.

(1) Every Ordinance made by the Legislative Council of the Cook Islands

---

[1] 1980.

under section 2 of the Cook Islands Amendment Act 1946, and in force immediately before Constitution Day, shall be deemed to be an Ordinance of the Legislative Assembly of the Cook Islands made before Constitution Day and shall continue in force as if it were such an Ordinance on and after Constitution Day.

(2) All Ordinances made by the Legislative Assembly of the Cook Islands under section 38 of the Cook Islands Amendment Act 1957, and in force immediately before Constitution Day, shall continue in force on and after Constitution Day.

82. The High Court.

(1) The High Court of the Cook Islands established by Article *47* hereof is hereby declared to be the same Court as the High Court of the Cook Islands established by the Cook Islands Act 1915.

(2) The Judges and Commissioners of that Court in office immediately before Constitution Day shall continue to hold office on and after Constitution Day as if they had been appointed under the provisions of this Constitution, and those Judges shall receive the salary to which they were entitled immediately before Constitution Day as if that salary had been fixed by enactment.

(3) All judgments, decrees, records, and acts of the High Court of the Cook Islands shall continue to have full force and effect on and after Constitution Day as judgments, decrees, records, and acts of the High Court established under this Constitution; and all proceedings, civil or criminal, pending in the High Court immediately before Constitution Day, and all appeals pending immediately before Constitution Day from decisions of the High Court, may be continued on and after Constitution Day.

83. The Land Court.

(1) The Land Court of the Cook Islands established by Article 52 hereof is hereby declared to be the same Court as the Native Land Court of the Cook Islands established by the Cook Islands Act 1915.

(2) The Land Court of the Cook Islands shall also be deemed for all purposes to be the same Court as that which existed at the commencement of the Cook Islands Act 1915 under the name of the Cook Islands Titles Court, and all orders theretofore made by the last-mentioned Court shall have effect accordingly.

(3) *Repealed.*

(4) All judgments, decrees, records, and acts of the Native Land Court of the Cook Islands shall continue in full force and effect on and after Constitution Day as judgments, decrees, records, and acts of the Land Court of the Cook Islands; and all proceedings pending in the Native Land Court of the Cook Islands immediately before Constitution Day may be continued in the Land Court of the Cook Islands on and after Constitution Day.

84. The Land Appellate Court.

(1) The Land Appellate Court of the Cook Islands established by Article *55* hereof is hereby declared to be the same Court as the Native Appellate Court of the Cook Islands established by section 19 of the Cook Islands Amendment Act 1946.

(2) All judgments, decrees, records, and acts of the Native Appellate Court of the Cook Islands shall continue in full force and effect on and after Constitution Day as judgments, decrees, records, and acts of the Land Appellate Court of the Cook Islands; and all proceedings pending in the Native Appellate Court of the Cook Islands immediately before Constitution Day may be continued in the Land Appellate Court of the Cook Islands on and after Constitution Day.

85. Justices of the Peace.

(1) Every person holding office immediately before Constitution Day as a Justice of the Peace for the Cook Islands other than Niue shall continue in office as a Justice of the Peace for the Cook Islands, as if he had been appointed to that office pursuant to Article 64 hereof.

(2) Subject to the provisions of sub-clause (3) of Article *64* hereof, every such person shall continue to hold office during the pleasure of the High Commissioner.

86. Cook Islands Government Account. The Cook Islands Government Account established by Article *67* hereof is hereby declared to be the same account as the Cook Islands Assembly Account established by section 15 of the Cook Islands Amendment Act 1957; and all money in the last-mentioned account immediately before Constitution Day shall on and after Constitution Day be deemed to form part of the Cook Islands Government Account.

87. Repealed.

88. Repealed.

SCHEDULES

Not Reproduced

XIV. Constitution of Niue[1]

August 29, 1974

PART I

THE EXECUTIVE GOVERNMENT OF NIUE

1. Executive authority vested in the Crown. The executive authority of Niue is vested in Her Majesty the Queen in right of New Zealand, and the Governor General of New Zealand is accordingly the representative of Her Majesty the Queen in relation to Niue.

The Cabinet

2. Cabinet of Ministers of Niue.

(1) There shall be a Cabinet of Ministers of Niue (hereinafter referred to as the Cabinet) which shall consist of the Premier of Niue (who shall be a member of the Niue Assembly) and 3 other members of the Niue Assembly.

(2) Subject to this Constitution, the executive authority of Niue may be exercised on behalf of Her Majesty by the Cabinet, which shall have the general direction and control of the executive government of Niue, and shall have such other functions and powers as are conferred on it by law.

3. Ministers to be collectively responsible.

(1) The members of the Cabinet (hereinafter referred to as Ministers) shall be collectively responsible to the Niue assembly.

(2) Subject to Article 7 of this Constitution, the Ministers shall continue in office until their successors are appointed pursuant to Article 5 (2) of this Constitution.

4. Premier of Niue.

(1) There shall be a Premier of Niue, who shall be elected to that office by an absolute majority of the members present and voting at a meeting of the Niue Assembly.

(2) The Niue Assembly shall proceed to elect the Premier at the first meeting of the Assembly after a general election, and also in each of the following circumstances:

(*a*) If the Premier ceases to be a member of the Assembly for any reason other than the dissolution thereof; or

(*b*) If the Premier tenders his resignation by writing under his hand addressed to the Speaker or is deemed to have tendered his resignation pursuant to Article 6 (3) or Article 7 (3) of this Constitution.

[1] An Act to make provision for self government by the people of Niue, and to provide a constitution for Niue. New Zealand Statutes 1974, No. 42.

5. *Appointment of Ministers after election of Premier.*

(1) As soon as practicable after his election to that office, the Premier elect shall nominate to the Speaker, with their consent, 3 other members of the Niue Assembly for appointment as Ministers.

(2) Upon receiving the nominations, the Speaker shall appoint as Ministers the Premier-elect and the members so nominated.

(3) Appointments under sub-clause (2) of this Article shall be made by the Speaker by instrument under the Seal of Niue.

(4) If the Premier-elect has not within 7 days after but excluding the date of his election to that office submitted to the Speaker his nominations for appointments to the Cabinet pursuant to this Article, his election to that office shall have no effect, and, subject to Article *26*(1)(*d*) of this Constitution, a meeting of the Niue Assembly shall be held as soon as practicable for the purpose of again electing a Premier.

6. *Vote of confidence in Cabinet.*

(1) At any meeting of the Niue Assembly

(*a*) The Premier, or another Minister acting on behalf of the Premier, may give notice of his intention to move a vote of confidence in the Cabinet, either generally or on any measure proposed by the Cabinet for adoption by the Assembly:

(*b*) Any 4 or more members of the Assembly who are not Ministers may give notice of their intention to move a vote of no confidence in the Cabinet.

(2) Any motion of which notice is given under sub-clause (1) of this Article shall be voted on at a meeting of the Niue Assembly held not earlier than 5 days nor later than 10 days after but excluding the date of the giving of the notice.

(3) If the motion of confidence is lost, or, as the case may be, the motion of no confidence is carried, the Premier shall be deemed to have tendered his resignation from his office at the expiration of 5 days after but excluding the date of the meeting of the Niue Assembly, unless before the expiration of that period he requests the Speaker to dissolve the Assembly.

7. *Vacation of office by Ministers.*

(1) Any Minister, other than the Premier, shall vacate his office if

(*a*) His appointment to that office is revoked by the Speaker, acting on the request of the Premier, by instrument under the Seal of Niue; or

(*b*) He ceases to be a member of the Niue Assembly for any reason other than the dissolution thereof; or

(*c*) He resigns his office by writing under his hand delivered to the Speaker.

(2) Within 7 days after the occurrence of any vacancy in the office of Minister, other than the Premier, the Premier shall nominate to the Speaker, with the consent of the member, a member of the Niue Assembly for appointment as a Minister, and the Speaker shall by instrument under the Seal of Niue appoint the member so nominated.

(3) If the Premier does not, within 7 days after but excluding the date of the occurrence of a vacancy in the office of a Minister, other than the Premier, nominate a Minister pursuant to sub-clause (2) of this Article, he shall be deemed to have tendered his resignation from his office as Premier at the expiration of that period of 7 days.

8. Temporary Ministers.

(1) Whenever it appears to the Premier that any Minister will, by reason of illness or absence from Niue, be unable to discharge his function in Niue for a period of 7 days or longer, the Premier shall nominate to the Speaker, with the consent of the member, a member of the Niue Assembly for appointment as a temporary Minister, and the Speaker shall, by instrument under the Seal of Niue, appoint that member accordingly.

(2) Every such temporary Minister shall be appointed in place of the Minister who is unable to discharge his functions in Niue, and, subject to subclause (3) of this Article, shall hold office, as if he had been appointed under Article 5 of this Constitution.

(3) Every such temporary Minister, unless he sooner vacates his office pursuant to Article 7 of this Constitution, shall remain in office until the Minister in whose place he is appointed is again able to discharge his functions in Niue.

9. Acting Premier.

(1) Whenever, by reason of illness or absence from Niue, the Premier is temporarily prevented from discharging his functions in Niue, the Speaker, acting on the request of the Cabinet, may, by instrument under the Seal of Niue, appoint another Minister to discharge the functions of Premier until such time as the Premier is capable of again discharging his functions or has vacated his office.

(2) Where the Premier dies or tenders his resignation to the Speaker after a dissolution of the Niue Assembly and before the appointment of the Ministers after the general election following that dissolution, the Speaker, acting on the request of the Cabinet, shall, by instrument under the Seal of Niue, appoint another minister to discharge the functions of Premier until the Ministers are appointed after that general election.

10. Official oath. Every Minister shall, before assuming the functions of his office, take and subscribe before the Speaker the following oath:

I, ... , being chosen and accepted as Premier of Niue (*or* a Minister), swear by Almighty God that I will to the best of my judgment, at all times when thereto required, freely give my counsel and advice for the good management of the affairs of Niue, and that I will not directly or indirectly reveal such matters as may be debated in the Cabinet or any committee of the Cabinet and committed to my secrecy, but that I will in all such things be a true and faithful Premier of Niue (*or* Minister). So help me God.

11. Allocation of responsibilities to Ministers.

(1) The Premier shall from time to time, by writing under his hand countersigned by the Clerk of the Cabinet and published in the *Niue Gazette,* allocate to any Minister (including himself) the primary responsibility for any Department or

or function of Government, and may from time to time in like manner vary any such allocation.

(2) The Premier shall have the primary responsibility for any Department or function of Government in respect of which, for the time being, no allocation under sub-clause (1) of this Article is in effect.

12. Meetings of Cabinet.

(1) No business shall be transacted at any meeting of the Cabinet unless at least 3 Ministers are present.

(2) The Cabinet shall not be disqualified for the transaction of business by reason only that there is a vacancy among its members, or that, in any case where Article *8* of this Constitution applies, no appointment has been made pursuant to that Article. No proceedings of the Cabinet shall be questioned on the ground that some person who acted as a Minister in relation to those proceedings was not qualified so to act.

(3) Notice of every meeting of the Cabinet and a copy of every paper to be considered at that meeting shall be given to each Minister, and to the Secretary to the Government.

(4) The Secretary to the Government shall have the right to attend any meeting of the Cabinet and to speak on any matter under consideration by the Cabinet, and he shall so attend if required to do so by the Premier.

(5) The decision of the Cabinet on any matter shall be taken only by the Ministers present at a meeting of the Cabinet.

(6) Subject to this Article, the Cabinet shall regulate its own procedure in such matters as it thinks fit.

13. Rules, other enactments, and decisions of Cabinet. Any rule or other enactment of the Cabinet shall have effect, and any other decision of the Cabinet shall be duly authenicated, when that rule or other enactment, or the record of that decision, has been signed by the Premier, whether or not he was present at the meeting of the Cabinet at which the rule or other enactment or decision was made, and by the Clerk of the Cabinet.

14. Clerk of the Cabinet. There shall be an officer of the Niue Public Service to be called the Clerk of the Cabinet, who shall be responsible for arranging the business for, and keeping the minutes of, meetings of the Cabinet, and for conveying decisions of the Cabinet to the appropriate person or authority, and shall perform with respect to the Cabinet such secretarial and other functions as may be required.

Seal of Niue

15. Seal of Niue.

(1) There shall be a Public Seal of Niue (in this Constitution referred to as the Seal of Niue), to be in such form or forms as the Cabinet from time to time approves.

(2) The Seal of Niue shall be in the custody of the Speaker.

(3) The Seal of Niue may be used by the Speaker for the authentication

of any public document in relation ot the Government of Niue or for the execution of any document required by law to be executed under the Seal of Niue.

(4) Judicial notice shall be taken of the Seal of Niue in all Courts.

PART II

THE LEGISLATIVE GOVERNMENT OF NIUE

The Niue Assembly

16. Niue Assembly.

(1) There shall be in and for Niue a legislative Assembly to be called the Niue Assembly.

(2) The Niue Assembly shall consist of

(*a*) The Speaker; and

(*b*) Twenty members to be elected by secret ballot under a system of universal suffrage in the following manner:

(i) Fourteen members, each of whom shall represent a village constituency, shall be elected by the electors of that constituency:

(ii) Six members shall be elected by the persons qualified to be electors of Niue voting on a common roll, which, for the purpose of electing those members, shall comprise the rolls of the several village constituencies.

(3) Subject to this Article and to Articles *17, 18, 19, 24,* and *25* of this Constitution, the boundaries of village constituencies, the qualifications and disqualification of electors and of candidates, the mode of electing members of the Niue Assembly, and the terms and conditions of their membership shall be as prescribed by law:

Provided that

(*a*) There shall be 14 village constituencies; and

(*b*) Every person qualified to be an elector for the election of members of the Niue Assembly shall be entitled to vote in one, and one only, village constituency; and

(*c*) Any determination or redetermination of the boundaries of any village constituency shall, so far as practicable, having due regard to local community interest, be made in accordance with the principle that the number of electors in that village constituency should not be substantially greater or smaller than the number of electors in any other village constituency.

(4) Unless the context otherwise requires, every reference in this Constitution to a member of the Niue Assembly shall be construed as a reference to a member elected pursuant to sub-clause (2)(*b*) of this Article, and shall, in any case where the Assembly has been dissolved, be read as a reference to a person who was a member of the Assembly immediately before that dissolution.

17. Nationality and residential qualifications of electors and candidates.

(1) Without limiting the provisions of any law prescribing any additional qualifications, a person shall be qualified to be an elector for the election of members of the Niue Assembly, or to be a candidate at any such election, if, and only if,

(*a*) He is a New Zealand citizen; and

(*b*) He has been ordinarily resident in Niue throughout the period of 3 months immediately preceding his application for enrolment as an elector or, as the case may be, his nomination as a candidate, and had at some period resided continuously in Niue for not less than 12 months.

(2) For the purposes of this Article, a person shall be deemed to be ordinarily resident in Niue if, and only if,

(*a*) He is actually residing in Niue; or

(*b*) Having been actually resident in Niue with the intention of residing there indefinitely, he is outside Niue but has, and has had ever since he left Niue, an intention to return and reside there indefinitely:

Provided that any person who has been outside Niue continuously for any period of more than 3 years shall be deemed not to have such an intention, unless during the whole or substantially the whole period of that absence he was undergoing a course of education or of technical training or instruction, or was in the service of the Government of Niue.

18. Public servants may become candidates or be elected.

(1) Employees of the Niue Public Service who become candidates for election as members of the Niue Assembly shall be granted leave of absence for the purposes of their candidature in accordance with such terms and conditions as may be prescribed by law.

(2) If any such employee is elected as a member of the Assembly, he shall, on being declared so elected, be deemed to have been granted leave of absence without salary from his employment in the Niue Public Service for the period during which he is a member.

19. Members disqualified from becoming public servants or interested in Government contracts. The seat of any member of the Niue Assembly shall become vacant

(*a*) If he becomes an employee of the Niue Public Service, or, being an employee of that Service at the time of his election, he accepts paid employment in that Service; or

(*b*) If he otherwise becomes interested in the execution or enjoyment of any contract under which any public money is payable, except to such extent as may be permitted by law.

20. Speaker of Niue Assembly.

(1) The Speaker of the Niue Assembly shall be elected to that office by an absolute majority of the members present and voting at a meeting of the Niue Assembly.

(2) Only a person who is qualified for election as a member of the Niue Assembly may be elected as Speaker.

(3) If any person elected as Speaker is, at the time of that election, a member of the Niue Assembly, he shall vacate his office as a member when he enters upon the duties of the office of Speaker.

(4) The election of the Speaker shall take place, before the despatch of any other business, at the first meeting of the Assembly after each general election, and, at a meeting of the Assembly called for that purpose, as soon as possible after any vacancy in the office of Speaker has occurred.

(5) Before a person who has been elected Speaker enters upon the duties of his office, he shall take and subscribe before the Clerk of the Niue Assembly at a meeting of the Assembly the Oath of Allegiance prescribed in Article *21* of this Constitution, and the provisions of that Article shall apply with the necessary modifications as if the references therein to a member were a reference to the Speaker.

(6) The Speaker may resign his office by writing under his hand addressed and delivered to the Clerk of the Niue Assembly, and shall vacate his office

(*a*) On the entry into office of a new Speaker elected when the Assembly first meets after a general election; or

(*b*) If he ceases to be qualified for election as a member of the Assembly; or

(*c*) If he becomes a candidate at any election of a member or members of the Assembly.

(7) If at any meeting of the Assembly the Speaker is absent or the office of Speaker is vacant, the members of the Assembly present at that meeting shall elect one of their number, not being a Minister, to preside over that meeting until the Speaker is again present, or, as the case may be, until a Speaker has been elected and has entered upon the duties of his office.

(8) If, at any time when the Assembly is not meeting, the Speaker is, by reason of illness or absence from Niue, temporarily prevented from performing his functions, or the office of Speaker is vacant, then, until the Assembly again meets, or, as the case may be, the Speaker is again able to perform his functions, those functions shall be performed by a member of the Assembly, not being a Minister, who has presided over a meeting of the Assembly pursuant to sub-clause (7) of this Article. If more than one member of the Assembly is so qualified and is available to perform the functions of the Speaker, those functions shall be performed by the member who most recently presided over a meeting of the Assembly, pursuant to that sub-clause.

(9) If it appears that no person is, for the time being, qualified and available to perform the functions of the Speaker,

(*a*) A meeting of the Assembly shall be called as soon as possible, and the Clerk of the Niue Assembly shall perform such of the functions of the Speaker as are required to be performed for the purpose of enabling that meeting to be held, and the provisions of Article *22*(6) of this Constitution shall not apply to that meeting; or (*b*) In any case where the Assembly has been dissolved and the ensuing general election has not taken place, a meeting of those persons who were members of the Assembly immediately before its dissolution shall be called as soon as possible for the purpose of electing one of their number to perform the functions of the Speaker until the Speaker is again able to perform his functions or, as the case may be, the new Assembly first meets; and the Clerk of the Niue Assembly shall do everything necessary to ensure that the meeting is called and to certify to the result of the election. The person elected shall, for the purpose of sub-clauses (7) and (8) of this Article, be deemed to be a person who has presided over a meeting of the Assembly.

(10) Every document, including the certificate on any Bill, signed by the Speaker in the performance of his functions shall be countersigned by the Clerk of the Niue Assembly, and, where, pursuant to this Article, any such document or certificate is signed by a member performing the functions of the Speaker, it shall be so stated on the document or in that certificate.

21. Members to take Oath of Allegiance. Except for the purpose of enabling this Article to be complied with and for the election of a Speaker, no member of the Niue Assembly shall be permitted to sit or vote therein until he has taken and subscribed the following oath before the Speaker namely:

I, ..., swear by Almighty God that I will be faithful and bear true allegiance to Her (*or* His) Majesty [*Specify the name of the reigning Soveriegn, as thus: Queen Elizabeth the Second*], Her (*or* His) heirs and successors, according to law, and that I will justly and faithfully carry out my duties as a member of the Niue Assembly. So help me God.

22. Procedure of Niue Assembly.

(1) The Niue Assembly shall meet at such places and at such times as the Speaker, acting on the request of the Premier, from time to time appoints in that behalf:

Provided that, if more than 6 weeks has elapsed since the time of the last meeting of the Assembly, any 4 or more members of the Assembly who are not Ministers may request the Speaker to appoint a place and time for a meeting of the Assembly, and the Speaker shall appoint a place and time in that behalf, such time to be not earlier than 5 days nor later than 10 days after but excluding the date of the making of the request.

(2) The Speaker shall preside at every meeting of the Niue Assembly at which he is present.

(3) Except where this Constitution otherwise provides, every question before the Niue Assembly shall be decided by a majority of the votes of the members present.

(4) Subject to any law requiring any member of the Assembly to refrain from voting on any matter concerning a contract in whose execution and enjoyment he is interested, every member present when any question is put to the Niue Assembly shall vote thereon.

(5) The Speaker or other presiding officer shall not have a casting vote and the Speaker shall not have a deliberative vote, but a member presiding in place of the Speaker shall have a deliberative vote.

(6) Subject to Article *20*(9)(*a*) of this Constitution, no business shall be transacted at any meeting of the Niue Assembly if the number of members then present, including any member presiding in place of the Speaker, is less than 10.

(7) The powers of the Niue Assembly shall not be affected by any vacancy in its membership.

(8) No Bill shall be passed unless it has been read 3 times in the Assembly.

(9) Any Bill or other business before the Assembly at its dissolution shall lapse.

(10) Subject to this Constitution, the Niue Assembly may from time to time make Standing Orders for the regulation and orderly conduct of its proceedings and the despatch of business.

23. Languages.

(1) The Speaker or any member of the Niue Assembly may speak in the Assembly either in Niuean language or in the English language:

Provided that the Clerk of the Niue Assembly shall, at the request of the Speaker or of any member made through the Speaker, arrange for the remarks of the Speaker or of any member to be translated into the English language or the Niuean language, as the case may be.

(2) Every Bill introduced into the Niue Assembly and every Act shall be in the Niuean language and also in the English language:

Provided that the Assembly may, be resolution, determine that any Bill or Act shall be in the Niuean language or the English language only.

(3) The records of proceedings in the Niue Assembly or in Committees thereof shall be in the Niuean language, and such of those records as are specified in the Standing Orders of the Assembly or as the Assembly may by resolution determine shall also be in the English language.

(4) The Niuean version and the English version of this Constitution and, subject to sub-clause (5) of this Article, the Niuean version and the English version of any record of proceedings in the Niue Assembly or any Committee thereof and of any enactment shall be equally authentic:

Provided that if in any case there is any apparent discrepancy between any provision of the Niuean version and of the Engligh version of this Constitution or of any such record or of any enactment, then, in construing that provision, regard shall be had to all the circumstances that tend to establish the true intent and meaning of that provision.

(5) In the case of any record of proceedings in the Niue Assembly or any Committee thereof the Assembly may be resolution determine, and in the case of any enactment it may be expressly provided, that where there is any conflict between the Niuean version and the English version of any such record or of any such enactment, one version only, being either the Niuean version or the English version, shall prevail.

24. Privileges of Niue Assembly and its members.

(1) The validity of any proceedings in the Niue Assembly or in any Committee thereof, and the validity of any certificate duly given by the Speaker under Article *34* or Article *35* of this Constitution shall not be questioned in any Court.

(2) Neither the Speaker nor any member or officer of the Niue Assembly in whom powers are vested for the regulation of procedure or the conduct of business or the maintenance of order shall in relation to the exercise by him of any of those powers be subject to the jurisdiction of any Court.

(3) Neither the Speaker nor any member of the Niue Assembly nor any person entitled to speak therein shall be liable to any proceedings in any Court in respect of anything said or any vote given by him in the Assembly or in any Committee thereof.

(4) No person shall be liable to any proceedings in any Court in respect of the publication by or under the authority of the Niue Assembly of any report, paper, vote, or proceeding.

(5) Subject to this Article, the privileges of the Niue Assembly and of the Committees thereof and the privileges of members and the Speaker of the Assembly and of the persons entitled to speak therein may be determined by Act; and any such Act may, subject to Article *31* of this Constitution, define offences relating to breach of privilege or contempt of the Assembly, and may make provision for the trial and punishment of such offences by the High Court, but not otherwise.

25. Remuneration of Premier, other Ministers, other members of the Niue Assembly, and the Speaker.

(1) The Niue Public Service Commission may from time to time, and shall when there is a general alteration of the levels of remuneration of employees of the Niue Public Service, report and make recommendations to the Assembly as to the levels of remuneration and other entitlements of the Premier, other Ministers, the members of the Assembly who are not Ministers, and the Speaker.

(2) The Premier, the other Ministers, the members of the Niue Assembly who are not Ministers, and the Speaker may receive such remuneration and allowances and such other benefits as may be prescribed by Act.

(3) If, in the opinion of the Speaker, any Bill, or any amendment to any Bill, deals with a matter to which this Article relates, that Bill or that amendment may not be introduced unless

(*a*) There is before the Assembly a report and recommendations made by the Niue Public Service Commission pursuant to this Article; and

(*b*) The issues raised by that Bill or by that amendment are, in the opinion of the Speaker, substantially similar to those considered in the Commission's report and recommendations.

26. Dissolution of Niue Assembly.

(1) The Speaker shall, by notice in the *Niue Gazette*, dissolve the Niue Assembly

(*a*) At the expiration of 3 years from the date of the last preceding general election, if it has not been sooner dissolved:

(*b*) At any time after the expiration of 2 years and 9 months from the date of the last preceding general election, if the Premier so requests:

(*c*) If, pursuant to Article *6*(3) of this Constitution, the Premier requests him to dissolve the Assembly:

(*d*) If a new election of Premier has been held pursuant to Article *5*(4) of this Constitution and that new election has become of no effect pursuant to that sub-clause.

(2) There shall be a general election of the members of the Niue Assembly at such time, being not less than 4 weeks nor more than 6 weeks after the date of every dissolution of the Assembly, as the Speaker shall, at the request of the Premier, appoint, or, if the Premier makes no such request within 7 days of any dissolution, as the Speaker acting in him own discretion, shall appoint, by notice in the *Niue Gazette.*

27. Clerk of the Niue Assembly.

(1) There shall be an officer of the Niue Public Service to be called the Clerk of the Niue Assembly, who shall be responsible for

(*a*) Arranging the business and keeping the records of the proceedings of the Niue Assembly; and

(*b*) Arranging for the signing of documents and giving of certificates by the Speaker, whenever any signature or certification by the Speaker is required pursuant to this Constitution or to any enactment, and keeping the records of all documents and certificates so signed or given.

(2) The Clerk of the Niue Assembly shall perform with respect to the Speaker and to the members of the Assembly such secretarial and other functions as may be required.

The Making of Laws

28. Power to make laws.

(1) Subject to this Constitution, the Niue Assembly may make laws for the peace, order, and good government of Niue.

(2) The powers of the Niue Assembly shall extend to the making, in relation to Niue, of laws having extra-territorial operation, that is to say, affecting or concerning any person or matter or thing outside Niue or any act done or omitted outside Niue.

(3) Without limiting the generality of the powers conferred by this Article, those powers shall inlcude the power to repeal or revoke or amend or modify or extend, in relaton to Niue, any law in force in Niue.

(4) Except to the extent to which it is inconsistent with this Constitution, no Act, and no provision of any Act shall be deemed to be invalid solely on the ground that it is inconsistent with any law in force in Niue.

29. Introduction of Bills, etc., into Niue Assembly. Subject to this Constitution and to the Standing Orders of the Niue Assembly, any member of the Assembly may introduce any Bill or propose any motion for debate in or present any petition to the Assembly, and the same shall be considered and disposed of in accordance with the Standing Orders.

30. Restrictions with regard to financial measures. Except with the recommendation or consent of the Premier or another Minister acting on behalf of the Premier, the Niue Assembly shall not proceed upon any bill (including an amendment to any Bill) which, in the opinion of the Speaker, would dispose of or charge any of the public revenues of Niue, or revoke or alter, otherwise than by way of reduction, any disposition thereof or charge thereon, or impose or alter or abolish any toll, due, fee, fine, or tax.

31. Special provisions with regard to measures affecting the criminal law or personal status.

(1) The Niue Assembly shall not proceed upon any Bill, or upon any amendment to a Bill, after its introduction, if, in the opinion of the Speaker, that Bill or that amendment makes provision concerning

(*a*) The constitution or jurisdiction of any Court other than the Land Court and the Land Appellate Court; or
(*b*) The definition of any criminal offence; or
(*c*) The sentence to be imposed on any person convicted of any criminal offence; or
(*d*) The arrest or release on bail of any person; or
(*e*) The procedure to be followed for the trial of any person charged with having committed any criminal offence; or
(*f*) The law of evidence; or
(*g*) The extradition of any offender or the return of any fugitive to or from Niue; or
(*h*) The law relating to marriage; or
(*i*) The law relating to divorce; or
(*j*) The law of adoption; or
(*k*) The law relating to maintenance and affiliation

unless the Chief Justice has been invited to comment on the legal, constitutional, and policy issues raised by that Bill or by that amendment, and there is before the Assembly the response of the Chief Justice to that invitation.

(2) If, pursuant to this Article, the Assembly by resolution decides to invite the Chief Justice to comment in relation to a Bill or to an amendment, the Speaker shall cause to be sent to the Chief Justice a copy of that resolution and an account of the Assembly's discussions thereon, together with a copy of that Bill or, as the case may be, of that amendment and of the Bill to which it relates; but if the Assembly takes a contrary decision, the Bill or the amendment to which that decision relates shall lapse.

(3) Whenever, pursuant to this Article, the Chief Justice is invited to comment in relation to a Bill or to an amendment, he shall, in responding to that invi-

tation, either furnish comments or state that there are no comments which he considers should be made.

(4) When pursuant to this Article the Assembly has received the response of the Chief Justice to any invitation to comment in relation to a Bill or an amendment to a Bill, and a new or revised amendment is thereafter introduced, the requirements of this Article shall not apply in relation to that new or revised amendment, unless, in the opinion of the Speaker, it raises legal, constitutional, or policy issues which were not raised by the previous invitation to the Chief Justice or by his response.

32. Special provisions with regard to measures affecting the Niue Public Service.

(1) The Niue Assembly shall not proceed upon any Bill or upon an amendment to any Bill, after its introduction, if, in the opinion of the Speaker, that Bill or that amendment makes provision concerning

- (*a*) The pay, allowances, discipline, control, and management of the Niue Public Service; or
- (*b*) The appointment, promotion, transfer, retirement, removal, suspension, and dismissal of employees of the Niue Public Service, including the review of or appeals against any decisions in relation thereto,

unless the Assembly has before it a report, made by the Niue Public Service Commission pursuant to this Article, on the legal, constitutional, and policy issues raised by that Bill or by that amendment.

(2) If, pursuant to this Article, the Assembly by resolution decides to request the Niue Public Service Commission to report in relation to a Bill or to an amendment, the Speaker shall cause to be sent to the Niue Public Service Commission a copy of that resolution, and an account of the Assembly's discussions thereon, together with a copy of that Bill or, as the case may be, of that amendment and of the Bill to which it relates; but, if the Assembly takes a contrary decision, the Bill or the amendment to which that decision relates shall lapse.

(3) When, pursuant to this Article, the Assembly has received the report of the Niue Public Service Commission in relation to a Bill or an amendment to a Bill, and a new or revised amendment is thereafter introduced, the requirements of this Article shall not apply in relation to that new or revised amendment, unless, in the opinion of the Speaker, it raises legal, constitutional, or policy issues which were not raised by the previous request to that Commission or by its report.

33. Special provisions with regard to measures affecting Niuean land.

(1) The Niue Assembly shall not proceed upon any Bill or upon an amendment to any Bill, after its introduction, if in the opinion of the Speaker, that Bill or that amendment makes provision concerning

- (*a*) The customary title to Niuean land; or
- (*b*) The alienation of Niuean land; or
- (*c*) The purchase, taking, or other acquistion of Niuean land for any public purpose; or
- (*d*) The constitution or jurisdiction of the Land Court or of the Land Appellate Court,

unless the Assembly has before it a report, made by a Commission of Inquiry, having such powers and authority to summon witnesses and to receive evidence as are conferred on a Commission of Inquiry by law, on the legal, constitutional, and policy issues raised by the Bill or by that amemdment.

(2) If the Assembly by resolution decides that any Bill or amendment to which this Article applies is worthy of consideration by a Commission of Inquiry pursuant to this Article, the Cabinet shall as soon as possible consider whether and in what manner it should act to enable effect to be given to the Assembly's decision; but, if the Assembly takes a contrary decision in relation to any such Bill or amendment, that Bill or that amendment shall lapse.

(3) Whenever the Assembly has by resolution decided that any Bill or amendment to which this Article applies is worthy of consideration by a Commission of Inquiry pursuant to this Article,

(*a*) The Cabinet may establish a Commission of Inquiry with appropriate terms of reference, or may make any necessary alteration in the terms of reference of a Commission of Inquiry already established to inquire into any matter affecting Niuean land; and the Premier shall as soon as possible inform the Assembly of any arrangement that has been made by the Cabinet to enable effect to be given to the Assembly's decision; and

(*b*) Whenever it appears that such an arrangement has been made by the Cabinet, the Speaker shall cause to be sent to the Commission of Inquiry designated by the Cabinet for the purpose of considering the Bill or the amendment to which the Assembly's resolution relates a copy of that resolution and an account of the Assembly's discussions thereon, together with a copy of the Bill or, as the case may be, a copy of the amendment and of the Bill to which it relates, and the Commission of Inquiry shall, pursuant to this Article, in due course make its report to the Assembly.

(4) When, pursuant to this Article, the Assembly has received the report of a Commission of Inquiry in relation to a Bill or to an amendment to a Bill and a new or revised amendment is thereafter introduced, the requirements of this Article shall not apply in relation to that new or revised amendment, unless, in the opinion of the Speaker, it raises legal, constitutional, or policy issues which were not raised by the previous report of that Commission of Inquiry.

(5) In this Article

'Alienation', in relation to the Niuean land, means the making or grant of any transfer, sale, gift, lease, licence, easement, profit, mortgage, charge, encumbrance, trust, or other disposition, whether absolute or limited, and whether legal or equitable; and includes a contract to make any such alienation; and also includes the surrender or variation of a lease, licence, easement, or profit and the variation of the terms of any other alienation as hereinbefore defined:

'Customary title' means title in accordance with the customs and usages of Niue:

'Niuean land' means land in Niue vested in the Crown but held by Niueans according to the customs and usages of Niue; and includes any land granted by the Crown in fee simple before the 1st day of April 1916 and any customary land declared to be Niuean freehold land or native freehold land by an order of any Court before the 1st day of November 1969.

34. When Bills become law.

(1) Subject to the requirements of Article *35* of this Constitution in those cases to which that Article applies, a bill shall become law if, and only if

(*a*) It has been passed by the Niue Assembly; and

(*b*) The Speaker, being satisfied that it has been passed in accordance with this Constitution and with the Standing Orders of the Assembly, has endorsed on a copy of the Bill a certificate of compliance with the requirements of this Article, and has, in the presence of the Clerk of the Niue Assembly, signed that certificate and sealed that copy with the Seal of Niue, and inscribed thereon the date of that signing and sealing; and

(*c*) The Clerk of the Niue Assembly has, in the presence of the Speaker countersigned the certificate on that copy of the Bill.

(2) A Bill which becomes law in accordance with the requirements of this Article, shall be an Act of the Niue Assembly.

(3) Subject to its provisions, an Act shall come into force on the date of its certification and sealing.

35. Power of the Niue Assembly to repeal or amend this Constitution.

(1) A Bill repealing or amending or modifying or extending any of the provisions of the Niue Constitution Act 1974 or of this Constitution or making any provision inconsistent with any of those provisions shall become law, if, and only if

(*a*) It has been passed by the Niue Assembly in compliance with the following requirements:

(i) On both the final reading, and on the reading which preceded it, the Bill receives the affirmative votes of not less than two thirds of the total membership of the Assembly, as provided in Article *16*(2)(*b*) of this Constitution; and

(ii) The vote on the final readings takes place at least 13 weeks after but excluding the day of the vote on the reading which preceded it; and

(*b*) It has thereafter been submitted to a poll, conducted in a manner prescribed by law, of the persons who at the time of that poll were entitled to vote as electors at a general election of members of the Niue Assembly, and has at that poll received the support

(i) In the case of any Bill repealing or amending or modifying or extending any of the provisions of sections 2 to 9 of the Niue Constitution Act 1974 or of Articles *1* to *69* of this Constitution or of this Article, by two thirds of the votes validly cast; and

(ii) In any other case, of a majority of the votes validly cast; and (*c*) The Speaker, being satisfied that it has been passed in accordance with this Constitution and with the Standing Orders of the Assembly, has endorsed on a copy of the Bill a certificate of compliance with the requirements of this Article, and has, in the presence of the Clerk of the Niue Assembly, signed that certificate and sealed that copy with the Seal of Niue, and inscribed thereon the date of that signing and sealing; and

(*d*) The Clerk of the Niue Assembly has, in the presence of the Speaker, countersigned the certificate on that copy of the Bill.

(2) A Bill which becomes law in accordance with the requirements of this Article shall be part of this Constitution and shall be described as a constitutional amendment.

(3) Subject to its provisions, a constitutional amendment shall come into force on the date of its certification and sealing.

36. New Zealand Parliament not to legislate for Niue, and New Zealand subordinate legislation not to apply to Niue, except with consent.

(1) No Act, and no provision of any Act, of the Parliament of New Zealand passed on or after Constitution Day shall extend to Niue as part of the law of Niue, unless

(*a*) The passing of that Act or the making of that provision, so far as it extends to Niue, has been requested and consented to by resolution of the Niue Assembly; and

(*b*) It is expressly declared in that Act that the Niue Assembly has requested and consented to the enactment of that Act or of that provision.

(2) No subordinate legislation made after Constitution Day pursuant to any Act of the Parliament of New Zealand shall extend to Niue as part of the law of Niue unless

(*a*) At the date of its making, the Act pursuant to which that subordinate legislation was made extends to Niue as part of the law of Niue; and

(*b*) The extension to Niue of that subordinate legislation has been requested and consented to by the Cabinet of Ministers of Niue; and

(*c*) It is expressly declared in that subordinate legislation that the Cabinet of Ministers of Niue has requested and consented to that extension.

(3) Any Act of the Parliament of New Zealand which, pursuant to this Article, extends to Niue as part of the law of Niue, shall have the same force and effect as if it were an Act of the Niue Assembly.

(4) In this Article the term 'subordinate legislation' means any Order in Council, Proclamation, regulations, rules, or other subordinate legislation.

PART III

THE JUDICIARY

The High Court of Niue

37. High Court established.

(1) There shall be a Court of record, to be called the High Court of Niue, for the administration of justice in Niue.

(2) The High Court shall have all such jurisdiction (both civil and criminal) as may be necessary to administer the law in force in Niue.

(3) No provision, except in an existing law, shall limit or restrict the jurisdiction or powers of the High Court, or confer exclusive jurisdiction on any other Court or tribunal, unless that provision is made by this Constitution or by Act.

38. Judges and Commissioners of the High Court.

(1) The High Court shall consist of the Chief Justice and such other Judges and such Commissioners as are from time to time appointed under this Constitution.

(2) A person shall not be qualified for appointment as Chief Justice or as another Judge or as a Commissioner of the High Court unless he possesses such qualifications as may, subject to this Constitution, be prescribed by Act.

39. Jurisdiction of Commissioners of the High Court.

(1) A Commissioner of the High Court shall possess and may exercise such of the functions of a Judge of the High Court (whether judicial or administrative, but excluding those vested exclusively in the Chief Justice) as may be prescribed by law, either generally or with respect to any particular Commissioner or Commissioners of that Court, and all references in any enactment to a Judge of the High Court shall be construed as applying to a Commissioner of the High Court within the limits of the jurisdiction so conferred on him.

(2) The office of Commissioner of the High Court may, with the approval of the Niue Public Service Commission, be held concurrently with the office of a Registrar of that Court or with any other office in the Niue Public Service, or may be held concurrently with any other position or employment, but a Commissioner of the High Court in the exercise of his functions shall not be under the control of the Niue Public Service Commission.

(3) Provision may be made by law for appeals from a Commissioner of the High Court to a Judge of that Court.

The Land Court of Niue

40. Land Court established. There shall be a Court of record, to be called the Land Court of Niue, which shall have the jurisdiction and powers conferred on it by existing law or by this Constitution or by Act.

41. Judges and Commissioners of the Land Court.

(1) The Land Court shall consist of a Chief Justice and such other Judges

and such Commissioners of that Court as are from time to time appointed under this Constitution.

(2) A person shall not be qualified for appointment as Chief Judge or as another Judge or as a Commissioner of the Land Court unless he possesses such qualifications as may, subject to this Constitution, be prescribed by Act.

42. Jurisdiction of Commissioners of the Land Court.

(1) A Commissioner of the Land Court shall possess and may exercise such of the functions of a Judge of the Land Court (whether judicial or administrative, but excluding those vested exclusively in the Chief Judge of that Court) as may be prescribed by law, either generally or with respect to any particular Commissioner or Commissioners of that Court, and all references in any enactment to a Judge of the Land Court shall be construed as applying to a Commissioner of the Land Court within the limits of the jurisdiction conferred upon him.

(2) The office of Commissioner of the Land Court may, with the approval of the Niue Public Service Commission, be held concurrently with any other office in the Niue Public Service other than the office of Registrar of that Court, or may be held concurrently with any other position or employment, but a Commissioner of the Land Court in the exercise of his functions shall not be under the control of the Niue Public Service Commission.

(3) Provision may be made by law for appeals from a Commissioner of the Land Court to a Judge of that Court.

The Land Appellate Court of Niue

43. Land Appellate Court of Niue. There shall be a Court of record, to be called the Land Appellate Court of Niue, which shall have the jurisdiction and powers conferred on it by existing law or by this Constitution or by Act.

44. Judges of the Land Appellate Court.

(1) The Chief Judge and the other Judges of the Land Court of Niue and the Chief Judge and the other Judges of the Maori Land Court of New Zealand shall be the Judges of the Land Appellate Court.

(2) Any 2 or more of the Judges (other than a Judge who determined the matter in dispute in the Land Court) shall have power to act as the Land Appellate Court but at least 2 Judges, or a majority of those Judges if the Court comprises more than 3 Judges, shall concur in every decision of that Court.

(3) The Chief Judge of the Land Court of Niue shall preside at any sitting of the Land Appellate Court at which he is present. In his absence the Chief Judge of the Maori Land Court of New Zealand, if present, shall preside, and in the absence of both of those Judges the Judge who is senior in terms of the date of his appointment to his present judicial office shall preside.

Appointment, Tenure of Office, and Salaries of Judges and Commissioners

45. Appointment of Judges and Commissioners.

(1) The Chief Justice and the other Judges of the High Court shall be appointed by the Governor General on the advice of the Cabinet.

(2) The Chief Judge and the other Judges of the Land Court and the Commissioners of the High Court or of the Land Court shall be appointed by the Cabinet.

(3) A person may be appointed as a Judge or Commissioner of the High Court or of the Land Court whether he holds any other judicial office, in Niue or elsewhere.

46. Tenure of office of Judges and Commissioners.

(1) Except in the case of an appointment made under Article *47* of this Constitution, no person who has attained the age of 68 years shall be appointed to or continue to hold office as a Judge or a Commissioner of the High Court or of the Land Court.

(2) Nothing done by a Judge or Commissioner of the High Court or of the Land Court in the performance of his functions shall be deemed to be invalid by reason only that he has reached the age at which he is required by this Article to retire, or, in the case of a Judge or Commissioner appointed under Article *47* of this Constitution, that his term of office has expired.

(3) A Judge or Commissioner of the High Court or of the Land Court may resign his office by writing under his hand addressed to the Premier.

47. Temporary Judges and Commissioners. The Cabinet may at any time appoint any person of any age who is otherwise qualified for appointment to hold office as Chief Justice or as another Judge or as a Commissioner of the High Court or as Chief Judge or as another Judge or as a Commissioner of the Land Court for such time, not exceeding one year, as is specified in his warrant of appointment.

48. Acting Chief Justice of the High Court and Acting Chief Judge of the Land Court.

(1) Where any vacancy exists in the office of Chief Justice, or it appears that the Chief Justice is, for any reason, for the time being unable to perform the functions of his office, those functions may be performed by another Judge of the High Court, and, if there is more than one such Judge who is able to perform those functions, then by the Judge who is senior in terms of the date of his appointment to that office, and that Judge may continue to perform those functions until a new Chief Justice is appointed and assumes office, or, as the case may be, until the Chief Justice is again able to perform the functions of his office.

(2) Where any vacancy exists in the office of Chief Judge of the Land Court or it appears that the Chief Judge is, for any reason, for the time being unable to perform the functions of his office, those functions may be performed by another Judge of the Land Court, and, if there is more than one such Judge who is able to perform those functions, then by the Judge who is senior in terms of the

date of his appointment to that office, and that Judge may continue to perform those functions until a new Chief Judge is appointed and assumes office, or, as the case may be, until the Chief Judge is again able to perform the functions of his office.

49. Removal of Judges and Commissioners from office.

(1) A Judge of the High Court shall not be removed from office except by the Governor General, acting on the advice of the Cabinet given in accordance with a recommendation contained in a resolution of the Niue Assembly.

(2) A Judge of the Land Court shall not be removed from office except by the Cabinet, acting in accordance with a recommendation contained in a resolution of the Niue Assembly.

(3) A Commissioner of the High Court or of the Land Court shall not be removed from office except by the Cabinet, acting in accordance with a recommendation of the Chief Justice.

(4) The only ground upon which any Judge or Commissioner may be removed from office is that of inability to discharge the functions of his office (whether arising from infirmity of body or mind or from any other cause) or of misbehavior.

50. Salaries of Judges and Commissioners.

(1) The Judges and Commissioners of the High Court or of the Land Court shall receive such salaries and allowances as may from time to time be prescribed by enactment; but, if any Judge or Commissioner is appointed on terms which do not require him to devote the whole of his time to performing the duties of that office, he shall receive, by way of salary and allowances, the amount that is appropriate, having regard to the extent of the duties he has performed and to the terms and conditions of his appointment.

(2) The salaries of the Judges and Commissioners shall be a charge upon the Niue Government Account.

(3) During the term of office of any Judge or Commissioner, his salary may be increased, whether to take account of any increase in general levels of remuneration or for any other reason, but his salary shall not during the term of his office be reduced, unless as part of a general reduction of salaries applied proportionately to all persons whose salaries are determined by enactments.

Appeals from the High Court

51. Appeal from High Court to Court of Appeal of New Zealand.

(1) Subject to this Constitution, an appeal shall lie to the Court of Appeal of New Zealand from a final judgment of the High Court

(*a*) As of right, if the High Court certifies that the case involves a substantial question of law as to the interpretation or effect of any provision of this Constitution:

(*b*) As of right, from any conviction by the High Court in the exercise of its criminal jurisdiction whereby the appellant has been sentenced to imprisonment for a term exceeding 6 months or to a fine of not less than $200, and from any such sentence (not being a sentence fixed by law) :

(*c*) As of right, when the matter in dispute on the appeal amounts to or is of the value of $400 or upwards:

(*d*) With the leave of the High Court in any other case, if in the opinion of that Court the question involved in the appeal is one which by reason of its general or public importance, or of the magnitude of the interests affected, or for any other reason, ought to be submitted to bhe Court of Appeal of New Zealand for decision.

(2) Notwithstanding anything in sub-clause (1) of this Article, the Court of Appeal of New Zealand may, in any case in which it thinks fit and at any time, grant leave to appeal to that Court from any final judgment of the High Court, subject to such conditions as to security for costs and otherwise as the Court of Appeal thinks fit.

52. Transmission of order of Court of Appeal on appeal. The determination of the Court of Appeal of New Zealand on any appeal from the High Court under Article *51* of this Constitution shall be transmitted to the Registrar of the High Court by the Registrar of the Court of Appeal under the Seal of the Court of Appeal, and judgment shall thereupon be entered by the High Court in conformity with that determination, or such other proceedings by way of new trial or otherwise shall be taken in the High Court as are required by that determination.

Justices of the Peace

53. Justices of the Peace.

(1) The Cabinet may appoint Justices of the Peace for Niue, who shall hold office for such time as may be prescribed in their warrants of appointment.

(2) Any 2 Justices of the Peace for Niue, acting together, shall possess and may exercise in Niue any of the functions that are by law conferred generally on Commissioners of the High Court; and Article *39* of this Constitution, with the necessary modifications, shall apply as if references therein to a Commissioner of the High Court were references to any 2 Justices of the Peace for Niue; but this subclause shall not apply in the case of any Justice of the Peace who is a member of the Niue Assembly or has attained the age of 68 years.

(3) A Justice of the Peace for Niue shall not be removed from office except by the Cabinet acting in accordance with a recommendation of the Chief Justice.

(4) Justices of the Peace for Niue shall receive, in respect of any duties they perform, such remuneration as may from time to time be prescribed by enactment.

Oath of Allegiance and Judicial Oath

54. Oath of Allegiance and Judicial Oath.

(1) Every Judge or Commissioner of the High Court, every Justice of the Peace for Niue, every Judge or Commissioner of the Land Court, and every Judge of the Land Appellate Court who is not also a Judge of the Land Court (being persons appointed to those offices on or after Constitution Day) shall, before performing the functions of his office, take and subscribe the Oath of Allegiance and the Judicial Oath prescribed in sub-clauses (2) and (3) of this Article, respectively, before the following person:

(*a*) In the case of the Chief Justice or of any other Judge or any Commissioner of the High Court, before a Judge of the High Court or before the Premier:

(*b*) In the case of the Chief Judge or any other Judge or any Commissioner of the Land Court, or of a Judge of the Land Appellate Court, before a Judge of the High Court of of the Land Court, or before the Premier:

(*c*) In the case of any Justice of the Peace for Niue, before any Judge or Commissioner of the High Court.

(2) The Oath of Allegiance shall be in the following form

I, ..., swear by Almighty God that I will be faithful and bear true allegiance to Her (*or* His) Majesty [*Specify the name of the reigning sovereign as thus: Queen Elizabeth the Second*] Her (*or* His) heirs and successors in accordance with the Constitution and the law. So help me God.

(3) The Judicial Oath shall be in the following form

I, ..., swear by Almighty God that I will well and truly serve Her (*or* His) Majesty [*Specify as above*] Her (*or* His) heirs and successors, in accordance with the Constitution and the law, in the office of ....; and I will do right to all manner of people, without fear or favor, affection or ill will. So help me God.

(4) No proceedings before any judicial officer or officers to whom this Article applies shall be questioned in any court solely on the ground that any one or more of those judicial officers have failed to comply with a requirement of this Article.

Comment by Chief Justice on Certain Bills

55. Chief Justice to comment on certain Bills. Whenever, pursuant to Article *31* of this Constitution, the Chief Justice is invited to comment on the legal, constitutional, and policy issues raised by any Bill or amendment, he shall as soon as possible, and in any case within one month after receiving the papers relating to the Bill or amendment, respond to that invitation, either by furnishing his comments to the Speaker, or by informing the Speaker that there are no comments which he considers should be made, or, if he requires further time or imformation before forming a final opinion, by making that known to the Speaker.

PART IV

THE PUBLIC REVENUES OF NIUE

56. Legislative control of public revenue and expenditure.

(1) No taxes shall be imposed except by law.

(2) All revenue received by the Government of Niue shall be paid into an appropriate public fund or account; and every such fund or account, unless established by existing law, shall be established by or pursuant to Act.

(3) All expenditure of public money, unless authorized by existing law, shall be authorized by Act.

57. Niue Government Account.

(1) There shall be a Niue Government Account.

(2) All taxes and other revenues and money raised or received by the Government of Niue shall be paid into the Niue Government Account, unless required or permitted by law to be paid into any other public fund or account.

58. Annual estimates and appropriations.

(1) Except as provided in Article *59*(4)(*b*) of this Constitution or where authorized by a specific appropriation contained in any existing law or in any Act, all expenditure of public money in any financial year shall be charged to votes specified in the Appropriation Act and in accordance with the estimates for that year.

(2) Each Appropriation Act shall relate to one financial year, and shall lapse at the end of that year.

59. Cabinet to supervise expenditure.

(1) It shall be the responsibility of the Cabinet to make proposals to the Assembly as to the projected levels of public revenue and of public expenditure in each financial year, and as to all other budgetary matters. In particular, the Premier or another Minister shall introduce or take responsibility in the Assembly for all Bills relating to financial measures, and for the submission of a detailed statement of estimated expenditure in respect of each financial year.

(2) The Cabinet shall also be accountable to the Assembly for all public expenditure, and for relating such expenditure to the appropriations made by the Assembly pursuant to Article *58* of this Constitution, or to any discretion to approve expenditure pursuant to sub-clause (4) of this Article, and shall lay the accounts for each financial year before the Assembly.

(3) Any delegation by the Cabinet, whether or not to one or more of its own members, of the power to approve public expenditure shall, subject to existing law, be made by or pursuant to Act, and shall be without prejudice to the generality of the Cabinet's continuing responsibilities under this Article.

(4) Subject to such lower limits and such restrictions as may from time to time be prescribed by any enactment, the Cabinet may approve the expenditure of such sums as it considers necessary

(*a*) In anticipation of provision to be made in the Appropriation Act for any financial year; but the total amount issued and paid under this paragraph in relation to any vote in any financial year shall not exceed the unexpended balance of the corresponding vote in the Appropriation Act for the preceding financial year, together with an amount equal to one fourth of that vote, and all money so spent shall be included in the estimates for that year; or

(*b*) Where, during the period between the passing of the Appropriation Act for any financial year and the end of that financial year, it is desirable that money should be expended in excess of or without the appropriation of the Niue assembly, but the total amount of all sums issued and paid under this paragraph in any financial year shall not exceed 1½ percent of the total amount of all sums appropriated by the Appropriation Act for that financial year.

(5) All expenditure made under sub-clause (4)(*b*) of this Article shall be charged as unauthorized expenditure to the appropriate fund or account.

(6) A statement of the unauthorized expenditure for any financial year shall be included in the accounts for that year laid before the Assembly.

60. Audit.

(1) The Audit Office of New Zealand shall be the auditor of the Niue Government Account and of all other public funds or accounts, and of the accounts of all Departments and Offices of executive government, and of such other public or statutory authorities or bodies as may be provided by law.

(2) The Audit Office shall, at least once annually, prepare and forward to the Speaker of the Niue Assembly for presentation to the Assembly a report containing such information as is required to be submitted by any enactment, together with such other information relating to the Niue Government Account, or to such other funds or accounts which under this Constitution or under any enactment are required to be audited by the Audit Office, as that office considers desirable.

PART V

HEALTH, EDUCATION, AND OTHER SOCIAL SERVICES

61. Health, education, and other social services.

(1) The Cabinet shall be responsible for establishing and maintaining in Niue such hospitals and other institutions and for providing such other services as it considers necessary for the public health.

(2) The Cabinet shall be responsible for establishing and maintaining in Niue such public schools and for making such other provision as it considers necessary to provide educational opportunities for the people of Niue.

(3) The Cabinet shall be responsible for establishing and maintaining such other institutions and services and for making such other provisions as it considers necessary to provide a reasonable standard of living for the people of Niue and to secure their economic, social, and cultural welfare.

(4) Nothing in this Article shall be construed as limiting the powers conferred on the Cabinet by Article *2* of this Constitution to exercise on behalf of Her Majesty the executive authority of Niue.

PART VI

THE NIUE PUBLIC SERVICE

62. Niue Public Service.

(1) There shall be a Niue Public Service comprising such employees as may be necessary to assist the Cabinet in exercising the executive authority of Niue and to perform such other functions or exercise such powers as may be prescribed by law.

(2) Except as provided in sub-clause (4) of this Article, no person shall be employed in the service of the Government of Niue unless he is an employee of the Niue Public Service.

(3) Except as may otherwise be provided by Act, employment by a public corporation or other statutory authority or public body constituted under the law of Niue shall, for the purposes of this Article, be considered as employment in the service of the Government of Niue.

(4) Sub-clause (2) of this Article shall not apply to service remunerated by way of fees or commission only, or honorary service, or service as

(*a*) A Judge or Commissioner of the High Court or of the Land Court, a Judge of the Land Appellate Court, a Justice of the Peace of Niue, or any other judicial officer appointed by or pursuant to existing law or Act; or

(*b*) A Minister, or any other member or the Speaker of the Niue Assembly; or

(*c*) A member of the Niue Public Service Commission.

63. Secretary to the Government.

(1) There shall be an officer of the Niue Public Service to be called the Secretary to the Government, who shall be the permanent head of the Niue Public Service and the chief administrative officer of the Government of Niue.

(2) In addition to the other functions and powers conferred upon him by law, the Secretary to the Government shall be responsible to the Cabinet for the general direction of the work of all departments and offices of the executive government. The head of each Department or office shall account for the work of that Department or office to the Secretary to the Government, as well as to the Minister primarily responsible for that Department or office or, as the case may be, for the function performed by that Department or office.

(3) Notwithstanding anything in Article *69*(2) of this Constitution, the Niue Public Service Commission shall consult the Premier and shall obtain the concurrence of the Cabinet before it appoints any person to be Secretary to the Government.

(4) Notwithstanding anything in any enactment, no appeal by any employee of the Niue Public Service shall lie against the promotion or appointment of any person to the office of Secretary to the Government.

Niue Public Service Commission

64. Niue Public Service Commission.

(1) There shall be a Public Service Commission for Niue, to be called the Niue Public Service Commission, which shall be constitued as follows

- (*a*) The Chairman of the New Zealand State Services Commission shall be the Chairman of the Niue Public Service Commission:
- (*b*) Another member of the New Zealand State Services Commission shall be appointed by that Commission to hold office as a member of the Niue Public Service Commission:
- (*c*) A person having special knowledge of Niue shall be appointed by the New Zealand State Services Commission with the concurrence of the Cabinet to hold office for a term of not more than 5 years but shall be eligible for reappointment.

(2) Notice of every appointment to the Niue Public Service Commission shall be published in the *Niue Gazette.*

(3) The following provisions shall apply with respect to the member of the Niue Public Service Commission appointed under sub-clause (1)(*c*) of this Article:

- (*a*) He shall be paid such remuneration as the Cabinet determines from time to time on the recommendation of the New Zealand State Services Commission:
- (*b*) He may resign his office by notice in writing to the New Zealand State Services Commission, or he may be removed from office by that Commission with the concurrence of the Cabinet on the ground that he is unable to discharge the functions of his office (whether by reason of infirmity of body or mind or from any other cause).

65. Acting members of Commission.

(1) In the event of the incapacity, by reason of illness or absence or any other cause, of the Chairman of the New Zealand State Services Commission, or if the office of the Chairman of that Commission is vacant, the member of the New Zealand State Services Commission for the time being acting as the Chairman of that Commission shall also act as the Chairman of the Niue Public Services Commission during that incapacity or vacancy.

(2) In the event of the incapacity, by reason of illness or absence or any other cause, of the other member of the New Zealand State Services Commission who is a member of the Niue Public Service Commission, the New Zealand State Services Commission may appoint another of its members to act for that member during that incapacity.

(3) In the event of the incapacity, by reason of illness or absence or any

other cause, of the member of the Niue Public Service Commission appointed under Article *64*(1)(*c*) of this Constitution, or if the office of that member is vacant, the New Zealand State Services Commission, with the concurrence of the Cabinet may appoint a person to act in place of that member during that incapacity or vacancy.

(4) Any person acting in place of a member of the Niue Public Service Commission pursuant to this Article shall be deemed for all purposes to be a member of the Commission, and no appointment of any such person, and no act done by him in his capacity as a member of the Commission, shall in any proceedings be questioned on the ground that the occasion for his appointment had not arisen or had ceased.

66. Procedure of Commission.

(1) At all meetings of the Niue Public Service Commission, 2 members shall form a quorum.

(2) The Commission shall have power to invite such other persons as it thinks fit to assist in its deliberations.

(3) At least 2 members of the Commission shall concur in any decision of the Commission.

(4) Any matter which may be decided by the Commission at a meeting may also be decided by a minute of the Commission signed by all the members.

(5) Subject to this Constitution, the Commission shall regulate its own procedure.

67. Delegation of powers.

(1) Without prejudice to its continuing responsibility for the organization and management of the Niue Public Service, the Commission may from time to time, either generally or particularly, delegate any of its powers in relation to the Niue Public Service (including this power of delegation) to any of its members or any other person who, in either case, is visiting Niue on the Commission's business or to the Secretary to the Government.

(2) Subject to any general or special directions given by the Commission, a person in the same manner and with the same effect as if they had been conferred on him directly by enactment and not be delegation.

(3) Every person purporting to act pursuant to any delegation under this Article shall, in the absence of proof to the contrary, be presumed to be acting in accordance with the terms of the delegation.

(4) Any delegation under this section may be made to a specified person or to persons of a specified class, or may be made to the holder for the time being of a specified office.

(5) The delegation of any powers under this section shall not prevent the exercise of those powers by the Commission or by any person making the delegation.

Management of Niue Public Service

68. Functions and powers of Commission.

(1) The Niue Public Service Commission shall be the employing authority for the Niue Public Service, and, subject to this Constitution, shall have the general oversight and control of its organization and management, and shall be responsible for reviewing the efficiency and economy of all departments and offices of the executive government.

(2) Subject to this Constitution and to any enactment, the Commission may prescribe and determine the terms and conditions of employment of members of the Niue Public Service, and may issue such instructions or exercise such other powers as may be necessary to enable it to perform the functions and carry out the duties described in this Constitution or conferred on it by law.

(3) In the performance or exercise of its functions, powers, and duties in relation to the Niue Public Service, the Commission may conduct such inquires and investigations as it considers necessary and, for the purpose of conducting any such inquiry or investigation, the Commission shall have such powers and authority to summon witnesses and to receive evidence as are conferred on a Commission of Inquiry by law.

(4) Except as provided in Article *69*(2) of this Constitution, the Commission shall be responsible to the Cabinet for the carrying out of its duties and the performance and exercise of its functions and powers, and the Commission shall, as necessary, inform and advise the Cabinet in relation to any matter affecting the Niue Public Service.

(5) The Commission shall as soon as practicable after the 31st day of March in each year furnish to the Cabinet a report on the state of the efficiency and economy of the Niue Public Service and on the work of the Commission for the year ending with that date. A copy of that report shall be laid before the Niue Assembly.

69. Appointments to Niue Public Service.

(1) All employees of the Niue Public Service shall be appointed by the Niue Public Service Commission and, subject to this Constitution and to any enactment, shall hold office on such terms and conditions as may from time to time be prescribed or determined by the Commission.

(2) In all matters relating to decisions about individual employees (whether thery relate to the appointment, promotion, demotion, transfer, disciplining, or cessation of employment of any employee or any other matter) the Commission shall not receive any direction from the Cabinet, but shall act independently.

(3) In establishing and revising the terms and conditions of employment in the Niue Public Service, the factors to be taken into account shall include

(*a*) The need for the Niue Public Service to recruit and retain an efficient staff, and, in particular, to provide varied careers and adequate advancement for Niueans with special skills:

(*b*) The need to afford reasonable opportunities of employment in

Niue for the people of Niue, and in so doing to have regard to the employment opportunities and levels of remuneration available in New Zealand:

(*c*) The need to act consistently with Government economic and social policy, bearing in mind that the terms and conditions of employment in the Niue Public Service are a major element in the general well-being of Niue.

(4) The pay and allowances of employees of the Niue Public Service shall be paid from the Niue Government Account out of money appropriated by the Niue Assembly.

Reports and Recommendations to Assembly

70. Commission to make certain reports and recommendations to Assembly.

(1) Pursuant to Article *25* of this Constitution, the Niue Public Service Commission shall from time to time consider whether circumstances require the making of a report and recommendations to the Assembly as to the levels of remuneration and other entitlements of the Premier, the other Ministers the members of the Assembly who are not Ministers, and the Speaker, and the Commission shall make such a report and recommendations, whenever there is a general alteration of the levels of remuneration of employees of the Niue Public Service.

(2) The Commission shall send to the Speaker any report and recommendations made under sub-clause (1) of this Article.

(3) Whenever, pursuant to Article *32* of this Constitution, the Niue Public Service Commission is requested to report on the legal, constitutional, and policy issues raised by any Bill or amendment, it shall as soon as possible, and in any case within one month after receiving the papers relating to the Bill or amendment, respond to that request either by furnishing its report to the Speaker, or, if it requires further time or imformation before forming a final opinion, by making that known to the Speaker.

PART VII

TRANSITIONAL PROVISIONS

71. Existing law to continue. Subject to this Constitution,

(*a*) The existing law shall, until repealed, and subject to any amendment thereof, continue in force on and after Consitution Day:

(*b*) All rights, obligations, and liabilities arising under the existing law shall continue to exist on and after Constitution Day, and shall be recognised, exercised, and enforced accordingly.

72. Premier and Cabinet.

(1) The Leader of Government holding office pursuant to section 9 of the Niue Act 1966 (as substituted by section 3 of the Niue Amendment Act 1971)

immediately before Constitution Day shall be deemed to have been duly elected under this Constitution as the Premier of Niue and appointed and sworn in as a Minister under this Constitution.

(2) The other appointed members of the Executive Committee of Niue holding office pursuant to section 10 of the Niue Act 1966 (as substituted by section 3 of the Niue Amendment Act 1971) immediately before Constitution Day shall be deemed to have been duly appointed and sworn in under this Constitution as Ministers.

73. Niue Assembly.

(1) The elected members of the Niue Island Assembly immediately before Constitution Day shall be deemed to have been duly elected and sworn in under this Constitution as members of the Niue Assembly, and, notwithstanding anything in Article *16* of this Constitution, the Niue Assembly shall consist, during the period commencing on Constitution Day and ending at the time of the first dissolution of the Assembly thereafter, of the Speaker and those members.

(2) Until provision is otherwise made by law, the seat of any member of the Niue Assembly to whom Article *19*(*b*) of this Constitution applies shall not become vacant if

(*a*) His interest in the execution or enjoyment of any contract under which any public money is payable is as a member of the general public or of any section or class of the general public; or

(*b*) On any occasion when he is present at a meeting of the Niue Assembly, any matter concerning a contract in whose execution or enjoyment he is interested comes before the Assembly, he discloses his interest to the Assembly and refrains from otherwise speaking and from voting on that matter.

(3) The Speaker of the Niue Island Assembly who is in office immediately before Constitution Day shall be deemed to have been duly elected and sworn in as Speaker of the Niue Assembly under this Constitution.

(4) Any person becoming a member of the Niue Assembly pursuant to sub-clause (1) of this Article who has, in the absence of the Speaker of the Niue Island Assembly, presided over any sitting of that Assembly shall, for the purposes of Article *20* of this Constitution, be deemed to be a member of the Niue Assembly who has presided over a meeting of the Assembly.

(5) Notwithstanding anything in Article *22*(6) of this Constitution, business may be transacted at any meeting of the Niue Assembly duirng the period referred to in sub-clause (1) of this Article if, but only if, the number of members present is not less than 7.

(6) Any Bill or other business before Niue Island Assembly immediately before Constitution Day shall not lapse, but shall become a Bill or other business before the Niue Assembly:

Provided that, where any Bill or amendment to a Bill before the Niue Island Assembly pursuant to this sub-clause has proceeded beyond its introduction and is one to which one or more of Articles, *25, 30, 31, 32,* and *33* of this Constitution applies, the Niue Assembly shall not proceed further upon a Bill or amendment unless the requirements of the applicable Article or Articles have first been met.

(7) Subject to this Constitution, the Standing Orders of the Niue Island Assembly in force immediately before Constitution Day shall be the Standing Orders of the Niue Assembly, and they may be amended, repealed, or added to under Article *22*(10) of this Constitution.

(8) Until an Act first passed pursuant to Article *25* of this Constitution comes into force, the Niue Civil List Regulations 1972 shalll continue in full force and effect and shall be deemed to be repealed on the date on which that Act comes into force.

(9) For the purposes of Article *26*(1) of this Constitution, the date of the last preceding general election shall be the date of the last preceding general election of the Niue Island Assembly in being on Constitution Day.

74. The High Court.

(1) The High Court of Niue established by Article *37* of this Constitution is hereby declared to be the same Court as the High Court of Niue established by section 53 of the Niue Act 1966.

(2) The High Court is hereby declared also to be the same Court as every other Court which, under existing law, was deemed to be the same Court as the High Court of Niue established by section 53 of the Niue Act 1966.

(3) All judgments, decrees, records, and acts of the High Court of Niue as established by the said section 53 and of every other Court to which sub-clause (2) of this Article applies shall continue to have full force and effect on and after Constitution Day as judgments, decrees. records, and acts of the High Court established by this Constitution; and all proceedings, civil or criminal, pending in the High Court of Niue immediately before Constitution Day may be continued on and after Constitution Day in the High Court established by this Constitution.

(4) The Judges and Commissioners of the High Court of Niue in office immediately before Consitution Day (other than the Resident Commissioner of Niue) shall continue to hold office on and after Constitution Day as Judges or Commissioners of the High Court establshed by this Constitution, as if they had been appointed under this Constitution, and those Judges and Commissioners shall receive the salaries and allowances to which they were entitled immediately before Constitution Day as if those salaries and allowances had been prescribed by enactment pursuant to Article *50* of this Constitution.

75. The Land Court.

(1) The Land Court of Niue established by Article *40* of this Constitution is hereby declared to be the same Court as the Land Court of Niue established by section 335 of the Niue Act 1966.

(2) The Land Court is hereby declared also to be the same Court as every other Court which, under existing law, was deemed to be the same Court as the Land Court of Niue established by the said section 335.

(3) All judgments, decrees, records, and acts of the Land Court of Niue as established by the said section 335 and of every other Court to which sub-clause (2)

of this Article applies shall continue to have full force and effect on and after Constitution Day as judgments, decrees, records, and acts of the Land Court established by this Constitution; and all proceedings pending in the Land Court of Niue established by the said section 335 immediately before Constitution Day may be continued on and after Constitution Day in the Land Court established by this Constitution.

(4) The Judges and Commissioners of the Land Court of Niue (other than the Resident Commissioner) in office immediately before Constitution Day shall hold office on and after Constitution Day as Judges or Commissioners of the Land Court established by this Constitution, as if they had been appointed under this Constitution, and those Judges and Commissioners shall receive the salaries and allowances to which they were entitled immediatley before Constitution Day as if those salaries and allowances had been prescribed by enactment pursuant to Article *50* of this Constitution.

76. The Land Appellate Court.

(1) The Land Appellate Court of Niue established by Article *43* of this Constitution is hereby declared to be the same Court as the Land Appellate Court of Niue established by section 386 of the Niue Act 1966.

(2) The Land Appellate Court is hereby declared also to be the same Court as every other Court which, under existing law, was deemed to be the same Court as the Land Appellate Court of Niue established by the said section 386.

(3) All judgments, decrees, records, and acts of the Land Appellate Court of Niue as established by the said section 386 and of every other Court to which sub-clause (2) of this Article applies shall continue in full force and effect on and after Constitution Day as judgments, decrees, records and acts of the Land Appellate Court established by this Constitution; and all proceedings pending in the Land Appellate Court of Niue established by the said section 386 immediately before Constitution Day may be continued on and after Constitution Day in the Land Appellate Court established by this Constitution.

77. Appeals from High Court.

(1) In any case in which, immediately before Constitution Day, an appeal to the Supreme Court of New Zealand from any final judgment of the High Court of Niue established by section 53 of the Niue Act 1966 was pending, that appeal may be continued on and after Constitution Day and shall otherwise in all respects be heard and disposed of in accordance with the existing law; and the determination of the Supreme Court on any appeal continued pursuant to this sub-clause shall be transmitted to the Registrar of the High Court by the Registrar of the Supreme Court under the seal of the Supreme Court, and the High Court shall act in respect thereof as if it were a determination of the Court of Appeal of New Zealand transmitted under Article *52* of this Constitution.

(2) In any other case where any final judgment of the High Court of Niue established by the said section 53 has been given before Constitution Day, the right of appeal from that final judgment shall be governed by the provisions of this Constitution as if that final judgment had been a final judgment of the High Court of Niue established by Article *37* of this Constitution.

78. Justices of the Peace.

(1) Every person holding office immediately before Constitution Day as a Justice of the Peace for Niue shall continue in office as if he had been appointed to that office pursuant to Article *53* of this Constitution.

(2) Subject to Article *53*(3) of this Constitution, every such person shall continue to hold office during the pleasure of the Cabinet and shall be paid the remuneration to which he was entitled immediately before Constitution Day as if that remuneration had been prescribed by enactment pursuant to Article *53*(4) of this Constitution.

79. Public revenues.

(1) The Niue Government Account established by Article *56* of this Constitution is hereby declared to be the same account as the Niue Assembly Account established by section 15 of the Niue Act 1966; and all money in the last-mentioned account immediately before Constitution Day shall on and after Constitution Day be deemed to form part of the Niue Government Account.

(2) The reference in Article *59*(4) of this Constitution to the Appropriation Act for the preceding financial year shall be read as if it included a reference to the Appropriation Ordinance of the Niue Island Assembly for the preceding financial year.

80. The Niue Public Service.

(1) The Niue Public Service established by Article *62* of this Constitution is hereby declared to be the same Service as the Niue Public Service constituted by Part XXXI of the Niue Act 1966.

(2) Every person who was an employee of the Niue Public Service immediately before Constitution Day shall continue to hold office as an employee of the Niue Public Service as if he had been appointed to that position by the Niue Public Service Commission pursuant to Article *69* of this Constitution.

(3) Where any public corporation or other statutory authority or public body has been constituted before Constitution Day under the law of Niue, nothing in Article *62*(3) of this Constitution shall, in the case of any appointment made before Constitution Day of any person as an employee of that public corporation or other statutory authority or public body, be construed as affecting the validity of that appointment or, in the case of any such appointment made after Constitution Day, be construed as requiring that appointment to be made by the Niue Public Service Commission, except to the extent that, under existing law that appointment was required to be made by the New Zealand State Services Commission.

(4) Where under this Constitution the holder of any office is required to be an employee of the Niue Public Serivce, any employee of the Niue Public Service holding the corresponding office immediately before Constitution Day shall be deemed to be the holder of that office; but this provision shall be without prejudice to the powers and discretions of the Niue Public Service Commission as the employing authority.

81. Seal of Niue. Until the Cabinet approves of a different form or forms, the

Seal of Niue established by Article *15* of this Constitution shall be in the form or forms approved by the Executive Committee for the Seal of Niue established by section 7 of the Niue Act 1966 (as substituted by section 3 of the Niue Amendment Act 1971).

PART VIII

INTERPRETATION

82. Interpretation.

(1) In this Constitution, unless the context otherwise requires,

'Act' means an Act of the Niue Assembly, as that term is used in Article *34* of this Constitution:

'Cabinet' means the Cabinet of Ministers of Niue established by Article *2* of this Constitution:

'Chief Justice' means the Chief Justice of the High Court of Niue appointed under Article *45* of this Constitution; and includes any other Judge of the High Court authorized under Article *48* of this Constitution to perform the office or exercise any function of the Chief Justice:

'Clerk of the Cabinet' means the Clerk of the Cabinet appointed pursuant to Article *14* of this Constitution:

'Clerk of the Niue Assembly' means the Clerk of the Niue Assembly appointed pursuant to Article *27* of this Constitution:

'Constitution' means this Constitution; and includes the Act of Parliament of New Zealand intituled the Niue Constitution Act 1974; and also includes any constitutional amendment, as that term is used in Article *35* of this Constitution, when that constitutional amendment has come into force:

'Constitution Day' means the date on which this Constitution comes into force:

'Enactment' means

(*a*) Any Act of the Niue Assembly and any Ordinance; and any regulation, rule, bylaw, or other instrument of a like nature made pursuant to any such Act or Ordinance:

(*b*) Any Act of the Parliament of New Zealand which extends to Niue as part of the law of Niue; and any Order in Council, Proclamation, regulation, rule, ministerial warrant, bylaw, or instrument of a like nature, made pursuant to any Act to which this paragraph applies, if that Order in Council, Proclamation, regulation, rule, ministrial warrant, bylaw, or other instrument extends to Niue as part of the law of Niue:

'Existing law' means any law in force in Niue immediately before Constitution Day; and includes any enactment passed or made before Constitution Day and coming into force on or after Constitution Day:

'High Court' means the High Court of Niue established by Article *37* of this Constitution:

'Judge', in relation to the High Court, means any Judge of that Court including the Chief Justice, and in relation to the Land Court, means any Judge of that Court including the Chief Judge of that Court:

'Land Appellate Court' means the Land Appellate Court of Niue established by Article *43* of this Constitution:

'Land Court' means the Land Court of Niue established by Article *40* of this Constitution:

'Law' means any law for the time being in force in Niue; and includes this Constitution and any enactment:

'Member of the Niue Assembly', or 'Member' used in relation to the Niue Assembly, means any person elected as a member of the Assembly pursuant to Article *16* of this Constitution; but does not include the Speaker; and, in any case where the Assembly has been dissolved, shall have the extended meaning given to that term by sub-clause (4) of that Article:

'Minister' means a member of the Cabinet; and includes the Premier; and also includes any member of the Niue Assembly appointed as a temporary Minister pursuant to Article *8* of this Constitution:

'Niue Assembly' or 'Assembly' means the Niue Assembly established by Article *16* of this Constitution:

'Niue Public Service' means the Niue Public Service established by Article *62* of this Constitution:

'Niue Public Service Commission' or 'Commission' means the Niue Public Service Commission established by Article *64* of this Constitution:

'Ordinance' means an Ordinance of the Niue Island Assembly or of the Island Council of Niue:

'Premier' means the member of the Niue Assembly elected as Premier pursuant to Article *4* of this Constitution after he has been appointed as a Minister pursuant to Article *5* of this Constitution; and includes the Minister discharging the functions of Premier pursuant to sub-clause (1) or sub-clause (2) of Article *9* of this Constitution:

'Secretary to the Government' means the Secretary to the Government of Niue appointed pursuant to Article *63* of this Constitution:

'Speaker' means the Speaker of the Niue Assembly elected pursuant to Article *20* of this Constitution; and includes any member of the Niue Assembly performing the functions of Speaker pursuant to that Article.

(2) Where in this Constitution any person is required to subscribe an oath, he shall be permitted, if he so desires, to comply with that requirement by making and subscribing an affirmation, and the form of oath prescribed by this Constitution shall be appropriately modified accordingly.

(3) Where under this Constitution the holder of any office is an employee of the Niue Public Service, any reference to the holder of that office shall be construed as including, to the extent of his authority, a reference to any other employee of the Niue Public Service for the time being authorized to exercise or perform all or any of the powers, duties, and functions of that office.

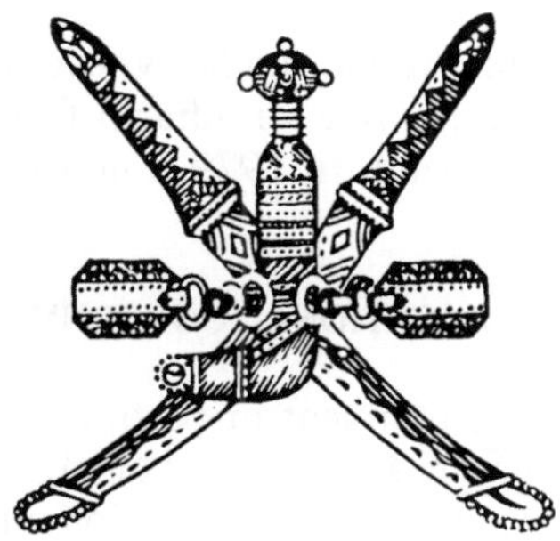

OMAN

SUMMARY

INTERNATIONAL STATUS

Oman is a member of the United Nations (October 7, 1971). It is a member of the Organization of Arab States, the Gulf Co-operation Council and of other international organizations.

Muscat and Oman (in 1970, the name became Oman) has been an independent sultanate since 1650, when it expelled the Portuguese who had established themselves in the coastal regions from 1508 onwards. The sultanate, which until the mid-nineteenth century was the most powerful state in Arabia, resisted Persian attempts at hegemony and extended its conquests to Zanzibar and the Portuguese east African settlements. These were separated from the sultanate in 1861, but continued to pay an annual subsidy until Zanzibar's independence in 1964. Since 1798, by a series of treaties, Oman was in a special relationship with Great Britain which provided military protection against external and internal enemies in exchange for control of foreign policy, commerce and petrol. By the 1951 treaty of friendship, commerce and navigation, the United Kingdom expressly recognized the sultanate as an independent state. The country was kept in strict isolation from all foreign or modernizing influences under the rule of the Sultan who reigned from 1932 to 1970, with only British military and petroleum personnel admitted into Oman, and Omans forbidden to travel abroad. The need for modernization subsequent to the development of petroleum production in the 1960's led to a conflict of interest between the petroleum companies and the sultan and he was deposed in favor of his son on July 23, 1970. The new sultan's first aims were to modernize the country and to liquidate the Dhofar rebellion. The latter had begun in 1965, in the southern province of Dhofar under the Marxist oriented People's Democratic Front for the Liberation of Oman. It was brought to an end with Iranian military assistance by the ceasefire arranged by Saudi Arabia, under which amnesty was granted to the PFLO fighters, and Iranian troops were withdrawn from Dhofar. In 1977, British troops withdrew from Masirah Island. In 1979, a new five year modernization plan was put into operation.

FORM OF NATIONAL GOVERNMENT

There is no constitution or parliament or parties in Oman. The sultan rules by decree and with the advice of an appointed cabinet. In pursuit of his policy of preparing his compatriots for decisive participation in the government's efforts to carry out its plans for the furtherance of social and economic growth in the country and for the sake of close co-operation between the government and civil sectors, Royal Decrees of October 18, 1981, established a Consultative Assembly of State. It is advisory in nature. Of the not more than 45 appointed representatives, 17 represent the government sector, 28 the civil sector of which 11 are from the private sector and 17 from the provinces. Their term of office is two years and is renewable. It meets in four sessions a year and *in camera*. Freedom of speech inside the Assembly is guaranteed. The organization of the Assembly is described.

Sharia courts apply Islamic law. The court of appeal is located in Muscat.

AREA, POPULATION, ETC.

The area of Oman is approximately 300,000 kilometres, the population 1,500,000 (1981 estimate). The capital is Muscat.

OMAN

ROYAL DECREE NO. 81/84 ON THE FORMATION OF A CONSULTATIVE ASSEMBLY OF STATE[1]

October 18, 1981

We, Qabus bin Sa'id, Sultan of Oman, further to establish our policy of preparing our compatriots for decisive participation in the Government's efforts to carry out its plans for the furtherance of social and economic growth in the country, in realization of the continuous expansion of this participation and for the sake of close co-operation between the Government and civil sectors; we have decreed the following:

Art. 1. A Consultative Assembly should be set up for the public good. It will have an advisory nature, will enjoy financial and administrative independence and will be called the Consultative Assembly of State. Its seat will be in the Capital.

Art. 2. The Assembly shall be formed from both the Government and civil sectors. Its members shall be chosen from people with experience and influence representing all the citizens. The number of these representatives, including the Speaker, shall not exceed 45, who shall be distributed as follows:

17 members to represent the government sector
28 members to represent the civil sector, of whom
11 from the private sector and 17 from the provinces.

It shall be a condition of every member that he shall be of Omani nationality and that his age at the time of his appointment shall not be less than 30 solar years.

Art. 3. A special Royal Decree will be issued concerning the nomination of the members and the choice of the Speaker, his Deputy and the Secretary-General, and the fixing of their qualifications.

Art. 4. The period of membership of the Assembly shall be 2 solar years from the date of appointment. Re-appointment shall be possible for all members.

Art. 5. The Assembly shall include the following support facilities:

(*a*) The Executive Office, which shall consist of the Speaker and his Deputy, 2 members from the government sector and 3 members from the civil sector, who shall be chosen by a majority of the votes of the members present at the first session of the Assembly.

(*b*) The General Secretariat which shall consist of the General Secretary of the Assembly, as well as such assistant-secretaries and technical, administrative and financial assistants as he may need.

Art. 6. The aims of the Assembly shall be to take a decisive part in the economic and social growth of the country. The Speaker shall be charged with submitting the Assembly's recommendations to His Majesty the Sultan.

Art. 7. In order to carry out these aims the Assembly shall enjoy the following powers:

[1] All decrees supplied by Oman Mission to the United Nations in September 1982. Translated from Arabic by P. A'C Bergne. Ed.

(*a*) Forming opinions on the economic and social laws of the Sultanate and advising on the development needed to cope with growth requirements which have emerged since the Sultan's accession to power.

(*b*) Expressing an opinion on the Government's proposals for general growth policy and advising how to perfect development plans and legislation intended by the Government.

(*c*) Proposing measures and new government development schemes in order that the process of growth may be hastened and the efficiency and capacity of internal production be raised.

(*d*) Identifying obstacles which the independent private sector may face in the economic and social fields and making recommendations for suitable curative measures within the limits of the possibilities available to the Government.

(*e*) Formulating an opinion on any other subjects His Majesty The Sultan sees fit to assign to the Assembly.

Art. 8. In the course of every year the Assembly will hold at least 4 ordinary sessions to consider the agenda the General Secretariat has prepared in agreement with the Executive Office. The Executive Office will manage the workings of the Assembly between sessions. The Assembly also has the right to form both permanent and temporary subcommittees from amongst its members, to study such subjects as are assigned to it.
the workings of the Assembly between sessions. The Assembly also has the right to form both permanent and temporary subcommittees from amongst its members, to study such subjects as are assigned to it.

Art. 9. A Royal Decree will be issued with regard to the internal organization of the Assembly, the Executive Office and the General Secretariat.

Art. 10. Work on Royal Decree No 79/19 and its modifications is herewith cancelled. This Decree concerns the establishment of a council to deal with agriculture, fishing and industry.

Art. 11. This Decree is to be published in the official Gazette and to come into force from the date of its publication.

Issued on the 19th of Dhu'ul Hijja 1401 corresponding to the 18th October 1981.

ROYAL DECREE NO 81/85 WITH REGARD TO THE CHOICE OF MEMBERS OF THE CONSULTATIVE ASSEMBLY OF STATE AND THE APPOINTMENT OF ITS SECRETARY-GENERAL

October 18, 1981

We, Qabus bin Sa'id, Sultan of Oman, in cognizance of the Royal Decree No 81/84 concerning the establishment of a Consultative Assembly of State and in accordance with the public interest, have decreed as follows:

Art. 1. The following are appointed members of the Consultative Assembly of State representing the government sector:

(1) The deputy ministers mentioned below by virtue of their appointments:

(*a*) Ministry of the Interior
(*b*) Ministry of Science and Education
(*c*) Ministry of Health
(*d*) Ministry of Social Affairs and Labor
(*e*) Ministry of Land Tenure and Local Government
(*f*) Ministry of Trade and Industry
(*g*) Ministry of Agriculture and Fisheries
(*h*) Ministry of Communications
(*i*) Ministry of Electricity and Water
(*j*) Ministry of Posts, Telegraphs and Telephones

(2) Seven members from the Government on the basis of their personal qualities, as follows:

(*a*) KHALFAN NASER AL WUHAIBI
(*b*) MUSALLAM 'ALI AL BU SA'IDI
(*c*) NASAR SAIF AL BU 'ALI
(*d*) MUHAMMAD 'ALI NASER AL 'ALAWI
(*e*) SA' ID NASER AL KHUSAIBI
(*f*) 'AMER SHAWIN AL HAWASNI
(*g*) 'ABD ULLAH SAQR AL 'AMER I

Art. 2. The following shall be nominated as members of the Consultative Assembly of State and representatives of the civil sector:

(1) From the private sector

(*a*) 'ALI SULTAN MUHAMMAD FADHIL
(*b*) SA'UD 'ALI AL KHALILI
(*c*) 'ALI MUHAMMAD MUSA
(*d*) MUHAMMAD 'ABD UL RASUL AL JAMALI
(*e*) HAMED 'ABDULLAH AL GHILANI
(*f*) NASER MUHAMMED 'UMAIR AL HINA'I
(*g*) MANSUR 'ALI MANSUR AL SALIMI
(*h*) NASER ABDULLAH AL SHAKU
(*i*) MUHSEN HAIDAR DARWISH
(*j*) HASAN 'ALI 'ABD UL LATIF
(*k*) AHMAD TAHER AL MUQAIBAL

(2) From the provinces

(*a*) MUHAMMAD SAIF AL 'AMURI
(*b*) SABA' HAMDAN AL SA'DI
(*c*) RASHED HAMDAN AL MUQBALI
(*d*) BADR SALEM AL 'ABRI
(*e*) NASER MUHAMMAD NASER AL GHAFERI
(*f*) HAMAD SALEM MUHAMMAD AL RUWAHI
(*g*) AHMAD MUHAMMAD AL SALEMI
(*h*) MUHAMMAD KHALIFAH AL HARETHI
(*i*) SA'ID AHMAD 'ALI AL BU SA'IDI
(*j*) HAMAD 'ALI SA'ID AL GHAFERI

(*k*) MUHAMMAD HAMDAN AL 'ALAWI
(*l*) MUHAMMAD HUMAID AL WA' ILI
(*m*) AHMAD 'ALI SUGHAIR AL SHEHHI
(*n*) 'ABD UL SATTAR AHMAD IBRAHIM AL KAMALI
(*o*) SALEM SA'ID ATIRUN JA'BUB
(*p*) MUSALLAM AHMAD JAMEDAH AL KATHIRI
(*q*) MUSALLAM SUHAIL JADAD BAIT KATHIR

ROYAL DECREE NO 81/86 CONCERNING THE INTERNAL ORGANIZATION OF THE CONSULTATIVE ASSEMBLY OF STATE

October 18, 1981

We, Qabus bin Sai'id, Sultan of Oman, further to the Royal Decree No 81/84 on the establishment of a Consultative Assembly of State, decree as follows:

PART 1

GENERAL PROVISIONS

Art. 1. The Consultative Assembly of State will take part in the formulation of opinion in the fields of economic and social development. This will be in accordance with the decree establishing the Assembly. The Speaker will be responsible for submitting recommendations to His Majesty the Sultan.

Art. 2. It is incumbent upon the departments of the government concerned, in cases where they cannot agree to adopt the Assembly's recommendations, to prepare for His Majesty the Sultan a report setting out the reasons.

Art. 3. These provisions guarantee freedom of speech inside the Assembly to all its members. In the discussions they hold and the recommendations they adopt, members are obliged to observe the laws of the land, their possibilities and the provisions of this order.

PART 2

THE PRINCIPAL OFFICES OF THE ASSEMBLY

Art. 4. The principal offices of the Assembly are:

(1) The Speaker
(2) The Executive Office
(3) The Permanent and Temporary Committees
(4) The General Secretariat

Section 1. The Speaker

Art. 5. The Speaker will ensure that the Assembly's business conforms with the provisions of the law of the land and of this order. In this he may draw on the help of his deputy or of the Executive Office.

Art. 6. The Speaker will generally supervise the good running of all the Assembly's activities. He will open its sessions, chair them, announce their termination and control debates, giving permission to speak and specifying the matters to be discussed. He will prevent speakers straying from the subject under discussion. He will also announce the recommendations issued by the Assembly in accordance with Article 43 of this order.

Art. 7. The Speaker may convene any committee to discuss an important or urgent subject. The Speaker will chair the sessions of such committees. Discussions between any of the Assembly's committees and the Government or any other authorities outside the Assembly will take place through the Speaker.

Art. 8. The Speaker will undertake the supervision of the General Secretariat and of all the administrative, financial and technical affairs of the Assembly.

Art. 9. Regarding the financial and administrative matters of the Assembly and its employees, the Speaker will enjoy the authority of a minister or the head of a government department.

Art. 10. In certain of his duties, the Speaker may delegate responsibiliy to his deputy. He may also appoint him to deputize for him in chairing certain sessions of the Assembly or its committees. Should the Speaker be absent, his deputy will assume chairmanship of the sessions. In such cases he will carry out the duties which this order lays down for the Speaker in administering the Assembly sessions.

Section 2. The Executive Office

Art. 11. The Assembly's Executive Office will comprise the Speaker, who will be its head, his deputy, 2 members from the government sector and 3 members from the civil sector, who shall be chosen in the Assembly by a majority of votes of the members present at its first meeting.

Art. 12. The Executive Office shall draw up a program for the activities of the Assembly and its committees in such a way as to ensure the efficient despatch of its duties. This programme will be submitted to the Assembly for approval. The Executive Office will undertake the supervision of the activities of the Assembly and its committees and will assist the Assembly members in carrying out their responsibilities. Likewise the Office will assist the Assembly's committees to lay down the rules governing their work and coordinate all aspects of their activity in accordance with the provisions of this order.

Art. 13. The Executive Office may instruct one of the committees to study a specific subject, to report on the results of its studies and make recommendations. Furthermore the Office may decide on the submission of the report to the Assembly.

Art. 14. The Executive Office will, together with the General Secretariat, participate in drawing up an agenda in accordance with the program of work which has been decided earlier. In this it shall have regard to the precedence accorded to subjects referred to the Assembly by His Majesty the Sultan and the Government and those bodies whose interests are to be given attention. The Secretary-General will announce the agenda and will inform the members of it at least 2 weeks in advance of each session.

Art. 15. In addition to the other duties referred to in this order, the Executive Office will supervise and organize all the Assembly's financial and administrative affairs. This shall be in accordance with the system adopted by the Office for this purpose which shall be approved by the Assembly.

Art. 16. The Speaker may call upon the Executive Office to attend regular meetings of the Assembly; he shall also have the right to summon them for emergency sessions.

No meeting of the Executive Office shall be valid unless attended by at least 5 of its members, amongst whom either the head of the Office or his deputy must also be present. The Office's decisions will be issued with the agreement of the majority of those present, provided that either the Office's head or, in his absence his deputy, is present. Noone shall be allowed to attend the Office's meetings who is not a member, with the exception of the General-Secretary and other members of the Assembly who receive permission to do so. The Secretary-General will draw up the minutes of the Office's meetings and these shall be confirmed by the Speaker of the Assembly or his deputy depending on the circumstances.

Section 3. The Assembly's Committees

Art. 17. The Assembly may form permanent and temporary subordinate committees from amongst its members. The Executive Office may charge these committees with studying any matters that have been submitted to it. Moreover, these committees shall assist the Assembly in exercising its functions in accordance with its constituent charter and the provisions of this order.

Art. 18. Each committee shall consist of a head and a number of members representing the state and civil sectors, in accordance with the proposal of the Executive Office and having regard to the committee's efficient functioning. Provided the agreement of the Executive Office is forthcoming, any member may participate in more than one committee so that his expertise and specialities can benefit their various activities.

Art. 19. For studying the matters submitted to it, any committee shall have the right to ask the Speaker of the Assembly to arrange meetings with delegates from specialist ministries so that explanations and information relating to the subject in hand may be heard. Furthermore, the Assembly's committees may, with its agreement, carry out field visits if these are pertinent for investigating the subject in hand.

Art. 20. Secret meetings of these committees shall be attended only by their members and other members of the Assembly whose help the committee may call on.

No committee shall be considered to have been convened correctly unless at least two-thirds of its members are present. A committee shall issue its decisions by a majority of votes of those members present. In all cases reference shall be made in the committee's report to the way in which all the members present have voted – whether for or against.

Section 4. The General Secretariat

Art. 21. The General Secretariat shall be composed of the General Secretary, his deputy and the employees of the offices and departments within the framework of whatever administrative mechanism shall be decided upon by the Assembly.

Art. 22. The General Secretary will afford the necessary help to the Assembly and all its sub-departments in carrying out their responsibilities and duties. This will be in accordance with the general organizational rules prepared by the Executive Office and ratified by the Assembly.

Art. 23. The Assembly will present a bill to regulate the conditions of work of the employees. This bill shall accord with the proposals of the Secretariat General working together with the Executive Office.

Art. 24. The Secretary General shall attend the Assembly's sessions and will supervise all the offices and departments of the Assembly's General Secretariat. He shall also be responsible to the Speaker for its efficient functioning.

The Secretary General shall undertake the preparation of the Assembly's minutes and shall announce them to the members in accordance with the instructions of the Speaker, or his deputy, according to the circumstances. In order that he may carry out his duties and supervise the financial and administrative offices of the Assembly, the General Secretary shall have the rank of an under-secretary in the Civil Service.

PART 3

THE SESSION OF THE ASSEMBLY AND ITS RECOMMENDATIONS

Section 1. The Correct Convocation of the Assembly

Art. 25. No meeting of the Assembly shall be valid unless attended by at least two thirds of its members including the Speaker or his deputy. If a meeting of the Assembly is convened correctly it shall be considered to continue correctly even if a number of the members present should leave the chamber after the beginning of the session.

Art. 26. Regarding matters about which any special stipulation may exist, the Assembly's decisions shall require a majority of two thirds of the votes of the members present.

Section 2. The Sessions

Art. 27. Sessions of the Assembly held *in camera*. These shall only be attended by the Assembly's members, the Secretary-General and any government official to whom permission is given to attend.

Art. 28. The Assembly shall convene 4 times a year during the first week of January, April, August and October. Each session shall not last longer than one week. The number of meetings and their times during each session shall be specified in the agenda of the Assembly.

With the agreement of the Assembly a session may be postponed *pro tem.* In this case the Speaker shall fix the date of the following session and will inform the members of the Assembly accordingly. The Speaker may convene the Assembly before the date fixed for the following session in case of urgent business.

Art. 29. Half an hour before the opening of each session the members shall be presented with a list to sign, to show that they have been present. Likewise they shall sign another list at the end of each session. This shall be in accordance with the procedure decided upon by the Executive Office.

Art. 30. The opening of any session shall be invalid unless attended by at least two thirds of the Assembly's members. If, at the time fixed for the opening of the session, there should not be a quorum, the Speaker shall postpone the opening by half an hour. If after the lapse of that time there shall still not be a quorum, the Speaker shall announce the postponement of the session and the date of the following one.

Art. 31. The General Secretary will undertake the recording of the session's minutes under the supervision of the Speaker, who will then sign them together with the Secretary General. Thereafter they shall be kept in the Assembly's General Secretariat. The minutes of the Assembly's sessions will only be available for reading by its members.

Art. 32. No member of the Assembly may speak during a session unless he has sought and received leave to do so from the Speaker. Permission to speak will not be given on any subject which has been referred to one of the committees except after the committee's report has been submitted and included in the Assembly's agenda. Only if a request has been made for reports on subjects that have been referred to the Assembly's committees to be expedited, shall permission be given for them to be raised in the Assembly.

Art. 33. No discussion will be permitted on any subject which is not included in the agenda, except if the Government or the Speaker should expressly request it.

Art. 34. Having regard to what any special ordinance may lay down concerning precedence in speaking, the Speaker will grant permission to speak in the order in which the requests were made, and having regard to the interests of orderly discussion. Anyone who requests permission to speak, may relinquish his turn in favor of another.

Art. 35. Responsible officials of the Government may attend the Assembly's meetings or those of its committees, should they request permission to do so or should the Assembly invite them to deliver statements and explanations concerning their ministry's or the Government's policies.

Such responsible officials of the Government shall have no right to vote in these sessions except if they are at the same time members of the Assembly.

Art. 36. If it should transpire that any member who has requested permission to speak, has in the past spoken in contravention of any of this order's provisions, the Speaker shall have the right to withdraw his permission to speak or to deprive him of the right to speak on any matter submitted to the Assembly until the end of the session.

Art. 37. Every speaker must express his opinions with due consideration for the dignity of the Government and the prestige of the Assembly. No speaker may wander from the subject under discussion or introduce any matter which infringes the order and dignity of the session.

Art. 38. Apart from the Speaker, nobody may interrupt a member who is speaking or make any comments. Only the Speaker has the right to warn a member during his speech that he has contravened the provisions of this order.

Art. 39. The Speaker shall order the erasure from the minutes of the session of any statement made by a member in contravention of the provisions of this order.

Art. 40. Any member shall have the right to request an explanation on a specific subject and to hear the reply given by whichever government official may be nominated to make a statement or offer an explanation in reply to his request or to an invitation from the Assembly; and this provided that the request for a statement shall be about a matter which is important.

Art. 41. The Assembly shall have the right, on the basis of a majority of two thirds of its members, to recommend the suspension of any member who neglects the duties of his office. The Speaker shall submit any such recommendation to His Majesty The Sultan for a final decision.

Section 3. The Voting and Publication of Recommendations

Art. 42. Voting will be undertaken either by a show of hands or by any other means that the Assembly may decide. Should there be any doubt as to the result of a vote taken by a show of hands it shall be retaken by a roll call.

Every member shall be obliged to vote on any subject which may be submitted to the vote.

Art. 43. The Speaker shall make the decision of the Assembly known to the members in accordance with the result of the vote. After this announcement no further comment shall be allowed upon the announcement. Likewise the Speaker shall announce the interruption or end of any session, the day fixed for the following session and the time of its opening.

Section 4. The Minutes of the Sessions

Art. 44. The Secretariat shall draw up minutes for every session in which all the business conducted, the subjects proposed, the decisions reached, and recommendations made shall be included in detail. The General Secretary shall also take the necessary steps to preserve the confidentiality of these minutes.

Art. 45. The Secretariat of the Assembly shall distribute the minutes to all the members as soon as they are printed and not later than 2 weeks after the date of the session in question; the Speaker shall then submit them to the Assembly for approval during the first session thereafter.

Art. 46. No request shall be entertained for any alteration in the minutes once they have been approved. Following their approval, the minutes shall be signed both by the Speaker and by the General Secretary and they shall be kept in the Assembly's archives.

PART 4

THE MEMBERS' RIGHTS AND DUTIES

Art. 47. The Royal Decree governing the nomination of the Assembly's members and the choice of the Speaker and his deputy and the General Secretary, shall also specify the different sorts of remuneration and allowances they shall receive.

Art. 48. The Assembly's members shall communicate in advance to the Speaker any action they resolve to take while the Assembly is in session.

Art. 49. Members must be regular in their attendance at the Assembly's meetings and those of its committees. Should any member have pressing grounds for absenting himself from one of the Assembly's sessions or meetins of its committees, he should inform the Speaker or the chairman of the committee in writing.

Art. 50. Any member who is obliged to leave the chamber during one of the sessions of the Assembly or one of its committees, shall obtain the permission of the Speaker or the committee's chairman to do so.

Art. 51. No member may commit actions, whether inside the Assembly or outside, which contravene the provisions of the law or of this order. Every member shall show due respect for the State.

Art. 52. All members are warned against exploiting their positions to obtain special privileges. All members should refrain from submitting any subject to the Assembly which touches upon their private interests.

PART 5

THE ASSEMBLY'S AFFAIRS

Section 1. Preservation of Order Within the Assembly.

Art. 53. The preservation of order within the Assembly is the exclusive concern of the Assembly. The Speaker shall specify the security measures he considers adequate for this purpose in coordination with the authorities concerned.

Art. 54. No one shall be allowed to enter the confines of the Assembly except with special permission. This will be given on condition that the instructions of those who fail in this shall be ejected.

Section 2. The Assembly's Budget and Accounts

Art. 55. The Assembly's budget shall be independent from the general budget of the State.

The Executive Office shall prepare the different headings of the budget, specify the way they shall be disbursed and submit an annual report to the Assembly. Final approval shall be given by His Majesty The Sultan.

Art. 56. The Executive Office shall lay down special regulations for ordering the Assembly's accounts, expenditure, stocktaking, and any other financial matters.

Art. 57. The Assembly shall look after its own accounts. In this respect the Assembly shall not be subordinate to the supervision of any other authority. However the Speaker must seek the help of the Office for the Inspection of Accounts in producing his report on the Assembly's accounts, the execution of the budget or on the Assembly's other financial matters.

PART 6

FINAL PROVISIONS

Art. 58. For the purpose of the application of the provisions of this order, by 'the Government' are meant the ministries, whether represented in the Assembly or not, the ministers and under-secretaries, as well as their representatives at Assembly sessions.

Art. 59. Excepting statements made by ministers of their representatives about their respective ministries' plans or those of the Government, no subject may be presented to the Assembly or entered in the agenda for one of its sessions before all the details and related studies have been submitted.

The Executive Office shall prepare any subject so submitted along with the details and explanations and make it available to the Assembly's members in good time before the session fixed to deal with it.

Art. 60. The Secretariat General shall be responsible for distributing the details, explanations and studies referred to in the previous article along with the agenda for the session in question. The only exception to this shall be if the Speaker should decide to the contrary for reasons which he shall explain to the Assembly.

Art. 61. This order shall not be altered except by Royal Decree and in accordance with a proposal of the executive office which shall include the articles whose alteration is desired and the justification for so doing, and which shall be presented by the Speaker to the Assembly which shall make its recommendation.

Art. 62. This order shall be published in the official Gazette and shall enter into force with effect from the date of its publication.

PAKISTAN

SUMMARY

INTERNATIONAL STATUS

Pakistan is a member of the United Nations (September 30, 1947). It is a member of other international organizations.

Pakistan became independent on August 14, 1947, under the India Independence Act 1947, which created the two dominions of India and Pakistan. On March 23, 1956, by a new Constitution it was proclaimed a federal Islamic republic.

The Moslem League was formed in 1906. Joint activity with the Indian Congress Party continued until communal disturbances followed the Moplah rebellion in 1921-1922. The Moslem League opposed the Government of India Act 1935, and in 1940 formally pronounced it unacceptable and adopted the policy of a separate autonomous Moslem state comprising areas with a predominately Moslem population. Hindi-Moslem clashes followed the formation of the interim Congress government in September 1946, and the Moslem League boycotted the Constituent Assembly of December 9 of that year. On February 20, 1947, Britain announced its intention to transfer power not later than June 1948. Consultations between the Viceroy and the Indian leaders led to the conclusion that the only solution was to divide India into two separate states. Partition was accompanied by mass migrations and massacres. Relations between India and Pakistan were further embittered by a dispute over the possession of Kashmir where a cease-fire arranged by the United Nations on January 1, 1949, resulted in the present division. Another war with India was ended with the Agreement of Tashkent of January 1966.

At its formation, Pakistan was composed of two areas united only by religion, West Pakistan where were the political and military power, and East Pakistan (formerly West Bengal) where lived the majority of the population. The latter declared its independence (see Bangladesh) in March 1971. After a period of civil war and repression, the Indian army intervened in December 1971 and forced the surrender and withdrawal of the Pakistan army. Pakistan recognized Bangladesh in 1974. The leader of the Pakistan People's Party which had gained the 1970 elections, became President of Pakistan, composed henceforth of the western province. Pakistan withdrew from the Commonwealth in 1972, and efforts to resume its membership in 1982 were blocked by India. In February 1973, direct presidential rule was imposed under emergency powers and the present constitution was adopted in August of that year. An army coup in July 1977, deposed President Bhutto (who was tried, condemned to death and executed in 1978). Martial law was imposed and has been in force since that time. The legislature was dissolved and many provisions of the 1973 constitution put in abeyance. In March 1981, a Provisional Constitutional Order which was promulgated retaining wholly or in part 119 articles of the 1973 Constitution, but giving the President power to change the Constitution, permits the martial law administrator to dissolve any political party and permits only the parties which registered for the 1979 elections (which did not take place), suspends political activity, and completes the erosion of the independence and authority of the judiciary with the imposition of Shariat law and the powers of the military courts. Serious incidents occurred in March 1982 with judges and lawyers in Sind and Baluchistan. A Consultative Committee, the Majlis-i-Shma, was set up in 1982, in place of the legislature dissolved in 1977.

Pakistan, since the U.S.S.R. occupation of Afghanistan, is faced with the problem of over a million refugees.

FORM OF NATIONAL GOVERNMENT

The Constitution of April 12, 1973, as modified up to April 1981, states that Pakistan is a federal Islamic republic and its territories are named.[1] It was preceded by the Constitutions of March 1, 1961 and March 23, 1956 (abrogated in 1958 and followed by a period of martial law). The articles in abeyance are indicated in the text of the Constitution and other articles are also affected by martial law orders since 1978. Islam is the state religion.[2] Sovereignty belongs to Allah alone and the authority exercised by the people of Pakistan within the limits prescribed by Him is a sacred trust.[3] The Tribal areas and their administration are described.[4] There is a provision relating to the state of Jammu and Kashmir.[5] Private armies are forbidden.[6] The 'Islamic Provisions' state that all existing laws must be brought into conformity with the Injunctions of Islam, and an Islamic Council is to make recommendations and give advice to Parliament and provincial assemblies.[7]

[1] Const., Art. 1.
[2] Id., Art. 2.
[3] Id., Art. Preamble.
[4] Id., Art. 246, 247.
[5] Id., Art. 257.
[6] Id., Art. 256.
[7] Id., Art. 227–230.

RIGHTS OF THE PEOPLE

Individuals have the right to protection of the law and to be treated in accordance with the law.[8] The remaining articles on rights are in abeyance under martial law orders of 1981.

LEGISLATIVE DEPARTMENT

The provisions concerning the legislature are in abeyance under martial law orders.

EXECUTIVE DEPARTMENT

The Constituton provides for a President who is Head of State and must be a Moslem.[9] The President may promulgate ordinances with the effect of law.[10] The executive authority of the Federation extends to matters where Parliament has the power to make laws, except where the provincial assemblies also have the power to make laws.[11] The President has the power of pardon.[12] Governors of the provinces are appointed by the President.[13] The Constitution provides for a Council of Common Interests composed of the chief ministers of the provinces with an equal number from the federal government appointed by the Prime Minister to consider economic and technical matters.[14] Immunities of the President, the governors and the Ministers are provided.[15] There are provisions regarding finance, and about property and ownership.[16]

JUDICIAL DEPARTMENT

The Constitution provides for a Supreme Court, a High Court for each province, and other courts.[17] The Chief Justice and justices of the Supreme Court and High Courts are appointed by the President, after consultation – in the case of the High Courts – with the Chief Justice and the Governor of the respective province.[18] The Supreme Court has original jurisdiction in in disputes between federal and provincial governments.[19] Its jurisdiction regarding fundamental rights is in abeyance since 1981.

Chapter 3A provides for the Federal Shariat Court and was introduced in June 1980. It is to have effect 'notwithstanding anything contained in the Constitution.' The Federal Shariat Court is composed of 5 Muslim members appointed by the President.[20] The Panel of Ulema and Ulema members, versed in Islamic law and

[8] Id., Art. 4.
[9] Id., Art. 45.
[10] Id., Art. 89.
[11] Id., Art. 97.
[12] Id., Art. 45.
[13] Id., Art. 101.
[14] Id., Art. 153.
[15] Id., Art. 248, 249.
[16] Id., Art. 160–174.
[17] Id., Art. 175.
[18] Id., Art. 176, 192, 193.
[19] Id., Art. 184.
[20] Id., Art. 203C.

associated with the Court is described.[21] The Court may decide, on the petition of a citizen or federal or provincial government, whether any law or provision thereof is repugnant to the Injunctions of Islam; if it so decides, such law or provision ceases to have effect.[22] Appeal may be had to the Shariat Appellate Bench of the Supreme Court, and other than that no court, including the Supreme Court or the High Court, may exercise any power or jurisdiction in respect of matters within the jurisdiction of the Federal Shariat Court.[23]

AREA, POPULATION, ETC.

The area is 803,943 square kilometres, the population (1981 estimate is 84,580,000. The capital is Islamabad. The national language is Urdu, which is to be used officially within 15 years, pending which English may be used.[24]

[21] Id., Art. 203CC.
[22] Id., Art. 203D.
[23] Id., Art. 203F, 203G.
[24] Id., Art. 251.

THE CONSTITUTION OF THE ISLAMIC REPUBLIC OF PAKISTAN[1]

April 12, 1973, as modified up to April 30, 1981

(In the name of Allah the Beneficent, the Merciful)

PREAMBLE

Whereas sovereignty over the entire Universe belongs to Almighty Allah alone, and the authority to be exercised by the people of Pakistan within the limits prescribed by Him is a sacred trust;

And whereas it is the will of the people of Pakistan to establish an order

Wherein the State shall exercise its powers and authority through the chosen representatives of the people;

Wherein the principles of democracy, freedom, equality, tolerance and social justice, as enunciated by Islam, shall be fully observed;

Wherein the Muslims shall be enabled to order their lives in the individual and collective spheres in accordance with the teachings and requirements of Islam as set out in the Holy Quran and Sunnah;

Wherein adequate provision shall be made for the minorities freely to profess and practise their religions and develop their cultures;

Wherein the territories now included in or in accession with Pakistan and such other territories as may hereafter be included in or accede to Pakistan shall form a Federation wherein the units will be autonomous with such boundaries and limitations on their powers and authority as may be prescribed;

Wherein shall be guaranteed fundamental rights, including equality of status, of opportunity and before law, social, economic and political justice, and freedom of thought, expression, belief, faith, worship and association, subject to law and public morality;

Wherein adequate provision shall be made to safeguard the legitimate interests of minorities and backward and depressed classes;

Wherein the independence of the judiciary shall be fully secured;

Wherein the integrity of the territories of the Federation, its independence and all its rights, including its sovereign rights on land, sea and air, shall be safeguarded;

So that the people of Pakistan may prosper and attain their rightful and honored place amongst the nations of the World and make their full contribution towards international peace and progress and happiness of humanity:

Now, therefore, we, the people of Pakistan.

Conscious of our responsibility before Almighty Allah and men;

[1]Prepared by Library Staff of the Lahore High Court under the guidance of Sheikh Ebrahim, Research and Reference Officer, Lahore High Court. Supplied by the Ministry of Law and Parliamentary Affairs in September 1982. Ed.

Cognizant of the sacrifices made by the people in the cause of Pakistan;

Faithful to the declaration made by the Founder of Pakistan, Quaid-i-Azam Muhammad Ali Jinnah, that Pakistan would be a democratice State on Islamic principles of social justice;

Dedicated to the preservation of democracy achieved by the unremitting struggle of the people against oppression and tyranny;

Inspired by the resolve to protect our national and political unity and solidarity by creating an egalitarian society through a new order;

Do hereby, through our representatives in the National Assembly, adopt, enact and given to ourselves, this Constitution.

PART I

INTRODUCTORY

1. The Republic and its territories.

(1) Pakistan shall be a Federal Republic to be known as the Islamic Republic of Pakistan, hereinafter referred to as Pakistan.

(2) The territories of Pakistan shall comprise

(*a*) the Provinçes of Baluchistan, the North-West Frontier, the Punjab and Sind;

(*b*) the Islamabad Capital Territory, hereinafter referred to as the Federal Capital;

(*c*) the Federally Administered Tribal Areas; and

(*d*) such States and territories as are or may be included in Pakistan, whether by accession or otherwise.

(3) Parliament may by law admit into the Federation new States or areas on such terms and conditions as it thinks fit.

2. Islam to be State Religion.

Islam shall be the State religion of Pakistan.

3. Elimination of exploitation.

The state shall ensure the elimination of all forms of exploitation and the gradual fulfilment of the fundamental principle, from each according to his ability to each according to his work.

4. Right of individuals to be dealt with in accordance with law, etc.

(1) To enjoy the protection of law and to be treated in accordance with law is the inalienable right of every citizen, wherever he may be, and of every other person for the time being within Pakistan.

(2) In particular

(*a*) no action detrimental to the life, liberty, body, reputation or property of any person shall be taken except in accordance with law;

(*b*) no person shall be prevented from or be hindered in doing that which is not prohibited by law; and

(*c*) no person shall be compelled to do that which the law does not require him to do.

5. Loyalty to State and obedience.

(1) Loyalty to the State is the basic duty of every citizen.

5. (2) 6. to 40. In abeyance.

41. The President.

(1) There shall be a President of Pakistan who shall be the Head of State and shall represent the unity of the Republic.

(2) A person shall not be qualified for election as President unless he is a Muslim of not less than forty-five years of age and is qualified to be elected as member of the National Assembly.

41. (3) to (6), to 44. In abeyance.

45. President's power to grant pardon etc.

The President shall have power to grant pardon, reprieve and respite, and to remit, suspend or commute any sentence passed by any court, tribunal or other authority.

46. to 77. In abeyance.

78. Federal Consolidated Fund and Public Account.

(1) All revenues received by the Federal Government, all loans raised by that Government, and all moneys received by it in repayment of any loan shall form part of a consolidated fund, to be known as the Federal Consolidated Fund.

(2) All other moneys

(*a*) received by or on behalf of the Federal Government; or

(*b*) received by or deposited with the Supreme Court or any other court established under the authority of the Federation;

shall be credited to the Public Account of the Federation.

79. Custody, etc., of Federal Consolidated Fund and Public Account.

The custody of the Federal Consolidated Fund the payment of moneys into that Fund, the withdrawal of moneys therefrom, the custody of other moneys received by or on behalf of the Federal Government, their payment into, and withdrawal from, the Public Account of the Federation, and all matters connected with or ancillary to the matters aforesaid shall be regulated by Act of Parliament or, until provision in that behalf is so made, by rules made by the President.

80 to 88. In abeyance.

89. Power of President to promulgate ordinances.

(1) The President may, except when the National Assembly is in session, if satisfied that circumstances exist which render it necessary to take immediate action, make and promulgate an Ordinance as the circumstances may require.

(2) An Ordinance promulgated under this Article shall have the same force and effect as an Act of Parliament and shall be subject to like restrictions as the power of Parliament to make law, but every such Ordinance

(*a*) shall be laid

(i) before the National Assembly if it is with respect to a matter in Part I of the Federal Legislative List, and shall stand repealed at the expiration of four months from its promulgation or, if before the expiration of that period a resolution disapproving it is passed by the Assembly, upon the passing of that resolution;

(ii) before both Houses if it is with respect to a matter in Part II of the Federal Legislative List or a matter in the Concurrent Legislative List, and shall stand repealed at the expiration of four months from its promulgation or, if before the expiration of that period a resolution disapproving it is passed by either House, upon the passing of that resolution; and

(*b*) may be withdrawn and at any time by the President.

(3) Without prejudice to the Provisions of clause (2), an Ordinance laid before the National Assembly shall be deemed to be a Bill introduced in the National Assembly.

90. to 96. In abeyance.

97. Extent of executive authority of Federation.

Subject to the Constitution, the executive authority of the Federation shall extend to the matters with respect to which Parliament has power to make laws, including exercise of rights, authority and jurisdiction in and in relation to areas outside Pakistan:

Provided that the said authority shall not, save as expressly provided in the Constitution or in any law made by Parliament, extend in any Province to a matter with respect to which the Provincial Assembly has also power to make laws.

98. Conferring of functions on subordinate authorities.

On the recommendation of the Federal Government, Parliament may by law confer functions upon officers or authorities subordinate to the Federal Government.

99. Conduct of Business of Federal Government.

(1) Orders and other instruments made and executed in the name of the President shall be authenticated in such manner as may be specified in rules to be made by the Federal Government, and the validity of an order or instrument which is so authenticated shall not be called in question on the ground that it is not an order or instrument made or executed by the President.

(2) The Federal Government may regulate the allocation and transaction of its business and may for the convenient transaction of that business delegate any of its functions to officers or authorities subordinate to it.

100. Attorney General for Pakistan.

(1) The President shall appoint a person, being a person qualified to be appointed a Judge of the Supreme Court, to be the Attorney General for Pakistan.

(2) The Attorney General shall hold office during the pleasure of the President.

(3) It shall be the duty of the Attorney General to give advice to the Federal Government upon such legal matters, and to perform such other duties of a legal character, as may be referred or assigned to him by the Federal Government, and in the performance of his duties he shall have the right of audience in all courts and tribunals in Pakistan.

(4) The Attorney General may, by writing under his hand addressed to the President, resign his office.

101. Appointment of Governor.

There shall be a Governor for each Province, who shall be appointed by President.

102. Oath of office.

Before entering upon office, the Governor shall make before the Chief Justice of the High Court oath in the form set out in the Third Schedule.

103. to 117. In abeyance.

118. Provincial Consolidated Fund and Public Account.

(1) All revenues received by the Provincial Government, all loans raised by that Government, and all moneys received by it in repayment of any loan, shall form part of a consolidated fund, to be known as the Provincial Consolidated Fund.

(2) All other moneys

(*a*) received by or on behalf of the Provincial Government; or

(*b*) received by or deposited with the High Court or any other court established under the authority of the Province;

shall be credited to the Public Account of the Province.

119. Custody, etc., of Provincial Consolidated Fund and Public Account.

The Custody of the Provincial Consolidated Fund, the payment of moneys into that Fund, the withdrawal of moneys therefrom, the custody of other moneys received by or on behalf of the Provincial Government, their payment into, and withdrawal from, the Public Account of the Province, and all matters connected with or ancillary to the matters aforesaid, shall be regulated by Act of the Provincial Assembly or, until provision in that behalf is so made, by rules made by the Governor.

120. to 127. In abeyance.

128. Power of Governor to promulgate ordinance.

(1) The Governor may, except when the Provincial Assembly is in session, if satisfied that circumstances exist which render it necessary to take immediate action, make and promulgate an Ordinance as the circumstances may require.

(2) An Ordinance promulgated under this Article shall have the same force and effect as an Act of the Provincial Assembly and shall be subject to like restrictions as the power of the Provincial Assembly to make laws, but every such Ordinance

(*a*) shall be laid before the Provincial Assembly and shall stand repealed at the expiration of three months from its promulgation if before the expiration of that period a resolution disapproving it is passed by the Assembly, upon the passing of that resolution; and

(*b*) may be withdrawn at any time by the Governor.

(3) Without prejudice to the provisions of clause (2), an Ordinance laid before the Provincial Assembly shall be deemed to be a Bill introduced in the Provincial Assembly.

129. to 136. In abeyance.

137. Extent of Executive Authority of Province.

Subject to the Constitution, the executive authority of the Province shall extend to the matters with respect to which the Provincial Assembly has power to make laws:

Provided that, in any matter with respect to which both Parliament and the Provincial Assembly of a Province have power to make laws, the executive authority of the Province shall be subject to, and limited by, the executive authority expressly conferred by the Constitution or by law made by Parliament upon the Federal Government or authorities therof.

138. Conferring of functions on subordinate authorities.

On the recommendation of the Provincial Government, the Provincial Assembly may by law confer functions upon officers or authorities subordinate to the Provincial Government.

139. Conduct of Business of Provincial Government.

(1) Order and other instruments made and executed in the name of the Governor shall be authenticated in such manner as may be specified in rules to be made by the Provincial Government, and the validity of an order or instrument which is so authenticated shall not be called in question on the ground that it is not an order or instrument made or executed by the Governor.

(2) The Provincial Government may regulate the allocation and transaction of its business and may for the convenient transaction of that business delegate any of its functions to officers or authorities subordinate to it.

140. Advocate General for a Province.

(1) The Governor of each Province shall appoint a person, being a person qualified to be appointed a Judge of the High Court, to be the Advocate General for the Province.

(2) It shall be the duty of the Advocate General to give advice to the Provincial Government upon such legal matters, and to perform such other duties of legal character, as may be referred or assigned to him by the Provincial Government.

(3) The Advocate General shall hold office during the pleasure of the Governor.

(4) The Advocate General may, by writing under his hand addressed to the Governor, resign his office.

141. Extent of Federal and Provincial Laws;

Subject to the Constitution, Parliament may make laws (including laws having extra-territorial operation) for the whole or any part of Pakistan, and a Provincial Assembly may make laws for the Province or any part thereof.

142. Subject-matter of Federal and Provincial Laws. Subject to the Constitution

(*a*) Parliament shall have exclusive power to make laws with respect to any matter in the Federal Legislative List;

(*b*) Parliament, and a Provincial Assembly also shall have power to make laws with respect to any matter in the Concurrent Legislative List;

(*c*) a Provincial Assembly shall, and Parliament shall not, have power to make laws with respect to any matter not enumerated in either the Federal Legislative List or the Concurrent Legislative List; and

(*d*) Parliament shall have exclusive power to make laws with respect to matters not enumerated in either of the Lists for such areas in the Federation as are not included in any Province.

143. Inconsistency between Federal and Provincial Laws.

If any provision of an Act of a Provincial Assembly is repugnant to any provision of an Act of Parliament which Parliament is competent to enact, or to any provision of any existing law with respect to any of the matters enumerated in the Concurrent Legislative List, then the Act of Parliament, whether passed before or after the Act of the Provincial Assembly, or, as the case may be, the existing law, shall prevail and the Act of the Provincial Assembly shall, to the extent of the repugnancy, be void.

144. In abeyance.

145. Power of President to direct Governor to discharge certain function as his agent.

(1) The President may direct the Governor of any Province to discharge as his Agent, either generally or in any particular matter, such functions relating to such areas in the Federation which are not included in any Province as may be specified in the direction.

(2) The provisions of Article 105 shall not apply to the discharge by the Governor of his functions under clause (1).

146. Power of Federation to confer powers etc., on Provinces, in certain cases.

(1) Notwithstanding anything contained in the Constitution, the Federal Government may with the consent of the Government of a Province, entrust either conditionally or unconditionally to that Government or to its officers; functions in relation to any matter to which the executive authority of the Federation extends.

(2) An Act of Parliament may, notwithstanding that it relates to a matter with respect to which a Provincial Assembly has no power to make laws confer powers and impose duties upon a Province or officers and authorities thereof.

(3) Where by virtue of this Article powers and duties have been conferred or imposed upon a Province or officers or authorities thereof, there shall be paid by the Federation to the Province such sum as may be agreed or, in default of agreement as may be determined by an arbitrator appointed by the Chief Justice of Pakistan, in respect of any extra costs of administration incurred by the Province in connection with the exercise of those powers or the discharge or those duties.

147. Power of the Provinces to entrust functions to the Federation.

Notwithstanding anything contained in the Constitution, the Government of a Province may, with the consent of the Federal Government, entrust, either conditionally or unconditionally, to the Federal Government, or to its officers, functions in relation to any matter to which the executive authority of the Province extends.

148. Obligation of Provinces and Federation.

(1) The executive authority of every Province shall be so exercised as to secure compliance with Federal laws which apply in that Province.

(2) Without prejudice to any other provision of this Chapter, in the exercise of the executive authority of the Federation in any Province regard shall be had to the interests of that Province.

(3) It shall be the duty of the Federation to protect every Province against external aggression and internal disturbances and to ensure that the Government of every Province is carried on in accordance with the provisions of the Constitution.

149. Directions to Provinces in certain cases.

(1) The executive authority of every Province shall be so exercised as not to impede or prejudice the exercise of the executive authority of the Federation, and the executive authority of the Federation shall extend to the giving of such directions to a Province as may appear to the Federal Government to be necessary for that purpose.

(2) The executive authority of the Federation shall also extend to the giving of directions to a Province as to the carrying into execution therein of any Federal law which relates to a matter specified in the Concurrent Legislative List and authorizes the giving of such directions.

(3) The executive authority of the Federation shall also extend to the giving of directions to a Province as to the construction and maintenance of means of communication declared in the direction to be of national or strategic importance.

(4) The executive authority of the Federation shall also extend to the giving of directions to a Province as to the manner in which the executive authority thereof is to be exercised for the purpose of preventing any grave menace to the peace or tranquillity or economic life of Pakistan or any part thereof.

150. Full faith and credit for public acts, etc.

Full faith and credit shall be given throughout Pakistan to public acts and records, and judicial proceedings of every Province.

151. Inter-provincial trade.

(1) Subject to clause (2), trade, commerce and intercourse throughout Pakistan shall be free.

(2) Parliament may by law impose such restrictions on the freedom of trade, commerce or intercourse between one Province and another or within any part of Pakistan as may be required in the public interest.

(3) A Provincial Assembly or a Provincial Government shall not have power to

(*a*) make any law, or take any executive action, prohibiting or restricting the entry into, or the export from, the Province of goods of any class or description, or

(*b*) impose a tax which, as between goods manufactured or produced in the Province and similar goods not so manufactured or produced, discriminates in favour of the former goods or which, in the case of goods manufactured or produced outside the Province discriminates between goods manufactured or produced in any area in Pakistan and similar goods manufactured or produced in other area in Pakistan.

(4) An Act of a Provincial Assembly which imposes any reasonable restriction in the interest of public health, public order or morality, or for the purpose of protecting animals or plants from disease or preventing or alleviating any serious shortage in the Province of an essential commodity shall not, if it was made with the consent of the President, be invalid.

152. Acquisition of land for Federal purposes.

The Federation may, if it deems necessary to acquire any land situated in a Province for any purpose connected with a matter with respect to which Parliment has power to make laws, require the Province to acquire the land on behalf, and at the expense, of the Federation or, if the land belongs to the Province, to transfer it to the Federation on such terms as may be agreed or, in default of agreement, as may be determined by an arbitrator appointed by the Chief Justice of Pakistan.

153. Council of Common Interests.

(1) There shall be a Council of Common Interests, in this Chapter referred to as the Council, to be appointed by the President.

(2) The members of the Council shall be

(*a*) the Chief Ministers of the Provinces, and

(*b*) an equal number from the Federal Government to be nominated by the Prime Minister from time to time.

(3) The Prime Minister, if he is a member of the Council, shall be the Chairman of the Council but, if at any time he is not a member, the President may nominate a Federal Minister who is a member of the Council to be its Chairman.

(4) The Council shall be responsible to Parliament.

154. Functions and rules of procedure.

(1) The Council shall formulate and regulate policies in relation to matters in Part II of the Federal Legislative List and, in so far as it is in relation to the affairs of the Federation, the matter in entry 34 (electricity) in the Concurrent Legislative List, and shall exercise supervision and control over related institutions.

(2) The decisions of the Council shall be expressed in terms of the opinion of the majority.

(3) Until Parliament makes provision by law in this behalf, the Council may make its rules of procedure.

(4) Parliament in joint sitting may from time to time by resolution issue directions through the Federal Government to the Council generally or in particular matter to take action as Parliament may deem just and proper and such directions shall be binding on the Council.

(5) If the Federal Government or a Provincial Government is dissatisfied with a decision of the Council, it may refer the matter to Parliament in a joint sitting whose decision in this behalf shall be final.

155. Complaints as to interference with water supplies.

(1) If the interests of a Province, the Federal Capital or the Federally Administered Tribal Areas, or any of the inhabitants thereof, in water from any natural source of supply have been or are likely to be affected prejudicially by

(*a*) any executive act or legislation taken or passed or proposed to be taken or passed, or

(*b*) the failure of any authority to exercise any of its powers with respect to the use and distribution or control of water from that source,

the Federal Government or the Provincial Government concerned may make a complaint in writing to the Council.

(2) Upon receiving such complaint, the Council shall, after having considered the matter, either give its decision or request the President to appoint a commission consisting of such persons having special knowledge and experience in irrigation, engineering, administration, finance or law as he may think fit, hereinafter referred to as the Commission.

(3) Until Parliament makes provision by law in this behalf, the provisions of the Pakistan Commissions of Inquiry Act, 1956, as in force immediately before the commencing day shall apply to the Council or the Commission as if the Council or the Commission were a commission appointed under that Act to which all the provision of section 5 thereof applied and upon which the power contemplated by section 10 A thereof had been conferred.

(4) After considering the report and supplementary report, if any, of the Commission, the Council shall record its decision on all matters referred to the Commission.

(5) Notwithstanding any law to the contrary, but subject to the provisions of clause (5) of Article 154, it shall be the duty of the Federal Government and the Provincial Government concerned in the matter in issue to give effect to the decision of the Council faithfully according to its terms and tenor.

(6) No proceeding shall lie before any court at the instance of any party to a matter which is or has been in issue before the Council, or of any person whatsoever, in respect of a matter which is actually or has been or might or ought to have been a proper subject of complaint to the Council under this Article.

156. National Economic Council.

(1) The President shall constitute a National Economic Council consisting of the Prime Minister who shall be its Chairman, and such other members as the President may detemine:

Provided that the President shall nominate one member from each Province on the recommendation of the Government of that Province.

(2) The National Economic Council shall review the overall economic condition of the country and shall, for advising the Federal Government and the Provincial Governments, formulate plans in respect of financial, commercial, social and economic policies; and in formulating such plans, it shall be guided by the Principles of Policy set out in Chapter 2 of Part II.

157. Electricity.

(1) The Federal Government may in any Province construct or cause to be constructed hydro-electric or thermal power installations or grid stations for the generation of electricity and lay or cause to be laid inter-provincial transmission lines.

(2) The Government of a Province may

(*a*) to the extent electricity is supplied to that Province from the national grid, require supply to be made in bulk for transmission and distribution within the Province;

(*b*) levy tax on consumption of electricity within the Province;

(*c*) construct power houses and grid station and lay transmission lines for use within the Province; and

(*d*) determine the tariff for distribution of electricity within the Province.

158. Priority of requirements of natural gas.

The Province in which a well-head of natural gas is situated shall have precedence over other parts of Pakistan in meeting the requirements from that well-head, subject to the commitments and obligations as on the commencing day.

159. Broadcasting and telecasting.

(1) The Federal Government shall not unreasonably refuse to entrust to a Provincial Government such functions with respect to broadcasting and telecasting as may be necessary to enable that Government

(*a*) to construct and use transmitters in the Province; and

(*b*) to regulate, and impose fees in respect of, the construction and use of transmitters and the use of receiving apparatus in the Province:

Provided that nothing in this clause shall be construed as requiring the Federal Government to entrust to any Provincial Government any control over the use of transmitters constructed or maintained by the Federal Government or by persons authorized by the Federal Government, or over the use of receiving apparatus by persons so authorized.

(2) Any functions so entrusted to a Provincial Government shall be exercised subject to such conditions as may be imposed by the Federal Government, including, notwithstanding anything contained in the Constitution, any conditions with respect to finance, but it shall not be lawful for the Federal Government so to impose any conditions regulating the matter broadcast or telecast by, or by authority of, the Provincial Government.

(3) Any Federal law with respect to broadcasting and telecasting shall be such as to secure that effect can be given to the foregoing provisions of this Article.

(4) If any question arises whether any conditions imposed on any Provincial Government are lawfully imposed, or whether any refusal by the Federal Government to entrust functions is unreasonable the queston shall be determined by an arbitrator appointed by the Chief Justice of Pakistan.

(5) Nothing in this Article shall be construed as restricting the powers of

the Federal Government under the Constitution for the prevention of any grave menace to the peace or tranquillity of Pakistan or any part thereof.

160. National Finance Commission.

(1) Within six months of the commencing day and thereafter at intervals not exceeding five years, the President shall constitute a National Finance Commission consisting of the Minister of Finance of the Federal Government, the Minister of Finance of the Provincial Government, and such other persons as may be appointed by the President after consultation with the Governors of the Provinces.

(2) It shall be the duty of the National Finance Commission to make recommendations to the President as to

(*a*) the distribution between the Federation and the Provinces of the net proceeds of the taxes mentioned in clause (3);

(*b*) the making of grant-in-aid by the Federal Government to the Provincial Government;

(*c*) the exercise by the Federal Government and the Provincial Governments of the borrowing powers conferred by the Constitution; and

(*d*) any other matter relating to finance referred to the Commission by the President.

(3) The taxes referred to in paragraph (*a*) of clause (2) are the following taxes raised under the authority of Parliament, namely:

(i) taxes on income, including corporation tax, but not including taxes on income consisting of remuneration paid out of the Federal Consolidated Fund;

(ii) taxes on the sales and purchases of goods imported, exported, produced, manufactured or consumed;

(iii) export duties on cotton, and such other export duties as may be specified by the President;

(iv) such duties of excise as may be specified by the President; and and

(v) such other taxes as may be specified by the President.

(4) As soon as may be after receiving the recommendations of the National Finance Commission, the President shall, by Order, specify, in accordance with the recommendations of the Commission under paragraph (*a*) of clause (2), the share of the net proceeds of the taxes mentioned in clause (3) which is to be allocated to each Province, and that share shall be paid to the Government of the Province concerned, and, notwithstanding the provision of Article 78 shall not form part of the Federal Consolidated Fund.
Federal Consolidated Fund.

(5) The recommendations of the National Finance Commission, together with an explanatory memorandum as to the action taken thereon, shall be laid before both Houses and the Provincial Assemblies.

(6) At any time before an Order under clause (4) is made, the President may, by Order, make such amendments or modifications in the law relating to the

distribution of revenues between the Federal Government and the Provincial Governments as he may deem necessary or expedient.

(7) The President may, by Order, make grants-in-aid of the revenues of the Province in need of assistance and such grants shall be charged upon the Federal Consolidated Fund.

161. Natural gas and hydro-electric power.

(1) Notwithstanding the provisions of Article 78 net proceeds of the Federal Duty of excise on natural gas levied at well-head and collected by the Federal Government, and of the royalty collected by the Federal Government, shall not form part of the Federal Consolidated Fund and shall be paid to the Province in which the well-head of natural gas is situated.

(2) The net profits earned by the Federal Government, or any undertaking established or administered by the Federal Government from the bulk generation of power at a hydro-electric station shall be paid to the province in which the hydro-electric station is situated.

Explanation.

For the purposes of this clause 'net profits' shall be computed by deducting from the revenues accruing from the bulk supply of power from the bus-bars of a hydro-electric station at a rate to be determined by the Council of Common Interests, the operating expenses of the Station, which shall include any sums payable as taxes, duties, interest or return on investment, and depreciations and element of obsolescence, and over-heads, and provision for reserves.

162. In abeyance.

163. Provincial taxes in respect of professions, etc.

A Provincial Assembly may by Act impose taxes, not exceeding such limits as may from time to time be fixed by Act of Parliament, on persons engaged in professions, trades, callings or employments, and no such Act of the Assembly shall be regarded as imposing a tax on income.

MISCELLANEOUS FINANCIAL PROVINCES

164. Grants out of Consolidated Fund.

The Federation or a Province may make grants for any purpose, notwithstanding that the purpose is not one with respect to which Parliament or, as the case may be, a Provincial Assembly may make laws.

165. Exemption of certain public property from taxation.

(1) The Federal Government shall not, in respect of its property or income, be liable to taxation under any Act of Provincial Assembly and, subject to clause (2), a Provincial Government shall not, in respect of its property or income, be liable to taxation under Act of Parliament or under Act of the Provincial Assembly of any other Province.

(2) If a trade or business of any kind is carried on by or on behalf of the Government of a Province outside that Province, that Government may, in respect of any property used in connection with that trade or business, or any income

arising from that trade or business, be taxed under Act of Parliament or under Act of the Provincial Assembly of the Province in which that trade or business is carried on.

(3) Nothing in this Article shall prevent the imposition of fees for services rendered.

Chapter 2. Borrowing and Audit

166. Borrowing by Federal Government.

The executing authority of the Federation extends to borrowing upon the security of the Federal Consolidated Fund within such limits, if any, as may from time to time be fixed by Act of Parliament, and to the giving of guarantees within such limits, if any, as may be so fixed.

167. Borrowing by Provincial Government.

(1) Subject to the provisions of this Article, the executive authority of a Province extends to borrowing upon the security of the Provincial Consolidated Fund within such limits, if any, as may from time to time be fixed by Act of the Provincial Assembly, and to the giving of guarantees within such limits, if any, as may be so fixed.

(2) The Federal Government may, subject to such conditions, if any, as it may think fit to impose, make loans to, or, so long as any limits fixed under Article 166 are not exceeded give guarantees in respect of loans raised by, any Province, and any sums required for the purpose of making loans to a Province shall be charged upon the Federal Consolidated Fund.

(3) A Province may not, without the consent of the Federal Government, raise any loan if there is still outstanding any part of a loan made to the Province by the Federal Government, or in respect of which guarantee has been given by the Federal Government; and consent under this clause may be granted subject to such conditions, if any, as the Federal Government may think fit to impose.

AUDIT AND ACCOUNTS

168. Auditor General of Pakistan.

(1) There shall be an Auditor General of Pakistan, who shall be appointed by the President.

(2) Before entering upon office, the Auditor General shall make before the Chief Justice of Pakistan oath in the form set out in the Third Schedule.

(3) The terms and conditions of service, including the term of office, of the Auditor General shall be determined by Act of Parliament and, until so determined, by Order of the President.

(4) A person who has held office as Auditor General shall not be eligible for further appointment in the service of Pakistan before the expiration of two years after he has ceased to hold that office.

(5) The Auditor General shall not be removed from office except in the like manner and on the like grounds as a Judge of the Supreme Court.

(6) At any time when the office of the Auditor General is vacant or the Auditor General is absent or is unable to perform the functions of his office due to any cause, such other person as the President may direct shall act as Auditor General and perform the functions of that office.

169. Functions and powers of Auditor General.

The Auditor General shall, in relation to

(*a*) the accounts of the Federation and of the Provinces; and

(*b*) the accounts of any authority or body established by the Federation or a Province,

perform such functions and exercise such powers as may be determined by or under Act of Parliament and, until so determined, by Order of the President.

170. Power of Auditor General to give directions as to accounts.

The accounts of the Federation and of the Provinces shall be kept in such form and in accordance with such principles and methods as the Auditor General may with the approval of the President, prescribe.

171. Reports of Auditor General.

The reports of the Auditor General relating to the accounts of the Federation shall be submitted to the President, who shall cause them to be laid before the National Assembly and the reports of the Auditor General relating to the accounts of a Province shall be submitted to the Governor of the Province, who shall cause them to be laid before the Provincial Assembly.

Chapter 3. Property, contracts, liabilities and suits.

172. Ownerless property.

(1) Any property which has no rightful owner shall, if located in a Province, vest in the Government of that Province, and in every other case, in the Federal Government.

(2) All lands, minerals and other things of value within the continental shelf or underlying the ocean within the territorial waters of Pakistan shall vest in the Federal Government.

173. Power to acquire property and to make contracts, etc.

(1) The executive authority of the Federation and of a Province shall extend, subject to any Act of the appropriate Legislature, to the grant, sale, disposition or mortgage of any property vested in, and to the purchase or acquisition of property on behalf of, the Federal Government or, as the case may be, the Provincial Goverment, and to the making of contracts.

(2) All property acquired for the purposes of the Federation or of a Province shall vest in the Federal Government or, as the case may be, in the Provincial Government.

(3) All contracts made in the exercise of the executive authority of the Federation or of a Province shall be expressed to be made in the name of the President or, as the case may be, the Governor of the Province, and all such contracts and all assurances or property made in the exercise of that authority shall be

executed on behalf of the President or Governor by such persons and in such manner as he may direct or authorize.

(4) Neither the President, nor the Governor of a Province, shall be personnally liable in respect of any contract or assurance made or executed in the exercise of the executive authority of the Federation or, as the case may be, the Province, nor shall any person making or executing any such contract or assurance on behalf of any of them be personally liable in respect thereof.

(5) Transfer of land by the Federal Government or a Provincial Government shall be regulated by law.

174. Suits and proceedings.

The Federation may sue or be sued by the name of Pakistan and a Province may sue or be sued by the name of the Province.

THE JUDICATURE

Chapter 1. The Courts

175. Establishment and jurisdiction of courts.

(1) There shall be a Supreme Court of Pakistan, a High Court for each Province and such other courts as may be established by law.

(2) No court shall have any jurisdiction save as is or may be conferred on it by the Constitution or by or under any law.

(3) The Judiciary shall be separated progressively from the Executive within eight years from the commencing day.

Chapter 2. The Supreme Court of Pakistan.

176. Constitution of Supreme Court.

The Supreme Court shall consist of a Chief Justice to be known as the Chief Justice of Pakistan and so many other Judges as may be determined by Act of Parliament or, until so determined, as may be fixed by the President.

177. Appointment of Supreme Court Judges.

(1) The Chief Justice of Pakistan shall be appointed by the President, and each of the other Judges shall be appointed by the President after consultation with the Chief Justice.

(2) A person shall not be appointed a Judge of the Supreme Court unless he is a citizen of Pakistan and

(*a*) has for a period of, or for periods aggregating, not less than five years been a judge of a High Court (including High Court which existed in Pakistan at any time before the commencing day); or

(*b*) has for a period of, or for periods aggregating, not less than fifteen years been an advocate of a High Court (including a High Court which existed in Pakistan at any time before the commencing day).

178. Oath of office.

Before entering upon office, the Chief Justice of Pakistan shall make before the President, and any other Judge of the Supreme Court shall make before the Chief Justice, oath in the form set out in the Third Schedule.

179. Retiring age.

A Judge of the Supreme Court shall hold office until he attains the age of sixty-five years, unless he sooner resigns or is removed from office in accordance with the Constitution.

180. Acting Chief Justice.

At any time when

(*a*) the office of Chief Justice of Pakistan is vacant; or

(*b*) the Chief Justice of Pakistan is absent or is unable to perform the functions of his office due to any other cause,

the President shall appoint one of the Judges of the Supreme Court who have not previously held the office of Chief Justice of Pakistan otherwise than under this Article to Act as Chief Justice of Pakistan.

181. Acting Judges.

(1) At any time when

(*a*) the office of a Judge of the Supreme Court is vacant; or

(*b*) a Judge of the Supreme Court is absent or is unable to perform the functions of his office due to any other cause,

the President may, in the manner provided in clause (1) of Article 177, appoint a Judge of a High Court who is qualified for appointment as a Judge of the Supreme Court to act temporarily as a Judge of the Supreme Court.

(2) An appointment under this Article shall continue in force until it is revoked by the President.

182. In abeyance.

183. Seat of the Supreme Court.

(1) The permanent seat of the Supreme Court shall, subject to clause (3), be at Islamabad.

(2) The Supreme Court may from time to time sit in such other places as the Chief Justice of Pakistan, with the approval of the President, may appoint.

(3) Until provision is made for establishing the Supreme Court at Islamabad, the seat of the Court shall be at such place as the President may appoint.[1]

184. Original jurisdiction of Supreme Court.

(1) The Supreme Court shall, to the exclusion of every other court, have original jurisdiction in any dispute between any two or more Governments.

Explanation.

In this clause, 'Governments' means the Federal Government and the Provincial Governments.

(2) In the exercise of the jurisdiction conferred on it by clause (1), the Supreme Court shall pronounce declaratory judgments only.

(3) Without prejudice to the provisions of Article 199, the Supreme Court shall, if it considers that a question of public importance with reference to the

---

[1] In 1974, Rawalpindi became the seat.

enforcement of any of the Fundamental Rights conferred by Chapter 1 of Part II is involved, have the power to make an order of the nature mentioned in the said Article.

185. Appellate jurisdiction of Supreme Court.

(1) Subject to this Article, the Supreme Court shall have jurisdiction to hear and determine appeals from judgements, decrees, final orders or sentences of a High Court.

(2) An appeal shall lie to the Supreme Court from any judgment, decree, final order or sentence of a High Court

(*a*) if the High Court has on appeal reversed an order of acquittal of an accused person and sentenced him to death or to transportation for life or imprisonment for life; or, on revision, has enhanced a sentence to a sentence as aforesaid; or

(*b*) if the High Court has withdrawn for trial before itself any case from any Court subordinate to it and has in such trial convicted the accused person and sentenced him as aforesaid; or

(*c*) if the High Court has imposed any punishment on any person for contempt of the High Court; or

(*d*) if the amount or value of the subject-matter of the dispute in the Court of first instance was, and also in dispute in appeal is, not less than fifty thousand rupees or such other sum as may be specified in that behalf by Act of Parliament and the judgment, decree of final order appealed from has varied or set aside the judgment, decree or final order of the court immediately below; or

(*e*) if the judgment, decree or final order involves directly or indirectly some claim or question respecting property of the like amount or value and the judgment, decree or final order appealed from has varied or set aside the judgment, decree or final order of the court immediately below; or

(*f*) if the High Court certifies that the case involves a substantial question of law as to the interpretation of the Constitution.

(3) An appeal to the Supreme Court from a judgment, decree, order or sentence of a High Court in a case to which clause (2) does not apply shall lie only if the Supreme Court grants leave to appeal.

186. Advisory jurisdiction.

(1) If, at any time, the President considers that it is desirable to obtain the opinion of the Supreme Court on any question of law which he considers of public importance, he may refer the question to the Supreme Court for consideration.

(2) The Supreme Court shall consider a question so referred and report its opinion on the question to the President.

187. Issue and execution of processes of Supreme Court.

(1) Subject to clause (2) of Article 175, the Supreme Court shall have power to issue such directions, orders or decrees as may be necessary for doing

complete justice in any case or matter pending before it, including an order for the purpose of securing the attendance of any person or the discovery or production of any document.

(2) Any such direction, order or decree shall be enforceable throughout Pakistan and shall, where it is to be executed in a Province, or a territory or any area not forming part of a Province, be executed as if it had been issued by the High Court of that Province.

(3) If a question arises as to which High Court shall give effect to a direction, order or decree of the Supreme Court, the decision of the Supreme Court on the question shall be final.

188. Review of judgments or orders by the Supreme Court.

The Supreme Court shall have power, subject to the provisions of any Act of Parliament and of any rules made by the Supreme Court, to review any judgment pronounced or any order made by it.

189. Decisions of Supreme Court binding on other courts.

Any decision of the Supreme Court shall, to the extent that it decides a question of law or is based upon or enunciates a principle of law, be binding on all other courts in Pakistan.

190. Action in aid of Supreme Court.

All executive and judicial authorities throughout Pakistan shall act in aid of the Supreme Court.

191. Rules of procedure.

Subject to the Constitution and law, the Supreme Court may make rules regulating the practice and procedure of the Court.

Chapter 3. The High Courts

192. Constitution of High Court.

(1) A High Court shall consist of a Chief Justice and so many other Judges as may be determined by law or, until so determined, as may be fixed by the President.

(2) The Sind and Baluchistan High Court shall cease to function as a common High Court for the Provinces of Baluchistan and Sind.

(3) The President shall, by Order, establish a High Court for each of the Provinces of Baluchistan and Sind and may make such provision in the Order for the principal seats of the two High Courts, transfer of the Judges of the common High Court, transfer of cases pending in the common High Court immediately before the establishment of two High Courts and, generally, for matters consequential or ancillary to the common High Court ceasing to function and the establishment of the two High Courts as he may deem fit.

(4) The jursidiction of a High Court may, by Act of Parliament, be extended to any area in Pakistan not forming part of a Province.

193. Appointment of High Court Judges.

(1) A Judge of a High Court shall be appointed by the President after consultation

(*a*) with the Chief Justice of Pakistan;
(*b*) with the Governor concerned; and
(*c*) except where the appointment is that of Chief Justice, with the Chief Justice of the High Court.

(2) A person shall not be appointed a Judge of a High Court unless he is a citizen of Pakistan, is not less than forty years of age, and

(*a*) he has for a period of, or for periods aggregating, not less than ten years been an advocate of a High Court (including a High Court which existed in Pakistan at any time before the commencing day); or
(*b*) he is, and has for a period of not less than ten years been, a member of a civil service prescribed by law for the purposes of this paragraph, and has for a period of not less than three years, served as or exercised the functions of a District Judge in Pakistan; or
(*c*) he has, for a period of not less than ten years, held a judicial office in Pakistan.

Explanation.

In computing the period during which a person has been an advocate of a High Court or held judicial office, there shall be included any period during which he has held judicial office after he became an advocate or, as the case may be, the period during which he has been an advocate after having held judicial office.

(3) In this Article, 'District Judge' means Judge of a principal civil court of original jurisdiction.

194. Oath of office.

Before entering upon office, the Chief Justice of a High Court shall make before the Governor, and any other Judge of the Court shall make before the Chief Justice, oath in the form set out in the Third Schedule.

195. Retiring age.

A Judge of a High Court shall hold office until he attains the age of sixty-two years, unless he sooner resigns or is removed from office in accordance with the Constitution.

196. In abeyance.

197. Additional judges.

At any time when

(*a*) the office of a Judge of a High Court is vacant; or
(*b*) a Judge of a High Court is absent or is unable to perform the functions of his office due to any other cause; or
(*c*) for any reason it is necessary to increase the number of Judges of a High Court,

the President may, in the manner provided in clause (1) of Article 193, appoint a person qualified for appointment as a Judge of the High Court to be Additional Judge of the Court for such period as the President may determine, being a period not exceeding such period, if any, as may be prescribed by law.

198. to 200. In Abeyance.

201. Decision of High Court binding on subordinate Courts.

Subject to Article 189, any decision of a High Court shall, to the extent that it decides a question of law or is based upon or enunciates a principle of law, be binding on all courts subordinate to it.

202. Rules of procedure.

Subject to the Constitution and law, a High Court may make rules regulating the practice and procedure of the Court or of any court subordinate to it.

203. High Court to superintend subordinate courts.

Each High Court shall supervise and control all courts subordinate to it.

Chapter 3A. Federal Shariat Court

203A. Provisions of Chapter to override other provisions of Constitution.

The provisions of this Chapter shall have effect notwithstanding anything contained in the Constitution.

203B. Definitions.

In this Chapter, unless there is anything repugnant in the subject or context,

(*a*) 'Chairman' means Chairman of the Court;

(*b*) 'Court' means the Federal Shariat Court constituted in pursuance of Article 203C;

(*c*) 'Law' includes any custom or usage having the force of law but does not include the Constitution Muslim personal law, any law relating to the procedure of any court or tribunal or, until the expiration of three years from the commencement of this Chapter, any fiscal law or any law relating to the levy and collection of taxes and fees or banking or insurance practice and procedure; and

(*d*) 'member' means member of the Court.

203C. The Federal Shariat Court.

(1) There shall be constituted for the purpose of this Chapter a court to be called the Federal Shariat Court.

(2) The Court shall consist of five Muslim members, including the chairman, to be appointed by the President.

(3) & (4). In abeyance.

(5) A Judge of a High Court who does not accept appointment as a member shall be deemed to have retired from his office and, on such retirement, shall be entitled to receive a pension calculated on the basis of the length of his service as Judge and total service, if any, in the service of Pakistan.

(6) The Principal seat of the Court shall be at Islamabad, but the Court may from time to time sit in such other places in Pakistan as the Chairman may, with the approval of the President, appoint.

(7) Before entering upon office, the Chairman and a member shall make before the President or a person nominated by him oath in the form set out, in the Third Schedule.

(8) At any time when the Chairman or a member is absent or is unable to perform the functions of his office, the President shall appoint another person qualified for the purpose to act as Chairman or, as the case may be, member.

(9) A Chairman who is not a Judge of the Supreme Court shall be entitled to the same salary, allowances and privileges as are admissible to a Judge of the Supreme Court and a member who is not a Judge of a High Court shall be entitled to the same salary, allowances and privileges as are admissible to a Judge of a High Court.

203CC. Panel of Ulema and Ulema members.

(1) The President may, in consultation with the Chairman, draw up a panel of Ulema who are well-versed in Islamic law for being associated with the Court in cases before it.

(2) The Chairman shall, in all cases before the Court, request the Ulema, not exceeding three, borne on the aforesaid panel to attend the sittings of the Court as Ulema members and, while so sitting, they shall have the same power and jurisdiction, and be entitled to the same privileges, as a member and such allowances as may be determined by the President.

203D. Powers, jurisdiction and functions of the Court.

(1) The Court may, on the petition of a citizen of Pakistan or the Federal Government or a Provincial Government, examine and decide the question whether or not any law or provision of law is repugnant to the Injunctions of Islam as laid down in the Holy Quran and the Sunnah of the Holy Prophet, hereinafter referred to as the Injunctions of Islam.

(2) If the Court decides that any law or provisions of Law is repugnant to the Injunctions of Islam, it shall set out in its decision

(*a*) the reasons for its holding that opinion; and

(*b*) the extent to which such law or provision is so repugnant;

and specify the day on which the decision shall take effect.

(3) If any law or provision of law is held by the Court to be repugnant to the Injunctions of Islam,

(*a*) the President in the case of a law with respect to a matter in the Federal Legislative List or the Concurrent Legislative List, or the Governor in the case of a law with respect to a matter not enumerated in either of those Lists, shall take steps to amend the law so as to bring such law or provision into conformity with the Injunctions of Islam; and

(*b*) such law or provision shall, to the extent to which it is held to be so repugnant, cease to have effect on the day on which the decision of the Court takes effect.

(4) *Omitted.*

203DD. Further Jurisdiction of the Court.

The Court shall have such other jurisdiction as may be conferred on it or under any law.

203E. Powers and procedure of the Court.

(1) For the purposes of the performance of its functions the Court shall have the powers of a Civil Court trying a suit under the Code of Civil Procedure, 1908 (Act V of 1908), in respect of the following matters, namely:

(*a*) summoning and enforcing the attendance of any person and examining him on oath;

(*b*) requiring the discovery and production of any document;

(*c*) receiving evidence on affidavits; and

(*d*) issuing commissions for the examination of witnesses or documents.

(2) The Court shall have power to conduct its proceedings and regulate its procedure in all respects as it deems fit.

(3) The Court shall have the power of a High Court to punish its own contempt.

(4) A party to any proceedings before the Court under clause (1) of Article *203D.* may be represented by a legal practitioner who is a Muslim and has been enrolled as an advocate of a High Court for a period of not less than five years or as an advocate of the Supreme Court or by a jurisconsult selected by the party from out of a panel of jurisconsults maintained by the Court for the purpose.

(5) For being eligible to have his name borne on the panel of jurisconsults referred to in clause (4), a person shall be an *aalim* who, in the opinion of the Court, is well-versed in Shariat.

(6) A legal practitioner or jurisconsult representing a party before the Court shall not plead for the party but shall state, expound and interpret the Injunctions of Islam relevant to the proceedings so far as may be known to him and submit to the Court a written statement of his interpretation of such Injunctions of Islam.

(7) The Court may invite any person in Pakistan or abroad whom the Court considers to be well-versed in Islamic law to appear before it and render such assistance as may be required of him.

(8) No court fee shall be payable in respect of any petition or application made to the Court under Article *203D.*

(9) The Court shall have power to review any decision given or order made by it.

203F. Appeal to Supreme Court.

(1) Any party to any proceedings before the Court under Article *203D* aggrieved by the final decision of the Court in such proceedings may, within sixty days of such decision, prefer an appeal to the Supreme Court.

(2) The provisions of clauses (2) and (3) of Article *203D* and clauses (4) and (8) of Article *203E* shall apply to and in relation to the Supreme Court as if reference in those provisions to Court were a reference to the Supreme Court.

(3) For the purpose of the exercise of the jurisdiction conferred by this Article, there shall be constituted in the Supreme Court a Bench consisting of three Muslim Judges of the Supreme Court, to be called the Shariat Appellate Bench, and reference in the proceedings clauses to 'Supreme Court' shall be construed as a reference to the Shariat Appellate Bench.

203G. Bar of Jurisdiction.

Save as provided in Article *203F*, no court or tribunal, including the Supreme Court and a High Court, shall entertain any proceedings or exercise any power or jurisdiction in respect of any matter within the power or jurisdiction of the Court.

203H. Pending proceedings to continue, etc.

(1) Subject to clause (2) nothing in this Chapter shall be deemed to require any proceedings pending in any Court or tribunal immediately before the commencement of this Chapter or initiated after such commencement, to be adjourned or stayed by reason only of a petition having been made to the Court for a decision as to whether or not a law or provision of law relevant to the decision of the point in issue in such proceedings is repugnant to the Injunctions of Islam; and all such proceedings shall continue, and the point in issue therein shall be decided, in accordance with the law for the time being in force.

(2) All proceedings under clause (1) of Article *203B* of the Constitution that may be pending before any High Court immediately before the commencement of this Chapter shall stand transferred to the Court and shall be dealt with by the Court from the stage from which they are so transferred.

(3) Neither the Court nor the Supreme Court shall in the exercise of its jurisdiction under this Chapter have power to grant an injunction or make any interim order in relation to any proceedings pending in any other court or tribunal.

203I. Administrative arrangements, etc.

The Federal Government shall make all such administrative arrangements, and make available to the Court the service of such officers and experts, as it may consider necessary for the convenient performance of the functions of the Court.

203J. Power to make rules.

(1) The Court may, by notification in the official Gazette, make rules for carrying out the purposes of this Chapter.

(2) In particular, and without prejudice to the generality of the foregoing power, such rules may make provision in respect of all or any of the following matters, namely:

(*a*) the scale of payment of honoraria to be made to jurisconsults, experts and witnesses summoned by the Court to defray the expenses, if any, incurred by them in attending for the purposes of the proceedings before the Court;

(*b*) the form of oath to be made by a jurisconsult expert or witness appearing before the Court;

(*c*) the powers and functions of the Court being exercised or performed by Benches consisting of one or more members constituted by the Chairman;

(*d*) the decision of the Court being expressed in terms of the opinion of the majority of its members or, as the case may be, of the members constituting a Bench; and

(*e*) the decision of cases in which the members constituting a Bench are equally divided in their opinion.

Chapter 4. General provisions relating to the Judicature

204. Contempt of Court.

(1) In this Article, 'Court' means the Supreme Court or a High Court.

(2) A court shall have the power to punish a person for contempt of Court in accordance with law.

205. Remuneration, etc., of Judges.

The remuneration and other terms and conditions of service of a Judge of the Supreme Court or of a High Court shall be as provided in the Fifth Schedule. the Fifth Schedule.

206. Resignation.

(1) A Judge of the Supreme Court or of a High Court may resign his office by writing under his hand addressed to the President.

(2) A Judge of a High Court who does not accept appointment as a Judge of the Supreme Court shall be deemed to have retired from his office and, on such retirement, shall be entitled to receive a pension calculated on the basis of the length of his service as Judge and total service, if any, in the service of Pakistan.

207. Judge not to hold office of profit, etc.

(1) A Judge of the Supreme Court of a High Court shall not

(*a*) hold any other office of profit in the service of Pakistan if his remuneration is thereby increased; or

(*b*) occupy any other position carrying the right to remuneration for the rendering of services.

(2) In abeyance.

(3) A person who has held office as a permanent Judge

(*a*) of the Supreme Court, shall not plead or act in any court or before any authority in Pakistan;

(*b*) of a High Court, shall not plead or act in any court or before any authority within its jurisdiction; and

(*c*) of the High Court of West Pakistan as it existed immediately before the coming into force of the Province of West Pakistan (Dissolution) Order, 1970, shall not plead or act in any court or before any authority within the jurisdiction of the principal seat of that High Court or, as the case may be, the permanent bench of that High Court to which he was assigned.

208. Officers and servants of Courts.

The Supreme Court, with the approval of the President and a High Court, with the approval of the Governor concerned, may make rules providing for the appointment by the Court of officers and servants of the Court and for their terms and conditions of employment.

209. Supreme Judicial Council.

(1) There shall be a Supreme Council of Pakistan, in this Chapter referred to as the Council.

(2) The Council shall consist of

(*a*) the Chief Justice of Pakistan;
(*b*) the two next most senior Judges of Supreme Court; and
(*c*) the two most senior Chief Justice of High Courts.

Explanation.

For the purpose of this clause, the *inter se* seniority of the Chief Justice of the High Courts shall be determined with reference to their dates of appointment as Chief Justice otherwise than as acting Chief Justice, and in case the dates of such appointment are the same, with reference to their dates of appointment as Judges of any of the High Courts.

(3) If at any time the Council is inquiring into the capacity or conduct of a Judge who is a member of the Council, or a member of the Council is absent or is unable to act due to illness or any other cause, then

(*a*) if such member is a Judge of the Supreme Court, the Judge of the Supreme Court who is next in seniority below the Judges referred to in paragraph (*b*) of clause (2), and
(*b*) if such member is the Chief Justice of a High Court, the Chief Justice of another High Court who is next in seniority amongst the Chief Justices of the remaining High Courts, shall act as a member of the Council in his place.

(4) If, upon any matter inquired into by the Council, there is a difference of opinion amongst its members, the opinion of the majority shall prevail, and the report of the Council to the President shall be expressed in terms of the view of the majority.

(5) If, on information received from the Council or from any other source, the President is of the opinion that a Judge of the Supreme Court or of a High Court,

(*a*) may be incapable of properly performing the duties of his office by reason of physical or mental incapacity; or
(*b*) may have been guilty of misconduct, the President shall direct the Council to inquire into the matter.

(6) If, after inquiring into the matter, the Council reports to the President that it is of the opinion

(*a*) that the Judge is incapable of performing the duties of his office or has been guilty of misconduct, and
(*b*) that he should be removed from office, the President may remove the Judge from office.

(7) A Judge of the Supreme Court or of a High Court shall not be removed from office except as provided by this Article.

(8) The Council shall issue a code of conduct to be observed by Judges of the Supreme Court and of the High Courts.

210. Power of Council to enforce attendance of persons, etc.

(1) For the purpose of inquiring into any matter, the Council shall have the same power as the Supreme Court has to issue directions or orders for securing the attendance of any person or the discovery or production of any document; and any such direction or order shall be enforceable as if it had been issued by the Supreme Court.

(2) The provisions of Article 204 shall apply to the Council as they apply to the Supreme Court and a High Court.

211. Bar of Jurisdiction.

The proceedings before the Council, its report to the President and the removal of a Judge under clause (6) of Article 209 shall not be called in question in any court.

212. Administrative Courts and Tribunals.

(1) Notwithstanding anything hereinbefore contained, the appropriate Legislature may by Act provide for the establishment of one or more Administrative Courts or Tribunals to exercise exclusive jurisdiction in respect of

(*a*) matters relating to the terms and conditions of persons who are or have been in the service of Pakistan, including disciplinary matters;

(*b*) matters relating to claims arising from tortious acts of Government, or any person in the service of Pakistan, or of any local or other authority empowered by law to levy any tax or cess and any servant of such authority acting in the discharge of his duties as such servant; or

(*c*) matters relating to the acquisition, administration and disposal of any property which is deemed to be enemy property under any law.

(2) Notwithstanding anything hereinbefore contained, where any Administrative Court or Tribunal is established under clause (1), no other Court shall grant an injunction, make any order or entertain any proceedings in respect of any matter to which the jurisdiction of such Administrative Court or Tribunal extends and all proceedings in respect of any such matter which may be pending before such other court immediately before the establishment of the Administrative Court or Tribunal other than an appeal pending before the Supreme Court, shall abate on such establishment:

Provided that the provisions of this clause shall not apply to an Administrative Court or Tribunal established under an Act of a Provincial Assembly unless, at the request of that Assembly made in the form of a resolution, Parliament by law extends the provisions to such a Court or Tribunal.

(3) An appeal to the Supreme Court from a judgment, decree, order or sentence of an Administrative Court or Tribunal shall lie only if the Supreme Court, being satisfied that the case involves a substantial question of law of public importance, grants leave to appeal.

227. Provisions relating to the Holy Quran and Sunnah.

(1) All existing laws shall be brought in conformity with the Injunctions of Islam as laid down in the Holy Quran and Sunnah, in this Part referred to as the Injunctions of Islam, and no law shall be enacted which is repugnant to such Injunctions.

Explanation.

In the application of this clause to the personal law of any Muslim sect, the expression 'Quran and Sunnah' shall mean the Quran and Sunnah as interpreted by that sect'.

(2) Effect shall be given to the provisions of clause (1) only in the manner provided in this Part.

(3) Nothing in this Part shall affect the personal laws of non-Muslim citizens or their status as citizens.

228. Composition, etc., of Islamic Council.

(1) There shall be constituted within a period of ninety days from the commencing day a Council of Islamic Ideology, in this part referred to as the Islamic Council.

(2) The Islamic Council shall consist of such members, being not less than eight and not more than twenty as the President may appoint from amongst persons having knowledge of the principles and philosophy of Islam as enunciated in the Holy Quran and Sunnah, or understanding of the economic, political, legal or administrative problems of Pakistan.

(3) While appointing members of the Islamic Council, the President shall ensure that

(*a*) so far as practicable various schools of thought are represented in the Council;

(*b*) not less than two of the members are persons each of whom is, or has been a Judge of the Supreme Court or of a High Court;

(*c*) not less than four of the members are persons each of whom has been engaged, for a period of not less than fifteen years, in Islamic research or instruction; and

(*d*) at least one member is a woman.

(4) The President shall appoint one of the members referred to in paragraph (*b*) of clause (3) to be the Chairman of the Islamic Council.

(5) Subject to clause (6), a member of the Islamic Council shall hold office for a period of three years.

(6) A member may, by writing under his hand addressed to the President, resign his office or may be removed by the President upon the passing of a resolution for his removal by a majority of the total membership of the Islamic Council.

229. Reference by Parliament, etc., to Islamic Council.

The President or the Governor of a Province may, or if two-fifths of its total membership so requires, a House or a Provincial Assembly shall, refer to the Islamic Council for advice any question as to whether a proposed law is or is not repugnant to the Injunctions of Islam.

230. Functions of the Islamic Council.

(1) The functions of the Islamic Council shall be

(*a*) to make recommendations to Parliament and the Provincial Assemblies as to the ways and means of enabling and encouraging the Muslims of Pakistan to order their lives individually and collectively in all respects in accordance with the principles and concepts of Islam as enunciated in the Holy Quran and Sunnah;

(*b*) to advise a House, a Provincial Assembly, the President or a Governor on any question referred, to the Council as to whether a proposed law is or is not repugnant to the Injunctions of Islam;

(*c*) to make recommendations as to the measures for bringing existing laws into conformity with the Injunctions of Islam and the stages by which such measures should be brought into effect; and

(*d*) to compile in a suitable form, for the guidance of Parliament and the Provincial Assemblies, such Injunctions of Islam as can be given legislative effect.

(2) When, under Article 229, a question is referred by a House, a Provincial Assembly, the President or a Governor to the Islamic Council, the Council shall, within fifteen days thereof, inform the House, the Assembly, the President or the Governor, as the case may be, of the period within which the Council expects to be able to furnish that advice.

(3) Where a House, a Provincial Assembly, the President or the Governor, as the case may be, considers that, in the public interest, the making of the proposed law in relation to which the question arose should not be postponed until the advice of the Islamic Council is furnished, the law may be made before the advice is furnished:

Provided that, where a law is referred for advice to the Islamic Council and the Council advises that the law is repugnant to the Injunctions of Islam, the House or, as the case may be, the Provincial Assembly, the President or the Governor shall reconsider the law so made.

(4) The Islamic Council shall submit its final report within seven years of its appointment, and shall submit an annual interim report. The report, whether interim or final, shall be laid for discussion before both Houses and each Provincial Assembly within six months of its receipt, and Parliament and the Assembly, after considering the report, shall enact laws in respect thereof within a period of two years of the final report.

231. Rules of procedure.

The Proceedings of the Islamic Council shall be regulated by rules of Procedure to be made by the Council with approval of the President.

EMERGENCY PROVISIONS

232. Proclamation of emergency on account of war, internal disturbance etc.

(1) If the President is satisfied that a grave emergency exists in which the security of Pakistan or any part thereof, is threatened by war or external aggression and by internal disturbance beyond the power of a Provincial Government to control he may issue a Proclamation of Emergency.

(2) Notwithstanding anything in the Constitution, while a Proclamation of Emergency is in force,

(*a*) Parliament shall have power to make laws for a Province, or any part thereof, with respect to any matter enumerated in Part II of the Federal List or the concurrent Legislative List or with respect to any matter not enumerated in either of those Lists, as if it were a matter specified in Part I of the Federal List;

(*b*) the executive authority of the Federation shall extend to the giving of directions to a Province as to the manner in which the ex-executive authority of the Province is to be exercised; and

(*c*) the Federal Government may be Order assume to itself, or direct the Governor of a Province to assume on behalf of the Federal Government, all or any of the functions of the Government of the Province, and all or any of the powers vested in, or exercisable by, any body or authority in the Province other than the Provincial Assembly, and make such incidental and consequential provisions as appear to the Federal Government to be necessary or desirable for giving effect to the objects of the Proclamation, including provisions for suspending, in whole or in part, the operation of any provisions of the Constitution relating to any body or authrority in the Province:

Provided that nothing in paragraph (*c*) shall authorize the Federal Government to assume to itself, or direct the Governor of the Province to assume on its behalf, any of the powers vested in or exercisable by a High Court, or to suspend either in whole or in part the operation of any provisions of the Constitution relating to High Courts.

(3) The power of Parliament to make laws for a Province with respect to any matter shall include power to make laws conferring powers and imposing duties, or authorizing the conferring or powers and the imposition of duties upon the Federation, or officers and authorities of the Federation, as respects that matter.

(4) Nothing in this Article shall restrict the power of a Provincial Assembly to make any law which under the Constitution it has power to make, but if any provision of a Provincial law is repugnant to any provision of an Act of Parliament which Parliament has under this Article power to make, the Act of Parliament, whether passed before or after the Provincial law, shall prevail and the Provincial law shall, to the extent of the repugnancy, but so long only as the Act of Parliament continues to have effect, be void.

(5) A law made by Parliament, which Parliament would not but for the issue of a Proclamation of Emergency have been competent to make, shall, to the extent of the incompetency, cease to have effect on the expiration of a period of six months after the Proclamation of Emergency has ceased to be in force, except as respects things done or omitted to be done before the expiration of the said period.

(6) While a Proclamation of Emergency is in force, Parliament may by law extend the term of the National Assembly for a period not exceeding one year and not extending in any case beyond a period of six months after the Proclamation has ceased to be in force.

(7) A Proclamation of Emergency shall be laid before a joint sitting

which shall be summoned by the President to meet within thirty days of the Proclamation being issued and

(*a*) shall cease to be in force at the expiration of two months unless before the expiration of that period it has been approved by a resolution of the joint sitting; and

(*b*) shall, subject to the provisions of paragraph (*a*), cease to be in force upon a resolution disapproving the Proclamation being passed by the votes of the majority of the total membership of the two Houses in joint sitting.

(8) Notwithstanding anything contained in clause (7), if the National Assembly stands dissolved at the time when a Proclamation of Emergency is issued, the Proclamation shall continue in force for a period of four months but, if a general election to the Assembly is not held before the expiration of that period, it shall cease to be in force at the expiration of that period unless it has earlier been approved by a resolution of the Senate.

233. In abeyance.

234. Power to issue proclamation in case of failure of Constitutional Machinery in a Province.

(1) If the President, on receipt of a report from the Governor of a Province or otherwise, is satisfied that a situation has arisen in which the Government of the Province cannot be carried on in accordance with the provisions of the Constitution, the President may, or if a resolution in this behalf is passed at a joint sitting shall, by Proclamation,

(*a*) assume to himself, or direct the Governor of the Province to assume on behalf of the President, all or any of the functions of the Government of the Province and all or any of the powers vested in, or exercisable by, any body or authority in the province, other than the Provincial Assembly;

(*b*) declare that the powers of the Provincial Assembly shall be exercisable by or under the authority of Parliament; and

(*c*) make such incidental and consequential provisions as appear to the President to be necessary or desirable for giving effect to the objects of the Proclamation, including provisions for suspending in whole or in part the operation of any provisions of the Constitution relating to any body or authority in the Province:

Provided that nothing in this Article shall authorize the President to assume to himself, or direct the Governor of the Province to assume on his behalf, any of the powers vested in, or exercisable by, a High Court, or to suspend either in whole or in part the operation of any provisions of the Constitution relating to High Court.

(2) The provisions of Article 105 shall not apply to the discharge by the Governor of his functions under clause (1).

(3) A Proclamation issued under this Article shall be laid before a joint sitting and shall cease to be in force at the expiration of two months, unless before the expiration of that period it has been approved by resolution of the joint sitting

and may by like resolution be extended for a further period not exceeding two months at a time; but no such Proclamation shall in any case remain in force for more than six months.

(4) Notwithstanding anything contained in clause (3), if the National Assembly stands dissolved at the time when a Proclamation is issued under this Article, the Proclamation shall continue in force for a period of three months but, if a general election to the Assembly is not held before the expiration of that period, it shall cease to be in force at the expiration of that period unless it has earlier been approved by a resolution in the Senate.

(5) Where by a Proclamation issued under this Article it has been declared that the powers of the Provincial Assembly shall be exercisable by or under the authority of Parliament, it shall be competent

- (*a*) to Parliament in joint sitting to confer on the President the power to make laws with respect to any matter within the legislative competence of the Provincial Assembly;
- (*b*) to Parliament in joint sitting, or the President, when he is empowered under paragraph (*a*), to make laws conferring powers and imposing duties, or authorizing the conferring of powers and the imposition of duties, upon the Federation, or officers and authorities thereof;
- (*c*) to the President, when Parliament is not in session, to authorize expenditure from the Provincial Consolidated Fund, whether the expenditure is charged by the Constitution upon that Fund or not, pending the sanction of such expenditure by Parliament in joint sitting; and
- (*d*) to Parliament in joint sitting by resolution to sanction expenditure authorized by the President under paragraph (*c*).

(6) Any law made by Parliament or the President which Parliament or the President would not, but for the issue of a Proclamation under this Article, have been competent to make, shall, to the extent of the incompetency, cease to have effect on the expiration of a period of six months after the Proclamation under this Article has ceased to be in force, except as to things, done or omitted to be done before the expiration of the said period.

235. Proclamation in case of financial emergency.

(1) If the President is satisfied that a situation has arisen whereby the economic life, financial stability or credit of Pakistan, or any part thereof, is threatened, he may, after consultation with the Governors of the Provinces or, as the case may be, the Governor of the Province concerned, by Proclamation make a declaration to that effect, and, while such a Proclamation is in force, the executive authority of the Federation shall extend to the giving of directions to any Province to observe such principles of financial propriety as may be specified in the directions, and to the giving of such other directions as the President may deem necessary in the interest of the economic life, financial stability or credit of Pakistan or any part thereof.

(2) Notwithstanding anything in the Constitution, any such directions may include a provision requiring a reduction of the salary and allowances of all or any class of persons serving in connection with the affairs of a Province.

(3) While a Proclamation issued under this Article is in force the President may issue directions for the reduction of the salaries and allowances of all or any class of persons serving in connection with the affairs of the Federation.

(4) The provisions of clauses (3) and (4) of Article 234 shall apply to a Proclamation issued under this Article as they apply to a Proclamation issued under that Article.

236. Revocation of Proclamation, etc.

(1) A Proclamation issued under this Part may be varied or revoked by a subsequent Proclamation.

(2) The validity of any Proclamation issued or Order made under this Part shall not be called in question in any court.

237. Parliament may make laws of indemnity, etc.

Nothing in the Constitution shall prevent Parliament from making any law indemnifying any person in the service of the Federal Government or a Provincial Government, or any other person, in respect of any act done in connection with the maintenance or restoration of order in any area in Pakistan.

238. and 239. In abeyance.

MISCELLANEOUS

240. Appointments to service of Pakistan and conditions of service.

Subject to the Constitution, the appointments to and the conditions of service of persons in the service of Pakistan shall be determined

(*a*) in the case of the service of the Federation, posts in connection with the affairs of the Federation and All-Pakistan Service, by or under Act of Parliament; and

(*b*) in the case of the service of a Province and posts in connection with affairs of a Province, by or under Act of the Provincial Assembly.

Explanation.

In this Article, 'All-Pakistan Service' means a service common to the Federation and the Province, which was in existence immediately before the commencing day or which may be created by Act of Parliament.

241. Existing rules, etc., to continue.

Until the appropriate Legislature makes a law under Article 240, all rules and orders in force immediately before the commencing day shall, so far as consistent with the provisions of the Constitution, continue in force and may be amended from time to time by the Federal Government or, as the case may be, the Provincial Government.

242. Public Service Commission.

(1) Parliament in relation to the affairs of the Federation, and the Provincial Assembly of a Province in relation to the affairs of the Province, may, by law,

provide for the establishment and constitution of a Public Service Commission.

(2) A Public Service Commission shall perform such functions as may be prescribed by law.

Chapter 2. Armed Forces

243. Command of Armed Forces.

(1) The Federal Government shall have control and command of the Armed Forces.

(2) The President shall subject to law, have power

(*a*) to raise and maintain the Military, Naval and Air Forces of Pakistan; and the Reserves of such Forces;

(*b*) to grant Commissions in such Forces; and

(*c*) to appoint the Chief of the Army Staff, the Chief of the Naval Staff, and the Chief of the Air Staff, and determine their salaries and allowances.

244. Oath of Armed Forces.

Every member of the Armed Forces shall make oath in the form set out in the Third Schedule.

245. Functions of Armed Forces.

(1) The Armed Forces shall, under the directions of the Federal Government defend Pakistan against external aggression or threat of war, and, subject to law, act in aid of civil power when called upon to do so.

(2) The validity of any direction issued by the Federal Government under clause (1) shall not be called in question in any Court.

(3) A High Court shall not exercise any jurisdiction under Article 199 in relation to any area in which the Armed Forces of Pakistan are, for the time being, acting in aid of civil power in pursuance of Article 245:

Provided that this clause shall not be deemed to affect the jurisdiction of the High Court in respect of any proceeding pending immediately before the day on which the Armed Forces start acting in aid of civil power.

(4) Any proceeding in relation to an area referred to in clause (3) instituted on or after the day the Armed Forces start acting in aid of civil power and pending in any High Court shall remain suspended for the period during which the Armed Forces are so acting.

Chapter 3. Tribal Areas

246. Tribal Areas.

In this Constitution,

(*a*) 'Tribal Areas' means the areas in Pakistan which, immediately before the commencing day, were Tribal Areas, and includes

(i) the Tribal Areas of Baluchistan and the North-West Frontier Province; and

(ii) the former States of Amb, Chitral, Dir and Swat;

(*b*) 'Provincially Administered Tribal Areas' means

(i) the districts of Chitral, Dir and Swat (which includes Kalam) (the Tribal Area in Kohistan district,) Malakand Protected Area, the Tribal Area adjoining Mansehra district and the former State of Amb; and

(ii) Zhob district, Loralai district (excluding Duki Tehsi), Dalbandin Tehsil of Chagai district and Marri and Bugti tribal territories of Sibi district; and

(*c*) 'Federally Administered Tribal Areas' includes

(i) Tribal Areas, adjoining Peshawar district;

(ii) Tribal Areas adjoining Kohat district;

(iii) Tribal Areas adjoining Bannu district;

(iv) Tribal Areas adjoining Dera Ismail Khan district;

(v) Bajaur Agency;

(vi) Orakzai Agency;

(vii) Khyber Agency;

(viii) Kurram Agency;

(ix) North Waziristan Agency; and

(x) South Waziristan Agency.

247. Administration of Tribal Areas.

(1) Subject to the Constitution, the executive authority of the Federation shall extend to the Federally Administered Tribal Areas; and the executive authority of a Province shall extend to the Provincially Administered Tribal Areas therein.

(2) The President may, from time to time, give such directions to the Governor of a Province relating to the whole or any part of a Tribal Area within the Province as he may deem necessary, and the Governor shall, in the exercise of his functions under this Article, comply with such directions.

(3) No Act of Parliament shall apply to any Federally Administered Tribal Area or to any part thereof, unless the President so directs, and no Act of Parliament or a Provincial Assembly shall apply to a Provincially Administered Tribal Area, or to any part thereof, unless the Governor of the Province in which the Tribal Area is situated, with the approval of the President, so directs; and in giving such a direction with respect to any law, the President or, as the case may be, the Governor, may direct that the law shall, in its application to a Tribal Area or to a specified part thereof, have effect subject to such exceptions and modifications as may be specified in the direction.

(4) Notwithstanding anything contained in the Constitution, the President may, with respect to any matter within the legislative competence of Parliament, and the Governor of a Province, with the prior approval of the President, may with respect to any matter within the legislative competence of the Provincial Assembly make regulations for the peace and good government of a Provincially Administered Tribal Area or any part thereof, situated in the Province.

(5) Notwithstanding anything contained in the Constitution, the President

may, with respect to any matter, make regulations for the peace and good government of a Federally Administered Tribal Area or any part thereof.

(6) The President may, at any time, by Order, direct that the whole or any part of a Tribal Area shall cease to be Tribal Area, and such Order may contain such incidental and consequential provisions as appear to the President to be necessary and proper:

Provided that before making any Order under this clause, the President shall ascertain, in such manner as he considered appropriate, the views of the people of the Tribal Area concerned, as represented in tribal jirga.

(7) Neither the Supreme Court nor a High Court shall exercise any jurisdiction under the Constitution in relation to a Tribal Area, unless Parliament by law otherwise provides;

Provided that nothing in this clause shall affect the jurisdiction which the Supreme Court or a High Court exercised in relation to a Tribal Area immediately before the commencing day.

Chapter 4. General

248. Protection to President, Governor, Minister, etc.

(1) The President, a Governor, the Prime Minister, a Federal Minister, a Minister of State, the Chief Minister and a Provincial Minister shall not be answerable to any Court for the exercise of powers and performance of functions of their respective offices or for any act done or purported to be done in the exercise of those powers and performance of those functions:

Provided that nothing in this clause shall be construed as restricting the right of any person to bring appropriate proceedings against the Federation or a Province.

(2) No criminal proceedings whatsoever shall be instituted or continued against the President or a Governor in any court during his term of office.

(3) No process for the arrest or imprisonment of the President or a Governor shall issue from any court during his term of office.

(4) No civil proceedings in which relief is claimed against the President or a Governor shall be instituted during his term of office in respect of anything done or not done by him in his personal capacity whether before or after he enters upon his office unless, at least sixty days before the proceedings are instituted, notice in writing has been delivered to him, or sent to him in the manner prescribed by law, stating the nature of the proceedings, the cause of action, the name, description and place of residence of the party by whom the proceedings are to be instituted and the relief which the party claims.

249. Legal proceedings.

(1) Any legal proceedings which, but for the Constitution, could have been brought by or against the Federation in respect of a matter which, immediately before the commencing day, was the responsiblility of the Federation and has, under the Constitution, become the responsibility of a Province, shall be brought by

or against the Province concerned; and if any such legal proceedings were pending in any court immediately before the commencing day then, in those proceedings, for the Federation the Province concerned shall, as from that day, be deemed to have been substituted.

(2) Any legal proceedings which, but for the Constitution, could have been brought by or against a Province in respect of a matter which, immediately before the commencing day, was the responsibility of the Federation, shall be brought by or against the Federation; and if any such legal proceedings were pending in any court immediately before the commencing day then, in those proceedings for the Province the Federation shall, as from that day, be deemed to have been substituted.

250. Salaries, allowances, etc., of the President, etc.

(1) Within two years from the commencing day, provision shall be made by law for determining the salaries, allowances and privileges of the President, the Speaker and Deputy Speaker and a member of the National Assembly or a Provincial Assembly, the Chairman and Deptuy Chariman and a member of the Senate, the Prime Minister, a Minister of State, a Chief Minister, a Provincial Minister and the Chief Election Commissioner.

(2) Until other provision is made by law,

(*a*) the salaries, allowances and privileges of the President, the Speaker or Deputy Speaker or a member of the National Assembly or a Provincial Assembly, a Federal Minister, a Minister of State, a Chief Minister, a Provincial Minister and the Chief Election Commissioner shall be the same as the salaries, allowances and privilleges to which the President, the Speaker or Deputy Speaker or member of the National Assembly of Pakistan or a Provincial Assembly, a Federal Minister of State, a Chief Minister, a Provincial Minister or, as the case may be, the Chief Election Commissioner was entitled immediately before the commencing day; and

(*b*) the salaries, allowances and privileges of the Chairman, the Deputy Chairman, the Prime Minister and a member of the Senate shall be such as the President may by Order determine.

(3) The salary, allowances and privileges of a person holding office as

(*a*) the President;
(*b*) the Chairman or Deputy Chairman;
(*c*) the Speaker or Deputy Speaker of the National Assembly or a Provincial Assembly;
(*d*) a Governor;
(*e*) the Chief Election Commissioner ; or
(*f*) the Auditor-General;

shall not be varied to his disadvantage during his term of office,

(4) At any time when the Chairman or Speaker is acting as President, he shall be entitled to the same salary, allowances and privileges as a President but

shall not exercise any of the functions of the office of Chairman or Speaker or a member of Parliament or be entitled to salary, allowances or privileges as Chairman, Speaker or such a member.

251. National language.

(1) The national language of Pakistan is Urdu, and arrangements shall be made for its being used for official and other purposes within fifteen years from the commencing day.

(2) Subject to clause (1), the English language may be used for official purposes until arrangements are made for its replacement by Urdu.

(3) Without prejudice to the status of the national language, a Provincial Assembly may by law prescribe measures for the teaching, promotion and use of a provincial language in addition to the national language.

252. Special provisions in relation to major ports and aerodromes.

(1) Nothwitstanding anything contained in the Constitution or in any law, the President may, by public notification, direct that, for a period not exceeding three months from a specified date, a specified law, whether a Federal law or a Provincial law, shall not apply to a specified major port or major aerodrome, or shall apply to a specified major port or major aerodrome subject to specified exceptions or modifications.

(2) The giving of a direction under this Article in relation to any law shall not affect the operation of the law prior to the date specified in the direction.

253. Maximum limits as to property, etc.

(1) Parliament may by law

(*a*) prescribe the maximum limits as to property or any class thereof which may be owned, held, possessed or controlled by any person; and

(*b*) declare that any trade, business, industry or service specified in such law shall be carried on or owned, to the exclusion, complete or partial, of other persons, by the Federal Government or a Provincial Government, or by a corporation controlled by any such Government.

(2) Any law which permits a person to own beneficially or possess beneficially an area of land greater than that which, immediately before the commencing day, he could have lawfully owned beneficially or possessed beneficially shall be invalid.

254. When any act or thing is required by the Constitution to be done within a particular period and it is not done within that period, the doing or the act of thing shall not be invalid or otherwise ineffective by reason only that it was not done within that period.

255. Oath of office.

(1) An oath required to be made by a person under the Constitution shall be made in a language that is understood by that person.

(2) Where, under the Constitution, an oath is required to be made before

a specified person and, for any reason, it is impracticable for the oath to be made before that person, it may be made before such other person as may be nominated by that person.

(3) Where, under the Constitution, a person is required to make an oath before he enters upon an office, he shall be deemed to have entered upon the office, on the day on which he makes the oath.

256. Private armies forbidden.

No private organization capable of functioning as a military organization shall be formed, and any such organization shall be illegal.

257. Provisions relating to the State of Jammu and Kashmir.

When the people of the State of Jammu and Kashmir decide to accede to Pakistan, the relationship between Pakistan and that State shall be determined in accordance with the wishes of the people of that State.

258. Government of territories outside Provinces.

Subject to the Constitution until Parliament by law otherwise provides, the President may, be order, make provision for peace and good government of any part of Pakistan not forming part of a Province.

259. Awards.

(1) No citizens shall accept any title, honor or decoration from any foreign State except with the approval of the Federal Government.

(2) No title, honor or decoration shall be conferred by the Federal Government or any Provincial Government on any citizen, but the President may award decorations in recognition of gallantry or meritorious service in the Armed Forces or academic distinction, as provided by Federal law.

Chapter 5. Interpretation

(3) All titles, honors and decorations awarded to citizens by any authority in Pakistan before the commencing day otherwise than in recognition of gallantry or meritorious service in the Armed Forces or academic distinction shall stand annulled:

260. Definitions.

(1) In the Constitution, unless the context otherwise requires, the following expressions have the meaning hereby respectively assigned to them, that is to say,

'Act of Parliament' means an Act passed by Parliament or the National Assembly and assented to, or deemed to have been assented to, by the President;

'Act of Provincial Assembly' means an Act passed by the Provincial Assembly of a Province and assented to, or deemed to have been assented to, by the Governor;

'agricultural income' means agricultural income as defined for the purposes of the law relating to income tax;

'Article' means Article of the Constitution;

'borrow' includes the raising of money by the grant of annuities, and 'loans' shall be construed accordingly;

'Chairman' means the Chairman of the Senate and, except in Article 49, includes a person acting as Chairman of the Senate;

'Chief Justice', in relation to the Supreme Court or a High Court, includes the Judge for the time being acting as Chief Justice of the Court;

'citizen' means a citizen of Pakistan as defined by law;

'clause' means clause of the Article in which it occurs;

'corporation tax' means any tax on income that is payable by companies and in respect of which the following conditions apply:

(*a*) the tax is not chargeable in respect of agricultural income;

(*b*) no deduction in respect of the tax paid by companies is, by any law which may apply to the tax, authorized to be made from dividends payable by the companies to individuals;

(*c*) no provision exists for taking the tax so paid into account in computing for the purposes of income-tax the total income of individuals receiving such dividends, or in computing the income tax payable by, or refundable to, such individuals;

'debt' includes any liability in respect of any obligation to repay capital sums by ways of annuities and any liability under any guarantee, and 'debt charges' shall be construed accordingly;

'estate duty' means a duty assessed on, or by reference to, the value of property passing upon death;

'existing law' has the same meaning as in clause (7) of Article 268;

'Federal law' means a law made by or under the authority of Parliament ;

'financial year' means a year commencing on the first day of July;

'goods' includes all materials, commodities and articles;

'Governor' means the Governor of a Province and includes any person for the time being acting as the Governor of a Province;

'guarantee' includes any obligation undertaken before the commencing day to make payments in the event of the profits of an undertaking falling short of a specified amount;

'House' means the Senate or the National Assembly;

'Joint sitting' means a joint sitting of the two Houses;

'Judge' in relation to the Supreme Court or a High Court, includes the Chief Justice of the Court and also includes

(*a*) in relation to the Supreme Court, a person who is acting as a Judge of the Court; and

(*b*) in relation to the High Court, a person who is an Additional Judge of the Court;

'members' of the Armed Forces' does not include persons who are not, for the time being, subject to any law relating to the members of the Armed Forces;

'net proceeds' means, in relation to any tax or duly, the proceeds

thereof, reduced by the cost of collection, as ascertained and certified by the Auditor-General;
'oath' includes affirmation;
'Part' means Part of the Constitution;
'pension' means a pension, whether contributory or not, of any kind whatsoever payable to, or in respect of, any person and includes retired pay so payable, a gratuity so payable, and any sum or sums so payable, by way of the return, with or without interest thereon or any addition thereto, of subscriptions to a provident fund;
'person' includes any body politic or corporate;
'President' means the President of Pakistan and includes a person for the time being acting as, or performing the functions of, the President of Pakistan and, as respects anything required to be done under the Constitution before the commencing day, the President under the Interim Constitution of the Islamic Republic of Pakistan;
'Property' includes any right, title or interest in property, movable or immovable, and any means and instruments of production;
'Provincial law' means a law made by or under the authority of the Provincial Assembly;
'remuneration' includes salary and pension;
'Schedule' means Schedule to the Constitution;
'security of Pakistan' includes the safety, welfare, stability and integrity of Pakistan and of each part of Pakistan, but shall not include public safety as such;
'service of Pakistan' means any service, post or office in connection with the affairs of the Federation or of a Province, and includes an All-Pakistan Service, service in the Armed Forces and any other service declared to be a service of Pakistan by or under Act of Parliament or of a Provincial Assembly, but does not include service as Speaker, Deputy Speaker, Chairman, Deputy Chairman, Prime Minister, Federal Minister, Minister of State, Chief Minister, Provincial Minister, Attorney-General, Advocate-General, Parliamentary Secretary or Chairman or member of a law commission, Chairman or member of the Council of Islamic Ideology, Special Assistant to the Prime Minister, Adviser to the Prime Minister, Special Assistant to a Chief Minister, Adviser to a Chief Minister or member of a House or a Provincial Assembly;
'Speaker' means the Speaker of the National Assembly or a Provincial Assembly, and includes any person acting as the Speaker of the Assembly;
'taxation' includes the imposition of any tax or duty, whether general, local or special, and 'tax' shall be construed accordingly;
'tax on income' includes a tax in the nature of an excess profits tax or a business profits tax.

(2) In the Constitution 'Act of Parliament' or 'Federal law' or 'Act of Provincial Assembly' or 'Provincial law' shall include an Ordinance promulgated by the President or, as the case may be, a Governor.

(3) A person who does not believe in the absolute and unqualified finality of the Prophethood of Muhammed (peace be upon him) the last of the Prophets or claims to be a prophet, in any sense of the word or of any description whatsoever, after Muhammed (peace be upon him), or recognizes such a claimant as a prophet or a religious reformer, is not a Muslim for the purposes of the Constitution or law.

261. Person acting in office not to be regarded as successor to previous occupant of office, etc.

For the purposes of the Constitution, a person who acts in an office shall not be regarded as the successor to the person who held that office before him or as the predecessor to the person who holds that office after him.

262. Gregorian calendar to be used.

For the purposes of the Constitution, periods of time shall be reckoned according to the Gregorian calendar.

263. Gender and number.

In the Constitution,

(*a*) words importing the masculin gender shall be taken to include females; and

(*b*) words in the singular shall include the plural, and words in the plural shall include the singular.

264. Effect of repeal of laws.

Where a law is repealed, or is deemed to have been repealed, by, under, or by virtue of the Constitution, the repeal shall not, except as otherwise provided in the Constitution.

(*a*) revive anything not in force or existing at the time at which the repeal takes effect;

(*b*) affect the previous operation of the law or anything duly done or suffered under the law;

(*c*) affect any right, privilege, obligation or liability acquired, accrued or incurred under the law;

(*d*) affect any penalty, forfeiture or punishment incurred in respect of any offence committed against the law; or

(*e*) affect any investigation, legal proceeding or remedy in respect of any such right, privilege, obligation, liability, penalty, forfeiture or punishment;

and any such investigation, legal proceeding or remedy may be instituted, continued or enforced, and any such penalty, forfeiture or punishment may be imposed, as if the law had not been repealed.

Chapter 6. Title, Commencement and Repeal

265. Title of Constitution and commencement.

(1) This Constitution shall be known as the Constitution of the Islamic Republic of Pakistan.

(2) Subject to clauses (3) and (4), the Constitution shall come into force on the fourteenth day of August, one thousand nine hundred and seventy-three or on such earlier day as the President may, by notification in the official Gazette, appoint, in the Constitution referred to as the 'commencing day'.

(3) The Constitution shall, to the extent necessary

(*a*) for the Constitution of the first Senate;

(*b*) for the first meeting of a House or a joint sitting to be held;

(*c*) for the election of the President and the Prime Minister to be held; and

(*d*) to enable any other thing to be done which, for the purposes of the Constitution, it is necessary to do before the commencing day,

come into force upon the enactment of the Constitution, but the person elected as President or Prime Minister shall not enter upon his office before the commencing day.

(4) Where by the Constitution a power is conferred to make rules or to issue orders with respect to the enforcement of any provision thereof, or with respect to the establishment of any court or office, or the appointment of any Judge or officer thereunder, or with respect to the person by whom, or the time when, or the place where or the manner in which, anything is to be done under any such provision, then that power may be exercised at any time between the enactment of the Constitution and its commencement.

266. Repeal.

The Interim Constitution of the Islamic Republic of Pakistan, together with the Acts and President's Orders making omissions from, additions to, modifications of, or amendments in, that Constitution is hereby repealed.

267. In abeyance.

268. Continuance in force, and adaptation of, certain laws.

(1) Except as provided by this Article, all existing laws shall, subject to the Constitution, continue in force, so far as applicable and with the necessary adaptations, until altered, repealed or amended by the appropriate Legislature.

(2) The laws specified in the Sixth Schedule shall not be altered, repealed or amended without the previous sanction of the President.

(3) For the purpose of bringing the provisions of any existing law into accord with the provisions of the Constitution (other than Part II of the Constitution), the President may by Order, within a period of two years from the commencing day, make such adaptations, whether by way of modification, addition or omission, as he may deem to be necessary or expedient, and any such Order may be made so as to have effect from such day, not being a day earlier than the commencing day as, may be specified in the Order.

(4) The President may authorize the Governor of a Province to exercise, in relation to the Province, the powers conferred on the President by clause (3) in respect of laws relating to matters with respect to which the Provincial Assembly has power to make laws.

(5) The powers exercisable under clauses (3) and (4) shall be subject to the provisions of an Act of the appropriate Legislature.

(6) Any court, tribunal or authority required or empowered to enforce an existing law shall, notwithstanding that no adaptations have been made in such law by an Order made under clause (3) or clause (4), construe the law with all such adaptations as are necessary to bring it into accord with the provisions of the Constitution.

(7) In this Article, 'existing laws' means all laws (including Ordinances, Orders-in-Council, Orders, rules, bye-laws, regulations and Letters Patent constituting a High Court, and any notifications and other legal instruments having the force of law) in force in Pakistan or any part thereof, or having extra-territorial validity, immediately before the commencing day.

Explanation.

In this Article, 'in force', in relation to any law, means having effect as law whether or not the law has been brought into operation.

269. Validation of laws, acts, etc.

(1) All Proclamations, President's Orders, Martial Law Regulations, Martial Law Orders and all other laws made between the twentieth day of December, one thousand nine hundred and seventy-one and the twentieth day of April, one thousand nine hundred and seventy-two (both days inclusive), are hereby declared notwithstanding any judgement of any court, to have been validly made by competent authority and shall not be called in question in any court on any ground whatsoever.

(2) All orders made, proceedings taken and acts done by any authority, or by any person, which were made, taken or done, or purported to have been made, taken or done, between the twentieth day of December, one thousand nine hundred and seventy-one, and the twentieth day of April, one thousand nine hundred and seventy-two (both days inclusive), in exercise of the powers derived from any President's Orders, Martial Law Regulations, Martial Law Orders, enactments, notifications, rules, orders or bye-laws, or in execution of any orders made or sentences passed by any authority in the exercise or purported exercise of power as aforesaid, shall, notwithstanding any judgment of any court, be deemed to be and always to have been validly made, taken or done and shall not be called in question in any court on any ground whatsoever.

(3) No suit or other legal proceedings shall lie in any court against any authority or any person for or on account of or in respect of any order made, proceedings taken or act done whether in the exercise or purported exercise of the powers referred to in clause (2) or in execution of or in compliance with orders made or sentences passed in exercise or purported exercise of such powers.

270. to 273. In abeyance.

274. Vesting of property, assets, rights liabilities and obligations.

(1) All property and assets which, immediately before the commencing day, were vested in the President or the Federal Government shall, as from that day, vest in the Federal Government unless they were used for purposes which, on that day, became purposes of the Government of a Province, in which case they shall, as from that day, vest in the Government of the Province.

(2) All property and assets which, immediately before the commencing day, were vested in the Government of a Province, shall, as from that day, continue to be vested in the Government of that Province, unless they were used for purposes, which on that day, became purposes of the Federal Government in which case they shall, as from that day, vest in the Federal Government.

(3) All rights, liabilities and obligations of the Federal Government or of the Government of a Province, whether arising out of contract or otherwise, shall as from the commencing day, continue to be respectively the rights, liabilities and obligations of the Federal Government or of the Government of the Province, except that

(*a*) all rights, liabilities and obligations relating to any matter which, immediately before that day, was the responsibility of the Federal Government, but which under the Constitution, has become the responsibility of the Government of a Province, shall devolve upon the Government of that Province; and

(*b*) all rights, liabilities and obligations relating to any matter which, immediately before that day, was the responsibility of the Government of a Province, but which under the Constitution, has become the responsibilty of the Federal Government, shall devolve upon the Federal Government.

275. Continuance in office of persons in service of Pakistan etc.

(1) Subject to the Constitution and until a law is made under Article 240 any person who, immediately before the commencing day, was in the service of Pakistan shall, as from that day, continue in the service of Pakistan on the same terms and conditions as were applicable to him under the Interim Constitution of the Islamic Republic of Pakistan immediately before that day.

(2) Clause (1) shall also apply in relation to a person holding office immediately before the commencing day as

(*a*) Chief Justice of Pakistan or other Judge of the Supreme Court, or Chief Justice or other Judge of a High Court;

(*b*) Governor of a Province;

(*c*) Chief Minister of a Province;

(*d*) Speaker or Deputy Speaker of the National Assembly or a Provincial Assembly;

(*e*) Chief Election Commissioner;

(*f*) Attorney-General for Pakistan or Advocate General of Pakistan.

(3) Notwithstanding anything contained in the Constitution, for a period of six months from the commencing day, a Federal Minister or a Minister of State or

the Chief Minister of a Province or a Provincial Minister may be a person who is not a member of Parliament or, as the case may be, the Provincial Assembly of that Province; and such Chief Minister and Provincial Minister shall have the right to speak and otherwise take part in the proceedings of the Provincial Assembly or any committee thereof of which he may be named a member, but shall not by virtue of this clause be entitled to vote.

(4) Any person who, under this Article, is continued in an office in respect of which a form of oath is set out in the Third Schedule shall, as soon as is practicable after the commencing day make before the appropriate person oath in that form.

(5) Subject to the Constitution and law

(*a*) all civil, criminal and revenue courts exercising jurisdiction and functions immediately before the commencing day shall, as from that day, continue to exercise their respective jurisdictions and functions; and

(*b*) all authorities and all offices (whether judicial, executive, revenue or ministerial) throughout Pakistan exercising functions immediately before the commencing day shall, as from that day, continue to exercise their respective functions.

276. In abeyance.

277. Transitional financial provisions.

(1) The schedule or authorized expenditure authenticated by the President for the financial year ending on the thirtieth day of June, one thousand nine hundred and seventy-four, shall continue to remain a valid authority for expenditure from the Federal Consolidated Fund for that year.

(2) The President may, in respect of expenditure of the Federal Government for any financial year preceding the financial year commencing on the first day of July, one thousand nine hundred and seventy-three (being expenditure in excess of the authorized expenditure for that year), authorized the withdrawal of moneys from the Federal Consolidated Fund.

(3) The provisions of clauses (1) and (2) shall apply to and in relation to a Province, and for the purpose

(*a*) any reference in those provisions to the President shall be read as a reference to the Governor of the Province;

(*b*) any reference in those provisions to the Federal Government shall be read as a reference to the Government of the Province; and

(*c*) any reference in those provisions to the Federal Consolidated Fund shall be read as a reference to the Provincial Consolidated Fund of the Province.

278. Accounts not audited before commencing day.

The Auditor-General shall perform the same functions and exercise the same powers in relation to account which have not been completed or audited before the commencing day as, by virtue of the Constitution, he is empowered to perform or exercise in relation to other accounts, and Article 171 shall, with the necessary modifications, apply accordingly.

279. Continuance of taxes.

Notwithstanding anything contained in the Constitution, all taxes and fees levied under any law in force immediately before the commencing day shall continue to be levied until they are varied or abolished by Act of the appropriate Legislature.

280. In abeyance.

SCHEDULES

(*Not reproduced*)

PAPUA NEW GUINEA

SUMMARY

INTERNATIONAL STATUS

Papua New Guinea is a member of the United Nations (October 10, 1975). It is a member of the Commonwealth of Nations and of other international governmental organizations.

Papua New Guinea became independent on September 16, 1975. Papua New Guinea was formed by merging the territory of Papua, under Australian rule from 1906, with the trust territory of New Guinea, formerly a German colony, administered by Australia from 1914. Both had been occupied by Japan during the second World War, after which they were set up as United Nations trusteeships and a joint administration established for the two areas in 1949, under the Papua New Guinea Act. A Legislative Council was established in 1951 and a House of Assembly, elected by the indigenous majority in 1964. Papua New Guinea received internal self government in 1973. Until the signing of a new border treaty in December 1979, relations with Indonesia had been strained because of the Indonesian annexation in December 1969, of Irian Jaya and its campaign against the Free Papua movement there. In December 1978, the Torres Strait border treaty with Australia was negotiated.

FORM OF NATIONAL GOVERNMENT

The Constitution of September 16, 1975, states that Papua New Guinea is a sovereign independent state and defines its territory.[1] It lists its goals and directive principles as integral human development, equality and participation, conservation, use and replenishment of natural resources and environment, the use of

[1] Constitution, Art. 1.

Papua New Guinea forms of social, political and economic organization.[2] All power belongs to the people.[3] The Constitution provides for a parliamentary form of government with the British sovereign, head of the Commonwealth, as Head of State. A section describes citizenship.[4]

RIGHTS OF THE PEOPLE

The basic rights are freedom under the law, the right to life, the prohibition of torture or inhuman treatment, protection of the law, liberty of the person, freedom from forced labor, from arbitrary search and entry, freedom of conscience, thought and religion, of assembly and association, of employment, the right to privacy; the right to vote and stand for public office, to freedom of information, movement, freedom from unjust deprivation of property, to equality, are stipulated.[5] Slavery and the slave trade are strictly prohibited.[6]

LEGISLATIVE DEPARTMENT

Legislative power is vested in the unicameral national Parliament, composed of members elected from single member open electorates, from single member provincial electorates, and of not more than 3 members appointed by Parliament by a two-thirds majority.[7] The term of office is 5 years subject to dissolution.[8] Privileges and immunities are described.[9] Incompatibilities of office are laid down.[10] Permanent parliamentary committees are provided for.[11] Sections refer to public finances[12] and the Ombudsman Commission.[13]

EXECUTIVE DEPARTMENT

The executive power is vested in the Head of State and the National Executive Council, composed of the Prime Minister and Ministers.[14] The British Queen is the Head of State and exercises those functions through a Governor General who must be a citizen of Papua New Guinea and is appointed by the Head of State with the advice of the Executive Council after decision of Parliament.[15] The Governor General's term of office is 6 years.[16] The Head of State, acting on the advice of the National Executive Council has the prerogative of mercy.[17] The Ministry is a parliamentary executive and the Prime Minister and Ministers must be members of Parliament.[18] They remain in office so long as they have the confidence of Parliament.[19] There are provisions for the Public Services Commission,[20] the Police Force,[21] the Defense Force.[22]

[2] Id., Preamble.
[3] Id., Art. Preamble.
[4] Id., Art. 64–81.
[5] Id., Art. 35–56.
[6] Id., Art. 253.
[7] Id., Art. 100–103.
[8] Id., Art. 104.
[9] Id., Art. 115.
[10] Id., Art. 130.
[11] Id., Art. 118–123.
[12] Id., Art. 209–216.
[13] Id., Art. 217–220.
[14] Id., Art. 138–140, 149.
[15] Id., Art. 82–88.
[16] Id., Art. 91.
[17] Id., Art. 15
[18] Id., Art. 14 142.
[19] Id., Art. 145.
[20] Id., Art. 190–195.
[21] Id., Art. 196–199.
[22] Id., Art. 200–208.

JUDICIAL DEPARTMENT

The judicial authority of the people is vested in the national judicial system, consisting of the Supreme Court, the National Court and other courts.[23] The independence of the national judicial system is guaranteed.[24] The Supreme Court is a superior court of record; it is composed of the Chief Justice appointed by the Head of State and the Deputy Chief Justice and other judges appointed by the Judicial and Legal Services Commission.[25] The Supreme Court has original jurisdiction as to any question relating to the interpretation or application of any provision of a constitutional law.[26]

AREA, POPULATION, ETC.

The area of Papua New Guinea is 462,840 square kilometres, its population 3,150,600 (1982 estimate). The capital is Port Moresby. English is used and there are some 300 dialects.

[23] Id., Art. 154–158.
[24] Id., Art. 157.
[25] Id., Art. 168–170.
[26] Id., Art. 18.

CONSTITUTION
OF
THE INDEPENDENT STATE OF PAPUA NEW GUINEA[1]

September 16, 1975

PREAMBLE

Adoption of Constitution

We, the people of Papua New Guinea, united in one nation, pay homage to th memory of our ancestors – the source of our strength and origin of our combinec heritage, acknowledge the worthy customs and traditional wisdoms of our people – which have come down to us from generation to generation, pledge ourselves tc guard and pass on to those who come after us our noble traditions and the Christian principles that are ours now.

By authority of our inherent right as ancient, free and independent peoples, we, the People, do now establish this sovereign nation and declare ourselves, under the guiding hand of God, to be the Independent State of Papua New Guinea.

And we assert, by virtue of that authority that all power belongs to the people – acting through their duly elected representatives, that respect for the dignity of the individual and community interdependence are basic principles of our society, that we guard with our lives our national identity, integrity and self-respect, that we reject violence and seek consensus as a means of solving our common problems, that our national wealth, won by honest, hard work be equitably shared by all.

We do now therefore declare that we, having resolved to enact a Constitution for the Independent State of Papua New Guinea, and acting through our Constituent Assembly on 15 August 1975, hereby establish, adopt and give to ourselves this Constitution to come into effect on Independence Day, that is 16 September 1975.

In doing we, the people of Papua New Guinea, set before ourselves these national goals and directive principles that underlie our constitution:

National Goals and Directive Principles

We hereby proclaim the following aims as our National Goals, and direct all persons and bodies, corporate and unincorporate, to be guided by these our declared Directives in pursuing and achieving our aims:

1. Integral human development.

We declare our first goal to be for every person to be dynamically involved in the process of freeing himself or herself from every form of domination or oppression so that each man or woman will have the opportunity to develop as a whole

[1] Published Port Moresby 1975. Supplied by the Department of Foreign Affairs and Trade in February 1982. Ed.

person in relationship with others.

We accordingly call for

(1) everyone to be involved in our endeavors to achieve integral human development of the whole person for every person and to seek fulfilment through his or her contribution to the common good; and

(2) education to be based on mutual respect and dialogue, and to promote awareness of our human potential and motivation to achieve our National Goals through self-reliant effort; and

(3) all forms of beneficial creativity, including sciences and cultures, to be actively encouraged; and

(4) improvement in the level of nutrition and the standard of public health to enable our people to attain self fulfilment; and

(5) the family unit to be recognized as the fundamental basis of our society, and for every step to be taken to promote the moral, cultural, economic and social standing of the Melanesian family; and

(6) development to take place primarily through the use of Papua New Guinean forms of social and political organization.

2. Equality and participation.

We declare our second goal to be for all citizens to have an equal opportunity to participate in, and benefit from, the development of our country.

We accordingly call for

(1) an equal opportunity for every citizen to take part in the political, economic, social, religious and cultural life of the country; and

(2) the creation of political structures that will enable effective, meaningful participation by our people in that life, and in view of the rich cultural and ethnic diversity of our people for those structures to provide for substantial decentralization of all forms of government activity; and

(3) every effort to be made to achieve an equitable distribution of incomes and other benefits of development among individuals and throughout the various parts of the country; and

(4) equalization of services in all parts of the country, and for every citizen to have equal access to legal processes and all services, governmental and otherwise, that are required for the fulfilment of his or her real needs and aspirations; and

(5) equal participation by women citizens in all political, economic, social and religious activities; and

(6) the maximization of the number of citizens participating in every aspect of development; and

(7) active steps to be taken to facilitate the organization and legal recognition of all groups engaging in development activities; and

(8) means to be provided to ensure that any citizen can exercise his personal creativity and enterprise in pursuit of fulfilment that is consistent with the common good, and for no citizen to be deprived of this opportunity because of the predominant position of another, and

(9) every citizen to be able to participate, either directly or through a

representative, in the consideration of any matter affecting his interests or the interests of his community; and

(10) all persons and governmental bodies of Papua New Guinea to ensure that, as far as possible, political and official bodies are so composed as to be broadly representative of citizens from the various areas of the country; and

(11) all persons and governmental bodies to endeavor to achieve universal literacy in *Pisin, Hiri Motu* or English, and in *'tok ples'* or *'via eda tano dado'*

(12) recognition of the principles that a complete relationship in marriage rests on equality of rights and duties of the partners, and that responsible parenthood is based on that equality.

3. National sovereignty and self-reliance.

We declare our third goal to be for Papua New Guinea to be politically and economically independent, and our economy basically self-reliant.

We accordingly call for

(1) our leaders to be committed to these National Goals and Directive Principles to ensure that their freedom to make decisions is not required by obligation to or relationship with others, and to make all of their decisions in the national interest; and

(2) all governmental bodies to base their planning for political, economic and social development on these Goals and Principles; and

(3) internal interdependence and solidarity among citizens, and between provinces, to be actively promoted; and

(4) citizens and governmental bodies to have control of the bulk of economic enterprise and production; and

(5) strict control of foreign investment capital and wise assessment of foreign ideas and values so that these will be subordinate to the goal of national sovereignty and self-reliance, and *in particular* for the entry of foreign capital to be geared to internal social and economic policies and to the integrity of the Nation and the People; and

(6) the State to take effective measures to control and actively participate in the national economy, and *in particular* to control major enterprises engaged in the exploitation of natural resources; and

(7) economic development to take place primarily by the use of skills and resources available in the country either from citizens or the State and not in dependence on imported skills and resources; and

(8) the constant recognition of our sovereignty, which must not be undermined by dependence on foreign assistance of any sort, and *in particular* for no investment, military or foreign-aid agreement or understanding to be entered into that imperils our self-reliance and self-respect, or our commitment to these National Goals and Directive Principles, or that may lead to substantial dependence upon or influence by any country, investor, lender or donor.

4. Natural resources and environment.

We declare our fourth goal to be for Papua New Guinea's natural resources and environment to be conserved and used for the collective benefit of us all, and be replenished for the benefit of future generations.

We accordingly call for

(1) wise use to be made of our natural resources and the environment in and on the land or seabed, in the sea, under the land, and in the air, in the interests of our development and in trust for future generation; and

(2) the conservation and replenishment, for the benefit of ourselves and posterity, of the environment and its sacred, scenic, and historical qualities; and

(3) all necessary steps to be taken to give adequate protection to our valued birds, animals, fish, insects, plants and trees.

5. Papua New Guinean ways.

We declare our fifth goal to be to achieve development primarily through the use of Papua New Guinean forms of social, political and economic organization.

We accordingly call for

(1) a fundamental re-orientation of our attitudes and the institutions of government, commerce, education and religion towards Papua New Guinean forms of participation, consultation, and consensus, and a continuous renewal of the responsiveness of these institutions to the needs and attitudes of the People; and

(2) particular emphasis in our economic development to be placed on small-scale artisan, service and business activity; and

(3) recognition that the cultural, commercial and ethnic diversity of our people is a positive strength, and for the fostering of a respect for, and appreciation of, traditional ways of life and culture, including language, in all their richness and variety, as well as for a willingness to apply these ways dynamically and creativily for the tasks of development; and

(4) traditional villages and communities to remain as viable units of Papua New Guinean society, and for active steps to be taken to improve their cultural, social, economic and ethical quality.

Basic Rights

We hereby acknowledge that, subject to any restrictions imposed by law on non-citizens, all persons in our country are entitled to the fundamental rights and freedoms of the individual, that is to say, the right, whatever their race, tribe, places of origin, political opinion, colour, creed or sex, but subject to respect for the rights and freedoms of others and for the legitimate public interest, to each of the following:

(*a*) life, liberty, security of the person and the protection of the law; and

(*b*) the right to take part in political activities; and

(*c*) freedom from inhuman treatment and forced labour; and

(*d*) freedom of conscience, of expression, of information and of assembly and association; and

(*e*) freedom of employment and freedom of movement; and

(*f*) protection for the privacy of their homes and other property and from unjust deprivation of property, and have accordingly included in this Constitution provisions designed to afford protection to those rights and freedoms, subject to such limitations on that protection as are contained in those provisions, being limitations primarily designed to ensure that the enjoyment of the acknowledged rights and freedoms by an individual does not prejudice the rights and freedoms of others or the legitimate public interest.

Basic social Obligations

We hereby declare that all persons in our country have the following basic obligations to themselves and their descendants, to each other, and to the Nation:

(*a*) to respect, and to act in the spirit of, this Constitution; and

(*b*) to recognize that they can fully develop their capabilities and advance their true interests only by active participation in the development of the national community as a whole; and

(*c*) to exercise the rights guaranteed or conferred by this Constitution, and to use the opportunities made available to them under it to participate fully in the government of the Nation; and

(*d*) to protect Papua New Guinea and to safeguard the national wealth, resources and environment in the interests not only of the present generation but also of future generations; and

(*e*) to work according to their talents in socially useful employment, and if necessary to create for themselves legitimate opportunities for such employment; and

(*f*) to respect the rights and freedoms of others, and to co-operate fully with others in the interests of interdependence and solidarity; and

(*g*) to contribute, as required by law, according to their means to the revenues required for the advancement of the Nation and the purposes of Papua New Guinea; and

(*h*) in the case of parents, to support, assist and educate their children (whether born in or out of wedlock), and in particlular to give them a true understanding of their basic rights and obligations and of the National Goals and Directive Principles; and

(*i*) in the case of the children, to respect their parents.

In addition, we hereby declare that all citizens have an obligation to themselves and their descendants, to each other and to the Nation to use profits from economic activities in the advancement of our country and our people, and that the law may impose a similar obligation on non-citizens carrying on economic activities in or from our country.

PART 1

INTRODUCTORY

Division 1. The Nation

1. (1) Papua New Guinea is a sovereign, independent State by the name of the independent State of Papua New Guinea.

(2) The name of the Independent State of Papua New Guinea and its variants shall be protected by an Act of the Parliament.

2. (1) The area of Papua New Guinea consists of the area that, immediately before Independence Day, constituted what was then known as Papua New Guinea, together with all internal waters and the territorial sea and underlying lands, and, subject to disclaimer by resolution of the Parliament at or before the end of its next meeting, includes such neighbouring waters and such lands underlying any such waters, and such additional lands and waters, as are declared by the Head of State, acting with, and in accordance with, the advice of the National Executive Council, to be part of that area.

(2) The sovereignty of Papua New Guinea over its territory, and over the natural resources of is territory, is and shall remain absolute, subject only to such obligations at international law as are freely accepted by Papua New Guinea in accordance with this Constitution.

3. (1) Acts of the Parliament may make provision for and in respect of

(*a*) a National Flag; and
(*b*) a National Emblem; and
(*c*) a National Motto; and
(*d*) a National Seal; and
(*e*) a National Anthem.

(2) Until such time as other provision is made in accordance with Subsection (1), the National Flag, National Emblem and National Seal are those that were in use immediately before Independence Day.

4. (1) There shall be a National Capital District.

(2) The Seat of Government shall be in the National Capital District.

(3) The boundaries of the National Capital District shall be as defined by an Organic Law.

(4) An Organic Law or an Act of the Parliament shall make provision in respect of the government of the National Capital District.

(5) In calculating the number of provincial electorates in accordance with Section 125 (*electorates*), the National Capital District shall be taken into account as if it were a province.

5. (1) An Organic Law may declare, or make provision in respect of the declaration of, part of the country as provinces.

(2) An Organic Law may provide for, or make provision in respect of, the creation of new provinces by the amalgamation or division of exisiting provinces or for the variation of the boundaries of a province.

6. Where a law requires a Declaration of Loyalty to be made, it shall be made in the following form:

'I, , realizing fully the responsibilities to which I am committing myself and the consequences of not living up to this Declaration and those responsibilities, freely and willingly declare my loyalty to the Independent State of Papua New Guinea and its People and to the Constitution of Papua New Guinea in accordance with its provisions, and promise that I will uphold the Constitution and the laws of Papua New Guinea.'

7. Where a law requires an Oath of Allegiance or Affirmation of Allegiance to be made, it shall be made in the following form:

Oath of Allegiance

I, , do swear that I will well and truly serve and bear true allegiance to Her Majesty Queen Elizabeth II, Her heirs and successors according to law.

So help me God!

Affirmation of Allegiance

I, , do promise and affirm that I will well and truly serve Her Majesty Queen Elizabeth II, Her heirs and successors according to law.'

Division 2. Interpretation

8. For the purpose of the interpretation of this Constitution and the Organic Law the provisions of Schedule 1 (Rules for Shortening and Interpretation of the Constitutional Laws) applies and, subject to that Schedule, the underlying law applies.

PART II

THE NATIONAL LEGAL SYSTEM

Division 1. The Laws of Papua New Guinea

9. The laws of Papua New Guinea consist of

(*a*) this Constitution; and
(*b*) the Organic Laws; and
(*c*) the Acts of the Parliament; and
(*d*) Emergency Regulations, and
(*e*) laws made under or adopted by or under this Constitution or any of those laws, including subordinate legislative enactments made under this Constitution or any of those laws; and
(*f*) the underlying law,

and none other.

10. All written laws (other than this Constitution) shall be read and construed subject to

(*a*) in any case – this Constitution; and

(*b*) in the case of Acts of the Parliament – any relevant Organic Laws; and

(*c*) in the case of adopted laws or subordinate legislative enactments – the Organic Laws and the laws by or under which they were enacted or made,

and so as not to exceed the authority to make them properly given, to the intent that where any such law would, but for this section, have been in excess of the authority so given it shall nevertheless be a valid law to the extent to which it is not in excess of that authority.

Division 2. Constitutional Laws

SUBDIVISION A. SUPREME LAW

11. (1) This Constitution and the Organic Laws are the Supreme Law of Papua New Guinea, and, subject to Section 10 (*construction of written laws*) all acts (whether legislative, executive or judicial) that are inconsistent with them are, to the extent of the inconsistency, invalid and ineffective.

(2) The provisions of this Constitution and of the Organic Laws are self-executing to the fullest extent that their respective natures and subject-matters permit.

12. (1) For the purposes of this Constitution, an Organic Law is a law made by the Parliament that is

(*a*) for or in respect of a matter provision for which by way of an Organic Law is expressly authorized by this Constitution; and

(*b*) not inconsistent with this Constitution; and

(*c*) expressed to be an Organic Law.

(2) An Organic Law may be altered only by another Organic Law, or by an alteration to this Constitution.

(3) Nothing in this section prevents an Organic Law from

(*a*) making any provision that might be made by an Act of the Parliament; or

(*b*) requiring any provision to be made by an Act of the Parliament that might otherwise be so made,

but any such provision may be altered by the same majority that is required for any other Act of the Parliament.

SUBDIVISION B. CONSTITUTIONAL ALTERATION AND ORGANIC LAWS

13. This Constitution may be altered only by law made by the Parliament that

(*a*) is expressed to be a law to alter this Constitution; and

(*b*) is made and certified in accordance with Section 14 (*making of alterations to the Constitution and Organic Laws*).

14. (1) Subject to Sections 12(3) (*Organic Laws*) and 15 (*urgent alterations*), a proposed law to alter this Constitution, or a proposed Organic Law, must be supported on a division in accordance with the Standing Orders of the Parliament by the prescribed majority of votes determined in accordance with Section 17 (*'prescribed majority of votes'*) expressed on at least two occasions after opportunity for debate on the merits.

(2) Subject to Section 15 (*urgent alterations*), the opportunities for debate referred to in Subsection (1) must have been

(*a*) during different meetings of the Parliament; and

(*b*) separated in time by at least two months.

and the proposed law must be published by the Speaker in full in the National Gazette, and circulated, in accordance with the Standing Orders of the Parliament, to all members of the Parliament not less than one month before it is formally introduced into the Parliament.

(3) Amendments to a proposed law to amend this Constitution or a proposed Organic Law shall not be moved unless they have been circulated to members of the Parliament before the end of the meeting of the Parliament at which the first opportunity for debate referred to in Subsection (1) occurs.

(4) Subject to Subsection (6), in his certificate given under Section 110 (*certification as to making of laws*), the Speaker must certify that the requirements of Subsections (1), (2) and (3) or Section 15 (*urgent alterations*), as the case may be, have been complied with.

(5) The certificate referred to in Subsection (4) shall state

(*a*) the date on which each vote was taken; and

(*b*) in relation to each vote

(i) the number of seats in the Parliament at the time; and

(ii) the respective numbers of members of the Parliament voting for and against the proposal, and where the requirements of Subsection (2) were waived under Section 15 (*urgent alterations*) for and against the motion for the waiver,

and is, in the absence of proof to the contrary, conclusive evidence of the matter so stated.

(6) Unless the Parliament decides otherwise in any particular case, Subsection (1) does not apply where the Speaker, after consultation with the Chief Justice or a Judge nominated by the Chief Justice for the purpose, certifies that the proposed law

(*a*) does not affect the substance of any provision to be altered by it; or

(*b*) is designed to correct a self-evident error or omission; or

(*c*) is merely incidental to or consequential on some other alteration of this Constitution or of any other law,

and such a law may be made in the same way as Acts of the Parliament.

(7) The Supreme Court may, on the application of any person made within four weeks after the date of a certificate under Subsection (6) or such further time

as a Judge, on application made within that period, considers reasonable in the particular circumstances, disallow the certificate, but otherwise the certificate is conclusive.

15. (1) The provisions of this section cease to have effect at the first moment of the fourth anniversary of Independence Day.

(2) Subject to Subsection (5), the requirements of Section 14(2) (*making of alterations to the Constitution and Organic Laws*) may be waived, on the ground of urgency, by the Parliament by a division in accordance with the Standing Orders of the Parliament by a two-thirds absolute majority vote.

(3) The requirements of Section 14(2) (*making of alterations to the Constitution and Organic Laws*) shall not be waived under Subsection (2) unless

(*a*) at least four days' notice of the intention in accordance with the standing Orders of the Parliament to invoke Subsection (2) has been given; and

(*b*) the proposed law has been circulated, in accordance with the Standing Orders of the Parliament, to all members of the Parliament and published in full by the Speaker in the National Gazette at least four days before the motion to invoke Subsection (2) is moved; and

(*c*) the opportunities for debate referred to in Section 14(1) (*making of alterations to the Constitution and Organic Laws*) have been separated in time by at least two weeks, but not necessarily during different meetings of the Parliament.

(4) Amendments to a proposed law to amend this Constitution or a proposed Organic Law to which this section applies shall not be moved unless they have been circulated to members of the Parliament before the end of the first debate on the matter.

(5) This section does not apply to proposed laws to alter the following provisions of the Constitution, or Organic Laws made for the purposes of any such provision:

(*a*) this section;
(*b*) the Preamble;
(*c*) Division II.2. (*Constitutional Laws*);
(*d*) Division III.1. (*National Goals and Directive Principles*);
(*e*) Division III.2. (*leadership code*);
(*f*) Division III.3. (*basic rights*);
(*g*) Division III.5. (*basic social obligations*);
(*h*) Part IV. (*citizenship*);
(*i*) Division VI.2. (*the National Parliament*);
(*j*) Division VI.3. (*special instances of the legislative powers*);
(*k*) Division VI.5. (*the administration of justice*);
(*l*) Division VII.2. (*the Public Services Commission*);
(*m*) Division VII.4. (*special provisions in relation to the Police Force*);
(*n*) Division VII.5. (*special provisions in relation to the Defence Force*);

(*o*) Part VIII. (*supervision and control*);
(*p*) Part IX. (*constitutional office-holders and constitutional institutions*);
(*q*) Part X. (*emergency powers*).

16. (1) No Constitutional Law takes effect so as to affect the operation of any provision of such a law in force immediately before the commencement of the first-mentioned law unless it was made in the manner and form required for the alteration of that provision.

(2) For the avoidance of doubt, it is hereby declared that subsection (1) extends to Schedule 1 (*Rules for Shortening and Interpretation of the Constitutional Laws*) in its application to any provisions of this Constitution.

17. (1) Subject to this section, in relation to a proposed law to alter any provision of this Constitution the prescribed majority of votes for the purposes of Section 14 (*making of alterations to the Constitution and Organic Laws*) is the majority of votes prescribed by this Constitution in relation to that provision, or if no majority is prescribed a two-thirds absolute majority vote.

(2) For the purposes of Subsection (1) the prescribed majority of votes for this subsection, Section 3, 6, 8, 20, 21, 23, 24, 26 to 31 (inclusive), 63, 68, 69, 73, 77 to 98 (inclusive), 101, 103, 104, 110, 117, 138, 139, 150, 156, 165, 167, 171, 184 to 187 (inclusive), 206, 248 to 252 (inclusive), 264 to 268 (inclusive), Sch. 1.21, Sch. 2.1 to Sch. 2.14 (inclusive), Schedules 3,4 and 5 is an abolute majority.

(3) For the purposes of Subsection (1) the prescribed majority of votes for this subsection, Sections 35, 36, 50, 57, 105, 106, 109, 113, 125, 126, 155, 157, 160, 163, 217, 235, 239, 243, 244, 245, and 269 is a three-quarters absolute majority.

(4) Subject to this section, for the purpose of a proposed law to add a new provision to this constitution the prescribed majority of votes is the same as the prescribed majority of votes that would be required to alter that provision if it was already enacted.

(5) Subject to Section 12(3) (*Organic Laws*), in relation to a proposed Organic Law the prescribed majority of votes is

(*a*) in the case of a proposed Organic Law to alter a provision of an Organic Law – the same as the majority that would be required for the making of the provision proposed to be altered; and
(*b*) in any other case
  (i) the majority of votes (not being less than an absolute majority) prescribed by this Constitution for the making of the Organic Law; and
  (ii) if no majority is prescribed, a two-thirds absolute majority.

(6) Where, by virtue of the operation of the preceding provisions of this section, there are different prescribed majorities in relation to different provisions of a proposed law, the prescribed majority of votes in relation to the law as a whole is the greatest of those majorities.

(7) Nothing in this section prevents different majorities being prescribed in respect of different aspects or subject-matters of a provision.

(8) No Organic Law may require a majority of votes for the alteration of a provision of an Organic Law greater than that by which the first-mentioned law was made.

(9) Notwithstanding anything in this section, until 16 September 1980

(*a*) for the purpose of a proposed law to add a new provision to this Constitution, the prescribed majority of votes is an absolute majority; and

(*b*) for the purpose of making an Organic Law for which there was provision in this Constitution when adopted the prescribed majority of votes is an absolute majority.

SUBDIVISION C. CONSTITUTIONAL INTERPRETATION

18. (1) Subject to this Constitution, the Supreme Court has original jurisdiction, to the exclusion of other courts, as to any question relating to the interpretation or application of any provision of a Constitutional Law.

(2) Subject to this Constitution, where any question relating to the interpretation or application of any provision of a Constitutional Law arises in any court or tribunal, other than the Supreme Court, the court or tribunal shall, unless the question is trivial, vexatious or irrelevant, refer the matter to the Supreme Court, and take whatever other action (including the adjournment of proceedings) is appropriate.

19. (1) Subject to Subsection (4), the Supreme Court shall, on application by an authority referred to in Subsection (3), give its opinion on any question relating to the interpretation or application of any provision of a Constitutional Law, including (but without limiting the generality of that expression) any question as to the validity of a law or proposed law.

(2) An opinion given under Subsection (1) has the same binding effect as any other decision of the Supreme Court.

(3) The following authorities only are entitled to make application under Subsection (1):

(*a*) the Parliament; and

(*b*) the Head of State, acting with, and in accordance with, the advice of the National Executive Council; and

(*c*) the Law Officers of Papua New Guinea; and

(*d*) the Law Reform Commission; and

(*e*) the Ombudsman Commission; and

(*f*) the Speaker, in accordance with Section 137(3) (*Acts of Indemnity*).

(4) Subject to any Act of the Parliament, the Rules of Court of the Supreme Court may make provision in respect of matters relating to the jurisdiction of the Supreme Court under this section, and in particular as to

(*a*) the form and contents of questions to be decided by the Court; and (*b*) The provision of counsel adequate to enable full argument before the Court of any question; and

(*c*) cases and circumstances in which the Court may decline to give an opinion.

(5) In this section, 'proposed law' means a law that has been formally placed before the relevant law-making body.

Division 3. Adoption, Reception and Development of Certain Laws

20. (1) An Act of Parliament shall

(*a*) declare the underlying law of Papua New Guinea; and

(*b*) provide for the development of the underlying law of Papua New Guinea.

(2) Until such time as an Act of Parliament provides otherwise

(*a*) the underlying law of Papua New Guinea shall be as prescribed in Schedule 2 (*adoption, etc., of certain laws*); and

(*b*) the manner of development of the underlying law shall be as prescribed by Schedule 2 (*adoption, etc., of certain laws*).

(3) Certain pre-Independence statutes are adopted and shall be adopted, as Acts of Parliament and subordinate enactments of Papua New Guinea, as prescribed by Schedule 2 (*adoption, etc., of certain laws*).

21. (1) The purpose of Schedule 2 (*adoption, etc., of certain laws*) and of the Act of the Parliament referred to in Section 20 (*underlying law and pre-Independence statutes*) is to assist in the development of our indigenous jurisprudence, adapted to the changing circumstances of Papua New Guinea.

(2) For the purpose set out in Subsection (1), a Law Reform Commission shall be established in accordance with Schedule 2 (*adoption, etc., of certain laws*), and certain special responsibilities are imposed by that Schedule on the National Judicial System (and in particular on the Supreme Court and the National Court) and on the Law Reform Commission.

Division 4. General

22. The provisions of this Constitution that recognize rights of individuals (including corporations and associations) as well as those that confer powers or impose duties on public authorities, shall not be left without effect because of the lack of supporting, machinery or procedural laws, but the lack shall, as far as practicable, be supplied by the National Court in the light of the National Goals and Directive Principles, and by way of analogy from other laws, general principles of justice and generally-accepted doctrine.

23. (1) Where any provision of a Constitutional Law prohibits or restricts an act, or imposes a duty, then unless a Constitutional Law or an Act of the Parliament provides for the enforcement of that provision the National Court may

(*a*) impose a sentence of imprisonment for a period not exceeding 10 years or a fine not exceeding K10 000.00; or (*b*) in the absence of any other equally effective remedy under the laws of Papua New Guinea, order the making of compensation by a person (including a governmental body) who is in default,

or both, for a breach of the prohibition, restriction or duty, and may make such further order in the circumstances as it thinks proper.

(2) Where a provision of a Constitutional Law prohibits or restricts an act or imposes a duty, the National Court may, if it thinks it proper to do so, make any order that it thinks proper for preventing or remedying a breach of the prohibition, restriction or duty, and Subsection (1) applies to a failure to comply with the order as if it were a breach of a provision of this Constitution.

(3) Where the National Court considers it proper to do so, it may include in an order under Subsection (2) an anticipatory order under Subsection (1).

24. (1) The official records of debates and of votes and proceedings

(*a*) in the pre-Independence House of Assembly on the report of the Constitutional Planning Committee; and

(*b*) in the Constituent Assembly on the draft of this Constitution,

together with that report and any other documents or papers tabled for the purposes of or in connection with those debates, may be used so far as they are relevant, as aids to interpretation where any question relating to the interpretation or application of any provision of a Constitutional Law arises.

(2) An Act of the Parliament may make provision for the manner of proof of the records and documents referred to in Subsection (1).

(3) In Subsection (1), 'the report of the Constitutional Planning Committee' means the Final Report of the pre-Independence Constitutional Planning Committee dated 13 August 1974 and presented to the pre-Independence House of Assembly on 16 August 1974.

PART III

BASIC PRINCIPLES OF GOVERNMENT

Division 1. National Goals and Directive Principles

25. (1) Except to the extent provided in Subsections (3) and (4), the National Goals and Directive Principles are non-justiciable.

(2) Nevertheless, it is the duty of all governmental bodies to apply and give effect to them as far as lies within their respective powers.

(3) Where any law, or any power conferred by any law (whether the power be of a legislative, judicial, executive, administrative or other kind), can reasonably be understood, applied, exercised or enforced, without failing to give effect to the intention of the Parliament or to this Constitution, in such a way as to give effect to the National Goals and Directive Principles, or at least not to derogate them, it is to be understood, applied or exercised, and shall be enforced, in that way.

(4) Subsection (1) does not apply to the jurisdiction of the Ombudsman

Commission or of any other body prescribed for the purposes of Division III.2 (*leadership code*), which shall take the National Goals and Directive Principles fully into account in all cases as appropriate.

Division 2. Leadership Code

26. (1) The provisions of this Division apply to and in relation to
(*a*) the Prime Minister, the Deputy Prime Minister and the other Ministers, and
(*b*) the Leader and Deputy Leader of the Opposition; and
(*c*) all other members of the Parliament; and
(*d*) heads of provincial government bodies; and
(*e*) all constitutional office-holders within the meaning of Section 221 (*definitions*); and
(*f*) all heads of Departments of the National Public Service; and
(*g*) all heads of or members of the boards or other controlling bodies of statutory authorities; and
(*h*) the Commissioner of Police; and
(*i*) the Commander of the Defence Force; and
(*j*) all ambassadors and other senior diplomatic and consular officials prescribed by an Organic Law or an Act of the Parliament; and
(*k*) the public trustee; and
(*l*) the personal staff of the Governor-General, the Ministers and the Leader and Deputy Leader of the Opposition; and
(*m*) executive officers of registered political parties as defined by Section 128 (*'registered political party'*); and
(*n*) persons holding such public offices as are declared under Subsection (3) to be offices to and in relation to which this Division applies.

(2) This Division applies to and in relation to a person referred to in Subsection (1) not only in the office referred to in that subsection but also in any other office or position that he holds under any law by virtue of that office.

(3) An Organic Law or an Act of the Parliament may declare any public office (including an office in a provincial government body or a local government body) to be an office to and in relation to which this Division applies.

(4) In the event of doubt as to whether a person is a person to whom this Division applies, the decision of the Ombudsman Commission is final.

27. (1) A person to whom this Division applies has a duty to conduct himself in such a way, both in his public or official life and his private life, and in his associations with other persons, as not
(*a*) to place himself in a position in which he has or could have a conflict of interests or might be compromised when discharging his public or official duties; or
(*b*) to demean his office or position; or

(*c*) to allow his public or official integrity, or his personal integrity, to be called into question; or

(*d*) to endanger or diminish respect for and confidence in the integrity of government in Papua New Guinea.

(2) In particular, a person to whom this Division applies shall not use his office for personal gain or enter into any transaction or engage in any enterprise or activity that might be expected to give rise to doubt in the public mind as to whether he is carrying out or has carried out the duty imposed by Subsection (1).

(3) It is the further duty of a person to whom this Division applies

(*a*) to ensure, as far as is within his lawful power, that his spouse and children and any other persons for whom he is responsible (whether morally, legally or by usage), including nominees, trustees and agents, do not conduct themselves in a way that might be expected to give rise to doubt in the public mind as to his complying with his duties under this section; and

(*b*) if necessary, to publicly disassociate himself from any activity or enterprise of any of his associates, or of a person referred to in paragraph (*a*), that might be expected to give rise to such a doubt.

(4) The Ombudsman Commission or other authority prescribed for the purpose under Section 28 (*further provisions*) may, subject to this Division and to any Organic Law made for the purposes of this Division, give directions, either generally or in a particular case, to ensure the attainment of the objects of this section.

(5) A person to whom this Division applies who

(*a*) is convicted of an offence in respect of his office or position or in relation to that performance of his functions or duties; or

(*b*) fails to comply with a direction under Subsection (4) or otherwise fails to carry out the obligations imposed by Subsections (1), (2) and (3).

is guilty of misconduct in office.

28. (1) For the purposes of this Division, an Organic Law

(*a*) may give to the Ombudsman Commission or some other authority any powers that are necessary or convenient for attaining the objects of this Division and of the Organic Law; and

(*b*) shall make provision for the disclosure to the Ombudsman Commission or some other authority of the personal and business incomes and financial affairs of persons to whom this Division applies, and of their families and associates, and in particular of interests in contracts with governmental bodies and of directorships and similar offices held by them (including powers to nominate directors, trustees or agents, or similar officers); and

(*c*) shall empower the Ombudsman Commission or some other authority to require a person to whom this Division applies to dispose of, or place under the control of the public trustee, any assets or income where this seems to be desirable for attaining the objects of this Division; and

(*d*) may prescribe specific acts that constitute misconduct in office, and

(*e*) may create offences (including offences by persons to whom this Division applies and offences by other persons); and

(*f*) shall provide for the investigation by the Ombudsman Commission or some other authority of cases of alleged or suspected misconduct in office, and confer on the Commission or authority any powers that are necessary or convenient for that purpose; and

(*g*) shall establish independent tribunals that

(i) shall investigate and determine any cases of alleged or suspected misconduct in office referred to them in accordance with the Organic Law: and

(ii) are required to recommend to the appropriate authority to dismiss from any office or position or, within limits fixed by law, otherwise make a recommendation to penalize a person found guilty of misconduct in office, unless they find both a lack of serious culpability and that public policy and the public good does not require dismissal; and

(*b*) may make any other provision that is necessary or convenient for attaining the objects of this Division.

(2) In the case of

(*a*) those persons referred to in Section 26(1) (*a*), (*b*), (*c*), and (*d*) (*application of Division 2*); and

(*b*) any other person holding an elective office that is declared under Section 26(1)(*n*) (*application of Division 2*) to be an office to which this Division applies,

the independent tribunal referred to in Subsection (1)(*g*) shall make any recommendation under Subsection (1)(*g*)(ii) to the Head of State, who shall act in accordance with the advice of the independent tribunal.

(3) In the case of

(*a*) those persons referred to in Section 26(1) (*application of Division 2*) other than those specified in Subsection (2); and

(*b*) any other person holding an appointed office that is declared under Section 26(1)(*n*) (*application of Division 2*) to be an office to which this Division applies,

the independent tribunal referred to in Subsection (1)(*g*) shall make any recommendation under Subsection (1)(*g*)(ii) to the appropriate appointing authority which shall act in accordance with the advice of the independent tribunal.

(4) An Organic Law may provide for the suspension from office of a person to whom this Division applies pending the investigation of any case of alleged or suspected misconduct in office by him.

(5) Proceedings under Subsection (1)(*g*) are not judicial proceedings but are subject to the principles of natural justice, and

(*a*) no such proceedings are a bar to any other proceedings provided for by law; and
(*b*) no other proceedings provided for by law are a bar to proceedings under that paragraph.

29. (1) Where the Ombudsman Commission or other authority referred to in Section 28(1)(*f*) (*further provisions*) is satisfied that there is a *prima facie* case that a person has been guilty of misconduct in office, it shall refer the matter to the Public Prosecutor for prosecution before a tribunal established under Section 28 (1)(*g*) (*further provisions*).

(2) If the Public Prosecutor fails to prosecute the matter within a reasonable period, the Commission may prosecute it in his stead.

30. Where another authority is prescribed under Section 28 (*further provisions*) that authority
(*a*) shall be composed of a person or persons who are declared under Section 222(1) (*definitions*) to be a constitutional office-holder, and
(*b*) is not subject to direction or control by any person or authority.

31. (1) A person who has been dismissed from office under this Division for misconduct in office is not eligible
(*a*) to election to any elective public office; or
(*b*) for appointment as Head of State or as a nominated member of the Parliament; or
(*c*) for appointment to a provincial government body or to a local government body,

for a period of three years after the date of his dismissal.

(2) In the event of doubt as to whether an office or position is an office or position to which Subsection (1) (*a*), (*b*) or (*c*) applies, the decision of the Ombudsman Commission is final.

Division 3. Basic Rights

SUBDIVISION A. INTRODUCTORY

32. (1) Freedom based on law consists in the least amount of restriction on the activities of individuals that is consistent with the maintenance and development of Papua New Guinea and of society in accordance with this Constitution and, in particular, with the National Goals and Directive Principles and the Basic Social Obligations.

(2) Every person has the right to freedom based on law, and accordingly has a legal right to do anything that
(*a*) does not injure or interfere with the rights and freedoms of others, and
(*b*) is not prohibited by law,

and no person
(*c*) is obliged to do anything that is not required by law; and

(*d*) may be prevented from doing anything that complies with the provisions of paragraphs (*a*) and (*b*).

(3) This section is not intended to reflect on the extra-legal existence, nature or effect of social, civic, family or religious obligations, or other obligations of an extra-legal nature, or to prevent such obligations being given effect to by law.

33. Nothing in this Division derogates the rights and freedoms of the individual under any other law and, in particular, an Organic Law or an Act of the Parliament may provide further guarantees of rights and freedoms and may further restrict the limitations that may be placed on, or on the exercise of, any right or freedom (including the limitations that may be imposed under Section 38 (*general qualifications on qualified rights*).

34. Subject to this Constitution, each provision of this Division applies, as far as may be

(*a*) as between individuals as well as between governmental bodies and individuals; and

(*b*) to and in relation to corporations and associations (other than governmental bodies) in the same way as it applies to and in relation to individuals,

except where, or to the extent that, the contrary intention appears in this Constitution.

SUBDIVISION B. FUNDAMENTAL RIGHTS

35. (1) No person shall be deprived of his life intentionally except

(*a*) in execution of a sentence of a court following his conviction of an offence for which the penalty of death is prescribed by law; or

(*b*) as the result of the use of force to such an extent as is reasonable in the circumstances of the case and is permitted by any other law

(i) for the defence of any person from violence; or

(ii) in order to effect a lawful arrest or to prevent the escape of a person lawfully detained; or

(iii) for the purpose of suppressing a riot, an insurrection or a mutiny; or

(iv) in order to prevent him from committing an offence, or

(*v*) for the purpose of suppressing piracy or terrorism or similar acts; or

(*c*) as the result of a lawful act of war.

(2) Nothing in Subsection (1)(*b*) relieves any person from any liability at law in respect of the killing of another.

36. (1) No person shall be submitted to torture (whether physical or mental), or to treatment or punishment that is cruel or otherwise inhuman, or is inconsistent with respect for the inherent dignity of the human person.

(2) The killing of a person in circumstances in which Section 35(1)(*a*) (*right to life*) does not, of itself, contravene Subsection (1), although the manner or the circumstances of the killing may contravene it.

37. (1) Every person has the right to the full protection of the law, and the succeeding provisions of this section are intended to ensure that that right is fully available, especially to persons in custody or charged with offences.

(2) Except, subject to any Act of the Parliament to the contrary, in the case of the offence commonly known as contempt of court, nobody may be convicted of an offence that is not defined by, and the penalty for which is not prescribed by, a written law.

(3) A person charged with an offence shall, unless the charge is withdrawn, be afforded a fair hearing within a reasonable time, by an independent and impartial court.

(4) A person charged with an offence

(*a*) shall be presumed innocent until proved guilty according to law, but a law may place upon a person charged with an offence the burden of proving particular facts which are, or would with the exercise of reasonable care be, peculiarly within his knowledge; and

(*b*) shall be informed promptly in a language which he understands, and in detail, of the nature of the offence with which he is charged; and

(*c*) shall be given adequate time and facilities for the preparation of his defence; and

(*d*) shall be permitted to have without payment the assistance of an interpreter if he cannot understand or speak the language used at the trial of the charge; and

(*e*) shall be permitted to defend himself before the court in person or, at his own expense, by a legal representative of his own choice, or if he is a person entitled to legal aid, by the Public Solicitor or another legal representative assigned to him in accordance with law; and

(*f*) shall be afforded facilities to examine in person or by his legal representative the witnesses called before the court by the prosecution, and to obtain the attendance and carry out the examination of witnesses and to testify before the court on his own behalf, on the same conditions as those applying to witnesses called by the prosecution.

(5) Except with his own consent, the trial shall not take place in his absence unless he so conducts himself as to render the continuance of the proceedings in his presence impracticable and the court orders him to be removed and the trial to proceed in his absence, but provision may be made by law for a charge that a person has committed an offence the maximum penalty for which does not include imprisonment, (except in default of payment of a fine), to be heard summarily in his absence if it is established that he has been duly served with a summons in respect of the alleged offence.

(6) Nothing in Subection (4)(*f*) invalidates a law which imposes reasonable

conditions that must be satisfied if witnesses called to testify on behalf of a person charged with an offence are to be paid their expenses out of public funds.

(7) No person shall be convicted of an offence on account of any act that did not, at the time when it took place, constitute an offence, and no penalty shall be imposed for an offence that is more severe in degree or description than the maximum penalty that might have been imposed for the offence at the time when it was committed.

(8) No person who shows that he has been tried by a competent court for an offence and has been convicted or acquitted shall again be tried for that offence or for any other offence of which he could have been convicted at the trial for that offence, except upon the order of a superior court made in the course of appeal or review proceedings relating to the conviction or acquittal.

(9) No person shall be tried for an offence for which he has been pardoned.

(10) No person shall be compelled in the trial of an offence to be a witness against himself.

(11) A determination of the existence or extent of a civil right or obligation shall not be made except by an independent and impartial court or other authority prescribed by law or agreed upon by the parties, and proceedings for such a determination shall be fairly heard within a reasonable time.

(12) Except with the agreement of the parties, or by order of the court in the interests of national security, proceedings in any jurisdiction of a court and proceedings for the determination of the existence or extent of any civil right or obligation before any other authority, including the announcement of the decision of the court or other authority, shall be held in public.

(13) Nothing in Subsection (12) prevents a court or other authority from excluding from the hearing of the proceedings before it persons, other than the parties and their legal representatives, to such an extent as the court or other authority

(*a*) is by law empowered to do and considers necessary or expedient in in the interest of public welfare or in circumstances where publicity would prejudice the interests of justice, the welfare of persons under voting age or the protection of the private lives of persons concerned in the proceedings; or

(*b*) is by law empowered or required to do in the interests of defence, public safety or public order.

(14) In the event that the trial of a person is not commenced within four months of the date on which he was committed for trial, a detailed report concerning the case shall be made by the Chief Justice to the Minister responsible for the National Legal Administration.

(15) Every person convicted of an offence is entitled to have his conviction and sentence reviewed by a higher court or tribunal according to law.

(16) No person shall be deprived by law of a right of appeal against his conviction or sentence by any court that existed at the time of the conviction or sentence, as the case may be.

(17) All person deprived of their liberty shall be treated with humanity and with respect for the inherent dignity of the human person.

(18) Accused persons shall be segregated from convicted persons and shall be subject to separate treatment appropriate to their status as unconvicted persons.

(19) Persons under voting age who are in custody in connection with an offence or alleged offence shall be separated from other persons in custody and be accorded treatment appropriate to their age.

(20) An offender shall not be transferred to an area away from that in which his relatives reside except for reasons of security or other good cause and, if such a transfer is made, the reason for so doing shall be endorsed on the file of the offender.

(21) Nothing in this section

(*a*) derogates Division III.4 (*principles of natural justice*); or

(*b*) affects the powers and procedures of village courts.

(2) Notwithstanding Subsection 21(*b*) the powers and procedures of villages courts shall be exercised in accordance with the principles of natural justice.

SUBDIVISION C. QUALIFIED RIGHTS

General

38. (1) For the purposes of this Subdivision, a law that complies with the requirements of this section is a law that is made and certified in accordance with Subsection (2), and that

(*a*) regulates or restricts the exercise of a right or freedom referred to in this Subdivision to the extent that the regulation or restriction is necessary

(i) taking account of the National Goals and Directive Principles and the Basic Social Obligations, for the purpose of giving effect to the public interest in

(A) defence, or

(B) public safety; or

(C) public order; or

(D) public welfare; or

(E) public health (including animal and plant health); or

(F) the protection of children and persons under disability (whether legal or practical); or

(G) the development of under-privileged or less advanced groups or areas; or

(ii) in order to protect the exercise of the rights and freedoms of others; or

(*b*) makes reasonable provision for cases where the exercise of one such right may conflict with the exercise of another,

to the extent that the law is reasonably justifiable in a democratic society having a proper respect for the rights and dignity of mankind.

(2) For the purposes of Subsection (1), a law must

(*a*) be expressed to be a law that is made for that purpose; and
(*b*) specify the right or freedom that it regulates or restricts; and
(*c*) be made, and certified by the Speaker in his certificate under Section 110 (*certification as to making of laws*) to have been made, by an absolute majority.

(3) The burden of showing that a law is a law that complies with the requirements of Subsection (1) is on the party relying on its validity.

39. (1) The question, whether a law or act is reasonably justifiable in a democratic society having a proper regard for the rights and dignity of mankind, is to be determined in the light of the circumstances obtaining at the time when the decision on the question is made.

(2) A law shall not be declared not to be reasonably justifiable in a society having a proper regard for the rights and dignity of mankind except by the Supreme Court or the National Court, or any other court prescribed for the purpose by or under an Act of the Parliament, and unless the court is satisfied that the law was never so justifiable such a declaration operates as a repeal of the law as at the date of the declaration.

(3) For the purposes of determining whether or not any law, matter or thing is reasonably justified in a democratic society that has a proper regard for the rights and dignity of mankind, a court may have regard to

(*a*) the provisions of this Constitution generally, and especially the National Goals and Directive Principles and the Basic Social Obligations; and
(*b*) the Charter of the United Nations; and
(*c*) the Universal Declaration of Human Rights and any other declaration, recommendation or decision of the General Assembly of the United Nations concerning human rights and fundamental freedoms; and
(*d*) the European Convention for the Protection of Human Rights and Fundamental Freedoms and the Protocols thereto, and any other international conventions, agreements or declarations concerning human rights and fundamental freedoms; and
(*e*) judgements, reports and opinions of the International Court of Justice, the European Commission of Human Rights, the European Court of Human Rights and other international courts and tribunals dealing with human rights and fundamental freedoms; and
(*f*) previous laws, practices and judicial decisions and opinions in the country; and
(*g*) laws, practices and judicial decisions and opinions in other countries; and
(*h*) the Final Report of the pre-Independence Constitutional Planning Committee dated 13 August 1974 and presented to the pre-Independence House of Assembly on 16 August 1974, as affected by decisions of that House on the report and by decisions of the

Constituent Assembly on the draft of this Constitution; and

(*i*) declarations by the International Commission of Jurists and other similar organizations; and

(*j*) any other material that the court considers relevant.

40. Nothing in this Part invalidates an emergency law as defined in Part X (*emergency powers*), but nevertheless so far as is consistent with their purposes and terms all such laws shall be interpreted and applied so as not to affect or derogate a right or freedom referred to in this Division to an extent that is more than is reasonably necessary to deal with the emergency concerned and matters arising out of it, but only so far as is reasonably justifiable in a democratic society having a proper regard for the rights and dignity of mankind.

41. (1) Notwithstanding anything to the contrary in any other provision of any law, any act that is done under a valid law but in the particular case

(*a*) is harsh or oppressive; or

(*b*) is not warranted by, or is disproportionate to, the requirements of the particular circumstances or of the particular case; or

(*c*) is otherwise not, in the particular circumstances, reasonably justifiable in a democratic society having a proper regard for the rights and dignity of mankind.

is an unlawful act.

(2) The burden of showing that Subsection (1)(*a*), (b) or (*c*) applies in respect of an act is on the party alleging it, and may be discharged on the balance of probabilities.

(3) Nothing in this section affects the operation of any other law under which an act may be held to be unlawful or invalid.

Rights of All Persons

42. (1) no person shall be deprived of his personal liberty except

(*a*) in consequence of his unfitness to plead to a criminal charge; or

(*b*) in the execution of the sentence or order of a court in respect of an offence of which he has been found guilty, or in the execution of the order of a court of record punishing him for contempt of itself or another court or tribunal; or

(*c*) by reason of his failure to comply with the order of a court made to secure the fulfilment of an obligation (other than a contractual obligation) imposed upon him by law; or

(*d*) upon reasonable suspicion of his having committed, or being about to commit, an offence; or

(*e*) for the purpose of bringing him before a court in execution of the order of a court; or

(*f*) for the purpose of preventing the introduction or spread of a disease or suspected disease, whether or humans, animals or plants, or for normal purposes of quarantine; or (*g*) for the purpose of preventing the unlawful entry of a person into Papua New Guinea, or for the purpose of effecting the expulsion, extradition or other lawful removal of a person from Papua New Guinea, or the taking of proceedings for any of those purposes; or

(*h*) in the case of a person who is, or is reasonably suspected of being of unsound mind

(i) or addicted to drugs or alcohol, for the purpose of his care or treatment or the protection of the community, under an order of a court; or

(ii) for the purpose of taking prompt legal proceedings to obtain an order of a court of a type referred to in Subparagraph (i).

(2) A person who is arrested or detained

(*a*) shall be informed promptly, in a language that he understands, of the reasons for his arrest or detention and of any charge against him; and

(*b*) shall be permitted whenever practicable to communicate without delay and in private with a member of his family or a personal friend, and with a lawyer of his choice (including the Public Solicitor if he is entitled to legal aid); and

(*c*) shall be given adequate opportunity to give instructions to a lawyer of his choice in the place in which he is detained,

and shall be informed immediately on his arrest of his rights under this subsection.

(3) A person who is arrested or detained

(*a*) for the purpose of being brought before a court in the execution of an order of a court; or

(*b*) upon reasonable suspicion of his having committed, or being about to commit, an offence,

shall, unless he is released, be brought without delay before a court or a judicial officer and, in a case referred to in paragraph (*b*), shall not be further held in custody in connection with the offence except by order of a court or judicial officer.

(4) The necessity or desirability of interrogating the person concerned or other persons, or any administrative requirement or convenience, is not a good ground for failing to comply with Subsection (3), but exigencies of travel which in the circumstances are reasonable may, without derogating any other protection available to the person concerned, be such a ground.

(5) Where complaint is made to the National Court or a Judge that a person is unlawfully or unreasonably detained

(*a*) the National Court or a Judge shall inquire into the complaint and order the person concerned to be brought before it or him; and

(*b*) unless the court or Judge is satisfied that the detention is lawful, and in the case of a person being detained on remand pending his trial does not constitute an unreasonable detention having regard, in particular, to its length, the Court or a Judge shall order his release either unconditionally or subject to such conditions as the Court or Judge thinks fit.

(6) A person arrested or detained for an offence (other than treason or wilful murder as defined by an Act of the Parliament) is entitled to bail at all times from arrest or detention to acquittal or conviction unless the interests of justice otherwise require.

(7) Where a person to whom Subsection (6) applies is refused bail

(*a*) the court or person refusing bail shall, on request by the person concerned or his representative, state in writing the reason for the refusal; and

(*b*) the person or his representative may apply to the Supreme Court or the National Court in a summary manner for his release.

(8) Subject to any other law, nothing in this section applies in respect of any reasonable act of the parent or guardian of a child, or a person into whose care a child has been committed, in the course of the education, discipline or upbringing of the child.

(9) Subject to any Constitutional Law or Act of the Parliament, nothing in this section applies in respect of a person who is in custody under the law of another country

(*a*) while in transit through the country; or

(*b*) as permitted by or under an Act of the Parliament made for the purposes of Section 206 (*visiting forces*).

43. (1) No person shall be required to perform forced labor.

(2) In Subsection (1), 'forced labor' does not include

(*a*) labor required by the sentence or order of a court; or

(*b*) labor required of a person while in lawful custody, being labor that, although not required by the sentence or order of a court, is necessary for the hygiene of, or for the maintenance of, the place in which he is in custody; or

(*c*) in the case of a person in custody for the purpose of his care, treatment, rehabilitation or welfare, labor reasonably required for that purpose; or

(*d*) labor required of a member of a disciplined force in pursuance of his duties as such a member; or

(*e*) subject to the approval of any local government body for the area in which he is required to work, labor reasonaby required as part of reasonable and normal communal or other civic duties; or

(*f*) labor of a reasonable amount and kind (including in the case of compulsory military service, labor required as an alternative to such service in the case of a person who has conscientious objections to military service) that is required in the national interest by an Organic Law that complies with Section 38 (*general qualifications on qualified rights*).

44. No person shall be subjected to the search of his person or property or to entry of his premises, except to the extent that the exercise of that right is regulated or restricted by a law.

(*a*) that makes reasonable provision for a search or entry
- (i) under an order made by a court; or
- (ii) under a warrant for a search issued by a court or judicial officer on reasonable grounds, supported by oath or affirmation, particularly describing the purpose of the search; or
- (iii) that authorizes a public officer or government agent of Papua New Guinea or an officer of a body corporate established by law for a public purpose to enter, where necessary, on the premises of a person in order to inspect those premises or anything in or on them in relation to any rate or tax or in order to carry out work connected with any property that is lawfully in or on those premises and belongs to the Government or any such body corporate; or
- (iv) that authorizes the inspection of goods, premises, vehicles, ships or aircraft to ensure compliance with lawful requirements as to the entry of persons or importation of goods into Papua New Guinea or departure of persons or exportation of goods from Papua New Guinea or as to standards of safe construction, public safety, public health, permitted use or similar matters, or to secure compliance with the terms of a licence to engage in manufacture or trade; or
- (v) for the purpose of inspecting or taking copies of documents relating to
  - (A) the conduct of a business, trade, profession or industry in accordance with a law regulating the conduct of that business, trade, profession or industry; or
  - (B) the affairs of a company in accordance with a law relating to companies; or
- (vi) for the purpose of inspecting goods or inspecting or taking copies of documents, in connection with the collection, or the enforcement of payment of taxes or under a law prohibiting or restricting the importation of goods into Papua New Guinea or the exportation of goods from Papua New Guinea; or

(*b*) that complies with Section 38 (*general qualifications on qualified rights*).

45. (1) Every person has the right to freedom of conscience, thought and religion and the practice of his religion and beliefs including freedom to manifest and propagate his religion and beliefs in such a way as not to interfere with the freedom of others, except to the extent that the exercise of that right is regulated or restricted by a law that complies with Section 38 (*general qualifications and qualified rights*).

(2) No person shall be compelled to receive religious instruction or to take part in a religious ceremony or observance, but this does not apply to the giving of religious instruction to a child with the consent of his parent or guardian or to

the inclusion in a course of study of secular instruction concerning any religion or belief.

(3) No person is entitled to intervene unsolicited into the religious affairs of a person of a different belief, or to attempt to force his or any religion (or irreligion) on another, by harassment or otherwise.

(4) No person may be compelled to take an oath that is contrary to his religion or belief, or to take an oath in a manner or form that is contrary to his religion or belief.

(5) A reference in this section to religion includes a reference to the traditional religious beliefs and customs of the peoples of Papua New Guinea.

46. (1) Every person has the right to freedom of expression and publication, except to the extent that the exercise of that right is regulated or restricted by a law

(*a*) that imposes reasonable restrictions on public office-holders; or
(*b*) that imposes restrictions on non-citizens; or
(*c*) that complies with Section 38 (*general qualifications on qualified rights*).

(2) In Subsection (1), 'freedom of expression and publication' includes

(*a*) freedom to hold opinions, to receive ideas and information and to communicate ideas and information, whether to the public generally or to a person or class of persons; and
(*b*) freedom of the press and other mass communications media.

(3) Notwithstanding anything in this section, an Act of the Parliament may make reasonable provision for securing reasonable access to mass communications media for interested persons and associations

(*a*) for the communication of ideas and information; and
(*b*) to allow rebuttal of false or misleading statements concerning their acts, ideas or beliefs,

and generally for enabling and encouraging freedom of expression.

47. Every person has the right peacefully to assemble and associate and to form or belong to, or not to belong to, political parties, industrial organizations or other associations, except to the extent that the exercise of that right is regulated or restricted by a law

(*a*) that makes reasonable provision in respect of the registration of all or any associations; or
(*b*) that imposes reasonable restrictions on public office-holders; or
(*c*) that imposes restrictions on non-citizens; or
(*d*) that complies with Section 38 (*general qualifications on qualified rights*).

48. (1) Every person has the right to freedom of choice of employment in any calling for which he has the qualifications (if any) lawfully required, except to the extent that that freedom is regulated or restricted voluntarily or by a law that complies with Section 38 (*general qualifications on qualified rights*), or a law that imposes restrictions on non-citizens.

(2) Subsection (1) does not prohibit reasonable action or provision for the encouragement of persons to join industrial organizations or for requiring membership of an industrial organization for any purpose.

49. Every person has the right to reasonable privacy in respect of his private and family life, his communications with other persons and his personal papers and effects, except to the extent that the exercise of that right is regulated or restricted by a law that complies with Section 38 (*general qualifications on qualified rights.*)

Special rights of Citizens

50. (1) Subject to the express limitations imposed by this Constitution, every citizen who is of full capacity and has reached voting age, other than a person who

(*a*) is under sentence of death or imprisonment for a period of more than nine months; or

(*b*) has been convicted, within the period of three years next preceding the first day of the polling period for the election concerned, of an offence relating to elections that is prescribed by an Organic Law or an Act of the Parliament for the purposes of this paragraph,

has the right, and shall be given a reasonable opportunity

(*c*) to take part in the conduct of public affairs, either directly or through freely chosen representatives; and

(*d*) to vote for, and to be elected to, elective public office at genuine, periodic, free elections; and

(*e*) to hold public office and to exercise public functions.

(2) The exercise of those rights may be regulated by a law that is reasonably justifiable for the purpose in a democratic society that has a proper regard for the rights and dignity of mankind.

51. (1) Every citizen has the right of reasonable access to official documents, subject only to the need for such secrecy as is reasonably justifiable in a democratic society in respect of

(*a*) matters relating to national security, defence or international relations of Papua New Guinea (including Papua New Guinea's relations with the Government of any other country or with any international organization); or

(*b*) records of meetings and decisions of the National Executive Council and of such executive bodies and elected governmental authorities as are prescribed by Organic Law or Act of the Parliament; or

(*c*) trade secrets, and privileged or confidential commercial or financial information obtained from a person or body; or

(*d*) parliamentary papers the subject of parliamentary privilege; or

(*e*) reports, official registers and memoranda prepared by governmental authorities or authorities established by government, prior to completion; or

(*f*) papers relating to lawful official activities for investigation and prosecution of crime; or

(*f*) papers relating to lawful official activities for investigation and prosecution of crime; or
(*g*) the prevention investigation and prosecution of crime; or
(*h*) the maintenance of personal privacy and security of the person; or
(*i*) matters contained in or related to reports prepared by, on behalf of or for the use of a governmental authority responsible for the regulation or supervision of financial institutions; or
(*j*) geological or geophysical information and data concerning wells and ore bodies.

(2) A law that complies with Section 38 (*general qualifications on qualified rights*) may regulate or restrict the right guaranteed by this section.

(3) Provision shall be made by law to establish procedures by which citizens may obtain ready access to official information.

(4) This section does not authorize

(*a*) withholding information or limiting the availability of records to the public except in accordance with its provisions; or
(*b*) withholding information from the Parliament.

52. (1) Subject to Subsection (3), no citizen may be deprived of the right to move freely throughout the country, to reside in any part of the country and to enter and leave the country, except in consequence of a law that provides for deprivation of personal liberty in accordance with Section 42 (*liberty of the person*).

(2) No citizen shall be expelled or deported from the country except by virtue of an order of a court made under a law in respect of the extradition of offenders, or alleged offenders, against the law of some other place.

(3) A law that complies with Section 38 (*general qualifications on qualified rights*) may regulate or restrict the exercise of the right referred to in Subsection (1), and in particular may regulate or restrict the freedom of movement of persons convicted of offences and of members of a disciplined force.

53. (1) Subject to Section 54 (*special provision in relation to certain lands*) and except as permitted by this section, possession may not be compulsorily taken of any property, and no interest in or right over property may be compulsorily acquired, except in accordance with an Organic Law or an Act of the Parliament, and unless

(*a*) the property is required for
  (i) a public purpose; or
  (ii) a reason that is reasonably justified in a democratic society that has a proper regard for the rights and dignity of mankind,

that is so declared and so described, for the purposes of this section, in an Organic Law or an Act of the Parliament; and

(*b*) the necessity for the taking of possession or acquisition for the attainment of that purpose or for that reason is such as to afford reasonable justification for the causing of any resultant hardship to any person affected.

(2) Subject to this section, just compensation must be made on just terms by the expropriating authority, giving full weight to the National Goals and Directive Principles and having due regard to the national interest and to the expression of that interest by the Parliament, as well as to the person affected.

(3) For the purposes of Subsection (2), compensation shall not be deemed not to be just and on just terms solely by reason of a fair provision for deferred payment, payment by instalments or compensation otherwise than in cash.

(4) In this section, a reference to the taking of possession of property, or the acquisition of an interest in or right over property, includes a reference to

- (*a*) the forfeiture; or
- (*b*) the extinction or determination (otherwise than by way of a reasonable provision for the limitation of actions or a reasonable law in the nature of prescription or adverse possession),

of any right or interest in property.

(5) Nothing in the preceding provisions of this section prevents

- (*a*) the taking of possession of property, or the acquisition of an interest in or right over property, that is authorized by any other provision of this Constitution; or
- (*b*) any taking of possession or acquisition
  - (i) in consequence of an offence or attempted offence against, or a breach or attempted breach of, or other failure to comply with a law; or
  - (ii) in satisfaction of a debt or civil obligation; or
  - (iii) subject to Subsection (6), where the property is or may be required as evidence in proceedings or possible proceedings before a court or tribunal,

in accordance with a law that is reasonably justifiable in a democratic society that has a proper regard for the rights and dignity of mankind; or

- (*c*) any taking of possession or acquisition that was an incident of the grant or acceptance of, or of any interest in or right over, that property or any other property by the holder or any of his predecessors in title; or
- (*d*) any taking of possession or acquisition that is in accordance with custom; or
- (*e*) any taking of possession or acquisition of ownerless or abandoned property (other than customary land); or
- (*f*) any restriction on the use of or on dealing with property or any interest in or right over any property that is reasonably necessary for the preservation of the environment or of the national cultural inheritance.

(6) Subsection (5)(*b*)(iii) does not authorize the retention of any property after the end of the period for which its retention is reasonably required for the purpose referred to in that paragraph.

(7) Nothing in the preceding provisions of this section applies to or in

relation to the property of any person who is not a citizen and the power to compulsorily take possession of, or to acquire an interest in, or right over, the property of any such person shall be as provided for by an Act of the Parliament.

54. Nothing in Section 37 (*protection of the law*) of 53 (*protection from unjust deprivation of property*) invalidates a law that is reasonably justifiable in a democratic society that has a proper regard for human rights and that provides

(*a*) for the recognition of the claimed title of Papua New Guinea to land where

(i) there is a genuine dispute as to whether the land was acquired validly or at all from the customary owners before Independence Day; and

(ii) if the land were acquired compulsorily the acquisition would comply with Section 53(1) (*Protection from unjust deprivation of property*); or

(*b*) for the settlement by extra-judicial means of disputes as to the ownership of customary land that appear not to be capable of being reasonably settled in practice by judicial means; or

(*c*) for the prohibition or regulation of the holding of certain interests in, or in relation to, some or all land by non-citizens.

55. (1) Subject to this Constitution, all citizens have the same rights, privileges, obligations and duties irrespective of race, tribe, place of origin, political opinion, colour, creed, religion or sex.

(2) Subsection (1) does not prevent the making of laws for the special benefit, welfare, protection or advancement of females, children and young persons, members of underprivileged or less advanced groups or residents of less advanced areas.

(3) Subsection (1) does not affect the operation of a pre-Independence law.

56. (1) Only citizens may

(*a*) vote in elections for, or hold, elective public offices; or

(*b*) acquire freehold land.

(2) An Act of the Parliament may

(*a*) define the offices that are to be regarded as elective public offices; and

(*b*) define the forms of ownership that are to be regarded as freehold; and

(*c*) define the corporations that are to be regarded as citizens,

for the purpose of Subsection (1).

(3) An Act of the Parliament may make further provision for rights and privileges to be reserved for citizens.

SUBDIVISION D. ENFORCEMENT

57. (1) A right or freedom referred to in this Division shall be protected by, and is enforceable in, the Supreme Court or the National Court or any other court prescribed for the purpose by an Act of the Parliament, either on its own initiative or on application by any person who has an interest in its protection and enforcement, or in the case of a person who is, in the opinion of the court, unable fully and freely to exercise his rights under the section by a person acting on his behalf, whether or not by his authority.

(2) For the purposes of this section

(*a*) the Law Officers of Papua New Guinea; and

(*b*) any other persons prescribed for the purpose by an Act of the Parliament; and

(*c*) any other persons with an interest (whether personal or not) in the maintenance of the principles commonly known as the Rule of Law such that, in the opinion of the court concerned, they ought to appear and be heard on the matter in question,

have an interest in the protection and enforcement of the rights and freedoms referred to in this Division, but this subsection does not limit, the persons or classes of persons who have such an interest.

(3) A court that has jurisdiction under Subsection (1) may make all such orders and declarations as are necessary or appropriate for the purposes of this section, and may make an order or declaration in relation to a statute at any time after it is made (whether or not it is in force).

(4) Any court, tribunal or authority may, on its own initiative or at the request of a person referred to in Subsection (1), adjourn, or otherwise delay a decision in, any proceedings before it in order to allow a question concerning the effect or application of this Division to be determined in accordance with Subsection (1).

(5) Relief under this section is not limited to cases of actual or imminent infringement of the guaranteed rights and freedoms, but may, if the court thinks it proper to do so, be given in cases in which there is a reasonable probability of infringement, or in which an action that a person reasonably desires to take is inhibited by the likelihood of, or a reasonable fear of, an infringement.

(6) The jurisdiction and powers of the courts under this section are in addition to, and not in derogation of, their jurisdiction and powers under any other provision of this Constitution.

58. (1) This section is in addition to, and not in derogation of, Section 57 (*enforcement of guaranteed rights and freedoms*).

(2) A person whose rights or freedoms declared or protected by this Division are infringed (including any infringement caused by a derogation of the restrictions specified in Part X.5 (*internment*) on the use of emergency powers in relation to internment is entitled to reasonable damages and, if the court thinks it proper, exemplary damages in respect of the infringement.

(3) Subject to Subsections (4) and (5), damages may be awarded against any person who committed, or was responsible for, the infringement.

(4) Where the infringement was committed by a governmental body, damages may be awarded either

(*a*) subject to Subsection (5), against a person referred to in Subsection (3); or

(*b*) against the governmental body to which any such person was responsible,

or against both, in which last case the court may apportion the damages between them.

(5) Damages shall not be awarded against a person who was responsible to a governmental body in respect of the action giving rise to the infringement if

(*a*) the action was an action made unlawful by Section 41(1) (*proscribed acts*); and

(*b*) the action taken was genuinely believed by that person to be required by law,

but the burden of proof of the belief referred to in Paragraph (*b*) is on the party alleging it.

59. (1) Subject to this Constitution and to any statute, the principles of natural justice are the rules of the underlying law known by that name developed for control of judicial and administrative proceedings.

(2) The minimum requirement of natural justice is the duty to act fairly and, in principle, to be seen to act fairly.

60. In the development of the rules of the underlying law in accordance with Sch. 2 (*Adoption, etc., of certain laws*) particular attention shall be given to the development of a system of principles of natural justice and of administrative law specifically designed for Papua New Guinea, taking special account of the National Goals and Directive Principles and of the Basic Social Obligations, and also of typically Papua New Guinean procedures and forms of organization.

61. For the avoidance of doubt, it is hereby declared that nothing in the preceding provisions of this Division derogates any of the rights and freedoms provided for by Division 3 (*basic rights*).

62. (1) Where a law provides or allows for an act to be done in the 'deliberate judgement' of a person, body or authority, the principles of natural justice apply only to the extent that the exercise of judgement must not be biassed, arbitrary or capricious.

(2) Except

(*a*) to the extent provided for by Subsection (1); and

(*b*) in accordance with Section 155(5) (*the National Judicial System*); and

(*c*) as provided by a Constitutional Law or an Act of the Parliament,

an act to which Subsection (1) applies is, to the extent to which it is done in the deliberate judgement of the person concerned, non-justiciable.

Division 5. Basic Social Obligations

63. (1) Except to the extent provided in Subsection (3) and (4), the Basic Social Obligations are non-justiciable.

(2) Nevertheless, it is the duty of all governmental bodies to encourage compliance with them as far as lies within their respective powers.

(3) Where any law, or any power conferred or duty imposed by any law (whether the power or duty be of a legislative, judicial, executive, administrative or other kind), can reasonably be understood, applied, exercised, complied with or enforced, without failing to give effect to the intention of the Parliament or to this Constitution, in such a way as to enforce or encourage compliance with the Basic Social Obligations, or at least not to derogate them, it is to be understood, applied, exercised, complied with or enforced in that way.

(4) Subsection (1) does not apply in the exercise of the jurisdiction of the Ombudsman Commission or other body prescribed for the purposes of Division III.2 (*leadership code*), which shall take the Basic Social Obligations fully into account in all cases as appropriate.

PART IV.

CITIZENSHIP

Division 1. Introductory

64. (1) Notwithstanding the succeeding provisions of this Part but subject to Subsection (2), no person who has a real foreign citizenship may be or become a citizen and the provisions of this Part shall be read subject to that prohibition.

(2) Subsection (1) does not apply to a person who has not yet reached the age of 19 years, provided that, before he reaches that age and in such manner as is prescribed by or under an Act of the Parliament, he renounces his other citizenship and makes the Declaration of Loyalty.

(3) A person who has a real foreign citizenship and fails to comply with Subsection (2) ceases to be a citizen of Papua New Guinea when he reached the age of 19 years.

(4) For the purposes of this section, a person who

(*a*) was, immediately before Independence Day, an Australian citizen or an Australian Protected Person by virtue of

(i) birth in the former Territory of Papua; or

(ii) birth in the former Territory of New Guinea and registration under Section 11 of the *Australian Citizenship* Act 1948-1975 of Australia;

and

(*b*) was never granted a right (whether revocable or not) to permanent residence in Australia,

has no real foreign citizenship.

Division 2. Acquistition of Citizenship

65. (1) A person born in the country before Independence Day who has two grandparents who were born in the country or an adjacent area is a citizen.

(2) A person born outside the country before Independence Day who has two grand-parents born in the country is a citizen as from Independence Day if

(*a*) within one year after Independence Day or such longer period as the Minister responsible for citizenship matters allows in a particular case, application is made by him or on his behalf for registration as a citizen; and

(*b*) he renounces any other citizenship and makes the Declaration of Loyalty

(i) if he has not reached the age of 19 years – in accordance with Section 64(2) (*dual citizenship*); or

(ii) if he has reached the age of 19 years – at or before the time when the application is made.

(3) In Subsection (1), 'adjacent area' means an area that immediately before Independence Day constituted

(*a*) the Solomon Islands; or

(*b*) the Province of the Republic of Indonesia known as Irian Jaya; or

(*c*) the islands in Torres Straits annexed to the then Colony of Queensland under Letters Patent of the United Kingdom of Great Britain and Ireland bearing date the 10th day of October in the forty-second year of the reign of Her Majesty Queen Victoria (that is, 1878),

not forming on Independence Day part of the area of Papua New Guinea.

(4) Subsection (1) and (2) do not apply to a person who

(*a*) has a right (whether revocable or not) to permanent residence in Austrialia; or

(*b*) is a naturalized Australian citizen; or

(*c*) is registered as an Australian citizen under Section 11 of the *Australian Citizenship* Act 1948-1975 of Australia; or

(*d*) is a citizen of a country other than Australia,

unless that person renounces his right to residence in Australia or his status as a citizen of Australia or of another country in accordance with Subsection (5).

(5) A person to whom Subsection (4) applies may, within the period of two months after Independence Day and in such manner as may be prescribed by or under an act of the Parliament, renounce his right to permanent residence in Australia or his status as an Australian citizen or as a citizen of another country and make the Declaration of Loyalty.

(6) Where in his opinion it is just to do so, the Minister responsible for citizenship matters may in his deliberate judgement (but subject to Division 4 (*Citizenship Advisory Committee*), extend the period of two months referred to in Subsection (4), but unless the Minister is satisfied that the applicant

(*a*) assumed in error that he was a citizen; or
(*b*) did not know that he was not a citizen; or
(*c*) had no reasonable opportunity or not enough time to determine his status,

the period may not be extended beyond a further two months.

66. (1) A person who
(*a*) is born in the country on or after Independence Day; and
(*b*) had one parent who was a citizen or who, if he had survived to Independence Day, would have been or would have been entitled to become, such a citizen,

is a citizen.

(2) A person
(*a*) who is born outside the country on or after Independence Day;
(*b*) who had one parent who was a citizen or who, if he had survived to Independence Day, would have been, or would have been entitled to become, such a citizen; and
(*c*) whose birth is registered as prescribed by or under an Act of the Parliament made for the purposes of this subsection,

is a citizen.

67. (1) A person who has resided continuously in the country for at least eight years may apply to the Minister responsible for citizenship matters to be naturalized as a citizen, and the Minister may, if he is satisfied as to the matters referred to in Subsection (2), in his deliberate judgement (but subject to Division 4 (*Citizenship Advisory Committee*), grant or refuse the application.

(2) To be eligible for naturalization, a person must
(*a*) be of good character; and
(*b*) intend to reside permanently in the country; and
(*c*) unless prevented by physical or mental disability, speak and understand *Pisin* or *Hiri Motu*, or a vernacular of the country, sufficiently for normal conversational purposes; and
(*d*) have a respect for the customs and cultures of the country; and
(*e*) be unlikely to be or become a charge on public funds; and
(*f*) have a reasonable knowledge and understanding of the rights, privileges, responsibilities and duties of citizenship; and
(*g*) renounce, in such manner as is prescribed by or under an Act ot the Parliament, any other citizenship and make the Declaration of Loyalty.

(3) If an applicant for naturalization so requests, any child of the applicant who is under voting age at the time when the applicant is naturalized becomes a citizen by naturalization of the applicant.

68. (1) A person who is eligible to become a citizen under Section 67(1) (*citizenship by naturalization*) and holds an executive office by virtue of being a member of an elective body shall cease to hold that office at the expiration of a period of two months after Independence Day unless within that time he makes application under that section to be naturalized and that application is granted.

(2) Without limiting the matters that may be taken into account in deciding on the application for naturalization under Section 67 (*citizenship by naturalization*) the following matters shall be taken into account in deciding on an application that is made during the first eight years after Independence Day:

(*a*) if the applicant is a person to whom Section 65(4) (*automatic citizenship on Independence Day*) applies, whether he acquired the right of permanent residence in Australia or became an Australian citizen otherwise than by reason of a voluntary act (other than marriage) on his part; and

(*b*) whether the applicant has at any time accepted pay and conditions of employment that were not in general applicable

(i) before Independence Day, to persons who qualify or would, if they had survived to that day, have qualified for citizenship under Section 65 (*automatic citizenship on Independence Day*); or

(ii) after Independence Day, to citizens; and

(*c*) whether the major part of the investment and business interests of the applicant are and have been in the country; and

(*d*) whether the applicant is or has been married to a citizen or to a person who, if he had survived to Independence Day, would have been entitled to become, a citizen, and the nature of the family ties of the applicant; and

(*e*) the length and nature of the residence of the applicant in the country; and

(*f*) any performance by the applicant of services beneficial to Papua New Guinea or its people; and

(*g*) any sacrifices made by the applicant in the interests of Papua New Guinea or its people; and

(*h*) the applicant's knowledge of *Pisin* or *Hiri Motu* or of a vernacular of the country; and

(*i*) whether or not the application of the applicant includes the children (if any) under voting age of the applicant; and

(*j*) any references given as to the good character and suitability for citizenship of the applicant; and

(*k*) the place of birth and the parentage of the applicant.

(3) Notwithstanding anything in a Constitutional law, a benefit, right or privilege, directly or indirectly, conferred upon 'Papua New Guineans' or 'natives'

or 'local persons' or 'non-overseas persons' or 'citizens' (where that term is to take effect after the making of a law relating to citizenship) by any pre-Independence law shall continue to be enjoyed only by persons who became citizens of Papua New Guinea under Section 65 (*automatic citizenship on Independence Day*) but only

(*a*) for a period of ten years after Independence Day; or

(*b*) until an Act of the Parliament takes away that benefit, right or privilege,

whichever first occurs.

(4) Notwithstanding anything in a Constitutional Law, during the five years after Independence Day only persons who become citizens of Papua New Guinea under Section 65 (*automatic citizenship on Independence Day*) shall have the rights conferred by Section 53 (*protection from unjust deprivation of property*) except that during this period the rights of a person who becomes a citizen otherwise than under Section 65 (*automatic citizenship on Independence Day*) in respect of his property shall not be less than those accorded by law to non-citizens.

(5) Notwithstanding anything in a Constitutional Law, but subject to Subsection (6), an Act of the Parliament made in the period of ten years after Independence Day may confer a benefit, right or privilege on persons who became citizens of Papua New Guinea under Section 65 (*automatic citizenship on Independence Day*).

(6) An Act of the Parliament referred to in Subsection (5)

(*a*) shall not derogate the rights conferred by Section 32 to 58 (*basic rights*) except the rights conferred by Section 55 (*equality of citizens*); and

(*b*) shall be for the purpose of giving advantage or assistance to persons who become citizens of Papua New Guinea under Section 65 (*automatic citizenship on Independence Day*).

69. (1) Subject to Subsection (2), an application for naturalization under Section 67 (*citizenship by naturalization*) must be made

(*a*) in the case of a person who has resided continuously in the country for eight years or more before Independence Day – within two months after Independence Day; and

(*b*) in the case of any other person – within two months after the completion by him of eight years continuous residence in the country.

(2) Where in his opinion it is just to do so, the Minister responsible for citizenship matters may in his deliberate judgement, (but subject to *Division* 4 (*Citizenship Advisory Committee*) extend the periods referred to in Subsection (1) where he is satisfied that

(*a*) the person was unaware of the provisions of Subsection (1); or

(*b*) there are special circumstances.

Division 3. Loss and Regaining of Citizenship

70. (1) A citizen who has reached voting age and is of full capacity who

(*a*) obtains the nationality or citizenship of another country by a voluntary act (other than marriage); or

(*b*) exercises a right that is exclusive to nationals or citizens of another country, unless the Minister responsible for citizenship matters is satisfied that the right was exercised inadvertently; or

(*c*) takes an oath or makes a declaration or affirmation of allegiance to another country or to the Sovereign or Head of State of another country; or

(*d*) does, agrees to or adopts any act (other than marriage) by which he becomes a national or citizen of another country; or

(*e*) enters or serves in the armed forces of another country, except with the express approval of the Head of State, acting with, and in accordance with, the advice of the National Executive Council; or

(*f*) except as permitted by an Act of the Parliament, votes in a national, provincial, state or local election, or accepts elective office, of another country; or

(*g*) subject to Subsection (3), travels under the protection of a passport or purported passport of another country in which he is described as a citizen or national of that country,

loses his citizenship.

(2) A person who is found by a court to have obtained citizenship by a false representation, fraud or concealment of a material fact on his part loses his citizenship, unless the Minister responsible for citizenship matters is satisfied that the offence was of a minor nature and that revelation of the true fact would not have affected the grant of naturalization.

(3) Subsection (1)(*g*) does not apply to

(*a*) a person who is absent from the country on Independence Day, continues to travel under the protection of a passport of another country, but only until

(i) the expiration of the then-current period of validity of the passport; or

(ii) his return to the country,

whichever first happens; or

(*b*) a person travelling under the protection of the passport of a parent or guardian; or

(*c*) a person travelling under the protection of a passport of another country with the approval of the Minister responsible for citizenship matters.

71. The preceding provisions of this Division do not apply to any act done under compulsion of law of another country.

72. (1) Subject to Subsections (2) and (3), a citizen who has reached voting age and is of full capacity may renounce his citizenship in such manner and on such conditions as are prescribed by or under an Act of the Parliament.

(2) A person may not renounce his citizenship unless

(*a*) he already holds some other nationality or citizenship; or

(*b*) the renunciation is for the purpose of his obtaining some other nationality or citizenship.

(3) During a time of war, citizenship may not be renounced without the prior consent of the Minister responsible for citizenship matters.

73. (1) Subject to Subsection (2), citizenship once lost can be regained

(*a*) in the case of citizenship by virtue of Section 65 (*automatic citizenship on Independence Day*) or 66 (*citizenship by descent*) – only after five years' continuous residence in the country after the loss of citizenship, and in the deliberate judgement (*but subject to Division* 4 (*Citizenship Advisory Committee*)) of the Minister responsible for citizenship matters; and

(*b*) in the case of citizenship by naturalization – only in accordance with the law relating to naturalization, for which purpose any period of residence in the country before the loss of citizenship shall be disregarded.

(2) Where a person

(*a*) was a citizen by virtue of Section 65 (*automatic citizenship on Independence Day*) or 66 (*citizenship by descent*); and

(*b*) married, before, on or after Independence Day, a person who was a national or citizen of another country; and

(*c*) became, on or during the marriage, a national or citizen of the country of which his spouse was at that time a national or citizen,

and the marriage has permanently broken up, the reference in Subsection (1)(*a*) to a period of five years shall be read as a reference to a period of three years commencing

(*d*) if the person was, at the time when the marriage broke up, resident in the country – on the date on which it broke up; or

(*e*) if the person was at that time resident outside the country – on his return to reside in the country.

74. (1) Where

(*a*) a parent of a child loses his citizenship; and

(*b*) the Minister is satisfied on application on behalf of the child that it is for the welfare of the child to do so,

the Minister responsible for citizenship matters may, by order, deprive the child of his citizenship.

(2) A person aggrieved by an order under Subsection (1) may appeal to the National Court.

(3) An Act of the Parliament may make special provision to facilitate the regaining of citizenship by persons who lose their citizenship by reason of the loss of citizenship by a parent.

Division 4. Citizenship Advisory Committee

75. (1) An Act of the Parliament shall make provision for a Citizenship Advisory Committee, all of the members of which must be citizens (other than naturalized citizens).

(2) The Committee shall consist of

(*a*) four permanent members, at least two of whom are members of the Parliament other than Ministers; and

(*b*) one ad hoc member to represent the community in which the person to whom a matter before the Committee relates resides.

76. (1) Before taking any action under this Part in relation to a person, the Minister responsible for citizenship matters shall refer the matter to the Citizenship Advisory Committee.

(2) If the Minister refuses to accept the advice of the Committee on any matter referred to it under Subsection (1), he shall, if so requested by a person affected or by the Committee, give to the Parliament, as soon as practicable, a statement on the matter setting out the reasons for his refusal, and the Parliament may reverse his decision on such conditions as it thinks proper.

(3) The reversal by the Parliament of a decision to grant or to allow the regaining citizenship, or to grant a certificate under Section 81 (*certificate as to citizenship*), takes effect, subject to any conditions to which it is made subject, as a deprivation of citizenship on the date of the reversal.

(4) The reversal by the Parliament of a decision to refuse to grant citizenship to a person, to deprive a person of citizenship or to refuse to grant a certificate under Section 81 (*certificate as to citizenship*) takes effect retrospectively to the date of the decision.

(5) The Committee has such powers and such other functions and duties as are conferred or imposed by or under an Act of the Parliament.

Division 5. General

77. (1) A foundling discovered at any time in the country shall, in the absence of proof to the contrary, be deemed to be the child of parents at least one of whom was, or if he had survived would have been, a citizen.

(2) Where the identity or the citizenship status of a parent of a child born in the country is unknown or doubtful, the parent shall be deemed to have been, in the absence of proof to the contrary, a person who was, or if he had survived would have been, a citizen.

(3) For the purposes of this Part, a posthumous child of a person has the same status as he would have had if he had been born immediately before the date of the death of his father.

78. (1) Where the citizenship status or entitlement of a person is to be determined by reference to a parent or grand-parent and the person, or a parent of the person, was adopted under a law at any time in force in the country or any other place, the status or entitlement shall be determined by reference to the natural parents or grand-parents, except that the Minister responsible for citizenship matters may, in his deliberate judgement (but subject to Division 4 (*Citizenship Advisory Committee*), allow an adoptive parent or grand-parent to be taken into account where the result would be to recognize citizenship or the entitlement to citizenship.

(2) In Subsection (1), a reference to adoption includes a reference to an adoption by custom.

79. For the purposes of this Part

(*a*) a person born on a registered ship or aircraft shall be deemed to have been born at the place where the ship or aircraft was registered; and

(*b*) a person born on an unregistered ship or aircraft belonging to the government of a country shall be deemed to have been born in that country.

80. Subject to any Act of the Parliament, a requirement in this Part of a period of residence in a place is not satisfied by

(*a*) residence in custody under sentence awaiting deportation or removal from the country; or

(*b*) residence as an unlawful immigrant.

81. (1) A person whose status or entitlement in relation to citizenship of Papua New Guinea is, or may be, in doubt may apply to the Minister responsible for citizenship matters for a certificate under this section.

(2) If the Minister is satisfied that the applicant is, or is entitled to become, a citizens, he may, in his deliberate judgement (but subject to Division 4 (*Citizenship Advisory Committee*)), grant a certificate stating that the person is or may become a citizen by virtue of a provision specified in the certificate.

(3) Subject to Section 76 (*functions of the Committee*), a certificate under this section is (unless it is proved that it was obtained by means of a false representation, fraud or concealment of a material fact) conclusive evidence that on the material date the person concerned was, is or may become a citizen in accordance with the terms of the certificate.

PART V

THE HEAD OF STATE

Division 1. The Head of State

82. (1) Her Majesty the Queen

(*a*) *having been* requested by the people of Papua New Guinea, through their Constituent Assembly, to become the Queen and Head of State of Papua New Guinea.

(*b*) having graciously consented so to become, is the Queen and Head of State of Papua New Guinea.

(2) Subject to and in accordance with this Constitution, the privileges,

powers, functions, duties and responsibilites of the Head of State may be had, exercised and performed through a Governor-General appointed in accordance with Division 3 (*appointment, etc., of Governor-General*) and, except where the contrary intention appears, reference in any law to the Head of State shall be read accordingly.

83. The provisions of this Constitution referring to the Queen extend to Her Majesty's heirs and successors in the sovereignty of the United Kingdom of Great Britain and Northern Ireland.

84. The Head of State takes precedence in rank over all other persons in Papua New Guinea, and the Governor-General takes precedence in rank immediately after the Head of State.

85. The Style and Titles of the Head of State are as determined by Act of the Parliament and until such an Act is made are

Elizabeth II, Queen of Papua New Guinea and Her other Realms and Territories, Head of the Commonwealth.

Division 2. Functions, etc., of the Head of State

86. (1) The privileges, powers, functions, duties and responsibilities of the Head of State are as prescribed by or under Constitutional Laws and Acts of the Parliament.

(2) Except as provided by Section 96(2) (*terms and conditions of employment*), in the exercise and performance of his privileges, powers, functions, duties and responsibilities the Head of State shall act only with, and in accordance with, the advice of the National executive Council, or of some other body or authority prescribed by a Constitutional Law or an Act of the Parliament for a particular purpose as the body or authority in accordance with whose advice the Head of State is obliged, in a particular case, to act.

(3) Any instrument made by or in the name of the Head of State shall recite that it is made with, and in accordance with, the advice of the National Executive Council or of any other body or authority in accordance with whose advice the Head of State is obliged, in the particular case, to act, but failure to comply with this subsection does not affect the validity of an instrument.

(4) The question, what (if any) advice was given to the Head of State, or by whom, is non-justiciable.

Division 3. Appointment, etc., of Governor-General

87. (1) The Governor-General must be a citizen who

(*a*) is qualified to be a member of the Parliament (except for the reason that he occupies the office of Governor-General); and

(*b*) is a mature person of good standing who enjoys the general respect of the community.

(2) The question, whether for the purposes of subsection (1) a person is a person to whom Subsection (1)(*b*) applies, is non-justiciable.

(3) The Governor-General must not hold any office or position or engage in any calling other than that of, or an office or position associated with, his office as Governor-General, except with the consent of the Head of State, acting with, and in accordance with, the joint advice of the National Executive Council and the Ombudsman Commission.

(4) A request for the consent of the Head of State under Subsection (3) shall not be made unless agreement on the matter in relation to which the consent is sought has been reached between the National Executive Council and the Ombudsman Commission.

(5) No person is eligible for appointment as Governor-General more than once unless the Parliament, by two-thirds absolute majority vote, approves appointment for a second term, but no person is eligible for appointment for a third term.

88. (1) Except in the case of the first Governor-General appointed before Independence Day the Governor-General shall be appointed by the Head of State, acting with, and in accordance with, the advice of the National Executive Council given in accordance with a decision of the Parliament.

(2) A decision of the Parliament to nominate a person for appointment as Governor-General shall be made by a simple majority vote, in an exhaustive secret ballot conducted in accordance with an Organic Law.

(3) Subject to Subsection (5), the speaker shall, within the period of three months before the completion of the normal term of office of the Governor-General, call a meeting of the Parliament to nominate the next Governor-General.

(4) Subject to Subsection (5), in the event of a casual vacancy in the office of Governor-General, the Speaker shall, as soon as practicable, call a meeting of the Parliament to nominate the next Governor-General.

(5) If

(*a*) at a time when a meeting of the Parliament should otherwise be called under Subsection (3) or (4) a general election to the Parliament has been ordered; or

(*b*) between the time when a meeting of the Parliament should otherwise be called under Subsection (3) and the date of the completion of the normal term of office of the outgoing Governor-General a general election to the Parliament is due to be held in accordance with this Constitution,

the Speaker shall not call a meeting of the Parliament in accordance with Subsection (3) or (4), as the case may be, and a nomination shall be made at the first meeting of the new Parliament as its first item of business after any formal business and the election of a Speaker.

89. Notwithstanding Section 90 (*Declaration of Loyalty, etc.*) for the purposes of this Constitution a person appointed as Governor-General takes office

(*a*) subject to paragraph (*b*), at the end of his predecessor's term of office; or

(*b*) if he is appointed to fill a casual vacancy – on the date of his appointment.

90. (1) Before entering upon the duties of his office, a Governor-General shall take the Oath of Allegiance and make the Declaration of Loyalty and the Declaration of Office before the Chief Justice and in the presence of the Parliament, but during a period of declared national emergency they may be taken and made in such manner as is directed by the National Executive Council.

(2) If the Governor-General has not complied with Subsection (1) before taking office

(*a*) he is suspended from office until such time as he does so; and

(*b*) if he does not do so at the first reasonably available opportunity, he may be dismissed from office by the Head of State, acting with, and in accordance with, the advice of the National Executive Council given in accordance with a decision of the Parliament, and in that event is not eligible for reappointment for a period of six years.

91. Unless he earlier dies, resigns, ceases to be qualified for office in accordance with Section 87 (*qualifications for appointment*), is dismissed under Section 90 (*Declaration of Loyalty, etc.,*) or 93 (*dismissal and removal from office*), or is removed from office under Section 93(2) (*dismissal and removal from office*), the Governor-General holds office for a term of six years from the date of his assumption of office in accordance with Section 89 (*assumption of office*), plus any period that is required, in accordance with Section 88(5) (*appointment to office*), for the appointment of the next Governor-General.

92. (1) The Governor-General may resign from office by notice in writing to the Head of State.

(2) The resignation takes effect on its acceptance by the Head of State, acting with, and in accordance with, the advice of the National Executive Council.

93. (1) The Governor-General may be dismissed from office by the Head of State, acting with, and in accordance with, the advice of the National Executive Council given in accordance with either

(*a*) a decision of the National Executive Council; or

(*b*) a decision made by an absolute majority of the Parliament.

(2) The Governor-General may be removed from office by the Head of State, acting with, and in accordance with, the advice of the National Executive Council given in accordance with a decision of the Parliament, if the Speaker advises the Parliament that two medical practitioners appointed for the purpose by the National authority responsible for the registration or licensing of medical practitioners have jointly reported to the Speaker that, in their professional opinions, the Governor-General is unfit, by reason of physical or mental incapacity, to carry out the duties of his office.

94. (1) The Governor-General may be suspended from office

(*a*) by the National Executive Council, if he refuses or fails to act in accordance with the advice of the National Executive Council or of any other body or authority in accordance with whose advice he is obliged, in the particular case, to act, or acts, or purports to act contrary to , or without, any such advice; or (*b*) in accordance with a Act of the Parliament pending an investigation for the purposes of Section 93(2) (*dismissal and removal from office*),

and pending any resultant action by the Parliament.

(2) If the Governor-General is suspended from office by the National Executive Council under Subsection (1)(*a*), the Prime Minister shall immediately inform the Speaker of the suspension and of the reason for it.

(3) If the Governor-General is suspended from office under Subsection (1)(*a*)

(*a*) the Speaker shall, as soon as practicable, call a meeting of the Parliament at which the matter of the suspension and of the possible dismissal of the Governor-General shall be the first item of business after any formal business and, if necessary, the appointment of a Speaker; and

(*b*) the suspension may be lifted at any time by decision of the Parliament; and

(*c*) unless before the end of the meeting a recommendation is made in accordance with Section 93(1) (*dismissal and removal from office*) that the Governor-General be dismissed from office, the suspension ceased at the end of the meeting.

(4) If the Governor-General is suspended from office under this section, the Prime Minister shall, as soon as practicable, inform the Head of State of the suspension and of the reasons for it.

(5) A period of suspension under this section shall be taken into account in calculating for the purposes of this Division, the length of the period of service in office of the Governor-General.

95. (1) In this section, a reference to the Speaker or to the Chief Justice shall be read as a reference to the substantive holder of that office.

(2) If

(*a*) there is a vacancy in the office of Governor-General; or

(*b*) the Governor-General is suspended from office; or

(*c*) the Governor-General is

(i) on leave of absence; or

(ii) absent from the country; or

(iii) out of speedy and effective communication; or

(iv) otherwise unable to perform, or is not readily available to perform, the duties of his office,

the Speaker is, subject to Subsection (3), the Acting Governor-General.

(3) If at any time to which Subsection (2) applies

(*a*) there is a vacancy in the office of Speaker; or

(*b*) the Speaker is suspended from office; or

(*c*) the Speaker is

(i) on leave of absence; or

(ii) absent from the country; or

(iii) out of speedy and effective communication; or
(iv) otherwise unable to perform, or is not readily available to perform duties of his office,

the Chief Justice (if he is a citizen) is the Acting Governor-General.

(4) During any period when he is the Acting Governor-General, the Speaker or the Chief Justice shall not exercise or perform any of the other powers, functions, duties and responsibilities of the office of Speaker or Chief Justice, as the case may be, except that the Chief Justice may complete any proceedings actually commenced before him unless other suitable arrangements can be made.

(5) When neither the Speaker nor the Chief Justice is available (or, in the case of the Chief Justice, qualified) to be the Acting Governor-General, the powers, functions, duties and responsibilities of the Governor-General shall be exercised and performed by a Minister appointed by the Head of State on the advice of the National Executive Council for the purpose.

(6) The question, whether the occasion for the exercise or performance of a power function, duty or responsibility by an Acting Governor-General or a Minister under this section has arisen or has ceased, is non-justiciable.

96. (1) Subject to this Constitution, the terms and conditions of employment of the Governor-General are as determined by or under an Organic Law.

(2) Except with the consent of the Governor-General the terms and conditions of employment of the Governor-General shall not be changed to his detriment during his term of office, and an Organic Law that so changes them shall recite the terms of the consent.

Division 4. General

97. Where any act is done, decision is made or advice is given by the Parliament or the National Executive Council under this Part, the Prime Minister shall immediately convey it to the Head of State.

98. Unless the contrary intention appears, any act by the Head of State takes effect when it is formally advised to the Prime Minister or the National Executive Council.

PART VI

THE NATIONAL GOVERNMENT

Division 1. General Principles

99. (1) Subject to and in accordance with this Constitution, the power, authority and jurisdiction of the People shall be exercised by the National Government.

(2) The National Government consists of three principal arms, namely:

(*a*) the National Parliament, which is an elective legislature with, subject to the Constitutonal Laws, unlimited powers of law-making; and

(*b*) the National Executive; and
(*c*) the National Judicial System, consisting of a Supreme Court of Justice and a National Court of Justice, of unlimited jurisdiction, and other courts.

(3) In principle, the respective powers and functions of the three arms shall be kept separate from each other.

(4) Subsection (2) is descriptive only and is non-justiciable.

Division 2. The National Parliament

SUBDIVISION A. THE LEGISLATIVE POWER

100. (1) Subject to this Constitution, the legislative power of the People is vested in the National Parliament.

(2) Subsection (1) does not prevent a law from conferring on an authority other than the Parliament legislative powers or functions (including, if the law so provides, a further power or further powers of delegation and subdelegation).

(3) Nothing in any Constitutional Law enables or may enable the Parliament to transfer permanently, or divest itself of, legislative power.

SUBDIVISION B. COMPOSITION OF THE NATIONAL PARLIAMENT

101. (1) Subject to this section, the Parliament is a single-chamber legislature, consisting of

(*a*) a number of members elected from single-member open electorates; and
(*b*) a number of members elected from single-member provincial electorates; and
(*c*) not more than three nominated members, appointed and holding office in accordance with Section 102 (*nominated members*).

(2) An Organic Law shall make provision for the number of open and provincial electorates.

(3) No member may represent two or more electorates at the same time.

(4) The precise number of open electorates and of provincial electorates and their boundaries shall be determined from time to time in accordance with Section 125 (*electorates*).

(5) An alteration to the number of electorates or to the boundaries of an electorate takes effect for the purposes of the next general election and of succeeding elections.

102. The Parliament may, from time to time, by a two-thirds absolute majority vote, appoint a person (other than a member) to be a nominated member of the Parliament.

103. (1) A member of the Parliament must be not less than 25 years of age.

(2) A candidate for election to the Parliament must have been born in the electorate for which he intends to nominate or have resided in the electorate

for a continuous period of two years immediately preceding his nomination or for a period of five years at any time.

(3) A person is not qualified to be, or to remain, a member of the Parliament if

(*a*) he is not entitled to vote in elections to the Parliament; or
(*b*) he is of unsound mind within the meaning of any law relating to the protection of the persons and property of persons of unsound mind; or
(*c*) subject to Subsections (4) to (7), he is under sentence of death or imprisonment for a period of more than nine months; or
(*d*) he is otherwise disqualified under this Constitution.

(4) Where a person is under sentence of death or imprisonment for a period exceeding nine months, the operation of Subsection (3)(*d*) is suspended until

(*a*) the end of any statutory period allowed for appeals against the conviction or sentence; or
(*b*) if an appeal is lodged within the period referred to in paragraph (*a*), the appeal is determined.

(5) The references in Subsection (4), to appeals and to the statutory period allowed for appeals shall, where there is provision for a series of appeals, be read as references to each appeal and to the statutory period allowed for each appeal.

(6) If a free pardon is granted, a conviction is quashed or a sentence is changed to a sentence of imprisonment for nine months or less, or some other form of penalty (other than death) is substituted, the disqualification ceases, and if at the time of the pardon, quashing, change of sentence of substitution of penalty the writ for the by-election has not been issued the member is restored to his seat.

(7) In this section

'appeal' includes any form of judicial appeal or judicial review;

'statutory period allowed for appeals' means a definite period allowed by law for appeals, whether or not it is capable of extension, but does not include an extension of such a definite period granted or that may be granted unless it is granted within that definite priod.

104. (1) An elected member of the Parliament takes office on the day immediately following the day fixed for the return of the writ for the election in his electorate.

(2) The seat of a member of the Parliament becomes vacant

(*a*) if he is appointed as Governor-General; or
(*b*) upon the expiry of the day fixed for the return of the writs, for the general election after he last became a member of the Parliament; or
(*c*) if he resigns his seat by notice in writing to the Speaker, or in the case of the Speaker to the Clerk of the Parliament; or

(*d*) if he is absent, without leave of the Parliament, during the whole of three consecutive meetings of the Parliament unless Parliament decides to waive this rule upon satisfactory reasons being given; or

(*e*) if, except as authorized by or under an Organic Law or an Act of the Parliament, he directly or indirectly takes or agrees to take any payment in respect of his services in the Parliament; or

(*f*) if he becomes disqualified under Section 103 (*qualifications for and disqualifications from membership*); or

(*g*) on his death; or

(*h*) if he is dismissed from office under Division III.2 (*leadership code*).

(3) For the purposes of Subsection (2)(*d*), a meeting of the Parliament commences when the Parliament first sits following a general election, prorogation of the Parliament or an adjourment of the Parliament otherwise than for a period of less than 12 days and ends when next the Parliament is prorogued or adjourned otherwise than for a period of less than 12 days.

105. (1) A general election to the Parliament shall be held

(*a*) within the period of three months before the fifth anniversary of the day fixed for the return of the writs for the previous general election; or

(*b*) if, during the last 12 months before the fifth anniversary of the day fixed for the return of the writs for the previous general election

(i) a vote of no confidence in the Prime Minister or the Ministry is passed in accordance with Section 145 (*motions of no confidence*); or

(ii) the Government is defeated on the vote on a question that the Prime Minister has declared to the Parliament to be a question of confidence; or

(*c*) if the Parliament, by an absolute majority vote, so decides.

(2) The Head of State, acting with, and in accordance with, the advice of the Electoral Commission, shall fix the first and last days of the period during which polling shall take place and the date by which the writs for a general election shall be returned.

(3) In advising the Head of State under Subsection (2), and in conducting the election, the Electoral Commission shall do its best to ensure that

(*a*) in a case to which Subsection (1)(*a*) applies – the date for the return of the writs is fixed as nearly as may reasonably be to the fifth anniversary of the date fixed for the return of the writs for the previous general election; and

(*b*) in a case to which Subsection (1)(*b*) or (*c*) applies – the date for the return of the writs is fixed as soon as may reasonably be after the date of the relevant decision of the Parliament.

106. If the office of an elected member of the Parliament becomes vacant otherwise than by virtue of Section 104(2)(*b*) (*normal term of office*), an election shall be held to fill the vacancy unless the vacancy occurs

(*a*) within the period of six months before the fifth anniversary of the date fixed for the return of the writs for the previous general election; or

(*b*) after the writ has been issued for an election under Section 105(1) (*general elections*) and before the day fixed for the return of that writ, writs for a general election are issued, the first-mentioned writ shall be deemed to have been revoked.

SUBDIVISION C. THE SPEAKER AND THE DEPUTY SPEAKER

107. (1) There shall be offices of Speaker and Deputy Speaker of the National Parliament.

(2) The Speaker and the Deputy Speaker must be members of the Parliament, and shall be elected by the Parliament by secret ballot in accordance with the Standing Orders of the Parliament.

(3) The Speaker and the Deputy Speaker hold office, and their offices become vacant, in accordance with the Constitutional Law and the Standing Orders of the Parliament.

(4) No Minister may be the Speaker or Deputy Speaker, and if a Speaker or Deputy Speaker becomes a Minister he vacates his office as Speaker or Deputy Speaker, as the case may be.

108. (1) The Speaker is responsible, subject to and in accordance with the Constitutional Laws, the Acts of the Parliament and the Standing Orders of the Parliament, for upholding the dignity of the Parliament, maintaining order in it, regulating its proceedings and administering its affairs, and for controlling the precincts of the Parliament as defined by or under an Act of the Parliament.

(2) In the event of a vacancy in the office of the Speaker or his absence from the country or from the Parliament, and otherwise as determined by or under a Constitutional Law, an Act of the Parliament or the Standing Orders of the Parliament, the Deputy Speaker has, subject to Section 95 (*Acting Governor-General*), all the rights, privileges, powers, functions, duties and responsibilities of the Speaker.

(3) A Constitutional Law, an Act of the Parliament or the Standing Orders of the Parliament may provide for other powers, functions, duties and responsibilities of the Speaker and the Deputy Speaker.

109. (1) Subject to this Constitution, the Parliament may make laws, having effect within and outside the country, for the peace, order and good government of Papua New Guinea and the welfare of the People.

(2) In particular, Acts of the Parliament, not inconsistent with the Constitutional Laws, may provide for all matters that are necessary or convenient to be prescribed for carrying out and giving effect to this Constitution.

(3) No law made by the Parliament is open to challenge in any court on the ground that

(*a*) it is not for the peace, order or good government of Papua New Guinea or the welfare of the People; or

(*b*) it purports to have extra-territorial effect.

(4) Each law made by the Parliament shall receive such fair, large and liberal construction and interpretation as will best ensure the attainment of the object of the law according to its true intent, meaning and spirit, and there is no presumption against extra-territoriality.

110. Certification as to making of laws.

(1) Subject to Section 137(3) (*Acts of Idemnity*) and to any Act of the Parliament made for the purpose of Subsection (3), the Speaker shall certify under the National Seal, in accordance with the Standing Orders of the Parliament, that a law has been made by the Parliament and, subject to Subsection (2), the law comes into operation on the date of the certificate.

(2) Nothing in Subsection (1) prevents a law

(*a*) being expressed to come, or to be deemed to have come, into force on a date specified by, or fixed in accordance with, law; or

(*b*) being retrospective or retroactive.

(3) An Act of the Parliament or the Standing Orders of the Parliament may make provision under which a law made by the Parliament may, at the direction of the Head of State, acting with, and in accordance with, the advice of the National Executive Council, be recommitted to the Parliament for the consideration of amendments proposed by the Head of State, acting with, and in accordance with, the advice of the National Executive Council.

111. (1) Subject to Section 210 (*executive initiative*), any member of the Parliament is entitled to introduce into the Parliament, in accordance with, and subject to any reasonable restrictions contained in, the Standing Orders of the Parliament, a petitition, question, bill, resolution or motion.

(2) The petition, question, bill, resolution or motion shall be dealt with as provided by the Standing Orders of the Parliament.

(3) The Standing Orders of the Parliament may make provision for priority to be given to Government business at certain times or in certain circumstances.

112. (1) Subject to Subdivision C (*the Speaker and the Deputy Speaker*) and to Subsection (2), the Standing Orders of the Parliament shall make provision in respect of the chairmanship of the Parliament and of Committees of the Whole.

(2) No Minister may preside in the Parliament or in a Committee of the Whole.

113. (1) The quorum for a sitting of the Parliament is one third of the number of seats in the Parliament at the time.

(2) The Standing Orders of the Parliament shall make provision for the action to be taken in the event of a lack of or loss of a quorum at any time.

114. (1) Except as otherwise provided by a Constitutional Law or the Standing Orders of the Parliament, all questions before a meeting of the Parliament shall be decided in accordance with the majority of votes of the members present and voting.

(2) The member presiding does not have a deliberative vote except

(*a*) on a motion of no confidence in the Prime Minister, the Ministry or a Minister, in accordance with an Organic Law referred to in Section 145 (*motions of no confidence*); or

(*b*) on any question which requires an affirmative vote greater than a simple majority.

(3) Except in a case where he has voted under Subsection (2), in the event of an equality of votes on a question, the member presiding has a casting vote, but if he fails to use it the motion shall be deemed to be withdrawn.

(4) The Standing Orders of the Parliament shall make provision for the manner in which a vote is to be taken and recorded.

115. (1) The powers (other than legislative powers), privileges and immunities of the Parliament and of its members and committees are as prescribed by or under this section and by any other provision of this Constitution.

(2) There shall be freedom of speech, debate and proceeding in the Parliament, and the exercise of those freedoms shall not be questioned in any court or in any proceedings whatever (otherwise than in proceedings in the Parliament or before a committee of the Parliament).

(3) No member of the Parliament is subject to the jurisdiction of any court in respect of the exercise of his powers or the performance of his functions, duties or responsibilities as such, but this subsection does not affect the operation of Division III.2 (*leadership code*).

(4) No member of the Parliament is liable to civil or criminal proceedings, arrest, imprisonment, fine, damages or compensation by reason of any matter or thing that he has brought by petition, question bill, resolution, motion or otherwise, or has said before or submitted to the Parliament or a committee of the Parliament.

(5) No member of the Parliament or other person is liable to civil or criminal proceedings, arrest, imprisonment, fine, damages or compensation by reason of

(*a*) an act done under the authority of the Parliament or under an order of the Parliament or a committee of the Parliament; or

(*b*) words spoken or used, or a document or writing made or produced, under an order or summons made or issued under the authority of the Parliament or a committee of the Parliament.

(6) Members of the Parliament are free from arrest for civil debt during meetings of the Parliament and during the period commencing three days before, and ending three days after, a meeting when they are travelling from their respective electorates to attend the meeting or are returning to their electorate from the meeting.

(7) No process issued by any court in the exercise of its civil jurisdiction shall be served or executed through the Speaker, an officer of the Parliament or a member of the Parliamentary Service, or within the precincts of the Parliament (as defined by or under an Act of the Parliament) while it is sitting.

(8) The powers conferred by Section 109 (*general powers of law-making*) extend to the making of laws

(*a*) declaring further powers (other than legislative powers), privileges and immunities of the Parliament, and of its members and committees; and

(*b*) providing for the manner in which powers, privileges and immunities provided for by or under this section may be exercised or upheld.

(9) The powers and privileges conferred by or under this section do not and shall not include the power to impose or provide for the imposition of a fine, imprisonment, forfeiture of property or other penalty of a criminal nature, but this subsection does not prevent the creation of offences for the purposes of this section that are triable within the National Judicial System.

116. (1) All subordinate legislative enactments made under an Act of the Parliament

(*a*) shall be tabled in the Parliament as soon as practicable, and in any event within seven sitting days of the Parliament, after being made; and

(*b*) are subject to disallowance in whole or in part by decision of the Parliament,

in accordance with Section Sch. 1.18 (*disallowance, etc.*) and the Standing Orders of the Parliament.

(2) Subject to Section Sch. 1.18 (*disallowance, etc.*) an Act of the Parliament may make further provision as to the disallowance of a subordinate legislative enactment or part of a subordinate legislative enactment under this section, and as to the effect of such a disallowance on or in respect of rights and liabilities under or affected by the disallowed enactment or part.

(3) Failure to comply with Subsection (1) does not invalidate a subordi-- nate legislative enactment.

117. (1) In this section, unless the contrary intention appears

'treaty' means an agreement between States that

(*a*) is governed by international law; and

(*b*) creates a relationship binding at international law on Papua New Guinea,

whether embodied in a single instrument or in two or more related instruments and whatever may be its designation, but does not include a visiting forces agreement entered into in accordance with Section 206(*visiting forces*);

'treaty document' means

(*a*) the text of a treaty that it is proposed to accept or to ratify; or

(*b*) a statement of the effect of such a treaty; or

(*c*) a copy of the document by which it is intended that Papua New Guinea will express its consent to be bound by such a treaty.

(2) Subject to Subsection (3), the consent of Papua New Guinea to be bound as a party to a treaty may be given only

(*a*) by the Head of State, acting with, and in accordance with, the advice of the National Executive Council; or

(*b*) by a Minister authorized either generally or specifically for the purpose by the Head of State, acting with, and in accordance with, the advice of the National Executive Council; or

(*c*) otherwise in accordance with international law, usage and practice,

and in accordance with this section.

(3) Subject to Subsection (5), the consent of Papua New Guinea to be bound as a party to a treaty shall not be given

(*a*) unless a treaty document relating to the treaty has been presented to the Parliament for at least 10 sitting days; or

(*b*) if within 10 sitting days of the Parliament after the day on which the treaty document was presented to the Parliament, by an absolute majority vote, disapproves the giving or the consent.

(4) The fact that the Parliament has disapproved the giving of the consent of Papua New Guinea to be bound as a party to a treaty does not prevent the re-presentation to the Parliament of a treaty document relating to the treaty, and in that event Subsection (3) once again applies.

(5) Subsection (3) does not apply if

(*a*) the Parliament has, by an absolute majority vote, waived the requirements of that subsection; or

(*b*) both the Speaker (acting on behalf of the Parliament) and the Prime Minister are satisfied that the giving of the consent of Papua New Guinea to be bound as a party to the treaty is too urgent a matter to allow of compliance with that subsection, or that compliance would not be in the national interest.

(6) A certificate of the Speaker as to any matter arising under this section is, before all courts and all persons acting judicially, conclusive evidence of the facts certified to.

(7) Notwithstanding the consent of Papua New Guinea to be bound as a party to a treaty, no treaty forms part of the municipal law of Papua New Guinea unless, and then only to the extent that, it is given the status of municipal law by or under a Constitutional Law or an Act of the Parliament.

(8) Legislative approval or ratification of a treaty does not, without more, give it the status of municipal law for the purposes of Subsection (7).

SUBSECTION E. THE COMMITTEE SYSTEM

118. (1) In order to ensure full and active participation by backbenchers in the work of the Parliament and of government, there shall be the following permanent Parliamentary Committees which, in principle, should cover all major fields of the activities of the National Government:

(*a*) a Public Accounts Committee, established in accordance with Subdivision VIII.1.C (*the Public Accounts Committee*); and

(*b*) such other committees as are determined by the Parliament from time to time.

(2) The Parliament shall, subject to this Constitution, make provision by Organic Law, by Act of the Parliament, Standing Order or otherwise, for the establishment, membership, jurisdiction, functions, powers and procedures of the Permanent Parliamentary Committees, and in particular for empowering such a Committee to call for persons, papers and records.

(3) No Minister shall be a member of a Permanent Parliamentary Committee.

(4) In principle, membership of the Permanent Parliamentary Committees should be spread as widely as practicable among the backbenchers.

119. (1) There shall be a Chairman and a Deputy Chairman of each Permanent Parliamentary Committee.

(2) In principle, either the Chairman or the Deputy Chairman of each Permanent Parliamentary Committee should be a member of the Parliament who is recognized by the Parliament as being generally committed to support the Government in the Parliament, and the other should be a member of the principal party or group, or coalition of parties or groups, that is recognized by the Parliament as being not so committed.

(3) Subject to any Act of the Parliament and to the Standing Orders of the Parliament, in the event of the absence or non-availability to act of the Chairman, the Deputy Chairman has all the rights, privileges, powers, functions, duties and responsibilities of the Chairman.

120. (1) The Chairman and Deputy Chairman of each Permanent Parliamentary Committee shall be granted full access to each Minister having responsibilities relevant to the jurisdiction and functions of his Committee and, by arrangement with the Minister, to the head of the Minister's department, and are entitled to be briefed and consulted on major policy issues.

(7) In relation to any information given to or obtained by them under Subsection (1), the Chairmen and the Deputy Chairman are under the same obligation, whether by law or by convention, as to confidentiality as is the Minister but this principle does not prevent the Chairman or Deputy Chairman from briefing the members of his Permanent Parliamentary Committee on major policy issues.

(3) In relation to any infomation given to him under Subsection (2), a member of a Permanent Parliamentary Committee is under the same obligation, whether by law or convention, as to confidentiality as is the Minister.

121. Nothing in this Subdivision prevents the Parliament from establishing Sessional or Select Committees or other committees for any purpose, or prevents the Parliament from sitting as a Committee of the Whole.

122. The business of the Parliament shall be so arranged as to allow reasonable time for committees of the Parliament to perform their functions adequately, and the Standing Order of the Parliament shall make provision to ensure that such time is allowed either within or outside the sitting hours of the Parliament.

123. Each committee of the Parliament shall consist only of members of the Parliament, but nothing in this section prevents the establishment, by statute or otherwise, of commissions or committees of any other kind.

SUBDIVISION F. CALLING, ETC., OF THE PARLIAMENT

124. (1) The Parliament shall be called to meet not more than 21 days after the day fixed for the return of the writs for a general election, and shall meet not less frequently than three times in each period of 12 months, and, in principle, for not less than nine weeks in each such period.

(2) An Organic Law shall make provision for the calling of meetings of the Parliament.

(3) Subject to Subsection (1) and (2), an Act of the Parliament or the Standing Orders of the Parliament may make provision in respect of the sittings of the Parliament.

SUBDIVISION G. ELECTORATES AND ELECTIONS

125. (1) The number of open electorates and of provincial electorates and their boundaries shall be determined by the Parliament in accordance with recommendations from a Boundaries Commission from time to time, at intervals determined by or under an Organic Law, being intervals of not more than 10 years.

(2) In recommending open electorates and open electorate boundaries, the Boundaries Commission shall taking into account any considerations laid down by an Organic Law, endeavour to ensure that all open electorates contain approximately the same population, within limits prescribed by an Organic Law.

(3) The Parliament may accept or reject, but may not amend, any recommendation of the Boundaries Commission under Subsection (1).

(4) The Boundaries Commission is not subject to direction or control by any person or authority.

(5) An Organic Law shall make further provision for and in respect of the appointment, constitution and procedures of the Boundaries Commission, and for safeguarding its independence, and in relation to the procedures for formulating and considering its recommendations.

(6) An Organic Law relating to provinces or to provincial government may confer or impose on the Boundaries Commission powers, functions, duties or responsibilities in relation to the boundaries of provinces and of provincial electorates.

126. (1) Elections to the Parliament shall be conducted, in accordance with an Organic Law, by an Electoral Commission.

(2) General elections shall be held in accordance with Sections 105 (*general elections*) and 106 (*by-elections*), as required.

(3) The members of the Parliament (other than the nominated members)

shall be elected under a system of universal, adult, citizen suffrage in accordance with Section 50 (*right to vote and stand for public office*) and to other Constitutional Laws, and the voting age is 18 years.

(4) A citizen's right to vote in an election to the Parliament is as provided by Section 50 (*right to vote and stand for public office*).

(5) No non-citizen may vote in an election for the Parliament.

(6) The Electoral Commission is not subject to direction or control by any person or authority.

(7) An Organic Law shall make provision for and in respect of

(*a*) the appointment, constitution and procedures of the Electoral Commission, and for safeguarding its independence; and

(*b*) the electoral system; and

(*c*) safeguarding the integrity of elections; and

(*d*) appeals to the National Court in electoral matters.

SUBDIVISION H. PROTECTION OF ELECTIONS FROM OUTSIDE OR HIDDEN INFLUENCE

127. The purpose of this Subdivision is to protect elections and to prevent candidates from being, or appearing to be or to have been, improperly or unduly influenced by outside (especially foreign) or hidden influences, and an Organic Law may make provision, in addition to the provisions expressly referred to in this Subdivision, for achieving that purpose.

128. In this Subdivision, 'registered political party' means a political party or organization registered under an Organic Law made for the purpose of Section 129(1)(*a*) (*integrity of political parties*).

129. (1) An Organic Law shall make provision

(*a*) requiring any political party or organization having political aims and desiring to nominate a candidate for election to the Parliament, or to publicly support such a candidate as representing its views, to register with the Electoral Commission such reasonable particulars as are precribed by Organic Law; and

(*b*) requiring any such party or organization to disclose to the Ombudsman Commission or some other authority prescribed by the law in such manner, at such times and with such details as are prescribed in or under the law

(i) its assets and income, and their sources; and

(ii) its expenditure on or connected with an election or the support of a candidate; and

(*c*) prohibiting non-citizens from membership of, and from contributing to the funds of, any such party or organization; and

(*d*) defining the corporations and organizations that are to be regarded as non-citizens for the purposes of a provision made for the purposes of paragraph (*e*); and (*e*) limiting the amount of contributions that such a party or organization may receive from any source or sources; and

(*f*) requiring persons who have made, or may have made, contributions to any such party or organization to given to the Ombudsman Commission, or some other authority, details of any such contribution.

(2) Where another authority is prescribed by the law under subsection (1) (*b*), that authority

(*a*) shall be composed of a person or persons who are declared under paragraph (i) of the definition of 'constitutional office-holder' in section 221 (*definitions*) to be a constitutional office-holder; and

(*b*) is not subject to direction or control by any person or authority.

(3) An Organic Law made for the purposes of Subsection (1) may provide that the value of any assistance given otherwise than in cash shall be taken into account as expenditure or contributions for any purpose of that subsection or of that law.

130. (1) An Organic Law shall make provision

(*a*) requiring a candidate for election to the Parliament to disclose to the Ombudsman Commission or some other authority prescribed by the law, in such manner, at such times and with such details as are prescribed by or under the law

(i) any assistance (financial or other) received by him in respect of his canditature, and its source; and

(ii) the amount or value of his electoral expenses; and

(*b*) prohibiting a candidate or former candidate for election to the Parliament from accepting from a non-citizen assistance (financial or other) in respect of his candidature; and

(*c*) defining the corporations and organizations that are to be regarded as non-citizens for the purposes of a provision made for the purposes of paragraph (*b*); and

(*d*) regulating or restricting the amount or kind of such assistance that may be received from any source other than a registered political party; and

(*e*) prohibiting a candidate for election to the Parliament from holding himself out as representing any party or organization other than a registered political party that has publicly adopted him as its candidate.

(2) Where another authority is prescribed by the law under Subsection (1)(*b*), that authority

(*a*) shall be composed of a person or persons who are declared under paragraph (i) of the definition of 'constitutional office-holder' in Section 221 (*definitions*) to be a constitutional office-holder; and

(*b*) is not subject to direction or control by any person or authority.

(3) An Organic Law made for the purposes of Subsection (1) may make provision for further defining what are to be regarded as assistance and electoral expenses for any purpose of that subsection or of that law, and in particular may provide that

(*a*) the value of hospitality (including meals, accommodation and transport) of a kind and to a degree recognized by custom in the country shall not be taken into account as assistance; and

(*b*) the personal expenses of a candidate shall not be taken into account as electoral expenses.

(4) In this section

'electoral expenses', in relation to a candidate, means expenses incurred (whether before, during or after an election to the Parliament, including expenses incurred before the issue of the writ for election) by him or on his behalf on account of or in respect of the election;

'personal expenses', in relation to a candidate, means any reasonable costs incurred by him personally for travel and for living away from his home for the purposes of the election.

SUBDIVISION 1. GENERAL

131. (1) A Parliamentary Salaries Tribunal is hereby established.

(2) The Tribunal shall consist of

(*a*) a judicial officer, appointed by the Judicial and Legal Services Commission, who shall be the Chairman; and

(*b*) a person with wide practical experience in wage fixation, appointed by the Public Services Commission; and

(*c*) a member of the Public Services Commission, appointed by that Commission.

(3) The Tribunal is responsible for fixing from time to time, at intervals determined by it, the salaries, allowances, pensions and other financial benefits for all or any members of the Parliament.

(4) An Act of the Parliament shall make provision for the powers and procedures of the Tribunal, and generally in respect of it.

132. (1) An Act of the Parliament shall make provision for and in respect of a Parliamentary Service, separate from the other State Services.

(2) Within the Service, there shall be an office of Clerk of the National Parliament who shall, subject to Subsection (3), be the head of the Service.

(3) The Service shall be subject to the direction and control of the Speaker and shall perform its functions impartially.

133. The Parliament may make Standing Orders and other rules and orders in respect of the order and conduct of its business and proceedings and the business and proceedings of its Committees, and of such other matters as by law are required or permitted to be prescribed or provided for by the Standing Orders of the Parliament.

134. Except as is specifically provided by a Constitutional Law, the question, whether the procedures prescribed for the Parliament or its committees have been complied with, is non-justiciable, and a certificate by the Speaker under Section 110 (*certification as to making of laws*) is conclusive as to the matters required to be set out in it.

135. The National Court has jurisdiction to determine any question as to

(*a*) the qualifications of a person to be or to remain a member of the Parliament; or

(*b*) the validity of an election to the Parliament.

136. Where a person who has purported to sit or vote as a member of the Parliament at a meeting of the Parliament or of a committee of the Parliament

(*a*) was not duly qualified to be elected or appointed, or to continue, as a member of the Parliament; or

(*b*) had vacated his office as a member of the Parliament,

all things done or purporting to have been done by the Parliament or by the committee, as the case may be, shall be deemed to have been as validly done as if that person had, when so sitting or voting, been duly qualified to be elected or appointed or to continue as a member of the Parliament, or had not vacated his office, as the case may be.

Division 3. Special Instances of the Legislative Power

137. (1) If

(*a*) a provision of a Constitutional Law has been contravened or not complied with; and

(*b*) the Parliament is satisfied that

(i) the contravention or non-compliance was made in good faith and in exceptional circumstances for the purpose, or with the intention, of upholding this Constitution or protecting Papua New Guinea, or of dealing with an emergency for which no provision or no adequate provision appeared to exist; and

(ii) no blameworthiness attaches to some person or some persons concerned in the contravention or non-compliance,

the Parliament may make a special law (to be known as an 'Act of Indemnity') in relation to that person or those persons.

(2) An Act of Idemnity shall

(*a*) specify the contravention or non-compliance; and

(*b*) certify as to the Parliament's satisfaction concerning the matters specified in Subsection (1)(*b*) (i) and (ii); and

(*c*) identify or provide for the identification of the person suffering injury as a result of the contravention or non-compliance; and

(*d*) provide for the making of full compensation to any person suffering injury as a result of the contravention or non-compliance; and

(*e*) be made in accordance with the procedures laid down by this Constitution for the making of Organic Laws; and (*f*) be passed by an absolute majority vote of the Parliament.

(3) Before the Speaker certifies under Section 110 (*certification as to making of laws*) as to the Act, he shall refer the question, whether the Act complies with this section, for the opinion of the Supreme Court in accordance with Section 19 (*special references to the Supreme Court*), and until the Court advises that the Act does so comply he shall not so certify it.

(4) An Act of Indemnity

(*a*) relieves, and shall be expressed to relieve, the person or persons concerned from all liability for, and from all legal consequences of, the contravention or non-compliance; and

(*b*) if a person concerned has been convicted of an offence in respect of or arising out of the contravention or non-compliance, takes effect as a free pardon,

but in respect only of acts done before the Parliament was formally advised of the intention to propose the Act.

(5) An Act of Indemnity does not take effect as a Constitutional Law.

(6) An Act of Indemnity shall not be amended or extended in any way, and its repeal does not affect the operation of Subsection (4).

Division 4. The National Executive

SUBDIVISION A. THE NATIONAL EXECUTIVE AND THE EXECUTIVE POWER

138. Subject to this Constitution, the executive power of the People is vested in the Head of State, to be exercised in accordance with Division V.2 (*functions, etc., of the Head of State*).

139. The National Executive consists of

(*a*) the Head of State acting in accordance with Division V.2 (*functions, etc., of the Head of State*); and

(*b*) the National Executive Council.

140. Except where the contrary intention appears, nothing in this Constitution prevents an Organic Law or a statute from conferring or imposing powers, functions, duties or responsibilities on a person or authority outside the National Executive.

SUBDIVISION B. THE MINISTRY

141. The Ministry is a Parliamentary Executive, and therefore

(*a*) no person who is not a member of the Parliament is eligible to be appointed to be a Minister, and, except as is expressly provided in this Constitution to the contrary, a Minister who ceases to be a member of the Parliament ceases to hold office as a Minister; and

(*b*) it is collectively answerable to the People, through the Parliament, for the proper carrying out of the executive government of Papua

New Guinea and for all things done by or under the authority of the National Executive; and

(*c*) it is liable to be dismissed from office, either collectively or individually, in accordance with this Subdivision.

142. (1) An office of Prime Minister is hereby established.

(2) The Prime Minister shall be appointed, at the first meeting of the Parliament after a general election and otherwise from time to time as the occasion for the appointment of a Prime Minister arises, by the Head of State, acting in accordance with a decision of the Parliament.

(3) If the Parliament is in session when a Prime Minister is to be appointed, the question of the appointment shall be the first matter for consideration, after any formal business and any nomination of a Governor-General or appointment of a Speaker, on the next sitting day.

(4) If the Parliament is not in session when a Prime Minister is to be appointed, the Speaker shall immediately call a meeting of the Parliament, and the question of the appointment shall be the first matter for consideration, after any formal business and any nomination of a Governor-General or appointment of a Speaker, on the next sitting day.

(5) The Prime Minister

(*a*) shall be dismissed from office by the Head of State if the Parliament passes, in accordance with Section 145 (*motions of no confidence*), a motion of no confidence in him or the Ministry, except where the motion is moved within the last 12 months before the fifth anniversary of the date fixed for the return of the writs at the previous general election; and

(*b*) may be dismissed from office in accordance with Division III.2 (*leadership code*); and

(*c*) may be removed from office by the Head of State, acting in accordance with a decision of the Parliament, if the Speaker advises the Parliament that two medical practitioners appointed by the National Authority responsible for the registration or licensing of medical practitioners have jointly reported in accordance with an Act of the Parliament that, in their professional opinions, the Prime Minister is unfit, by reason of physical or mental incapacity, to carry out the duties of his office.

(6) The Prime Minister may be suspended from office

(*a*) by the tribunal appointed under an Organic Law made for the purposes of Section 28 (*further provisions*), pending an investigation into a question of misconduct in office within the meaning of Division III.2 (*leadership code*), and any resultant action; or

(*b*) in accordance with an act of the Parliament, pending an investigation for the purposes of Subsection (5)(*c*), and any resultant action by the Parliament.

143. (1) Subject to Subsection (2) an Act of the Parliament shall make provision for and in respect of the appointment of a Minister to be Acting Prime Minister to exercise and perform the powers, functions, duties and responsibilities of the Prime Minister when

(*a*) there is a vacancy in the office of Prime Minister; or
(*b*) the Prime Minister is suspended from office; or
(*c*) the Prime Minister is
(i) absent from the country; or
(ii) out of speedy and effective communications; or
(iii) otherwise unable or not readily available to perform the duties of his office.

(2) Where a Prime Minister is dismissed under section 142(5)(*a*) (*the Prime Minister*) the person nominated under Section 145(2)(*a*) (*motions of no confidence*)

(*a*) becomes the Acting Prime Minister until he is appointed a Prime Minister in accordance with Section 142(2) (*the Prime Minister*); and
(*b*) may exercise and perform all the powers, functions, duties and responsibilities of a Prime Minister.

(3) The question whether the occasion for the appointment of an Acting Prime Minister or for the exercise or performance of a power, function, duty or responsibility by an Acting Prime Minister, under this section has arisen or has ceased, is non-justiciable.

144. (1) There shall be such number of Ministers (other than the Prime Minister), not being less than six or more than one quarter of the number of members of the Parliament from time to time, as is determined by or under an Organic Law.

(2) The Ministers, other than the Prime Minister, shall be appointed by the Head of State, acting with, and in accordance with, the advice of the Prime Minister.

(3) A Minister, other than the Prime Minister, may be suspended from office in accordance with an Organic Law made for the purposes of Section 28(2) (*further provisions*).

(4) A Minister other than the Prime Minister

(*a*) shall be dismissed from office by the Head of State if the Parliament passes, in accordance with Section 145 (*motions of no confidence*), a motion of no confidence in him; and
(*b*) may be dismissed from office
(i) by the Head of State, acting with, and in accordance with, the advice of the Prime Minister; or
(ii) in accordance with Division III.2 (*leadership code*).

145. (1) For the purposes of Sections 142 (*the Prime Minister*) and 144 (*other Ministers*), a motion of no confidence is a motion

(*a*) that is expressed to be a motion of no confidence in the Prime Minister, the Ministry or a Minister, as the case may be; and (*b*) of which not less than one weeks's notice, signed by a number of members of the parliament being not less than one tenth of the total number of seats in the Parliament, has been given in accordance with the Standing Orders of the Parliament.

(2) A motion of no confidence in the Prime Minister or the Ministry

(*a*) moved during the first four years of the life of Parliament shall not be allowed unless it nominates the next Prime Minister; and

(*b*) moved within 12 months before the fifth anniversary of the date fixed for the return of the writs at the previous general election shall not be allowed if it nominates the next Prime Minister.

(3) A motion of no confidence in the Prime Minister or the Ministry moved in accordance with Subsection (2)(*a*) may not be amended in respect of the name of the person nominated as the next Prime Minister except by substituting the name of some other person.

(4) A motion of no confidence in the Prime Minister or in the Ministry may not be moved during the period of six months commencing on the date of the appointment of the Prime Minister.

146. (1) The Prime Minister may resign from office by notice in writing to the Head of State.

(2) A Minister other than the Prime Minister may resign from office by notice in writing to the Prime Minster.

147. Normal term of office.

(1) Unless he earlier

(*a*) dies; or

(*b*) subject to Subsection (2), resigns; or

(*c*) subject to Subsection (3), ceases to be qualified to be a Minister; or

(*d*) is dismissed or removed from office,

a Minister (including the Prime Minister) holds office until the next appointment of a Prime Minister.

(2) Notwithstanding Subsection (1)(*b*)

(*a*) a Prime Minister who resigns; and

(*b*) a Ministry that resigns collectively,

shall continue in office until the appointment of the next Prime Minister.

(3) Notwithstanding Subsection (1)(*c*), a Minister who

(*a*) ceases, by reason of a general election, to be a member of the Parliament; but

(*b*) remains otherwise qualified to be a member of the Parliament,

shall continue in office until the next appointment of a Prime Minister.

148. (1) Ministers (including the Prime Minister) have such titles, portfolios and responsibilities as are determined from time to time by the Prime Minister.

(2) Except as provided by a Constitutional Law or an Act of the Parliament, all departments, sections, branches and functions of government must be the political responsibility of a Minister, and the Prime Minister is politically

responsible for any of them that are not specifically allocated under this Section.

(3) Subsection (2) does not confer on a Minister any power of direction or control.

SUBDIVISION C. THE NATIONAL EXECUTIVE COUNCIL

149. (1) A National Executive Council is hereby established.

(2) The Council shall consist of all the Ministers (including the Prime Ministers when he is present as Chairman).

(3) The functions of the Council are

(*a*) to be responsible, in accordance with this Constitution, for the executive government of Papua New Guinea; and

(*b*) such other functions as are allocated to it by this Constitution or any other law.

(4) Except where the contrary intention appears, nothing in this Constitution prevents the powers, functions, duties or responsibilities of the Council from being exercised, as determined by it, through a Minister.

(5) Subject to any Organic Law or Act of Parliament, the procedures of the Council are as determined by it.

150. (1) An office of Secretary to the National Executive Council is hereby established.

(2) Subject to any Act of the Parliament, the functions and responsibilities of the Secretary of the Council shall be as determined by the Council.

SUBDIVISION D. THE POWER OF MERCY

151. (1) Subject to this Subdivision, the Head of State, acting with, and in accordance with, the advice of the National Executive Council, may grant to a person convicted of an offence or held in penal detention under a law of Papua New Guinea

(*a*) a pardon, either free or conditional; or

(*b*) a remission or commutation of sentence; or

(*c*) a respite of the execution of sentence; or

(*d*) a less severe form of punishment for that imposed by any sentence,

and may remit or refund, in whole or in part, any fine, penalty or forfeiture paid or payable to a governmental body.

(2) Where an offence has been committed, the Head of State, acting with, and in accordance with, the advice of the National Executive Council, may grant a pardon, either free or conditional, to an accomplice who gives evidence that leads to the conviction of a principal offender.

(3) Except in a case referred to in Subsection (2) or as otherwise permitted by or under an Act of the Parliament, the exercise of the power conferred by Subsection (1) shall not be held out, offered or promised in advance of conviction.

(4) Nothing in this section prevents the establishment by law of systems of probation, parole or release on licence, or any similar systems.

152. (1) An Organic Law shall make provision for and in respect of an Advisory Committee on the Power of Mercy, and for and in respect of its appointment, constitution, powers and procedures.

(2) Before giving any advice to the Head of State under Section 151(1) (*grant of pardon, etc.,*) the National Executive Council shall consider a report from the Advisory Committee.

SUBDIVISION E. GENERAL

153. (1) Subsection (2), (3) and (4) are subject to any Constitutional Law or Act of the Parliament.

(2) The question, whether the procedures prescribed for the National Executive Council have been or are being complied with, is non-justiciable.

(3) The question, whether any, and if so what report has been given to the National Executive Council by the Advisory Committee on the Power of Mercy, is non-justiciable.

(4) No act of a Minister is open to challenge on the ground that he was not empowered to perform the act, if some other Minister, or any Minister, was so empowered.

(5) This section does not limit the jurisdiction or powers of the Ombudsman Commission, or of an authority or tribunal established under Division III.2 (*leadership code*).

Division 5. The Administration of Justice

SUBDIVISION A. GENERAL STRUCTURE AND PRINCIPLES OF THE NATIONAL JUSTICE ADMINISTRATION

154. The National Justice Administration consists of
- (*a*) the National Judicial System; and
- (*b*) the Minister responsible for the National Justice Administration; and
- (*c*) the Law Officers of Papua New Guinea.

155. (1) The National Judicial System consists of
- (*a*) the Supreme Court; and
- (*b*) the National Court; and
- (*c*) such other courts as are established under Section 172 (*establishment of other courts*).

(2) The Supreme Court
- (*a*) is the final court of appeal; and
- (*b*) has an inherent power to review all judicial acts of the National Court; and
- (*c*) has such other jurisdiction and powers as are conferred on it by this Constitution or any other law.

(3) The National Court
(*a*) has an inherent power to review any exercise of judicial authority; and
(*b*) has such other jurisdiction and powers as are conferred on it by this Constitution or any law,

except where
(*c*) jurisdiction is conferred upon the Supreme Court to the exclusion of the National Court; or
(*d*) the Supreme Court assumes jurisdiction under Subsection (4); or
(*e*) the power of review is removed or restricted by a Constitutional Law or an Act of the Parliament.

(4) Both the Supreme Court and the National Court have an inherent power to make, in such circumstances as seem to them proper, orders in the nature of prerogative writs and such other orders as are necessary to do justice in the circumstances of a particular case.

(5) In a case referred to in Subsection (3)(*e*), the National Court has nevertheless an inherent power of review where, in its opinion, there are over-riding considerations of public policy in the special circumstances of a particular case.

(6) Subject to any right of appeal or power of review of a decision, it is the duty of all persons (including the Law Officers of Papua New Guinea and other public officers in their respective official capacities), and of all bodies and institutions, to comply with and, so far as is within their respective lawful powers, to put into effect all decisions of the National Judicial System.

156. (1) The Law Officers of Papua New Guinea are
(*a*) the principal legal adviser to the National Executive, and
(*b*) the Public Prosecutor; and
(*c*) the Public Solicitor.

(2) An Act of the Parliament shall make provision for and in respect of the office referred to in Subsection (1)(*a*).

157. Except to the extent that this Constitution specifically provides otherwise, neither the Minister responsible for the National Justice Administration nor any other person or authority (other than the Parliament through legislation) outside the National Judicial System has any power to give directions to any court, within that System in respect of the exercise of judicial power or functions.

SUBDIVISION B. THE JUDICIAL POWER

158. (1) Subject to this Constitution, the Judicial authority of the People is vested in the National Judicial System.

(2) In interpreting the law the courts shall give paramount consideration to the dispensation of justice.

159. (1) Subject to Subsection (3), nothing in this Constitution prevents an Organic Law or a statute from conferring judicial authority on a person or body outside the National Judicial System, or the establishment by or in accordance with law, or by consent of the parties, of arbitral or conciliatory tribunals, whether ad hoc or other, outside the National Judicial System.

(2) Nothing in, or done in accordance with, Subsection (1) affects the operation of Section 155(4) or (5) (*the National Judicial System*).

(3) No person or body outside the National Judicial System, has, or may be given, power to impose a sentence of death or imprisonment, or to impose any other penalty as for a criminal offence, but nothing in this subsection prevents

(*a*) the impositition, in accordance with law, of disciplinary detention or any other disciplinary punishment (other than death) by a disciplinary authority of a disciplined force on persons subject to the disciplinary law of the force; or

(*b*) the imposition, in accordance with law, of disciplinary punishments (other than death or detention) on members of other State or provincial services; or

(*c*) the imposition of reasonable penalties (other than death or detention) by an association on its members for breaches of its rules.

(4) In Subsection (3)(*a*), 'disciplined force' has the same meaning as in Section 207 (*definition of 'disciplined force'*).

SUBDIVISION C. THE SUPREME COURT OF JUSTICE

160. (1) A Supreme Court of Justice is hereby established.

(2) The Supreme Court is a superior court of record and accordingly, subject to any Act of the Parliament, has the power to punish the offence against itself commonly known as contempt of court.

161. (1) The Supreme Court shall consist of the Chief Justice, the Deputy Chief Justice and the other Judges of the National Court (excluding the acting Judges).

(2) Subject to Section 162(2) (*jurisdiction of the Supreme Court*) and for the purposes of any hearing, the Supreme Court shall consist of at least three Judges.

(3) In a hearing that consists of at least three Judges, the Chief Justice, the Deputy Chief Justice or the most senior Judge available shall preside over the Court.

162. (1) The Jurisdiction of the Supreme Court is as set out in

(*a*) Subdivision II.2.C (*constitutional interpretation*); and

(*b*) Subdivision III.3.D (*enforcement*); and

(*c*) Section 155 (*the National Judicial System*),

and otherwise as provided by this Constitution or any other law.

(2) In such cases as are provided for by or under an Act of the Parliament or the Rule of Court of the Supreme Court, the jurisdiction of the Surpeme Court may be exercised by a single Judge of that Court, or by a number of Judges sitting together.

(3) The jurisdiction of the Supreme Court may be exercised by a Judge or Judges of that Court notwithstanding that it is being exercised at the same time by another such Judge or Judges.

(4) The jurisdiction of the Supreme Court may be exercised either in court or in chambers, as provided by or under an Act of the Parliament or the Rules of Court of the Supreme Court.

SUBDIVISION D. THE NATIONAL COURT OF JUSTICE

163. (1) A National Court of Justice is hereby established.

(2) The National Court is a superior court of record and accordingly, subject to any Act of the Parliament, has the power to punish the offence against itself commonly known as contempt of court.

164. The National Court shall consist of

(*a*) the Chief Justice; and

(*b*) the Deputy Chief Justice; and

(*c*) subject to Section 165(2) (*Acting Judges*) not less than four or more than six other Judges, or such greater number as is determined by or under a Act of the Parliament.

165. (1) A person who is qualified under Section 168 (*qualifications*) for appointment may be appointed to be an acting Judge of the National Court

(*a*) to fill temporarily a vacancy; or

(*b*) in the case of the absence from duty for any reason of a Judge of that Court; or

(*c*) to meet a temporary unexpected workload or other exigency of the business of the Court.

(2) An appointment under Subsection (1)(*c*) may be made without reference to the numerical limit imposed by Section 164 (*composition of the National Court*).

166. (1) Subject to this Constitution, the National Court is a court of unlimited jurisdiction.

(2) In particular, the National Court has the jurisdiction set out in

(*a*) Section 22 (*enforcement of the Constitution*); and

(*b*) Subdivision III.3.D (*enforcement*); and

(*c*) Section 155 (*the National Judicial System*),

and otherwise as provided by this Constitution or any other law.

(3) Subject to any Act of the Parliament and to the Rules of Court of the National Court, the jurisdiction of the National Court may be exercised by a single Judge of that Court, or by a number of Judges sitting together.

(4) The jurisdiction of the National Court may be exercised by a Judge or Judges of that Court notwithstanding that it is being exercised at the same time by another Judge or other Judges.

(5) The jurisdiction of the National Court may be exercised either in court or in chambers, as provided by or under an Act of the Parliament or the Rules of Court of the National Court.

167. Subject to this section, an Act of the Parliament may make provision for and in respect of the appointment of Assistant Judges of the National Court, and for and in respect of their qualifications, privileges, powers, functions, duties and responsibilities, and of their terms and conditions of employment.

SUBDIVISION E. APPOINTMENT, ETC., OF JUDGES

168. The qualifications for appointment as a Judge are as determined by or under an Act of the Parliament.

169. (1) An office of Chief Justice of Papua New Guinea is hereby established.

(2) The Chief Justice shall be appointed by the Head of State, acting with and in accordance with, the advice of the National Executive Council given after consultation with the Minister responsible for the National Justice Administration.

(3) In addition to his other powers, functions, duties and responsibilities, the Chief Justice, after consultation with the other Judges, is responsible for the organization of the affairs and the administration of the business of the Supreme Court and the National Court (other than, except to the extent allowed by or under an Act of the Parliament, matters relating to the National Public Service).

(4) Where

(*a*) there is a vacancy in the office of Chief Justice; or

(*b*) the Chief Justice is absent from the country or is absent from duty; or

(*c*) the Chief Justice is unable or unavailable to act, or

(*d*) the Chief Justice so directs,

the powers, functions, duties and responsibilities (other than as acting Governor-General) of the Chief Justice may be exercised and performed by the next most senior Judge who is available.

(5) The question, whether the occasion for the exercise or performance of the powers, functions, duties and responsibilities of the Chief Justice by another Judge under this section has arisen or has ceased, is non-justiciable.

170. (1) An office of Deputy Chief Justice of Papua New Guinea is hereby established.

(2) The Deputy Chief Justice and the other Judges of the National Court (other than the Chief Justice) and acting Judges shall be appointed by the Judicial and Legal Services Commission.

(3) No appointment of an acting Judge shall continue for a period of more than 12 months, but one extension for a period of not more than 12 months may be granted by the Judicial and Legal Services Commission.

(4) The question, whether the occasion for the appointment of an acting Judge has arisen or has ceased, is non-justiciable.

171. (1) Subject to Subsection (2), the Chief Justice is the most senior Judge, the Deputy Chief Justice is the second senior Judge and the other Judges (other than acting Judges) have seniority according to the dates of their respective appointments, unless otherwise stated in an instrument of appointment.

(2) Unless otherwise stated in an instrument of appointment, acting Judges

(*a*) rank in seniority after the other Judges; and

(*b*) have seniority as between themselves according to the dates of their respective appointments or last appointments, as the case requires.

SUBDIVISION F. INFERIOR COURTS, THE MAGISTERIAL SERVICE, ETC.

172. (1) Subject to this Constitution, Acts of the Parliament may establish, or provide the establishment of, courts within the National Judicial System in addition to the Supreme Court and the National Court, and may define, or provide for the definition of, their respective powers, functions and jurisdictions and their relationship with other components of the National Judicial System.

(2) Courts established under Subsection (1) may include courts intended to deal with matters primarily by reference to custom or in accordance with customary procedures, or both.

(3) Full-time members of courts established under Subsection (1) (other than courts referred to in Subsection (2) shall be appointed by the Judicial and Legal Services Commission, and may be removed from office in accordance with an Act of the Parliament, but only for incapacity or misbehaviour (including, if applicable, misconduct in office).

(4) Acts of the Parliament may make provision for or in respect of the appointment and removal from office of members of courts referred to in Subsection (2).

173. (1) A service to be known as the Magisterial Service is hereby established.

(2) The Magisterial Service consists of

(*a*) the Chief Magistrate; and

(*b*) subject to Section 174 (*magistrates, etc., outside the magisterial Service*), all other members of courts established under Section 172 (*establishment of other courts*); and

(*c*) such other persons employed in connection with the National Judicial System as are prescribed by or under Acts of the Parliament.

(3) The Chief Magistrate is responsible to the Judicial and Legal Services Commission for the efficient functioning and operation of the Magisterial Service.

(4) Subject to the Constitutional Laws, an Act of the Parliament shall make provision for and in respect of the Magisterial Service.

174. (1) Unless and except to the extent that an Act of the Parliament makes provision to the contrary, members of village courts are not, as such, members of the Magisterial Service.

(2) An Act of the Parliament may provide for part-time members of courts established under Section 172 (*establishment of other courts*), who need not be members of the Magisterial Service.

175. (1) An office of Chief Magistrate is hereby established.

(2) The Chief Magistrate shall be appointed by the Judicial and Legal Services Commission.

(3) Unless and except to the extent that an Act of the Parliament makes provision to the contrary, the Chief Magistrate is *ex officio* a member of all courts (other than village courts) established under Section 172 (*establishment of other courts*), and, if provision is made for grades of powers, functions or jurisdiction within any such courts, has all the powers, functions and jurisdiction of the highest grades.

(4) In the performance of his functions under Section 173(3) (*establishment of the Magisterial Service*), the Chief Magistrate shall carry out any directions or instructions of the Judicial and Legal Services Commission.

SUBDIVISION G. THE PUBLIC PROSECUTOR AND THE PUBLIC SOLICITOR

176. (1) Offices of Public Prosecutor and Public Solicitor are hereby established.

(2) The Public Prosecutor and the Public Solicitor shall be appointed by the Judicial and Legal Services Commission.

(3) Subject to this Constitution

(*a*) in the performance of his functions under this Constitution the Public Prosecutor is not subject to direction or control by any person or authority; but

(*b*) nothing in paragraph (*a*) prevents the Head of State, acting with, and in accordance with, the advice of the National Executive Council, giving a direction to the Public Prosecutor on any matter that might prejudice the security, defense or international relations of Papua New Guinea (including Papua New Guinea's relations with the Government of any other country or with any international organization).

(4) The Prime Minister shall table in the National Parliament any direction to the Public Prosecutor at the next sitting of the Parliament after the direction is given unless, after consultation with the Leader of the Opposition, he considers that tabling of the direction is likely to prejudice the security, defence or international relations of Papua New Guinea.

(5) Subject to Section 177(2) (*functions of the Public Prosecutor and the Public Solicitor*), in the performance of his functions under this Constitution the Public Solicitor is not subject to direction or control by any person or authority.

177. (1) The functions of the Public Prosecutor are

(*a*) in accordance with an Act of the Parliament and the Rules of Court of the Supreme Court and the National Court, to control the exercise and performance of the prosecution function (including appeals and the refusal to initiate and the discontinuance of prosecutions) before the Supreme Court and the national Court, and before other Courts as provided by or under Acts of the Parliament; and

(*b*) to bring or to decline to bring proceedings under Division III.2 (*leadership code*) for misconduct in office.

(2) The functions of the Public Solicitor are to provide legal aid, advice and assistance for persons in need of help by him, and in particular

(*a*) to provide legal assistance to a person in need of help by him who has been charged with an offence punishable by imprisonment for more than two years; and

(*b*) notwithstanding the provisions of Section 176(5) (*establishment of offices*) he shall provide legal aid, advice and assistance to any person when directed to do so by the Supreme Court or the National Court; and

(*c*) in his discretion in any matter, whether of a criminal or civil nature provided that such assistance shall be

(i) limited to advice and preparation of documents in any proceedings in respect of which an Act of the Parliament prohibits legal representation of any party to the proceedings; and

(ii) granted in accordance with an order of priorities relative to the resources of the Public Solicitor laid down by an Act of the Parliament.

(3) A person aggrieved by a refusal of the Public Solicitor to provide legal aid may apply to the Supreme Court or the National Court for a direction under Subsection (2)(*b*).

(4) For the purposes of this section the need of a person is to be interpreted in relation to each particular case and, without limiting the generality of this expression, account shall be taken of the means of the person to meet the probable cost of obtaining alternative legal assistance, the availability of such assistance and the hardship which might result to the person if compelled to obtain legal assistance other than by the Public Solicitor.

(5) An Act of Parliament may make provision for the Public Solicitor to make a reasonable charge for services provided by him to persons in need of his help whom he considers are able to make a contribution towards the cost of these services.

(6) An Act of the Parliament may confer, or may provide for the conferring of, additional functions, not inconsistent with the performance of the functions conferred by Subsection (1) and (2), on the Public Prosecutor or the Public Solicitor.

SUBDIVISION H. REMOVAL FROM OFFICE OF SENIOR JUDICIAL AND LEGAL OFFICE-HOLDERS

178. A Judge, the Public Prosecutor, the Public Solicitor or the Chief Magistrate may, during his term of office, be removed from office only

(*a*) for inability (whether arising from physical or mental infirmity or otherwise) to perform the functions and duties of his office; or

(*b*) for misbehaviour; or

(*c*) in accordance with Division III.2 (*leadership code*), for misconduct in office.

179. (1) If the National Executive Council is satisfied that the question of the removal from office of the Chief Justice should be investigated, the Head of State, acting with, and in accordance with, the advice of the National Executive Council, may

(*a*) appoint a tribunal under Section 181 (*constitution, etc., of tribunals*); and

(*b*) refer the matter, together with a statement of the reasons for its opinion, to the tribunal for investigation and report to it.

(2) If the tribunal reports that there are good grounds for removing the Chief Justice from office, the Head of State, acting with, and in accordance with, the advice of the National Executive Council, may, by notice in writing to the Chief Justice, remove him from office.

(3) The Prime Minister shall send a copy of the notice, together with a copy of the report of the tribunal, to the Speaker for presentation to the Parliament, and shall also forward copies to the Judicial and Legal Services Commission.

180. (1) If the Judicial and Legal Services Commission is satisfied that the question of the removal from office of a Judge (other than the Chief Justice), the Public Prosecutor, the Public Solicitor or the Chief Magistrate should be investigated, it may

(*a*) appoint a tribunal under Section 181 (*constitution, etc., of tribunals*); and

(*b*) refer the matter, together with a statement of the reasons for its opinion, to the tribunal for investigation and report to it.

(2) If the tribunal reports that there are good grounds for removing the Judge, Public Prosecutor, Public Solicitor or Chief Magistrate from office, the Judicial and Legal Services Commission, may, by notice in writing to the Judge, Public Prosecutor, Public Solicitor or Chief Magistrate, as the case may be, remove him from office.

(3) The Commission shall send a copy of the notice, together with a copy of the report of the tribunal, to the Speaker for presentation to the Parliament.

181. (1) A tribunal for the purposes of Section 179 (*removal from office of Chief Justice*) or 180 (*removal from office of other Judges, etc.*) shall consist of a Chairman and two other members, each of whom must be

(*a*) a Judge or former Judge of the Supreme Court or of the National Court; or (*b*) a former Judge or acting Judge of the pre-Independence Supreme Court; or

(*c*) a Judge or former Judge of a court of unlimited jurisdiction of a country with a legal system similar to that of Papua New Guinea, or of a court to which an appeal from such a court lies.

(2) The tribunal shall make due inquiry into any matter referred to it without regard to legal formalities or the rules of evidence, and shall inform itself in such manner as it thinks proper, subject to compliance with the principles of natural justice.

182. (1) Where a question has been referred to a tribunal under this Subdivision

(*a*) the Head of State, acting with, and in accordance with, the advice of the National Executive Council, in the case of the Chief Justice; or

(*b*) the Judicial and Legal Services Commission, in any other case,

may suspend the person concerned from office pending the report of the tribunal, and may remove the suspension at any time.

(2) Unless otherwise determined by the Head of State, acting with, and in accordance with, the advice of the National Executive Council, or by the Judicial and Legal Services Commission, as the case may be, the suspension shall be on full pay.

(3) Where at the time of the suspension, a suspended Judge or Chief Magistrate was dealing with any judicial proceedings, he may continue and complete those proceedings, unless the Judicial and Legal Services Commission in the case of the Chief Justice in any other case, otherwise orders.

SUBDIVISION I. THE JUDICIAL AND LEGAL SERVICES COMMISSION

183. (1) A Judicial and Legal Services Commission is hereby established.

(2) Subject to Subsection (3), the Commission consists of

(*a*) the Minister responsible for the National Justice Administration, or a person nominated by him, who is the Chairman; and

(*b*) the Chief Justice; and

(*c*) the Deputy Chief Jusitce; and

(*d*) the Chief Ombudsman; and

(*e*) a member of the Parliament appointed by the Parliament.

(3) When the Commission is considering a matter relating to the appointment or removal from office of a member of the Magisterial Service, or any other matter relating to the Magisterial Service prescribed for the purposes of this subsection by or under an Act of the Parliament, the Chief Magistrate is (except in a matter involving himself) an additional member of the Commission.

(4) The Commission is not subject to direction or control by any person or authority.

(5) An Organic Law may make further provision in respect of the

constitution, powers, functions, duties and responsibilities of the Commission, and for guaranteeing its independence.

SUBDIVISION J. MISCELLANEOUS

184 (1) The Judges of the Supreme Court or of the National Court may make rules of court, not inconsistent with a Constitutional Law or an Act of the Parliament, with respect to the practice and procedure in and in relation to the Supreme Court or the National Court, as the case may be.

(2) Without limiting the generality of Subsection (1), the rules may make provision for and in respect of

(*a*) the practice and procedures in the office of the Supreme Court and the National Court; and
(*b*) the service and execution of process and judgments of the Supreme Court and the National Court; and
(*c*) the service and execution within the country of process and judgment of foreign courts; and
(*d*) the issue by the Supreme Court or the National Court of letters of request for the service in a foreign country of process of the Supreme Court or the National Court, as the case may be, or for the examination of witnesses in a foreign country; and
(*e*) the costs of and relating to proceedings in the Supreme Court or the National Court; and
(*f*) the methods of pleading; and
(*g*) the attendance of witnesses and the taking of evidence; and
(*h*) the means by which particular facts may be proved, and the manner in which evidence of particular facts may be given, in any proceedings or in any application in connection with, or at any stage of, any proceedings.

(3) The Rules of Court may require or permit legal argument to be submitted in writing.

(4) If an Act of the Parliament comes into force that is inconsistent with a rule of court, the rule ceases to have effect to the extent of the inconsistency.

(5) All rules of court shall be forwarded by the Chief Justice to the Speaker, for presentation to the Parliament, as soon as practicable after being made, and may be disallowed by the Parliament.

185. If in the circumstances of a particular case before a court no provision, or no adequate provision, is made in respect of a matter of practice or procedure, the court shall give ad hoc directions to remedy the lack or inadequacy.

186. Nothing in this Division prevents the establishment, by or under an Act of the Parliament, of a system of juries or assessors.

187. (1) The Judges shall, at least once in each period of 12 months, at such times as are fixed by or under an Act of the Parliament or, subject to any such Act, by the Head of State, acting with, and in accordance with, the advice of the National

Executive Council, give to the Head of State, for presentation to the Parliament, a report on the Work of the National Judicial System, with such recommendations as to improvement as they think proper.

(2) Nothing in Subsection (1) prevents the Judges from making, on their own initiative or at the request of the Parliament or of the National Executive, other reports on any aspect of the work of the National Judicial System.

PART VII

THE STATE SERVICES

Division 1. Introductory

188. (1) The following State Services are hereby established:

(*a*) the National Public Service; and

(*b*) the Police Force; and

(*c*) the Papua New Guinea Defence Force; and

(*d*) the Parliamentary Service.

(2) Acts of the Parliament may make provision for or in respect of other State Services.

189. All of the state Services other than the Defence Force shall be civilian services, and all of the State Services shall be subject at all times to ultimate civilian control.

Division 2. The Public Services Commission

190. (1) A Public Services Commission is hereby established.

(2) The Commission shall consist of not less than four members, who shall be appointed by the Head of State, acting with, and in accordance with, the advice of the National Executive Council given after consultation with any appropriate Permanent Parliamentary Committee.

(3) All of the members of the Commission must be citizens.

(4) Subject to this Constitution, an Organic Law shall make provision for and in respect of the appointment and the terms and conditions of employment of the members of the Commission, and for and in respect of its constitution, powers and procedures.

191. (1) Subject to this Constitution, the Public Services Commission shall be responsible, in accordance with an Act of the Parliament, for

(*a*) the efficient management and control of the National Public Service; and

(*b*) all personnel matters connected with the National Public Service; and

(*c*) such other matters in relation to the other State Services and the services of other governmental bodies as are prescribed by Constitutional Laws or Acts of the Parliament.

(2) It is a special function of the Commission to keep under continuous review the State Services (other than the Defence Force) and the service of other governmental bodies, and to advise, either on its own initiative or on request, the National Executive and any authority responsible for any of those services on organizational matters and the co-ordination of effort, and in particular on conditions of employment, with a special view to avoiding wasteful duplication of effort and competition.

(3) Nothing in Subsection (2) gives the Commission any power of direction or control.

192. The Public Services Commission is responsible to the National Executive Council, but, subject to Section 193 (*appointments to certain offices*), in personnel matters

(*a*) it shall comply with any general directions as to policy from the Head of State, acting with, and in accordance with, the advice of the National Executive Council; and

(*b*) it is otherwise not subject to direction or control by any person or authority.

193. (1) This section applies to and in respect of the following offices and positions:

(*a*) all offices in the National Public Service the occupants of which are directly responsible to the National Executive Council or to a Minister; and
(*b*) the offices of the members of the Boundaries Commission; and
(*c*) the office the occupant of which is responsible for the administration of the Government broadcasting service, or, if that responsibility rests with a board or commission, the chairman or president of the board or commission; and
(*d*) the offices of the persons (including members of boards or commissions) responsible for the administration of any of the State Services; and
(*e*) the office of Commissioner of Police; and
(*f*) the office of Commander of the Defence Force; and
(*g*) the office of Secretary to the National Executive Council; and
(*h*) such other offices and positions as are prescribed by an Act of the Parliament for the purpose,

other than the offices of the members of the Public Services Commission.

(2) All appointment (whether temporary or substantive) to offices to which Subsection (1)(*b*), (*c*), (*e*) and (*h*) apply shall be made by the Head of State, acting with, and in accordance with, the advice of the National Executive Council given after consultation with the Public Services Commission and any appropriate Permanent Parliamentary Committee, and a report concerning each of them shall be given to the Parliament by the responsible Minister as soon as possible after it has been made.

(3) All appointments (whether temporary or substantive) to which

Subsection (1)(*a*), (*d*), (*f*) and (*g*) apply and such other offices and positions as are prescribed by an Act of the Parliament for the purpose of this subsection, shall be made by the Head of State, acting with, and in accordance with, the advice of the National Executive Council given after consultation with the Public Services Commission.

(4) An Act of the Parliament may make provision for and in respect of a temporary appointment to an office to which this section applies until such time as it is practicable to make an appropriate substantive appointment in accordance with Subsection (2).

194. In this Division, 'personnel matters' means decisions and other service matters concerning an individual whether in relation to his appointment, promotion, demotion, transfer, suspension, diciplining or cessation or termination of employment (except cessation or termination at the end of his normal period of employment as determined in accordance with law), or otherwise.

Division 3. The State Services Generally

195. Subject to this Part, Acts of the Parliament may make provision for or in respect of the State Services, and in particular for and in respect of

(*a*) the structures and organization of the State Services; and
(*b*) the employment of persons in the State Services; and
(*c*) the terms and conditions of appointment to, and of employment in, the State Services.

Division 4. Special Provisions in Relation to the Police Force

196. (1) The Police Force is subject to the control of the National Executive Council through a Minister.

(2) The Minister has no power of command within the Police Force, except to the extent provided for by a Constitutional Law or an Act of the Parliament.

197. (1) The primary functions of the Police Force are, in accordance with the Constitutional Laws and Acts of the Parliament

(*a*) to preserve peace and good order in the country; and
(*b*) to maintain and, as necessary, enforce the law in an impartial and objective manner.

(2) Insofar as it is a function of the Police Force to lay, prosecute or withdraw charges in respect of offences, the members of the Police Force are not subject to direction or control by any person outside the Force.

198. There shall be, within the Police Force, an office of Commissioner of Police, who shall be responsible for the superintendence, efficient organization and control of the Force in accordance with an Act of the Parliament.

199. There shall be only one Police Force in Papua New Guinea, but this section does not prevent (*a*) the creation of reserve or special forces, or other similar forces (by whatever name known); or

(*b*) the creation of special bodies, or the authorization of persons than members of the Police Force, for the Administration or enforcement of Particular laws; or

(*c*) the conferring of police powers on persons who are not members of the Police Force,

by or under an Act of the Parliament.

Division 5. Special Provisions in Relation to the Defence Force

200. (1) It is strictly forbidden to establish, organize, equip, train or take part in or associate with a military or para-military force, or to organize or take part in military or para-military training, except such as is provided for by this Constitution, or to plan, prepare for or assist in the raising or training of such a force or in such training.

(2) Subsection (1) does not prevent

(*a*) the establishment of a reserve, auxiliary or special force (by whatever name known) as part of the Defence Force; or

(*b*) the establishment of civilian components of the Defence Force, or the establishment or recognition of non-combatant units or or organizations within, attached to or associated with the Defence Force,

in accordance with an Act of the Parliament.

(3) An Act of the Parliament may provide that Subsection (1) does not apply to the armed forces of any other country specified in or under the Act, or to the civilian components of, or to the non-combatant units or organizations whether attached to or associated with such forces.

201. (1) There shall be no office of Commander-in-Chief of the Defence Force, whether honorary or otherwise.

(2) The Defence Force is subject to the superintendence and control of the National Executive Council, through the Minister responsible for the Defence Force.

(3) No serving member of the Defence Force may be the Minister responsible for the Defence Force.

(4) The Minister responsible for the Defence Force shall not use any military rank or title, and, except to the extent provided for by Constitutional Law or an Act of the Parliament, has no power of command within the Defence Force.

(5) There shall be

(*a*) within the Defence Force, an office of Commander of the Defence Force, who shall be the principal military adviser to the Minister responsible for the Defence Force on matters relating to the Defence Force; and (*b*) within the National Public Service, an officer of the Service, who shall be the principal civilian adviser to the Minister on matters relating to the Defence Force,

and each of whom shall have such other powers, function, duties and responsibilities as are prescribed by or under an Act of the Parliament.

202. The functions of the Defence Force are

(*a*) to defend Papua New Guinea and its territory; and

(*b*) to assist in the fulfilment by Papua New Guinea of its international obligations; and

(*c*) to provide assistance to civilian authorities

(i) in a civil disaster; or

(ii) in the restoration of public order and security on being called out in accordance with Section 204 (*call-out in aid to the civil power*) or

(iii) in accordance with an Act of the Parliament during a period of declared national emergency under Part X. (*emergency powers*); and

(*d*) to perform, as directed, functions and services of a civil nature so as to participate to the maximum in the task of national development and improvement,

either within the country or outside it, in accordance with this Constitution and Acts of the Parliament.

203. Since it is necessary that the Defence Force and the members of the Defence Force have no special position under the law except to such extent as is required by the nature of the Force as a disciplined force and its peculiar functions, duties and responsibilities, it is hereby declared that, except as is specifically provided by a Constitutional Law or an Act of the Parliament, the Defence Force and the members of the Defence Force are subject to all laws in the same way as other bodies and persons.

204. Call-out in aid to the civil power.

(1) The Defence Force or a part of the Defence Force may be called out to perform functions under Section 202(*c*)(ii) (*functions of the Defence Force*) only by the Head of State acting with, and in accordance with, the advice of the National Executive Council.

(2) When called out in accordance with Subsection (1), the Defence Force or a part of the Defence Force

(*a*) does not have, and shall not be given, any power or protection that would not be possessed by the Police Force or the members of the Police Force in similar circumstances; and

(*b*) shall support the Police Force for so long and so far as is necessary to enable the Police Force to restore public order and security; and

(*c*) in so doing shall act only on, and to the extent specified in, a request by the appropriate civilian authority in accordance with an Act of the Parliament; and (*d*) shall cease to act in support of the Police Force when directed to do so by the Head of State, acting with, and in accordance with, the advice of the National Executive Council.

205. (1) Except for the purposes of defence against attack, the Defence Force or a part of the Defence Force

(*a*) may be ordered on active service only by the Head of State, acting with, and in accordance with, the advice of the National Council; and

(*b*) may be sent out of the country only by the authority of and on conditions imposed by the Head of State, acting with, and in accordance with, the advice of the National Executive Council.

(2) The Defence Force or a part of the Defence Force may not be ordered on, or committed to

(*a*) active service; or

(*b*) an international peace-keeping or relief operation,

outside the country without the prior approval of the Parliament.

(3) If practicable before, and in any event as soon as practiceable after, action is taken under Subsection (1) or the Defence Force becomes engaged in war or warlike operations, or in defence against attack, the Parliament shall be advised of the action taken, or likely to be taken, and of the reasons for it, and shall be given an opportunity to debate the matter.

(4) Subsection (1)(*b*) does not prevent

(*a*) the Defence Force or a part of the Defence Force being sent out of the country for normal administrative or training purposes; or

(*b*) any action that is required or permitted by an Act of the Parliament for the purposes of enforcing a law.

206. (1) An Act of the Parliament may make provision for or in respect of

(*a*) the presence in the country, by arrangement with the National Executive, of forces of another country; and

(*b*) the presence in another country of the Defence Force or a part of the Defence Force,

and in particular for or in respect of

(*c*) the concession to courts or tribunals, and to service authorities, of the other country of jurisdiction over members of its forces (other than citizens of Papua New Guinea) in relation to some or all civil and criminal matters; or

(*d*) the assertion of the exclusive jurisdiction of courts and tribunals of Papua New Guinea, and of Defence Force authorities, over members of the Defence Force in another country.

(2) Except in relation to its own members or to civilian components of, or civilians accompanying, the force, a visiting force of another country shall not be used in the country in any role in which the Defence Force may not be used, and accordingly any law that restricts the role, powers or functions of the Defence Force or of members of the Defence Force applies equally to visiting forces and members of visiting forces.

(3) A law made for the purposes of Subsection (1) may apply, in whole or in part, to civilian components of, or civilians accompanying, the Defence Force or a part of the Defence Force, or to civilian components of, or civilians accompanying a visiting force.

Division 6. Special Provisions relating to Disciplined Forces

207. (1) The following are, for the purposes of this Division, disciplined forces:

(*a*) the Police Force; and

(*b*) the Defence Force; and

(*c*) any other force or service that

(i) is established by or under a statute; and

(ii) is declared by an Organic Law to be a disciplined force for the purpose of this Division.

(2) For the purposes of any Organic Law made for the purposes of this Division, a person acting, as required or authorized by law, under the direction of a member of a diciplined force, for the purpose of assisting in the performance of the functions or duties of the member or of the force, shall be deemed to be a member of that force.

208. (1) Because of the special nature of disciplined forces and of their operations, it is a primary duty of their members to obey lawful orders, and accordingly an Organic Law shall make special provision for relieving a member of such a force from responsibility for the consequences of

(*a*) carrying out a lawful order; or

(*b*) carrying out an order which he honestly, and on reasonable grounds believed to be a lawful order, in which case the onus of establishing his belief and the reasonable grounds on which it was based, shall be upon him.

(2) Without derogating any other right to compensation from an authority responsible for the disciplined force concerned, an Organic Law made for the purpose of Subsection (1) shall make provision for any liability to make compensation that would otherwise lie on a member of a disciplined force to lie on the authority responsible for the force.

PART VIII

SUPERVISION AND CONTROL

SUBDIVISION A. THE PARLIAMENT AND FINANCE

209. (1) Notwithstanding anything in this Constitution, the raising and expenditure of finance by the National Government, including the imposistion of taxation and the raising of loans, is subject to authorization and control by the Parliament, and shall be regulated by an Act of the Parliament.

(2) For each fiscal year, there shall be a National Budget comprising estimates of finance proposed to be raised, and estimates of proposed expenditure, by the National Government in respect of the fiscal year, and appropriations for the service of that year, and such other supplementary Budgets and appropriations as are necessary.

(3) Before any Budget or appropriation is prepared for submission to the Parliament, the National Executive Council shall consult with any appropriate Permanent Parliamentary Committee, but this subsection does not confer any right or impose any duty of consultation after the initial stages of the preparation of the Budget or appropriation.

210. (1) The Parliament shall not provide for the imposition of taxation, the raising of loans or the expenditure of public moneys of Papua New Guinea except on the recommendation of the Head of State, acting with, and in accordance with, the advice of the National Executive Council.

(2) The Parliament may reduce, but shall not increase or re-allocate, the amount or incidence of, or change the purpose of, any proposed taxation, loan or expenditure.

211. (1) All moneys of or under the control of the National Government shall be expended except as provided by this Constitution or by or under an Act of the Parliament.

212. (1) If at the beginning of a fiscal year the Parliament has not made provision for public expenditure for that year, the National Executive may, in accordance with an Act of the Parliament, expend out of the Consolidated Revenue Fund, without authorization other than this section, amounts not exceeding in total one third of the budgetted expenditure by the National Government during the immediately preceding fiscal year.

(2) The authority conferred by Subsection (1) lapses when the Parliament has made provision for the public expenditure for the fiscal year in question, and any amounts expended by virtue of that subsection are a charge against the expenditure so provided for and shall be properly brought to account accordingly.

213. (1) An office of Auditor-General is hereby established.

(2) The Auditor-General shall be appointed by the Head of State, acting with, and in accordance with, the advice of the National Executive Council given after receiving reports from the Public Services Commission and the Public Accounts Committee.

(3) In the performance of his functions under this Constitution, the Auditor-General is not subject to the control or direction of any person or authority.

214. (1) The primary functions of the Auditor-General are to inspect and audit, and to report at least once in every fiscal year (as provided by an Act of the Parliament) to the Parliament on the Public accounts of Papua New Guinea, and on the control of and on transactions with or concerning the public moneys and property of Papua New Guinea, and such other functions as are prescribed by or under a Constitutional Law.

(2) Unless other provision is made by law in respect of the inspection and audit of them, Subsection (1) extends to the accounts, finances and property of

(*a*) all arms, departments, agencies and instrumentalities of the National Government; and

(*b*) all bodies set up by an Act of the Parliament, or by executive or administrative act of the National Executive, for governmental or official purposes.

(3) Notwithstanding that other provision for inspection or audit is made as provided for by Subsection (2), the Auditor-General may, if he thinks it proper to do so, inspect and audit, and report to the Parliament on, any accounts, finances or property of an institution referred to in that subsection, insofar as they relate to, or consist of or are derived from, public moneys or property of Papua New Guinea.

(4) An Act of the Parliament may expand, and may provide in more detail for, the functions of the Auditor-General under Subsections (1), (2) and (3), and may confer on the Auditor-General additional functions and duties not inconsistent with the performance of the functions and duties conferred and imposed by those subsections.

SUBDIVISION C. THE PUBLIC ACCOUNTS COMMITTEE

215. There shall be a Public Accounts Committee, which is a Permanent Parliamentary Committee for the purposes of Subdivision VI.2.E (*the Committee system*).

216. (1) The primary function of the Public Accounts Committee is, in accordance with an Act of the Parliament, to examine and report to the Parliament on the public accounts of Papua New Guinea and on the control of and on transactions with or concerning, the public moneys and property of Papua New Guinea.

(2) Subsection (1) extends to any accounts, finances and property that are subject to inspection and audit by the Auditor-General under Section 214(2) (*functions of the Auditor-General*), and to reports by the Auditor-General under that subsection or Section 214(3) (*functions of the Auditor-General*).

(3) An Act of the Parliament may expand and may provide in more detail for, the functions of the Committee under Subsection (1) and (2), and may confer on the Committee additional functions and duties not inconsistent with the performance of the functions and duties conferred and imposed by those subsections.

Division 2. The Ombudsman Commission

217. (1) There shall be an Ombudsman Commission, consisting of a Chief Ombudsman and two Ombudsmen.

(2) The members of the Commission shall be appointed by the Head of State, acting with, and in accordance with, the advice of an Ombudsman Appointments Committee consisting of,

(*a*) the Prime Minister, who shall be Chairman; and
(*b*) the Chief Justice; and
(*c*) the Leader of the Opposition; and
(*d*) the Chairman of the appropriate Permanent Parliamentary Committee, or, if the Chairman is not a member of the Parliament who is recognized by the Parliament as being generally committed to support the Government in the Parliament, the Deputy Chairman of that Committee; and
(*e*) the Chairman of the Public Services Commission.

(3) The salary and other conditions of employment of the Ombudsman shall be not less than or inferior to the salary and other conditions of employment of a Judge other than the Chief Justice and the Deputy Chief Justice without taking into account any conditions of employment personal to that Judge.

(4) The salary and other conditions of employment of the Ombudsman shall be not less than or inferior to the salary and other conditions of employment of the Public Prosecutor, without taking into account any conditions of employment personal to any particular Public Prosecutor.

(5) In the performance of its functions under Section 219 (*functions of the Commission*) the Commission is not subject to direction or control by any person or authority.

(6) The proceedings of the Commission are not subject to review in any way, except by the Supreme Court or the National Court on the ground that it has exceeded its jurisdiction.

(7) An Organic Law shall make further provision in respect of the appointment, powers, procedures and immunity of the Commission.

(8) In this section 'conduct' includes
(*a*) any action or inaction relating to a matter of administration; and
(*b*) any alleged action or inaction relating to a matter of administration.

218. The purposes of the establishment of the Ombudsman Commission are
(*a*) to ensure that all governmental bodies are responsibe to the needs and aspirations of the People; and
(*b*) to help in the improvement of the work of governmental bodies and the elimination of unfairness and discrimination by them; and
(*c*) to help in the elimination of unfair or otherwise defective legislation and practices affecting or administered by governmental bodies; and
(*d*) to supervise the enforcement of Division III.2 (*leadership code*).

219. (1) Subject to this section and to any Organic Law made for the purpose of Subsection (7), the functions of the Ombudsman Commission are
(*a*) to investigate, on its own initiative or on complaint by a person affected, any conduct on the part of
(i) any State Service or a member of any such service; or

(ii) any other governmental body, or an officer or employee of a governmental body; or
(iii) any local government body or provincial government body, or an officer or employee of any such body; or
(iv) any other body set up by statute
(A) that is wholly or mainly supported out of public moneys of Papua New Guinea; or
(B) all of, or the majority of, the members of the controlling authority of which are appointed by the National Executive,

or an officer or employee of any such body; and
(v) any member of the personal staff of the Governor-General, a Minister or the Leader or Deputy Leader of the Opposition; or
(vi) any other body or person prescribed for the purpose by an Act of the Parliament,

specified by or under an Organic Law in the exercise of a power or function vested in it or him by law in cases where the conduct is or may be wrong, taking into account, amongst other things, the National Goals and Directive Principles, the Basic Rights and the Basic Social Obligations; and

(*b*) to investigate any defects in any law or administrative practice appearing from any such investigation; and
(*c*) to investigate, either on its own initiative or on complaint by a person affected, any case of an alleged or suspected discriminatory practice within the meaning of a law prohibiting such practices; and
(*d*) any functions conferred on it under Division III.2 (*leadership code*); and
(*e*) any other functions conferred upon it by or under an Organic Law.

(2) Subject to Subsections (3), (4) and (5), and without otherwise limiting the generality of the expression, for the purposes of Subsection (1)(*a*) conduct is wrong if it is

(*a*) contrary to law; or
(b) unreasonable, unjust, oppressive or improperly discriminatory, whether or not it is in accordance with law or practice; or
(*c*) based wholly or partly on improper motives, irrelevant grounds or irrelevant considerations; or
(*d*) based wholly or partly on a mistake of law or of fact; or
(*e*) conduct for which reasons should be given but were not,

whether or not the act was supposed to be done in the exercise of deliberate judgement within the meaning of Section 62 (*decisions in 'deliberate judgement'*).

(3) The Commission shall not inquire into the jusifiability of a policy of the National Government or a Minister, except insofar as the policy may be contrary

to law or to the National Goals and Directive Principles, the Basic Rights or the Basic Social Obligations, or of any act of the Parliament.

(4) The Commission shall not inquire into the exercise of a rule-making power by a local government body.

(5) The Commission shall not inquire into a decision by a court, except insofar as the decision may show an apparent defect in law or administrative practice to which Subsection (1)(*b*) would apply.

(6) Except as provided by or under Division III.2 (*leadership code*), the Commission's powers of enforcement are limited to publicity for its proceedings, reports and recommendations, to the making of reports and recommendations to the Parliament and other appropriate authorities as provided by an Organic Law, and to the giving of advice.

(7) An Organic Law shall make provision in respect of the powers and procedures of the Commission, and in particular

(*a*) shall, subject to paragraph (*b*), make provision for the Commission to have access to all available relevant information; and

(*b*) may impose reasonable restrictions on the availability of information; and

(*c*) shall make provision to ensure the secrecy or confidentiality of secret or confidential information made available to the Commission or to a member of the Commission or of its staff; and

(*d*) may limit or restrict to a reasonable extent and in a reasonable manner the jurisdiction of the Commission in relation to any matters, and in particular in relation to national security; and

(*e*) shall make provision for and in respect of publicity for the proceedings, reports and recommendations of the Commission.

(8) In this section, 'conduct' includes

(*a*) any action or inaction relating to a matter of administration; and

(*b*) any alleged action or inaction relating to a matter of administration.

220. (1) The Ombudsman Commission shall, at least once in each period of 12 months, at such time as is fixed by or under an Act of the Parliament or, subject to any such act, by the Head of State, acting with, and in accordance with, the advice of the National Executive Council, give to the Head of State, for presentation to the Parliament, a report on the functions and workings of the Commission, with such recommendations as to improvement as the Commission thinks proper.

(2) Nothing in Subsection (1) prevents the Commission from making, on its own initiative or at the request of the Parliament or of the National Executive, other reports on any aspect of the functions and workings of the Commission.

PART IX

CONSTITUTIONAL OFFICE-HOLDERS AND CONSTITUTIONAL INSTITUTIONS

221. In this Part
'constitutional institution' means any office or institution established or provided for by this Constitution, other than an office of Head of State or of a Minister, or the National Executive
(*a*) a Judge; or
(*b*) the Public Prosecutor or the Public Solicitor; or
(*c*) the Chief Magistrate; or
(*d*) a member of the Ombudsman Commission; or
(*e*) a member of the Electoral Commission; or
(*f*) the Clerk of the Parliament; or
(*g*) a member of the Public Services Commission; or
(*h*) the Auditor-General; or
(*i*) the holder of any other office declared by an Organic Law or an Act of the Parliament to be a constitutional office for the purposes of this Part.

222. This Part shall be read subject to any other provisions of this Constitution relating to particular constitutional office-holders or particular constitutional institutions.

223. (1) Subject to this Constitution, Organic Laws shall make provision for and in respect of the qualifications, appointment and terms and conditions of employment of constitutional office-holders.

(2) In particular, Organic Laws shall make provision guaranteeing the rights and independence of constitutional office-holders by, amongst other things
(*a*) specifying the grounds on which, and the procedures by which, they may be dismissed or removed from office, but only by, or in accordance with the recommendation of, an independent and impartial tribunal; and
(*b*) providing that at the end of their periods of office they are entitled, unless they have been dismissed from office, to suitable further employment by a governmental body, or to adequate and suitable pensions or other retirement benefits, or both, subject to such reasonable requirements and conditions (if any) as are laid down by an Organic Law.

(3) A constitutional office-holder may not be suspended, dismissed or removed from office during his term of office except in accordance with a Constitutional Law.

(4) The total emoluments of a constitutional office-holder shall not be reduced while he is in office, except

(*a*) as part of a general reduction applicable equally or proportionately to all constitutional office-holders or, if he is a member of a State Service, to members of that service; or

(*b*) as a result of taxation that does not discriminate against him as a constitutional office-holder, or against constitutional office-holders generally.

(5) The office of a constitutional office-holder may not be abolished while there is a substantive holder of the office but this subsection does not apply to the abolition of any additional constitutional office created by an Act of the Parliament.

(6) Nothing in this section prevents the making by or under an Organic Law or an Act of the Parliament of reasonable provision for the appointment of a person to act temporarily in the office of a constitutional office-holder.

224. (1) Subject to this Constitution, Organic Laws and Acts of the Parliament shall provide, or shall make provision for, the powers and procedures of constitutional institutions, and generally for facilitating the performance of their functions, duties and responsibilities.

(2) Subject to this Constitution, if no próvision is made under Subsection (1) a constitutional institution

(*a*) may provide, to the extent of the deficiency, for its own procedures; and

(*b*) has all reasonable powers that are necessary or convenient for the exercise and performance of its powers, functions, duties and responsibilities.

225. Without limiting the generality of any other provision of this Constitution, it is the duty of the National Government and of all other governmental bodies, and of all public office-holders and institutions, to ensure, as far as is within their respective legal powers, that all arrangements are made, staff and facilities provided and steps taken to enable and facilitate, as far as may reasonably be, the proper and convenient performance of the functions of all constitutional institutions and of the offices of all constitutional office-holders.

PART X

EMERGENCY POWERS

Division 1. Introductory

226. In this Part, unless the contrary intention appears

'declaration of a national emergency' means a declaration under Section 228 (*declaration of national emergency*);

'emergency' includes, without limiting the generality of the expression

(*a*) imminent danger of war between Papua New Guinea and another country, or of warlike operations threatening national security; and (*b*) an earthquake, volcanic eruption, storm, tempest, flood, fire or outbreak of pestilence or infectious disease, or any other natural calamity whether similar to any such occurrence or not on such an extensive scale as to be likely to endanger the public safety or to deprive the community or any substantial proportion of the community of supplies or services essential to life; and

(*c*) action taken, or immediately threatened, by any person that is of such a nature, and on so extensive a scale, as to be likely to endanger the public safety or to deprive the community or any substantial portion of the community of supplies or services essential to life;

'Emergency Act' means an Act of the Parliament made for the purposes of this Part and in accordance with Section 230 (*Emergency Acts*);

'Emergency Committee' means an Emergency Committee appointed under Section 240 (*Emergency Committees*), and includes a Temporary Emergency Committee appointed and in office under Section 241 (*Temporary Emergency Committees*);

'emergency law' means

(*a*) an Emergency Act; or

(*b*) an Emergency Regulation;

'Emergency order' means an order made under an emergency law, as provided for by Section 232 (*emergency orders*);

'Emergency Regulation' means a law that is made in accordance with Section 231 (*Emergency Regulations*);

'internment' means detention that is authorized by or under a law the validity of which depends solely on this Part, but does not include the detention of a member of the armed forces of another country as a prisoner of war;

'period of declared national emergency' means any period during which

(*a*) Papua New Guinea is at war with another country by virtue of a declaration under Section 227 (*declaration of war*); or

(*b*) a declaration of a national emergency is in force under Section 228 (*declaration of national emergency*).

Division 2. Periods of Declared National Emergency

227. The Head of State, acting with, and in accordance with, the advice of the National Executive Council, may publicly declare that Papua New Guinea is at war with another country.

228. (1) If the National Executive Council is of the opinion that an emergency exists or is about to come into being such that it is necessary that the powers conferred by the succeeding provisions of this Part be available, the Head of State, acting with, and in accordance with, the advice of the National Executive Council, may publicly declare the existence of a national emergency in relation to the whole or part of the country.

(2) Unless it is impracticable to do so, a declaration under Subsection (1) shall be made in relation to a part of the country only after prior consultation with the Emergency Committee.

229. A declaration of war or of a national emergency may be revoked at any time

(*a*) by the Head of State, acting with, and in accordance with, the advice of the National Executive Council; or

(*b*) by decision of the Parliament.

Division 3. Emergency Measures

230. (1) Before or during a period of declared national emergency, the Parliament may make Acts of the Parliament (to be known as 'Emergency Acts') to make provision for dealing with the emergency, and with matters arising out of it.

(2) An Emergency Act shall be expressed to be an Emergency Act.

(3) Except to the extent necessary to bring it into effective operation at the time when it otherwise comes into operation, an Emergency Act made before the commencement of a period of declared national emergency shall not come into operation until the commencement of the period.

231. (1) Subject to this Part, at any time before the end of the period of 24 hours after the Parliament first meets after commencement of a period of declared national emergency the Head of State, acting with, and in accordance with, the advice of the National Executive Council, may make laws (to be known as 'Emergency Regulations') to make provision for dealing with the emergency concerned, and with matters arising out of it if, and to the extent that, the nature of the emergency or its requirements necessitate the making of the provision before the Parliament can reasonably consider the matter.

(2) An Emergency Regulation shall be immediately forwarded to

(*a*) the Speaker for presentation to the Parliament; and

(*b*) an Emergency Committee in accordance with Section 242(1)(*a*) (*functions, etc., of Emergency Committees*) or where no Emergency Committee established under Section 241 (*Temporary Emergency Committees*).

(3) Unless earlier extended by decision of the Parliament, an Emergency Regulation expires at the end of the period of 28 days after the making of the declaration of the emergency, or at the end of the period of 14 days after the Parliament first meets after the commencement of the period of declared national emergency, whichever first happens.

232. (1) An emergency law may make provision for the giving of orders, not inconsistent with the emergency law, by persons authorized to do so by or under the law.

(2) No emergency law shall purport to confer powers to make orders that could not be made in the form of an emergency law.

(3) An order shall, if practicable, be in writing and be notified to the appropriate authority appointed by law.

(4) As far as practicable, details of, or copies of, all orders given in accordance with this section shall immediately be forwarded to

(*a*) the Speaker for presentation to the Parliament; and

(*b*) the Emergency Committee in accordance with Section 242(1)(*a*) (*functions, etc., of Emergency Committees*) or where no Emergency Committee has been established, to the Temporary Emergency Committee established under Section 241 (*Temporary Emergency Committees*).

233. (1) Subject to this Part, an emergency law may make provision for the peace, order and good government of the country to the extent reasonably required for achieving its purpose.

(2) Notwithstanding the provisions of Section 12 and 13 but subject to Subsections (3) and (4), an emergency law may alter, wholly or partly, and absolutely or subject to conditions, any provision of Division III.3 (*basic rights*), any Organic Law made for the purposes of any such provision or any other law (other than a Constitutional Law) to the extent reasonably necessary to deal with the emergency concerned, and with matters arising out of it, but only so far as is reasonably justifiable in a democratic society having a proper regard for the rights and dignity of mankind.

(3) An emergency law

(*a*) may not alter

(i) Section 35 (*right to life*); or

(ii) Section 36 (*freedom from inhuman treatment*); or

(iii) Section 45 (*freedom of conscience, thought and religion*); or

(iv) Section 50 (*right to vote and stand for public office*); or

(v) Section 55 (*equality of citizens*); or

(vi) Section 56 (*other rights and privileges of citizens*); and

(*b*) may provide for internment only in accordance with Division 5 (*internment*); and

(*c*) may alter Section 37 (*protection of the Law*) or Section 42 (*Liberty of the person*) only to the extent allowed by paragraph (*b*).

(4) In addition, an Emergency Regulation may not alter

(*a*) Section 46 (*freedom of expression*); or

(*b*) Section 47 (*freedom of assembly and association*); or

(*c*) Section 49 (*right to privacy*); or

(*d*) Section 51 (*right to freedom of information*),

and may not provide for a sentence of imprisonment for a period exceeding nine months.

(5) In the case of an inconsistency between a valid emergency law and any other law, the law made later prevails.

234. Subject to any Act of the Parliament made for the purpose of dealing with the effect of the expiry or revocation of a particular Emergency Regulation, any person held in custody under or for the purposes of an Emergency Regulation shall be released from custody on its expiry or repeal, unless he is also held in custody under some other law.

235. If a member of the Parliament is held in custody under an Emergency Regulation, or is an internee, he shall, at all times when the Parliament is in session or when a committee (of which he is a member) of the Parliament is meeting, be released, on such conditions (if any) as are prescribed by an Act of the Parliament into the custody of the Parliament in order to allow him to attend to his parliamentary duties, unless he is also held in custody under some other law.

236. (1) An Emergency Act may be altered

(*a*) by an Act of the Parliament; or

(*b*) in an urgent case, where to do so would not be contrary to the positive intention expressed by a resolution of the Parliament dealing with the particular emergency, by an Emergency Regulation.

(2) An Emergency Regulation may be altered at any time

(*a*) by the Head of State, acting with, and in accordance with, the advice of the National Executive Council; or

(*b*) by an Emergency Act; or

(*c*) by decision of the Parliament.

(3) An emergency order may be disallowed at any time by decision of the Parliament.

237. (1) Subject to Section 238 (*extension of Emergency Acts*) an emergency law, unless it has expired under Section 231(3) (*Emergency Regulations*) or unless earlier repealed shall be deemed to be repealed immediately after the end of the day on which the period of declared national emergency ends.

(2) Where an Emergency Regulation which has amended or repealed any law in force immediately before the regulation took effect, is deemed to be repealed under Subsection (1), the repeal of that regulation shall revive the previous law from the date of that repeal as if the repealed regulation had not been made.

238. (1) Subject to Subsection (2), to the extent that its extension is necessary to deal with the results or aftermath of the period of declared national emergency and is reasonably justifiable in a democratic society that has a proper regard for the rights and dignity of mankind, the operation of an Emergency Act may be extended from time to time, after the end of the period of declared national emergency, by decision of the Parliament by an absolute majority vote, for a period or periods each not exceeding two months.

(2) After the end of the period of declared national emergency, internment may be continued only in accordance with Section 244(6) (*laws providing for internment*).

Division 4. Parliamentary Supervision and Control

239. (1) Unless the Parliament is in session at the commencement of a period of declared national emergency, it shall be called to meet as soon as practicable, and in any event not more than 15 days, after the commencement of the period and thereafter during the period at intervals each not exceeding two months.

(2) At each meeting of the Parliament during a period of declared national emergency the Prime Minister shall present to the parliament a statement setting out

(*a*) the reasons for the declaration of war or of the national emergency, or for the continuance of the period; and

(*b*) the reasons for any new Emergency Regulations; and

(*c*) a report on the operation of the emergency laws.

(3) Unless earlier revoked, a declaration of a national emergency expires at the end of the period of 21 days after its making, but may be extended from time to time by decision of the Parliament by an absolute majority vote, for a period or periods each not exceeding two months.

240. (1) An Act of the Parliament shall provide for and in respect of the appointment of committees of the Parliament (to be known as 'Emergency Committees') in respect of a period or periods of declared national emergency.

(2) No Minister may be a member of a Committee.

(3) A Committee shall be available to meet at all times during the period in respect of which it was appointed.

(4) Subject to the availability of members to meet in accordance with Subsection (3), a Committee should, in principle, be broadly representative of the various parts of the country and of parties and groups in the Parliament.

241. (1) An Act of the Parliament or the Standing Orders of the Parliament shall make provision for and in respect of the appointment of a Temporary Emergency Committee to hold office if a period of declared national emergency commences at a time when the Parliament is not in session and an Emergency Committee has not been established in accordance with Section 240 (*Emergency Committees*) in respect of the period.

(2) A Temporary Emergency Committee ceases to hold office (except for the purpose of making a report in accordance with Section 242(2) (*functions, etc., of Emergency Committees*) as to events occurring during its term of office)

(*a*) at the time of the establishment of an Emergency Committee in accordance with Section 240 (*Emergency Committees*) in respect of the period of declared national emergency; or

(*b*) at the end of the first meeting of the Parliament after its establishment,

whichever first occurs.

242. (1) The Prime Minister shall ensure that

(*a*) copies of all emergency laws and, so far as is practicable, of all emergency orders, are forwarded immediately to the Emergency Committee; and (*b*) subject ot any Emergency Act, the Committee is fully provided with information concerning, and is fully consulted concerning, developments in the situation and in particular concerning proposed emergency laws and the operation of existing emergency laws.

(2) At each meeting of the Parliament during a period of declared national emergency the Emergency Committee shall present to the Parliament a statement as to

(*a*) whether or not the period of declared national emergency should continue; and

(*b*) the justification for and the operation of the emergency laws; and

(*c*) whether or not any emergency law should be altered,

and such other related matters as it thinks fit.

(3) As soon as practicable after receipt by him of a request to do so from the Emergency Committee, and in any event not more than 15 days afterwards, the Speaker shall call a meeting of the Parliament to consider

(*a*) any statements by the Committee under Subsection (2) and by the Prime Minister under Section 239(2) (*Parliamentary control*); and

(*b*) whether or not the period of declared national emergency should be allowed to continue; and

(*c*) whether or not an emergency law should be altered,

and such other matters as the Parliament thinks fit.

243. During a period of declared national emergency, and while any emergency law is in force, first priority shall, subject to any express provision of this Constitution to the contrary, be given to any question, notice, motion or other Parliamentary process relating to the emergency or to an emergency law.

Division 5. Internment

244. (1) The internment of persons may be permitted only by an Act of the Parliament.

(2) An Act referred to in Subsection (1)

(*a*) must be made by an absolute majority vote; and

(*b*) takes effect on a date fixed by an absolute majority vote of the Parliament made after the commencement of a period of declared national emergency and, after at least four days' notice of the relevant motion has been given; and

(*c*) subject to Subsection (6), authorizes internment only during a period of declared national emergency.

(3) Subject to Subsection (4), at least four days' notice of the intention to introduce to the Parliament a proposed law to permit internment must be given, and the proposed law must be circulated, in accordance with the Standing Orders of the Parliament, to all members of the Parliament at least four days before the proposed law is made.

(4) During a time of war, the periods of four days prescribed in Subsection (3) are reduced to 24 hours.

(5) In his certificate given under Section 110 (*certification as to making of laws*) the Speaker must certify that the requirements of Subsection (2)(*a*) and (*b*), and of Subsection (3) or (4), as the case may be, have been complied with.

(6) Internment may continue after the end of the period of declared national emergency only to the extent that is reasonably required for the orderly and peaceful repatriation, resettlement or re-establishment of internees.

245. (1) The following provisions apply to and in relation to an internee:

(*a*) an internee and his next-of-kin or other close relative in the country shall, as soon as practicable and in any case not more than seven days after the commencement of his internment, be furnished with a statement in writing in a language that he understands specifying in detail the grounds upon which he is interned; and

(*b*) subject to Section 244(6) (*laws providing for internment*), an internee (other than an alien enemy) shall be released from detention at the end of the period of two months after his internment unless an independent and impartial tribunal established under paragraph (*e*) has reviewed his case and found that sufficient cause has been shown for his internment; and

(*c*) subject to Section 244(6), (*laws providing from internment*) an internee (other than an alien enemy) shall be released from detention at the end of the period of six months after his internment; and

(*d*) an internee (other than an alien enemy) is entitled to have his case reviewed by an independent and impartial tribunal under paragraph (*e*) as soon as practicable after he has been interned, and in any case not more than one month after the commencement of his internment, and afterwards at intervals not exceeding two months; and

(*e*) an Organic Law shall provide for the establishment of the independent and impartial tribunal referred to in this section and that the Chairman of the tribunal shall be a person qualified to be a Judge of the National Court, and

(*f*) the Organic Law referred to in paragraph (*e*) shall provide that as far as practicable where the case of an internee is being reviewed on a second or subsequent occasion, a majority of the members (including the Chairman) of any tribunal referred to in that paragraph which conducts that review shall be different from the members of any such tribunal which previously reviewed the case of that detainee; and

(*g*) subject to Subsection (5), where a tribunal established under paragraph (*e*) finds that a citizen has been interned wrongly or without sufficient reason

(i) the Head of State, acting with, and in accordance with, the advice of the National Executive Council shall order that he be released; and

(ii) he is entitled to compensation, in accordance with law, for the internment and any consequences of it; and

(*h*) subject to Subsection (5), where a tribunal established in accordance with paragraph (*e*) finds that there are no longer sufficient grounds for the internment of a citizen, the Minister responsible for national security shall order that he be released immediately; and

(*i*) a person released from internment in accordance with paragraphs (*c*) (*g*) or (*h*) shall not again be interned substantially on the same facts unless a change in circumstances relating to the grounds of the original internment gives these facts a new significance; and

(*j*) internees shall be kept separated, as far as practicable, from other persons in custody, and shall receive treatment not less favourable than that afforded to persons in custody awaiting trial for offences; and

(*k*) the names and places of residence of internees shall be published in the National Gazette and in any newspaper which has a national circulation, within 14 days of the internment, and at monthly intervals afterwards; and

(*l*) the Minister responsible for national security shall present to the Parliament at each meeting of the Parliament during the period of declared national emergency, but in any event, at intervals not exceeding six months, reports concerning all internees, their treatment, the review of their cases and action taken in regard to them.

(2) An internee shall be given adequate facilities to prepare and make representations to the review tribunal referred to in Subsection (1)(*e*) either personally or through a lawyer, and in particular shall be allowed full access to a lawyer (and if necessary to legal aid) and the services of a competent interpreter if required.

(3) An internee shall

(*a*) be permitted to appear in person before the review tribunal; and

(*b*) be permitted to be represented by a lawyer and a friend before the review tribunal.

(4) The Tribunal shall forward copies of its findings and recommendations to the internee and to his next-of-kin or other close relative in the country when they are furnished to the Minister responsible for national security.

(5) Where in his opinion it is necessary to do so in the interests of national security or public order, the Head of State, acting with, and in accordance with, the advice of the National Executive Council may refuse to make an order in accordance with Subsection (1)(*g*) or (*b*) for the release of an internee, but in that event, except in time of war

(*a*) he shall promptly present to the Parliament a report stating that he has refused to release the internee and setting out the reasons for his refusal; and

(*b*) the Parliament may order that the internee be released.

(6) Where an order is made in accordance with Subsection (5)

(*a*) the internee shall be released in accordance with the order; and

(*b*) Subsection (1)(*i*) applies as though the order were an order under Subsection (1)(*g*) or (*h*), as appropriate.

(7) An Organic Law, an Act of the Parliament or an emergency law may make further provision, not inconsistent with this section, in respect of the treatment, security and discipline of internees.

(8) The provisions of the Geneva Convention Relative to the Protection of Civilian Persons in Time of War of August 14, 1949, and any other international convention relating to interned persons, shall be complied with in relation to persons protected by them, and in addition such of those provisions that are of general application and can appropriately be applied to interned citizens shall be complied with in relation to such internees.

Division 6. Miscellaneous

246. During a period of declared national emergency the Parliament may, by an absolute majority vote, extend its term of office, or the term of office of the Governor-General, or both, for a term not exceeding the length of the period and such time afterwards as is necessary to allow a general election to be arranged and held, or for a Governor-General to be appointed, as the case requires.

PART XI

MISCELLANEOUS

247. (1) Papua New Guinea has power to acquire, hold and dispose of property of any kind, and to make contracts, in accordance with an Act of the Parliament.

(2) Papua New Guinea may sue and be sued, in accordance with an Act of the Parliament.

248. All property that was, immediately before Independence Day, vested in the body corporate at that time known as 'The Government of Papua New Guinea' is, on that day, vested in Papua New Guinea, and all rights and liabilities (actual or contingent) of that body immediately before that day are, on that day, rights and liabilities of Papua New Guinea.

249. Subject to any Organic Law, every person who is subject to Division III.2 (*leadership code*) before entering upon the duties of or exercising any of the powers of his office, shall make

(*a*) unless he has made it on a previous occasion or is exempt from making it under

(i) Section 251(1) (*taking certain oaths, etc., by non-citizens*); or

(ii) Section 272 (*oaths, affirmation, etc.*),

the Declaration of Loyalty; and

(*b*) in the case of

(i) a judicial officer—the Judicial Declaration; or

(ii) an office-holder other than a judicial officer—the Declaration of Office.

250. (1) Subject to any provision of a Constitutional Law making special provision for the purpose, the Oath of Allegiance, the Declaration of Loyalty, the Judicial Declaration or the Declaration of Office (or any other oath, affirmation or declaration that is required or permitted to be taken or made by or for the purposes of a Constitutional Law) may be taken or made before any person appointed for the purpose by or under an Act of the Parliament, or in the absence of any such Act, before a person appointed for the purpose by the Head of State, acting with, and in accordance with, the advice of the National Executive Council.

(2) Notwithstanding the provisions of Subsection (1), an oath, affirmation or declaration referred to in that subsection is binding and effectual no matter before whom it is taken or made.

251. (1) If

(*a*) it is desirable that a non-citizen be appointed to an office under a statute; and

(*b*) it is a requirement that in order to be qualified for appointment, or to enter upon the duties or exercise the powers of the office, a person must take the Oath of Allegiance or make the Declaration of Loyalty, or take or make some oath, affirmation or declaration; and

(*c*) the National Executive Council is satisfied that, by reason of the law of some other country, to take the Oath of Allegiance or make the Declaration of Loyalty, or to take or make the other oath, affirmation or declaration, in the prescribed manner or form would or might adversely affect the nationality or citizenship status of the person concerned,

the Head of State, acting with, and in accordance with, the advice of the National Executive Council, may, by order, substitute some oath, affirmation or declaration or, if thought necessary, exempt the person from the requirement.

(2) Notwithstanding Subsection (1), the non-citizen is subject to all laws as if he had made the Declaration of Loyalty, or had taken or made the other oath, affirmation or declaration, as the case may be.

(3) Nothing in Subsection (1) applies to or in respect of the Judicial Declaration.

252. There shall be an official journal of the National Government, which shall be known as the National Gazette or by such other name as is given by or under an Act of the Parliament.

253. Slavery, and the slave trade in all their forms, and all similar institutions and practices, are strictly prohibited.

254. In principle

(*a*) no constitutional office shall be left unfilled on a substantive basis for longer than is necessary for it to be filed by an appropriate appointee; and

(*b*) no person shall hold more than one public office at the same time except where one such office is so much associated with, or related to, another, or where the holding of one such office is so relevant to the holding of another, as to make it desirable that the offices be held jointly; and

(*c*) public offices of similar importance or standing, and in particular offices in any statutory board or committee, should be filled by persons from the various areas of the country.

255. In principle, where a law provides for consultation between persons or bodies, or persons and bodies, the consultation must be meaningful and allow for a genuine interchange and consideration of views.

256. Subject to this Constitution, an Act of the Parliament may make provision for and in respect of annual and other reports by a constitutional office-holder or any other public office-holder, or by a constitutional institution or any other statutory body.

257. (1) All courts, Judges and persons acting judicially shall take judicial notice of all acts and proceedings of the Constituent Assembly.

(2) An Act of, or the proceedings of, the Constituent Assembly may be proved for any purpose by the production of

(*a*) a certificate under the hand, or purporting to be under the hand, of the Speaker of the pre-Independence House of Assembly; or

(*b*) a document under the hand, or purporting to be under the hand, of the Clerk or other proper officer of the pre-Independence House of Assembly and purporting to be the minutes or other official record of the proceedings of the Constituent Assembly.

258. (1) The Head of State, acting with, and in accordance with, the advice of the National Executive Council, may make regulations, not inconsistent with a Constitutional Law or an Act of the Parliament, prescribing all matters that by a Constitutional Law are required or permitted to be prescribed or provided for by Constitutional Regulation.

(2) All Constitutional Regulation shall be tabled in the Parliament as soon as practicable after being made, and may be disallowed by the Parliament at any time.

259. Unless otherwise provided for by a Constitutional Law, in any case where a Constitutional law requires the appointment of an independent tribunal, the members of that tribunal shall be appointed from a list of names approved by the Judicial and Legal Services Commission.

PART XII

CONSTITUTIONAL REVIEW

260. (1) An Act of the Parliament shall make provision for and in respect of the establishment, at or after the end of the period of three years commencing on Independence Day, of a General Constitutional Commission.

(2) The members of the Commission shall

(*a*) be appointed by the Head of State, acting with, and in accordance with, the advice of the National Executive Council given after consultation with any appropriate parliamentary committee; and

(*b*) be broadly representative of the different areas of the country; and

(*c*) give balanced representation of the major parties and groups in Parliament.

(3) Each member of the General Constitutional Commission must be

(*a*) a member of the Parliament; or

(*b*) a member of a provincial government or local government body; or

(*c*) a member of a State Service; or

(*d*) some other citizen with relevant expertise.

(4) The General Constitutional Commission shall inquire into the working of this Constitution and the Organic Laws.

(5) As soon as is reasonably practicable after its appointement, the General Constitutional Commission shall forward a report of its findings to the Speaker for presentation to the Parliament, together with its recommendations (if any) as to amendment of this Constitution, and new or amended Organic Laws or other laws or administrative procedures.

261. (1) An Act of Parliament shall provide that until the Constitutional Commission is established there shall be an Interim Constitutional Commission the membership of which is in accordance with Section 260(2) and (3) (*General Contitutional Commission*).

(2) The Interim Constitutional Commission shall consider proposed alteration of this Constitution or of any Organic Law, and report to Parliament before there is an opportunity for debate of the proposed legislation.

262. (1) Acts of the Parliament may make provision for and in respect of other commissions and committees to investigate such other aspects of the working of this Constitution as the Parliament thinks desirable.

(2) The commissions and committees established in accordance with Subsection (1)(*b*) shall report to the General Constitutional Commission on the subject matters of their respective investigations, with such recommendations (if any) as they think desirable, in time to allow the General Constitutional Commission to report to the Parliament in accordance with Section 260 (*General Constitutional Commission*).

(3) The General Constitutional Commission shall ensure that any reports of commissions or committees established in accordance with Subsection (1)(*b*) are forwarded to the Speaker for presentation to the Parliament before or at the same time as its report is so forwarded.

263. Acts of the Parliament may make provision for further defining the terms of reference of the General Constitutional Commission and any other commissions or committees established in accordance with Section 262 (*subordinate commissions and committees*).

PART XII

IMMEDIATE AND TRANSITIONAL PROVISIONS

264. The provisions of this Part, and of any Provisional Organic Law or Organic Law made for the purposes of Section 267 (*transitional laws*), have effect notwithstanding anything in the preceding provisions of this Constitution.

265. The Constituent Assembly, having performed its duty to frame and adopt, on behalf of the People, a Constitution, and its other duties, is dissolved.

266. (1) If before Independence Day the Constituent Assembly has made an instrument expressed to be a Provisional Organic Law, the instrument takes effect, on Independence Day, as if it were an Organic Law made and coming into effect on that day.

(2) If before Independence Day the Constituent Assembly has made an instrument expressed to be a Provisional Act of the Parliament made for the purpose of bringing any provision of this Constitution into effective operation on Independence Day, the instrument takes effect, on Independence Day, as if it were an Act of the Parliament made and coming into effect on that day.

267. (1) A Provisional Organic Law or an Organic Law may make whatever provison seems necessary or desirable for a smooth transition from pre-Independence arrangements to arrangements under this Constitution and, in particular, but without limiting the generality of the foregoing, for securing

(*a*) the immediate filling of offices, and the immediately effective operation of institutions under this Constitution where there were corresponding pre-Independence offices or institutions; and

(*b*) the continued effect of acts done or commenced before Independence Day under pre-Independence laws.

(2) A Provisional Organic Law or an Organic Law made for the purposes of Subsection (1) may declare what were the pre-Independence offices and institutions that correspond with offices and institutions under this Constitution.

268. If before Independence Day

(*a*) the Constituent Assembly has nominated by a simple majority vote, in an exhaustive secret ballot a person to be the first Governor-General; and (*b*) Her Majesty, Elizabeth II, having consented to become Queen and Head of Papua New Guinea has signified her approval to that person becoming the Governor-General,

that person becomes the first Governor-General on Independence Day.

269. (1) Notwithstanding anything in this Constitution, but subject to Subsection (6), the open and regional electorates for the pre-Independence House of Assembly established immediately before Independence Day are the first open and provincial (as the case may be) electorates for the Parliament.

(2) Notwithstanding anything in this Constitution but subject to any Organic Law on national electoral matters

(*a*) each member of the pre-Independence House of Assembly in office immediately before Independence Day (including a member who although he is or may be disqualified under Section 37 (4)(*a*) of the *Papua New Guinea Act* 1949-1975 of Australia has been confirmed in his membership by resolution of the House of Assembly) is the first member of the Parliament for his electorate and shall continue to hold office unless or until

(i) his seat becomes vacant by virtue of Section 104(2)(*a*), (*b*), (*c*), (*d*), (*e*), (*g*) or (*h*) (*normal term of office*); or

(ii) he becomes a person who has been convicted of and is under sentence of imprisonment, or is subject to be sentenced (other than a person who has been released on recognizance to appear and receive judgement when called upon), for an offence punishable by imprisonment for one year or longer, as in Section 50(1)(*a*) (*right to vote and stand for public office*); or

(iii) he becomes disqualified under Section 103(3)(*b*) or (*d*) (*qualifications for and disqualifications from membership*); and

(*b*) the pre-Independence Speaker and Chairman of Committees in office immediately before Independence Day are the first Speaker and Deputy Speaker, respectively, of the Parliament; and

(*c*) the electoral rolls in effect immediately before Independence Day are the first electoral rolls for the first open and provincial electorates (as the case may be).

(3) The Boundaries Commission shall recommend to the Parliament the number of open electorates and their boundaries for determination by the Parliament under Section 125(1) (*electorates*) as soon as possible after Independence Day.

(4) Unless a general election to the Parliament is held earlier under Section 105 (*general elections*) the term of the first Parliament is

(*a*) the balance of the term of the pre-Independence House of Assembly remaining unexpended immediately after Independence Day; and (*b*) the period up to the first general election held after Independence Day and the first general elections shall be held, as directed by the Head of State, acting with, and in accordance with, the advice of the Electoral Commission, in the months May and June 1977.

(5) If the Parliament has not made a determination under Section 125(1) (*electorates*) in time for the first general elections held after Independence Day

(*a*) the number and boundaries of the open electorates shall remain the same as for the previous general elections; and

(*b*) the number of provincial electorates shall be as determined by an Organic Law; and

(*c*) the boundaries of the provincial electorates shall be as detemined by the Head of State, acting with, and in accordance with, the advice of the Boundaries Commission, but so that the boundaries of the provincial electorates

(i) enclose all the territory of open electorates within each province; and

(ii) so near as may be, coincide with the boundaries of the provinces as defined in the Organic Law on Provincial Boundaries and the boundaries of the National Capital District as defined in the Organic Law on the Boundaries of the National Capital District.

(6) If a provincial electorate consists of two or more provinces, an Organic Law shall make adequate provision for

(*a*) the declaration of each province as a provincial electorate; and

(*b*) each electorate to be represented by a provincial member, as soon as practicable after Independence Day.

270. (1) The pre-Independence Chief Minister in office immediately before Independence Day is the first Prime Minister.

(2) The other Ministers of the pre-Independence House of Assembly in office immediately before Independence Day are the other first Ministers.

271. Notwithstanding anything in this Constitution

(*a*) the pre-Independence Chief Justice in office immediately before Independece Day is the first Chief Justice of Papua New Guinea; and

(*b*) the Senior Puisne Judge in office immediately before Independence Day is the First Deputy Chief Justice of Papua New Guinea; and

(*c*) each Judge in office immediately before Independence Day is a Judge of the National Court; and

(*d*) each acting Judge in office immediately before Independence Day is an Acting Judge of the National Court,

on the same terms and conditions that were applicable to him before Independence Day but in no case shall his term of office exceed three years from the date of his present appointment.

272. (1) Notwithstanding anything in this Constitution, but subject to Section 250 (*making of Declaration of Loyalty, etc.*) and Section 251 (*taking certain oaths, etc., by non-citizens*)

(*a*) the first Governor-General shall take the Oath of Allegiance and make the Declaration of Loyalty and the Declaration of Office; and

(*b*) the first Prime Minister and other Ministers, and the first Speaker and Deputy Speaker, shall make the Declaration of Loyalty and the Declaration of Office; and

(*c*) the first Chief Justice and other Judges shall make the Judicial Declaration,

in public on Independence Day, at such place, and in such manner and form, as are directed by the Prime Minister.

(2) If it is not practicable for a person referred to in Subsection (1)(*a*), (*b*) or (*c*) to comply with the requirements of Subsection (1), he shall take and make the necessary oath or declarations, or both, as the case requires, at such time and place, and in such manner and form, as are directed by the Head of State, acting with, and in accordance with, the advice of the Prime Minister.

(3) Any provision of this Constitution preventing a person referred to in Subsection (1)(*a*), (*b*) or (*c*) from entering upon the duties of his office until he has taken the Oath of Allegiance or made the Declaration of Loyalty, the Declaration of Office or the Judicial Declaration (as the case requires) is suspended pending compliance with the preceding provisions of this section.

273. The provisions of Section 117 (*treaties, etc.*) do not prevent the Head of State, acting with, and in accordance with, the advice of the National Executive Council, from making a declaration that an international commitment, that, immediately before Independence Day, applied to the territory at that time known as Papua New Guinea or a component part of that territory may, by agreement, be treated as if it were binding on Papua New Guinea for a period not exceeding five years after that day.

274. Except where expressly provided otherwise in a Constitutional Law, until 16 September 1985, where a constitutional institution other than the Supreme Court or the National Court is composed of more than one person, the majority of those persons must be citizens, but failure to comply with this section does not invalidate any act of the institution.

275. Until 16 September 1985, in addition to persons who are qualified to be appointed as Judges of the National Court, a person who holds office as a magistrate of the highest grade or classification is eligible for appointment as Chairman of a tribunal appointed in accordance with Section 245(1)(*e*) (*internment*).

SCHEDULES
(*Not reproduced*)

PHILIPPINES

SUMMARY

INTERNATIONAL STATUS

The Philippines is a member of the United Nations (October 24, 1945). It is a member of other international organizations. It ratified in 1974 the International Convention on Social, Economic and Cultural Rights.

The Philippines became independent on July 4, 1946, pursuant to an Act of the United States Congress signed on March 24, 1934, which established a ten years transitional period at the end of which independence would automatically be effective.

The Philippines were a Spanish colony from 1565. Nationalism and movements for independence began in the mid-nineteenth century. On August 26, 1896, an insurrection broke out and on June 12, 1898, the Philippines proclaimed their independence and the establishment of a provisional republic. The Spanish-American war had begun in the meanwhile, and by the treaty between the United States and Spain of December 10, 1898 the islands were ceded to the United States. The Filipinos continued to maintain their independence, proclaimed the Malolos Constitution of January 23, 1899 and continued fighting the United States forces until 1901. Their continuing campaign for independence resulted in the Tydings-McDuffie Act of 1934 making the country a self-governing Commonwealth and providing for independence in ten years. The Act was ratified by the Philippine legislature on May 1, 1934, and the Constitution drawn up by a Constituent Convention on May 14, 1935. From 1942 to 1945, the islands were occupied by Japan.

Economic misery and the continuing will to independence favored the peasant rebellion of 1930 to 1940, and developed into the Huk rebellion against the Japanese occupiers. After the end of the war, guerilla activity continued under the leadership of the communist New People's Army. During the 1970's, a Moslem movement for secession, originating in the age-long conflict between Christians and Moslems who consider themselves, as the Moro nation, the original Filipinos, gained amplitude in southern Mindanao where in five of the thirteen provinces the Moslems are the majority of the population. The Moslem National Liberation Front has led that rebellion.

Ferdinand Marcos won the 1965 presidential elections and, in 1972, before the expiration of his second and constitutionally last term, proclaimed martial law, suspended the legislature, imposed press censorship, arrested the leaders of the opposition and disbanded the private armies of the landed oligarchy. Elections were held for a constitutional assembly in 1970 and the new Constitution was approved by a referendum of January 1973. A referendum held in December 1977 approved the President's policies and the continuation of martial law. The April 1978 elections to the interim legislative assembly were followed by the arrest of opposition leaders and the reimposition of martial law. President Marcos under the transitional articles of the Constitution (Article XVII), continued as President under the 1935 Constitution with the powers granted by that Constitution and also occupied the post of Prime Minister under the 1973 one. The Constitutional amendments approved by referendum on April 7 1981, restored the powers of the President and provided for his direct election. For the elections held in June 1981, martial law was lifted and President Marcos was reelected. He has announced an end to the transitional period and elections for the legislature in 1984.

FORM OF NATIONAL GOVERNMENT

The Constitution of January 17, 1973, was approved by referendum of January 10 to 15, 1973 and provided a parliamentary system in the place of the presidential system of the preceding Constitution of February 8, 1935. The amendments of 1976 and 1981 restored the powers of the President in the Constitution itself, while under the transitional provisions (Article XVII), which continued operative during the state of martial law, it is provided that the provisions of the 1935 Constitution concerning the President continue to be applicable.

The Constitution provides that the Philippines is a republican State; sovereignty resides in the people; the defense of the State is a prime duty of the Government and the people.[1] The Philippines renounce war as an instrument of national policy will promote and strengthen the family, youth, social justice, protection of labor, autonomy of local government units; civilian authority is superior to military.[2] A chapter concerning the national economy and patrimony of the nation provides for the regulation of monopolies, the limitation of foreign investors, lands of the public domain, conservation, agrarian reform.[3] The separation of church and state

[1] Const., Art. II. [2] Id., Art. II: 3–10. [3] Id., Art. XIV.

is inviolable.[4] No religious sect may be registered as a political party and no party seeking its goal through violence may be accredited.[5]

RIGHTS OF THE PEOPLE

The Constitution guarantees due process of law. the right to property, security against search and seizure, freedom of residence and travel, privacy of communications and correspondence. freedom of association, religion, speech, press, assembly, petition; it forbids titles, *ex post facto* laws, imprisonment for debt, involuntary servitude, witnessing against oneself, excessive fines, cruel and unusual punishment and double jeopardy; it ensures the right of *habeas corpus* and free access to the courts for all.[6] The duties and obligations of citizens include loyalty to the Republic, defense of the State, co-operation with the authorities in the attainment and preservation of a just and orderly society; voting is obligatory.[7]

LEGISLATIVE DEPARTMENT

Legislative power is vested in the *Batasang Pambansa*, composed of not more than 200 members including representatives elected from regions of the Philippines, those elected or selected from various sectors as provided by law, and those chosen by the President from members of the Cabinet.[8] The *Batasang Pambansa* is elected for a term of 6 years and is subject to dissolution.[9] It convenes once a year in regular session.[10] Privileges and immunities are provided and incompatibilities of office described.[11] There are provisions concerning finance bills.[12] Bills passed by the *Batasang Pambansa* are presented to the President for signature; if vetoed, the bill can become law only if passed again by a two-thirds majority vote.[13] The *Batasang Pambansa* may withhold its confidence from the Prime Minister and the President submits a nominee to be elected by it.[14] The 1976 and 1981 amendments to the Constitution provide an interim *Batasang Pambansa* (the legislature had been suspended by martial law) of not more than 120 members and the incumbent President of the Philippines.

EXECUTIVE DEPARTMENT

Executive power is exercised by the President, Head of State and Chief Executive, elected by direct vote for a renewable term of 6 years.[15] The President has control of the ministries, is Commander-in-Chief and when public safety so requires may suspend *habeas corpus* and place the Philippines or any part of it under martial law.[16] He has the power of appointment, the right of pardon.[17] There is provision

[4] Id., Art. XV: 15.
[5] Id., Art. XII: 8.
[6] Id., Art. IV.
[7] Id., Art. V.
[8] Id., Art. VIII: 1, 2.
[9] Id., Art. VIII: 3, 13.
[10] Id., Art. VIII: 6.
[11] Id., Art. VIII: 9, 10, 11.
[12] Id., Art. VIII: 16–18.
[13] Id., Art. VIII: 20.
[14] Id., Art. VIII: 13.
[15] Id., Art. VII: 1–3.
[16] Id., Art. VII: 8, 9.
[17] Id., Art. VII: 10, 11.

for a Cabinet of Ministers appointed by the President and a Prime Minister nominated by the President from among the members of the *Batasang Pambansa* and elected by a majority of its members.[18] An Executive Committee is stipulated, designated by the President and composed of the Prime Minister and not more than 14 other members, at least half of which must be members of the legislature, to assist the President in the exercise of his powers.[19]

There are provisions concerning local government,[20] the Constitutional Commissions on the civil service, elections and the audit,[21] the accountability of public officers,[22] the National Economic and Development Authority.[23]

Under the 1976 and 1981 amendments the incumbent President is also Prime Minister and exercises his powers under the 1935 Constitution and legislative powers until the lifting of martial law.

JUDICIAL DEPARTMENT

Judicial power is vested in the Supreme Court and inferior courts.[24] The Supreme Court is composed of a Chief Justice and 14 Associate Justices appointed by the President and holding office during good behavior until the age of 70.[25] Its powers include pronouncing on the constitutionality of treaties and laws.[26] The Supreme Court has administrative supervision over all courts and the personnel thereof.[27]

AREA, POPULATION, ETC.

The area of the Philippines (land area composed of 7000 islands of which 9 are the large main islands) is 299,681 square kilometres, its population (1981 census) 48,098,460. The official languages are English and Pilipino and the latter is to be developed into a common national language.[28]

[18] Id., Art. IX: 1, 2.
[19] Id., Art. IX: 3.
[20] Id., Art. XI.
[21] Id., Art. XII.
[22] Id., Art. XIII.
[23] Id., Art. XIV.
[24] Id., Art. X: 1.
[25] Id., Art. X: 2, 3, 4, 7.
[26] Id., Art. X: 2, 5.
[27] Id., Art. X: 6.
[28] Id., Art. XV: 3.

CONSTITUTION OF THE REPUBLIC OF THE PHILIPPINES[1]

January 7, 1973, as amended 1976 and 1981

PREAMBLE

We, the sovereign Filipino people, imploring the aid of Divine Providence, in order to establish a Government that shall embody our ideals, promote the general welfare, conserve and develop the patrimony of our Nation, and secure for ourselves and our posterity the blessings of democracy under a regime of justice, peace, liberty, and equality, do ordain and promulgate this Constitution.

ARTICLE I

THE NATIONAL TERRITORY

Sec. 1. The National territory comprises the Philippine archipelago, with all the islands and water embraced therein, and all the other territories belonging to the Philippines by historic right or legal title including the territorial sea, the air space, the subsoil, the sea-bed, the insular shelves, and the other submarine areas over which the Philippines has sovereignty or jurisdiction. The waters around, between, and connecting the islands of the archipelago, irrespective of their breadth and dimensions, form part of the internal waters of the Philippines.

ARTICLE II

DECLARATION OF PRINCIPLES AND STATE POLICIES

Sec. 1. The Philippines is a republican state. Sovereignty resides in the people and all government authority emanates from them.

Sec. 2. The defense of the State is a prime duty of the Government and the people, and in the fulfilment of his duty all citizens may be required by law to render personal military or civil service.

Sec. 3. The Philippines renounces war as an instrument of national policy, adopts the generally accepted principles of international law as part of the law of the land and adheres to the policy of peace, equality, justice, freedom, co-operation, and amity with all nations.

Sec. 4. The State shall strengthen the family as basic social institution. The natural right and duty of the parents in the rearing of the youth for civic efficency and the development of moral character shall receive the aid and support of the Government.

[1] 'The Philippine Foreign Service Reader – 1981', published by the Foreign Service Institute, Manila. Supplied by Ministry of Foreign Affairs in March 1982. Ed.

Sec. 5. The State recognizes the vital role of the youth in nation-building and shall promote their physical, intellectual, and social well-being.

Sec. 6. The State shall promote social justice to ensure the dignity, welfare, and security of all the people. Towards this end, the State shall regulate the acquisition, ownership, use, enjoyment, and disposition of private property, and equitably diffuse property ownership and profits.

Sec. 7. The State shall establish, maintain, and ensure adequate social services in the field of education, health, housing, employment, welfare, and social security to guarantee the enjoyment by the people of a decent standard of living.

Sec. 8. Civilian authority is at all times supreme over the military.

Sec. 9. The State shall afford protection to labor, promote full employment and equality in employment, ensure equal work opportunities regardless of sex, race or creed, and regulate the relations between workers and employers. The State shall assure the rights of workers to self-organization, collective bargaining, security of tenure and just and humane conditions of work. The State may provide for compulsory arbitration.

Sec. 10. The State shall guarantee and promote the autonomy of local government units, especially the barrio, to ensure their fullest development as self-reliant communities.

ARTICLE III

CITIZENSHIP

Sec. 1. The following are citizens of the Philippines:

(1) Those who are citizens of the Philippines at the time of the adoption of the Constitution.

(2) Those whose fathers or mothers are citizens of the Philippines.

(3) Those who elect Philippine citizenship pursuant to the provision of the Constituton of nineteen hundred and thirty-five.

(4) Those who are naturalized in accordance with law.

Sec. 2. A female citizen of the Philippines who marries an alien shall retain her Philippine citizenship, unless by her act or omission she is deemed, under the law, to have renounced her citizenship.

Sec. 3. Philippine citizenship may be lost or reacquired in the manner provided by law.

Sec. 4. A natural-born citizen is one who is a citizen of the Philippines from birth without having to perform any act to acquire or perfect his Philippine citizenship.

ARTICLE IV

BILL OF RIGHTS

Sec. 1. No person shall be deprived of life, liberty, or property without due process of law, nor shall any person be denied the equal protection of the law.

Sec. 2. Private property shall not be taken for public use without just compensation.

Sec. 3. The right of the people to be secure in their person, houses, papers and effects against unreasonable searches and seizures of whatever nature and for any purpose shall not be violated, and no search warrant or warrant of arrest shall issue except upon probable cause to be determined by the judge, or such other responsible officer as may be authorized by law, after examination under oath or affirmation of the complainant and the witnesses he may produce, and particularly describing the place to be searched, and the persons or things to be seized.

Sec. 4. (1) The privacy of communication and correspondence shall be inviolable except upon lawful order of the court, or when public safety and order require otherwise.

(2) Any evidence obtained in violation of this or the preceding section shall be inadmissible for any purpose in any proceeding.

Sec. 5. The liberty of abode and of travel shall not be impaired except upon lawful order of the court, or when necessary in the interest of national security, public safety, or public health.

Sec. 6. The right of the people to information on matters of public concern shall be recognized. Access to official records, and to documents and papers pertaining to official acts, transactions, or decisions, shall be afforded the citizen subject to such limitations as may be provided by law.

Sec. 7. The right to form associations or societies for purposes not contrary to law shall not be abridged.

Sec. 8. No law shall be made respecting an establishment of religion, or prohibiting the free exercise thereof. The free exercise and enjoyment of religious profession and worship, without discrimination or preference, shall forever be allowed. No religious test shall be required for the exercise of civil or political rights.

Sec. 9. No law shall be passed abridging the freedom of speech, or of the press, or the right of the people peaceably to assemble and petition the Government for redress of grievances.

Sec. 10. No law granting a title of royalty or nobility shall be enacted.

Sec. 11. No law impairing the obligation of contracts shall be passed.

Sec. 12. No *ex post facto* law or bill or attainder shall be enacted.

Sec. 13. No person shall be imprisoned for debt or non-payment of a poll tax.

Sec. 14. No involuntary servitude in any form shall exist as a punishment for a crime whereof the party shall have been duly convicted.

Sec. 15. The privilege of the writ of *habeas corpus* shall not be suspended except in case of invasion, insurrection, rebellion, or imminent danger thereof, when the public safety requires it.

Sec. 16. All persons have the right to a speedy disposition of their cases before all judicial, quasi-judicial, or administrative bodies.

Sec. 17. No person shall be held to answer for a criminal offense without due process of law.

Sec. 18. All persons except those charged with capital offenses when evidence of guilt is strong, shall before conviction, be bailable by sufficient sureties. Excessive bail shall not be required.

Sec. 19. In all criminal prosecutions, the accused shall be presumed innocent until the contrary is proved, and shall enjoy the right to be heard by himself and counsel, to be informed of the nature and cause of the accusation against him, to have a speedy, impartial, and public trial, to meet the witnesses face to face, and to have compulsory process to secure the attendance of witnesses and the production of evidence in his behalf. However, after arraignment, trial may proceed notwithstanding the absence of the accused provided that he has been duly notified and his failure to appear is unjustified.

Sec. 20. No person shall be compelled to be a witness against himself. Any person under investigation for the commission of an offense shall have the right to remain silent and to counsel, and to be informed of such right. No force, violence, threat, intimidation or any other means which violates the free will shall be used against him. Any confession obtained in violation of this section shall be inadmissible as evidence.

Sec. 21. Excessive fines shall not be imposed, nor cruel or unusual punishment inflicted.

Sec. 22. No person shall be twice put in jeopardy of punishment for the same offense. If an act is punished by a law and an ordinance, conviction or acquittal under either shall constitute a bar to another prosecution for the same act.

Sec. 23. Free access to the courts shall not be denied to any person by reason of poverty.

ARTICLE V

DUTIES AND OBLIGATIONS OF CITIZENS

Sec. 1. It shall be the duty of the citizen to be loyal to the Republic and to honor the Philippine flag, to defend the State and contribute to its development and welfare, to uphold the Constitution and obey the laws, and to cooperate with the duly constituted authorities in the attainment and preservation of a just and orderly society.

Sec. 2. The rights of the individual impose upon him the correlative duty to exercise them responsibly and with due regard for the rights of others.

Sec. 3. It shall be the duty of every citizen to engage in gainful work to assure himself and his family a life worthy of human dignity.

Sec. 4. It shall be obligation of every citizen qualified to vote to register and cast his vote.

ARTICLE VI

SUFFRAGE

Sec. 1. Suffrage shall be exercised by citizens of the Philippines not otherwise disqualified by law, who are eighteen years of age or over, and who shall have resided in the Philippines for at least one year and in the place wherein they propose to vote for at least six months preceding the election. No literacy, property, or other substantive requirement shall be imposed on the exercise of suffrage. The *Batasang Pambansa* shall provide a system for the purpose of securing the secrecy and sanctity of the vote.

ARTICLE VII

THE PRESIDENT

Sec. 1. The President shall be the head of state and chief executive of the Republic of the Philippines.

Sec. 2. No person may be elected President unless he is a natural-born citizen of the Philippines, a registered voter, able to read and write, at least fifty years of age on the day of election for President, and a resident of the Philippines for at least ten years immediately preceding such election.

Sec. 3. The President shall be elected by direct vote of the people for a term of six years which shall begin at noon on the thirtieth day of June following the day of the election and shall end at noon of the same date six years thereafter when the term of his successor shall begin.

The returns of every election for President, duly certified by the board of canvassers of each province or city, shall be transmitted to the Speaker at the *Batasang Pambansa*, who shall, not later than thirty days after the day of the election, and in the presence of the *Batasang Pambansa*, open all the certificates and the votes shall then be counted.

The person having the highest number of votes shall be proclaimed elected; but in case two or more shall have an equal and the highest number of votes, one of them shall forthwith be chosen by a vote of a majority of all the Members of the *Batasang Pambansa* in session assembled.

Sec. 4. If, at the time fixed for the beginning of his term, the President-elect shall have died or shall have failed to qualify or if the President shall not have been chosen, the Executive Committee, headed by the Prime Minister as hereinafter provided, shall exercise the power and discharge the duties of the President until a President shall have been elected and qualified. If the *Batasang Pambansa* withdraws its confidence in the Prime Minister the Speaker shall preside over the Executive Committee. In the absence of an Executive Committee, the Speaker of the *Batsang Pambansa* shall act as President until a President shall have been elected and qualified.

In the event of death or failure to qualify as herein provided, the *Batasang Pambansa* shall call a special election in the manner prescribed in Section 7 hereof.

Sec. 5. The President, on assuming office, shall take the following oath or affirmation.

'I do solemnly swear (or affirm) that I will faithfully and conscientiously fulfil my duties as President of the Philippines, preserve and defend its Constitution, execute its laws, do justice to every man and consecrate myself to the service of the nation. So help me God.' (In case of affirmation, the last sentence is omitted).

Sec. 6. (1) The President shall have an official residence and shall receive a compensation to be fixed by law, which shall not be increased or decreased during his term of office. He shall not receive during his tenure any other emoluments from the Government or any other source. Until the *Batasang Pambansa* shall provide otherwise, the President shall receive an annual salary of one hundred thousand pesos.

(2) The President shall not, during his tenure, hold any other office, practice any profession, participate directly in the management of any business, or be financially interested directly or indirectly in any contract with, or in any franchise or special privilege granted by the Government or any subdivision, agency, or instrumentality thereof, including any Government-owned or controlled corporation.

Sec. 7. In case of permanent disability, death, removal from office or resignation of the President, the Executive Committee headed by the Prime Minister as hereinafter provided shall exercise the powers of the President until a President shall have been elected and qualified. If the permanent disability, death, removal from office or resignation of the President occurs earlier than eighteen months before the expiration of his term, the *Batasang Pambansa* shall, within thirty days from the time the vacancy occurs, call a special election to be held not earlier than forty five days nor later than sixty days from the time of such call, to elect a President to serve the unexpired term.

In the absence of an Executive Committee, the Speaker shall act as President until the President shall have been elected and qualified.

Sec. 8. The President shall have control of the ministries.

Sec. 9. The President shall be Commander-in-Chief of all Armed Forces of the Philippines and, whenever it becomes necessary, he may call out such armed forces to prevent or suppress lawless violence, invasion, insurrection or rebellion. In case of invasion, insurrection or rebellion, or imminent danger thereof, when the public safety requires it, he may suspend the privilege of the writ of *habeas corpus*, or place the Philippines or any part thereof under martial law.

Sec. 10. The President shall appoint the heads of bureaus and offices, the officers of the armed forces of the Philippines from the rank of brigadier general or commodore, and all other officers of the Government whose appointments are not otherwise provided for, and those whom he may be authorized by law to appoint. However, the *Batasang Pambansa* may by law vest in the Prime Minister, members of the Cabinet, the Executive Committee, courts, heads of agencies, commissions, and boards the power to appoint inferior offices.

Sec. 11. The President may, except in cases of impeachment, grant reprieves, commutations and pardons, remit fines and forfeitures, and with the concurrence of the *Batasang Pambansa*, grant amnesty.

Sec. 12. The President may contract and guarantee foreign and domestic loans on behalf of the Republic of the Philippines subject to such limitations as may be provided by law.

Sec. 13. The President shall formulate the guidelines of national policy.

Sec. 14. The President shall address the *Batasang Pambansa* at the opening of its regular session. He may also appear before it at any other time.

Sec. 15. The President shall be immune from suit during his tenure. Thereafter, no suit whatsoever shall lie for official acts done by him or by others pursuant to his specific orders during his tenure.

The immunities herein provided shall apply to the incumbent President referred to in Article XVII of this Consitution.

Sec. 16. All powers vested in the President of the Philippines under the 1935 Constitution and the laws of the land which are not herein provided for or conferred upon any official shall be deemed and are hereby vested in the President unless the *Batasang Pambansa* provides otherwise.

ARTICLE VIII

BATASANG PAMBANSA

Sec. 1. The Legislative power shall be vested in a *Batasang Pambansa.*

Sec. 2. The *Batasang Pambansa*, which shall be composed of not more than 200 Members unless otherwise provided by law, shall include representatives elected from the different regions of the Philippines, those elected or selected from various sectors as may be provided by law, and those chosen by the President from the members of the Cabinet. Regional representatives shall be appointed among the regions in accordance with the number of their respective inhabitants and on the basis of a uniform and progressive ratio.

The number of representatives from each region and the manner of their election shall be prescribed by law. The number of representatives from each sector and the manner of their election or selection shall be prescribed by law.

Sec. 3. (1) The Members of the *Batasang Pambansa* shall have a term of six years which shall begin, unless otherwise provided by law, at noon on the thirieth day of June next following their election.

(2) In case the *Batasang Pambansa* is dissolved, the newly elected Members shall serve the unexpired portion of the term from the time the President convokes the Assembly, which shall not be later than thirty days immediately following their election.

Sec. 4. No person shall be a Member of the *Batasang Pambansa* as a regional representative unless he is a natural-born citizen of he Philippines and, on the day of the election, is at least twenty-five years of age, able to read and write, a registered voter in the Region in which he shall be elected, and a resident thereof for a period of not less than one year immediately preceding the day of the election.

A sectoral representative shall be a natural-born citizen, able to read and write, and shall have such other qualifications as may be provided by law.

Sec. 5. (1) The regular election of the Members of the *Batasang Pambansa* shall be held on the second Monday of May 1984 and every six years thereafter.

(2) In case a vacancy arises in the *Batasang Pambansa* eighteen months or more before a regular election the Commission on Elections shall call a special election to be held within sixty days after the vacancy occurs to elect the Member to serve the unexpired term.

Sec. 6. The *Batasang Pambansa* shall convene once every year on the fourth Monday of July for its regular session, unless a different date is fixed by law. and shall continue to be in session for such number of days as it may determine. However, it may be called to session at any time by the President to consider such subjects or legislation as he may designate.

Sec. 7. (1) The *Batasang Pambansa* shall, by a majority vote of all its Members, elect its Speaker from the Members thereof. It shall choose such other officers at it may deem necessary.

(2) A majority of all the Members of the *Batasang Pambansa* shall constitute a quorum to dó business, but a smaller number may adjourn from day to day and may compel the attendance of absent Members in such manner, and under such penalties, as the *Batasang Pambansa* may provide.

(3) The *Batasang Pambansa* may determine the rules of its proceedings punish its Members for disorderly behavior, and with the concurrence of two thirds of all its Members, suspend or expel a Member, but if the penalty is suspension, this shall not exceed sixty days.

(4) The *Batasang Pambansa* shall keep a Journal of its proceedings, and from time to time publish the same, excepting such parts as may, in its judgment, affect national security; and the yeas and nays on any question shall, at the request of one fifth of the Members present, be entered in the Journal.

Sec. 8. (1) Unless otherwise provided by law, each Member of the *Batasang Pambansa* shall receive an annual salary of sixty thousand pesos. The Speaker of the *Batasang Pambansa* shall receive an annual salary of seventy five thousand pesos. No increase in salary shall take effect until after the expiration of the term of the Members of the *Batasang Pambansa* approving such increase.

(2) The records and books of accounts of the *Batasang Pambansa*, shall be open to the public in accordance with law, and such books shall be audited by the Commission on Audit which shall publish annually the itemized expenditures for each Member.

Sec. 9. A Member of the *Batasang Pambansa* shall, in all offenses punishable by not more than six years imprisonment, be privileged from arrest during his attendance at its sessions, and in going to and returning from the same; but the *Batasang*

Pambansa shall surrender the Member involved to the custody of the law within twenty four hours after its adjournment for a recess or for its next session, otherwise such privilege shall cease upon its failure to do so. A Member shall not be questioned nor be held liable in any other place for any speech or debate in the Batasang or in any committee thereof.

Sec. 10. A Member of the *Batasang Pambansa* shall not hold any other office or employment in the Government, or any subdivision, agency or instrumentality thereof, including Government-owned or controlled corporations during his tenure except that of the Prime Minister, Deputy Prime Minister, member of the Cabinet or the Executive Committee, or Deputy Minister. Neither shall he, during the term for which he was elected, be appointed to any civil office which may have been created or the emoluments thereof increased while he was a Member of the *Batasang Pambansa.*

Sec. 11. No Member of the *Batasang Pambansa* shall appear as counsel before any court without appellate jurisdiction, before any court in any civil case wherein the Government, or any subdivision, agency or instrumentality thereof is the adverse party, or in any criminal case wherein any officer or employee of the Government is accused of an offense committed in relation to his office, or before any administrative body. Neither shall he, directly or indirectly, be interested financially in any contract with, or in any subdivision, agency or instrumentality thereof, including any Government-owned or controlled corporation, during his term of office. He shall not accept employment to intervene in any cause of matter where he may be called upon to act on account of his office.

Sec. 12. (1) There shall be a question hour at least once a month or as often as the Rules of the *Batasang Pambansa* may provide, which shall be included in its agenda, during which the Prime Minister, the Deputy Prime Minister or any Minister may be required to appear and answer questions and interpellations by Members of the *Batasang Pambansa.* Written questions shall be submitted to the Speaker at least three days before a scheduled question hour. Interpellation shall not be limited to the written questions, but may cover matters related thereto. The agenda shall specify the subjects of the question hour. When the security of he State so requires and the President so states in writing, the question hour shall be conducted in executive session.

(2) The *Batasang Pambansa* or any of its committees may conduct inquiries in aid of legislation in accordance with its duly published rules of procedure. The rights of persons appearing in or affected by such inquires shall be respected.

Sec. 13. (1) The *Batasang Pambansa* may withdraw its confidence in the Prime Minister by a majority vote of all its Members. The motion for a vote of no confidence shall be calendared for debate if it is signed by at least one fifth of the Members of the *Batasang Pambansa.* No such motion shall be debated and voted upon until after the lapse of seven days after its submission.

Within ten days from receipt of the written advice of the approval of the motion of no confidence the President may submit a nominee for a Prime Minister to be elected by the *Batasang Pambansa.*

(2) The Prime Minister may advise the President in writing to dissolve the *Batasang Pambansa* whenever the need arises for a popular vote of confidence on fundamental issues, but not on a matter involving his own personal intergrity. Whereupon, the President may dissolve the *Batasang Pambansa* not earlier than seven nor later than fourteen days from his receipt of the advice, and call for an election on a date set by him which shall not be earlier than forty five nor later than sixty days from the date of such dissolution. However, no dissolution of the *Batasang Pambansa* shall take place within eighteen months immediately preceding a regular election of the *Batasang Pambansa* or within eighteen months immediately following such election, or during the pendency of impeachment proceedings against the President, or when the powers of the President are exercised by the Executive Committee or the Speaker. The *Batasang Pambansa* shall not be dissolved oftener than once every twelve months.

Sec. 14. (1) Except as otherwise provided in this Constitution, no treaty shall be valid and effective unless concurred in by a majority of all the Members of the *Batasang Pambansa.*

(2) The *Batasang Pambansa*, by vote of two thirds of all its Members shall have the sole power to declare the existence of a state war.

Sec. 15. In times of war or other national emergency, the *Batasang Pambansa* may by law authorize the President for a limited period and subject to such restrictions as it may prescribe, to exercise powers necessary and proper to carry out a declared national policy. Unless sooner withdrawn by resolution of the *Batasang Pambansa*, such powers shall cease upon its next adjournment.

Sec. 16. (1) The Prime Minister shall submit to the *Batasang Pambansa* within thirty days from the opening of each regular session, as the basis of the general appropriations bill, a budget of receipts based on existing and proposed revenue measures, and of expenditures. The form, content and manner of preparation of the budget shall be prescribed by law.

(2) No provision or enactment shall be embraced in the general appropriations bill unless it relates specifically to some particular appropriation therein. Any such provision or enactment shall be limited in its operation to the appropriation to which it relates.

(3) The procedure in approving appropriations for the *Batasang Pambansa* shall strictly follow the procedure for approving appropriations for other departments and agencies.

(4) A special appropriations bill shall specify the purpose for which it is intended, and shall be supported by funds actually available as certified to by the National Treasurer, or to be raised by a corresponding revenue proposal included therein.

(5) No law shall be passed authorizing any transfer of appropriations; however, the President, the Prime Minister, the Speaker, the Chief Justice of the Supreme Court, and the heads of Constitutional Commissions may by law be authorized to augment any items in the general appropriations law for their respective offices from savings in other items of their respective appropriations.

(6) If, by the end of any fiscal year, the *Batasang Pambansa* shall have failed to pass the general appropriations bill for the ensuing fiscal year, the general appropriations law for the preceding fiscal year shall be deemed re-enacted and shall remain in force and effect until the general appropriations bill is passed by the *Batasang Pambansa.*

Sec. 17. (1) The rule of taxation shall be uniform and equitable. The *Batasang Pambansa* shall evolve a progressive system of taxation.

(2) The *Batasang Pambansa* may by law authorize the President to fix within specified limits, and subject to such limitations and restrictions as it may impose, tariff rates, import and export quotas, tonnage and wharfage dues, and other duties or imposts.

(3) Charitable institutions, churches, parsonages or convents appurtenant thereto, mosques, and non-profit cemeteries, and all lands, buildings and improvements actually, directly and exclusively used for religious or charitable purposes shall be exempt from taxation.

(4) No law granting any tax exemption shall be passed without concurrence of a majority of all the Members of the *Batasang Pambansa.*

Sec. 18. (1) No money shall be paid out of the Treasury except in pursuance of an appropriation made by law.

(2) No public money or property shall ever be appropriated, applied, paid or used directly or indirectly, for the use, benefit or support of any sect, church, denomination, sectarian institution or system of religion, or for the use, benefit or support of any priest, preacher, minister or other religious teacher or dignitary as such, except when such priest, preacher, minister or dignitary is assigned to the armed forces, or to any penal institution, or government orphanage or leprosarium.

Sec. 19. (1) Every bill shall embrace only one subject which shall be expressed in the title thereof.

(2) No bill shall become a law unless it has passed three readings on separate days, and printed copies thereof in its final form have been distributed to the Members three days before its passage, except when the Prime Minister certifies to the necessity of its immediate enactment to meet a public calamity or emergency. Upon the last reading of a bill, no amendment thereto shall be allowed, and the vote thereon shall be taken immediately thereafter, and the yeas and nays entered in the Journal.

Sec. 20. (1) Every bill passed by the *Batasang Pambansa* shall, before it becomes a law, be presented to the President. If he approves the same, he shall sign it; otherwise, he shall veto it and return the same with his objections to the *Batasang Pambansa.* The bill may be reconsidered by the *Batasang Pambansa* and, if approved by two thirds of all the Members, shall become a law. The President shall act on every bill passed by the *Batasang Pambansa* within thirty days after the date of receipt thereof, otherwise, it shall become a law as if he had signed it.

(2) The President shall have the power to veto any particular item or items in an appropriation, revenue or tariff bill, but the veto shall not affect the item or items to which he does not object.

ARTICLE IX

THE PRIME MINISTER, THE CABINET AND THE EXECUTIVE COMMITTEE

Sec. 1. There shall be a Cabinet which shall be composed of Ministers with or without portfolio appointed by the President. At least a majority of the Members of the Cabinet who are heads of ministries shall come from the Regional representatives of the *Batasang Pambansa.*

The Prime Minister shall be the head of the Cabinet. He shall, upon the nomination of the President from among the Members of the *Batasang Pambansa*, be elected by a majority of all the Members thereof.

Sec. 2. The Prime Minister and the Cabinet shall be responsible to the *Batasang Pambansa* for the program of government approved by the President.

Sec. 3. There shall be an Executive Committee to be designated by the President, composed of the Prime Minister as Chairman, and not more than fourteen other members, as least half of whom shall be Members of the *Batasang Pambansa.* The Executive Committee shall assist the President in the exercise of his powers and functions and in the performance of his duties as he may prescribe.

The Members of the Executive Committee shall have the same qualifications as those of the Members of the *Batasang Pambansa.*

Sec. 4. The term of office of the Prime Minister shall commence from the date of his election by the *Batasang Pambansa* and shall end on the date that the nomination of his successor is submitted by the President to the *Batasang Pambansa.* Any other member of the Cabinet or the Executive Committee may be removed at the discretion of the President.

Sec. 5. (1) The President may nominate from among the Members of the *Batasang Pambansa* a Deputy Prime Minister who shall be elected by a majority of the Members thereof. The Deputy Prime Minister shall perform such functions as may be assigned to him by the Prime Minister.

(2) The President shall also appoint the Deputy Ministers who shall perform such functions as may be assigned to them by law or by respective heads of ministries.

Sec. 6. The Prime Minister, Deputy Prime Minister, the Members of the Cabinet, and the Members of the Executive Committee, on assuming office, shall take the following oath or affirmation:

'I do solemnly swear (or affirm) that I will faithfully and conscientiously fulfil my duties as (name of position) of the Philippines, preserve and defend its Constitution, execute its laws, do justice to every man and consecrate myself to the service of the Nation. So help me God.' (In case of affirmation, the last sentence will be omitted).

Sec. 7. The salaries and emoluments of the Prime Minister, Deputy Prime Minister, Members of the Cabinet and of the Executive Committee shall be fixed by law which shall not be increased or decreased during their tenure of office. Until otherwise provided by law, the Prime Minister shall receive the same salary as that of the President.

Sec. 8. The Prime Minister, the Members of the Cabinet and the Members of the Executive Committee shall be subject to the provisions of Section 11, Article VIII hereof and may not appear as counsel before any court or administrative body, or manage any business, or practice any profession, and shall also be subject to such other disqualifications as may be provided by law.

Sec. 9. The Prime Minister, Deputy Prime Minister, any Member of the Cabinet or the Executive Committee may resign for any cause without vacating his seat as Regional or Sectoral Representative in the *Batasang Pambansa*, or any other government position.

Sec. 10. The Prime Minister shall have supervision of all ministries.

ARTICLE X

THE JUDICIARY

Sec. 1. The Judicial power shall be vested in one Supreme Court and in such inferior courts as may be established by law. The *Batasang Pambansa* shall have the power to define, prescribe, and apportion the jurisdiction of the various courts, but may not deprive the Supreme Court of its jurisdiction over cases enumerated in Section five hereof.

Sec. 2. (1) The Supreme Court shall be composed of a Chief Justice and fourteen Associate Justice. It may sit *en banc* or in two divisions.

(2) All cases involving the constitutionality of a treaty, executive agreement, or law shall be heard and decided by the Supreme Court *en banc*, and no treaty, executive agreement, or law may be declared unconstitutional without concurrence of at least ten Members. All other cases, which under its rules are required to be heard *en banc*, shall be decided with the concurrence of at least eight members.

(3) Cases heard by a division shall be decided with the concurrence of at least five Members, but if such required number is not obtained, the case shall be decided *en banc:* Provided, that no doctrine or principle of law laid down by the Court in a decision rendered *en banc* or in division may be modified or reversed except by the Court sitting *en banc.*

Sec. 3. (1) No person shall be appinted Member of the Supreme Court unless he is a natural born- citizen of the Philippines, at least forty years of age and has for ten years or more been a judge of a court of record or engaged in the practice of law in the Philippines.

(2) The *Batasang Pambansa* shall prescribe the qualifications of judges of inferior courts, but no person may be appointed judge thereof unless he is a natural-born citizen of the Philippines and a member of the Philippine Bar.

Sec. 4. The Members of the Supreme Court and judges of inferior courts shall be appointed by the President.

Sec. 5. The Supreme Court shall have the following powers:

(1) Exercise original jurisdiction over cases affecting ambassadors other public ministers, and consuls and over petitions for *certiorari,* prohibition, *mandamus, quo warranto,* and *habeas corpus.*

(2) Review and revise, reverse, modify, or affirm on appeal of *certiorari,* as the law or the Rules of Court may provide, final judgments and decrees of inferior courts in

a. All cases in which the constitutionality or validity of any treaty, executive agreement, law, ordinance, or executive order of regulation is in question.

b. All cases involving the legality of any tax, impost, assessment, or toll, or any penalty imposed in relation thereto.

c. All cases in which the jurisdiction of any inferior court is issue.

d. All criminal cases in which the penalty imposed is death or life imprisonment.

e. All cases in which only an error or question of law is involved.

(3) Assign temporily judges of inferior courts to other stations as public interest may require. Such temporary assignment will not last longer than six months without the consent of the judge concerned.

(4) Order a change of venue or place of trial to avoid a miscarriage of justice.

(5) Promulgate rules concerning pleading, practice, and procedure in all courts, the admission to the practice of law, and the integration of the Bar which, however may be repealed, altered, or supplemented by the *Batasang Pambansa.* Such rules shall provide a simplified and inexpensive procedure for the speedy diposition of cases, shall be uniform for all courts of the same grade, and shall not diminish, increase, or modify substantive rights.

(6) Appoint its officials and employees in accordance with Civil Service Law.

Sec. 6. The Supreme Court shall have administrative supervision over all courts and the personnel thereof.

Sec. 7. The Members of the Supreme Court and judges of inferior courts shall hold office during good behavior until they reach the age of seventy years or become incapacitated to discharge the duties of their office. The Supreme Court shall have the power to discipline judges of inferior courts and, by a vote of at least eight Members, order their dismissal.

Sec. 8. The conclusion of the Supreme Court in any case submitted to it for decision *en banc* or in division shall be reached in consultation before the case is assigned to a Member for the writing of the opinion of the Court. Any Member dissenting from a decision shall state the reason for his dissent. The same requirements shall be observed by all inferior collegiate courts.

Sec. 9. Every decision of a court of record shall clearly and distinctly state the facts and the law on which it is based. The Rules of Court shall govern the promulgation of minute resolutions.

Sec. 10. The salary of the Chief Justice and of the Associate Justices of the Supreme Court, and of judges of inferior courts shall be fixed by law, which shall not be decreased during their continuance in office. Until the *Batasang Pambansa* shall provide otherwise, the Chief Justice shall receive an annual salary of seventy five thousand pesos, and each Associate Justice, sixty thousand pesos.

Sec. 11. (1) Upon the effectivity of this Constitution, the maximum period within which a case or matter shall be decided or resolved from the date of its submission, shall be eighteen months for the Supreme Court, and, unless reduced by the Supreme Court, twelve months for all inferior collegiate courts, and three months for all other inferior courts.

(2) With respect to the Supreme Court and other collegiate appellate courts, when the applicable maximum period shall have lapsed without the rendition of the corresponding decision or resolution because the necessary vote cannot be had, the judgment, or order, or resolution appealed from shall be deemed affirmed, except in those cases where a qualified majority is required and in appeals from conviction in criminal cases; and in original special civil actions and proceedings for *habeas corpus*, the petition in such cases shall be deemed dismissed; and a certification to this effect signed by the Chief Magistrate of the court shall be issued and a copy thereof attached to the record of the case.

Sec. 12. The Supreme Court shall, within thirty days from the opening of each regular session of the *Batasang Pambansa* submit to the President, the Prime Minister, and the *Batasang Pambansa* an annual report on the operations and activities of the Judiciary.

ARTICLE XI

LOCAL GOVERNMENT

Sec. 1. The territorial and political subdivisions of the Philippines are the provinces, cities, municipalities, and barrios.

Sec. 2. The *Batasang Pambansa* shall enact a local government code which may not thereafter be amended except by a majority vote of all its Members defining a more responsive and accountable local government structure with an effective system of recall, allocating among the different local government units their powers, responsibilities, and resources, and providing for the qualifications, election and removal, term, salaries, powers, functions, and duties of local officals, and all other matters relating to the organization and operation of local units. However any change in the existing form of local government shall not take effect until ratified by a majority of the votes cast in a plebiscite called for the purpose.

Sec. 3. No province, city, municipality or barrio may be created, divided, merged, abolished, or its boundary substantially altered, except in accordance with the criteria established in the local government code, and subjected to the approval by a majority of the votes cast on a plebiscite in the unit or units affected.

Sec. 4. (1) Provinces with respect to component cities and municipalities with respect to component barrios, shall ensure that the acts of their component units are within the scope of their assigned powers and functions. Highly urbanized cities, as determined by standards established in the local government code shall be independent of the province.

(2) Local government units may group themselves, or consolidate or coordinate their efforts, service, and resources for purposes commonly beneficial to them.

Sec. 5. Each local government unit shall have the power to create its own sources of revenue and to levy taxes, subject to such limitations as may be provided by law.

ARTICLE XII

THE CONSTITUTIONAL COMMISSIONS

A. Common Provisions

Sec. 1. The Constitutional Commissions shall be the Civil Service Commission, the Commission on Elections, and the Commission on Audit.

Sec. 2. Unless otherwise provided by law, the Chairman and each Commissioner of a Constitutional Commission shall receive an annual salary of sixty thousand pesos and fifty thousand pesos, respectively, which shall not be decreased during their continuances in office.

Sec. 3. No Member of a Constitutional Commission shall, during his tenure in office, engage in the practice of any profession or in the management of any business, or be financially interested directly or indirectly in any contract with, or in any franchise or privilege granted by, the Government or any subdivision, agency, or instrumentality thereof, including government-owned or controlled corporations.

Sec. 4. The Constitutional Commission shall appoint their officials and employees in accordance with the Civil Service Law.

B. The Civil Service Commission

Sec. 1. (1) The Civil Service embraces every branch, agency, subdivision, and instrumentality of the government, including every government-owned or controlled corporation. It shall be administered by an independent Civil Service Commission composed of a Chairman and two Commissioners who shall be natural-born citizens of the Philippines, and, at the time of their appointment, are at least thirty five years of age and holders of a college degree, and must not have been candidates for any elective position in the election immediately preceeding their appointment. The Chairman and the Commissioner shall be appointed by the President for a term of seven years without reappointment. Of the Commissioners first appointed, one shall hold office for seven years, another for five years and the third for three years. Appointment to any vacancy shall be only for the unexpired portion of the term of the predecessor.

(2) The Commission, shall, subject to such limitations as may be provided by law, establish a career service and adopt measures to promote morale, efficiency, and integrity in the Civil Service.

Sec. 2. Appointments in the Civil Service, except as to those which are policy-determining, primarily confidential, or highly technical in nature, shall be made only according to merit and fitness, to be determined as far as practicable by competitive examination.

Sec. 3. No officer or employee in the Civil Service shall be suspended or dismissed except for cause as provided by law.

Sec. 4. (1) Unless otherwise provided by law, no elective official shall be eligible for appointment to any office or position during his tenure, except as Member of the Executive Committee referred to in Section 3, Article IX hereof.

(2) No candidate who lost in an election shall be eligible for appointment or reappointment to any office in the government, or in any government-owned or controlled corporation, within one year following such election.

Sec. 5. No officer or employee in the Civil Service, including members of the armed forces, shall engage directly or indirectly in any partisan political activity or take part in any election except to vote.

Sec. 6. The *Batasang Pambansa* shall provide for the standardization of compensation-owned or controlled corporations, taking into account the nature of the responsibilities pertaining to, and the qualifications required for, the positions concerned.

C. The Commission on Elections

Sec. 1. (1) There shall be an independent Commission on Elections composed of a Chairman and eight Commissioners who shall be natural-born citizens of the Philippines and, at the time of their appointment, at least thirty five years of age and holders of a college degree. However, a majority thereof, including the Chairman, shall be members of the Philippine Bar who have been engaged in the practice of law for at least ten years.

(2) The Chairman and the Commissioners shall be appointed by the President for a term of seven years without reappointment. Of the Commissioners first appointed, three shall hold office for seven years, three for five years, and the last three for three years. Appointment to any vacancy shall be only for the unexpired portion of the term of the predecessor.

Sec. 2. The Commission on Elections shall have the following powers and functions.

(1) Enforce and administer all laws relative to the conduct of elections.

(2) Be the sole judge of all contests relating to the elections, returns, and qualifications of all Members of the *Batasang Pambansa* and elective provincial and city officials.

(3) Decide, save those involving the right to vote, administrative questions affecting elections, including the determination of the number and location of polling places, the appointment of election officials and inspectors and the registration of voters.

(4) Deputize, with the consent or at the instance of the President, law enforcement agencies and instrumentalities of the Government, including the Armed Forces of the Philippines, for the purpose of ensuring free, orderly, and honest elections.

(5) Register and accredit political parties subject to the provisions of Section eight hereof.

(6) Recommend to the *Batasang Pambansa* effective measures to minimize election expenses and prohibit all forms of election frauds and malpractices, political opportunism, guest or nuisance candidacy, or other similar acts.

(7) Submit to the President, the Prime Minister, and the *Batasang Pambansa* a report on the conduct and manner of each election.

(8) Perform such other functions as may be provided by law.

Sec. 3. The Commission on Elections may sit *en banc* or in three divisions. All election cases may be heard and decided by divisions, except contests involving Members of the *Batasang Pambansa,* which shall, be heard and decided *en banc*. Unless otherwise provided by law, all election cases shall be decided within ninety days from the date of their submission for decision.

Sec. 4. The Commission may recommend to the President the removal of, or any other disciplinary action against, any officer or employee it has deputized, for violation or disregard of, or disobedience to, its decision, order or directive.

Sec. 5. The enjoyment or utilization of all franchises or permits for the operation of transportation and other public utilities, media of communication or information, all grants, special privileges, or concessions granted by the Government, or any subdivision, agency, or instrumentality thereof, including any government owned or controlled corporation, may be supervised or regulated by the Commission during the election period for the purpose of ensuring free, orderly, and honest elections.

Sec. 6. Unless otherwise fixed by the Commission in special cases, the election period shall commence ninety days before the day of election and shall end thirty days thereafter.

Sec. 7. No pardon, parole, or suspension of sentence for violation of the law or rules and regulations concerning elections shall be granted without the recommendation of the Commission.

Sec. 8. The political parties whose respective candidates for President have obtained the first and second highest number of votes in the last preceding election for President under this Constitution shall be entitled to accreditation if each has obtained at least ten percent of the total number of votes cast in such election. If the candidates for President obtaining the two highest number of votes, do not each obtain at least ten percent of the total number of votes cast, or in the case no election for President shall as yet have been held, the Commission on Elections shall grant accreditation to political parties as may be provided by law.

No religious sect shall be registered as a political party, and no political party which seeks to achieve its goal through violence shall be entitled to accreditation.

Sec. 9. (1) *Bona fide* candidates for any public office shall be free from any form of harassment and discrimination.

(2) Accredited political parties shall be represented in the registration board, board of election inspectors, board of canvassers, or other similar bodies as may be provided by law.

Accredited political parties may by law be granted other rights or privileges.

Sec. 10. No elective public officer may change his political party affiliation during his term of office, and no candidate for any elective office may change his political party affiliation within six months immediately preceding or following an election, unless otherwise provided by law.

Sec. 11. Any decision, order, or ruling of the Commission may be brought to the Supreme Court on *certiorari* by the aggrieved party within thirty days from his receipt of a copy thereof.

D. The Commission of Audit

Sec. 1. (1) There shall be an independent Commission on Audit composed of a Chairman and two Commissioners, who shall be natural-born citizens of the Philippines, and at the time of their appointment, at least forty years of age and certified public accountants or members of the Philippine Bar for at least ten years.

(2) The Chairman and the Commissioners shall be appointed by the President for a term of seven years without reappointment. Of the Commissioners first appointed, one shall hold office for seven years, another for five years, and the third for three years. Appointment to any vacancy shall be only for the unexpired portion of the term of the predecessor.

Sec. 2. The Commission on Audit shall have the following powers and functions:

(1) Examine, audit, and settle, in accordance with law and regulations all accounts pertaining to the revenues and receipts of, and expenditures or uses of funds and property, owned or held in trust by, or pertaining to, the Government, or any of its subdivisions, agencies, or instrumentalities, including government-owned or controlled corporations; keep the general accounts of the Government and, for such period as may be provided by law, perserve the vouchers, pertaining thereto: and promulgate accounting and auditing rules and regulations including those for the prevention of irregular, unnecessary, excessive, or extravagant expenditures or uses of funds and property.

(2) Decide any case brought before it within sixty days from the date of its submission for resolution. Unless otherwise provided by law, any decision, or ruling of the Commission may be brought to the Supreme Court on *certiorari* by the aggrieved party within thirty days from his receipt of a copy thereof.

(3) Submit to the President, the Prime Minister, and the *Batasang Pambansa* within the time fixed by law, an annual financial report of the Government, its subdivisions, agencies, and instrumentalities, including government-owned or

controlled corporations, and recommend measures necessary to improve their efficiency and effectiveness. It shall submit such other reports as may be required by law.

(4) Perform such other duties and functions as may be prescribed by law.

ARTICLE XIII

ACCOUNTABILITY OF PUBLIC OFFICERS

Sec. 1. Public Office is a public trust. Public officers and employees shall serve with the highest degree of responsibility, integrity, loyalty, and efficiency, and shall remain accountable to the people.

Sec. 2. The President, the Members of the Supreme Court, and the Members of the Consititutional Commission shall be removed from office on impeachment for, and conviction of, culpable violation of the Constitution, treason, bribery, other high crimes, or graft and corruption.

Sec. 3. The *Batasang Pambansa* shall have the exclusive power to initiate, try and decide all cases of impeachment. Upon the filing of a verified complaint, the *Batasang Pambansa* may initiate impeachment by a vote of at least one fifth of all its Members. No official shall be convicted without the concurrence of at least two thirds of all the Members thereof. When the *Batasang Pambansa* sits in impeachment cases, its members shall be on oath or affirmation.

Sec. 4. Judgments in cases of impeachment shall be limited to removal from office and disqualification to hold any office of honor, trust, or profit under the Republic of the Philippines, but the party convicted shall nevertheless be liable and subject to prosecution, trial, and punishment, in accordance with law.

Sec. 5. The *Batasang Pambansa* shall create a special court, to be known as *Sandiganbayan*, which shall have jurisdiction over criminal and civil cases involving graft and corruption practices and such other offenses committed by public officers and employees, including those in government-owned or controlled corporations, in relation to their offices as may be determined by law.

Sec. 6. The *Batasang Pambansa* shall create an office of the Ombudsman, to be known as *Tanodbayan,* which shall receive and investigate complaints relative to public office, including those in government owned or controlled corporations, make appropriate recommedations, and in case of failure of justice as defined by law, file and prosecute the corresponding criminal, civil, or administrative case before the proper court or body.

ARTICLE XIV

THE NATIONAL ECONOMY AND THE PATRIMONY OF THE NATION

Sec. 1. The *Batasang Pambansa* shall establish a National Economic and Development Authority, to be headed by the President, which shall recommend to the *Batasang Pambansa* after consultation with the private sector, local government units, and other appropriate public agencies, continuing, coordinated, and fully integrated social and economic plans and programs.

Sec. 2. The State shall regulate or prohibit private monopolies when the public interest so requires. No combinations in restraint of trade or unfair competition shall be allowed.

Sec. 3. The *Batasang Pambansa* shall, upon recommendation of the National Economic and Development Authority, reserve to citizens of the Philippines or to corporations or associations wholly owned by such citizens, certain traditional areas on investments when the national interest so dictates.

Sec. 4. The *Batasang Pambansa* shall not, except by general law, provide for the formation, organization, or regulation of private corportations, unless such corporations are owned and controlled by the Government or any subdivision or instrumentality thereof.

Sec. 5. No franchise, certificate, or any other form of authorization for the operation of a public utility shall be granted except to citizens of the Philippines or to corporations or associations organized under the laws of the Philippines at least sixty *per centum* of the capital of which is owned by such citizens, nor shall such franchise, certificate, or authorization be exlcusive in character of for a longer period than fifty years. Neither shall any such franchise or right be granted except under the condition that it shall be subject to amendment, alteration, or repeal by the *Batasang Pambansa* when the public interest so requires. The State shall encourage equity participation in public utilities by the general public. The participation of foreign investors in the governing body of any public utility enterprise shall be limited to their proportionate share in the capital thereof.

Sec. 6. The State may, in the interest of national welfare or defense, establish and operate industries and means of transportation and communication, and, upon payment of just compensation, transfer to public ownership utilities and other private enterprises to be operated by the Government.

Sec. 7. In times of national emergency when the public interest so requires, the State may temporarily take over or direct the operation of any privately owned public utility or business affected with the public interest.

Sec. 8. All lands of the public domain, waters, minerals, coal, petroleum and other mineral oils, all forces of potential energy, fisheries, wildlife, and other natural resources of the Philippines belong to the State. With the exception of agricultural, industrial, or commercial, residential, and resettlement lands of the public domain, natural resources shall not be alienated, and no license, concession, or lease for the exploration, development, exploitation, or utilization of any of the natural resources shall be granted for a period exceeding twenty five years, renewable for not more than twenty five years, except as to water rights for irrigation, water supply, fisheries, or industrial use other than the development of water power, in which cases, beneficial use may be the measure and the limit of the grant.

Sec. 9. The disposition, exploration, development, exploitation, or utilization of any of the natural resources of the Philippines shall be limited to citizens of the Philippines, or to corporations or associations at least sixty *per centum* of the capital of which is owned by such citizens. The *Batasang Pambansa,* in the national interest, may allow such citizens, corporations, or associations to enter into service contracts for financial, technical, management, or other forms of assistance with any foreign person or entity for the exploration, development, exploitation, or utilization of any of the natural resources. Existing valid and binding service contracts for financial, technical, management, or other forms of assistance are hereby recognized as such.

Sec. 10. Lands of the public domain are classified into agricultural, industrial or commercial, residential, resettlement, mineral, timber or forest and grazing lands, and such other classes as may be provided by law.

Sec. 11. The *Batasang Pambansa,* taking into account conservation, ecological, and developmental requirements of the natural resources, shall determine by law the size of lands of the public domain which may be developed, held or acquired by, or leased to, any qualified individual, corporation or association, and the conditions therefor. No private corporation or association may hold alienable lands of the public domain except by lease not to exceed one thousand hectares in area; nor may any citizen hold such lands by lease in excess of five hundred hectares or acquire by purchase or homestead in excess of twenty four hectares. No private corporation or association may hold by lease, concession, license, or permit, timber or forest lands and other timber or forest resources in excess of one hundred thousand hectares; however, such area may be increased by the *Batasang Pambansa* upon recommendation of the National Economic and Development Authority.

Sec. 12. The State shall formulate and implement an agrarian reform program aimed at emancipating the tenant from the bondage of the soil and achieving the goals enunciated in this Constitution.

Sec. 13. The *Batasang Pambansa* may authorize, upon payment of just compensation, the expropriation of private lands to be subdivided into small lots and conveyed at cost to deserving citizens.

Sec. 14. Save in cases of hereditary succession, no private land shall be transferred or conveyed except to individuals, corporations, or associations qualified to acquire or hold lands of the public domain.

Sec. 15. Notwithstanding the provisions of Section 14 of this Article, a natural-born citizen of the Philippines who has lost his Philippine citizenship may be a transferee of private land, for use by him as his residence, as the *Batasang Pambansa* shall provide.

Sec. 16. Any provision of paragraph one, Section Fourteen, Article Eight and of this Article notwithstanding, the President may enter into international treaties or agreements as the national welfare and interest may require.

ARTICLE XV

GENERAL PROVISIONS

Sec. 1. The flag of the Philippines shall be red, white, and blue, with a sun and three stars, as consecreated and honored by the people and recognized by law.

Sec. 2. The *interim Batasang Pambansa* may by law adopt a new name for the country, a national anthem, and a national seal, which shall all be truly reflective and symbolic of the ideals, history, and traditions of the People. Thereafter the national name, anthem, and seal so adopted shall not be subject to change except by constitutional amendment.

Sec. 3. (1) This Constitution shall be officially promulgated in English and in Pilipino and translated into each dialect spoken by over fifty thousand people, and into Spanish and Arabic. In case of conflict, the English text shall prevail.

(2) The *Batasang Pambansa* shalll take steps towards the development and formal adoption of a common national language to be known as Pilipino.

(3) Until otherwise provided by law, English and Pilipino shall be the official languages.

Sec. 4. All public officers and employees and members of the armed forces shall take an oath to support and defend the Constitution.

Sec. 5. No elective or appointive public officer or employee shall receive additional or double compensation unless specifically authorized by law, nor accept, without the consent of the *Batasang Pambansa,* any present, emolument, office, or title of any kind from any foreign state.

Sec. 6. No salary or any form of emolument of any public officer or employee, including constitutional officers, shall be exempt from payment of income tax.

Sec. 7. (1) The ownership and management of mass media shall be limited to citizens of the Philippines or to corporations or associations wholly owned and managed by such citizens.

(2) The governing body of every entity engaged in commercial telecommunications shall in all cases be controlled by citizens of the Philippines.

Sec. 8. (1) All educational institutions shall be under the supervision of, and subject to regulation by, the State. The State shall establish and miantain a complete, adequate, and integrated system of education relevant to the goals of naational development.

(2) All institutions of higher learning shall enjoy academic freedom.

(3) The study of the Constitution shall be part of the curricula in all schools.

(4) All educational institutions shall aim to inculcate love of country, teach the duties of citizenship, and develop moral character, personal discipline, and scientific, technological, and vocational efficiency.

(5) The State shall maintain a system of free public elementary education and, in area where finances permit, establish and maintain a system of free public education at least up to the secondary level.

(6) The State shall provide citizenship and vocational training to adult citizens and out-of-school youth, and create and maintain scholarships for poor and deserving students.

(7) Educational institutions, other than those established by religious orders, mission boards, and charitable organizations, shall be owned solely by citizens of the Philippines, or corporations or associations sixty *per centum* of the capital of which is owned by citizens. The control and administration of educational institutions shall be vested in citizens of the Philippines. Nó educational institution shall be exclusively for aliens, and no group of aliens shall comprise more than one third of the enrolment in any school. The provisions of this sub-section shall not apply to schools established for foreign diplomatic personnel and their dependents and, unless otherwise provided by law, for other foreign temporary residents.

(8) At the option expressed in writing by the parents or guardians and without cost to them and the Government, religion shall be taught to their children or wards in public elementary and high schools as may be provided by law.

Sec. 9. (1) The State shall promote scientific research and invention. The advancement of science and technology shall have priority in the national development.

(2) Filipino culture shall be preserved and developed for national identity. Arts and letters shall be under the patronage of the State.

(3) The exclusive right to inventions, writings, and artistic creations shall be secured to inventors, authors, and artists for a limited period. Scholarships, grants-in-aid, or other forms of incentives shall be provided for specially gifted citizens.

Sec. 10. It shall be the responsibility of the State to achieve and maintain population levels most conducive to the national welfare.

Sec. 11. The State shall consider the customs, traditions, beliefs, and interests of national cultural communities in the formulation and implementation of state policies.

Sec. 12. The State shall establish and maintain an integrated national police force whose organization, administration, and operation shall be provided by law.

Sec. 13. (1) The Armed Forces of the Philippines shall include a citizen army composed of all able-bodied citizens of the Philippines who shall undergo military training, as may be provided by law. It shall keep a regular force necessary for the security of the State.

(2) The citizen army shall have a corps of trained officers and men in active duty status as may be necessary to train, service, and keep it in reasonable prepardness at all times.

Sec. 14. The *Batasang Pambansa* shall establish a central monetary authority which shall provide policy direction in the areas of money, banking, and credit. It shall have supervisory authority as may be provided by law over the operations of finance companies and other institutions performing similar functions. Until the *Batasang Pambansa* shall otherwise provide, the Central Bank of the Philippines, operating under existing law, shall function as the central monetary authority.

Sec. 15. The separation of Church and State shall be inviolable.

Sec. 16. The State may not be sued without its consent.

ARTICLE XVI

AMENDMENTS

Sec. 1. (1) Any amendment to, or revision of, this Constitution may be proposed by the *Batasang Pambansa* upon a vote of three fourths of all its Members, or by a constitutional convention.

(2) The *Batasang Pambansa* may, by a vote of two thirds of all its Members, call a constitutional convention or, by a majority vote of all its Members, submit the question of calling such a convention to the electorate in an election.

Sec. 2. Any amendment to, or revision of, this Constitution shall be valid when ratified by a majority of the votes cast in a plebiscite which shall be held not later than three months after the approval of such amendment or revision.

ARTICLE XVII

TRANSITORY PROVISIONS

Sec. 1. There shall be an *interim* National Assembly which shall exist immediately upon the ratification of this Constitution and shall continue until the Members of the regular National Assembly shall have been elected and shall have assumed office following an election called for the purpose by the *interim* National Assembly. Except as otherwise provided in this Constitution, the *interim* National Assembly shall have the same powers and its Members shall have the same functions, responsibilities, rights, privileges, and disqualifications as the regular National Assembly and the Members thereof.

Sec. 2. The Members of the *interim* National Assembly shall be the incumbent President and Vice President of the Philippines, those who served as President of the nineteen hundred and seventy one Constitutional Convention, those Members of the Senate and the House of Representatives who shall express in writing to the Commission on Elections within thirty days after the ratification of this Constitution their option to serve therein, and those Delegates to the nineteen hundred and seventy one Constitutional Convention who have opted to serve therein by voting affirmatively for this Article. They make their oath of office before any officer authorized to administer oath and qualify thereto, after the ratification of this Constitution.

Sec. 3. (1) The incumbent President of the Philippines shall iniatially convene the *interim* National Assembly and shall preside over its sessions until the *interim*

Speaker shall have been elected. He shall continue to exercise his powers and prerogatives under the nineteen hundred and thirty five Constitution and the powers vested in the President and the Prime Minister under this Constitution until he calls upon the *interim* National Assembly to elect the *interim* President and the *interim* Prime Minister, who shall then exercise their respective powers vested by this Constitution.

(2) All proclamations orders, decrees, instructions, and acts promulgated, issued or done by the incumbent President shall be part of the law of the land, and shall remain valid, legal, binding, and effective even after lifting of martial law or the ratification of this Constitution, unless modified, revoked, or superseded by subsequent proclamations, orders, decrees, instructions, or other acts of the incumbent President, or unless expressly and explicitly modified or repealed by the regular National Assembly.

Sec. 4. The *interim* Prime Minister and his Cabinet shall exercise all the powers and functions, and discharge the responsibilities of the regular Prime Minister and his Cabinet, and shall be subject to the same disqualifications provided in this Constitution.

Sec. 5. The *interim* National Assembly shall give priority to measures for the orderly transition from the presidential to the parliamentary system, the reorganization of the Government, the eradication of graft and corruption, the effective maintenance of peace and order, the implementation of declared agrarian reforms, the standardization of compensation of government employees, and such other measures as shall bridge the gap between the rich and the poor.

Sec. 6. The *interim* National Assembly shall reapportion the Assembly seats in accordance with Section Two, Article Eight, of this Constitution.

Sec. 7. All existing laws not inconsistent with this Constitution shall remain operative until amended, modified, or repealed by the National Assembly.

Sec. 8. All courts existing at the time of the ratification of this Constitution shall continue and exercise their jurisdiction, until otherwise provided by law in accordance with this Constitution, and all cases pending in said courts shall be heard, tried, and determined under the laws then in force. The provisions of the existing Rules of Court not inconsistent with this Constitution shall remain operative unless amended, modified, or repealed by the Supreme Court or the National Assembly.

Sec. 9. All officials and employees in the existing Government of the Republic of the Philippines shall continue in office until otherwise provided by law or decreed by the incumbent President of the Philippines, but all officials whose appointments are by this Constitution vested in the Prime Minister shall vacate their respective offices upon the appointment and qualification of their successors.

Sec. 10. The incumbent members of the Judiciary may continue in office until they reach the age of seventy years, unless sooner replaced in accordance with the preceding section hereof.

Sec. 11. The rights and privileges granted to citizens of the United States or to corporations or associations owned or controlled by such citizens under the Ordinance appended to the nineteen hundred and thirty five Constitution shall automatically terminate on the third day of July, nineteen hundred and seventy four. Titles to private lands acquired by such person before such date shall be valid as against other private persons only.

Sec. 12. All treaties, executive agreements, and contracts, entered into by the Government, or any subdivision, agency, or instrumentality thereof, including government-owned or controlled corporations, are hereby recognized as legal, valid, and binding. When the national interest so requires, the incumbent President of the Philippines or the *interim* Prime Minister may review all contracts, concessions, permits or other forms of privileges, for the exploration, development, exploitation, or utilization of natural resources entered into, granted, issued, or acquired before the ratification of this Constitution.

Sec. 13. Any public officer or employee separated from the service as a result of the reorganization effected under this Constitution shall, if entitled under the laws then in force, receive the retirement and other benefits accruing thereunder.

Sec. 14. All records, equipment, building, facilities, and properties of any office or body abolished or reorganized under this Constitution shall be transferred to the office or body to which its powers, functions, and responsibilities substantially pertain.

Sec. 15. The *interim* National Assembly, upon special call by the *interim* Prime Minister, may, by a majority vote of all its Members, propose amendments to this Constitution. Such amendments shall take effect when ratified in accordance with Article Sixteen hereof.

Sec. 16. This Constitution shall take effect immediately upon its ratification by a majority of the votes case in a plebiscite called for the purpose and, except as herein provided, shall supersede the Constitution of nineteen hundred and thirty five and all amendments thereto.

Amendments of October 27, 1976 and April 10, 1981

1. There shall be, in lieu of the interim National Assembly, an interim *Batasang Pambansa.* Members of the interim *Batasang Pambansa* which shall not be more than 120, unless otherwise provided by law, shall include the incumbent President of the Phillipines, representatives elected from the different regions of the nation, those who shall not be less than eighteen years of age elected by their respective sectors, and those chosen by the incumbent President from the Members of the Cabinet. Regional representatives shall be apportioned among the regions in accordance with the number of their respective inhabitants and on the basis of a uniform and progressive ratio, while the sector shall be determined by law. The number of representatives from each region or sector and the manner of their election shall be prescribed and regulated by law.

2. The interim *Batasang Pambansa* shall have the same powers and it Members shall have the same functions, responsibilites, rights, privileges, and disqualifications as the interim National Assembly and the regular National Assembly and the Members thereof.

3. The incumbent President of the Philippines shall, within 30 days from the election and selection of the Members, convene the interim *Batasang Pambansa* and preside over its sessions until the Speaker shall have been elected. The incumbent President of the Philippines shall be the Prime Minister and he shall continue to exercise all his powers even after the interim *Batasang Pambansa* is organized and ready to discharge its function, and likewise he shall continue to exercise his powers and prerogatives under the 1935 Constitution and the powers vested in the President and the Prime Minister under this Constitution.

4. The President (Prime Minister) and his Cabinet shall exercise all the powers and functions, and discharge the responsibilities of the regular President (Prime Minister) and his Cabinet, and shall be subject only to such disqualifications as the President (Prime Minister) may prescribe. The President (Prime Minister), if he so desires, may appoint a Deputy Prime Minister or as many Deputy Prime Ministers as he may deem necessary.

5. The incumbent President shall continue to exercise legislative powers until martial law shall have been lifted.

6. Whenever in the judgment of the President (Prime Minister), there exists a grave emergency or a threat of imminence thereof, or whenever the *interim Batasang Pambansa* or the Regular National Assembly fails or is unable to act adequately on any matter for any reason that in his judgment requires immediate action, he may, in order to meet the exigency, issue the necessary decrees, orders, or letters of instructions, which shall form part of the law of the land.

7. The *barangays* and *sanggunians* shall continue as presently constituted but their functions, powers, and compositions may be altered by law.

Referenda conducted through the *barangays* and under the supervision of the Commission on Elections may be called at any time the Government deems it necessary to ascertain the will of the people regarding any important matter, whether of national or local interest.

8. All provisions of this Constitution not inconsistent with any of these amendments shall continue in full force and effect.

9. These amendments shall take effect after the incumbent President shall have proclaimed that they have been ratified by a majority of the votes cast in the referendum-plebiscite.

SUMMARY

INTERNATIONAL STATUS

Qatar is a member of the United Nations (September 21, 1971). It is a member of the League of Arab States, the Gulf Co-operation Council and other internationa. organizations.

Qatar, like the other Persian Gulf states was an emirate important in the commerce of the area and coveted by Persians, Arabs, Portuguese, Turks and British in turn. Special treaty regulations came to govern relations between Great Britain and the Persian Gulf states during the nineteenth century. Qatar became a British protected state in 1916, with Great Britain responsible for its foreign relations and defense. On February 27, 1968, after the British announcement of its imminent withdrawal from the Persian Gulf, the rulers of Bahrain, Qatar and the 7 Trucial States decided to form a union and a provisional constitution was promulgated in July 1970. Qatar decided to withdraw from the union and become separately independent on September 1, 1971.

Oil was discovered in 1940 and exploited commercially from 1949. In 1972, the Sheik Khalifa Bin Hamad Al Thani acceded to the throne after a bloodless coup, ended the period of absolute monarchy and instituted a program of modernization and industrialization and exploitation of the rich petroleum and natural gas resources.

FORM OF NATIONAL GOVERNMENT

The Provisional Constitution of April 19, 1972, was promulgated by the Amir in whom all power is vested as Head of State. The Provisional Constitution states that Qatar is an independent, sovereign, democratic Arab state; its religion is Islam and Sharia law is the source of its legislation.[1] The State must preserve its integrity and sovereignty.[2] It must support the Union of Arab States, strengthen their solidarity and support the untiy of the Arab nations.[3] Offensive war is prohibited.[4]

RIGHTS OF THE PEOPLE

Property, capital and labor are basic elements in the social structure of the State and they are individual rights; the State guarantees free enterprise; it has the right to supervise the national economy and direct economic advancement.[5] The family is the basis of society, and the State endeavors to instil Islamic religious principles,

[1] Prov. Const., Art. 1.
[2] Id., Art. 2, 5.
[3] Id., Art. 5.
[4] Id., Art. 25.
[5] Id., Art. 6.

to provide care and guidance, health, social security, equal opportunities, education.[6] All persons enjoy equal public rights and duties without discrimination.[7] Laws may not be retroactive.[8] Guaranteed are the rights to fair trial, sanctity of the home, freedom of publication and the press, the right of ownership.[9]

LEGISLATIVE DEPARTMENT

The Amir promulgates laws on the basis of recommendations of the Council of Ministers and after taking the opinion of the Advisory Council.[10] The latter expresses its opinions in the form of recommendations.[11] It consists of 20 members appointed by the Amir for a term of one year which may be extended, and after the initial period members are to be elected by direct secret ballot.[12] The Advisory Council debates draft laws, government policy, the budget.[13] It may be dissolved by the Amir.[14] It meets in one annual session of at least 8 months.[15]

EXECUTIVE DEPARTMENT

Executive power is vested in the Amir who is Head of State, his person inviolable; rulership of the State is hereditary in the family of Al-Thani.[16] He is assisted by Ministers appointed by him who must be Qatari citizens.[17] The Council of Ministers is jointly and individually responsible to the Amir.[18] Incompatibilities for holding the office of Minister are described.[19] The Amir commands the Armed Forces, has the power of appointment, the prerogative of mercy, is the fount of honor.[20] He concludes treaties and may declare defensive war.[21]

JUDICIAL DEPARTMENT

Judges are independent in the exercise of their power; the organization of the judiciary is determined by law.[22]

AREA, POPULATION, ETC.

The area is 11,400 square kilometres, the population (1981 estimate) is 244,534. The capital is Doha.[23] The language is Arabic.[24]

[6] Id., Art. 7,8.
[7] Id., Art. 9.
[8] Id., Art. 10.
[9] Id., Art. 11–13, 16.
[10] Id., Art. 17.
[11] Id., Art. 40.
[12] Id., Art. 41, 45, 46.
[13] Id., Art. 51.
[14] Id., Art. 61.
[15] Id., Art. 53.
[16] Id., Art. 18, 20, 21.
[17] Id., Art 28–30.
[18] Id., Art. 35.
[19] Id., Art. 38.
[20] Id., Art. 23.
[21] Id., Art. 24, 25.
[22] Id., Art. 65, 66.
[23] Id., Art. 2.
[24] Id., Art. 1.

THE AMENDED PROVISIONAL CONSTITUTION OF THE STATE OF QATAR[1]

April 19, 1972

We, Khalifa Bin Hamad Al-Thani, the Amir of Qatar State.

Whereas our great aspiration, for whose realization we have pledged to God to exert every possible effort, declaring before our people that we will devote ourselves for it, is the advancement of our dear country in its present stage of progressive setting-out towards the building-up of a better society wherein all citizens will enjoy greater welfare, justice, equality, learning and health, and wherein both they and the public authorities shall together practice their rights and carry out their duties in the best manner that guarantees the realization of this aspiration;

And whereas the former Provisional Constitution was laid down at a time when the State of Qatar was a member of the Union of Arab Emirates, and had not attained complete independence and full sovereignity, and whereas these factors necessitated the amendment – by addition, deletion and substitution – of the provisions of aforesaid constitution so that they may – through the stage of gradual development requisite and convenient for the transitional period conform with the wide and deep changes resultant from both the country's attainment of full independence from one side and the rise of the new era of comprehensive reformist renaissance from the other side.

And whereas the laying down of sound bases for the desired comprehensive reform through the transitional period requires the re-organization of the state by the execution of convenient measures, and the enactment of suitable legislation, regualtions and decisions at the proper speed, especially as we are determined to reduce the aforesaid transitional period to the minimum time necessitated by the State's higher interest and imposed by its needs, therefore the amendment included the provisions organizing the Advisory Council, stipulating its formation, for the first time, of twenty members appointed by an Amiri Edict with the possibility of adding four other members by a similar edict should His Highness find out that public interest justifies such step. The amendment did not alter the Council's authority which shall remain the same. It provided that the Council's term of office shall in principle be for one year. It also simultaneously stipulated the setting up of a new Advisory Council at the end of the First Advisory Council's term of office. The new Council shall be elected by direct secret ballot in compliance with the regulations that shall be issues in a Special Law organizing such public ballot and issued within thirty days following the end of aforesaid interval. The electoral procedure shall be completed within thirty days following the issuance of aforementioned Special Law. There is no need to confirm that fact that the principle of members appointment applicable to the First Advisory Council of the sort that the country has ever known is generally applicable in all countries of newly-introduced constitutions especially in the earlier stages of such constitutions application.

[1] Provided by the Ministry of Foreign Affairs, Doha, in September 1981. Ed.

For all said considerations, we take pleasure to proclaim this Amended Provisional Constitution revising the former Provisional Constitution for Qatar State for the sake of its application in pursuance of same previously stipulated basic principles governing the State's general policies in economical, social and cultural fields through the transitional period. This Amended Provisional Constitution shall continue to be in force until the issuance of a thorough and permanent constitution to be laid down in the light of the first factual experience of applying such constitution in our country. The thorough and permanent constitution shall be applicable immediately after the expiry of the transitional period.

We pray to God to enable us to adopt best methods that secure with the assistance and support of our people the realization of our mutual expectations of positive and fruitful participation, for the accomplishment of the strong edifice of our new state on most modern and sound bases.

Such steps, we hope, shall lead to the securement of the high position which our country deserves to occupy in the Arab World in particular, and the world community in general, in such a manner that qualifies the country to play its full role in collaboration with sister Arab States, and in such a fruitful and efficient method as may realize what we all look for, namely, the advancement and strength of our immortal Arab people and the peace and security of the whole world at large.

PART ONE

THE FORM OF GOVERNMENT

Art. 1. Qatar is an independent sovereign Arab State. Its religion is Islam, and Islamic Shari'a Law shall be the fundamental source of its legislation. Its regime is democratic and its official language is Arabic.

The people of Qatar are a part of the Arab Nation.

Art. 2. The Capital of Qatar is the City of Doha.

The sovereignty of the State extends over all lands and territorial waters lying within its international boundaries.

The State may not relinquish its sovereignty, or cede any part of its territory or its waters.

Art. 3. The flag, emblem, official medals and national anthem of the State shall be determined by law.

Art. 4. Citizenship of the State shall be determined by law.

Citizenship may not be taken away or withdrawn from a citizen save in the cases prescribed by law.

PART TWO

ESSENTIAL GUIDING PRINCIPLES OF STATE POLICY

Art. 5. Political Principles.

(*a*) The State shall preserve its integrity, and shall maintain its safety, security and stability, and repel any agression against it by all possible means within its power.

(*b*) The State believes that the Union or Arab State in the region is a fatal requirement necessitated by high Arab mutual interests of the region in particular, and the whole Arab World in general. The State shall devote all possible efforts to supplement such Union and shall strive to have it realized in the best mode that unites it with those Arab States to whom it is tied by deeply-rooted, most strong and genuine relations.

(*c*) The State believes in the brotherhood of all Arabs, and shall direct its efforts to the strengthening of ties of solidarity with sister Arab States, and shall endeavor to consolidate the unity of the Arab Nation, and support with all its power the joint effort to serve and promote Arab causes and interests. The State fully supports the League of Arab States and the ideals which the charter of the League aims at realizing.

(*d*) The State shall direct its efforts in all fields to the consolidation of a proper basis for the establishment of true democracy, and the creation of a proper administrative organization that will ensure justice, tranquillity and equality for its citizens, and respect for public order, and shall safeguard security, stability and the best interests of the country.

(*e*) The foreign policy of the State shall aim at strengthening the ties of friendship with all Islamic States and peoples in particular, and with all peace-loving States and peoples in general, on a basis of mutual respect, common interests and non-interference in internal affairs.

The State shall adhere to the principles of the United Nations Charter which aim at supporting the right of peoples to decide their own future, promoting international co-operation for the good of all mankind, spreading peace and security in all parts of the worlds, adherence by states to the principle of settling their disputes by peaceful means and establishing their relations with each other on a basis of justice and equality in accordance with the principles of international law.

Art. 6. Economic Principles:

(*a*) Property, capital and labor shall be basic elements in the social structure of the State, and they are individual rights serving social ends as prescribed by law.

(*b*) The State shall guarantee free enterprise within the limits of public interest.

The State shall have the right to supervise the national economy in a manner that will ensure its safety for the good of the country. Such supervision shall be regulated, and its limits shall be defined by law, as may be required in the public interest.

(*c*) The State shall direct economic advancement through scientific planning and technical co-operation with specialized international organizations, in a manner that will realise such prosperity in the country as will ensure honorable life for its citizens.

Art. 7. Social Principles:

(*a*) The basis of society is the family, based on religion, morality and patriotism. The law shall prescribe the means for the protection of the family against such elements as may weaken its ties, and for supporting its structure, and strengthening its bonds and fostering motherhood and child care within the family.

(*b*) The State shall endeavor to instil proper Islamic religious principles in society, and to purify it from all manifestations of moral disintegration.

(*c*) The State shall provide care and guidance for the rising generations, and shall protect them from immorality and corruption, exploitation and the evils of physical and spiritual neglect.

(*d*) The State shall endeavor to provide equal opportunities for all citizens, and to make it possible for them to exercise the right to work under laws that will ensure social justice.

(*e*) The State shall do everything in its power to protect its citizens against the causes of ignorance and poverty.

(*f*) The State shall provide means for the care of the health of its citizens.

(*g*) The State shall adopt a social security plan that will ensure assistance to citizens in case of old age, sickness, disasters and other causes of disability.

Art. 8.

(*a*) Education is a basic factor in the progress and well-being of society, and is the right of every citizen. The State shall endeavor to realize the implementation of compulsory general education, free of charge at all levels.

(*b*) Education is the means to culture. It shall be guaranteed and fostered by the State.

(*c*) The goal of education is the creation of citizens who are strong in body, mind and character believing in God, possessing good morals, proud of their Arab-Islamic heritage, enlightened with knowledge, aware of their responsibilities and mindful of their rights.

(*d*) The State shall foster, preserve and assist in the spreading of the cultural heritage of the nation, and shall promote science, arts, literature and scientific research.

PART THREE

PUBLIC RIGHTS AND DUTIES

Art. 9. All persons shall enjoy equal rights and shall be subject to equal public duties without distinction on grounds of race, sex or religion.

Art. 10.

(*a*) The provisions of the laws shall only apply to acts or events which take place on or after the date on which such laws come into effect, and they shall not affect any acts or events which take place prior to that date. However subject to the provisions of the next following paragraph, a law may contain a provision to the contrary.

(*b*) No act may be considered a criminal offence, and no criminal penalty may be imposed except under a law that has been previously enacted.

Art. 11. A person who is accused of a criminal offence shall be considered innocent until he is proven guilty. He shall have the right to be fairly tried before a court, and to defend himself either personally or through an attorney.

Art. 12. The sancitity of homes shall be guaranteed and entry thereto without the permission of the persons residing therein shall be prohibited except in the cases determined by law, and in the manner prescribed therein.

Art. 13. The freedom of publication and the press shall be guaranteed in accordance with the law.

Art. 14. The holding of public office is a national service to be rendered by the office holder. The goal of a civil servant in the discharge of the duties of his office shall be the promotion of the public interest exclusively.

Art. 15. Maintenance of public order and respect of public morals is the duty of every person living in the State.

Art. 16. Individual and collective ownership of property shall be respected, and this right of ownership may not be taken away except in the public interest and in accordance with the law.

PART FOUR

THE AUTHORITIES

Chapter 1. General Provisions

Art. 17. The Amir shall promulgate laws on the basis of the recommendations of the Council of Ministers, and after taking the opinion of the Advisory Council in the manner prescribed by this Provisional Constitution.

Art. 18. The executive power shall be vested in the Amir, who shall be assisted by the Council of Ministers, in the manner prescribed by this Provisional Constitution.

(*There is no Article 19 in the published text. Ed.*)

Chapter II. The Head of the State

Art. 20. The Amir shall be the Head of the State. His person shall be accorded inviolability and it shall be a duty to respect him.

Art. 21. The rulership of the State is hereditary in the family of Al-Thani.

The heir apparent shall be nominated during a maximum interval of one year following the issuance of this Provisional Constitution. His appointment shall be effected by an Amiri Edict following consultations with responsible notables in the country and their majority's acceptance of said nomination.

The provisions regulating accession to the reign of the state shall be defined in a Special Law to be issued within an interval not exceeding one year as from the issuance date of this constitution. This Special Law shall not be subjected to any revision other than that stipulated in its text.

Art. 22. In cases of the Amir's absence outside the State he appoints by an Amiri Edict a deputy who exercises his authorities by deputization during the Amir's absence. Such an Amiri Edict can detail limitations of said authorities and organization of their practice.

Art. 23. The Amir exercises the following powers:

1. He represents the State internally and towards other states in all international relations.

2. He ratifies and promulgates the laws and decrees. Such laws and decrees shall not come into effect until they are published in the official Gazette. Such publication following their ratification and promulgation shall come into effect after one month from the date of their publication in the Official Gazette unless another date is stipulated in the law itself.

3. He presides over the Council of Ministers.

4. He assumes supreme command and supervision of the Armed Forces.

5. He appoints and dismisses civil and military servants in accordance with the law.

6. He accepts the credentials of the heads of diplomatic and consular corps.

7. He may waive or reduce any penalty by decree.

8. He bestows medals of honor in accordance with the law.

9. Any other powers with which he is vested under this Provisional Constitution or with which he may be vested under the law.

Art. 24. The Amir concludes treaties by a decree and communicates same to the Advisory Council attached with appropriate explanation. Such treaties shall have the power of law following their conclusion, ratification and publishing in the Official Gazette.

In no case shall such treaties include secret provisions in contradiction with their declared provisions.

Art. 25. The Amir shall by a decree declare a defensive war. Offensive war shall be prohibited.

Art. 26. (*a*) The Amir will be assisted in the discharge of the duties referred to in paragraph 4 of Article 23 by a Defence Council, which shall come directly under him.

(*b*) The Defence Council shall be established by a decree.

(*c*) The Defence Council shall be prescribed for the duties of submitting opinion and advice for the Amir on all matters relating to defence, the preservation of the integrity and the security of the State, the preparation, training, equipment and development of the armed forces and the siting of their location and camps.

Art. 27. In exceptional circumstances which require the adoption of urgent measures without delay, and which require the promulgation of laws at a time when the Advisory Council is not in session, the Amir may issue decrees, which shall have the force of laws, regarding such matters provided that such decrees do not conflict with the essential guiding principles of State Policy.

Such decrees shall be submitted to the Advisory Council for its opinion, at its first meeting.

Chapter III. The Council of Ministers

Art. 28. A Council of Ministers shall be formed to assist the Amir in the discharge of his duties and the exercise of his powers in accordance with this constitution and with the law.

Art. 29. The Amir shall appoint the ministers and relieve them of their posts by an Amiri decree.

Art. 30. No person may assume a ministerial post unless he is a citizen of Qatar originally.

Art. 31. The formation of the Council of Ministers shall be effected by an Amiri Edict.

The law shall determine the authority of the ministers and the powers of ministers and other Government organs.

Art. 32. The Ministers shall take the following oath before the Amir prior to assuming office.

> 'I swear by the Almighty God to be loyal to the State of Qatar and the Amir, and to respect the Islamic Shari'a Law and this Provisional Constitution and the laws of the country, and to discharge my duties as a minister faithfully, conscientiously and honorably, and to look after the interests of the people fully, and to safeguard completely the safety and territoral integrity of the State.'

Art. 33. The Amir, in his capacity as Prime Minister, shall preside over the meetings of the Council, and shall direct the activities of the ministers and supervise the coordination of work among all ministries and Government organs, and ensure the unity of these organs, and issue general instructions for the direction of the Government. He issues directives to the Government and signs in the name of the Council, and on its behalf, the decisions which it promulgates.

Art. 34. The Council of Ministers, in its capacity as the highest executive organ of the State, shall be responsible for the administration of all the internal and external affairs which fall within its competence in accordance with this basic constitution and the law.

1. The preparation of a comprehensive plan which secures for the State the utmost possible economical, social, cultural and administrative revival and in accordance with the basic principles directing the State's policy as stipulated in this constitution.

2. Propose draft laws and decrees. Draft laws shall be submitted to the Advisory Council for discussion and for its opinion with regard thereto prior to their sub-

mission to the Amir for ratification and promulgation in accordance with this Provisional Constitution.

3. Ratification of regulations and decisions prepared by ministries, each in its own field for the implementation of laws in accordance with the provisions prescribed therein.

4. Supervise the implementation of laws, decrees, regulations, orders and court judgments.

5. Establish and organize, in accordance with the provisions of the law, the organs and departments of the Government.

6. Higher supervision of the financial and administrative system of the government.

7. Appointment and discharge of government officials where such measures do not lie within authority of the Amir or concerned ministries in accordance with law.

8. Supervise the external interests of the State, and conduct its international relations and external affairs in general, in accordance with the provisions of the law.

9. Formulate the general principles that will ensure the maintenance of internal security, and the preservation of public order in all parts of the State, in accordance with the provisions of the law.

10. Administer the finance of the State and prepare the draft of the general budget of the State in accordance with this Provisional Constitution and the provisions of the law.

11. Exercise supreme supervision over the conduct of civil servants, and the progress of State work in general.

12. The preparation of a report at the beginning of every financial year, including a detailed report on the major work accomplished internally and externally, together with a plan detailing the best means of ensuring the realization of the comprehensive advancement of the State and ensuring its progress and prosperity and the maintenance of its security and stability.

13. Any other powers with which it may be vested under this Provisional Constitution or the law.

Art. 35. The Council of Ministers shall be jointly responsible politically to the Amir for the implementation of the general policy in the State.

Every minister shall be individually responsible to the Amir for the manner in which he discharges his duties and exercises his powers in his ministry.

Art. 36. (*a*) The discussions of the Council of Ministers shall be held in camera. No decision shall be adopted unless a majority of its members are present and unless the majority of votes of those present are in its favor. Should a tie happen the Prime Minister shall have a casting vote. The opinion of the majority shall be binding on the minority.

The Council shall lay down its own internal rules, necessary for the regulation of its work and all its other procedures.

(*b*) A General Secretariat for the Council of Ministers shall be established, comprising the necessary number of employees.

Art. 37. The Office of a minister shall become vacant in the following cases:
(*a*) On the death of the office-holder.
(*b*) If he is relieved of his post or if his resignation is accepted by the Amir.
(*c*) If he is convicted of a moral crime.

Art. 38. The Ministers may not, while holding office, practice any profession, or engage in any commercial business, or enter into any commercial transaction with the State.

The personal conduct of each of them must be aimed at upholding the public interest and the complete renunciation of self-interest. They may not exploit their official positions in any manner for their personal benefit, or for the benefit of persons with whom they may be connected by a special relationship.

The law defines those acts performed by the Ministers during their term of office which would call for an enquiry and it stipulates the way in which this enquiry shall be carried out.

Art. 39. The emoluments of ministers shall be determined by law.

Chapter IV. Advisory Council

Art. 40. An Advisory Council shall be established to assist, through the expression of its opinions, the Amir and the Council of Ministers in the discharge of their respective duties. This Council shall be known as 'The Advisory Council', and it shall express its opinions in the form of recommendations.

Art. 41. The Advisory Council shall be composed of twenty members, appointment of whom shall be effected by an Amiri Edict.

The Amir may issue a decision to appoint not more than four additional members if he deems this necessary in the public interest.

Art. 42. A member of the Advisory Council must posses the following qualifications:
(*a*) His original citizenship must be that of the State of Qatar.
(*b*) His age should not be less than twenty-four solar years on the date of his appointment.
(*c*) He should not have been previously convicted for normal crime. unless he has been rehabilitated in accordance with the law.

Art. 43. In selecting the members of the Advisory Council consideration shall be given to the fact that they should be persons of respectable social standing, of good judgment and of competence in various fields.

Art. 44. The Advisory Council shall elect annually from among its members, by secret ballot, and on the basis of a proportional majority, a President and a Vice-President, at the first meeting in its ordinary annual session. The senior member by age shall preside at this first meeting.

The President and the Vice-President of the Advisory Council may be re-elected after the expiry of thier terms of office.

Art. 45. The term of office of the Advisory Council shall be one calendar year commencing from the date of its first meeting. The term of office may be extended if necessary in the public interest.

Art. 46. On the expiry of the term of office of the Advisory Council in accordance with the provision of the previous Article, a new Advisory Council shall be formed by direct secret ballot in accordance with the provisions of a Special Law to be issued regulating such ballot. Such Special Law shall be issued within thirty days following the expiry of the Advisory Council's term of office referred to in the previous Article. The electoral procedure shall be executed within sixty days from the date of issuance of the Special Law.

Art. 47. If the seat of an elected member of the Advisory Council becomes vacant prior to the expiry of his term of office, for any reason whatsoever, the Amir, shall appoint another member to that vacant seat within one month from the date on which the Council announces such vacancy. The term of office of the new member shall be up to the end of his predecessor's term.

If the vacancy occurs during the last two months preceding the expiry of the term of office of the Council no substitute member shall be appointed to such vacancy.

Art. 48. A member of the Advisory Council shall take the following oath before the Council at an open meeting, prior to assuming office:

> 'I swear by the Almightly God to be loyal to the State of Qatar and the Amir, and to preserve the safety of the State and look after the interests of the people, and to respect the constitution and the laws of the country, and to discharge my work in the Council and its committees faithfully and honestly'.

Art. 49. The Advisory Council shall have a bureau that shall consist of he President, the Vice-President and two controllers. A general secretariat for the Council shall also be established, and to which the necessary number of employees shall be appointed.

Art. 50. The Amir opens the annual session of the Advisory Council, and delivers a speech at the opening meeting which includes a statement regarding the state of affairs in the country, the major achievements, and the projects and reforms which the State intends to implement during the coming year.

Art. 51. The Advisory Council shall have the power to:

1. Debate the draft laws proposed by the Government before their submission to the Amir for ratification and promulgation.

2. Debate the general policy of the State on such political, economic, cultural, social or administrative affairs as may be referred to it by the Government.

3. Debate the draft budget of the major public projects.

4. Submit recommendations regarding the matters mentioned in the above-preceding paragraphs of this Article.

5. Request statements regarding any of the aspects mentioned in paragraphs 1, 2, 3, of this article from the Council of Ministers, if the matter relates to the general policy of the Government; or from the Minister concerned if the matter relates to the affairs falling within the competence of his Ministry.

Art. 52. The Advisory Council shall hold its meetings in the Capital. The Amir may, however, convene a meeting of the Council at any other place. Any meeting of the Advisory Council that is held at a place other than the legally prescribed place shall not be legal, and its proceedings shall be considered automatically null and void by operation of the law.

Art. 53. The Advisory Council session duration shall be eight months at least, during which period it shall hold monthly meetings.

Art. 54. The Amir convenes the first meeting of the first Advisory Council within a period not exceeding thirty days from the date of publication in the Official Gazette of the Amiri Edict announcing the names of the members of the Advisory Council.

Art. 55. The Amir may postpone, by decree, the meeting of the Advisory Council for a period not exceeding one month.

Art. 56. The Amir shall convene an extraordinary meeting of the Advisory Council in case of necessity, or on the basis of a request signed by a majority of the members of the Advisory Council.

The Advisory Council may not hold any meetings without an invitation, except when it is in session, otherwise such meeting shall not be legal, and any recommendation adopted thereat shall be considered null and void by operation of the law.

The Advisory Council may not consider at an extra-ordinary session any matters other than those which it was convened to consider.

Art. 57. The Advisory Council shall form the necessary committees for conducting its work from among its members, within the first week of its annual session. Such committees may carry out their functions when the Council is not in session in order to submit the results to the Council when it meets.

Art. 58. No subject whatsoever may be submitted or discussed at any meeting of the Advisory Council unless it has been included in the agenda of that meeting which has been approved by the Council.

Art. 59. The presence of a majority of the members of the Advisory Council at any of its meetings is necessary to constitute a legal quorum. If a majority of the members is not present, the meeting shall be postponed for a period that is not less than two days and not exceeding eight days. Resolutions shall be adopted by an absolute majority of the votes of the members who are present. Should a tie occur, the President shall have a casting vote.

Art. 60. The ministers shall attend the meetings of the Advisory Council wherever the agenda includes any subject related to the matters falling within the competence of their respective ministries.

Art. 61. The Amir may dissolve the Advisory Council if the highest interest of the Station so require, and he shall state the reasons therefor.

If the Advisory Council is dissolved, a new Council shall be formed provided that the first meeting of the new council shall be held within a period not exceeding one month from the date of dissolution of the outgoing council.

Art. 62. If a member loses confidence and respect, the Amir may decide to terminate his membership.

Art. 63. The members of the Council, shall be remunerated; the amount of such remuneration shall be determined by law, and shall start to accrue as from the date on which the oath is taken by a member before the Council.

Art. 64. The Advisory Council shall formulate and adopt its own internal rules, which shall prescribe the procedure to be adopted in the conduct of its work, and the work of any committees which it may form, as well as the rules of procedure for debates, voting, submission of motions and the conduct of meetings.

Chapter V. The Judiciary

Art. 65. Judicial justice is a fundamental principle of Government in the State.

Judges shall be independent in the exercise of their power, and no party whatsoever may interfere in the administration of justice.

Art. 66. The general organization of the Judiciary in the State shall be determined by law in accordance with the provisions of this Provisional Constitution.

PART FIVE

GENERAL AND TRANSITIONAL PROVISIONS

Art. 67. The Amir may revise this Provisional Constitution by amendment, deletion or addition if he deems such revision necessary in the public interest.

Art. 68. All matters prescribed by the laws, regulations, decrees and orders that are in force on the date of coming into effect of this Provisional Constitution, and that do not conflict with any of its provisions shall continue to be in effect unless amended or revoked in accordance with the principles prescribed by this Provisional Constitution.

Where this Provisional Constitution provides that a specific matter shall be determined by law and where no such law is actually in force on the date of coming into effect of this Provisional Constitution, the existing Administrative procedures on that date regarding such matters, shall continue to be adopted until such time as the necessary law is enacted.

The laws required under this Provisional Constitution shall be promulgated within a period of two years from the date on which it comes into effect, unless otherwise expressly provided in this Provisional Constitution.

Art. 70. This Provisional Constitution shall remain in force until the date on which the complete Permanent Constitution which is referred to in the previous Article of this Provisional Constitution come into effect.

With the exception of provisions for which a stipulation fixing a specific date for their application is hereby mentioned, this Provisional Constitution shall come into effect as from the date of its publication in the Official Gazette, and it shall be published in the Official Gazette within a period of one week from the date of its promulgation.

SAMOA

SUMMARY

INTERNATIONAL STATUS

Samoa is a member of the United Nations (December 15, 1976). It is a member of the Commonwealth of Nations and of other international organizations.

Samoa, as Western Samoa, became independent on January 1, 1962, by the Western Samoa Act of November 24, 1961, of the New Zealand Parliament, to make provision in connection with the attainment of independence by the people of Western Samoa.

The Kingdom of Samoa granted trading and coaling rights to the United States, Germany and Great Britain in the 1870's. The Congress of Berlin in 1889, in an act providing for the neutrality of the islands, established, in effect, a tripartite protectorate. Under conventions of 1900 the United States annexed Eastern Samoa and Germany Western Samoa. New Zealand troops occupied the latter in 1914, and the country became a League of Nations mandate and then a United Nations trust territory administered by New Zealand. In May 1961, a plebiscite approved independence on the basis of the Constitution which the Legislative Assembly had adopted on October 28, 1960. By treaty with New Zealand, the latter acts as the official channel of communication with other governments and international organizations outside the Pacific islands area.

FORM OF NATIONAL GOVERNMENT

The Constitution of October 28, 1960, amended 1963, 1965, 1969, provides that Samoa is an independent and sovereign state based on Christian principles and Samoan custom and tradition; it names the islands forming the nation.[1] The source of sovereign power is not stated.

RIGHTS OF THE PEOPLE

The Constitution provides the right to life, liberty, fair trial, freedom of religion, speech, assembly, association, movement, residence, property, and equality before the law.[2] It forbids torture, inhuman treatment, forced labor, expropriation except by law.[3]

LEGISLATIVE DEPARTMENT

Parliament is unicameral consisting of the Head of State and the Legislative Assembly.[4] The Legislative Assembly is composed of members elected, one each, by the 45 territorial constituencies and of members elected by the individual voters' roll, for a term of three years subject to dissolution.[5] Immunities of members are provided.[6] There are provisions relating to finance.[7]

EXECUTIVE DEPARTMENT

Executive power is vested in the Head of State or *O le Ao o le Malo*, elected by the Legislative Assembly for a term of five years.[8] There is a Council of Deputies composed of at most three persons, elected by the Legislative Assembly, to act during the absence or incapacity of the Head of State.[9] The Head of State acts on the advice of the Prime Minister or Cabinet, which is composed of the Prime Minister and eight other members of Parliament and which directs and controls the executive government and is responsible to Parliament.[10]

There are provisions regarding the public service,[11] land and titles,[12] emergency powers.[13]

JUDICIAL DEPARTMENT

The Constitution provides a Supreme Court which is a superior court of record, the Chief Justice of which is appointed by the Head of State on the advice of the Prime Minister.[14] The Supreme Court may determine questions as to the interpretation or effect of provisions of the Constitution,[15] and it has the power to enforce the application of the rights provided in the Constitution.[16] There is a Court of Appeal to which appeals may lie from decisions of the Supreme Court in respect of the foregoing.[17]

[1] Const., Art. 1, Preamble.
[2] Id., Art. 5–15.
[3] Id., Art. 7, 8.
[4] Id., Art. 42.
[5] Id., Art. 44, 46, 63, 64.
[6] Id., Art. 62.
[7] Id., Art. 90–99.
[8] Id., Art. 16–19, 31.
[9] Id., Art. 23–25.
[10] Id., Art. 26, 32.
[11] Id., Art. 83–89.
[12] Id., Art. 100–104.
[13] Id., Art. 105, 106.
[14] Id., Art. 65.
[15] Id., Atr. 73.
[16] Id., Art. 4.
[17] Id., Art. 80, 81.

AREA, POPULATION, ETC.

The area of Samoa is 2835 square kilometres, its population (1981 estimate) is 156,893. The capital is Apia and the languages of Parliament are Samoan and English.[18]

[18] Id., Art. 54.

CONSTITUTION OF THE INDEPENDENT STATE OF WESTERN SAMOA[1]

October 28, 1960, amended 1963, 1965, 1969

In the Holy Name of God, the Almighty, the Ever Loving

Whereas sovereignty over the Universe belongs to the Omnipresent God alone, and the authority to be exercised by the people of Western Samoa within the limits prescribed by His commandments is a sacred heritage;

Whereas the Leaders of Western Samoa have declared that Western Samoa should be an Independent State based on Christian principles and Samoan custom and tradition;

And whereas the Constitutional Convention, representing the people of Western Samoa, has resolved to frame a constitution for the Independent State of Western Samoa;

Wherein the State should exercise its powers and authority through the chosen representatives of the people;

Wherein should be secured to all the people their fundamental rights;

Wherein the impartial administration of justice should be fully maintained;

And wherein the integrity of Western Samoa, its independence, and all its rights should be safeguarded;

Now therefore, we the people of Western Samoa in our Constitutional Convention, this twenty-eighth day of October 1960, do hereby adopt, enact, and give to ourselves this Constitution.

PART I

THE INDEPENDENT STATE OF WESTERN SAMOA AND ITS SUPREME LAW

1. (1) The Independent State of Western Samoa (hereinafter referred to as Western Samoa) shall be free and sovereign.

(2) Western Samoa shall comprise the islands of Upolu, Savai'i Manono and Apolima in the South Pacific Ocean, together with all other islands adjacent thereto and lying between the 13th and 15th degrees of south latitude and the 171st and 173rd degrees of longitude west of Greenwich.

2. (1) This Constitution shall be the supreme law of Western Samoa.

(2) Any existing law and any law passed after the date of coming into force of this Constitution which is inconsistent with this Constitution shall, to the extent of the inconsistency, be void.

[1] Published by the Government Printer, Apia, 1974. Supplied by them January 1980.

PART II

FUNDAMENTAL RIGHTS

3. In this Part, unless the context otherwise requires, 'the State' includes the Head of State, Cabinet, Parliament and all local and other authorities established under any law.

4. (1) Any person may apply to the Supreme Court by appropriate proceedings to enforce the rights conferred under the provisions of this Part.

(2) The Supreme Court shall have power to make all such orders, as may be necessary and appropriate to secure to the applicant the enjoyment of any of the rights conferred under the provisions of this Part.

5. (1) No person shall be deprived of his life intentionally, except in the execution of a sentence of a court following his conviction of an offence for which this penalty is provided by Act.

(2) Deprivation of life shall not be regarded as having been inflicted in contravention of the provisions of this Article when it results from the use of force to such extent and in such circumstances as are prescribed by law and as are reasonably justifiable

(*a*) in defence of any person from violence; or

(*b*) in order to effect an arrest or to prevent the escape of a person detained, if the person who is being arrested or who is escaping is believed on reasonable grounds to be in possession of a firearm or

(*c*) for the purpose of suppressing a riot, insurrection or mutiny.

6. (1) No person shall be deprived of his personal liberty except in accordance with law.

(2) Where complaint is made to the Supreme Court that a person is being unlawfully detained, the Court shall inquire into the complaint and, unless satisfied that the detention is lawful, shall order him to be produced before the Court and shall release him.

(3) Every person who is arrested shall be informed promptly of the grounds of his arrest and of any charge against him and shall be allowed to consult a legal practitioner of his own choice without delay.

(4) Every person who is arrested or otherwise detained shall be produced before a Judge of the Supreme Court, some other judicial officer, the Registrar of the Supreme Court or of any subordinate Court or any Deputy Registrar of the Supreme Court or of any subordinate Court from time to time approved in writing for this purpose by the Registrar of the Supreme Court (hereinafter collectively referred to as 'remanding officer') within a period of twenty-four hours (excluding the time of any necessary journey), and no such person shall be detained beyond that period without the authority of one of the remanding officers.'

7. No person shall be subjected to torture or to inhuman or degrading treatment or punishment.

8. (1) No person shall be required to perform forced or compulsory labor.

(2) For the purposes of this Article, the term 'forced or compulsory labor' shall not include

(*a*) any work required to be done in consequence of a sentence of a court; or

(*b*) any service of a military character or, in the case of conscientious objectors, service exacted instead of compulsory military service; or

(*c*) any service exacted in case of an emergency or calamity threatening the life or well-being of the community; or

(*d*) any work or service which is required by Samoan custom or which forms part of normal civic obligations.

9. (1) In the determination of his civil rights and obligations or of any charge against him for any offence, every person is entitled to a fair and public hearing within a reasonable time by an independent and impartial tribunal established under the law. Judgment shall be pronounced in public, but the public and representatives of news service may be excluded from all or part of the trial in the interests of morals, public order or national security, where the interests of juveniles or the protection of the private life of the parties so require, or to the extent strictly necessary in the opinion of the court in special circumstances where publicity would prejudice the interests of justice.

(2) Nothing in Clause (1) shall invalidate any law by reason only that it confers upon a tribunal, Minister or other authority power to determine questions arising in the administration of any law that affect or may affect the civil rights of any person.

(3) Every person charged with an offence shall be presumed innocent until proved guilty according to law.

(4) Every person charged with an offence has the following minimum rights.

(*a*) To be informed promptly, in a language which he understands and in detail, of the nature and cause of the accusation against him:

(*b*) To have adequate time and facilities for the preparation of his defence:

(*c*) To defend himself in person or through legal assistance of his own choosing and, if he has not sufficient means to pay for legal assistance, to be given it free when the interests of justice so require:

(*d*) To examine or have examined witnesses against him and to obtain the attendance and examination of witnesses on his behalf under the same conditions as witnesses against him:

(*e*) To have the free assistance of an interpreter, if any doubt exists as to whether he can understand or speak the language used in court.

(5) No person accused of any offence shall be compelled to be a witness against himself.

10. (1) No person shall be convicted of an offence other than an offence defined by law.

(2) No person shall be held guilty of any offence on account of any act or omission which did not constitute an offence at the time when it was committed; nor shall a heavier penalty be imposed than the one that was applicable at the time that the offence was committed.

(3) No person who has been tried for any offence shall, after conviction or acquittal, again be tried for any offence except

(*a*) where a retrial is ordered or conducted by a court or judicial officer exercising a jurisdiction superior to that under which that person was acquitted or convicted; or

(*b*) in the case of a conviction entered in a trial conducted by a Judge or Judges of the Supreme Court, where a retrial is ordered by a Judge of that Court on an application made within fourteen days of that conviction.

11. (1) Every person has the right to freedom of thought, conscience and religion; this right includes freedom to change his religion or belief, and freedom, either alone or in community with others, and, in public or private, to manifest and propagate his religion or belief in worship, teaching, practice and observance.

(2) Nothing in Clause (1) shall affect the operation of any existing law or prevent the State from making any law in so far as that existing law or the law so made imposes reasonable restrictions on the exercise of the right conferred under the provisions of that Clause in the interests of national security or of public order, health or morals, or for protecting the rights and freedom of others, including their rights and freedom to observe and practice their religion without the unsolicited interference of members of other religions.

12. (1) No person attending any educational institution shall be required to receive religious instruction or take part in any religious ceremony or attend religious worship, if that instruction, ceremony or worship relates to a religion other than his own.

(2) Every religious community or denomination shall have the right to establish and maintain educational institutions of its own choice and to provide therein religious instruction for pupils of that community or denomination.

(3) Nothing in Clause (2) shall prevent the State from making any law requiring the inspection of educational institutions and the maintenance therein of standards in keeping with the general educational level in Western Samoa.

13. (1) All citizens of Western Samoa shall have the right

(*a*) to freedom of speech and expression; and

(*b*) to assemble peaceably and without arms; and

(*c*) to form associations or unions; and

(*d*) to move freely throughout Western Samoa and to reside in any part thereof.

(2) Nothing in sub-clause (*a*) of Clause (1) shall affect the operation of any existing law or prevent the State from making any law in so far as that existing law or the law so made imposes reasonable restriction on the exercise of the right conferred under the provisions of that sub-clause in the interests of national security, friendly relations with other states, or public order or morals, for protecting

the privileges of the Legislative Assembly, for preventing the disclosure of information received in confidence, or for preventing contempt of court, defamation or incitement to any offence.

(3) Nothing in sub-clauses (*b*) or (*c*) of Clause (1) shall affect the operation of any existing law or prevent the State from making any law in so far as that existing law or the law so made imposes reasonable restrictions on the exercise of either or both of the rights conferred under the provisions of those sub-clauses in the interests of national security or public order, health or morals.

(4) Nothing in sub-clause (*d*) of Clause (1) shall affect the operation of any existing law or prevent the State from making any law in so far as that existing law or the law so made imposes reasonable restrictions on the exercise of the right conferred under the provisions of that sub-clause in the interests of national security, the economic well-being of Western Samoa, or public order, health or morals, for detaining persons of unsound mind, for preventing any offence, for the arrest and trial of persons charged with offences, or for punishing offenders.

14. (1) No property shall be taken possession of compulsorily, and no right over or interest in any property shall be acquired compulsorily, except under the law which, of itself or when read with any other law

(*a*) requires the payment within a reasonable time of adequate compensation therefor; and

(*b*) gives to any person claiming that compensation a right of access, for the determination of his interest in the property and the amount of compensation, to the Supreme Court; and

(*c*) gives to any party to proceedings in the Supreme Court relating to such a claim the same rights of appeal as are accorded generally to parties to civil proceedings in that Court sitting as a court of original jurisdiction.

(2) Nothing in this Article shall be construed as affecting any general law

(*a*) for the imposition or enforcement of any tax, rate or duty; or

(*b*) for the imposition of penalties or forfeitures for breach of the law, whether under civil process or after conviction of an offence; or

(*c*) relating to leases, tenancies, mortgages, charges, bills of sale, or any other rights or obligations arising out of contracts; or

(*d*) relating to the vesting and administration of the property or persons adjudged bankrupt or otherwise declared insolvent, of infants or persons suffering under some physical or mental disability, of deceased persons, and of companies, other corporate bodies and unincorporated societies, in the course of being wound up; or

(*e*) relating to the execution of judgments or orders of courts; or

(*f*) providing for the taking of possession of property which is in a dangerous state or is injurious to the health of human beings, plants or animals; or

(*g*) relating to trusts and trustees; or

(*h*) relating to the limitation of actions; or
(*i*) relating to property in statutory corporation; or
(*j*) relating to the temporary taking of possession of property for the purposes of any examination, investigation or inquiry; or
(*k*) providing for the carrying out of work on land for the purpose of soil conservation or for the protection of water catchment areas.

15. (1) All persons are equal before the law and entitled to equal protection under the law.

(2) Except as expressly authorized under the provisions of this Constitution, no law and no executive or administrative action of the State shall, either expressly or in its practical application, subject any person or persons to any disability or restriction or confer on any persons or persons any privilege or advantage on grounds only of descent, sex language, religion, political or other opinion, social origin, place of birth, family status, or any of them.

(3) Nothing in this Article shall
(*a*) prevent the prescription of qualifications for the service of Western Samoa or the service of a body corporate directly established under the law; or
(*b*) prevent the making of any provision for the protection or advancement of women or children or of any socially or educationally retarded class of persons.

(4) Nothing in this Article shall affect the operation of any existing law or the maintenance by the State of any executive or administrative practice being observed on Independence Day:

Provided that the State shall direct its policy towards the progressive removal of any disability or restriction which has been imposed on any of the grounds referred to in Clause (2) and of any privilege or advantage which has been conferred on any of those grounds.

PART III

THE HEAD OF STATE

16. There shall be a Head of State of Western Samoa to be known as O le Ao o le Malo.

17. (1) Notwithstanding anything to the contrary contained in this Part and subject to the provisions of this Article, Tupua Tamasese Mea'ole and Malietoa Tanumafili II shall on Indpendence Day assume jointly the office of Head of State. They shall be known jointly as O Ao o le Malo and severally as O le Ao o le Malo.

(2) On the death on or after Independence Day of either of the persons named in Clause (1), the survivor shall continue to hold the office of Head of State.

(3) In the event of the death before Independence Day of either of the

persons named in Clause (1), the survivor shall on Independence Day assume the office of Head of State.

(4) The provisions of this Part, except the provisions of Articles 18 and 19, shall apply to each of Tupua Tamasese Mea'ole or Malietoa Tanumafili II as a joint holder or as sole holder of the office of Head of State, as the case may be.

(5) On the death, resignation or removal from office of both the persons named in Clause (1) or of the survivor or either of them, this Article shall cease to be in force.

18. (1) The Head of State shall be elected by the Legislative Assembly under the provisions of the First Schedule.

(2) A person shall not be qualified to be elected to the office of Head of State

(*a*) if he is not a person qualified to be elected as a Member of Parliament; or

(*b*) if he does not possess such other qualifications as the Legislative Assembly may determine from time to time by resolution; or

(*c*) if he has previously been removed from the office of Head of State under the provisions of Clause (2) of Article 21.

(3) The validity of the election of the Head of State shall not be contested in any court.

19. (1) Subject to the provisions of Article 17 and 21, the Head of State shall hold office for a term of five years from the date on which he assumes the functions of his office:

Provided that, notwithstanding the expiry of his term, he shall continue to hold office until his successor assumes the functions of his office or for a period of three months, whichever is the shorter period.

(2) Subject to the provisions of this Constitution, a person who holds or who has held, office as Head of State, shall be eligible for re-election to that office.

(3) An election to fill a vacancy in the office of Head of State caused by the death, resignation or removal of the Head of State or by the expiry of the term of his office shall be held under the provisions of the First Schedule, and, subject to the provisions of this Constitution, the person elected to that office shall hold office for a term of five years from the date on which he assumes the functions of his office.

20. The Head of State shall not hold any other office of profit or any other position carrying the right to remuneration for the rendering of services, or engage in any occupation for reward outside the functions of his office; but nothing in this Clause shall prevent him from holding the *pule* over any customary land, from holding any freehold land or other private property, or from disposing of the produce of any customary or freehold land.

21. (1) The Head of State may resign his office by writing under his hand addressed to the Prime Minister, who shall forthwith advise the Speaker of the Legislative Assembly of that resignation.

(2) The Head of State may be removed from office by the Legislative Assembly on the ground of misbehaviour or of infirmity of body or mind.

(3) No proposal for the removal from office of the Head of State under the provisions of Clause (2) shall be effective unless

(*a*) notice of motion setting out the grounds for the proposed removal has been given in writing and signed by not less than one fourth of the total number of Members of Parliament (including vacancies); and

(*b*) a period of at least fourteen days has elapsed between that notice and the debate on the motion; and

(*c*) the motion has been agreed to by not less than two thirds of the total number of Members of Parliament (including vacancies),

(4) A resolution carried under the provisions of Clause (3), shall have the effect of removing the Head of State from his office as from the date on which the resolution is so carried.

22. The salary of the Head of State shall be determined by Act and shall be charged on the Treasury Fund, and that salary shall not be diminished during the period of office of the Head of State, unless as part of a general reduction of salaries applied proportionately to all persons whose salaries are determined by Act.

23. (1) While any vacancy exists in the office of Head of State or during the absence from Western Samoa of the Head of State, the Council of Deputies shall perform the functions of the office of Head of State.

(2) Whenever the Chief Justice declares in writing that he is satisfied by evidence, which shall include, where possible, the evidence of the wife and of at least two physicians, that the head of State is by reason of infirmity of body or mind incapable for the time being of performing his functions as Head of State, or that he is satisfied by evidence that the Head of State is from some definite cause not available for the performance of those functions, then, until it is declared in like manner that the Head of State has so far recovered his health as to warrant his resumption of the functions of the office of Head of State or has become available for the performance thereof, as the case may be, those functions shall be performed by the Council of Deputies.

24. While Tupua Tamasese Mea'ole and Malietoa Tanumafili II hold jointly the office of Head of State, the following provisions shall apply:

(*a*) During any period for which one joint holder of office is absent from Western Samoa or is incapable of, or not available for, the performance of his functions as Head of State, the other joint holder shall perform those functions.

(*b*) During any period for which neither of the joint holders is able to perform the functions of the office of Head of State, whether by reason of absence from Western Samoa, incapacity or unavailability, the Council of Deputies shall perform those functions.

(*c*) For the purposes of this Article, the Chief Justice shall determine, under the provisions of Clause (2) of Article 23, the period during which a joint holder is incapable of, or not available for, the performance of his functions as Head of State.

25. (1) There shall be a Council of Deputies, which shall consist of one, two or three persons elected by the Legislative Assembly:

Provided that, if the Assembly shall not have elected a Council of Deputies, the Chief Justice shall assume the functions of the Council.

(2) A person shall not be qualified to be elected as, or to continue to be, a member of the Council of Deputies unless he is qualified to be elected as Head of State under the provisions of Article 18.

(3) An election of members of the Council of Deputies shall be held as soon as possible after each election of a Head of State:

Provided that, while the provisions of Article 17 are in force, an election of members of the Council of Deputies shall be held as soon as possible after Independence Day and, thereafter, at intervals of not less than four years and nine months and not more than five years and three months.

(4) If at any time the number of members of the Council of Deputies is less than three, the Legislative Assembly may elect as a member of the council a person qualified to be elected under the provisions of Clause (2), and any person so elected shall hold office until the next ensuing election held under the provisions of Clause (3).

(5) Subject to the provisions of Clause (2), a member of the Council of Deputies shall be eligible for re-election.

(6) A member of the Council of Deputies may resign his office by writing under his hand addressed to the Prime Minister, who shall forthwith advise the Speaker of the Legislative Assembly of that resignation.

(7) The Legislative Assembly may, on a motion carried by not less than two thirds of the total number of Members of Parliament (including vacancies), remove from office a member of the Council of Deputies on the ground of stated misbehaviour or of infirmity of body or mind.

(8) The salaries of members of the Council of Deputies shall be determined by Act and shall be charged on the Treasury Fund but an Act may provide that no such salary shall be payable to such a member for any period for which he is a full-time salaried employee of the Government. The salaries of such members shall not be diminished during their period of office, unless as part of a general reduction of salaries applied proportionately to all persons whose salaries are determined by Act.

(9) A member of the Council of Deputies shall not be qualified to be elected as a Member of Parliament:

Provided that the provisions of this Clause shall not disqualify a member of the Council from being elected to the office of Head of State.

(10) The Council of Deputies shall determine which of its members shall, from time to time, preside over the Council.

(11) Subject to the provisions of this Constitution, the Council of Deputies may regulate its procedure in such manner as it thinks fit.

26. (1) Except as otherwise provided in this Constitution, the Head of State in the performance of his functions shall act on the advice of Cabinet, the Prime Minister or the appropriate Minister as the case may be.

(2) If Cabinet, the Prime Minister or an appropriate Minister tenders advice to the Head of State as to the performance of any functions of the Head of State and, if the Head of State does not, within seven days after the date on which the tendering of that advice comes to the notice of the Secretary to the Head of State, accept that advice or take some other action in relation thereto which he is entitled to take under the provisions of this Constitution or of any Act, the Head of State shall be deemed to have accepted that advice; and an instrument under the hand of the Secretary to Cabinet, acting on the instruction of the Prime Minister, to that effect shall operate as the performance of the function concerned in accordance with that advice.

27. It shall be the duty of the Prime Minister

(*a*) to arrange for the circulation to the Head of State of copies of the agenda and minutes of Cabinet and of all other papers laid before Cabinet at the time when they are circulated to Ministers; and

(*b*) to furnish such information relating to the administration of the affairs of Western Samoa and proposals for legislation as the Head of State may call for.

28. The Head of State and each member of the Council of Deputies shall, before assuming the functions of his office, take and subscribe before the Chief Justice an oath in the form set out in the Third Schedule.

29. The Head of State shall keep and use the Public Seal of Western Samoa.

30. There shall be a Secretary to the Head of State.

PART IV

THE EXECUTIVE

31. (1) The executive power of Western Samoa shall vest in the head of State and shall be exercised by him under the provisions of this Constitution.

(2) Nothing in Clause (1) shall prevent Parliament from conferring by Act functions on authorities other than the Head of State.

32. (1) There shall be a Cabinet of Ministers, who shall have the general direction and control of the executive government of Western Samoa and shall be collectively responsible therefor to Parliament..

(2) Cabinet shall be appointed as follows:

(*a*) The Head of State shall appoint as Prime Minister to preside over Cabinet a Member of Parliament who commands the confidence of a majority of the Members of Parliament.

(*b*) The Head of State shall, acting on the advice of the Prime Minister, appoint eight other Members of Parliament to be Ministers.

(*c*) If an appointment is to be made while the Legislative Assembly is dissolved, a person who was a Member of Parliament immediately before the Assembly was last dissolved may be appointed to be Prime Minister or a Minister.

(*d*) Appointments under the provisions of this Clause shall be made by the Head of State by instrument under the Public Seal.

(*e*) The Head of State shall, acting on the advice of the Prime Minister, appoint another Member or Members of Parliament to be a Minister or Ministers as soon as possible after the number of Ministers falls below eight by reason of the office of any Minister or Ministers becoming vacant, so that the number of Ministers (in addition to the Prime Minister) shall be restored to eight as soon as possible.

33. (1) The appointment of the Prime Minister who is in office at the commencement of the first session of the Legislative Assembly following a dissolution thereof shall be terminated by the Head of State on the seventh day of that session if the Prime Minister has not sooner resigned.

(2) The appointment of the Prime Minister shall also be terminated by the Head of State

(*a*) if the Prime Minister ceases to be a Member of Parliament for any reason other than a dissolution of the Legislative Assembly; or

(*b*) if the Legislative Assembly passes a motion in express words of no confidence in Cabinet or if Cabinet is defeated on any question or issue which the Prime Minister has declared to be a question or issue of confidence:

Provided that, if after the passing of such a motion or after that defeat the Prime Minister so requests, the Head of State may dissolve the Legislative Assembly instead of terminating the appointment of the Prime Minister; or

(*c*) if the Prime Minister resigns his office by writing under his hand addressed to the Head of State; or

(*d*) if the Prime Minister is absent from Western Samoa without written permission given by the Head of State, acting in his discretion.

(3) The office of any other Minister shall become vacant

(*a*) if the appointment of the Prime Minister has been terminated under the provisions of Clause (1) or Clause (2); or

(*b*) if the appointment of the Minister to that office is revoked by the Head of State, acting on the advice of the Prime Minister, by instrument under the Public Seal; or

(*c*) if the Minister ceases to be a Member of Parliament for any reason other than a dissolution of the Legislative Assembly; or

(*d*) if the Minister resigns his office by writing under his hand addressed to the Head of State; or

(*e*) if the Minister is absent from Western Samoa without written permission given by the Head of State, acting on the advice of the Prime Minister.

(4) Whenever, by reason of illness or of absence from Western Samoa with the written persmission of the Head of State, the Prime Minister is temporarily prevented from performing, in Western Samoa, the functions of his office, the Head of State may, by instrument under the Public Seal, appoint another Minister to perform those functions until such time as the Prime Minister is capable of again performing them or has vacated his office.

(5) The power conferred on the Head of State under the provisions of Clause (4) shall be exercised by the Head of State, acting in his discretion, if in his opinion it is impracticable to obtain the advice of the Prime Minister by reason of the illness or absence of the Prime Minister and, in any other case, shall be exercised by the Head of State, acting on the advice of the Prime Minister.

(6) The Head of State, acting on the advice of the Prime Minister, may by instrument under the Public Seal

(*a*) declare a Minister to be by reason of illness temporarily incapable of performing his functions as a Minister; or

(*b*) suspend a Minister during the period of any investigation or inquiry into the conduct of that Minister.

(7) Any Minister in respect of whom action has been taken under the provisions of Clause (6) shall not perform any of the functions of his office or sit in or otherwise take part in the proceedings of Cabinet until the Head of State, acting on the advice of the Prime Minister, has revoked the aforesaid instrument under the Public Seal.

34. Every Minister shall, before assuming the functions of his office, take and subscribe before the Head of State an oath in the form set out in the Third Schedule.

35. (1) The Prime Minister may, by direction in writing under his hand

(*a*) charge any Minister with the responsibility for any Department or subject; and

(*b*) revoke or vary any direction given under the provisions of this Clause.

(2) The Prime Minister may retain in his charge any Department or subject.

36. Cabinet shall be summoned only by the Prime Minister or, in his absence, by such Minister as the Prime Minister shall appoint in that behalf.

37. (1) Subject to the provisions of this Constitution, Cabinet may regulate its procedure (including the fixing of a quorum) in such manner as it thinks fit.

(2) There shall be a Secretary to Cabinet.

(3) Cabinet shall not be disqualified for the transaction of business by reason of any vacancy in the number of its members, and any proceedings of Cabinet shall be valid notwithstanding that some person who was not entitled to do so sat or voted in Cabinet or otherwise took part in the proceedings.

(4) It shall be the duty of the Prime Minister, if the Head of State so requires, to submit for the consideration of Cabinet any matter on which a decision has been taken by a Minister (including the Prime Minister) but which has not been considered by Cabinet.

(5) A decision of Cabinet shall be recorded in minutes which shall, under the hand of the Secretary to Cabinet, be communicated to the Secretary to the Head of State within twenty-four hours of the making of the decision.

(6) A decision of Cabinet shall not take effect except under the provisions of Article 38.

38. (1) A decision of Cabinet shall take effect

(*a*) on its approval by the Head of State, acting in his discretion; or

(*b*) on the expiry of four days after the date of the decision, unless a meeting of the Executive Council is sooner held under the provisions of Article 40; or

(*c*) if the issue involved in the decision is, in the opinion of a majority of Ministers present and voting at the meeting at which the decision is taken, of extreme urgency, on the expiry of one day after the date of the decision, unless a meeting of the Executive Council is sooner held under the provisions of Article 40; or

(*d*) under the provisions of Article 40.

(2) For the purposes of subclauses (*b*) and (*c*) of Clause (1), the date of a decision of Cabinet shall be the date on which the minutes in which the decision is recorded are communicated to the Secretary to the Head of State under the provisions of Clause (5) of Article 37.

(3) An instrument under the hand of the Secretary to Cabinet certifying that a decision of Cabinet has taken effect shall be conclusive evidence that that decision has taken effect.

39. (1) There shall be an Executive Council of Western Samoa, which shall consist of:

(*a*) The Head of State:

(*b*) The Prime Minister and Ministers holding office under the provisions of Article 32 and 33.

(2) Subject to the provisions of this Constitution, the Executive Council may regulate its procedure (including the fixing of a quorum) in such manner as it thinks fit.

(3) The Secretary to Cabinet shall be Clerk of the Executive Council.

40. (1) The Head of State, acting in his discretion, or the Prime Minister may summon a meeting of the Executive Council to consider any decision recorded in the minutes of a Cabinet meeting.

(2) If at a meeting of the Executive Council thus summoned the Head of State supports the decision concerned, that decision shall take effect as a decision of Cabinet.

(3) If at a meeting of the Executive Council thus summoned the Head of State opposes the decision concerned or requests any amendment thereto, Cabinet shall thereupon be summoned under the provisions of Article 36 and requested to reconsider that decision.

(4) If Cabinet after that reconsideration reaffirms its original decision or accepts the amendment requested by the Head of State, the original decision or

the decision as so amended, as the case may be, shall forthwith take effect as a decision of Cabinet.

(5) If Cabinet after that reconsideration adopts a decision which incorporates an amendment to its original decision, other than an amendment requested by the Head of State under the provisions of Clause (3), the decision as so amended shall operate as a new decision of Cabinet to which the provisions of Clauses (5) and (6) of Article 37 shall apply.

41. (1) The Head of State, acting on the advice of the Prime Minister, shall appoint an Attorney General, who shall be a person qualified to be a Judge of the Supreme Court.

(2) The Attorney General shall advise on legal matters referred to him by the Head of State, Cabinet, the Prime Minister or a Minister and shall have power, exercisable in his discretion, to institute, conduct or discontinue any proceedings for an offence alleged to have been committed.

(3) The Attorney General shall have a right of audience in, and shall take precedence over any other person appearing before, any court or tribunal.

(4) The powers of the Attorney General may be exercised by him in person or by officers subordinate to him, acting under and in accordance with his general or special instructions.

(5) The Attorney General shall hold office for such term or terms and under such conditions as may be determined by the Head of State, acting on the advice of the Prime Minister.

PART V

PARLIAMENT

42. There shall be a Parliament of Western Samoa, which shall consist of the Head of State and the Legislative Assembly.

43. Subject to the provisions of this Constitution, Parliament may make laws for the whole or any part of Western Samoa and laws having effect outside as well as within Western Samoa.

44. (1) The Legislative Assembly shall consist of:

(*a*) One member elected for each of forty-one territorial constituencies having such names and boundaries and including such villages or sub-villages or villages and sub-villages as are prescribed from time to time by Act:

(*aa*) Four additional members being one additional member elected for each of such four of those territorial constituencies as are prescribed from time to time by Act.

(*b*) Members elected by those persons whose names appear on the individual voters' roll.

(2) The number of members to be elected under the provisions of subclause (*b*) of Clause (1) shall be determined under the provisions of the Second Schedule.

(3) Subject to the provisions of this Constitution, the mode of electing members of the Legislative Assembly, the terms and condition of their membership, the qualifications of electors, and the manner in which the roll for each territorial constituency and the individual voters' roll shall be established and kept shall be prescribed by law.

(4) Members of the Legislative Assembly shall be known as Members of Parliament.

45. (1) Any person shall be qualified to be elected as a Member of Parliament who

(*a*) is a citizen of Western Samoa; and

(*b*) is not disqualified under the provisions of this Constitution or of any Act.

(2) If any person other than a person qualified under the provisions of Clause (1) is elected as a Member of Parliament, the election of that person shall be void.

46. (1) Every Member of Parliament shall cease to be a Member at the next dissolution of the Legislative Assembly after he has been elected or previously thereto if his seat becomes vacant under the provisions of Clause (2).

(2) The seat of a Member of Parliament shall become vacant

(*a*) upon his death; or

(*b*) if he resigns his seat by writing under his hand addressed to the Speaker; or

(*c*) if he ceases to be a citizen of Western Samoa; or

(*d*) if he becomes disqualified under the provisions of this Constitution or of any Act.

47. All questions that may arise as to the right of any person to be or to remain a Member of Parliament shall be referred to and determined by the Supreme Court.

48. Whenever the seat of a Member of Parliament becomes vacant under the provisions of Clause (2) of Article 46, the Speaker shall, by writing under his hand, report that vacancy to the Head of State, and the vacancy shall be filled by election in the manner provided by law.

49. (1) The Legislative Assembly shall, immediately when it first meets after a general election and as soon as possible after any vacancy occurs in the office of Speaker otherwise than by reason of a dissolution of the Assembly, elect a Member of Parliament to be Speaker of the Legislative Assembly.

(2) The Speaker, upon being elected and before assuming the functions of his office, shall take and subscribe before the Head of State an Oath of Allegiance in the form set out in the Third Schedule.

(3) The Speaker may at any time resign his office by writing under his hand addressed to the Clerk of the Legislative Assembly and shall vacate his office

(*a*) if he ceases to be a Member of Parliament; or

(*b*) if he is appointed to be a Minister.

50. (1) The Legislative Assembly may elect a Member of Parliament not being a Minister, to be Deputy Speaker.

(2) The Deputy Speaker may at any time resign his office by writing under his hand addressed to the Clerk of the Legislative Assembly and shall vacate his office

(*a*) if he ceases to be a Member of Parliament; or

(*b*) if he is appointed to be a Minister; or

(*c*) if he is elected to be Speaker.

(3) Subject to the provisions of this Constitution, the functions conferred under the provisions of this Constitution upon the Speaker shall, if there is no person holding the office of Speaker or if the Speaker is absent from Western Samoa or is otherwise unable to perform those functions, be performed by the Deputy Speaker.

51. There shall be a Clerk of the Legislative Assembly.

52. The Legislative Assembly shall meet at such times and at such places as the Head of State appoints from time to time in that behalf, by notice published in the Western Samoa Gazette and recorded in the *Savali*:

Provided that the Assembly shall meet not later than forty-five days after the holding of a general election and at least once in every year thereafter, so that a period of twelve months shall not intervene between the last sitting of the Assembly in one session and the first sitting thereof in the next session.

53. Subject to the provisions of this Constitution, the Legislative Assembly may make amend and repeal standing orders regulating its procedure.

54. (1) All debates and discussions in the Legislative Assembly shall be conducted in the Samoan language and the English language.

(2) The Minutes and the debates of the Legislative Assembly, every bill introduced therein, every paper presented thereto, and all minutes of proceedings, minutes of evidence and reports of committees of the Assembly shall be in the Samoan language and the English language.

55. The Speaker, or in his absence the Deputy Speaker, shall preside over sittings of the Legislative Assembly. In the absence from any sitting of both the Speaker and the Deputy Speaker, the Members of Parliament present shall choose one of their number (not being a Minister) to preside over that sitting.

56. The Legislative Assembly shall not be disqualified for the transaction of business by reason of any vacancy among the Members of Parliament, including any vacancy not filled at a general election, and any proceedings therein shall be valid notwithstanding that some person who was not entitled to do so sat or voted in the Assembly or otherwise took part in the proceedings.

57. No business shall be transacted at any sitting of the Legislative Assembly if objection is taken by any Member of Parliament present that the number of Members present is (besides of Speaker or other Member presiding) fewer than one half of the total number of Members of Parliament (excluding vacancies).

58. (1) Except as otherwise provided in this Constitution, every question before the Legislative Assembly shall be decided by a majority of the votes of the Members of Parliament present.

(2) The Speaker, or the Deputy Speaker or any other Member of Parliament

while presiding over a sitting of the Legislative Assembly in the absence of the Speaker, shall not have a deliberative vote but, in the case of an equality of votes, shall have a casting vote.

59. Subject to the provisions of this Part and of the Standing Orders of the Legislative Assembly, any Member of Parliament may introduce any bill or propose any motion for debate in the Assembly or present any petition to the Assembly, and the same shall be considered and disposed of under the provisions of the Standing Orders.

Provided that, except upon the recommendation or with the consent of the Head of State, the Assembly shall not proceed upon any bill which, in the opinion of the Speaker, the Deputy Speaker or other Member of Parliament presiding would dispose of or charge the Treasury Fund or any other public fund or account, or revoke or alter any disposition thereof or charge thereon, or impose, alter or repeal any tax, rate or duty.

60. (1) No bill shall become a law until the Head of State has given his assent thereto.

(2) Whenever a bill which has been passed by the Legislative Assembly is presented to the Head of State for his assent, he shall, acting on the advice of the Prime Minister, declare that he assents to the bill or that he refuses his assent to the bill.

(3) A law assented to by the Head of State as herein provided shall be known as an Act of Parliament and shall come into force whether on the day on which it is assented to, or on any date (whether earlier or later than the date on which it is assented to) specified in that behalf in the Act.

61. Except for the purpose of enabling this Article to be complied with and for the election of a Speaker, no Member of Parliament shall sit or vote in the Legislative Assembly until he shall have taken and subscribed before the Assembly an Oath of Allegiance in the form set out in the Third Schedule.

62. The privileges, immunities and powers of the Legislative Assembly, of the committees thereof and of Members of Parliament may be determined by Act:

Provided that no such privilege or power may extend to the imposition of a fine or to committal to prison for contempt or otherwise, unless provision is made by Act for the trial and punishment of the person concerned by the Supreme Court.

63. (1) The Head of State may at any time, by notice published in the Western Samoa Gazette, prorogue the Legislative Assembly.

(2) If, at any time, the office of Prime Minister is vacant, the Head of State shall, by notice published in the Western Samoa Gazette, dissolve the Legislative Assembly as soon as he is satisfied, acting in his discretion, that a reasonable period has elapsed since that office was last vacated and that there is no Member of Parliament likely to command the confidence of a majority of the Members.

(3) The Head of State may at any time, by notice published in the Western Samoa Gazette, dissolve the Legislative Assembly, if he is advised by the Prime Minister to do so, but shall not be obliged to act in this respect in accordance with the advice of the Prime Minister unless he is satisfied, acting in his discretion, that, in tendering that advice, the Prime Minister commands the confidence of a majority of the Members of Parliament.

(4) The Head of State shall dissolve the Legislative Assembly at the expiry of three years from the date of the last preceding general election, if it has not been sooner dissolved.

64. There shall be a general election of the Legislative Assembly at such time within three months after every dissolution of the Assembly as the Head of State appoints by notice in the Western Samoa Gazette.

PART VI

THE JUDICIARY

65. (1) There shall be a Supreme Court of Western Samoa, which shall be a superior court of record and shall consist of a Chief Justice and such number of other Judges as may be determined by Act.

(2) The Chief Justice of the Supreme Court shall be appointed by the Head of State, acting on the advice of the Prime Minister.

(3) A person shall not be qualified for appointment as a Judge of the Supreme Court unless

(*a*) he possesses such qualifications as the Head of State, acting on the advice of the Judicial Service Commission, may prescribe and

(*b*) he has been in practice as a barrister in Western Samoa, or in an approved country, or partly in the one and partly in the other, for a period of or periods amounting in the aggregate to, not less than eight years.

(4) In computing, for the purposes of sub-clause (*b*) of Clause (3), the period or periods during which any person has been in practice as a barrister, any period or periods during which he has held judicial office in a court of superior or subordinate jurisdiction in Western Samoa or an approved country shall be included.

(5) For the purpose of this Article or of Clause (4) of Article 75 or of both of them, the Head of State, acting on the advice of the Judicial Service Commission, may designate as an approved country any country which, in the opinion of the Commission, has a legal system similar to that existing in Western Samoa.

66. Each Judge of the Supreme Court or any two or more Judges may, in any part of Western Samoa and at any time or place, exercise all the powers of the Supreme Court.

67. Every Judge of the Supreme Court shall, before assuming the functions of his office, take and subscribe before the Head of State an oath in the form set out in the Third Schedule.

68. (1) Except in the case of an appointment made under the provisions of Clause (2), a Judge of the Supreme Court shall hold office until he reaches the age of sixty-two years:

Provided that the Head of State, acting (in the case of the Chief Justice) on the advice of the Prime Minister or (in the case of any other Judge of the Supreme Court) on the advice of the Judicial Service Commission, may extend the period of office of a Judge who has reached the age of sixty-two years.

(2) Any person of any age who is not a citizen of Western Samoa and who is qualified for appointment under the provisions of Clause (3) of Article 65 may be appointed to hold office as a Judge of the Supreme Court for a term of years.

(3) Nothing done by a Judge of the Supreme Court in the performance of his functions shall be deemed to be invalid by reason only that he has reached the age at which he is required by this Article to retire or that his term of office has expired, as the case may be.

(4) A Judge of the Supreme Court may resign his office by writing under his hand addressed to the Head of State.

(5) A Judge of the Supreme Court shall not be removed from office, except by the Head of State on an address of the Legislative Assembly carried by not less than two thirds of the total number of Members of Parliament (including vacancies), praying for his removal from office on the ground of stated misbehavior or of infirmity of body or mind.

(6) The Head of State, acting (in the case of the Chief Justice) on the advice of the Prime Minister or (in the case of any other Judge of the Supreme Court) on the advice of the Judicial Service Commission, may at any time when the Legislative Assembly is not meeting suspend a Judge of the Supreme Court from his office, and such suspension, unless previously revoked, shall continue in force until the end of the next ensuing session and no longer.

69. The salaries of Judges of the Supreme Court to whom Clause (1) of Article 68 applies shall be determined by Act and shall be charged on the Treasury Fund. The salaries of such Judges shall not be diminished during their period of office, unless as part of a general reduction of salaries applied proportionately to all persons whose salaries are determined by Act.

70. (1) While any vacancy exists in the office of Chief Justice or during any absence from Western Samoa of the Chief Justice, the senior Judge of the Supreme Court shall have authority to act as Chief Justice and to perform the functions of the office of Chief Justice.

(2) Wherever by reason of illness or any cause other than absence from Western Samoa the Chief Justice is unable to perform the functions of the office of Chief Justice, the Head of State, acting of the advice of the Prime Minister may authorize the senior Judge of the Supreme Court to act as Chief Justice until the Chief Justice resumes those functions and, during that period, to perform those functions.

(3) The authority conferred on the Acting Chief Justice under the provisions of this Article shall not include power to preside over the Court of Appeal unless he is qualified by virtue of his seniority to preside thereover under the provisions of Clause (3) of Article 75.

71. (1) If the office of any Judge of the Supreme Court (other than the Chief Justice) is vacant or if any such Judge is unable to perform the functions of his office, the Head of State, acting on the advice of the Judicial Service Commission may appoint a person qualified under the provisions of Clause (3) of Article 65 to be temporarily a Judge of the Supreme Court:

Provided that a person may be so appointed notwithstanding that he has attained the age of sixty-two years.

(2) Any person appointed under the provisions of Clause (1) to be temporarily a Judge of the Supreme Court shall hold office for the period of his appointment or, if no such period is specified, until his appointment is revoked by the Head of State, acting on the advice of the Judicial Service Commission:

Provided that he may at any time resign his office by writing under his hand addressed to the Head of State.

72. (1) There shall be a Judicial Service Commission which shall consist of:

(*a*) The Chief Justice, as President:

(*b*) The Attorney General or, if for any reason the Attorney General is unable to act, the Chairman of the Public Service Commission:

(*c*) A person nominated from time to time by the Minister of Justice.

(2) No business shall be transacted by the Judicial Service Commission unless three members are present, and all questions proposed for decisions by the Commission shall be decided by a majority of the votes of the members.

(3) The power of appointing, promoting and transferring any judicial officer, other than the Chief Justice, and of dismissing any judicial officer, other than a Judge of the Supreme Court, is hereby vested in the Head of State, acting on the advice of the Judicial Service Commission.

73. (1) The Supreme Court shall have such original, appellate and revisional jurisdiction as may be provided by Act.

(2) Without prejudice to any appellate or revisional jurisdiction of the Supreme Court, where in any proceedings before another court (except the Court of Appeal) a question arises as to the interpretation or effect of any provision of this Constitution, the Supreme Court may, on the application of any party to the proceedings, determine that question and either dispose of the case or remit it to that other court to be disposed of in accordance with the determination.

(3) The Head of State, acting on the advice of the Prime Minister, may refer to the Supreme Court for its opinion any question as to the interpretation or effect of any provision of this Constitution which has arisen or appears likely to arise, and the Court shall pronounce its opinion on any question so referred to it.

74. There shall be such subordinate courts possessing such jurisdiction and powers as may be provided by Act.

75. (1) There shall be a Court of Appeal of Western Samoa, which shall be a superior court of record.

(2) Subject to the provisions of this Part, the Judges of the Court of Appeal shall be:

(*a*) The Chief Justice and the other Judges of the Supreme Court

(*b*) Such persons, possessing the qualifications prescribed under the provisions of Clause (3) of Article 65, as may be appointed from time to time by the Head of State, acting on the advice of the Judicial Service Commission.

(3) The Chief Justice shall be President of the Court of Appeal, but, in

his absence, the senior Judge of the Court present at the appeal or, if the Judges so present are of the same seniority, a Judge designated by the Chief Justice shall preside.

(4) Judges of the Court of Appeal shall take seniority according to the respective dates of their first appointment as Judges of a superior court in Western Samoa or in any approved country.

(5) An appointment under the provisions of sub-clause (*b*) of Clause (2) shall be for a period of time or for the trial or hearing of particular causes or matters, as may be specified in the instrument of appointment.

76. (1) Any three Judges of the Court of Appeal may exercise all the powers of the Court:

Provided that the Court may have its judgment delivered by any one of it members who is also a Judge of the Supreme Court, and if there is no such member then through the Registrar of the Court of Appeal.

(2) The judgment of the Court of Appeal shall be in accordance with the opinion of the majority of the Judges present.

77. A Judge of the Court of Appeal shall not sit on the hearing of an appeal from any decision made by him or by a court on which he sat as a member.

78. Any person appointed under the provisions of sub-clause (*b*) of Clause (2) of Article 75 to be a Judge of the Court of Appeal shall, on first appointment, take and subscribe before the Head of State an oath in the form set out in the Third Schedule.

79. Subject to the provisions of this Constitution, the Court of Appeal shall have jurisdiction to hear and determine such appeals (including proceedings removed by order of the Supreme Court to the Court of Appeal) as may be provided by Act.

80. (1) An appeal shall lie to the Court of Appeal from any decision of the Supreme Court in any proceeding, if the Supreme Court certifies that the case involves a substantial question of law as to the interpretation or effect of any provision of this Constitution.

(2) Where the Supreme Court has refused to give such a certificate, the Court of Appeal may, if it is satisfied that the case involves a substantial question of law as to the interpretation or effect of any provision of this Constitution, grant special leave to appeal from that decision.

(3) Where such a certificate is given or such leave is granted, any party in the case may appeal to the Court of Appeal on the ground that any such question as aforesaid has been wrongly decided and, with the leave of that Court, on any other ground.

81. An appeal shall lie to the Court of Appeal from any decision of the Supreme Court in any proceedings under the provisions of Article 4.

82. In Article 77, 80, 81 and 119, 'decision' includes judgment, decree, order, writ, declaration, conviction, sentence, opinion or other determined.

PART VII

THE PUBLIC SERVICE

83. The 'Public Service' means the service of Western Samoa; but does not include service remunerated by way of fees or commission only, honorary service, or service in any of the following capacities, namely as

(*a*) Head of State; or
(*b*) a member of the Council of Deputies; or
(*c*) Prime Minister or a Minister; or
(*d*) Speaker or Deputy Speaker; or
(*e*) a Member of Parliament; or
(*f*) a Judge of the Supreme Court or any other judicial officer; or
(*g*) Attorney General; or
(*h*) Controller and Chief Auditor or
(*i*) a member of the Public Service Commission who is not an employee of the Public Service at the time of his appointment to be a member of the Public Service Commission; or
(*j*) an officer of police or an officer of prisons; or
(*k*) a member of any uniformed branch of any defence force; or
(*l*) a *Pulenu'u.*

84. (1) There shall be a Public Service Commission of Western Samoa, which shall consist of not more than three persons appointed by the Head of State, acting on the advice of the Prime Minister.

(2) The Head of State, acting on the advice of the Prime Minister shall appoint one of the members of the Public Service Commission to be Chairman.

(3) No person shall be appointed to be or shall remain a member of the Public Service Commission

(*a*) if he is not or ceases to be a citizen of Western Samoa; or
(*b*) if he is or becomes a Member of Parliament.

(4) No member of the Public Service Commission shall hold concurrently any other office in the Public Service.

(5) The powers of the Public Service Commission shall not be affected by any vacancy in the number of its members, and any proceedings of the Commission shall be valid notwithstanding that some person who was not entitled to do so took part in those proceedings.

85. (1) A member of the Public Service Commission shall be appointed to hold office for a term of not more than three years but shall be eligible for reappointment.

(2) A member of the Public Service Commission may at any time resign his office by writing under his hand addressed to the Prime Minister but shall not be removed from office except on the like grounds and in the like manner as a Judge of the Supreme Court.

(3) The Head of State, acting on the advice of the Prime Minister, may at

any time when the Legislative Assembly is not meeting suspend a member of the Public Service Commission from his office, and such suspension, unless previously revoked, shall continue in force until the end of the next ensuing session and no longer.

86. The salaries of members of the Public Service Commission shall be determined by the Head of State, acting on the advice of the Prime Minister.

87. (1) Subject to the provisions of Clause (3), the Public Service Commission shall be responsible for the appointment, promotion, transfer, termination of appointment, dismissal and disciplinary control of the Public Service and shall have such other functions as may be provided by Act.

(2) In the performance of its functions, the Public Service Commission shall have regard to the general policy of Cabinet relating to the Public Service, and shall give effect to any decision of Cabinet defining that policy conveyed to the Commission in writing by the Prime Minister.

(3) An Act of Parliament may designate as a special post any post of head of department or any post of a corresponding grade; and the Head of State, acting on the advice of Cabinet after Cabinet has consulted the Public Service Commission, shall be responsible, in respect of any post so designated, for appointments, grading, salaries, promotions, transfers, retirements, terminations of appointments, dismissals and discipline.

88. (1) Subject to the provisions of this Constitution and of any law, the Public Service Commission may

(*a*) regulate its procedure (including the fixing of a quorum) in such manner as it thinks fit; and

(*b*) delegate any of its functions to any of its members or to any person or persons.

(2) The Commission shall make an annual report on its activities to the Head of State, who shall cause a copy of that report to be laid before the Legislative Assembly.

89. (1) There shall be a Public Service Board of Appeal, which shall consist of:

(*a*) The Chief Justice or a judicial officer nominated by the Chief Justice;

(*b*) One person appointed by, and holding office at the pleasure of, the Head of State, acting on the advice of the Prime Minister;

(*c*) One person, being an officer of the Public Service, elected by the officers of the Public Service and holding office for a term not exceeding three years.

(2) The Chief Justice or the person nominated by the Chief Justice shall be Chairman of the Public Service Board of Appeal.

(3) An Act of Parliament may

(*a*) prescribe the manner of election of the person to be elected under the provisions of sub-clause (*c*) of Clause (1);

(*b*) provide for the appointment of deputies to act for members of the Public Service Board of Appeal appointed under the provisions of sub-clauses (*b*) and (*c*) of Clause (1);

(*c*) prescribe the jurisdiction of the Board of Appeal to hear and determine appeals from decisions of the Public Service Commission.

PART VIII

FINANCE

90. There shall be a Treasury Fund and such other public funds or accounts as may be provided by Act.

91. No taxation shall be imposed except by Parliament.

Public Revenue

92. All taxes and other revenues and moneys raised or receipted by Western Samoa shall be paid into the Treasury Fund unless required or permitted by Act to be paid into any other public fund or account.

93. No money shall be issued out of the Treasury Fund or any other public fund or account except in pursuance of a warrant under the hand of the Head of State.

94. (1) The Minister responsible for finance shall, in respect of every financial year, cause to be laid before the Legislative Assembly a statement of the estimated receipts and expenditure for that year, and unless Parliament in respect of any year otherwise provides, that statement shall be so laid before the commencement of that year.

(2) The proposals for all expenditure contained in the estimates (other than statutory expenditure) shall be submitted to the vote of the Legislative Assembly by means of an Appropriation Bill.

(3) If, in respect of any financial year, it is found

(*a*) that any expenditure is incurred or is likely to be incurred upon any service which is in excess of the sum provided for that service by the Appropriation Act relating to that year; or

(*b*) that any expenditure (other than statutory expenditure) is incurred or is likely to be incurred upon any service not provided for by the Appropriation Act relating to that year,

the Minister responsible for finance shall cause to be laid before the Legislative Assembly supplementary estimates in respect to that expenditure and the proposals for expenditure therein contained shall be submitted to the vote of the Assembly by means of a Supplementary Appropriation Bill.

(4) Statutory expenditure, which shall not be submitted to the vote of the Legislative Assembly under the provisions of this Article means

(*a*) the expenditure charged on the Treasury Fund under the provisions of Articles 22, 25, 69 and 98; and

(*b*) such other expenditure as may by Act be charged upon the Treasury Fund or any other public fund or account and in such Act be expressly stated to be statutory expenditure.

(5) The Legislative Assembly may approve or refuse its approval to any proposal for expenditure contained in an Appropriation or Supplementary Appropriation Bill, but may not increase the amount or alter the destination of any proposed expenditure.

95. If an Appropriation Bill has not become law by the first day of the financial year to which it relates, the Minister responsible for finance may, with the prior approval of Cabinet, authorize such expenditure (not otherwise authorized by Act) as he may consider essential for the continuance of any services, until an Appropriation Bill becomes law:

Provided that the expenditure so authorized shall not exceed the amount of any unexpended balance of the vote in the Appropriation law for the preceding year together with an amount equal to one-fourth of that vote.

96. Where, during the period between the passing of the Appropriation Act for any financial year and the end of that year, it is desirable that money should be expended in excess of or without the appropriation of the Legislative Assembly, Cabinet, or, to the extent that Cabinet so authorizes, the Minister responsible for finance may authorize the expenditure of such sums as are considered necessary:

Provided that the total amount of all sums issued and paid under the provisions of this Article shall not exceed one percent of the total amount of all sums appropriated by the Appropriation Act for that year.

97. (1) There shall be a Controller and Chief Auditor, who shall be appointed by the Head of State, acting on the advice of the Prime Minister.

(2) A person who has held the office of Controller and Chief Auditor shall not be eligible for appointment to any other office in the service of Western Samoa within a period of three years of his having ceased to hold the office of Controller and Chief Auditor.

(3) The Controller and Chief Auditor shall hold office until he reaches the age of sixty years:

Provided that the Legislative Assembly may by resolution extend the period of office of a Controller and Chief Auditor who has reached the age of sixty years:

(4) The Controller and Chief Auditor may at any time resign his office by writing under his hand addressed to the Prime Minister but shall not be removed from office except on the like grounds and in the like manner as a Judge of the Supreme Court.

(5) The Head of State, acting on the advice of the Prime Minister, may at any time when the Legislative Assembly is not meeting suspend the Controller and Chief Auditor from his office, and such suspension, unless previously revoked, shall continue in force until the end of the next ensuing session and no longer.

98. The salary of the Controller and Chef Auditor shall be determined by Act and shall be charged on the Treasury Fund, and that salary shall not be diminished during the period of office of the controller and Chief Auditor, unless as part of a general reduction of salaries applied proportionately to all persons whose salaries are determined by Act.

99. (1) The Controller and Chief Auditor shall audit the Treasury Fund, such other public funds or accounts as may be established, the accounts of all Departments and offices of executive government and the accounts of such other public statutory or local authorities and bodies as may be provided by Act.

(2) The Controller and Chief Auditor shall report at least once annually to the Legislative Assembly on the performance of his functions under this Article and shall in his report draw attention to any irregularities in the accounts audited by him.

PART IX

LAND AND TITLES

100. A *matai* title shall be held in accordance with Samoan custom and usage and with the law relating to Samoan customs and usage.

101. (1) All land in Western Samoa is customary land, freehold land or public land.

(2) Customary land means land held from Western Samoa in accordance with Samoan custom and usage and with the law relating to Samoan custom and usage.

(3) Freehold land means land held from Western Samoa for an estate in fee simple.

(4) Public land means land vested in Western Samoa being land that is free from customary title and from any estate in fee simple.

102. It shall not be lawful or comptetent for any person to make any alienation or disposition of customary land or of any interest in customary land, whether by way of sale, mortgage or otherwise howsoever, nor shall customary land or any interest therein be capable of being taken in execution or be assets for the payments of the debts of any person on his decease or insolvency:

Provided that an Act of Parliament may authorize

(*a*) the granting of a lease or licence of any customary land or of any interest therein;

(*b*) the taking of any customary land or any interest therein for public purposes.

103. There shall be a Land and Titles Court with such composition and with such jurisdiction in relation to *matai* titles and customary land as may be provided by Act.

104. (1) Subject to the provisions of any act, all land lying below the line of high-water mark shall be public land.

(2) For the purposes of this Article, the term 'high-water mark' means the line of median high tide between the spring and neap tides.

PART X

EMERGENCY POWERS

105. (1) If the Head of State is satisfied, acting in his discretion, after consultation with Cabinet, that a grave emergency exists whereby the security or economic life of Western Samoa or of any part thereof is threatened, whether by war, external agression, internal disturbance or natural catastrophe, he may by proclamation (hereinafter referred to as a Proclamation of Emergency) declare that a state of emergency exists.

(2) A Proclamation of Emergency shall remain in force for a period of thirty days, if not sooner revoked, but the provisions of this Clause shall not preclude the issue of a further Proclamation before the expiry of the period for which the immediately preceding Proclamation is in force.

(3) If the Legislative Assembly is meeting at the time the Proclamation of Emergency is made, the Proclamation shall forthwith be laid before the Assembly.

(4) If the Legislative Assembly is not meeting at the time the Proclamation of Emergency is made, the Head of State shall appoint a time for the Assembly to meet which time shall be as soon as the Head of State, acting in his discretion, considers that conditions make it practicable, and the Proclamation shall forthwith be laid before the Assembly.

Provided that, if not less than one-half of the total number of Members of Parliament (excluding vacancies) by notice in writing to the Head of State require that a time for the meeting of the Assembly be appointed for the purposes of this Clause, the Head of State shall appoint such a time which shall be not later than seven days after the date of receipt of that notice.

106. (1) When a Proclamation of Emergency has been made and so long as it remains in force, the Head of State may from time to time make such orders (hereinafter referred to as Emergency Orders) as appear to him to be necessary or expedient for securing the public safety, the defence of Western Samoa and the efficient prosecution of any action in which Western Samoa may be engaged, for maintaining public order and the supplies and services essential to the life of the community, and generally for safe-guarding the interests and maintaining the welfare of the community.

(2) Emergency Orders may empower or provide for empowering such authorities, persons or classes of persons as may be specified in the Orders to make regulation, rules or by-laws for any of the purposes for which Emergency Orders are authorized under the provisions of this Article to be made, and may contain such incidental and supplementary provisions as appear to the Head of State to be necessary or expedient for making effective the powers conferred under the provisions of Clause (1).

(3) Every Emergency Order, if otherwise valid, shall have effect notwithstanding anything contained in Part II.

(4) No provision of any Emergency Order, and no regulation, rule or by law duly made under the provisions of any such Order, shall be invalid because it

deals with any matter already provided for under any law or because of any inconsistency with any such law.

107. (1) If the Legislative Assembly is meeting at the time an Emergency Order is made under the provisions of Article 106, the Order shall forthwith be laid before the Assembly; and, if the Assembly is not then meeting, the Order shall be laid before the Assembly as soon as the next meeting thereof commences.

(2) When an Emergency Order has been laid before the Legislative Assembly under the provisions of Clause (1), a notice of motion, signed by six Members of Parliament and made within ten days of the day the Order was laid before the Assembly, praying that the Order be revoked shall be debated in the Assembly at the first convenient opportunity within four sitting days next after the day on which notice of motion was given and, if the Assembly resolves that the Order be revoked, it shall cease to be in force.

(3) All Emergency Orders made under the provisions of Article 106, if not sooner revoked, shall expire on the date on which the Proclamation of Emergency ceases to be in force or, where more than one such Proclamation is made in respect of the emergency, when the last of those Proclamations ceases to be in force.

(4) The revocation or expiry of an Emergency Order shall not affect the previous operation thereof, the validity of anything done or omitted to be done thereunder, or any offence committed or any penalty or punishment incurred.

108. (1) For the purposes of this Article, there shall be an advisory board, which shall consist of:

(*a*) A Chairman appointed by the Head of State from among the persons who are or have been Judges of the Supreme Court or are qualified to be Judges of the Supreme Court:

(*b*) Two other members appointed by the Head of State, acting in his discretion after consultation with the Chief Justice.

(2) Where an Emergency Order made under the provisions of Article 106 authorizes the detention of any person

(*a*) any person detained under the provisions of that Order shall, as soon as possible, be informed of the grounds for his detention and, subject to the provisions of Clause (3), of the allegations of fact on which it is based, and be given an opportunity of making representations to the advisory board against his detention; and

(*b*) no person shall be detained under the provisions of that Order for a period exceeding three months unless the advisory board has considered any representations made by him under the provisions of sub-clause (*a*) and has reported, before the expiry of of that period, that there is in its opinion sufficient cause for the detention.

(3) This Article shall not require any authority or person who is authorized to detain any person under any Emergency Order made under the provisions of Article 106 to disclose facts whose disclosure would in its or his opinion be against the national interest.

PART XI

GENERAL AND MISCELLANEOUS

109. (1) Any of the provisions of this Constitution may be amended or repealed by Act, and new provisions may be inserted in this Constitution by Act, if a bill for any such purpose is supported at its third reading by the votes of not less than two thirds of the total number of Members of Parliament (including vacancies) and if not fewer than ninety days elapse between the second and third readings of that bill:

Provided that no bill amending, repealing or adding to the provisions of Article 102 or the provisions of this proviso shall be submitted to the Head of State for assent until it has been submitted to a poll of the electors on the rolls for the territorial constituencies established under the provisions of Article 44 and unless it has been supported by two thirds of the valid votes cast in such a poll.

(2) A certificate under the hand of the Speaker that a bill has been passed under the provisions of Clause (1) shall be conclusive and shall not be questioned in any court.

110. (1) The Head of State shall have power to grant pardons, reprieves and respites, and to remit, suspend or commute any sentence passed by any court, tribunal or authority established under the law.

(2) In the exercise of the powers conferred upon him under the provisions of Clause (1), the Head of State shall act in his discretion after consultation with such Minister as the Prime Minister shall designate from time to time.

111. (1) In this Constitution, unless it is otherwise provided or the context otherwise requires

'Act' or Act of Parliament' means an Act of the Parliament of Western Samoa; and includes any Ordinance of the Legislative Assembly of the Trust Territory constituted under the provisions of the Samoa Amendment Act 1957:

'Cabinet' means the Cabinet of Ministers:

'Chief Justice' means the Chief Justice of the Supreme Court of Western Samoa;

'Court of Appeal' means the Court of Appeal of Western Samoa:

'Employee of the Public Service' means a person employed in the Public Service:

'Existing law' means any law in force in the Trust Territory of Western Samoa or any part thereof immediately before Independence Day;

'Head of State' means the Head of State of Western Samoa:

'High Court' means the High Court of Western Samoa constituted under the provisions of the Samoa Act 1921.:

'Independence Day' means the day on which this Constitution comes into force under the provisions of Article 113:

'Judicial officer' means the holder of any judicial office but does not include an employee of the Public Service who exercises all or any of the functions of a judicial office:

'Law' means any law for the time being in force in Western Samoa and includes this Constitution, any Act of Parliament and any proclamation, regulation, order, by-law or other act of authority made thereunder, the English common law and equity for the time being in so far as they are not excluded by any other law in force in Western Samoa, and any custom or usage which has acquired the force of law in Western Samoa or any part thereof under the provisions of any Act or under a judgment of a Court of competent jurisdiction:

'Legislative Assembly' means the Legislative Assembly constituted under the provisions of Article 44:

'Legislative Assembly of the Trust Territory' means the Legislative Assembly constituted under the provisions of the Samoa Amendment Act 1957 and in being immediately before Independence Day:

'Minister' includes the Prime Minister:

'Office of profit' means any office in the service of Western Samoa carrying the right to salary, and includes any office declared by Act to be an office of profit:

'Officer of the Public Service'means an employee of the Public Service other than a person employed in a temporary capacity or on probation:

'Parliament' means the Parliament of Western Samoa:

'Proclamation' means a proclamation made by the Head of State under his hand and the Public Seal of Western Samoa and published in the Western Samoa Gazette:

'Property' includes real and personal property, any estate or interest in any other right or interest:

'Public Seal' means the Public Seal of Western Samoa:

'Public service Commission' means the Public Service Commission of Western Samoa;

'Salary' includes salary or wages, allowances, superannuation rights, free or subsidized housing, free or subsidized transport, and other privileges capable of being valued in money:

'Service of Western Samoa' means service in any capacity of Western Samoa; and includes service in any of the capacities named in subclauses (*a*) to (*k*) inclusive of Article 83, but not service in respect of the Western Samoa Trust Estates Corporation:

'Speaker' means the Speaker of the Legislative Assembly:

'Supreme Court' means the Supreme Court of Western Samoa:

'Western Samoa Trust Estates Corporation' means the corporation constituted under that name on Independence Day.

(2) Where in this Constitution reference is made to the Samoa Act 1921

or to any amendment to that Act, that reference shall be construed as a reference to the Act of the Parliament of New Zealand bearing the short title 'the Samoa Act 1921' or to the relevant amendment thereto, including any amendment to that Act of the Parliament of New Zealand or that relevant amendment.

(3) Unless the context otherwise requires, where in this Constitution reference is made to a specified Part, Article or Schedule that reference shall be construed as a reference to that Part or Article of, or that Schedule to, this Constitution; and, where reference is made to a specified Clause, sub-clause or paragraph, that reference shall be construed as a reference to that Clause of the Article, that sub-clause of the Clause or that paragraph of the sub-clause in which the reference occurs.

(4) Where under the provisions of this Constitution a person is required to take and subscribe an oath, he shall be permitted, if he so desires, to comply with that requirement by taking and subscribing an affirmation.

(5) Where in this Constitution reference is made to the functions of any office, that reference shall, unless the context otherwise requires, be construed as a reference to the functions of that office and to any powers and authorities that may lawfully be exercised by, and any duties that may be required to be performed by, the holder of that office.

(6) Where in this Constitution reference is made to any officer by the term designating his office, that reference shall, unless the context otherwise requires be construed as a reference to the officer for the time being lawfully performing the functions of that office.

(7) Where this Constitution confers any power to make any appointment to any office, the person or authority having power to make the appointment shall, unless the context otherwise requires, have power, exercisable in a like manner

(*a*) to direct that a person other than the person appointed shall, during any period that the person appointed is unable to perform the functions of his office owing to absence or inablility to act from illness or any other cause, perform the functions of that office;

(*b*) to appoint another person substantively to an office notwithstanding that there is a substantive holder thereof, when that substantive holder is on leave of absence pending relinquishment of his office.

(*c*) to direct that a person shall perform the functions of that office when no person has been appointed thereto, either until a contrary direction shall be given by the person or authority having power to make the appointment or until a person shall have been appointed substantively thereto, whichever shall be the earlier.

112. The Samoan and English texts of this Constitution are equally authoritative but, in case of difference, the English text shall prevail.

113. This Constitution shall come into force on the day approved by the General Assembly of the United Nations as the date of the termination of the Trusteeship Agreement for the Territory of Western Samoa approved by the General Assembly on 13 December 1946.

PART XII

TRANSITIONAL

114. Subject to the provisions of this Constitution

(*a*) the existing law shall, until repealed by Act, continue in force on and after Independence Day; and

(*b*) all rights, obligations and liabilities arising under the existing law shall continue to exist on and after Independence Day and shall be recognized, exercised and enforced accordingly; and

(*c*) proceedings in respect of offences committed against the existing law may be instituted on and after Independence Day in that court, established under the provisions of this Constitution, having the appropriate jurisdiction, and offenders shall be liable to the punishments provided by the existing law.

115. Where the existing law confers any function on the Council of State of Western Samoa constituted under the provisions of the Samoa Amendment Act 1959, that function shall be performed by the Head of State and where any such function is to be performed by the Council of State, acting by and with the advice of the Executive Council, that function shall be performed by the Head of State acting by and with the advice of Cabinet.

116. Any person holding office as Prime Minister or as a Minister immediately before Independence Day shall be deemed to have been duly appointed thereto under the provisions of Part IV.

117. (1) The Legislative Assembly of the Trust Territory shall continue in being on and after Independence Day as the Legislative Assembly, and the members of the Legislative Assembly of the Trust Territory shall be deemed to have been duly elected as Members of Parliament under the provisions of this Constitution.

(2) The Speaker and the Deputy Speaker of the Legislative Assembly of the Trust Territory who are in office immediately before Independence Day shall be deemed to have been duly elected as Speaker and Deputy Speaker, respectively, under the provisions of this Constitution.

(3) The first session of the Legislative Assembly shall commence within three months of Independence Day.

(4) For the purposes of the provisions of Clause (4) of Article 63, the general election at which the Legislative Assembly of the Trust Territory was elected shall be the date of the last preceding election in respect of the Legislative Assembly in being on and after Independence Day.

(5) Subject to the provisions of this Constitution, the Standing Orders of the Legislative Assembly of the Trust Territory in force immediately before Independence Day shall be the Standing Orders of the Legislative Assembly, and they may be amended, repealed or added to under the provisions of Article 53.

(6) If the seat of a Member of Parliament becomes vacant before the date of the first general election to be held after Independence Day, that vacancy

shall be filled under the law in force immediately before Independence Day in relation to the filling of vacancies in the membership of the Legislative Assembly of the Trust Territory.

118. Subject to the provisions of this Constitution, a person holding office as a Judge of the High Court immediately before Independence Day shall, on and after that day, hold the office of Judge of the Supreme Court on the same terms and conditions as were applicable to him immediately before Independence Day.

119. (1) All legal proceedings pending in the High Court immediately before Independence Day shall, on and after that day, stand transferred to, and be deemed to be pending for determination before that court, established under the provisions of this Constitution, having the appropriate jurisdiction.

(2) All appeals from the High Court which immediately before Independence Day lay to, or were pending in, any court having jurisdiction to hear such appeals shall, on and after that day, lie to or stand transferred to, and be deemed to be pending for determination before, the Court of Appeal.

(3) Any decision of the High Court or of any court having jurisdiction to hear appeals from the High Court shall have the same force and effect as if it had been delivered or made by the Supreme Court or the Court of Appeal, respectively.

120. Subject to the provisions of this Constitution

(*a*) a person who, immediately before Independence Day, holds the office of Attorney General or of a member of the Public Service Commission shall, on and after that day, hold the corresponding office established under the provisions of this Constitution on the same terms and conditions as were applicable to him immediately before Independence Day; and

(*b*) a person who, immediately before Independence Day, is an employee of Western Samoan Public Service referred to in the Samoa Amendment Act 1949 shall, on and after that day, hold the like employment in the Public Service.

121. Where any Ordinance was enacted or made by the Legislative Assembly of the Trust Territory and the coming into force of that Ordinance was suspended, that Ordinance may, on or after Independence Day, come into force on the date specified therein or as may be specified by any authority empowered to bring it into force; and, in such case, the Ordinance shall, on and after that date, take effect as an Act of Parliament.

122. Where in the existing law reference is made to Her Majesty the Queen in right of the Trust Territory of Western Samoa, to the Crown in right of the Trust Territory of Western Samoa, to the Trust Territory of Western Samoa, to Western Samoa or to Samoa, that reference shall, unless the context otherwise requires, be construed as a reference to Western Samoa.

123. (1) All property which immediately before Independence Day is vested in Her Majesty the Queen in right of the Trust Territory of Western Samoa or in the Crown in right of the Trust Territory of Western Samoa shall, on Independence Day vest in Western Samoa.

(2) Subject to the provisions of Clause (3), land which immediately before Independence Day, is under the provisions of the Samoa Act 1921; Samoan land, European land or Crown land shall, on and after Independence Day, be held, under the provisions of this Constitution, as customary land freehold land or public land, respectively.

(3) All land in Western Samoa which immediately before Independence Day is vested in the Crown in right of the Government of New Zealand shall, on Independence Day, become freehold land held by Her Majesty the Queen in right of the Government of New Zealand for an estate in fee simple.

124. No amendments to the provisions of this Constitution shall be made before Parliament is constituted under the provisions of Part V, except such as the Legislative Assembly of the Trust Territory may make by Ordinance to remove any difficulties in the transition from the constitutional arrangements in force immediately before Independence Day to those provided for in this Constitution; and any Ordinance made under the provisions of this Article shall, unless sooner repealed, cease to be in force at the expiry of a period of nine months beginning with the day on which the Legislative Assembly first meets.

SCHEDULES

(*Not reproduced*)

SAUDI ARABIA

NOTE

Saudi Arabia is a member of the United Nations (October 24, 1945). It is a member of the League of Arab States, the Gulf Co-operation Council and other international organizations. Hejaz, now part of Saudi Arabia, was one of the original members of the League of Nations.

The Wahhabi movement began in Arabia in the mid-eighteenth century, and the Wahhabi empire reached its peak in 1802, after capturing Mecca and Medina. A period of Turkish control through Egyptian garrisons lasted from 1812 to 1824, when a Wahhabi state established itself with its capital at Ryadh. By 1842, the last Egyptian garrisons were ejected. A period of anarchy and dynastic struggles ended when Abdulla-Aziz-Al Saud, in 1901, captured Riyadh and through the following years recovered the outlying provinces until he captured the Hejaz and entered Mecca in 1927. He became King of Hejaz and Nejd and their dependencies, the two being united under a Decree of January 29, 1927. The Kingdom's name was changed to Saudi Arabia in September 1923, and a Decree of September 18, 1932 established the Kingdom of Saudi Arabia.

Oil was discovered in the 1930's and large scale production began after the second world war, together with economic and social development. The two 'neutral zones' with Iraq and Kuwait created during the 1920's years of border settlements, were equally partitioned and their oil wealth equally shared, the former in 1975 and the latter in 1971.

There is no Constitution of Saudi Arabia which is an absolute monarchy. The King appoints and leads the Council of Ministers and the members of the Wahhabi dynasty control the administration of the state. In March 1980, a 60 member Consultative Council was announced to draw up a 200 article system of rule based on Islamic principles. By the end of 1982, it had not yet been set up.

AREA, POPULATION, ETC.

Tha area of Saudi Arabia is 2,149,690 square kilometres, the population (1980 estimate) 8.960.000. The royal capital is Riyadh, the administrative capital is Jeddah. Mecca is the religious capital of the Moslem world.

VOLUME II – ASIA, AUSTRALIA, OCEANIA

SINGAPORE

SUMMARY

INTERNATIONAL STATUS

Singapore is a member of the United Nations (September 21, 1965). It is a member of the Commonwealth of Nations and of other international organizations.

Singapore became independent on August 9, 1965, when it withdrew from the Federation of Malaysia of which it had been a member since its establishment on September 16, 1963. The United Kingdom relinquished sovereignty over Singapore on that date, having granted full internal self-government to Singapore by a Constitution of June 3, 1959.

Singapore became a British colony on April 1, 1867; prior to that it was the seat of the Resident in charge of the Straits Settlements under the Government of Bengal, from 1819.

FORM OF NATIONAL GOVERNMENT

The Constitution of the State of Singapore of September 16, 1963, was amended in 1965 and 1966 to provide for Singapore's new status as an independent nation; it was further amended in 1968, 1969, 1970, 1971, 1972, 1973. It is a republic.[1] The source of sovereign power is not stated. There are provisions concerning citizenship.[2]

[1] Const., Art. 91.
[2] Id., Art. 53–69.

RIGHTS OF THE PEOPLE

There are no provisions concerning the rights of the people. There are provisions for the care of the interests of racial and religious minorities and the special position of the Malays.[3] A Council is provided to advise the President relating to the Muslim religion.[4]

LEGISLATIVE DEPARTMENT

The legislature is unicameral consisting of the President and Parliament.[5] Parliament is composed of 51 members, elected for a term of five years, subject to dissolution.[6] It meets in at least one session a year.[7] The legislature determines the immunities of Parliament.[8] There are provisions concerning finance.[9] Money bills cannot be introduced except on the recommendation of the President and signified by a Minister.[10]

EXECUTIVE DEPARTMENT

Executive authority is vested in the President, elected by Parliament for a term of four years, and the Cabinet, composed of a Prime Minister and other Ministers, which is collectively responsible to Parliament.[11] There are provisions relating to the public service; the Constitution states that every person who is a member of the public service holds office during the pleasure of the President; a Public Service Commission is provided.[12] There is a Presidential Council for Minority Rights whose members are appointed by the President to consider and report on such matters affecting persons of any racial or religious community as are referred to it by Parliament or the Government.[13]

JUDICIAL DEPARTMENT

Judicial power is vested in a Supreme Court and subordinate courts as provided by law.[14] Judges are appointed by the President on the advice of the Prime Minister and hold office until the age of 65.[15]

AREA, POPULATION, ETC.

The area of Singapore is 618 square kilometres, the population (1981 estimate) is 2,443,300. The languages of debate in the legislature are English, Malay, Mandarin, or Tamil.[16]

[3] Id., Art. 89.
[4] Id., Art. 6.
[5] Id., Art. 22.
[6] Id., Art. 23, 49, 50.
[7] Id., Art. 48.
[8] Id., Art. 47.
[9] Id., Art. 82–88.
[10] Id., Art. 43.
[11] Id., Art. 1, 7, 8.
[12] Id., Art. 70–81.
[13] Id., Art. 81A–Y.
[14] Id., Art. 52A.
[15] Id., Art. 52C, 52F.
[16] Id., Art. 37.

THE CONSTITUTION OF SINGAPORE[1]

September 16, 1963, as amended 1965, 1966, 1968, 1969, 1970, 1971 1972, 1973

PART I

THE GOVERNMENT

Chapter I. The President

1. (1) There shall be a President of Singapore, who shall be elected by Parliament.

(2) The President shall not be liable to any proceedings whatsoever in any court.

(3) The President shall hold office for a term of four years from the date on which he enters upon his office but may at any time resign his office by writing under his hand addressed to the Speaker of Parliament, and may be removed from office pursuance of a resolution of Parliament supported by the votes of not less than two thirds of the total number of the Members thereof.

(4) The Cabinet may appoint a person to exercise the functions of the President for any period during which the President is unable to do so himself owing to illness, absence from Singapore or any other cause; but no person shall be so appointed unless he would be qualified to be appointed as President.

1A. (1) Parliament may elect a Vice-President of Singapore.

(2) No person shall be so elected unless he would be qualified to be elected President.

(3) The Vice-President shall hold office for a term of three years from the date on which he enters upon his office but may at any time resign his office by writing under his hand addressed to the Speaker of Parliament, and may be removed from office in pursuance of a resolution of Parliament supported by the votes of not less than two thirds of the total number of the Members thereof.

(4) The Vice-President shall assist the President in the exercise of such of his functions as the President may from time to time delegate to him, but in making such delegation the President shall act in accordance with the advice of the Cabinet.

(5) Nothing in clause (4) of this Article shall be construed as prohibiting the President from exercising at any time any function delegated to the Vice-President under the said clause.

(6) The Cabinet may, instead of appointing a person to exercise the functions of the President for any period during which the President is unable to do so himself as provided in clause (4) of Article 1 of this Constitution appoint the Vice-

[1] Reprint of the Constitution of Singapore Government Gazette No. 14, 1966; also Government Gazettes Acts Supplements 9:1968, 22:1968, 6:1970, 26:1970, 55:1970, 26:1971, 41:1972, 29:1972, 23:1973. Supplied by Ministry of Foreign Affairs, Singapore, October 1979. Ed.

President to exercise all the functions of the President during any such period, notwithstanding any delegation that may already have been made under the provisions of clause (4) of this Article.

(7) The Vice-President shall before exercising any functions under this Article take and subscribe in the presence of the Chief Justice or of another Judge of the High Court an oath, *mutatis mutandis,* in the form set out in the First Schedule to this Constitution.

(8) The Legislature may by law make provision for the remuneration of the Vice-President, and any such remuneration shall be charged on and paid out of the Consolidated Fund.

2. (1) A person who is not a citizen of Singapore born in Malaya shall not be elected President.

(2) The President shall not hold any office of profit and shall not actively engage in any commercial enterprise.

3. The President or person appointed to exercise the functions of the President under clause (4) of Article 1 of this Constitution shall before exercising his functions take and subscribe in the presence of the Chief Justice of Singapore or of another Judge of the Supreme Court an oath in the form set out in the First Schedule to this Constitution.

4. (1) The Legislature shall by law provide a Civil List for the President.

(2) Any other person authorized under this Constitution to exercise the functions of the office of President shall, during any period during which he exercises those functions, be entitled to such remuneration as the Legislature may by law provide.

(3) The Civil List of the President and the remuneration to which any person is entitled under the preceding clause shall be charged on and paid out of the Consolidated Fund and shall not be diminished during the continuance in office of the President or, as the case may be, during the period during which the said person exercises the functions of the office of President.

(4) Subject to the provisions of the following clause, the appointment, terms of service, disciplinary control, termination of appointment and dismissal of the personal staff of the President shall be matters for the President acting in his discretion.

(5) The President, if he so desires, may appoint to his personal staff such public officers as he may select, after consultation with the Prime Minister, from a list submitted by the Public Service Commission and the provisions of the preceding clause (except in so far as they relate to appointment) shall apply in relation to a person so appointed as respects his service on the personal staff of the President but not as respects his service as a public officer.

(6) The remuneration of the personal staff of the President, other than a person appointed under the preceding clause, shall be defrayed out of the Civil List of the President.

5. (1) In the exercise of his functions under this Constitution or any law the President shall act in accordance with the advice of the Cabinet or of a Minister acting under the general authority of the Cabinet, except as otherwise provided by this Constitution; but shall be entitled, at his request, to any information concerning the Government which is available to the Cabinet.

(2) The President may act in his discretion in the performance of the following function (in addition to those in the performance of which he may act in his discretion under the other provisions of this Constitution) that is to say

(*a*) the appointment of the Prime Minister;

(*b*) the withholding of consent to a request for the dissolution of Parliament.

(3) The Legislature may by law make provision for requiring the President to act after consultation with or on the recommendation of any person or body of persons other than the Cabinet in the exercise of his functions other than

(*a*) functions exercisable in his discretion;

(*b*) functions with respect to the exercise of which provision is made in any other provision of this Constitution or in the Constitution of Malaysia.

Chapter 2. Muslim Religion

6. (1) [*Deleted 1966*].

(2) The Legislature shall by law make provision for regulating Muslim religious affairs and for constituting a Council to advise the President in matters relating to the Muslim religion.

Chapter 3. The Executive

7. (1) The executive authority of Singapore shall be vested in the President and exercisable subject to the provisions of this Constitution by him or by the Cabinet or any Minister authorized by the Cabinet.

(2) The Legislature may by law confer executive functions on other persons.

8. (1) There shall be in and for Singapore a Cabinet which shall consist of the Prime Minister and such other Ministers as may be appointed in accordance with the provisions of the following Article.

(2) Subject of the provisions of this Constitution, the Cabinet shall have the general direction and control of the Government and shall be collectively responsible to Parliament.

9. (1) The President shall appoint as Prime Minister a Member of Parliament who in his judgment is likely to command the confidence of the majority of the Members of Parliament, and shall, acting in accordance with the advice of the Prime Minister, appoint other Ministers from among the Members of Parliament:

Provided that, if an appointment is made while Parliament is dissolved, a person who was a Member of the last Parliament may be appointed but shall not continue to hold office after the first sitting of the next Parliament unless he is a Member thereof.

(2) Appointments under this Article shall be made by the President by instrument under the public seal.

10. (1) The President shall, by writing under the public seal, declare the office of Prime Minister vacant

(*a*) if the Prime Minister resigns his office by writing under his hand addressed to the President; or

(*b*) if the President acting in his discretion is satisfied that the Prime Minister had ceased to command the confidence of a majority of the Members of Parliament:

Provided that, before declaring the office of Prime Minister vacant under this paragraph, the President shall inform the Prime Minister that he is satisfied as aforesaid and, if the Prime Minister so requests, the President may dissolve Parliament instead of making such a declaration.

(2) A Minister other than the Prime Minister shall vacate his office

(*a*) if his appointment to that office is revoked by the President, acting in accordance with the advice of the Prime Minister, by instrument under the public seal; or

(*b*) if he resigns his office by writing under his hand addressed to the President.

(3) A person who has vacated his office as Minister may, if qualified, be again appointed as Minister from time to time.

(4) (*a*) Whenever the Prime Minister is ill or absent from Singapore or has been granted leave of absence from his duties under Article 16 of this Constitution, the functions conferred on him by this Constitution shall be exercisable by any other Minister authorized by the President, by instrument under the public seal, in that behalf.

(*b*) The President may, by instrument under the public seal, revoke any authority given under this clause.

(*c*) The powers conferred upon the President by this clause shall be exercised by him acting in his discretion, if in his opinion it is impracticable to obtain the advice of the Prime Minister owing to the Prime Minister's illness or absence, and in any other case shall be exercised by the President in accordance with the advice of the Prime Minister.

(*d*) [*Deleted 1966*].

11. The Prime Minister and every other Minister shall, before entering on the duties of his office, take and subscribe before the President the Oath of Allegiance and the appropriate Oath for the due execution of his office in the forms set out in the First Schedule to this Constitution.

12. (1) The Cabinet shall not be summoned except by the authority of the Prime Minister.

(2) The Prime Minister shall, so far as is practicable, attend and preside at meetings of the Cabinet and, in his absence, such other Minister shall preside as the Prime Minister shall appoint.

13. Any proceedings in the Cabinet shall be valid notwithstanding that some person who was not entitled so to do sat or voted therein or otherwise took part in the proceedings.

14. (1) The Prime Minister may, by directions in writing

(*a*) charge any Minister with responsibility for any department or subject;

(*b*) revoke or vary any directions given under this clause.

(2) The Prime Minister may retain in his charge any department or subject.

15. (1) The President, acting in accordance with the advice of the Prime Minister, may by instrument under the public seal, appoint Parliamentary Secretaries from among the Members of Parliament to assist Ministers in the discharge of their duties and functions:

Provided that, if an appointment is made while Parliament is dissolved, a person who was a Member of the last Parliament may be appointed a Parliamentary Secretary but shall not continue to hold office after the first sitting of the next Parliament unless he is a Member thereof.

(2) The provisions of clauses (2) and (3) of Article 10 and the provisions of Article 11 of this Constitution shall apply to Parliamentary Secretaries as they apply to Ministers.

16. The President, acting in accordance with the advice of the Prime Minister, may grant leave of absence from his duties to the Prime Minister, to any other Minister and to any Parliamentary Secretary.

17. A member of the Cabinet or Parliamentary Secretary shall not hold any office of profit and shall not actively engage in any commercial enterprise.

18. (1) There shall be for each Ministry one or more Permanent Secretaries who shall be persons who are public officers.

(2) (*a*) Appointments to the grade of Permanent Secretary shall be made by the President acting in accordance with the advice of the Prime Minister, from a list of names submitted by the Public Service Commission.

(*b*) The responsibility for the allocation of each Permanent Secretary to a Ministry shall be vested in the Prime Minister.

(3) Every Permanent Secretary shall, subject to the general direction and control of the Minister, exercise supervision over the department or departments to which he is allocated.

19. (1) The office of Attorney General is hereby constituted and appointments thereto shall be made by the President, acting in accordance with the advice of the Prime Minister, from among persons who are qualified for appointment as a Judge of the Supreme Court.

(2) When it is necessary to make an appointment to the office of Attorney General otherwise than by reason of the death of the holder of that office or his removal from office under clause (6) of this Article, the Prime Minister shall, before tendering advice to the President under the preceding clause, consult the person holding the office of Attorney General or, if that office is then vacant, the person

who has last vacated it, and the Prime Minister shall, in every case, before tendering such advice, consult the Chief Justice of Singapore and the Chairman of the Public Service Commission.

(3) The Prime Minister shall not be obliged to consult any person under the provisions of the preceding clause if he is satisfied that by reason of the infirmity of body or mind of that person or for any other reason it is impracticable so to do.

(4) The Attorney General may be appointed for a specific period and, if he was so appointed, shall, subject to the provisions of clause (6) of this Article, vacate his office (without prejudice to his eligibility for re-appointment) at the expiration of that period, but, subject as aforesaid, shall otherwise hold office until he attains the age of fifty five years:

Provided that

(*a*) he may at any time resign his office by writing under his hand addressed to the President; and

(*b*) the President, acting in accordance with the advice of the Prime Minister, may permit an Attorney General who has attained the age of fifty five years to remain in office for such fixed period as may have been agreed between the Attorney General and the Government.

(5) Nothing done by the Attorney General shall be invalid by reason only that he has attained the age at which he is required by this Article to vacate his office.

(6) (*a*) The Attorney General may be removed from office by the President, acting in accordance with the advice of the Prime Minister, but the Prime Minister shall not tender such advice except for inability of the Attorney General to discharge the functions of his office (whether arising from infirmity of body or mind or any other cause) or for misbehavior and except with the concurrence of a tribunal consisting of the Chief Justice of Singapore and two other Judges of the Supreme Court nominated for that purpose by the Chief Justice of Singapore.

(*b*) The tribunal constituted under this clause shall regulate its own procedure and may make rules for that purpose.

(7) It shall be the duty of the Attorney General to advise the Government upon such legal matters and to perform such other duties of a legal character, as may from time to time be referred or assigned to him by the President or the Cabinet and to discharge the functions conferred on him by or under this Constitution or any other written law.

(8) The Attorney General shall be paid such remuneration and allowances as may from time to time be determined and such remuneration and allowances shall be charged on and paid out of the Consolidated Fund.

(9) Subject to the provisions of this Article, the terms of service of the Attorney General shall either

(*a*) be determined by or under any law made under this Constitution; or (*b*) (in so far as they are not determined by or under any such law) be determined by the President.

(10) The terms of service of the Attorney General shall not be altered to his disadvantage during his continuance in office.

(11) For the purposes of the preceding clause, in so far as the terms of service of the Attorney General depend upon his option any terms for which he opts shall be taken to be more advantageous to him than any for which he might have opted.

20. (1) The President acting in accordance with the advice of the Prime Minister may appoint a public officer to be the Secretary to the Cabinet.

(2) The Secretary to the Cabinet shall be responsible, in accordance with such instructions as may be given to him by the Prime Minister, for arranging the business for, and keeping the minutes of, the meetings of the Cabinet and for conveying the decisions of the Cabinet to the appropriate person or authority and shall have such other functions as the Prime Minister may from time to time direct.

Chapter 4. Capacity as regards property, contract and suits

21. (1) The Government shall have power to acquire, hold and dispose of property of any kind and to make contracts.

(2) The Government may sue and be sued.

PART II

THE LEGISLATURE

22. The Legislature of Singapore shall consist of the President and Parliament.

23. (1) The Parliament shall consist of such number of elected Members as the Legislature may by law provide, and until other provision is so made, the number of Members shall be fifty one.

(2) If any person who is not a Member of Parliament is elected as Speaker or Deputy Speaker, he shall by virtue of holding the office of Speaker or Deputy Speaker, be a Member of Parliament in addition to the Members aforesaid, except for the purposes of Chapter 3 of Part I and of Article 30 of this Constitution.

24. (1) When Parliament first meets after any general election and before it proceeds to the despatch of any other business, it shall elect a person to be Speaker, and, whenever the office of Speaker is vacant otherwise than by reason of a dissolution of Parliament, shall not transact any business other than the election of a person to fill that office.

(2) The Speaker may be elected, in such manner as Parliament may from time to time decide, either from among the Members of Parliament who are neither Ministers nor Parliamentary Secretaries or from among persons who are not Members of Parliament:

Provided that a person who is not a Member of Parliament shall not be elected as

Speaker if, under any of the provisions of this Constitution, he is not qualified for election as a Member of Parliament.

(3) Upon the Speaker being elected and before he enters upon the duties of his office, he shall (unless he has already done so in accodance with the provisions of Article 45 of this Constitution) take and subscribe before Parliament the Oath of Allegiance in the form set out in the First Schedule to this Constitution.

(4) The Speaker may at any time resign his office by writing under his hand addressed to the Clerk of Parliament, and shall vacate his office

(*a*) when Parliament first meets after a general election; or

(*b*) in the case of a Speaker elected from among the Members of Parliament, if he ceases to be a Member of Parliament otherwise than by reason of a dissolution thereof or if he is appointed to be a Minister or a Parliamentary Secretary; or

(*c*) in the case of a Speaker elected from among persons who are not Members of Parliament, if any circumstances arises that, if he had been elected to a seat in Parliament, would cause him to vacate his seat by virtue of paragraph (*a*) or paragraph (*e*) of clause (2) of Article 30 of this Constitution.

25. The Speaker shall be paid such salary as Parliament may from time to time determine, and that salary, which is hereby charged on the Consolidated Fund, shall not be diminished during his continuance in office.

26. (1) When Parliament first meets after any general election, it shall, as soon as practicable, elect a person to be Deputy Speaker; and whenever the office of Deputy Speaker becomes vacant otherwise than by reason of a dissolution of Parliament, Parliament shall, as soon as convenient, elect another person to that office.

(2) (*a*) The Deputy Speaker may be elected, in such manner as Parliament may from time to time decide, either from among the Members of Parliament who are neither Ministers nor Parliamentary Secretaries or from among persons who are not Members of Parliament:

Provided that a person who is not a Member of Parliament shall not be elected as Deputy Speaker if, under any of the provisions of this Constitution, he is not qualified for election as a Member of Parliament.

(*b*) Upon the Deputy Speaker being elected and before he enters upon his duties of his office, he shall (unless he has already done so in accordance with the provisions of Article 45 of this Constitution) take and subscribe before Parliament the Oath of Allegiance in the form set out in the First Schedule to this Constitution.

(*c*) The Deputy Speaker may at any time resign his office, by writing under his hand addressed to the Clerk of Parliament, and shall vacate his office

(i) when Parliament first meets after a general election; or

(ii) in the case of a Deputy Speaker elected from among the Members of Parliament, if he ceases to be a Member of Parliament otherwise than by reason of a dissolution thereof or if he is appointed to be a Minister or a Parliamentary Secretary; or

(iii) in the case of a Deputy Speaker elected from among persons who are not Members of Parliament, if any circumstance arises that, if he had been elected to a seat in Parliament, would cause him to vacate his seat by virtue of paragraph (*a*) or paragraph (*e*) of clause (2) of Article 30 of this Constitution.

(3) The Deputy Speaker shall be paid such salary or allowance as Parliament may from time to time determine, and that salary or allowance, which is hereby charged on the Consolidated Fund, shall not be diminished during his continuance in office.

27. The functions conferred by this Constitution upon the Speaker shall, if there is no person holding the office of Speaker or if the Speaker is absent from a sitting of Parliament or is otherwise unable to perform those functions, be performed by the Deputy Speaker, or if there be no Deputy Speaker or if he is likewise absent or unable to perform those functions, by some other person to be elected by Parliament for the purpose.

28. (1) Members of Parliament shall be persons qualified for election in accordance with the provisions of this Constitution and elected in the manner provided by or under any law for the time being in force in Singapore.

(2) A person shall be qualified to be elected as a Member of Parliament if

(*a*) he is a citizen of Singapore;

(*b*) he is of the age of twenty one years or upwards on the day of nomination;

(*c*) his name appears in a current register of electors;

(*d*) he is resident in Singapore at the date of his nomination for election;

(*e*) he is able, with a degree of proficiency sufficient to enable him to take an active part in the proceedings of Parliament, to speak and, unless incapacitated by blindness or other physical cause, to read and write at least one of the following languages, that is to say, English, Malay, Mandarin and Tamil; and

(*f*) he is not disqualified from being a Member of Parliament under the provisions of Article 29 of this Constitution.

(3) Any question whether any person possesses the qualifications mentioned in paragraph (*e*) of the preceding clause shall be determined in such manner as may be prescribed by or under any law for the time being in force in Singapore or, in so far as not so prescribed, as may be provided by Order made by the President and published in the *Gazette*.

29. (1) Subject to the provisions of this Article, a person shall not be qualified to be a Member of Parliament who

(*a*) is and has been found or declared to be of unsound mind;

(*b*) is an undischarged bankrupt;

(*c*) holds an office of profit;

(*d*) having been nominated for election to Parliament or having acted as election agent to a person so nominated, has failed to lodge any return of election expenses required by law within the time and in the manner so required;

(*e*) has been convicted of an offence by a court of law in Singapore or Malaysia and sentenced to imprisonment for a term of not less than one year or to a fine of not less than two thousand dollars and has not received a free pardon:

Provided that where the conviction is by a court of law in Malaysia, the person shall not be so disqualified unless the offence is also one which, had it been committed in Singapore, would have been punishable by a court of law in Singapore;

(*f*) has voluntarily acquired citizenship of, or exercised rights of citizenship in a foreign country or has made a declaration of allegiance to a foreign country;

(*g*) is disqualified under any law relating to offences in connection with elections to Parliament by reason of having been convicted of such offence or having in proceedings relating to such an election been proved guilty of an act constituting such an offence.

(2) The disqualification of a person under paragraph (*d*) or paragraph (*e*) of clause (1) of this Article may be removed by the President and shall, if not so removed, cease at the end of five years beginning from the date on which the return mentioned in the said paragraph (*d*) was required to be lodged or, as the case may be, the date on which the person convicted as mentioned in the said paragraph (*e*) was released from custody or the date on which the fine mentioned in the said paragraph (*e*) was imposed on such person; and a person shall not be disqualified under paragraph (*f*) of clause (1) of this Article by reason only of anything done by him before he became a citizen.

(3) In paragraph (*f*) of clause (1) of this Article, the expression 'foreign country' does not include any part of the Commonwealth or the Republic of Ireland.

30. (1) Every Member of Parliament shall cease to be a Member at the next dissolution of Parliament after he has been elected, or previously thereto if his seat becomes vacant, under the provisions of this Constitution.

(2) The seat of a Member of Parliament shall become vacant

(*a*) if he ceases to be a citizen of Singapore; or

(*b*) in the case of a Member elected after the coming into force of this Constitution, if he ceases to be a Member of, or is expelled or resigns from, the political party for which he stood in the election; or

(*c*) if, by writing under his hand addressed to the Speaker, he resigns his seat in Parliament; or

(*d*) if during two consecutive months in each of which sittings of Parliament (or any committee of Parliament to which he has been appointed) are held, he is absent from all such sittings without having obtained from the Speaker before the termination of such sitting permission to be or to remain absent therefrom; or

(*e*) if he becomes subject to any of the disqualifications specified in Article *29* of this Constitution.

(3) Any person whose seat in Parliament has become vacant may, if qualified, again be elected as a Member of Parliament from time to time.

31. A person shall not be at the same time a Member of Parliament for more than one constituency.

32. Any question whether

(*a*) any Member of Parliament has vacated his seat therein;

(*b*) in the case of any person who has been elected as Speaker or Deputy Speaker from among persons who are not Members of Parliament, any circumstance has arisen that, if he had been elected to a seat in Parliament, would cause him to vacate his seat by virtue of paragraph (*a*) or paragraph (*e*) of clause (2) of Article *30* of this Constitution.

shall be determined by Parliament whose decision shall be final.

Provided that this Article shall not be taken to prevent the practice of Parliament postponing a decision in order to allow for the taking or determination of any proceedings that may affect the decision (including proceedings for the removal of the disqualification).

33. Whenever the seat of a Member has become vacant for any reason other than a dissolution, the vacancy shall be filled by election in the manner provided by or under any law for the time being in force in Singapore.

34. (1) Any person who sits or votes in Parliament, knowing or having reasonable ground for knowing that he is not entitled to do so, shall be liable to a penalty not exceeding two hundred dollars for each day on which he so sits or votes.

(2) The said penalty shall be recoverable by action in the High Court at the suit of the Attorney General.

35. (1) The staff of Parliament shall consist of a Clerk of Parliament, and such other officers as may from time to time be appointed under Part IV of this Constitution to assist him.

(2) The Clerk of Parliament shall be appointed by the President after consultation with the Speaker and the Public Service Commission.

(3) The Clerk of Parliament may at any time resign his office by writing under his hand addressed to the Speaker and, subject to the provisions of the following clause, may be removed from office by the President after consultation with the Speaker.

(4) The Clerk of Parliament shall not be removed from office under the preceding clause unless Parliament by a resolution which has received the affirmative vote of not less than two thirds of all the Members thereof, has resolved that he ought to be so removed for inability to discharge the functions of his office (whether arising from infirmity of body or mind or any other cause) or for misbehaviour.

(5) The staff of Parliament shall not be eligible for promotion or transfer to any other office in the public service without the consent of the Speaker.

(6) Subject to the provisions of Article 101 of this Constitution, the terms of service of the staff of Parliament may be determined by Parliament after receiving the advice of a Commission consisting of the following persons, that is to say:

(*a*) the Speaker, as Chairman;

(*b*) not more than three Ministers nominated by the Prime Minister, of whom one shall be the Minister responsible for finance; and

(*c*) a member of the Public Service Commission.

36. Subject to the provisions of this Constitution, Parliament may from time to time make, amend and revoke Standing Orders for the regulation and orderly conduct of its own proceedings and the despatch of business.

37. Until the Legislature otherwise provides all debates and discussions in Parliament shall be conducted in the Malay, English, Mandarin or Tamil languages.

38. The Speaker shall preside at each sitting of Parliament.

39. Parliament shall not be disqualified for the transaction of business by reason of any vacancy among the Members thereof, including any vacancy not filled when Parliament is first constituted or is reconstituted at any time; and any proceedings therein shall be valid notwithstanding that some person who was not entitled so to do sat or voted in Parliament or otherwise took part in the proceedings.

40. If objection is taken by any Member present that there are present (besides the Speaker or other Member presiding) fewer than one quarter of the total number of Members and, after such interval as may be prescribed in the Standing Orders of Parliament, the Speaker or other Member presiding ascertains that the number of Members present is still less than one quarter of the total number of Members, he shall thereupon adjourn Parliament.

41. (1) Save as otherwise provided in this Constitution, all questions proposed for decision in Parliament shall be determined by a majority of the votes of the Members present and voting; and if, upon any question before Parliament, the votes of the Members are equally divided, the motion shall be lost.

(2) If the Speaker has been elected from among persons who are not Members of Parliament, he shall not vote, but subject to this provision, the Speaker or other person presiding shall have an original vote but no casting vote.

42. (1) Subject to the provisions of Part IVA of this Constitution the power of the Legislature to make laws shall be exercised by Bills passed by Parliament and assented to by the President.

(2) A Bill shall become law on being assented to by the President and such law shall come into operation on the date of its publication in the *Gazette* or, if it is enacted either in such law or in any other law for the time being in force in Singapore that it shall come into operation on some other date, on that date.

43. (1) Subject to the provisions of this Constitution and of Standing Orders of Parliament, any Member may introduce any Bill or propose any motion for debate in, or may present any petition to Parliament, and the same shall be debated and disposed of according to the Standing Orders of Parliament.

(2) A Bill or amendment making provision (whether directly or indirectly) for

(*a*) imposing or increasing any tax or abolishing, reducing or remitting any existing tax; or

(*b*) the borrowing of money, or the giving of any guarantee, by the Government, or the amendment of the law relating to the financial obligations of the Government; or

(*c*) the custody of the Consolidated Fund, the charging of any money on the Consolidated Fund or the abolition or alteration of any such charge; or

(*d*) the payment of moneys into the Consolidated Fund or the payment, issue or withdrawal from the Consolidated Fund of any moneys not charged thereon, or any increase in the amount of such a payment, issue or withdrawal; or

(*e*) the receipt of any moneys on account of the Consolidated Fund or the custody or issue of such moneys;

being provision as respects which the Minister charged with responsibility for finance signifies that it goes beyond what is incidental only and not of a substantial nature having regard to the purposes of the Bill or amendment, shall not be introduced or moved except on the recommendation of the President signified by a Minister.

(3) A Bill or amendment shall not be deemed to make provision for any of the said matters by reason only that it provides for the imposition or alteration of any fine or other pecuniary penalty or for the payment or demand of a licence fee or a fee or charge for any service rendered.

44. In every Bill presented for assent the words of enactment shall be as follows: "Be it enacted by the President with the advice and consent of the Parliament of Singapore, as follows:–".

45. No Member of Parliament shall be permitted to take part in the proceedings thereof (other than proceedings necessary for the purpose of this Article) until he has taken and subscribed before Parliament the Oath of Allegiance in the form set out in the First Schedule to this constitution:

Provided that the election of a Speaker may take place before the Members of Parliament have taken and subscribed such Oath.

46. The President may address Parliament and may send messages thereto.

47. It shall be lawful for the Legislature by law to determine and regulate the privileges, immunities or powers of Parliament.

48. (1) There shall be a session of Parliament once at least in every year and a period of six months shall not intervene between the last sitting of Parliament in any one session and the first sitting thereof in the next session.

(2) The sessions of Parliament shall be held in such places and shall commence at such times as the president may from time to time appoint by Proclamation in the *Gazette.*

49. (1) The President may at any time, by Proclamation in the *Gazette,* prorogue Parliament.

(2) If, at any time, the office of Prime Minister is vacant, the President shall, by proclamation in the *Gazette,* dissolve Parliament as soon as he is satisfied, acting in his discretion, that a reasonable period has elapsed since that office was last vacated and that there is no Member of Parliament likely to command the confidence of a majority of the Members thereof.

(3) The President may at any time, by Proclamation in the *Gazette,* dissolve Parliament if he is advised by the Prime Minister so to do, but he shall not be obliged to act in this respect in accordance with the advice of the Prime Minister unless he is satisfied that, in tendering that advice, the Prime Minister commands the confidence of a majority of the Members of Parliament.

(4) Parliament unless sooner dissolved shall continue for five years from the date of its first sitting and shall then stand dissolved.

50. There shall be a general election at such time within three months after every dissolution of Parliament as the President shall appoint by Proclamation published in the *Gazette.*

51. The Legislature may by law make provisions for the remuneration of Members of Parliament.

52. Any law enacted by the Legislature after the coming into operation of this Constitution which inconsistent with this Constitution shall, to the extent of the inconsistency, be void.

PART IIA

JUDICIARY

52A. The judicial power of Singapore shall be vested in a Supreme Court and in such subordinate courts as may be provided by any written law for the time being in force.

52B. (1) The Supreme Court shall consist of a Chief Justice and such other Judges as may from time to time be appointed:

Provided that the office of a Judge of the Supreme Court shall not be abolished during his continuance in office.

(2) A person qualified for appointment as a Judge of the Supreme Court or a person who has ceased to hold the office of a Judge of the Supreme Court may sit as a Judge of that Court, if designated for the purpose (as occasion requires) in accordance with Article *52C* of this Constitution, and such person shall hold office for such period or periods as the President, acting on the advice of the Prime Minister, shall direct.

52C. (1) The Chief Justice and the other Judges of the Supreme Court shall be appointed by the President, acting on the advice of the Prime Minister.

(2) Before tendering his advice as to the appointment under clause (1) of this Article of a Judge, other than the Chief Justice, the Prime Minister shall consult the Chief Justice.

(3) This Article shall apply to the designation of a person to sit as a Judge

of the Supreme Court under clause (2) of Article 52B of this Constitution as it applies to the appointment of a Judge of that Court other than the Chief Justice.

52D. A person is qualified for appointment as a Judge of the Supreme Court if he has for an aggregate period of not less than ten years been a qualified person within the meaning of section 2 of the Legal Profession Act, 1966, or a member of the Legal Service in Singapore or both.

52E. The Chief Justice and every person appointed to be a Judge of the Supreme Court shall, before he enters on the execution of his office, take, in the presence of the President, the oath of office and allegiance in the form set out in the First Schedule to this Constitution.

52F. (1) Subject to the provisions of this Article, a Judge of the Supreme Court shall hold office until he attains the age of sixty five years or such later time not being later than six months after he attains that age, as the President may approve.

(2) A Judge of the Supreme Court may at any time resign his office by writing under his hand addressed to the President, but shall not be removed from office except in accordance with the following provisions of this Article.

(3) If the Prime Minister, or the Chief Justice after consulting the Prime Minister, represents to the President that a Judge of the Supreme Court ought to be removed on the ground of misbehavior or of inability, from infirmity of body or mind or any other cause, to properly discharge the functions of this office, the President shall appoint a tribunal in accordance with clause (4) of this Article and shall refer that representation to it; and may on the recommendation of the tribunal remove the Judge from office.

(4) The tribunal shall consist of not less than five persons who hold or have held office as a Judge of the Supreme Court or the High Court in Singapore, or, if it appears to the President expedient to make such an appointment, persons who hold or have held equivalent office in any part of the Commonwealth, and the tribunal shall be presided over by the member first in the following order, namely, the Chief Justices according to their precedence among themselves and other members according to the order of their appointment to an office qualifying them for membership (the older coming before the younger of two members with appointments of the same date).

(5) Pending any reference and report under clause (3) of this Article, the President may, on the recommendation of the Prime Minister and, in the case of any other Judge, after consulting the Chief Justice, suspend a Judge of the Supreme Court from the exercise of his functions.

(6) Parliament shall by law provide for the remuneration of the Judges of the Supreme Court and the remuneration so provided shall be charged on the Consolidated Fund.

(7) Subject to the provisions of this Article, Parliament may by law provide for the terms of office of the Judges of the Supreme Court, other than their remuneration.

(8) The remuneration and other terms of office (including pension rights)

of a Judge of the Supreme Court shall not be altered to his disadvantage after his appointment.

(9) Notwithstanding clause (1) of this Article, the validity of anything done by a Judge of the Supreme Court shall not be questioned on the ground that he had attained the age on which he was required to retire.

(10) The President may in his discretion grant leave of absence from his duties to the Chief Justice and, acting on the advice of the Chief Justice, to any other Judge of the Supreme Court.

52G. The conduct of a Judge of the Supreme Court shall not be discussed in Parliament except on a substantive motion of which notice has been given by not less than one quarter of the total number of Members of Parliament.

52H. (1) The President may make arrangements with Her Majesty for reference to the Judicial Committee of Her Britannic Majesty's Privy Council of appeals from the Supreme Court.

(2) Any appeal under this Article shall be subject to such conditions as to leave or otherwise as may be prescribed by any written law or by or under the enactments regulating the proceedings of the Judicial Committee of Her Britannic Majesty's Privy Council.

52I. (1) The Chief Justice of Singapore and other Judges of the Federal Court and the High Court in Singapore holding office immediately before the appointed day shall, as from that day, become the Chief Justice and the Judges of the Supreme Court respectively, and the provisions of this Part of this Constitution shall, subject to clause (2) of this Article, apply to them accordingly.

(2) The persons becoming the Chief Justice and the other Judges of the Supreme Court under clause (1) of this Article shall continue to hold office on terms and conditions not less favourable than those applicable to them immediately before the appointed day.

(3) For the purposes of this Article, 'appointed day' means the day appointed for the coming into operation of this Part of this Consitution.

PART IIB

PROTECTION OF THE SOVEREIGNTY OF THE REPUBLIC OF SINGAPORE

52J. (1) There shall be

(*a*) no surrender or transfer, either wholly or in part, of the sovereignty of the Republic of Singapore as an independent nation, whether by way of merger or incorporation with any other sovereign state or with any Federation, Confederation, country or territory or in any other manner whatsoever; and

(*b*) no relinquishment of control over the Singapore Police Force or the Singapore Armed Forces,

unless such surrender, transfer or relinquishment has been supported, at a national referendum, by not less than two thirds of the total number of votes cast by the electors registered under the Parliamentary Elections Act.

(2) For the purposes of this Article, the expression

(*a*) the 'Singapore Police Force' shall mean the Singapore Police Force and the Special Constabulary established under the Police Force Act and any Auxiliary Police Force created in accordance with Part X of the said Act, and shall include the Vigilante Corps established under the Vigilante Corps Act and such other force as the President may, by notification in the *Gazette,* declare to be a police force for the purposes of this Article; and

(*b*) the 'Singapore Armed Forces' shall mean the Singapore Armed Forces raised and maintained under the Singapore Armed Forces Act, 1972, and shall include any civil defence force formed under the Civil Defence Act and such other force as the President may, by notification in the *Gazette,* declare to be an armed force for the purpose of this Article.

52K. Without in any way derogating from the force and effect of Article 52J of this Constitution, nothing in that Article shall be construed as precluding Singapore or any association, body or organization therein from

(*a*) participating or co-operating in, or contributing towards, any scheme, venture, project, enterprise or undertaking of whatsoever nature, in conjunction or in concert with any other sovereign state or with any Federation, Confederation, country or countries or any association, body or organization therein, where such scheme, venture, project, enterprise or undertaking confers, has the effect of conferring or is intended to confer, on Singapore or any association, body or organization therein, any economic, financial, industrial, social, cultural, educational or other benefit of any kind or is, or appears to be, advantageous in any way to Singapore or any association, body or organization therein; or

(*b*) entering into any treaty, agreement, contract, pact or other arrangement with any other sovereign state or with any Federation, Confederation, country or countries or any association, body or organization therein, where such treaty, agreement, contract, pact or arrangement provides for mutual or collective security or any other object or purpose whatsoever which is, or appears to be, beneficial or advantageous to Singapore in any way.

52L. (1) A Bill for making an amendment to this Part shall not be passed by Parliament unless it has been supported, as a national referendum, by not less than two thirds of the total number of votes cast by the electors registered under the Parliamentary Elections Act.

(2) In this Article 'amendment' includes addition and repeal.

PART III

CITIZENSHIP

53. (1) There shall be a status known as 'citizen of Singapore'.

(2) The status of a citizen of Singapore may be acquired

(*a*) by birth;

(*b*) by descent;

(*c*) by registration or, before the 9th day of August, 1965, by enrolment; or

(*d*) under the provisions of the constitution of Malaysia, by naturalization.

(3) [*Deleted 1966*].

54. (1) Subject to the provisons of this Article, every person born in Singapore after the coming into operation ot this Constitution shall be a citizen of Singapore by birth.

(2) A person shall not be a citizen of Singapore by virtue of clause (1) of this Article if at the time of his birth

(*a*) his father, not being a citizen of Singapore, possessed such immunity from suit and legal process as is accorded to an envoy of a sovereign power accredited to the President; or

(*b*) his father was an enemy alien and the birth occurred in a place then under the occupation of the enemy; or

(*c*) neither of his parents was a citizen of Singapore and neither of them was a permanent resident in Singapore:

Provided that paragraph (*c*) of this clause shall not apply to any person if, as a result of the application of that paragraph, he would not be a citizen of any country.

55. (1) A person born outside Singapore after the coming into operation of this Constitution shall be a citizen of Singapore by descent if at the time of the birth his father is a citizen of Singapore by birth or by registration:

Provided that such person shall not be such a citizen unless his birth is registered at a Consulate of Singapore or with the Government in the prescribed manner within one year of its occurrence or with the permission of the Government later. And Provided further that where such person is born of a father who is a citizen of Singapore by registration at the time of the birth, he would not acquire the citizenship of that country in which he was born by reason of his birth in that country.

(2) [*Deleted 1966*].

56. [*Repealed 1966*].

57. (1) Subject to the provisions of this Constitution, any person of or over the age of twenty one years who was resident in Singapore on the coming into operation of this Constitution may, on application being made therefor in the prescribed form be registered as a citizen of Singapore if he satisfies the Government that he

(*a*) is of good character;
(*b*) has resided in Singapore throughout the twelve months immediatley preceding the date of his application;
(*c*) has during the twelve years immediately preceding the date of his application resided in Singapore for periods amounting in the aggregate to not less than ten years;
(*d*) intends to reside permanently in Singapore; and
(*e*) has an elementary knowledge of the national language:

Provided that the Government may exempt an applicant who has attained the age of forty five years or who is deaf or dumb from compliance with the provisions of paragraph (*e*) of this clause.

(2) Subject to the provisions of this Constitution any woman who is married to a citizen of Singapore may, on making application therefor in the prescribed manner, be registered as a citizen of Singapore if she satisfies the Government

(*a*) that she has resided continuously in Singapore for a period of not less than two years immediately preceding the date of the application;
(*b*) that she intends to reside permanently in Singapore; and
(*c*) that she is of good character.

58. (1) The Government may if satisfied that a child under the age of twenty one years

(*a*) is the child of a citizen of Singapore; and
(*b*) is residing in Singapore,

cause such child to be registered as a citizen of Singapore on application being made therefor in the prescribed manner by the parent or guardian of such child.

(2) The Govenment may, in such special circumstances as it thinks fit, cause any child under the age of twenty one years to be registered as a citizen of Singapore.

59. Subject to the provisions of Article 60 of this Constitution a person registered as a citizen of Singapore under Article 57 or 58 of this Constitution shall be a citizen of Singapore from the date on which he is so registered.

60. (1) No person shall be registered as a citizen of Singapore under Article 57 of this Constitution until he has taken the oath of allegiance and loyalty in the form prescribed in the Second Schedule to this Constitution.

(2) Except with the approval of the Government, no person who has renounced or has been deprived of citizenship of Singapore under this Constitution or the Singapore Citizenship Ordinance, 1975, or the Constitution of Malaysia, as the case may be, shall be registered as a citizen of Singapore under the provisions of this Constitution.

61. (1) A citizen of Singapore who is a citizen by registration or by naturalization shall cease to be such a citizen if he is deprived of his citizenship by an order of the Government made in accordance with the provisions of this Article.

(2) The Government may, by order, deprive any such citizen of his citizenship if the Government is satisfied that the registration or certificate of naturalization

(*a*) was obtained by means of fraud, false representation or the concealment of any material fact; or

(*b*) was effected or granted by mistake.

(3) The Government may, by order, deprive any such citizen of his citizenship if the government is satisfied that that citizen has, within the period of five years after registration or naturalization, been sentenced in any country to imprisonment for a term of not less than twleve months or to a fine of not less than five thousand dollars or the equivalent in the currency of that country and has not received a free pardon in respect of the offence for which he was sentenced.

(4) No person shall be deprived of citizenship under this Article unless the Government is satisfied that it is not conducive to the public good that that person should continue to be a citizen of Singapore; and no person shall be deprived of citizenship under paragraph (*b*) of clause (2) or under clause (3) of this Article if the Government is satisfied that as a result of the deprivation he would not be a citizen of any country.

(5) [*Deleted 1966*].

62. (1) Where a person has been enrolled as a citizen of Singapore before the 9th day of August, 1965, and the Government is satisfied that the enrolment

(*a*) was obtained by means of fraud, false representation or the concealment of any material fact; or

(*b*) was effected by mistake,

the Government may by order cancel the enrolment.

(2) Where under this Article a person's enrolment as a citizen of Singapore is cancelled that shall not discharge him from liability in respect of anything done or omitted before the cancellation.

63. (1) Before making an order under Article 61 or 62 of this Constitution, the Government shall give the person against whom the order is proposed to be made notice in writing informing him of the ground on which the order is proposed to be made and of his right to have the case referred to a committee of inquiry under this Article.

(2) If any person to whom such notice is given applies within such time as may be prescribed to have the case referred to a committee of inquiry, the Government shall, and in any other case may, refer the case to a committee of inquiry consisting of a Chairman, who shall be a person qualified to be appointed as a Judge of the Supreme Court, and two other members chosen from a panel to be appointed by the Government in that behalf.

(3) The committee of inquiry shall, on such reference, hold an inquiry in such manner as may be prescribed and submit a report to the Government and the Government shall have regard to such report in making the order.

64. Where a person who is a citizen of Singapore has renounced his citizenship of Malaysia or been deprived of his citizenship of Malaysia by the Government of Malaysia before the 9th day of August, 1965, such person shall be deemed to have renounced or been deprived of his citizenship of Singapore under this Constitution and such person shall cease to be a citizen of Singapore.

65. (1) Where a person has been deprived of his citizenship or his enrolment as a citizen has been cancelled under the provisions of this Part of this Constitution, the Government may by order deprive of his citizenship or, as the case may be, cancel the enrolment of any child of that person under the age of twenty one years who has been registered or enrolled as a citizen under the provisions of this Constitution or the Singapore Citizenship Ordinance, 1957, and was so registered or enrolled as being the child of that person or of that person's wife or husband.

(2) No person shall be deprived of his citizenship under clause (1) of this Article unless the Government is satisfied that it is not conducive to the public good that he should continue to be a citizen; and no person shall be deprived of his citizenship under clause (1) of this Article if the Government is satisfied that as a result of such deprivation he would not be a citizen of any country.

66. Upon application made in that behalf in the prescribed manner the Government may grant in the form prescribed a certificate of citizenship to a person with respect to whose citizenship a doubt exists, whether of fact or of law.

Provided that where the Government is satisfied that such a certificate was obtained in circumstances set out in paragraph (*a*) or (*b*) of clause (1) of Article 62 of this Constitution, the Government may by order cancel such certificate.

67. [*Repealed 1966*].

68. Until the Legislature otherwise provides by law, the supplementary provisions contained in the Third Schedule to this Constitution shall have effect for the purposes of this Part of this Constitution.

69. (1) The Singapore Citizenship Ordinance, 1957 is hereby repealed.

(2) Any person who immediately before the coming into operation of this Constitution, was by virtue of the Singapore Citizenship Ordinance, 1957, a citizen of Singapore by birth, descent, registration or naturalization, shall as from the coming into operation of this Constitution continue, subject to the provisions of this Constitution, to possess that status.

(3) Where a person would have been a citizen of Singapore by descent immediately before the coming into operation of this Constitution if his birth had been registered under the provisions of the Singapore Citizenship Ordinance, 1957, he shall become a citizen of Singapore by descent if his birth is registered at a consulate of Singapore or with the Government in the prescribed manner within one year of its occurrence or with the permission of the Government later.

(4) Notwithstanding the repeal of the Singapore Citizenship Ordinance, 1957, where a person who has become a citizen of Singapore was liable in respect of things done before the coming into operation of this Constitution to be deprived of that statue under the Ordinance, then the Government may by order deprive him of his citizenship, if proceedings for that purpose are begun during the period of two years after the commencement of this Constitution.

(5) Where a person is liable to be deprived of citizenship under clause (4) of this Article and proceedings had before the coming into operation of this Constitution been begun to deprive him of citizenship of Singapore under the provisions of the Singapore Citizenship Ordinance, 1957, those proceedings shall be

treated as proceedings to deprive him of citizenship under that clause and shall be continued as such in accordance with the provisions of the Singapore Citizenship Ordinance, 1957, in force immediately before the coming into operation of this Constitution.

PART IV

THE PUBLIC SERVICE

70. For the purposes of this Constitution and except as hereinafter in this Part provided, the public service shall be

(*a*) the Singapore Armed Forces;
(*b*) the civil service of Singapore;
(*c*) the legal service; and
(*d*) the Police Force.

71. Except for the purposes of Articles 79, 80A and 80B of this Constitution, and except where the context otherwise requires, in the interpretation of this Part of this Constitution

(*a*) the expression 'the public service' shall not include service otherwise than in a civil capacity;
(*b*) the expression 'public office' shall not include the following offices, that is to say
 (i) the office of the Chief Justice;
 (ii) the office of the Attorney General;
 (iii) the office of Judge of the Supreme Court;
 (iv) the office of member of the Public Service Commission;
 (v) the office of any police officer below the rank of Inspector; or
 (vi) any office the remuneration of the holder of which is calculated on a daily rate,

and the expression 'public officer' shall be construed accordingly.

72. Except as expressly provided by this Constitution, every person who is a member of the public service shall hold office during the pleasure of the President.

73. (1) There shall be a Public Service Commission which shall consist of a Chairman and not less than five and not more than nine other members, each of whom shall be appointed in writing under the hand of the President, acting in accordance with the advice of the Prime Minister.

(2) The Chairman shall be a citizen of Singapore.

(3) There shall be a Deputy Chairman who shall be a person chosen by the members of the Public Service Commission from among their own number.

(4) A person appointed to be a member of the Public Service Commission shall thereafter be ineligible for appointment to any public office.

(5) At any meeting of the Public Service Commission, three members who shall include either the Chairman or the Deputy Chairman, and may include both of

them, shall form a quorum. If the quorum is present, the Commission shall not be disqualified for the transaction of business by reason of any vacancy among its members, and any proceeding of the Commission shall be valid notwithstanding that some person not entitled so to do took part therein.

(6) Before assuming the duties of his office the Chairman and every other member of the Public Service Commission shall take and subscribe before the Chief Justice or some other Judge of the Supreme Court the appropriate oath for the due execution of his office in the form set out in the First Schedule to this Constitution.

74. A person shall not be appointed to be a member of the Public Service Commission if he is, and shall cease to be a member if he becomes

(*a*) a public officer;

(*b*) an employee of any corporation incorporated by or under the provisions of any law for the time being in force in Singapore other than the repealed Companies Ordinance and the Companies Act, 1967, or any other law replacing the said Act;

(*c*) A Member of Parliament or a duly nominated candidate for election as such Member;

(*d*) a member of any trade union or of any body or association affiliated to a trade union; or

(*e*) the holder of any office in any political association.

75. (1) Subject to the provisions of Article 74 of this Constitution, every member of the Public Service Commission shall, unless he earlier resigns his office by writing under his hand addressed to the President or is removed therefrom under this Article, hold office for a period of five years from the date of his appointment, but shall be eligible for re-appointment.

(2) If the Prime Minister, or the Chairman of the Public Service Commission after consulting with the Prime Minister, represents to the President that a member of the Public Service Commission ought to be removed from office for inability to discharge the functions of his office (whether arising from infirmity of body or mind or any other cause) or for misbehavior, the President shall refer that representation to a tribunal consisting of the Chief Justice and two other Judges of the Supreme Court nominated for that purpose by the Chief Justice and shall, if that tribunal so recommends, remove that member from office by writing under his hand.

(3) The tribunal constituted under clause (2) of this Article shall regulate its own procedure and may make rules for that purpose.

76. (1) The Chairman and other members of the Public Service Commission shall be paid such salary and allowances as may from time to time be determined, and such salary and allowances shall be charged on and paid out of the Consolidated Fund.

(2) Subject to the provisions of this Constitution, the terms of service of the members of the Public Service Commission may either

(*a*) be prescribed by or under any law made under this Constitution; or (*b*) (in so far as they are not prescribed by or under any such law) be prescribed by the President.

(3) The terms of service of any member of the Public Serivce Commission shall not be altered to his disadvantage during his continuance in office.

(4) For the purposes of clause (3) of this Article, in so far as the terms of service of a member of the Public Service Commission depend upon his option, any terms for which he opts shall be taken to be more advantageous to him than any for which he might have opted.

77. (1) There shall be a Secretary to the Public Service Commission who shall be a person who is a public officer and who shall be appointed by the President in accordance with the advice of the Commission.

(2) The Secretary to the Public Service Commission shall be responsible, in accordance with such instruction as may be given to him by the Chairman of the Commission, for arranging the business for, and keeping the minutes of, the meetings of the Commission and for conveying the decisions of the Commission to the appropriate person or authority and shall have such other functions as the Chairman may from time to time direct.

78. (1) Subject to the provisions of this Constitution, it shall be the duty of the Public Service Commission to appoint, confirm, emplace on the permanent or pensionable establishment, promote, transfer, dismiss and exercise disciplinary control over public officers.

(2) The promotion of public officer shall be on the basis of official qualifications, experience and merit.

(3) No public officer shall be dismissed or reduced in rank under the provisions of this Article without being given a reasonable opportunity of being heard.

(4) In clause (1) of this Article

'appoint' does not include an appointment to act in an office for two months or less;

'transfer' does not include transfer without a change of rank within a department of the Government.

79. (1) The law applicable to any pension, gratuity or other like allowance (in this Article referred to as an 'award') granted to any public officer or to his widow, children, dependent or personal representatives shall be that in force on the relevant day or any later law not less favorable to the person concerned.

(2) For the purposes of this Article, the relevant day is

(*a*) in relation to an award made before the 16th day of September, 1963, the date on which the award was made;

(*b*) in relation to an award made after the 16th day of September, 1963, to or in respect of any person who was a public officer before that day, the day immediately before that day;

(*c*) in relation to an award made to or in respect of any person who first became a public officer on or after the 19th day of September, 1963, the date on whch he first became a public officer.

(3) For the purposes of this Article, where the law applicable to an award

depends on the option of the person to whom it is made, the law for which he opts shall be taken to be more favorable to him than any other law for which he might have opted.

80. (1) Where under any written law any person or authority has a discretion

(*a*) to decide whether or not any award shall be made; or

(*b*) to withhold, reduce in amount or suspend any such award that has been made,

that award shall be made and may not be withheld, reduced in amount or suspended unless the Public Service Commission or the Legal Service Commission, as the case may be, concurs in the refusal to grant the award or, as the case may be, in the decision to withhold, reduce in amount or suspend it.

(2) Where the amount of any award that may be made to any person is not fixed by law, the amount of the award to be made to him shall be the greatest amount for which he is eligible unless the Public Service Commission or the Legal Service Commission, as the case may be, concurs in the making of an award of a smaller amount.

(3) In this Article, 'award' has the same meaning as in Article 79 of this Constitution.

80A. Pensions, gratuities and other like allowances granted in respect of the public service shall be charged on and paid out of the Consolidated Fund.

80B. (1) Notwithstanding any provision of this Constitution relating to the circumstances in which a public officer may vacate his office, any public officer may, with the consent of the Government (which consent shall not be unreasonably withheld), relinquish his office for the purpose of transfer to some other public office or to an office in any other public service, and if he so relinquishes his office, his claim to any pension, gratuity or other like allowance shall not thereby be prejudiced.

(2) For the purposes of this Article, the expression 'other public service' has the meaning given to it by the Pensions Ordinance, 1956, as in force immediately before the date of the coming into operation of this Constitution.

80C. (1) Subject to the provisions of any written law for the time being in force in Singapore, the President may make regulations for all or any of the following matters, that is to say:

(*a*) the division of public officers into Divisions and Services;

(*b*) the prescribing of Schemes regulating the recruitment, service and promotion of members of such Services; and

(*c*) the conduct and discipline of the public service.

(2) The Public Service Commission may, subject to the provisions of this Constitution, regulate its own procedure and make rules for that purpose, and may, in connection with the discharge of its functions, confer powers and impose duties on any person or any authority of the Government.

(3) The Public Service Commission may, by directions in writing and subject to such conditions as it thinks fit, delegate any of its functions under clause (1) of Article 78 of this Constitution to any member of the Commission, to any public

officer or other person, or to any board consisting of public officers and other persons appointed by it or to any person who is a member of a panel appointed by the Commission for the purposes of representing the public in any disciplinary proceedings in respect of any grade of the public service and that member, officer, board or person shall exercise those functions under the direction and control of the Public Service Commission.

80D. (1) No legal proceedings whatsoever shall lie or be instituted or maintained in any court of law for or on account of or in respect of any act, decision or thing done or taken by the Public Service Commission or by any member, committee or delegate thereof or by any person acting under the authority of the Public Service Commission during the period from the 16th day of September, 1963, to the date of the coming into operation of the Constitution (Amendment) Act, 1970, if done or taken in good faith in the execution of duty or for the purpose of regulating conduct or enforcing discipline in the public service.

(2) No legal proceedings in respect of any such act, decision or thing which is alleged to have been done or taken in bad faith in the execution of duty or for the purpose of regulating conduct or enforcing discipline in the public service during the period from the 16th day of September, 1963, to the date of the coming into operation of the Constitution (Amendment) Act, 1970, shall be instituted or maintained in any court of law unless a certificate of the Attorney General shall first have been obtained sanctioning the institution of such legal proceedings.

(3) In the exercise of purported exercise of any the powers conferred upon the Public Service Commission pursuant to clause (1) of Article 75 of the Constitution [which is repealed by the Constitution (Amendment Act, 1970], all acts or things done, exercised or performed by the Public Service Commission or by any member, committee or delegate thereof or by any person acting under the authority of the Public Service Commission during the period from the 16th day of September, 1963 to the date of the coming into operation of the Constitution (Amendment) Act, 1970, shall be deemed to be and always to have been within the competence and jurisdiction of the Public Service Commission or such member, committee, delegate or person, as the case may be, and shall be deemed to be and always to have been validly done, exercised or performed.

(4) All rules, regulations, orders or notifications whatsoever made during the period from the 16th day of September, 1963, to the date of the coming into operation of the Constitution (Amendment) Act, 1970, by or in the name of the Public Service Commission or any committee thereof shall be deemed to be and always to have been validly made, notwithstanding that any such rules, regulations, orders or notifications have been revoked or amended or are or have been inconsistent with, or in conflict with, or contrary to any written law or law previously in force.

81. Parliament may by law provide for the exercise of other functions by the Public Service Commission.

PART IVA

PRESIDENTIAL COUNCIL FOR MINORITY RIGHTS

81A. In this Part, unless the context otherwise requires

'adverse report' means a report of the Council stating that, in the opinion of the Council, some specified provision of a Bill or of a subsidiary legislation would be a differentiating measure;

'Chairman' means the Chairman of the Council;

'Council' means the Presidential Council for Minority Rights established under Article 81B of this Constitution;

'differentiating measure' means any measure which is, or is likely in its practical application to be, disadvantageous to persons of any racial or religious community and not equally disadvantageous to persons of other such communities, either directly by prejudicing persons of that community or indirectly by giving advantage to persons of another community;

'member' means a member of the Council and includes the Chairman;

'Money Bill' means a Bill which contains only provision dealing with all or any of the following matters, namely:

(*a*) the imposition, repeal, remission, alteration or regulation of taxation;

(*b*) the imposition, for the payment of debt or other financial purposes, of charges on the Consolidated Fund or any other public funds, or the variation or repeal of any such charges;

(*c*) the grant of money to the Government or to any authority or person, or the variation or revocation of any such grant;

(*d*) the appropriation, receipt, custody, investment, issue or audit of accounts of public money;

(*e*) the raising or guarantee of any loan or the repayment thereof, or the establishment, alteration, administration or abolition of any sinking fund provided in connection with any such loan;

(*f*) subordinate matters which are ancillary or incidental to any of the foregoing matters;

'sitting day' means any date on which Parliament meets.

81B. (1) There shall be a Presidential Council for Minority Rights which shall consist of

(*a*) a Chairman appointed for a person of three years;

(*b*) not more than ten permanent members appointed for life; and

(*c*) not more than ten other members appointed for a period of three years.

(2) The Chairman and the members shall be appointed by the President on the advice of the Cabinet.

(3) The Chairman and the members appointed under paragraph (*c*) of clause (1) of this Article shall be eligible for re-appointment.

81C. Whenever a member informs the Chairman that he is or will be incapable, for a period of three months or more, of taking part in the proceedings of the Council by reason of illness, absence or other cause, the Chairman shall convey the information to the President who may, on the advice of the Cabinet, appoint a person to serve as a member for that period.

81D. No person shall be qualified to be appointed as a member unless

(*a*) he is a citizen of Singapore;

(*b*) he is not less than thirty five years of age;

(*c*) he is resident in Singapore; and

(*d*) he is not liable to any of the disqualifications provided by Article 81E of this Constitution.

81E. A person shall be disqualified for appointment as a member who

(*a*) is or has been found or declared to be of unsound mind;

(*b*) is insolvent or an undischarged bankrupt;

(*c*) has been convicted of an offence by a court in Singapore or Malaysia and sentenced to inprisonment for a term of not less than one year or to a fine of not less than two thousand dollars and has not received a free pardon:

Provided that where the conviction is by a court in Malaysia, the person shall not be so disqualified unless the offence is also one which, had it been committed in Singapore, would have been punishable by a court in Singapore; or

(*d*) has voluntarily acquired citizenship of, or exercised the rights of citizenship in, a foreign country or has made a declaration of allegiance to a foreign country.

81F. A member shall vacate his seat in the Council

(*a*) if he ceases to be a citizen of Singapore;

(*b*) if by writing under his hand addressed to the Chairman he resigns his seat; or

(*c*) if he becomes subject to any of the disqualifications provided in Article 81E of this Constitution.

81G. (1) Any question whether any person has become a member or has vacated his seat as such member shall be referred to and determined by a tribunal consisting of a Judge of the Supreme Court appointed by the Chief Justice and two members appointed by the Council.

(2) Any tribunal constituted under clause (1) of this Article shall

(*a*) sit in private;

(*b*) afford the person concerned adequate opportunity to call witnesses and be heard; and

(*c*) report its decision to the Chairman.

(3) The decision of the tribunal shall be final and shall not be open to question in any court.

81H. Before any person who has been appointed Chairman or a member enters upon the duties of his office, he shall take and subscribe before a Judge of the Supreme Court the Oath of Allegiance and the Oath of Secrecy in the forms set out respectively at paragraphs 2 and 7 in the First Schedule to this Consitution.

81I. (1) It shall be the general function of the Council to consider and report on such matters affecting persons of any racial or religious community in Singapore as may be referred to the Council by Parliament or the Goverment.

(2) A reference to the Council by Parliament may be made by the Speaker, and a reference to the Council by the Government may be made by a Minister.

81J. It shall be the particular function of the Council to draw attention to any Bill or to any subsidiary legislation if that Bill or subisdiary legislation is in the opinion of the Council a differentiating measure.

81K. (1) Immediately after any Bill to which this Article applies has been given a final reading and passed by Parliament and before it is presented to the President for assent, the Speaker shall cause an authenticated copy of the Bill to be sent to the Council.

(2) The Council shall consider the Bill and shall, within thirty days of the date on which the Bill was sent to the Council, make a report ot the Speaker stating whether or not in the opinion of the Council any and, if so, which provision of the Bill would, if enacted, be a differentiating measure.

(3) Whenever after the receipt of an adverse report from the Council, the Bill to which it relates is amended by Parliament, the Speaker shall cause the Bill in its amended form to be sent again to the Council.

(4) On the application of the Chairman, the Speaker may extend, as he thinks fit, the period of thirty days prescribed by clause (2) of this Article, where he considers it proper to do so on account of the length or complexity of any Bill or the number of matters for the time being under consideration by the Council or for any sufficient reason.

(5) The Speaker shall cause every report received by him from the Council in pursuance of Clause (2) of this Article to be presented to Parliament without undue delay. Where the Speaker receives no such report on the Bill within the time provided in clause (2) of this Article, or any extension thereof granted under clause (4) of this Article, it shall be conclusively presumed that the Council is of the opinion that no provision of the Bill would, if enacted, be a differentiating measure.

(6) No Bill to which this Article applies shall be presented to the President for assent unless it is accompanied by a certificate under the hand of the Speaker stating that

(*a*) in the opinion of the Council no provision of the Bill would, if enacted, be a differentiating measure;

(*b*) no report having been received from the Council within the time prescribed or any extenstion thereof, the Council is presumed to be of the opinion that no provision of the Bill would, if enacted be a differentiating measure; or

(*c*) notwithstanding the opinion of the Council that some specified provision of the Bill would, if enacted, be a differentiating measure, a motion for the presentation of the Bill to the President for assent has been passed by the affirmative vote of not less than two thirds of the total membership of Parliament.

(7) The provisions of this Article shall not apply to

(*a*) a Money Bill;

(*b*) a Bill certified by the Prime Minister as being one which affects the defence or the security of Singapore or which relates to public safety, peace or good order in Singapore; or

(*c*) a Bill certified by the Prime Minister to be so urgent that it is not in the public interest to delay its enactment.

(8) A Bill shall be deemed to be a Money Bill if the Speaker certifies in writing that, in his opinion, it is a Bill to which the definition of 'Money Bill' contained in Article 81A of this Constitution applies. No Money Bill shall be presented to the President for assent, unless it is accompanied by the Speaker's certificate which shall be conclusive for all purposes and shall not be open to question in any court.

81L. (1) Where the President assents to a Bill which has been certified as urgent by the Prime Minister under clause (7) of Article 81K of this Constitution, it shall nevertheless be the duty of the Speaker to cause an authenticated copy of the Act to be sent as soon as may be to the Council.

(2) The Council shall thereupon consider the Act and shall, within thirty days of the date on which the Act was sent to the Council, make a report to the Speaker stating whether or not in the opinion of the Council and and, if so, which provision of the Act is a differentiating measure.

(3) The Speaker shall cause any such report to be presented to Parliament as soon as may be.

81M. (1) An authenticated copy of every subsidiary legislation shall be sent to the Council by the appropriate Minister within fourteen days of the publication of such subsidiary legislation.

(2) The Council shall thereupon consider such subsidiary legislation and shall, within thirty days of the date on which the subsidiary legislation was sent to the Council, make a report to the Speaker and to the appropriate Minister, stating whether or not in the opinion of the Council and and, if so, which provision of the subsidiary legislation is a differentiating measure.

(3) The Speaker shall cause every report of the Council on a subsidiary legislation to be presented to Parliament on the next sitting day after receiving the Council's report.

(4) Where an adverse report in respect of any provision of any subsidiary legislation is presented to Parliament in pursuance of clause (3) of this Article, then, within six months after the presentation of that report, unless either

(*a*) the provision has been revoked or amended by the appropriate Minister; or

(*b*) Parliament has passed a resolution confirming that provision.

the appropriate Minister shall revoke such provision and cause a notice of revocation to be published in the *Gazette*.

(5) If no report on any subsidiary legislation is received from the Council within the time provided in clause (2) of this Article, it shall be conclusively pre-

sumed that the Council is of the opinion that no provision in such subsidiary legislation is a differentiating measure.

81N. (1) The Council may examine any written law in force on the 9th day of January, 1970, and may make a report in regard to any provision in such written law shich in the opinion of the Council is a differentiating measure.

(2) The Council shall send such report to the Speaker and the Speaker shall cause such report to be presented to Parliament as soon as may be.

(3) In the case of a report on any subsidiary legislation the Council shall also cause a copy of the report to be sent to the appropriate Minister.

81O. (1) The Council shall meet on the summons of the Chairman.

(2) The Chairman, if present, shall preside at all meetings of the Council.

(3) Whenever the office of Chairman is vacant or the Chairman for any reason is unable to attend, some other member of the Council shall be elected by the Council to act as Chairman.

81P. (1) The Council shall not transact any business unless a quorum of eight members, including the Chairman or member presiding, is present.

(2) Any decision of the Council shall be made by a majority of the votes of the members present and voting.

(3) The Chairman or member presiding shall have an original vote but not a casting vote.

(4) If upon any question before the Council the votes of the members are equally divided, the motion shall be deemed to be lost.

81Q. The proceedings of the Council shall be conducted in private and the Council shall not be entitled to hear objectors or examine witnesses in regard to any Bill or law which is being considered by the Council in pursuance of the provisions of this Part.

81R. In reporting the opinion of the Council under the provisions of this Part, the Council shall state

(*a*) either that the report is unanimous or the number of votes for and against it; and

(*b*) in the case of an adverse report, the grounds on which the Council has reached its conclusion.

81S. Subject to the provisions of clause (1) of Article 81P of this Constitution, the Council shall not be disqualified for the transaction of business by reason of any vacancy among the members thereof; and any proceedings therein shall be valid notwithstanding that some person who was not entitled to do so took part in those proceedings.

81T. Any Minister, Minister of State or Parliamentary Secretary specially authorized by the Prime Minister for this purpose shall be entitled to attend and take part in the proceedings of the Council as if he were a member but shall not have the right to vote in the Council.

81U. Subject to the provisions of this Constitution, the Council may make rules with respect to the regulation and conduct of its proceedings and the despatch of its business but no such rules shall have effect until they have been approved by the President.

81V. (1) Once in every year it shall be the duty of the Council to compile and present to the President a report on the work of the Council during the preceding twelve months.

(2) The President shall cause such report to be presented to Parliament as soon as may be.

81W. (1) There shall be paid to the Chairman and the other members such salaries and fees as may be determined by the President.

(2) The salaries and fees payable under clause (1) of this Article shall be defrayed out of monies provided by Parliament.

81X. The Council shall have power to appoint a Secretary to the Council and such other officers as may be required to enable the Council to carry out its functions under this Part.

81Y. The President may make rules for the conduct of business between the Council and Parliament and between the Council and any authority empowered to make subsidiary legislation, and generally for carrying out the purposes of this Part.

PART V

FINANCIAL PROVISIONS

82. No tax or rate shall be levied by or for the purposes of Singapore except by or under the authority of law.

83. There shall be in and for Singapore a Consolidated Fund into which, subject to the provisions of any law for the time being in force in Singapore, shall be paid all revenues of Singapore not allocated to specific purposes.

84. (1) The Minister responsible for finance shall, before the end of each financial year, cause to be prepared annual estimates of revenue and expenditure for public services of Singapore during the succeeding financial year which, when approved by the Cabinet, shall be laid before Parliament.

(2) The estimates of expenditure shall show separately

(*a*) the total sums required to meet expenditure charged in the Consolidated Fund; and

(*b*) subject to clause (3) of this Article the sums respectively required to meet the heads of other expenditure proposed to be met from the Consolidated Fund.

(3) The estimates of revenue to be shown in the estimates shall not include any sums received by way of *Zakat, Fitrah* and *Batt-ul-Mal* or similar Muslim revenue; and the sums to be shown under paragraph (*b*) of clause (2) of this Article shall not include

(*a*) sums representing the proceeds of any loan raised by the Government for specific purposes and appropriated for those purposes by the law authorizing the raising of the loan;

(*b*) sums representing any money or interest on money received by the Government subject to a trust and to be applied in accordance with the terms of the trust;

(*c*) sums representing any money held by the Government which has been received or appropriated for the purpose of any trust fund established by or in accordance with any written law.

(4) The Minister responsible for finance shall also lay before Parliament together with the estimates of expenditure, a statement showing as far as is practicable the assets and liabilities of Singapore at the end of the last completed financial year, the manner in which those assets are invested or held and the general heads in respect of which those liabilities are outstanding.

85. (1) The heads of expenditure to be met from the Consolidated Fund other than statutory expenditure and other than expenditure to be met by such sums as are mentioned in clause (3) of Article 84 of this Constitution shall be included in a Bill to be known as a Supply Bill, providing for the issue from the Consolidated Fund of the sums necessary to meet that expenditure and the appropriation of those sums for the purposes specified therein.

(2) Whenever

(*a*) any moneys are expended or are likely to be expended in any financial year upon any service which are in excess of the sum provided for that service by the Supply law relating to that year; or

(*b*) any moneys are expended or are likely to be expended (otherwise than by way of statutory expenditure) in any financial year upon any new service not provided for by the Supply law relating to that year,

supplementary estimates (or, as the case may be, statements of excess) shall be prepared by the Minister responsible for finance and, when approved by the Cabinet, shall be laid before and voted on by Parliament; in respect of all supplementary expenditure so voted the Minister responsible for finance may, at any time before the end of the financial year, introduce into Parliament a Supplementary Supply Bill containing, under appropriate heads, the estimated sums so voted and shall, as soon as possible after the end of each financial year, introduce into Parliament a Final Supply Bill containing any such sums which have not yet been included in any Supply Bill.

(3) That part of any estimate of expenditure laid before Parliament which shows statutory expenditure shall not be voted on by Parliament, and such expenditure shall, without further authourity of Parliament, be paid out of the Consolidated Fund.

(4) For the purposes of this Article and the preceding Article statutory expenditure means expenditure charged on the Consolidated Fund or on the general revenues and assets of Singapore by virtue of the provisions of clause (3) of Article 4, clause (8) of Article 19, Article 25, clause (3) of Article 26, clause (1) of Article 74, Article 78 and Article 88 of this Constitution or by virtue of the provisions of any other law for the time being in force in Singapore.

86. (1) Subject to the following provisions of this Article, no moneys shall be withdrawn from the Consolidated Fund unless they are

(*a*) charged on the Consolidated Fund; or

(*b*) authorized to be issued by a Supply or Supplementary Supply law.

(2) No moneys shall be withdrawn from the Consolidated Fund except in the manner provided by law.

(3) Clause (1) of this Article shall not apply to any such sums as are mentioned in clause (3) of Article 84 of this Constitution.

(4) Parliament may by resolution approving estimates containing a vote on account, authorize expenditure for part of any year before the passing of the Supply law for that year, but the aggregate sums so voted shall be included, under the appropriate heads, in the Supply Bill for that year.

(5) If a Supply Bill has not become law by the first day of the financial year to which it relates, the Minister responsible for finance may, with the prior approval of the Cabinet, authorize such expenditure (not otherwise authorized by law) from the Consolidated Fund or other Government funds as he may consider essential for the continuance of the public services shown in the estimates until the Supply Bill becomes law:

Provided that the expenditure so authorized for any service shall not exceed one quarter of the amount voted for that service in the Supply law for the preceding year.

(6) Parliament may, by a resolution approving a vote of credit, authorize expenditure for the whole or part of the year, otherwise than in accordance with Articles 84 and 85 of this Constitution, if owing to the magnitude or indefinite character of any service or to circumstances of unusual urgency, it appears to Parliament desirable to do so.

87. (1) The Legislature may by law create a Contingencies Fund and authorise the Minister responsible for finance to make advances from that Fund if he is satisfied that there is an urgent and unforeseen need for expenditure for which no provision or no sufficient provision has been made by a Supply law.

(2) Where any advance is made by virtue of the authority conferred under the preceding clause, a supplementary estimate of the sum required to replace the amount so advanced shall as soon as practicable be laid before and voted on by Parliament and the sum so voted shall be included in a Supplementary Supply Bill or a Final Supply Bill.

88. (1) The following are hereby charged on the Consolidated Fund

(*a*) all debt charges for which the Government is liable; and

(*b*) any moneys required to satisfy any judgment, decision or award against the Government by any court or tribunal.

(2) For the purposes of this Article debt charges include interest, sinking fund charges, repayment or amortisation of debt and all expenditure in connection with the raising of loans on the security of the Consolidated Fund and the service and redemption of debt created thereby.

PART VI

GENERAL PROVISIONS

89. (1) It shall be the responsibility of the Government constantly to care for the interests of the racial and religious minorities in Singapore.

(2) The Government shall exercise its functions in such manner as to recognise the special position of the Malays, who are the indigenous people of Singapore, and accordingly it shall be the responsibility of the Government to protect, safeguard, support, foster and promote their political, educational, religious, economic, social and cultural interests and the Malay language.

90. (1) The provisions of this Constitution may be amended by a law enacted by the Legislature.

(2) In this Article 'amendment' includes addition and repeal.

91. (1) In this Constitution unless it is otherwise provided or the context otherwise requires

'Cabinet' means the Cabinet constituted under this Constitution;

'Civil List' means the provision made under Article 4 of this Cosntitution for the maintenance of the President;

'citizen of Singapore' means any person who, under the provisions of this Constitution, has the status of a citizen of Singapore;

'Consolidated Fund' means the Consolidated Fund established by this Constitution;

'existing law' means any law having effect as part of the law of Singapore immediately before the coming into operation of this Constitution;

'Constitution of Malaysia' includes the Malaysia Act;

'Government' means the Government of Singapore;

'law' includes written law and any legislation of the United Kingdom or other enactment or instrument whatsoever which is in operation in Singapore and the common law in so far as it is in operation in Singapore and any custom or usage having the force of law in Singapore:

'Legislature' means the Legislature of Singapore;

'Malaya' means Singapore and the Malay Peninsula;

'Minister' means a Minister appointed under this Constitution;

'office of profit' means, subject to the provisions of clause (5) of this Article, any whole time office in the public service;

'Parliament' means the Parliament of Singapore;

'Prime Minister' means the Prime Minister of Singapore appointed under the provisions of this Constitution;

'public office' means, subject to the provisions of clause (5) of this Article, an office of emolument in the public service;

'public officer' means the holder of any public office.

'the public seal' means the public seal of Singapore;

'public service' means service under the Government;

'Public Service Commission' means the Public Service Commission constituted under this Constitution.

'reigister of electors' means the register of electors prepared under the provisions of any written law for the time being in force relating to election;

'remuneration' in respect of any public officer means only the emoluments of that officer, the whole or any part of which count for pension in accordance with the provisions of any law relating to the grant of pensions in respect of the public service;

'session' means the sittings of Parliament commencing when it first meets after being constituted, or after its prorogation or dissolution at any time, and terminating when Parliament is prorogued or is dissolved without having been prorogued;

'Singapore' means the Republic of Singapore;

'sitting' means a period during which Parliament is sitting continuously without adjourment, including any period during which Parliament is in committee;

'Speaker' and 'Deputy Speaker' mean, respectively, the Speaker and Deputy Speaker of Parliament;

'terms of service' in respect of any officer include the remuneration to which that officer is entitled by virtue of his office, and any pension, gratuity or other like allowance payable to or in respect of that officer;

'written law' means this Constitution and the Constitution of Malaysia and all Acts and Ordinances and subsidiary legislation for the time being in force in Singapore and includes rules and regulations made under the Singapore (Constitution) Order in Council, 1958, so long as they are in force in Singapore.

(2) Save where this Constitution otherwise provides or where the context otherwise requires

(*a*) the person or authority having power to make substantive appointments to any public officer may appoint a person to perform the functions of that office during any period during which it is vacant or during which the holder thereof is unable (whether by reason of absence or infirmity of body or mind or any other cause) to perform those functions;

(*b*) every appointment to perform the functions of an office made under the preceding paragraph shall be made in the same manner as and subject to the same conditions as apply to a substantive appointment to that office;

(*c*) any reference in this Constitution to the holder of any office by the term designating his office shall be construed as including a reference to any person for the time being lawfully performing the functions of that office;

(*d*) any reference in this Constitution to an appointment to any office shall be construed as including a reference to an appointment to perform the functions of that office.

(3) Where in this Constitution power is conferred on any person or authority to appoint a person to perform the functions of any office if the holder thereof

is unable himself to perform its functions, any such appointment shall not be called in question on the ground that the holder of that office was not unable to perform those functions.

(4) For the purposes of this Constitution, the resignation of a member of any body or the holder of any office constituted by this Constitution that is required to be addressed to any person shall be deemed to have effect from the time that it is received by that person:

Provided that, in the case of a resignation that is required to be addressed to the Speaker, the resignation shall, if the office of Speaker is vacant or the Speaker is absent from Singapore, be deemed to have effect from the time that it is received by the Deputy Speaker on behalf of the Speaker.

(5) For the purposes of this Constitution, a person shall not be considered as holding a public office or an office or profit by reason of the fact that he is in receipt of any remuneration or allowances (including a pension or other like allowance) in respect of his tenure of the office of President, Vice-President, Prime Minister, Chief Justice, Speaker, Deputy Speaker, Minister, Parliamentary Secretary, Political Secretary, Member of Parliament, Ambassador, High Commissioner or such other office as the President may from time to time by order prescribe.

(6) (*a*) Without prejudice to the provisions of clause (2) of this Article, when the holder of any public office is on leave of absence pending relinquishment of that office, the person or authority having power to make appointments to that office may appoint another person thereto.

(*b*) Where two or more persons are holding the same office by reason of any appointment made pursuant to the preceding paragraph, the person last appointed shall, in respect of any function conferred on the holder of that office, be deemed to be the sole holder of that office.

(7) Where a person is required by the Constitution to take an oath, he shall be permitted, if he so desires, to comply with that requirement by making an affirmation.

(8) References in this Constitution to any period shall, so far as the context admits be construed as including references to a period beginning before the date of the coming into operation of this Constitution.

(9) Subject to the provisions of this Article, the Interpretation Act, 1965, shall apply for the purposes of interpreting this Constitution and otherwise in relation thereto as it applies for the purpose of interpreting and otherwise in relation to any written law within the meaning of that Act.

92. Subject to the provisions of this Constitution, all persons of whatever race in the same grade of the service of the government shall, subject to the terms and conditions of their employment, be treated impartially.

93. The President may from time to time authorize the Government Printer to print copies of this Constitution including all amendments in force at the date of such authorization; and any such copy so printed shall be deemed for all purposes to be a true and correct copy.

94. Subject to the provisions of Part VII of this Constitution, this Constitution shall come into operation immediately before the 16th day of September, 1963.

*PART VII

TEMPORARY AND TRANSITIONAL PROVISIONS

95. (1) The person holding the office of Yang di-Pertuan Negara on the coming into operation of this Constitution shall continue to hold the office and to carry out the functions of the Yang di-Pertuan Negara under this Constitution, as if appointed under this Constitution for a term of years expiring on the 3rd of December, 1963.

(2) The person holding the office of Yang di-Pertuan Negara shall before exercising the functions of the Yang di-Pertuan Negara under this Constitution take and subscribe in the presence of the Chief Justice of Singapore or a Judge of the High Court the oath in the form set out in the First Schedule to this Constitution.

96. (1) The Legislative Assembly established by the Singapore (Constitution) Order in Council, 1958, shall remain in being and shall be deemed to be the Legislative Assembly established by this Constitution, and accordingly

(*a*) the persons who immediately before the coming into operation of this Constitution hold the offices of Speaker and Deputy Speaker or Members of the Legislative Assembly shall, on the coming into operation of this Constitution, continue to hold those offices or their seats as Members in accordance with the provisions of this Constitution; and

(*b*) the Legislative Assembly shall, unless sooner dissolved, stand dissolved on the expiration of five years from the date of the first sitting of the Legislative Assembly under the Singapore (Constitution) Ording in Council, 1958.

(2) The Speaker shall not exercise the functions of his office and no member of the Legislative Assembly shall take part in the proceedings thereof after the coming into operation of this Constitution (other than proceedings necessary for the purposes of this clause) until he has taken and subscribed before the Legislative Assembly an oath of allegiance in the form set out in the First Schedule to this Constitution.

97. The Standing Orders of the Legislative Assembly established by the Singapore (Consitution) Order in Council, 1958, which are in force immediately before the coming into operation of this Constitution shall, subject to amendment or revocation under Article 36 of the Constitution, be the Standing Orders of the Legislative Assembly established by this Constitution, but shall be construed with such modifications, adaptations, qualifications and exceptions as may be necessary to bring them into conformity with the provisions of this Constitution.

*This Part has been left unamended.

98. (1) The Cabinet established by the Singapore (Constitution) Order in Council, 1958, shall remain in being and shall be deemed to be the Cabinet established by this Constitution, and accordingly the persons who immediately before the coming into operation of this Constitution hold the office of Prime Minister and other Ministers shall on the coming into operation of this Constitution continue to hold those offices in accordance with the provisions of this Constitution.

(2) Any person who continues to hold office of Prime Minister or other Minister as from the coming into operation of this Constitution by virtue of clause (1) of this Article shall, before entering on the duties of his office after the coming into operation of this Constitution, take and subscribe before the Yang di-Pertuan Negara an oath of allegiance in the form set out in the First Schedule to the Constitution.

99. The persons who, immediately before the coming into operation of this Constitution, were the Chairman and other members of the Public Service Commission established by the Singapore (Constitution) Order in Council 1958, shall on the coming into operation of this Constitution be deemed to have been appointed as Chairman and members of the Commission under Article 71 of this Constitution and shall hold their offices in accordance with the provisions of this Constitution and in relation to any such person, the reference in clause (1) of Article 73 of this Constitution to the date of his appointment shall be construed as a reference to the date of his appointment to the Public Service Commission established by the Singapore (Constitution) Order in Council, 1958.

100. Subject to the provisions of this Constitution and the Federal Constitution, every person who immediately before the coming into operation of this Constitution holds a public office shall on its coming into operation continue to hold the like office in the public service.

101. (1) Save where other provisions is made by this Constitution, any person who, under the provisions of this Part of this Constitution, holds any office as from the coming into operation of this Constitution by virtue of having been the holder of any office immediately before the coming into operation shall, as from its coming into operation, be entitled to the same terms of service as were applicable to him immediately before its coming into operation, and those terms, in so far as they relate to remuneration, shall not be altered to his disadvantage during his continuance in the public service thereafter.

(2) For the purposes of this Article, in so far as the terms of service of any person depend upon his option, any terms for which he opts shall be taken to be more advantageous to him than any for which he might have opted.

102. (1) Where on Malaysia Day or any day thereafter any post in the public service becomes a post in the general public service or the judicial and legal service of the Federation any person serving in that post immediately before that day shall on that day be seconded to the general public service or the judicial and legal service of the Federation, as the case may be.

(2) Clause (1) of this Article shall not apply to persons in such grades of service as the Yang di-Pertuan Negara may, with the consent of the Yang di-Pertuan Agong, direct.

(3) The power confered by clause (2) of this Article may be exercised at any time after the publication of this Constitution in the *Gazette.*

(4) A person seconded to the General Public Service or the Judicial and Legal Service of the Federation under this Article, shall not, unless and until he elects to the contrary, be liable to be transferred without his consent to a post outside the State.

103. (1) Subject to the provisions of this Article, all property and assets which immediately before the coming into operation of this Constitution were vested in Her Majesty for the purposes of ths State shall on its coming into operation vest in the State.

(2) Subject to the provsions of the Federal Constitution any land in the State which immediately before the coming into operation of this Constitution was vested in Her Majesty shall on its coming into operation vest in the State.

(3) Any property which was immediately before the coming into operation of this Constitution liable to escheat to Her Majesty in respect of the Government shall on its coming into operation be liable to escheat to the State.

104. (1) All rights, liabilities and obligations of Her Majesty in respect of the Government shall on and after the coming into operation of this Constitution be rights, liabilities and obligations of the State.

(2) In this Article, rights, liabilities and obligations include rights, liabilities and obligations arising from contract or otherwise, other than rights to which Article 103 of this Constitution applies.

105. (1) Subject to the provisions of this Article and to any provision made on or after Malaysia Day by or under Federal law or State law, all existing laws shall continue in force on and after the coming into operation of this Constitution and all laws which have not been brought into force by the coming into operation of this Constitution may, subject as aforesaid, be brought into force on or after its coming into operation, but all such laws shall, subject to the provisons of this Article, be construed as from the coming into operation of this Constitution with such modifications, adaptations, qualifications and exceptions as may be necessary to bring them into conformity with this Constitution and the Malaysia Act.

(2) (*a*) The Yang di-Pertuan Negara may, by order made at any time during the period of two years after the commencement of this Constitution and published in the *Gazette,* make such modifications in any existing law to the extent that it is by virtue of the provisions of the Federal Constitution treated as a State law as appear to him to be necessary or expedient in consequence of the promulgation of this Constitution or the passing of the Malaysia Act.

(*b*) Any order made under this clause may be amended or repealed by a further order so made.

(*c*) An Order made under this clause shall have effect from such date, not being earlier than the date of the coming into operation of this Constitution, as may be specified therein.

(*d*) An Order made under this clause shall be presented to the Legislative Assembly as soon as may be after it is made.

(3) In clause (2) of this Article, 'modification' includes amendment, adaptation and repeal.

(4) In this Article, 'existing law' includes the Retirement from the Public Service (Compensation) Ordinance, 1956, as modified by sub-section (1) of section 118 of the Singapore (Constitution) Order in Council, 1958.

SCHEDULES

(*Not reproduced*)

SOLOMON ISLANDS

SUMMARY

INTERNATIONAL STATUS

Solomon Islands is a member of the United Nations (September 19, 1978). It is a member of the Commonwealth of Nations and of other international organizations. It ratified in 1982 the International Convention of Social, Economic and Cultural Rights.

Solomon Islands became independent on July 7, 1978, under the Solomon Islands Independence Order of May 31, 1978. The Solomon Islands, a scattered Melanesian archipelago, come under British and German protection in the 1890's (the South and North Solomons respectively), and after German cessions, entirely under British protection under the jurisdiction of the West Pacific High Commission with headquarters in Fiji. Invaded and occupied by Japan in 1942, they were largely recaptured by the United States during 1943. After the war, elected local councils were set up on most of the islands, the 1960 constitution set up appointed legislatative and executive councils which from 1964 onwards were increasingly elected. A legislative assembly of 24 members was established under the 1974 constitution and the islands officially named the Solomon Islands in 1975. In 1976, internal self government was granted and a constitutional conference was held in London in September 1977.

FORM OF NATIONAL GOVERNMENT

The Constitution of May 31, 1978, states that Solomon Islands is a sovereign democratic state with a government based of the principle of universal suffrage and the responsibility of executive authorities to elected assemblies.[1] All power belongs to the people.[2] The system is parliamentary. A chapter relates to citizenship,[3] another to land and customary land,[4] one to provincial government,[5] one to the public service.[6] There is a chapter entitled 'Leadership Code', which describes the responsibilities of office, conflict of interest, the obligation not to use office for personal gain, the duty not to demean office or endanger respect and confidence in the government of Solomon Islands.[7]

RIGHTS OF THE PEOPLE

The Constitution provides in detail for the rights without discrimination and subject to respect of the rights of others, to life, liberty, security, protection of the law, freedom of conscience, expression, association, assembly, privacy of the home and property including protection of ownership.[8] Slavery and forced labor are forbidden.[9] Torture and inhuman or degrading treatment are forbidden.[10]

LEGISLATIVE DEPARTMENT

The Legislature is a unicameral Parliament, composed of members elected by constituencies; the rules for elections and qualifications for candidates and voters are detailed.[11] Parliament meets in at least one session a year, and its term is four years subject to dissolution.[12] There are provisions for the Governor General appointing, with the advice of the Speaker, a Leader of the Official Opposition and a Leader of the Independent Members.[13] Parliament prescribes its privileges and immunities.[14] The Constitution provides for an Ombudsman with a term of 5 years.[15] There is a chapter on finance.[16]

EXECUTIVE DEPARTMENT

Executive authority is vested in the Head of State who is the Queen of the United Kingdom.[17] It is exercised by the Governor General who must be a citizen of Solomon Islands.[18] He is appointed by Her Majesty for a five year term renewable once.[19] He acts on the advice of the Cabinet composed of the Prime Minister elected by the members of Parliament from among their number and not more than 11 Ministers.[20] The Cabinet is collectively responsible to Parliament.[21] The Governor General has the power of appointment and the prerogative of mercy.[22]

[1] Const., Art. 1 and Preamble.
[2] Id., Preamble.
[3] Id., Art. 20–26.
[4] Id., Art. 110–113.
[5] Id., Art. 114.
[6] Id., Art. 115–133.
[7] Id., Art. 93–95.
[8] Id., Art. 3–15.
[9] Id., Art. 6.
[10] Id., Art. 7.
[11] Id., Art. 46–58.
[12] Id., Art. 72, 73.
[13] Id., Art. 66.
[14] Id., Art. 69.
[15] Id., Art. 96–99.
[16] Id., Art. 100–109.
[17] Id., Art. 1, 30.
[18] Id., Art. 27, 48.
[19] Id., Art. 27.
[20] Id., Art. 31–33.
[21] Id., Art. 35.
[22] Id., Art. 45, 127.

JUDICIAL DEPARTMENT

The Constitution provides for a High Court with unlimited original jurisdiction including constitutional questions, composed of a Chief Justice and Puisne Judges, appointed by the Governor General on the advice of the Judicial and Legal Services Commission.[23] They hold office until the age of 60; thereafter non-Solomon Islands citizens may be appointed for specific terms[24] A Court of Appeal is provided formed of a President and Justices of Appeal, appointed in the same way, and *ex officio* of the Chief Justice and Puisne Judges of the High Court.[25] The same term of office applies.

AREA, POPULATION, ETC.

The area is 27,556 square kilometres, the estimated population (1981) 234,000. The capital is Honiara on Guadalcanal Island.

[23] Id., Art. 77–79.
[24] Id., Art. 80.
[25] Id., Art. 85–87.

THE CONSTITUTION OF SOLOMON ISLANDS[1]

May 31, 1978

We the people of Solomon Islands, proud of the wisdom and the worthy customs of our ancestors, mindful of our common and diverse heritage and conscious of our common destiny, do now, under the guiding hand of God, establish the sovereign democratic State of Solomon Islands;

As a basis of our united nation

DECLARE that

(*a*) all power in Solomon Islands belongs to its people and is exercised on their behalf by the legislature, the executive and the judiciary established by this Constitution;

(*b*) the natural resources of our country are vested in the people and the government of the Solomon Islands;

AGREE AND PLEDGE that

(*a*) our government shall be based on democratic principles of universal suffrage and the responsibility of executive authorities to elected assemblies;

(*b*) we shall uphold the principles of equality, social justice and the equitable distribution of incomes;

(*c*) we shall respect and enhance human dignity and strengthen and build on our communal solidarity;

(*d*) we shall cherish and promote the different cultural traditions within Solomon Islands;

(*e*) we shall ensure the participation of our people in the governance of their affairs and provide within the framework of our national unity for the decentralization of power;

AND for these purposes we now give ourselves this Constitution.

CHAPTER I

THE STATE AND THE CONSTITUTION

1. (1) Solomon Islands shall be a sovereign democratic State.

(2) Her Majesty shall be the Head of State of Solomon Islands.

2. This Constitution is the supreme law of Solomon Islands and if any other law is inconsistent with this Constitution, that other law shall, to the extent of the inconsistency, be void.

[1]Solomon Islands Independence Order 1978. Statutory Instruments, Legal Notice No. 43. Supplied by New Zealand Embassy Athens in October 1982. Ed.

CHAPTER II

PROTECTION OF FUNDAMENTAL RIGHTS AND FREEDOMS OF THE INDIVIDUAL

3. Whereas every person in Solomon Islands is entitled to the fundamental rights and freedoms of the individual, that is to say, the right, whatever his race, place of origin, political opinions, color, creed or sex, but subject to respect for the rights and freedoms of others and for the public interest, to each and all of the following namely:

(*a*) life, liberty, security of the person and the protection of the law;

(*b*) freedom of conscience, of expression and of assembly and association; and

(*c*) protection for the privacy of his home and other property and from deprivation of property without compensation,

the provisions of this Chapter shall have effect for the purpose of affording protection to those rights and freedoms subject to such limitations of that protection as are contained in those provisions, being limitations designed to ensure that the enjoyment of the said rights and freedoms by any individual does not prejudice the rights and freedoms of others or the public interest.

4. (1) No person shall be deprived of his life intentionally save in execution of the sentence of a court in respect of a criminal offence under the law in force in Solomon Islands of which he has been convicted.

(2) A person shall not be regarded as having been deprived of his life in contravention of this section if he dies as the result of the use, to such extent and in such circumstances as are permitted by law, of such force as is reasonably justifiable

(*a*) for the defence of any person from violence or for the defence of property;

(*b*) in order to effect a lawful arrest or to prevent the escape of a person lawfully detained;

(*c*) for the purposes of suppressing a riot, insurrection or mutiny; or

(*d*) in order to prevent the commission by that person of a criminal offence.

or if he dies as the result of a lawful act of war.

5. (1) No person shall be deprived of his personal liberty save as may be authorized by law in any of the following cases, that is to say

(*a*) in consequence of his unfitness to plead to a criminal charge;

(*b*) in execution of the sentence or order of a court, whether established for Solomon Islands or some other country, in respect of a criminal offence of which he has been convicted;

(*c*) in execution of the order of a court of record punishing him for contempt of that court or of a court inferior to it;

(*d*) in execution of the order of a court made to secure the fulfilment of any obligation imposed on him by law;

(*e*) for the purpose of bringing him before a court in execution of the order of a court;

(*f*) upon reasonable suspicion of his having committed, or being about to commit, a criminal offence under the law in force in Solomon Islands;

(*g*) in the case of a person who has not attained the age of eighteen years, under the order of a court or with the consent of his parent or guardian, for the purpose of his education or welfare;

(*h*) for the purpose of preventing the spread of an infectious or contagious disease;

(*i*) in the case of a person who is, or is reasonably suspected to be, of unsound mind, addicted to drugs or alcohol, or a vagrant, for the purpose of his care or treatment or the protection of the community;

(*j*) for the purpose of preventing the unlawful entry of that person into Solomon Islands, or for the purpose of effecting the expulsion, extradition or other lawful removal of that person from Solomon Islands or for the purpose of restricting that person while he is being conveyed through Solomon Islands in the course of his extradition or removal as a convicted prisioner from one country to another; or

(*k*) to such extent as may be necessary in the execution of a lawful order of a court requiring that person to remain within a specified area within the Solomon Islands or prohibiting him from being within such an area, or to such extent as may be reasonably justifiable for the taking of proceedings against that person relating to the making of any such order, or to such extent as may be reasonably justifiable for restraining that person during any visit that he is permitted to make to any part of Solomon Islands in which, in consequence of any such order, his presence would otherwise be unlawful.

(2) Any person who is arrested or detained shall be informed as soon as reasonably practicable, and in a language that he understands, of the reasons for his arrest or detention.

(3) Any person who is arrested or detained

(*a*) for the purpose of bringing him before a court in execution of the order or a court; or

(*b*) upon reasonable suspicion of his having committed, or being about to commit, a criminal offence under the law in force in Solomon Islands,

and who is not released, shall be brought without undue delay before a court; and if any person arrested or detained upon reasonable suspicion of his having committed or being about to commit a criminal offence is not tried within a reasonable time, then, without prejudice to any further proceedings that may be brought against him, he shall be released either unconditionally or upon reasonable conditions, including in particular such conditions as are reasonably necessary to ensure that he appears at a later date for trial or for proceedings preliminary to trial.

6. (1) No person shall be held in slavery or servitude.

(2) No person shall be required to perform forced labor.

(3) For the purposes of this section, the expression 'forced labor' does not include

(*a*) any labor required in consequence of the sentence or order of a court;

(*b*) any labor required of any person while he is lawfully detained that, though not required in consequence of the sentence or order of a court, is reasonably necessary in the interests of hygiene or for the maintenance of the place at which he is detained;

(*c*) any labor required of a member of a disciplined force in pursuance of his duties as such or, in the case of a person who has conscientious objections to service as a member of a naval, military or air force, any labor that that person is required by law to perform in place of such service;

(*d*) any labor required during any period of public emergency or in the event of any other emergency or calamity that threatens the life and well-being of the community, to the extent that the requiring of such labor is reasonably justifiable in the circumstances of any situation arising or existing during that period or as a result of that other emergency or calamity, for the purpose of dealing with that situation; or

(*e*) any labor reasonably required as part of reasonable and normal communal or other civic obligations.

7. No person shall be subjected to torture or to inhuman or degrading punishment or other treatment.

8. (1) No property of any description shall be compulsorily taken possession of, and no interest in or right over property of any description shall be compulsorily acquired, except where the following conditions are satisfied, that is to say

(*a*) the taking of possession or acquisition is necessary or expedient in the interests of defence, public safety, public order, public morality, public health, town or country planning or the development or utilization of any property in such a manner as to promote the public benefit; and

(*b*) there is reasonable justification for the causing of any hardship that may result to any person having an interest in or right over the property; and

(*c*) provision is made by a law applicable to that taking of possession or acquisition

(i) for the payment of reasonable compensation (the valuable consideration of which may take the form of cash or some other form and may be payable by way of lump sum or by instalments) within a reasonable period of time having due regard to all the relevant circumstances; and

(ii) securing to any person having an interest in or right over the property a right of access to the High Court, whether direct or on appeal from any other authority, for the determination of his interest or right, the legality of the taking of possession or aquisition of the property, interest or right, and the reasonableness of the compensation and the period of time within which it shall be paid.

(2) Nothing contained in or done under the authority of any law shall be held to be inconsistent with or in contravention of this section

(*a*) to the extent that the law in question makes provision for the taking possession or acquisition of any property

(i) in satisfaction of any tax, rate or duty;

(ii) by way of penalty for breach of the law or forfeiture in consequence of a breach of the law;

(iii) as an incident of a lease, tenancy, mortgage, charge, bill of sale, pledge or contract;

(iv) in the execution of judgments or orders of a court in proceedings for the determination of civil rights or obligations;

(v) in circumstances where it is reasonably necessary so to do because of the property is in a dangerous state or injurious to the health of human beings, animals or plants;

(vi) in consequence of any law with respect to the limitation of actions or acquistive prescription; or

(vii) for so long only as may be necessary for the purposes of any examination, investigation, trial or enquiry or, in the case of land, the carrying out thereon

(A) of work of soil conservation or of conservation of other natural resources; or

(B) of work relating to agricultural development or improvement which the owner or occupier of the land has been required, and has without reasonable excuse refused or failed, to carry out,

except so far as that provision or, as the case may be, the thing done under the authority thereof is shown not to be reasonably justifiable in a democratic society; or

(*b*) to the extent that the law in question makes provision for the taking of possession or acquisition of

(i) enemy property;

(ii) property of a deceased person, a person of unsound mind, a person who has not attained the age of twenty-one years or a person who is absent from Solomon Islands, for the purpose of its administration for the benefit of the persons entitled to the beneficial interest therein;

(iii) property of a person declared to be insolvent or a body corporate in liquidation, for the purpose of its administration for the benefit of the creditors of the insolvent or body corporate and, subject thereto, for the benefit of other persons entitled to the beneficial interest in the property; or

(iv) property subject to a trust, for the purpose of vesting the property in persons appointed as trustees under the instrument creating the trust or by a court or, by order of a court, for the purpose of giving effect to the trust.

(3) Nothing in this section shall be construed as affecting the making or operation of any law for the compulsory taking of possession in the public interest of any property, or the compulsory acquisition in the public interest of any interest in or right over property, where that property, interest or right is held by a body corporate established for public purposes by any law and in which no moneys have been invested other than moneys provided by the Government.

9. (1) Except with his own consent, no person shall be subjected to the search of his property or the entry by others on his premises.

(2) Nothing contained in or done under the authority of any law shall be held to be inconsistent with or in contravention of this section to the extent that that law in question makes provision

(*a*) in the interests of defence, public safety, public order, the prevention and investigation of breaches of the law, public morality, public health, town or country planning, the development and utilization of mineral resources, or the development or utilization of any other property in such a manner as to promote the public benefit;

(*b*) for the purpose of protecting the rights or freedoms of other persons,

(*c*) for the purpose of authorizing an officer or agent of the Government, a provincial government authority or a body corporate established by law for a public purpose to enter on the premises of any person in order to inspect those premises or anything thereon for the purpose of any tax, rate or duty or in order to carry out work connected with any property that is lawfully on those premises and that belongs to the Government, that authority or that body corporate, as the case may be;

(*d*) for the purpose of authorizing the entry upon any premises in pursuance of an order of a court for the purpose of enforcing the judgment or order of a court in any proceedings; or

(*e*) for the purpose of authorizing the entry upon any premises for the purpose of preventing or detecting criminal offences,

and except so far as that provision or, as the case may be, anything done under the authority thereof is shown not be to reasonably justifiable in a democratic society.

10. (1) If any person is charged with a criminal offence, then, unless the charge is withdrawn, that person shall be afforded a fair hearing within a reasonable time by an independent and impartial court established by law.

(2) Every person who is charged with a criminal offence

(*a*) shall be presumed to be innocent until he is proved or has pleaded guilty;

(*b*) shall be informed as soon as reasonably practicable, in detail and in a language that he understands, of the nature of the offence charged;

(*c*) shall be given adequate time and facilities for the preparation of his defence;

(*d*) shall be permitted to defend himself before the court in person or, at his own expense, by a legal representative of his own choice;

(*e*) shall be afforded facilities to examine in person or by his legal representative the witnesses called by the prosecution before the court, and to obtain the attendance and carry out the examination of witnesses to testify on his behalf before the court on the same conditions as those applying to witnesses called by the prosecution; and

(*f*) shall be permitted to have without payment the assistance of an interpreter if he cannot understand the language used at the trial of the charge,

and, except with his own consent, the trial shall not take place in his absence unless he so conducts himself as to render the continuance of the proceedings in his presence impracticable and the court has ordered him to be removed and the trial to proceed in his absence.

(3) When a person is tried for any criminal offence, the accused person or any person authorized by him in that behalf shall, if he so requires and subject to payment of such reasonable fee as may be prescribed by law, be given within a reasonable time after judgment a copy for the use of the accused person of any record of the proceedings made by or on behalf of the court.

(4) No person shall be held to be guilty of a criminal offence on account af any act or omission that did not, at the time it took place, constitute such an offence, and no penalty shall be imposed for any criminal offence that is severer in degree or description than the maximum penalty that might have been imposed for that offence at the time when it was committed.

(5) No person who shows that he has been tried by a competent court for a criminal offence and either convicted or acquitted shall again be tried for that offence or for any other criminal offence of which he could have been convicted at the trial for that offence, save upon the order of a superior court in the course of appeal or review proceedings relating to the conviction or acquittal.

(6) No persons shall be tried for a criminal offence if he shows that he has been pardoned for that offence.

(7) No person who is tried for a criminal offence shall be compelled to give evidence at the trial.

(8) Any court or other authority prescribed by law for the determination of the existence or extent of any civil right or obligation shall be established or recognized by law and shall be independent and impartial; and where proceedings for such a determination are instituted by any person before such a court or other adjudicating authority, that person shall be given a fair hearing within a reasonable time.

(9) Except with the agreement of all the parties thereto, all proceedings of every court and proceedings for the determination of the existence or extent of any civil right or obligation before any other adjudicating authority, including the announcement of the decision of the court or authority, shall be held in public.

(10) Nothing in the preceding sub-section shall prevent the court or other adjudicating authority from excluding from the proceedings persons other than the parties thereto and their legal representatives to such extent as the court or other authority

(*a*) may by law be empowered so to do and may consider necessary or expedient in circumstances where publicity would prejudice the interests of justice or in interlocutory proceedings or in the interests of decency, public morality, the welfare of persons under the age of eighteen years or the protection of the private lives of persons concerned in the proceedings; or

(*b*) may by law be empowered or required so to do in the interests of defence, public safety or public order.

(11) Nothing contained in or done under the authority of any law shall be held to be inconsistent with or in contravention of

(*a*) sub-section (2)(*a*) of this section to the extent that the law in question imposes upon any person charged with a criminal offence the burden of proving particular facts;

(*b*) sub-section (2)(*e*) of this section to the extent that the law in question imposes reasonable conditions that must be satisfied if witnesses called to testify on behalf of an accused person are to be paid their expenses out of public funds; or

(*c*) sub-section (5) of this section to the extent that the law in question authorizes a court to try a member of a disciplined force for a criminal offence notwithstanding any trial and conviction or acquittal of that member under the disciplinary law of that force, so, however, that any court so trying such a member and convicting him shall in sentencing him to any punishment take into account any punishment awarded him under that disciplinary law.

11. (1) Except with his own consent, no person shall be hindered in the enjoyment of his freedom of conscience, and for the purposes of this section the said freedom includes freedom of thought and of religion, freedom to change his religion or belief, and freedom either alone or in community with others, and both in public and in private, to manifest and propagate his religion or belief in worship, teaching, practice and observance.

(2) Every religious community shall be entitled, at its own expense, to establish and maintain places of education and to manage any place of education which it wholly maintains.

(3) No religious community shall be prevented from providing religious instruction for persons of that community in the course of any education provided at any place of education which it wholly maintains or in the course of any education which it otherwise provides.

(4) Except with his own consent (or, if he is a person who has not attained the age of eighteen years, the consent of his guardian) no person attending any place of education shall be required to receive religious instruction or take part in or attend any religious ceremony or observance if that instruction, ceremony or observance relates to a religion other than his own.

(5) No person shall be compelled to take any oath which is contrary to his religion or belief or to take any oath in a manner which is contrary to his religion or belief.

(6) Nothing contained in or done under the authority of any law shall be held to be inconsistent with or in contravention of this section to the extent that the law in question makes provision which is reasonably required

(*a*) in the interest of defence, public safety, public order, public morality or public health; or

(*b*) for the purpose of protecting the rights and freedoms of other persons, including the right to practise and observe any religion without the unsolicited intervention of members of any other religion.

and except so far as that provision or, as the case may be, the thing done under the authority thereof is shown not to be reasonably justifiable in a democratic society.

(7) Nothing in this section shall affect the power of Parliament to prescribe the curriculum and related matters in all places of education within the Solomon Islands.

(8) References in this section to a religion shall be construed as including references to a religious denomination, and cognate expressions shall be construed accordingly.

12. (1) Except with his own consent, not person shall be hindered in the enjoyment of his freedom of expression, and for the purposes of this section the said freedom includes the freedom to hold opinions without interference, freedom to receive ideas and information without interference, freedom to communicate ideas and information without interference and freedom from interference with his correspondence.

(2) Nothing contained in or done under the authority of any law shall be held to be inconsistent with or in contravention of this section to the extent that the law in question makes provision

(*a*) in the interests of defence, public safety, public order, public morality or public health;

(*b*) for the purpose of protecting the reputations, rights and freedoms of other persons or the private lives of persons concerned in legal proceedings, preventing the disclosure of information received in confidence, maintaining the authority and independence of the courts, or regulating the administration or the technical operation of telephony, telegraphy, posts, wireless, broadcasting or television; or

(*c*) that imposes restriction upon public officers,

and except so far as that provision or, as the case may be, the thing done under the authority thereof is shown not to be reasonably justifiable in a democratic society.

13. (1) Except with his own consent, no person shall be hindered in the enjoyment of his freedom of assembly and association, that is to say, his right to assemble freely and associate with other persons and in particular to form or belong to political parties or to form or belong to trade unions or other associations for the protection of his interests.

(2) Nothing contained in or done under the authority of any law shall be held to be inconsistent with or in contravention of this section to the extent that the law in question makes provision

(*a*) in the interests of defence, public safety, public order, public morality or public health;

(*b*) for the purpose of protectiong the rights or freedoms of other persons; or

(*c*) that imposes restrictions upon public officers,

and except so far as that provisions or, as the case may be, the thing done under the authority thereof is shown not to be reasonably justifiable in a democratic society.

14. (1) No person shall be deprived of his freedom of movement, and for the purposes of this section the said freedom means the right to move freely throughout Solomon Islands, the right to reside in any part of Solomon Islands, the right to enter Solomon Islands and immunity from expulsion from Solomon Islands.

(2) Any restriction on a persons's freedom of movement that is involved in his lawful detention shall not be held to be inconsistent with or in contravention of this section.

(3) Nothing contained in or done under the authority of any law shall be held to be inconsistent with or in contravention of this section to the extent that the law in question makes provision

(*a*) for the imposition of restrictions on the movement or residence within Solomon Islands of any person or on any person's right to leave Solomon Islands that are reasonably required in the interests of defence, public safety or public order;

(*b*) for the imposition of restriction on the movement of residence within Solomon Islands or on the right to leave Solomon Islands of persons generally or any class of persons that are reasonably required in the interest of defence, public safety, public order, public morality or public health;

(*c*) for the imposition of restrictions on the movement or residence within Solomon Islands of any person who is not a citizen of Solomon Islands or the exclusion or expulsion from Solomon Islands of any such person;

(*d*) for the imposition of restriction on the acquisition or use by any person of land or other property in Solomon Islands;

(*e*) for the imposition of restriction upon the movement or residence within Solomon Islands of public officers;

(*f*) for the removal of a person from the Solomon Islands to be tried or punished in some other country for a criminal offence under the law of that other country or to undergo imprisonment in that other country in execution of the sentence of a court in respect of a criminal offence under the law in force in Solomon Islands of which he has been convicted; or

(*g*) for the imposition of restrictions, by order of a court, on the movement or residence within Solomon Islands of any person or on any person's right to leave Solomon Islands either in consequence of his having been found guilty of a criminal offence under the law in force in Solomon Islands or for the purpose of ensuring that he appears before a court at a later date for trial or for proceedings relating to his extradition or lawful removal from Solomon Islands,

and except so far as that provision or, as the case may be, the thing done under the authority thereof is shown not to be reasonably justifiable in a democratic society.

(4) If any person whose freedom of movement has been restricted by virtue only of such a provision as is referred to in sub-section (3)(*a*) or (*b*) of this section so requests at any time during the period of that restriction not earlier than six months after he last made such a request during that period, his case shall be reviewed by an independent and impartial tribunal presided over by a person, qualified to be admitted to practise in Solomon Islands as an advocate or as a barrister and solicitor, appointed by the Chief Justice.

(5) On any review by a tribunal in pursuance of the preceding sub-section of the case of a person whose freedom of movement has been restricted, the decision of the tribunal concerning the necessity or expediency of continuing the restriction shall be binding on the authority by which it was ordered.

15. (1) Subject to the provisions of sub-sections (5), (6) and (9) of this section, no law shall make any provisions that is discriminatory either of itself or in its effect.

(2) Subject to the provisions of sub-sections (7), (8) and (9) of this section, no person shall be treated in a discriminatory manner by any persons acting by virtue of any written law or in the performance of the functions of any public office or any public authority.

(3) Subject to the provisions of sub-section (9) of this section, no person shall be treated in a discriminatory manner in respect of access to shops, hotels, lodging-houses, public restaurants, eating-houses or places of public entertainment

or in respect of access to places of public resort maintained wholly or partly out of public funds or dedicated to the use of the general public.

(4) In this section, the expression 'discriminatory' means affording different treatment to different persons attributable wholly or mainly to their respective descriptions by race, place of origin, political opinions, color, creed or sex whereby persons of one such description are subjected to disabilities or restriction to which persons of another such description are not made subject or accorded privileges or advantages which are not accorded to persons of another such description.

(5) Sub-section (1) of this section shall not apply to any law so far as that law makes provision

(*a*) for the imposition of taxation or the appropriation of revenue by the government or any provincial government or assembly for local purposes;

(*b*) with respect to persons who are not citizens of Solomon Islands;

(*c*) for the application, in the case of persons of any such description as is mentioned in the preceding sub-section (or of persons connected with such persons), of the law with respect to adoption, marriage, divorce, burial, devolution or property on death or other like matters that is the personal law applicable to persons of that description;

(*d*) for the application of customary law;

(*e*) with respect to land, the tenure of land, the resumption and acquisition of land and other like purposes;

(*f*) for the advancement of the more disadvantaged members of the community; or

(*g*) whereby persons of any such description as is mentioned in the preceding sub-section may be subjected to any disability or restriction or may be accorded ay privilege or advantage which, having regard to its nature and to special circumstances pertaining to those persons or to persons of any other such description, is reasonably justifiable in a democratic society.

(6) Nothing contained in any law shall be held to be inconsistent with or in contravention of sub-section (1) of this section to the extent that is makes provision with respect to standards or qualifications (not being standards or qualifications specifically relating to race, place of origin, political opinions, color, creed or sex) to be required of any person who is appointed to any office in the public service, any office in a disciplined force, any office in the service of a provincial government or any office in a body corporate established directly by any law for public purposes, or who wishes to engage in any trade or business.

(7) Sub-section (2) of this section shall not apply to anything which is expressly or by necessary implication authorized to be done by any such provision or law as is referred to in sub-section (5) or (6) of this section.

(8) Sub-section (2) of this section shall not affect any discretion relating to the institution, conduct or discontinuance of civil or criminal proceedings of any court that is vested in any person by or under this Constitution or any other law.

(9) Nothing contained in or done under the authority of any law shall be held to be inconsistent with or in contravention of this section to the extent that the law in question makes provision whereby persons of any such description as is mentioned in sub-section (4) of this section may be subjected to any restriction on the rights and freedoms guaranteed by section 9, 11, 12, 13 and 14 of this Constitution, being such a restriction as is authorized by section 9(2), 11(6), 12(2), 13(2) or 14(3), as the case may be.

16. (1) In this Chapter 'period of public emergency' means any period during which

(*a*) Solomon Islands is at war; or

(*b*) there is in force a declaration made under the provisions of this section.

(2) The Governor General may at any time by proclamation declare that a state of public emergency exists and as soon as practicable shall publish such proclamation in the *Gazette*.

(3) A declaration made under sub-section (2) of this section shall cease to have effect on the expiration of a period of seven days commencing with the day on which the declaration is made unless before the expiration of that period it has been approved by a resolution of Parliament supported by the votes of at least two thirds of all the members thereof;

Provided that, if a declaration is made during any period when Parliament is not sitting, Parliament shall be convened not later than two weeks after the day on which the declaration is made and the period of seven days referred to in this sub-section shall commence on the day on which Parliament convened.

(4) A declaration made under sub-section (2) of this section may at any time before it has been approved by a resolution of Parliament be revoked by the Governor General by a proclamation published in the *Gazette*.

(5) A declaration made under sub-section (2) of this section and approved by a resolution of Parliament under sub-section (3) shall continue in force until the expiration of a period of four months commencing with the day on which the declaration is made or until such earlier date as may be specified in the resolution.

(6) Notwithstanding the provisions of sub-section (5) of this section, a declaration made under sub-section (2) and approved by a resolution of Parliament under sub-section (3) may at any time be revoked by a resolution of Parliament supported by the votes of a majority of all the members thereof.

(7) Nothing contained in or done under the authority of any law shall be held to be inconsistent with or in contravention of section 5, 6(2), 9, 11, 12, 13, 14 or 15 of this Constitution to the extent that the law in question makes in relation to any period of public emergency provision, or authorizes the doing during any such period of anything, that is reasonably justifiable in the circumstances of any situation arising or existing during the period for the purpose of dealing with that situation.

(8) Where a person is detained by virtue of a law that authorizes the taking during a period of public emergency of measures that are reasonably justifiable for

the purpose of dealing with the situation that exists in Solomon Islands during that period, the following provisions shall apply, that is to say

(*a*) he shall, as soon as reasonably practicable, be furnished with a statement in writing, in a language that he understands, specifying in detail the grounds upon which he is detained;

(*b*) the announcement of his detention shall be made as soon as possible, and not more than fourteen days after the commencement of his detention a notification shall be published in the *Gazette* stating that he has been detained and giving particulars of the provision of law under which his detention is authorized;

(*c*) not more than one month after the commencement of his detention and thereafter during his detention at intervals of not more than six months, his case shall be reviewed by an independent and impartial tribunal established by law consisting of a Chairman appointed by the Chief Justice and two other persons appointed by the Judicial and Legal Service Commission;

(*d*) he shall be afforded reasonable facilities to consult a legal representative of his own choice who shall be permitted to make representations to the tribunal; and

(*e*) at the hearing of his case by the tribunal he shall be permitted to appear in person or by a legal representative of his own choice.

(9) On any review by a tribunal in pursuance of sub-section (8) of this section of the case of a detained person, the decision of the tribunal concerning the necessity or expediency of continuing his detention shall be binding on the authority by which it was ordered.

(10) Nothing contained in paragraph (*d*) or (*e*) of sub-section (8) of this section shall be construed as entitling a person to legal representation at public expense.

17. Any persons of whose rights or freedoms under this Chapter has been contravened shall be entitled to compensation for the contravention thereof from the person or authority which contravened it.

18. (1) Subject to the provisions of sub-section (6) of this section, if any person alleges that any of the provisions of sections 3 to 16 (inclusive) of this Constitution has been, is being or is likely to be contravened in relation to him (or, in the case of a person who is detained, if any other person alleges such a contravention in relation to the detained person) then, without prejudice to any other action with respect to the same matter which is lawfully available, that person (or that other person) may apply to the High Court for redress.

(2) The High Court shall have original jurisdiction

(*a*) to hear and determine any application made by any person in pursuance of the preceding sub-section;

(*b*) to determine any question arising in the case of any person which is referred to it in pursuance of the next following sub-section,

and may make such orders, issue such writs and give such directions, including the payment of compensation, as it may consider appropriate for the purpose of enforcing or securing the enforcement of any of the provisions of sections 3 to 16 (inclusive) of this Constitution:

Provided that the High Court may decline to exercise its powers under this subsection if it is satisfied that adequate means of redress for the contravention alleged are or have been available to the person concerned under any other law.

(3) If in any proceedings in any subordinate court any question arises as to the contravention of any of the provisions of sections 3 to 16 (inclusive) of this Constitution, the person presiding in that court may, and shall if any party to the proceedings so requests, refer the question to the High Court unless, in his opinion, the raising of the question is merely frivolous or vexatious.

(4) Any person aggrieved by any determination of the High Court under this section may appeal therefrom to the Court of Appeal:

Provided that no appeal shall lie from a determination of the High Court under this section dismissing an application on the ground that it is frivolous or vexatious.

(5) Parliament may confer upon the High Court powers additional to those conferred by this section for the purpose of enabling that court more effectively to exercise the jurisdiction conferred upon it by this section.

(6) Rules of court making provisions with respect to the practice and procedure of the High Court in relation to the jurisdiction conferred on it by or under this section (including rules with respect to the time within which any application or reference shall or may be made or brought) may be made by the person or authority for the time being having power to make rules of court with respect to the practice and procedure of that court generally.

19. (1) In this Chapter, unless the context otherwise requires

'contravention', in relation to any requirement, includes a failure to comply with that requirement, and cognate expressions shall be construed accordingly;

'court' means any court of law having jurisdiction in Solomon Islands, other than a court established by a disciplinary law, and includes in section 4 and 6 of this Constitution a court established by a disciplinary law;

'disciplinary law' means a law regulating the discipline of any disciplined force;

'disciplined force' means

(*a*) any naval, military or air force;

(*b*) the Solomon Islands Fire Service;

(*c*) the Prisons Service;

(*d*) the Marine Division;

(*e*) the Police Force;

(*f*) the Special Constabulary; or

(*g*) any other constabulary or police force established by Parliament;

'member', in relation to a disciplined force, includes any person who, under the law regulating the discipline of that force, is subject to that discipline.

(2) Nothing contained in sections 12, 13 and 14 of this Constitution shall be construed as precluding the inclusion in the terms and conditions of service of

public officers of reasonable requirements as to their communication or association with other persons or as to their movements or residence.

(3) In relation to any person who is a member of a disciplined force of Solomon Islands, nothing contained in or done under the authority of the disciplinary law of that force shall be held to be inconsistent with or in contravention of any of the provisions of this Chapter other than sections 4, 6, 7, 8 and 15.

(4) In relation to any person who is a member of a disciplined force that is not a disciplined force of Solomon Islands and who is present in Solomon Islands in pursuance of arrangements made between the Government of Solomon Islands and another Government or an international organization, nothing contained in or done under the authoriy of the disciplinary law of that force shall be held to be inconsistent with or in contravention of any of the provisions of this Chapter.

(5) No measure taken in relation to a person who is a member of a disciplined force of a country with which Solomon Islands is at war and no law, to the extent that it authorizes the taking of any such measures, shall be held to be inconsistent with or in contravention of any of the provisions of this Chapter.

CHAPTER III

CITIZENSHIP

20. (1) (*a*) Every person who is immediately before Independence Day an indigenous Solomon Islander shall become a citizen of Solomon Islands on Independence Day.

(*b*) Every person who was born in Solomon Islands before Independence Day and who has or had two grandparents who are or were members of a group, tribe or line indigenous to Papua New Guinea or the New Hebrides shall become a citizen of Solomon Islands on Independence Day.

(2) Every person who before Independence Day has made, or been included in, an application to the Government for citizenship of Solomon Islands containing the information specified in sub-section (4) of this section and who at the time of making such application possessed any of the qualifications specified in subsection (3) of this section shall become a citizen of Solomon Islands on Independence Day.

(3) The qualifications referred to in sub-section (2) of this section and subsection (1) of the next following section are that the person concerned, not being an indigenous Solomon Islander, is

(*a*) a woman married to an indigenous Solomon Islander; or

(*b*) a citizen of the United Kingdom and Colonies or a British protected person who was born in Solomon Islands; or

(*c*) a citizen of the United Kingdom and Colonies or a British protected person having acquired such status under the British Nationality Acts 1948 to 1965 by virtue of his having been naturalized or or registered under those acts, or naturalized as a British subject before 1949, by the Governor of the former protectorate of the Solomon Islands; or

(*d*) a citizen of the United Kingdom and Colonies or a British protected person whose father possesses, or at his death possessed, one of the qualifications specified in paragraph (*b*) or (*c*) of this sub-section; or

(*e*) a woman who has been married to a person who possesses, or at his death possessed, one of the qualifications specified in paragraph (*b*), (*c*) or (*d*) of this sub-section; or

(*f*) a citizen of the United Kingdom and Colonies or a British protected person who was deemed to belong to Solomon Islands because such person

(i) has lawfully resided in Solomon Islands for any period of seven years during which he has not been absent therefrom for a period or periods amounting in all to more than eighteen months and since the completion of such period of residence has not been ordinarily resident continuously for a period of two years or more in any other territory within the Commonwealth in circumstances in which he has acquired or retained a right of residence in that territory; or

(ii) is the wife of a person to whom the foregoing subparagraph applies not living apart from such person under a decree of a court or a deed of separation; or

(iii) is the child, step-child or child adopted in a manner recognised by law under the age of eighteen years of a person to whom either of the foregoing subparagraphs applies.

(4) The information required to be contained in an application for the purposes of this section and the next following section is as follows

(*a*) the name, date and place of birth (so far as is known) of the applicant, of any other person included in the application or of a minor on whose behalf the application is made, together with, where applicable, the date of naturalization or registration;

(*b*) a statement by the applicant whether or not he is including in his application his wife and minor children, if any, and in the case of an application including a wife, a statement by her that she consents to her inclusion in the application;

(*c*) if the applicant is applying on grounds that his father was born, naturalized or registered in Solomon Islands, also the father's name, place and date of birth (so far as is known) and, if relevant, the date of the father's naturalization or registration;

(*d*) if the application is made by or on behalf of a woman on grounds of marriage to a man who, or whose father, was born, naturalized or registered in Solomon Islands, also the name, place and date of birth (so far as is known) and, if relevant, the date of naturalization or registration or the man and, if necessary, his father;

(*e*) a statement by the applicant that, if he is resident in Solomon Islands at the time of making application, he intends to continue such residence, or that, if he is not so resident at that time, he regards Solomon Islands as his home country;

(*f*) a declaration by the applicant of his allegiance to Solomon Islands and his respect for the culture, the language and the way of life of Solomon Islands; and

(*g*) a statement by the applicant that he intends to renounce any other nationality that he may hold at the time of making application.

(5) The reference in paragraph (*c*) of sub-section (3) of this section to the Governor of the former protectorate of the Solomon Islands shall, in relation to any certificate of naturalization granted or registration effected by some other officer in his capacity as the officer for the time being administering the Government of the former protectorate of the Solomon Islands, be construed as a reference to that officer.

(6) Every person who becomes a citizen of Solomon Islands on Independence Day by virtue of sub-section (2) of this section shall receive a certificate of his acquisition of such citizenship as soon as practicable after Independence Day.

21. (1) Every person who immediately before Independence Day possessed any of the qualifications specified in subsection (3) of the preceding section and who within the prescribed period has made, or been included in, an application to the Government for citizenship of Solomon Islands containing the information specified in sub-section (4) of the preceding section shall be registered as a citizen of Solomon Islands.

(2) For the purposes of sub-section (1) of this section, 'the prescribed period' means the period beginning on Independence Day and expiring two years thereafter:

Provided that the Minister responsible for citizenship matters may extend that period in respect of such application or classes of application where the applicant was, by reason of his absence from Solomon Islands or other reasonable cause, unaware of his right to apply, as he may think fit.

22. Every person born on or after Independence Day, whether within or outside Solomon Islands, shall become a citizen of Solomon Islands at the date of his birth if at that date either of his parents is, or would but for his death have been, a citizen of Solomon Islands.

23. (1) Subject to the provisions of sub-section (2) of this section, any citizen of Solomon Islands who is a national of some other country shall cease to be a citizen of Solomon Islands at the expiry of two years after the date on which he acquired citizenship of Solomon Islands or attained the age of eighteen years, whichever is the later, or such longer period as may be prescribed by Parliament, unless before the expiry of that period he has renounced or lost the nationality of that other country or, if the law of that other country does not permit him to renounce that nationality, made such declaration as may be prescribed.

(2) Any person who, being aged eighteen years or more, acquired citizen-

ship of Solomon Islands by virtue of section (20(2) or 21 of this Constitution and who is a national of some other country shall cease to be a citizen of Solomon Islands at the expiry of six months after the date on which he acquired citizenship of Solomon Islands or such longer period as may be prescribed by Parliament, unless before the expiry of that period he has renounced or lost the nationality of that other country or, if the law of that other country does not permit him to renounce that nationality, made such declaration as may be prescribed.

24. (1) Every person who under this Chapter or any other law is a citizen of Solomon Islands or under any enactment for the time being in force in any country to which this section applies is a citizen of that country shall, by virtue of that citizenship, have the status of a Commonwealth citizen.

(2) Every person who is a British subject without citizenship under the British Nationality Act 1948, who continues to be a British subject under section 2 of that Act or is a British subject under the British Nationality Act 1965 shall, by virtue of that status, have the status of a Commonwealth citizen.

(3) Save as may be otherwise provided by Parliament, the countries to which this section applies are Australia, The Bahamas, Bangladesh, Barbados, Botswana, Canada, Cyprus, Fiji, The Gambia, Ghana, Grenada, Guyana, India, Jamaica, Kenya, Lesotho, Malawi, Malaysia, Malta, Mauritius, Nauru, New Zealand, Nigeria, Papua New Guinea, Seychelles, Sierra Leone, Singapore, Southern Rhodesia, Sri Lanka, Swaziland, Tanzania, Tonga, Trinidad and Tobago, Uganda, The United Kingdom and Colonies, Western Samoa and Zambia.

25. Parliament nay make provision

(*a*) for the acquisition of citizenship of Solomon Islands by persons who are not eligible or who are no longer eligible to become citizens of Solomon Islands by virtue of the provisions of this Chapter;

(*b*) for the deprivation and renunciation of citizenship of Solomon Islands held by any person who has attained the age of eighteen years.

26. (1) In this Chapter

'British protected persons' means a person who is a British protected person for the purposes of the British Nationality Act 1948;

'indigenous Solomon Islander' means any person who is, or one of whose parents is or was, a British protected person and of a group, tribe or line indigenous to Solomon Islands.

(2) Any reference in this Chapter to the father of a person shall, in relation to a person born out of wedlock, be construed as a reference to the mother of that person.

(3) For the purposes of this Chapter, a person born aboard a registered ship or aircraft, or aboard an unregistered ship or aircraft of the government of any country, shall be deemed to have been born in the place in which the ship or aircraft was registered or, as the case may be, in that country.

(4) For the purposes of this Chapter, an application shall be deemed to have been made on the date on which it is lodged with the Government or with any person who has been appointed by the Government to receive applications.

CHAPTER IV

THE GOVERNOR GENERAL

27. (1) There shall be a Governor General of Solomon Islands who shall be appointed by the Head of State in accordance with an address from Parliament and who shall be the representative of the Head of State in Solomon Islands.

(2) A person shall not be qualified for appointment to the office of Governor General unless he is qualified for election as a member of Parliament under Chapter VI of this constitution.

(3) The office of Governor General shall become vacant

(*a*) at the expiration of five years from the date of his appointment; or

(*b*) if he is removed from office by the Head of State, in accordance with an address from Parliament supported by the votes of at least two thirds of all the members thereof, for misbehaviour or for such other cause as may be prescribed by parliament.

(4) No person may be appointed as Governor General for more than two terms of office.

28. Whenever the office of Governor General is vacant or the holder of the office is absent from Solomon Islands or is for any other reason unable to perform the functions of his office, those functions shall be performed by the Speaker or, if the office of Speaker is vacant or the holder of that office is likewise absent or unable to perform those functions, by the Chief Justice.

29. A person appointed to the office of Governor General or assuming the functions of that office under the preceding section shall, before entering upon the duties of that office, take and subscribe the oath of allegiance and the oath of office as prescribed in Schedule 1 to this Constitution, such oaths being administered by the Chief Justice or such other judge of the High Court or the Court of Appeal as may be designated by the Chief Justice.

CHAPTER V

THE EXECUTIVE

30. (1) The executive authority of the people of Solomon Islands is vested in the Head of State.

(2) Save as otherwise provided in this Constitution, that authority may be exercised on behalf of the Head of State by the Governor General either directly or through officers subordinate to him.

(3) Nothing in this section shall preclude persons or authorities other than the Governor General from exercising such functions as may be conferred upon them by any law.

31. (1) In the exercise of his functions under this Constitution or any other law, the Governor General shall act in accordance with the advice of the Cabinet or of a Minister acting under the general authority of the Cabinet except in case where he is required by this Constitution to act in accordance with the advice of, or after consultation with, any person or authority other than the Cabinet or in his own deliberate judgment.

(2) Where the Governor General is required by this Constitution to exercise any function after consultation with any person or authority other than the Cabinet, he shall not be obliged to exercise that function in accordance with the advice of that person or authority.

(3) Where the Governor General is required by this Constitution to act in accordance with the advice of, or after consultation with, any person or authority, the question whether he has in any matter so acted shall not be called in question in any court of law.

32. The Prime Minister shall keep the Governor General fully informed concerning the general conduct of the government of Solomon Islands and shall furnish the Governor General with such information as he may request with respect to any particular matter relating to the government of Solomon Islands.

33. (1) There shall be a Prime Minister who shall be elected as such by the members of Parliament from amongst their number in accordance with the provisions of Schedule 2 to this Constitution.

(2) There shall be, in addition to the office of Prime Minister, such other offices of Minister of the Government, not exceeding eleven or such greater number as Parliament may prescribe, as may be established by the Governor General, acting in accordance with the advice of the Prime Minister:

Provided that one of such offices of Minister of the Government shall be that of Deputy Prime Minister.

(3) The Ministers other than the Prime Minister shall be appointed by the Governor General, acting in accordance with the advice of the Prime Minister, from among the members of Parliament:

Provided that if occasion arises for making an appointment while Parliament is dissolved a person who was a member of Parliament immediately before the dissolution may be appointed.

34. (1) If a resolution of no confidence in the Prime Minister is passed by Parliament by an absolute majority of the votes of members thereof the Governor General shall remove the Prime Minister from office, whereupon the members of Parliament shall meet as soon as possible during the same session of parliament to elect a new Prime Minister in accordance with the provisions of Schedule 2 to this Constitution.

(2) A motion for a resolution of no confidence in the Prime Minister shall not be passed by Parliament unless notice of the motion has been given to the Speaker at least seven clear days before it is introduced.

(3) The office of Prime Minister shall also become vacant

(*a*) when, after a general election, the members of Parliament meet to elect a Prime Minister in accordance with the provisions of Schedule 2 to this Constitution;

(*b*) if he ceases to be a member of Parliament for any reason other than a dissolution of Parliament;
(*c*) if he is elected as Speaker or Deputy Speaker; or
(*d*) if he resigns such office by writing under his hand addressed to the Governor General.

(4) Subject to the next following subsection, during any period when the office of Prime Minister is vacant, the person who held that office immediately before the vacancy arose shall continue to perform the functions of Prime Minister until a person is elected to the office of Prime Minister in accordance with the provisions of Schedule 2 to this Constitution.

(5) If the person holding the office of Prime Minister dies, the Governor General shall, after consultation with the other Ministers, appoint one of them to perform the functions of Prime Minister until a person is elected to the office of Prime Minister in accordance with the provisions of Schedule 2 to this Constitution.

(6) The office of a Minister other than the Prime Minister shall become vacant

(*a*) upon the election of any person to the office of Prime Minister in accordance with the provisions of Schedule 2 to this Constitution;
(*b*) if he ceases to be a member of Parliament for any reason other than a dissolution of Parliament;
(*c*) if he is elected as Speaker or Deputy Speaker;
(*d*) if he resigns such office by writing under his hand addressed to the Governor General; or
(*e*) if his appointment to the office of a Minister is revoked by the Governor General, acting in accordance with the advice of the Prime Minister.

35. (1) There shall be a Cabinet for Solomon Islands, consisting of the Prime Minister and the other Ministers.

(2) The functions of the Cabinet shall be to advise the Governor General in the government of Solomon Islands and the Cabinet shall be collectively responsible to Parliament for any advice given to the Governor General by or under the general authority of the Cabinet and for all things done by or under the authority of any Minister in the execution of his office.

(3) The provisions of the preceding subsection shall not apply in relation to

(*a*) the appointment and removal from office of Ministers, the assigning of responsibility to any Minister under section 37 of this Constitution, or the authorisation of another Minister to perform the functions of the Prime Minister during illness or absence; or
(*b*) the matters referred to in section 45 of this Constitution (which relate to the Prerogative of Mercy).

(4) The Attorney General shall be the legal adviser to the Cabinet and as such shall attend the meetings of the Cabinet unless otherwise directed by the Cabinet.

36. (1) The Cabinet shall be summoned by the Prime Minister.

(2) The Prime Minister shall, so far as is practicable, attend and preside at all meetings of the Cabinet.

(3) No business except that of adjournment shall be transacted in the Cabinet if objection is taken by any member present that there are present less than a majority of the members for the time being of the Cabinet.

(4) Subject to the preceding subsection, the Cabinet shall not be disqualified for the transaction of business by reason of any vacancy in its membership, and any proceedings of the Cabinet shall be valid notwithstanding that some person who was not entitled to do so took part in those proceedings.

(5) The Prime Minister shall decide what business shall be considered at any meeting of the Cabinet.

(6) The person presiding in the Cabinet may summon any person to a meeting of the Cabinet, notwithstanding that that person is not a member of the Cabinet, when in the opinion of the person presiding the business of the Cabinet makes the presence of that person desirable:

Provided that a person shall not be under any obligation to answer any question put to him by any member of the Cabinet at such meeting.

37. The Governor General, acting in accordance with the advice of the Prime Minister, may, by directions in writing, assign to the Prime Minister or any other Minister responsibility for the conduct (subject to the provisions of this Constitution and any other law) of any business of the Government, including responsibility for the administration of any department of the Government.

38. (1) Whenever the Prime Minister is unable, by reason of illness or absence from Solomon Islands, to perform the functions conferred on him by this Constitution, those functions shall be performed by the Deputy Prime Minister or, if he too is unable to do so, the Governor General may, by directions in writing, authorise some other Ministers to perform those functions (other than the functions conferred by this section) and that Minister may perform those functions until his authority is revoked by the Governor General.

(2) The powers of the Governor General under this section shall be exercised by him in accordance with the advice of the Prime Minister:

Provided that if the Governor General, acting in his own deliberate judgment, considers that it is impracticable to obtain the advice of the Prime Minister owing to the Prime Minister's illness or absence, the Governor General may exercise those powers without that advice and in his own deliberate judgment.

39. Before assuming the functions of his office every member of the Cabinet shall make before the Governor General, or some person authorised in that behalf by the Governor General, oaths of allegiance and for the due execution of his office in the forms set out in Schedule 1 to this Constitution.

40. Where any Minister has been charged with responsibility for the administration of any department of the Government, he shall exercise general direction and control over that department and, subject to such direction and control, any department in the charge of a Minister (including the office of the Prime Minister or any other Minister) shall be under the supervision of a Permanent Secretary or some other supervising officer whose office shall be a public office:

Provided that

(*a*) any such department may be under the joint supervision of two or more supervising officers; and

(*b*) different parts of any such department may respectively be under the supervision of different supervising officers.

41. (1) There shall be a Secretary to the Cabinet whose office shall be that of a Permanent Secretary.

(2) The Secretary to the Cabinet shall have charge of the office of the Cabinet and shall be responsible, in accordance with such instructions as may be given to him by the Prime Minister, for arranging the business for, and keeping the minutes of, the meetings of the Cabinet and for conveying the decisions of the Cabinet to the appropriate person or authority, and shall have such other functions as the Prime Minister may from time to time direct.

42. (1) There shall be an Attorney General whose office shall be a public office and who shall be the principal legal adviser to the Government.

(2) The Attorney General shall be appointed by the Judicial and Legal Service Commission acting in accordance with the advice of the Prime Minister.

(3) No person shall be qualified to hold the office of Attorney General unless he is entitled to practice in Solomon Islands as an advocate or as a barrister and solicitor.

(4) If the Minister responsible for justice is not a person entitled to practise in Solomon Islands as an advocate or as a barrister and solictor, the person holding the office of Attorney General shall be entitled to take part in the proceedings of Parliament as adviser to the Government:

Provided that he shall not be entitled to vote in Parliament or in any election for the office of Prime Minister.

43. (1) There shall be a Commissioner of Police, whose office shall be a public office.

(2) The Commissioner of Police shall be appointed by the Governor General, acting in accordance with the advice of the Prime Minister tendered after the Prime Minister has consulted the Police and Prisons Service Commission.

(3) The Police Force shall be under the command of the Commissioner of Police.

(4) The Prime Minister, or such other Minister as may be authorized in that behalf by the Prime Minister, may give to the Commissioner of Police such general directions of policy with regard to the maintenance of public safety and public order as he may consider necessary and the Commissioner shall comply with such directions or cause them to be complied with.

(5) Nothing in this section shall be construed as precluding the assignment to a Minister of responsibility under section 37 of this Constitution for the organization, maintenance and administration of the Police Force, but the Commissioner of Police shall be responsible for determining the use and controlling the operations

of the Force and, except as provided in the preceding subsection, the Commissioner shall not, in the exercise of his responsibilities and powers with respect to the use and operational control of the Force, be subject to the direction or control of any person or authority.

44. Subject to the provisions of this Constitution and of any other law, the Governor General, acting on the advice of the Prime Minister, may constitute offices for Solomon Islands, make appointments to any such office and terminate any such appointment.

45. (1) The Governor General may, in the name and on behalf of the Head of State

(*a*) grant to any person convicted of any offence under the law of Solomon Islands a pardon, either free or subject to lawful conditions;

(*b*) grant to any person a respite, either indefinite or for a specified period, of the execution of any punishment imposed on that person for such an offence;

(*c*) substitute a less severe form of punishment for any punishment imposed on any person for such an offence; or

(*d*) remit the whole or any part of any punishment imposed on any person for such an offence or any penalty or forfeiture otherwise due to the Crown on account of such an offence.

(2) There shall be a Committee on the Prerogative of Mercy (in this section referred to as 'the Committee') which shall consist of the following members

(*a*) a Chairman and two other persons, one of whom shall be a qualified medical practitioner and the other of whom shall be a social worker, appointed by the Governor General in his own deliberate judgment; and

(*b*) one person nominated by the provincial assembly of the province in which the person whose case is being reviewed ordinarily resides.

(3) The provincial assembly of every province shall as soon as it is elected nominate a person for the purposes of subsection (2) (*b*) of this section for such period as it deems appropriate.

(4) A member of the Committee appointed under subsection (2) (*a*) of this section shall vacate his seat on the Committee

(*a*) at the expiration of the term of his appointment (if any) specified in the instrument of his appointment; or

(*b*) if his appointment is revoked by the Governor General, acting in his own deliberate judgment.

(5) In the exercise of the powers conferred upon him by subsection (1) of this section, the Governor General shall act in accordance with the advice of the Committee.

(6) The validity of the transaction of any business by the Committee shall not be affected by reason only of the fact that some person who was not entitled to do so took part in the proceedings.

(7) Whenever any person has been sentenced to death (otherwise than by a court-martial) for an offence, a report on the case by the judge who presided at the trial (or, if a report cannot be obtained from that judge, a report on the case by the Chief Justice), together with such other information derived from the record of the case or elsewhere as may be required by or furnished to the Committee shall be taken into consideration at a meeting of the Committee, which shall then advise the Governor General whether or not to exercise his powers under sub-section (1) of this section in that case.

CHAPTER VI

THE NATIONAL LEGISLATURE

Part I. Parliament

46. There shall be a national legislature for Solomon Islands, which shall consist of a single chamber and shall be known as the National Parliament of Solomon Islands.

47. (1) Parliament shall consist of persons elected in accordance with the provisions of this Constitution and, subject thereto, in such manner as may be prescribed.

(2) Each of the constituencies prescribed under section 54(1) of this Constitution shall return one member of Parliament.

48. Subject to the provisions of the next following section, a person shall be qualified for election as a member of Parliament if, and shall not be so qualified unless

(*a*) he is a citizen of Solomon Islands; and
(*b*) he has attained the age of twenty-one years.

49. (1) No person shall be qualified for election as a member of Parliament who

(*a*) is, by virtue of his own act, under any acknowledgement of allegiance, obedience or adherence to a foreign power or state;
(*b*) holds, or is acting in, any public office;
(*c*) is an undischarged bankrupt, having been adjudged or otherwise declared bankrupt under any law for the time being in force in any part of the Commonwealth;
(*d*) is certified to be insane or otherwise adjudged to be of unsound mind under any law for the time being in force in Solomon Islands;
(*e*) is under sentence of death imposed on him be a court in any part of the world, or is under a sentence of imprisonment (by whatever name called) for a term of, or exceeding, six months, other than a sentence in lieu of a fine, but including a suspended sentence, imposed on him by such a court or substituted by competent authority for some other sentence imposed on him by such a court;

(*f*) is disqualified from membership of Parliament or from registration as an elector or from voting at elections under any law for the time being in force in Solomon Islands relating to offences connected with elections; or

(*g*) holds, or is acting in, any office the functions of which involve any responsibility for, or in connection with, the conduct of any election to Parliament or the compilation or revision of any electoral register for that purpose.

(2) For the purpose of paragraph (*e*) of the preceding sub-section two or more terms of imprisonment that are required to be served consecutively shall be regarded as a single term of inprisonment for the aggregate period of those terms.

50. A member of Parliament shall vacate his seat

(*a*) on a dissolution of Parliament;

(*b*) if he resigns his seat by writing under his hand addressed to the Speaker;

(*c*) if he is elected as Speaker;

(*d*) if he is appointed as Governor General;

(*e*) if he is absent from two consecutive meetings of Parliament without having obtained from the person presiding, before the termination of either meeting, permission to be or to remain absent therefrom unless, in the opinion of the Speaker (or, if the office of Speaker is vacant or he is for any reason unable to perform the functions of his office, the Deputy Speaker), such absence was due to causes beyond the member's control;

(*f*) if any circumstances arises that, if he were not a member of Parliament, would cause him to be disqualified from election thereto by virtue of paragraph (*a*), (*b*), (*d*), (*f*) or (*g*) of sub-section (1) of this preceding section; or

(*g*) in the circumstances mentioned in the next following section.

51. (1) Subject to the provisions of this section, if a member of Parliament is sentenced by a court in any part of the world to death or to imprisonment (by whatever name called) for a term of, or exceeding, six months, including a suspended sentence, he shall forthwith cease to perform his functions as a member of Parliament, and his seat in Parliament shall become vacant at the expiration of a period of thirty days thereafter:

Provided that the Speaker (or, if the office of Speaker is vacant or he is for any reason unable to perform the functions of his office, the Deputy Speaker) may, at the request of the member, from time to time extend that period for thirty days to enable the member to pursue any appeal in respect of his conviction or sentence so however that extensions of time exceeding in the aggregate one hundred and fifty days shall not be given without approval of Parliament signified by resolution.

(2) If at any time before the member vacates his seat he is granted a free pardon or his conviction is set aside or his sentence is reduced to a term of imprisonment of less than six months or a punishment other than imprisonment is substituted, his seat in Parliament shall not become vacant under the provisions of this section, and he may again perform his functions as a member of Parliament.

(3) For the purposes of this section

(*a*) two or more terms of imprisonment that are required to be served consecutively shall be regarded as a single term of imprisonment for the aggregate period of those terms; and

(*b*) no account shall be taken of a sentence of imprisonment imposed as an alternative to or in default of the payment of a fine.

52. (1) The High Court shall have jurisdiction to hear and determine any question whether

(*a*) any person has been validly elected as a member of Parliament; or

(*b*) any member of Parliament has vacated his seat therein or is required by virtue of section 51 of this Constitution to cease to perform his functions as a member.

(2) No appeal shall lie from any decision of the High Court in proceedings under the preceding sub-section.

53. (1) There shall be a Constituency Boundaries Commission consisting of

(*a*) a Chairman and two other members (in this section referred to as 'the appointed members') appointed by the Governor General, acting in accordance with the advice of the Judicial and Legal Service Commission; and

(*b*) the persons for the time being holding the offices of Chief Surveyor and Head of the Government's Statistical Services, who shall be members of the Commission *ex officio.*

(2) A person shall not be qualified to be an appointed member of the Commission if he is a member of, or a candidate for election to, Parliament or any provincial assembly.

(3) Subject to the provisions of the next following sub-section, an appointed member of the Commission shall vacate his office

(*a*) at the expiration of the period specified in the instrument by which he was apponted; or

(*b*) if any circumstances arise that, if he were not a member of the Commission, would cause him to be disqualified from appointment as such.

(4) The provisions of section 126 of this Constitution shall apply to an appointed member of the Constituency Boundaries Commission as they apply to a member of the Public Service Commission except that sub-section (7) shall apply as if for the words 'in accordance with the advice of the Prime Minister' there were substituted the words 'in accordance with the advice of the Judicial and Legal Service Commission'.

54. (1) For the purposes of the election of members of Parliament, Solomon Islands shall be divided into such number of constituencies, being not less than thirty and not more than fifty, and each constituency shall have such boundaries, as may be prescribed by Parliament by resolution on a recommendation of the Constituency Boundaries Commission in accordance with sub-section (4) of this section.

(2) The Constituency Boundaries Commission shall make recommendations to Parliament with respect to the number and boundaries of constituencies as soon as practicable after the commencement of this Constitution; and thereafter the Commission may review the number and boundaries of the constituencies whenever they consider this to be desirable and shall do so not later than ten years after they last reviewed them, and may make recommendations to Parliament for alterations in the number and boundaries of the constituencies.

(3) In making recommendations under the preceding sub-section, the Constituency Boundaires Commission shall have regard to the principle that the number of inhabitants of each constituency shall be as nearly equal as is reasonably practicable:

Provided that the Commission may depart from the foregoing principle to such extent as they consider expedient in order to take account of the distribution of the population, the means of communication, and ethnic affiliations.

(4) Parliament may, by resolution, approve or reject the recommendations of the Constituency Boundaries Commission but may not vary them; and, if so approved, the recommendations shall have effect as from the next dissolution of Parliament.

55. (1) Subject to the provisions of this section, a person shall be entitled to be registered as an elector if, and shall not be so entitled unless

(*a*) he is a citizen of Solomon Islands; and

(*b*) he has attained the age of eighteen years.

(2) No person shall be entitled to be registered as an elector

(*a*) in more than one constituency; or

(*b*) in any constituency in which he is not ordinarily resident.

(3) No person shall be entitled to be registered as an elector who

(*a*) is under sentence of death imposed on him by a court in any part the world, or us under a sentence of imprisonment (by whatever name called) for a term of, or exceeding, six months, other than a sentence in lieu of a fine, but including a suspended sentence, imposed on him by such a court or substituted by competent authority for some other sentence imposed on him by such a court;

(*b*) is certified to be insane or otherwise adjudged to be of unsound mind under any law for the time being in force in Solomon Islands; or

(*c*) is disqualified from registration as an elector or from voting at elections under any law for the time being in force in Solomon Islands relating to offences connected with elections.

(4) For the purposes of paragraph (*a*) of the preceding sub-section two or more terms of imprisonment that are required to be served consecutively shall be regarded as as single term of imprisonment for the aggregate period of those terms.

56. (1) Any person who is registered as an elector in any constituency shall be entitled to vote in such manner as may be prescribed at any election for that constituency unless (*a*) on the date appointed for polling he is under such sentence of death or serving such sentence of imprisonment as is referred to in paragraph (*a*) of section 55(3) of this Constitution or (except in so far as may be otherwise prescribed) he is for any other reason unable to attend in person at the place and time appointed for polling; or

(*b*) he is prohibited from so voting by any law in force in Solomon Islands because he holds or is acting in any office the functions of which involve any responsibility for, or in connection with, the conduct of that election or because he has been convicted of any offence connected with elections.

(2) No person shall vote at any election for any constituency who is not registered as an elector in that constituency.

57. (1) There shall be an Electoral Commission consisting of

(*a*) the Speaker, who shall be Chairman of the Commission; and

(*b*) two other members (in this section referred to as 'the appointed members') appointed by the Governor General, acting in accordance with the advice of the Judicial and Legal Service Commission.

(2) A person shall not be qualified to be an appointed member of the Commission if he is a member of, or a candidate for election to, Parliament or any provincial assembly.

(3) Subject to the provisions of the next following sub-section, an appointed member of the Commission shall vacate his office

(*a*) at the expiration of the period specified in the instrument by which he was appointed; or

(*b*) if any circumstances arise that, if he were not a member of the Commission, would cause him to be disqualified from appointment as such.

(4) The provisions of section 126 of this Constitution shall apply to an appointed member of the Electoral Commission as they apply to a member of the Public Service Commission except that sub-section (7) shall apply as if for the words 'in accordance with the advice of the Prime Minister' there were substituted the words 'in accordance with the advice of the Judicial and Legal Service Commission'.

58. (1) The Electoral Commission shall have general responsibility for, and shall supervise, the registration of electors for the election of members of Parliament and the conduct of elections of such members and the Commission shall have such powers and other functions relating to such registration and such elections as may be prescribed.

(2) Every proposed Bill and every proposed regulation or other instrument having the force of law relating to the registration of electors for the election of members of Parliament or to the election of such members shall be referred to the Electoral Commission at such time as shall give them sufficient opportunity to make comments thereon before the Bill is introduced in Parliament or, as the case may be, the regulation or other instrument is made.

(3) The Electoral Commission may make such reports to the Governor General concerning the matters under their supervision, or any draft Bill or instrument that is referred to them, as they may think fit, and if the Commission so request in any such report other than a report on a draft Bill or instrument that report shall be laid before Parliament.

Part II. Legislation and Procedure in Parliament

59. (1) Subject to the provisions of this Constitution, Parliament may make laws for the peace, order and good government of Solomon Islands.

(2) The laws referred to in this section shall take the form of Bills passed by Parliament; and when a Bill has been passed by Parliament it shall be presented to the Governor General who shall assent to it forthwith on behalf of the Head of State, and when such assent is given the Bill shall become law.

(3) No law shall come into operation until it has been published in the *Gazette* but Parliament may postpone the coming into operation of any such law and may make laws, subject to section 10(4) of this Constitution, with retrospective effect.

(4) All laws made by Parliament shall be styled 'Acts of Parliament' and the words of enactment shall be 'Enacted by the National Parliament of Solomon Islands'.

60. Except on the recommendation of the Cabinet signified by a Minister, Parliament shall not

(*a*) proceed upon any Bill (including any amendment to a Bill) which, in the opinion of the person presiding, makes provision for imposing or increasing any tax, for imposing or increasing any charge on the Consolidated Fund or other funds of Solomon Islands, or for altering any such charge otherwise than by reducing it, or for compounding or remitting any debt due to Solomon Islands;

(*b*) proceed upon any motion (including any amendment to a motion) which would, in the opinion of the person presiding, if the motion were carried, require the introduction of such a Bill as is referred to in paragraph (*a*) to give effect to the motion; or

(*c*) receive any petition which, in the opinion of the person presiding, requests that provision be made for any of the purposes aforesaid.

61. (1) Subject to the provisions of this section, Parliament may alter this Constitution.

(2) A Bill for an Act of Parliament to alter any of the following provisions of this Constitution, that is to say

(*a*) this section;

(*b*) Chapters II, VII and IX;

(*c*) sections 46 to 58 (inclusive), and 108; and

(*d*) Chapter XIV to the extent that it relates to any of the provisions specified in the preceding paragraphs, shall not be passed by Parliament unless it is supported at the final voting on two separate readings in Parliament by the votes of not less than three quarters of all the members of Parliament.

(3) A Bill for an Act of Parliament to alter any provisions of this Constitution (but which does not alter any of the provisions of this Constitution as specified in sub-section (2) of this section) shall not be passed by Parliament unless it is supported at the final voting on two separate readings in Parliament by the votes of not less than two thirds of all the members of Parliament.

(4) Without prejudice to the provisions of sub-sections (2) and (3) of this section, a Bill for an Act of Parliament under this section shall not be passed by Parliament unless

(*a*) notice of the Bill has been given to the Speaker at least four weeks before the first reading of the Bill in Parliament; and

(*b*) the Bill is clearly expressed to be a Bill for an Act of Parliament to alter the Constitution.

(5) In this section

(*a*) references to this Constitution or to any particular provision thereof include references to any other law in so far as that law alters the Constitution or, as the case may be, that provision; and

(*b*) references to altering this Constitution or any particular provision thereof include references

(i) to repealing it, with or without re-enactment thereof or the making of different provision in lieu thereof;

(ii) to modifying it, whether by omitting or amending any of its provisions or inserting additional provisions in it or otherwise;

(iii) to suspending its operation for any period, or terminating any such suspension; and

(iv) to making any other provision that is repugnant to or otherwise inconsistent with it.

62. Subject to the provisions of this Constitution, Parliament may from time to time make, amend and revoke rules and orders for the regulation and orderly conduct of its proceedings and the despatch of business, and for the passing, intituling and numbering of Bills.

63. No member of Parliament shall be permitted to take part in the proceedings of Parliament (other than proceedings necessary for the purpose of this section) until he has made before Parliament an oath of allegiance in the form set out in Schedule 1 to this Constitution.

64. (1) Parliament shall at its first sitting after any general election elect

(*a*) from among persons who are qualified for election as a member of Parliament, a Speaker; and

(*b*) from among its members, a Deputy Speaker.

(2) The office of the Speaker or the Deputy Speaker shall become vacant

(*a*) if he announces the resignation of his office to Parliament or if, by writing under his hand addressed to Parliament and received by the Clerk to the Legislature, he resigns that office;

(*b*) if Parliament passes a resolution supported by the votes of not less than two thirds of all the members thereof requiring his removal;
(*c*) in the case of the Speaker
(i) if any circumstances arise that would cause him to be disqualified from election as a member of Parliament; or
(ii) when Parliament first sits after a general election; or
(*d*) in the case of the Deputy Speaker
(i) if he ceases to be a member of Parliament or if, under the provisions of section 51 of this Constitution, he is required to cease to perform his functions as a member of Parliament;
(ii) if he becomes a Minister;
(iii) if he is elected as Speaker; or
(iv) if he becomes a recognized leader in Parliament of any political party.

(3) If the office of Speaker or Deputy Speaker becomes vacant Parliament shall, unless it is sooner dissolved, elect a person qualified under this section to fill the vacancy at its next sitting after the occurrence of the vacancy or as soon as practicable thereafter.

(4) No business shall be transacted in Parliament (other than the election of a Speaker) at any time when the office of Speaker is vacant.

(5) Save as otherwise provided in this Constitution or any other law, the Speaker shall not hold any other office.

65. The Speaker or in his absence the Deputy Speaker or in their absence a member of Parliament (not being a Minister) elected by Parliament for the sitting, shall preside at any sitting of Parliament:

Provided that at the first sitting of Parliament after any general election, until a Speaker is elected there shall preside the person who last held office as Speaker or, in his absence, the person who last held office as Deputy Speaker.

66. (1) If at any time it appears to the Governor General, acting in accordance with the advice of the Speaker, that the leader of an opposition group, by reason of the numerical strength of that opposition group or by reason of the support which he receives from the members of opposition groups generally, should be appointed as Leader of the Official Opposition, the Governor General shall appoint him as such leader.

(2) If at anytime it appears to the Governor General, acting in accordance with the advice of the Speaker, that the leader of an independent group, by reason of the numerical strength of that independent group or by reason of the support which he receives from the members of independent groups generally, should be appointed as Leader of the Independent Members, the Governor General shall appoint him as such leader.

(3) If the Governor General, acting in accordance with the advice of the Speaker, considers that the Leader of the Official Opposition is no longer the person who, if the office of Leader of the Official Opposition were vacant would be appointed thereto under sub-section (1) of this section, the Governor General shall remove the Leader of the Official Opposition from office.

(4) If the Governor General, acting in accordance with the advice of the Speaker, considers that the Leader of the Independent Members is no longer the person who, if the office of Leader of the Independent Members were vacant, would be appointed thereto under sub-section (2) of this section, the Governor General shall remove the Leader of the Independent Members from office.

(5) Before tendering advice to the Governor General under sub-sections (1) and (3) of this section, the Speaker shall consult with the leaders and members of the opposition groups and such other persons as he deems appropriate, and before tendering advice under sub-sections (2) and (4) of this section, the Speaker shall consult with the leaders and members of the independent groups and such other persons as he deems appropriate.

(6) If the Leader of the Official Opposition or the Leader of the Independent Members

(*a*) is required under section 51 of this Constitution to cease to perform his functions as a member of Parliament;

(*b*) otherwise ceases to be such a member; or

(*c*) is elected as Deputy Speaker,

his office shall become vacant.

(7) For the purposes of this section

'opposition group' means a group of members of Parliament in opposition to the Government, whose number includes a leader who commands their support;

'independent group' means a group of members of Parliament whose members are independent both of the Government and of any opposition group and whose number includes a leader who commands their support.

(8) Parliament may by resolution supported by an absolute majority of the members thereof prescribe the minimum number of members of opposition or independent groups there must be before the Leader of the Official Opposition or of the Independent Members, as the case may be, is appointed under this section.

67. If objection is taken by any member of Parliament present that there are present in Parliament (besides the person presiding) less than half of all the members thereof and, after such interval as may be prescribed in the rules of procedure of Parliament, the person presiding ascertains that the number of members present is still less than half of all the members, he shall thereupon adjourn Parliament.

68. Subject to the provisions of the preceding section, Parliament shall not be disqualified from the transaction of business by reason of any vacancy in its membership, and any proceedings in Parliament shall be valid notwithstanding that some person who was not entitled to do so took part in those proceedings.

69. Parliament may prescribe the privileges, immunities and powers of Parliament and its members.

70. The proceedings of Parliament shall be held in public except in so far as its rules of procedure otherwise provide.

71. (1) Subject to the provisions of this Constitution, all questions proposed for decision in Parliament shall be determined by a majority of the votes of the members present and voting.

(2) If the person presiding is

(*a*) the Speaker, he shall have neither an original nor a casting vote;

(*b*) the Deputy Speaker or a member elected by Parliament for the sitting under section 65 of this Constitution, he shall not have an original vote but shall have and shall exercise a casting vote if on any question the votes are equally divided.

(3) Subject to the provisions of sub-section (2)(*b*) of this section, if upon any question the votes are equally divided the motion shall be declared lost.

72. (1) Subject to the provisions of this section, each session of Parliament shall be held at such place within Solomon Islands and shall commence at such time as the Governor General may appoint by proclamation published in the *Gazette.*

(2) Sessions of Parliament shall be held so that a period of twelve months does not intervene between the end of one session and the first sitting of Parliament in the next session.

73. (1) If at any time Parliament decides by resolution supported by the votes of an absolute majority of the members of Parliament that Parliament should be prorogued or dissolved, the Governor General shall forthwith prorogue or, as the case may be, dissolve Parliament by proclamation published in the *Gazette.*

(2) A motion for a resolution under the preceding sub-section shall not be passed by Parliament unless notice of the motion has been given to the Speaker at least seven days before it is introduced.

(3) Parliament, unless sooner dissolved under sub-section (1) of this section, shall continue for four years from the date of the first sitting of Parliament after any general election and shall then stand dissolved.

74. There shall be a general election at such time within four months of every dissolution of Parliament as the Governor General shall appoint by proclamation published in the *Gazette.*

CHAPTER VII

THE LEGAL SYSTEM

Part I. The Application of Laws

75. (1) Parliament shall make provision for the application of laws. including customary laws.

(2) In making provision under this section, Parliament shall have particular regard to the customs, values, and aspirations of the people of Solomon Islands.

76. Until Parliament makes other provisions under the preceding section, the provisions of Schedule 3 to this Constitution shall have effect for the purpose of determining the operation in Solomon Islands

(*a*) of certain Acts of the Parliament of the United Kingdom mentioned therein;

(*b*) of the principles and rules of the common law and equity;

(*c*) of customary law; and

(*d*) of the legal doctrine of judicial precedent.

Part II. The Judiciary

(A) THE HIGH COURT

77. (1) There shall be a High Court for Solomon Islands which shall have unlimited original jursidiction to hear and determine any civil or criminal proceedings under any law and such jurisdiction and powers as may be conferred on it by this Constitution or by Parliament.

(2) The judges of the High Court shall be the Chief Justice and such number of puisne judges, if any, as may be prescribed by Parliament:

Provided that the office of a judge shall not be abolished while any person is holding that office unless he consents to its abolition.

78. (1) The Chief Justice shall be appointed by the Governor General, acting in accordance with the advice of the Judicial and Legal Service Commission.

(2) The puisne judges shall be appointed by the Governor General, acting in accordance with the advice of the Judicial and Legal Service Commission.

(3) A person shall not be qualified for appointment as a judge of the High Court unless

(*a*) he holds, or has held, high judicial office in any country in the Commonwealth or in any country outside the Commonwealth that may be prescribed by Parliament; or

(*b*) he is qualified to practise as a barrister or solicitor in such a country and he has been so qualified for not less than five years.

(4) In computing, for the purposes of the preceding sub-section, the period during which any person has been qualified to practise as a barrister or solicitor, any period during which he has held judicial office after becoming so qualified shall be included.

79. (1) If the office of Chief Justice is vacant or if the person holding that office is for any reason unable to perform the functions of his office, the Governor General, acting in accordance with the advice of the Judicial and Legal Service Commission, may appoint a puisne judge or some other person qualified for appointment as a judge of the High Court to act as Chief Justice.

(2) If the office of a puisne judge is vacant or if a person holding the office of puisne judge is acting as Chief Justice or is for any reason unable to perform the functions of his office, the Governor General, acting in accordance with the advice of the Judicial and Legal Service Commission, may appoint a person qualified for appointment as a judge of the High Court to act as a puisne judge.

(3) Any person appointed under the provisions of this section to act as a judge of the High Court shall, unless he earlier resigns his acting office or is removed therefrom under the next following section, continue so to act until the end of the period for which he was appointed or, if he was not appointed for a specified period, until his appointment is revoked by the Governor General, acting in accordance with the advice of the Judicial and Legal Service Commission.

Provided that a person whose appointment has expired or whose appointment has been revoked may continue to act as such for so long thereafter as may be necessary to enable him to deliver judgment or to do any other thing in relation to any proceedings that were commenced before him previously thereto.

(4) Whenever he is satisfied that no judge of the High Court is available to attend to the business of the Court, the Governor General, acting in accordance with the advice of the Judicial and Legal Service Commission, may appoint some other person to perform

(*a*) all or any of the functions of a judge, either generally or in respect of any particular case or class of cases;

(*b*) such functions of a judge as it shall appear to that person require to be performed without delay.

subject to such limitations and conditions, if any, as may be specifed in the instrument of appointment.

(5) Any person appointed under the provisions of the preceding sub-section shall be styled a Commissioner of the High Court; all things done by him in accordance with the terms of his appointment shall have the same validity and effect as if they had been done by a judge of the High Court; in respect thereof he shall have the same powers and enjoy the same immunities as if he had been a judge of the High Court; and, notwithstanding that the period of his appointment has expired or his appointment has been revoked, he may sit as a Commissioner of the High Court for the purpose of delivering judgment or doing any other thing in relation to any proceedings that were commenced before him whilst his appointment was subsisting.

80. (1) Subject to the provisions of this section, a judge of the High Court shall hold office until he attains the age of sixty years.

(2) Notwithstanding the preceding sub-section, a person who is not a citizen of Solomon Islands and is over the age of sixty years may be appointed as a judge of the High Court for a term of years and shall cease to hold office at the expiration of that term, and shall not otherwise cease to hold office except in accordance with this section.

(3) Nothing done by a judge of the High Court shall be invalid by reason only that he has attained the age at which he is required by this section to vacate his office.

(4) A judge of the High Court may be removed from office only for inability to discharge the functions of his office (whether arising from infirmity of body or mind or any other cause) or for misbehavior and shall not be so removed except in accordance with the provisions of this section.

(5) A judge of the High Court shall be removed from office by the Governor General if the question of the removal of that judge from office has been referred to a tribunal appointed under the next following sub-section and the tribunal has advised the Governor General that he ought to be removed from office for inability as aforesaid or for misbehavior.

(6) If the Governor General considers that the question of removing a judge of the High Court from office for inability as aforesaid or for misbehavior ought to be investigated, then

(*a*) the Governor General shall appoint a tribunal which shall consist of a chairman and not less than two other members, selected by the Governor General from among persons who hold or have held high judicial office in some part of the Commonwealth; and

(*b*) the tribunal shall enquire into the matter and report on the facts thereof to the Governor General and advise the Governor General whether that judge should be removed under this section.

(7) If the question of removing a judge of the High Court from office has been referred to a tribunal under the preceding sub-section, the Governor General may suspend the judge from performing the functions of his office, and any such suspension may at any time be revoked by the Governor General and shall in any case cease to have effect if the tribunal advises the Governor General that that judge should not be removed from office.

(8) Except as provided in sub-section (5) of this section, the functions of the Governor General under this section shall be exercised by him in his own deliberate judgment.

81. A judge of the High Court whose appointment has terminated otherwise than by reason of his removal from office may sit as a judge of that Court for the purpose of delivering judgment or doing any other thing in relation to any proceedings that were commenced before him while his appointment was subsisting.

82. The High Court shall have a seal bearing on it the words 'The High Court of Solomon Islands' and such device as Parliament may approve by resolution.

83. (1) Subject to the provisions of sections 31(3) and 98(1) of, and paragraph 10 of Schedule 2 to, this Constitution, if any person alleges that any provision of this Constitution (other than Chapter II) has been contravened and that his interests are being or are likely to be affected by such contravention, then, without prejudice to any other action with respect to the same matter which is lawfully available, that person may apply to the High Court for a declaration and for relief under this section.

(2) The High Court shall have jurisdiction, in any application made by any person in pursuance of the preceding sub-section or in any other proceedings lawfully brought before the Court, to determine whether any provisions of this Constitution (other than Chapter II) has been contravened and to make a declaration accordingly:

Provided that the High Court shall not make a declaration in pursuance of the jurisdiction conferred by this sub-section unless it is satisfied that the interests of the person by whom the application under the preceding sub-section is made or, in the case of other proceedings before the Court, a party to those proceedings, are being or are likely to be affected.

(3) Where the High Court makes a declaration in pursuance of the preceding sub-section that any provision of the Constitution has been contravened and the person by whom the application under sub-section (1) of this section was made or, in the case of other proceedings before the Court, the party in those proceedings in respect of whom the declaration is made, seeks relief, the High Court may grant to

that person such remedy, being a remedy available against any person in any proceedings in the High Court under any law for the time being in force in Solomon Islands, as the Court considers appropriate.

(4) Nothing in this section shall confer jurisdiction on the High Court to hear or determine any such question as is referred to in section 52 of this Constitution otherwise than upon an application made in accordance with the provisions of that section.

84. (1) The High Court shall have jurisdiction to supervise any civil or criminal proceedings before any subordinate court and may make such orders, issue such writs and give such directions as it may consider appropriate for the purpose of ensuring that justice is duly administered by any such court.

(2) Where any question as to the interpretation of any provision of this Constitution other than Chapter II arises in any subordinate court and the court is of opinion that the question involves a substantial question of law, the court shall refer the question to the High Court.

(3) Where any question is referred to the High Court in pursuance of the preceding sub-section, the High Court shall give its decision upon the question and the court in which the question arose shall dispose of the case in accordance with that decision or, if that decision is the subject of an appeal to the Court of Appeal, in accordance with the decision of the Court of Appeal.

(B) THE COURT OF APPEAL

85. (1) There shall be a Court of Appeal for Solomon Islands which shall have such jurisdiction and powers to hear and determine appeals in civil and criminal matters as may be conferred on it by this Constitution or by Parliament.

(2) The judges of the Court of Appeal shall be

(*a*) a President and such number of other Justices of Appeal, if any, as may be prescribed by Parliament; and

(*b*) the Chief Justice and the puisne judges of the High Court, who shall be judges of the Court *ex officio*.

86. (1) The President of the Court of Appeal shall be appointed by the Governor General, acting in accordance with the advice of the Judicial and Legal Service Commission.

(2) The other Justices of Appeal shall be appointed by the Governor General, acting in accordance with the advice of the Judicial and Legal Service Commission.

(3) A person shall not be qualified to be appointed under sub-section (1) or (2) of this section unless he is qualified for appointment as a judge of the High Court.

(4) A judge of the Court of Appeal shall not sit as a Judge of the Court on the hearing of an appeal

(*a*) from any decision given by himself or any decision given by any court of which he was sitting as a member; or (*b*) against a conviction or sentence if he was the judge by or before whom the appellant was convicted.

(5) If the office of President of the Court of Appeal is vacant or if the person holding that office is for any reason unable to perform the functions of his office, then until a person has been appointed to and has assumed the functions of that office or until the holder thereof has resumed those functions, as the case may be, the Governor General, acting in accordance with the advice of the Judicial and Legal Service Commission, may appoint one of the other judges of the Court of Appeal or some other person qualified for appointment to that office to act as President of the Court of Appeal:

Provided that a person appointed under this sub-section who is not a judge of the Court of Appeal may, notwithstanding the assumption or resumption of the functions of the office of President of the Court of Appeal by the holder of that office, continue to act as a judge of the Court of Appeal for so long thereafter as may be necessary to enable him to deliver judgment or do any other thing in relation to any proceedings that were commenced before him previously thereto.

(6) Nothing in this section or the preceding section shall preclude the offices of Chief Justice and President of the Court of Appeal from being held by the same person.

87. (1) Subject to the provisions of this section, a judge of the Court of Appeal shall hold office until he attains the age of sixty years.

(2) Notwithstanding the preceding sub-section, a person who is not a citizen of Solomon Islands and is over the age of sixty years may be appointed as a judge of the Court of Appeal for a term of years and shall cease to hold office at the expiration of that term, and shall not otherwise cease to hold office except in accordance with this section.

(3) Nothing done by a judge of the Court of Appeal shall be invalid by reason only that he has attained the age at which he is required by this section to vacate his office.

(4) A judge of the Court of Appeal may be removed from office only for inability to discharge the functions of his office (whether arising from infirmity of body or mind or any other cause) or for misbehavior, and shall not be so removed except in accordance with the provisions of this section.

(5) A judge of the Court of Appeal shall be removed from office by the Governor General if the question of the removal of that judge from office has been referred to a tribunal appointed under the next following sub-section and the tribunal has advised the Governor General that he ought to be removed from office for inability as aforesaid or for misbehavior.

(6) If the Governor General considers that the question of removing a judge of the Court of Appeal from office for inability as aforesaid or for misbehavior ought to be investigated, then

(*a*) the Governor General shall appoint a tribunal which shall consist of a chairman and not less than two other members, selected by the Governor General from among persons who held or have held high judicial office in some part of the Commonwealth; and (*b*) the tribunal shall enquire into the matter and report on the facts thereof to the Governor General and advise the Governor General whether that judge should be removed under this section.

(7) If the question of removing a judge of the Court of Appeal from office has been referred to a tribunal under the preceding sub-section, the Governor General may suspend the judge from performing the functions of his office, and any such suspension may at any time be revoked by the Governor General and shall in any case cease to have effect if the tribunal advises the Governor General that that judge should not be removed from office.

(8) Except as provided in sub-section (5) of this section, the functions of the Governor General under this section shall be exercised by him in his own deliberate judgment.

88. A judge of the Court of Appeal whose appointment has terminated otherwise than by reason of his removal from office may sit as a judge of that Court for the purpose of delivering judgment of doing any other thing in relation to any proceedings that were commenced before him while his appointment was subsisting.

89. The Court of Appeal shall have a seal bearing on it the words 'The Court of Appeal of Solomon Islands' and such device as Parliament shall approve by resolution.

(C) RULES OF COURT

90. There shall be a Rules Committee, consisting of the Chief Justice, the President of the Court of Appeal and the Attorney General (who shall constitute a quorum) and such other persons as the Governor General, acting after consultation with the Chief Justice, may appoint, which may make rules of court regulating the practice and procedure of the High Court and the Court of Appeal, prescribing the fees to be paid in respect of any proceeding and generally for making provision for the proper and effectual exercise of the jurisdiction of the High Court and the Court of Appeal, including the procedure for the making and hearing of appeals to the High Court from subordinate courts and for the making and hearing of appeals to the Court of Appeal from the High Court:

Provided that rules regulating the admission of legal practitioners to practise as barristers and solicitors or in either of these capacties, or prescribing or affecting the amount of any fees or the recovery thereof, shall not come into operation unless approved, either before or after being made, by Parliament.

Part III. The Director of Public Prosecutions and the Public Solicitor

91. (1) There shall be a Director of Public Prosecutions whose office shall be a public office.

(2) The Director of Public Prosecutions shall be appointed by the Governor General, acting in accordance with the advice of the Judicial and Legal Service Commission.

(3) A person shall not be qualified to hold or act in the office of Director of Public Prosecutions unless he is entitled to practise in Solomon Islands as an advocate or as a barrister and solicitor.

(4) The Director of Public Prosecutions shall have power in any case in which he considers it desirable to do so

(*a*) to institute and undertake criminal proceedings against any person before any court (other than a court-martial) in respect of any offence alleged to have been committed by that person;

(*b*) to take over and continue any such criminal proceedings that have been instituted or undertaken by any other person or authority; and

(*c*) to discontinue at any stage before judgment is delivered any such criminal proceedings instituted or undertaken by himself or any other criminal person or authority.

(5) The powers of the Director of Public Prosecutions under the preceding sub-section may be exercised by him in person or through other persons acting in accordance with his general or specific instructions.

(6) The powers conferred on the Director of Public Prosecutions by paragraphs (*b*) and (*c*) of sub-section (4) of this section shall be vested in him to the exclusion of any other person or authority:

Provided that where any other person or authority has instituted criminal proceedings, nothing in this sub-section shall prevent the withdrawal of those proceedings by or at the instance of that person or authority and with the leave of the court.

(7) In the exercise of the powers conferred on him by this section the Director of Public Prosecutions shall not be subject to the direction or control of any other person or authority.

Provided that, where any case in any way concerns the defence, security or international relations of Solomon Islands, the Director of Public Prosecutions shall bring the matter to the attention of the Minister responsible for justice and shall, in the exercise of his powers in relation to that case, act in accordance with any directions that Minister may give to him.

(8) For the purposes of this section, any appeal from any judgment in any criminal proceedings before any court, or any case stated or question of law reserved for the purpose of any such proceedings to any other court, shall be deemed to be part of those proceedings:

Provided that the power conferred on the Director of Public Prosecutions by paragraph (*c*) of sub-section (2) of this section shall not be exercised in relation to any appeal by a person convicted in any criminal proceedings or to any case stated or question of law reserved at the instance of such a person.

(9) During any period when the office of Director of Public Prosecutions is vacant or the holder of that office is for any reason unable to perfrom the functions of his office, those functions shall be performed by the Attorney General.

92. (1) There shall be a Public Solicitor, whose office shall be a public office.

(2) The Public Solicitor shall be appointed by the Governor General, acting in accordance with the advice of the Judicial and Legal Service Commission.

(3) A person shall not be qualified to hold or act in the office of Public Solicitor unless he is entitled to practise in Solomon Islands as an advocate or as a barrister and solicitor.

(4) The functions of the Public Solicitor are to provide legal aid, advice and assistance to persons in need in such circumstances and subject to such conditions as may be prescribed by Parliament, and in particular

(*a*) to provide legal aid, advice and assistance to any person in need who has been charged with a criminal offence; and

(*b*) to provide legal aid, advice and assistance to any person when directed to do so by the High Court.

(5) A person aggrieved by a refusal of the Public Solicitor to provide legal aid, advice and assistance to him may apply to the High Court for a direction under paragraph (*b*) of the preceding sub-section.

(6) Parliament may make provision for the Public Solicitor to make a reasonable charge for services provided by him to persons in need whom he considers are able to make a contribution towards the cost of those services.

(7) Except as provided in paragraph (*b*) of sub-section (4) of this section, in the exercise of the functions conferred on him by or under this section the Public Solicitor shall not be subject to the direction or control of any other person or authority.

CHAPTER VIII

LEADERSHIP CODE

93. The provisions of this Chapter apply to and in relation to

(*a*) the Governor General;

(*b*) the Prime Minister and other Ministers;

(*c*) the Leader of the Official Opposition and the Leader of the Independent Members;

(*d*) all other members of Parliament;

(*e*) the Speaker;

(*f*) members of any Commission established by this Constitution;

(*g*) public officers;

(*h*) provincial government officers and members of provincial assemblies;

(*i*) officers of statutory corporations and Government agencies; and

(*j*) such other officers as Parliament may prescribe.

94. (1) A person to whom this Chapter applies has a duty to conduct himself in such a way, both in his public or official life and his private life, and in his associations with other persons, as not

(*a*) to place himself in a position in which he has or could have a conflict of interests or in which the fair exercise of his public or official duties might be compromised;

(*b*) to demean his office or position;
(*c*) to allow his integrity to be called into question; or
(*d*) to endanger or diminish respect for and confidence in the integrity of the government of Solomon Islands.

(2) In particular, a person to whom this Chapter applies shall not use his office for personal gain or enter into any transaction or engage in any enterprise or activity that might be expected to give rise to doubt in the public mind as to whether he is carrying out or has carried out the duty imposed by the preceding sub-section.

(3) It is the further duty of a person to whom this Chapter applies
(*a*) to ensure, as far as it within his lawful power, that his spouse and children and any other persons for whom he is responsible, including nominees, trustees and agents, do not conduct themselves in a way that might be expected to give rise to doubt in the public mind as to his complying with his duties under this section; and
(*b*) if necessary, publicly to dissociate himself from any activity or enterprise of any of his associates, or of a person referred to in paragraph (*a*) of this sub-section, that might be expected to give rise to such a doubt.

(4) A person to whom this Chapter applies who
(*a*) is convicted of an offence in respect of his office or position or in relation to the performance of his functions or duties;
(*b*) fails to carry out the obligations imposed by the preceding sub-sections of this section; or
(*c*) commits any act or omission prescribed under section 95 of this Constitution as constituting misconduct in office,

is guilty of misconduct in office.

95. Subject to the provisions of this Constitution, for the purposes of this Chapter, Parliament
(*a*) may make provision for the disclosure of the personal and business incomes and financial affairs of persons to whom this Chapter applies, and of their families and associates, and in particular of interests in contracts with governmental bodies and of directorships and similar offices held by them (including powers to nominate directors, trustees or agents, or similar officers);
(*b*) may make provision for the disposal or temporary control of the assets or income of a person to whom this Chapter applies where this seems to be desirable for attaining the objects of this Chapter;
(*c*) may prescribe specific acts or omissions as constituting misconduct in office;
(*d*) may create offences (including offences by persons to whom this Chapter applies and offences by other persons) and prescribe penalties for such offences;
(*e*) shall provide for the investigation of cases of alleged or suspected misconduct in office;

(*f*) shall provide for the reference of cases of alleged or suspected misconduct in office to such independent courts or tribunals as may be prescribed, and for the investigation and determination by such courts or tribunals of any such cases that may be referred to them in the manner prescribed;

(*g*) shall make provision with respect to the powers and procedure of such courts or tribunals as may be prescribed under the preceding paragraph and shall prescribe the penalties or other consequences that may result from a lawful determination by any such court or tribunal that a person to whom this Chapter applies is guilty of misconduct in office; and

(*h*) may make such other provision as may appear necessary or expedient for attaining the objects of this Chapter.

CHAPTER IX

THE OMBUDSMAN

96. (1) There shall be an Ombudsman, whose office shall be a public office.

(2) the Ombudsman shall be appointed by the Governor General, acting in accordance with the advice of a committee consisting of the Speaker, the Chairman of the Public Service Commission and the Chairman of the Judicial and Legal Service Commission.

(3) If the person appointed as Ombudsman is a member of Parliament or a provincial assembly, he shall forthwith cease to be such a member.

(4) The Ombudsman shall not perform the functions of any other public or provincial government office, and shall not, without the approval of the Governor General in each particular case, hold any other office of emolument than the office of the Ombudsman or engage in any occupation for reward outside the duties of his office.

(5) Subject to the provisions of the next following sub-section, the Ombudsman shall vacate his office at the expiration of five years from the date of his appointment.

(6) The Ombudsman may be removed from office only for inability to discharge the functions of his office (whether arising from infirmity of body or mind or any other cause) or for misbehavior and shall not be so removed except in accordance with the procedure for the removal of a judge of the High Court as set out in sub-sections (4) to (7) of section 80 of this Constitution.

97. (1) The functions of the Ombudsman shall be to

(*a*) enquire into the conduct of any person to whom this section applies in the exercise of his office or authority, or abuse thereof;

(*b*) assist in the improvement of the practices and procedure of public bodies; and

(*c*) ensure the elimination of arbitrary and unfair decisions.

(2) Parliament may confer additional functions on the Ombudsman.

(3) This section applies to members of the public service, the Police Force, the Prisons Service, provincial governments, and such other offices, commissions, corporate bodies or public agencies as may be prescribed by Parliament:

Provided that it shall not apply to the Governor General or his personal staff or to the Director of Public Prosecutions or any person acting in accordance with his instructions.

(4) Nothing in this section or in any Act of Parliament enacted for the purposes of this Chapter shall confer on the Ombudsman any power to question or review any decision of any judge, magistrate or registrar in the excercise of his judicial functions.

98. (1) In the discharge of his functions the Ombudsman shall not be subject to the direction or control of any other person or aurhority and no proceedings of the Ombudsman shall be called in question in any court of law.

(2) The Ombudsman shall not conduct an investigation in respect of any matter if he has been given notice by the Prime Minister that the investigation of that matter would not be in the interests of the security of Solomon Islands.

(3) The Ombudsman shall make an annual report and may make such additional reports to Parliament as he deems appropriate concerning the discharge of his functions, and may draw attention to any defects which appear to him to exist in the administration or any law.

99. Parliament may make provision for such supplementary and ancillary matters as may appear necessary or expedient to give effect to the provision of this Chapter.

CHAPTER X

FINANCE

100. (1) All revenues or other moneys raised or received by or for the purposes of the Government (not being revenues or other moneys that are payable by or under any law into some other fund established for any specific purpose or that may, by or under any law, be retained by the authority that received them for the purposes of defraying the expenses of that authority) shall be paid into and form one Consolidated Fund.

(2) Parliament may make provision for the establishment of Special Funds, which shall not form part of the Consolidated Fund.

(3) The receipts, earnings and accruals of Special Funds established under this section and the balance of such funds at the close of each financial year shall not be paid into the Consolidated Fund but shall be retained for the purposes of those funds.

101. (1) No money shall be issued from the Consolidated Fund except upon the authority of a warrant under the hand of the Minister of Finance.

(2) No warrant shall be issued by the Minister of Finance for the purpose of meeting any expenditure unless

(*a*) the expenditure has been authorized for the financial year during which the issue is to take place by an Appropriation Act;

(*b*) the expenditure has been authorized in accordance with the provisions of section 103 or 104 of this Constitution; or

(*c*) it is statutory expenditure.

102. (1) The Minister of Finance shall cause to be prepared and laid before Parliament before the commencement of each financial year estimates of the revenues and expenditure of the Government for that year, provided that in exceptional circumstances which shall be explained to Parliament the Minister may cause the estimates to be laid before Parliament not later than ninety days after the commencement of the financial year.

(2) The heads of expenditure contained in the estimates (other than statutory expenditure) shall be included in a bill to be known as an Appropriation Bill which shall be introduced into Parliament to provide for the issue from the Consolidated Fund of the sums necessary to supply those heads and the appropriation of those sums for the purposes specified therein.

(3) If in respect of any financial year it is found that the sum appropriated by the Appropriation Act for any purpose is insufficient or that a need has arisen for expenditure for a purpose for which no sum has been appropriated by that law, a supplementary estimate showing the sums required shall be included in a Supplementary Appropriation Bill for appropriation.

(4) If at the close of account for any financial year it is found that any moneys have been expended on any head in excess of the sum appropriated for that head by an Appropriation Act or for a purpose for which no money has been appropriated, the excess or the sum expended but not appropriated as the case may be shall be included in a statement of heads in excess which, together with the report of the Public Accounts Committee thereon, shall be presented to Parliament.

(5) Statutory expenditure shall not be voted on by Parliament but, without further authority of Parliament, shall be paid out of the Consolidated Fund by warrant under the hand of the Minister of Finance.

103. (1) If the Appropriation Act in respect of any financial year has not come into operation by the beginning of that financial year, Parliament by resolution may empower the Minister of Finance to authorize the issue of moneys from the Consolidated Fund for the purpose of meeting expenditure necessary to carry on the public services at a level not exceeding the level of these services in the previous financial year, until the expiration of four months from the beginning of that financial year or the coming into operation of the Appropriation Act, whichever is the earlier.

(2) Where in respect of any financial year the Minister is satisfied that an urgent and unforeseen need has arisen to authorize for any purpose issue from the Consolidated Fund for expenditure in excess of the sum appropriated for that purpose by an Appropriation Act, or for a purpose for which no sum has been so appropriated, he may, subject to the provisions of any law or regulations for the time being in force in that regard, authorize, with the prior approval of the Cabinet,

such issues by warrant and shall include such amount in a Supplementary Appropriation Bill for appropriation at the meeting of Parliament next following the date on which the warrant was issued:

Provided that if there shall be no further meeting in the same financial year, the Bill may be deferred to any meeting held before the end of the following financial year.

(3) No expenditure shall be authorized or incurred under the preceding sub-section unless Parliament has specified in advance of the expenditure the maximum amount of expenditure that may be incurred under that sub-section.

104. Where at any time Parliament has been dissolved before any provision or any sufficient provision is made under this Chapter of this Constitution for the carrying on of the government of Solomon Islands, the Minister of Finance may issue a warrant for the payment out of the Consolidated Fund of such sums as he may consider necessary for the continuance of the public services until the expiry of a period of three months commencing with the date on which Parliament first meets after that dissolution, but a statement of the sums so authorized shall, as soon as practicable, be laid before Parliament and the aggregate sums shall be included, under the appropriate heads, in the next Appropriation Bill.

105. (1) There shall be charged on the consolidated Fund all debt charges for which the Government is liable.

(2) For the purposes of this section debt charges include interest, sinking fund charges, the repayment or amortisation of debt, and all expenditure in connection with the raising of loans on the security of the revenue of the Government or the Consolidated Fund and the service and redemption of debt thereby created.

(3) The Government shall not borrow money nor enter into a guarantee involving any financial liability except in accordance with such provisions as may be prescribed by Parliament.

106. No taxation shall be imposed or altered except by or under an Act of Parliament.

107. (1) There shall be paid to the holders of the offices to which this section applies such salary or other remuneration and such allowances as may be prescribed by Parliament.

(2) The remuneration and allowances payable to the holders of those offices are hereby charged on and shall be paid out of the Consolidated Fund.

(3) The remuneration prescribed in pursuance of this section in respect of the holder of any such office and his other terms of service (other than allowances that are not taken into account in computing, under any law in that behalf, any pension payable in respect of his service in that office) shall not be altered to his disadvantage after his appointment except as part of any alteration generally applicable to holders of offices specified in this section.

(4) Where a person's remuneration or other terms of service depend upon his option, the remuneration or terms for which he opts shall, for the purposes of the preceding sub-section, be deemed to be more advantageous to him than any others for which he might have opted.

(5) This section applies to the offices of Governor General, any judge of the High Court or the Court of Appeal, Speaker, Ombudsman, Director of Public Prosecutions, Public Solicitor, Auditor General, Commissioner of Police, and member of any Commission established by this Constitution.

108. (1) There shall be an Auditor General whose office shall be a public office.

(2) The Auditor General shall be appointed by the Governor General, acting in accordance with the advice of the Public Service Commission.

(3) The public accounts of Solomon Islands, of all Ministries, offices, courts and authorities of the Government, and of all provincial governments, shall be audited and reported on annually by the Auditor General, and for that purpose the Auditor General or any person authorized by him in that behalf shall at all times be entitled to access to all books, records, returns and other documents relating to such accounts.

(4) The Auditor General shall submit his reports to the Speaker who shall cause them to be laid before Parliament; and he shall also send a copy of each report to the Minister of Finance and the Minister concerned.

(5) In the exercise of his functions under this section, the Auditor General shall not be subject to the direction or control of any other person or authority.

(6) Nothing in this section shall prevent the performance by the Auditor General of

(*a*) such other functions in relation to the accounts of the Government and the accounts of other public authorities and other bodies administering public funds in Solomon Islands as may be prescribed by Parliament; or

(*b*) such other functions in relation to the supervision and control of expenditure from public funds in Solomon Islands as may be so prescribed.

109. In this Chapter of this Consitution

'financial year' means the twelve months ending on the 31st December in any year or on such other date as may from time to time be prescribed by Parliament;

'statutory expenditure' means expenditure charged on the Consolidated Fund or on the general revenues and assets of Solomon Islands by virtue of any of the provisions of this Constitution or by virtue of any provision of any other law for the time being in force in Solomon Islands.

CHAPTER XI

LAND

110. The right to hold or acquire a perpetual interest in land shall vest in any person who is a Solomon Islander and only in such other person or persons as may be prescribed by Parliament.

111. Parliament may, in regard to land which has ceased to be customary land:

(*a*) provide for the conversion into a fixed-term interest of any perpetual interest in such land held by a person who is not entitled under the preceding section to hold such a perpetual interest;
(*b*) provide for the compulsory acquisition where necessary of such land or any right over or interest in such land;
(*c*) prescribe the criteria to be adopted in regard to the assessment and payment of compensation for such conversion or compulsory acquisition (which may take account of, but need not be limited to, the following factors: the purchase price, the value of improvements made between the date of purchase and the date of acquisition, the current use value of the land, and the fact of its abandonment or dereliction).

112. Parliament shall provide, in relation to any compulsory acquisition of customary land or any right over or interest in it, that:
(*a*) before such land is compulsorily acquired, there shall be prior negotiations with the owner of the land, right or interest;
(*b*) the owner shall have a right of access to independent legal advice; and
(*c*) so far as practicable the interest so acquired shall be limited to a fixed-term interest.

113. (1) Nothing in this Chapter shall be construed as enabling Parliament to make any provision which is inconsistent with the provisions of section 8(1)(*c*) of this Constitution.

(2) In this Chapter 'Solomon Islander' has the same meaning as in the Land and Titles Ordinance.

CHAPTER XII

PROVINCIAL GOVERNMENT

114. (1) Solomon Islands shall be divided into provinces, the number and boundaries of which shall be prescribed by Parliament after considering the advice of the Constituency Boundaries Commission.

(2) Parliament shall make provision for the government of the provinces established under this section and consider the role of traditional chiefs therein.

CHAPTER XIII

THE PUBLIC SERVICE

115. (1) There shall be a Public Service Commission for Solomon Islands which shall consist of a Chairman and not less than four other members appointed by the Governor General for such period, being not less than three nor more than six years, as may be specified in their respective instruments of appointment.

(2) A person shall be disqualified for appointment as a member of the Public Service Commission if he is a member of Parliament or a public officer or an

officer of any society or association which the Governor General, in his own deliberate judgment, is satisfied is of a political nature.

(3) A person shall not, while he holds or is acting in the office of member of the Public Service Commission or within a period of five years commencing with the date on which he last held or acted in that office, be eligible for appointment to or to act in any public office.

(4) The office of a member of the Public Service Commission shall become vacant

(*a*) at the expiration of the period specified in the instrument by which he was appointed;

(*b*) if he becomes a member of Parliament;

(*c*) if he becomes an officer of any society or association which the Governor General, in his own deliberate judgment, is satisfied is of a political nature; or

(*d*) if he is removed from office in accordance with section 126 of this Constitution.

(5) Whenever the office of the Chairman of the Public Service Commission is vacant or the holder thereof is for any reason unable to perform the functions of his office, such one of the other members of he Public Service Commission as the Governor General shall appoint may act in the office of the Chairman.

(6) If the office of a member of the Public Service Commission other than the Chairman is vacant or the holder thereof is acting as the Chairman or is for any reason unable to perform the functions of his office, the Governor General may appoint a person who is qualified for appointment as a member of the Commission to act as such a member; and any person so appointed may, subject to the provisions of sub-section (4) of this section, continue to act until he is notified by the Governor General that the circumstances giving rise to the appointment have ceased to exist.

(7) Except as provided in sub-section (2) and (4)(*c*) of this section, the powers conferred on the Governor General by this section shall be exercised by him acting in accordance with the advice of the Prime Minister.

116. (1) Subject to the provisions of this Constitution, power to make appointments to public offices (including power to confirm appointments) and to remove and to exercise disciplinary control over persons holding or acting in such offices is vested in the Public Service Commission.

(2) The Public Service Commission may, subject to such conditions as it thinks fit, delegate any of its powers under this section by directions in writing to any member of the Commission or to any public officer.

(3) The provisions of this section shall not apply in relation to

(*a*) the office of any judge of the High Court or the Court of Appeal;

(*b*) the office of Ombudsman, Director of Public Prosecutions, Public Solicitor or Auditor General;

(*c*) any office to which section 118 of this Constitution applies;

(*d*) the office of any member of the Police Force or the Prisons Service; or

(*e*) any office to which section 127 of this Constitution applies.

(4) The Public Service Commission shall not exercise any of its powers in relation to any office on the personal staff of the Governor General or in relation to any person holding or acting in any such office without the concurrence of the Governor General, acting in his own deliberate judgment.

(5) Before making any appointment to any office on the staff of the Ombudsman, the Public Service Commission shall consult the Ombudsman.

(6) Before making any appointment to the office of Clerk to the Legislature, the Public Service Commission shall consult the Speaker.

117. (1) There shall be a Judicial and Legal Service Commission for Solomon Islands.

(2) The members of the Commission shall be

(*a*) the Chief Justice, who shall be Chairman of the Commission;

(*b*) the Attorney General; and

(*c*) the Chairman of the Public Service Commission.

(3) An additional member may be appointed if the Governor General, acting in his own deliberate judgment, so decides, and if he so decides he shall appoint such a member acting in accordance witht he advice of the Prime Minister.

(4) The office of the member of the Commission appointed under the preceding sub-section shall become vacant

(*a*) at the expiration of three years from the date of his appointment;

(*b*) if he becomes a member of Parliament or a public officer other than a judge of the High Court or the Court of Appeal; or

(*c*) he is removed from office in accordance with section 126 of this Constitution.

118. (1) Power to make appointments to the offices to which this section applies (including power to confirm appointments) and to remove and to exercise disciplinary control over persons holding or acting in such offices is vested in the Judicial and Legal Service Commission.

(2) This section applies to

(*a*) all public offices for which a legal qualification is required, except those of Attorney General, judge of the High Court or the Court of Appeal, Director of Public Prosecutions and Public Solicitor;

(*b*) magistrates engaged in full time judicial and related duties; and

(*c*) such other officers, including registrars of the High Court and the Court of Appeal, as may be prescribed.

119. (1) There shall be a Police and Prisons Service Commission for Solomon Islands

(2) The members of the Commission shall be

(*a*) the Chairman and the Public Service Commission, who shall be Chairman of the Commission;

(*b*) the Chairman of the Judicial and Legal Service Commission; and

(*c*) a person appointed by the Governor General, acting in accordance with the advice of the Prime Minister.

(3) If the office of the member of the Commission appointed under sub-section (2)(*c*) of this section is vacant or the holder thereof is for any reason unable to perform the functions of his office, the Governor General, acting in accordance with the advice of the Prime Minister, may appoint some other person to act in the office of that member; and any person so appointed may continue to act until he is notified by the Governor General, acting as aforesaid, that the circumstances giving rise to the appointment have ceased to exist.

120. (1) Save as provided in section 43(2) of this Constitution, power to make appointments (including power to confirm appointments) to offices in the Police Force of or above the rank of Inspector is vested in the Police and Prisons Service Commission.

(2) Power to make appointments (including power to confirm appoinments) in the Police Force below the rank of Inspector is vested in the Commissioner of Police.

(3) There shall be in the Police Force such number of Police Promotion Boards, each consisting of officers in the Police Force above the rank of Inspector, as may be prescribed by regulations made under sub-section (5) of this section.

(4) In the exercise of the powers to make appointments to offices in the Police Force vested in him, the Commissioner of Police may refer any question relating to the promotion of an officer in the Police Force to a rank below that of Inspector to a Police Promotion Board for their advice, but he shall not be obliged to act in accordance with the advice given him by any such Board.

(5) The Police and Prisons Service Commission may by regulations make provisions for all or any of the following matters

(*a*) the number of Police Promotion Boards which shall be established for the Police Force;

(*b*) the composition of any Police Promotion Board and the method of appointment and tenure of office of the members thereof; and

(*c*) the manner in which a Police Promotion Board shall perform its functions.

(6) The power to make appointments under sub-section (1) of this section shall not extend to postings or transfers within the Police Force of officers in that Force, and the power to make such postings and transfers is vested in the Commissioner of Police.

121. (1) Save as provided in section 129 of this Constitution and sub-section (2) of this section, power to remove and to exercise disciplinary control over persons holding or acting in offices in the Police Force is vested in the Police and Prisons Service Commission.

(2) The following powers are vested in the Commissioner of Police

(*a*) in respect of officers of or above the rank of Assistant Superintendent, the power to administer reprimands;

(*b*) in respect of Inspectors, the power to exercise disciplinary control other than removal or reduction in rank; and

(*c*) in respect of officers below the rank of Inspector, the power to exercise disciplinary control including the power of removal.

(3) The Commissioner of Police may, by directions in writing, and subject to such conditions as he thinks fit, delegate to any officer in the Police Force of or above the rank of Inspector any of his powers under sub-section (2)(*c*) of this section other than the power of removal, but an appeal from any award of punishment by such an officer shall lie to the Commissioner.

122. Any police officer upon whom the Commissioner has imposed any punishment which includes

(*a*) reduction in rank; or

(*b*) removal,

may appeal to the Police and Prisons Service Commission against either the finding or the punishment or both, and the Commission may confirm, set aside or vary the finding and confirm, set aside, reduce, suspend or otherwise vary the punishment:

Provided that nothing in this section shall be construed as empowering the award of any greater punishment than could have been awarded by the officer inflicting the punishment.

123. (1) Power to make appointments (including power to confirm appointments) to offices in the Prisons Service of or above the rank of Assistant Prison Officer is vested in the Police and Prisons Service Commission.

(2) Power to make appointments (including power to confirm appointments) in the Prison Service below the rank of Assistant Prison Officer is vested in the Superintendent of Prisons.

(3) The power to make appointments under sub-section (1) of this section shall not extend to postings or transfers within the Prisons Service of officers in that Service, and the power to make such postings and tranfers is vested in the Superintendent of Prisons.

124. (1) Save as provided in sub-section (2) of this section, power to remove and to exercise disciplinary control over persons holding or acting in offices in the Prisons Service is vested in the Police and Prisons Service Commission.

(2) The following powers are vested in the Superintendent of Prisons

(*a*) in respect of officers of or above the rank of Prison Officer, the power to administer reprimands;

(*b*) in respect of Assistant Prison Officers, the power to exericse disciplinary control other than removal or reduction in rank; and

(*c*) in respect of officers below rank of Assistant Prison Officer, the power to exercise disciplinary control including the power of removal.

(3) The Superintendent of Prisons may, bv directions in writing, and subject to such conditions as he thinks fit, delegate to any officer in the Prisons Service of or above the rank of Assistant Prison Officer any of his powers under sub-section (2)(*c*) of this section other than the power of removal, but an appeal from any award of punishment by such an officer shall lie to the Superintendent of Prisons.

125. Any officer in the Prisons Service upon whom the Superintendent of Prisons has imposed any punishment which includes:

(*a*) reduction in rank; or

(*b*) removal.

may appeal to the Police and Prisons Service Commission against either the finding or the punishment or both, and the Commission may confirm, set aside or vary the finding and confirm, set aside, reduce, suspend or otherwise vary the punishment:

Provided that nothing in this section shall be construed as empowering the award of any greater punishment than could have been awarded by the officer inflicting the punishment.

126. (1) A person holding an office to which this section applies (in this section referred to as 'a Commissioner') may be removed from office only for inability to discharge the functions of his office (whether arising from infirmity of body or mind or any other cause) or for misbehavior and shall not be so removed except in accordance with the provisions of this section.

(2) A Commissioner shall be removed from office by the Governor General if the question of his removal from that office has been referred to a tribunal appointed under the next following sub-section and the tribunal has advised the Governor General that he ought to be removed from office for inability as aforesaid or for misbehavior.

(3) If the Governor General considers that the question of removing a Commissioner ought to be investigated, then

(*a*) the Governor General shall appoint a tribunal in accordance with the provisions of sub-section (6) of this section; and

(*b*) that tribunal shall inquire into the matter and report on the facts thereof to the Governor General and advise the Governor General whether the Commissioner ought to be removed under this section.

(4) If the question of removing a Commissioner has been referred to a tribunal under this section, the Governor General may suspend the Commissioner from performing the functions of his office, and any such suspension may at any time be revoked by the Governor General, and shall in any case cease to have effect if the tribunal advises the Governor General that the Commissioner should not be removed.

(5) The officers to which this section applies are those of members of the Public Service Commission, member of the Judicial and Legal Service Commission appointed under section 117(*g*) of this Constitution, and member ofthe Police and Prisons Service Commission appointed under section 119(3) of this Constitution.

(6) A tribunal appointed under this section shall consist of a chairman and two other members. and

(*a*) in the case of a tribunal to investigate the removal of the member of the Judicial and Legal Serivce Commission appointed under section 117(3) of this Constitution, all members of the tribunal shall be persons who hold or have held high judicial office in some part of the Commonwealth; and (*b*) in any case, the chairman shall be a person who holds or has held such office.

(7) Except as provided in sub-section (2) of this section, the functions of the Governor General under this section shall be exercised by him in accordance with the advice of the Prime Minister.

127. (1) Power to make appointments to the offices to which this section applies (including power to confirm appointments) and to remove and to exercise disciplinary control over persons holding or acting in such offices is vested in the Governor General, acting in accordance with the advice of the Prime Minister tendered after the Prime Minister has consulted the Public Service Commission.

(2) The offices to which this section applies are those of Ambassador, High Commissioner or other principal representative of Solomon Islands in any other country or accredited to any international organization.

128. (1) Power to make appointments to the office of Permanent Secretary shall vest in the Public Service Commission acting with the concurrence of the Prime Minister.

(2) Power of posting or transfer of a person holding the office of Permanent Secretary shall vest in the Prime Minister, acting after consultation with the Public Serivce Commission.

129. (1) The provisions of this section shall apply in relation to persons holding the offices of Auditor General, Director of Public Prosecutions, Public Solicitor and Commissioner of Police.

(2) Subject to the provisions of this section, a person to whom this section applies shall vacate his office when he attains the age of fifty-five years:

Provided that the Governor General may permit a person to whom this section applies who attains the age of fifty-five years to continue in office until he has attained such later age as may have been agreed between the Governor General and that person.

(3) A person to whom this section applies may be removed from office only for inability to discharge the functions of his office (whether arising from infirmity of body or mind or any other cause) or for misbehavior and shall not be so removed except in accordance with the provisions of this section.

(4) A person to whom this section applies shall be removed from office by the Governor General if the question of his removal from office has been referred to a tribunal appointed under sub-section (5) of this section and the tribunal has recommended to the Governor General that he ought to be removed from office for inability as aforesaid or for misbehavior.

(5) If the Governor General considers that the question of removing a person to whom this section applies from office for inability as aforesaid or for misbehavior ought be be investigated, or if the Prime Minister represents to the Governor General that that question ought to be investigated, then

(*a*) the Governor General shall appoint a tribunal, which shall consist of a Chairman who is a person who holds or has held high judicial office in some part of the Commonwealth, and not less than two other members; and (*b*) the tribunal shall inquire into the matter and report on the facts thereof to the Governor General and recommend to the Governor General whether the person ought to be removed from office for inability as aforesaid or for misbehavior.

(6) If the question of removing a person to whom this section applies has been referred to a tribunal under sub-section (5) of this section, the Governor General may suspend the person from performing the functions of his office, and any such suspension may at any time be revoked by the Governor General and shall in any case cease to have effect if the tribunal recommends to the Governor General that the person should not be removed.

(7) Except as provided in sub-section (4) of this section, the functions of the Governor General under this section shall be exercised by him

(*a*) in relation to the office of Auditor General, in accordance with the advice of the Public Service Commission;

(*b*) in relation to the office of Director of Public Prosecutions of Public Solicitor, in accordance with the advice of the Judicial and Legal Service Commission; and

(*c*) in relation to the office of Commissioner of Police, in his own deliberate judgment.

(8) The provisions of this section shall not apply in relation to a person appointed to act in any office referred to in sub-section (1) of this section during any period when that office is vacant or the holder thereof is unable to perform the functions of his office; and the appointment of such a person may be revoked by the Governor General at any time before the expiration of that period.

(9) (*a*) nothing in this section shall prevent the appointment of a person who is not a citizen of Solomon Islands to any office to which this section applies for a term of years.

(*b*) A person appointed to an office to which this section applies under this sub-section shall cease to hold office on the expiration of the term for which he was appointed but shall otherwise be removed from office only in accordance with the provisions of this section.

130. (1) Subject to the provisions of section 132 of this Constitution, the law applicable to the grant and payment to any officer, or to his widow, children, dependants or personal representatives, or any pension, gratuity or other like allowance (in this section and in sections 131 and 132 of this Constitution referred to asn an 'award') in respect of the service of that officer in a public office shall be that in force on the relevant day or any later law not less favorable to the person concerned.

(2) For the purposes of this section the relevant day is

(*a*) in relation to an award granted before Independence Day, the day on which the award was granted;

(*b*) in relation to an award granted or to be granted on or after Independence Day to or in respect of a person who was a public officer before that day, the day immediately before that day;

(*c*) in relation to an award granted or to be granted to or in respect of a person who first becomes a public officer on or after Independence Day, the day on which he becomes a public officer.

(3) For the purposes of this section, in so far as the law applicable to an award depends on the option of the persons to or in respect of whom it is granted or to be granted, the law for which he opts shall be taken to be more favorable to him than any other law for which he might have opted.

131. Awards granted under any law for the time being in force in Solomon Islands are (except so far as they are a charge on some other fund and are duly paid out of that fund to the person to whom payment is due) hereby charged on and shall be paid out of the Consolidated Fund.

132. (1) The power to grant any award under any pensions law for the time being in force in Solomon Islands (other than an award to which, under that law, the person to whom it is payable is entitled as of right) and, in accordance with any provisions in that behalf in any such law, to withhold, reduce in amount or suspend any award payable under any such law shall vest in the Governor General.

(2) The power vested in the Governor General by sub-section (1) of this section shall be exercised by him

(*a*) in the case of an award payable in respect of the services of any person who, having been a public officer, was, immediately before the date on which he ceased to hold public office, serving as a judge of the High Court or the Court of Appeal, or Commissioner of Police, in his own deliberate judgment;

(*b*) in the case of an award payable in respect of the services of any person who, having been a public officer, was, immediately before the date aforesaid, serving as Ombudsman, Director of Public Prosecutions, or Public Solicitor, or in any office to which section 118 of this Constitution applies at the date of the exercise of the power, in accordance with the advice of the Judicial and Legal Service Commission;

(*c*) in the case of an award payable in respect of the services of any person who, having been a public officer, was, immediately before the date aforesaid, serving in any office in the Prisons Service or in the Police Force other than the office of Commissioner of Police, in accordance with the advice of the Police and Prisons Service Commission; and

(*d*) in the case of an award payable in respect of the services of any other person for whom no other statutory or other provisions has been made, in accordance with the advice of the Public Service Commission.

(3) In this section, 'pensions law' means any law relating to the grant to any person, or to the widow, children, dependants or personal representatives of that person, of an award in respect of the services of that person in a public office.

CHAPTER XIV

MISCELLANEOUS

133. (1) Any reference in this Constitution to power to make appointments to any public office shall be construed as including a reference to power to make appointments on promotion and transfer to that office and to power to appoint a person to act in that office during any period during which it is vacant or the holder thereof is unable to perform the functions of that office.

(2) In this Constitution, unless the context otherwise requires, a reference to the holder of an office by the term designating his office shall be construed as including a reference to any person who is for the time being lawfully acting in or performing the functions of that office.

(3) Where by this Constitution any person is directed, or power is conferred on any person or authority to appoint a person, to act in or otherwise to perform the functions of an office if the holder thereof is unable to perform the functions of that office, the validity of any performance of those functions by the person so directed or of any appointment made in exercise of that power shall not be called in question in any court on the ground that the holder of the office is not unable to perform the functions of the office.

134. (1) Where any person has vacated any office established by this Constitution, he may, if qualified, again be appointed or elected to hold that office in accordance with the provisions of this Constitution.

(2) Whenever the holder of any office constituted by or under this Constitution, or any public office otherwise constituted, is on leave of absence pending relinquishment of his office

(*a*) another person may be appointed to that office; and

(*b*) that person shall, for the purpose of any function of that office, be deemed to be the sole holder of that office.

135. (1) References in this Constitution to the power to remove a public officer from his office shall be construed as including references to any power conferred by any law to require or permit that officer to retire from the public service and to any power or right to terminate a contract on which a person is employed as a public officer and to determine whether any such contract shall or shall not be renewed:

Provided that

(*a*) nothing in this sub-section shall be construed as conferring on any person or authority power to require any judge of the High Court or the Court of Appeal, the Ombudsman, the Director of Public Prosecutions, the Public Solicitor, the Commissioner of Police or the Auditor General to retire from the public service; and

(*b*) any power conferred by any law to permit a person to retire from the public service shall, in the case of any officer mentioned in the preceding paragraph or an officer who may be removed from office by some person or authority other than a Commission established by this Constitution, vest in the Commission or other authority that, if that officer had retired, would be the appropriate Commission or authority in relation to the awards of that officer under section 132 of this Constituion.

(2) Any provision of this Constitution that vests in any person or authority power to remove any public officer from his office shall be without prejudice to the power of any person or authority to abolish any office or to any law providing for the compulsory retirement of public officers generally or any class of public officer on attaining an age specified therein.

136. Save as othewise provided in sections 34, 50 and 64 of this Constitution, any person who is appointed to or to act in any office established by this Constitution may resign from that office by writing under his hand addressed to the person by whom he was apponted; and the resignation of any person from any such office (including any seat in Parliament) by writing under his hand addressed in accordance with this Constitution to any other person shall take effect, and the office shall accordingly become vacant

(*a*) at such time or on such date (if any) as may be specified in the writing; or

(*b*) when the writing is received by that other person,

whichever is the later:

Provided that the resignation may be withdrawn before it takes effect if the person to whom the resignation is addressed consents to its withdrawal.

137. (1) Any Commission established by this Constitution may by regulations make provision for regulating and facilitating the performance by the Commission of their functions under this Constitution.

(2) Any decision by any such Commission shall require the concurrence of a majority of all the members thereof and, subject as aforesaid, the Commission may act notwithstanding the absence of any member:

Provided that if in any particular case a vote of all the members is taken to decide the question and the votes cast are equally divided the chairman shall have and shall exercise a casting vote.

(3) Subject to the provisions of this section, any such Commission may regulate their own procedure.

(4) In the exercise of their functions under this Constitution, no such Commission shall be subject to the direction or control of any other person or authority, except where otherwise provided by this Constitution.

(5) In addition to the functions conferred upon them by or under this Constitution any such Commission shall have such powers and other functions (if any) as may be prescribed.

(6) The validity of the transaction of business of any such Commission shall not be affected by the fact that some person who was not entitled to do so took part in the proceedings.

(7) The provisions of sub-sections (1), (2), (3) and (4) of this section shall

apply in relation to the Committe on the Prerogative of Mercy as they apply in relation to a Commission established by this Constitution.

(8) The provisions of sub-sections (1), (2), (3) and (4) of this section shall apply in relation to a tribunal established for the purposes of section 14(4), 16(8), 80(6), 87(6), 126(3) and 129(5) of this Constitution, as they apply in relation to a Commission established by this Constitution, and any such tribunal shall have the same powers as the High Court in respect of the attendance and examination of witnesses (including the administration of oaths and the examination of witnesses abroad) and in respect of the production of documents.

138. No provision of this Constitution that any person or authority shall not be subject to the direction or control of any other person or authority in the exercise of any functions under this Constitution shall be construed as precluding a court of law from exercising jurisdiction in relation to any question whether that person or authority had performed those functions in accordance with this Constitution or any other law or should not perform those functions.

139. Where any power is conferred by this Constitution to make any proclamation, regulation, order or rule, or to give any direction or instructions, the power shall be construed as including the power, exercisable in like manner, to amend or revoke any such proclamation, regulation, order, rule, direction or instructions.

140. (1) Where any person or authority other than the Governor General is directed by this Constitution to exercise any function after consultation with any other person or authority, that person or authority shall not be obliged to exercise that function in accordance with the advice of that other person or authority.

(2) Where any person or authority is directed by any law to consult any other person or authority before taking any decision or action, that other person or authority must be given a genuine opportunity to present his or its views before the decision or action, as the case may be, is taken.

141. (1) Before entering upon the functions of his office a person to whom this section applies shall take and subscribe the oath of allegiance and such other oath (if any) as may be prescribed by Parliament.

(2) This section applies to any person appointed to hold or to act in

(*a*) the office of any judge of the High Court or the Court of Appeal;

(*b*) such other public offices as may be prescribed by Parliament; and

(*c*) the office of member of any Commission established by this Constitution or of the Committee on the Prerogative of Mercy.

141. There shall be a national seal bearing on it such device as Parliament shall approve by resolution.

143. The offices specified in sections 91 (Director of Public Prosecutions), 92 (Public Solicitor) and 96 (Ombudsman) shall be established no later than 8th July 1981.

144. (1) In this Constitution, unless the context otherwise requires

'absolute majority' means at least one half of all the member plus one;

'the Commonwealth' means Solomon Islands and any country to which section 24 of this Constitution for the time being applies, and includes the dependencies of any such country;

'the Crown' means the Crown in right of Solomon Islands;

'customary law' means the rules of customary law prevailing in an area of Solomon Islands;

'functions' includes rights, duties and powers;

'the *Gazette*' means the Solomon Islands *Gazette*;

'the Government' means Her Majesty's Government of Solomon Islands;

'the Governor General' means the Governor General of Solomon Islands;

'the High Court' and 'the Court of Appeal' mean respectively the High Court and the Court of Appeal established by this Constitution;

'high judicial office' menas the office of judge of a court having unlimited jurisdiction in civil and criminal matters or a court having jurisdiction in appeals from any such court;

'Independence Day' means 7th July 1978;

'legal representative' means a person entitled to practise as an advocate or a barrister and solicitor in Solomon Islands;

'meeting' in relation to Parliament means any sittings of Parliament commencing when Parliament first meets after being summoned at any time, and terminating when Parliament is adjourned *sine die* or at the conclusion of a session;

'oath' includes affirmation;

'oath of allegiance' means such oath of allegiance as is prescribed in Schedule 1 to this Constitution;

'Parliament' means the National Parliament of Solomon Islands established by this Constitution;

'the Police Force' means the Solomon Islands Police Force;

'prescribed' means prescribed in a law:

Provided that

(*a*) in relation to anything that may be prescribed only by Parliament, it means prescribed in an Act of Parliament; and

(*b*) in relation to anything that may be prescribed only by some other specified person or authority, it means prescribed in an order made by that other person or authority;

'the Prisons Service' means the Solomon Islands Prisons Service;

'provincial government officer' means a person holding or acting in any office of emolument in the service of a provincial government authority;

'public office' means, subject to the provisions of the next following section, an office of emolument in the public service;

'public officer' means a person holding or acting in any public office;

'public service' means the service of the Crown in a civil capacity in respect of the government of Solomon Islands;

'session' means the sittings of Parliament commencing when Parliament first meets after its prorogation or dissolution at any time and ending when Parliament is prorogued or dissolved without having been prorogued;

'sitting' means, in relation to Parliament, a period during which Parliament sits without adjournment and includes any period during which Parliament is in committee;

'Solomon Islands' means the territory which immediately before Independence Day constituted the territory under Her Majesty's protection known as the Solomon Islands;

'the Speaker' means the Speaker of Parliament;

(2) The provisions referring to Her Majesty shall extend to Her Majesty's Heirs and Successors in the sovereignty of the United Kingdom of Great Britain and Northern Ireland.

(3) Save as otherwise provided in this Constitution, the Interpretation Act 1889(a) shall apply, with the necessary adaptations, for the purpose of interpreting this Constitution, and otherwise in relation thereto, as it applies for the purpose of interpreting, and in relation to, Acts of the Parliament of the United Kingdom.

145. (1) In this Constitution the expression 'public office' shall be construed

(*a*) as including the office of any judge of the High Court or the Court of Appeal and the office of member of any other court of law in Solomon Islands, unless the context otherwise requires;

(*b*) as not including

(i) the office of any Minister, Leader of the Official Opposition, Leader of the Independent Members, Speaker or member of Parliament; or

(ii) the office of member of any Commission established by this Constitution or of the Committee on the Prerogative of Mercy.

(2) For the purposes of this Constitution a person shall not be treated as holding, or acting in, a public office by reason only that he

(*a*) is on leave of absence pending relinquishment of a public office, or is on leave of absence without salary from a public office;

(*b*) is receiving a pension or other like allowance from the Crown;

(*c*) is a special constable or a retired or reserve member of Her Majesty's forces;

(*d*) is a provincial government officer; or

(*e*) is the holder of an office in the service or appointment of the Crown, or is performing any functions on behalf of the Crown, if the only payments he receives in respect of that office or those functions are by way of travelling or subsistence allowances or a refund of out-of-pocket expenses.

SCHEDULES

(*Not reproduced*)

SRI LANKA

SUMMARY

INTERNATIONAL STATUS

Sri Lanka is a member of the United Nations (December 14, 1955, as Ceylon). It is a member of the Commonwealth of Nations and of other international organizations. It ratified in 1980 the International Conventions on Economic, Social and Cultural Rights and on Civil and Political Rights.

Ceylon, Buddhist from ancient times, was composed of Buddhist Sinhalese in the south and west with the Kingdom of Kandy as their heartland, and of Dravidian Hindu Tamils in the north and east with a separate kingdom at Jaffna in the seventeenth century. The island was repeatedly invaded by Indian princes; the first Europeans were the Portuguese who established themselves on the coasts from 1501 until the Dutch took their place in the seventeenth century, warring with and conquering all the kingdoms except Kandy. It became a crown colony of Great Britain at the Peace of Amiens in 1802, and the British established their rule over the whole country with the fall of Kandy in 1815.

The Ceylon National Congress was formed in 1919, by Low Country Sinhalese and Tamils. The Tamils withdrew in 1921, and in 1931, opposed the single electorate (rather than by communities) adopted together with universal suffrage under the new constitution which created a State Council with legislative and executive functions. The 1946 Soulbury Constitution provided for fully responsible internal government.

Ceylon became independent on February 4, 1948, under the Ceylon independence Act 1947. In 1956, a revival of Buddhist nationalism began under the Sri Lanka Freedom Party based on the Sinhalese rural masses. Its leader, Solomon Bandaranaika, was assasinated in 1959, but his wife became Prime Minister with the 1960 elections and instituted a program of socialist and land reforms and the expansion of the state sector during the five years of its term of office. The party together with other left wing and communist parties returned to power in the 1970 elections. The 1972 Constitution made the country a republic under the name of Sri Lanka, and instituted a presidential system. Tensions between Tamils and Sinhalese and demands by the Tamil minority (18% of the population) for a separate state led to an armed revolt in 1971 and the imposition of martial law from 1971 to 1977. The first Tamil party had been formed in 1948, claiming parity of language and autonomy for the Tamil provinces. It frequently held the balance between the two major political parties which alternated in office. After the 1977 elections, the new government attempted to meet some of the Tamil demands in the new constitution promulgated in 1978. Greater power was given to local government, economic development and an improved inter-communal climate were striven for, the Tamil language was given equality with Sinhala as a national language. But violent outbreaks have continued since 1979 and emergency rule has been imposed at various times on different parts of the country.

FORM OF NATIONAL GOVERNMENT

The Constitution of August 31, 1978, replaced that of 1972, which had superseded the various constitutional documents of 1946 and 1947. It states that Sri Lanka is a free, sovereign, independent, democratic, socialist republic and a unitary state.[1] Sovereignty resides with the people.[2] Buddhism is given foremost place.[3] There is a chapter on public security providing that the Public Security Ordinance shall be deemed a law enacted by Parliament.[4] The 1982 Prevention of Terrorism Act suspends a number of legal safeguards provided under the Constitution.

RIGHTS OF THE PEOPLE

The Constitution provides freedom of thought, conscience, religion, freedom from torture, from arbitrary arrest, detention and punishment, equality before the law, freedom of speech, assembly, association, occupation and movement.[5]

LEGISLATIVE DEPARTMENT

Parliament consists of 196 members elected from electoral districts for a term of six years subject to dissolution.[6] Suffrage is universal.[7] Parliament meets at least once a year.[8] Privileges and immunities are provided for.[9] Money bills may only be introduced by a Minister.[10] A chapter relates to finance.[11] There are provisions for referenda.[12]

[1] Const., Art. 1, 2.
[2] Id., Art. 3.
[3] Id., Art. 9.
[4] Id., Art. 155.
[5] Id., Art. 10–17.
[6] Id., Art. 62.
[7] Id., Art. 30.
[8] Id., Art. 70
[9] Id., Art. 67.
[10] Id., Art. 152.
[11] Id., Art. 148–154.
[12] Id., Art. 85–87.

EXECUTIVE DEPARTMENT

The Constitution provides for a President, Head of State, Head of the Executive and the Governmental and Commander-in-Chief of the Armed Forces.[13] He is elected by universal suffrage for a term of 6 years.[14] The President is responsible to Parliament.[15] There is a Cabinet of Ministers, the Prime Minister appointed by the President as the member of Parliament commanding the confidence of Parliament.[16] There are provisions for the public service and a Public Service Commission.[17] The President has the prerogative of mercy.[18]

JUDICIAL DEPARTMENT

The Supreme Court is the highest and final superior Court of record in the Republic.[19] It consists of the Chief Justice and not less than six nor more than 10 other judges appointed by the President and holding office during good behaviour who may not be removed except by a majority of the total members of Parliament after a resolution to such effect signed by no less than one third of the total.[20] It has the sole and exclusive jurisdiction to determine whether bills are inconsistent with the Constitution, and as to interpretation of the Constitution.[21] There is provisions for a Court of Appeal.[22]

AREA, POLULATION, ETC.

The area of Ceylon is 65,610 square kilometres, the population (1981 census) 14,850,001. The capital is Colombo. The official language is Sinhalese, the national languages Sinhala and Tamil, with Tamil as official in the northern and eastern provinces.[23]

[13] Id., Art. 30.
[14] Id., Art. 30, 88, 89.
[15] Id., Art. 34.
[16] Id., Art. 42.
[17] Id., Art. 42, 43.
[18] Id., Art. 54–61.
[18a] Id., Art. 118.
[19] Id., Art. 118.
[20] Id., Art. 119, 107.
[21] Id., Art. 120–123, 125.
[22] Id., Art. 137.
[23] Id., Art. 18, 19.

THE CONSTITUTION OF THE DEMOCRATIC SOCIALIST REPUBLIC OF SRI LANKA[1]

SVASTI

August 31, 1978

The people of Sri Lanka having, by their Mandate freely expressed and granted on the sixth day of the waxing moon in the month of Adhi Nikini in the year two thousand five hundred and twenty-one of the Buddhist Era (being Thursday the twenty-first day of the month of July in the year one thousand nine hundred and seventy-seven), entrusted to and empowered their Representatives elected on that day to draft, adopt and operate a new Republican Constitution in order to achieve the goals of a Democratic Socialist Republlic, and having solemnly resolved by the grant of such Mandate and the confidence reposed in their said Representatives who were elected by an overwhelming majority, to constitute Sri Lanka into a Democratic Socialist Republic, whilst ratifying the immutable republican principles of Representative Democracy, and assuring to all peoples freedom, equality, justice, fundamental human rights and the independence of the judiciary as the intangible heritage that guarantees the dignity and well being of succeeding generations of the People of Sri Lanka and of all the people of the World, who come to share with those generations the effort of working for the creation and preservation of a just and free society:

We, the freely elected representatives of the people of Sri Lanka, in pursuance of such Mandate, humbly acknowledging our obligations to our People and gratefully remembering their heroic and unremitting struggle to regain and preserve their rights and privileges so that the Dignity and Freedom of the Individual may be assured, Just, Social, Economic and Cultural Order attained, the Unity of the Country restored, and Concord established with other Nations, do hereby adopt and enact this Constitution as the Supreme Law of the Democratic Socialist Republic of Sri Lanka.

CHAPTER I

THE PEOPLE, THE STATE AND SOVEREIGNTY

1. Sri Lanka (Ceylon) is a Free Sovereign, Independent and Democratic Socialist Republic and shall be known as the Democratic Socialist Republic of Sri Lanka.

2. The Republic of Sri Lanka is a Unitary State.

3. In the Republic of Sri Lanka sovereignty is in the People and is inalienable. Sovereignty includes the powers of government, fundamental rights and the franchise.

[1] Published by Department of Government Printing, Colombo, 1978. Received 1978 Ed.

4. The Sovereignty of the People shall be exercised and enjoyed in the following manner:

(*a*) the legislative power of the People shall be exercised by Parliament, consisting of elected representatives of the People and by the People at a Referendum;

(*b*) the executive power of the People, including the defence of Sri Lanka, shall be exercised by the President of the Republic elected by the People;

(*c*) the judicial power of the People shall be exercised by Parliament through courts, tribunals and institutions created and established, or recognized, by the Constitution, or created and established by law, except in regard to matters relating to the privileges, immunities and powers of Parliament and of its Members, wherein the judicial power of the People may be exercised directly by Parliament according to law;

(*d*) the fundamental rights which are by the Constitution declared and recognized shall be respected, secured and advanced by all the organs of government, and shall not be abridged, restricted or denied, save in the manner and to the extent hereinafter provided; and

(*e*) the franchise shall be exercisable at the election of the President of the Republic and of the Members of Parliament, and at every Referendum by every citizen who has attained the age of eighteen years, and who, being qualified to be an elector as herinafter provided, has his name entered in the register of electors.

5. The territory of the Republic of Sri Lanka shall consist of the twenty-four administrative districts, the names of which are set out in the First Schedule, and its territorial waters.

6. The National Flag of the Republic of Sri Lanka shall be the Lion Flag depicted in the Second Schedule.

7. The National Anthem of the Republic of Sri Lanka shall be 'Sri Lanka Matha', the words and music of which are set out in the Third Schedule.

8. The National Day of the Republic of Sri Lanka shall be the fourth day of February.

CHAPTER II

BUDDHISM

9. The Republic of Sri Lanka shall give to Buddhism the foremost place and accordingly it shall be the duty of the State to protect and foster the Buddha *Sasana*, while assuring to all religions the rights granted by Articles 10 and 14(*e*).

CHAPTER III

FUNDAMENTAL RIGHTS

10. Every person is entitled to freedom of thought, conscience and religion, including the freedom to have or to adopt a religion or belief of his choice.

11. No person shall be subjected to torture or to cruel, inhuman or degrading treatment or punishment.

12. (1) All persons are equal before the law and are entitled to the equal protection of the law.

(2) No citizen shall be discriminated against on the grounds of race, religion, language, caste, sex, political opinion, place of birth or any one of such grounds:

Provided that it shall be lawful to require a person to acquire within a reasonable time sufficient knowledge of any language as a qualification for any employment or office in the Public, Judicial or Local Government Service or in the service of any public corporation, where such knowledge is reasonably necessary for the discharge of the duties of such employment or office:

Provided further that it shall be lawful to require a person to have a sufficient knowledge of any language as a qualification for any such employment or office where no function of that employment or office can be discharged otherwise than with a knowledge of that language.

(3) No person shall, on the grounds of race, religion, language, caste, sex or any one of such grounds, be subject to any disability, liability, restriction or condition with regard to access to shops, public restaurants, hotels, places of public entertainment and places of public worship of his own religion.

(4) Nothing in this Article shall prevent special provision being made, by law, subordinate legislation or executive action, for the advancement of women, children or disabled persons.

13. (1) No person shall be arrested except according to procedure established by law. Any person arrested shall be informed of the reason for his arrest.

(2) Every person held in custody, detained or otherwise deprived of personal liberty shall be brought before the judge of the nearest competent court according to procedure established by law, and shall not be further held in custody, detained or deprived of personal liberty except upon and in terms of the order of such judge made in accordance with procedure established by law.

(3) Any person charged with an offence shall be entitled to be heard, in person or by an attorney-at-law, at a fair trial by a competent court.

(4) No person shall be punished with death or imprisonment except by order of a competent court, made in accordance with procedure established by law. The arrest, holding in custody, detention or other deprivation of personal liberty of a person, pending investigation or trial, shall not constitute punishment.

(5) Every person shall be presumed innocent until he is proved guilty:

Provided that the burden of proving particular facts may, by law, be placed on an accused person.

(6) No person shall be held guilty of an offence on account of any act or omission which did not, at the time of such act or omission, constitute such an offence, and no penalty shall be imposed for any offence more severe than the penalty in force at the time such offence was committed.

Nothing in this Article shall prejudice the trial and punishment of any person for any act or omission which, at the time when it was committed, was criminal according to the general principles of law recognized by the community of nations.

It shall not be a contravention of this Article to require the imposition of a minimum penalty for an offence provided that such penalty does not exceed the maximum penalty prescribed for such offence at the time such offence was committed.

(7) The arrest, holding in custody, detention or other deprivation of personal liberty of a person, by reason of a removal order or a deportation order made under the provisions of the Immigrants and Emigrants Act or the Indo-Ceylon Agreement (Implementation) Act, No. 14 of 1967, or such other law as may be enacted in substitution therefor, shall not be a contravention of this Article.

14. (1) Every citizen is entitled to

(*a*) the freedom of speech and expression including publication;

(*b*) the freedom of peaceful assembly;

(*c*) the freedom of association;

(*d*) the freedom to form and join a trade union;

(*e*) the freedom, either by himself or in association with others, and either in public or in private, to manifest his religion or belief in worship, observance, practice and teaching;

(*f*) the freedom by himself or in association with others to enjoy and promote his own culture and to use his own language;

(*g*) the freedom to engage by himself or in association with others in any lawful occupation, profession, trade, business or enterprise;

(*h*) the freedom of movement and of choosing his residence within Sri Lanka; and

(*i*) the freedom to return to Sri Lanka.

(2) A person who, not being a citizen of any other country, has been permanently and legally resident in Sri Lanka immediately prior to the commencement of the Constitution and continues to be so resident shall be entitled, for a period of ten years from the commencement of the Constitution, to the rights declared and recognized by paragraph (1) of this Article.

15. (1) The exercise and operation of the fundamental rights declared and recognized by Articles 13 (5) and 13 (6) shall be subject only to such restrictions as may be prescribed by law in the interests of national security. For the purposes of this paragraph 'law' includes regulations made under the law for the time being relating to public security.

(2) The exercise and operation of the fundamental right declared and recognized by Article 14(1)(*a*) shall be subject to such restrictions as may be prescribed by law in the interests of racial and religious harmony or in relation to

Parliamentary privilege, contempt of court, defamation or incitement to an offence.

(3) The exercise and operation of the fundamental right declared and recognized by Article 14(1)(*b*) shall be subject to such restrictions as may be prescribed by law in the interests of racial and religious harmony.

(4) The exercise and operation of the fundamental right declared and reccognized by Article 14(1)(*c*) shall be subject to such restrictions as may be prescribed by law in the interests of racial and religious harmony or national economy.

(5) The exercise and operation of the fundamental right declared and recognized by Article 14(1)(*g*) shall be subject to such restrictions as may be prescribed by law in the interests of national economy or in relation to

(*a*) the professional, technical, academic, financial and other qualifications necessary for practising any profession or carrying on any occupation, trade, business or enterprise, and the licensing and disciplinary control of the person entitled to such fundamental right, and

(*b*) the carrying on by the State, a State agency or a public corporation of any trade, business, industry, service or enterprise whether to the exclusion, complete or partial, of citizens or otherwise.

(6) The exercise and operation of the fundamental right declared and recognized by Article 14(1)(*h*) shall be subject to such restrictions as may be prescribed by law in the interests of national economy.

(7) The exercise and operation of all the fundamental rights declared and recognized by Articles 12, 13, (1), 13 (2) and 14 shall be subject to such restrictions as may be prescribed by law in the interests of national security, public order and the protection of public health or morality, or for the purpose of securing due recognition and respect for the rights and freedoms of others, or of meeting the just requirements of the general welfare of a democratic society. For the purposes of this paragraph 'law' includes regulations made under the law for the time being relating to public security.

(8) The exercise and operation of the fundamental rights declared and recognized by Articles 12 (1), 13 and 14 shall, in their application to the members of the Armed Forces, Police Force and other Forces charged with the maintenance of public order, be subject to such restrictions as may be prescribed by law in the interests of the proper discharge of their duties and the maintenance of discipline among them.

16. (1) All existing written law and unwritten law shall be valid and operative notwithstanding any inconsistency with the preceding provisions of this Chapter.

(2) The subjection of any person on the order of a competent court to any form of punishment recognized by any existing written law shall not be a contravention of the provisions of this Chapter.

17. Every person shall be entitled to apply to the Supreme Court, as provided by Article 126, in respect of the infringement or imminent infringement, by executive or administrative action, of a fundamental right to which such person is entitled under the provisions of this Chapter.

CHAPTER IV

LANGUAGE

18. The Official Language of Sri Lanka shall be Sinhala.

19. The National Languages of Sri Lanka shall be Sinhala and Tamil.

20. A Member of Parliament or a member of a local authority shall be entitled to perform his duties and discharge his functions in Parliament or in such local authority in either of the National Languages.

21. (1) A person shall be entitled to be educated through the medium of either of the National Languages:

Provided that the provisions of this paragraph shall not apply to an institution of higher education where the medium of instruction is a language other than a National Language.

(2) Where one National Language is a medium of instruction for or in any course, department or faculty of any University directly or indirectly financed by the State, the other National Language shall also be made a medium of instruction for or in such course, department or faculty for students who prior to their admission to such University, were educated through the medium of such other Nationnal Language:

Provided that compliance with the preceding provisions of this paragraph shall not be obligatory if such other National Language is the medium of instruction for or in any like course, department or faculty either at any other campus or branch of such University or of any other like University.

(3) In this Article 'University' includes any institution of higher education.

22. (1) The Official Language shall be the language of administration throughout Sri Lanka:

Provided that the Tamil Language shall also be used as the language of administration for the maintenance of public records and the transaction of all business by public institutions in the Northern and Eastern Provinces.

(2) A person, other than an offical acting in his official capacity, shall be entitled

(*a*) to receive communications from, and to communicate and transact business with, any official in his offical capacity, in either of the National Languages;

(*b*) if the law recognizes his right to inspect or to obtain copies of or extracts from any official register, record, publication or other document, to obtain a copy of, or an extract from such register, record, publication or other document or a translation thereof, as the case may be, in either of the National Languages; and

(*c*) where a document is executed by any official for the purpose of being issued to him, to obtain such document or a translation thereof, in either of the National Languages.

(3) A local authority in the Northern or Eastern Province which conducts

its busines in either of the National Languages shall be entitled to receive communications from, and to communicate and transact business with, any official in his official capacity, in such National Language.

(4) All Orders, Proclamations, rules, by-laws, regulations and notifications made or issued under any written law, the *Gazette*, and all other official documents including circulars and forms issued or used by any public institution or local authority, shall be published in both National Languages.

(5) A person shall be entitled to be examined through the medium of either of the National Languages at any examination for the admission of persons to the Public Service, Judicial Service, Local Government Service, a public corporation or statutory institution, subject to the condition that he may be required to acquire a sufficient knowledge of the Offical Language within a reasonable time after admission to any such Service, public corporation or statutory institution where such knowledge is reasonably necessary for the discharge of his duties:

Provided that a person may be required to have a sufficient knowledge of the Official Language as a condition for admission to any such Service, public corporation or statutory institution where no function of the office or employment for which he is recruited can be discharged otherwise than with a sufficient knowledge of the Official Language.

(6) In this Article

'offical' means the President, any Minister, Deputy Minister, or any officer of a public institution or local authority; and

'public institution' means a department or institution of the Government, a public corporation or a statutory institution.

23. (1) All laws and subordinate legislation shall be enacted or made, and published, in both National Languages together with a translation in the English Language. In the event of any inconsistency between any two texts, the text in the Official Language shall prevail.

(2) All laws and subordinate legislation in force immediately prior to the commencement of the Constitution, shall be published in the *Gazette* in both National Languages as expeditiously as possible.

(3) The law published in Sinhala under the provisions of paragraph (2) of this Article, shall, as from the date of such publication, be deemed to be the law and supersede the corresponding law in English.

24. (1) The Official Language shall be the language of the courts throughout Sri Lanka and accordingly their records and proceedings shall be in the Official Language:

Provided that the language of the courts exercising original jurisdiction in the Northern and Eastern Provinces shall also be Tamil and their records and proceedings shall be in the Tamil Language. In the event of an appeal from any such court, records in both National Languages shall be prepared for the use of the court hearing such appeal:

Provided further that

(*a*) the Minister in charge of the subject of Justice may, with the concurrence of the Cabinet of Ministers, direct that the record of any such court shall also be maintained and proceedings conducted in the Official Language; and

(*b*) the record of any particular proceeding in such court shall also be maintained in the Official Language if so required by the judge of such court, or by any party or applicant or any person legally entitled to represent such party or applicant in such proceeding, where such judge, party, applicant or person is not conversant with the Tamil Language.

(2) Any party or applicant or any person legally entitled to represent such party or applicant may initiate proceedings, and submit to court pleadings and other documents, and participate in the proceedings in court, in either of the National Languages.

(3) Any judge, juror, party or applicant or any person legally entitled to represent such party or applicant, who is not conversant with the language used in a court, shall be entitled to interpretation and to translation into the appropriate National Language, provided by the State, to enable him to understand and participate in the proceedings before such court, and shall also be entitled to obtain in either of the National Languages, any such part of the record or a translation thereof, as the case may be, as he may be entitled to obtain according to law.

(4) The Minister in charge of the subject of Justice may, with the concurrence of the Cabinet of Ministers, issue directions permitting the use of a language other than a National Language in or in relation to the records and proceedings in any court for all purposes or for such purposes as may be specified therein. Every judge shall be bound to implement such directions.

(5) In this Article

'court' means any court or tribunal created and established for the administration of justice including the adjudication and settlement of industrial and other disputes, or any other tribunal or institution exercising judicial or quasi-judicial functions or any tribunal or institution created and established for the conciliation and settlement of disputes;

'judge' includes the President, Chairman presiding officer and member of any court; and

'record' includes pleadings, judgments, orders and other judicial and ministerial acts.

25. The State shall provide adequate facilities for the use of the languages provided for in this Chapter.

CHAPTER V

CITIZENSHIP

26. (1) There shall be one status of citizenship known as 'the status of a citizen of Sri Lanka'.

(2) A citizen of Sri Lanka shall for all purposes be described only as a 'citizen of Sri Lanka', whether such person became entitled to citizenship by descent or by virtue of registration in accordance with the law relating to citizenship.

(3) No distinction shall be drawn between citizens of Sri Lanka for any purpose by reference to the mode of acquisition of such status, as to whether acquired by descent or by virtue of registration.

(4) No citizen of Sri Lanka shall be deprived of his status of a citizen of Sri Lanka, except under and by virtue of the provisions of sections 19, 20, 21 and 22 of the Citizenship Act:

Provided that the provisions of sections 23 and 24 of that Act shall also be applicable to a person who became entitled to the status of a citizen of Sri Lanka by virtue of registration under the provisions of section 11, 12, or 13 of that Act.

(5) Every person who immediately prior to the commencement of the Constitution was a citizen of Sri Lanka, whether by descent or by virtue of registration in accordance with any law relating to citizenship, shall be entitled to the status and to the rights of a citizen of Sri Lanka as provided in the preceding provisions of this Article.

(6) The provisions of all existing written laws relating to citizenship and all other existing written laws wherein reference is made to citizenship shall be read subject to the preceding provisions of this Article.

CHAPTER VI

DIRECTIVE PRINCIPLES OF STATE POLICY AND FUNDAMENTAL DUTIES

27. (1) The Directive Principles of State Policy herein contained shall guide Parliament, the President and the Cabinet of Ministers in the enactment of laws and the governance of Sri Lanka for the establishment of a just and free society.

(2) The State is pledged to establish in Sri Lanka a democratic socialist society, the objectives of which include

- (*a*) the full realization of the fundamental rights and freedoms of all persons;
- (*b*) the promotion of the welfare of the People by securing and protecting as effectively as it may, a social order in which justice (social, economic and political) shall guide all the institutions of the national life;
- (*c*) the realization by all citizens of an adequate standard of living for themselves and their families, including adequate food, clothing and housing, the continuous improvement of living conditions and the full enjoyment of leisure and social and cultural opportunities;
- (*d*) the rapid development of the whole country by means of public and private economic activity and by laws prescribing such planning

and controls as may be expedient for directing and co-ordinating such public and private economic activity towards social objectives and the public weal;

(*e*) the equitable distribution among all citizens of the material resources of the community and the social product, so as best to subserve the common good;

(*f*) the establishment of a just social order in which the means of production, distribution and exchange are not concentrated and centralized in the State, State agencies or in the hands of a privileged few, but are dispersed among, and owned by, all the People of Sri Lanka;

(*g*) raising the moral and cultural standards of the People, and ensuring the full development of human personality; and

(*h*) the complete eradication of illiteracy and the assurance to all persons of the right to universal and equal access to education at all levels.

(3) The State shall safeguard the independence, sovereignty, unity and the territorial integrity of Sri Lanka.

(4) The State shall strengthen and broaden the democratic structure of government and the democratic rights of the People by decentralizing the administration and by affording all possible opportunities to the People to participate at every level in national life and in government.

(5) The State shall strengthen national unity by promoting co-operation and mutual confidence among all sections of the People of Sri Lanka, including the racial, religious, linguistic and other groups, and shall take effective steps in the fields of teaching, education and information in order to eliminate discrimination and prejudice.

(6) The State shall ensure equality of opportunity to citizens, so that no citizen shall suffer any disability on the ground of race, religion, language, caste, sex, political opinion or occupation.

(7) The State shall eliminate economic and social privilege and disparity, and the exploitation of man by man or by the State.

(8) The State shall ensure that the operation of the economic system does not result in the concentration of wealth and the means of production to the common detriment.

(9) The State shall ensure social security and welfare.

(10) The State shall assist the development of the cultures and the languages of the People.

(11) The State shall create the necessary economic and social environment to enable people of all religious faiths to make a reality of their religious principles.

(12) The State shall recognize and protect the family as the basic unit of society.

(13) The State shall promote with special care the interests of children and youth, so as to ensure their full development, physical, mental, moral, religious and social, and to protect them from exploitation and discrimination.

(14) The State shall protect, preserve and improve the environment for the benefit of the community.

(15) The State shall promote international peace, security and co-operation, and the establishment of a just and equitable international economic and social order, and shall endeavor to foster respect for international law and treaty obligations in dealings among nations.

23. The exercise and enjoyment of rights and freedoms is inseparable from the performance of duties and obligations, and accordingly it is the duty of every person in Sri Lanka

(*a*) to uphold and defend the Constitution and the law;
(*b*) to further the national interest and to foster national unity;
(*c*) to work conscientiously in his chosen occupation;
(*d*) to preserve and protect public property, and to combat misuse and waste of public property;
(*e*) to respect the rights and freedoms of others; and
(*f*) to protect nature and conserve its riches.

29. The provisions of this Chapter do not confer or impose legal rights or obligations, and are not enforceable in any court or tribunal. No question of inconsistency with such provisions shall be raised in any court or tribunal.

CHAPTER VII

THE EXECUTIVE

The President of the Republic

30. (1) There shall be a President of the Republic of Sri Lanka, who is the Head of the State, the Head of the Executive and of the Government, and the Commander-in-Chief of the Armed Forces.

(2) The President of the Republic shall be elected by the People, and shall hold office for a term of six years.

31. (1) Any citizen who is qualified to be elected to the office of President may be nominated as a candidate for such office

(*a*) by a recognized political party, or
(*b*) if he is or has been an elected member of the legislature, by any other political party or by an elector whose name has been entered in any register of electors.

(2) No person who has been twice elected to the office of President by the People shall be qualified thereafter to be elected to such office by the People.

(3) The poll for the election of the President shall be taken not less than one month and not more than two months before the expiration of the term of office of the President in office.

(4) The term of office of the President shall commence on the fourth day of February next succeeding the date of his election:

Provided that the president in office, notwithstanding anything to the contrary in Article 30, shall continue to exercise, perform and discharge the powers, duties and functions of the office of President until the assumption of office by the person declared elected as President. If the office of President becomes vacant, by reason of the person declared elected as President failing to assume office, the President in office shall continue to exercise, perform and discharge the powers, duties and functions of the office of President, until the Prime Minister or if the office of Prime Minister be then vacant or if the Prime Minister be unable to act, the Speaker commences to act in the office of President in terms of Article 40.

(5) The election of the President shall be conducted by the Commissioner of Elections who shall fix the date for the nomination of candidates for such election and the date on which the poll shall be taken.

(6) Parliament shall by law make provisions for

(*a*) the nomination of candidates for the election of President;

(*b*) the register of electors to be used at and the procedure for the election of the President;

(*c*) the creation of offences relating to such election and the punishment therefor;

(*d*) the grounds and manner of avoiding such election and of determining any disputed election; and

(*e*) all other matters necessary or incidental thereto.

32. (1) The person elected or succeeding to the office of President shall assume office upon taking and subscribing the oath or making and subscribing the affirmation, set out in the Fourth Schedule, in Sri Lanka before the Chief Justice or any other Judge of the Supreme Court.

(2) Upon such assumption of office the President shall cease to hold any other office created or recognized by the Constitution and if he is a Member of Parliament, shall vacate his seat in Parliament. The President shall not hold any other office or place of profit whatsoever.

(3) The President shall, by virtue of his office, have the right at any time to attend, address and send messages to Parliament. In the exercise of such right the President shall be entitled to all the privileges, immunities and powers, other than the right to vote, of a Member of Parliament and shall not be liable for any breach of the privileges of Parliament, or of its Members.

33. In addition to the powers and functions expressly conferred on or assigned to him by the Constitution or by any written law whether enacted before or after the commencement of the Constitution, the President shall have the power

(*a*) to make the Statement of Government Policy in Parliament at the commencement of each session of Parliament;

(*b*) to preside at ceremonial sittings of Parliament;

(*c*) to receive and recognize, and to appoint and accredit, Ambassadors, High Commissioners, Plenipotentiaries and other diplomatic agents;

(*d*) to keep the Public Seal of the Republic, and to make an execute under the Public Seal, the Acts of Appointment of the Prime Minister and other Ministers of the Cabinet of Ministers, the Chief Justice and other Judges of the Supreme Court, such grants and dispositions of lands and immovable property vested in the Republic as he is by law required or empowered to do, and to use the Public Seal for sealing all things whatsoever that shall pass that Seal;

(*e*) to declare war and peace; and

(*f*) to do all such acts and things, not being inconsistent with the provisions of the Constitution or written law, as by international law, custom or usage he is required or authorized to do.

34. (1) The President may in the case of any offender convicted of any offence in any court within the Republic of Sri Lanka

(*a*) grant a pardon, either free or subject to lawful conditions;

(*b*) grant any respite, either indefinite or for such period as the President may think fit, of the execution of any sentence passed on such offender;

(*c*) substitute a less severe form of punishment for any punishment imposed on such offender; or

(*d*) remit the whole or any part of any punishment imposed or of any penalty or forfeiture otherwise due to the Republic on account of such offence:

Provided that where any offender shall have been condemned to suffer death by the sentence of any court, the President shall cause a report to be made to him by the Judge who tried the case and shall forward such report to the Attorney General with instructions that after the Attorney General has advised thereon, the report shall be sent together with the Attorney General's advice to the Minister in charge of the subject of Justice, who shall forward the report with his recommendation to the President.

(2) The President may in the case of any person who is or has become subject to any disqualification specified in paragraph (*d*), (*e*), (*f*), (*g*), or (*h*) of Article 89 or sub-paragraph (*g*) of paragraph (1) of Article 91.

(*a*) grant a pardon, either free or subject to lawful conditions, or

(*b*) reduce the period of such disqualification.

(3) When any offence has been committed for which the offender may be tried within the Republic of Sri Lanka, the President may grant a pardon to any accomplice in such offence who shall give such information as shall lead to the conviction of the principal offender or of any one of such principal offenders, if more than one.

35. (1) While any person holds office as President, no proceedings shall be instituted or continued against him in any court or tribunal in respect of anything done or omitted to be done by him either in his official or private capacity.

(2) Where provisions is made by law limiting the time within which proceedings of any description may be brought against any person, the period of time during which such person holds the office of President shall not be taken into account in calculating any period of time prescribed by that law.

(3) The immunity conferred by the provisions of paragraph (1) of this

Article shall not apply to any proceedings in any court in relation to the exercise of any power pertaining to any subject or function assigned to the President or remaining in his charge under paragraph (2) of Article 44 or to proceedings in the Supreme Court under paragraph (2) of Article 129 or to proceedings in the Supreme Court under Article 130 (*a*) relating to the election of the President:

Provided that any such proceedings in relation to the exercise of any power pertaining to any such subject or function shall be instituted against the Attorney-General.

36. (1) Within one month of the commencement of the Constitution, Parliament shall by resolution determine the salary, allowances and pension entitlement of the holders of the office of President. Such pension shall be in addition to any other pension to which such person is entitled by virtue of any prior service.

(2) Upon the assumption of the office of President the holder of such office shall become entitled to the receipt of such salary and allowances and thereafter, of such pension as may be determined by Parliament. Any subsequent amendment, repeal or replacement of this Article, and any subsequent law or any provision thereof inconsistent with this Article shall not have retrospective operation.

(3) The salary, allowances and pension of the President shall be charged on the Consolidated Fund.

(4) Parliament may by resolution increase, but shall not reduce, the salary, allowances or pension entitlement of the holders of the office of President.

37. (1) If the President is of the opinion that by reason of illness, absence from Sri Lanka or any other cause he will be unable to exercise, perform and discharge the powers, duties and functions of his office, he may appoint the Prime Minister to exercise, perform and discharge the powers, duties and functions of the office of President during such period, and may also appoint one of the other Ministers of the Cabinet to act in the office of Prime Minister during such period:

Provided that if the office of Prime Minister be then vacant or the Prime Minister is unable to act, the President may appoint the Speaker to exercise, perform and discharge the powers, duties and functions of the office of President during such period.

(2) If the Chief Justice in consultation with the Speaker is of the opinion that the President is temporarily unable to exercise, perform and discharge the powers, duties and functions of his office and is unable to make an appointment in terms of paragraph (1) of this Article, he shall communicate in writing his opinion to the Speaker and thereupon the Prime Minister shall exercise, perform and discharge the powers, duties and functions of the office of President during such period, notwithstanding the absence of such appointment as is provided for in paragraph (1) of this Article:

Provided that if the office of Prime Minister be then vacant or the Prime Minister is unable to act, the Speaker shall exercise, perform and discharge the powers, duties and functions of the office of President during such period.

(3) The provisions of the Constitution relating to the President (other than the provisions of paragraph (2) of Article 32) shall apply, in so far as they can be

applied, to the person so exercising, performing and discharging the powers, duties and functions of the office of President.

(4) In this Article and in Articles 38 (1) (*b*) and 40 (1), 'the Speaker' includes, during any period when Parliament is dissolved, the person who held the office of Speaker immediately before the dissolution of Parliament.

38. (1) The office of President shall become vacant

(*a*) upon his death;

(*b*) if he resigns his office by a writing under his hand addressed to the Speaker;

(*c*) if he ceases to be a citizen of Sri Lanka;

(*d*) if the person elected as President wilfully fails to assume office within one month from the date of commencement of his term of office;

(*e*) if he is removed from office as provided in the next succeeding paragraph; or

(*f*) if the Supreme Court in the exercise of its powers under Article 130 (*a*) determines that his election as President was void and does not determine that any other person was duly elected as President.

(2) (*a*) Any Member of Parliament may, by a writing addressed to the Speaker, give notice of a resolution alleging that the President is permanently incapable of discharging the functions of his office by reason of mental or physical infirmity or that the President has been guilty of

(i) intentional violation of the Constitution,

(ii) treason,

(iii) bribery,

(iv) misconduct or corruption involving the abuse of the powers of his office, or

(v) any offence under any law, involving moral turpitude,

and setting out full particulars of the allegation or allegations made and seeking an inquiry and report thereon by the Supreme Court.

(*b*) No notice of such resolution shall be entertained by the Speaker or placed on the Order Paper of Parliament unless it complies with the provisions of sub-paragraph (*a*) and

(i) such notice of resolution is signed by not less than two thirds of the whole number of Members of Parliament, or

(ii) such notice of resolution is signed by not less than one half of the whole number of Members of Parliament, and the Speaker is satisfied that such allegation or allegations merit inquiry and report by the Supreme Court.

(*c*) Where such resolution is passed by not less than two thirds of the whole number of Members (including those not present) voting in its favor, the allegation or allegations contained in such resolution shall be referred by the Speaker to the Supreme Court for inquiry and report.

(*d*) The Supreme Court shall, after due inquiry at which the President shall have the right to appear and to be heard, in person or by an attorney-at-law, make a report of its determination to Parliament together with the reasons therefor.

(*e*) Where the Supreme Court reports to Parliament that in its opinion the President is permanently incapable of discharging the functions of his office by reason of mental or physical infirmity or that the President has been guilty of any of the other allegations contained in such resolution, as the case may be, Parliament may by a resolution passed by not less than two thirds of the whole number of Members (including those not present) voting in its favor remove the President from office.

39. (1) Where the Supreme Court in the exercise of its jurisdiction under Article 130 determines

(*a*) that the election of the President was void and does not determine that any other person was duly elected, then, a poll for the election of the President shall be taken not later than three months from the date of the determination; or

(*b*) that any other person was duly elected as President, then, such other person shall assume the office of President within one month of the date of the determination.

For the purposes of Article 38 (1) (*d*), the date of commencement of the term of office of the new President shall be the date of his election or the date of the determination, as the case may be.

(2) Upon the Supreme Court making any such determination as is referred to in paragraph (1) of this Article, the person who was exercising, performing and discharging the powers, duties and functions of the office of President shall forthwith cease to exercise, perform and discharge such powers, duties and functions. During the period intervening between the date of such determination and the assumption of office by the new President, the Prime Minister shall act in the office of President and shall appoint one of the other Ministers of the Cabinet to act in the office of the Prime Minister:

Provided that if the office of Prime Minister be then vacant or the Prime Minister is unable to act, the Speaker shall act in the office of the President.

(3) For the purposes of Article 30 (2) and notwithstanding the provisions of Article 31 (4), the term of office of the new President shall be deemed to have commenced on the date on which the term of office of the person whose election was determined to have been void or undue would, but for such determination, have commenced.

(4) The exercise, performance and discharge by any person of the powers, duties and function of the office of President shall not be invalid by reason only of the fact that the Supreme Court subsequently determines that the election of such person as President was void or undue.

(5) The provisions of this Article shall apply notwithstanding anything to the contrary in Article 40.

40. (1) (*a*) If the office of President shall become vacant prior to the expiration of his term of office, Parliament shall elect as President one of its Members who is qualified to be elected to the office of President. Any person so succeeding to the office of President shall hold office only for the unexpired period of the term of office of the President vacating office.

(*b*) Such election shall be held as soon as possible after, and in no case later than one month from, the date of occurrence of the vacancy. Such election shall be by secret ballot and by an absolute majority of the votes cast in accordance with such procedure as Parliament may by law provide:

Provided that if such vacancy occurs after the dissolution of Parliament, the President shall be elected by the new Parliament within one month of its first meeting.

(*c*) During the period between the occurrence of such vacancy and the assumption of office by the new President, the Prime Minister shall act in the office of President and shall appoint one of the other Ministers of the Cabinet to act in the office of Prime Minister:

Provided that if the office of Prime Minister be then vacant or the Prime Minister is unable to act, the Speaker shall act in the office of President.

(2) The provisions of the Constitution relating to the President (other than the provisions of paragraph (2) of Article 32) shall apply, in so far as they can be applied, to an acting President.

(3) Parliament shall by law provide for all matters relating to the procedure for the election of the President by Parliament and all other matters necessary or incidental thereto.

41. (1) The President shall have the power to appoint such Secretaries, and, in consultation with the Cabinet of Ministers, such other officers and staff as are in his opinion necessary to assist him in the exercise, performance and discharge of the powers, duties and functions of his office, and to determine their terms and conditions of service.

(2) The salaries of such Secretaries, officers and staff shall be charged on the Consolidated Fund.

(3) Such Secretaries, officers and staff shall be deemed to be public officers except that the dismissal and disciplinary control of such Secretaries, officers and staff shall be vested in the President, who may delegate to any such Secretary his powers of dismissal and disciplinary control in respect of any such officers or staff.

(4) Every such Secretary, officer or member of the staff shall cease to hold office upon a new President assuming office.

(5) Where any such Secretary, officer or member of the staff so ceases to hold office, the Cabinet of Ministers may appoint such Secretary, officer or member of the staff to any post in the Public Service;

Provided that any such secretary, officer or member of the staff who immediately prior to his appointment as Secretary, officer or member of the staff was in the Public or Local Government Service or in the service of a public corporation shall be entitled to revert to such service without loss of seniority upon a new President assuming office.

(6) The proviso to paragraph (5) of this Article shall, *mutatis mutandis*, apply to any person referred to in that proviso upon

(*a*) the President terminating the services of such person, otherwise than by dismissal on disciplinary grounds; or

(*b*) the resignation of such person, unless disciplinary proceedings are pending or contemplated against such person on the date of his resignation.

(7) For the purposes of paragraphs (5) and (6) of this Article any person who has continuously held the office of Secretary to the President, Secretary to any Ministry or any office in the President's staff or any one or more of such offices shall be deemed to have continuously held the office which such person last held.

CHAPTER VIII

THE EXECUTIVE

The Cabinet of Ministers

42. The President shall be responsible to Parliament for the due exercise, performance and discharge of his powers, duties and functions under the Constitution and any written law, including law for the time being relating to public security.

43. (1) There shall be a Cabinet of Ministers charged with the direction and control of the Government of the Republic, which shall be collectively responsible and answerable to Parliament.

(2) The President shall be a member of the Cabinet of Ministers, and shall be the Head of the Cabinet of Ministers:

Provided that notwithstanding the dissolution of the Cabinet of Ministers under the provisions of the Constitution the President shall continue in office.

(3) The President shall appoint as Prime Minister the Member of Parliament who in his opinion is most likely to command the confidence of Parliament.

44. (1) The President shall, from time to time, in consultation with the Prime Minister, where he considers such consultation to be necessary

(*a*) determine the number of Ministers of the Cabinet of Ministers and the Ministries and the assignment of subjects and functions to such Ministers; and

(*b*) appoint from among the Members of Parliament, Ministers to be in charge of the Ministries so determined.

(2) The President may assign to himself any subject or function and shall remain in charge of any subject or function not assigned to any Minister under the provisions of paragraph (1) of this Article or the provisions of paragraph (1) of

Article 45, and may for that purpose determine the number of Ministries to be in his charge, and accordingly, any reference in the Constitution or any written law to the Minister to whom such subject or function is assigned, shall be read and construed as a reference to the President.

(3) The President may, at any time, change the assignment of subjects and functions and the composition of the Cabinet of Ministers. Such changes shall not affect the continuity of the Cabinet of Ministers, and the continuity of its responsibility to Parliament.

45. (1) The President may, from time to time, in consultation with the Prime Minister where he considers such consultation to be necessary

(*a*) appoint from among Members of Parliament, Ministers who shall not be Members of the Cabinet of Ministers; and

(*b*) determine the assignment of subjects and functions to, and the Ministries, if any, which are to be in charge of, such Ministers.

(2) The President may at any time change any appointment or assignment made under paragraph (1) of this Article.

(3) Every Minister appointed under this Article shall be responsible and answerable to the Cabinet of Ministers and to Parliament.

(4) Any Minister of the Cabinet of Ministers may, by Notification published in the *Gazette*, delegate to any Minister who is not a member of the Cabinet of Ministers any power or duty pertaining to any subject or function assigned to him, or any power or duty conferred or imposed on him by any written law and it shall be lawful for such other Minister to exercise and perform any power or duty delegated to him under this paragraph, notwithstanding anything to the contrary in written law by which that power or duty is conferred or imposed.

46. (1) The President may, from time to time, in consultation with the Prime Minister, where he considers such consultation to be necessary, appoint from among the Members of Parliament, Deputy Ministers to assist the Ministers of the Cabinet of Ministers in the performance of their duties.

(2) Any Minister of the Cabinet of Ministers may, by Notification published in the *Gazette*, delegate to his Deputy Minister any power or duty pertaining to any subject or function assigned to him, or any power or duty conferred or imposed on him by any written law and it shall be lawful for the Deputy Minister to exercise and perform any power or duty delegated to him under this paragraph notwithstanding anything to the contrary in the written law by which that power or duty is conferred or imposed on such Minister.

47. The Prime Minister, a Minister of the Cabinet of Ministers, any other Minister or Deputy Minister shall continue to hold office throughout the period during which the Cabinet of Ministers continues to function under the provisions of the Constitution unless he

(*a*) is removed by a writing under the hand of the President;

(*b*) resigns his office by a writing under his hand addressed to the President; or

(*c*) ceases to be a Member of Parliament.

48. (1) The Cabinet of Ministers functioning immediately prior to the dissolution of Parliament shall notwithstanding such dissolution continue to function and shall cease to function upon the conclusion of the General Election, and accordingly, the Prime Minister, Ministers of the Cabinet of Ministers, other Ministers and Deputy Ministers shall continue to function unless they cease to hold office as provided in paragraph (*a*) or (*b*) of Article 47.

(2) Notwithstanding the death, removal from office or resignation of the Prime Minister, during the period intervening between the dissolution of Parliament and the conclusion of the General Election, the Cabinet of Ministers shall continue to function with the other Ministers of the Cabinet as its members until the conclusion of the General Election. The President may appoint one such Minister to exercise, perform and discharge, or may himself exercise, perform and discharge the powers, duties and functions of the Prime Minister. If there is no such other Minister the President shall himself exercise perform and discharge the powers, duties and functions of the Cabinet of Ministers until the conclusion of the General Election.

(3) On the death, removal from office or resignation, during the period intervening between the dissolution of Parliament and the conclusion of the General Election, of a Minister of the Cabinet of Ministers or any other Minister, the President may appoint any other Minister to be the Minister in charge of such Ministry or to exercise, perform and discharge the powers, duties and functions of such Minister or may himself take charge of such Ministry or exercise, perform and discharge such powers, duties and functions.

49. (1) On the Prime Minister ceasing to hold office by removal, resignation or otherwise, except during the period intervening between the dissolution of Parliament and the conclusion of the General Election, the Cabinet of Ministers shall, unless the President has in the exercise of his powers under Article 70, dissolved Parliament, stand dissolved and the President shall appoint a Prime Minister, Ministers of the Cabinet of Ministers, other Ministers and Deputy Ministers in terms of Articles 43, 44, 45 and 46:

Provided that if after the Prime Minister so ceases to hold office Parliament is dissolved, the Cabinet of Ministers shall continue to function with the other Ministers of the Cabinet as its members, until the conclusion of the General Election. The President may appoint one such Minister to exercise, perform and discharge or may himself exercise, perform and discharge the powers, duties and functions of the Prime Minister, and the provisions of Article 48 shall, *mutatis mutandis*, apply.

(2) If Parliament rejects the Statement of Government Policy or the Appropriation Bill or passes a vote of no-confidence in the Government, the Cabinet of Ministers shall stand dissolved, and the President shall, unless he has in the exercise of his powers under Article 70, dissolved Parliament, appoint a Prime Minister, Ministers of the Cabinet of Ministers, other Ministers and Deputy Ministers in terms of Articles 43, 44, 45 and 46.

50. Whenever a Minister of the Cabinet of Ministers, other Minister or Deputy Minister is unable to discharge the functions of his office, the President may appoint any Member of Parliament to act in place of the said Minister of the Cabinet of Ministers, other Minister or Deputy Minister.

51. There shall be a Secretary to the Cabinet of Ministers who shall be appointed by the President. The Secretary shall, subject to the direction of the President, have charge of the office of the Cabinet of Ministers, and shall discharge and perform such other functions and duties as may be assigned to him by the President or the Cabinet of Ministers.

52. (1) There shall be for each Ministry a Secretary who shall be appointed by the President.

(2) The Secretary to the Ministry shall, subject to the direction and control of his Minister, exercise supervision over the department of Government or other institutions in the charge of his Minister.

(3) The Secretary to a Ministry shall cease to hold office upon the dissolution of the Cabinet of Ministers under the provisions of the Constitution or upon a determination by the President under Article 44 or Article 45 which results in such Ministry ceasing to exist.

(4) Where the Secretary to a Ministry so ceases to hold office, the Cabinet of Ministers may appoint such Secretary to any other post in the Public Service:

Provided that a person who immediately prior to his appointment as Secretary was in the Public or Local Government Service or in the service of any public corporation shall be deemed to have been temporarily released from such service and shall be entitled to revert to such service without loss of seniority upon his so ceasing to hold office as Secretary.

(5) The proviso to paragraph (4) of this Article shall, *mutatis mutandis*, apply to a Secretary to a Ministry upon

(*a*) the President terminating his services, otherwise than by dismissal on disciplinary grounds, or

(*b*) his resignation, unless disciplinary proceedings are pending or contemplated against him on the date of his resignation.

(6) For the purposes of paragraphs (4) and (5) of this Article any person who has continuously held the office of Secretary to the President, Secretary to a Ministry or any other office in the President's staff or any one or more of such offices shall be deemed to have continuously held the office which such person last held.

(7) For the purposes of this Article, the Office of the Parliamentary Commissioner for Administration, the Office of the Secretary-General of Parliament, the Department of the Commissioner of Elections, the Department of the Auditor-General and the Office of the Secretary to the Cabinet of Ministers shall be deemed not to be departments of Government.

53. A person appointed to any office referred to in this Chapter shall not enter upon the duties of his office until he takes and subscribes the oath or makes and subscribes the affirmation set out in the Fourth Schedule.

CHAPTER IX

THE EXECUTIVE

The Public Service

54. The President shall appoint all public officers required by the Constitution or other written law to be appointed by the President, as well as the Attorney-General and the Heads of the Army, the Navy, the Air Force and the Police Force.

55. (1) Subject to the provisions of the Constitution, the appointment, transfer, dismissal and disciplinary control of public officers is hereby vested in the Cabinet of Ministers, and all public officers shall hold office at pleasure.

(2) The Cabinet of Ministers shall not delegate its powers of appointment, transfer, dismissal and disciplinary control in respect of Heads of Departments.

(3) The Cabinet of Ministers may from time to time delegate its powers of appointment, transfer, dismissal and disciplinary control of other public officers to the Public Service Commission:

Provided that the Cabinet of Ministers may, from time to time and notwithstanding any delegation under this Article, delegate to any Minister its power of transfer in respect of such categories of officers as may be specified, and upon such delegation, the Public Service Comission or any Committee thereof shall not exercise such power in respect of such categories of officers.

For the purposes of this proviso, 'transfer' means the moving of a public officer from one post to another post in the same service or in the same grade of the same Ministry or Department with no change in salary.

(4) Subject to the provisions of the Constitution, the Cabinet of Ministers shall provide for and determine all matters relating to public officers, including the formulation of schemes of recruitment and codes of conduct for public officers, the principles to be followed in making promotions and transfers, and the procedure for the exercise and the delegation of the powers of appointment, transfer, dismissal and disciplinary control of public officers.

(5) Subject to the jurisdiction conferred on the Supreme Court under paragraph (1) of Article 126 no court or tribunal shall have power or jurisdiction to inquire into, pronounce upon or in any manner call in question, any order or decision of the Cabinet of Ministers, a Minister, the Public Service Commission, a Committee of the Public Service Commission or of a public officer, in regard to any matter concerning the appointment, transfer, dismissal or disciplinary control of a public officer.

(6) For the purposes of this Article and Articles 56 to 59 (both inclusive) 'public officer' does not include a member of the Army, Navy or Air Force.

56. (1) There shall be a Public Service Commission which shall consist of not less than five persons appointed by the President. The President shall nominate one of the members of the Commission to be the Chairman.

(2) No person shall be appointed or continue as a member of the Public Service Commission if he is a Member of Parliament.

(3) Every person who, immediately before his appointment as a member of the Public Service Commission, was a public officer or a judicial officer shall, when such appointment takes effect, cease to hold such office, and shall be ineligible for further appointment as a public officer or judicial officer:

Provided that any such person shall, until he ceases to be a member of the Public Service Commission, or while continuing to be such a member, attains the age at which he would if he were a public officer or a judicial officer, as the case may be, be required to retire, be deemed to be a public officer or a judicial officer, and to hold a pensionable office in the service of the State, for the purposes of any provision relating to the grant of pensions, gratuities or other allowances in respect of such service.

(4) Every member of the Public Service Commission shall hold office for a period of five years from the date of his appointment, unless he earlier resigns his office by a writing under his hand addressed to the President, or is removed from office by the President for cause assigned, but shall be eligible for reappointment.

(5) The President may grant leave from his duties to any member of the Public Service Commission and may appoint a person qualified to be a member of the Public Service Commission to be a temporary member for the period of such leave.

(6) A member of the Public Service Commission shall be paid such salary as may be determined by Parliament. The salary payable to any such member shall be charged on the Consolidated Fund and shall not be diminished during his term of office.

(7) There shall be a Secretary to the Public Service Commission who shall be appointed by the Commission.

(8) The quorum for any meeting of the Commission shall be three members.

(9) The Public Service Commission shall have power to act notwithstanding any vacancy in its membership, and no act or proceeding of the Commission shall be, or be deemed to be, invalid by reason only of any such vacancy or any defect in the appointment of a member.

(10) For the purposes of Chapter IX of the Penal Code, a member of the Public Service Commission shall be deemed to be a public servant.

57. (1) Whenever the Cabinet of Ministers so directs the Chairman of the Public Service Commission shall appoint a Committee of the Public Service Commission to exercise the powers of the Commission in respect of such categories of public officers as are specified in such direction.

(2) Upon a direction being made under paragraph (1) of this Article, the Chairman of the Public Service Commission shall appoint a Committee consisting of three members of the Public Service Commission. Where such Chairman is a member of the Committee so appointed, he shall be the Chairman of the Committee, and where he is not a member of the Committee so appointed, then such member of that Committee as may be nominated in writing by such Chairman, shall be the Chairman of that Committee.

(3) Upon the appointment of any such Committee, the Public Service Commission shall cease to exercise its powers of appointment, transfer, dismissal and disciplinary control in respect of the categories of public officers specified in the direction for the appointment of such Committee.

(4) There shall be a Secretary to each such Committee who shall be appointed by the Public Service Commission.

(5) The quorum for any meeting of any such Committee shall be two members.

(6) Any such Committee shall have power to act notwithstanding any vacancy in its membership and any act or proceeding of any such Committee shall not be, or be deemed to be, invalid by reason only of any such vacancy or any defect in the appointment of a member.

58. (1) The Public Service Commission or any Committee thereof may delegate to a public officer, subject to such conditions as may be prescribed by the Cabinet of Ministers, its powers of appointment, transfer, dismissal or disciplinary control of any category of public officers.

(2) Any public officer aggrieved by any order of transfer or dismissal, or any other order relating to a disciplinary matter made by a public officer to whom the Public Service Commission or any Committee thereof has delegated its powers under the preceding paragraph shall have a right of appeal to the Public Service Commission or such Committee, as the case may be.

59. The Cabinet of Ministers shall have the power to alter, vary or rescind

(*a*) any appointment, order of transfer or dismissal or any other order relating to a disciplinary matter made, on appeal or otherwise, by the Public Service Commission or a Committee thereof;

(*b*) any order of transfer made by a Minister; or

(*c*) any appointment made by a public officer to whom the Public Service Commission or any Committee thereof has delegated its powers under Article 58 (1).

60. Every person who, otherwise than in the course of his duty, directly or indirectly, by himself or by any other person, in any manner whatsoever, influences or attempts to influence any decision of the Public Service Commission, or of any Committee thereof, or of any member of such Commission or of any public officer exercising any powers delegated by such Commission or Committee, shall be guilty of an offence, and shall, on conviction by the High Court after trial without a jury be liable to a fine not exceeding one thousand rupees or to imprisonment for a term not exceeding one year or to both such fine and such imprisonment and fine:

Provided that nothing in this Article shall prohibit any person from giving a certificate or testimonial to any applicant or candidate for any public office.

61. A person appointed to any office referred to in this Chapter shall not enter upon the duties of his office until he takes and subscribes the oath or makes and subscribes the affirmation set out in the Fourth Schedule.

CHAPTER X

THE LEGISLATURE

Parliament

62. (1) There shall be a Parliament which shall consist of one hundred and ninety-six Members elected by the electors of the several electoral districts constituted in accordance with the provisions of the Constitution.

(2) Unless Parliament is sooner dissolved, every Parliament shall continue for six years from the date appointed for its first meeting and no longer, and the expiry of the said period of six years shall operate as a dissolution of Parliament.

63. Except for the purpose of electing the Speaker, no Member shall sit or vote in Parliament until he has taken and subscribed the following oath, or made and subscribed the following affirmation, before Parliament:

'I . . . . do solemnly declare and affirm/swear that I will uphold and defend the Constitution of the Democratic Socialist Republic of Sri Lanka.'

64. (1) Parliament shall, at its first meeting after a General Election, elect three Members to be respectively the Speaker, the Deputy Speaker and Chairman of Committees (hereinafter referred to as the 'Deputy Speaker') and the Deputy Chairman of Committees thereof.

(2) A Member holding office as the Speaker or the Deputy Speaker or the Deputy Chairman of Committees shall, unless he earlier resigns his office by a writing under his hand addressed to the President or ceases to be a Member, vacate his office on the dissolution of Parliament.

(3) Whenever the office of Speaker, Deputy Speaker or Deputy Chairman of Committees becomes vacant otherwise than as a result of a dissolution of Parliament, Parliament shall at its first meeting after the occurrence of the vacancy elect another Member to be the Speaker, the Deputy Speaker or the Deputy Chairman of Committees, as the case may be.

(4) If Parliament, after having been dissolved, is summoned under paragraph (7) of Article 70, each of the Members mentioned in paragraph (2) of this Article shall, notwithstanding anything therein, resume and continue to hold his office while that Parliament is kept in session.

(5) The Speaker, or in his absence the Deputy Speaker, or in their absence the Deputy Chairman of Committees, shall preside at sittings of Parliament. If none of them is present, a Member elected by Parliament for the sitting shall preside at that sitting of Parliament.

65. (1) There shall be a Secretary-General of Parliament who shall be appointed by the President and who shall hold office during good behavior.

(2) The salary of the Secretary-General shall be determined by Parliament, shall be charged on the Consolidated Fund and shall not be diminished during his term of office.

(3) The members of the staff of the Secretary-General shall be appointed by him with the approval of the Speaker.

(4) The salaries of the members of the staff of the Secretary-General shall be charged on the Consolidated Fund.

(5) The office of the Secretary-General shall become vacant

(*a*) upon his death;

(*b*) on his resignation in writing addressed to the President;

(*c*) on his removal by the President on account of ill health or physical or mental infirmity; or

(*e*) on his removal by the President upon an address of Parliament.

(6) Whenever the Secretary-General is unable to discharge the functions of his office, the President may appoint a person to act in the place of the Secretary-General.

66. The seat of a Member shall become vacant

(*a*) upon his death;

(*b*) if, by a writing under his hand addressed to the Secretary-General of Parliament, he resigns his seat;

(*c*) upon his assuming the office of President consequent to his election to such office, either by the People or by Parliament;

(*d*) if he becomes subject to any disqualification specified in Article 89 or 91;

(*e*) if he becomes a member of the Public Service or an employee of a public Corporation or, being a member of the Public Service or an employee of a public corporation, does not cease to be a member of such Service or an employee of such corporation, before he sits in Parliament;

(*f*) if, without the leave of Parliament first obtained, he absents himself from the sittings of Parliament during a continuous period of three months;

(*g*) if his election as a Member is declared void under the law in force for the time being;

(*h*) upon the dissolution of Parliament; or

(*i*) upon a resolution for his expulsion being passed in terms of Article 81.

67. The privileges, immunities, and powers of Parliament and of its Members may be determined and regulated by Parliament by law, and until so determined and regulated, the provisions of the Parliament (Powers and Privileges) Act, shall, *mutatis mutandis*, apply.

68. (1) Ministers, Deputy Ministers and Members, including the Speaker, the Deputy Speaker and the Deputy Chairman of Committees, shall be paid such remuneration or allowance as may be provided by Parliament, by law or by resolution, and the receipt thereof shall not disqualify the recipient from sitting or voting in Parliament.

(2) Until Parliament so provides, the remuneration payable to Ministers, Deputy Ministers and Members, including the Speaker, the Deputy Speaker and

the Deputy Chairman of Committees, shall be the same as the remuneration paid to Ministers, Deputy Ministers and Members including the Speaker, the Deputy Speaker and the Deputy Chairman of Committees of the National State Assembly immediately prior to the commencement of the Constitution.

69. Parliament shall have power to act notwithstanding any vacancy in its membership, and its proceedings shall be valid notwithstanding that it is discovered subsequently that a person who was not entitled so to do that or voted or otherwise took part in the proceedings.

CHAPTER XI

THE LEGISLATURE

Procedure and Powers

70. (1) The President may, from time to time, by Proclamation summon, prorogue and dissolve Parliament:

Provided that

(*a*) subject to the provisions of sub-paragraph (*d*), when a General Election has been held consequent upon a dissolution of Parliament by the President, the President shall not thereafter dissolve Parliament until the expiration of a period of one year from the date of such General Election, unless Parliament by resolution requests the President to dissolve Parliament;

(*b*) the President shall not dissolve Parliament on the rejection of the Statement of Government Policy at the commencement of the first session of Parliament after a General Election;

(*c*) subject to the provisions of sub-paragraph (*d*), the President shall not dissolve Parliament after the Speaker has entertained a resolution complying with the requirements of sub-paragraphs (*a*) and (*b*) of paragraph (2) of Article 38, unless

(i) such resolution is not passed as required by sub-paragraph (*c*) of paragraph (2) of Article 38;

(ii) The Supreme Court determines and reports that the President has not become permanently incapable of discharging the functions of his office or that the President has not been guilty of any of the other allegations contained in such resolution;

(iii) the consequent resolution for the removal of the President is not passed as required by sub-paragraph (*e*) of paragraph (2) of Article 38; or

(iv) Parliament by resolution requests the President to dissolve Parliament;

(*d*) where the President has not dissolved Parliament consequent upon the rejection by Parliament of the Appropriation Bill, the President shall dissolve Parliament if Parliament rejects the next Appropriation Bill.

(2) Parliament shall be summoned to meet once at least in every year.

(3) A Proclamation proroguing Parliament shall fix a date for the next session, not being more than two months after the date of the Proclamation;

Provided that, at any time while Parliament stands prorogued, the President may by Proclamation

(i) summon Parliament for an earlier date, not being less than three days from the date of such Proclamation, or

(ii) subject to the provisions of this Article, dissolve Parliament.

(4) All matters which, having been duly brought before Parliament, have not been disposed of at the time of the prorogation of Parliament, may be proceeded with during the next session.

(5) (*a*) A Proclamation dissolving Parliament shall fix a date or dates for the election of Members of Parliament, and shall summon the new Parliament to meet on a date not later than three months after the date of such Proclamation.

(*b*) Upon the dissolution of Parliament by virtue of the provisions of paragraph (2) of Article 62, the President shall forthwith by Proclamation fix a date or dates for the election of Members of Parliament, and shall summon the new Parliament to meet on a date not later than three months after the date of such Proclamation.

(*c*) The date fixed for the first meeting of Parliament by a Proclamation under sub-paragraph (*a*) or sub-paragraph (*b*) may be varied by a subsequent Proclamation, provided that the date so fixed by the subsequent Proclamation shall be a date not later than three months after the date of the original Proclamation.

(6) Where the poll for the election of the President is to be taken on a date which falls between the date of dissolution of Parliament and the date before which Parliament is required by paragraph (5) of this Article to be summoned to meet, Parliament shall, notwithstanding anything in that paragraph, be summoned to meet on a date not later than four months after the date of dissolution of Parliament.

(7) If at any time after the dissolution of Parliament, the President is satisfied that an emergency has arisen of such a nature that an earlier meeting of Parliament is necessary, he may by Proclamation summon the Parliament which has been dissolved to meet on a date not less than three days from the date of such Proclamation and such Parliament shall stand dissolved upon the termination of the emergency or the conclusion of the General Election, whichever is earlier.

71. Parliament may adjourn from time to time as it may determine by resolution or Standing Order, until it is prorogued or dissolved.

72. (1) Save as otherwise provided in the Constitution any question proposed for decision by Parliament shall be decided by the majority of votes of the Members present and voting.

(2) The person presiding shall not vote in the first instance but shall have and exercise a casting vote in the event of an equality of votes.

73. If at any time during a meeting of Parliament the attention of the person presiding is drawn to the fact that there are fewer than twenty Members present, the persons presiding shall, subject to any Standing Order, adjourn the sitting without question put.

74. (1) Subject to the provisions of the Constitution, Parliament may by resolution or Standing Order provide for

(i) the election and retirement of the Speaker, the Deputy Speaker and the Deputy Chairman of Committees, and

(ii) the regulation of its business, the preservation of order at its sittings and any other matter for which provision is required or authorized to be so made by the Constitution.

(2) Until Parliament otherwise provides by law or by resolution, the Standing Orders of the National State Assembly, operative immediately prior to the commencement of the Constitution, shall, *mutatis mutandis*, be the Standing Orders of Parliament.

75. Parliament shall have power to make laws, including laws having retrospective effect and repealing or amending any provision of the Constitution, or adding any provision to the Constitution:

Provided that Parliament shall not make any law

(*a*) suspending the operation of the Constitution or any part thereof, or

(*b*) repealing the Constitution as a whole unless such law also enacts a new Constitution to replace it.

76. (1) Parliament shall not abdicate or in any manner alienate its legislative power, and shall not set up any authority with any legislative power.

(2) It shall not be a contravention of the provisions of paragraph (1) of this Article for Parliament to make, in any law relating to public security, provision empowering the President to make emergency regulations in accordance with such law.

(3) It shall not be a contravention of the provisions of paragraph (1) of this Article for Parliament to make any law containing any provision empowering any person or body to make subordinate legislation of prescribed purposes, including the power

(*a*) to appoint a date on which any law or any part thereof shall come into effect or cease to have effect;

(*b*) to make by order any law or any part thereof applicable to any locality or to any class of persons; and

(*c*) to create a legal person, by an order or an act.

In sub-paragraph (*a*) and (*b*) of this paragraph, 'law' includes existing law.

(4) Any existing law containing any such provision as aforesaid shall be valid and operative.

77. (1) It shall be the duty of the Attorney-General to examine every Bill for any contravention of the requirements of paragraphs (1) and (2) of Article 82 and for any provision which cannot be validly passed except by the special majority prescribed by the Constitution; and the Attorney-General or any officer assisting the Attorney-General in the performance of his duties under this Article shall be afforded all facilities necessary for the performance of such duties.

(2) If the Attorney-General is of the opinion that a Bill contravenes any of the requirements of paragraphs (1) and (2) of Article 82 or that any provision in a Bill cannot be validly passed except by the special majority prescribed by the Constitution, he shall communicate such opinion to the President:

Provided that in the case of an amendment proposed to a Bill in Parliament, the Attorney-General shall communicate his opinion to the Speaker at the stage when the Bill is ready to be put to Parliament for its acceptance.

78. (1) Every Bill shall be published in the *Gazette* at least seven days before it is placed on the Order Paper of Parliament.

(2) The passing of a Bill or a resolution by Parliament shall be in accordance with the Constitution and the Standing Orders of Parliament. Any one or more of the Standing Orders may be suspended by Parliament in the circumstances and in the manner prescribed by the Standing Orders.

79. The Speaker shall endorse on every Bill passed by Parliament a certificate in the following form:

'This Bill (here state the short title of the Bill) has been duly passed by Parliament.'

Such certificate may also state the majority by which such Bill was passed:

Provided that where by virtue of the provisions of Article 82 or Article 83 or Article 84 or Article 123 (2) a special majority is required for the passing of a Bill, the Speaker shall certify such Bill only if such Bill has been passed with such special majority:

Provided further that where by virtue of Article 83, the Bill or any provision thereof requires the approval of the People at a Referendum, such certificate shall further state that the Bill or such provision shall not become law until approved by the People at a Referendum.

80. (1) Subject to the provisions of paragraph (2) of this Article, a Bill passed by Parliament shall become law when the certificate of the Speaker is endorsed thereon.

(2) Where the Cabinet of Ministers has certified that any Bill or any provision thereof is intended to be submitted for approval by the People at a Referendum or where the Supreme Court has determined that a Bill or any Provision thereof requires the approval of the People at a Referendum or where any Bill is submitted to the People by Referendum under paragraph (2) of Article 85, such Bill or such provision shall become law upon being approved by the People at a Referendum in accordance with paragraph (3) of Article 85 only when the President certifies that the Bill or provision thereof has been so approved. The President shall endorse on every Bill so approved a certificate in the following form:

'This Bill/provision has been duly approved by the People at a Referendum.'

Every such certificate shall be final and conclusive, and shall not be called in question in any court.

(3) Where a Bill becomes law upon the certificate of the President or the Speaker, as the case may be, being endorsed thereon, no court or tribunal shall inquire into, pronounce upon or in any manner call in question, the validity of such Act on any ground whatsoever.

81. (1) Where a Special Presidential Commission of Inquiry established under the Special Presidential Commissions of Inquiry Law, No. 7 of 1978, and consisting of a member or members each of whom is a Judge of the Supreme Court, Court of Appeal, High Court or the District Court recommends that any person should be made subject to civic disability by reason of any act done or omitted to be done by such person before or after the commencement of the Constitution, Parliament may by resolution passed by not less than two thirds of the whole number of Members (including those not present) voting in its favor.

- (*a*) impose civic disability on such person for a period not exceeding seven years, and
- (*b*) expel such person from Parliament, if he is a Member of Parliament.

Where a Special Presidential Commission of Inquiry consists of more than one member, a recommendation made by the majority of such members, in case of any difference of opinion, shall be, and shall be deemed for all purposes to be, the recommendation of such Commission of Inquiry.

(2) No such resolution shall be entertained by the Speaker or placed on the Order Paper of Parliament unless introduced by the Prime Minister with the approval of the Cabinet of Ministers.

(3) The Speaker shall endorse on every resolution passed in accordance with the preceding provisions of this Article a certificate in the following form:

'This resolution has been duly passed by Parliament in accordance with the provisions of Article 81 of this Constitution.

Every such certificate shall be conclusive for all purposes and shall not be questioned in any court, and no court or tribunal shall inquire into, or pronounce upon or in any manner call in question, the validity of such resolution on any ground whatsoever.

(4) In this Article, 'District Court' means a District Court created and established by existing law and includes a court that may be created by Parliament to exercise and perform powers and functions corresponding or substantially similar to the powers and functions exercised and performed by the District Court.

CHAPTER XII

THE LEGISLATURE

Amendment of the Constitution

82. (1) No Bill for the amendment of any provision of the Constitution shall be placed on the Order Paper of Parliament, unless the provision to be repealed, altered or added, and consequential amendments, if any, are expressly specified in the Bill and is described in the long title thereof as being an Act for the amendment of the Constitution.

(2) No Bill for the repeal of the Constitution shall be placed on the Order Paper of Parliament unless the Bill contains provisions replacing the Constitution and is described in the long title thereof as being an Act for the repeal and replacement of the Constitution.

(3) If in the opinion of the Speaker, a Bill does not comply with the requirements of paragraph (1) or paragraph (2) of this Article, he shall direct that such Bill be not proceeded with unless it is amended so as to comply with those requirements.

(4) Notwithstanding anything in the preceding provisions of this Article, it shall be lawful for a Bill which complies with the requirements of paragraph (1) or paragraph (2) of this Article to be amended by Parliament provided that the Bill as so amended shall comply with those requirements.

(5) A Bill for the amendment of any provision of the Constitution or for the repeal and replacement of the Constitution shall become law if the number of votes cast in favor thereof amounts to not less than two thirds of the whole number of Members (including those not present) and upon a certificate by the President or the Speaker, as the case may be, being endorsed thereon in accordance with the provisions of Article 80 or 79.

(6) No provision in any law shall, or shall be deemed to, amend, repeal or replace the Constitution or any provision thereof, or be so interpreted or construed, unless enacted in accordance with the requirements of the preceding provisions of this Article.

(7) In this Chapter, 'amendment' includes repeal, alteration and addition.

83. Notwithstanding anything to the contrary in the provisions of Article 82

(*a*) a Bill for the amendment or for the repeal and replacement of or which is inconsistent with any of the provisions of Articles 1, 2, 3, 6, 7, 8, 9, 10, and 11, or of this Article, and

(*b*) a Bill for the amendment or for the repeal and replacement of or which is inconsistent with the provisions of paragraph (2) of Article 30 or of paragraph (2) of Article 62 which would extend the term of office of the President or the duration of Parliament, as the case may be, to over six years,

shall become law if the number of votes cast in favor thereof amounts to not less than two thirds of the whole number of Members (including those not present), is approved by the People at a Referendum and a certificate is endorsed thereon by the President in accordance with Article 80.

84. (1) A Bill which is not for the amendment of any provision of the Constitution or for the repeal and replacement of the Constitution, but which is inconsistent with any provision of the Constitution may be placed on the Order Paper of Parliament without complying with the requirements of paragraph (1) or paragraph (2) of Article 82.

(2) Where the Cabinet of Ministers has certified that a Bill is intended to

be passed by the special majority required by this Article or where the Supreme Court has determined that a Bil requires to be passed by such special majority, such Bill shall become law only if the number of votes cast in favor thereof amounts to not less than two thirds of the whole number of Members (including those not present) and a certificate by the President or the Speaker, as the case may be, is endorsed thereon in accordance with the provisions of Article 80 or 79.

(3) Such a Bill when enacted into law shall not, and shall not be deemed to, amend, repeal or replace the Constitution or any provision thereof, and shall not be so interpreted or construed, and may thereafter be repealed by a majority of the votes of the Members present and voting.

CHAPTER XIII

THE REFERENDUM

85. (1) The President shall submit to the People by Referendum every Bill or any provision in any Bill which the Cabinet of Ministers has certified as being intended to be submitted to the People by Referendum, or which the Supreme Court has determined as requiring the approval of the People at a Referendum if the number of votes cast in favor of such Bill amounts to not less than two thirds of the whole number of Members (including those not present).

(2) The President may in his discretion submit to the People by referdum any Bill (not being a Bill for the repeal or amendment of any provision of the Constitution, or for the addition of any provision to the Constitution, or which is inconsistent with any provision of the Constitution), which has been rejected by Parliament.

(3) Any Bill or any provision in any Bill submitted to the People by Referendum shall be deemed to be approved by the People if approved by an absolute majority of the valid votes cast at such Referendum:

Provided that when the total number of valid votes cast does not exceed two thirds of the whole number of electors entered in the register of electors, such Bill shall be deemed to be approved only if approved by not less than one third of the whole number of such electors.

86. The President may, subject to the provisions of Article 85, submit to the People by Referendum any matter which in the opinion of the President is of national importance.

87. (1) Every Referendum shall be conducted by the Commissioner of Elections who shall communicate the result thereof to the President.

(2) Parliament shall by law provide for all matters relating to the procedure for the submission of Bills and of matters of national importance to the People by Referenda, the register of electors to be used at a Referendum, the creation of offences relating thereto and the punishment therefor, and all other matters necessary or incidental thereto.

CHAPTER XIV

THE FRANCHISE AND ELECTIONS

88. Every person shall, unless disqualified as hereinafter provided, be qualified to be an elector at the election of the President and of the Members of Parliament or to vote at any Referendum:

Provided that no such person shall be entitled to vote unless his name is entered in the appropriate register of electors.

89. No person shall be qualified to be an elector at an election of the President, or of the Members of Parliament or to vote at any Referendum, if he is subject to any of the following disqualifications, namely

(*a*) if he is not a citizen of Sri Lanka;

(*b*) if he has not attained the age of eighteen years on the qualifying date specified by law under the provisions of Article 101;

(*c*) if he is under any law in force in Sri Lanka found or declared to be of unsound mind;

(*d*) if he is serving or has during the period of seven years immediately preceding completed serving of a sentence of imprisonment (by whatever name called) for a term not less than six months imposed after conviction by any court for an offence punishable with imprisonment for a term not less than two years or is under sentence of death or is serving or has during the period of seven years immediately preceding completed the serving of a sentence of imprisonment for a term not less than six months awarded in lieu of execution of such sentence:

Provided that if any person disqualified under this paragraph is granted a free pardon such disqualification shall cease from the date on which the pardon is granted;

(*e*) if a period of seven years has not elapsed since

(i) the last of the dates, if any, of his being convicted of any offence under section 52 (1) or 53 of the Ceylon (Parliamentary Elections) Order in Council, 1946, or of such offence under the law for the time being relating to Referenda or to the election of the President or of Members of Parliament as would correspond to an offence under either of the said two sections;

(ii) the last of the dates, if any, of his being convicted of a corrupt practice under the Ceylon (Parliamentary Elections) Order in Council, 1946, or of such offence under the law for the time being relating to Referenda or to the election of the President or of Members of Parliament as would correspond to the said corrupt practice:

(iii) the last of the dates, if any, being a date after the commencement of the Constitution, of a report made by a Judge finding him guilty of any law for the time being relating to Referenda or to the election of the President or of Members of Parliament;

(iv) the last of the dates, if any, of his being convicted or found guilty of bribery under the provisions of the Bribery Act or of any future law as would correspond to the Bribery Act;

(*f*) if a period of five years has not elapsed since

(i) the last of the dates, if any, of his being convicted of any offence under the provisions of section 77 to 82 (both inclusive) of the Local Authorities Elections Ordinance or for such offence under any future law as would correspond to any offence under the said sections; or

(ii) the last of the dates, if any, of his being convicted of an offence under the provisions of section 2 and 3 of the Public Bodies (Prevention of Corruption) Ordinance or of such offence under any future law as would correspond to the said offence;

(*g*) if a period of three years has not elapsed since

(i) the last of the dates, if any, of his being convicted of an illegal practice under the Ceylon (Parliamentary Elections) Order in Council, 1946, or of such offence under the law for the time being relating to Referenda or to the election of the President or of Members of Parliament as would correspond to the said illegal practice;

(ii) the last of the dates, if any, being a date after the commencement of the Constitution, of a report made by a Judge finding him guilty of any illegal practice under the Ceylon (parliamentary Elections) Order in Council, 1946, or under any law for the time being relating to Referenda or to the election of the President or of Members of Parliament;

(*h*) if a resolution for the imposition of civic disability upon him has been passed in terms of Article 81, and the period of such civic disability specified in such resolution has not expired;

(*i*) if a period of seven years has not elapsed since

(i) the date of his being convicted of any offence under the provisions of sections 188 to 201 (both inclusive) of the Penal Code or for such other offence under any future law as would correspond to any offence under the said sections, or

(ii) the date of his being convicted of an offence of contempt against, or in disrespect of, the authority of any Special Presidential Commission of Inquiry consisting of such member or members specified in Article 81 by reason of

(1) the failure of such person, without cause which in the opinion of such Commission is reasonable, to appear before such Commission at the time and place mentioned in any summons which such Commission is empowered by law to issue, or

(2) the refusal of such person to be sworn or affirmed, or the refusal or failure of such person, without cause which in the opinion of such Commission is reasonable, to answer any

question put to such person touching the matters directed to be inquired into by such Commission, or

(3) the refusal or failure of such person, without cause which in the opinion of such Commission is reasonable, to produce and show to such Commission any document or thing which is in the possession or power of such person and which in the opinion of such Commission is necessary for arriving at the truth of the matters to be inquired into by such Commission.

(*j*) if the period of his disqualification imposed under Article 116 has not elapsed.

90. Every person who is qualified to be an elector shall be qualified to be elected as a Member of Parliament unless he is disqualified under the provisions of Article 91.

91. (1) No person shall be qualified to be elected as a Member of Parliament or to sit and vote in Parliament

(*a*) if he is or becomes subject to any of the disqualifications specified in Article 89;

(*b*) if he

(i) stands nominated as a candidate for election for more than one electoral district at a General Election,

(ii) stands nominated as a candidate for election by more than one recognized political party or independent group in respect of any electoral district,

(iii) stands nominated as a candidate for election for an electoral district and before the conclusion of the election for that electoral district, he stands nominated as a candidate for election for any other electoral district, or

(iv) being a Member of Parliament, except in the circumstances referred to in Article 70 (7) or Article 155 (4) (i), stands nominated as a candidate for election for any electoral district;

(*c*) if he is the President of the Republic;

(*d*) if he is

(i) a judicial officer,

(ii) the Parliamentary Commissioner for Administration,

(iii) the Secretary-General of Parliament or a member of his staff

(iv) a member of the Public Service Commission,

(v) the Commissioner of Elections,

(vi) the Auditor-General,

(vii) a public officer holding any office, the initial of the salary scale of which is not less than Rs. 6,720 per annum,

(viii) an officer in any public corporation holding any office the initial of the salary scale of which is not less than Rs. 7,200 per annum,

(ix) a member of the Regular Force of the Army, Navy or Air Force, or

(x) a police officer or a public officer exercising police functions;

(*e*) if he has any such interest in any such contract made by or on behalf of the State or a public corporation as Parliament shall by law prescribe;

(*f*) if he is an undischarged bankrupt or insolvent, having been declared bankrupt or insolvent;

(*g*) if during the preceding seven years he has been adjudged by a competent court or by a Special Presidential Commission of Inquiry to have accepted a bribe or gratification offered with a view to influencing his judgment as a Member of Parliament or as a member of the legislature prior to the commencment of the Constitution.

(2) For the purposes of sub-paragraph (*g*) of paragraph (1) of this Article, the acceptance by a Member of Parliament of any allowance or other payment made to him by any trade union or other organization solely for the purpose of his maintenance shall be deemed not to be the acceptance of a bribe or gratification.

92. Every person who is qualified to be an elector shall be qualified to be elected to the office of President unless he is subject to any of the following disqualifications

(*a*) if he has not attained the age of thirty years;

(*b*) if he is not qualified to be elected as a Member of Parliament under sub-paragraph (*d*), (*e*), (*f*) or (*g*) of paragraph (1) of Article 91;

(*c*) if he has been twice elected to the office of President by the People; and

(*d*) if he has been removed from the office of President under the provisions of sub-paragraph (*e*) of paragraph (2) of Article 38.

93. The voting for the election of the President of the Republic and of the Members of Parliament and at any Referendum shall be free, equal and by secret ballot.

94. (1) At the election of the President every voter while casting his vote for any candidate may

(*a*) where there are three candidates for election, specify his second preference; and

(*b*) where there are more than three candidates for election, specify his second and third preferences.

(2) The candidate, if any, who receives more than one-half of the valid votes cast shall be declared elected as President.

(3) Where no candidate is declared elected under paragraph (2) of this Article, the candidate or candidates, other than the candidates who received the highest and second highest number of such votes, shall be eliminated from the contest, and

(*a*) the second preference of each voter whose vote had been for a candidate eliminated from the contest, shall, if it is for one or the other of the remaining two candidates, be counted as a vote for such candidate and be added to the votes counted in his favor under paragraph (2), and (*b*) the third preferency of each voter referred to in sub-paragraph (*a*) whose second preference is not counted under that sub-paragraph shall, if it is for one or the other of the remaining two candidates, be counted as a vote for such candidate and be added to the votes counted in his favor under sub-paragraph (*a*) and paragraph (2),

and the candidate who receives the majority of the votes so counted shall be declared elected as President.

(4) Where an equality is found to exist between the votes received by two or more candidates and the addition of one vote would determine

(*a*) which candidate is to be declared elected under this Article; or

(*b*) which candidate is not to be eliminated under this Article.

then the determination of the candidate to whom such additional vote shall be deemed to have been given for the purpose of such determination shall be made by lot.

95. (1) Within three months of the commencement of the Constitution the President shall for the delimitation of electoral districts, establish a Delimitation Commission consisting of three persons appointed by him who he is satisfied are not actively engaged in politics. The President shall appoint one of such persons to be the Chairman.

(2) If any member of the Delimitation Commission shall die or resign or if the President is satisfied that any such member has become incapable of discharging his functions as such, the President shall, in accordance with the provisions of paragraph (1) of this Article, appoint another person in his place.

96. (1) The Delimitation Commission shall divide Sri Lanka into not less than twenty and not more than twenty-four electoral districts, and shall assign names thereto.

(2) Each Province of Sri Lanka may itself constitute an electoral district or may be divided into two or more electoral districts.

(3) Where a Province is divided into a number of electoral districts the Delimitation Commission shall have regard to the existing administrative districts so as to ensure as far as is practicable that each electoral district shall be an administrative district or a combination of two or more administrative districts or two or more electoral districts together constitute an administrative district.

(4) The electoral districts of each Province shall together be entitled to return four members, (independently of the number of members which they are entitled to return by reference to the number of electors whose names appear in the registers of electors of such electoral districts), and the Delimitation Commission shall apportion such entitlement equitably among such electoral districts.

(5) In the event of a differemce of opinion among the members of the Delimitation Commission, the opinion of the majority thereof shall prevail and shall be deemed to be the decision of the Commission. Where each member of the Commission is of a different opinion, the opinion of the Chairman shall be deemed to be to the decision of the Commission. Any dissentient member may state his reasons for such dissent.

(6) The Chairman of the Delimitation Commission shall communicate the decisions of the Commission together with the reasons, if any, stated by a dissentient member to the President.

97. The President shall by Proclamation publish the names and boundaries of the electoral districts and the number of members, which each such electoral district is entitled to return by virtue of the provisions of paragraph (4) of Article 96 in accordance with the decision of the Delimitation Commission. The electoral districts specified in the Proclamation shall come into operation at the next ensuing General Election of Members of Parliament and shall thereafter be the electoral districts of Sri Lanka for all the purposes of the Constitution and of any law for the time being in force relating to the election of Members of Parliament.

98. (1) The several electoral districts shall together be entitled to return one hundred and ninety-six members.

(2) The apportionment of the number of members that each electoral district shall be entitled to return shall, in the case of thirty-six members, be determined in accordance with the provisions of paragraph (4) of Article 96.

(3) The apportionment of the number of members that each electoral district shall be entitled to return out of the balance number of one hundred and sixty members shall be determined in accordance with the succeeding provisions of this Aricle.

(4) The total number of electors whose names appear in the registers of electors of all the electoral districts shall be divided by one hundred and sixty. The whole number resulting from such division (any fraction not being taken into account) is hereinafter referred to as the 'qualifying number'.

(5) The total number of electors whose names appear in the register of electors of each electoral district shall be divided by the qualifying number and each electoral district shall be entitled to return such number of members as is equivalent to the whole number resulting from the division of the total number of such electors in that electoral district by the qualifying number and the balance number of such electors, if any, after such division shall be dealt with, if necessary, in accordancy with paragraph (6) of this Article.

(6) Where the total number of members to be returned by all the electoral districts ascertained by reference to the qualifying number in accordance with paragraph (5) of this Article is less than one hundred and sixty members, the apportionment of the entitlement among the electoral districts of the balance number of members shall be by reference to the balance number of such electors and in the case of any electoral district not entitled to return a single member according to the determination made under paragraph (5), the total number of electors whose names appear in the register of electors of such electoral district, the electoral district having the highest of such balance number of such electors or such total number of such electors, being entitled to return one more member and so on until the total number of members to be returned number one hundred and sixty.

(7) Where in making an apportionment under paragraph (6) of this Article an equality is found to exist between two or more balance number of such electors

or two or more total number of such electors or any combination of them and the addition of one such elector would entitle one electoral district to return an additional member, the determination of the electoral district to which one such elector shall be deemed to be added shall be determined by lot.

(8) The Commissioner of Elections, as soon as possible after the certification of the registers of electors for all the electoral districts, shall by Order published in the *Gazette* certify the number of members which each electoral district is entitled to return by virtue of the Proclamation under Article 97 and this Article and the number of candidates required under Article 99 (2) to be set out in the nomination paper.

(9) For the purposes of this Article 'the register of electors' means the register of electors for the time being in operation on the basis of which an election is being held.

99. (1) At any election of Members of Parliament, the total number of members which an electoral district is entitled to return shall be the number specified by the Commissioner of Elections in the Order published in accordance with the provisions of paragraph (8) of Article 98.

(2) Any recognized political party or any group of persons contesting as independent candidates (hereinafter referred to as an 'independent group') may for the purpose of any election of Members of Parliament for any electoral district, submit one nomination paper setting out the names, in order of priority, of such number of members to be elected for that electoral district, increased by one third. Where one third of the number of members to be elected for any electoral district is an integer and fraction the integer immediately higher to that integer and fraction shall be deemed to be the one third for the purposes of this paragraph.

(3) Each elector whose name appears in the register of electors shall be entitled to only one vote notwithstanding that his name appears in the electoral register in more than one electoral district.

(4) The recognized political party or independent group which polls the highest number of votes in any electoral district shall be entitled to have the candidate whose name appears first in the nomination paper of that recognized political party or independent group declared elected.

(5) (*a*) Every recognized political party and independent group polling less than one eighth of the total votes polled at any election in any electoral district shall be disqualified from having any candidates of such party or group being elected for that electoral district.

(*b*) The votes polled by the disqualified parties and independent groups, if any, shall be deducted from the total vote polled at the election in that electoral district and the number of votes resulting from such deduction is hereinafter referred to as the 'relevant number of votes.'

(6) The relevant number of votes shall be divided by the number of members to be elected for that electoral district reduced by one. If the number resulting from such division is an integer, that integer, or if that number is an integer and

fraction, the integer immediately higher to that integer and fraction is hereinafter referred to as the 'resulting number'.

(7) The number of votes polled by each recognized political party and independent group (other than those parties or groups disqualified under paragraph (5) of this Article), beginning with the party or group which polled the highest number of votes, shall then be divided by the resulting number and such number of candidates (excluding the candidate declared elected under paragraph (4) of this Article) as is equivalent to the whole number resulting from the division by the resulting number of the votes polled by such party or group shall be declared elected from each such party or group in the order in which their names appear in the nomination paper. The remainder of the votes, if any, after such division, shall be dealt with, if necessary, under paragraph (8) of this Article.

(8) Where after the declaration of the election of members as provided in paragraph (7) of this Article there are one or more members yet to be declared elected, such member or number of members shall be declared elected by reference to the remainder of the votes referred to in paragraph (7) to the credit of each party or group after the declaration made under that paragraph and the votes polled by any party or group not having any of its candidates declared elected under paragraph (7), the candidate next in the order of priority in the nomination paper of the party or group having the highest of such votes being declared elected the next member and so on until all the members to be elected are declared elected.

(9) (*a*) Where the number of votes polled by each recognized political party or independent group is less then the resulting number referred to in paragraph (6) of this Article the party or group which has polled the highest number of votes shall be entitled to have the candidate whose name appears first in the nomination paper of that party or group (excluding the candidate declared elected under paragraph (4) of this Article) declared elected and if there are one or more members yet to be declared elected, the party or group having the next highest number of votes polled shall be entitled to have the member whose name appears first in the nomination paper of that party or group to be declared elected and so on, until all the members to be elected for that electoral district are declared elected under the provisions of this paragraph.

(*b*) After the determination under paragraph (*a*) if there are one or more members yet to be declared elected in respect of that electoral district the provisions of that paragraph shall, *mutatis mutandis*, apply to the election of such members.

(10) Where under paragraph (4) or (8) or (9) of this Article an equality is found to exist between the votes polled by two or more recognized political parties or two or more independent groups or any combination of them and the addition of a vote would entitle the candidate of one such party or group to be elected, the determination of the party or group to which such additional vote shall be deemed to have been given shall be made by lot.

(11) For the purposes of this Article the number of votes polled shall be deemed to be the number of votes counted other than rejected votes.

(12) A recognized political party shall have the right, from time to time after all the members for an electoral district have been declared elected under the preceding provisions of this Article, to change the order of priority of the persons whose names appear in the nomination paper submitted by it and to substitute the names of other persons in place of those who have died or ceased to be members of such party.

(13) (*a*) Where a Member of Parliament ceases, by resignation, expulsion or otherwise, to be a member of a recognized political party, or independent group on whose nomination paper (hereinafter referred to as the 'relevant nomination paper') his name appeared at the time of his becoming such Member of Parliament, his seat shall become vacant upon the expiration of a period of one month from the date of his ceasing to be such member:

Provided that in the case of the expulsion of a Member of Parliament his seat shall not become vacant if prior to the expiration of the said period of one month he applies to the Supreme Court by petition in writing, and the Supreme Court upon such application determines that such expulsion was invalid. Such petition shall be inquired into by three Judges of the Supreme Court who shall make their determination within two months of the filing of such petition. Where the Supreme Court determines that the expulsion was valid the vacancy shall occur from the date of such determination.

(*b*) Where the seat of a Member of Parliament becomes vacant as provided in Article 66 (other than paragraph (*g*) of that Article) or by virtue of the preceding provisions of this paragraph, the person whose name appears first in order of priority in the relevant nomination paper (excluding the names of any person who have previously been declared elected) shall be declared elected to fill such vacancy.

100. Any person who

(*a*) having been elected a Member of Parliament but not having been at the time of such election qualified to be so elected, shall sit or vote in Parliament; or

(*b*) shall sit or vote in Parliament after his seat therein has become vacant or he has become disqualified from sitting or voting therein,

knowing or having reasonable grounds for knowing that he was so disqualified or that his seat has become vacant, as the case may be, shall be liable to a penalty of five hundred rupees for every day upon which he so sits or votes to be recovered as a debt due to the Republic by an action instituted by the Attorney-General in the District Court of Colombo.

101. (1) Parliament may by law make provision for

(*a*) the registration of electors;

(*b*) the prescribing of a qualifying date on which a person should be resident in any electoral district to be entered in the register of electors of that electoral district;

(*c*) the prescribing of a qualifying date on which a person should have attained the age of eighteen years to qualify for the purposes of registration as an elector;
(*d*) the preparation and revision of registers of electors;
(*e*) the procedure for the election of Members of Parliament;
(*f*) the creation of offences relating to such elections and the punishment therefor;
(*g*) the grounds for avoiding such elections, and where an election has been held void the manner of holding fresh elections;
(*h*) the form and manner in which vacancies shall be filled when all the candidates whose names appearing in the nomination paper of a recognized political party or independent group have been exhausted by election or otherwise; and
(*i*) the manner of determination of disputed elections and such other matters as are necessary or incidental to the election of Members of Parliament:

Provided that no such law shall add to the disqualifications specified in Articles 89 and 91.

(2) Until Parliament by law makes provision for such matters, the Ceylon (Parliamentary Elections) Order in Council, 1946 as amended from time to time, shall, subject to the provisions of the Consititution, *mutatis mutandis*, apply.

102 When a public officer or an officer of a public corporation is a candidate at any election, he shall be deemed to be on leave from the date on which he stands nominated as a candidate until the conclusion of the election. Such a public officer or an officer of a public corporation shall not during such period exercise, perform or discharge any of the powers, duties or functions of his office.

103 (1) There shall be a Commissioner of Elections who shall be appointed by the President and who shall hold office during good behavior.

(2) The salary of the Commissioner of Elections shall be determined by Parliament, shall be charged on the Consolidated Fund and shall not be diminished during his term of office.

(3) The office of the Commissioner of Elections shall become vacant
(*a*) upon his death;
(*b*) on his resignation in writing addressed to the President;
(*c*) on his attaining the age of sixty years;
(*d*) on his removal by the President on account of ill health or physical or mental infirmity; or
(*e*) on his removal by the President upon an address of Parliament.

(4) Whenever the Commissioner of Elections is unable to discharge the functions of his office, the President may appoint a person to act in the place of the Commissioner of Elections.

(5) The President may in exceptional circumstances permit a Commissioner of Elections who has reached the age of sixty years to continue in office for a period not exceeding twelve months.

104. The Commissioner of Elections shall exercise, perform or discharge all such powers, duties or functions as may be conferred or imposed on or vested in him by the law for the time being in force relating to elections to the office of President of the Republic and of Members of Parliament, and to Referenda, or by any other written law.

CHAPTER XV

THE JUDICIARY

105. (1) Subject to the provisions of the Constitution, the institutions for the administration of justice which protect, vindicate and enforce the rights of the People shall be

(*a*) the Supreme Court of the Republic of Sri Lanka,

(*b*) the Court of Appeal of the Republic of Sri Lanka,

(*c*) the High Court of the Republic of Sri Lanka and such other Courts of First Instance, tribunals or such institutions as Parliament may from time to time ordain and establish.

(2) All courts, tribunals and institutions created and established by existing written law for the administration of justice and for the adjudication and settlement of industrial and other disputes, other than the Supreme Court, shall be deemed to be courts, tribunals and institutions created and established by Parliament. Parliament may replace or abolish, or, amend the powers, duties, jurisdiction and procedure of, such courts, tribunals and institutions.

(3) The Supreme Court of the Republic of Sri Lanka and the Court of Appeal of the Republic of Sri Lanka shall each be a superior court of record and shall have all the powers of such court including the power to punish for contempt of itself, whether committed in the court itself or elsewhere, with imprisonment or fine or both as the court may deem fit. The power of the Court of Appeal shall include the power to punish for contempt of any other court, tribunal or institution referred to in paragraph 1 (*c*) of this Article, whether committed in the presence of such court or elsewhere:

Provided that the preceding provisions of this Article shall not prejudice or affect the rights now or hereafter vested by any law in such other court, tribunal or institution to punish for contempt of itself.

(4) Parliament may by law provide for the creation and establishment of courts, tribunals or institutions for the adjudication and settlement of matters relating to the discipline of *bhikkus* or any dispute between *bhikkus* or any other dispute relating to the performance of services in, or in relation to, temples. Such law may, notwithstanding anything to the contrary in this Chapter or Chapter XVI, make provision

(*a*) for the appointment, transfer, dismissal and disciplinary control of the member or members of such courts, tribunals or institutions by the President or by such other person or body of persons as may be provided for in such law;

(*b*) for the exclusion of the jurisdiction of any other institution referred to in paragraph (1) of this Article in relation to such matters and disputes.

In this paragraph the expressions '*bhikku*' and '*temple*' shall have the same meanings as in the Buddhist Temporalities Ordinance, as at the commencement of the Constitution.

106. (1) The sittings of every court, tribunal or other institution established under the Constitution or ordained and established by Parliament shall subject to the provisions of the Constitution be held in public, and all persons shall be entitled freely to attend such sittings.

(2) A judge or presiding officer of any such court, tribunal or other institution may, in his discretion, whenever he considers it desirable

(*a*) in proceedings relating to family relations,

(*b*) in proceedings relating to sexual matters,

(*c*) in the interests of national security or public safety, or

(*d*) in the interests of order and security within the precincts of such court, tribunal or other institution,

exclude therefrom such persons as are not directly interested in the proceedings therein.

Independence of the Judiciary

107. (1) The Chief Justice, the President of the Court of Appeal and every other Judge of the Supreme Court and Court of Appeal shall be appointed by the President of the Republic by warrant under his hand.

(2) Every such Judge shall hold office during good behavior, and shall not be removed except by an order of the President made after an address of Parliament, supported by a majority of the total number of Members of Parliament (including those not present) has been presented to the President for such removal on the ground of proved misbehavior or incapacity:

Provided that no resolution for the Presentation of such an address shall be entertained by the Speaker or placed on the Order Paper of Parliament, unless notice of such resolution is signed by not less than one third of the total number of Members of Parliament and sets out full particulars of the alleged misbehavior or incapacity.

(3) Parliament shall be law or by Standing Orders provide for all matters relating to the presentation of such an address, including the procedure for the passing of such resolution, the investigation and proof of the alleged misbehavior or incapacity and the right of such Judge to appear and to be heard in person or by representative.

(4) Every person appointed to be or to act as Chief Justice, President of the Court of Appeal or a Judge of the Supreme Court or Court of Appeal shall not enter upon the duties of his office until he takes and subscribes or makes and subscribes before the President, the oath or the affirmation set out in the Fourth Schedule.

(5) The age of retirement of Judges of the Supreme Court shall be sixty-five years and of Judges of the Court of Appeal shall be sixty-three years.

108. (1) The salaries of the Judges of the Supreme Court and of the Court of Appeal shall be determined by Parliament and shall be charged on the Consolidated Fund.

(2) The salary payable to, and the pension entitlement of, a Judge of the Supreme Court and a Judge of the Court of Appeal shall not be reduced after his appointment.

109. (1) If the Chief Justice or the President of the Court of Appeal is temporarily unable to exercise, perform and discharge the powers, duties and functions of his office, by reason of illness, absence from Sri Lanka or any other cause, the President shall appoint another Judge of the Supreme Court, or of the Court of Appeal, as the case may be, to act in the office of Chief Justice, or President of the Court of Appeal, respectively, during such period.

(2) If any Judge of the Supreme Court or of the Court of Appeal is temporarily unable to exercise, perform and discharge the powers, duties and functions of his office, by reason of illness, absence from Sri Lanka or any other cause, the President may appoint another person to act as a Judge of the Supreme Court or Court of Appeal, as the case may be, during such period.

110. (1) A Judge of the Supreme Court or Court of Appeal may be required by the President of the Republic to perform or discharge any other appropriate duties or functions under any written law.

(2) No Judge of the Supreme Court or Court of Appeal shall perform any other office (whether paid or not) or accept any place of profit or emolument, except as authorized by the Constitution or by written law or with the written consent of the President.

(3) No person who has held office as a permanent Judge of the Supreme Court or of the Court of Appeal may appear, plead, act or practise in any court, tribunal or institution as an attorney-at-law at any time without the written consent of the President.

111. (1) The highest Court of First Instance exercising criminal jurisdiction and created by law shall be called and known as 'The High Court of the Republic of Sri Lanka' and shall exercise such jurisdiction and powers as Parliament may by law vest or ordain.

(2) The Judges of the High Court shall be appointed by the President of the Republic by warrant under his hand and be removable and be subject to disciplinary control by the President on the recommendation of the Judicial Service Commission established under this Chapter.

(3) Subject to the provisions of paragraph (2) of this Article, Parliament may by law provide for matters relating to the retirement of the Judges of such High Court.

112. (1) There shall be a Judicial Service Commission (in this Chapter referred to as the 'Commission') which shall consist of the Chief Justice who shall be the Chairman, and two Judges of the Supreme Court appointed by the President of the Republic.

(2) The quorum for any meeting of the Commission shall be two members.

(3) The Commission shall have power to act notwithstanding any vacancy in its membership, and no act or proceeding by the Commission shall be, or be deemed to be, invalid by reason only of any such vacancy or any defect in the appointment of a member.

(4) A Judge of the Supreme Court appointed as a member of the Commission shall, unless he earlier resigns his office, or is removed therefrom as hereinafter provided or ceases to be a Judge of the Supreme Court, hold office for a period of five years from the date of his appointment, but shall be eligible for reappointment.

(5) The President may for cause assigned remove from office any member of the Commission appointed by him.

(6) The President may grant to any member of the Commission leave from his duties, and may appoint a person qualified to be a member of the Commission to be a temporary member for the period of such leave.

(7) A member of the Commission may be paid such salary or allowance as may be determined by Parliament. Any salary or allowance payable to a member shall be charged on the Consolidated Fund and shall not be diminished during his term of office. The salary so payable shall be in addition to the salary or other emoluments attached to, and received from, his substantive appointment.

(8) The Judicial Service Commission may make

(*a*) rules regarding schemes for recruitment and procedure for the appointment of judicial officers; and

(*b*) provision for such matters as are necessary or expedient for the exercise, performance and discharge of the powers, duties and functions of such Commission.

113. (1) There shall be a Secretary to the Commission who shall be appointed by the President in consultation with the Cabinet of Ministers.

(2) No person holding the office of Secretary of the Commission shall be a judge of any Court of First Instance, either during or after his tenure of office as Secretary.

114. (1) The appointment, transfer, dismissal and disciplinary control of judicial officers, and (notwithstanding anything to the contrary in Chapter IX) of scheduled public officers, is vested in the Commission.

(2) It shall be competent to the Judicial Service Commission by Order published in the *Gazette*, to delegate its powers under paragraph (1) of this Article in respect of such class or category of judicial officers or scheduled public officers as may be specified, to a Committee of not less than three Judges, each of whom shall be a Judge of the Supreme Court or of the Court of Appeal, and one of whom shall be nominated by the Chief Justice as Chairman.

(3) Any judicial officer or scheduled public officer may resign his office by writing under his hand addressed to the Chairman of the Commission.

(4) The Commission may, by Order published in the *Gazette*, delegate to the Secretary to the Commission the power to make all transfers, other than

transfers involving increase of salary, or to make acting appointments in such cases and subject to such limitations as may be specified in the Order.

(5) The Chairman of the Judicial Service Commission or any Judge or of the Supreme Court authorized by the Chairman of the Commission shall have full power and authority to inspect any Court of First Instance or the records, registers or other documents maintained in such court and to hold such inquiry as may be necessary.

(6) In this Article

'appointment' includes an acting or temporary appointment;

'Judicial officer' does not include a Judge of the Supreme Court or of the Court of Appeal or of the High Court;

'scheduled public officer' means the Registrar of the Supreme Court, the Registrar of the Court of Appeal, the Registrar of any Court employed in the Registry of the Supreme Court, the Court of Appeal or any Court of First Instance, included in a category specified in the Fifth Schedule or in such other categories as may be specified by Order made by the Minister in charge of the subject of Justice, and approved by Parliament, and published in the *Gazette*.

115. Every person who, otherwise than in the course of his duty, directly or indirectly, by himself or by any other person, in any manner whatsoever, influences or attempts to influence any decision of the Commission or of any member thereof, shall be guilty of an offence and shall, on conviction by the High Court after trial without a jury, be liable to a fine not exceeding one thousand rupees or to imprisonment for a term not exceeding one year or to both such fine and such imprisonment:

Provided that nothing in this Article shall prohibit any person from giving a certificate or testimonial to any applicant or candidate for any judicial office.

116. (1) Every judge, presiding officer, public officer or other person entrusted by law with judicial powers or functions or with functions under this Chapter or with similar functions under any law enacted by Parliament shall exercise and perform such powers and functions without being subject to any direction or other interference proceeding from any other person except a superior court, tribunal, institution or other person entitled under law to direct or supervise such judge, presiding officer, public officer or such other person in the exercise or performance of such powers or functions.

(2) Every person who, without legal authority, interferes or attempts to interfere with the exercise or performance of the judicial powers or functions of any judge, presiding officer, public officer or such other person as is referred to in paragraph (1) of this Article, shall be guilty of an offence punishable by the High Court on conviction after trial without a jury with imprisonment of either description for a term which may extend to a period of one year or with fine or with both such imprisonment and fine and may, in addition, be disqualified for a period not exceeding seven years from the date of such conviction from being an elector of the President of the Republic or at any election of a Member of Parliament or any

local authority or from holding any public office and from being employed as a public officer.

117. No suit or proceeding shall lie against any member of the Commission for any act which in good faith is done or is purported to be done by him in the performance of his duties or discharge of his functions under the Constitution.

CHAPTER XVI

THE SUPERIOR COURTS

The Supreme Court

118. The Supreme Court of the Republic of Sri Lanka shall be the highest and final superior Court of record in the Republic and shall subject to the provisions of the Constituion exercise

(*a*) jurisdiction in respect of constitutional matters;
(*b*) jurisdiction for the protection of fundamental rights;
(*c*) final appellate jurisdiction;
(*d*) consultative jurisdiction;
(*e*) jurisdiction in election petitions;
(*f*) jurisdiction in respect of any breach of the privileges of Parliament, and
(*g*) jurisd·ction in respect of such other matters which Parliament may by law vest or ordain.

119. (1) The Supreme Court shall consist of the Chief Justice and of not less than six and not more than ten other Judges who shall be appointed as provided in Article 107.

(2) The Supreme Court shall have power to act notwithstanding any vacancy in its membership, and no act or proceeding of the Court shall be, or shall be deemed to be, invalid by reason only of any such vacancy or any defect in the appointment of a Judge.

120. The Supreme Court shall have sole and exclusive jurisdiction to determine any question as to whether any Bill or any provision thereof is inconsistent with the Constitution:

Provided that

(*a*) in the case of a Bill described in its long title as being for the amendment of any provision of the Constitution, or for the repeal and replacement of the Constitution, the only question which the Supreme Court may determine is whether such Bill requires approval by the People at a Referendum by virtue of the provisions of Article 83;

(*b*) where the Cabinet of Ministers certifies that a Bill, which is described in its long title as being for the amendment of any provisions of the Constitution, or for the repeal and replacement of the Constitution, is intended to be passed with the special majority required by Article 83 and submitted to the People by Referendum, the Supreme Court shall have and exercise no jurisdiction in respect of such Bill;

(*c*) where the Cabinet of Ministers certifies that a Bill which is not described in its long title as being for the amendment of any provision of the Constitution, or for the repeal and replacement of the Constitution, is intended to be passed with the special majority required by Article 84, the only question which the Supreme Court may determine is whether such Bill requires approval by the People at a Referendum by virtue of the provisions of Article 83 or whether such Bill is required to comply with paragraphs (1) and (2) of Article 82; or

(*d*) where the Cabinet of Ministers certifies that any provision of any Bill which is not described in its long title as being for the amendment of any provision of the Constitution or for the repeal and replacement of the Constitution, is intended to be passed with the special majority required by Article 84, the only question which the Supreme Court may determine is whether any other provision of such Bill requires to be passed with the special majority required by Article 84 or whether any provision of such Bill requires the approval by the People at a Referendum by virtue of the provisions of Article 83 or whether such Bill is required to comply with the provisions of paragraphs (1) and (2) of Article 82.

121. (1) The jurisdiction of the Supreme Court to ordinarily determine any such question as aforesaid may be invoked by the President by a written reference addressed to the Chief Justice, or by any citizen by a petition in writing addressed to the Supreme Court. Such reference shall be made, or such petition shall be filed, within one week of the Bill being placed on the Order Paper of the Parliament, and a copy thereof shall at the same time be delivered to the Speaker. In this paragraph 'citizen' includes a body, whether incorporated or unincorporated, if not less than three fourths of the members of such body are citizens.

(2) Where the jurisdiction of the Supreme Court has been so invoked no proceedings shall be had in Parliament in relation to such Bill until the determination of the Supreme Court has been made, or the expiration of a period of three weeks from the date of such reference or petition, whichever occurs first.

(3) The Supreme Court shall make and communicate its determination to the President and to the Speaker within three weeks of the making of the reference or the filing of the petition, as the case may be.

122. (1) In the case of a Bill which is, in the view of the Cabinet of Ministers, urgent in the national interest, and bears an endorsement to that effect under the hand of the Secretary to the Cabinet

(*a*) the provisions of Article 78 (1) and of Article 121, shall subject to the provisions of paragraph (2) of this Article, have no application;

(*b*) the President shall by a written reference addressed to the Chief Justice, require the special determination of the Supreme Court as to whether the Bill or any provision thereof is inconsistent with the Constitution. A copy of such reference shall at the same time be delivered to the Speaker;

(*c*) the Supreme Court shall make its determination within twenty-four hours (or such longer period not exceeding three days as the President may specify) of the assembling of the Court, and shall communicate its determination only to the President and the Speaker.

(2) The provisions of paragraph (2) of Article 121 shall, *mutatis mutandis*, apply to such Bill.

123. (1) The determination of the Supreme Court shall be accompanied by the reasons therefor, and shall state whether the Bill or any provision thereof is inconsistent with the Constitution and if so, which provision or provisions of the Constitution.

(2) Where the Supreme Court determines that the Bill or any provision thereof is inconsistent with the Constitution, it shall also state

(*a*) whether such Bill is required to comply with the provisions of paragraphs (1) and (2) of Article 82; or

(*b*) whether such Bill or any provision thereof may only be passed by the special majority required under the provisions of paragraph (2) of Article 84; or

(*c*) whether such Bill or any provision thereof requires to be passed by the special majority required under the provisions of paragraph (2) of Article 84 and approved by the People at a Referendum by virtue of the provisions of Article 83,

and may specify the nature of the amendments which would make the Bill or such provision cease to be inconsistent.

(3) In the case of a Bill endorsed as provided in Article 122, if the Supreme Court entertains a doubt whether the Bill or any provision thereof is inconsistent with the Constitution, it shall be deemed to have been determined that the Bill or such provision of the Bill is inconsistent with the Constitution, and the Supreme Court shall comply with the provisions of paragraphs (1) and (2) of this Article.

(4) Where any Bill, or the provision of any Bill, has been determined, or is deemed to have been determined, to be inconsistent with the Constitution, such Bill or such provision shall not be passed except in the manner stated in the determination of the Supreme Court:

Provided that it shall be lawful for such Bill to be passed after such amendment as would make the Bill cease to be inconsistent with the Constitution.

124. Save as otherwise provided in Articles 120, 121 and 122, no court or tribunal created and established for the administration of justice, or other institution, person or body of persons shall in relation to any Bill, have power or jurisdiction to inquire into, or pronounce upon, the constitutionality of such Bill or its due compliance with the legislative process, on any ground whatsoever.

125. (1) The Supreme Court shall have sole and exclusive jurisdiction to hear and determine any question relating to the interpretation of the Constitution, and accordingly, whenever any such question arises in the course of any proceedings in any other court or tribunal or other institution empowered by law to administer justice or to exercise judicial or quasi-judicial functions, such question shall forthwith be referred to the Supreme Court for determination. The Supreme Court may direct that further proceedings be stayed pending the determination of such question.

(2) The Supreme Court shall determine such question within two months of the date of reference and make any such consequential order as the circumstances of the case may require.

126. (1) The Supreme Court shall have sole and exclusive jurisdiction to hear and determine any question relating to the infringement or imminent infringement by executive or administrative action of any fundamental right or language right declared and recognized by Chapter III or Chapter IV.

(2) Where any person alleges that any such fundamental right or language right relating to such person has been infringed or is about to be infringed by executive or administrative action, he may himself or by an attorney-at-law on his behalf, within one month thereof, in accordance with such rules of court as may be in force, apply to the Supreme Court by way of petition in writing addressed to such Court praying for relief or redress in respect of such infringement. Such application may be proceeded with only with leave to proceed first had and obtained from the Supreme Court, which leave may be granted or refused, as the case may be, by not less than two Judges.

(3) Where in the course of hearing in the Court of Appeal into an application for orders in the nature of a writ of habeas corpus, *certiorari*, prohibition, *procedendo, mandamus* or *quo warranto*, it appears to such Court that there is prima facie evidence of an infringement of the provisions of Chapter III or Chapter IV by a party to such application, such Court shall forthwith refer such matter for determination by the Supreme Court.

(4) The Supreme Court shall have power to grant such relief or make such directions as it may deem just and equitable in the circumstance in respect of any petition or reference referred to in paragraphs (2) and (3) of this Article if in its opinion there is no infringement of a fundamental right or language right.

(5) The Supreme Court shall hear and finally dispose of any petition or reference under this Article within two months of the filing of such petition or the making of such reference.

127. (1) The Supreme Court shall, subject to the Constitution, be the final Court of civil and criminal appellate jurisdiction for and within the Republic of Sri Lanka for the correction of all errors in fact or in law which shall be committed by the Court of Appeal or any Court of First Instance, tribunal or other institution and the judgments and orders of the Supreme Court shall in all cases be final and conclusive in all such matters.

(2) The Supreme Court shall, in the exercise of its jurisdiction, have sole

and exclusive cognizance by way of appeal from any order, judgment, decree, or sentence made by the Court of Appeal, where any appeal lies in law to the Supreme Court and it may affirm, reverse or vary any such order, judgment, decree or sentence of the Court of Appeal and may issue such directions to any Court of First Instance or order a new trial or further hearing in any proceedings as the justice of the case may require, and may also call for and admit fresh or additional evidence if the interests of justice so demands and may in such event, direct that such evidence be recorded by the Court of Appeal or any Court of First Instance.

128. (1) An appeal shall lie to the Supreme Court from any final order, judgment, decree or sentence, of the Court of Appeal in any matter or proceedings, whether civil or criminal, which involves a substantial question of law, if the Court of Appeal grants leave to appeal to the Supreme Court *ex mero motu* or at the instance of any aggrieved party to such matter or proceedings;

(2) The Supreme Court may, in its discretion, grant special leave to appeal to the Supreme Court from any final or interlocutory order, judgment, decree, or sentence made by the Court of Appeal in any matter or proceedings, whether civil or criminal, where the Court of Appeal has refused to grant leave to appeal to the Supreme Court, or where in the opinion of the Supreme Court, the case or matter is fit for review by the Supreme Court:

Provided that the Supreme Court shall grant leave to appeal in every matter or proceedings in which it is satisfied that the question to be decided is of public or general importance.

(3) Any appeal from an order or judgement of the Court of Appeal, made or given in the exercise of its jurisdiction under Article 139, 140, 141, 142 or 143 to which the President, a Minister, a Deputy Minister or a public officer in his official capacity is a party, shall be heard and determined within two months of the date of filing thereof.

(4) An appeal shall lie directly to the Supreme Court on any matter and in the manner specifically provided for by any other law passed by Parliament.

129. (1) If at any time it appears to the President of the Republic that a question of law or fact has arisen or is likely to arise which is of such nature and of such public importance that it is expedient to obtain the opinion of the Supreme Court upon it, he may refer that question to that Court for consideration and the Court may, after such hearing as it thinks fit, within the period specified in such reference or within such time as may be extended by the President, report to the President its opinion thereon.

(2) Where the Speaker refers to the Supreme Court for inquiry and report all or any of the allegation or allegations, as the case may be, contained in any such resolution as is referred to in Article 38 (2) (*a*), the Supreme Court shall in accordance with Article 38 (2) (*d*) inquire into such allegation or allegations and shall report its determination to the Speaker within two months of the date of reference.

(3) Such opinion, determination and report shall be expressed after consideration by at least five Judges of the Supreme Court, of whom, unless he otherwise directs, the Chief Justice shall be one.

(4) Every proceeding under paragraph (1) of this Article shall be held in private unless the Court for special reasons otherwise directs.

130. The Supreme Court shall have the power to hear and determine and make such orders as provided for by law on

(*a*) any legal proceeding relating to the election of the President;

(*b*) any appeal from an order or judgment of the Court of Appeal in an election petition case:

Provided that the hearing and determination of a proceeding relating to the election of the President shall be by at least five Judges of the Supreme Court of whom, unless he otherwise directs, the Chief Justice shall be one.

131. The Supreme Court shall have according to law the power to take cognizance of and punish any person for the breach of the privileges of Parliament.

132. (1) The several jurisdictions of the Supreme Court shall be ordinarily exercised at Colombo unless the Chief Justice otherwise directs.

(2) The jurisdiction of the Supreme Court may be exercised in different matters at the same time by the several Judges of that Court sitting apart:

Provided that its jurisdiction shall, subject to the provisions of the Constitution, be ordinarily exercised at all times by not less than three Judges of the Court sitting together as the Supreme Court.

(3) The Chief Justice may

(i) of his own motion; or

(ii) at the request of two or more Judges hearing any matter; or

(iii) on the application of a party to any appeal, proceeding or matter if the question involved is in the opinion of the Chief Justice one of general and public importance,

direct that such appeal, proceeding or matter be heard by a Bench comprising five or more Judges of the Supreme Court.

(4) The judgment of the Supreme Court shall, when it is not an unanimous decision, be the decision of the majority.

133. (1) If at any time there should not be quorum of the Judges of the Supreme Court available to hold or continue any sittings of the Court, the Chief Justice may with the previous consent of the President request in writing the attendance at the sittings of the Court as an *ad hoc* Judge, for such period as may be necessary, of the President of the Court of Appeal or any Judge of the Court of Appeal.

(2) It shall be the duty of such a Judge who had been so requested, in priority to other duties of his office, to attend the sittings of the Supreme Court at the time and for the period for which his attendance is required, and while so attending he shall have all the jurisdictions, powers and privileges, and shall perform the duties, of a Judge of the Supreme Court.

134. (1) The Attorney-General shall be noticed and have the right to be heard in all proceedings in the Supreme Court in the exercise of its jurisdiction under Articles 120, 121, 122, 125, 126, 129 (1) and 131.

(2) Any party to any proceedings in the Supreme Court in the exercise of

its jurisdiction shall have the right to be heard in such proceedings either in person or by representation by an attorney-at-law.

(3) The Supreme Court may in its discretion grant to any other person or his legal representative such hearing as may appear to the Court to be necessary in the exercise of its jurisdiction under this Chapter.

135. The Registry of the Supreme Court shall be in charge of an officer designated the Registrar of the Supreme Court who shall be subject to the supervision, direction and control of the Chief Justice.

136. (1) Subject to the provisions of the Constitution and of any law the Chief Justice with any three Judges of the Supreme Court nominated by him, may, from time to time, make rules regulating generally the practice and procedure of the Court including

(*a*) rules as to the procedure for hearing appeals and other matters pertaining to appeals including the terms under which appeals to the Supreme Court and the Court of Appeal are to be entertained and provision for the dismissal of such appeals for non-compliance with such rules;

(*b*) rules as to the proceedings in the Supreme Court and Court of Appeal in the exercise of the several jurisdictions conferred on such Courts by the Constitution or by any law, including the time within which such matters may be instituted or brought before such Courts and the dismissal of such matters for non-compliance with such rules;

(*c*) rules as to the granting of bail;

(*d*) rules as to the stay of proceedings;

(*e*) rules providing for the summary determination of any appeal or any other matter before such Court by petition or otherwise, which appears to the Court to be frivolous and vexatious or brought for the purpose of delay;

(*f*) the preparation of copies of records for the purpose of appeal or other proceedings in the Supreme Court and Court of Appeal;

(*g*) the admission, enrollment, suspension and removal of attorneys-at-law and the appointment of senior attorneys-at-law and the rules of conduct and etiquette for such attorneys-at-law;

(*h*) the attire of Judges, attorneys-at-law, officers of court and persons attending the courts in Sri Lanka whether established by the Constitution, or by Parliament or by existing law;

(*i*) the manner in which panels of jurors may be prepared, and the mode of summoning, empanelling and challenging of jurors;

(*j*) proceedings of Fiscals and other ministerial officers of such courts and the process of such courts and the mode of executing the same;

(*k*) the binding effect of the decision of the Supreme Court;

(*l*) all matters of practice and procedure including the nature and extent of costs that may be awarded, the manner in which such costs may be taxed and the stamping of documents in the Supreme Court, Court of Appeal, High Court and Courts of First Instance not specially provided by or under any law.

(2) Every rule made under this Article shall be published in the *Gazette* and shall come into operation on the date of such publication or on such later date as may be specified in such rule.

(3) All rules made under this Article shall as soon as convenient after their publication in the *Gazette* be brought before Parliament for approval. Any such rule which is not so approved shall be deemed to be rescinded as from the date it was not so approved, but without prejudice to anything previously done thereunder.

(4) The Chief Justice and any three Judges of the Supreme Court nominated by him may amend, alter or revoke any such rules of court and such amendment, alteration or revocation of the rules will operate in the like manner as set out in the preceding paragraph with reference to the making of the rules of court.

The Court of Appeal

137. The Court of Appeal shall consist of the President of the Court of Appeal and not less than six and not more than eleven other Judges who shall be appointed as provided in Article 107.

138. (1) The Court of Appeal shall have and exercise subject to the provisions of the Constitution or of any law, an appellate jurisdiction for the correction of all errors in fact or in law which shall be committed by any Court of First Instance, tribunal or other institution and sole and exclusive cognizance, by way of appeal, revision and *restitutio in integrum*, of all causes, suits, actions, prosecutions, matters and things of which such Court of First Instance, tribunal or other institution may have taken cognizance:

Provided that no judgment, decree or order of any court shall be reversed or varied on account of any error, defect or irregularity, which has not prejudiced the substantial rights of the parties or occasionad a failure of justice.

(2) The Court of Appeal shall also have and exercise all such powers and jurisdiction, appellate and original, as Parliament may by law vest or ordain.

139. (1) The Court of Appeal may in the exercise of its jurisdiction, affirm, reverse, correct or modify any order, judgment, decree or sentence according to law or it may give directions to such Court of First Instance, tribunal or other institution or order a new trial or further hearing upon such terms as the Court of Appeal shall think fit.

(2) The Court of Appeal may further receive and admit new evidence additional to, or supplementary of, the evidence already taken in the Court of First Instance touching the matters at issue in any original case, suit, prosecution or action, as the justice of the case may require.

140. Subject to the provisions of the Constitution, the Court of Appeal shall have full power and authority to inspect and examine the records of any Court of First Instance or tribunal or other institution, and grant and issue, according to law, orders in the nature of writs of *certiorari*, prohibition, *procedendo, mandamus* and *quo warranto* against the judge of any Court of First Instance or tribunal or other institution or any other person.

141. The Court of Appeal may grant and issue orders in the nature of writs of habeas corpus to bring up before such Court

(*a*) the body of any person to be dealt with according to law; or

(*b*) the body of any person illegally or improperly detained in public or private custody,

and to discharge or remand any person so brought up or otherwise deal with such person according to law:

Provided that it shall be lawful for the Court of Appeal to require the body of such person to be brought up before the most convenient Court of First Instance and to direct the judge of such court to inquire into and report upon the acts of the alleged imprisonment or detention and to make such provision for the interim custody of the body produced as to such court shall seem right; and the Court of Appeal shall upon the receipt of such report, make order to discharge or remand the person so alleged to be imprisoned or detained or otherwise deal with such person according to law, and the Court of First Instance shall conform to, and carry into immediate effect, the order so pronounced or made by the Court of Appeal:

Provided further that if provision be made by law for the exercise by any court, of jurisdiction in respect of the custody and control of minor children, then the Court of Appeal, if satisfied that any dispute regarding the custody of any such minor child may more properly be dealt with by such court, direct the parties to make application in that court in respect of the custody of such minor child.

142. The Court of Appeal may direct

(i) that a prisoner detained in any prison be brought before a court martial or any Commissioners acting under the authority of any Commission from the President of the Republic for trial or to be examined relating to any matters pending before any such court-martial or Commissioners respectively; or

(ii) that a prisoner detained in prison be removed from one custody to another for purposes of trial.

143. The Court of Appeal shall have the power to grant and issue injunctions to prevent any irremediable mischief which might ensue before a party making an application for such injunction could prevent the same by bringing an action in any Court of First Instance;

Provided that it shall not be lawful for the Court of Appeal to grant an injunction to prevent a party to any action in any court from appealing to or prosecuting an appeal to the court of Appeal or to prevent any party to any action in any court from insisting upon any ground of action, defence or appeal, or to prevent any person from suing or prosecuting in any court, except where such person has instituted two separate actions in two different courts for and in respect of the same cause of action, in which case the Court of Appeal shall have the power to intervene by restraining him from prosecuting one or other of such actions as to it may seem fit.

144. The Court of Appeal shall have and exercise jurisdiction to try election petitions in respect of the election to the membership of Parliament in terms of any law for the time being applicable in that behalf.

145. The Court of Appeal may, *ex mero motu* or on any application made, call for, inspect and examine any record of any Court of First Instance and in the exercise of its revisionary powers may make any order thereon as the interests of justice may require.

146. (1) The Court of Appeal shall ordinarily exercise its jurisdiction at Colombo:

Provided however that the Chief Justice may from time to time when he deems it so expedient direct that the Court of Appeal shall hold its sittings and exercise its jurisdiction in any judicial zone or district, specified in the direction.

(2) The jurisdiction of the Court of Appeal may be exercised in different matters at the same time by the several Judges of the Court sitting apart:

Provided that

(i) its jurisdiction in respect of judgments and orders of the High Court shall be exercised by at least three Judges of the Court;

(ii) its jurisdiction in respect of judgment and orders of all other Courts of First Instance, tribunals and other institutions shall be exercised by at least two Judges of the Court;

(iii) its jurisdiction in respect of its powers as contained in Articles 140, 141, 142, and 143 shall be exercised by not less than two Judges of the Court, unless the President of the Court of Appeal by general or special order otherwise directs;

(iv) its jurisdiction in respect of its powers under Article 144 shall be exercised by the President of the Court of Appeal or any Judge of that Court nominated by such President or one or more of such Judges nominated by such President, of whom such President may be one.

(3) In the event of any difference of opinion between two Judges constituting the Bench, the decision of the Court shall be suspended until three Judges shall be present to review such matter.

(4) The judgment of the Court of Appeal, shall when it is not an unanimous decision, be the decision of the majority.

147. The Registry of the Court of Appeal shall be in charge of an officer designated as the Registrar of the Court of Appeal who shall be subject to the supervision, direction and control of the President of the Court of Appeal.

CHAPTER XVII

FINANCE

148. Parliament shall have full control over public finance. No tax, rate or any other levy shall be imposed by any local authority or any other public authority, except by or under the authority of a law passed by Parliament or of any existing law.

149. (1) The funds of the Republic not allocated by law to specific purposes shall form one Consolidated Fund into which shall be paid the produce of all taxes, imposts, rates and duties and all other revenues and receipts of the Republic not allocated to specific purposes.

(2) The interest on the public debt, sinking fund payments, the costs, charges and expenses incidental to the collection, management and receipt of the Consolidated Fund and such other expenditure as Parliament may determine shall be charged on the Consolidated Fund.

150. (1) Save as otherwise expressly provided in paragraphs (3) and (4) of this Article, no sum shall be withdrawn from the Consolidated Fund except under the authority of a warrant under the hand of the Minister in charge of the subject of Finance.

(2) No such warrant shall be issued unless the sum has by resolution of Parliament or by any law been granted for specified public services for the financial year during which the withdrawal is to take place or is otherwise lawfully charged on the Consolidated Fund.

(3) Where the President dissolves Parliament before the Appropriation Bill for the financial year has passed into law, he may, unless Parliament shall have already made provision, authorize the issue from the Consolidated Fund and the expenditure of such sums as he may consider necessary for the public services until the expiry of a period of three months from the date on which the new Parliament is summoned to meet.

(4) Where the President dissolves Parliament and fixes a date or dates for a General Election the President may, unless Parliament has already made provison in that behalf, authorize the issue from the Consolidated Fund and the expenditure of such sums as he may, after consultation with the Commissioner of Elections, consider necessary for such elections.

151. (1) Notwithstanding any of the provisions of Article 149, Parliament may by law create a Contingencies Fund for the purpose of providing for urgent and unforeseen expenditure.

(2) The Minister in charge of the subject of Finance, if satisfied

(*a*) that there is need for any such expenditure, and

(*b*) that no provision for such expenditure exists,

may, with the consent of the President, authorize provision to be made therefor by an advance from the Contingencies Fund.

(3) As soon as possible after every such advance, a Supplementary

Estimate shall be presented to Parliament for the purpose of replacing the amount so advanced.

152. No Bill or motion, authorizing the disposal of, or the imposition of charges upon, the Consolidated Fund or other funds of the Republic, or the imposition of any tax or the repeal, augmentation or reduction of any tax for the time being in force shall be introduced in Parliament except by a Minister, and unless such Bill or motion has been approved either by the Cabinet of Ministers or in such manner as the Cabinet of Ministers may authorize.

153. (1) There shall be an Auditor-General who shall be appointed by the President and who shall hold office during good behavior.

(2) The salary of the Auditor-General shall be determined by Parliament, shall be charged on the Consolidated Fund and shall not be diminished during his term of office.

(3) The office of the Auditor-General shall become vacant

(*a*) upon his death;

(*b*) on his resignation in writing addresses to the President;

(*c*) on his attaining the age of sixty years;

(*d*) on his removal by the President on account of ill health or physical or mental infirmity; or

(*e*) on his removal by the President upon an address of Parliament.

(4) Whenever the Auditor-General is unable to discharge the functions of his office, the President may appoint a person to act in the place of the Auditor-General.

154. (1) The Auditor-General shall audit the accounts of all departments of Government, the Offices of the Cabinet of Ministers, the Judicial Service Commission, the Public Service Commission, the Parliamentary Commissioner for Administration, the Secretary-General of Parliament and the Commissioner of Elections, local authorities, public corporations and business or other undertakings vested in the Government under any written law.

(2) Notwithstanding the provisions of paragraph (1) of this Article, the Minister in charge of any such public corporation or business or other undertaking may, with the concurrence of the Minister in charge of the subject of Finance, and in consultation with the Auditor-General, appoint a qualified auditor or auditors to audit the accounts of such public corporation or business or other undertaking. Where such appointment has been made by the Minister, the Auditor-General may, in writing, inform such auditor or auditors that he proposes to utilize his or their services for the performance and discharge of the Auditor-General's duties and functions in relation to such public corporation, business or other undertaking and thereupon such auditor or auditors shall act under the direction and control of the Auditor-General.

(3) The Auditor-General shall also perform and discharge such duties and functions as may be prescribed by Parliament by law.

(4) (*a*) The Auditor-General may for the purpose of the performance and discharge of his duties and functions engage the services of a

qualified auditor or auditors who shall act under his direction and control.

(*b*) If the Auditor-General is of opinion that it is necessary to obtain assistance in the examination of any technical, professional or scientific problem relevant to the audit, he may engage the services of

(i) a person not being an employee of the department, body or authority the accounts of which are being audited, or

(ii) any technical or professional or scientific institution which has any interest in the management of the affairs of such department, body or authority,

and such person or institution shall act under his direction and control.

(5) (*a*) The Auditor-General or any person authorized by him shall in the performance and discharge of his duties and functions be entitled

(i) to have access to all books, records, returns and other documents;

(ii) to have access to stores and other property; and

(iii) to be furnished with such information and explanations as may be necessary for the performance of such duties and functions.

(*b*) Every qualified auditor appointed to audit the accounts of any public corporation, or business or other undertaking, or any person authorized by such auditor shall be entitled to like access, information and explanations in relation to such public corporation, or business or other undertaking.

(6) The Auditor-General shall within ten months after the close of each financial year and as and when he deems it necessary report to Parliament on the performance and discharge of his duties and functions under the Constitution.

(7) Every qualified auditor appointed under the provision of paragraph (2) of this Article shall submit a copy thereof to the Auditor-General.

(8) In this Article, 'qualified auditor' means

(*a*) an individual who, being a member of the Institute of Chartered Accountants of Sri Lanka, or of any other Institute established by law, possesses a certificate to practise as an Accountant issued by the Council of such Institute; or

(*b*) a firm of Accountants each of the resident partners of which, being a member of the Institute of Chartered Accountants of Sri Lanka or of any other Institute established by law, possesses a certificate to practise as an Accountant issued by the Council of such Institute.

CHAPTER XVIII

PUBLIC SECURITY

155. (1) The Public Security Ordinance as amended and in force immediately prior to the commencement of the Constitution shall be deemed to be a law enacted by Parliament.

(2) The power to make emergency regulations under the Public Security Ordinance or the law for the time being in force relating to public security shall include the power to make regulations having the legal effect of over-riding, amending or suspending the operation of the provisions of any law, except the provisions of the Constitution.

(3) The provisions of any law relating to public security, empowering the President to make emergency regulations which have the legal effect of over-riding, amending or suspending the operation of the provisions of any law, shall not come into operation, except upon the making of a Proclamation under such law, bringing such provisions into operation.

(4) Upon the making of such a Proclamation, the occasion thereof shall, subject to the other provisions of this Article, be forthwith communicated to Parliament, and, accordingly

(i) if such Proclamation is issued after the dissolution of Parliament such Proclamation shall operate as a summoning of Parliament to meet on the tenth day after such Proclamation, unless the Proclamation appoints an earlier date for the meeting which shall not be less than three days from the date of the Proclamation; and the Parliament so summoned shall be kept in session until the expiry, or revocation of such or any further Proclamation or until the conclusion of the General Election whichever event occurs earlier and shall thereupon stand dissolved;

(ii) if Parliament is at the date of the making of such Proclamation, separated by any such adjournment or prorogation as will not expire within ten days, a Proclamation shall be issued for the meeting of Parliament within ten days.

(5) Where the provision of any law relating to public security have been brought into operation by the making of a Proclamation under such law, such Proclamation shall, subject to the succeeding provisions of this Article, be in operation for a period of one months from the date of the making thereof, but without prejudice to the earlier revocation of such Proclamation or to the making of a further Proclamation at or before the end of that period.

(6) Where such provisions as are referred to in paragraph (3) of this Article, of any law relating to public security, have been brought into operation by the making of a Proclamation under such law, such Proclamation shall expire after a period of fourteen days from the date on which such provisions shall have come

into operation, unless such Proclamation is approved by a resolution of Parliament:

Provided that if

(*a*) Parliament stands dissolved at the date of the making of such Proclamation, or

(*b*) Parliament is at such date separated by any such adjournment or prorogation as is referred to in paragraph (4) (ii) of this Article; or

(*c*) Parliament does not meet when summoned to meet as provided in paragraphs (4) (i) and (4) (ii) of this Article,

then such Proclamation shall expire at the end of ten days after the date on which Parliament shall next meet and sit, unless approved by a resolution at such meeting of Parliament.

(7) Upon the revocation of a Proclamation referred to in paragraph (6) of this Article within a period of fourteen days from the date on which the provisions of any law relating to public security shall have come into operation or upon the expiry of such a Proclamation in accordance with the provisions of paragraph (6), no Proclamation made within thirty days next ensuing shall come into operation until the making thereof shall have been approved by a resolution of Parliament.

(8) Where such provisions as are referred to in paragraph (6) of this Article, of any law relating to public security, shall have been in operation for a period of ninety consecutive days or a period of ninety days in the aggregate during six consecutive calendar months, no Proclamation bringing such provisions of any law into operation, shall, if made at any time during the succeeding six calendar be in operation for more than ten days from the date on which such provisions are brought into operation by such Proclamation, unless such Proclamation is approved by a resolution of Parliament passed by at least two thirds of the whole number of Members of Parliament (including those not present) voting in favor of such resolution:

(*a*) Parliament stands dissolved at the date of the making of such Proclamation, or

(*b*) Parliament is, at such date, separated by any such adjournment or prorogation, as is referred to in paragraph (4) (ii) of this Article, or;

(*c*) Parliament does not meet when summoned to meet as provided by paragraph (4) (i) of this Article,

then such Proclamation shall expire at the end of ten days after the date on which Parliament shall next meet and sit unless approved by Parliament by a resolution passed by at least two thirds of the whole number of Members of Parliament (including those not present) voting in favor of such resolution.

(9) Upon the revocation of a Proclamation referred to in paragraph (8) of this Article within a period of ten days from the date on which the provisions of any law relating to public security shall have come into operation or upon the expiry of such a Proclamation in accordance with the provisions of paragraph (8) of this Article, no Proclamation made within ninety days next ensuing shall come

into operation until making thereof shall have been approved by a resolution of Parliament passed by at least two thirds of the whole number of Members of Parliament (including those not present) voting in favor of such resolution.

(10) If Parliament does not approve any Proclamation bringing such provisions as are referred to in paragraph (3) of this Article into operation, such Proclamation shall, immediately upon such disapproval, cease to be valid and of any force in law but without prejudice to anything lawfully done thereunder.

(11) If the making of a Proclamation cannot be communicated to and approved by Parliament by reason of the fact that Parliament does not meet when summoned, nothing contained in paragraph (6), (7), (8) or (9) of this Article, shall affect the validity or operation of such Proclamation:

Provided that in such event, Parliament shall again be summoned to meet as early as possible thereafter.

CHAPTER XIX

THE PARLIAMENTARY COMMISSIONER FOR ADMINISTRATION

156. (1) Parliament shall by law provide for the establishment of the office of the Parliamentary Commissioner for Administration (Ombudsman) charged with the duty of investigating and reporting upon complaints or allegations of the infringements of fundamental rights and other injustices by public officers and officers of public corporations, local authorities and other like institutions, in accordance with and subject to the provisions of such law.

(2) The Parliamentary Commissioner for Administration shall be appointed by the President and shall hold office during good behavior.

(3) The salary of the Parliamentary Commissioner for Administration shall be determined by Parliament and shall not be diminished during his term of office.

(4) The office of the Parliamentary Commissioner for Administration shall become vacant

(*a*) upon his death;

(*b*) on his resignation in writing addressed to the President;

(*c*) on his attaining the age fixed by law;

(*d*) on his removal by the President on account of ill health or physical or mental infirmity; or

(*e*) on his removal by the President on an address of Parliament.

(5) Whenever the Parliamentary Commissioner for Administration is unable to perform and discharge the duties and functions of his office, the President shall appoint a person to act in his place.

CHAPTER XX

GENERAL

157. Where parliament by resolution passed by not less than two thirds of the whole number of Members of Parliament (including those not present) voting in its favor, approves as being essential for the development of the national economy, any Treaty or Agreement between the Government of Sri Lanka and the Government of any foreign State for the promotion and protection of the investments in Sri Lanka of such foreign State, its nationals, or of corporations, companies and other associations incorporated or constituted under its laws, such Treaty or Agreement shall have the force of law in Sri Lanka, and otherwise than in the interests of national security no written law shall be enacted or made, and no executive or administrative action shall be taken, in contravention of the provisions of such Treaty or Agreement.

158. Where any person is empowered under the provisions of the Constitution to delegate any power, duty or function to any other person, such person delegating such power, duty or function may, notwithstanding such delegation, exercise, perform or discharge such power, duty or function and may at any time revoke such delegation.

In this Article, 'person' includes any body of persons or any authority.

159. Where the Speaker is unable to discharge the functions of his office, the powers, duties and functions conferred or imposed on, or assigned to, the Speaker by any provision of the Constitution, other than by Articles 31 (4), 37, 38 (2) (*b*), (39 (2) and 40, may be exercised, performed or discharged by the Deputy Speaker.

CHAPTER XXI

TRANSITIONAL PROVISIONS

160. Notwithstanding anything to the contrary in any other provision of the Constitution, the person holding the office of President immediately before the commencement of the Constitution shall be the first President under the Constitution and shall be deemed for all purposes to have been elected as the President of the Republic, and shall hold office for a period of six years from February 4, 1978.

The President shall, notwithstanding the provisions of Article 32, be deemed to have assumed office immediately upon the commencement of the Constitution and shall be entitled thereupon to exercise, perform and discharge all the powers, duties and functions conferred or imposed on, or assigned to, the President by the constitution or otherwise. The President shall, as soon as possible thereafter at a sitting of Parliament, take and subscribe the oath or make and subscribe the affirmation set out in the Fourth Schedule.

161. Notwithstanding anything to the contrary in any other provision of the Constitution

(*a*) the first Parliament shall consist of one hundred and sixty-eight members, and subject to the succeeding provisions of this Article all persons who immediately before the commencement of the Constitution were members of the National State Assembly shall be deemed to have been elected as Members of Parliament;

(*b*) (i) if the election, as a Member of the National State Assembly, of a person deemed to have been elected to the first Parliament is declared void under the law for the time being in force and no other person is determined to have been duly returned or elected, the seat of such Member shall be vacant, and an election to the electoral district as existing immediately prior to the commencement of the Constitution, shall be held in accordance with the law relating to elections to the National State Assembly in force immediately before the commencement of the Constitution and on the basis of the register of electors applicable to such electoral district which was operative on the day immediately preceding the commencement of the Constitution;

(ii) the law applicable to election petitions in relation to an election held as provided in sub-paragraph (i) shall be the law in force upon the commencement of the Constitution and in the event of such an election being declared void the provisions of sub-paragraph (i) shall, *mutatis mutandis*, apply;

(*c*) if the election as a Member of the National State Assembly of a person who is deemed to have been elected to the first Parliament is declared void or undue and any other person is determined to have been duly returned or elected such other person shall be deemed to have been duly elected as a Member of the first Parliament;

(*d*) (i) where immediately before the commencement of the Constitution there was a vacancy in the membership of the National State Assembly or where a vacancy in the membership of the first Parliament occurs otherwise than under the provisions of paragraph (*b*) of this Article, such vacancy shall be filled in the manner provided in sub-paragraph (iii) hereof;

(ii) where a Member ceases by resignation, expulsion or otherwise to be a member of the recognized political party to which he belonged upon the commencement of the Constitution, his seat shall become vacant upon the expiration of one month from the date he ceased to be a member of such party. The Secretary of such party shall, in every case where a Member ceases to be a member of such party, inform the Secretary-General of Parliament of the fact and date thereof:

Provided, however, that in the case of the expulsion of a Member the provisions of the proviso to paragraph (13) (*a*) of Article 99 shall, *mutatis mutandis*, apply;

(iii) where a vacancy as is referred to in sub-paragraph (i) or (ii) has occurred, the Secretary-General of Parliament shall forthwith inform the Commission of Elections of such vacancy. The Commissioner of Elections shall thereupon require the Secretary of the political party to which such Member belonged to nominate a member of such party to fill such vacancy. Upon receipt of such nomination the Commissioner shall declare such person to be the Member for the electoral district in respect of which the vacancy occurred;

(*e*) unless sooner dissolved, the first Parliament shall continue for six years from August 4, 1977, and no longer, and the expiry of the aforesaid period of six years shall operate as a dissolution of Parliament, and the provisions of Article 70 (5) (*b*) shall apply.

162. (1) The provisions of Article 98, other than paragraphs (8) and (9) thereof, and Article 99 shall not come into operation until the General Election held upon the dissolution of the first Parliament.

(2) If at the time of such dissolution the notification of electoral districts has not been proclaimed as required by Article 97, the electoral districts for the first General Election to be held upon the dissolution of the first Parliament, and the number of Members which each such district shall be entitled to return by virtue of the provisions of paragraph (4) of Article 96, shall be as set out in the Sixth Schedule and accordingly, registers of electors shall be prepared and certified for each such electoral district, and unless Parliament otherwise provides, such registers shall be prepared on the basis of the register of electors in force immediately before the commencement of the Constitution.

163. All Judges of the Supreme Court and the High Courts established by the Administration of Justice Law, No. 44 of 1973, holding office on the day immediately before the commencement of the Constitution cease to hold office.

164. Subject to the provisions of Article 163 every person who immediately before the commencement of the Constitution

(*a*) held office in any court or tribunal deemed, by virtue of the provisions of paragraph (2) of Article 105, to be a court or tribunal created and established by Parliament,

(*b*) was in the service of the Republic, any local authority or any public corporation,

(*c*) held office in any local authority or public corporation, or

(*d*) held any appointment under any existing written law,

shall continue in such service or hold such office or appointment under the same terms and conditions.

165. (1) Every public officer, judicial officer and every other person as is required by the Constitution to take an oath or make an affirmation on entering upon the duties of his office, every holder of an office required under the existing law to take an official oath and every person in the service of every local authority and of every public corporation shall take and subscribe the affirmation set out in the Fourth Schedule. Any such public officer, judicial officer, person or holder of an office failing to take and subscribe such oath or make and subscribe such affirmation after the commencement of the Constitution on or before such date as may be prescribed by the Prime Minister by Order published in the *Gazette* shall cease to be in service or hold office.

(2) The Minister in charge of the subject of Public Administration may, in his sole discretion, permit any public officer, judicial officer, person or holder of an office referred to in paragraph (1) of this Article, to take the oath or make the affirmation referred to in that paragraph after the prescribed date if he is satisfied that the failure to take the oath or make the affirmation within the time prescribed was occasioned by illness or some other unavoidable cause. On his taking such oath or making such affirmation, he shall continue in service or hold office as if he had taken such oath or made such affirmation in the time prescribed under paragraph (1) of this Article.

(3) The President may by Proclamation

(*a*) exclude the application of the provisions of paragraph (1) of this Article to any category of public officers,

(*b*) prescribe the persons or categories of persons who may administer such oath or affirmation in addition to the persons who are empowered under the existing law to administer oaths or affirmations.

166. Unless Parliament otherwise provides, the Republic of Sri Lanka shall continue to possess and exercise all powers, privileges, immunities and rights whatsoever possessed, exercised or exercisable immediately prior to the commencement of the Constitution.

167. All rights and all duties or obligations, howsoever arising, of the Government of Sri Lanka and subsisting immediately prior to the commencement of the Constitution shall be rights, duties and obligations of the Government of the Republic of Sri Lanka under the Constitution.

168. (1) Unless Parliament otherwise provides, all laws, written laws and unwritten laws, in force immediately before the commencement of the Constitution, shall, *mutatis mutandis*, and except as otherwise expressly provided in the Constitution, continue in force.

(2) Save as otherwise provided in the Constitution, existing laws, written laws and unwritten laws are not and shall not in any manner be deemed to be provisions of the Constitution.

(3) Wherever the Constitution provides that any law, written law or unwritten law or any provision of the Constitution shall continue in force until or unless Parliament otherwise provides, any law enacted by Parliament so providing may be passed by a majority of the Members present and voting.

(4) Whenever the Constitution provides that any provision of any existing written law shall continue in force until or unless Parliament otherwise provides and the exising written law referred to consists of subordinate legislation, the provision that such existing written law shall continue in force until or unless

Parliament otherwise provides shall not in any manner be deemed to derogate from the power of the person or body on whom the power to make and, when made, to amend, vary, rescind or revoke such subordiante legislation is conferred, to exercise the power so conferred until or unless Parliament otherwise provides.

(5) Unless the Constitution otherwise provides, the past operation of any law in force prior to the commencement of the Constitution or anything duly done or suffered or any offence committed or any right, liberty, obligation or penalty acquired or incurred under any law in force prior to the commencement of the Constitution shall not in any manner be affected or be deemed to be affected by the Constitution coming into force.

(6) All actions, prosecutions, proceedings, matters or things, including proceedings of Commissions appointed or established by or under any existing written law, pending or uncompleted on the commencement of the Constitution shall, subject to the provisions of the Constitution and, *mutatis mutandis*, be deemed to continue and may be carried on and completed after the commencement of the Constitution.

169. Unless Parliament otherwise provides

(1) any provisions of the Administration of Justice Law, No. 44 of 1973, which are inconsistent with the provisions of the Constitution, shall, to the extent of such inconsistency, be deemed to be repealed;

(2) the Supreme Court established by the Administration of Justice Law, No. 44 of 1973, shall, on the commencement of the Constitution, cease to exist, and accordingly the provisions of that Law relating to the establishment of the said Supreme Court, shall be deemed to have been repealed. Unless otherwise provided in the Constitution, every reference in any existing written law to the Supreme Court shall be deemed to be a reference to the Court of Appeal;

(3) all appellate proceedings including proceedings by way of revision, case stated and *restitutio in integrum* pending in the Supreme Court established under the Administration of Justice Law, No. 44 of 1973, on the day preceding the commencement of the Constitution, shall stand removed to the Court of Appeal and the Court of Appeal shall have jurisdiction to take cognizance of and to hear and determine the same; and the judgments and orders of the Supreme Court aforesaid delivered or made before the commencement of the Constitution in appellate proceedings shall have the same force and effect as if they had been delivered or made by the Court of Appeal;

(4) all original proceedings by way of applications for the issue of high prerogative Writs and application for any other relief pending in the Supreme Court as well as all applications for injunctions pending in the High Court established under the Administration of Justice Law No. 44 of 1973, on the date immediately preceding the commencement of the Constitution shall stand removed to the Court of Appeal and such Court shall have jurisdiction to take cognizance of, hear and determine or to continue and complete the same, and the judgments and orders of the Supreme Court established under the Administration of Justice Law, No. 44 of 1973, delivered or made before the commencement of the Constitution

in original proceedings shall have the same force and effect as if they had been delivered or made by the Court of Appeal:

Provided that any proceedings in relation to any alleged breach of privileges of Parliament pending in the Supreme Court shall stand removed to the Supreme Court created and established by the Constitution;

(5) no appeal shall lie from any judgment, order or decree of the Supreme Court established under the Administration of Justice Law, No. 44 of 1973, to the Supreme Court created and established under the Constitution but such judgment, order or decree, as the case may be, shall be final as between the parties to the action, application or other proceeding in which judgment, order or decree was made:

Provided that it shall be competent for the Court of Appeal and all officers of such Court to take all such steps as may be necessary, including the entering of decrees if not already entered and taxation and recovery of costs so as to ensure that such judgments, orders and decrees are completely and effectively complied with, as if they had been delivered or made by the Court of Appeal created and established by the Constitution;

(6) the several High Courts established under Chapter I of the Administration of Justice Law, No. 44 of 1973, shall be deemed for all purposes to constitute a single court created and established by Parliament called the High Court of the Republic of Sri Lanka having jurisdiction throughout the Republic of Sri Lanka to be exercised in the several Zones in accordance with the law for the time being in force. Accordingly, subject to the provisions of the Constitution, and of any existing written law, all provisions relating to High Courts contained in such Law shall, *mutatis mutandis*, apply to the High Court of the Republic of Sri Lanka;

(7) all criminal and admiralty cases, proceedings or matters, other than applications for injunctions, pending in the High Courts established under the Administration of Justice Law, No. 44 of 1973, on the day preceding the commencement of the Constitution shall stand removed to the said High Court of the Republic of Sri Lanka and such Court shall have jurisdiction to take cognizance of, hear and determine or to continue and complete the same, and the judgments and orders of the aforesaid High Courts delivered or made before the commencement of the Constitution shall have the same force and effect as if they had been delivered or made by the High Court of the Republic of Sri Lanka;

(8) the President of the Court of Appeal shall from time to time as he may deem expedient nominate the Judges of the High Court of the Republic of Sri Lanka to exercise the jurisdiction of the High Court in such zones as he may determine and the provisions of Chapter II of the Administration of Justice Law, No. 44 of 1973, shall, *mutatis mutandis*, apply to the hearing and disposal of all proceedings pending in or hereafter instituted in the High Court;

(9) all indictments filed hereafter in the High Court of the Republic of Sri Lanka shall be in the name of the Republic of Sri Lanka and shall be signed by the Attorney-General or any person authorized under section 189 of the Administration of Justice Law, No. 44 of 1973;

(10) all election petition proceedings relating to the election of any person to the membership of the National State Assembly pending in the High Courts established under the Administration of Justice Law, No. 44 of 1973, on the day

preceding the commencement of the Constitution, shall stand removed to the Court of Appeal and the Court of Appeal shall have the same jurisdiction to take cognizance of, hear and determine or to continue and complete the same, and the judgments and orders of the Supreme Court established by the Administration of Justice Law, No. 44 of 1973, and of the High Courts aforesaid delivered or made before the commencement of the Constitution in such election petition proceedings shall have the same force and effect as if they had been delivered or made by the Supreme Court and the Court of Appeal established by the Constitution, as the case may be. The President of the Court of Appeal is hereby vested with the power to nominate a Judge of the Court of Appeal to hear and determine any election petition in respect of which the Court of Appeal is vested with jurisdiction by the Constitution;

(11) all attorneys-at-law admitted and enrolled or deemed to have been admitted and enrolled as attorneys-at-law under the provisions of the Administration of Justice Law, No. 44 of 1973, shall subject to the provisions of the Constitution be deemed to have been admitted and enrolled as attorneys-at-law of the Supreme Court created and established by the Constitution;

(12) after the date fixed by the Minister in charge of the subject of Justice, by Order published in the *Gazette*, no attorney-at-law shall be entitled to represent any party to a proceeding or be given the right of audience in any court, tribunal or other institution until or unless he has taken and subscribed the oath or made and subscribed the affirmation set out in the Fourth Schedule, before a Judge of the Supreme Court, Court of Appeal, High Court or any other judicial officer as defined in Article 114; and its shall be the duty of any such Judge or judicial officer, as the case may be, to forward such oath or affirmation so taken and subscribed or made and subscribed to the Registrar of the Supreme Court who shall cause the same to be entered in the rolls of such Court. Such entry shall be the only proof that such attorney-at-law has taken and subscribed or made and subscribed such oath or affirmation;

(13) the provisions of the Administration of Justice Law, No. 44 of 1973, relating to the Attorney-General, the legal profession, State Attorneys and State Counsel, shall be deemed for all purposes to be in operation, and every reference to the Supreme Court in section 33 to 36 of the Administration of Justice Law, No. 44 of 1973, and in the rules and regulation relating thereto shall be deemed to be a reference to the Supreme Court established by the Constitution;

(14) if any matter or question shall arise with regard to any procedure or practice to be followed in any court in consequence of the coming into operation of the Constitution, not provided for in the Constitution or any written law, the Chief Justice shall have the power to give such directions as he may consider necessary to prevent injustice or as the justice of the case may require and to ensure that the provisions of Chapters XV and XVI of the Constitution are given full and complete effect;

(15) (i) any reference in section 2 of the Special Presidental Commissions of Inquiry Law, No. 7 of 1978, to the Supreme Court shall be deemed to be a

reference to the Supreme Court established by the Constitution;

(ii) where any person has been appointed as a member of a Special Presidential Commission of Inquiry established under the Special Presidential Commissions of Inquiry Law, No. 7 of 1978, then, such person shall notwithstanding the provisions of the Constitution, continue to be such member and shall be deemed for the purposes of Article 81 (1) to be a Judge of a Court referred to therein unless he resigns, or refuses or becomes unable to act, or is discharged by the President from the performance of his duties as such member in accordance with the provisions of the Special Presidential Commissions of Inquiry Law, No. 7 of 1978;

(iii) any such member specified in the Warrant establishing such Special Presidential Commission of Inquiry as Chairman, shall, subject to the provisions of sub-paragraph (ii) of this paragraph, continue to be the Chairman of such Special Presidential Commission of Inquiry;

(16) (i) any breach of the privileges of the National State Assembly functioning, immediately prior to the commencement of the Constitution, shall be deemed to be a breach of the privileges of Parliament and accordingly, Parliament and the Supreme Court, shall have the power to take cognizance of and punish any person for such breach of privileges of Parliament;

(ii) where prior to the commencement of the Constitution, any step required or authorized by the Parliament (Powers and Privileges) Act has been taken in respect of, or in relation to, any act or omission alleged to constitute such a breach of the privileges of Parliament as is referred to in sub-paragraph (i) of this paragraph, such step shall be deemed to have been validly taken and any further steps as are required or authorized under such Act, may be taken, in respect of, or in relation to, such alleged breach of the privileges of Parliament, as if the act or omission alleged to constitute such breach of privileges of Parliament had been committed or had occurred after the commencement of the Constitution.

CHAPTER XXII

INTERPRETATION

170. In the Constitution

'civic disability' shall have the same meaning as in the Special Presidential Commissions of Inquiry Law, No. 7 of 1978, as on the commencement of the Constitution;

'commencement of the Constitution' means the date appointed by the Proclamation made under Article 172;

'conclusion of the General Election' means the time at which Members of Parliament for all the electoral districts in respect of which a poll has been taken on the date or dates specified in the Proclamation made under Article 70 (5) have been declared elected by the respective returning officers, or when on the results declared more than half the total membership of Parliament consists of Members belonging to any single recognized political party or independent group, whichever event occurs earlier;

'existing law' and 'existing written law' mean any law and written law, respectively, in force immediately before the commencement of the Constitution which under the Constitution continue in force;

judicial officer', other than in Article 114, means any person who holds office as

(*a*) a Judge of the Supreme Court or a Judge of the Court of Appeal;

(*b*) any other Court of First Instance, tribunal or institution created and established for the administration of justice or for the adjudication of any labour or other dispute but does not include a person who performs arbitral functions or a public officer whose principal duty or duties is or are not the performance of functions of a judicial nature.

No Court or tribunal or institution shall have jurisdiction to determine the question whether a person is a judicial officer within the meaning of the Constitution but such question shall be determined by the Judicial Service Commission whose decision thereon shall be final and conclusive.

No act of such person or proceeding held before such person, prior to such determination, shall be deemed to be invalid by reason of such determination.

'law' means any Act of Parliament, and any law enacted by any legislature at any time prior to the commencement of the Constitution and includes an Order in Council;

'local authority' means any Municipal Council, Urban Council, Town Council or Village Council and includes any Authority created and established by or under any law to exercise, perform and discharge powers, duties and functions corresponding to or similar to the powers, duties and functions exercised, performed and discharged by any such Council;

'public corporation' means any corporation, board or other body which was or is established by or under any written law other than the Companies Ordinance, with funds or capital wholly or partly provided by the Government by way of grant, loan or otherwise;

'public officer' means a person who holds any paid office under the Republic, other than a judicial officer but does not include

(*a*) the President;

(*b*) the Speaker;

(*c*) a Minister;

(*d*) a member of the Judicial Service Commission;

(*e*) a member of the Public Service Commission;
(*f*) a Deputy Minister;
(*g*) a Member of Parliament;
(*h*) the Secretary-General of Parliament;
(*i*) a member of the President's staff;
(*j*) a member of the staff of the Secretary-General of Parliament;

'recognized political party' means unless Parliament otherwise provides, every political party which is treated as a recognized political party under the Ceylon (Parliamentary Elections) Order in Council, 1946;

'territorial waters' includes the territorial sea and the historic waters of Sri Lanka;

'written law' means any law and subordinate legislation and includes Orders, Proclamation, Rules, By-laws and Regulations made or issued by any body or person having power or authority under any law to make or issue the same.

CHAPTER XXIII

REPEAL

171. The Constitution adopted and enacted on the 22nd day of May, 1972, is hereby repealed.

CHAPTER XXIV

PROMULGATION OF THE CONSTITUTION

172. (1) The provisions of Chapter I to Chapter XXIII shall come into force on the day appointed by the President by Proclamation.

(2) Parliament shall meet on the day so appointed and the President may, in such Proclamation, specify the time at which Parliament shall so meet.

SCHEDULES

(Not reproduced)

SYRIA

SUMMARY

INTERNATIONAL STATUS

Syria is a member of the United Nations (October 24, 1945). It is a member of the League of Arab States and of other international organizations. It ratified in 1969 the International Conventions on Social, Economic and Cultural Rights and on Civil and Political Rights.

Syria became fully independent with the departure of the last French troops in April 1946. It was invited as an independent state to the United Nations Conference at San Francisco in March 1945. Syria and Lebanon had been under Islam for some 900 years when they were conquered by the Ottomans in 1516. Ottoman rule was based on the Millet system of a sort of autonomy for non-Muslim religious communities under their religious leaders, on delegation of administrative powers to local leaders in areas not of special military importance, and of capitulations which – beginning with the privileges granted to the King of France in 1535 – came to cover legal, religious, economic and even political rights for almost all non-Ottoman nationals resident in the Empire. Militarily, Ottoman rule protected the Arab areas against conquest. During the eighteenth century, Greater Syria was divided into the four pashaliks of Aleppo, Tripoli, Damascus and Sidon.

Napoleon's invasion of Egypt in 1798, brought world political rivalries into the area and a series of interventions and occupations, military or economic, by Britain, France, Austria and Germany as well as Italy and Russia. In the second half of the nineteenth century, movements for Arab nationalism and constitutional government became important. The first Arab Conference was held in Paris in June 1913, and demanded immediate reforms, guarantees for Arab autonomy for the Arab provinces of the Ottoman Empire, and Arabic as an official language of the Ottoman

Parliament. The outbreak of World War I enabled the Young Turks to pursue their own Turkification and centralized administration. Severe repression throughout Greater Syria reinforced the movement for complete independence. But, at the 1919 Paris Peace Conference, England and France under the secret 1916 Sykes-Picot Agreement divided the whole area of the Fertile Crescent between themselves. The French League of Nations mandate began on September 29, 1923, after the independence movements in Syria had been crushed by the French army in 1920. A renewed struggle for independence began (in 1927 the French bombarded Damascus) and a Constitution was proclaimed in 1930, only to be withdrawn in 1933. In 1936, under the Popular Front Government in France, the 1936 Treaty providing for the eventual independence of both Syria and Lebanon was drawn up. The fall of the Blum government meant that it was never ratified. In 1936, violating the territorial integrity terms of the mandate, France permitted the cession of the Sanjak of Alexandretta to Turkey.

After the fall of France in World War II, the British supported the entry of Free French troops into the area in June 1941, and proclaimed the two countries independent. The reality of independence was only achieved by continued struggle against the French desire to maintain its privileged position, by the United Nations decision, and under the 1945 treaty with France.

The failure of the Arab intervention in Palestine in 1948 aroused great discontent in both Syria and Lebanon. In March 1949, the army took over the government, dissolved the Chamber and imposed martial law. In 1950 Syria denounced the economic union (of 1943) with Lebanon. A period of political upheaval ensued. Union with Egypt as the United Arab Republic lasted from February 1, 1958 until October 1961. In March 1963, the National Revolutionary Command Council came to power and formed the first Baath government. The Baath Party (Arab Socialist Renaissance Party) was founded in 1941. In February 1966, a violent coup brought in the 'progressive' wing of the party, which was replaced, after a bloodless coup in 1970, by a new Regional Command under General Hafez Assad. The first legislative body since 1965, the People's Council, was formed in 1971 and approved the Constitution of January 31, 1973, replacing the provisional Constitution of 1964.

Hafez Assad was reelected to the Presidency in February 1978. In October 1978, Syria and Iraq signed the 'National Charter for Joint Action', and in June 1979, a 'unified political leadership' was announced to lead toward constitutional unity.

Syria has been in a state of war with Israel since the latter's independence. In the 1967 Arab-Israeli war, Syria lost the Golan Heights which have remained under Israeli occupation since. In October 1973, there was another Arab-Israeli war. In June 1976, Syria intervened militarily in the civil war in Lebanon and maintains troops there in the Arab Deterrent Force.

FORM OF NATIONAL GOVERNMENT

The Constitution of March 1973, states its main principles in the Preamble, that total Arab revolution is required to achieve the aims of the Arab Nation of Unity, Liberty and Socialism and that the Revolution of the Syrian Arab Region is part of the total Arab revolution, that present achievements cannot be secure until pro-

tected by Arab unity and any threat to a single Arab country from socialism and Zionism is a threat to the Arab Nation, that establishment of a socialist regime is a basic need, that freedom is a sacred right and a people's democracy the ideal formula to guarantee it, that the Arab revolutionary movement is part of the world liberation movement. The Syrian Arab Republic is a democratic people's state, sovereign and socialist, a member of the Federation of Arab Republics.[1]
The system of government is republican; sovereignty belongs to the people.[2] Islam is the religion of the President and Islamic jurisprudence a principle source of legislation.[3] The Baath Arab Socialist Party is the leader party and leads a National Progressive Front.[4] The state economy is socialist and planned, property is composed of people's property, collective property and private property.[5] The principles of education and culture are set out.[6].

RIGHTS OF THE PEOPLE

The Constitution guarantees personal freedom, supremacy of the law, equality before the law, due process of law; torture is forbidden; laws may not be retroactive; inviolability of the home, privacy of correspondence, freedom of movement, of belief are provided and the state guarantees the performance of all religious rituals consonant with public order; protection of political refugees; citizens may not be expelled from the homeland.[7] The state protects work as the right and duty of citizens, defines hours of work and guarantees social security benefits.[8] Education is a right, free in all stages and compulsory in the elementary stages.[9] Freedom of speech and the press, the right of assembly is guaranteed.[10] Military service is obligatory.[11] Protection is provided for the family, women's rights and opportunities, health, the formation of unions and professional, social and co-operative organizations.[12]

LEGISLATIVE DEPARTMENT

Legislative power is exercised by the People's Council composed of members elected by secret, direct, equal and universal suffrage for a term of 4 years.[13] Members represent the entire people.[14] It meets in 3 regular sessions annually.[15] Immunities of members are provided.[16] It may pass a vote of no-confidence in the Cabinet or one of its members.[17]

EXECUTIVE DEPARTMENT

Candidature for the post of President of the Republic is made by the People's Council at the suggestion of the Regional Leadership of the Baath Arab Socialist

[1] Const., Art. 1.
[2] Id., Art. 2.
[3] Id., Art. 3.
[4] Id., Art. 8.
[5] Id., Art. 13, 14.
[6] Id., Art. 21–24.
[7] Id., Art. 25–33.
[8] Id., Art. 36.
[9] Id., Art. 37.
[10] Id., Art. 38, 39.
[11] Id., Art. 40.
[12] Id., Art. 44, 45.
[13] Id., Art. 46–49.
[14] Id., Art. 50, 51.
[15] Id., Art. 61.
[16] Id., Art. 67.
[17] Id., Art. 71, 72.

Party; the President is elected by referendum where he must receive an absolute majority of the votes; his term is 7 years.[18] He nominates one or more Vice-Presidents, the President of the Council of Ministers and the ministers.[19] He has the power to declare war and conclude peace with the assent of the People's Council, the right of pardon, commands the Armed Forces, he may dissolve the People's Council and assume legislative power when the Council is not in session or if required by national necessity or security, provided such legislation be referred to the Council in its first subsequent meeting.[20] The Council of Ministers is the highest executive and administrative body of the state, its members are responsible to the President.[21]

There are provisions for People's Local Councils.[22]

JUDICIAL DEPARTMENT

The judicial power is independent and judges are subject to no authority other than the law.[23] A High Constitutional Court is provided whose members are appointed by the President for a renewable term of 4 years.[24] It may decide upon the constitutionality of laws.[25]

AREA, POPULATION, ETC.

The area of Syria is 185,180 square kilometres, its population (1980 estimate) 8,979,000 (including 174,000 Palestinian refugees). The capital is Damascus. The language is Arabic.[26]

[18] Id., Art. 83–85.
[19] Id., Art. 95.
[20] Id., Art. 100–111.
[21] Id., Art. 115–117.
[22] Id., Art. 129, 130.
[23] Id., Art. 133.
[24] Id., Art. 139–141.
[25] Id., Art. 145, 146.
[26] Id., Art. 4.

CONSTITUTION OF THE SYRIAN ARAB REPUBLIC[1]

March 1973

PREAMBLE

When united, the Arab Nation played a great role in the development of human civilization; but when its national solidarity weakened, its civilization role receded and waves of colonial invasions were able to shatter its unity, occupy its lands and plunder its resources.

Faced with this challenge, the Arab Nation firmly rejected the imposed realities of dismemberment, exploitation, and regression, prompted thereto by the belief in its ability to overcome those realities and to reenter history and play, alongside other liberated nations, a special role in building up civilization and progress.

Close to the end of the first half of the present century the struggle of the Arab people, in various countries was extended and intensified to achieve liberation from the direct colonialism of occupation.

The Arab masses, however, did not consider political independence a final objective and the end of all struggle and sacrifices. They regarded it rather as a means of enhancing their struggle and an advanced stage in the battle against colonialism, Zionism and exploitation – a battle which was led by progressive national forces and directed to achieve the aims of the Arab Nation: Unity, Freedom and Socialism.

In the Syrian Arab Region, after the achievement of independence, the masses of our people continued their struggle and were able, through a strenuous and intensified endeavor to achieve the great victory of launching the Revolution of the 8th of March of 1963, under the leadership of the Baath Arab Socialist Party, which harnessed power to serve the endeavor to build up the united socialist Arab society.

The Baath Arab Socialist party was the first movement in the Arab Homeland to give Arab unity its true revolutionary meaning, to combine the national and the socialist struggles and to represent the will of the Arab Nation and its aspiration to a future, linking it with its glorious past and qualifying it to play an appropriate part in the victory of the cause of the liberation of all peoples.

In the course of the militant march of the party came the corrective movement of the 16th November 1970, in response to the needs and aspirations of our people. This movement represented an important specific development and a true embodiment of the spirit, principles and aims of the Party. It created the atmosphere favorable to the realization of a number of important achievements in the interests of the masses. First among these was the establishment of the Federation of the Arab Republics in response to the call for unity, a call which occupies a privileged place in the Arab conscience and which has been enhanced by the common Arab struggle against colonialism, Zionism and provincial and separatist trends and has

[1]Supplied by the Ministry of Foreign Affairs, Damascus, August 1979. Ed.

been confirmed by the contemporary Arab revolution against domination and exploitation.

Under the auspices of the corrective movement an important step in the direction of consolidating the national unity of our masses has been accomplished. Led by the Baath Arab Socialist Party, a Progressive National Front has been established in a developed framework satisfying the needs and interests of the people and oriented to make of the masses, who are the instrument of the Arab revolution, a unified political organization.

The establishment of this constitution represents the crowning achievement of the struggle of our people to implement the principle of the adoption of a people's democracy, providing clear guidance to the future march of the people, a directive for the acts of the various establishments of the state and a source of its legislation.

This Constitution is based upon the following main principles:

1. That the total Arab revolution represents a continuing and standing need to achieve the aims of the Arab Nation of Unity, Liberty and Socialism. The Revolution of the Syrian Arab Region is part of the total Arab revolution. Its policies in all fields derive from the general strategy of the Arab Revolution.

2. All achievements which have been, or may be, attained by any Arab country in the present state of dismemberment are bound to be inadequate and incapable of reaching their full dimensions, as well as subject to deformation and setbacks unless enhanced and protected by Arab unity. Likewise, any danger from colonialism and Zionism menacing any Arab country is a danger that threatens the entire Arab Nation.

3. The drive towards establishing a socialist regime in addition to its being a necessity emanating from the needs of Arab society, also represents a basic need to mobilize all the potentialities of the Arab masses in the battle against Zionism and Imperialism.

4. Freedom is a sacred right, and a people's democracy is the ideal formula to guarantee for citizens the exercise of their freedom, which makes of them dignified human beings, capable of giving and achieving constructive work and of defending the homeland in which they live, and ready to offer sacrifices for the benefit of the nation to which they belong, inasmuch as the liberty of the homeland is only safeguarded by free citizens and the freedom of citizens is never complete unless they enjoy economic and social freedom.

5. The Arab revolutionary movement is a basic part of the world liberation movement, and the struggle of the Arab people is part of the struggle of peoples who are fighting to achieve freedom, independence and progress.

This Constitution will serve as a guideline for the masses of our people spurring them to continue the battle of liberation and construction in the light of its principles and provisions, to consolidate their struggle and to hasten their steps towards the looked for future.

PART ONE

FUNDAMENTAL PRINCIPLES

Chapter I. Political Principles

Art. 1. (1) The Syrian Arab Republic is a democratic people's state, sovereign and socialist. No part of its territory may be ceded. It is a member of the Federation of Arab Republics.

(2) The Syrian Arab Region is part of the Arab Homeland.

(3) The people of the Syrian Arab Region are part of the Arab Nation, who work and struggle to achieve all-embracing unity.

Art. 2. (1) The system of government of the Syrian Arab Region is republican.

(2) Sovereignty belongs to the people, and shall be exercised by them in the manner defined by the Constitution.

Art. 3. (1) Islam is the religion of the President of the Republic.

(2) Islamic Jurisprudence is a principal source of legislation.

Art. 4. Arabic is the official language.

Art. 5. Damascus is the Capital of the State.

Art. 6. The flag, emblem and anthem of the state are those of the Federation of Arab Republics.

Art. 7. The constitutional oath of office shall be as follows: 'I swear by Almighty God, loyally to safeguard the people's republican and democratic regime, to respect the laws and the Constitution, to watch over the interests of the people and the security of the Homeland, and to work and struggle to achieve the aim of the Arab Nation, of Unity, Liberty and Socialism.'

Art. 8. The Baath Arab Socialist Party shall be the leader party in society and the state and shall lead a National Progressive Front that works to unite the capacities of the masses of the people to serve the interests of the Arab Nation.

Art. 9. The people's organizations and co-operative societies are institutions embodying the active forces of the people, with the aim of developing society and serving the interests of their members.

Art. 10. The Councils of the People are democratically elected institutions through which citizens exercise their rights of administering the state and directing society.

Art. 11. The Armed Forces and other Defence Organizations are responsible for the security of the Homeland and the safeguarding of the aims of the Revolution, of Unity, Liberty and Socialism.

Art. 12. The State shall serve the people, and its institutions shall endeavor to safeguard the fundamental rights of the citizens and develop their lives. They also shall give support to the people's organizations to enable them to develop themselves by themselves.

Chapter II. Economic Principles

Art. 13. (1) The economy of the state shall be socialist and planned and shall aim to abolish all forms of exploitation.

(2) Economic planning in Syria shall take into consideration the objective of realizing the economic integration of the Arab Homeland.

Art. 14. The law shall organize property, which is of three kinds:

(1) People's property: this shall include natural resources, public services, and the establishments and institutions which are nationalized, or created, operated and supervised by the state in the interest of the people. These shall be protected by citizens.

(2) Collective property: This includes property owned by popular and professional organizations, by production units, co-operative societies and other social establishments. The law shall ensure protection and support for such property.

(3) Private property: includes property owned by individuals. The law shall define its social role in the service of national economy and within the development plan. Its manner of utilization shall not be directed against the interests of the people.

Art. 15. (1) Private property shall not be expropriated except for a public benefit and against a just compensation in accordance with the law.

(2) General confiscation of property shall be prohibited.

(3) Special confiscation may not be imposed except by a judicial decisions.

(4) Private confiscation may be imposed through a provision of the law and against a just compensation.

Art. 16. The law shall fix maximum limits for agrarian ownership, in a manner ensuring the protection of peasants and agricultural workers against exploitation and guaranteeing increased production.

Art. 17. The right of inheritance shall be guaranteed in accordance with the law.

Art. 18. 'Saving' is a national duty, protected, encouraged and regulated by the state.

Art. 19. Taxes shall be imposed on just and progressive bases and in accordance with principles of equality and social justice.

Art. 20. The utilization of private and 'mixed' economic enterprise shall aim to meet economic needs, to increase the national income and to ensure the welfare of the people.

Chapter III. Principles of Education and Culture

Art. 21. The educational and cultural system shall aim to bring up a national Arab generation, who are socialist and scientific in their manner of thinking, attached to their land and history, proud of their heritage, and imbued with the spirit of struggling to realize the aims of the nation of Unity, Liberty and Socialism, and of contributing to the service and progress of humanity.

Art. 22. The educational system shall ensure the continued progress of the people and shall meet the needs of their continued social, economic and cultural development.

Art. 23. (1) The national socialist culture shall be the basis of building up the unified socialist Arab society. It shall aim at enhancing moral values, realizing the ideals of the Arab Nation, developing society, and serving human causes; the state shall encourage and protect this culture.

(2) Encouraging artistic talents and capacities is a basis of the development and progress of society.

Artistic creation shall maintain contact with the life of the people. The state shall endeavor to develop the artistic talents and propensities of all citizens.

(3) Physical education is a basic factor in building up society. It shall be encouraged by the State in order to bring up a generation, strong in body, character and thought.

Art. 24. (1) Science, scientific research and all scientific achievements constitute a main prop for the progress of Arab socialist society. The state shall give them full support.

Chapter IV. Freedoms: Public Rights and Obligations

Art. 25. (1) Freedom is a sacred right. The state shall guarantee the personal freedom of citizens and safeguard their dignity and security.

(2) Supremacy of the law shall be a basic principle of society and the state.

(3) Citizens shall be equal before the law in rights and obligations.

(4) The state shall guarantee to citizens the principle of equal opportunities.

Art. 26. Every citizen shall have the right to participate in the political, economic, social and cultural life of the country. The law shall organize their participation.

Art. 27. Citizens shall exercise their rights and enjoy their freedoms within the limits of the law.

Art. 28. (1) Every accused person shall be presumed to be innocent until he is condemned by a final judicial decision.

(2) No one shall be subjected to a search or inquiry, or taken into custody, except as provided by the law.

(3) No one shall be subjected to physical or moral torture, or to treatment outrageous to dignity. The law shall define the penalties of such actions.

(4) The right of litigation, of recourse to a court of law and of defence before it, are guaranteed by law.

Art. 29. There shall be no crime or punishment except as laid down by provisions of the law.

Art. 30. Provisions of the law shall not apply except to acts that follow the date of their coming into effect. They shall not have retroactive effect. The law, however, may provide otherwise in non-penal matters.

Art. 31. Houses are inviolable and shall not be entered, or searched except in cases defined by the law.

Art. 32. Privacy of postal correspondence and telephonic communications shall be guaranteed in accordance with provisions of the law.

Art. 33. (1) A citizen may not be expelled from the territories of the Homeland.

(2) Every citizen shall have the right of free movement within the territories of the state, unless restricted by a judicial decision or by the implementation of laws or public health and safety.

Art. 34. Political refugees shall not be surrendered because of their political principles or of actions they may take in defense of the cause of freedom.

Art. 35. (1) Freedom of belief shall be guaranteed. The State shall respect all religions.

(2) The state shall guarantee the performance of all religious rituals provided this does not violate public order.

Art. 36. (1) Work is the right and duty of every citizen. The state shall endeavor to ensure it for all citizens.

(2) Every citizen shall have the right to be paid for his work on the basis of kind and efficiency. The state shall guarantee this right.

(3) The state shall define hours of work, shall guarantee social security benefits for workers, shall regulate their right to rest and holidays, as well as to indemnities and gratuities.

Art. 37. Education shall be a right guaranteed by the state. It shall be free in all stages and compulsory in the elementary stage. The state shall endeavor to make other stages compulsory, and shall supervise education and direct it in a manner ensuring adapting it to the needs of society and production.

Art. 38. Every citizen shall have the right to express his opinion publicly and freely, in speech, writing and other forms of expression and to participate in the work of control and the voicing of constructive criticism aimed to ensure the safety of the structure of the Homeland and the Nation and to enhance the socialist regime. The state shall guarantee the freedom of the press and of printing and publishing, in accordance with the law.

Art. 39. Citizens shall have the right of assembly and peaceful demonstration within the principles of the Constitution. Exercising this right shall be regulated by law.

Art. 40. (1) All citizens shall be required to carry out the sacred duty of defending the security of the Homeland and of respecting the country's constitution and its unionist and socialist regime.

(2) Military service shall be compulsory and regulated by law.

Art. 41. Payment of taxes and public charges shall be a duty required by law.

Art. 42. Safeguarding national unity and the secrets of the state shall be the duty of every citizen.

Art. 43. Syrian Arab nationality shall be regulated by law. Special facilities shall be granted to Syrian Arab emigrants and their descendants, and to citizens of other countries of the Arab Homeland.

Art. 44. (1) The family is the basic cell of society; it shall have the protection of the state.

(2) The state shall protect and encourage marriage and shall act to remove material and social impediments hindering it; it shall protect maternity and children, look after youth and ensure them of conditions favorable to the development of their faculties.

Art. 45. The state shall guarantee to women all opportunities enabling them to make complete and full contribution to the political, social, cultural and economic life of society. It shall endeavor to remove impediments that hinder their development and their participation in the building up of Arab socialist society.

Art. 46. (1) The state shall guarantee assistance to all citizens and their families in cases of accidents, disease, disability, orphanage and old age.

(2) The state shall protect the health of citizens and shall provide them with means of prevention of disease, with medical treatment and with medication.

Art. 47. The state shall ensure cultural, social and health services and shall make these service available to villages in order to raise their standards.

Art. 48. The popular sectors shall have the right to form trade unions, social or professional organizations and co-operative societies for production services. The law shall determine the frameworks of these organizations, their interrelations, and the limits of their activities.

Art. 49. Popular organizations shall participate effectively in the various sectors, and in the councils established by law to achieve the following objectives:

(1) Building up the Arab socialist society and protecting its regime.

(2) Planning and guiding the country's socialist economy.

(3) Developing conditions of labor and management for the prevention of disease and the promotion of health and culture, and for other matters serving the interests of members of these organizations.

(4) Ensuring scientific and technical progress and developing means of production.

(5) Keeping watch over government machinery.

PART TWO

POWERS OF THE STATE

Chapter I. Legislative Power

Art. 50. (1) The People's Council shall exercise legislative power in the manner defined by the Constitution.

(2) Members of the People's Council shall be elected by universal suffrage in secret, direct and equal ballot in conformity with provisions of the Electoral law.

Art. 51. Period of mandate of the People's Council shall be four years; it shall begin on the day of the first meeting of the Council and may not be extended except in case of war and by virtue of a law.

Art. 52. A member of the People's Council shall represent the entire people. His mandate may not be restricted by any condition or limitation and shall be exercised by him in accordance with the dictates of honor and conscience.

Art. 53. The law shall determine the electoral constituencies and the number of members of the People's Council, provided one half of the members are peasants and workers. The law shall define the terms 'a worker' and 'a peasant'.

Art. 54. The electors shall be those citizens who have completed 19 years of age, who are registered in the state's 'Civil Status Register' and who fulfil the conditions prescribed in the electoral law.

Art. 55. The law shall determine the rules of elections and the referendum, as well as the conditions required in a member of the People's Council.

Art. 56. State employees, including employees of the Public Sector, may become candidates for membership of the People's Council except and apart from cases defined by law, an elected member shall devote the whole of his time to the duties of membership. Moreover, he shall retain his right to his former post or employment, in connection with which the time he spends as Council member will be regarded as effective service for him.

Art. 57. The electoral law shall include provisions ensuring:

(1) Freedom of choice for electors and the integrity of elections.

(2) The right of candidates to supervise election operations.

(3) Punishment for those interfering with the will of the electors.

Art. 58. (1) Elections shall take place within 90 days following the date of expiry of the mandate of the People's Council.

(2) The council shall resume after the prescribed 90 days elapse if a new council is not elected, and shall continue to function until a new council is elected.

Art. 59. If a Council seat becomes vacant, for any reason and the remaining period of the mandate of the Council is not less than six months, a new member shall be elected within 90 days of the day when the seat became vacant. Membership of the new member shall end with the expiry of the period of the Council's mandate. The law shall define cases when the Council's membership shall be considered 'vacant'.

Art. 60. (1) The People's Council shall be convened by a decree issued by the President of the Republic within 15 days following the day on which the results of the elections are announced; and in all cases shall meet on the 16th day, if such decree is not issued.

(2) The Council shall elect its Speaker and members of its Bureau in its first meeting.

Art. 61. The Council shall be convened in three regular sessions annually; and it may also be convened in extraordinary sessions. The Council's Internal Rules shall specify the dates and durations of regular sessions. Extraordinary sessions are convened either by a decision of the Speaker of the Council or at a written request by the President of the Republic or by one third of members of the Council.

Art. 62. The Council shall decide on the legality of the election of its members in the light of an enquiry conducted by the High Constitutional Court, within one month of receipt by the Council of the court's ruling. Membership of the Council shall not be annulled except by a vote of the majority of its members.

Art. 63. Before assuming office, members of the People's Council shall publicly take the oath prescribed in Article (7) of this Constitution.

Art. 64. Salaries and allowances of members of the People's Council shall be fixed by law.

Art. 65. The People's Council shall adopt Internal Rules to regulate the manner in which it shall conduct its work and fulfil its functions.

Art. 66. Members of the Council shall not be answerable, in criminal or civil action, for facts mentioned or opinions expressed by them, or for voting in the public or secret meetings of the Council or Committees.

Art. 67. During the whole period of the mandate of the Council, its members shall enjoy immunity. Except in cases when a member is caught in the act, no criminal or civil proceedings may be initiated against him, except by the prior consent of the Council. When the Council is not in session, the authorization of the Speaker of the Council shall be required, of which the Council shall be informed in its first meeting following the action taken in relation thereto.

Art. 68. (1) A member of the Council may not take advantage of his membership in any activity.

(2) The Speaker of the People's Council shall determine the activities which are incompatible with membership of the Council.

Art. 69. (1) The Speaker of the People's Council shall represent the Council, sign for it, and speak on its behalf.

(2) The Council shall have a special guard, who takes orders from the Speaker of the Council. No other armed force may enter the precincts of the Council except with the permission of the Speaker.

Art. 70. Members of the People's Council may suggest laws and direct questions or interpellations to the Council of Ministers, or to a Minister, in accordance with the Internal Rules of the Council.

Art. 71. The People's Council shall have the following functions:

(1) Nomination of the President of the Republic.

(2) Passing laws.

(3) Discussing the Policy of the Cabinet.

(4) Approving the General Budget and Development Plans.

(5) Ratifying international treaties and agreements relating to the security of the state, that is treaties of peace and alliance, all treaties relating to sovereignty, agreements granting concessions to companies or foreign establishments, and treaties and agreements incurring expenditure from the treasury of the state other than those allocated in the budget; also treaties contrary to provisions of laws in effect, and treaties the enforcement of which requires the passing of a new legislation.

(6) Passing a general amnesty.

(7) Accepting or rejecting the resignation of a member of the Council.

(8) Passing a vote of no-confidence in the Cabinet or in one of its members.

Art. 72. A vote of no-confidence may not be passed except after addressing a question to the Cabinet or one of the Ministers; the vote of no-confidence shall be proposed by at least one fifth of the members of the Council and approved by a majority of members. When a vote of no confidence in the Cabinet is passed, the President of the Council of Ministers shall tender his resignation to the President of the Republic. A minister against whom a vote of no-confidence is passed shall resign.

Art. 73. The Council may set up *ad hoc* fact finding committees to collect information and facts regarding subjects related to the exercise of its functions.

Art. 74. The budget bill shall be submitted to the People's Council at least two months before the beginning of the financial year. The budget shall not take effect until it is approved by the Council.

Art. 75. Voting on the budget shall be taken chapter by chapter. The manner of preparing the budget shall be regulated by law.

Art. 76. There shall be only one budget for each financial year; the beginning of the financial year shall be fixed by a law.

Art. 77. If the Council does not finish approving the budget before the beginning of the new financial year, the budget of the previous year shall continue to be effective until the new budget is approved. Meanwhile revenues shall continue to be levied in accordance with the law in force.

Art. 78. Transfer from one budget allocation to another may not be made except in accordance with the laws in force.

Art. 79. The Council may not, during its discussion of the budget, increase the estimates of the total of the revenues or of the expenditures.

Art. 80. After approving the budget, the People's Council may adopt laws involving new expenditure and providing to meet such expenditure.

Art. 81. No tax shall be created, amended or abolished except by a law.

Art. 82. The final accounts for the financial year shall be submitted to the People's Council within two years following the end of the financial year. The closing of the year's account shall be effected by virtue of a law. The procedure followed in approving the budget shall be likewise followed in approving the closure of accounts.

CHAPTER II

EXECUTIVE POWER

(I) PRESIDENT OF THE REPUBLIC

Art. 83. A candidate for the Presidency of the Republic shall be a Syrian Arab, enjoying civil and political rights, who has completed 40 years of age.

Art. 84. (1) Candidature for the post of President of the Republic shall be made by the People's Council at the suggestion of the Regional Leadership of the the Baath Arab Socialist Party. It shall be submitted to citizens in a referendum.

(2) The referendum shall be held at the request of the Speaker of the People's Council.

(3) Election of the new President must take place not later than 30 days and not earlier than 60 days before the expiry of the term of office of the incumbent President.

(4) The candidate for the Presidency of the Republic shall become President on obtaining an absolute majority of the votes of electors participating in the referendum; failing this, the Council shall nominate another candidate. In the nomination and election of the new candidate, the prescribed procedure shall be followed, and election shall take place within one month following the date of the announcement of results of the first referendum.

Art. 85. The President of the Republic shall be elected for a term of seven years beginning on the day of the expiry of the term of office of the incumbent President.

Art. 86. Should a temporary hindrance prevent the President of the Republic from exercising the duties of his office, he shall ask the Vice President to act on his behalf.

Art. 87. When resigning his office, the President shall address the letter of resignation to the Speaker of the People's Council.

Art. 88. The first Vice President of the Republic, or the Vice President nominated by the President, shall exercise the functions of the President of the Republic when he is unable to exercise these functions. If the hindrances are permanent and in cases of death or resignation, a referendum shall be held in connection with the election of the new president in accordance with the procedures set out in Article (84) of this Constitution. This shall be done within a period of no more than 90 days. Should the Council be in a state of dissolution, or should the period of office remaining for the President be less than 90 days, the First Vice President shall assume the functions of the President of the Republic until the new Council is convened.

Art. 89. Should the post of the President of the Republic become vacant when there is no Vice-President, the President of the Council of Ministers shall exercise the duties and powers of the President of the Republic pending the holding of a referendum to elect a new President within 90 days.

Art. 90. Prior to assuming office, the President of the Republic shall take, before the People's Council, the Constitutional oath provide for in Article (7) of this Constitution.

Art. 91. The President of the Republic shall not be responsible for acts performed by him in the exercise of the functions of his office except in the case of high treason. Impeachment of the President shall then be made at the suggestion of at least one third of members of the People's Council and by a decision of the Council based on a vote made publicly and resulting in a two-thirds majority, taken at a special secret meeting of the Council. Trial of the President shall take place before the High Constitutional Court only.

Art. 92. The prerogatives and protocol of the office of the President of the Republic shall be defined by a law. Its allocations shall be fixed by a law.

Art. 93. (1) The President of the Republic shall watch over adherence to the Constitution and shall guarantee the regular functioning of the public authorities and the upholding of the state.

(2) The President of the Republic shall exercise the executive power on behalf of the people within the limits defined in this Constitution.

Art. 94. The President of the Republic shall draw up the general policy of the state and shall supervise its implementation in consultation with the Council of Ministers.

Art. 95. The President of the Republic nominates one or more Vice-Presidents and delegates to them some of his powers. He also nominates the President of the Council of Ministers and his deputies, the ministers and deputy ministers, accepts their resignation and dismisses them from office.

Art. 96. Prior to assuming the duties of their office, the Vice President of the Republic shall take before the President of the Republic the oath prescribed in Article (7) of this Constitution.

Art. 97. The President of the Republic may call the Council of Ministers to a meeting presided over by him. He may also ask Ministers to report to him.

Art. 98. The President of the Republic shall issue the laws passed by the People's Council; he may object to such laws by a decision giving reasons for the objection, within a month of the receipt of such laws by the Presidency of the Republic. However, should the Council adopt the laws a second time by a two-thirds majority, the President of the Republic shall issue them.

Art. 99. The President of the Republic shall issue Decrees, Decisions and Orders in accordance with legislation in force.

Art. 100. The President of the Republic shall have the power to declare war, order general mobilization and conclude peace with the assent of the People's Council.

Art. 101. The President of the Republic may declare a state of emergency and may cancel it in the manner defined by law.

Art. 102. The President of the Republic shall accredit the heads of political missions to foreign governments and receive the credentials of heads of political missions accredited to him.

Art. 103. The President of the Republic shall be the Supreme Commander of the Army and the Armed Forces. He shall issue all decisions and orders required in the exercise of this power, which he may partially delegate.

Art. 104. The President of the Republic shall conclude international treaties and agreements and shall cancel them in accordance with the provisions of the Constitution.

Art. 105. The President of the Republic shall have the power to order a special pardon and a recovery of civil rights.

Art. 106. The President of the Republic shall have the power to confer medals and decorations.

Art. 107. (1) The President of the Republic may order the dissolution of the People's Council by a decision issued by him giving reasons for the dissolution. Elections shall take place within 90 days of the dissolution.

(2) Dissolution of the People's Council may not be effected more than once for the same reason.

Art. 108. (1) The President of the Republic may call a meeting of the People's Council in an extraordinary session.

(2) He also has the right to address messages to the Council and make statements before it.

Art. 109. The President of the Republic shall appoint the civil and military officials and shall terminate their services in accordance with the law.

Art. 110. The President of the Republic may draw up bills of law and may refer them to the People's Council to deliberate on their approval.

Art. 111. (1) The President of the Republic shall assume legislative power when the People's Council is not in session. All legislation issued by the President shall be referred to the Council in the course of the first session held by the Council.

(2) The President of the Republic shall assume legislative power when the Council is in session if this is required by an extreme necessity relating to the country's national interests or requirements of the national security, provided that all legislation so issued shall be referred to the Council in the first meeting held by the council after the issuance of the legislation.

(3) The People's Council may abolish or amend the legislation issued under the two previous paragraphs by a law. This shall be done by a vote of a two-thirds majority of the Council's members registered as attending the meeting, provided their number is no less than the absolute majority of members. Such abolishment or amendment shall not have a retroactive effect. If the Council does not abolish or amend the legislation referred to it, it shall be considered approved; and there shall be no need to vote on it.

(4) The President of the Republic shall assume legislative power in the interval between the terms of two Councils. Legislation so passed shall not be referred to the People's Council. Its amendment and abrogation shall be effected through the same procedure prescribed for amending and abrogating laws in force.

Art. 112. The President of the Republic may refer to the people in a referendum important matters relating to the higher interests of the country, which shall be published by the President of the Republic, shall be binding and effective from the day of their announcement.

Art. 113. Should a grave danger arise threatening national unity or the safety and security of the homeland or impeding the state institutions from the performance of their constitutional functions, the President of the Republic shall take speedy measures to face the imminent danger.

Art. 114. The President of the Republic may set up bodies, councils and specialized committees, whose competence and functions shall be defined in the Decisions providing for their formation.

(2) THE COUNCIL OF MINISTERS

Art. 115. (1) The Council of Ministers is the highest executive and administrative body of the State. It consists of the President of the Council of Ministers, his Deputies and the Ministers. It supervises the enforcement of laws and regulations and controls the establishments and the machinery of the state.

(2) The President of the Council of Ministers supervises the work of the Ministers.

(3) The salaries and allowances of the President of the Council of Ministers, of his Deputies and of the Ministers, shall be fixed by a law.

Art. 116. Whenever a new cabinet is formed the President of the Council of Ministers and his Deputies, the Ministers and Deputy Ministers shall take, before the President of the Republic and before assuming office, the constitutional oath prescribed in Article (7) of this Constitution. In the case of a reshuffle, the new Ministers only shall take the oath.

Art. 117. The President of the Council of Ministers and the Ministers are responsible before the President of the Republic.

Art. 118. (1) Following its formation, the Cabinet shall submit to the People's Council a statement concerning the Cabinet's general policy and program of work.

(2) The Cabinet shall submit to the People's Council a statement on the implementation of plans of development and the increase of production.

Art. 119. A Minister shall be the administrative head of his Ministry with regard to which he shall undertake the carrying out of the general policy of the state.

Art. 120. During the mandate of their office, Ministers may not become members of the Board of Directors of a private co-operation or the agents of such corporation. They shall also be prohibited from engaging in any commercial or industrial work, or practising any liberal profession. During the mandate of their office, Ministers may not, directly or indirectly, compete for contracts or submit tenders to Ministries, Departments or establishment of the state, or to companies of the public sector.

Art. 121. The law shall define the limits of the penal and civil responsibilities of Ministers.

Art. 122. When the term of office of the President of the Republic expires or when he is permanently disabled from the discharge of the duties of his office for any reason, the Council of Ministers shall continue to run the affairs of the Government pending the nomination of a new cabinet by the new President of the Republic.

Art. 123. The President of the Republic shall have the power to have a Minister tried for crimes committed by him while discharging the functions of his office or because of these functions. The trial shall be conducted in accordance with provisions of the law and the Constitution.

Art. 124. The accused Minister shall be suspended from exercising his functions immediately on the accusation. His resignation or dismissal from office shall not impede his trial, the procedure of which shall take place as prescribed by the law.

Art. 125. The office of Minister and the membership of the People's Council may be held simultaneously.

Art. 126. Provisions relating to Ministers shall apply to Deputy Ministers.

Art. 127. The Council of Ministers shall have the following powers:

(1) Participating with the President of the Republic in the drawing up and implementation of the general policy of the State.

(2) Directing, coordinating and following up the work of the Ministries and of all public institutions and services attached to the State.

(3) Drawing up the general budget of the State.

(4) Drafting bills of law.

(5) Preparing plans of economic development, developing production, utilization of national resources, and all that may enhance and develop economy and increase the national income.

(6) Receiving loans and granting them in accordance with provisions of the Constitution.

(7) Concluding agreements and treaties in accordance with provisions of the Constitution.

(8) Following up the enforcement of laws, maintaining the security of the State and protecting the rights of citizens and the interests of the State.

(9) Issuing executive and administrative orders and supervising their enforcement.

Art. 128. In addition to the powers of the Council of Ministers, the President of the Council of Ministers and the Ministers shall have the powers defined by laws in force, provided these do not conflict with the powers granted by this Constitution to the other authorities of the State.

(3) PEOPLE'S LOCAL COUNCILS

Art. 129. (1) The People's Local Councils exercise their power in the administrative units in accordance with the provisions of the law.

(2) Administrative Units shall be determined by provisions of the law.

Art. 130. The law shall determine the competence of the People's Local Councils, the manner of their elections and formation and the rights and duties of their members and all other provisions relating to them.

Chapter III. Judicial Power

(1) JUDGES OF THE BENCH AND THE PROSECUTION

Art. 131. The Judicial Power is independent. The President of the Republic, assisted by the Supreme Judicial Council; shall guarantee this independence.

Art. 132. The President of the Republic shall preside over the Supreme Judicial Council; the law shall determine the powers, method of formation and rules of procedure of this Council.

Art. 133. (1) Judges are independent. They are subject to no authority other than that of the law in the discharge of their functions.

(2) The honor, conscience and impartiality of judges shall be a guarantee of the rights and freedoms of individuals.

Art. 134. Judgements are passed in the name of the Arab people of Syria.

Art. 135. The law shall organize the judicial machinery in all its kinds and degrees and shall determine the competence of the various courts.

Art. 136. The law shall determine conditions relating to the appointment, promotion, transfer, disciplinary action against, or dismissal of, judges.

Art. 137. The Public Prosecution is the judicial institution presided over by the Minister of Justice. The law shall determine its functions and powers.

Art. 138. The Council of State shall exercise judgment in administrative matters. The law shall determine conditions relating to the appointment, promotion, transfer, disciplinary action against, and the dismissal of, its judges.

(2) THE HIGH CONSTITUTIONAL COURT

Art. 139. The High Constitutional Court shall consist of five members, one of whom shall be President of the Court. Members are appointed by a decree issued by the President of the Republic.

Art. 140. A member of the High Constitutional Court may not be a Minister or a member of the People's Council. The law shall determine the other activities which are incompatible with membership of the Court.

Art. 141. The period of membership of the High Constitutional Court is four years. This period is renewable.

Art. 142. Members of the High Constitutional Court may not be dismissed from office except in accordance with provisions of the law.

Art. 143. Before assuming office, the President and members of the High Constitutional Court shall take, before the President of the Republic and in the presence of the Speaker of the People's Council, the following oath:

'I swear by Almighty God to respect the Constitution and laws of the country and to discharge my duties faithfully and impartially'.

Art. 144. The High Constitutional Court shall investigate charges relating to the legality of the election of members of the People's Council and shall report to the Council on results of the investigation.

Art. 145. The High Constitutional Court shall investigate and decide upon the constitutionality of laws in the following manner:

(1) If the President of the Republic, or one fourth of members of the People's Council, question the legality of a law before its promulgation, this promulgation shall be suspended until the Court decides the issue within 15 days from the date on which the objection to the law is submitted to the Court in writing. If the law is of an urgent nature, the Constitutional Court shall decide the issue within seven days.

(2) If one fourth of members of the People's Council challenges the constitutionality of a legislative Decree within 15 days of the commencement of a session of the Council, the High Constitutional Court has to decide the issue within 15 days from the date on which the objection to the law is submitted to the Court in writing.

(3) If the High Constitutional Court decides that a law or a legislative decree is contrary with the provisions of the Constitution, the part of it which is so judged by the Court shall be abrogated with retroactive effect and shall have no consequence.

Art. 146. The High Constitutional Court shall not have the power to investigate the constitutionality of laws referred by the President of the Republic to the people and approved by them in a popular referendum.

Art. 147. At the request of the President of the Republic, the High Constitutional Court shall give its opinion regarding the constitutionality of bills of law and legislative Decrees and the legality of Decrees.

Art. 148. The law shall regulate the procedure of deliberating on, and deciding matters within the competence of the High Constitutional Court, and shall determine its 'cadre', the conditions prerequisite in members of the Court as well as their salaries, immunitites, prerogatives and responsibilities.

PART THREE

AMENDMENT OF THE CONSTITUTION

Art. 149. (1) The President of the Republic, or one third of members of the People's Council, shall have the right to suggest an amendment of the Constitution.

(2) The amendment proposal shall give the text of the provisions proposed for amendment and the reasons for moving the proposal.

(3) Immediately on receipt of the amendment proposal, the People's Council shall refer it to a special Committee to study it.

(4) The Council shall debate the amendment proposal and if it is approved by three quarters of its members, the amendment shall be regarded as final provided it is ratified by the President of the Republic and incorporated in the Constitution.

PART FOUR

GENERAL AND TRANSITIONAL PROVISIONS

Art. 150. The Preamble to this Constitution shall be regarded as an integral and inseparable part of it.

Art. 151. This Constitution shall not be amended before 18 months from the date on which it becomes effective.

Art. 152. Pending the formation of the High Constitutional Court, the General body of the Court of Cassation shall investigate the legality of the election of members of the People's Council, after referring cases to it by the Speaker of the Council and shall report to the Speaker on results of the investigation.

Art. 153. All legislation in force issued before the proclamation of this Constitution shall remain effective until amended in conformity with its provisions.

Art. 154. The term of office of the incumbent President of the Republic expires after seven years from the date of the announcement of his election as President of the Syrian Arab Republic.

Art. 155. Election of the first People's Council in accordance with provisions of this Constitution shall be held within 90 days of the announcement of its approval by the people in a referendum.

Art. 156. The President of the Republic shall publish this Constitution in the 'Official Gazette', and its provisions shall become effective as from the date of its approval by the people in a referendum.

TAIWAN

SUMMARY

INTERNATIONAL STATUS

Taiwan, the Republic of China, the island of Formosa, is not a member of the United Nations. It retained the name and the claim to represent all China when the Nationalist (Kuomintang) government retreated from mainland China in 1949. It held the seat of China in the United Nations and other international bodies until 1971, when the government of the People's Republic of China was recognized as the government of China by the United Nations.

The Republic was founded in 1911 by Sun Yat-sen, who had founded the national party, the Kuomintang, in 1900. On February 12, 1912, the last emperor of the Manchu dynasty (1644–1911) was forced to abdicate and a provisional constitution was proclaimed in March. In 1915, a provisional Kuomintang government was set up in Canton under Sun Yat-sen. The Kuomintang and Communist parties co-operated from 1923 to 1927, and again during the period of the Japanese occupation from 1937 to the end of the Second World War. The civil war resumed in March 1946, and the Constituent Assembly met in Peking on November 15, 1946, without the participation of the Communists, and granted virtually absolute power to Chaing Kai-shek. By the middle of 1949, all of mainland China had fallen to the Communist forces under Mao.

Taiwan had been under Japanese occupation from the end of the Sino-Japanese war in 1895. It became again a Chinese province at the end of the second World War in 1945. The Kuomintang instituted rule from the mainland and suppressed with brutality a revolt in February 1947 of the Taiwanese against the maladministration of this rule. Before the Nationalist government retreated to Taiwan, they had proclaimed a state of siege and martial law in the island to last as long as 'communist rebellion' existed on the Chinese mainland. On December 8, 1949, the seat of government of the Republic of China was formally transferred to Taipeh. The island prospered economically with the imposition of agrarian reform and with American and Japanese aid. The state of siege continued with the suspension of a number of constitutional provisions including those guaranteeing individual rights. From 1948 to 1969, no elections to the legislature were held. After 1969, partial elections have been held approximately every three year to fill the 71 supplementary seats allotted to districts of Taiwan. The Kuomintang exercises a virtual monopoly of political power since the only parties authorized are those which existed in China before 1948. Opposition candidates may not form political parties.

After its expulsion in 1971 from the United Nations and the recognition by most countries of the People's Republic as the government of China, Taiwan is recognized diplomatically by 22 countries while more than 100 countries have commercial relations with Taiwan. Taiwan had rejected offers of the Chinese government in 1973, 1978 and 1981 to hold talks on reunification.

FORM OF NATIONAL GOVERNMENT

The Constitution of December 25, 1946, which entered into force on December 25, 1947, provides that China is a democratic republic of the people. by the people and for the people.[1] Sovereignty resides in the whole body of citizens.[2] Temporary Provisions effective during the period of Communist Rebellion were adopted on April 18, 1948, and amended in 1960 and 1966. They suspend most of the provisions concerning human rights and the legislature and provide for the President to promulgate regulations without being subject to the constitutional provisions concerning emergencies (Articles 39 and 43) or to the restrictions of Article 27 concerning the rights of initiative and referendum.

RIGHTS OF THE PEOPLE

The Consitution provides equality before the law, personal freedom and due process of law, freedom of residence, speech, teaching, writing, publication, privacy of correspondence, freedom of religious belief, of association and assembly.[3] The rights to work and property, to petition, to elections and to holding public office are guaranteed.[4]

[1] Const., Art. 1.
[2] Id., Art. 2.
[3] Id., Art. 7–14.
[4] Id., Art. 15–19.

LEGISLATIVE DEPARTMENT

The legislature is unicameral, composed of the Legislative Yuan. The Constitution provides for members to be elected, 5 to each province or municipality of all China with a population up to 3 million, and an additional member for each additional million of population; other members are elected by the Mongolian Leagues and Banners, Tibet, racial groups in frontier regions, Chinese abroad and occupational groups.[5] The term of office provided is 3 years.[6] It meets in two sessions a year.[7] Parliamentary immunities are provided.[8] The Constitution provides for a National Assembly of delegates elected every 6 years to elect the President and Vice-President, to amend the Constitution or vote on amendments submitted by the Legislative Yuan.[9]

EXECUTIVE DEPARTMENT

The President is the Head of State, supreme commander of the Armed Forces, has the power of appointment; the Constitution provides for the President and the Vice-President to be elected by the National Assembly for a term of six years, once renewable.[10] The Temporary Provisions provide that the President and Vice-President may be re-elected without being subject to the later restriction. The Executive Yuan, composed of a President appointed by the President of the Republic with the consent of the Legislative Yuan and ministers, is the highest administrative organ; it is responsible to the Legislative Yuan.[11] Chapters deal with the Examination Yuan,[12] the Control Yuan,[13] the powers of the central and local governments,[14] and the system of local government.[15]

JUDICIAL DEPARTMENT

The Judicial Yuan is the highest judicial organ. It has the power to interpret the Constitution and laws and orders.[16] Its President and Vice-President are appointed by the President of the Republic for life.[17]

AREA, POPULATION, ETC.

The area of Taiwan is 36,003 square Kilometres. The population (1982 estimate) is 18,325,852. The capital is Taipeh.

[5] Id., Art. 64.
[6] Id., Art. 65.
[7] Id., Art. 68.
[8] Id., Art. 73, 74.
[9] Id., Art. 26–28.
[10] Id., Atr. 47.
[11] Id., Art. 53–57.
[12] Id., Art. 83–89.
[13] Id., Art. 90–106.
[14] Id., Art. 107–111.
[15] Id., Art. 112–128.
[16] Id., Art. 78.
[17] Id., Art. 79, 81.

THE CONSTITUTION OF THE REPUBLIC OF CHINA[1] (TAIWAN)

December 25, 1946

the National Constituent Assembly of the Republic of China, by virtue of the mandate received from the whole body of citizens, in accordance with the teachings bequeathed by Dr. Sun Yat-sen in founding the Republic of China, and in order to consolidate the authority of the State, safeguard the rights of the people, ensure social tranquillity, and promote the welfare of the people, do hereby adopt this Constitution to be promulgated throughout the land for faithful and perpetual observance by one and all.

CHAPTER I

GENERAL PROVISIONS

Art. 1. The Republic of China, founded on the Three Principles of the People, shall be a democratic republic of the people, by the people and for the people.

Art. 2. The sovereignty of the Republic of China shall reside in the whole body of citizens.

Art. 3. Persons with the nationality of the Republic of China shall be citizens of the Republic of China.

Art. 4. The territory of the Republic of China within its existing national boundaries shall not be altered except by a resolution of the National Assembly.

Art. 5. There shall be complete equality among the various groups in the Republic of China.

Art. 6. The national flag of the Republic of China shall show a red fish with a blue sky and a white sun in the upper left corner.

CHAPTER II

RIGHTS AND DUTIES OF THE PEOPLE

Art. 7. All citizens of the Republic of China, irrespective of sex, religion, ethnic origin, class, or party affiliation, shall be equal before the law.

Art. 8. Personal freedom shall be guaranteed to the people. In no case except that of *flagrante delicto*, which shall be separately prescribed by law, shall any person be arrested or detained other than by a judicial or police organ in accordance with the procedure prescribed by law. No person shall be tried or punished other than by a law court in accordance with the procedure prescribed by law. Any arrest, detention, trial, or punishment not carried out in accordance with the procedure prescribed by law may be resisted.

[1] Supplied by Ministry of Foreign Affairs in June 1979. Ed

When a person is arrested or detained on suspicion of having committed a crime, the organ making the arrest or detention shall inform him in writing, and any relative or friend of his designated by him, of the grounds for his arrest or detention, and shall turn him over, not later than twenty-four hours after his arrest, to a competent court for trial. The said person, or any other person may petition the competent court to serve a writ on the organ making the arrest to surrender within twenty-four hours the said person for trial.

The court shall not reject the petition referred to in the preceding paragraph, nor shall it first of all order the organ concerned to make an investigation and submit a report thereon. The organ concerned shall not refuse to comply, or delay in complying, with the writ of the court for the surrender of the said person for trial.

When a person is unlawfully arrrested or detained by any organ, he or any other person may petition the court to make an investigation. The court shall not reject such a petition and shall, within twenty-four hours, investigate the action taken by the organ concerned and deal with the matter in accordance with law.

Art. 9. Except those in active military service, no person shall be liable to court-martial.

Art. 10. The people shall have freedom of residence and of change of residence.

Art. 11. The people shall have freedom of speech, teaching, writing, and publication.

Art. 12. The people shall have freedom of privacy of correspondence.

Art. 13. The people shall have freedom of religious belief.

Art. 14. The people shall have freedom of assembly and of association.

Art. 15. The right to live, the right to work, and the right to own property shall be guaranteed to the people.

Art. 16. The people shall have the right to present petitions, lodge complaints, and institute legal proceedings.

Art. 17. The people shall have the rights of election, recall, initiative, and referendum.

Art. 18. The people shall have the right to take public examinations and hold public offices.

Art. 19. The people shall have the duty to pay taxes in accordance with law.

Art. 20. The people shall have the duty to render military service in accordance with law.

Art. 21. The people shall have the right and duty to receive elementary education.

Art. 22. All other freedoms and rights of the people that are not detrimental to social order or public welfare shall be guaranteed under the Constitution.

Art. 23. All the freedoms and rights enumerated in the preceding Articles shall not be abridged by law except such as may be necessary to prevent infringement upon the freedoms of others, to avert an imminent danger, to maintain social order, or to promote public welfare.

Art. 24. Any public employee who, in violation of law, infringes upon the freedom or right of any person shall, in addition to being subject to disciplinary punishment in accordance with law, be liable to criminal and civil action. The victim may, in accordance with law, claim damages from the State for any injury sustained therefrom.

CHAPTER III

THE NATIONAL ASSEMBLY

Art. 25. The National Assembly shall, in accordance with the provisions of this Constitution, exercise political rights on behalf of all the citizens of the country.

Art. 26. The National Assembly shall be composed of the following Delegates:

1. One Delegate shall be elected from each County, Municipality, or area of equivalent status. In case the population of the electoral district exceeds 500,000. one additional Delegate shall be elected for each additional 500,000. The election of Delegates representing areas equivalent in status to the County or Municipality shall be prescribed by law.

2. Delegates to represent Mongolia shall be elected on the basis of four for each League and one for each Special Banner.

3. The number of Delegates to be elected from Tibet shall be prescribed by law.

4. The number of Delegates to be elected by various ethnic groups in frontier regions shall be prescribed by law.

5. The number of Delegates to be elected by Chinese citizens residing abroad shall be prescribed by law.

6. The number of Delegates to be elected by occupational groups shall be presecribed by law.

7. The number of Delegates to be elected by women's organizations shall be prescribed by law.

Art. 27. The functions of the National Assembly shall be as follows:

1. To elect the President and the Vice-President.

2. To recall the President and the Vice-President.

3. To amend the Consitution.

4. To vote in the exercise of its right of referendum on proposed constitutional amendments originating in the Legislative Yuan.

With respect to the rights of initiative and referendum, except as is provided in Items 3 and 4 of the preceding paragraph, the National Assembly shall adopt regulations pertaining thereto and put them into effect after one half of the Counties and Municipalities of the country shall have exercised their rights of initiative and referendum in their respective jurisdictions.

Art. 28. A new election for Delegates to the National Assembly shall be held every six years.

The term of office of the Delegates to each National Assembly shall terminate on the day the next National Assembly convenes.

No incumbent government official may be elected a Delegate to the National Assembly to represent the electoral district in which he holds office.

Art. 29. The National Assembly shall be convoked by the President to meet ninety days prior to the expiration of each Presidential term.

Art. 30. An extraordinary session of the National Assembly shall be convoked in any one of the following circumstances:

1. When, in accordance with the provisions of Article 49 of the Constitution, a new President and a new Vice-President are to be elected.
2. When, by a resolution of the Control Yuan, an impeachment of the President or the Vice-President is instituted.
3. When, by a resolution of the Legislative Yuan, an amendment ot the Constitution is proposed.
4. When over two fifths of the Delegates to the National Assembly request that an extraordinary session be convoked.

When an extraordinary session of the National Assembly is to be convoked in accordance with Item 1 or Item 2 of the preceding paragraph, the President of the Legislative Yuan shall issue the notice of convocation; when it is to be convoked in accordance with Item 3 or Item 4, it shall be convoked by the President of the Republic.

Art. 31. The National Assembly shall meet at the seat of the Central Government.

Art. 32. No Delegate to the National Assembly shall be held responsible outside the Assembly for opinions expressed or votes cast at meetings of the Assembly.

Art. 33. While the Assembly is in session, no Delegate to the National Assembly shall, except in case of *flagrante delicto*, be arrested or detained without the permission of the National Assembly.

Art. 34. The organization of the National Assembly, the election and recall of Delegates to the National Assembly, and the procedure whereby the National Assembly carries out its functions shall be prescribed by law.

CHAPTER IV

THE PRESIDENCY

Art. 35. The President shall be the Chief of State and shall represent the Republic of China in foreign relations.

Art. 36. The President shall have supreme command of the army, navy, and air force of the country.

Art. 37. The President shall, in accordance with law, promulgate laws and issue mandates with the countersignature of the President of the Executive Yuan or with the countersignatures of both the President of the Executive Yuan and the Ministers or Chairmen of Commissions concerned.

Art. 38. The President shall, in accordance with the provisions of this Constitution, exercise the powers of concluding treaties, declaring war, and making peace.

Art. 39. The President may, in accordance with law, declare martial law with the approval of, or subject to confirmation by, the Legislative Yuan. When the Legislative

Yuan deems it necessary, it may, by a formal resolution, request the President to lift the martial law already declared.

Art. 40. The President shall, in accordance with law, exercise the powers of amnesty, pardon, remission of sentence, and restitution of civil rights.

Art. 41. The President shall, in accordance with law, appoint and dismiss civil and military officers.

Art. 42. The President may, in accordance with law, confer honors and decorations.

Art. 43. In case of a natural disaster, an epidemic, or a national financial or economic crisis that calls for emergency action, the President, if the Legislative Yuan happens to be in recess, may, by a resolution of the Executive Yuan Council and in accordance with the Law on Emergency Orders, issue emergency orders and take such measures as may be necessary to cope with the situtation. But the action thus taken shall be submitted to the Legislative Yuan for confirmation within one month after issuance of the emergency orders. In case the Legislative Yuan withholds confirmation, the said orders shall immediately become null and void.

Art. 44. In case of disputes, involving two or more Yuan, other than those for which provisions are made in this Constitution, the President may call a meeting of the Presidents of the Yuan concerned to work out a solution therefor.

Art. 45. Any citizen of the Republic of China who has reached the age of forty may be elected President or Vice-President.

Art. 46. The election of the President and the Vice-President shall be prescribed by law.

Art. 47. The President and the Vice-President shall serve a term of six years. If re-elected, they may serve one more term.

Art. 48. On assuming office, the President shall take an oath, which shall read as follows:

> 'I do solemnly and with all sincerity swear before the people of the whole country that I will observe the Constitution, faithfully perform my duties, promote the welfare of the people. and safeguard the security of the State so as not to betray the people's trust. Should I break my oath, I will submit myself to severe punishment by the State. This is my solemn oath.'

Art. 49. In case the office of the President should become vacant, the Vice-President shall succeed to it until the expiration of the original Presidential term. In case the office of both the President and Vice-President should become vacant, the President of the Executive Yuan shall act for the President and, in accordance with the provisions of Article 30 of this Constitution, convoke an extraordinary session of the National Assembly to elect a new President and a new Vice-President to serve out the unfinished term of the preceding President. In case the President should, for any cause, be unable to attend to his official duties, the Vice-President shall act for him. In case both the President and the Vice-President should be unable to attend their official duties, the President of the Executive Yuan shall act for the President.

Art. 50. The President shall be relieved of his duties on the day his term of office expires. If, by that time, the next President has not yet been elected, or if the President-elect and the Vice-President-elect have not yet assumed office, the President of the Executive Yuan shall act for the President.

Art. 51. The period during which the President of the Executive Yuan acts for the President shall not exceed three months.

Art. 52. Unless the President is guilty of rebellion or treason, he shall not be liable to criminal prosecution without having been recalled or relieved of his duties as President.

CHAPTER V

ADMINISTRATION

Art. 53. The Executive Yuan shall be the highest administrative organ of the State.

Art. 54. The Executive Yuan shall have a President, a Vice-President, and a number of Ministers and Chairmen of Commissions, and Ministers without Portfolio.

Art. 55. The President of the Executive Yuan shall be nominated and, upon confirmation by the Legislative Yuan, appointed by the President of the Republic.

If the President of the Executive Yuan should resign or his office should become vacant when the Legislative Yuan is not in session, his duties and functions shall be performed for him by the Vice-President of the Executive Yuan. But the President of the Republic shall, within forty days, request the Legislative Yuan to convoke a meeting for the confirmation of the nominee he has selected as the next President of the Executive Yuan. Pending confirmation of the nominee, the Vice-President of the Executive Yuan shall temporarily perform the duties and functions of the President of the said Yuan.

Art. 56. The Vice-President of the Executive Yuan, Ministers and Chairman of Commissions, and Ministers without Portfolio shall be appointed by the President of the Republic upon the recommendation of the President of the Executive Yuan.

Art. 57. The Executive Yuan shall be responsible to the Legislative Yuan in accordance with the following provisions:

1. The Executive Yuan has the duty to present to the Legislative Yuan a policy statement and an administrative report. When the Legislative Yuan is in session, its Members have the right to interpellate the President of the Executive Yuan and Ministers and Chairmen of Commissions of the said Yuan.

2. In case of the Legislative Yuan does not agree with any major policy of the Executive Yuan, it may, by a formal resolution, request the Executive Yuan to change it. Confronted with the Legislative Yuan's resolution, the Executive Yuan may, with the approval of the President of the Republic, request the Legislative Yuan for reconsideration. If, during reconsideration, two thirds of the members of the Legislative Yuan present at the meeting uphold the original resolution, the President of the Executive Yuan shall either accede to the Legislative Yuan's view or tender his resignation.

3. In case the Executive Yuan deems an enactment, a budget, or a treaty passed by the Legislative Yuan difficult to enforce, it may, with the approval of the President of the Republic and within ten days after the transmission of the Legislative Yuan's message, request the latter for reconsideration. If, during reconsideration, two thirds of the members of the Legislative Yuan present at the meeting uphold the original resolution, the President of the Executive Yuan shall either abide by the Legislative Yuan's resolution or tender his resignation.

Art. 58. In the Executive Yuan there shall be an Executive Yuan Council to be composed of its President, Vice-President, Ministers and Chairmen of Commissions, and Ministers without Portfolio, with its President as Chairman.

Bills on proposed laws, budgets, martial law, amnesty, declaration of war, conclusion of peace, treaties, and other important matters to be submitted to the Legislative Yuan, as well as matters of common concern to all the ministries and commissions, shall be laid before the Executive Yuan Council by the President of the Executive Yuan and by the various Ministers and Chairmen of Commissions for its consideration and decision.

Art. 59. The Executive Yuan shall, three months before the beginning of each fiscal year, submit to the Legislative Yuan a budgetary bill for the following fiscal year.

Art. 60. The Executive Yuan shall, within four months after the end of each fiscal year, submit to the Control Yuan a final financial statement of the year.

Art. 61. The organization of the Executive Yuan shall be prescribed by law.

CHAPTER VI

LEGISLATION

Art. 62. The Legislative Yuan shall be the highest legislative organ of the State. It shall be composed of Members elected by the people and shall exercise legislative power on their behalf.

Art. 63. The Legislative Yuan shall have the power to pass bills on laws, budgets, martial law, amnesty, declaration of war, conclusion of peace, treaties, and other important matters of State.

Art. 64. Members of the Legislative Yuan shall be elected in accordance with the folowing provisions:

1. Those to be elected from the Provinces or Municipalities under the direct jurisdiction of the Executive Yuan shall be five for each Province or Municipality with a population of not more than 3,000,000, one additional Member shall be elected for each additional 1.000,000.
2. Those to be elected from Mongolian Leagues and Banners.
3. Those to be elected from Tibet.
4. Those to be elected by the ethnic groups in frontier regions.
5. Those to be elected by Chinese citizens residing abroad.
6. Those to be elected by occupational groups.

The election of Members of the Legislative Yuan and the number of those to be elected under items 2 to 6 of the preceding paragraph shall be prescribed by law. The number of women to be elected under all the items of the preceding paragraph shall be prescribed by law.

Art. 65. Members of the Legislative Yuan shall serve a term of three years and shall be re-elegible. Their election shall be completed within three months prior to the expiration of each term.

Art. 66. The Legislative Yuan shall have a President and a Vice-President to be elected from among its Members.

Art. 67. The Legislative Yuan may set up various committees.

The various committees of the Legislative Yuan may invite government officials and concerned individuals in society at large to be present at the committee meetings to present their views.

Art. 68. The Legislative Yuan shall hold two sessions each year and shall convene of its own accord. The first session shall be from February to the end of May, and the second from September to the end of December. Any session may be prolonged, if necessary.

Art. 69. An extraordinary session of the Legislative Yuan may be held in either of the following circumstances:

1. At the request of the President of the Republic.
2. At the request of over one fourth of its own Members.

Art. 70. The Legislative Yuan shall not propose any increase in the budget estimates submitted by the Executive Yuan.

Art. 71. At meetings of the Legislative Yuan, the Presidents of the various Yuan concerned and the various Ministers and Chairmen of Commissions concerned may be present to present their views.

Art. 72. Law bills passed by the Legislative Yuan shall be transmitted to the President of the Republic and the Executive Yuan. The President shall, within ten days after receipt of the bills, promulgate them, but he may also deal with them in accordance with the provisions of Article 57 of this Constitution.

Art. 73. No Member of the Legislative Yuan shall be held responsible outside the Yuan for opinions expressed or votes cast in the Yuan.

Art. 74. No Member of the Legislative Yuan shall, except in case of *flagrante delicto*, be arrested or detained without the permission of the Legislative Yuan.

Art. 75. No Member of the Legislative Yuan shall concurrently hold a government post.

Art. 76. The organization of the Legislative Yuan shall be prescribed by law.

CHAPTER VII

THE JUDICIARY

Art. 77. The Judicial Yuan shall be the highest judicial organ of the State. It shall be responsible for the trial of civil, criminal, and administrative cases and the disciplinary punishment of public employees.

Art. 78. The Judicial Yuan shall interpret the Constitution and shall have the power to unify the interpretation of laws and ordinances.

Art. 79. The Judicial Yuan shall have a President and a Vice-President. The President and the Vice-President of the Judicial Yuan shall be nominated and, upon confirmation by the Control Yuan, appointed by the President of the Republic.

The Judicial Yuan shall have a number of Grand Justices to be responsible for the matters specified in Article 78 of this Constitution. The Grand Justices shall be nominated and, upon confirmaton by the Control Yuan, appointed by the President of the Republic.

Art. 80. Judges shall be non-partisan. They shall try cases independently, in accordance with law, and be free from any interference.

Art. 81. Judges shall hold office for life. No judge shall be removed from office unless he has been guilty of a criminal offense or subjected to disciplinary action, or declared to be under interdiction. No judge shall, except in accordance with law, be suspended from office, transferred, or liable to salary cuts.

Art. 82. The organization of the Judicial Yuan and the different grades of law courts shall be prescribed by law.

CHAPTER VIII

EXAMINATION

Art. 83. The Examination Yuan shall be the highest examination organ of the State. It shall be responsible for matters relating to examination, employment, official grading, service rating, salary scales, promotion and transfer, security of tenure, commendation, pension for the deceased's family, retirement, and old-age pension.

Art. 84. The Examination Yuan shall have a President, a Vice-President, and a number of Members. They shall be nominated and, upon confirmation by the Control Yuan, appointed by the President of the Republic.

Art. 85. Public employees shall be selected through a system of open, competitive examination. Provincial and area quotas shall be fixed and examinations shall be held in different areas. No person shall be appointed to a public office unless he has successfully passed such an examination.

Art. 86. The following qualifications shall be determined by examination and screening by the Examination Yuan in accordance with law:

1. Qualifications for appointment as public employees.
2. Qualifications for practice in specialized professions and as technicians.

Art. 87. The Examination Yuan may, with respect to matters for which it is responsible, submit draft law bills to the Legislative Yuan.

Art. 88. Members of the Examination Yuan shall be non-partisan and shall exercise their functions independently, in accordance with law.

Art. 89. The organization of the Examination Yuan shall be prescribed by law.

CHAPTER IX

CONTROL

Art. 90. The Control Yuan shall be the highest control organ of the State. It shall exercise the powers of consent, impeachment, censure, and auditing.

Art. 91. The Control Yuan shall be composed of Members to be elected by Provincial and Municipal Councils, the local Councils of Mongolia and Tibet, and Chinese citizens residing abroad. Their quotas shall be allotted according to the following provisions:

1. Five Members for each Province.
2. Two Members for each Municipality under the direct jurisdiction of the Executive Yuan.
3. Eight Members for the Mongolian Leagues and Banners.
4. Eight Members for Tibet.
5. Eight Members for Chinese citizens residing abroad.

Art. 92. The Control Yuan shall have a President and a Vice-President to be elected from among its Members.

Art. 93. Members of the Control Yuan shall serve a term of six years and may be re-eligible.

Art. 94. In exercising its power of confirmation in accordance with this Constitution, the Control Yuan shall do so by a majority vote of the Members present at the meeting.

Art. 95. In exercising its power of control, the Control Yuan may request the Executive Yuan and its Ministries and Commissions to make available to it any orders they have issued and all other relevant documents.

Art. 96. The Control Yuan may, according to the work of the Executive Yuan and its Ministries and Commissions, set up a number of committees to look into all aspects of their activities to see whether there is any violation of law or dereliction of duty.

Art. 97. The Control Yuan may, on the basis of the findings and resolutions of its committees, propose corrective measures and transmit them to the Executive Yuan and its Ministries and Commissions concerned with the request that corrective action be taken.

In case the Control Yuan deems a public employee in the Central Government or in a local government guilty of dereliction of duty or violation of law, it may propose corrective measures or institute an impeachment. If it involves a criminal offense, the case shall be turned over to a law court.

Art. 98. Impeachment by the Control Yuan of a public employee in the Central Government or in a local government shall be instituted upon the proposal of one or more than one Member of the Control Yuan and the decision, after careful consideration, by a committee composed of nine or more than nine Members.

Art. 99. In case of Impeachment of the personnel of the Judicial Yuan or of the Examination Yuan for dereliction of duty or violation of law, the provisions of Articles 95, 97, and 98 of this Constitution shall apply.

Art. 100. Impeachment proceedings initiated by the Control Yuan against the President or the Vice President shall be instituted upon the proposal of one fourth or more than one fourth of all Members of the Control Yuan and the resolution, after careful consideration, by a majority of all Members of the Control Yuan. The impeachment proceedings thus instituted shall be transmitted to the National Assembly for action.

Art. 101. No Member of the Control Yuan shall be held responsible outside the Yuan for opinions expressed or votes cast in the Yuan.

Art. 102. No Member of the Control Yuan shall, except in case of *flagrante delicto,* be arrested or detained without the permission of the Control Yuan.

Art. 103. No member of the Control Yuan shall concurrently hold any other public office or engage in any profession.

Art. 104. The Control Yuan shall have an Auditor-General who shall be nominated and, upon confirmation by the Legislative Yuan, appointed by the President of the Republic.

Art. 105. The Auditor-General shall, within three months after submission by the Executive Yuan of the final financial statement, complete the auditing thereof in accordance with law and submit an audit to the Legislative Yuan.

Art. 106. The organization of the Control Yuan shall be prescribed by law.

CHAPTER X

POWERS OF THE CENTRAL AND LOCAL GOVERNMENTS

Art. 107. The Central Government shall be competent to legislate and execute the following matters:

1. Foreign affairs.
2. National defense and military affairs bearing on national defense.
3. Nationality law and criminal, civil, and commercial laws.
4. The judiciary.
5. Aviation, national highways, State-owned railways, navigation, and postal and telecommunication services.
6. Central Government finance and national taxes.
7. Demarcation of national, provincial, and county taxes.
8. State-operated economic enterprises.
9. The currency system and State banks.
10. Weights and measures.
11. Foreign trade policy.
12. Financial and economic matters affecting aliens or foreign countries.
13. Other matters of the Central Government as provided by this Constitution.

Art. 108. The Central Government shall be competent to legislate and execute the following matters, which, however, may also be delegated to the provincial or county government to execute:

1. General principles of provincial and county self-government.

2. Demarcation of administrative areas.
3. Forestry, industry, mining, and commerce.
4. The educational system.
5. Banking and stock exchange.
6. Shipping and deep-sea fishery.
7. Public utilities.
8. Cooperative enterprises.
9. Interprovincial water and land communication and transportation.
10. Interprovincial water conservancy, waterways, agriculture, and animal husbandry.
11. Official grading, employment, surveillance, and security of tenure of officials in the Central and local governments.
12. Land legislation.
13. Labor legislation and other social legislation.
14. Right of eminent domain.
15. Census taking and compilation of population statistics for the whole country.
16. Population migration and land reclamation.
17. The police system.
18. Public health.
19. Disaster relief, pension for the deceased's family, and unemployment relief.
20. Preservation of ancient books, ancient relics, and ancient monuments of cultural value.

With respect to the various items referred to in the preceding paragraph, the Provinces may enact separate rules and regulations provided they do not contravene national laws.

Art. 109. The Provincial Government shall be competent to legislate and execute the following matters, which, however, may also be delegated to the county governments to execute:

1. Provincial education, public health, industry, and communications.
2. Management and disposal of provincial property.
3. Administration of cities under provincial jurisdiction.
4. Provincial public enterprises.
5. Provincial cooperative enterprises.
6. Provincial agriculture, forestry, water conservancy, fishery, animal husbandry, and public works.
7. Provincial finance and provincial taxes.
8. Provincial debts.
9. Provincial banks.
10. Provincial police administration.
11. Provincial philanthropic and public welfare work.
12. Other matters delegated to the Provinces in accordance with national laws.

Unless otherwise provided by law, any of the matters referred to in the various items of the preceding paragraph, if it involves two or more Provinces, may be jointly undertaken by the Provinces concerned.

In case any of the Provinces lacks sufficient funds to undertake any of the matters referred to in the various items of the preceding paragraph, subsidies may be granted from the National Treasury by a resolution of the Legislative Yuan.

Art. 110. The county government shall be competent to legislate and execute the following matters:

1. County education, public health, industry, and communications.
2. Management and disposal of county property.
3. County public enterprises.
4. County co-operative enterprises.
5. County agriculture, forestry, water conservancy, fishery, animal husbandry, and public works.
6. County finance and taxes.
7. County debts.
8. County banks.
9. County police administration.
10. County philanthropic and public welfare work.
11. Other matters delegated to the County in accordance with national laws and Provincial Self-Government Regulations.

Unless otherwise provided by law, any of the matters referred to in the various items of the preceding paragraph, if it involves two or more Counties, may be jointly undertaken by the Counties concerned.

Art. 111. Any matter not specifically mentioned in Articles 107, 108, 109 and 110 shall fall within the jurisdiction of the Central Government if it is national in nature, within that of the Province if it is provincial in nature, and within that of the County if it is county in nature. In case of dispute, the matter shall be settled by the Legislative Yuan.

CHAPTER XI

SYSTEM OF LOCAL GOVERNMENT

Section 1. The Province

Art. 112. A Province may convoke a Provincial People's Representatives Conference to draw up, in accordance with the General Principles of Provincial and County Self-Government, a set of Provincial Self-Government Regulations which, however, shall not contravene the Constitution.

The organization of the Provincial People's Representatives Conference and the election of the Representatives shall be prescribed by law.

Art. 113. The Provincial Self-Government Regulations shall include the following provisions:

1. There shall be a Provincial Assembly; Members of the Provincial Assembly shall be elected by the people of the Province.

2. There shall be a Provincial Government and a Provincial Governor; the Provincial Governor shall be elected by the people of the Province.

3. Relationship between the Province and the Counties.

The legislative powers of the Province shall be exercised by the Provincial Assembly.

Art. 114. The Provincial Self-Government Regulations, after being enacted, shall be submitted to the Judicial Yuan. If the Judicial Yuan deems any part of the Regulations unconstitutional, it shall declare the relevant provisions null and void.

Art. 115. If, in the course of implementing the Provincial Self-Government Regulations, there should arise any serious obstacle in the application of any of the articles contained therein, the Judicial Yuan shall first summon the various parties concerned to present their views. Then, the Presidents of the Executive Yuan, the Legislative Yuan, the Judicial Yuan, the Examination Yuan, and the Control Yuan shall form themselves into a committee under the chairmanship of the President of the Judicial Yuan to propose a formula for solution.

Art. 116. Provincial rules and regulations that contravene national laws shall be null and void.

Art. 117. In case of doubt as to whether any provincial rule or regulation contravenes national laws, the matter shall be settled by interpretation by the Judicial Yuan.

Art. 118. The self-government of Municipalities under the direct jurisdiction of the Executive Yuan shall be prescribed by law.

Art. 119. The local self-government system of the Mongolian Leagues and Banners shall be prescribed by law.

Art. 120. The system of self-government in Tibet shall be safeguarded.

Section 2. The County

Art. 121. The County shall practise county self-government.

Art. 122. A County may convoke a County People's Representatives Conference to draw up, in accordance with the General Principles of Provincial and County Self-Government, a set of County Self-Government Reguations which, however, shall not contravene the Constitution and the Provincial Self-Government Regulations.

Art. 123. The people of the County shall, in accordance with law, exercise the rights of initiative and referendum in matters relating to county self-government and shall, in accordance with law, exercise the rights of election and recall of the Magistrate and other county self-government officials.

Art. 124. There shall be a County Council. Members of the County Council shall be elected by the people of the County.

The legislative power of the County shall be exercised by the County Council.

Art. 125. County rules and regulations that contravene national laws or provincial rules and regulations shall be null and void.

Art. 126. There shall be a County Government and a Magistrate; the Magistrate shall be elected by the people of the County.

Art. 127. The Magistrate shall have charge of all matters relating to county self-government and shall administer such matters as are delegated to the County by the Central and Provincial Governments.

Art. 128. The provisions governing the County shall apply *mutatis mutandis* to the Municipality.

CHAPTER XII

ELECTION, RECALL, INITIATIVE, AND REFERENDUM

Art. 129. The various kinds of election provided in this Constitution, unless otherwise stipulated in this Constitution, shall be by universal, equal, and direct suffrage and by secret ballot.

Art. 130. Any citizen of the Republic of China who has attained the age of twenty shall have the right of election in accordance with law. Unless otherwise provided by this Constitution or by law, any citizen who has attained the age of twenty-three shall have the right of being elected in accordance with law.

Art. 131. All candidates in the various kinds of election prescribed in this Constitution shall openly conduct their electoral campaigns.

Art. 132. Intimidation or offer of pecuniary inducements shall be strictly forbidden in elections. Electoral litigations shall be settled by law courts.

Art. 133. A person duly elected may be recalled by his constituency in accordance with law.

Art. 134. In the various kinds of election, quotas of successful candidates shall be assigned to women; methods of implementation shall be prescribed by law.

Art. 135. The number of Delegates to the National Assembly to be elected by people in interior areas with special ways of living and habits and the methods of their election shall be prescribed by law.

Art. 136. The exercise of the rights of initiative and referendum shall be prescribed by law.

CHAPTER XIII

FUNDAMENTAL NATIONAL POLICIES

Section 1. National Defense

Art. 137. It shall be the objective of the national defense of the Republic of China to safeguard national security and preserve world peace.

The organization of national defense shall be prescribed by law.

Art. 138. The army, navy, and air force of the nation shall rise above personal, regional, and party affiliations and shall be loyal to the State and love and protect the people.

Art. 139. No political party and no individual shall make use of armed forces as an instrument in the struggle for political power.

Art. 140. No person in active military service shall concurrently hold a civil office.

Section 2. Foreign Policy

Art. 141. The foreign policy of the Republic of China shall be conceived in a spirit of independence and self-reliance and based on the principles of equality and reciprocity to promote friendly relations with other nations and abide by treaties and the Charter of the United Nations so as to protect the rights and interests of Chinese citizens residing abroad, foster international cooperation, advance international justice, and insure world peace.

Section 3. The National Economy

Art. 142. The national economy shall be based on the Principle of People's Livelihood and shall seek to effect the equalization of land rights and regulation of private capital in order to assure an equitable distribution of national wealth and sufficiency for the people's livelihood.

Art. 143. All land within the territoral limits of the Republic of China shall belong to the entire body of citizens. Private ownership of land, acquired by the people in accordance with law, shall be protected and restricted by law. Privately owned land shall pay taxes according to its value and may be purchased by the Government according to its value.

Mineral ores embedded in the land and natural forces which can be economically utilized for public benefit shall belong to the State, even if ownership of the land may have been acquired by private individuals.

The State shall levy a land value increment tax on any land whose value has increased not through the application of labor or capital, and the proceeds therefrom shall be used for the people at large.

In the distribution and readjustment of land, the State shall, in principle, assist owner-farmers and owner-users of land and shall also regulate their appropriate areas of operation.

Art. 144. Public utilities and other enterprises of monopolistic nature, in principle, shall be under public operation. In cases permitted by law, they may be operated by private citizens.

Art. 145. With respect to private wealth and privately operated enterprises, the State shall restrict them by law if they are deemed detrimental to the balanced development of national wealth and people's livelihood.

Co-operative enterprises shall receive encouragement and assistance from the State.

Private citizens productive enterprises and foreign trade shall recieve encouragement, guidance, and protection by the State.

Art. 146. The State shall, by use of scientific techniques, develop water conservancy, increase the productivity of land, improve agricultural conditions, develop agricultural resources, and foster the industrialization of agriculture.

Art. 147. The Central Government, in order to achieve a balanced development of the economy of the various Provinces, shall extend appropriate financial assistance to the poorer and less productive Provinces.

The Provincial Government, in order to achieve a balanced development of the economy of the various Counties, shall extend appropriate financial assistance to the poorer and less productive Counties.

Art. 148. Within the territory of the Republic of China, all commodities shall be permitted to move freely from place to place.

Art. 149. Financial institutions shall, in accordance with law, be subject to State control.

Art. 150. The State shall widely establish financial institutions for the common people so as to relieve unemployment.

Art. 151. With respect to Chinese citizens residing abroad, the State shall foster and protect the development of their economic enterprises.

Section 4. Social Security

Art. 152. The State shall provide suitable opportunities for work to those persons who have the ability to work.

Art. 153. The State shall enact laws and carry out policies for the protection of laborers and farmers so as to better their livelihood and improve their productive skills.

Special protection shall be provided for women and children doing manual labor, according to their age and physical conditions.

Art. 154. Management and labor shall act in accordance with the principles of harmony and cooperation for the development of productive enterprises. Conciliation and arbitration of disputes between capital and labor shall be prescribed by law.

Art. 155. The State shall establish a system of social insurance to promote social welfare. To the aged and the physically disabled who are unable to make a living, and to victims of extraordinary calamities, the State shall provide appropriate assistance and relief.

Art. 156. The State, in order to consolidate the foundation of national existence and development, shall protect motherhood and carry out a policy for the promotion of the welfare of women and children.

Art. 157. The State, in order to improve national health, shall establish extensive services for sanitation and health protection and a system of public medical care.

Section 5. Education and Culture

Art. 158. Education and culture shall aim at the development, among the citizens, of the national spirit, the spirit of self-government, national morality, a healthy physique, scientific knowledge, and the ability to earn a living.

Art. 159. All citizens shall have an equal opportunity to receive education.

Art. 160. All children of school age from six to twelve years shall receive free elementary education. Those from poor families shall be supplied with books by the Government.

All citizens above school age who have not received elementary education shall receive supplementary education free of charge and shall also be supplied with books by the Government.

Art. 161. The various levels of government shall provide a large number of scholarships to assist students of good scholastic standing and exemplary conduct who lack the means to continue their school education.

Art. 162. All public and private education and cultural institutions in the country shall, in accordance with law, be subject to State supervision.

Art. 163. The State shall pay due attention to the balanced development of education in different regions and shall promote social education to elevate the cultural standards of the citizens in general. Grants from the National Treasury shall be made to frontier regions and economically poor areas to help them meet their educational and cultural expenses. The Central Government may either itself undertake the more important educational and cultural enterprises in such regions and areas or render them financial assistance.

Art. 164. Funds earmarked for education, science, and culture shall be, in respect of the Central Government, not less than fifteen percent of the total national budget; in respect of the Provincial Government, not less than twenty-five percent of the total Provincial budget; and in respect of the Municipal or County Government, not less than thirty-five percent of the total Municipal or County budget. Educational and cultural foundations established in accordance with law, and their property, shall be protected.

Art. 165. The State shall safeguard the livelihood of educational, scientific, and artistic workers and shall, as the national economy develops, increase their remuneration from time to time.

Art. 166. The State shall encourage scientific discoveries and inventions and shall protect ancient monuments and ancient relics of historical, cultural, or artistic value.

Art. 167. The State shall encourage or subsidize the following enterprises or individuals:

1. Private educational enterprises with outstanding records.
2. Overseas Chinese education enterprises with outstanding records.
3. Individuals who have made scholarly or technical inventions.
4. Educational workers who have rendered long and meritorious services.

Section 6. The Frontier Regions

Art. 168. The State shall accord to the various ethnic groups in the frontier regions legal protection of thier status and shal give special assistance to their work in local self-government.

Art. 169. The State shall actively undertake and foster the development of education, culture, communications, water conservancy, public health, and other economic and social enterprises among the various ethnic groups in the frontier regions. With respect to land utilization, the State shall, in the light of climatic conditions, nature of the soil, and the life and habits of the people, adopt measures for its protection and assist in its development.

CHAPTER XIV

ENFORCEMENT AND AMENDMENT OF THE CONSITUTION

Art. 170. The term 'law' referred to in this Constitution shall mean any legislative bill duly passed by the Legislative Yuan and promulgated by the President of the Republic.

Art. 171. Laws that contravene the Constitution shall be null and void.

In case of doubt as to whether a given law contravenes the Constitution, the matter shall be settled by interpretation by the Judicial Yuan.

Art. 172. Any ordinance that contravenes the Constitution or laws shall be null and void.

Art. 173. The Constitution shall be interpreted by the Judicial Yuan.

Art. 174. The Constitution shall be amended in accordance with either one of the following procedures:

1. The Constitution may be amended upon the proposal of one fifth of the total number of Delegates to the National Assembly and by a resolution of three fourths of the Delegates present at a meeting with a quorum of two thirds of all Delegates to the National Assembly.

2. An amendment to the Constitution may be drawn up by the Legislative Yuan and submitted by it to the National Assembly for concurrence through referendum upon the proposal of one fourth of the Members of the Legislative Yuan and by a resolution of three fourths of the Members present at a meeting with a quorum of three fourths of all Members of the Yuan. Such a proposed amendment to the Constitution shall be publicly announced half a year before the National Assembly meets.

Art. 175. Whenever necessary, enforcement procedures in regard to any matter referred to in this Constitution shall be separately prescribed by law.

The preparatory procedures for the enforcement of this Constitution shall be adopted by a resolution of the National Constituent Assembly which has drawn up this Constitution.

TEMPORARY PROVISIONS EFFECTIVE DURING THE PERIOD OF COMMUNIST REBELLION

(Adopted by the National Assembly on April 18, 1948, and promulgated by the National Government on May 10, 1948. Successively amended by the National Assembly on March 11, 1960, on February 7 and March 19, 1966, and promulgated by the National Government on March 22, 1966).

Assembly on March 11, 1960, on February 7 and March 19, 1966, and promulgated by the National Government on March 22, 1966).

In accordance with the procedure prescribed in paragraph 1 of Article 174 of the Consitution, the following Temporary Provisions to be effective during the period of Communist Rebelling are hereby enacted:

1. During the period of Communist Rebellion, the President may, by a resolution of the Executive Yuan Council, take emergency measures to avert an imminent danger to the security of the State or the people, or to cope with any serious financial or economic crisis, without being subject to the restrictions prescribed in Article 39 or Article 43 of the Constitution.

2. The emergency measures mentioned in the preceding paragraph may be modified or abrogated by the Legislative Yuan in accordance with the provisions of paragraph 2 of Article 57 of the Constitution.

3. During the period of Communist Rebellion, the President and the Vice-President may be re-elected without being subject to the two-term restriction prescribed in Article 47 of the Constitution.

4. During the period of Communist Rebellion, the President is hereby authorized under the constitutional system to set up an *ad hoc* organization to decide major policies on national mobilization and suppression of Communist Rebellion and to handle administrative matters in the war zone.

5. To meet the needs of national mobilization and suppression of Communist Rebellion, the President may make readjustments in the administrative and personnel agencies of the Central Government and in their organization.

6. During the period of Communist Rebellion, the President may, in accordance with the following provisions, promulgate regulations governing the election of additional representatives to the central parliamentary bodies without being subject to the restrictions of Articles 26, 64, and 91 of the Constitution:

(*a*) In areas under government control the number of representatives of the central parliamentary bodies shall be increased and a date shall be set for election. For the election of overseas members of the Legislative Yuan and the Control Yuan by Chinese citizens residing abroad, the President may, if such election cannot be held owing to factual circumstances, promulgate regulations for their selection.

(*b*) the original representatives of the central parliamentary bodies have all been duly elected by the people in a nation-wide election and have exercised their functions and powers according to law. So do those representatives of the same bodies later elected in by-elections either through a subsequent increase in the number of representative or to fill vacancies created by deaths.

In areas on the mainland, as they are recovered, there shall be held elections, in one area after another, of representatives of the central parliamentary bodies.

(*c*) Representatives of the central parliamentary bodies to be added and elected shall exercise the same functions and powers as the original repressentatives.

Those members of the National Assembly to be added and elected shall serve six years; those of the Legislative Yuan three years; and those of the Control Yuan six years.

7. During the period of Communist Rebellion, the National Assembly may, without being subject to the restrictions of paragraph 2 of Article 27 of the Constitution draw up measures to intitiate general principles of national legislation and call for a referendum of specific national laws.

8. During the period of Communist Rebellion, the President may, when he deems it necessary, convoke an extraordinary session of the National Assembly to consider any pending case of initiative or referendum.

9. When the National Assembly is not in session, it may set up a Commission for the Study of Constitutional Problems.

10. The termination of the period of Communist Rebellion shall be declared by the President.

11. Amendments to, or the abrogation of, the Temporary Provisions shall be decided by resolutions of the National Assembly.

THAILAND

SUMMARY

INTERNATIONAL STATUS

Thailand is a member of the United Nations (December 16, 1946). It is a member of the Association of Southeast Asian Nations and of other international organizations. The name of Siam was changed to Thailand on June 24, 1939.

The Thais established themselves as an organized state in the thirteenth century, Siam became a strong kingdom in the seventeenth and early eighteenth centuries. After a further period of Burmese invasions and occupation, the present dynasty of Bandkok, or of the Cakri, was founded in 1782. Two exceptional kings, from 1851 to 1910, succeeded in maintaining the independence of Siam in the face of western colonial expansion. An 'open door' policy and extraterritorial rights were granted to France and England, frontier questions were settled and the monarchy was progressively modernized. The first legislative council was established in 1895. In 1932, a *coup d'état* ended the period of absolute monarchy, and a Constitution and Parliament were imposed. From June 1933 to 1944, Siam was ruled by a military regime which imposed a child as king following the abdication of the reigning monarch in March 1935, in protest against the military. This regime, nationalist and militarist, allied itself to Japan soon after the declaration of war. In 1944, it was replaced by a civilian regime which repudiated the declaration of war and restored the territories Thailand had acquired during it. In March 1946, a new Constitution was adopted. The military returned to power from November 1947 to December 1951, when the 1932 Constitution was restored. The military again returned to power in 1957, imposed martial law, abrogated the Constitution, dissolved the National Assembly and the political parties. Ten years of military rule followed. 1968 saw a new constitution and a civilian government which lasted until 1971.

1968 saw a new constitution and a civilian government which lasted until 1971. During that period there was a rise in communist insurgency and civilian unrest in the country. In November 1971, the military returned with martial law and its consequences. Their rule was brought down by violent student uprisings in 1973. Civilian rule was restored, a new Constitution proclaimed in 1974, elections held in January 1975 and April 1976. Violent student demonstrations in October 1976 brought back the military who installed a civilian government and a constitution which they annulled a year later. The December 1978 Constitution was drawn up by a nominated National Legislative Assembly, and elections were held under it in April 1979. The role of the Armed Forces in government is predominant, although a bill to assign them a permanent role through a constitutional amendment was rejected by the Legislative Assembly in March 1983. Thailand faces a serious refugee problem on its frontier with Kampuchea.

FORM OF NATIONAL GOVERNMENT

The Constitution of December 22, 1978, replacing the Constitution of 1977 and previous ones, provides that Thailand is a unified and indivisible Kingdom with a democratic regime of government with the King as Head of State.[1] Sovereign power is derived from the Thai people.[2] The provisions of any law inconsistent with the Constitution are unenforceable.[3] Directive principles of state policies are listed and include the promotion of friendly relations with other countries, the manner and use of the Armed Forces, the promotion of education, securing of land ownership and rights to farmers, prevention of economic monopolies by individuals, fair protection of labor, promotion of public health.[4]

LEGISLATIVE DEPARTMENT

The bicameral National Assembly consists of the Senate and the House of Representatives.[5] The Senate is composed of members, their number not to exceed three quarters of the House of Representatives, appointed by the King for a term of 6 years; they may not belong to any political party.[6] The House of Representatives is composed of members elected for a term of 4 years from constituencies (*Changwats*) by direct suffrage and secret ballot and by group voting according to the lists of candidates supported by the political parties.[7] The King may dissolve the House of Representatives.[8] Incompatibilities of office are listed.[9] Members of the legislature represent the Thai people.[10] Immunities of members are provided.[11] The Leader of the Opposition is appointed by the King after the constitution of the Council of Ministers.[12] The National Assembly meets in one or two ordinary sessions a year.[13] Bills may only be introduced by the Council of Ministers or

[1] Const., Sec. 1, 2.
[2] Id., Sec. 3.
[3] Id., Sec. 5.
[4] Id., Sec. 53–73.
[5] Id., Sec. 74.
[6] Id., Sec. 84, 85.
[7] Id., Sec. 89–93, 99.
[8] Id., Sec. 101.
[9] Id., Sec. 97.
[10] Id., Sec. 106.
[11] Id., Sec. 121–123.
[12] Id., Sec. 105.
[13] Id., Sec. 115.

members of the House of Representatives, and money bills only with the endorsement of the Prime Minister.[14]

EXECUTIVE DEPARTMENT

The King is 'enthroned in a position of revered worship and shall not be violated'.[15] He is the Head of State, [16] the head of the Armed Forces,[17] he has the prerogative of declaring and lifting martial law, the right of pardon.[18] He is Buddhist and the upholder of religions.[19] He has a Privy Council appointed by him whose members may not be members of the legislature, government officials not attached to any political party.[20]

The Council of Ministers, composed of the Prime Minister and not more than 44 other Ministers appointed by the King, must state policy to the National Assembly but no vote of confidence is required.[21] Ministers vacate office upon a no-confidence vote of the House of Representatives, expiration or dissolution of the House or termination of the Prime Minister.[22]

RIGHTS OF THE PEOPLE

The Constitution provides equality before the law, freedom of religion, due, process of law, liberty of the person, forbids forced labor, provides freedom of residence and inviolability of domicile, the right of property and succession, freedom of speech and the press, assembly, association; the liberty to form political parties which must conform to the law on political parties and disclose the sources of their income and expenditures.[23] Freedom of communication, of travel, family rights, petition are stipulated.[24] The duties of upholding the nation, defending the country, paying taxes are laid down.[25]

JUDICIAL DEPARTMENT

Courts are established only by Acts.[26] Judges are independent in conducting trials and rendering judgments.[27] They are appointed and removed by the King.[28] The Constitution Tribunal, composed of the President of the National Assembly, the President of the Senate, the Director of Public Prosecutions and four other National Assembly appointees gives opinions on the consistency of bills with the Constitution.[29]

AREA, POPULATION, ETC.

Thailand has an area of 542.373 square kilometres, a population (1982 estimate) of 48,490,000. The capital is Bangkok and the language Siamese.

[14] Id., Sec. 125.
[15] Id., Sec. 6.
[16] Id., Sec. 2.
[17] Id., Sec. 8
[18] Id., Sec. 157–160, 163.
[19] Id., Sec. 7.
[20] Id., Sec. 10–12.
[21] Id., Sec. 146–151.
[22] Id., Sec. 154.
[23] Id., Sec. 22–38.
[24] Id., Sec. 39–42.
[25] Id., Sec. 46–52.
[26] Id., Sec. 170.
[27] Id., Sec. 173.
[28] Id., Sec. 175.
[29] Id., Sec. 184–193.

CONSTITUTION OF THE KINGDOM OF THAILAND[1]

December 22, 1978

SOMDET PHRA PARAMINTHARAMAHA BHUMIBOL ADULYADEJ SAYAMINTHARATHIRAT BOROMMANATTHABOPHIT

Enacted on the 22nd day of December B.E. 2521
Being the 33rd Year of the Present Reign.

May there be virtue. Today is the eighth day of the waxing moon in the first month of the year of Goat under the lunar calendar, being Friday, the twenty second day of December under the solar calendar, in the 2521st year of the Buddhist Era.

Phrabat Somdet Phra Paramintharamaha Bhumibol Adulyadej Mahitalathibet Ramathibodi Chakkri Narubodin Sayamintharathirat Borommanatthabophit is graciously pleased to proclaim that He was advised by the National Legislative Council that since the grant of the Constitution of the Kingdom of Thailand B.E. 2475 by His Majesty King Prajadhipok Phra Pok Klao Chao Yu Hua, His Majesty's Uncle, there had been amendment to the Constitution and promulgation of New Constitutions on several occasions, and sometimes the changes of situation in the country had resulted in the promulgation of an Interim Constitution, pending the drafting of a permanent Constitution. All Constitutions and Interim Constitutions that had been promulgated were in unity with one another in adhering to the democratic regime of government with the King as Head of the State who should exercise the legislative power through the National Assembly, the executive power through the Council of Ministers, and the judicial power through the Courts. The essential differences between them lay in the forms of the National Assembly and in the relationship between the legislative and the executive powers, depending on the changing situation of the country for the time being. This revealed the faithful adherence of the Thai people to the democratic regime of government with the King as Head of the State, which was in accordance with the will of His Majesty's Uncle, King Prajadhipok Phra Pok Klao Chao Yu Hua, in granting the power to administer the State affairs to the Thai people. The adherence to the democratic regime of government with the King as Head of the State had been inherited until the present time. Even the Constitution for the Administration of the Kingdom B.E. 2520 had demonstrated such will and entrusted the task of drafting the Constitution to the National Legislative Council so that a general election should be held within the 2521st year of the Buddhist Era.

The National Legislative Council had appointed a Committee charged with the duty of drafting the Constitution. When the Constitution had been completely drafted, the National Legislative Council considered the Draft Constitution in three readings in accordance with the common will of the Thai people in upholding

[1]Published in the Government Gazette Vol. 95, Part 146, Special Issue, dated 22nd December B.E. 2521 (1978). Translation supplied by the Ministry of Foreign Affairs in January 1980. Ed.

the independence and security of the Nation, preserving the religion to become everlasting, enthroning the King as Head of the State and in the hearts of the Thai people, adhering to the democratic regime of government with the King as Head of the State as the means of administering the State affairs, upholding and protecting the right and liberties of the Thai people, and uniting to secure justice, prosperity and happiness for all Thai people.

Having carefully determined and revised the Draft Constitution in the light of the situation of the country, the National Legislative Council passed a resolution approving the presentation of the Draft Constitution to the King for His Royal Signature to promulgate it as the Constitution of the Kingdom of Thailand.

Having thoroughly examined the Draft Constitution, the King deemed it expedient to grant His Royal assent in accordance with the resolution of the National Legislative Council.

Be it, therefore, commanded by the King that the Constitution of the Kingdom of Thailand be promulgated to replace, as from the date of its promulgation, the Interim Constitution for the Administration of the Kingdom B.E. 2520 promulgated on the 9th November B.E. 2520.

May the Thai people unite in protecting the Constitution of the Kingdom of Thailand in order to maintain the democratic regime of government and the sovereign power of the Thai people in the province of the Kingdom, and to bring about happiness, prosperity and dignity to His Majesty's subjects according to the will of His Majesty in every respect.

CHAPTER I

GENERAL PROVISIONS

Sec. 1. Thailand is a unified and indivisible Kingdom.

Sec. 2. Thailand adopts a democratic regime of government with the King as Head of the State.

Sec. 3. The sovereign power is derived from the Thai people. The King as Head of the State shall exercise such power through the National Assembly, the Council of Ministers and the Courts in accordance with the provisions of this Constitution.

Sec. 4. The Thai people, irrespective of their birth or religion, shall enjoy equal protection under this Constitution.

Sec. 5. The provisions of any law, which is contrary to or inconsistent with this Constitution, shall be unenforceable.

CHAPTER II

THE KING

Sec. 6. The King shall be enthroned in a position of revered worship and shall not be violated.

No person shall expose the King to any sort of accusation or action.

Sec. 7. The King is a Buddhist and Upholder of religions.

Sec. 8. The King holds the position of Head of the Thai Armed Forces.

Sec. 9. The King has the prerogative power to create titles and confer decorations.

Sec. 10. The King selects and appoints qualified persons President of the Privy Council and not more than fourteen Privy Councillors to constitute the Privy Council.

The Privy Council has a duty to render such advices to the King on all matters pertaining to His functions as He may consult, and has other duties as provided in this Constitution.

Sec. 11. The selection and appointment as well as the removal of a Privy Councillor shall depend entirely upon the Royal prerogative.

The President of the National Assembly shall countersign the Royal Command appointing or removing the President of the Privy Council.

The President of the Privy Council shall countersign the Royal Command appointing or removing other Privy Councillors.

Sec. 12. A Privy Councillor shall not be a senator, member of the House of Representatives, government official holding a permanent position or receiving a salary, official of a State enterprise, or member or official of a political party, and must not manifest loyalty to any political party.

Sec. 13. Before taking office, a Privy Councillor must make a solemn declaration before the King in the following words:

> 'I, (name of the declarer), do solemnly declare that I will be loyal to the King and will faithfully perform my duties in the interests of the country and of the people. I will also uphold and observe the Constitution of the Kingdom of Thailand in every respect.'

Sec. 14. A Privy Councillor vacates his office upon death, resignation, or removal by a Royal Command.

Sec. 15. The appointment and the removal of officials of the Royal Household and of the Royal Chief Aide-de-Camp shall depend entirely upon the Royal prerogative.

Sec. 16. Whenever the King is absent from the Kingdom or unable to perform His functions for whatever reason, He will appoint a person Regent with the approval of the National Assembly, and the President of the National Assembly shall countersign the Royal Command.

Sec. 17. In the case where the King does not appoint a Regent under section 16, or in the case where the King is unable to appoint a Regant owing to His not being *sui juris* or to any other reason whatever, the Privy Council shall submit the name of a person suitable to hold the office of Regent to the National Assembly for approval. Upon approval by the National Assembly, the President of the National Assembly shall make an announcement in the name of the King, of the appointment of such person as Regent.

Sec. 18. In the absence of the Regent under section 16 or section 17 , the President of the Privy Council shall be Regent *pro tempore.*

In the case where the Regent appointed under section 16 or section 17 is unable to perform his duties, the President of the Privy Council shall temporarily act as Regent.

While being Regent under paragraph one or acting as Regent under paragraph two, the President of the Privy Council shall not perform his duties as President of the Privy Council. In such case, the Privy Council shall select a Privy Councillor to act temporarily as President of the Privy Council.

Sec. 19. Before taking office, the Regent appointed under section 16 or section 17 shall make a solemn declaration before the National Assembly in the following words:

'I (name of the declarer), do solemnly declare that I will be loyal to His Majesty King (name of the King) and will faithfully perform my duties in the interests of the country and of the people. I will also uphold and observe the Constitution of the Kingdom of Thailand in every respect.'

Sec. 20. The succession to the Throne shall be in accordance with the Palace Law on Succession B.E. 2467 and in accordance with the approval of the National Assembly. In the absence of a Prince, the National Assembly may approve the succession by a Princess.

The amendment of the Palace Law on Succession B.E. 2467 shall be made in the same manner as an amendment of the Constitution.

Sec. 21. In the case where the Throne becomes vacant, the Privy Council shall, in accordance with section 20, submit the name of the Heir to the Throne to the National Assembly for approval. Upon the approval of the National Assembly, the President of the National Assembly shall invite such Heir to ascend the Throne and proclaim him King.

Pending the proclamation of the name of the Heir to the Throne under paragraph one, the President of the Privy Council shall temporarily be Regent. In the case where the Throne becomes vacant while the Regent has been appointed under section 16 or section 17 or while the President of the Privy Council is acting as Regent under section 18 paragraph one, such Regent, as the case may be, shall continue to be Regent until the proclamation of the name of the Heir to the Throne.

In the case where the Regent who has been appointed and continues to be Regent under paragraph two is unable to preform his duties, the President of the Privy Council shall act temporarily as Regent.

In the case where President of the Privy Council is Regent under paragraph two or acts temporarily as Regent under paragraph three, the provision of section 18 paragraph three shall apply.

CHAPTER III

RIGHTS AND LIBERTIES OF THE THAI PEOPLE

Sec. 22. All persons shall enjoy rights and liberties subject to the provisions of the Constitution.

Sec. 23. All persons are equal before the law and shall enjoy equal protection under the law.

Sec. 24. All persons shall enjoy political rights.

The exercise of political rights shall be in accordance with the provision of law.

Sec. 25. Every person shall enjoy full liberty to profess a religion, a religious sect or creed, and to exercise a form of worship in accordance with his belief; provided that it is not contrary to his civil duties or to public order or good morals.

In exercising the liberty referred to in paragraph one, every person is protected from any act of the State, which is derogatory to his rights or detrimental to his due benefits, on the ground of professing a religion, a religious sect or creed, or of exercising a form of worship in accordance with his belief different from that of others.

Sec. 26. No person shall be inflicted with a criminal punishment unless he has committed an act which the law in force at the time of commission provides it to be an offence and imposes a punishment therefor, and the punishment to be inflicted on such person shall not be heavier than that provided by the law in force at the time of commission.

Sec. 27. An alleged offender or an accused in a criminal case shall be presumed innocent.

Before the passing of a final judgment convicting a person of having committed an offence, such person shall not be treated as a convict.

Sec. 28. Every person shall enjoy the liberty of this person.

The arrest, detention or search of a person, irrespective of the circumstances, shall not be made except by virtue of law.

Sec. 29. In the case where the alleged offender or the accused is poor and unable to pay for his own advocate, that person is entitled to obtain legal aid from the State as provided by law.

Sec. 30. In the case where any person was inflicted with a criminal punishment by a final judgment, if it appears in the judgment of the court re-opening the case thereafter that he did not commit the alleged offence, he shall be entitled to compensation and to recover any right he had lost by virtue of the results of the judgment upon the condition and in the manner provided by law.

Sec. 31. Forced labor shall not be imposed except by virtue of law specifically enacted for the purpose of averting imminent public calamity or by virtue of the law which provides for its imposition during the time when the country is in a state of armed conflict or war, or when a state of emergency or martial law is declared.

Sec. 32. Every person shall enjoy the liberty of dwelling.

Every person is protected for his peaceful habitation in and for possession of his dwelling. The entry into a dwelling without the consent of its possessor or the search thereof shall not be made except by virtue of law.

Sec. 33. The property right of a person is protected. The extent and restriction of such right shall be in accordance with the provision of law.

The succession is protected. The right of succession of a person shall be in accordance with the provision of law.

The expropriation of immovable property shall not be made except by virtue of law specifically enacted for the purpose of public utility, national defence, exploitation of national resources, town and country planning, agricultural or industrial development, land reform, or other public interests, and fair compensation shall be paid in due time to the owner thereof as well as to the person having the right thereto, who suffers loss by such expropriation, as to be specified by law.

The amount of compensation under paragraph three shall be assessed with due regard to the mode of acquisition, nature and situation of the immovable property as well as the cause and purpose of the expropriation so as to secure social justice.

The immovable property, acquired by way of expropriation for a certain purpose, if not being used to fulfil that purpose within the period of time prescribed by law, shall be returned to the original owner or his heir unless it is used for other purposes according to paragraph three pursuant to the provision of law.

The return of immovable property to the original owner or his heir under paragraph five and the claim of compensation paid shall be in accordance with the provision of law.

Sec. 34. Every person shall enjoy the liberty of speech, writing, printing and publication.

The restriction on such liberty shall not be imposed except by virtue of law specifically enacted for the purpose of maintaining the security of State or safereguarding the liberties, dignity or reputation of other persons or maintaining public order or good morals or preventing deterioration of the mind or health of the public.

The press owner shall be a Thai national subject to the conditions prescribed by law.

No grant of money or other properties shall be made by the State as subsidy to a private newspaper.

Sec. 35. Every person shall enjoy the liberty of education; provided that such education is not contrary to his civic duties under the Constitution, and to the law relating to compulsory education and the law relating to the organization of educational establishments.

Sec. 36. Every person shall enjoy the liberty to assembly peacefully and without arms.

The restrictions on such liberty shall not be imposed except by virtue of law specifically enacted for the case of public meetings and for securing public conveniences in the use of public places or for maintaining public order during the time when the country is in a state of armed conflict or war, or when a state of emergency or martial law is declared.

Sec. 37. Every person shall enjoy the liberty to form an association, union, league, co-operative or any other group.

The formation, incorporation, management and dissolution of an association, union, league, co-operative or any other group shall be in accordance with the provision of law.

Sec. 38. Every person shall enjoy the liberty to form a political party for the purpose of performing the political activities through the means of a democratic regime as provided in this Constitution.

The formation, incorporation, management and dissolution of a political party shall be in accordance with the provision of the law on political parties.

A political party shall openly disclose its sources of income and the expenditure.

Sec. 39. Every person shall enjoy the liberty of communication by lawful means.

The censorship, detention or disclosure of communication between persons including any other act disclosing a statement in the communication between persons, shall not be effected except by virtue of law specifically enacted for public order or good morals, public safety, or for maintaining the security of the State.

Sec. 40. Every person shall enjoy the liberty of travelling and the liberty of making the choice of his residence withing the Kingdom.

The restriction on such liberties shall not be imposed except by virtue of law specifically enacted for the purpose of maintaining the security of the country, public order, public welfare, town and country planning or welfare of the youth.

No person of Thai nationality shall be deported or prohibited from entering the Kingdom.

Sec. 41. Family rights are protected.

Sec. 42. Every person shall have a right to present a petition upon the conditions and in the manner provided by law.

Sec. 43. The right of a person to sue a Government agency which is a juridical person to be liable for an act done by its official is protected.

Sec. 44. Persons who are in the armed forces and the police force, government officials, local government officials and employees of State organizations shall enjoy the same rights and liberties under the Constitution as those accorded to the people unless such enjoyment is restricted by law, by-law or regulation issued by virtue of law specifically enacted in so far as it is concerned with policies, efficiency or discipline.

Sec. 45. No person shall exercise the rights and liberties under the Constitution against the Nation, religion, the King and Constitution.

CHAPTER IV

DUTIES OF THE THAI PEOPLE

Sec. 46. Every person shall have a duty to uphold the Nation, religion, the King and the Democratic Regime of Government under this Constitution.

Sec. 47. Every person shall have a duty to defend the country.

Sec. 48. Every person shall have a duty to serve in the armed forces as provided by law.

Sec. 49. Every person shall have a duty to comply with the law.

Sec. 50. Every person shall have a duty to pay taxes and duties imposed by law.

Sec. 51. Every person shall have a duty to render assistance to the official service as provided by law.

Sec. 52. Every person shall have a duty to receive education and training under the conditions and in the manner provided by law.

CHAPTER V

DIRECTIVE PRINCIPLES OF STATE POLICIES

Sec. 53. The provisions of this Chapter are intended to be used as directive principles for legislating and determining the policies, and shall not give rise to any cause of action against the State.

Sec. 54. The State shall maintain the institution of kingship, the independence and integrity of its territories.

Sec. 55. The State should promote friendly relations with other countries and adopt the principle of reciprocity.

Sec. 56. The State shall arrange for the maintenance of the armed forces for safeguarding its independence, security of the State and national interest.

The armed forces shall be employed in an armed conflict or a war, for the protection of the institution of kingship, for suppressing a rebellion and a riot, for maintaining the security of the State and for national development.

Sec. 57. The State shall enforce the law and order so that the people may be assured of the safety in their lives, persons and property as well as in their peaceful existence.

Sec. 58. The State should organize the systems of official service and other State affairs for the achievement of efficiency and should take every measure to prevent and suppress corruption.

Sec. 59. The State should organize the system of judicial process to ensure justice to the people and to meet the requirement of expediency.

Sec. 60. The State should promote and support education and professional training according to the suitability and to the demand of the country.

The organization of educational system is an exclusive duty of the State. All educational establishments shall be under the control and supervision of the State.

The State should provide the indigent person with grants and requisites in their education and occupational training.

Compulsory education in the educational establishments of the State is to be provided without charge.

As for higher education, the State should allow educational establishments to manage their own affairs within the limits provided by law.

Sec. 61. The State should encourage researches in arts and sciences and should promote the application of science and technology in the development of the country.

Sec. 62. The State should support and promote national youth development so that they may be physically, mentally and intellectually sound for the purpose of economic and social development and for the security of the State.

Sec. 63. The State should promote public understanding of, and public belief in, the democratic regime of government with the King as its Head as well as the local government.

The State should ensure the local people to enjoy the right of self-government as provided by law.

Sec. 64. The State should promote and conserve the national culture.

Sec. 65. The State should conserve the balance of environment and eliminate pollution with jeopardizes the health and hygiene of the people.

Sec. 66. The State should proceed to raise the economic and social status of individuals to the level of comfortable livelihood.

Sec. 67. The State should, by means of land reform or by other means, secure land ownership or rights in land to all farmers for engaging in agriculture.

The State should protect and preserve the interests of the farmers in the production and in the disposition of their produce by means of price guarantee, or price maintenance as well as organizing the system and control of production and disposition appropriate to the demand of the market or by other means, and should promote the assembling of farmers in the form of co-operatives or other forms.

Sec. 68. The State should support economic initiative in the private sector.

The State should engage in an enterprise in the nature of public utility in such a way as to be beneficial to the people as a whole. An enterprise in the nature of public utility shall be engaged by individuals only if done by virtue of law.

The State should impose measures to prevent direct or indirect economic monopoly by individuals, which is not created by virtue of law.

Sec. 69. The State should have a demographic policy appropriate for natural resources, economic and social conditions, and technological progress for the purpose of economic and social development and for the security of the State.

Sec. 70. The State should give aid to persons suffering from performing duties for the Nation, or rendering assistance to the official service or performing a moral duty, or from natural calamities.

Sec. 71. The State should promote and support the State and private social works for the welfare and happiness of the people.

Sec. 72. The State should support the people of working age to obtain suitable employments, ensure the fair protection of labor, and provide for the system of labor relations including the settlement of fair wages.

Sec. 73. The State should promote public health and provide the indigent persons with free medical treatment.

The State shall prevent and suppress harmful contagious diseases in the interest of the public without charge.

CHAPTER VI

THE NATIONAL ASSEMBLY

Part 1. General Provisions

Sec. 74. The National Assembly consists of the Senate and the House of Representatives.

Joint or separate sittings of the National Assembly shall be in accordance with the provisions of this Constitution.

Sec. 75. The President of the Senate is President of the National Assembly. The President of the House of Representatives is Vice-President of the National Assembly.

The President of the National Assembly has the power and duty to conduct the proceedings of the National Assembly at joint sittings in accordance with the rules of procedure and has other powers and duties as provided in this Constitution.

In the case where the President of the National Assembly is absent or is unable to perform his duties, the Vice-President shall act in his place.

Sec. 76. A bill may be enacted as law only by and with the advice and consent of the National Assembly.

Sec. 77. After a bill has been approved by the National Assembly, the Prime Minister shall present it to the King for signature and it shall come into force upon its publication in the Government Gazette.

Sec. 78. If the King refuses His assent to a bill and either returns it to the National Assembly or does not return it within ninety days, the National Assembly must re-deliberate such bill. If the National Assembly resolves to reaffirm the bill with the votes of not less than two thirds of the total number of members of both Houses, the Prime Minister shall present such bill to the King for signature once again. If the King does not sign and return the bill within thirty days, the Prime Minister shall cause the bill to be promulgated as an Act in the Government Gazette as if the King had signed it.

Sec. 79. The President and the Vice-President of the Senate, the President and the Vice-President of the House of Representatives, senators and members of the House of Representatives shall receive emoluments and other considerations in accordance with the law.

Sec. 80. No person shall be a senator and a member of the House of Representatives simultaneously.

Sec. 81. Senators or members of the House of Representatives of not less than one tenth of the total number of members of each House have a right to lodge with the President of the House of which they are members a complaint asserting that the membership of any member of the House has terminated under section 87(3), (4), (5), (6), (9) or (10) or section 103(3), (4), (5), (6), (9), (10) or (11), as the case may be, and the President of the House with whom the complaint is lodged shall refer it to the Constitutional Tribunal for decision as to whether the membership of such person has terminated.

When the Constitutional Tribuanl has made its decision, the Constitutional Tribunal shall inform the President of the House with whom the complaint is lodged under paragraph one of such decision.

Sec. 82. In the case where any senator or member of the House of Representatives does in act jeopardizing the dignity of membership of the Senate or the House of Representatives, senators or members of the House of Representaives, as the case may be, of not less than one fourth of the total number of members of each House have the right to lodge with the President of the House of which they are members a complaint in order to have the Senate or the House of Represenatives decide to terminate the membership of that member.

Sec. 83. The vacation of the office of a senator or a member of the House of Representatives after the day on which his membership terminates or after the decision of the Constitutional Tribunal that the membership of any person terminates does not affect any act done by such person in the capacity of a member including the receipt of emoluments or other considerations by such member before he vacates his office, or the President of the House of which such person is a member has been informed of the decision of the Constitutional Tribunal, as the case may be.

Part 2. The Senate

Sec. 84. The Senate is composed of members to be appointed by the King from qualified persons possessing knowledge and experience in various branches of learning or affairs which will be useful to the administration of the State, being of Thai nationality by birth, being not less than thirty-five years of age, and not being a member of any political party.

The number of senators shall not exceed three fourths of the total number of members of the House of Representatives.

Sec. 85. The membership of the Senate is six years from the date of appointment by the King. As for the initial stage, one third of the total number of senators shall retire by drawing lots after two years in office. At the end of the period of four years from the date of appointment by the King, one half of the senators who remain in office after drawing lots at the end of the period of the first two years shall retire by drawing lots. If the number so calculated has any fraction, the fraction shall be disregarded. The termination of membership by drawing lots shall be regarded as retirement at the expiration of term of office.

The King shall have the prerogative to re-appoint the persons retiring at the expiration of term of office.

Sec. 86. Section 97 except (1) shall apply *mutatis mutandis* to senators.

Paragraph one shall not apply to cases where a senator takes or holds the position of a committee member appointed in the course of the administration of State affairs or State enterprise.

Sec. 87. The membership of a senator terminates upon:

(1) The expiration of term of office;

(2) death;
(3) resignation;
(4) loss of Thai nationality;
(5) becoming a member of any political party;
(6) acting in contravention of the prohibition under section 86;
(7) disenfranchisement under section 96(1), (2) or (3);
(8) the Senate passing a resolution terminating the membership in accordance with Section 82. In such case, the membership shall be terminated at the date of the resolution;
(9) having been absent throughout a session, which is not less than ninety days without the permission of the President of the Senate;
(10) being sentenced to imprisonment by a final judgment except that the sentence is for an offence committed through negligence or for a petty offence.

Sec. 88. If the office of a senator becomes vacant for any reason other than the expiration of his term of office, the King will appoint a person properly qualified under section 84 to fill the vacancy. The Senator so appointed may serve only for the remainder of his predecessor's term of office.

Part 3. The House of Representatives

Sec. 89. The House of Representatives is composed of members to be elected by the people of the number determined on the basis provided in section 90.

Sec. 90. The number of members of the House of Representatives to be elected shall be determined by the number of inhabitants in each *Changwat* as evidenced in the census announced in the year preceding the year of the election on the basis of the ratio of one member of the House of Representatives to one hundred and fifty thousand inhabitants. A *Changwat* with the inhabitants less than one hundred and fifty thousand shall elect one member, while a *Changwat* with the inhabitants exceeding one hundred and fifty thousand shall elect an additional member for every one hundred and fifty thousand inhabitants; any fraction thereof, if amounting to seventy-five thousand or more, shall be counted as one hundred and fifty thousand.

For the election of member of the House of Representatives, the area of a *Changwat* shall be regarded as one constituency, except that Bangkok Metropolis shall be divided into three constituencies and each constituency shall have equal or approximately equal number of members of the House of Representatives; the boundaries of each constituency shall be adjoining and the ratio of the number of inhabitants to the number of members of the House of Representatives to be elected in one constituency must be close to that in another constituency.

Sec. 91. The election of members of the House of Representatives shall be conducted by group voting in accordance with the lists of names of the candidates supported by the political parties to stand in the constituencies.

The election shall be conducted by direct suffrage and secret ballot.

Sec. 92. A person having the following qualifications has the right to vote at an election:

(1) being of Thai nationality by birth; privided that a Thai national having alien father must also possess qualifications stipulated by the law on election of members of the House of Representatives;

(2) being not less than twenty years of age on 1st January of the year of the election;

(3) having his name appearing on the house register in the constituency.

Sec. 93. A person under any of the following prohibitions on the date of the election is disenfranchised;

(1) being of unsound mind or of mental infirmity;

(2) being deaf and dumb and illiterate;

(3) being a Buddhist priest, novice, monk or clergy;

(4) being detained by a warrant of the Court or by a lawful order;

(5) being in the state of disenfranchisement by a judgment.

Sec. 94. A person having the following qualifications has the right to be a candidate at an election:

(1) being of Thai nationality by birth; provided that a Thai national having alien father must also possess the qualifications stipulated by the law on election of members of the House of Representatives;

(2) being not less than twenty-five years of age on the date of the election;

(3) being a member either of the political party sending members to stand for election under section 95 or of the political party under section 104 paragraph two;

(4) having other qualifications, if any, as stipulated by the law on election of members of the House of Representatives.

Sec. 95. In the general election, the political party, the members of which shall have a right to stand as candidates under section 94(3), must be the party sending members of not less than one half of the total number of members of the House of Representatives to stand as candidates at the election. And in each constituency where the said political party sends its members to stand for election, the members shall stand as a group of candidates equal in number to that of the members of the House of Representatives and each political party shall send only one group in each constituency.

When any political party has sent the candidates to stand for election, that political party or its candidates cannot withdraw the candidatures.

When any political party has sent the candidates in the requried number according to paragraph one, and thereafter the number of the candidates of that political party has reduced below the required number for any reason whatever, that political party shall be regarded as having sent the candidates for the required number according to paragraph one.

Sec. 96. A person under any of the following prohibitions shall have no right to be a candidate at an election:

(1) being addicted to harmful habit-forming drugs;

(2) being an undischarged bankrupt;

(3) being disfranchised under 93(1), (2), (3) and (5);

(4) having been sentenced by a judgment or ordered by a lawful order for imprisonment and having been detained by a warrant of the Court or the order;

(5) having been discharged for a period of less than five years on the election day after being sentenced or ordered by a judgment or lawful order to imprisonment for a term of two years or over except for an offence committed through negligence;

(6) being a government official or local government official holding a permanent position or receiving a salary except a political official;

(7) being an official of a State agency or State enterprise.

Sec. 97. A member of the House of Representatives shall not:

(1) hold any postition or have any duty in any government agency or State agency or State enterprise, or a position of member of local assembly, local administrator or local official, except the position of the Minister or any other political official;

(2) receive any concession from the State or government agency or state agency or State enterprise or become a party to the contract of the nature of economic monopoly with the State or a government agency or State agency or State enterprise, whether directly or indirectly;

(3) receive any special money or benefit from any government agency or State agency or State enterprise apart from what the government agency or State agency or State enterprise gives to other persons in the ordinary course of business.

The provisions of (2) shall not apply in the case where a member of the House of Representatives received the concession or became a party to the contract before he is elected.

The provision of this section shall not apply in the case where a member of the House of Representatives receives *Bia Wad,* gratuities, pensions, or annuities or any other form of payments of the same nature, and shall not apply in the case where a member of the House of Representatives accepts or holds the position of committee member of the National Assembly or the House of Representatives, or committee member appointed as a qualified person under the provision of law, or committee member appointed in the course of the administration of the State affairs in case he holds a position of political official.

Sec. 98. Subject to the provisions of this Constitution, the rules and procedure of election shall be in accordance with the law on election of members of the House of Representatives.

Sec. 99. The term of the House of Representatives is four years from the date of the election.

Sec. 100. Upon expiration of the term of the House of Representatives, the King will issue a Royal Decree calling for a general election of members of the House of Representatives in which the election day must be fixed within sixty days from from the date of expiration of the term of the House of Representatives and the election day must be the same all over the Kingdom.

Sec. 101. The King has the prerogative of dissolving the House of Representatives for a new election of members of the House of Representatives.

The dissolution of the House of Representatives shall be made in the form of a Royal Decree in which the election day for the general election must be fixed within ninety days and such election day must be the same all over the Kingdom.

The dissolution of the House of Representatives may be only once under the same circumstances.

Sec. 102. The membership of the House of Representatives commences on the election day.

Sec. 103. The membership of the House of Representatives terminates upon:

(1) the expiration of the term or dissolution of the House of Representatives;

(2) death;

(3) resignation;

(4) being disqualified under section 94(1), (2) or (4);

(5) being under any prohibition provided in section 96(1), (2), (3), (6) and (7);

(6) having done an act prohibited by section 97;

(7) the resignation from membership of his political party or his political party passing a resolution of not less than three fourths of the joint meeting of the executive committee of the political party and members of the House of Representatives belonging to that political party terminating his membership of the political party. In such cases, his membership shall be deemed to have terminated from the date of resignation or the resolution of the political party;

(8) the House of Representatives passing a resolution terminating the membership under section 82. In such case, his membership shall be deemed to have terminated from the date of the resolution of the House of Representatives.

(9) the loss of membership of the political party in the case where the political party of which he is a member is dissolved by an order of the Court and he is unable to become a member of another political party within sixty days from the date on which the Court issues its order. In such case, his membership shall be deemed to have terminated on the day following the date on which sixty days have elapsed.

(10) having been absent throughout a session which is not less than ninety days without the permission of the President of the House of Representatives;

(11) having been imprisoned by a final judgment of imprisonment except for an offence committed through negligence or a petty offence.

Sec. 104. If the office of member of the House of Representatives becomes vacant for any reason other than the expiration of the term or the dissolution of the House of Representatives, an election of a member of the House of Representatives to fill the vacancy shall be held within ninety days unless the remainder of the term of the House of Representatives is less than one hundred and eighty days.

In the election under paragraph one, the candidate for an election shall be member of the political party having its members being members of the House of Representatives elected at the general election, and section 95 shall apply *mutatis mutandis.*

The replacing member of the House of Representatives may serve only for the remainder of the term of the House of Representatives.

Sec. 105. After the Council of Ministers has assumed the administration of the State affairs, the King will appoint as Leader of the Opposition in the House of Representatives a member of the House of Representatives who is leader of the political party having its members of the House of Representatives holding no ministerial position, and having the largest number of members of the House of Representatives among the political parties having their members of the House of Representatives holding no ministerial position, and such number must not be less than one fifth of the total number of members of the House of Representatives.

The President of the House of Representatives shall countersign the Royal Command appointing the Leader of the Opposition in the House of Representatives.

The Leader of the Opposition in the House of Representatives shall vacate office upon being disqualified as referred to in paragraph one, and section 109 shall apply *mutatis mutandis,* and in such case, the King will appoint a new Leader of the Oppposition in the House of Representativs to fill the vacancy.

Part 4. Provisions Applicable to both Houses

Sec. 106. Senators and members of the House of Representatives are representatives of the Thai people.

Sec. 107. Before taking office, a senator and a member of the House of Representatives must make a solemn declaration in a sitting of the House of which he is a member in the following words:

> 'I, (name of the declarer), do solemnly declare that I will perform my duties in accordance with the honest dictates of my conscience for the common interest of the Thai people. I will also uphold and observe the Constitution of the Kingdom of Thailand in every respect.'

Sec. 108. The Senate and the House of Representatives shall each have one President and one or two Vice-Presidents who are appointed by the King from the members of such House in accordance with its resolution.

Sec. 109. The President and the Vice-President of the Senate hold office until the day preceding the date of election of the new President and Vice-President, which must be held every two years.

The President and the Vice-President of the House of Representatives hold office until the expiration of the term or the dissolution of the House.

The President and the Vice-President of the Senate and the President and the Vice-President of the House of Representatives vacate office before the expiration of term of office under paragraph one or paragraph two, as the case may be, upon:

(1) the loss of membership of the House of which he is a member;
(2) resignation from office;
(3) holding a position of Minister or of other political official;
(4) being sentenced by a judgment of imprisonment;

Sec. 110. The President of the Senate and the President of the House of Representatives have the power and duty to carry out the business of the Houses in accordance with their rules of procedure. The Vice-President has the power and duty to act on behalf of the President when the President is absent or unable to perform his duty.

Sec. 111. When the President and the Vice-President of the Senate or the President and the Vice-President of the House of Representatives are absent from any sitting, the members of each House shall elect one among themselves to preside over such sitting.

Sec. 112. At a sitting of the Senate or of the House of Representatives, the presence of not less than one half of the total number of members of each House is required to constitute a quorum.

Sec. 113. A resolution on any issue shall be made by a majority of votes unless it is otherwise provided in this Constitution.

In casting the vote, each member has one vote. In case of an equality of votes, the presiding member shall have an additional vote as a casting vote.

Sec. 114. At a sitting of the Senate or of the House of Representatives or at a joint sitting of the National Assembly, words expressed in giving a statement of fact or opinion or in casting the vote by any member are absolutely privileged. No charge or action in any manner whatever shall be brought against such member.

This privilege also extends to printers and publishers of the minutes of sittings in accordance with the regulations of the Senate or of the House of Representatives, as the case may be, and to persons permitted by the presiding member to give a statement of fact or opinion at such sittings.

Sec. 115. The National Assembly shall, within thirty days from the date of the election of members of the House of Representatives, be summoned for the first sitting.

Each year, there shall be one or two ordinary sessions of the National Assembly as may be determined by the House of Representatives.

The day on which the first sitting referred to in paragraph one is held shall be considered as the first day of the annual ordinary session, and the first day of the succeeding annual ordinary session shall be fixed by the House of Representatives.

Sec. 116. An ordinary session of the National Assembly shall last ninety days but the King may prolong it.

An ordinary session may be prorogued before the end of ninety days only with the approval of the National Assembly.

Sec. 117. The King convokes the National Assembly. He opens and prorogues its session.

The King may be present to perform the opening ceremony of the first annual ordinary session or may command the Heir to the Throne who is *sui juris* or any person to perform the ceremony as His Representative.

Sec. 118. When it is necessary for the interests of the State, the King may convoke an extraordinary session of the National Assembly.

Sec. 119. Senators and members of the House of Representatives collectively, or members of the Houser of Representatives, of not less than one third of the total number of members of both Houses have the right to present their petition to the King for the issue of a Royal Command convoking an extraordinary session of the National Assembly.

The petition referred to in paragraph one shall be lodged with the President of the National Assembly.

The President of the National Assembly shall present the petition to the King and countersign the Royal Command.

Sec. 120. Subject to section 119, the convocation, the prolongation of session and the prorogation of the National Assembly shall be made by a Royal Decree.

Sec. 121. No senator or member of the House of Representatives shall, during a session, be arrested or detained or summoned by a warrant for inquiry as an alleged offender in a criminal case unless permission of the House of which he is a member is obtained or he is arrested in *flagrante delicto.*

In the case where a senator or a member of the House of Representatives has been arrested in *flagrante delicto,* it shall be forthwith reported to the President of the House of which he is a member and the President of the House of which he is a member may order the release of the person so arrested.

Sec. 122. In the case where a criminal charge is brought against a senator or a member of the House of Representatives, whether the House is in session or not, the Court shall not try the case during a ssession unless permission of the House of which he is a member is obtained; provided that the proceedings of the Court shall not hinder such member from attending the sitting of the House.

The proceedings of the Court before the invocation of membership of either House of the accused are valid.

Sec. 123. If a senator or member of the House of Representatives is detained during the inquiry or trial before the beginning of a session, where the session begins, the inquiry official or the Court, as the case may be, must order his release as soon as the House of which he is a member has so requested.

The order of release under paragraph one shall be effective as from the date of such order until the last day of the session.

Sec. 124. Subject to section 161, the Senate shall not hold its sitting during the expiration of the term or the dissolution of the House of Representatives.

Sec. 125. Bills may be introduced only by the Council of Ministers or members of the House of Representatives, but money bills may be introduced by members of the House of Representatives only with the endorsement of the Prime Minister.

A member of the House of Representatives may introduce a bill only if the political party of which he is a member has passed a resolution approving the introduction thereof, and the bill is endorsed by not less than twenty members of the House of Representatives who are members of that political party.

A money bill means a bill with provision dealing with one or all of the following matters:

(1) imposition, repeal, reduction, alteration, modification, remission, or regulation of taxes or duties;

(2) allocation, receipt, custody, or payment of the State funds or transfer of expenditure estimates of the State;

(3) raising of loans, or guarantee or redemption of loans;

(4) currency;

In case of doubt as to whether a bill is a money bill which requires the endorsement of the Prime Minister, it shall be the power of the President of the House of Representatives to make a decision thereon.

Sec. 126. A bill shall be first submitted to the House of Representatives.

Sec. 127. Subject to section 133, when the House of Representatives has considered a bill submitted under section 126 and resolves to approve it, the House of Representatives shall submit such bill to the Senate. The Senate must finish the consideration of the bill within sixty days; if it is a money bill, the consideration thereof must be finished within thirty days; provided that the House of Representatives may resolve to extend the period as a special case. The said period shall mean the period during a session and shall be counted as from the day on which such bill reaches the Senate.

The period referred to in paragraph one shall not include the period during which the bill is under the consideration of the Constitutional Tribunal under section 130.

If the Senate has not finished the consideration of the bill within the period referred to in paragraph one, it shall be deemed that the Senate has approved such bill.

In the case where the House of Representatives submits a money bill to the Senate, the President of the House of Representatives shall also advise the Senate that the bill so submitted is a money bill. The advice of the President of the House of Representatives shall be deemed final.

In the case where the President of the House of Representatives does not advise the Senate that the bill is a money bill, such bill shall not be deemed a money bill.

Sec. 128. Subject to section 133, after the Senate has finished the consideration of a bill:

(1) if it agrees with the House of Representatives, further proceedings under section 77 shall be taken;

(2) if it disagrees with the House of Representatives, such bill shall be withheld and returned to the House of Representatives;

(3) if there is an amendment, the amended bill shall be returned to the House of Representatives; in such case, each House shall appoint its members or other persons in equal number as may be fixed by the House of Representatives to constitute a joint committee for consideration of the bill; the joint committee shall prepare a report thereon and submit the bill which it has already considered to both Houses; if both Houses approve the bill considered by the joint committee, further proceedings under section 77 shall be taken; if either House disapproves the bill, such bill shall be withheld.

The joint committee has the power to demand documents from any person or summon any person to give a statement of fact or opinion in respect of the consideration of the bill and the privilege provided in section 114 shall also extend to the person performing his duties under this section.

At a meeting of the joint committee, the presence of not less than one-half of the total number of its members is required to consititute a quorum and the rules of procedure of the House of Representatives in so far as the committee is concerned shall apply *mutatis mutandis.*

Sec. 129. A bill withheld under section 128 may be reconsidered by the House of Representatives only after the lapse of one hundred and eighty days from the date the bill is returned to the House of Representatives by the Senate in case of withholding under section 128(2) and from the date either House disapproves the bill in case of withholding under section 128(3). In such cases, if the House of Representatives resolves to reaffirm the original bill or the bill considered by the joint committee by the votes of more the one half of the total number of members of the House, such bill shall be deemed to have been approved by the National Assembly and further proceedings under section 77 shall be taken.

If the bill withheld is a money bill, the House of Representatives may forthwith proceed to reconsider it. In such case, if the House of Representatives resolves to reaffirm the original bill or the bill considered by the joint committee by the votes of more than one half of the total number of members of the House, such bill shall be deemed to have been approved by the National Assembly and further proceedings under section 77 shall be taken.

Sec. 130. While a bill is being withheld under section 128, the Council of Ministers or members of the House of Representatives may not introduce a bill having the same or similar principle as that of the bill so withheld.

In the case where the Senate or the House of Representatives is of the opinion that the bill so introduced or referred to for consideration has the same or similar principle as that of the bill being withheld, the President of the Senate or the President of the House of Representatives shall refer the said bill to the Constitutional Tribunal for decision. If the Constitutional Tribunal decides that it is a bill having the same or similar principle as that of the bill so withheld, such bill shall lapse.

Sec. 131. In the case where the term of the House of Representatives expires or the House of Representatives is dissolved, all bills which have not yet been approved by the National Assembly, those to which the King has refused assent and those which have not been returned by the King within ninety days shall lapse.

Sec. 132. The expenditure estimates of State shall be made in the form of an Act. If the Annual Appropirations Act for the following fiscal year is not enacted in time, the law on annual appropriations for the preceding fiscal year shall apply for the time being.

Sec. 133. The House of Representatives must finish the consideration of the annual appropriations bill, the supplementary appropriations bill and the transfer of appropriations bill within ninety days from the date the bills reach the House of Representatives.

If the House of Representatives has not finished the consideration of the bill within the period referred to in paragraph one, such bill shall be deemed to have been approved by the House of Representatives and shall be submitted to the Senate.

In the consideration of the bill, the Senate must approve or disapprove it within fifteen days from the date the bill reaches the Senate. After such period, such bill shall be deemed to have been approved; in such case and in the case where the Senate approves it, further proceedings under section 77 shall be taken.

If the Senate disapproves the bill, section 129 paragraph two shall apply *mutatis mutandis.*

In the consideration of the annual appropriations bill, the supplementary appropriations bill and the transfer of appropriations bill, a member of the House of Representatives shall not submit a motion adding any item or amount to the bill, but may submit a motion reducing or abridging the expenditures which are not expenditures according to any one of the following obligations:

(1) money for payment of the principle of a loan;

(2) interest on a loan;

(3) money payable in accordance with the law.

Sec. 134. The payment of State funds shall be made only when it has been authorized by the law on appropriations, the law on budgetary procedure, the law on transfer of appropriations or the law on treasury balance, except that it may be prepaid in the case of urgent necessity under the rules and procedure provided by the law. In such case, the expenditure estimates for reimbursement must be set aside in the Transfer of Appropriations Act, the Supplementary Appropriations Act, or the Annual Appropriations Act for the following fiscal year.

Sec. 135. The Senate and the House of Representatives are, by virtue of this Constitution, vested with the power to control the administration of the State affairs.

Sec. 136. At a sitting of the Senate or of the House of Representatives, every member has the right to interpellate a Minister on any matter within the scope of his authority but the Minister has the right to decline to answer if the Council of Ministers is of the opinion that the matter should not yet be disclosed on the ground of safety or vital interest of the State.

Sec. 137. Members of the House of Representatives of not less than one fifth of the total number of members of the House of Representatives have the right to submit a motion for a general debate for the purpose of passing a vote of no-confidence in an individual Minister or in the Council of Ministers.

If the general debate is concluded with a resolution not to pass over the agenda of the general debate, the House of Representatives shall pass a vote of confidence or no-confidence. Voting in such case shall not take place on the same day as that of the conclusion of the debate. The vote of no-confidence must be passed by more than one half of the total number of members of the House.

In the case where a vote of no-confidence is passed by not more than one half of the total number of members of the House, the members of the House of Representatives who submit the motion for the general debate shall no longer have the right to submit another motion for the general debate for the purpose of passing a vote of no-confidence in an individual Minister or in the Council of Ministers throughout the session.

Sec. 138. The sittings of the Senate and of the House of Representatives and the joint sittings of the National Assembly are public under the conditions stipulated in the rules of procedure of each House. A sitting *in camera* shall be held at the request of the Council of Ministers or members of not less than a quarter of the total number of members of each House or of both Houses, as the case may be.

Sec. 139. The Senate and the House of Representatives have the power to select and appoint members of each House to constitute a standing committee and have the power to select and appoint members or other persons to constitute an *ad hoc* committee in order to perform any act, inquire into, or study any matter as may be assigned by the House and report its findings to the House. The said committee may demand documents from any person or summon any person to give a statement of fact or opinion on the act or the matter under its inquiry or study.

The privilege provided in section 114 shall also extend to the persons performing their duties under this section.

The number of members of a standing committee to be appointed shall be in proportion to or in close proportion to the number of members of the House of Representatives of each political party or group of political parties in the House of Representatives.

In the absence of the rules of procedure of the House of Representatives under section 142, the President of the House of Representatives shall determine the proportion under paragraph three.

Sec. 140. At a meeting of the committee, the presence of not less than one-half of the total number of members of the committee is required to constitute a quorum.

Sec. 141. Subject to section 191, if there is a problem, which requires an interpretation of the Constitution in relation to the power and duty of the National Assembly, it shall be within the power of the National Assembly to make the interpretation and the interpretation shall be regarded as final.

Sec. 142. The Senate and the House of Representatives have the power to make the rules of procedure governing the selection and performance of duties of the Presidents and the Vice-Presidents of the Houses, and members of committees, sittings, introduction and consideration of bills, presentation of motions, consultation, debate, passing of resolution, interpellation, general debate, observation of the rules and order as well as other matters for the execution of this Constitution.

Part 5. Joint sittings of the National Assembly

Sec. 143. The National Assembly shall hold a joint sitting in the following cases:

(1) approval of the appointment of the Regent under section 16 and section 17;

(2) making of a solemn declaration by the Regent before the National Assembly under section 19;

(3) amendment of the Palace Law on Succession, D.E. 2467 under section 20;

(4) approval of the Succession to the Throne under section 21;

(5) reconsideration of a bill under section 78;

(6) approval of the prorogation of session under section 116;

(7) opening of the session of the National Assembly under section 117;

(8) interpretation of the Constitution under section 141;

(9) announcement of policies under section 151;

(10) general debate under section 153;
(11) approval of the declaration of war under section 161;
(12) approval of a treaty under section 162;
(13) appointment of members of the Constitutional Tribunal under section 184;
(14) amendment of the Constitution under section 194.

Sec. 144. At a joint sitting of the National Assembly, the rules of procedure of the Senate shall apply *mutatis mutandis.*

Sec. 145. Subject to section 20, section 78, section 161 paragraph two and section 194, the provisions applicable to both Houses shall apply *mutatis mutandis* to the joint sitting of the National Assembly; provided that, in so far as the appointment of a committee is concerned, the number of members of committee appointed from the members of each House must be in proportion to or in close proportion to the number of members of each House.

CHAPTER VII

THE COUNCIL OF MINISTERS

Sec. 146. The King appoints the Prime Minister and not more than forty four other Ministers to constitute the Council of Ministers having the duty to carry out the administration of the State Affaris.

The President of the National Assembly shall countersign the Royal Command appointing the Prime Minister.

Sec. 147. Before taking office, a Minister must make a solem declaration before the King in the following words:

"I, (name of declarer), do solemnly declare that I will be loyal to the King and will faithfully perform my duties in the interests of the country and the people. I will also uphold and observe the Constitution of the Kingdom of Thailand in every respect."

Sec. 148. A Minister shall not be a government official holding a permanent position or receiving a salary except a political official.

Sec. 149. A Minister shall not hold a position or perform an act, which a member of the House of Representatives is prohibited to hold or perform under section 97, except the position required to be held by law, and shall neither be a manager, director, advisor, agent, nor employee of any person, partnership, company, or organization, which engages in a business for profit.

Sec. 150. A Minister has the right to attend and give a statement of fact or opinion at a sitting of the House of which he is not a member, but he has no right to vote.

Sec. 144. Governing privileges shall apply *mutatis mutandis.*

Sec. 151. The Council of Ministers which will assume the administration of the State affairs must state its policy to the National Assembly but no vote of confidence is required.

Sec. 152. In the implementation of the policy on the administration of the State

Affairs, the Ministers shall be responsible individually to the House of Representatives for the performance of their duties and shall be responsible collectively for the general policy of the Council of Ministers.

Sec. 153. If there is a problem in the administration of the State affairs, on which the Council of Ministers deems it advisable to take opinion of the Senators and the members of the House of Representatives, the Prime Minister may give a notice to the President of the National Assembly requesting that a general debate be held at a sitting of the National Assembly. In such case, no resolution shall be passed by the National Assembly on the issue put in the debate.

Sec. 154. Ministers shall vacate office *en masse* upon:

(1) the passing of a vote of no-confidence by the House of Representatives under section 137;

(2) the expiration of the term or the dissolution of the House of Representatives;

(3) the resignation of the Council of Ministers;

(4) the termination of ministership of the Prime Minister under section 155.

The outgoing Council of Ministers shall remain in office and carry on the administration until the newly appointed Council of Ministers takes the office.

Sec. 155. The ministership of an individual Minister terminates upon:

(1) death;

(2) resignation;

(3) being disqualified as a candidate at an election of members of the House of Representatives under section 94(1), (2) or (4) in case of a Minister not being a member of the House of Representatives or under section 94 (1), (2), (3) or (4) in case of a Minister being a member of the House of Representatives, or being under any prohibition provided in section 96 (1), (2), (3), (5) or (6);

(4) being sentenced by a judgment to imprisonment;

(5) the passing of a vote of no-confidence by the House of Representatives under section 137;

(6) having done an act prohibited by section 149;

(7) a Royal Command issued under section 156.

Section 81, section 82 and section 83 shall apply *mutatis mutandis* to the termination of the ministership under (2), (3), (4) or (6).

Sec. 156. The King has the prerogative of relieving a Minister of his office upon the advice of the Prime Minister.

Sec. 157. In case of an emergency when there is an urgent necessity to maintain national or public safety or national economic security or to avert public calamity, the King may issue an Emergency Decree which shall have the force as an Act.

In the next succeeding sitting of the National Assembly, the Council of Ministers shall submit the Emergency Decree to the National Assembly for consideration without delay. If the House of Representatives disapproves it or approves it but the Senate disapproves it and the House of Representatives reaffirms its approval by the votes of not more than one-half of the total number of its members, the Emergency Decree shall lapse; provided that it shall not affect any act done during the enforcement of such Emergency Decree.

If the Senate and the House of Representatives approve the Emergency Decree, or if the Senate disapproves it but the House of Representatives reaffirms its approval by the votes of more than one-half of the total number of its members, such Emergency Decree shall continue to have the force as an Act.

The Prime Minister shall cause the approval or disapproval of the Emergency Decree to be published in the Government Gazette. In case of disapproval, it shall be effctive as from the day following the date of its publication in the Government Gazette.

The consideration of an Emergency Decree by the Senate and by the House of Representatives in case of reaffirmation of approval of the Emergency Decree must take place on the first opportunity when such Houses hold their sitting.

Sec. 158. If, during a session, it is necessary to have a law on taxes, duties or currency, which, in the interests of the State, requires an urgent and confidential consideration, the King may issue an Emergency Decree which shall have the force as an Act.

The Emergency Decree issued under paragraph one must be submitted to the House of Representatives within three days after the date of its publication in the Government Gazette, and section 157 shall apply *mutatis mutandis.*

Sec. 159. The King has the prerogative of issuing a Royal Decree which is not contrary to the law.

Sec. 160. The King has the prerogative of declaring and lifting the martial law in accordance with the conditions and manner under the martial laws.

In the case where it is necessary to declare the martial laws in a certain locality without delay, the military authority may do so under the martial laws.

Sec. 161. The King has the prerogative of declaring war with the approval of the National Assembly.

The resolution of approval of the National Assembly must be passed by a majority of votes of not less than two thirds of the total number of members of both Houses.

After the expiration of the term or the dissolution of the House of Representatives, the Senate shall perform the function of the National Assembly in making the approval under paragraph one.

Sec. 162. The King has the prerogative of concluding a peace treaty, armistice and other treaties with other countries or international organizations.

A treaty which provides for a change in the Thai territories or the national territorial sovereignty or requires the enactment of an Act for its implementation must be approved by the National Assembly.

Sec. 163. The King has the prerogative of granting pardon.

Sec. 164. The King has the prerogative of removing titles and recalling decorations.

Sec. 165. The King appoints and removes officials in the military service and in the civil service holding the positions of Under-Secretary of State, Director General and their equivalent.

Sec. 166. Subject to section 165, the requirement of qualifications, recruitment, appointment, promotion, increase of salaries, punishment and retirement of government officials shall be in accordance with the provisions of law.

Sec. 167. A government official holding a permanent position or receiving a salary, except political official, shall not be a political official.

Sec. 168. All laws, Royal Rescripts and Royal Commands relating to the State affairs must be countersigned by a Minister unless otherwise provided in this Constitution.

CHAPTER VIII

THE COURTS

Sec. 169. The trial and adjudication of cases are the power of the Courts, which must proceed in accordance with the law and in the name of the King.

Sec. 170. All Courts may be established only by Acts.

Sec. 171. A new Court for the trial and adjudication of any particular case or a case of any particular charge in place of an ordinary Court existing under the law and having jurisdiction over such case shall not be established.

Sec. 172. A law having an effect of changing or amending the law on organization of courts or law on judicial procedure for the purpose of applying it to a particular case shall not be enacted.

Sec. 173. Judges are independent in the trial and adjudication of cases in accordance with the law.

Sec. 174. Judges shall not be political officials.

Sec. 175. The King appoints and removes judges.

Before taking office for the first time, a judge is required to make a solemn declaration before the King with the words prescribed by the Judicial Commission under the law on judicial service.

Sec. 176. The appointment and removal from office of a judge of a Court of Justice must be approved by the Judicial Commission under the law on judicial service before they are tendered to the King.

The promotion, increase of salaries and punishment of judges of Court of Justice must be approved by the Judicial Commission under the law on judicial service.

Sec. 177. Military Courts have the power to try and adjudicate cases as provided by the law.

The appointment and removal of a military judge shall be in accordance with the law.

Sec. 178. The appointment and removal of a judge of a Court other than the Court of Justice or Military Court as well as the juridsiction and the procedure of such Court shall be in accordance with the law on the establishment of such Court.

Sec. 179. In the case where there is a dispute on the jurisdiction between the Court of Justice and any other Court or between other Courts, the Constitutional Tribunal shall decide it.

CHAPTER IX

LOCAL GOVERNMENT

Sec. 180. The administration of local government shall, subject to the law, be in accordance with the principle of self-government according to the will of the people in the locality.

Sec. 181. Local government shall consist of a local assembly and a local administrative committee or local administrators.

The powers and duties of a local assembly, local administrative committee or local administrator shall be in accordance with the provision of law.

Sec. 182. Members of a local assembly shall be basically elected. Members shall be appointed only in case of necessity in accordance with the provision of law, and whose number must be less than the number of elected members.

The election of members of a local assembly shall be by direct suffrage and secret ballot.

A candidate standing for the election of member of a local assembly must at least possess the qualifications in accordance with section 94 (1) and (2).

The rules and procedure of election under this section shall be in accordance with the law on such purpose.

Sec. 183. A local administrative committee or local administrator shall be basically elected. A local administrative committee or local administrators shall be appointed only in case of necessity as provided by the law.

The rules and procedure of election under this section shall be in accordance with the law on such purpose.

CHAPTER X

THE CONSTITUTIONAL TRIBUNAL

Sec. 184. The Constitutional Tribunal is composed of the President of the National Assembly, the President of the Supreme Court, the Director General of the Public Prosecution Department and four other persons appointed by the National Assembly from qualified persons.

The President of the National Assembly shall be President of the Constitutional Tribunal.

Sec. 185. A member of the Constitutional Tribunal appointed by the National Assembly shall not be a senator, member of the House of Representatives, member of a local assembly, local administrators, government official holding a permanent position or receiving a salary, official of a State enterprise, or local government official.

Sec. 186. A member of the Constitutional Tribunal may receive emoluments and other considerations in accordance with the provision of law.

Sec. 187. At each general election, the National Assembly shall appoint, from qualified persons, new members of the Constitutional Tribunal within the period of thirty days from the opening of the first session of the National Assembly.

The period of time referred to in paragraph one means the period during session.

In the appointment of new members of the Constitutional Tribunal under paragraph one, the National Assembly may re-appoint the retiring members.

Sec. 188. A member of the Constitutional Tribunal vacates office upon:

(1) the opening of the first session of the National Assembly after the general election;

(2) death;

(3) resignation;

(4) being a senator, member of the House of Representatives, member of a local assembly, local administrator, government official holding a permanent position or receiving a salary, official of a State enterprise, or local government official;

(5) being sentenced by a judgment to imprisonment.

Sec. 189. If the office of a member of the Constitutional Tribunal becomes vacant upon any reason except upon reason referred to in section 168(1), the National Assembly shall appoint a new member of the Constitutional Tribunal to fill the vacancy within a period of thirty days.

The period of time referred to in paragraph one means the period during the session.

Sec. 190. After a bill has been approved by the National Assembly and before the Prime Minister presents it to the King for signature under section 77.

(1) if the senators and the members of the House of Representatives or members of each House of not less than one fifth of the total number of members of both Houses are of the opinion that the provision of the said bill is contrary to or inconsistent with the Constitution, they shall submit their opinion to the President of the National Assembly, the President of the Senate, or the President of the House of Representatives, as the case may be, and the President of the House who receives the said opinion shall then refer it to the Constitutional Tribunal for consideration and decision and inform the Prime Minister of it;

(2) if the Prime Minister is of the opinion that the provision of the said bill is contrary to or inconsistent with the Constitution, he shall refer such opinion to the Constitutional Tribunal for consideration and decision and then inform the President of the Senate and the President of the House of Representatives of it.

During the consideration of the Constitutional Tribunal, the Prime Minister shall suspend the proceedings in respect of the promulgation of the bill referred to in paragraph one until the Constitutional Tribunal gives a decision thereon. If the Constitutional Tribunal decides that the provision of such bill is contrary to or inconsistent with the Constitution, the Prime Minister shall return the bill to the National Assembly.

Sec. 191. In applying a law to any case, if the Court is of the opinion that the provision of such law comes under section 5 and there has not yet been a decision of the Constitutional Tribunal relating to such provision, the Court shall stay its trial and adjudication of the case and submit its opinion through proper channel to the Constitutional Tribunal for consideration and decision.

The decision of the Constitutional Tribunal shall apply to all cases but shall not affect the judgments of the Courts which have been final.

Sec. 192. The decision of the Constitutional Tribunal shall be deemed final and shall be published in the Government Gazette.

Sec. 193. The procudure of the Constitutional Tribunal shall be in accordance with the law.

CHAPTER XI

AMENDMENT OF THE CONSTITUTION

Sec. 194. An amendmentof the Constitution may be made only under the rules and procedure as follows:

(1) a motion for amendment must be proposed either by the Council of Ministers or members of the House of Representatives of not less than one third of the total number of members of the House of Representatives; provided that the motion of members of the House of Representatives may be made only in accordance with the resolution of the political party to which they belong;

(2) a motion for amendment must be proposed in the form of a draft Constitution Amendment and the National Assembly shall consider it in three readings;

(3) the voting in the first reading for acceptance in principle shall be by roll call and the amendment must be approved by the votes of not less than one half of the total number of members of both Houses;

(4) the voting in the second reading for consideration section by section shall be decided by simple majority of votes;

(5) at the conclusion of the second reading, there shall be an intervening period of fifteen days after which the National Assembly shall proceed with its third reading;

(6) the voting in the third and final reading shall be by roll call and the promulgation of it as the Constitution must be approved by the votes of more than one half of the total number of members of both Houses;

(7) after the resolution has been passed in accordance with the above rules and procedure, the draft Constitution Amendment shall be presented to the King and section 77 and section 78 shall apply *mutatis mutandis.*

TRANSITORY PROVISIONS

Sec. 195. As from the date of the promulgation of this Constitution until the date of the election of members of the House of the House of Representatives under section 202, the National Legislative Assembly under the Constitution for the Administration of the Kingdom B.E. 2520 shall act as the National Assembly in accordance with this Constitution, but the members of the National Assembly shall not introduce a bill under section 125 or exercise the right of interpellation under section 136 or submit motion for a general debate under section 137, and the provision of section 86 and section 97 shall not apply to the holding of office of the members of the National Legislative Council under this section.

Sec. 196. Section 114, section 121, section 122 and section 123 shall apply *mutatis mutandis* to members of the National Legislative Council under section 195.

Sec. 197. The Privy Council holding office before the date of the promulgation of this Constitution shall be the Privy Council under this Constitution.

Sec. 198. The Council of Ministers administering the State affairs before the date of the promulgation of this Constitution or the Council of Ministers, if formed prior to the election of members of the House of Representatives under section 202, shall be the Council of Ministers administering the State affairs under this Constitution, and section 148, section 149 and section 151 shall not apply to the holding of office of the Ministers under this section.

After the election of members of the House of Representatives under section 202, the Council of Ministers referred to in paragraph one shall vacate office; provided that it shall remain in office until the new Council of Ministers takes office.

Section 167 and 174 shall not apply to the officials holding the postition of political officials before the date the new Council of Ministers takes office.

Sec. 199. The National Policy Council acting before the date of the promulgation of this Constitution shall give advice to the Council of Ministers so as to make the administration of State affairs being in accordance with the Directive Principles of State policy and in accordance with the duty under section 200 until the new Council of Ministers takes office.

Sec. 200. Since the date of the promulgation of this Constitution until the new Council of Ministers takes office in the case where the Prime Minister deems it necessary for the prevention, aversion or suppression of an act subverting the security of the Kingdom, the Throne, the national economy or the State affairs or of an act endangering or jeopardizing public order or good morals or of an act destroying the natural resources or detrimental to public health, whether such act has occurred before or after the date of the promulgation of this Constitution, either within or outside the Kingdom, the Prime Minister shall, with the approval of the Council of Ministers and the National Policy Council, have the power to issue any order, or take any action, and such order or action as well as acts performed in compliance therewith shall be considered lawful according to the laws in force and to this Constitution.

Having issued any order or raken any action under paragraph one, the Prime Minister shall inform the National Assembly of it.

After the end of the period of time under paragraph one, all orders of the Prime Minister issued under this section which are still in force shall continue to be in force, and the repeal or modification of the said orders shall be made by an Act.

Sec. 201. At the initial stage, the King will appoint senators in accordance with this Constitution on the date of the election of members of the House of Representatives under section 202.

Sec. 202. The election of members of the House of Representatives under the provision of this Constitution shall be carried out within the 2521st year of the Buddhist Era, the period of time for holding the election shall be extended; provided that the extension is not beyond one hundred and twenty days as from the end of the 2521st year of the Buddhist Era.

Sec. 203. At the initial stage when the Constitution has been promulgated, apart from the cases provided in section 143, the following acts shall also be done in the joint sitting of the National Assembly:

(1) the consideration of the annual appropriation bill, the supplementary appropriations bill and the transfer of appropriations bill;

(2) the general debate under section 137;

(3) the consideration of the bill which the Council of Ministers has notified that it is an important bill relating to the security of the Kingdom, the Throne or the national economy, and the President of the National Assembly has approved the notification;

(4) the consideration of the Emergency Decree under section 157 and section 158,

provided that senators shall have the same right as members of the House of Representatives, but they shall not submit or join to submit a motion for a general debate under section 137, and the phrase 'the House of Representatives or the Senate' as stipulated in section 133, section 137 paragraphs two and three, section 157 and section 158 shall mean the National Assembly.

Sec. 204. At the initial stage when the Constitution has been promulgated:

(1) Section 90 paragraph two, section 91 paragraph one, section 94(3), section 95 and section 103(7) and (9) shall not apply to the election, holding of office and termination of membership of members of the House of Representatives elected under this Constitution.

Whether the election of members of the House of Representatives is to be done by means of combining or dividing the constituencies shall be determined in accordance with the law on election of members of the House of Representatives, and a person qualified to vote shall have the right to vote for a number of candidates equal to the total number of members of the House of Representatives for that constituency.

(2) Section 79, section 105, and section 139 paragraph three shall not apply to the appointment, holding of office and the vacation of Leader of the Opposition, and the appointment of the standing committee.

(3) Section 148, section specifically related to the prohibition referred to in section 97 (1) and (3) and section 167 shall not apply to the holding of office, of Minister and other political officials.

(4) Section 125 paragraph two and section 194 (1) specifically related to the political party shall not apply to the introduction of a bill and the submission of motion to amend the Constitution.

(5) The introduction of a bill by members of the House of Representatives shall be done only with the endorsement of the *ad hoc* Committee considering bills composing of seventeen members, three of whom are appointed by the Council of Ministers, six of whom by the Senate, and eight of whom by the House of Representatives.

Sec. 205. At the end of the period of four years from the date of the appointment of senators under section 201, section 203 and section 204 shall be repealed; provided that section 204 (3) shall continue to be in force until the new Council of Ministers takes office.

Sec. 206. All orders issued by the Prime Minister under section 21 of the Constitution of the Kingdom of Thailand B.E. 2519 or under the provision of section 27 of the Constitution for the Administration of the Kingdom B.E. 2520, and which are in force on the date of the promulgation of this Constitution, shall continue to be in force, the repeal or modification of the said orders shall be made by an Act.

TONGA

SUMMARY

INTERNATIONAL STATUS

Tonga is not a member of the United Nations. It is a member of the Commonwealth of Nations and of other international organizations.

An archipelago of 171 islands, Tongan power, both temporal and spiritual had reached a height in the thirteenth century and extended over much of Polynesia and as far as Hawaii. European explorers, Tasman in 1643, Captain Cook in 1773, gave the name of the Friendly Islands. In 1797, the first missionaries arrived and exploited the civil strife in Tonga to implant themselves. In 1845, the islands were united and the present dynasty founded under Taufa'ahau or King George Tupou I. In 1862 he abolished the system of semi-serfdom and established a system of land tenure. In 1875 he granted a constitution. In 1900 it became a British protected state. By an exchange of letters of May 19, 1970, the United Kingdom was no longer responsible for external relations and complete independence was declared on June 4, 1970.

FORM OF NATIONAL GOVERNMENT

The Constitution of November 1, 1875, was consolidated with all its amendments on January 1, 1967, and has been amended at times since up to 1981. It provides for a constitutional government under King Taufa'ahau Tupou IV and his heirs; the system of succession is described.[1] All land is the property of the King who may grant to nobles and chiefs hereditary estates; land may only be leased not sold and the system of leases is described.[2]

[1] Const. Art. 30, 31. [2] Id., Art. 105–110.

RIGHTS OF THE PEOPLE

The Constitution guarantees the right to freedom, prohibits slavery, provides one law for all, freedom of worship, speech, publication, correspondence and petition.[3] Habeas corpus shall apply.[4] No one may be punished without trial or tried without indictment, or tried twice for the same offence, or tried on another charge than that for which summoned.[5] The Sabbath day is to be kept holy.[6] Sanctity of domicile is provided.[7] Retrospective laws are forbidden.[8]

LEGISLATIVE DEPARTENT

The Legislative Assembly is composed of representatives of the people and representatives of the nobles sitting as one house.[9] Its members are the Ministers who sit as nobles,7 nobles elected by the nobles of the Kingdom and 7 representatives of the people elected by all subjects over 21 who pay taxes and are literate.[10] Only the nobles may discuss or vote on matters relating to the royal family or the nobles.[11] Immunities of members are provided.[12] The term of office is three years subject to dissolution, and it meets in one session a year.[13]

EXECUTIVE DEPARTMENT

The Kingdom is hereditary, the King is Commander-in-Chief of land and sea forces, is the fount of honor and has the prerogative of pardon.[14] His person is sacred, he governs the country but his Ministers are responsible.[15] There is a Privy Council appointed by the King, composed of members of the Cabinet, Governors and others.[16] The Ministers of the Cabinet are appointed by the King and participate in the Legislative Assembly as nobles.[18]

JUDICIAL DEPARTMENT

Judicial power vests in the Court of Appeal, the Supreme Court, the Magistrates Court and the Land Court.[18] The first two are composed of Chief Justices and other judges appointed by the King with the consent of the Privy Council.[19] Judges hold office during good behavior.[20] The Supreme Court has jurisdiction in cases in law and equity arising under the Constitution and laws, and in matters concerning treaties, Ministers, maritime cases.[21]

AREA, POPULATION, ETC.

The area of Tonga is 748 square kilometres, the population (1982) 100,069. There are 171 islands. The capital is Nuku'alofa, Tongatapu Island.

[3] Id., Art. 1–8.
[4] Id., Art. 9.
[5] Id., Art. 10–13.
[6] Id., Art. 6.
[7] Id., Art. 16.
[8] Id., Art. 20.
[9] Id., Art. 56.
[10] Id., Art. 60, 64
[11] Id., Art. 67.
[12] Id., Art. 73.
[13] Id., Art. 58, 77.
[14] Id., Art. 32–37, 44.
[15] Id., Art. 41.
[16] Id., Art. 50.
[17] Id., Art. 51.
[18] Id., Art. 84.
[19] Id., Art. 85.
[20] Id., Art. 87.
[21] Id., Art. 90

THE CONSTITUTION OF TONGA[1]

November 1, 1875, amended to 1981

Granted by His Majesty King George Tupou I on the fourth day of November One thousand eight hundred and seventy-five and amended in accordance with the law on divers dates in and between the year One thousand eight hundred and eighty and the year One thousand nine hundred and sixty-six and revised in accordance with the Laws Consolidation Act on the first day of January, 1967.

PART I

DECLARATION OF RIGHTS

1. Since it appears to be the will of God that man should be free as He has made all men of one blood therefore shall the people of Tonga and all who sojourn or may sojourn in this Kingdom be free for ever. And all men may use their lives and persons and time to acquire and possess property and to dispose of their labor and the fruit of their hands and to use their own property as they will.

2. No person shall serve another against his will except he be undergoing punishment by law and any slave who may escape from a foreign country to Tonga (unless he be escaping from justice being guilty of homicide or larceny or any great crime or involved in debt) shall be free from the moment he sets foot on Tongan soil for no person shall be in servitude under the protection of the flag of Tonga.

3. Whoever may wish to bring persons from other islands to work for him may make an agreement with them for the number of years they will work for him and a copy of the written agreement he makes with them shall be deposited in the Public Offices stating the amount of payment they shall receive the period they shall work and a promise to take them back to their own land. And the Government shall cause such contract to be carried out both on behalf of those who engage and those who are engaged. And such persons being so introduced shall be subject to the laws of the land and shall pay the same Customs duties as all the people in the Kingdom and taxes as shall be ordained by the King and his Cabinet.

4. There shall be but one law in Tonga for chiefs and commoners for non-Tongans and Tongans. No laws shall be enacted for one class and not for another class but the law shall be the same for all the people of this land.

5. All men are free to practise their religion and to worship God as they may deem fit in accordance with the dictates of their own consciences and to assemble for religious service in such places as they may appoint. But it shall not be lawful to use this freedom to commit evil and licentious acts or under the name of worship to do what is contrary to the law and peace of the land.

[1] Volume I of the Law of Tonga, published 1967, and subsequent Acts of Amendment incorporated. Supplied by New Zealand Embassy, Athens, in October 1982. Ed.

6. The Sabbath Day shall be kept holy in Tonga and no person shall practice his trade or profession or conduct any commercial undertaking on the Sabbath Day except according to law; and any agreement made or witnessed on that day shall be null and void and of no legal effect.

7. It shall be lawful for all people to speak write and print their opinions and no law shall ever be enacted to restrict this liberty. There shall be freedom of speech and of the press for ever but nothing in this clause shall be held to outweigh the law of slander or the laws for the protection of the King and the Royal Family.

8. All people shall be free to send letters or petitions to the King or Legislative Assembly and to meet and consult concerning matters about which they think it right to petition the King or Legislative Assembly to pass or repeal enactments provided that they meet peaceably without arms and without disorder.

9. The law of the writ of Habeas Corpus shall apply to all people and it shall never be suspended excepting in the case of war or rebellion in the land when it shall be lawful for the King to suspend it.

10. No one shall be punished because of any offence he may have committed until he has been sentenced according to law before a Court having jurisdiction in the case.

11. No one shall be tried or summoned to appear before any court or punished for failing to appear unless he has first received a written indictment (except in cases of impeachment or for small offences within the jurisdiction of the magistrate or for contempt of court while the court is sitting). Such written indictment shall clearly state the offence charged against him and the grounds for the charge. And at his trial the witnesses against him shall be brought face to face with him and he shall hear their evidence and shall be allowed to question them and to bring forward any witness of his own and to make his own statement regarding the charge preferred against him. But whoever shall be indicted for any offence if he shall so elect shall be tried by jury and this law shall never be repealed. And all claims for large amounts shall be decided by a jury and the Legislative Assembly shall determine what shall be the amount of claim that may be decided without a jury.

12. No one shall be tried again for any offence for which he has already been tried whether he was acquitted or convicted except in cases where the accused shall confess after having been acquitted by the court and when there is sufficient evidence to prove the truth of his confession.

13. No one shall be tried on any charge but that which appears in the indictment summons or warrant and for which he was brought to trial:

Save and except that

(*a*) where the complete commission of the offense charged is not proved but the evidence establishes an attempt to commit that offence the accused may be convicted of this attempt and punished accordingly; and

(*b*) where an attempt to commit an offence is charged but the evidence establishes the commission of the full offence the accused may be convicted of the attempt; and (*c*) on the trial of any person for embezzlement the jury shall be at liberty to find such person not guilty of embezzlement but guilty of larceny and on the trial of any person for larceny the jury shall be at liberty to find such person guilty of embezzlement.

14. No one shall be intimidated into giving evidence against himself nor shall the life or property or liberty of anyone be taken away except according to law.

15. It shall not be lawful for any judge or magistrate to adjudicate or for any juryman to sit in any case in which one of his relations is concerned either as a plaintiff defendant or witness: Nor shall any judge or magistrate sit in any case which concerns himself: Nor shall any judge or magistrate or juryman on any pretence receive any present or money or anything else from anyone who is about to be tried nor from any of the defendant's friends but all judges, magistrates and juryman shall be entirely free and shall in no case whatever be interested or biased in the discharge of their duties.

16. It shall not be lawful for anyone to enter forcibly the houses or premises of another or to search for anything or to take anything the property of another except according to law: And should any person lose any property and believe it to be concealed in any place whether house or premises it shall be lawful for him to make an affidavit before a magistrate that he believes it to be concealed in that place in which he believes it to be concealed and the magistrate shall issue a search warrant to the police to search for the property according to the affidavit so made.

17. The King shall govern on behalf of all his people and not so as to enrich or benefit any one man or any one family or any one class but without partiality for the good of all the people of his Kingdom.

18. All the people have the right to expect that the Government will protect their life, liberty and property and therefore it is right for all the people to support and contribute to the Government according to law. And if at any time there should be a war in the land and the Government should take the property of anyone the Government shall pay the fair value of such property to the owner. And if the Legistature shall resolve to take from any person or persons their premises or a part of their premises or their houses for the purpose of making Government roads or other work of benefit to the Government the Government shall pay the fair value.

19. (*a*) No money shall be paid out of the Treasury nor borrowed nor debts contracted by the Government but by the prior vote of the Legislative Assembly, except in the following cases:

(i) Where an Act duly passed by the Legislative Assembly gives power to pay out money or borrow or contract debts, then money may be paid out, or borrowing carried out or debts contracted in terms of said Act; and

(ii) In cases of war or rebellion or dangerous epidemic or a similar emergency, then it may be done by the Treasurer with the consent of Cabinet, and the King shall at once convoke the Legislative Assembly and the Treasurer shall state the grounds for the expenditure and the amount.

(*b*) The Treasurer, with the approval of Privy Council, shall have power to increase or decrease the taxes and/or customs duties and shall have power to levy new taxes and/or customs duties, and all such increases or decreases or new taxes or customs duties shall be published in the Gazette and shall be placed before the next session of the Legislative Assembly and shall have full force and shall remain effective from the date of publication in the Gazette until rescinded by the Legislative Assembly or by the Treasurer with the approval of Privy Council.

20. It shall not be lawful to enact any retrospective laws in so far as they may curtail or take away or affect rights or privileges existing at the time of the passing of such laws.

21. Every soldier shall be subject to the laws of the land whether he belongs to the Guards, the Artillery or to the Militia in accordance with the twenty-second clause and any soldier who breaks the law of the land shall be tried in the courts as any other person. And it shall not be lawful for any officer to quarter any soldier upon the premises of anyone except in time of war and then only as may be resolved by the Legislative Assembly.

22. The Royal Guards shall have the right to vote for representatives to the Legislative Assembly although they are exempt from taxes in accordance with the provisions of this Constitution. It shall be lawful for the King to command any taxpayer to join the militia for the purpose of instruction or for parade on public occasions should he think fit and also in time of war to call out all those capable of bearing arms and to make orders and regulations for their control and provisioning.

23. No person having been convicted of a criminal offence punishable by imprisonment for more than two years, shall hold any office under the Government whether of emolument or honor nor shall he be qualified to vote for nor to be elected a representative of the Legislative Assembly unless he has received from the King a pardon together with a declaration that he is freed from the disabilities to which he would otherwise be subject under the provisions of this clause.

24. It shall not be lawful for anyone holding any office under the Government whether of emolument or otherwise to hold any appointment under or receive an emolument from another Government without first obtaining permission from the King. And it shall not be lawful for anyone holding an office of emolument under the Government to engage in trade or work for anyone else except with the prior consent of Cabinet.

25. (Repealed).

26. Whoever shall be really poor whether owing to sickness or old age may be exempted from paying taxes but it shall not be lawful to exempt any person who receives rents from leased land or any person who receives any emolument or pension from the Government.

27. No person may succeed to any *tofia* or any title until he has attained the age of twenty-one years save for members of the Royal Family who shall be deemed to have attained maturity at eighteen years of age.

28. Every male Tongan who has arrived at the age of twenty-one years and can read and write and is not disabled by the twenty-third clause of this Constitution shall be liable to serve on juries and the names of all those who are liable to serve shall be published once every year and anyone who neglects to serve shall be punished as shall be enacted by the Legislature. But members of the Legislative Assembly, ministers of religion, assistant ministers, schoolmasters, collegians, public servants, guardsmen, artillerymen and all officials of the Government shall be exempt from serving on juries.

29. Any foreigner after he has resided in the Kingdom for the space of five years or more may with the consent of the King take the oath of allegiance and he may be granted Letters of Naturalization and all naturalized subjects shall have the same rights and privileges as native born subjects of Tonga with the exception that they shall not be entilted to the rights of hereditary tax allotments.

PART II

FORM OF GOVERNMENT

30. The Government of this Kingdom is divided into three Bodies

1st. The King Privy Council and Cabinet (Ministry);

2nd. The Legislative Assembly;

3rd. The Judiciary.

31. The form of Government for this Kingdom is a Constitutional Government under His Majesty King Taufa'ahau Tupou IV his heirs and successors.

32. The right and title of King George Tupou I to the Crown and Throne of this Kingdom were confirmed by the Constitution of 1875 and it was further declared in the said Constitution that the succession to the Crown and Throne should devolve upon David Uga and then upon Wellington Gu and then upon them begotten by him in marriage and if at any time there be no heirs of Wellington Gu the Crown and Throne shall descend in accordance with the following law of succession: It shall be lawful only for those born in marriage to succeed. The succession shall be to the eldest male child and the heirs of his body but if he should have no children to the second male child and the heirs of his body and so on until all the male line shall be ended. Should there be no male child the eldest female child shall succeed and the heirs of her body and if she should have no children it shall descend to the second female child and the heirs of her body until the female line is ended. And if there shall be none of this line of David Uga lawful descendants by marriage to succeed to the Crown of Tonga it shall descend to William Tungi and his lawful heirs begotten by him in marriage and to their heirs begotten by them. And if there should be no lawful heir the King shall appoint his heir if the House of Nobles consent to it (the representatives of the people having no voice in the matter) and he shall be publicly declared heir to the Crown during the King's life. Should there be no heir to the Crown or successor who has been so publicly proclaimed the Premier or in his absence the Cabinet ministers shall convoke the nobles of the Legislative

Assembly (the representatives of the people having no voice in the matter) and when they meet the House of Nobles shall choose by ballot some one of the chiefs whom they wish to succeed as King. And he shall succeed as the first of a new dynasty and he and the heirs of his body born in marriage shall possess the Crown according to law. And in the event of there being none to succeed according to this law the Premier or in his absence the Cabinet ministers shall again convoke the nobles of the Legislative Assembly in accordance with this law and they shall choose one to succeed to the Throne as the first of a new dynasty and so on according to this law for ever.

33. (1) It shall not be lawful for any member of the Royal Family who is likely to succeed to the throne to marry any person without the consent of the King. And if any person should thus marry the marriage shall not be considered legal and it shall be lawful for the King to cancel the right of such person and his heirs to succeed to the Crown of Tonga. And the next person in succession to him who so marries shall be declared the heir and the offender shall be regarded as dead.

(2) The expression 'any member of the Royal Family who is likely to succeed to the throne' in the last preceding sub-clause shall be construed to include all persons born in lawful marriage and related by descent either lineally or collaterally to the King but not more than twenty times removed from the King.

34. The following oath shall be taken by those who shall succeed to the throne

'I solemnly swear before Almighty God to keep in its integrity the Constitution of Tonga and to govern in conformity with the laws thereof.'

35. No person shall succeed to the Crown of Tonga who has been found guilty of a felony or who is insane or imbecile.

36. The King is the Commander-in-Chief of the forces on land and sea. He shall appoint all officers and make such regulations for the training and control of the forces as he may think best for the welfare of the country but it shall not be lawful for the King to make war without the consent of the Legislative Assembly.

37. It shall be lawful for the King with the consent of the Privy Council to pardon any person who has been convicted of a breach of law, or to remit or mitigate any sentence, or any part of any sentence, imposed by any court for a breach of law:

Provided that he shall not pardon any person convicted of maladministration in accordance with the fifty-first clause. It shall not be lawful to pardon any person convicted of this offence.

38. The King may convoke the Legislative Assembly at any time and may dissolve it at his pleasure and command that new representatives of the nobles and people be elected to enter the Assembly. But it shall not be lawful for the Kingdom to remain without a meeting of the Assembly for a longer period than one year. The Assembly shall always meet at Nukui'alofa and at no other place except in time of war.

39. It shall be lawful for the King to make treaties with Foreign States provided that such treaties shall be in accordance with the laws of the Kingdom. It shall not be lawful for the King to alter the customs duties without the consent of the Legislative Assembly. The King may appoint his representatives to other nations according to the custom of nations.

40. The King shall receive Foreign Ministers and may address the Legislative Assembly in writing regarding the affairs of the Kingdom and matters which he may wish to bring before the Assembly for deliberation.

41. The King is the Sovereign of all the Chiefs and all the people. The person of the King is sacred. He governs the country but his ministers are responsible. All Acts that have passed the Legislative Assembly must bear the King's signature before they become law.

42. Should the King die before his heir is eighteen years of age a Prince Regent shall be appointed in accordance with the forty-third clause.

43. Should the King wish to travel abroad it shall be lawful for him to appoint a Prince Regent who shall administer the affairs of the Kingdom during his absence And if the King should die whilst his heir is not yet arrived at the age of eighteen years and he has not declared in his will his wishes regarding a Prince Regent during his heir's minority the Premier of the Cabinet shall at once convoke the Legislative Assembly and they shall choose by ballot a Prince Regent who shall administer the affairs of the Kingdom in the name of the King until the heir shall have attained his majority (but the representatives of the people shall have no voice in such election).

44. It is the King's prerogative to give titles of honor and to confer honorable distinctions but it shall not be lawful for him to deprive anyone who has an hereditary title of his title such as chiefs of hereditary lands and nobles of the Legislative Assembly who possess hereditary lands except in cases of treason. And if anyone shall be tried and found guilty of treason the King shall appoint a member of that family to succeed to the name and inheritance of the guilty person.

45. It is the prerogative of the King with the advice of his Cabinet to decree the coinage which shall be legal tender in this Kingdom and to make regulations for the coining of money.

46. In the event of civil war or war with a foreign state it shall be lawful for the King to proclaim martial law over any part or over the whole of the country.

47. The Flag of Tonga (the flag of King George) shall never be altered but shall always be the flag of this Kingdom and the present Royal Ensign shall always be the ensign of the Royal Family of Tonga.

48. The lands of the King and the property of the King are his to dispose of as he pleases. The Government shall not touch them nor shall they be liable for any Government debt. But the houses built for him by the Government and any inheritance which may be given to him as King shall descend to his successors as the property and inheritance of the Royal line.

49. It shall not be lawful to sue the King in any court for a debt without the consent of the Cabinet.

50. The King shall appoint a Privy Council to assist him in the discharge of his important functions. The Privy Council shall be composed of the Cabinet in accordance with the fifty-first clause and the Governors in accordance with the fifty-fourth clause and any others whom the King shall see fit to call to his Council. No Ordinance which may be passed by the King and Privy Council shall have any effect until the signature of the minister to whose department such Ordinance relates is affixed thereto and if such Ordinance shall be illegal such minister alone shall be responsible and when the Legislative Assembly shall meet it may confirm such Ordinances and make them law or rescind them.

Cabinet

51. The Cabinet or ministers of the King shall consist of the Prime Minister, Minister of Foreign Affairs, the Minister of Lands, the Minister of Police and any other ministers whom His Majesty may be pleased to appoint. It is the King's prerogative to appoint the ministers and they shall hold office during the King's pleasure or for such period as may be specified in their commissions and any one minister may hold two or more offices. It shall be lawful to impeach the ministers before the Legislative Assembly if their administration is not in accordance with law. The ministers shall be members of the Privy Council and of the Legislative Assembly as nobles. Each minister shall draw up a report once every year acquainting the King with the affairs of his department and such report shall answer all questions put to him by the Legislative Assembly and report everything in connection with his department.

52. Each member of the Cabinet shall have an office in Nuku'alofa the capital of the Kingdom and he shall satisfy himself that all the subordinates in his department faithfully perform their duties. And the Government shall build or rent offices suitable for the work of each minister.

53. When the Legislative Assembly shall meet the Treasurer shall present to the Legislative Assembly on behalf of the Cabinet an account of all moneys which have been received and expended during the current year or since the last meeting of the Assembly and the nature of the receipts and expenditure.

54. The King with the consent of the Cabinet shall appoint Governors to Ha' apai and Vava'u. The Governors shall in virtue of their office hold seats in the Legislative Assembly and shall also be members of the Privy Council whilst they hold the office of Governor and they shall hold office only during the Kings's pleasure.

55. It shall not be lawful for a Governor to enact any law but he shall be responsible that the law is enforced in his district. If the administration of any Governor be contrary to law it shall be lawful to impeach him in the Legislative Assembly.

The Legislative Assembly

56. The King and the Legislative Assembly shall have power to enact laws, and the representatives of the nobles and the representatives of the people shall sit as one House. When the Legislative Assembly shall have agreed upon any Bill which has been read and voted for by a majority three times it shall be presented to the King for his sanction and after receiving his sanction and signature it shall become law upon publication. Votes shall be given by raising the hand or by standing up in division or by saying 'Aye' or 'No'.

57. The Legislative Assembly shall be called the Legislative Assembly of Tonga

58. The Legislative Assembly shall meet at least once in every twelve calendar months but it shall be lawful to summon the same at any time.

59. The Legislative Assembly shall be composed of the Privy Councillors and Cabinet ministers, who shall sit as nobles, the representatives of the nobles, and representatives of the people.

60. There shall be elected by the nobles of the Kingdom from among their number seven nobles as representatives of the nobles and there shall be elected by electors duly qualified seven representatives of the people. The Legislative Assembly shall determine how both classes of representatives shall be apportioned amongst the various districts.

61. The King shall appoint the Speaker of the Assembly but all other officers shall be appointed by the Assembly.

62. The Assembly shall make its own rules of procedure for the conduct of its meetings.

63. (1) No person shall succeed to the position of a noble who is insane or imbecile or who is disabled by the twenty-third clause.

(2) Every noble shall be competent to vote in an election for representatives of the nobles and to sit in the Assembly if chosen according to law.

64. Every Tongan subject of twenty-one years of age or more who being a male and not a noble pays taxes and being a male or female can read and write and is not insane or imbecile and is not disabled by the twenty-third clause shall be entitled to vote in an election for representatives of the people to the Legislative Assembly and on the day appointed for election shall be exempt for summons from debt.

65. Representatives of the people shall be chosen by ballot and any person who is qualified to be an elector may be chosen as a representative, save that no person may be chosen against whom an order has been made in any Court in the Kingdom for the payment of a specific sum of money the whole or any part of which remains outstanding or if ordered to pay by instalments the whole or any part of such instalments remain outstanding on the day on which such person submits his nomination paper to the Returning Officer or on the day on which this Act comes into force whichever is the latter.

Provided that no person holding an office of emolument under the Crown shall enter the Assembly except the Ministers, and the Governors.

66. Any person elected as a representative who shall be proved to the satisfaction of the Assembly to have used threats or offered bribes for the purpose of persuading any person to vote for him shall be unseated by the Assembly.

67. It shall be lawful for only the nobles of the Legislative Assembly to discuss or vote upon laws relating to the King or the Royal Family or the titles and inheritance of the nobles and after any such bill has been passed three times by a majority of the nobles of the Legislative Assembly it shall be submitted to the King for his sanction.

68. Should the king withhold his sanction from any law passed by the Legislative Assembly and submitted to him for approval it shall be unlawful for the Legislative Assembly again to discuss such law until the following session.

69. It shall be lawful for the Legislative Assembly to pass judgment upon its members for their acts or conduct as members of the Legislative Assembly and although all the members may not be present it shall be lawful for the Legislative Assembly to discuss and pass laws and transact business should one-half of its members be present but should there be less than one half present the Legislative Assembly shall stand adjourned to another day and if at such adjourned meeting there should be still less than half the members present it shall be lawful for the King or the Speaker of the Assembly to command the presence of all the members and if any fail to attend on such command it shall be lawful to inflict punishment for such disobedience such punishment to be determined by the Legislative Assembly.

70. If anyone shall speak or act disrespectfully in the presence of the Legislative Assembly it shall be lawful to imprison him for thirty days and whoever shall publish any libel on the Legislative Assembly, or threaten any member or his property, or rescue any person whose arrest has been ordered by the Legislative Assembly, may be imprisoned for not exceeding thirty days.

his position whether during the session of the Legislative Assembly or not he may be tried and deprived of his office by the nobles of the Legislative Assembly but the representatives of the people shall not take part in his trial and if he be deposed another noble shall be elected to succeed to his seat in the Legislative Assembly but his title and hereditary estates shall not be confiscated except for treason or sedition.

72. A journal of the proceedings of the Legislative Assembly shall be kept and the votes of each member present for and against every motion or resolution shall be recorded in the journal.

73. The members of the Legislative Assembly shall be free from arrest and judgment whilst it is sitting except for indictable offences and no member of the House shall be liable for anything he may have said or published in the Legislative Assembly.

74. Any representative of the nobles or of the people who may wish to resign his seat in the Legislative Assembly may tender his resignation in writing to the Speaker and his connection with the Legislative Assembly shall cease when he tenders his resignation.

75. (1) It shall be lawful for the members of the Legislative Assembly to impeach any Privy Councillor, Minister, Governor, or Judge for any of the following offences

Breach of the laws or the resolutions of the Legislative Assembly, maladministration, incompetency, destruction or embezzlement of Government property, or the performance of acts which may lead to difficulties between this and another country.

(2) The impeached person shall be given a copy of the accusation in writing seven days before the day of trial.

(3) The trial shall be conducted in accordance with the eleventh clause.

(4) The Chief Justice shall preside but if the Chief Justice is impeached the King shall appoint some other member of the Assembly to preside.

(5) After the witnesses have been heard the impeached person shall withdraw and the Assembly shall consider their decision and upon a decision being made he shall be brought before the Assembly and the decision announced to him. If he be found guilty it shall be lawful to dismiss him from office but if acquitted it shall not be lawful to impeach him again on the same charge as is provided in the twelfth clause.

76. Upon the death or resignation of any representative of the nobles or of the people the Speaker shall immediately command that the nobles or the electors of the district which he represented shall elect a representative in his place. But the Legislative Assembly shall have the power to sit and act although its number be not complete.

77. New elections shall be held for all the representatives of the nobles and the people at least once every three years but it shall be lawful for the King at his pleasure to dissolve the Legislative Assembly although three years from the last election may not have expired and to command that new elections be held according to law throughout the Kingdom.

78. The Legislative Assembly shall assess the amount of taxes to be paid by the people and the customs duties and fees for trading licences and shall pass the estimates of expenditure for the Public Service in accordance with the nineteenth clause and upon the report of the Minister of Finance upon the expenditure and revenue received during the year succeeding the last meeting of the Assembly the Legislative Assembly shall determine the estimates for the expenditure of the Government until the next meeting of the Legislative Assembly. And the ministers shall be guided by the estimates of public expenditures so authorized by the Legislative Assembly.

79. It shall be lawful for the Legislative Assembly to discuss amendments to the Constitution provided that such amendments shall not affect the law of liberty, the succession to the Throne and the titles and hereditary estates of the nobles. And if the Legislative Assembly wish to amend any clause of the Constitution such amendment shall after it has passed the Legislative Assembly three times be submitted to the King and if the Privy Council and the Cabinet are unanimously in favor of the amendment it shall be lawful for the King to assent and when signed by the King it shall become law.

80. The formula for enacting laws shall be 'Be it enacted by the King and Legislative Assembly of Tonga in the Legislature of the Kingdom as follows:'

81. To avoid confusion in the making of laws every law shall embrace but one subject which shall be expressed by its title.

82. The present law shall be in force until repealed by the Legislative Assembly excepting such laws as are at variance with this Constitution. And it shall be lawful for the Chief Justice to suspend the operation of any law passed by the Legislative Assembly or Privy Council which is at variance with the Constitution until the next meeting of the Legislative Assembly.

83. The following oath shall be taken by the members of the Privy Council: 'I solemnly swear before God that I will be truly loyal to His Majesty King Taufa' ahau Tupou IV the rightful King of Tonga and that I will keep righteously and perfectly the Constitution of Tonga and assist to the end of my power and ability in all things in connection with the Privy Council.' The following oath shall be taken by the ministers: 'I solemnly swear before God that I will be truly loyal to His Majesty King Taufa'ahau Tupou IV the rightful King of Tonga and that I will keep righteously and perfectly the Constitution of Tonga and discharge the duties of may department to the end of my ability for the benefit of the King and his Government.' The following oath shall be taken by the nobles and representatives of the people: 'I solemnly swear before God that I will be truly loyal to His Majesty King Taufa'ahau Tupou IV the rightful King of Tonga and that I will righteously and perfectly conform to and keep the Constitution of Tonga and zealously discharge my duties as a member of the Legislative Assembly.' The members of the Privy Council shall sign their names to the oath and read it in the presence of the King. The ministers shall sign their names to the oath and read it in the presence of the King. The nobles and representatives of the people shall sign their names to the oath and read it in the presence of the Legislative Assembly.

The Judiciary

84. The judicial power of the Kingdom shall be vested in the Court of Appeal, the Supreme Court, the Magistrate's Court, and the Land Court.

85. The Court of Appeal shall consist of the Chief Justice of Tonga and of such other judges as may be appointed from time to time by the King with the consent of Privy Council:

Provided that no person shall be appointed unless

(*a*) he holds, or has held, high judicial office; or

(*b*) (i) he is qualified to practise as an advocate in a court in some part of Her Britannic Majesty's dominions having unlimited jurisdiction in civil or criminal matters; and

(ii) he has been qualified so to practise for not less than ten years.

86. The Supreme Court shall consist of a judge called the Chief Justice and such other judges as may be appointed from time to time by the King with the consent of the Privy Council sitting with or without a jury.

87. The judges shall hold office during good behavior and shall receive such salaries as the Legislature may determine and the Legislature may increase but shall not decrease such salaries during their tenure of office:

Provided that it shall be lawful to appoint Judges of the Court of Appeal for limited periods, or for the purposes of a particular sitting of the Court of Appeal, or of particular proceedings to come before the Court, on such terms as to salary, or other remuneration, as may be approved by the King with the consent of Privy Council.

88. (1) It shall be lawful for the Premier with the consent of Cabinet in the name and on behalf of His Majesty, at any time during the illness or absence of any judge, or for any other temporary purpose to appoint an acting judge for the period during which the judge is ill or absent or for the period necessary to effect the temporary purpose.

(2) An acting judge shall have the jurisdiction and powers of, and may exercise all the authorities which are vested in or may be exercised by a judge and shall be paid such salary as may be detemined by Cabinet.

89. The judges shall have power to direct the form of indictments to control the procedure of the lower Courts, and to make rules of procedure.

90. The Supreme Court shall have jurisdiction in all cases in Law and Equity arising under the Constitution and Laws of the Kingdom (except indictable offences where the accused elected to be tried by jury and except also cases concerning titles to land which shall be detemined by a Land Court subject to an appeal to the Privy Council) and in all matters concerning Treaties with Foreign States and Ministers and Consuls and in all cases affecting Public Ministers and Consuls and all Maritime Cases.

91. (1) Subject to the provisions of any Act of the Legislative Assembly regulating appeals to the Court of Appeal, a party to any proceedings in the Supreme Court who is aggrieved by a decision given in those proceedings by that Court, or a judge thereof, sitting in first instance, may appeal to the Court of Appeal against such decision.

(2) Except as may be provided by any Act of the Legislative Assembly, or by rules in respect of limited classes of appeals, no appeal shall be finally determined by less than three members of the Court of Appeal.

92. The Court of Appeal shall have exclusive power and jurisdiction to hear and determine all appeals which by virtue of this Constitution or of any Act of the Legislative Assembly lie from the Supreme Court or any judge thereof and shall have such further or other jurisdiction as may be conferred upon it by any such Act.

93. The judges shall give opinions upon important or difficult matters when requested so to do by the King, the Cabinet or the Legislative Assembly.

94. It shall not be lawful for any judge to sit or adjudicate upon an appeal from any decision which he may have given.

95. The Chief Justice and any other judge shall take the following oath: 'I swear in the presence of God that I will be loyal to His Majesty King Taufa'ahau Tupou IV the lawful King of Tonga and that I will perform truly and with impartiality my duties as a judge in accordance with the Constitution and the Laws of the Kingdom'. The judge shall read and sign this oath in the presence of the Cabinet:

Provided that a Chief Justice or any other judge, who is not a Tongan subject, shall take the following oath in lieu of the foregoing oath: 'I swear in the presence of God that I will perform truly and with impartiality my duties as a judge in accordance with the Constitution and the Laws of the Kingdom'.

96. The Legislature shall determine the fees payable to the various Courts. The Registrar of the Supreme Court shall keep the Court records.

97. It shall not be lawful for any judicial officer to receive any portion of a fine paid by any person convicted of an offence or for the Government to allot prisoners to serve any judicial officer, police officer, juror, or any other person as payment for duties discharged by them.

98. The Legislature shall regulate the summoning of jurors and the fees (if any) they shall receive.

99. Any person committed for trial before the Supreme Court on a charge of having committed any criminal offence punishable by a term of imprisonment exceeding two years or a fine of fifty pounds or both such penalties shall if he shall so elect be tried by a jury; and whenever any issue of fact is raised in any civil action may claim the right of trial by jury; and the law of trial by jury shall never be repealed.

100. It is the duty of the jury in criminal cases to pronounce whether the person accused is guilty or not guilty according to the evidence given before the Court. In civil cases the jury shall give judgment for payment or compensation as the case may be and according to the merits of the case.

101. In civil and criminal cases the judge shall direct the jury upon the law bearing upon the case and assist them in arriving at a just decision upon the case before them. The judge shall have power to refuse to admit evidence which he may deem to be irrelevant or improper.

102. The Chief Justice shall report once a year to the King upon the administration of justice and the criminal statistics of the country and upon any amendments in the law which he may recommend. And the King shall lay this report before the Assembly at its next meeting in the same manner as the reports of the ministers.

103. The Legislature shall determine the time and place for holding the Courts and shall limit the powers of the magistrates in criminal and civil matters and shall determine what cases shall be committed for trial to the Supreme Court.

PART III

THE LAND

104. All the land is the property of the King and he may at pleasure grant to the nobles and titular chiefs or matabules one or more estates to become their hereditary estates. It is hereby declared by this Constitution that it shall not be lawful for anyone at any time hereafter whether he be the King or any one of the chiefs or the people of this country to sell any land whatever in the Kingdom of Tonga but they may lease it only in accordance with this Constitution and mortgage it in accordance with the Land Act. And this declaration shall become a covenant binding on the King and chiefs of this Kingdom for themselves and their heirs and successors for ever.

105. The Cabinet shall determine the terms for which leases shall be granted and the Cabinet shall determine the amount of rent for all Government lands but no lease shall be granted for any longer period than ninety- nine years without the consent of His Majesty in Council.

106. The forms of deed transfer and permit which shall from time to time be sanctioned by His Majesty in Privy Council are hereby appointed to be the forms according to which all deeds of leases transfers and permits shall be made.

107. This Constitution shall not affect any leases which have been granted by the Government or any leases which have been promised whether leases of land in the interior or of town allotments. Such leases will be recognized by the Government but this exception shall not refer to any leases which may be granted after the granting of this Constitution.

108. No leases of any town site shall in future be granted to any religious body for any purpose unless there are thirty adults, male and female, of such church in that town, and it shall not be lawful for any religious body to use such leased lands for other than religious purposes or to sub-let to any person without the prior consent of Cabinet, and upon satisfactory proof before a Court that any such land has been sub-let without consent, such land shall revert to the person from whom the land was leased, to his successor in title as the case may be.

109. All the beach frontage of this Kingdom belongs to the Crown from fifty feet above high-water mark and it shall be lawful for the Government to lease any portion of the beach frontage for erecting a store jetty or wharf and the Minister of Lands with the consent of the Cabinet shall have power to grant such lease.

110. All leases unless signed by the King himself shall be signed by the Minister of Lands and sealed with the seal of his office and countersigned by one of the Cabinet ministers who shall affix the seal of his office and no lease or transfer will be considered valid or recognized by the Government unless registered in the office of the Minister of Lands.

111. The following is the law of succession to hereditary estates and titles: Children lawfully born in wedlock only may inherit and the eldest male child shall succeed and the heirs of his body but if he has no descendants then the second male child and the heirs of his body and so on until all the male line is ended. Should there be no male child the eldest female child shall succeed and the heirs of her body and if she should have no descendants the second female child and the heirs of her body and so on until the female line is ended. And failing direct heirs the property shall revert to the eldest brother of the owner of the property beginning with the eldest and his heirs in succession to the youngest and their heirs in accordance with the law of inheritance. And if the brothers have no descendants it shall descend to the eldest sister and the female line as provided in the case of the male line. And if these should have no descendants and there should be no legitimate heir it shall revert to the Crown in accordance with the one hundred and twelfth clause. But should a female be next in succession to the title of a noble or of an hereditary chief the next male heir shall inherit the title and estates. But should such female afterwards have a legitimate male issue the title and estates shall revert to the male issue of the female upon the death of the male in possession of the estate:

Provided that the female that is the heir shall occupy the town allotment and the plantation lands appertaining to such title but the hereditary estates that is the lands occupied by the people shall be held by the inheritor of the title.

Whereas by Tongan custom provision has always been made that an adopted child might succeed to the estates and titles of his adoptive father now therefore it is decreed that upon the death of the holder of an estate or title who has inherited such estate or title by virtue of his blood descent from such adopted child the estate and title shall revert to the descendant by blood of the original holder of the estate and title in accordance with the provisions of this clause and should there be alive no such descendant by blood the provisions of the one hundred and twelfth clause shall apply.

112. Should there be no legitimate heirs to an estate such estate shall revert to the King. But the King may confer the title and estate upon any other person and the person so appointed and his heirs shall possess such title and estates for ever.

113. A widow shall have the right to succeed to her deceased husband's tax and town allotment. Every person who holds a tax and town allotment shall pay such rents therefore as may be determined by the Legislature. Every taxpayer shall have the right to hold an hereditary tax and town allotment upon and subject to such conditions as to the area thereof and the rent to be paid therefore as may be determined from time to time by the Legislature.

114. No lease, sub-lease, transfer of a lease or of a sub-lease shall be granted

(*a*) without the prior consent of Cabinet where the term is ninety-nine years, or less, or

(*b*) without the prior consent of Privy Council where the term is over ninety-nine years,

Provided that no consent shall be granted to a lease by a widow of the land of her deceased husband.

115. This Constitution may be cited as The Act of Constitution of Tonga.

TURKEY

SUMMARY

INTERNATIONAL STATUS

Turkey is a member of the United Nations (October 24, 1945). It is a member of the North Atlantic Treaty Organization and of other international organizations.

The Turkish revolution of 1908 led to the restoration on July 24th of that year of the Constitution promulgated on December 23, 1876, which had remained in effect for only two years. Slavery was abolished but there were no other serious reforms, and the Balkan Wars and First World War achieved the collapse of the Ottoman Empire. From 1918 to 1922, Mustafa Kemal Ataturk fought against all foreign presences in the country and for the establishment of a republic, which was proclaimed on October 29, 1923. The Sultanate had been abolished on October 1, 1922, and the Caliphate was abolished on March 3, 1924, as part of the process of making Turkey an entirely secular state. The Treaty of Lausanne of July 24, 1923, fixed the present boundaries of Turkey.

Radical social, political, linguistic, religious and economic reforms were introduced by Ataturk and Ataturkism became the ideological basis of modern Turkey. The one party system with Ataturk's Republican People's Party, lasted until the 1950 elections. On May 27, 1960, a military coup d'etat overthrew the government and dissolved Parliament. Civilian rule was restored in October 1961, with a new constitution. In 1971, a wave of strikes and unrest caused the Armed Forces to demand the resignation of the government. A 'guided democracy', under military supervision with martial law and the suppression of left wing activities, lasted until the October 1973 elections. The civilian government was unable to control the internal problems arising out of a demographic explosion combined with urbanization and a political life divided into extremes, and the consequent violence throughout the country. In September 1979, martial law was imposed in 19 provinces. Violence and killings continued to escalate and on September 12, 1980, the Armed Forces in a bloodless coup took power, imposed martial law throughout the country, dissolved parliament and banned all political activities. A provisional constitution was promulgated in October 1980 by the National Security Council which received unlimited powers until December 1980.

On October 16, 1981, all political parties were dissolved and a Constitutional Assembly was formed of appointed members to draw up a new constitution. Elections were announced for November 6, 1983, under the restrictions concerning political parties contained in the provisional articles of the Constitution and the April 1983 law on political parties. The draft constitution was circulated for discussion in July 1982, and approved by referendum on November 7, 1982. It entered into force immediately.

In July and August 1974, Turkey invaded Cyprus and occupied one third of its territory. United Nations resolutions since that date have called for the withdrawal of its forces.

FORM OF NATIONAL GOVERNMENT

The Constitution of November 7, 1982, replaces the provisional constitution of 1980, which superseded that of July 9, 1961, as amended. The latter had replaced the constitution of April 20, 1924. The 1982 Constitution provides that Turkey ia a republic, a democratic, secular and social state governed by the rule of law.[1] Sovereignty is vested in the nation which exercises it through the authorized organs.[2] It is loyal to the nationalism of Ataturk.[3] The Turkish state with its territory and nation is an indivisible entity.[4] Citizenship is described.[5] The formation of political parties and the principles they must observe are stipulated.[6] The provisional articles restrict all political activity of officers of political parties dissolved in 1981, during ten years after the coming into force of the constitution, and of deputies and senators of the Grand National Assembly dissolved in 1980 for five years.[7]

RIGHTS OF THE PEOPLE

The Constitution provides equality before the law without any discrimination; no privileges may be granted.[8] Everyone has the right to life, no one may be subject to torture or ill treatment, forced labor is forbidden.[9] The right to liberty and security of the person together with the conditions for deprivation of liberty are described.[10] The Constitution guarantees inviolability of private and family life and

[1] Const., Art. 1, 2.
[2] Id., Art. 6.
[3] Id., Art. 2.
[4] Id., Art. 3.
[5] Id., Art. 66.
[6] Id., Art. 68, 69.
[7] Id., Prov. Art. 4.
[8] Id., Art. 10.
[9] Id., Art. 17, 18.
[10] Id., Art. 19.

domicile, thought, opinion, expression, speech, science, the arts.[11] Press and publication are free subject to being held responsible under the law in case of threats to state security or tending to incite offense, riot or insurrection.[12] The right to use mass media and means of communication other than the press is provided.[13] The Constitution guarantees freedom of association and assembly, under the proviso that associations may not pursue, engage in or support political aims or activities.[14] The right of property is provided, retroactive punishment and self-incrimination forbidden, criminal responsibility is personal and general confiscation may not be imposed.[15] The social and economic rights include protection of the family, the right to education, sea, lake and river shores at the disposal of the State, determination by the State of efficient land use, possibility in the national interest of nationalization of private enterprises, the right, duty and freedom to work, to rest and leisure.[16] The right to form labor unions and employers associations and to strike is provided; labor unions may not engage in political activity nor support or be supported by political parties.[17] The State supervises health services, supports public housing, protects youth, encourages sport.[18] It will provide social security; protect Turkish nationals working abroad.[19] Citizens have the right to vote, to be elected, to engage in political activity.[20] The right of petition is stipulated.[21] The fundamental rights and freedoms include duties and responsibilities and may be restricted by law with the aim of safeguarding the indivisible integrity of the State, the republic, national security, general peace and the public interest.[22]

LEGISLATIVE DEPARTMENT

Legislative power is vested in the Grand National Assembly and may not be delegated.[23] The Grand National Assembly is composed of 400 deputies, elected by free, equal, secret, direct, universal suffrage for a term of five years, subject to dissolution.[24] It meets in one regular annual session.[25] Members of the Assembly represent the whole nation.[26] Incompatibilities and immunities of members are stated.[27] The functions and powers are described.[28] There are provisions concerning finance,[29] and economic planning and development.[30]

EXECUTIVE DEPARTMENT

Executive power and functions is exercised and carried out by the President, Head of State, and the Council of Ministers.[31] The President is elected from among

[11] Id., Art. 20–27.
[12] Id., Art. 28.
[13] Id., Art. 31.
[14] Id., Art. 33.
[15] Id., Art. 35, 38.
[16] Id., Art. 41–50.
[17] Id., Art. 51, 52.
[18] Id., Art. 56–59.
[19] Id., art. 60–62.
[20] Id., Art. 67.
[21] Id., Art. 74.
[22] Id., Art. 12, 13.
[23] Id., Art. 7.
[24] Id., Art. 75, 77, 67, 116.
[25] Id., Art. 93.
[26] Id., Art. 80.
[27] Id., Art. 76, 82, 83.
[28] Id., Art. 87–100.
[29] Id., Art. 161–165.
[30] Id., Art. 166–173.
[31] Id., Art. 8.

and by the members of the Grand National Assembly for a non-renewable term of seven years.[32] If a member of a political party, he shall sever his relations with his party.[33] The Council of Ministers is composed of the Prime Minister appointed by the President from among the members of the Grand National Assembly and Ministers nominated by the Prime Minister from among deputies or those eligible to be deputies.[34] The powers of the President are described.[35] There are provisions concerning national defense, emergency rule,[37] the administration,[38] civil servants,[39] higher educational institutions,[40] broadcasting and news agencies,[41] professional organizations,[42] religious affairs.[43]

JUDICIAL DEPARTMENT

The judicial power is exercised by independent courts.[44] Judges are independent and may not be dismissed.[45] There are provisions for State Security Courts to deal with certain defined offenses and with offenses directly involving the security of the State; military justice is provided for.[46] The Constitutional Court, composed of 11 regular and 4 substitute members appointed by the President, examines the constitutionality of laws, decrees, constitutional amendments.[47] There is a High Court of Appeals,[48] a Council of State,[49] the Military High Court of Appeals and Administrative Court,[50] the Jurisdictional Court,[51] the Supreme Council of Judges and Public Prosecutors,[52] the audit Court.[53]

AREA, POPULATION, ETC.

Turkey has an area of 779,452 square kilometres, a population (1980 census) of 44,736,957. The capital is Ankara and the language Turkish, and no other language may be taught Turkish citizens as mother tongue.[54]

[32] Id., Art. 101, 102.
[33] Id., Art. 101.
[34] Id., Art. 109.
[35] Id., Art. 104.
[36] Id., Art. 117, 118.
[37] Id., Art. 119–122.
[38] Id., Art. 123–127.
[39] Id., Art. 128, 129.
[40] Id., Art. 130–132.
[41] Id., Art. 133.
[42] Id., Art. 135.
[43] Id., Art. 136.
[44] Id., Art. 9.
[45] Id., Art. 138, 139.
[46] Id., Art. 143–145.
[47] Id., Art. 146–148.
[48] Id., Art. 154.
[49] Id., Art. 155.
[50] Id., Art. 156, 157.
[51] Id., Art. 158.
[52] Id., Art. 159.
[53] Id., Art. 160.
[54] Id., Art. 3, 42.

THE CONSTITUTION OF THE REPUBLIC OF TURKEY[1]

November 7, 1982

PREAMBLE

Following the operation carried out on 12 September 1980 by the Turkish Armed Forces in response to a call from the Turkish nation, of which they form an inseparable part, at a time when the approach of a separatist, destructive and bloody civil war unprecedented in the Republican era threatened the integrity of the eternal Turkish nation and motherland and the existence of the sacred Turkish state,

This Constitution was prepared by the Consultative Assembly, given final form by the Council of National Security, which are the legitimate representatives of the Turkish nation, and adopted, approved and directly enacted by the Turkish nation,

And is entrusted for safekeeping by the Turkish Nation to the patriotism of its democracy – loving sons and daughters, in order that it may be understood to embody the Ideas, Beliefs and Resolutions set forth below and be interpreted and implemented accordingly, commanding respect for, and absolute loyalty to, its letter and spirit :

The direction of the concept of nationalism as outlined by Atatürk, the founder of the Republic of Turkey, its immortal leader and unrivalled hero; and in line with the reforms and principles introduced by him;

– The determination to safeguard the everlasting existence, prosperity and material and spiritual well-being of the Republic of Turkey, and to ensure that it attains the standards of contemporary civilization, as a full and honorable member of the world family of nations;

– Recognition of the absolute supremacy of the will of the nation, and of the fact that sovereignty is vested fully and unconditionally in the Turkish Nation and that no individual or body empowered to exercise it on behalf of the nation shall deviate from democracy based on freedom, as set forth in the Constitution and the rule of law instituted according to its requirements;

– The understanding that separation of powers does not imply an order of precedence among the organs of state, but reflects a civilized division of labor and mode of co-operation restricted to the exercise of specific state powers, and that supremacy is vested solely in the Constitution and the laws;

– The determination that no protection shall be afforded to thought or opinions contrary to Turkish national interests, the principle of the existence of Turkey as an indivisible entity with its state and territory, Turkish historical and moral values, or the nationalism, principles, reforms and modernism of Atatürk, and that as

[1]Published by Directorate General of Press and Information, Ankara, 1983. Supplied by Turkish Embassy, Athens, in April 1983. Ed.

required by the principle of secularism, there shall be no interference whatsoever of sacred religious feelings in state affairs and politics;

– The understanding that it is the birthright of every Turkish citizen to lead an honorable life and develop his material and spiritual resources under the aegis of national culture, civilization and the rule of law, through the exercise of the fundamental rights and freedoms set forth in this Constitution, in conformity with the requirements of equality and social justice;

– The recognition that all Turkish citizens are united in national honor and pride, in national joy and grief, in their rights and duties towards their existence as a nation, in blessings and in burdens, and in every manifiestation of national life, and that they have the right to demand a peaceful life based on absolute respect for one another's rights and freedoms, mutual love and fellowship, and the desire for, and belief in, 'Peace at home, peace in the world'.

PART ONE

GENERAL PRINCIPLES

Art. 1. The Turkish State is a Republic.

Art. 2. The Republic of Turkey is a democratic, secular and social State governed by the rule of law; bearing in mind the concepts of public peace, national solidarity and justice; respecting human rights; loyal to the nationalism of Atatürk and based on the fundamental tenets set forth in the Preamble.

Art. 3. The Turkish State, with its territory and nation, is an indivisible entity. Its language is Turkish.

Its flag, the form of which is prescribed by the relevant law, is composed of a white crescent and star on a red background.

Its national anthem is the 'Independence March'.

Its capital is Ankara.

Art. 4. the provisions of Article 1 of the Constitution establishing the form of the State as a Republic, the provisions in Article 2 on the characteristics of the Republic, and the provision of Article 3 shall not be amended, nor shall their amendment be proposed.

Art. 5. The fundamental aims and duties of the State are: to safeguard the independence and integrity of the Turkish Nation, the indivisibility of the country, the Republic and democracy; to ensure the welfare, peace, and happiness of the individual and society; to strive for the removal of political, social and economic obstacles which restrict the fundamental rights and freedoms of the individual in a manner incompatible with the principles of justice and of the social State governed by the rule of law; and to provide the conditions required for the development of the individual's material and spiritual existence.

Art. 6. Sovereignty is vested in the nation without reservation or condition.

The Turkish nation shall exercise its sovereignty through the authorized organs as prescribed by the principles laid down in the Constitution.

The right to exercise sovereignty shall not be delegated to any individual, group or class. No person or agency shall exercise any State authority which does not emanate from the Constitution.

Art. 7. Legislative power is vested in the Grand National Assembly of Turkey on behalf of the Turkish Nation. This power cannot be delegated.

Art. 8. Executive power and function shall be exercised and carried out by the President of the Republic and the Council of Ministers in conformity with the Constitution and the laws.

Art. 9. Judicial power shall be exercised by independent courts on behalf of the Turkish Nation.

Art. 10. All individuals are equal without any discrimination before the law, irrespective of language, race, color, sex, political opinion, philosophical belief, religion and sect, or any such considerations.

No privilege shall be granted to any individual, family, group or class.

State organs and administrative authorities shall act in compliance with the principle of equality before the law in all their proceedings.

Art. 11. The provisions of the Constitution are fundamental legal rules binding upon legislative, executive and judicial organs, and administrative authorities and other agencies and individuals.

Laws shall not be in conflict with the Constitution.

PART TWO

FUNDAMENTAL RIGHTS AND DUTIES

Chapter one. General Provisions

Art. 12. Everyone possesses inherent fundamental rights and freedoms which are inviolable and inalienable.

The fundamental rights and freedoms also include the duties and responsibilities of the individual towards society, his family, and other individuals.

Art. 13. Fundamental righs and freedoms may be restricted by law, in conformity with the letter and spirit of the Constitution, with the aim of safeguarding the indivisible integrity of the State with its territory and nation, national sovereignty, the Republic, national security, public order, general peace, the public interest, public morals and public health, and also for specific reasons set forth in the relevant articles of the Constitution.

General and specific grounds for restrictions of fundamental rights and freedoms shall not conflict with the requirements of the democratic order of society and shall not be imposed for any purpose other than those for which they are prescribed.

The general grounds for restriction set forth in this article shall apply for all fundamental rights and freedoms.

Art. 14. None of the rights and freedoms embodied in the Constitution shall be exercised with the aim of violating the indivisible integrity of the State with its territory and nation, of endangering the existence of the Turkish State and Republic, of destroying fundamental rights and freedoms, of placing the government of the State under the control of an individual or a group of people, or establishing the hegemony of one social class over others, or creating discrimination on the basis of language, race, religion or sect, or of establishing by any other means a system of govenment based on these concepts and ideas.

The sanctions to be applied against those who violate these prohibitions, and those who incite and provoke others to the same end shall be determined by law.

No provision of this Constitution shall be interpreted in a manner that would grant the right of destroying the rights and freedoms embodied in the Constitution.

Art. 15. In times of war, mobilization, martial law, or state of emergency the exercise of fundamental rights and freedoms can be partially or entirely suspended, or measures may be taken to the extent required by the exingecies of the situation, which derogate the guarantees embodied in the Constitution, provided that obligations under international law are not violated.

Even under the circumstances indicated in the first paragraph, the individual's right to life, and the integrity of his material and spiritual entity shall be inviolable except where death occurs through lawful acts of warfare and execution of death sentences; no one may be compelled to reveal his religion, conscience, thought or opinion, nor be accused on account of them; offences and penalties may not be made retroactive, nor may anyone be held guilty until so proven by a court judgment.

Art. 16. The fundamental rights and freedoms of aliens may be restricted by law in a manner consistent with international law.

Chapter Two. The Rights and Duties of the Individual

Art. 17. Everyone has the right to life and the right to protect and develop his material and spiritual entity.

The physical integrity of the individual shall not be violated except under medical necessity and in cases prescribed by law; he shall not be subject to scientific or medical experiments without his consent.

No one shall be subjected to torture or ill-treatment; no one shall be subjected to penalty or treatment incompatible with human dignity.

The cases of carrying out of death penalties under court sentences, the act of killing in self-defense, the occurrences of death as a result of the use of a weapon permitted by law as a necessary measure in cases of: apprehension, or the execution of warrants of arrest, the prevention of escape of lawfully arrested or convicted persons, the quelling of a riot or insurrection, the execution of the order of authorized bodies during martial law or state of emergency are outside of the provision of paragraph 1.

Art. 18. No one shall be required to perform forced labor. Unpaid compulsory work is prohibited.

The term forced labor does not include work required of an individual while serving a court sentence or under detention, services required from citizens during a state of emergency, and physical or intellectual work necessitated by the requirements of the country as a civic obligation, provided that the form and conditions of such labor are prescribed by law.

Art. 19. Everyone has the right to liberty and security of person.

No one shall be deprived of his liberty except in the following cases where procedure and conditions are prescribed by law: Execution of sentences restricting liberty and the implementation of security measures decided by courts, apprehension or detention of a person as a result of a court order or as a result of an obligation upon him designated by law; execution of an order for the purposes of the educational supervision of a minor or for bringing him before the competent authority; execution of measures taken in conformity with the relevant legal provision for the treatment, education or correction in institutions of a person of unsound mind, an alcoholic or drug addict or vagrant or a person spreading contagious diseases, when such persons constitute a danger to the public; apprehension or detention of a person who enters or attempts to enter illegaly into the country or concerning whom a deportation or extradition order has been issued.

Individuals against whom there are strong indications of having committed an offence can be arrested by decision of a judge solely for the purposes of preventing escape, or preventing the destruction or alteration of evidence as well as in similar other circumstances which necessitate detention and are prescribed by law. Apprehsion of a person without a decision by a judge shall be resorted to only in case when a person is caught in the act of committing an offence or in cases where delay is likely to thwart justice; the conditions for such apprehension shall be defined by law.

Individuals arrested or detained shall be promptly notified, and in all cases in writing, or orally, when the former is not possible, of the grounds for their arrest or detention and the charges against them; in case of offences committed collectively this notification shall be made, at the latest, before the individual is brought before the judge.

The person arrested or detained shall be brought before a judge within 48 hours and within fifteen days in the case of offences committed collectively, excluding the time taken to send him to the court nearest to the place of seizure. No one can be deprived of his liberty without the decision of a judge after the expiry of the above-specified periods. These periods may be extended during a state of emergency, under martial law or in time of war.

Notification of the situation of the person arrested or detained shall be made to the next of kin, except in cases of definite necessities pertaining to the risks of revealing the scope and subject of the investigation compelling otherwise.

Persons under detention shall have the right to request to be tried within a reasonable time or to be released during investigation or prosecution. Release may be made conditional on the presentation of an appropriate guarantee with a view to securing the presence of the person at the trial proceedings and the execution of the court sentence.

Persons deprived of their liberty under any circumstances are entitled to apply to the appropriate judicial authority for speedy conclusion of proceedings regarding their situation and for their release if the restriction placed upon them is not lawful.

Damages suffered by persons subjected to treatment contrary to the above provisions shall be compensated for according to law, by the State.

Art. 20. Everyone has the right to demand respect for his private and family life. Privacy of individual and family life cannot be violated. Exceptions necessitated by judiciary investigation and prosecution are reserved.

Unless there exists a decision duly passed by a judge in cases explicitly defined by law, and unless there exists an order of an agency authorized by law in cases where delay is deemed prejudicial, neither the person nor the private papers, nor belongings of an individual shall be searched nor shall they be seized.

Art. 21. The domicile of an individual shall not be violated. Unless there exists a decision duly passed by a judge in cases explicitly defined by law, and unless there exists an order of an agency authorized by law in cases where delay is deemed prejudicial, no domicile may be entered or searched, or the property therein seized.

Art. 22. Everyone has the right to freedom of communication.

Secrecy of communication is fundamental.

Communication shall not be impeded nor its secrecy be violated, unless there exists a decision duly passed by a judge in cases explicitly defined by law, and unless there exists an order of an agency authorized by law in cases where delay is deemed prejudicial.

Public establishments or institutions where exceptions to the above may be applied will be defined by law.

Art. 23. Everyone has the right to freedom of residence and movement.

Freedom of residence may be restricted by law for the purpose of preventing offences, promoting social and economic development, ensuring sound and orderly urban growth, and protecting public property; freedom of movement may be restricted by law for the purpose of investigation and prosecution of an offence, and prevention of offences. A citizen's freedom to leave the country may be restricted on account of the national economic situation, civic obligations, or criminal investigation or prosecution.

Citizens may not be deported, or deprived of their right of entry into their homeland.

Art. 24. Everyone has the right to freedom of conscience, religious belief and conviction.

Acts of worship, religious services, and ceremonies shall be conducted freely, provided that they do not violate the provisions of Article 14.

No one shall be compelled to worship, or to participate in religious ceremonies and rites, to reveal religious beliefs and convictions, or be blamed or accused because of his religious beliefs and convictions.

Education and instruction in religion and ethics shall be conducted under State supervision and control. Instruction in religious culture and moral education shall be compulsory in the curricula of primary and secondary schools. Other religious education and instruction shall be subject to the individual's own desire, and in the case of minors, to the request of their legal representatives.

No one shall be allowed to exploit or abuse religion or religious feelings, or things held sacred by religion, in any manner whatsoever, for the purpose of personal or political influence, or for even partially basing the fundamental, social, economic, political, and legal order of the State on religious tenets.

Art. 25. Everyone has the right to freedom of thought and opinion.

No one shall be compelled to reveal his thoughts and opinions for any reason or purpose; nor shall anyone be blamed or accused on account of his thoughts and opinions.

Art. 26. Everyone has the right to express and disseminate his thought and opinion by speech, in writing or in pictures or through other media, individually or collectively. This right includes the freedom to receive and impart information and ideas without interference from official authorities. This provision shall not preclude subjecting transmission by radio, television, cinema, and similar means to a system of licencing.

The exercise of these freedoms may be restricted for the purposes of preventing crime, punishing offenders, withholding information duly classified as a State secret protecting the reputation and rights and the private and family life of others, or protecting professional secrets as prescribed by law, or ensuring the proper functioning of the judiciary.

No language prohibited by law shall be used in the expression and dissemination of thought. Any written or printed documents, phonograph records, magnetic or video tapes, and other means of expression used in contravention of this provision shall be seized by a duly issued decision of judge or, in cases where delay is deemed prejudicial, by the competent authority designated by law. The authority issuing the seizure order shall notify the competent judge of its decision within twenty-four hours. The judge shall decide on the matter within three days.

Provisions regulating the use of means of disseminating information and ideas shall not be interpreted as a restriction of the freedom of expression and dissemination and thoughts.

Art. 27. Everyone has the right to study and teach freely, explain, and disseminate science and arts and to carry out research in these fields.

The right to disseminate shall not be exercised for the purpose of changing the provisions of Article 1, 2 and 3 of this Constitution.

The provisions of this Article shall not preclude regulation by law of the entry and distribution of foreign publications in the country.

Art. 28. The Press is free, and shall not be censored. The establishment of a printing house shall not be subject to prior permission and to the deposit of a financial guarantee.

Publication shall not be made in any language prohibited by law.

The State shall take the necessary measures to ensure the freedom of the Press and freedom of information.

In the limitation of freedom of the press, Articles 26 and 27 of the Constitution are applicable.

Anyone who writes or prints any news or articles which threaten the internal or external security of the State or the indivisible integrity of the State with its territory and nation, which tend to incite offence, riot or insurrection, or which refer to classified State secrets and anyone who prints or transmits such news or articles to others for the above purposes, shall be held responsible under the law relevant to these offences. Distribution may be suspended as a preventive measure by a decision of a judge, or in the event delay is deemed prejudicial by the competent authority designated by law. The authority suspending distribution shall notify the competent judge within forty-eight hours at the latest.

No ban shall be placed on the reporting of events, except by a decision of a judge issued to ensure proper functioning of the judiciary, within the limits to be specified by law.

Periodical and non-periodical publications may be seized by a decision of a judge in cases of ongoing investigation or prosecution of offences prescribed by law; and, in situations where delay could endanger the indivisible integrity of the State with its territory and nation, national security, public order or public morals, and for the prevention of offence, by order of the competent authority designated by law. The authority issuing the seizure order shall notify the competent judge of its decision within twenty-four hours at the latest. The seizure order shall become null and void unless upheld by the competent court within forty-eight hours at the latest.

The general common provisions shall apply when seizure and confiscation of periodicals and non-periodicals for reasons of criminal investigation and prosecution take place.

Periodicals published in Turkey may be temporarily suspended by court sentence if found guilty of publishing material which contravenes the indivisible integrity of the State with its territory and nation, the fundamental principles of the Republic, national security and public morals. Any publication which clearly bears the characteristics of being the continuation of the suspended periodical is prohibited; and shall be seized by a decision of a judge.

Art. 29. Publication of periodicals or non-periodicals shall not be subject to prior authorization or to the deposit of a financial guarantee.

To publish a periodical it shall suffice to submit the information and documents prescribed by law to the competent authority designated by law. If the information and documents submitted are found to be in contravention of law, the competent authority shall apply to the appropriate court for suspension of publication.

The publication of periodicals, the conditions of publication, the financial resources and rules relevant to the profession of journalism shall be regulated by law. The law shall not impose any political, economic, financial, and technical conditions obstructing or making difficult the free dissemination of news, thought, or beliefs.

Periodicals shall have equal access to the means and facilities of the State, other public corporate bodies, and their agencies.

Art. 30. A printing press or its annexes duly established as a publishing house under law shall not be seized, confiscated, or barred from operation on the grounds of being an instrument of crime, except in cases where it is convicted of offences against the indivisible integrity of the State with its territory and nation, against the fundamental principles of the Republic or against the national security.

Art. 31. Individuals and political parties have the right to use mass media and means of communication other than the Press owned by public corporations. The conditions and procedures for such use shall be regulated by law.

The law shall not impose restrictions preventing the public from receiving information or forming ideas and opinions through these media, or preventing public opinion from being freely formed, on grounds other then the general restrictions set forth in Article 13.

Art. 32. The right of rectification and reply shall be accorded only in cases where personal reputation and honor is attacked or in cases of unfounded allegation and shall be regulated by law.

If a rectification or reply is not published, the judge will decide, within seven days of appeal by the individual involved, whether this publication is required.

Art. 33. Everyone has the right to form associations without prior permission.

Submitting the information and documents stipulated by law to the competent authority designated by law shall suffice to enable an association to be formed. If the information and documents submitted are found to contravene the law, the competent authority shall apply to the appropriate court for the suspension of activities or dissolution of the association involved.

No one shall be compelled to become or remain a member of an association. The formalities, conditions, and procedures governing the exercise of freedom of association shall be prescribed by law.

Associations shall not contravene the general grounds of restriction in Article 13, nor shall they pursue political aims, engage in political activities, receive support from or give support to political parties, or take joint action with labor unions, with public professional organizations or with foundations.

Associations deviating from their original aims or conditions of establishment, or failing to fulfil the obligations stipulated by law shall be considered dissolved.

Associations may be dissolved by decision of a judge in cases prescribed by law. They may be suspended from activity by the competent authority designated by law pending a court decision in cases where delay endangers the indivisible integrity of the State with its territory and nation, national security or sovereignty, public order, the protection of the rights and freedoms of others, or the prevention of crime.

Provisons of the first paragraph of this Article shall not prevent imposition of restrictions on the rights of Armed Forces officials and civil servants to form associations, or the prohibition of the exercise of this right.

This article shall apply equally to foundations and other organizations of the same nature.

Art. 34. Everyone has the right to hold unarmed and peaceful meetings and demonstration marches without prior permission.

The competent administrative authority may determine a site and route for the demonstration march in order to prevent disruption of order in urban life.

The formalities, conditions, and procedures governing the exercise of the right to hold meetings and demonstration marches, shall be prescribed by law.

The competent authority designated by law may prohibit a particular meeting and demonstration march, or postpone it for not more than two months in situations where there is a strong possibility that disturbances may arise which would seriously upset public order, where the requirement of national security may be violated, or where acts aimed at destroying the fundamental characteristics of the Republic may be committed. In cases where the law forbids all meetings or demonstration marches in districts of a province for the same reasons, the postponement may not exceed three months.

Associations, foundation, labor unions, and public professional organisations shall not hold meetings or demonstration marches exceeding their own scope and aims.

Art. 35. Everyone has the right to own and inherit property.

These rights may be limited by law only in view of public interest.

The exercise of the right to own property shall not be in contravention of the public interest.

Art. 36. Everyone has the right of litigation either as plaintiff or defendant before the courts through lawful means and procedure.

No court shall refuse to hear a case within its jurisdiction.

Art. 37. No one may be tried by an judicial authority other than the legally designated court.

Extraordinary tribunals with jurisdiction that would in effect remove a person from the jurisdiction of his legally designated court shall not be established.

Art. 38. No one shall be punished for any act which did not constitute a criminal offence under the law in force at the time it was committed; no one shall be given a heavier penalty for an offence than the penalty applicable at the time when the offence was committed.

The provision of the above paragraph shall also apply to the statute of limitations on offences and penalties and on the results of conviction.

Penalties, and security measures in lieu of penalties, shall be prescribed only by law.

No one shall be compelled to make a statement that would incriminate himself or his legal next of kin, or to present such incriminating evidence.

Criminal responsibility shall be personal.

General confiscation shall not be imposed as penalty.

The Administration shall not impose any sanction resulting in restriction of personal liberty. Exceptions to this provision may be introduced by law regarding inttemal order of the Armed Forces.

No citizen shall be extradited to a foreign country on account of an offence.

Art. 39. In libel and defamation suits involving allegations against persons in the public service in connection with their functions or services, the defendant has the right to prove the allegations. A plea for presenting proof shall not be granted in any other case unless proof would serve the public interest or unless the plaintiff consents.

Art. 40. Everyone whose constitutional rights and freedoms are violated has the right to request prompt access to the competent authorities.

Damages incurred by any person through unlawful treatment by holders of public office shall be compensated by the State. The State reserves the right of recourse to the official responsible.

Chapter Three. Social and Economic Rights and Duties

Art. 41. The family is the foundation of Turkish society.

The State shall take the necessary measures and establish the necessary organisation to ensure the peace and welfare of the family, especially the protection of the mother and children, and for family planning education and application.

Art. 42. No one shall be deprived of the right of learning and education.

The scope of the right to education shall be defined and regulated by law.

Training and education shall be conducted along the lines of the principles and reforms of Atatürk, on the basis of contemporary science and education methods, under the supervision and control of the State. Institutions of training and education contravening these provisions shall not be established.

The freedom of training and education does not relieve the individual from loyalty to the Constitution.

Primary education is compulsory for all citizens of both sexes and is free of charge in State schools.

The principles governing the functioning of private primary and secondary schools shall be regulated by law in keeping with the standards set for State schools.

The State shall provide scholarships and other means of assistance to enable students of merit lacking financial means to continue their education. The State shall take necessary measures to rehabilitate those in need of special training so as to render such people useful to society.

Training, education, research, and study are the only activities that shall be pursued at institutions of training and education. These activities shall not be obstructed in any way.

No language other than Turkish shall be taught as mother tongue to Turkish citizens at any institutions of training or education. Foreign languages to be taught in institutions of training and education and the rules to be followed by schools conducting training and education in a foreign language shall be determined by law. The provisions of international treaties are reserved.

Art. 43. The coasts are under the sovereignty and at the disposal of the State.

In the utilisation of the sea coast, lake shores or river banks, and of the coastal strip along the sea and lakes, public interest shall be taken into consideration with priority.

The width of coasts, and coastal strips to be determined according to the purpose of utilization, and the conditions and possibilities of such utilization by individuals shall be determined by law.

Art. 44. The State shall take the necessary measures to maintain and develop efficient land cultivation, to prevent its loss through erosion, and to provide land to farmers with insufficient land of their own, or no land. For this purpose, the law may define the size of appropriate land units, according to different agricultural regions and types of farming. Providing of land to farmers with no or insufficient land shall not lead to a fall in production, or to the depletion of forests and other land and underground resources.

Lands distributed for this purpose shall neither be divided nor be transferred to others, except through inheritance, and shall be cultivated only by farmers, to whom they have been distributed, and their heirs. The principles relating to the recovery by the State of the land thus distributed in the event of loss of these conditions shall be prescribed by law.

Art. 45. The State shall assist farmers and livestock breeders in acquiring machinery, equipment and other inputs in order to prevent improper use and destruction of agricultural land, meadows and pastures and to increase crop and livestock production in accordance with the principles of agricultural planning.

The State shall take necessary measures to promote the values of crop and livestock products, and to enable producers to be paid their real value.

Art. 46. The State and public corporations shall be entitled, where the public interest requires it, to expropriate privately owned real estate wholly or in part or impose administrative servitude on it in accordance with the principles and procedures prescribed by law, provided that compensation is paid in advance.

The method and procedure for calculating compensation for expropriation shall be prescribed by law. In determining the compensation, the law shall take into account tax declarations, current value established by official assesment at the time of expropriation, unit prices and construction costs for real estate, and other objective criteria.

The procedure for taxing and difference between the sum due in compensation and the value declared in the tax declaration shall be prescribed by law.

Compensation shall be paid in cash and in advance. However, the procedure to be applied in paying compensation for land expropriated in order to carry out land reform, major energy and irrigation projects, and housing and resettlement schemes and afforestation, and to protect the coasts and to build tourist facilities shall be regulated by law. In the previous cases where the law may allow payment in instalments, the payment period shall not exceed five years; whence payment shall be made in equal instalments, and an interest rate equivalent to the highest interest paid on the public debt shall be paid for the remainder of instalments.

Compensation for land expropriated from the small farmer who cultivates his own land shall in all cases be paid in advance.

Art. 47. Private enterprises performing public service may be nationalized when this is required by the exigencies of public interest.

Nationalization shall be carried out on the basis of real value. The methods and procedures for calculating real value shall be prescribed by law.

Art. 48. Everyone has the freedom to work and conclude contracts in the field of his choice. The establishment of private enterprises is free.

The State shall take measures to ensure that private enterprises operate in accordance with national economic requirements and social objectives and in conditions of security and stability.

Art. 49. Everyone has the right and duty to work.

The State shall take the necessary measures to raise the standard of living of workers, to protect them in order to improve the general conditions of labor, to promote labor, and to create suitable economic conditions for prevention of unemployment.

The State shall take facilitating and protecting measures in order to secure labor peace in worker – employer relations.

Art. 50. No one shall be required to perform work unsuited to his age, sex, and capacity.

Minors, women and persons with physical or mental disabilities, shall enjoy special protection with regard to working conditions.

All workers have the right to rest and leisure.

Rights and conditions relating to paid weekends and holidays, together with paid annual leave, shall be regulated by law.

Art. 51. Workers and employers have the right to form labor unions and employers' associations and higher organizations, without prior permission, in order to safeguard and develop their economic and social rights and the interests of their members in their labor relations.

In order to form unions and their higher bodies, it shall suffice to submit the information and documents prescribed by law to the competent authority designated by law. If this information and documentation is not in conformity with law, the competent authority shall apply to the appropriate court for the suspension of activities or the dissolution of the union or the higher body.

Everyone shall be free to become a member of or withdraw from memberhip in a union.

No one shall be compelled to become a member, remain a member, or withdraw from membership of a union.

Workers and employers cannot hold concurrent memberships in more than one labor union or employers' association.

Employment in a given work-place shall not be made conditional on being, or not being a member of a labor union.

To become an executive in a labor union or in higher organizations of them it is a prerequisite condition that the worker should have held the status of a laborer for at least ten years.

The status, the administration, and the functioning of the labor unions and their higher bodies should not be inconsistent with the characteristics of the Republic as defined in the Constitution, or with democratic principles.

Art. 52. Labor Unions, in addition to being under the general restrictions set forth in Article 13, also shall not pursue a political cause, engage in political activity receive support from political parties or give support to them and shall not act jointly for these purposes with associations, public professional organizations, and foundations.

The fact of engaging in labor union activities in a work-place shall not justify failure to perform one's work.

The administrative and financial supervision of labor unions by the State, and their revenues and expenditures, and the method of payment of memberhip dues to the labor union, shall be regulated by law.

Labor Unions shall not use their revenues beyond the scope of their professional aims, and shall keep all their funds in State banks.

Art. 53. Workers and employers have the right to conclude collective bargaining agreements in order to regulate reciprocally their economic and social position and conditions of work.

The procedure to be followed in concluding collective bargaining agreements shall be regulated by law.

More than one collective bargaining agreement at the same place of work for the same period shall not be concluded or put into effect.

Art. 54. Workers have the right to strike if a dispute arises during the collective bargaining process. The procedures and conditions governing the exercise of this right and the employer's recourse to a lockout, the scope of both actions, and the exceptions to which they are subject shall be regulated by law.

The right to strike, and lockout shall not be exercised in a manner contrary to the principle of goodwill, to the detriment of society, and in a manner damaging national wealth.

During a strike, the labor union is liable for any material damage caused in a place where the strike is being held, as a result of deliberate negligent behavior by the workers and the labor union.

The circumstances and places in which strikes and lockouts may be prohibited or postponed shall be regulated by law.

In cases where a strike or a lockout is prohibited or postponed, the dispute shall be settled by the Supreme Arbitration Board at the end of the period of postponement. The disputing parties may apply to the Supreme Arbitration Board by mutual agreement at any state of the dispute.

The decisions of the Supreme Arbitration Board shall be final and have the force of a collective bargaining agreement.

The organization and functions of the Supreme Arbitration Board shall be regulated by law.

Politically motivated strikes and lockouts, solidarity strikes and lockouts, occupation of work premises, labor go-slows, production decreasing and other forms of obstruction are prohibited.

Those who refuse to go on strike, shall in no way be barred from working at their work place by strikers.

Art. 55. Wages shall be paid in return for work.

The State shall take the necessary measures to ensure that workers earn a fair wage suitable for the work they perform and that they enjoy other social benefits.

In determining the minimum wage, the economic and social conditions of the country shall be taken into account.

Art. 56. Everyone has the right to live in a healthy, balanced environment.

It is the duty of the State and the citizens to improve the natural environment, and to prevent environmental pollution.

To ensure that everyone lead their lives in conditions of physical and mental health and to secure co-operation in terms of human and material resources through economy and increased productivity, the State shall regulate central planning and functioning of the health services.

The State shall fulfil this task by utilizing and supervising the health and social assistance institutions, in both the public and private sectors.

In order to establish widespread health services general health insurance may be introduced by law.

Art. 57. The State shall take measures to meet the needs for housing, within the framework of a plan which takes into account the characteristics of cities and environmental conditions and supports community housing projects.

Art. 58. The State shall take measures to ensure the training and development of youth into whose keeping our State, independence, and our Republic are entrusted, in the light of contemporary science, in line with the principles and reforms of Atatürk, and in opposition to ideas aiming at the destruction of the indivisible integrity of the State with its territory and nation.

The State shall take necessary measures to protect youth from addiction to alcohol, drug addiction, crime, gambling, and similar vices, and ignorance.

Art. 59. The State shall take measures to develop the physical and mental health of Turkish citizens of all ages, and encourage the spread of sports among the masses.

The State shall protect successful athletes.

Art. 60. Everyone has the right to social security.

The State shall take the necessary measures and establish the organization for the provision of social security.

Art. 61. The State shall protect the widows and orphans of those killed in war and in the line of duty, together with the disabled and war veterans, and ensure that they enjoy a decent standard of living.

The State shall take measures to protect the disabled and secure their integration into community life.

The aged shall be protected by the State. State assistance to the aged, and other rights and benefits shall be regulated by law.

The State shall take all kinds of measures for social resettlement of children in need of protection.

To achieve these aims the State shall establish the necessary organizations or facilities, or arrange for their establishment by other bodies.

Art. 62. The State shall take the necessary measures to ensure the family unity, the education of the children, the cultural needs, and the social security of Turkish nationals working abroad, and shall take the necessary measures to safeguard their ties with the country, and to help them on their return home.

Art. 63. The State shall ensure the conservation of the historical, cultural and natural assets and wealth, and shall take supporting and promoting measures towards this end.

Any limitation to be imposed on such assets and wealth which are privately owned, and the compensation and exemptions to be accorded to the owners of such, as a result of these limitations, shall be regulated by law.

Art. 64. The state shall protect artistic activities and artists. The State shall take the necessary measures to protect, promote and support works of art and artists, and encourage the spread of art appreciation.

Art. 65. The State shall fulfil its duties as laid down in the Constitution in the social and economic fields, within the limits of its financial resources, taking into consideration the maintenance of economic stability.

Art. 66. Everyone bound to the Turkish State through the bond of citizenship is a Turk.

The child of a Turkish father or a Turkish mother is a Turk. The citizenship of a child of a foreign father and a Turkish mother shall be defined by law.

Citizenship can be acquired under the conditions stipulated by law, and shall be forfeited only in cases determined by law.

No Turk shall be deprived of citizenship, unless he commits an act incompatible with loyalty to the motherland.

Recourse to the courts, against the decisions and proceedings related to the deprivation of citizenship, shall not be denied.

Art. 67. In conformity with the conditions set forth in the law, citizens have the right to vote, to be elected, and to engage in political activities independently or in a political party, and to take part in a referendum.

Elections and referendums shall be held under the direction and supervision of the judiciary, according to the principles of free, equal, secret, direct, universal suffrage, and public counting of the votes.

All Turkish citizens over 21 years of age shall have the right to vote in elections and to take part in a referendum.

The exercise of these rights shall be regulated by law.

Privates and corporals serving in the Armed Services, students in military schools, and detainees and convicts in prisons cannot vote.

Art. 68. Citizens have the right to form political parties, and to join and withdraw from them in accordance with the established procedure. To become a member of a party one must be over 21 years of age.

Political parties are indispensable elements of the democratic political system.

Political parties shall be founded without prior permission and shall pursue their activities in accordance with the provisions set forth in the Constitution and law.

The statutes and programs of political parties shall not be in conflict with the indivisible integrity of the State with its territory and nation, human rights, national sovereignty, and the principles of the democratic and secular Republic.

Political parties whose aim is to support and to set up the domination of a class or groups, or any kind of dictatorship cannot be formed.

Political parties shall not organize and function abroad, shall not form discriminative auxiliary bodies such as women's or youth branches, nor shall they establish foundations.

Judges and prosecutors, members of higher judicial organs, members of the teaching staff at institutions of higher education, members of the Higher Education Council, civil servants in public organizations and corporations, and other public servants who are not considered to be laborers by virtue of the services they perform, students, and members of the Armed Forces, shall not become members of political parties.

Art. 69. Political parties shall not engage in activities outside the lines of their statutes and programs, and shall not contravene the restrictions set forth in Article 14 of the Constitution; those that contravene them shall be dissolved permanently.

Political parties shall not have political ties and engage in political co-operation with associations, unions, foundations, co-operatives, and public professional organizations and their higher bodies in order to implement and strengthen their party policies, nor shall they receive material assistance from these bodies.

The internal functioning and the decisions of political parties shall not be contrary to the principles of democracy.

The auditing of political parties shall be carried out by the Constitutional Court.

The Office of the Chief Public Prosecutor shall examine, with priority, the conformity of the statutes and programs of new parties and of the status of their founders in view of the Constitution and the law; and shall also follow their activities.

The dissolution of political parties shall be decided the Constitutional Court after the filing of a suit by the Office of the Chief Public Prosecutor of the Republic.

The founding members and administrators at every level of a political party which has been permanently dissolved shall not become founding members administrators, or comptrollers of a new political party; nor shall any new political party be founded, the majority of whose members are former members of a political party previously dissolved.

Political parties shall not receive assistance in kind or cash from foreign States, international organizations, associations and groups in foreign countries, nor shall they take orders from these groups in foreign countries, nor shall they take orders from these bodies, or participate in their decisions and activities which are prejudicial to the independence and territorial integrity of Turkey. Political parties contravening the provisions of this paragraph shall also be dissolved permanently.

The formulation and activities, supervision, and dissolution of political parties shall be regulated by law within the above-mentioned provisions.

Art. 70. Every Turk has the right to enter the public service.

No criteria other than the qualifications for the office concerned shall be taken into consideration for recruitment into the public service.

Art. 71. Declaration of assets by persons entering public service, and the frequency of such declaration, shall be determined by law. Those serving in the legislative and executive organs shall not be exempted from this requirement.

Art. 72. National service is the right and duty of every Turk. The manner in which this service shall be performed, or considered as performed, either in the Armed Forces or in the public service shall be regulated by law.

Art. 73. Everyone is under the obligation to pay taxes according to his financial resources, in order to meet public expenditures.

An equitable and balanced distribution of the tax burden is the social objective of fiscal policy.

Taxes, fees, duties, and other such financial impositions shall be imposed, amended, or revoked by law.

The Council of Ministers may be empowered to amend the percentages of exemtion, exceptions and reductions in taxes, fees, duties and other such financial impositions, within the minimum and maximum limits prescribed by law.

Art. 74. Citizens have the right to apply in writing to the competent authorities and to the Grand National Assembly of Turkey with regard to requests and complaints concerning themselves or the public.

The result of the application concerning himself shall be made known to the petitioner in writing.

The way of exercising this right shall be determined by law.

PART THREE

FUNDAMENTAL ORGANS OF THE REPUBLIC

Chapter one. Legislative Power

1. GRAND NATIONAL ASSEMBLY OF TURKEY

Art. 75. The Grand National Assembly of Turkey shall be composed of four hundred deputies elected by universal suffrage by the nation.

Art. 76. Every Turk over the age of 30 is eligible to be a deputy.

Persons who have not completed their primary education, who have been deprived of legal capacity, who have failed to perform compulsory military service, who are banned from public service, who have been sentenced to a prison term totalling one year or more excluding involuntary offences, or to a heavy imprisonment; those who have been convicted for dishonorable offences such as embezzlement, corruption, bribery, theft, fraud, forgery, breach of trust, fraudulent bankruptcy; and persons convicted of smuggling, conspiracy in official bidding tender, or purchases, of offences related to the disclosure of State secrets, of involvement in ideological and anarchistic activities, and incitement and encouragement of such activities, shall not be elected deputies, even if they have been pardoned.

Judges and prosecutors, members of the higher judicial organs, members of the teaching staff at institutions of higher education, members of the Higher Education Council, employees of public institutions and agencies who have the status of civil servants, other public employees not regarded as laborers on account of the duties they perform, and members of the Armed Forces, shall not stand for election or be eligible to be a deputy unless they resign from office.

Art. 77. Elections for the Grand National Assembly of Turkey shall be held every five years.

The Assembly may decide to hold new elections before the termination of this period, and new elections may also be decided upon according to a decision, taken in accordance with the conditions set forth in the Constitution, by the President of the Republic. A deputy whose term of office expires may be eligible for re-election.

In the event of a decision to hold new elections, the powers of the Assembly shall continue until the election of a new Assembly.

Art. 78. If the holding of new elections is found impossible because of war, the Grand National Assembly of Turkey may decide to defer elections for a year.

If the grounds for deferment do not disappear this measure may be repeated under the procedure for deferment.

By-elections shall be held when vacancies arise in the membership of the Grand National Assembly of Turkey. By-elections shall be held once in every election term and cannot be held until 30 months have elapsed from the date of the previous general elections. However, in cases where the number of vacant seats reaches five percent of the total number of seats, by-elections shall be held within three months.

By-elections shall not be held within one year before general elections.

Art. 79. Elections shall be held under the general administration and supervision of the judicial organs.

The Supreme Election Council shall execute all the functions to ensure the fair and orderly conduct of the elections from the beginning to the end of polling, carry out investigations take final decisions on all irregularities, complaints and objections concerning the elections during and after the polling, and verify the election returns of the members of the Grand National Assembly of Turkey. No appeal shall be made to any authority against the decisions of the Supreme Election Council.

The functions and powers of the Supreme Election Council and other election councils shall be detemined by law.

The Supreme Election Council shall be composed of seven regular members and four substitutes. Six of the members shall be elected by the Plenary Assembly of the High Court of Appeals, and five members shall be elected by the Plenary Assembly of the Council of State from amongst its own members, by secret ballot and by an absolute majority of the total number of members. These members shall elect a Chairman and a Vice-Chairman from amongst themselves, by absolute majority and secret ballot.

Amongst the members elected to the Supreme Election Council by the High Court of Appeals and by the Council of State, two members from each group shall be designated, by lot, as substitute members. The Chairman and Vice-Chairman of the Supreme Election Council shall not take part in this procedure.

The general conduct and supervision of a referendum on legislation amending the Constitution shall be subject to the same provisions as those relating to the election of deputies.

Art. 80. Members of the Grand National Assembly of Turkey represent, not merely their own constituencies or constituents, but the Nation as a whole.

2. OATH TAKING

Art. 81. Members of the Grand National Assembly of Turkey, on assuming office, shall take the following oath :

'I swear upon my honor and integrity, before the great Turkish Nation, to safegurard the existence and independence of the State, the indivisible integrity of the country and the Nation, and the absolute sovereignty of the Nation; to remain loyal to the supremacy of law, to the democratic and secular Republic, and to Atatürk's principles and reforms; not to deviate from the ideal according to which everyone is entitled to enjoy human rights and fundamental feedoms under peace and prosperity in society, national solidarity and justice, and loyalty to the Constitution.'

3. ACTIVITIES INCOMPATIBLE WITH MEMBERSHIP

Art. 82. Members of the Grand National Assembly of Turkey shall not hold office in State departments and other public corporate bodies and their subsidiaries; in corporations and enterprises affiliated with the State and other public corporate bodies; in the executive or supervisory organs of enterprises and corporations where there is direct or indirect participation of the State and public corporate bodies; in the executive and supervisory organs of public benefit associations, whose special resources of revenue and privileges are provided by law; in the executive and supervisory organs of foundations which enjoy tax exemption and receive financial subsidies from the State; and in the executive and supervisory organs of labor unions and public professional organizations, and in the enterprises and corporations in which the above-mentioned unions and associations or their higher bodies have a share; nor can they be appointed as representatives of the above-mentioned bodies or be party to a business contract, directly or indirectly, and be arbitrators of representatives in their business transactions.

Members of the Grand National Assembly of Turkey shall not be entrusted with any official or private duties involving recommendation, appointment, or approval by the Executive organ. Acceptance by a deputy of a temporary assignment given by the Council of Ministers on a specific matter, and not exceeding a period of six months, is subject to the approval of the Assembly.

Other functions and activities incompatible with membership in the Grand National Assembly of Turkey shall be regulated by law.

4. PARLIAMENTARY IMMUNITY

Art. 83. Members of the Grand National Assembly of Turkey shall not be liable for their votes and statements concerning parliamentary functions, for the views they express before the Assembly, or unless the Assembly decides otherwise on the proposal of the Bureau for that sitting, for repeating or revealing these outside the Assembly.

A deputy who is alleged to have committed an offence before or after election, shall not be arrested, interrogated, detained or tried unless the Assembly decides otherwise. This provision shall not apply in cases where a member is caught in the act of committing a crime punishable by a heavy penalty and in case subject to Article 14 of the Constitution if an investigation has been initiated before the election. However, in such situations the competent authority shall notify the Grand National Assembly of Turkey immediately and directly.

The execution of a criminal sentence imposed on a member of the Grand National Assembly of Turkey either before or after his election shall be suspended until he ceases to be a member; the statute of limitations does not apply during the term of memberhip.

Investigation and prosecution of a re-elected deputy shall be subject to the renewed waiver of immunity by the Assembly.

Political party groups in the Grand National Assembly of Turkey shall not hold discussions or take decisions regarding parliamentary immunity.

5. LOSS OF MEMBERSHIP

Art. 84. The loss of membership by deputies shall be decided by an absolute majority of the total number of members in respect of deputies who resign, who are convicted of an offence precluding election to the Grand National Assembly of Turkey, who are deprived of their legal capacity, who resign from their party in order to join another party, or take up a ministerial post in the Council of Ministers other than a provisional ministerial post during the election period, who assume a function incompatible with membership, or who failed to attend without excuse, five meetings in a period of one month.

A deputy who resigns from his party shall not be nominated as a candidate in the following elections by the central organs of any party existing at the time of his resignation.

The membership of a deputy, whose acts and statements are cited in a judgement of the Constitutional Court as having caused the dissolution of a political party and that of other deputies who belonged to the party on the date when the action for dissolution was brought, shall end on the date when the Presidency of the Grand National Assembly of Turkey is notified of the dissolution order.

6. APPLICATION FOR ANNULMENT

Art. 85. If the Grand National Assembly of Turkey decides to waive the parliamentary immunity of a member or disqualify him from membership, the member concerned or any member of the Grand National Assembly of Turkey, may, within a week of the decision, appeal to the Constitutional Court for the decision to be annulled on the grounds that it is contrary to the Constitution or to the Rules of Procedure of the Assembly. The Constitutional Court shall decide on the appeal within fifteen days.

7. SALARIES AND ALLOWANCES

Art. 86. The salaries and allowances of the members of the Grand National Assembly of Turkey shall be regulated by law. The monthly amount of the salary shall not exceed the salary of the most senior civil servant; the travel allowance shall not exceed half of that salary.

The salaries and allowances paid to the members of the Grand National Assembly of Turkey shall not necessitate the suspension of payments of pensions and similar benefits by social security agencies.

A maximum of three months' salaries and allowances may be paid in advance.

II. FUNCTIONS AND POWERS OF THE GRAND NATIONAL ASSEMBLY OF TURKEY

Art. 87. The functions and powers of the Grand National Assembly of Turkey comprise the enactment, amendment, and repeal of laws; the supervision of the Council of Ministers and the Ministers; authorization of the Council of Ministers to issue governmental decrees having force of law on certain matters; debating and approval of the budget draft and the draft law of the final accounts; making decisions regarding printing of currency and declaration of war; ratifying international agreements, deciding on the proclamation of amnesties and pardons excluding those who have been convicted for activities set out in Article 14 of the Constitution; confirming death sentences passed by the courts; and exercising the powers and executing the functions envisaged in the other articles of the Constitution.

Art. 88. The Council of Ministers and deputies are empowered to introduce laws.

The procedure and principles relating to the debating of draft bills and proposals of law in the Grand National Assembly of Turkey shall be regulated by the Rules of Procedure.

Art. 89. The President of the Republic shall promulgate the laws adopted by the Grand National Assembly of Turkey within fifteen days.

He shall, within the same period, refer to the Grand National Assembly of Turkey for further consideration laws which he deems unsuitable for promulgation, together with a statement of his reasons. Budget laws shall not be subject to this provision.

If the Grand National Assembly of Turkey adopts in its unchanged form the law referred back, the President of the Republic shall promulgate it; if the Assembly amends the law which was referred back, the President of the Republic may again refer back the amended law to the Assembly.

Provisions relating to constitutional amendments are reserved.

Art. 90. The ratification of treaties concluded with foreign states and international organizations on behalf of the Republic of Turkey, shall be subject to adoption by the Grand National Assembly of Turkey by a law approving the ratification.

Agreements regulating economic, commercial and technical relations, and covering a period of no more than one year, may be put into effect through promulgation, provided they do not entail any financial commitment by the State, and provided they do not infringe upon the status of individuals or upon the property rights of Turkish citizens abroad. In such cases, these agreements must be brought to the knowledge of the Grand National Assembly of Turkey within two months of their promulgation.

Agreements in connection with the implementation of an international treaty, and economic, commercial, technical, or administrative agreements which are concluded depending on an authorization given by law shall not require approval by the Grand National Assembly of Turkey. However, agreements concluded under the provision of this paragraph and affecting the economic, or commercial relations and private rights of individuals shall not be put into effect unless promulgated.

Agreements resulting in amendments to Turkish laws shall be subject to the provisions of the first paragraph.

International agreements duly put into effect carry the force of law. No appeal to the Constitutional Court can be made with regard to these agreements, on the ground that they are unconstitutional.

Art. 91. The Grand National Assembly of Turkey may empower the Council of Ministers to issue decrees having force of law. However, the fundamental rights, individual rights and duties included in the first and second Chapter of the Second Part of the Constitution and the political rights and duties listed in the Fourth Chapter, cannot be regulated by decrees having force of law except during periods of martial law and states of emergency.

The empowering law shall define the purpose, scope, principles, and operative period of the decree having force of law, and whether more than one decree will be issued within the same period.

Resignation or fall of the Council of Ministers, or expiration of the legislative term shall not cause the termination of the power conferred for the given period.

When approving a decree having force of law before the end of the prescribed period, the Grand National Assembly of Turkey shall also state whether the power has terminated or will continue until the expiry of the said period.

Provisions relating to the decrees having force of law issued by the Council of Ministers meeting under the chairmanship of the President of the Republic in time of martial law or states of emergency, are reserved.

Decrees having force of law shall come into force on the day of their publication in the Official Gazette. However, a later date may be indicated in the decree as the date of entry in to force.

Decrees are submitted to the Grand National Assembly of Turkey on the day of their publication in the Official Gazette.

Laws of empowering and decrees having force of law which are based on these, shall be discussed in the committees and in the plenary of the Grand National Assembly of Turkey with priority and urgency.

Decrees not submitted to the Grand National Assembly of Turkey on the day of their publication shall cease to have effect on that day and decrees rejected by the Grand National Assembly shall cease to have effect on the day of the publication of the decision in the Official Gazette. The amended provisions of the decrees which are approved as amended shall go into force on the day of their publication in the Official Gazette.

Art. 92. The power to authorize the declaration of the state of war in cases deemed legitimate by international law and, except where required by international treaties to which Turkey is a party or by the rules of international courtesy, to send Turkish Armed Forces to foreign countries and to allow foreign armed forces to be stationed in Turkey, is vested in the Grand National Assembly of Turkey.

If the country is subjected, while the Grand National Assembly of Turkey is adjourned or in recess, to sudden armed aggression and it thus becomes imperative to decide immediately on the use of armed forces, the President of the Republic can decide on the use of the Turkish Armed Forces.

III. PROVISIONS RELATING TO THE ACTIVITIES OF THE GRAND NATIONAL ASSEMBLY OF TURKEY

Art. 93. The Grand National Assembly of Turkey shall convene of its own accord on the first day of September each year.

The Assembly may be in recess for a maximum of three months in the course of a legislative year. During an adjournment and recess it may be summoned by the President of the Republic either on his own initiative or at the request of the Council of Ministers.

The President of the Assembly may also summon the Assembly either on his own initiative or at the written request of one-fifth of the members.

If the Grand National Assembly of Turkey is convened during an adjournment or recess, it shall not adjourn or go into recess again before having given priority consideration to the matter requiring the summons.

Art. 94. The Bureau of the Assembly of the Grand National Assembly of Turkey shall be composed of the President, the Deputy Presidents, Secretary Members, and the Administrative Members elected from among the Assembly members.

The Bureau of the Assembly shall be so composed as to ensure proportionate representation to the number of members of each political party in the Assembly. Political party groups shall not nominate candidates for the Presidency.

Two elections to the Bureau of the Grand National Assembly of Turkey shall be held in the course of one legislative term. The term of office of those elected in the first round is two years and the term of office of those elected in the second round is three years.

The candidates from among the members of the Assembly for the President of the Grand National Assembly of Turkey shall be announced, within ten days of the convening of the Assembly, to the Bureau of the Assembly. Election of the President shall be held by secret ballot. In the first two ballots, a two-thirds majority of the total number of members, and in the third ballot an absolute majority of the total number of members is required. If the absolute majority cannot be obtained in the third ballot a fourth ballot shall be held between the two candidates who have received the greatest number of votes in the third ballot; the member who receives the greatest number of votes in the fourth ballot shall be elected President. The election of the President, shall be completed within ten days of the expiry of the period for the nomination of candidates.

The quorum required for election, the number of ballots and its procedure, the number of Deputy Presidents, Secretary Members and Administrative Members, shall be stipulated by the Rules of Procedure of the Assembly.

The President and Deputy Presidents of the Grand National Assembly of Turkey cannot participate in the activities of the political party or party group of which they are a member nor in debates, within or outside the Assembly, except in cases required by their functions; the President and the Deputy President who is presiding over the session shall not vote.

Art. 95. The Grand National Assembly of Turkey shall carry out its activities in accordance with the provisions of the Rules of Procedures drawn up by itself.

The provisions of the Rules of Procedure shall be drawn up in such a way as to ensure the participation of each political party group in all the activities of the Assembly in proportion to its number of members. Political party groups shall only be constituted if they have at least twenty members.

All security and administrative services of the Grand National Assembly of Turkey regarding all buildings, installations, annexes and its grounds shall be organized and directed by the office of the President of the Assembly.

Sufficient forces to ensure security and other such services shall be allocated to the Office of the President of the Assembly by the relevant authorities.

Art. 96. Unless otherwise stipulated in the Constitution, the Grand National Assembly of Turkey shall convene with at least one third of the total number of members and shall take decisions by an absolute majority of those present; however, the quorum for decisions can under no circumstances, be less than a quarter plus one of the total number of members.

Members of the Council of Ministers may delegate a minister to vote on their behalf in sessions of the Grand National Assembly of Turkey which they are unable to attend. However, a minister shall not cast more than two votes including his own.

Art. 97. Debates held in the Plenary of the Grand National Assembly of Turkey shall be public and shall be published verbatim in the Journal of Records.

The Grand National Assembly of Turkey may hold closed sessions in accordance with the provisions of its Rules of Procedure; the publication of debates of such sessions shall be subject to the decision of the Grand National Assembly of Turkey.

Public proceedings of the Assembly may be freely published through all means, unless a decision to the contrary is adopted by the Assembly upon a proposal of the Bureau of the Assembly.

IV. WAYS OF COLLECTING INFORMATION AND SUPERVISION BY THE NATIONAL ASSEMBLY OF TURKEY

Art. 98. The Grand National Assembly of Turkey shall exercise its supervisory power by means of questions, Parliamentary inquiries, general debates, interpellation and Parliamentary investigations.

A question is a request for information addressed to the Prime Minister or Ministers to be answered orally or in writing on behalf of the Council of Ministers.

A Parliamentary inquiry is an examination conducted to obtain information on a specific subject.

A general debate is the consideration of a specific subject relating to the community and the activities of the State at the Plenary session of the Grand National Assembly of Turkey.

The form of presentation, content, and scope of the motions concerning questions, Parliamentary inquiries and general debates, and the procedures for answering, debating and investigating them, shall be regulated by the Rules of Procedure.

Art. 99. A motion for interpellation may be tabled either on behalf of a political party group, or by the signature of at least twenty deputies.

The motion for interpellation shall be circulated in printed form to the members within three days of its being tabled; inclusion of a motion of interpellation in the agenda shall be debated within ten days of its circulation. In this debate, only one of the signatories to the motion, one deputy from each political party group, and the Prime Minister or one Minister on behalf of the Council of Ministers, may take the floor.

Together with the decision to include the motion of interpellation on the agenda, the date for debating it will also be decided; however, the debate shall not take place less than two days after the decision to place it on the agenda and shall not be deferred more than seven days.

In the course of the debate on the motion of interpellation, a motion of no-confidence with a statement of reasons tabled by deputies or party groups, or the request for a vote of confidence by the Council of Ministers, shall be put to vote only after a full day has elapsed.

In order to unseat the Council of Ministers or a Minister, an absolute majority of the total number of members shall be required in the voting, in which only the votes of no-confidence shall be counted.

Other provisions concerning interpellations, provided that they are consistent with the smooth functioning of the Assembly, and with the above-mentioned principles shall be designed by the Rules of Procedure.

Art. 100. Parliamentary investigation concerning the Prime Minister or other Ministers may be requested with a motion tabled by at least one tenth of the total number of members of the Grand National Assembly of Turkey. The Assembly shall consider and decide on this request within one month at the latest.

In the event of a decision to initiate an investigation, this investigation shall be conducted by a commission of fifteen members chosen by lot on behalf of each party from among three times the number of members the party is entitled to have on the commission, representation being proportional to the parliamentary membership of the party. The commission shall submit its report on the result of the investigation to the Assembly within two months. If the investigation is not completed within the time alloted, the commission shall be granted a further and final period of two months.

The Assembly shall debate the report with priority and, if found necessary, may decide to bring the person involved before the Supreme Court. The decision to bring a person before the Supreme Court shall be taken only by an absolute majority of the total number of members.

Political party groups in the Assembly shall not hold discussions or take decisions regarding Parliamentary investigation.

Chapter two. Executive

I. PRESIDENT OF THE REPUBLIC

Art. 101. The President of the Republic shall be elected for a term of office of seven years by the Grand National Assembly of Turkey from among its own members who are over forty years of age and who have completed their higher education or from among Turkish citizens who fulfil these requirements and are eligible to be deputies.

The nomination of a candidate for the Presidency of the Republic from outside the Grand National Assembly of Turkey shall require a written proposal by at least one fifth of the total number of members of the Assembly.

The President of the Republic cannot be elected for a second time.

The President-elect, if a member of a party, shall sever his relations with his party and his status as a member of the Grand National Assembly of Turkey shall cease.

Art. 102. The President of the Republic shall be elected by a two-thirds majority of the total number of members of the Grand National Assembly of Turkey and by secret ballot. If the Grand National Assembly of Turkey is not in session, it shall be summoned immediately to meet.

The election of the President of the Republic shall begin thirty days before the term of office of the incumbent President of the Republic expires or ten days after the Presidency falls vacant, and shall be completed within thirty days of the beginning of the election. Candidates shall be declared to the Bureau of the Assembly within the first ten days of this period, and elections shall be completed within the remaining twenty days.

If a two-thirds majority of the total number of members cannot be obtained in the first two ballots, between which there shall be at least a three day interval, a third ballot shall be held and the candidate who receives the absolute majority of votes of the total number of members shall be elected President of the Republic. If an absolute majority of votes of the total number of members is not obtained in the third ballot, a fourth ballot will be held between the two candidates who receive the greatest number of votes in the third ballot; if the President of the Republic cannot be elected by an absolute majority of the total number of members in this ballot, new general elections for the Grand National Assembly of Turkey shall be held immediately.

The term of office of the incumbent President of the Republic shall continue until the President-elect takes office.

Art. 103. On assuming office, the President of the Republic shall take the following oath before the Grand National Assembly of Turkey:

'In my capacity as President of the Republic I swear upon my honor and integrity before the Grand National Assembly of Turkey and before history to safeguard the existence and independence of the State, the indivisible integrity of the country and the nation and the absolute sovereignty of the nation, to abide by the Constitution, the rule of law, democracy, the principles and reforms of Atatürk and the principles of the secular republic, not to deviate from the ideal according to which everyone is entitled to enjoy human rights and fundamental freedoms under conditions of national peace and prosperity and in a spirit of national solidarity and justice, and to do my utmost to preserve and exalt the glory and honor of the Republic of Turkey and perform without bias the functions that I have assumed.'

Art. 104. The President of the Republic is the Head of the State. In this capacity he shall represent the Republic of Turkey and the unity of the Turkish nation; he shall ensure the implementation of the Constitution, and the regular and harmonious functioning of the organs of State.

To this end, the duties he shall perform, and the powers he shall exercise, in accordance with the conditions stipulated in the relevant articles of the Constitution are as follows:

a) Those relating to legislation:

To deliver, if he deems it necessary, the opening address of the Grand National Assembly of Turkey on the first day of the legislative year,

To summon the Grand National Assembly of Turkey to meet, when necessary,

To promulgate laws,

To return laws to the Grand National Assembly of Turkey to be reconsidered,

To submit to referendum, if he deems it necessary, legislation regarding the amendments of the Constitution,

To appeal to the Constitutional Court for the annulment in part or entirety of certain provision of laws, decrees having force of law, and the Rules of Procedure of the Grand National Assembly of Turkey on the grounds that they are unconstitutional in form or in content.

To call new elections for the Grand National Assembly of Turkey.

b) Those relating to the executive functions:

To appoint the Prime Minister and to accept his resignation,

To appoint and dismiss Ministers on the proposal of the Prime Minister,

To preside over the Council of Ministers or to call the Council of Ministers to meet under his chairmanship whenever he deems it necessary,

To accredit representatives of the Turkish State to foreign States and to receive the representatives of foreign States to the Republic of Turkey,

To ratify and promulgate international treaties,

To represent the office of the Commander-in-Chief of the Turkish Armed Forces on behalf of the Grand National Assembly of Turkey,

To decide to use the Turkish Armed Forces,

To appoint the Chief of the General Staff,

To call the National Security Council to meet,

To preside over the National Security Council,

To proclaim martial law or state of emergency, and to issue decrees having force of law, in accordance with the decisions of the Council of Ministers under his chairmanship.

To sign decrees,

To remit, on grounds of chronic illness, disability, or old age, all or part of the sentences imposed on certain individuals,

To appoint the members and the chairman of the State Supervisory Council,

To instruct the State Supervisory Council to carry out enquiries, investigations and inspections,

To appoint the members of the Higher Education Council,

To appoint rectors of universities

c) Those relating to the judiciary:

To appoint the members of the Constitutional Court, one fourth of the members of the Council of State, the Chief Public Prosecutor and the Deputy Chief Public Prosecutor of the High Court of Appeals, the members of the Military High Court of Appeals, the members of the Supreme Military Administrative Court and the members of the Supreme Council of Judges and Public Prosecutors.

The President of the Republic shall also exercise powers of election and appointment, and perform the other duties conferred on him by the Constitution and laws.

Art. 105. All presidential decrees except those which the President of the Republic is empowered to enact by himself without the signatures of the Prime Minister and the minister concerned, in accordance with the provisions of the Constitution and other laws, shall be signed by the Prime Minister, and the Ministers concerned. The Prime Minister and the Ministers concerned shall be accountable for these decrees.

No appeal shall be made to any legal authority, including the Constitutional Court, against the decisions and orders signed by the President of the Republic on his own initiative.

The President of the Republic may be impeached for high treason on the proposal of at least one third of the total number of members of the Grand National Assembly of Turkey, and by the decision of at least three quarters of the total number of members.

Art. 106. In the event of a temporary absence of the President of the Republic on account of illness, travel abroad or similar circumstances, the President of the Grand National Assembly of Turkey shall serve as Acting President of the Republic until the President of the Republic resumes his functions; and in the event that the Presidency falls vacant as a result of death or resignation or for any other reason, until the election of a new President of the Republic.

Art. 107. The establishment, the principles of organization and functioning, and the appointment of personnel of the General Secretariat of the Presidency of the Republic shall be regulated by Presidential decrees.

Art. 108. The State Supervisory Council which shall be established attached to the office of the Presidency of the Republic with the purpose of performing and furthering the regular and efficient functioning of the administration and its observance of law, will be empowered to conduct upon the request of the President of the Republic all enquiries, investigations and inspections of all public bodies and organizations, all enterprises in which those public bodies and organizations share more than half of the capital, public professional organizations, employers' associations and labor unions at all levels, and public benefit associations and foundations.

The Armed Forces and all judicial organs are outside the jurisdiction of the State Supervisory Council.

The members and the Chairman to be designated from among the members of the State Supervisory Council shall be appointed by the President of the Republic from among those with the qualifications set forth in the law.

The functioning of the State Supervisory Council, the term of office of its mem bers, and other matters relating to their status shall be regulated by law.

II. COUNCIL OF MINISTERS

Art. 109. The Council of Ministers shall consist of the Prime Minister and the Ministers.

The Prime Minister shall be appointed by the President of the Republic from among the members of the Grand National Assembly of Turkey.

The Ministers shall be nominated by the Prime Minister and appointed by the President of the Republic, from among the members of the Grand National Assembly of Turkey, or from among those eligible for election as deputies; and they can be dismissed, by the President of the Republic upon the proposal of the Prime Minister when deemed necessary.

Art. 110. The complete list of members of the Council of Ministers shall be submitted to the Grand National Assembly of Turkey. If the Grand National Assembly of Turkey is in recess, it shall be summoned to meet.

The Government Program of the Council of Ministers shall be read by the Prime Minister or by one of the Ministers before the Grand National Assembly of Turkey within a week of the formation of the Council of Ministers, following which a vote of confidence shall be taken. Debate on the vote of confidence shall begin two full days after the reading of the program and the vote shall be taken one full day after the end of debate.

Art. 111. If the Prime Minister deems it necessary, and after discussing the matter in the Council of Ministers he may ask for a vote of confidence in the Grand National Assembly of Turkey.

The request for a vote of confidence shall not be debated before one full day has elapsed from the time it was submitted to the Grand National Assembly of Turkey and shall not be put to vote until one full day has passed after debate.

A request for a vote of confidence shall be rejected only by an absolute majority of the total number of members.

Art. 112. The Prime Minister, as Chairman of the Council of Ministers, shall ensure cooperation among the ministers, and supervise the implementation of the government's general policy. The members of the Council of Ministers are jointly responsible for the implementation of this policy.

Each minister shall be responsible to the Prime Minister and shall also be responsible for the conduct of affairs under his jurisdiction and for the acts and activities of his subordinates.

The Prime Minister shall ensure that the ministers exercise their functions in accordance with the Constitution and the laws and shall take corrective measures to this end.

The members of the Council of Ministers who are not deputies shall take their oath before the Grand National Assembly of Turkey as written in Article 81, and during their term of office as ministers they shall abide by the rules and conditions to which deputies are subject and shall enjoy parliamentary immunity. They receive the same salaries and allowances as members of the Grand National Assembly of Turkey.

Art. 113. The formation, abolition, functions, powers and organization of the Ministries shall be regulated by law.

A minister may act for another if a ministry is vacant or if the minister is on leave or absent for a valid reason. However, a minister shall not act for more than one other minister.

A minister who is brought before the Supreme Court by decision of the Grand National Assembly of Turkey, shall lose his ministerial status. If the Prime Minister is brought before the Supreme Court, the Government shall be considered to have resigned.

If a ministry falls vacant for any reason, an appointment shall be made to it within fifteen days.

Art. 114. The Ministers of Justice, Internal Affairs and Communications shall resign prior to general elections to the Grand National Assembly of Turkey.

Three days before the beginning of the elections or, in the event of a decision to hold new elections before the end of the election term, within five days of this decision, the Prime Minister shall appoint independent persons from within or outside of the Grand National Assembly of Turkey to these Ministries.

In the event of a decision to hold new elections under Article 116, the Council of Ministers shall resign and the President of the Republic shall appoint a Prime Minister to form a Provisional Council of Ministers.

The Provisional Council of Ministers shall be composed of members of the political party groups in proportion to their parliamentary membership with the exception of the Ministers of Justice, Internal Affairs, and Communications, who shall be independent persons appointed from within or outside the Grand National Assembly of Turkey.

The number of members to be taken from political party groups shall be determined by the President of the Grand National Assembly of Turkey, and shall be communicated to the Prime Minister. Party members who do not accept the ministerial posts offered them, or who resign subsequently, shall be replaced by independent persons from within or outside of the Grand National Assembly of Turkey.

The provisional Council of Ministers shall be formed within five days of the publication in the Official Gazette of the decision to hold new elections.

The Provisional Council of Ministers shall not be subject to a vote of confidence.

The Provisional Council of Ministers shall remain in office for the duration of the elections, and until the new Assembly convenes.

Art. 115. The Council of Ministers may issue regulations governing the mode of implementation of laws or designating matters ordered by law, provided that they do not conflict with existing laws and are examined by the Council of State.

Regulations shall be signed by the President of the Republic and promulgated in the same manner as laws.

Art. 116. In cases where the Council of Ministers fails to receive a vote of confidence under Article 110 or is compelled to resign by a vote of no-confidence under Articles 99 or 111, and if a new Council of Ministers cannot be formed within forty five days or the new Council of Ministers fails to receive a vote of confidence, the President of the Grand National Assembly of Turkey, may call new elections.

If a new Council of Ministers cannot be formed within forty five days of the resignation of the Prime Minister without being defeated by a vote of confidence, or also within forty five days of elections for the Bureau of the President of the Grand National Assembly of Turkey, the President of the Republic may likewise, in consultation with the President of the Grand National Assembly of Turkey, call new elections.

The decision to call new elections shall be published in the Official Gazette and the election shall be held thereafter.

II.[1] NATIONAL DEFENCE

Art. 117. The office of the Commander in Chief is inseparable from the spiritual existence of the Grand National Assembly of Turkey and is represented by the President of the Republic.

The Council of Ministers shall be responsible to the Grand National Assembly of Turkey for national security and for the preparation of the Armed Forces for the defence of the country.

The Chief of the General Staff is the commander of the Armed Forces, and, in time of war exercises the duties of Commander in Chief on behalf of the President of the Republic.

The Chief of the General Staff shall be appointed by the President of the Republic on the proposal of the Council of Ministers; his duties and powers shall be regulated by law. The Chief of the General Staff shall be responsible for the Prime Minister in the exercise of his duties and powers.

The functional relations and the scope of jurisdiction of the Ministry of National Defence with regard to the chief of the General Staff and the Commanders of the Armed Forces shall be regulated by law.

Art. 118. The National Security Council shall be composed of the Prime Minister the Chief of the General Staff, the Minister of National Defence, Internal Affairs, and Foreign Affairs, the Commanders of the Army, Navy and the Air Force and the General Commander of the Gendarmerie, under the chairmanship of the President of the Republic.

Depending on the particulars of the Agenda, Ministers and other persons concerned may be invited to meetings of the Council and their views be heard.

The National Security Council shall submit to the Council of Ministers its views on taking decisions and ensuring necessary coordination with regard to the formulation, establishment and implementation of the National Security policy of the State. The Council of Ministers shall give priority consideration to the decisions of the National Security Council concerning the measures that it deems necessary for the preservation of the existence and independence of the State, the integrity and indivisibility of the country, and the peace and security of society.

The Agenda of the National Security Council shall be drawn up by the President of the Republic taking into account the proposals of the Prime Minister and the Chief of the General Staff.

In the absence of the President of the Republic, the National Security Council shall meet under the chairmanship of the Prime Minister.

The organization and duties of the General Secretariat of the National Security Council shall be regulated by law.

III. PROCEDURE GOVERNING EMERGENCY RULE

Art. 119. In the event of natural disaster, dangerous epidemic diseases or a serious economic crisis, the Council of Ministers, meeting under the chairmanship

[1] In the original text there are 2 chapter headings numbered II, this one and that preceding Article 109. Ed.

of the President of the Republic, may declare a state of emergency in one or more regions or throughout the country for a period not exceeding six months.

Art. 120. In the event of the emergence of serious indications of widespread acts of violence aimed at the destruction of the free democratic order established by the Constitution or of fundamental rights and freedoms, or serious deterioration of public order because of acts of violence, the Council of Ministers, meeting under the chairmanship of the President of the Republic, after consultation with the National Security Council, may declare a state of emergency in one or more regions or throughout the country for a period not exceding six months.

Art. 121. In the event of a declaration of a state of emergency under the provisions of Articles 119 and 120 of the Constitution this decision shall be published in the Official Gazette and shall be submitted immediately to the Grand National Assembly of Turkey for approval. If the Grand National Assembly of Turkey is in recess, it shall be summoned immediately. The Assembly may alter the duration of the state of emergency, extend the period for a maximum of four months each time at the request of the Council of Ministers, or may lift the state of emergency.

The financial, material, and labor obligations which are to be imposed on citizens in the event of the declaration of a state of emergency under Article 119, and, applicable according to the nature of each kind of state of emergency, the procedure as to how fundamental rights and freedoms shall be restricted or suspended in line with the principles of Article 15, how and by what means the measures necessitated by the situation shall be taken, what sort of powers shall be conferred on public servants, what kind of changes shall be made in the status of officials, and the procedure governing emergency rule, shall be regulated by the Law on State of Emergency.

During the state of emergency, the Council of Ministers meeting under the chairmanship of the President of the Republic, may issue decrees having force of law on matters necessitated by the state of emergency. These decrees shall be published in the Official Gazette, and shall be submitted to the Grand National Assembly of Turkey on the same day for approval; the time limit and procedure for their approval by the Assembly shall be indicated in the Rules of Procedure.

Art. 122. The Council of Ministers, under the chairmanship of the President of the Republic, after consultation with the National Security Council, may declare martial law in one or more regions or throughout the country for a period not exceeding six months, in the event of widespread acts of violence which are more dangerous than the cases necessitating a state of emergency and which are aimed at the destruction of the free democratic order or the fundamental rights and freedoms embodied in the Constitution; or in the event of war, the emergence of a situation necessitating war, an uprising, or the spread of violent and strong rebellious actions against the motherland and the Republic, or widespread acts of violence of either internal or external origin threatening the indivisibility of the country and the nation. This decision shall be published immediately in the Official Gazette, and shall be submitted for approval to the Grand National Assembly of Turkey, on the same day. If the Grand National Assembly of Turkey is in recess, it shall be summoned immediately. The Grand National Assembly of Turkey may, when it deems necessary, reduce or extend the period of martial law or lift it.

During the period of martial law, the Council of Ministers meeting under the chairmanship of the President of the Republic may issue decrees having force of law on matters necessitated by the state of martial law.

These decrees shall be published in the Official Gazette and shall be submitted for approval to the Grand National Assembly of Turkey on the same day. The time limit and procedure for their approval by the Assembly shall be indicated in the Rules of Procedure.

Extension of the period of martial law for a maximum of four months each time, shall require a decision of the Grand National Assembly of Turkey. In the event of state of war, the limit of four months does not apply.

In the event of martial law, mobilization and state of war, the provisions to be applied and conduct of affairs, the relations with the administration, the manner in which freedoms are to be restricted or suspended and the obligations to be imposed on the citizens in a state of war or in the event of emergence of a situation necessitating war shall be regulated by law.

The Martial Law Commanders shall exercise their duties under the authority of the Office of the Chief of the General Staff.

IV. ADMINISTRATION

Art. 123. The administration forms a whole with regard to its structure and functions, and shall be regulated by law.

The organization and functions of the administration are based on the principles of centralization and local administration.

Public corporate bodies shall be established only by law, or on the authority expressly granted by law.

Art. 124. The Prime Ministry, the ministries, the public corporate bodies may issue by-laws in order to ensure the application of laws and regulations relating to their particular fields of operation, provided that they are not contrary to these laws and regulations. The law shall designate which by-laws are to be published in the Official Gazette.

Art. 125. Recourse to judicial review shall be open against all actions and acts of the administration.

The acts of the President of the Republic in his own competence, and the decisions of the Supreme Military Council are outside the scope of judicial review.

In suits filed against administrative acts, statute of limitations shall start from the date of written notification.

Judicial power is limited to the verification of the conformity of the actions and acts of the administration with law. No judicial ruling shall be passed which restricts the exercise of the executive function in accordance with the forms and principles prescribed by law, which has the quality of an administrative action and act, or which removes discretionary powers.

If the implementation of an administrative act would result in damages which are difficult or impossible to compensate, and at the same time this act is clearly unlawful, then a stay of execution may be decided upon, stating the reasons therefore.

The law may restrict the issuing of stay of execution orders in cases of state of emergency, martial law, mobilization and state of war, and for reasons of national security, public order and public health.

The administration shall be liable to compensate for damages resulting from its actions and acts.

Art. 126. In terms of central administrative structure, Turkey is divided into provinces on the basis of geographical situation and economic conditions, and public service requirements; provinces are further divided into lower steps of administrative districts.

The administration of the provinces is based on the principle of devolution of wide powers.

Central administrative organizations comprising several provinces may be established to ensure efficiency and coordination of public services. The functions and powers of this organization shall be regulated by law.

Art. 127. Local administrative bodies are public corporate entities established to meet the common local needs of the inhabitants of provinces municipal districts and villages, whose decision-making organs are elected by the electorate described in law, and whose principles of structure are also determined by law.

The formation, duties and powers of the local administrations shall be regulated by law in accordance with the principle of local administration.

The elections for local administrative bodies shall be held every five years in accordance with the principles set forth in Article 67 of the Constitution. Special administrative arrangements may be introduced for larger urban areas.

The procedures dealing with objections to the acquisition by elected organs of local government of their status as an organ, and their loss of such status shall be resolved by the judiciary. However as a provisional measure, the Minister of Internal Affairs may remove from office those organs of local administration or their members against whom investigation or prosecution has been initiated on grounds of offences related to their duties, pending judgment.

The central administration has the power of administrative trusteeship over the local governments in the framework of principles and procedures set forth by law with the objective of ensuring the functioning of local services in conformity with the principle of the integral unity of the administration, securing uniform public service, safeguarding the public interest and meeting local needs, in an appropriate manner.

The formation of local administrative bodies into a union with the permission of the Council of Ministers for the purpose of performing specific public services; and the functions, powers, financial and security arrangements of these unions, and their reciprocal ties and relations with the central administration, shall be regulated by law. These administrative bodies shall be allocated financial resources in porportion to their functions.

Art. 128. The fundamental and permanent functions required by the public services that the State economic enterprises and other public corporate bodies are assigned to perform, in accordance with principles of general administration, shall be carried out by public servants and other employees.

The qualifications of public servants and other public employees, procedures governing their appointments, duties and powers, their rights and responsibilities, salaries and allowances, and other matters related to their status shall be regulated by law.

The procedure and principles governing the training of senior administrators shall be specially regulated by law.

Art. 129. Public servants and other public employees are obliged to carry out their duties within loyalty to the Constitution and the laws.

Public servants, other public employees and members of public professional organizations or their higher bodies shall not be subjected to disciplinary penalty without their being granted the right of defence.

Disciplinary decisions shall be subject to judicial review, with the exception of warnings and reprimands.

Provisions concerning the members of the Armed Forces, judges and prosecutors are reserved.

Actions for damages arising from faults committed by public servants and other public employees in the exercise of their duties shall be brought only against the administration in accordance with the procedure and conditions prescribed by law, and subject to recourse to them.

Prosecution of public servants and other public employees for alleged offences shall be subject, except in cases prescribed by law, to the permission of the administrative authority designated by law.

Art. 130. For the purpose of training manpower under a system of contemporary education and training principles and meeting the needs of the nation and the country, universities comprising several units will be established by the State and by law as public corporations having autonomy in teaching, assigned to educate, and conduct research, to act as consultants, to issue publications and to serve the country and humanity.

Institutions, of higher education under the supervision and control of the State, can be established by foundations in accordance with the procedures and principles set forth in the law provided that they do not pursue lucrative aims.

The law shall provide for a balanced geographical distribution of universities throughout the country.

Universities, members of the teaching staff and their assistants may freely engage in all kinds of scientific research and publication. However, this shall not include the liberty to engage in activities directed against the existence and independence of the State, and against the integrity and indivisibility of the nation and the country.

Universities and units attached to them are under the control and supervision of the State and their security is ensured by the State.

University rectors shall be appointed by the President of the Republic, and faculty deans by the Higher Education Council, in accordance with the procedures and provisions of the law.

The administrative and supervisory organs of the universities and the teaching staff may not for any reason whatsoever be removed from their office by authorities other than those of the competent organs of the university or by the Higher Education Council.

The budgets drawn up by universities, after being examined and approved by the Higher Education Council shall be presented to the Ministry of National Education, and shall be put into effect and supervised in conformity with the principles applied to general and subsidiary budgets.

The establishment of institutions of higher education and their organs, their functioning and elections, their duties, authorities and responsibilities, the procedures to be followed by the State in the exercise of the right to supervise and inspect the universities, the duties of the teaching staff, their titles, appointments, promotions and retirement, the training of the teaching staff, the relations of the universities and the teaching staff with public institutions and other organizations, the level and duration of education, admission of students into institutions of higher education, attendance requirements and fees, principles relating to assistance to be provided by the State, disciplinary and penalty matters, financial affairs, personnel rights, conditions to be conformed with by the teaching staff, the assignment of the teaching staff in accordance with inter-university requirements, the pursuance of training and education in freedom and under guarantee in accordance with the requirements of contemporary science and technology, and the use of financial resources provided the State to the Higher Education Council and the Universities, shall be regulated by law.

Institutions of higher education established by foundations, shall be subject to the provisions set forth in the Constitution for State institutions of higher education, as regards the academic activities, recruitment of teaching staff and security, excepting the financial and administrative matters.

Art. 131. The Higher Education Council shall be established, to plan, organize, administer, and supervise the education provided by institutions of higher education, to orient the activities of teaching, education and scientific research, to ensure the establishment and development of these institutions in conformity with the objectives and principles set forth by law, to ensure the effective use of the resources alloted to the universities, and to plan the training of the teaching staff.

The Higher Education Council is composed of members appointed by the President of the Republic from among the candidates who are nominated by the Council of Ministers, the Chief of the General Staff and the Universities, and in accordance with the numbers, qualifications and procedure prescribed by law, priority being given to those who have served successfully as Faculty members or Rectors, and of members directly appointed by the President of the Republic himself.

The organization, functions, authority, responsibility and operating principles of the Council shall be regulated by law.

Art. 132. Institutions of Higher Education attached to the Turkish Armed forces and to the security organization are subject to the provisions of their respective special laws.

Art. 133. Radio and television stations shall be established only by the State, and shall be administered by an impartial public corporate body.

The law shall provide that broadcasts are made in a manner to safeguard the existence and independence of the Turkish State, the indivisible integrity of the country and the nation, the peace of society, public morals, and the fundamental characteristics of the Republic as outlined in Article 2 of the Constitution; and, it shall observe the principle of impartiality in the administration and supervision of the Corporation, in the formation of its administrative organs, and in all radio and television broadcasts.

The principles governing the selection, treatment and presentation of news and programs, the fulfilment of the task to aid the national culture and education, and the principles ensuring the accuracy of the news; and the election, functions, and responsibilities of the organs shall be regulated by law.

The provisions of paragraph 2 above shall also apply to those news agencies having the character of state economic enterprises and to those receiving financial aid from the State or other public corporate bodies.

Art. 134. The 'Atatürk High Institution of Culture, Language and History' shall be established, as a public corporate body, under the moral aegis of Atatürk, under the supervision and with the support of the President of the Republic, attached to the office of the Prime Minister, and composed of the Atatürk Center of Research, the Turkish Language Society, the Turkish Historical Society and the Atatürk Cultural Center, in order to conduct scientific research, to produce publications and to disseminate information on the thought, principles, and reforms of Atatürk, Turkish culture, Turkish history and the Turkish language.

The financial income of the Turkish Language Society and Turkish Historical Society, bequeathed to them by Atatürk in his will are reserved and shall be allocated to them accordingly.

The establishment, organs, operating procedures, and personnel matters of the Atatürk High Institution of Culture, Language and History, and its authority over the Institutions within it, shall be regulated by law.

Art. 135. Public professional organizations and their higher organizations are public corporate bodies established by law, with the objectives to meet the common needs of the members of a given profession, to facilitate their professional activities, to ensure the development of the profession in keeping with the common interests, to safeguard professional discipline and ethics in order to ensure integrity and trust in relations among its members and with the public; their organs shall be elected by secret ballot by their members in accordance with the procedure set forth in the law, and under judicial supervision.

Persons regularly employed in public institutions, or in state economic enterprises shall not be required to become members of public professional organizations.

Public professional organizations shall not engage in activities outside the aims for which they were established, nor shall they engage in political activities or take joint action with political parties, labour unions or associations.

Political parties, labor unions and their higher bodies shall not nominate candidates in elections for the organs of public professional organizations or their higher bodies, nor shall they engage in activities or propaganda for or against particular candidates.

Public professional organizations shall be subject to administrative and financial supervision of the State as prescribed by law.

The responsible organs of public professional organizations which engage in activities beyond their objectives or in political activities, shall be dissolved by a court decision, at the request of the authority designated by law; and new organs shall be elected in their place.

In respect of safeguarding the existence and independence of the Turkish State, the indivisible integrity of the country and nation, the peace of society, and, preventing the activities threatening the fundamental characteristics of the State as defined in the Constitution, the highest local administrator, may, in the event delay is deemed prejudicial, temporarily remove these organs from office.

The decision to remove from office shall be communicated to the court within three days. The court shall decide within ten days at the latest whether the decision of removal from office is justified.

Art. 136. The Department of Religious Affairs, which is within the general administration, shall exercise its duties prescribed in its particular law, in accordance with the principles of secularism, removed from all political views and ideas, and aiming at national solidarity and integrity.

Art. 137. A person employed in public services, irrespective of his position or status when he finds an order given by his superiors to be contrary to the provisions of by-laws, regulations, laws, or the Constitution shall not carry it out, and shall inform the person giving the order of this inconsistency. However, if his superior insists on the order and renews it in writing, this order shall be executed; in this case the person executing the order shall not be held responsible.

An order which in itself constitutes an offence shall under no circumstances be executed; the person who executes such an order shall not evade responsibility.

Exceptions designated by law relating to the execution of military duties and the protection of public order or public security in urgent situations are reserved.

PART THREE

JUDICIAL POWER

I. GENERAL PROVISIONS

Art. 138. Judges shall be independent in the discharge of their duties; they shall give judgement in accordance with the Constitution, law, and their personal conviction conforming with the Law.

No organ, authority, office or individual may give orders or instructions to courts or judges relating to the exercise of judicial power, or send them circulars, make recommendations or suggestions.

No question shall be asked, debates held, or statements made in the Legislative Assembly relating to the exercise of judicial power concerning a case under trial.

Legislative and executive organs and the administration shall comply with court decisions; these organs and the administration shall neither alter them in any respect, nor delay their execution.

Art. 139. Judges and public prosecutors shall not be dismissed, or retired before the age prescribed by the Constitution; nor shall they be deprived of their salaries, allowances or other rights relating to their status, even as a result of the abolition of court or post.

Exceptions indicated in law relating to those convicted for an offence requiring dismissal from the profession, those who are definitely established as unable to perform their duties on account of ill-health, and those determined unsuitable to remain in the profession, are reserved.

Art. 140. Judges and public prosecutors shall serve as judges and public prosecutors of courts of justice and of administrative courts. These duties shall be carried out by career judges and public prosecutors.

Judges shall discharge their duties in accordance with the principles of the independence of the courts and the security of tenure of judges.

The qualification, appointment, rights and duties, salaries and allowances of judges and public prosecutors, their promotion, temporary or permanent change of their duties or posts, the initiation of disciplinary proceedings against them and the subsequent imposition of disciplinary penalties, the conduct of investigation concerning them and the subsequent decision to prosecute them on account of offences committed in connection with, or in the course of their duties; the conviction for offences or instances of incompetence requiring their dismissal from the profession, their in-service training and other matters relating to their personnel status shall be regulated by law in accordance with the principles of the independence of the courts and the security of tenure of judges.

Judges and public prosecutors shall exercise their duties until they complete the age of sixty-five; the age limit, promotion and the retirement of military judges shall be prescribed by law.

Judges and public prosecutors shall not assume official or public functions other than those prescribed by law.

Judges and public prosecutors shall be attached to the Ministry of Justice in so far as their administrative functions are concerned.

Those judges and public prosecutors working in administrative posts of the justice service shall be subject to the same provisions as other judges and public prosecutors. Their categories and grades shall be determined according to the principles applying to judges and public prosecutors, and they shall enjoy all the rights accorded to judges and public prosecutors.

Art. 141. Court hearings shall be open to the public. It may be decided to conduct all or part of the hearings in closed session only in cases where required absolutely for reasons of public morality or public security.

Special provisions shall be provided in the law with respect to the trial of minors.

The decisions of all courts shall be made in writing with a statement of justification.

It is the duty of the judiciary to conclude trials as quickly as possible and at minimum cost.

Art. 142. The organization, functions and jurisdictions of the courts, their functioning and trial procedures shall be regulated by law.

Art. 143. Courts of the Security of the State shall be established to deal with offences against the indivisible integrity of the State with its territory and nation, the free democratic order, or against the Republic whose characteristics are defined in the Constitution, and offences directly involving the internal and external security of the State.

The Court of the Security of the State shall consist of a President, two regular and two substitute members, one public prosecutor and a sufficient number of deputy prosecutors.

The President, one regular and one substitute member and the public prosecutor from among first category judges and public prosecutors; one regular and one substitute member from among first category military judges; and deputy public prosecutors from among public prosecutors of the Republic and military judges shall be appointed in accordance with procedures prescribed by their special laws.

The President, members and substitute members, and public prosecutors and deputy public prosecutors of the Court of the Security of the State shall be appointed for four years; those whose term of office expires may be reappointed.

The High Court of Appeals is the competent authority to examine appeals against the verdicts of the Court of the Security of the State.

Other provisions relating to the functioning, the duties and jurisdiction and the trial procedure of the Court of the Security of the State shall be prescribed by law.

In the event of declaration of martial law within the regions under the jurisdiction of a Court of the Security of the State, the latter may be transformed, in accordance with the provisions prescribed by law, into a Martial Law Military Tribunal with jurisdiction restricted to these regions.

Art. 144. Supervision of judges and public prosecutors with regard to the performance of their duties in accordance with laws, regulations, by-laws and circulars (administrative circulars, in the case of judges), investigation into whether they have committed offences in connection with, or in the course of, their duties, whether their behavior and attitude are in conformity with their status and duties and if necessary, inquiry and investigations concerning them shall be made by judiciary inspectors with the permission of the Ministry of Justice. The Minister of Justice may request the investigation or inquiry to be conducted by a judge or public prosecutor who is senior to the judge or public prosecutor to be investigated.

Art. 145. Military justice shall be exercised by military courts and military disciplinary courts. These courts shall have jurisdiction to try military personnel: for military offences, for offences committed by them against other military personnel or in military places, or for offences connected with military service and duties.

Military courts also have jurisdiction to try non-military persons for military offences specified in the special law; and for offences committed while performing their duties specified by law, or against military personnel on military places specified by law.

The offences and persons falling within the jurisdiction of military courts in time of war or under martial law, their organization and appointment, where necessary, of judges and public prosecutors from courts of justice to military courts shall be regulated by law.

The organization of military judicial organs, their functions, matters relating to the status of military judges, relations between military judges acting as military prosecutors and the office of commander under which they serve, shall be regulated by law in accordance with the principles of the independence of courts and the security of tenure of judges and with the requirements of military service. Relations between military judges and the office of commander under which they serve, regarding the requirements of military service apart from the judicial functions, shall also be prescribed by law.

II. HIGHER COURTS

A. The Constitutional Court

Art. 146. The Constitutional Court shall be composed of eleven regular and four substitute members.

The President of the Republic shall appoint two regular and two substitute members from the High Court of Appeals, two regular and one substitute member from the Council of State, and one member each from the Military High Court of Appeals, the High Military Administrative Court and the Audit Court, three candidates being nominated for each vacant office by the Plenary Assemblies of each court from among their respective presidents and members, by an absolute majority of the total number of members; the President of the Republic shall also appoint one member from a list of three candidates nominated by the Council of Higher Education from among members of the teaching staff of Institutions of higher education who are not members of the Council, and three members of one substitute member from among senior administrative officers and lawyers.

To qualify for appointments as regular or substitute members of the Constitutional Court members of the teaching staff of institutions of higher education, senior administrative officers and lawyers shall be required to be over the age of forty and to have completed their higher education, or to have served at least fifteen years as a member of the teaching staff of institutions of higher education or to have worked actually at least fifteen years in public service or to have practiced as a lawyer for at least fifteen years.

The Constitutional Court shall elect a President and Deputy President from among its regular members for a term of four years by secret ballot and by an absolute majority of the total number of members. They may be re-elected at the end of their term of office.

The Members of the Constitutional Court shall not assume other official and private functions, besides their main functions.

Art. 147. The members of the Constitutional Court shall retire on reaching the age of sixty-five.

Membership in the Constitutional Court shall terminate automatically if a member is convicted of an offence requiring his dismissal from the judicial profession; it shall terminate by a decision of an absolute majority of the total number of members of the Constitutional Court if it is definitely established that he is unable to perform his duties on account of ill health.

Art. 148. The Constitutional Court shall examine the constitutionality in respect of both form and substance of laws, decrees having force of law, and the Rules of Procedure of the Grand National Assembly of Turkey. Constitutional amendments shall be examined and verified only with regard to their form. However, no action shall be brought before the Constitutional Court alleging the unconstitutionality as to the form or substance of decrees having force of law, issued during a state of emergency, martial law or in time of war.

The verification of laws as to form shall be restricted to consideration of whether the requisite majority was obtained in the last ballot; the verification of constitutional amendments shall be restricted to consideration of whether the requisite majorities were obtained for the proposal and in the ballot, and whether the prohibition on debates under urgent procedure was compiled with. Verification as to the form may be requested by the President of the Republic or by one fifth of the members of the Grand National Assembly of Turkey. Applications for annulment on the grounds of defect in form shall not be made more than ten days after the date on which the law was promulgated; nor shall objection be raised.

The President of the Republic, members of the Council of Ministers, Presidents and members of the Constitutional Court, of the High Court of Appeals of the Council of State, of the Military High Court of Appeals, of the High Military Administrative Court of Appeals, their Chief Public Prosecutors, Deputy Public Prosecutors of the Republic, and the Presidents and members of the Supreme Council of Judges and Public Prosecutors, and of the Audit Court shall be tried for offences relating to their functions by the Constitutional Court in its capacity as the Supreme Court.

The Chief Public Prosecutor of the Republic or Deputy Chief Public Prosecutor of the Republic shall act as public prosecutor in the Supreme Court.

The judgments of the Supreme Court shall be final.

The Constitutional Court shall also perform the other functions given to it by the Constitution.

Art. 149. The Constitutional Court shall convene with its President and ten members, and shall take decisions by absolute majority. Decision of annulment of Constitutional amendments shall be taken by a two-thirds majority.

The Constitutional Court shall give priority to the consideration of, and to decisions on, applications for annulment on the ground of defect in form.

The organization and trial procedures of the Constitutional Court shall be determined by law; its method of work and the division of labour among its members shall be regulated by the Rules of Procedure made by the Court.

The Constitutional Court shall examine cases on the basis of files, except where it acts as the Supreme Court. However when it deems necessary, it may call on those concerned and those having knowledge relevant to the case to present oral explanations.

Art. 150. The President of the Republic, Parliamentary Groups of the Party in power and of the main opposition party, and a minimum of one fifth of the total number of members of the Grand National Assembly of Turkey shall have the right to apply for annulment action to the Constitutional Court, based on the assertion of the unconstitutionality of laws in form and in substance, of decrees having force of law, of Rules of Procedure of the Grand National Assembly of Turkey or of specific articles or provisions thereof. If more than one political party is in power, the right of the parties in power to apply for annulment action shall be exercised by the party having the greatest number of members.

Art. 151. The right to apply for annulment directly to the Constitutional Court shall lapse sixty days after the publication in the Official Gazette of the contested law, the decree having force of law, or the Rules of Procedure.

Art. 152. If a court which is trying a case, finds that the law or the decree having force of law to be applied is unconstitutional, or if it is convinced of the seriousness of a claim of unconstitutionality submitted by one of the parties, it shall postpone the consideration of the case until the Constitutional Court decides on this issue.

If the court is not convinced of the seriousness of the claim of unconstitutionality, such a claim together with the main judgment shall be decided upon by the competent authority of appeal.

The Constitutional Court shall decide on the matter and make public its judgment within five months of receiving the contention. If no decision is reached within this period, the trial court shall conclude the case under existing legal provisions. However, if the decision of the Constitutional Court is announced before the decision on the merits of the case becomes final, the trial court is obliged to comply with it.

No allegation of unconstitutionality shall be made with regard to the same legal provision until ten years elapse after the publication in the Official Gazette of the decision of the Constitutional Court dismissing the application on its merit.

Art. 153. The decisions of the Constitutional Court are final. Decisions of annulment cannot be made public without a written statement of reasons.

In the course of anulling the whole or a provision of laws or decrees having force of law, the Constitutional Court shall not act as a law-maker and pass judgement leading to new implementation.

Laws, decrees having force of law, or Rules of Procedure of the Grand National Assembly of Turkey or provisions thereof, shall cease to have effect from the date of publication in the Official Gazette of the annulment decision. Where necessary, the Constitutional Court may also decide on the date on which the annulment decision shall come into effect. The date shall not be more than one year from the date of the publication of the decision in the official Gazette.

In the event of the postponement of the date on which an annulment decision is to come into effect, the Grand National Assembly of Turkey shall debate and decide with priority on the draft bill or a law proposal, designed to fill the legal void arising from the annulment decision.

The annulment decision cannot have retroactive effect.

Decisions of the Constitutional Court shall be published immediately in the Official Gazette, and shall be binding on the legislative, executive, and judicial organs, on the administrative authorities, and on persons and corporate bodies.

Art. 154. The High Court of Appeals is the last instance for reviewing decisions and judgements given by courts of justice and which are not referred by law to other judicial authority. It shall also be the first and last instance for dealing with specific cases prescribed by law.

Members of the High Court of Appeals shall be appointed by the Supreme Council of Judges and Public Prosecutors from among the first category of judges and public prosecutors of the Republic of the Courts of Justice, or those considered to be members of this profession, by secret ballot and by an absolute majority of the total number of members.

The First President, first deputy presidents and heads of division shall be elected by the Plenary Assembly of the High Court of Appeals from among its own members, for a term of four years, by secret ballot and by an absolute majority of the total number of members; there may be re-elected at the end of their term of office.

The Chief Public Prosecutor of the Republic and the Deputy Chief Public Prosecutor of the Republic of the High Court of Appeals shall be appointed by the President of the Republic for a term of four years from among five candidates nominated for each office by the Plenary Assembly of the High Court of Appeals from among its own members by secret ballot. They may be re-elected at the end of their term of office.

The organization, the functioning, the qualifications and procedures of election of the President, deputy presidents, the heads of division and members and the Chief Public Prosecutor of the Republic and the deputy chief public prosecutor of the Republic of the High Court of Appeals shall be regulated by law in accordance with the principles of the independence of courts and the security of tenure of judges.

Art. 155. The Council of State is the last instance for reviewing decisions and judgments given by administrative courts and which are not referred by law to other administrative courts. It shall also be the first and last instance for dealing with specific cases prescribed by law.

The Council of State shall try administrative cases, give its opinions on draft legislation submitted by the Prime Minister and the Council of Ministers, examine draft regulations and the conditions and contracts under which concessions are granted, settle administrative disputes and discharge other duties as prescribed by law.

Three fourths of the members of the Council of State shall be appointed by the Supreme Council of Judges and Public Prosecutors from among the first category administrative judges and public prosecutors, or those considered to be of this profession; and the remaining one fourth of the members by the President of the Republic from among officials meeting the requirements designated by law.

The President, Chief Public Prosecutor, deputy presidents, and heads of division of the Council of State shall be elected by the Plenary Assembly of the Council of State from among its own members for a term of four years by secret ballot and by an absolute majority of the total number of members. They may be re-elected at the end of their term of office.

The organization, the functioning, the qualifications and procedures of elections of the President, the Chief Public Prosecutor, the deputy presidents and the heads of division and the members of the Council of State, shall be regulated by law in accordance with the principles of specific nature of the administrative jurisdiction, and of the independence of the courts and the security of tenure of judges.

D. Military High Court of Appeals

Art. 156. The Military High Court of Appeals is the last instance for reviewing decisions and judgements given by military courts. It shall be the first and last instance for dealing with specific cases designated by law concerning military personnel.

Members of the Military High Court of Appeals shall be appointed by the President of the Republic from among three candidates nominated for each vacant office by the Plenary Assembly of the Military High Court of Appeals from among military judges of the first category, by secret ballot and by an absolute majority of the total number of members.

The President, Chief Public Prosecutor, Second Presidents and heads of division of the Military High Court of Appeals shall be appointed according to rank and seniority from among the members of the Military High Court of Appeals.

The organization, the functioning of the Military High Court of Appeals, disciplinary and personnel matters relating to the status of its members shall be regulated by law in accordance with the principles of the independence of the courts and the security of tenure of judges and with the requirements of military service.

E. High Military Administrative Court of Appeals

Art. 157. The High Military Administrative Court of Appeals shall be the first and last instance for the judicial supervision of disputes arising from administrative acts and actions involving military personnel or relating to military service, even if such acts and actions have been carried out by civilian authorities. However in disputes arising from the obligation to perform military service, there shall be no condition that the person concerned be a member of the military body.

Members of the High Military Administrative Court of Appeals who are military judges shall be appointed by the President of the Republic from a list of three candidates nominated for each vacant office by the President and members of the Court, who are also military judges, by secret ballot and by an absolute majority of the total number of such members, from among military judges of the first category; members who are not military judges shall be appointed by the President of the Republic from a list of three candidates nominated for each vacant office by the Chief of the General Staff from among officers holding the rank and qualifications prescribed by law.

The term of office of members who are not military judges shall not exceed four years.

The President, Chief Public Prosecutor and heads of division of the Court shall be appointed from among military judges according to rank and security.

The organization and functioning of the High Military Administrative Court, its procedure, disciplinary affairs and other matters relating to the status of its members shall be regulated by law in accordance with the principles of the independence of the courts and the security of tenure of judges and with the requirements of military service.

F. Jurisdictional Conflict Court

Art. 158. The Jurisdictional Conflict Court shall be empowered to deliver final judgments in disputes between courts of justice, and administrative and military courts concerning their jurisdiction and decisions.

The organization of the Jurisdictional Conflict Court, the qualifications of its members and the procedure for their election, and its functioning shall be regulated by law. The office of President of this Court shall be held by a member delegated by the Constitutional Court from among its own members.

Decisions of the Constitutional Court shall take precedence in jurisdictional disputes between the Constitutional Court and other courts.

III. SUPREME COUNCIL OF JUDGES AND PUBLIC PROSECUTORS

Art. 159. The Supreme Council of Judges and Public Prosecutors shall be established and shall exercise its functions in accordance with the principles of the independence of the courts and the security of tenure of judges.

The President of the Council is the Minister of Justice. The Undersecretary to the Minister of Justice shall be an *ex-officio* member of the Council. Three regular and three substitute members of the Council shall be appointed by the President of the Republic for a term of four years from a list of three candidates nominated for each vacant office by the Plenary Assembly of the High Court of Appeals from among its own members and two regular and two substitute members shall be similarly appointed from a list of three candidates nominated for each vacant office by the Plenary Assembly of the Council of State. They may be re-elected at the end of their term of office. The Council shall elect a deputy president from among its elected regular members.

The Supreme Council of Judges and Public Prosecutors shall deal with the admission of judges and public prosecutors of courts of justice and of administrative courts into the profession, appointments, transfers to other posts, the delegation of temporary powers, promotion, and promotion to the first category, the allocation of posts, decisions concerning those whose continuation in the profession is found to be unsuitable, the imposition of disciplinary penalties and removed from office. It shall take final decisions on proposals by the Ministry of Justice concerning the abolition of a court or an office of judge or public prosecutor, or changes in the jurisdiction of a court. It shall also exercise the other functions given to it by the Constitution and laws.

There shall be no appeal to any judicial instance against the decisions of the Council.

The functioning of the Council and methods of performing its duties, the procedure governing election and working methods, the principles relating to the examination of objections within the Council shall be regulated by law.

The Minister of Justice is empowered to appoint judges and public prosecutors with their consent, to temporary or permanent functions in the central offices of the Ministry of Justice.

The Minister of Justice may, in cases where delay is deemed prejudicial, confer temporary powers on judges or public prosecutors to prevent the disruption of services, subject to approval of the Supreme Council of Judges and Public Prosecutors at its first meeting thereafter.

IV. AUDIT COURT

Art. 160. The Audit Court shall be charged with auditing, on behalf of the Grand National Assembly of Turkey, all the accounts relating to the revenue, expenditure and property of government departments financed by the general and subsidiary budgets, with taking final decisions on the acts and accounts of the responsible officials, and with exercising the functions required of it by law in matters of inquiry, auditing and judgment. Parties concerned may file a single request for reconsideration of a final decision of the Audit Court within fifteen days of the date of written notification of the decision. No applications for judicial review of such decisions shall be filed in administrative courts.

In the event of a dispute between the Council of State and the Audit Court concerning decisions on matters of taxation or similar financial obligations and duties, the decision of the Council of State shall take precedence.

The organization, functioning and auditing procedure of the Audit Count, the qualifications, appointments, duties and powers, rights and obligations of its members, other matters relating to their personnel status, and the security of tenure of the President and members shall be regulated by law. The procedure for auditing, on behalf of the Grand National Assembly of Turkey, of State property in possession of the Armed Forces shall be regulated by law in accordance with the principles of secrecy required by National Defence.

PART FOUR

FINANCIAL AND ECONOMIC PROVISIONS

Chapter one. Financial provisions

Art. 161. The expenditures of the State and those of public corporations other than state economic enterprises shall be determined by annual budgets.

The beginning of the fiscal year and the preparation and implementation of the general and subsidiary budgets shall be defined by law.

The law may prescribe special periods and procedures for investments relating to development plans, or for business and service expected to last more than one year.

No provisions other than those pertaining to the budget shall be included in the Budget Act.

Art. 162. The Council of Ministers shall submit the draft of general and subsidiary budgets and the report containing the national budgetary estimates to the Grand National Assembly of Turkey at least seventy-five days before the beginning of the financial year.

The draft budgets and the report shall be considered by the Budget Committee, which shall be composed by forty members. In the composition of this Committee, the proportional representation of the various political party groups and independent members in the Assembly, shall be taken into consideration subject to the allocation of at least twenty five seats to members of the party or parties in power.

The draft budget, which shall be adopted by the Budget Committee within fifty five days shall thereafter be considered by the Assembly and shall be decided on before the beginning of the fiscal year.

Members of the Grand National Assembly of Turkey shall express their opinions on ministerial, departmental and subsidiary budgets during the debates held in Plenary Session on each budget as a whole; the various headings and motions for amendments shall be read out and put to the vote without separate debate.

During debates in the Plenary Session on the draft Budget Act, members of the Grand National Assembly of Turkey shall not make proposals which entail an increase in expenditure or a decrease in revenue.

Art. 163. The appropriations granted under the general and subsidiary budgets shall indicate the limit of expenditure allowed. No provisions shall be included in the budget to the effect that the limit of expenditure may be exceeded in pursuance of a decision of the Council of Ministers. The Council of Ministers shall not be empowered to amend the budget by a decree having force of law. In draft amendments entailing an increase in appropriations under the budget for the current fiscal year and, in draft laws and law proposals providing for additional financial commitments in the budgets for the current or following year, the financial resources which would meet the stated expenditure shall be indicated.

Art. 164. Draft final accounts shall be submitted to the Grand National Assembly of Turkey by the Council of Ministers within seven months of the end of the relevant fiscal year, unless a shorter period is prescribed by law. The Audit Court shall submit its notice of conformity to the Grand National Assembly of Turkey within seventy five days of the submission of the draft final accounts in question.

The draft final accounts shall be placed on the agenda of the budget Committee together with the Draft Budget Act for the new fiscal year. The Budget Committee shall submit the draft Budget Act to the Plenary Assembly in conjunction with the draft final accounts; the Plenary Assembly shall consider, and decide on, the draft final accounts in conjunction with the draft Budget Act for the new fiscal year.

The submission of the draft final accounts and the notice of conformity to the Grand National Assembly of Turkey shall not preclude the auditing of accounts for the relevant year which have not already been dealt with by the Audit Court and shall not indicate that a final decision has been taken on these accounts.

Art. 165. The principles governing the auditing, by the Grand National Assembly of Turkey of the accounts of public establishments and partnerships in which more than half of the capital directly or indirectly belongs to the State, shall be regulated by law.

Chapter two. Economic provisions

Art. 166. The planning of economic, social and cultural development, in particular the speedy, balanced and harmonious development of industry and agriculture throughout the country, and the efficient use of national resources on the basis of detailed analysis and assessment and the establishment of the necessary organization for this purpose are the duty of the State.

Measures to increase national thriftiness and production, to ensure stability in prices and balance in foreign trade transactions, to promote investment and employment, shall be included in the plan; in investments, public benefit and requirements shall be taken into account; the efficient use of resources shall be aimed at. Development activities shall be realized according to this plan.

The procedure and principles governing the preparation of development plans, their approval by the Grand National Assembly of Turkey, their implementation and their revision, and of the prevention of amendments liable to affect the unity of the plan shall be regulated by law.

Art. 167. The State shall take measures to ensure and promote the sound, orderly functioning of the money, credit, capital, goods and services markets;

and shall prevent the formation, in practice or by agreement of monopolies and cartels in the markets.

In order to regulate foreign trade for the benefit of the economy of the country, the Council of Ministers may be empowered by law to introduce or lift additional financial impositions on imports, exports and other foreign transactions in addition to tax and similar impositions.

Art. 168. Natural wealth and resources shall be placed under the control and at the disposal of the State. The right to explore and exploit them belongs to the State. The State may delegate this right to individuals or public corporations for specific periods. Of the natural wealth and resources, those to be explored and exploited by the State in partnership with individuals or public corporations, and those to be directly explored and exploited by individuals, or public corporations shall be subject to the explicit permission of the law. The conditions to be observed in such cases by individuals and public corporations, the procedure and principles governing supervision and control by the State, and the sanctions to be applied shall be prescribed by law.

Art. 169. The State shall enact the necessary legislation and take the necessary measures for the protection of forests and the extension of their areas. Forest areas destroyed by fire shall be reafforested; other agricultural and stock-breeding activities shall not be allowed in such areas. All forests shall be under the care and supervision of the State.

The ownership of the State forests shall not be transferred to others. State forests shall be managed and exploited by the State in accordance with the law. Ownership of these forests cannot be acquired through prescription, nor shall servitude other than that in the public interest be imposed in respect of such forests.

Acts and actions which might damage forests shall not be permitted. No political propaganda which might lead to the destruction of the forests shall be made; no amnesties or pardons to be specifically granted for offences against forests shall be legislated. Offences committed with the intention of burning or destroying forests or reducing forest areas shall not be included within the scope of amnesties or pardons on other occasions.

The restraining of forest boundaries shall be prohibited, except in respect of areas whose preservation as forests is considered technically and scientifically useless but whose conversion into agricultural land has been found definately advantageous, and in respect of fields, vineyards, orchards, olive groves or similar areas which technically and scientifically ceased to be forest before 31 December 1981 and whose use for agricultural or stock-breeding purposes has been found advantageous, and in respect of built-up areas in the vicinity of cities, towns or villages.

Art. 170. Measures shall be introduced by law to secure cooperation between the State and the inhabitants of villages located in or near forests in the supervision and exploitation of forests for the purpose of ensuring their conservation and improving the living conditions of their inhabitants; the law shall also regulate the development of areas which technically and scientifically ceased to be forests before 31 December 1981, the identification of areas whose preservation as forest is considered technically and scientifically useless, their exclusion from forest boundaries, their improvement by the State for the purpose of settling all or some of the inhabitants of forest villages in them, and their allocation to these villages.

The State shall take measures to facilitate the acquisition, by these inhabitants, of farming equipment and other inputs.

The land owned by villagers resettled outside a forest shall immediately be reafforested as a state forest.

Art. 171. The State shall take measures, in keeping with national and economic interests, to promote the development of co-operatives, which shall be primarily designed to increase production and protect consumers.

Co-operatives shall be subject in all respects to the supervision and inspection of the State, and shall not engage in political activities and shall not co-operate with political parties.

Art. 172. The State shall take measures to protect and inform consumers; shall encourage their initiatives to protect themselves.

Art. 173. The State shall take measures to protect and support small traders and craftsmen.

PART FIVE

MISCELLANEOUS PROVISIONS

Art. 174. No provision of the Constitution shall be construed or interpreted as rendering unconstitutional the Reform Laws indicated below, which aim to raise Turkish society above the level of contemporary civilisation and to safeguard the secular character of the Republic, and which were in force on the date of the adoption by referendum of the Constitution of Turkey.

1. Act No. 430 of 3 March 1340 (1924) on the Unification of the Educational System;
2. Act No. 671 of 25 November 1341 (1925) on the Wearing of Hats;
3. Act No. 677 of 30 November 1341 (1925) on the Closure of Dervish Convents and Tombs, the Abolition of the Office of Keeper of Tombs and the Abolition and Prohibition of Certain Titles;
4. The principle of Civil marriage according to which the marriage act shall be concluded in the presence of the competent official, adopted with the Turkish Civil Code No. 743 of 17 February 1926, and Article 110 of the Code;
5. Act No. 1288 of 20 May 1928 on the Adoption of International Numerals;
6. Act No. 1353 of 1 November 1928 on the Adoption and Application of the Turkish Alphabet;
7. Act No. 2590 of 26 November 1934 on the Abolition of Titles and Appellations such as Efendi, Bey or Pasa;
8. Act No. 2596 of 3 December 1934 on the Prohibition of the Wearing of Certain Garments.

PART SIX

PROVISIONAL ARTICLES

Prov. Art. 1. On the Proclamation, under lawful procedure, of the adoption by referendum of the Constitution as the Constitution of the Republic of Turkey, the Chairman of the Council of National Security and Head of State at the time of the referendum, shall assume the title of President of the Republic and shall exercise the constitutional functions and powers of the President and the Republic for a period of seven years. The oath he took as Head of State on 18 September 1980 shall remain valid. At the end of the period of seven years the election for the Presidency of the Republic shall be held in accordance with the provisions set forth in the Constitution.

The President of the Republic shall also hold the chairmanship of the Council of National Security formed on 12 December 1980 under Act No. 2356, until the convening of the Grand National Assembly of Turkey and the formation of the Bureau of the Assembly following the first general elections.

If the Presidency of the Republic falls vacant for any reason before the Grand National Assembly of Turkey convenes and assumes its functions at the end of the first general elections, the most senior members of the Council of National security shall act as President of the Republic and shall exercise all his constitutional functions and powers until the convening of the Grand National Assembly of Turkey and its election of a new President of the Republic in Accordance with the provisions of the Constitution.

Prov. Art. 2. The Council of National Security formed on 12 December 1980 under Act No. 2356 shall continue to exercise its functions under Act No. 2324 on the Constitutional Order and Act No. 2485 on the Constituent Assembly until the convening of the Grand National Assembly of Turkey and the formation of the Bureau of the Assembly following the first general elections held under the Political Parties Act and the Election Act prepared in accordance with the Constitution.

After the adoption of the Constitution, Article 3 of Act No. 2356 relating to the procedure for filling a seat on the Council of National Security which falls vacant for any reason, shall cease to apply.

After the Grand National Assembly of Turkey has convened and assumed its functions, the Council of National Security shall become the Presidential Council for a period of six years, and the members of the Council of National Security shall acquire the title of members of the Presidential Council. The oath they took on 18 September 1980 as members of the Council of National Security shall remain valid. Members of the Presidential Council shall enjoy the rights and immunity conferred by the Constitution on members of the Grand National Assembly of Turkey. The legal existence of the Presidential Council shall terminate on the expiry of the period on six years.

The functions of the Presidential Council shall be as follows:

a. To examine laws adopted by the Grand National Assembly of Turkey and submitted to the President of the Republic concerning: the fundamental rights and freedoms and duties, the principle of secularism, the preservation of the reforms of Atatürk, national security and public order, set forth in the Constitution, the Turkish Radio and Television Corporation, International Treaties, the sending of Armed Forces to foreign countries and the stationing of foreign forces in Turkey, emergency rule, martial law and the state of war, and other laws deemed necessary by the President of the Republic, within the first ten days of the period of fifteen days granted to the President of the Republic for his consideration;

b. On the request of the President of the Republic and within the period specified by him:

To consider and give an opinion on matters relating to: the holding of new general elections, the exercise of emergency powers and the measures to be taken during a state of emergency, the management and supervision of the Turkish Radio and Television Corporation, the training of youth and the conduct of Religious affairs;

c. According to the request of the President of the Republic, to consider and investigate matters relating to internal or external security and such other matters relating to internal or external security and such other matters as are deemed necessary, and to submit its findings to the President of the Republic.

Prov. Art. 3. With the convening of the Grand National Assembly of Turkey and the formation of the Bureau of the Assembly following the first general elections held in accordance with the Constitution:

a. Act No. 2324 of 27 October 1980 on the Constitutional Order;

b. Act No. 2356 of 12 December 1980 on the Council of National Security;

c. Act No. 2485 of 29 June 1981 on the Constituent Assembly.

shall cease to have effect and the legal existence of the Council of National Security and the Consultative Assembly shall terminate.

Prov. Art. 4. (1) Of those political parties dissolved on 16 October 1981 under Act No. 2533:

Those against whose legal personality, or against one of whose central executive officers or one of whose members of Parliament a penal action was brought after 11 September 1980 for any of the offences against the personality of the State set forth in Part II, Chapter 1 of the Turkish Penal Code, and of those political parties which were the party in power, and main opposition party on 11 September 1980:

a. Persons who were chairman, deputy or acting chairman, general secretaries deputy general secretaries and members of the central executive committee or similar organs of those parties on 1 January 1980 and thereafter shall not form political parties for a period of ten years following the adoption by referendum of the Constitution, nor shall they become members of political parties formed under the provisions set forth in the Constitution, or be nominated as candidates by these parties or stand for election either on behalf of such parties or as independent candidates in either general elections by-elections or local elections. They shall not establish relations of any kind with political parties or assume any functions whatsoever in political parties even on an honorary basis.

b. Persons who were members of the Grand National Assembly of Turkey as deputies and senators on 1 January 1980 shall not form political parties for a period of five years following the adoption by referendum of the Constitution, nor shall they hold office in the central executive organs or similar organs of political parties to be formed.

(2) Of those who were senators appointed under the presidential quota *ex-officio* members of the Senate or independent members of the Grand National Assembly of Turkey on 1 January 1980: persons against whom a penal action has been brought for any of the offences against the personality of the State set forth in Part II, Chapter I of the Turkish Penal Code or those who had become members of one of the political parties defined in the first paragraph shall be subject to the provisions of sub-paragraph b.

Prov. Art. 5. On the tenth day following the proclamation by the Supreme Election Council of the results of the first general elections, the Grand National Assembly of Turkey shall convene of its own accord at the premises of the Grand National Assembly of Turkey in Ankara at 15.00 hrs. The eldest Deputy shall take the Chair for this session. At this session the deputies shall take their oaths.

Prov. Art. 6. Until the Grand Natinal Assembly of Turkey formed in accordance with the Constitution, adopts the Rules of Procedure which shall govern its sessions and proceedings, those provisions of the Rules of Procedure of the National Assembly which were in force before 12 September 1980 and which are not contrary to the Constitution shall apply.

Prov. Art. 7. The present Council of Ministers shall continue in office until the convening of the Grand National Assembly of Turkey and the formation of the new Council of Ministers following the first general elections.

Prov. Art. 8. Legislation relating to the organization, duties, powers and functioning of the new organs, institutions and agencies established under the Constitution and other legislation whose introduction of amendment is provided for in the Constitution, shall be enacted during the period of the Constituent Assembly, starting from the date of the adoption of the Constitution; legislation which cannot be dealt with during this period shall be enacted within the year following the first session of the newly elected Grand National Assembly of Turkey.

Prov. Art. 9. Within a period of six years following the formation of the Bureau of the Grand National Assembly of Turkey which is to convene after the first general elections, the President of the Republic may refer to the Grand National Assembly of Turkey for further consideration any Constitutional amendments adpted by the Assembly. In this case the re-submission of the Constitutional amendment draft in its unchanged form to the President of the Republic by the Grand National Assembly of Turkey, is only possible with a three-fourths majority of the votes of the total number of members.

Prov. Art. 10. Local elections shall be held within a year of the first session of the Grand National Assembly of Turkey.

Prov. Art. 11. Regular and substitute members of the Constitutional Court who were in office on the date of the adoption by referendum of the Constitution shall continue to hold office and exercise their functions. Those previously elected by the Constitutional Court to specific functions shall retain the status thus acquired.

No election shall be held to fill the vacant seats of the regular members of the Constitutional Court until the number of these members falls to eleven, nor shall an election be held to fill the vacant seats of substitute members until the total number of regular and substitute members falls to fifteen. Until the Constitutional Court adapts to the new system, the principles and order of precedence set forth in the Constitution shall be observed in the elections which are to be held because the number of regular members has fallen below eleven, or because the total number of regular and substitute members has fallen below fifteen.

Until the number of regular members of the Constitutional Court falls to eleven, the quorum prescribed by Act No. 44 of 22 April 1962 shall be observed in all cases and proceedings.

Prov. Art. 12. Persons appointed by the Head of State as regular and substitute members of the Supreme Judges and Public Prosecutors from among the members of the High Court of Appeals and the Council of State under Provisional Article 1 of Act No. 2461 of 13 May 1981 on the Supreme Council of Judges and Public Prosecutors; as Chief Public Prosecutor and Deputy Chief Public Prosecutor in accordance with the Provisional Article appended to Act No. 1730 on the High Court of Appeals under Act No. 2483 of 25 June 1981; and as President, Chief Public Prosecutor, deputy-presidents and heads of division of the Council of State under Provisional Article 14, paragraph 2 of Act No. 2575 of 6 January 1982 on the Council of State shall continue to exercise their functions until the end of the term of office for which they were elected.

The Provisions of the Provisional Articles of Act No. 2576 of 6 January 1982 which concern the appointment of the Presidents and members of Administrative Courts shall also remain in force.

Prov. Art. 13. The elections of one regular and one substitute member to be elected to the Supreme Council of Judges and Public Prosecutors from among the members of the High Court of Appeals shall take place within twenty days of the entry into force of the Constitution.

Until the assumption of office by the elected members, the quorum for meetins of the Council shall be met with the participation of substitute members.

Prov. Art. 14. The obligation of the labor unions to deposit their revenues in the State banks shall be fulfilled within two years of the entry into force of the Constitution, at the latest.

Prov. Art. 15. No allegation of criminal, financial or legal responsibility shall be made, nor shall an application be filed with a court for this purpose in respect of any decisions or measures whatsoever taken by: the Council of National Security formed under Act No. 2356 which will have exercised legislative and executive power on behalf of the Turkish nation from 12 September 1980 to the date of the formation of the Bureau of the Grand National Assembly of Turkey which is to convene following the first general elections; the governments formed during the term of office of the Council; or the Consultative Assembly which has exercised its function under Act No. 2485 on the Constituent Assembly.

The provisions of the above paragraphs shall also apply in respect of persons who have taken decisions and adopted or implemented measures as part of the implementation of such decisions and measures by the administration or by the competent organs authorities and officials.

No allegation of unconstitutionality shall be made in respect of decisions or measures taken under laws or decrees having force of law enacted during this perior or under Act No. 2324 on the Constitutional Order.

Prov. Art. 16. Persons who fail to participate in the referendum on the Constitution without valid legal or actual reasons despite being entitled to vote and being included on the register of electors and the polling station register compiled for the referendum, shall neither participate nor stand for election in general elections, by-elections, local elections or referendums for a period of five years following the referendum on the Constitution.

PART SEVEN

FINAL PROVISIONS

I. AMENDMENT OF THE CONSTITUTION

Art. 175. Constitutional amendments shall be proposed in writing by at least one third of the total number of members of the Grand National Assembly of Turkey. Proposals to amend the Constitution shall not be considered under urgent procedure. The adoption of a proposal for an amendment shall require a two-thirds majority of the total number of members of the Assembly.

The consideration and adoption of proposals for the amendment of the Constitution shall be subject to the provisions governing the consideration and adoption of legislation, with the exception of the conditions set forth in the first paragraph of this Article.

If the Assembly adopts unchanged a draft law amending the Constitution which has been referred back to it for further consideration by the President of the Republic, the President may submit the law to referendum.

II. PREAMBLE AND HEADINGS OF ARTICLES

Art. 176. The Preamble, which states the basic views and principles underlying the Constitution, shall form an integral part of the Constitution.

The headings of articles merely indicate the subject matter of the articles, their order, and the connections between them. These headings shall not be regarded as a part of the text of the Constitution.

III. ENTRY INTO FORCE OF THE CONSTITUTION

Art. 177. On its adoption by referendum and its publication in the Official Gazette, this Constitution shall become the Constitution of the Republic of Turkey and shall come into force in its entirety, subject to the following exceptions and the provisions relating to their entry into force:

a. The provisions of Part II, Chapter II relating to personal liberty and security, the Press, publication and the media, and the right and freedom of assembly.

The provisions of Chapter III, relating to labor, collective agreements, the right to strike, and lockout.

These provisions shall come into force when the relevant legislation is promulgated, or when the existing legislation is amended, and at the latest, when the Grand National Assembly of Turkey assumes its functions. However until their entry into force, existing legislation and the decrees and decisions of the Council of National Security shall apply.

b. The provisions of Part II relating to political parties and the right to engage in political activities, shall come into force on the promulgation of the new Political Parties Act which is to be prepared in accordance with these provisions;

The right to vote and stand for election shall come into force on the promulgation of the Elections Act, also to be prepared in accordance with these provisions.

c. The provisions of Part III, relating to legislative power:

These provisions shall come into force on the proclamation of the results of the first general elections. However, the provisions relating to the functions and powers of the Grand National Assembly of Turkey which take place in this section shall be exercised by the Council of National Security until the Grand National Assembly of Turkey assumes its functions, the provisions of Act No. 2485 of 29 June 1981 on the Constituent Assembly being reserved.

d. The provisions of Part III relating to the functions and powers of the President of the Republic and to the State Supervisory Council under the heading 'President of the Republic'; to regulations, National Defence, procedures governing the emergency rule under the heading 'Council of Ministers'; to all other provisions under the heading 'Administration' except local administration, and except the Atatürk High Institution of Culture, Language and History; and all the provisions relating to the judiciary power, except the Courts of the Security of the State, shall come into force on the publication in the Official Gazette of the adoption by referendum of the Constitution. The provisions relating to the President of the Republic and the Council of Ministers which do not come into force shall come into force when the Grand National Assembly of Turkey assumes its functions, and the provisions relating to local administrations and to the Courts of the Security of the State shall come into force on the promulgation of the relevant legislation.

e. If new legislation, or amendments to existing legislation are required in connection with the constitutional provisions which are to come into force on the proclamation of the adoption by referendum of the Constitution or in connection with existing or future institutions, organizations and agencies, the procedure to be followed shall be subject to those provisions of existing laws which are not unconstitutional, or to the provisions of the Constitution in accordance with Article 11 of the Constitution.

The second paragraph of Article 164 regulating the procedure for the consideration of draft final accounts shall come into force in 1984.

TUVALU

SUMMARY

INTERNATIONAL STATUS

Tuvalu came under British jurisdiction under the name of the Ellice Islands in 1877. It became a British protectorate in September 1892 and, together with the Gilbert Islands, became the Gilbert (Micronesian) and Ellice (Polynesian) Islands
Tuvalu came under British Jurisdiction under the name of the Ellice Islands in 1877. It became a British protectorate in September 1892 and, together with the Gilbert Islands, became the Gilbert (Micronesian) an Ellice (Polynesian) Islands Colony on January 12, 1916. A referendum in 1974, declared for separation of the two territories and the Ellice Islands were established as a separate colony on October 1, 1975, under their ancient name of Tuvalu.[1]

FORM OF NATIONAL GOVERNMENT

The Constitution of July 25, 1978, provides in the Preamble that the independent state of Tuvalu is based on Christian principles, the rule of law and Tuvaluan custom and tradition, and the people of Tuvalu affirm their allegiance to the Queen of England and her heirs and successors. Tuvalu is a sovereign democratic state.[2] The source of sovereign power is not stated.

RIGHTS OF THE PEOPLE

The Constitution provides protection of the right to life, personal liberty and habeus corpus, protection from slavery and forced labor, from inhuman treatment,

[1] Const., Preamble.
[2] Id., Art. 1.
[3] Id., Art. 3–15.

deprivation of property; protection of the home and other property, fair trial freedom of conscience, expression, assembly, association, movement, freedom from discrimination on grounds of race, origin, political opinions, color or creed.[3] There is a chapter on citizenship.[4]

LEGISLATIVE DEPARTMENT

The Constitution provides for a Parliament of 12 members, directly elected for a term of four years subject to dissolution.[5] Legislation and procedure in Parliament is described.[6] Bills for imposing or increasing taxes or other charges may only be proceeded upon on the recommendation of a Minister.[7] Privileges and immunities of members of Parliament are provided for.[8]

EXECUTIVE DEPARTMENT

The executive authority of Tuvalu is vested in Her Majesty (of Great Britain) and is exercised by a Governor General who is 'Her Majesty's representative in Tuvalu', appointed by the Queen on the advice of the Prime Minister of Tuvalu, and who must be a citizen of Tuvalu.[9] There is a Prime Minister elected by Parliament, and a Cabinet of not more than 4 Ministers appointed by the Governor General on the advice of the Prime Minister from the members of Parliament.[10] The Governor General, has the prerogative of mercy.[11]

JUDICIAL DEPARTMENT

The Constitution provides for a High Court which is a superior court of record.[12] The Chief Justice is appointed by the Governor General acting on the advice of the Prime Minister for such period as is specified in his instrument of appointment.[13] The High Court has original jurisdiction to hear and determine any question as to the interpretation of the Constitution.[14]

AREA, POPULATION, ETC.

The land of Tuvalu, which comprises 9 islands (8 of them inhabited) is 26 square kilometres; these extend over 580 kilometres and its territorial waters cover 1.3 million square kilometres. Its population (1979 census) is 7,349.

[4] Id., Art. 19–27.
[5] Id., Art. 46, 71.
[6] Id., Art. 57–72.
[7] Id., Art. 60.
[8] Id., Art. 69.
[9] Id., Art. 28, 31.
[10] Id., Art. 32–39
[11] Id., Art. 45.
[12] Id., Art. 73.
[13] Id., Art. 74.
[14] Id., Art. 81.

CONSTITUTION OF TUVALU[1]

July 25, 1978

PREAMBLE

Whereas the Islands in the Pacific Ocean then known as the Ellice Islands came under the protection of Her Most Gracious Majesty Queen Victoria in September 1892 and on 12th January 1916 in conjunction with the Gilbert Islands became known as the Gilbert and Ellice Islands Colony;

And whereas on 1st October 1975 Her Most Excellent Majesty Queen Elizabeth II was graciously pleased to establish the Ellice Islands as a separate colony under their ancient name of Tuvalu;

And whereas the people of Tuvalu, acknowledging God as the Almighty and Everlasting Lord and giver of all good things, humbly place themselves under His good providence and seek His blessing upon themselves and their lives;

And whereas the people of Tuvalu desire to constitute themselves as an Independent State based on Christian principles, the Rule of Law, and Tuvaluan custom and tradition;

Now therefore the people of Tuvalu hereby affirm their allegiance to Her Most Excellent Majesty Queen Elizabeth II, Her Heirs and Successors, and do hereby proclaim the establishment of a free and democratic sovereign nation, of which the following provisions shall form the Constitution.

CHAPTER I

THE STATE AND THE CONSTITUTION

1. Tuvalu shall be a sovereign democratic State.

2. This Constitution is the supreme law of Tuvalu and if any other law is inconsistent with this Constitution, that other law shall, to the extent of the.inconsistency be void.

CHAPTER II

FUNDAMENTAL RIGHTS AND FREEDOMS OF THE INDIVIDUAL

3. Whereas every person in Tuvalu is entitled to the fundamental rights and freedoms of the individual, that is to say, the right, whatever his race, place of origin, political opinions, color, creed or sex, but subject to respect for the rights and freedoms of others and for the public interest, to each and all of the following, namely

[1] Tuvalu Gazette Supplement. No. 3 of 1978. December 31, 1978. Supplied by the Office of the Prime Minister June 1979. Ed.

(*a*) life, liberty, security of the person and the protection of the law;
(*b*) freedom of conscience, of expression and of assembly and association; and
(*c*) protection for the privacy of his home and other property and from deprivation of property without compensation,

the provisions of this Chapter shall have effect for the purpose of affording protection to those rights and freedoms subject to such limitations on that protection as are contained in those provisions, being limitations designed to ensure that the enjoyment of the said rights and freedoms by any individual does not prejudice the rights and freedoms of other or the public interest.

4. (1) No person shall be deprived of his life intentionally.

(2) A person shall not be regarded as having been deprived of his life in contravention of this section if he dies as the result of the use, to such extent and in such circumstances as are permitted by law, of such force as is reasonably justifiable

(*a*) for the defence of any person from violence or for the defence of property;
(*b*) in order to effect a lawful arrest or to prevent the escape of a person lawfully detained;
(*c*) for the purpose of suppressing a riot, insurrection or mutiny; or
(*d*) in order to prevent the commission by that person of a criminal offence,

or if he dies as the result of a lawful act of war.

5. (1) No person shall be deprived of his personal liberty save as may be authorized by law in any of the following cases, that is to say

(*a*) in consequence of his unfitness to plead to a criminal charge;
(*b*) in execution of the sentence or order of a court, whether established for Tuvalu or some other country, in respect of a criminal offence of which he has been convicted;
(*c*) in execution of the order of a court of record punishing him for contempt of that court or of a court inferior to it;
(*d*) in execution of the order of a court made to secure the fulfilment of any obligation imposed on him by law;
(*e*) for the purpose of bringing him before a court in execution of the order of a court;
(*f*) upon reasonable suspicion of his having committed, or being about to commit, a criminal offence under the law in force in Tuvalu;
(*g*) in the case of a person who has not attained the age of 18 years, under the order of a court or with the consent of his parent or guardian, for the purpose of his education or welfare;
(*h*) for the purpose of preventing the spread of an infectious or contagious disease;
(*i*) in the case of a person who is, or is reasonably suspected to be, of unsound mind, addicted to drugs or alcohol, or a vagrant, for the purpose of his care or treatment or the protection of the community;
(*j*) for the purpose of preventing the unlawful entry of that person into

Tuvalu, or for the purpose of effecting the expulsion, extradition or other lawful removal of that person from Tuvalu or for the purpose of restricting that person while he is being conveyed through Tuvalu in the course of his extradition or removal as a convicted prisoner from one country to another; or

(*k*) to such extent as may be necessary in the execution of a lawful order requiring that person to remain within a specified area within Tuvalu or prohibiting him from being within such an area, or to such extent as may be reasonably justifiable for the taking of proceedings against that person relating to the making of any such order, or to such extent as may be reasonably justifiable for restraining that person during any visit that he is permitted to make to any part of Tuvalu in which, in consequence of any such order, his presence would otherwise be unlawful.

(3) any person who is arrested or detained

(*a*) for the purpose of bringing him before a court in execution of the order of a court; or

(*b*) upon reasonable suspicion of his having committed, or being about to commit, a criminal offence under the law in force in Tuvalu,

and who is not released, shall be brought without undue delay before a court; and if any person arrested or detained upon reasonable suspicion of his having committed or being about to commit a criminal offence is not tried within a reasonable time, then, without prejudice to any further proceedings that may be brought against him, he shall be released either unconditionally or upon reasonable conditions, including in particular such conditions as are reasonably necessary to ensure that he appears at a later date for trial or for proceedings preliminary to trial.

(4) Any person who is unlawfully arrested or detained by any other person shall be entitled to compensation therefor from that other person.

6. (1) No person shall be held in slavery or servitude.

(2) No person shall be required to perform forced labor.

(3) For the purposes of this section, the expression 'forced labor' does not include

(*a*) any labor required in consequence of the sentence or order of a court;

(*b*) any labor required of any person while he is lawfully detained that, though not required in consequence of the sentence or order of a court, is reasonably necessary in the interests of hygiene or for the maintenance of the place at which he is detained.

(*c*) any labor required of a member of a disciplined force in pursuance of his duties as such or, in the case of a person who has conscientious objections to service as a member of a naval, military or air force, any labor that person is required by law to perform in place of such service;

(*d*) any labor required during any period of public emergency or in the event of any other emergency or calamity that threatens the life and well-being of the community, to the extent that the requiring of such labor is reasonably justifiable in the circumstances of any situation arising or existing during that period or as a result of that other emergency or calamity, for the purpose of dealing with that situation; or

(*e*) any labor reasonably required as part of reasonable and normal communal or other civic obligations.

7. No person shall be subjected to torture or to inhuman or degrading punishment or other treatment.

8. (1) No property of any description shall be compulsorily taken possession of, and no interest in or right over property of any description shall be compulsorily acquired, except where the following conditions are satisfied, that is to say

(*a*) the taking of possession or acquisition is necessary or expedient in the interests of defence, public safety, public order, public morality, public health, town or country planning or the development of utilization of any property in such a manner as to promote the public benefit;

(*b*) there is reasonable justification for the causing of any hardship that may result to any person having an interest in or right over the property; and

(*c*) provision is made by a law applicable to that taking of possession or acquisition

(i) for the prompt payment of adequate compensation; and

(ii) securing to any person having an interest in or right of access to a court of competent jurisdiction, whether direct or on appeal from any other authority, for the determination of his interest or right, the legality of the taking of possession or acquisition of property, interest or right and the amount of any compensation to which he is entitled, and for the purpose of obtaining payment of that compensation.

(2) Nothing contained in or done under the authority of any law shall be held to be inconsistent with or in contravention of this section

(*a*) to the extent that the law in question makes provisions for the taking of possession or acquisition of any property

(i) in satisfaction of any tax, rate or duty;

(ii) by way of penalty for breach of the law or forfeiture in consequence of a breach of the law;

(iii) as an incident of a lease, tenancy, mortgage, charge, bill of sale, pledge or contract;

(iv) in the execution of judgments or orders of a court in proceedings for the determination of civil rights or obligations;

(v) in circumstances where it is reasonably necessary so to do because the property is in a dangerous state or injurious to the health of human beings, animals or plants;

(vi) in consequence of any law with respect to the limitation of actions or acquisitive prescription; or

(vii) for so long only as may be necessary for the purposes of any examination, investigation, trial or inquiry or, in the case of land, the carrying ot thereon

(A) of work of soil conservation or of conservation of other natural resources; or

(B) of work relating to agricultural development or improvement which the owner or occupier of the land has been required, and has without reasonable excuse refused or failed, to carry out,

except so far as that provision or, as the case may be, the thing done under the authority thereof is shown not to be reasonably justifiable in a democratic society; or

(*b*) to the extent that the law in question makes provision for the taking of possession or acquisition of

(i) enemy property;

(ii) property of a deceased person, a person of unsound mind, a person who has not attained the age of 21 years or a person who is absent from Tuvalu, for the purpose of its administration for the benefit of the persons entitled to the beneficial interest therein;

(iii) property of a person declared to be insolvent or a body corporate in liquidation, for the purpose of its administration of the benefit of the creditors of the insolvent or body corporate and, subject thereto, for the benefit of other persons entitled to the beneficial interest in the property; or

(iv) property subject to a trust for the purpose of vesting the property in persons appointed as trustees under the instrument creating the trust or by a court or, by order of a court, for the purpose of giving effect to the trust.

(3) Nothing in this section shall be construed as affecting the making or operation of any law for the compulsory taking of possession in the public interest of any property, or the compulsory acquisition in the public interest of any interest in or right over property, where that property, interest or right is held by a body corporate establshed for public purposes by any law and in which no moneys have been invested other than moneys provided by the Government.

9. (1) Except with his own consent, no person shall be subjected to the search of his person or his property or the entry by others on his premises.

(2) Nothing contained in or done under the authority of any law shall be held to be inconsistent with or in contravention of this section to the extent that the law in question makes provision

(*a*) in the interest of defence, public safety, public order, public morality, public health, town or country planning, the development or utilization of mineral resources, or the development or utilization of any other property in such a manner as to promote the public benefit;

(*b*) for the purpose of protecting the rights or freedoms of other persons;

(*c*) for the purpose of authorizing an officer or agent of the Government, a local government council or a body corporate established by law for a public purpose to enter on the premises of any person in order to inspect those premises or anything thereon for the purpose of any tax, rate or duty or in order to carry out work connected with any property that is lawfully on those premises and that belongs to that Government, council or body corporate, as the case may be;

(*d*) for the purpose of authorizing the entry upon any premises in pursuance of an order of a court for the purpose of enforcing the judgment or order of a court in any proceedings; or

(*e*) for the purpose of authorizing the entry upon any premises for the purpose of preventing or detecting criminal offences,

and except so far as that provision or, as the case may be, anything done under the authority thereof is shown not to be reasonably justifiable in a democratic society.

10. (1) If any person is charged with a criminal offence, then, unless the charge is withdrawn, the case shall be afforded a fair hearing within a reasonable time by an independent and impartial court established by law.

(2) Every person who is charged with a criminal offence

(*a*) shall be presumed to be innocent until he is proved or has pleaded guilty;

(*b*) shall be informed as soon as reasonably practicable, in detail and in a language that he understands, of the nature of the offence charged;

(*c*) shall be given adequate time and facilities for the preparation of his defence;

(*d*) shall be permitted to defend himself before the court in person or, at his own expense, by a representative of his own choice;

(*e*) shall be afforded facilities to examine in person or by his representative the witnesses called by the prosecution before the court, and to obtain the attendance and carry out the examination of witnesses to testify on his behalf before the court on the same conditions as those applying to witnesses called by the prosecution; and

(*f*) shall be permitted to have without payment the assistance of an interpreter if he cannot understand the language used at the trial of the charge,

and, except with his own consent, the trial shall not take place in his absence unless he so conducts himself as to render the continuance of the proceedings in his presence impracticable and the court has ordered him to be removed and the trial to proceed in his absence.

(3) When a person is tried for any criminal offence, the accused person or any person authorized by him in that behalf shall, if he so requires and subject to payment of such reasonable fee as may be prescribed by law, be given within a reasonable time after judgment a copy for the use of the accused person of any record of the proceedings made by or on behalf of the court.

(4) No person shall be held to be guilty of a criminal offence on account of any act or omission that did not, at the time it took place, constitute such an offence, and no penalty shall be imposed for any criminal offence that is severer in degree or description than the maximum penalty that might have been imposed for that offence at the time when it was omitted.

(5) No person who shows that he has been tried by a competent court for a criminal offence and either convicted or acquitted shall again be tried for that offence or for any other criminal offence of which he could have been convicted at the trial for that offence, save upon the order of superior court in the course of appeal or review proceedings relating to the conviction or acquittal.

(6) No person shall be tried for a criminal offence if he shows that he has been pardoned for that offence.

(7) No person who is tried for a criminal offence shall be compelled to give evidence at the trial.

(8) Any court or other adjudicating authority prescribed by law for the determination of the existence or extent of any civil right or obligation shall be established or recognized by law and shall be independent and impartial; and where proceedings for such determination are instituted by any person before such a court or other adjudicating authority, the case shall be given a fair hearing within a reasonable time.

(9) Except with the agreement of all the parties thereto, all proceedings of every court and proceedings for the determination of the existence or extent of any civil right or obligation before any other adjudicating authority, including the announcement of the decision of the court or other authority, shall be held in public.

(10) Nothing in the last preceding sub-section shall prevent the court or other adjudicating authority from excluding from the proceedings persons other than the parties thereto and their representatives in those proceedings to such extnet as the court or other authority

(*a*) may by law be empowered so to do and may consider necessary or expedient in circumstances where publicity would prejudice the interests of justice or in interlocutory proceedings or in the interests of decency, public morality, the welfare of persons under the age of 18 years or the protection of the privacy of persons concerned in the proceedings; or

(*b*) may by law be empowered or required so to do in the interests of defence, public safety or public order.

(11) Nothing contained in or done under the authority of any law shall be held to be inconsistent with or in contravention of

(*a*) sub-section (2)(*a*) of this section to the extent that the law in question imposes upon any person charged with a criminal offence the burden of proving particular facts;

(*b*) sub-section (2)(*e*) of this section to the extent that the law in question imposes reasonable conditions that must be satisfied if witnesses called to testify on behalf of an accused person are to be paid their expenses out of public funds; or

(*c*) sub-section (5) of this section to the extent that the law in question authorizes a court to try a member of a disciplined force for a criminal offence notwithstanding any trial and conviction or acquittal of that member under the disciplinary law of that force, so, however that any court so trying such a member and convicting him shall in sentencing him to any punishment take into account any punishment awarded him under that disciplinary law.

(12) In this section 'criminal offence' means a criminal offence under the law in force in Tuvalu.

11. (1) Except with his own consent, no person shall be hindered in the enjoyment of his freedom of conscience, and for the purposes of this section the said freedom includes freedom of thought and of religion, freedom to change his religion or belief, and freedom, either alone or in community with others, and both in public and in private, to manifest and propagate his religion or belief in worship, teaching, practice and observance.

(2) Every religious community shall be entitled, at its own expense, to establish and maintain places of education and to manage any place of education which it wholly maintains, subject to the maintenance of minimum prescribed educational standards in such places of education.

(3) No religious community shall be prevented from providing religious instruction for persons of that community in the course of any education provided at any place of education which it wholly maintains or in the course of any education which it otherwise provides.

(4) Except with his own consent (or, if he is a person who has not attained the age of 21 years, the consent of his guardian) no person attending any place of education shall be required to receive religious instruction or to take part in or attend any religious ceremony or observance if that instruction, ceremony or observance relates to a religion other than his own.

(5) No person shall be compelled to take any oath which is contrary to his religion or belief or to take any oath in a manner which is contrary to his religion or belief.

(6) Nothing contained in or done under the authority of any law shall be held to be inconsistent with or in contravention of this section to the extent that the law in question makes provision which is reasonably required

(*a*) in the interests of defence, public safety, public order, public morality or public health; or
(*b*) for the purpose of protecting the rights and freedoms of other persons, including the right to observe and practise any religion without the unsolicited intervention of members of any other religion,

and except so far as that provision or, as the case may be, the thing done under the authority thereof is shown not to be reasonably justifiable in a democratic society.

(7) References in this section to a religion shall be construed as including references to a religious denomination, and cognate expressions shall be construed accordingly.

12. (1) Except with his own consent, no person shall be hindered in the enjoyment of his freedom of expression, and for the purposes of this section the said freedom includes the freedom to hold opinions without interference, freedom to receive ideas and information without interference and freedom from interference with his correspondence.

(2) Nothing contained in or done under the authority of any law shall be held to be inconsistent with or in contravention of this section to the extent that the law in question makes provision

(*a*) in the interests of defence, public safety, public order, public morality or public health;
(*b*) for the purpose of protecting the reputations, rights and freedoms of other persons or the privacy of persons concerned in legal proceedings, preventing the disclosure of information received in confidence, maintaining the authority and independence of the courts, or regulating the administration or the technical operation of telephony, telegraphy, posts, wireless, broadcasting or television; or
(*c*) for the imposition of restrictions upon public officers,

and except so far as that provision or, as the case may be, the thing done under the authority thereof is shown not to be reasonalby justifiable in a democratic society.

13. (1) Except with his own consent, no person shall be hindered in the enjoyment of his freedom of assembly and association, that is to say, his right to assemble freely and associate with other persons and in particular to form or belong to political parties or to form or belong to trade unions or other associations for the protection of his interests.

(2) Nothing contained in or done under the authority of any law shall be held to be inconsistent with or in contravention of this section the extent that the law in question makes provision

(*a*) in the interest of defence, public safety, public order, public morality or public health;
(*b*) for the purpose of protecting the rights or freedoms of other persons; or
(*c*) for the imposition of restrictions upon public officers,

and except so far as that provision or, as the case may be, the thing done under the authority thereof is shown not to be reasonably justifiable in a democratic society.

14. (1) No person shall be deprived of his freedom of movement, and for the purposes of this section the said freedom means the right to move freely throughout Tuvalu, the right to reside in any part of Tuvalu, the right to enter and to leave Tuvalu and immunity from expulsion from Tuvalu.

(2) Any restriction on a person's freedom of movement that is involved in his lawful detention shall not be held to be inconsistent with or in contravention of this section.

(3) Nothing contained in or done under the authority of any law shall be held to be inconsistent with or in contravention of this section to the extent that the law in question makes provision

(*a*) for the imposition of restrictions on the movement or residence within Tuvalu of any person or on any person's right to leave Tuvalu that are reasonably required in the interests of defence, public safety or public order;

(*b*) for the imposition of restrictions on the movement or residence within Tuvalu or on the right to leave Tuvalu of persons generally or any class of persons that are reasonably required in the interests of defence, public safety, public order, public morality, public health or environmental conservation;

(*c*) for the imposition of restrictions of the movement of residence within Tuvalu of any person who is not a citizen of Tuvalu or the exclusion or expulsion from Tuvalu of any such person;

(*d*) for the imposition of restrictions on the acquisition or use by any person of land or other property in Tuvalu;

(*e*) for the imposition of restrictions upon the movement or residence within Tuvalu of public officers that are reasonably required for the purpose of ensuring the proper performance of their functions;

(*f*) for the removal of a person from Tuvalu to be tried or punished in some other country for a criminal offence under the law of that other country or to undergo imprisonment in that other country in execution of the sentence of a court in respect of a criminal offence under law in force in Tuvalu of which he has been convicted;

(*g*) for the imposition of restriction , by order of a court, on the movement or residence within Tuvalu of any person or on any person's right to leave Tuvalu either in consequence of his having been found guilty of a criminal offence under the law of Tuvalu or for the purpose of ensuring that he appears before a court at a later date for trial or for proceedings relating to his extradition or lawful removal from Tuvalu; or

(*h*) for the imposition of restrictions on the right of any person to leave Tuvalu in order to secure the fulfilment of any obligations imposed upon that person by law, except so far as the provision or, as the case may be, the thing done under the authority thereof is shown not to be reasonably justifiable in a democratic society.

(4) If any person whose freedom of movement has been restricted by virtue only of such a provision as is referred to in sub-section (3)(*a*) of this section so requests at any time during the period of that restriction not earlier than 6 months after he last made such a request during that period, his case shall be reviewed by an independent and impartial tribunal presided over by a person, qualified to be admitted to practise as an advocate in the High Court in Tuvalu, appointed by the Chief Justice.

(5) On any review by a tribunal in pursuance of the preceding sub-section of the case of a person whose freedom of movement has been restricted, the tribunal may make recommendations concerning the necesity or expediency of continuing the restriction to the authority by which it was ordered but, unless it is otherwise provided by law, that authority shall not be obliged to act in accordance with any such recommendations.

15. (1) Subject to the provisions of sub-sections (4), (5) and (8) of this section, no law shall make any provisions that is discriminatory either of itself or in its effect.

(2) Subject to the provisions of sub-sections (6), (7) and (8) of this section, no person shall be treated in a discriminatory manner by any person acting by virtue of any written law or in the performance of the functions of any public office or any public authority.

(3) In this section, the expression 'discriminatory' means affording different treatment to different persons attributable wholly or mainly to their respective descriptions by race, place of origin, political opinions, color or creed whereby persons of one such description are subjected to disabilities or restrictions to which persons of another such description are not made subject or are accorded privileges or advantages which are not accorded to persons of another such description.

(4) Sub-section (1) of this section shall not apply to any law so far as that law makes provision

(*a*) for the imposition of taxation or the appropriation of revenue by the Government or any local authority or body for local purposes;

(*b*) with respect to persons who are not citizens of Tuvalu;

(*c*) for the application of the law with respect to adoption, marriage, divorce, burial, devolution of property or other like matters that is the personal law applicable to any person;

(*d*) with respect to land, the tenure of land, the resumption and acquisition of land and other like purposes; or

(*e*) where any person or class of persons may be subjected to any disability or restriction or may be accorded any privilege or advantage which, having regard to its nature and to special circumstances pertaining to such person or class of persons, is reasonably justifiable in a democratic society.

(5) Nothing contained in any law shall be held to be inconsistent with or in contravention of sub-section (1) of this section to the extent that it makes provision with respect to standards or qualifications (not being standards or qualifications

specifically relating to race, place of origin, political opinions, color or creed) to be required of any person who is appointed to any office in the public service, any office in a disciplined force, any office in the service of a local authority or any office in a body corporate established directly by any law for public purposes.

(6) Sub-section (2) of this section shall not apply to anything which is expressly or by necessary implication authorized to be done by any such provision of law as is referred to in sub-section (4) or (5) of this section.

(7) Sub-section (2) of this section shall not affect any discretion relating to the institution, conduct or discontinuance of civil or criminal proceedings in any court that is vested in any person by or under this Constitution or any other law.

(8) Nothing contained in or done under the authority of any law shall be held to be inconsistent with or in contravention of this section to the extent that the law in question makes provision whereby any person or class of persons may be subjected to any restriction of the rights and freedoms guaranteed by sections 9, 11, 12, 13 and 14 of this Constitution, being such a restriction as is authorized by section 9(2), 11(6), 12(2), 13(2) or 14(3) respectively, as the case may be.

(9) Nothing contained in or done under the authority of any law shall be held to be inconsistent with the provisions of this section

(*a*) if that law was in force in Tuvalu immediately before Independence Day and has continued in force at all times since that day; or

(*b*) to the extent that the law repeals and re-enacts any provision which has been contained in any enactment in force in Tuvalu at all times since immediately before Independence Day.

16. (1) Nothing contained in or done under the authority of any law shall be held to be inconsistent with or in contravention of section 5, 6(2), 9, 11, 12, 13, 14 or 15 of this Constitution to the extent that the law in question makes in relation to any period of public emergency provision, or authorizes the doing during any such period of any thing, that is reasonably justifiable in the circumstances of any situation arising or existing during the period for the purpose of dealing with that situation.

(2) Where a person is detained by virtue of a law that authorizes the taking during a period of public emergency of measures that are reasonably justifiable for the purpose of dealing with the situation that exists in Tuvalu during that period, the following provisions shall apply, that is to say

(*a*) he shall, as soon as reasonably practicable and in any case not more than 10 days after the commencement of his detention, be furnished with a statement in writing, in a language that he understands, specifying in detail the grounds upon which he is detained;

(*b*) not more than 14 days after the commencement of his detention, a notification shall be published in the *Gazette* stating that he has been detained and giving particulars of the provision of law under which his detention is authorized;

(*c*) not more than one month after the commencement of his detention and thereafter during his detention at intervals of not more than 6 months, his case shall be reviewed by an independent and impartial tribunal established by law and presided over by a person appointed by the Chief Justice from among persons qualified to practise as advocates in the High Court in Tuvalu;

(*d*) he shall be afforded reasonable facilities to consult a representative of his own choice who shall be permitted to make representations to the tribunal; and

(*e*) at the hearing of his case by the tribunal he shall be permitted to appear in person or by a representative of his own choice.

(3) On any review by a tribunal in pursuance of this section of the case of a detained person, the tribunal may make recommendations concerning the necessity or expediency of continuing his detention to the authority by which it was ordered but, unless it is otherwise provided by law, that authority shall not be obliged to act in accordance with any such recommendations.

(4) Nothing contained in sub-sections (2)(*d*) or (*c*) of this section shall be construed as entitling a person to representation at public expense.

17. (1) Subject to the provisions of sub-section (6) of this section, if any person alleges that any of the provisions of sections 3 to 16 (inclusive) of this Constitution has been, is being or is likely to be contravened in relation to him (or, in the case of a person who is detained, if any other person alleges such a contravention in relation to the detained person) then, without prejudice to any other action with respect to the same matter which is lawfully available, that person (or that other person) may apply to the High Court for redress.

(2) The High Court shall have original jurisdiction

(*a*) to hear and determine any application made by any person in pursuance of the preceding sub-section;

(*b*) to determine any question arising in the case of any person which is referred to in pursuance of the next following sub-section,

and may make such orders, issue such writs and give such directions as it may consider appropriate for the purpose of enforcing or securing the enforcement of any of the provisions of sections 3 to 16 (inclusive) of this Constitution:

Provided that the High Court may decline to exercise its powers under this subsection if it is satisfied that adequate means of redress for the contravention alleged are or have been available to the person concerned under any other law.

(3) If in any proceedings in any subordinate court any question arises as to the contravention of any of the provisions of sections 3 to 16 (inclusive) of this Constitution, the person presiding in that court may, and shall if any part to the proceedings so requests, refer the question to the High Court unless, in his opinion, the raising of the question is merely frivolous or vexatious.

(4) Any person aggrieved by any determination of the High Court under this section may appeal therefrom to the Court of Appeal:

Provided that no appeal shall lie from a determination of the High Court under this section dismissing an application on the ground that it is frivolous or vexatious.

(5) Parliament may confer upon the High Court powers additional to those

conferred by this section for the purpose of enabling that court more effectively to exercise the jurisdiction conferred upon it by this section.

(6) Rules of court making provisions with respect to the practice and procedure of the High Court in relation to the jurisdiction conferred on it by or under this section (including rules with respect to the time within which any application or reference shall or may be made or brought) may be made by the person or authority for the time being having power to make rules of court with respect to the practice and procedure of that court generally.

18. (1) In this Chapter, unless the context otherwise requires

'contravention', in relation to any requirement, includes a failure to comply with that requirement, and cognate expressions shall be construed accordingly;

'court' means any court of law having jurisdiction in Tuvalu, other than a court established by a disciplinary law, and includes Her Majesty in Council and in sections 5 and 6 of this Constitution a court established by a disciplinary law;

'disciplinary law' means a law regulating the discipline of any disciplined force;

'disciplined force' means

(*a*) any naval, military or air force;

(*b*) the Tuvalu Police; or

(*c*) any other constabulary or police force or any prison service established by Parliament;

'member', in relation to a disciplined force, includes any person who, under the law regulating the discipline of that force, is subject to that discipline.

(2) Nothing contained in section 12, 13 or 14 of this Constitution shall be construed as precluding the inclusion in the terms and conditions of service of public officers of reasonable requirements as to their communication or association with other persons or as to their movements or residence.

(3) In relation to any person who is a member of a disciplined force of Tuvalu, nothing contained in or done under the authority of the disciplinary law of that force shall be held to be inconsistent with or in contravention of any of the provisions of this Chapter other than sections 4, 6 and 7.

(4) In relation to any person who is a member of a disciplined force that is not a disciplined force of Tuvalu and who is present in Tuvalu in pursuance of arrangements made between the Government of Tuvalu and another Government or an international organization, nothing contained in or done under the authority of the disciplinary law of that force shall be held to be inconsistent with or in contravention of any of the provisions of this Chapter.

(5) No measures takin in relation to a person who is a member of a disciplined force of a country with which Tuvalu is at war and no law, to the extent that it authorizes the taking of any such measures, shall be held to be inconsistent with or in contravention of any of the provisions of this Chapter.

(6) In this Chapter 'period of public emergency' means any period during which

(*a*) Tuvalu is engaged in any war; or

(*b*) there is in force a proclamation by the Governor General, acting in accordance with the advice of the Prime Minister, declaring that a state of public emergency exists.

(7) Without prejudice to the power of the Governor General, acting as aforesaid, to revoke at any time a proclamation made for the purpose of the preceding sub-section, such a proclamation shall lapse at the expriation of 3 days (or, in the case of a proclamation made otherwise than during a session of Parliament, 14 days) from the date it was made unless it has in the meantime been approved by a resolution of Parliament, and a proclamation that has been so approved shall remain in force so long as the resolution remains in force and no longer.

(8) A resolution of Parliamen passed for the purposes of the preceding sub-section shall remain in force for such period not exceeding 6 months as may be specified therein:

Provided that any such resolution may be extended from time to time by a further such resolution, each extension being for such period not exceeding 6 months from the date of the resolution effecting the extension as may be specified therein.

CHAPTER III

CITIZENSHIP

19. (1) Every person who, having been born in Tuvalu, is on the day prior to Independence Day a citizen of the United Kingdom and Colonies or a British protected person shall become a citizen of Tuvalu on Independence Day.

(2) Every person who, havng been born outside Tuvalu, is on the day prior to Independence Day a citizen of the United Kingdom and Colonies or a British protected person shall, if one of his parents was born in Tuvalu, become a citizen of Tuvalu on Independence Day.

(3) Every person who on the day prior to Independence Day was deemed to belong to Tuvalu by section 18 of the Constitution set out in Schedule 2 to the Tuvalu Order 1975 shall become a citizen of Tuvalu on Independence Day.

(4) Every person who on the day prior to Independence Day is the wife or child of a person who becomes, or would but for this death have become, a citizen of Tuvalu by virtue of sub-section (3) of this section shall become a citizen of Tuvalu on Independence Day.

(5) Every person who before Independence Day has in accordance with Tuvalu customary law been adopted by a person who becomes, or would but for his death have become, a citizen of Tuvalu by virtue of sub-section (1), (2), (3) or (4) of this section shall become a citizen of Tuvalu on Independence Day.

(6) Every person who, on the day prior to Independence Day, is a citizen of the United Kingdom and Colonies or a British protected person

(*a*) having acquired such status under the British Nationality Acts 1948 to 1965 by virtue of his having been naturalized or registered under those Acts, or naturalized as a British subject before 1949, while resident in Tuvalu; or

(*b*) one of whose parents was so naturalized or registered,

shall become a citizen of Tuvalu on Independence Day.

(7) Every woman who, having been married to a person who becomes, or would but for this death have become, a citizen of Tuvalu by virtue of sub-section (1), (2) or (6) of this section, acquired the status of citizen of the United Kingdom and Colonies or British Protected person, automatically or by registration on the grounds of that marriage, and who possesses that status on the day prior to Independence Day, shall become a citizen of Tuvalu on Independence Day.

20. Every person who does not become a citizen of Tuvalu on Independence Day by virtue of section 19 of this Constitution but who on the day prior to Independence Day was deemed to belong to Tuvalu pursuant to section 16 of the Constitution set out in Schedule 2 to the Tuvalu Orders 1975 shall be entitled, upon making application in such manner as may be prescribed within two years after Independence Day, to be registered as a citizen of Tuvalu:

Provided that no person who is a national of another country shall be registered as a citizen of Tuvalu under this section unless at the time of this application he renounces his nationality of that other country or, if the law of that other country does not permit him to renounce his nationality of that other country, makes such declaration as may be prescribed.

21. any person who

(*a*) has attained the age of 18 years before Independence Day;

(*b*) becomes a citizen of Tuvalu by virtue of section 19 of this Constitution; and

(*c*) is a national of some other country.

shall cease to be a citizen of Tuvalu at the expiry of a period of two years after Independence Day or such longer period as may be prescribed, unless before the expiry of that period he has renounced or lost his nationality of that other country or, if the law of other country does not permit him to renounce his nationality of that other country, made such declaration as may be prescribed.

22. Every person born in Tuvalu after the day prior to Indepencence Day shall become a citizen of Tuvalu at the date of his birth:

Provided that a person shall not become a citizen of Tuvalu by virtue of this section if at the time of his birth

(*a*) his father possesses such immunity from suit and legal process as is accorded to any envoy of a foreign sovereign power accredited to Tuvalu and neither of his parents is a citizen of Tuvalu; or

(*b*) his father is a citizen of a country with which Tuvalu is at war and the birth occurs in a place then under occupation by such country.

23. A person born outside Tuvalu after the day prior to Independence Day shall become a citizen of Tuvalu at the date of his birth if at that date either of his parents is, or would but for his death have been, a citizen of Tuvalu.

24. Any person who after the day prior to Independence Day marries a person who is or becomes a citizen of Tuvalu shall be entitled, upon making application in such manner as may be prescribed, to be registered as a citizen of Tuvalu:

Provided that the right to be registered as a citizen of Tuvalu under this section shall be subject to such exceptions and qualifications as may be prescribed in the interests of national security or public policy.

25. (1) Every person who under this Constitution or any other law is a citizen of Tuvalu or under any enactment for the time being in force in any country to which this section applies is a citizen of that country shall, by virtue of that citizenship, have the status of a Commonwealth citizen.

(2) Every person who is a British subject without citizenship under the British Nationality Act 1948, continues to be a British subject under section 2 of that Act or is a British subject under the British Nationality Act 1965 shall, by virtue of that status, have the status of a Commonwealth citizen.

(3) Save as may be otherwise provided by Parliament, the countries to which this section applies are Australia, The Bahamas, Bangladesh, Barbados, Botswana, Canada, Cyprus, Fiji, The Gambia, Ghana, Grenada, Guyana, India, Jamaica, Kenya, Lesotho, Malawi, Malaysia, Malta, Mauritius, Nauru, New Zealand, Nigeria, Papua New Guinea, Seychelles, Sierra Leone, Singapore, Solomon Islands, Southern Rodesia, Sri Lanka, Swaziland, Tanzania, Tonga, Trinidad and Tobago, Uganda, The United Kingdom and Colonies, Western Samoa and Zambia.

26. Parliament may make provision

(*a*) for the acquisition of citizenship of Tuvalu by persons who are not eligible or who are no longer eligible to become citizens of Tuvalu by virtue of the provisions of this Chapter;

(*b*) for depriving of his citizenship of Tuvalu any person who is a citizen of Tuvalu otherwise than by virtue of section 19, 22 or 23 of this Constitution;

(*c*) for the renunciation by any person of his citizenship of Tuvalu;

(*d*) for the maintenance of a register of citizens of Tuvalu who are also nationals of other countries;

(*e*) for depriving of his citizenship of Tuvalu any citizen of Tuvalu who has attained the age of 18 years after the day prior to Independence Day and who, being a national of some other country, has not, within such period after his attainment of that age as may be prescribed, renounced his nationality of that other country or, if the law of that other country does not permit him to renounce his nationality of that other country, made such declaration as may be prescribed; or

(*f*) for prescribing anything which under this Chapter needs to be prescribed.

27. (1) In this Chapter, 'British protected person' means a person who is a British protected person for the purposes of the British Nationality Act 1948.

(2) Any reference in this Chapter to the father of a person shall, in relation to a person born out of wedlock, be construed as a reference to the mother of that person.

(3) For the purposes of this Chapter, a person born aboard a registered ship or aircraft, or aboard an unregistered ship or aircraft of the government of any country, shall be deemed to have been born in the place in which the ship or aircraft was registered or, as the case may be, in that country.

CHAPTER IV

THE GOVERNOR GENERAL

28. (1) There shall be a Governor General of Tuvalu who shall be Her Majesty's representative in Tuvalu.

(2) The Governor General shall be appointed, and may be removed from office, by Her Majesty acting in accordance with the advice of the Prime Minister tendered after the Prime Minister has in confidence consulted the members of Parliament.

(3) No person shall be appointed to the office of Governor General unless he is a citizen of Tuvalu.

29. Whenever the office of Governor General is vacant or the holder of the office is absent from Tuvalu or is for any other reason unable to perform the functions of his office, those functions shall be performed by such person as Her Majesty, acting in accordance with the advice of the Prime Minister tendered after the Prime Minister has in confidence consulted the members of Parliament, may appoint or, if there is no such person in Tuvalu so appointed and able to perform those functions, by the Speaker.

30. A person appointed to the office of Governor General or assuming the functions of that office under the preceding section shall, before entering upon the duties of that office, take and subscribe the oath of allegiance and the oath of office as prescribed by Annex 2 to this Constitution, such oaths being administered by the Chief Justice or such other person as may be designated by the Chief Justice.

CHAPTER V

THE EXECUTIVE

31. (1) The executive authority of Tuvalu is vested in Her Majesty.

(2) Save as otherwise provided in this Constitution, that authority may be exercised on behalf of Her Majesty by the Governor General either directly or through officers subordinate to him.

(3) Nothing in this section shall preclude persons or authorities other than the Governor General from exercising such functions as may be conferred upon them by any law.

32. (1) There shall be a Prime Minister who shall be elected as such in accordance with the provisions of Annex 1 to this Constitution.

(2) There shall be, in addition to the office of Prime Minister, such other offices of Minister of the Government, not exceeding 4 as may be established by the Governor General, acting in accordance with the advice of the Prime Minister.

(3) The Ministers other than the Prime Minister shall be appointed by the Governor General, acting in accordance with the advice of the Prime Minister, from among the members of Parliament:

Provided that if occasion arises for making an appointment while Parliament is dissolved a person who was a member of Parliament immediately before the dissolution may be appointed.

33. (1) The office of Prime Minister shall become vacant

(*a*) upon the happening of any of the events specified in paragraph (*a*), (*b*) or (*c*) of sub-section (2) of this section; or

(*b*) if a motion of no confidence in the Government receives in Parliament the affirmative votes of a majority of all the members.

(2) The office of a Minister other than the Prime Minister shall become vacant

(*a*) when, after a general election, the members of Parliament meet, in accordance with the provisions of Annex 1 to this Constitution, to elect the Prime Minister;

(*b*) if he ceases to be a member of Parliament for any reason other than a dissolution of Parliament;

(*c*) if he resigns such office by writing under his hand addressed to the Governor General;

(*d*) if his appointment to the office of Minister is revoked by the Governor General, acting in accordance with the Prime Minister; or

(*e*) upon the election of any person to the office of Prime Minister in accordance with the provisions of Annex 1 to this Constitution.

(3) Subject to the next following sub-section, during any period when the office of Prime Minister is vacant, the person who held that office immediately before the vacancy arose shall continue to perform the functions of Prime Minister until a person is elected to the office of Prime Minister in accordance with the provisions of Annex 1 to this Constitution:

Provided that a person performing the functions of Prime Minister under this sub-section shall not have the power to advise Her Majesty to remove the Governor General from office.

(4) If the person holding the office of Prime Minister dies, the Governor General shall, after consultation with the other Ministers, appoint one of them to perform the functions of Prime Minister until a person is elected to the office of Prime Minister in accordance with the provisions of Annex 1 to this Constitution.

(5) Any question whether the office of Prime Minister or of a Minister has become vacant shall be determined by the Governor General, *acting in his own deliberate judgment.*

34. (1) Whenever the Prime Minister is unable, by reason of illness or absence from Tuvalu, to perform the functions conferred on him by this Constitution, the Governor General may, by directions in writing, authorize some other Minister to perform those functions (other than the functions conferred by this section) and that Minister may perform those functions until his authority is revoked by the Governor General.

(2) Whenever a Minister is unable, by reason of illness or absence from Tuvalu, to perform his functions as a Minister, or has been authorized under the

preceding sub-section to perform the functions of Prime Minister, the Governor General may, by directions in writing, appoint a member of Parliament who is not already a Minister to be temporarily a Minister and that member may act as a Minister until his authority is revoked by the Governor General:

Provided that if occasion arises for making an appointment while Parliament is dissolved a person who was a member of Parliament immediately before the dissolution may be appointed.

(3) Subject to the provisions of this section, the provisions of this Constitution shall apply to a person appointed to be temporarily a Minister under the preceding sub-section as they apply in relation to the Minister in whose place he has been temporarily appointed.

(4) The powers of the Governor General under this section shall be exercised by him in accordance with the advice of the Prime Minister:

Provided that if the Governor General, *acting in his own deliberate judgment*, considers that it is impracticable to obtain the advice of the Prime Minister owing to the Prime Minister's illness or absence, the Governor General may exercise those powers without that advice and in his own deliberate judgment.

35. (1) There shall be a Cabinet for Tuvalu, consisting of the Prime Minister and the other Ministers.

(2) The functions of the Cabinet shall be to advise the Governor General upon the government of Tuvalu and the Cabinet shall be collectively responsible to Parliament for any adivce given to the Governor General by or under the general authority of the Cabinet and for all things done by or under the authority of any Minister in the execution of his office.

(3) The provisions of the preceding sub-section shall not apply in relation to the appointment and removal from office of Ministers, the assigning of responsibility to any Minister under section 38 of this Constitution, the authorization of any Minister to perform the functions of Prime Minister, or the appointment of a member of Parliament to be temporarily a Minister.

36. Before assuming the functions of his office every member of the Cabinet shall make before the Governor General, or some person authorized in that behalf by the Governor General, an oath of allegiance and an oath for the due execution of his office in the form set out in Annex 2 to this Constitution.

37. (1) The Cabinet shall be summoned by the Prime Minister.

(2) The Prime Minister shall, so far as is practicable, attend and preside at all meetings of the Cabinet.

(3) No business except that of adjournment shall be transacted in the Cabinet if objection is taken by any member present that there are less than 3 members present.

(4) Subject to the provisions of the preceding sub-section, the Cabinet shall not be disqualified for the transaction of business by reasons of any vacancy in its membership, and any proceedings of the Cabinet shall be valid notwithstanding that some person who was not entitled to do so took part in those proceedings.

(5) The Prime Minister shall decide what business shall be considered at any meeting of the Cabinet.

(6) The person presiding in the Cabinet may summon any person to a meeting of the Cabinet, notwithstanding that that person is not a member of the Cabinet, when in the opinion of the person presiding the business before the Cabinet makes the presence of that person desirable.

38. The Governor General, acting in accordance with the advice of the Prime Minister, may, by directions in writing, assign to the Prime Minister or any other Minister responsibility for the conduct (subject to the provisions of this Constitution and any other law) of any business of the Government, including responsibility for the administration of any ministry in the Government.

39. (1) in the exercise of his functions under this Constitution or any other law, the Governor General shall act in accordance with the advice of the Cabinet or of a Minister acting under the general authority of the Cabinet except in cases where he is required by this Constitution to act in accordance with the advice of, or after consultation with, any person or authority other than the Cabinet or in his own deliberate judgment.

(2) Where the Governor General is required by this Constitution to exercise any function after consultation with any person or authority other than the Cabinet, he shall not be obliged to exercise that function in accordance with the advice of that person or authority.

(3) Where the Governor General is required by this Constitution to act in accordance with the advice of, or after consultation with, any person or authority, the question whether he has in any matter so acted shall not be called in question in any court of law.

40. The Prime Minister shall keep the Governor General informed concerning the general conduct of the government of Tuvalu and shall furnish the Governor General with such information as he may request with respect to any particular matter relating to the government of Tuvalu.

41. Where any Minister has been charged with responsibility for the administration of any ministry in the Government, he shall exercise direction and control over that ministry and, subject to such direction and control, any ministry in the charge of a Minister shall be under the supervision of a Secretary whose office shall be a public office:

Provided that the office of the Prime Minister and any ministry for which the Prime Minister has direct responsibility shall be under the supervision of the Secretary to Government.

42. (1) There shall be a Secretary to Government, whose office shall be a public office.

(2) The Secretary to Government shall be responsible, in accordance with such instructions as may be given to him by the Cabinet, for coordinating the work of all ministries and offices of the Government, for arranging the business for, and keeping the minutes of, the Cabinet and for conveying the decisions of the Cabinet to the appropriate person or authority, and shall have such other functions as the Cabinet or the Prime Minister may direct.

43. (1) There shall be an Attorney General for Tuvalu whose office shall be a public office and who shall be the principal legal adviser to the Government.

(2) The Attorney General shall be appointed, and may be removed from office, by the Governor General acting in accordance with the advice of the Prime Minister.

(3) No person shall be qualified to hold or to act in the office of Attorney General unless he is entitled to practise in Tuvalu as an advocate in the High Court.

(4) Unless he has been excused by or under the authority of Parliament, the Attorney General shall attend all sittings of Parliament, and shall be entitled to take part in the proceedings of Parliament but shall not have a vote.

(5) Unless he has been excused by or under the authority of the Prime Minister, the Attorney General shall attend all meetings of the Cabinet.

(6) The Attorney General shall have power in any case in which he considers it desirable to do so

(*a*) to institute and undertake criminal proceedings against any person before any court (other than a court-martial) in respect of any offence alleged to have been committed by that person;

(*b*) to take over and continue any such criminal proceedings that have been instituted or undertaken by any other person or authority; and

(*c*) to discontinue at any stage before judgment is delivered any such criminal proceedings instituted or undertaken by himself or any other person or authority.

(7) The powers of the Attorney General under the preceding sub-section may be exercised by him in person or by officers subordinate to him acting in accordance with his general or specific instructions.

(8) Subject to the provisions of the preceding sub-section, the powers conferred on the Attorney General by sub-section (6)(*b*) and (*c*) of this section shall be vested in him to the exclusion of any other person or authority:

Provided that where any other person or authority has instituted criminal proceedings, nothing in this sub-section shall prevent the withdrawal of those proceedings by or at the instance of that person or authority and with the leave of the court.

(9) In the exercise of the functions vested in him by sub-section (6) of this section the Attorney General shall not be subject to the direction or control of any other person or authority.

(10) For the purposes of this section, any appeal from any judgment in any criminal proceedings before any court, or any case stated or question of law reserved for the purpose of any such proceedings, to any other court or to Her Majesty in Council shall be deemed to be part of those proceedings:

Provided that the power conferred on the Attorney General by sub-section (6) (*c*) of this section shall not be exercised in relation to any appeal by a person convicted in any criminal proceedings or to any case stated or question of law reserved at the instance of such a person.

44. Subject to the provisions of this Constitution and of any other law, the

Governor General may constitute offices for Tuvalu, make appointments to any such office and terminate any such appointment.

45. The Governor General may, in Her Majesty's name and on Her Majesty's behalf

(*a*) grant to any person a pardon for any offence under the law of Tuvalu, either free or subject to lawful conditions;

(*b*) grant to any person a respite, either indefinite or for a specified period, of the execution of any punishment imposed on that person for such an offence;

(*c*) substitute a less severe form of punishment for any punishment imposed on any person for such an offence; or

(*d*) remit the whole or part of any punishment imposed on any person for such an offence or of any penalty of forfeiture otherwise due to the Crown on account of such an offence.

CHAPTER VI

PARLIAMENT

Part I. Composition of Parliament

46. There shall be a Parliament for Tuvalu, which shall consist of 12 members who shall be directly elected in accordance with the provisions of this Constitution and, subject thereto, in such manner as may be prescribed by Parliament.

47. For the purpose of the election of the members of Parliament, electoral districts shall be established within Tuvalu having such boundaries and such number of elected representatives as may be prescribed by Parliament.

48. Subject to the provisions of the next following section, a person shall be qualified to be elected as a member of Parliament if, and shall not be so qualified unless,

(*a*) he is a citizen of Tuvalu; and

(*b*) he has attained the age of 21 years.

49. (1) No person shall be qualified to be elected as a member of Parliament who

(*a*) is, by virtue of his own act, under any acknowledgement of allegiance, obedience or adherence to a foreign power or state;

(*b*) has been adjudged or otherwise declared bankrupt under any law for the time being in force in any part of the Commonwealth and has not been discharged;

(*c*) is certified to be insane or otherwise adjudged to be of unsound mind under any law for the time being in force in Tuvalu;

(*d*) is under sentence of death imposed on him by a court in any part of the Commonwealth, or is serving a sentence of imprisonment by whatever name called) for a term of or exceeding 12 months, imposed on him by such a court or substituted by competent authority for some other sentence imposed on him by such a court;

(*e*) is disqualified from membership of Parliament under any law for the time being in force in Tuvalu relating to offences connected with elections; or

(*f*) subject to such exemptions as may be prescribed by any law in force in Tuvalu, holds, or is acting in, any public office.

(2) For the purposes of paragraph (*d*) of the preceding sub-section

(*a*) 2 or more terms of imprisonment that are required to be served consecutively shall be regarded as a single term of imprisonment for the aggregate period of those terms; and

(*b*) no account shall be taken of a sentence of imprisonment imposed as an alternative to or in default of the payment of a fine.

50. The seat of a member of Parliament shall become vacant

(*a*) on a dissolution of Parliament;

(*b*) if he is absent from the sittings of Parliament for such period and in such circumstances as may be prescribed in the rules of procedure of Parliament;

(*c*) if he resigns his seat by writing under his hand addressed to the Speaker;

(*d*) if, being the Speaker, he announces the resignation of his seat to Parliament or, by writing under his hand addressed to Parliament and received by the Clerk of Parliament, he resigns his seat;

(*e*) if any circumstances arise which, if he were not a member of Parliament, would cause him not to be qualified for election thereto under paragraph (*a*) of section 48 of this Constitution or to be disqualified for election thereto by virtue of paragraph (*a*), (*b*), (*c*), (*e*) or (*f*) of sub-section (1) of the preceding section;

(*f*) if, having a pecuniary interest in any matter under discussion in Parliament, he votes on that matter or, without first having disclosed the full nature of his interest to Parliament, he takes part in discussion of that matter; or

(*g*) in the circumstances specified in the next following section.

51. (1) Subject to the provisions of this section, if a member of Parliament is sentenced by a court in any part of the Commonwealth to death or to imprisonment (by whatever name called) for a term of or exceeding 12 months, he shall forthwith cease to discharge his functions as a member of Parliament, and his seat in Parliament shall become vacant at the expiration of a period of 30 days thereafter:

Provided that the Speaker may, at the request of the member, from time to time extend that period of 30 days to enable the member to pursue any appeal in respect of his conviction or sentence, so however that extensions of time exceeding in the aggregate 150 days shall not be granted without the approval of Parliament signified by resolution.

(2) If at any time before the member vacates his seat he receives a free pardon or his conviction is set aside or his sentence is reduced to a term of imprisonment of less than 12 months or a punishment other than imprisonment is substi-

tuted, his seat in Parliament shall not become vacant under the provisions of the preceding sub-section and he may again discharge his functions as a member of Parliament.

(3) For the purposes of this section

(*a*) 2 or more terms of imprisonment that are required to be served consecutively shall be regarded as a single term of imprisonment for the aggregate period of those terms; and

(*b*) no account shall be taken of a sentence of imprisonment imposed as an alternative to or in default of the payment of a fine.

52. (1) The High Court shall have jurisdiction to hear and determine any question whether

(*a*) any person has been validly elected as a member of Parliament; or

(*b*) any member of Parliament has vacated his seat therein or is required by virtue of the preceding section to cease to perform his functions as a member.

(2) An application to the High Court for the determination of

(*a*) any question under paragraph (*a*) of the preceding sub-section may be made by any person entitled to vote in the electoral district, and at the election, to which the application relates or by any person who was a candidate in that district at that election or by the Attorney General;

(*b*) any question under paragraph (*b*) of the preceding sub-section may be made by any person entitled to vote at an election in the electoral district for which the member concerned was returned or by any member of Parliament or by the Attorney General:

Provided that if such an application is made by a person other than the Attorney General, the Attorney General may intervene and may then appear or be represented in the proceedings.

(3) Parliament may make provision with respect to

(*a*) the circumstances and manner in which and the imposition of conditions upon which any application may be made to the High Court for the determination of any question under sub-section (1) of this section; and

(*b*) the powers, practice and procedure of the High Court in relation to any such application.

(4) No appeal shall lie from any decision of the High Court in proceedings under sub-section (1) of this section.

53. (1) Any person who sits or votes in Parliament knowing or having reasonable grounds for knowing that he is not entitled to do so shall be liable to a penalty not exceeding $20 for each day upon which he so sits or votes.

(2) Any such penalty shall be recoverable by civil action in the High Court at the suit of the Attorney General.

54. (1) Subject to the provisions of the next following section, a person shall be entitled to be registered as an elector if, and shall not be so entitled unless

(*a*) he is a citizen of Tuvalu;
(*b*) he has attained the age of 18 years; and
(*c*) he satisfies such other requirements, whether as to residence or otherwise, as may be prescribed.

(2) No person shall be registered as an elector in more than one electoral district.

55. No person shall be entitled to be registered as an elector who

(*a*) has been sentenced by a court in any part of the Commonwealth to death or to imprisonment (by whatever name called) for a term exceeding 12 months and has not been granted a free pardon:

Provided that if 3 years or more have elapsed since the termination of the imprisonment the person convicted shall not be disqualified from registration as an elector by reason only of such conviction; or

(*b*) is certified to be insane or otherwise adjudged to be of unsound mind under any law for the time being in force in Tuvalu; or

(*c*) is disqualified for registering as an elector or from voting under any law for the time being in force in Tuvalu relating to offences connected with elections.

56. (1) Any person who is registered as an elector in an electoral district shall be entitled to vote in such manner as may be prescribed by Parliament at any election for the electoral district unless he is prohibited from so voting by any law in force in Tuvalu because

(*a*) he is a returning officer; or
(*b*) he has been concerned in any offence connected with elections:

Provided that no such person shall be entltled so to vote if on the date prescribed for polling his is in lawful custody or (except so far as may be otherwise presecribed) he is for any other reason unable to attend in person at the place and time prescribed for polling.

(2) No person shall vote at any election for any electoral district who is not registered as an elector in that district.

Part II. Legislation and Procedure in Parliament

57. Subject to the provisions of this Constitution, Parliament may make laws for the peace, order and good government of Tuvalu.

58. (1) The power of Parliament to make laws shall be exercisable by Bills passed by Parliament and assented to by the Governor General on behalf of Her Majesty.

(2) When a Bill is submitted to the Governor General for assent in accordance with the provisions of this Constitution he shall signify that he assents or that he withholds assent.

(3) When the Governor General assents to a Bill that has been submitted to him in accordance with the provisions of this Constitution the Bill shall become law and the Governor General shall thereupon cause it to be published in the *Gazette* as a law.

(4) No law made by Parliament shall come into operation until it has been published in the *Gazette* but Parliament may postpone the coming into operation of any such law and may make laws with retrospective effect.

(5) All laws made by Parliament shall be styled 'Ordinances' and the words of enactment shall be 'Enacted by the Parliament of Tuvalu'.

59. Subject to the provisions of this Constitution, Parliament may make rules of procedure for the regulation and orderly conduct of its proceedings and the discharge of business at sittings of Parliament and for the passing, intituling and numbering of Bills and for the presentation thereof to the Governor General for assent.

60. (1) Subject to the provisions of this Constitution and the rules of procedure of Parliament, any member may introduce any Bill or propose any motion for debate in, or may present any petition to, Parliament, and the same shall be debated and disposed of according to the rules of procedure of Parliament.

(2) With the exception of Bills which have been certified by the Governor General, acting in accordance with the advice of the Prime Minister, as urgent or as not of general public importance, Parliament shall not proceed upon any Bill after its first reading in Parliament until the next following session of Parliament so as to permit consideration of the Bill by Island Councils.

(3) Except on the recommendation of a Minister, Parliament shall not

(*a*) proceed upon any bill (including any amendment to a Bill) which, in the opinion of the person presiding in Parliament, makes provision for imposing or increasing any tax, for imposing or increasing any charge on the Consolidated Fund or other funds of Tuvalu, or for altering any such charge otherwise than by reducing it, or for compounding or remitting any debt due to the Government; or

(*b*) proceed upon any motion (including any amendment to a motion) the effect of wich, in the opinion of the person presiding in Parliament, is that provision would be made for any of the purposes aforesaid.

61. (1) Subject to the provisions of this section, Parliament may by Ordinance alter this Constitution.

(2) A Bill for an Ordinance to alter any provision of this Constitution shall not be passed by Parliament unless it is supported at its second reading in Parliament by the votes of not less than 8 members of Parliament.

(3) In this section

(*a*) references to this Constitution include references to any other law in so far as that law alters the Constitution;

(*b*) references to altering this Constitution include references

(i) to repealing it, with or without re-enactment or the making of different provision in lieu thereof;

(ii) to modifying it, whether by omitting or amending any of its provisions or inserting additonal provisions in it or otherwise;

(iii) to suspending its operation for any period, or terminating any such suspension; and

(iv) to making any other provision that is repugnant to or otherwise inconsistent with it.

62. No member of Parliament shall be permitted to take part in the proceedings of Parliament (other than proceedings necessary for the purpose of this section) until he has made before Parliament an oath of allegiance in the form set out in Annex 2 to this Constitution.

63. (1) There shall be a Speaker of Parliament who shall be elected as such by the members of Parliament from among their number.

(2) A person shall not be qualified for election as Speaker if he is a Minister.

(3) A person shall vacate the office of Speaker

(*a*) when Parliament first meets after a dissolution of Parliament;

(*b*) if he announces the resignation of his office to Parliament or if, by writing under his hand addressed to Parliament and received by the Clerk of Parliament, he resigns that office;

(*c*) if he ceases to be a member of Parliament for any reason other than a dissolution of Parliament;

(*d*) if he becomes a Minister;

(*e*) if Parliament so resolves by resolution supported by the votes of not less than 8 members; or

(*f*) if he was at the date of his appointment a party to (or a partner in a firm or a director or manager of a company which was a party to) any contract with the Government for or on account of the public service and if, before the expiration of a period of 30 days from the date of his appointment, he has not disclosed to Parliament the nature of such contract and his interest, or the interest of such firm or company, therein and Parliament has not exempted him from vacating his office under this paragraph.

64. The Speaker or, in his absence or when his office is vacant, a member of Parliament (not being a Minister) elected by Parliament for that sitting, shall preside at each sitting of Parliament.

65. (1) Subject to the provisions of this Constitution, all questions proposed for decision in Parliament shall be determined by a majority of the votes of the members present and voting.

(2) Subject to the provisions of the next following sub-section, the Speaker or other member presiding in Parliament shall not have an original vote but shall have and shall exercise a casting vote if in any question the votes are equally divided.

(3) The Speaker shall have an original vote on

(*a*) any motion of no confidence in the Government; and

(*b*) any Bill for an Ordinance to alter any provision of this Constitution.

66. If objection is taken by any member of Parliament present that there are present in Parliament (besides the person presiding) less than 6 members of Parliament and, after such interval as may be prescribed in the rules of procedure of Parliament, the person presiding ascertains that the number of members present other than himself is still less than 6, he shall thereupon adjourn Parliament.

67. At the request of a Minister, the person presiding in Parliament may summon any person to a sitting of Parliament, notwithstanding that that person is not a member of Parliament, and a person so summoned shall be entitled to take part in the proceedings of Parliament as if he were a member but shall not have a vote:

Provided that a person shall not be under any obligation to answer any question put to him by any member of Parliament, or by the person presiding at such sitting.

68. Parliament shall not be disqualified for the transaction of business by reason of any vacancy in its membership, and any proceedings in Parliament shall be valid notwithstanding that some person who was not entitled to do so took part in those proceedings.

69. (1) Subject to the provisions of sub-section (2) and (3) of this section, Parliament may determine the privileges, immunities and powers of Parliament and of its members.

(2) No civil or criminal proceedings may be instituted against any member of Parliament for words spoken before, or written in a report to, Parliament or a committee of Parliament, or by reason of any matter or thing brought by him in Parliament or in a committee of Parliament.

(3) No process issued by any court in the exercise of its civil jurisdiction shall be served or executed within the precincts of Parliament while Parliament is sitting.

Part III. Summoning, Prorogation and Dissolution

70. (1) Subject to the provisions of this section, each session of Parliament shall be held at such place within Tuvalu and shall commence at such time as the Governor General, acting in accordance with the advice of the Prime Minister, may by proclamation appoint.

(2) Sessions of Parliament shall be held so that a period of 12 months does not intervene between the end of one session and the first sitting of Parliament in the next session.

(3) A session of Parliament shall be appointed to commence within one month of the date prescribed for polling at any general election.

71. (1) The Governor General, acting in accordance with the advice of the Prime Minister, may at any time prorogue Parliament.

(2) Subject to the provisions of the next following sub-section, the Governor General, acting in accordance with the advice of the Prime Minister, may at any time dissolve Parliament:

Provided that the Prime Minister shall not advise the Governor General to dissolve Parliament under this sub-section unless Parliament has resolved that he should do so.

(3) If the office of Prime Minister is vacant and no person has been elected to that office within such period as the Governor General, acting in his own deliberate judgment, may consider reasonable, the Governor General, acting in his own deliberate judgment, may dissolve Parliament.

(4) Parliament, unless sooner dissolved, shall continue for 4 years from the date of the first sitting of Parliament after any general election and shall then stand dissolved.

72. There shall be a general election on such day or days within 2 months of every dissolution of Parliament as the Governor General, acting in accordance with the advice of the Prime Minister, shall by proclamation appoint.

CHAPTER VII

THE JUDICIARY

Part I. The High Court

73. There shall be a High Court of Tuvalu which shall be a superior court of record with such jurisdiction and powers as may be prescribed by this Constitution or by any law for the time being in force in Tuvalu.

74. (1) There shall be a judge of the High Court who shall be styled Chief Justice and shall be appointed by the Governor General, acting in accordance with the advice of the Prime Minister, for such period as may be specified in his instrument of appointment.

(2) A person shall not be qualified for appointment as Chief Justice unless

(*a*) he is or has been a judge of a court having unlimited jurisdiction in civil and criminal matters in some part of the Commonwealth or in the Republic of Ireland, or a court having jurisdiction in appeals from any such court; or

(*b*) he is qualified to practise as an advocate in such a court and he has been qualified for not less than 5 years to practise as an advocate or solicitor in such a court.

75. (1) Whenever he is satisfied that the Chief Justice is not available to attend to the business of the High Court the Governor General, acting in accordance with the advice of the Prime Minister, may appoint a person qualified to be appointed as Chief Justice to perform

(*a*) all or any of the functions of the Chief Justice either generally or in respect of any particular case or class of cases; or

(*b*) such functions of the Chief Justice as it shall appear to the person appointed under this sub-section require to be performed without delay,

subject to such limitations and conditions, if any, as may be specified in the instrument of appointment.

(2) A person appointed under the preceding sub-section shall be styled a Commissioner of the High Court, and all things done by him in accordance with the terms of his appointment shall have the same validity and effect as if they had been done by the Chief Justice and in respect thereof he shall have the same powers and enjoy the same immunities as if he had been the Chief Justice.

76. (1) Subject to the provisions of this section, the office of Chief Justice shall become vacant upon the expiration of the period of his appointment to that office.

(2) The Chief Justice may at any time resign his office by writing under his hand addressed to the Governor General.

(3) The Chief Justice may be removed from office only for inability to discharge the functions of his office (whether arising from infirmity of body or mind or any other cause) or for misbehavior and shall not be removed except in accordance with the provisions of the next following sub-section.

(4) The Chief Justice may be removed from office by Parliament by resolutions if the question of his removal from office has been referred to a tribunal appointed under the next following sub-section and the tribunal has advised the Parliament that he ought to be removed from office for inability as aforesaid or for misbehavior.

(5) If the Governor General considers, or Parliament resolves, that the question of removing the Chief Justice from office for inability as aforesaid or for misbehavior ought to be investigated, then,

(*a*) the Governor General, acting after consultation with the Prime Minister, shall appoint a tribunal which shall consist of a chairman and not less than one other member, selected by the Governor General from among persons who are qualified for appointment as Chief Justice; and

(*b*) the tribunal shall enquire into the matter and report on the facts thereof to Parliament and advise Parliament whether the Chief Justice should be removed under this section.

(6) If the question of removing the Chief Justice from office has been referred to a tribunal under the preceding sub-section, the Governor General may suspend the Chief Justice from performing the functions of his office, and any such suspension may at any time be revoked by the Governor General and shall in any case cease to have effect if the tribunal advises Parliament that the Chief Justice should not be removed from office.

77. The Chief Justice may, even though his appointment has terminated (otherwise than by reason of his removal from office), sit as such for the purpose of giving judgment or otherwise in relation to any proceedings summoned before him while his appointment was subsisting.

78. The High Court shall have, and use as occasion requires, a seal bearing on it the words 'The High Court of Tuvalu' and such device as Parliament shall approve.

79. (1) There shall be such registrars and other officers of the High Court as the Governor General, subject to any law in force in Tuvalu, may appoint, and every such registrar or other officer shall discharge such duties as may be prescribed by law or by rules of court or as the Chief Justice may direct:

Provided that the Chief Justice may, subject to any directions given by the Governor General, appoint a person temporarily to discharge such duties accordingly.

(2) Any appointment made under the provisions of this preceding sub-section may, at any time, be determined by the Governor General.

(3) The functions of the Governor General under this section shall be exercised by him in accordance with the advice of the Public Service Commission.

80. There shall be a Rules Committee, consisting of the Chief Justice and the Attorney General (who shall constitute a quorum) and such other persons, not exceeding 2 in number, as the Governor General, acting after consultation with the Chief Justice, may appoint, which may make rules of court regulating the practice and procedure of the High Court, the admission of legal practitioners to practise as advocates or barristers and solicitors or in any of these capacities, prescribing the fees to be paid in respect of any proceeding and generally for making provision for the proper and effectual exercise of the jurisdiction of the High Court, including the procedure for the making and hearing of appeals to the High Court from subordinate courts and, with the concurrence of the President of the Court of Appeal, for the making of appeals from the High Court in accordance with the provisions of this Constitution:

Provided that rules prescribing or affecting the amount of any fees or the recovery thereof shall not come into operation unless approved, either before or after being made, by Parliament.

81. (1) Subject to the provisions of this Constitution, the High Court shall have original jurisdiction to hear and determine any question as to the interpretation of this Constitution.

(2) Where any question as to the interpretation of this Constitution arises in any proceedings in any subordinate court and the court is of the opinion that the question involves a substantial question of law, the court may, and shall if any party to the proceedings so requests, refer the question to the High Court.

(3) Where any question is referred to the High Court in pursuance of the preceding sub-section, the High Court shall give its decision upon the question and the court in which the question arose shall dispose of the case in accordance with that decision, or if that decision is the subject of an appeal to the Court of Appeal or to Her Majesty in Council, in accordance with the decision of the Court of Appeal or, as the case may be, Her Majesty in Council.

Part II. Appeals

82. The High Court shall have jurisdiction to hear and determine such appeals from the judgments (including reserved questions of law and cases stated) of any other courts established in Tuvalu and for that purpose to exercise such powers and authorities as may be prescribed by or under any law for the time being in force in Tuvalu; and subject to the provisions of any such law for all purposes of and incidental to the hearing and determination of any appeal within its jurisdiction, the High Court shall have the power, authority and jurisdiction vested in the court from which the appeal is brought.

83. (1) Subject to any provisions contained in any law which applies to the cause or matter concerned, an appeal shall lie, in accordance with rules of court made under section 80 of this Constitution, from a judgment of the High Court, whether in the exercise of original or appellate jurisdiction, in any civil or criminal cause or matter, to the Court of Appeal, and, subject to the provisions of any such law for all purposes of and incidental to the hearing and determination of any appeal within its jurisdiction under this section, the Court of Appeal shall have the power, authority and jurisdiction vested in the High Court.

(2) In the exercise of appellate jurisdiction under this section, the process of the Court of Appeal shall run and any judgment of the Court shall have full force and effect in Tuvalu, and may be executed and enforced in like manner as if it were an original judgment of the court from which the appeal is brought.

84. (1) An appeal shall lie from decisions of the Court to Her Majesty in Council as of right in the following cases:

(*a*) final decisions, in any civil or criminal proceedings, on questions as to the interpretation of this Constitution;

(*b*) final decisions in any civil proceedings where the matter in dispute on the appeal is of the value of $1,000 or upwards or where the appeal involves, directly or indirectly, a claim to or question respecting property or a right of the value of $1,000 or upwards;

(*c*) final decisions in proceedings under section 17 of this Constitution;

(*d*) final decision in proceedings for dissolution or nullity of marriage; and

(*e*) such other cases as may be prescribed by Parliament.

(2) An appeal shall lie from decisions of the Court of Appeal to Her Majesty in Council with the leave of the Court in the following cases:

(*a*) final or interlocutory decisions in any civil proceedings where in the opinion of the Court the question involved in the appeal is one which, by reason of its great general or public importance or otherwise, ought to be submitted to Her Majesty in Council; and

(*b*) such other cases as may be prescribed by Parliament.

(3) Nothing in this section shall affect any right of Her Majesty to grant special leave to appeal to Her Majesty in Council from the decision of any court in any civil or criminal matter.

Part III. Jurisdiction of Courts

85. Subject to the provisions of this Constitution and of any other law for the time being in force in Tuvalu, the civil and criminal jurisdiction of the courts in Tuvalu shall be exercised in accordance with the rules which governed the exercise of that jurisdiction immediately before Independence Day:

Provided that in the exercise of their jurisdiction the courts shall, to the extent that circumstances and the justice of any particular case may permit, modify or adapt such rules to take account of Tuvalu custom and tradition.

CHAPTER VIII

THE PUBLIC SERVICE

86. (1) There shall be a Public Service Commission for Tuvalu which shall consist of a Chairman and 3 other members appointed by the Governor General.

(2) A person shall be disqualified for appointment as a member of the Public Service Commission if he is a member of Parliament or a public officer.

(4) The office of a member of the Public Service Commission shall become of the Public Service Commission or within a period of 3 years commencing with the date on which he last held or acted in that office, be eligible for appointment to or to act in any public office.

(4) The office of a member of the Public Service Commission shall become vacant

(*a*) at the expiration of 4 years from the date of his appointment;

(*b*) if he becomes a member of Parliament; or

(*c*) if he is removed from office in accordance with section 90 of this Constitution.

(5) The provisions of sub-sections (2), (3), (4) and (5) of section 90 of this Constitution shall apply to a person holding the office of member of the Public Service Commission.

(6) Whenever the office of Chairman of the Public Service Commission is vacant or the Chairman is for any reason unable to perform the functions of his office, those functions shall be performed by such one of the other members of the Commission as the Governor General may appoint.

(7) If the office of a member of the Public Service Commission other than the Chairman is vacant or the holder thereof is acting as Chairman or is for any reason unable to perform the functions of his office, the Governor General may appoint a person qualified for appointment as a member of the Commission to act as such a member; and any person so appointed may, subject to the provisions of sub-section (4)(*b*) of this section, continue to act until his appointment is revoked by the Governor General.

(8) The Secretary to Governemnt shall act as secretary to the Commission:

Provided that, whenever the Commission has occasion to consider the position of the Secretary to Government, it shall appoint some other person to act in his stead for so long as it thinks fit.

(9) The functions of the Governor General under this section shall be exercised by him in accordance with the advice of the Prime Minister.

87. (1) Subject to the provisions of this Constitution, power to make appointments to public offices (including power to confirm appointments) and to remove and to exercise disciplinary control over persons holding or acting in such offices is vested in the Governor General, acting in accordance with the advice of the Public Service Commission.

(2) The Public Service Commission may, subject to such conditions as it

thinks fit, delegate any of its powers under this section by directions in writing to any member of the Commission or to any public officer.

(3) The provisions of this section shall not apply in relation to

(*a*) the office of Chief Justice, Attorney General, Principal Auditor or Chief of Police;

(*b*) the office of any member of the Tuvalu Police below the rank of Inspector.

(4) No appointment to hold or act in the office of Secretary to Government shall be made unless the Prime Minister concurs in the appointment.

(5) No appointment to hold or act in the office of a Secretary to a ministry in the Government shall be made unless the Minister for the time being charged with responsibility for the administration of that ministry concurs in the appointment.

(6) The powers of the Governor General under this section in relation to any office on the personal staff of the governor General or in relation to any person holding or acting in any such office shall be exercised by the Governor General acting in his own deliberate judgment.

88. Power to make appointments to the office of Magistrate or Island Magistrate and to remove and to exercise disciplinary control over persons holding or acting in such offices is vested in the Governor General, acting in accordance with the advice of the Public Service Commission.

(2) The Governor General, acting in accordance with the advice of the Chairman of the Public Service Commission, may at any time suspend the Chief of Police from performing the functions of his office and may likewise revoke any such suspension.

(3) Power to make appointments to any office in the Tuvalu Police below the rank of Inspector and to remove and to exercise disciplinary control over persons holding or acting in such offices is vested in the Chief of Police:

Provided that there shall be a right of appeal to the Public Service Commission from any decision of the Chief of Police in exercise of his power of removal or disciplinary control.

90. (1) Subject to the provisions of this section, the office of a person to whom this section applies shall become vacant upon the expiration of the period of his appointment to that office.

(2) A person holding an office to which this section applies may be removed from office only for inability to discharge the functions of his office (whether arising from infirmity of body or mind or any other cause) or for misbehavior and shall not be so removed except in accordance with the provisions of this section.

(3) A person to whom this section applies shall be removed from office by the Governor General if the question of his removal from office has been referred to a tribunal appointed under the next following sub-section and the tribunal has recommended to the Governor General that he ought to be removed from office for inability as aforesaid or for misbehavior.

(4) If the Governor General considers that the question of removing a

a person to whom this section applies from office for inability as aforesaid or for misbehavior ought to be investigated, then

(*a*) the Governor General, acting after consultation with the Prime Minister, shall appoint a tribunal, which shall consist of a chairman who is qualified for appointment as Chief Justice and not less than one other member; and

(*b*) the tribunal shall inquire into the matter and report on the facts thereof to the Governor General and recommend to the Governor General whether the person ought to be removed from office for inability as aforesaid or for misbehavior.

(5) If the question or removing a person to whom this section applies has been referred to a tribunal under the preceding sub-section, the Governor General may suspend the person from performing the functions of his office, and any such suspension may at any time be revoked by the Governor General and shall in any case cease to have effect if the tribunal recommends to the Governor General that the person should not be removed.

(6) This section applies to person holding the offices of Principal Auditor and Chief of Police.

91. (1) Subject to the provisions of section 93 of this Constitution, the law applicable to the grant and payment to any officer, or to his widow, children, dependents or personal representatives, of any pension, gratuity or other like allowance (in this section and in sections 92 and 93 of this Constitution referred to as an 'award') in respect of the service of that officer in a public office shall be that in force on the relevant day or any later law not less favorable to the person concerned.

(2) For the purposes of this section the relevant day is

(*a*) in relation to an award granted before Independence Day, the day on which the award was granted;

(*b*) in relation to an award granted or to be granted on or after Indepedence Day to or in respect of a person who was a public officer before that day, the day immediately before that day;

(*c*) in relation to an award granted or to be granted to or in respect of a person who first becomes a public officer on or after Independence Day, the day on which he becomes a public officer.

(3) For the purposes of this section, in so far as the law applicable to an award depends on the option of the person to or in respect of whom it is granted or to be granted, the law for which he opts shall be taken to be more favorable to him than any other law for which he might have opted.

92. Awards granted under any law for the time being in force in Tuvalu are (except so far as they are a charge on some other fund and are duly paid out of that fund to the person to whom payment is due) hereby charged on and shall be paid out of the Consolidated Fund.

93. (1) The power to grant any award under any pensions law for the time being in force in Tuvalu (other than an award to which, under that law, the person to whom it is payable is entitled as of right) and, in accordance with any provisions in that behalf in any such law, to withhold, reduce in amount or suspend any award payable under any such law shall vest in the Governor General.

(2) The power vested in the Governor General by the preceding subsection shall be exercised by him

(*a*) in the case of an award payable in respect of the services of any person who, having been a public officer, was, immediately before the date on which he ceased to hold public office, serving as Chief Justice, Chief of Police, Principal Auditor or member of the personal staff of the Governor General, in his own deliberate judgment; and

(*b*) in the case of an award payable in respect of the services of any other person, in accordance with the advice of the Public Service Commission.

(3) In this section, 'pensions law' means any law relating to the grant to any person, or to the widow, children, dependents or personal representatives of that person, of an award in respect of the services of that person in a public office.

CHAPTER IX

FINANCE

94. (1) There shall be in and for Tuvalu a Consolidated Fund into which, subject to the provisions of any law for the time being in force in Tuvalu, shall be paid all revenues of the Government.

(2) Parliament may make provision for the establishment of Special Funds, which shall not form part of the Consolidated Fund.

(3) The receipts, earnings and accruals of Special Funds established under this section and the balance of such funds at the close of each financial year shall not be paid into the Consolidated Fund but shall be retained for the purposes of those funds.

95. (1) No money shall be issued from the Consolidated Fund except upon the authority of a warrant under the hand of the Minister of Finance.

(2) No warrant shall be issued by the Minister of Finance for the purpose of meeting any expenditure unless

(*a*) the expenditure has been authorized for the financial year during which the issue is to take place by an Appropriation Ordinance;

(*b*) the expenditure has been authorized in accordance with the provisions of section 96(4), 97 or 98 of this Constitution; or

(*c*) it is statutory expenditure.

96. (1) The Minister of Finance shall cause to be prepared and laid before Parliament before or not later than 60 days after the commencement of each financial year estimates of the revenues and expenditure of the Government for that year.

(2) The heads of expenditure contained in the estimates (other than statutory expenditure) shall be included in a Bill to be known as an Appropriation Bill which shall be introduced into Parliament to provide for the issue from the Consolidated Fund of the sums necessary to supply those heads and the appropriation of those sums for the purpose specified therein.

(3) If in respect of any financial year it is found that the sum appropriated by the Appropriation Ordinance for any purpose is insufficient or that a need has arisen for expenditure for a purpose for which no sum has been appropriated by that law, a supplementary estimate showing the sums required shall be included in a Supplementary Appropriation Bill for appropriation.

(4) Where in respect of any financial year the Minister of Finance is satisfied that an urgent and unforeseen need has arisen to authorize for any purpose advances from the Consolidated Fund for expenditure in excess of the sum appropriated for that purpose by an Appropriation Ordinance, or for a purpose for which no sum has been so appropriated, he may, subject to the provisions of any law for the time being in force in that regard, authorize such advances by warrant and shall include such amount in a Supplementary Appropriation Bill for appropriation at the meeting of Parliament next following the date on which the warrant was issued.

(5) If at the close of account for any financial year it is found that any moneys have been expended on any head in excess of the sums appropriated for that head by an Appropriation Ordinance or for a purpose for which no money has been appropriated, the excess or the sum expended but not appropriated as the case may be shall be included in a statement of heads in excess which shall be presented to Parliament.

(6) Statutory expenditure shall not be voted on by Parliament but, without further authority of Parliament, shall be paid out of the Consolidated Fund by warrant under the hand of the Minister of Finance.

97. If the Appropriation Ordinance in respect of any financial year has not come into operation by the beginning of that financial year, Parliament by resolution may empower the Minister of Finance to authorize the issue of moneys from the Consolidated Fund for the purpose of meeting expenditure necessary to carry on the public service at a level of these services in the previous financial year, until the expiration of 4 months from the beginning of that financial year or the coming into operation of the Appropriation Ordinance, whichever is the earlier.

98. Where at any time Parliament has been dissolved before any provision or any sufficient provision is made under this Chapter for the carrying on of the government of Tuvalu, the Minister of Finance may issue a warrant for the payment out of the Consolidated Fund of such sums as he may consider necessary for the continuance of the public services until the expiry of a period of 3 months commencing with the date on which Parliament first meets after that dissolution, but a statement of the sums so authorized shall, as soon as practicable, be laid before Parliament and the aggregate sums shall be included, under the appropriate heads, in the next Appropriation Bill.

99. (1) There shall be charged on the Consolidated Fund all debt charges for which the Government is liable.

(2) For the purposes of this section debt charges include interest, sinking fund charges, the repayment or amortisation of debt, and all expenditure in connection with the raising of loans on the security of the revenue of the Government or the Consolidated Fund and the service and redemption of debt thereby created.

100. (1) There shall be paid to the holders of the offices to which this section applies such salary or other remuneration and such allowances as may be prescribed by Parliament.

(2) The remuneration and allowances payable to the holder of those offices are hereby charged on and shall be paid out of the Consolidated Fund.

(3) The remuneration prescribed in pursuance of this section in respect of the holder of any such office and his other terms of service (other than allowances that are not taken into account in computing, under any law in that behalf, any pension payable in respect of his service in that office) shall not be altered to his disadvantage after his appointment.

(4) Where a person's remuneration or other terms of service depend upon his option, the remuneration or terms for which he opts shall, for the purposes of the preceding sub-section, be deemed to be more advantageous to him than any others for which he might have opted.

(5) This section applies to the offices of Governor General, Speaker, Prime Minister or other Minister, any other member of Parliament, Chief Justice, Attorney General, Principal Auditor, Chief of Police, and member of the Public Serivce Commission.

101. (1) There shall be a Principal Auditor whose office shall be a public office.

(2) The Principal Auditor shall be appointed by the Governor General, acting in accordance with the advice of the Public Service Commission.

(3) The public accounts of Tuvalu and of all ministries, offices, courts and authorities of the Government shall be audited and reported on annually by the Principal Auditor, and for tht purpose the Principal Auditor or any person authorized by him in that behalf shall at all times be entitled to access to all books, records, returns and other documents relating to such accounts.

(4) The Principal Auditor shall submit his reports made under the preceding sub-section to the Minister of Finance who shall cause them to be laid before Parliament.

(5) In the exercise of his functions under this section, the Principal Auditor shall not be subject to the direction or control of any other person or authority.

(6) Nothing in this section shall prevent the performance by the Principal Auditor of

(*a*) such other functions in relation to the accounts of the Government and the accounts of other public authorities and other bodies administering public funds in Tuvalu as may be prescribed by Parliament; or

(*b*) such other functions in relation to the supervision and control of expenditure from public funds in Tuvalu as may be so prescribed.

102. A committee of Parliament consisting of members of Parliament shall

(*a*) consider the accounts of the Government in conjunction with the report of the Principal Auditor;

(*b*) consider the accounts of any corporation, statutory board, body or commission where a report on the examination and audit of any such accounts is requred by law to be laid before Parliament.

103. In this Chapter of this Constitution

'financial year' means the 12 months ending on the 31st December in any year or on such other date as may from time to time be prescribed by Parliament;

'statutory expenditure' means expenditure charged on the Consolidated Fund or on the general revenues and assets of Tuvalu by virtue of any provision of any other law for the time being in force in Tuvalu.

CHAPTER X

MISCELLANEOUS

104. (1) In this Constitution, unless the context otherwise requires

'the Commonwealth' means Tuvalu and any country to which section 25 of this Constitution for the time being applies, and includes the dependencies of any such country;

'the Court of Appeal' means such court in any part of the Commonwealth as may be designated by Parliament by resolution:

Provided that, until any other court is so designated, it means the Court of Appeal established for Fiji by the Constitution of Fiji set out in the Schedule to the Fiji Independence Order 1970 or by any law modifying or replacing that Constitution;

'the Crown' means the Crown in right of Tuvalu;

'functions' includes rights, duties and powers;

'the *Gazette*' means the official *Gazette* of Tuvalu;

'general election' means a general election of the members of Parliament;

'the Government' means Her Majesty's Government of Tuvalu;

'the Governor General' means the Governor General of Tuvalu;

'the High Court' means the High Court of Tuvalu established by this Constitution;

'Independence Day' means 1st October 1978;

'oath' includes affirmation;

'oath of allegiance' means such oath of allegiance as is prescribed in Annex 2 to this Constitution;

'Parliament' means the Parliament of Tuvalu established by this Constitution;

'prescribed' means prescribed in a law;

Provided that

(*a*) in relation to anything that may be prescribed only by Parliament, it means prescribed in an Ordinance; and

(*b*) in relation to any thing that may be prescribed only by some other specified person or authority, it means prescribed in an order or regulation made by that other person or authority;

'public office' means, subject to the provisions of the next following section, an office of emolument in the public service;

'public officer' means a person holding or acting in any public office;

'public service' means the service of the Crown in a civil capacity in respect of the government of Tuvalu;

'session' means the sittings of Parliament commencing when Parliament first meets after its prorogation or dissolution at any time and ending when Parliament is prorogued or dissolved without having been prorogued;

'sitting' means, in relation to Parliament. any period during which Parliament is sitting continuously without adjournment and includes any period during which Parliament is in committee;

'the Speaker' means the Speaker of Parliament;

'Tuvalu' means the territories which immediately before Independence Day comprised the colony of Tuvalu.

(2) Save as otherwise provided in this Constitution, the Interpretation Act 1889 shall apply, with the necessary adaptations, for the purpose of interpreting this Constitution, and otherwise in relation thereto, as it applies for the purpose of interpreting, and in relation to, Acts of the Parliament of the United Kingdom.

105. (1) In this Constitution the expression 'public office' shall be construed

(*a*) as including the office of Chief Justice;

(*b*) as not including

(i) the office of Speaker, Prime Minister, any Minister referred to in section 32(2) of this Constitution, or any other member of Parliament;

(ii) the office of member of the Public Service Commission.

(2) For the purposes of this Constitution a person shall not be treated as holding, or acting in, a public office by reason only that he

(*a*) is on leave of absence pending relinquishment of a public office, or is on leave of absence without salary from a public office;

(*b*) is receiving a pension or other like allowance from the Crown;

(*c*) is a retired or reserve member of Her Majesty's forces or a special constable;

(*d*) is a member, officer or servant of any local government council; or

(*e*) is the holder of an office in the service or appointment of the Crown, or is performing any functions on behalf of the Crown, if the only payments he receives in respect of that office or those functions are by way of travelling or subsistence allowances or a refund of out-of-pocket expenses.

106. (1) Any reference in this Constitution to power to make appointments to any public office shall be construed as including a reference to power to make appointment on promotion and transfer to that office and to power to appoint a person to act in that office during any period during which it is vacant or the holder thereof is unable to perform the functions of that office.

(2) In this Constitution, unless the context otherwise requires, a reference to the holder of an office by the term designating his office shall be construed as including a reference to any person who is for the time being lawfully acting in or performing the functions of that office.

(3) Where by this Constitution any person is directed, or power is conferred on any person or authority to appoint a person, to act in or otherwise to perform the functions of an office if the holder thereof is unable to perform the functions of that office, the validity of any performance of those functions by the person so directed or of any appointment made in exercise of that power shall not be called in question in any court in the ground that the holder of the office is not unable to perform the functions of the office.

107. (1) Where any person has vacated any office established by this Constitution, he may, if qualified, again be appointed or elected to hold that office in accordance with the provisions of this Constitution.

(2) Whenever the holder of any office constituted by or under this Constitution, or any public office otherwise constituted, is on leave of absence pending relinquishment of his office

(*a*) another person may be appointed to that office; and

(*b*) that person shall, for the purpose of any function of that office, be deemed to be the sole holder of that office.

108. (1) Reference in this Constitution to the power to remove a public officer from his office shall be construed as including references to any power conferred by any law to require or permit that officer to retire from the public service and to any power or right to terminate a contract on which a person is employed as a public officer and to determine whether any such contract shall or shall not be renewed.

Provided that

(*a*) nothing in this sub-section shall be construed as conferring on any person or authority power to require the Chief Justice, the Chief of Police or the Principal Auditor to retire from the public service; and

(*b*) any power conferred by any law to permit a person to retire from the public service shall, in the case of any officer mentioned in the preceding paragraph or an officer who may be removed from office by some person or authority other than the Public Service Commission, vest in the authority that, if that officer had retired, would be the appropriate authority in relation to the awards of that officer under section 93 of this Consitution.

(2) Any provisions of this Constitution that vests in any person or authority power to remove any public officer from his office shall be without prejudice to the power of any person or authority to abolish any office or to any law providing for the compulsory retirement of public officers generally or any class of public officer on attaining an age specified therein.

109. Save as otherwise provided in section 33, 50 and 63 of this Constitution, any person who is appointed to or to act in any office established by this Constitution may resign from that office by writing under his hand addressed to the person by whom he was appointed; and the resignation of any person from any such office by writing under his hand addressed in accordance with this Constitution to any other person shall take take effect, and the office shall accordingly become vacant.

(*a*) at such time or on such date (if any) as may be specified in the writing; or

(*b*) when the writing is received by that other person, whichever is the later:

Provided that the resignation may be withdrawn before it take effect if the person to whom the resignation is addressed consents to its withdrawal.

110. (1) The Public Service Commission (in this section referred to as 'the Commission') may by regulations make provision for regulating and facilitating the performance by the Commission of its functions under this Constitution.

(2) Any decision by the Commission shall require the concurrence of a majority of all the members thereof and, subject as aforesaid, the Commission may act notwithstanding the absence of any member:

Provided that if in any particular case a vote of all the members is taken to decide the question and the votes cast are equally divided the chariman shall have and shall exercise a casting vote.

(3) Subject to the provisions of this section, the Commission may regulate its own procedure.

(4) In the exercise of its functions under this Constitution, the Commission shall not be subject to the direction or control of any other person or authority.

(5) In addition to the functions conferred upon it by or under this Constitution the Commission shall have such other functions (if any) as may be prescribed.

(6) The validity of the transaction of business of the Commission shall not be affected by the fact that some person who was not entitled to do so took part in the proceedings.

(7) The provisions of sub-sections (1), (2), (3) and (4) of this section apply in relation to a tribunal established for the purposes of section 14(4), 16(2), 76(5) or 90(4) of this Constitution as they apply in relation to the Commission, and any such tribunal shall have the same powers as the High Court in respect of the attendance and examination of witnesses (including the administration of oaths and the examination of witnesses abroad) and in respect of the production of documents.

111. No provisions of this Constitution that any person or authority shall not be subject to the direction or control of any other person or authority in the exercise of any functions under this Constitution shall be construed as precluding a court of law from exercising jurisdiction in relation to any question whether that person or authority has performed those functions in accordance with this Constitution or any other law or should not perform those functions.

112. Where any power is conferred by this Constitution to make any proclamation, regulation, order or rule, or to give any direction or instructions, the power shall be construed as including the power, exercisable in like manner, to amend or revoke any such proclamation, regulation, order, rule, direction or instructions.

113. Where any person or authority other than the Governor General is directed by this Constitution to exercise any function after consultation with any other person or authority, that person or authority shall not be obliged to exercise that function in accordance with the advice of that other person or authority.

114. Where anything is required by this Constitution to be published in the *Gazette,* it may instead by published in such other manner as the Governor General shall determine.

ANNEXES
(*Not reproduced*)

UNITED ARAB EMIRATES

SUMMARY

INTERNATIONAL STATUS

The United Arab Emirates is a member of the United Nations (December 9, 1971). It is a member of the Organization of Arab States, the Persian Gulf Co-operative Council and of other international organizations.

The United Arab Emirates was proclaimed on December 2, 1971, as a union of the emirates of Abu Dhabi, Dubai, Sharjah, Ajman, Umm Al Qawain and Fujairah. On February 10, 1972, Ras El Khaima joined the Union. From the time of the first Arab implantation two thousand years ago, the entrance to the Persian Gulf was important for navigation and for the ports along the coast. Rivalries between the north and south Arabs facilitated European penetration of the area from the first Portuguese in the sixteenth centruy to the British truces in 1806 and 1835, whence the name, the Trucial Coast. In 1892, the British became the sole foreign agents with authority to handle foreign relations; in 1911 and 1922, they received sole authority to grant oil or pearl fishing concessions. In return, they protected the sheikdoms against Ottoman, French and Persian encroachments. Discovery of oil after the second World War and the subsequent oil boom ended the economic misery consequent upon the change of trade routes after the opening of the Suez Canal and the ruin of the Arab pearl fisheries by the Japanese cultured pearl.

In 1968, The United Kingdom announced the withdrawal of its forces from the Persian Gulf. The Emirates decided to unite and the first agreement between Abu Dhabi and Dubai was signed on February 19, 1968. Bahrain and Qatar were included in the original project but decided upon separate independence. In 1973, the Union adopted a single currency; in 1974, a long standing frontier conflict with Saudi Arabia was settled. In 1976, the Emirates decided to unify their military forces, but each retains for the present its own. On May 26, 1981, the statutes of the Persian Gulf Co-operative Council were signed and the organization, composed of Saudi Arabia, Kuwait, Oman, Qatar, Bahrain, the United Arab Emirates, set up with headquarters at Ryadh.

FORM OF NATIONAL GOVERNMENT

The Provisional Constitution was extended in 1976 and 1981 for further five year periods beyond the transitional period of five years indicated in the Preamble during which the foundations for federal rule are to be laid and a permanent Constitution to be prepared. The members of the Union are listed and the Union declared an independent, sovereign, federal state.[1] The Union exercises sovereignty within the international borders and the seven member Emirates sovereignty over their own territories and territorial waters on all matters not otherwise assigned in the Consitution.[2] The Union is part of the Great Arab Nation.[3] Islam is the official religion, the Islamic Shariah the main source of legislation.[4] The Emirates of the Union are to form an economic and customs entity by progressive stages.[5] The fundamental social and economic bases to be striven for are equality, social justice, safety and security, the protection of the family, childhood and motherhood, education and the eradication of illiteracy, medical care, the provision of employment, protection of private property, inviolability of public property.[6] The Emirates exercise all powers not assigned to the Union.[7] The distribution of legislative, executive and international jurisdiction between the Union and the emirates is laid down.[8]

RIGHTS OF THE PEOPLE

The Consitution provided equality before the law, personal liberty, prohibits torture or degrading treatment, penalties may be imposed only by law; stipulated are freedom of movement and residence, of opinion and expression, secrecy of correspondence, freedom of worship in accordance with established customs, freedom of assembly and association, prohibition of slavery.[9] The domicile is inviolable, citizens may not be banished, neither citizens nor political refugees may be extradited.[10] Confiscation of property is forbidden.[11] The defense of the Union is the duty of all citizens.[12] Death sentences imposed by Union judicial authorities may not be carried out without the confirmation of the President of the Union.[13]

LEGISLATIVE DEPARTMENT

The Constitution provides for a National Assembly composed of 40 members, distributed 8 each to Abu Dhabi and Dubai, 6 each to Sharjah and Ras Al-Khaimah, and 4 each to Ajman, Umm Al Qawain and Fujairah, each Emirate deciding upon the method of selection of its representatives.[14] The term of office is two years subject to dissolution, and members may be reelected. Members represent the whole people of the Union.[15] It meets in one regular session of six months at least.[16] Immunities of members are provided.[17] Union bills are submitted to the National Assembly before their submission to the President and Supreme Council.[18] Laws may be promulgated over the objections of the National Assembly by the President of the Union after ratification by the Supreme Council.[19] The National Assembly is informed of international treaties.[20] It may discuss subject pertaining to the Union unless the Council of Ministers objects.[21]

[1] Const., Art. 1, 2.
[2] Id., Art. 3,4.
[3] Id., Art. 6.
[4] Id., Art. 7.
[5] Id., Art. 11.
[6] Id., Art. 13–24.
[7] Id., Art. 116.
[8] Id., Art. 120.
[9] Id., Art. 25–34.
[10] Id., Art. 36–38.
[11] Id., Art. 39.
[12] Id., Art. 43.
[13] Id., Art. 108.
[14] Id., Art. 68, 69.
[15] Id., Art. 77.
[16] Id., Art. 78.
[17] Id., Art. 81, 82.
[18] Id., Art. 89.
[19] Id., Art. 110.
[20] Id., Art. 91.
[21] Id.. Art. 92.

EXECUTIVE DEPARTMENT

The Supreme Council of the Union is the highest authority and formulates general policy, sanctions Union laws and decrees, ratifies international agreements, has the power of appointment.[22] It is composed of the Rulers of all the Emirates, each Emirate having a single vote.[23] Decisions are by a majority of 5, provided the majority includes Abu Dhabi and Dubai.[24] The Supreme Council elects the President and Vice-President of the Union for a term of five Gregorian years.[25] The President has the power of appointment, supervises the implementation of Union laws, has the right of pardon, is the fount of honor.[26] The Council of Ministers is composed of the Prime Minister, Deputy Prime Minister and Ministers chosen from among citizens of the Union known for their competence and experience.[27] The Council of Ministers is the executive authority of the Union under the supreme control of the President and the Supreme Council; it supervises the implementation of laws and policy, initiates federal laws for submission to the Union National Assembly, draws up the budget, supervises the execution of court judgments, controls the administration.[28] Its deliberations are secret and the Prime Minister has the casting vote.[29] Incompatibilities of office are listed.[30] The Prime Minister and Ministers are responsible to the President and Supreme Council of the Union.[31] The management of financial affairs is laid down.[32] There are provisions concerning the Armed Forces.[33]

JUDICIAL DEPARTMENT

Judges are independent in the performance of their duties.[34] The Constitution provides for a Union Supreme Court and Union Primary Tribunals.[35] The Union Supreme Court is composed of a President and not more than 5 judges appointed by the President; they may only be removed for certain reasons.[36] The Union Supreme Court has jurisdiction in disputes between Emirates or between the Emirates and the Union, examines the constitutionality of Union or Emirate legislation, interprets the Constitution, tries Ministers and senior officials and has jurisdiction over crimes directly affecting the Union and conflicts of jursidiction.[37] The jurisdiction of Union Primary Tribunals is stipulated.[38] In all matters not assigned to the Union the local judicial authorities of each Emirate have jurisdiction.[39]

AREA, POPULATION, ETC,

The area of the Union is 77,700 square kilometres, the population (1980 census) 1,040,275. The official language is Arabic.[40] The provisional capital is Abu Dhabi, the capital to be established on the borders of Abu Dhabi and Dubai and called Al Karama.[41]

[22] Id., Art. 46, 47.
[23] Id., Art. 46.
[24] Id., Art. 49.
[25] Id., Art. 51, 52.
[26] Id., Art. 54.
[27] Id., Art. 55, 56.
[28] Id., Art. 60.
[29] Id., Art. 61.
[30] Id., Art. 62.
[31] Id., Art. 64.
[32] Id., Art. 126–136.
[33] Id., Art. 137–143.
[34] Id., Art. 94.
[35] Id., Art. 95.
[36] Id., Art. 96, 97.
[37] Id., Art. 99.
[38] Id., Art. 102.
[39] Id., Art. 104.
[40] Id., Art. 7.
[41] Id., Art. 9.

THE PROVISIONAL CONSTITUTION OF THE UNITED ARAB EMIRATES[1]

July 18, 1971, amended 1972

We, the Rulers of the Emirates of Abu Dhabi, Dubai, Sharjah, Ajman, Umm Al Qawain and Fujairah;[2]

Whereas it is out desire and the desire of the people of our Emirates to establish a Union between these Emirates, to promote a better life, more enduring stability and a higher international status for the Emirates and their people;

Desiring to create closer links between the Arab Emirates in the form of an independent, sovereign, federal state, capable of protecting its existence and the existence of its members, in co-operation with the sister Arab states and with all other friendly states which are members of the United Nations Organization and of the family of nations in general, on a basis of mutual respect and reciprocal interests and benefits;

Desiring also to lay the foundation for federal rule in the coming years on a sound basis, corresponding to the realities and the capacities of the Emirates at the present time, enabling the Union, so far as possible, freely to achieve its goals, sustaining the identity of its members providing that this is not inconsistent with those goals and preparing the people of the Union at the same time for a dignified and free constitutional life, and progressing by steps towards a comprehensive, representative, democratic regime in an Islamic and Arab society free from fear and anxiety;

And whereas the realization of the foregoing was our dearest desire, towards which we have bent our strongest resolution, being desirous of advancing our country and our people to the status of qualifying them to take appropriate place among civilized states and nations;

For all these reasons and until the preparation of the permanent Constitution for the Union may be completed, we proclaim before the Supreme and Omnipotent Creator, and before all the peoples, our agreement to this provisional Constitution, to which our signatures were appended, which shall be implemented during the transitional perod indicated in it;

May Allah, our Protector and Defender, grant us success.

PART ONE

THE UNION, ITS FUNDAMENTAL CONSTITUENTS AND AIMS

Art. 1. The United Arab Emirates is an independent, sovereign, federal state and is referred to hereafter in this Constitution as the Union.

[1] Published by the Ministry of Information, Abu Dhabi. Supplied by them in January 1982. Ed.
[2] Ras El Khaima joined the Union on the 10th of February, 1972. Ed.

The Union shall consist of the following Emirates:

Abu Dhabi – Dubai – Sharjah – Ajman – Umm Al Qawain – Fujairah – Ras Al – Khaimah.

Any other independent Arab country may join the Union provided that the Supreme Council agrees unanimously to this.

provided that the Supreme Council agrees unanimously to this.

In the event of the acceptance of a new member joining the Union, the Supreme Council of the Union shall determine the number of seats which will be allocated to that member in the National Assembly of the Union, being in addition to the number stipulated in Article 68 of this Constitution.

Art. 2. The Union shall exercise sovereignty in matters assigned to it in accordance with this Constitution over all territory and territorial waters lying within the international boundaries of the member Emirates.

Art. 3. The member Emirates shall exercise sovereignty over their own territories and territorial waters in all matters which are not within the jurisdiction of the Union as assigned in this Constitution.

Art. 4. The Union may not cede its sovereignty or relinquish any part of its territories or waters.

Art. 5. The Union shall have a Flag, an Emblem and a National Anthem. The Flag and the Emblem shall be prescribed by Law. Each Emirate shall retain its own flag for use within its territories.

Art. 6. The Union is a part of the Great Arab Nation, to which it is bound by the ties of religion. language, history and common destiny.

The people of the Union are one people, and one part of the Arab Nation.

Art. 7. Islam is the official religion of the Union. The Islamic Shari'ah shall be a main source of legislation in the Union. The official language of the Union is Arabic.

Art. 8. The citizens of the Union shall have a single nationality which shall be prescribed by law. When abroad, they shall enjoy the protection of the Union Government in accordance with accepted international principles.

No citizen of the Union may be deprived of his nationality nor may his nationality be withdrawn save in exceptional circumstances which shall be defined by Law.

Art. 9. 1. The Capital of the Union shall be established in an area allotted to the Union by the Emirates of Abu Dhabi and Dubai on the borders between them and it shall be given the name 'Al Karama'.

2. There shall be allocated in the Union budget for the first year the amount necessary to cover the expenses of technical studies and planning for the construction of the Capital. However, construction work shall begin as soon as possible and shall be completed in not more than seven years from the date of entry into force of this Constitution.

3. Until the construction of the Union Capital is complete, Abu Dhabi shall be the provisional headquarters of the Union.

Art. 10. The aims of the Union shall be the maintenance of its independence and sovereigenty, the safeguard of its security and stability, the defence against any agression upon its existence or the existence of its member states, the protection of the rights and liabilities of the people of the Union. the achievement of close co-operation between the Emirates for their common benefit in realising these aims and in promoting their prosperity and progress in all fields, the provision of a better life for all citizens together with respect by each Emirate for the independence and sovereignty of the other Emirates in their internal affairs within the framework of this Constitution.

Art. 11. 1. The Emirates of the Union shall form an economic and customs entity. Union Laws shall regulate the progressive stages appropriate to the achievement of this entity.

2. The free movement of all capital and goods between the Emirates of the Union is guaranteed and may not be restricted except by a Union Law.

3. All taxes, fees, duties and tolls imposed on the movement of goods from one member Emirate to the other shall be abolished.

Art. 12. The foreign policy of the Union shall be directed towards support for Arab and Islamic causes and interests and towards the consolidation of the bonds of friendship and co-operation with all nations and peoples on the basis of the principles of the Charter of the United Nations and ideal international standards.

PART TWO

THE FUNDAMENTAL SOCIAL AND ECONOMIC BASIS OF THE UNION

Art. 13. The Union and the member Emirates shall co-operate, within the limits of their jurisdiction and abilities, in executing the provisions of this Part.

Art. 14. Equality, social justice, ensuring safety and security and equality of opportunity for all citizens shall be the pillars of the Society. Co-operation and mutual mercy shall be a firm bond between them.

Art. 15. The family is the basis of society. It is founded on morality, religion, ethics and patriotism. The law shall guarantee its existence, safeguard and protect it from corruption.

Art. 16. Society shall be responsible for protecting childhood and motherhood and shall protect minors and others unable to look after themselves for any reason, such as illness or incapacity or old age or forced unemployment. It shall be responsible for assisting them and enabling them to help themselves for their own benefit and that of the community.

Such matters shall be regulated by welfare and social security legislations.

Art. 17. Education shall be a fundamental factor for the progress of society. It shall be compulsory in its primary stage and free of charge at all stages, within the Union. The law shall prescribe the necessary plans for the propagation and spread of education at various levels and for the eradication of illiteracy.

Art. 18. Private schools may be established by individuals and organizations in accordance with the provisions of the law, provided that such schools shall be subject to the supervision of the competent public authorities and to their directives.

Art. 19. Medical care and means of prevention and treatment of diseases and epidemics shall be ensured by the community for all citizens.

The community shall promote the establishment of public and private hospitals, dispensaries and cure-houses.

Art. 20. Society shall esteem work as a corner-stone of its development. It shall endeavor to ensure that employment is available for citizens and to train them so that they are prepared for it. It shall furnish the appropriate facilities for that by providing legislation protecting the rights of the employees and the interests of the employers in the light of the developing international labor legislations.

Art. 21. Private property shall be protected. Conditions relating thereto shall be laid down by Law. No one shall be deprived of his private property except in circumstances dictated by the public benefit in accordance with the provisions of the Law and on payment of a just compensation.

Art. 22. Public property shall be inviolable. The protection of public property shall be the duty of every citizen. the Law shall define the cases in which penalties shall be imposed for the contravention of that duty.

Art. 23. The natural resources and wealth in each Emirate shall be considered to be public property of that Emirate. Society shall be responsible for the protection and proper exploitation of such natural resources and wealth for the benefit of the national economy.

Art. 24. The basis of the national economy shall be social justice. It is founded on sincere co-operation between public and private activities. Its aim shall be the achievement of economic development, increase of productivity, raising the standards of living and the achievement of prosperity for citizens, all within the limits of Law.

The Union shall encourage co-operation and savings.

PART THREE

FREEDOM, RIGHTS AND PUBLIC DUTIES

Art. 25. All persons are equal before the law, without distinction between citizens of the Union in regard to race, nationality, religious belief or social status.

Art. 26. Personal liberty is guaranteed to all citizens. No person may be arrested, searched, detained or imprisoned except in accordance with the provisions of law.

No person shall be subjected to torture or to degrading treatment.

Art. 27. Crimes and punishments shall be defined by the law. No penalty shall be imposed for any act of commission or omission committed before the relevant law has been promulgated.

Art. 28. Penalty is personal. An accused shall be presumed innocent until proved guilty in a legal and fair trial. The accused shall have the right to appoint the person who is capable to conduct his defence during the trial. The law shall prescribe the cases in which the presence of a counsel for defence shall be assigned.

Physical and moral abuse of an accused person is prohibited.

Art. 29. Freedom of movement and residence shall be guaranteed to citizens within the limits of law.

Art. 30. Freedom of opinion and expressing it verbally, in writing or by other means of expression shall be guaranteed within the limits of law.

Art. 31. Freedom of communication by post, telegraph or other means of communication and the secrecy thereof shall be guaranteed in accordance with law.

Art. 32. Freedom to exercise religious worship shall be guaranteed in accordance with established customs, provided that it does not conflict with public policy or violate public morals.

Art. 33. Freedom of assembly and establishing association shall be guaranteed within the limits of law.

Art. 34. Every citizen shall be free to choose his occupation, trade or profession within the limits of law. Due consideration being given to regulations organizing some of such professions and trades. No person may be subjected to forced labor except in exceptional circumstances provided for by the law and in return for compensation.

No person may be enslaved.

Art. 35. Public office shall be open to all citizens on a basis of equality of opportunity in accordance with the provisions of law. Public office shall be a national service entrusted to those who hold it. The public servant shall aim, in the execuion of his duties, at the public interest alone.

Art. 36. Habitations shall be inviolable. They may not be entered without the permission of their inhabitants except in accordance with the provisions of the law and in circumstances laid down therein.

Art. 37. Citizens may not be deported or banished form the Union.

Art. 38. Extradition of citizens and of political refugees is prohibited.

Art. 39. General confiscation of property shall be prohibited. Confiscation of an individual's possessions as a penalty may not be inflicted except by a court judgment in the circumstances specified by law.

Art. 40. Foreigners shall enjoy, within the Union, the rights and freedom stipulated in international charters which are in force or in treaties and agreements to which the Union is party. They shall be subject to the corresponding obligations.

Art. 41. Every person shall have the right to submit complaints to the competent authorities, concerning the abuse or infringement of the rights and freedom stipulated in this Part.

Art. 42. Payment of taxes and public charges determined by law is a duty of every citizen.

Art. 43. Defence of the Union is a sacred duty of every citizen and military service an honor for citizens which shall be regulated by law.

Art. 44. Respect of the Constitution, laws and orders issued by public authorites in execution thereof, observance of public order and respect of public morality are duties incumbent upon all inhabitants of the Union.

PART FOUR

THE UNION AUTHORITIES

Art. 45. The Union authorities shall consist of:
1. The Supreme Council of the Union.
2. The President of the Union and his Deputy.
3. The Council of Ministers of the Union.
4. The National Assembly of the Union.
5. The Judiciary of the Union.

Chapter I. The Supreme Council of the Union

Art. 46. The Supreme Council of the Union shall be the highest authority in the Union. It shall consist of the Rulers of all the Emirates composing the Union, or of those who deputise for the Rulers in their Emirates in the event of their absence or if they have been excused from attending.

Each Emirate shall have a single vote in the deliberations of the Council.

Art. 47. The Supreme Council of the Union shall exercise the following matters:

1. Formulation of general policy in all matters invested in the Union by this Constitution and consideration of all matters which leads to the achievement of the goals of the Union and the common interest of the member Emirates.

2. Sanction of various Union laws before their promulgation, including the Laws of the Annual General Budget and the Final Accounts.

3. Sanction of decrees relating to matters which by virtue of the provisions of this Constitution are subject to the ratification or agreement of the Supreme Council. Such sanction shall take place before the promulgation of these decrees by the President of the Union.

4. Ratification of treaties and international agreements. Such ratification shall be accomplished by decree.

5. Approval of the appointment of the Chairman of the Council of Ministers of the Union, acceptance of his resignation and his removal from office upon a proposal from the President of the Union.

6. Approval of the appointment of the President and Judges of the Supreme Court of the Union, acceptance of their resignations and their dismissal in the circumstances stipulated by this Constitution. Such acts shall be accomplished by decrees.

7. Supreme Control over the affairs of the Union in general.

8. Any other relevant matters stipulated in this Constitution or in the Union laws.

Art. 48. 1. The Supreme Council shall lay down its own bye-laws which shall include its procedure for the conduct of business and the procedure for voting on its decisions. The deliberations of the Council shall be secret.

2. The Supreme Council shall establish a general Secretariat which shall consist of an adequate number of officials to assist it in the execution of its duties.

Art. 49. Decisions of the Supreme Council on substantive matters shall be by a majority of five of its members provided that this majority includes the votes of the Emirates of Abu Dhabi and Dubai. The minority shall be bound by the view of the said majority.

But, decisions of the Council on procedural matters shall be by a majority vote. Such matters shall be defined in the bye-laws of the Council.

Art. 50. Sessions of the Supreme Council shall be held in the Union capital. Sessions may be held in any other place agreed upon beforehand.

Chapter II. The President of the Union and his Deputy

Art. 51. The Supreme Council of the Union shall elect from among its members a President, and a Vice-President of the Union. The Vice-President of the Union shall exercise all the powers of the President in the event of his absence for any reason.

Art. 52. The term of office of the President and the Vice-President shall be five Gregorian years. They are eligible for re-election to the same offices.

Each of them shall, on assuming office, take the following oath before the Supreme Council:

'I swear by Almighty God that I will be faithful to the United Arab Emirates; that I will respect its Constitution and its laws; that I will protect the interests of the people of the Union; that I will discharge my duties faithfully and loyally and that I will safeguard the independence of the Union and its territorial integrity.'

Art. 53. Upon vacancy of the office of the President or his Deputy for death or resignation, or because either one of them ceases to be Ruler in his Emirate for any reason, the Supreme Council shall be called into session within one month of that date to elect a successor to the vacant office for the period stipulated in Article 52 of this Constitution.

In the event that the two offices of the President of the Supreme Council and his Deputy become vacant simultaneously, the Council shall be immediately called into session by any one it its members or by the Chairman of the Council of Ministers of the Union, to elect a new President and Vice-President to fill the two offices.

Art. 54. The President of the Union shall assume the following powers:

1. Presiding the Supreme Council and directing its discussions.

2. Calling the Supreme Council into session, and terminating its sessions according to the rules of procedure upon which the Council shall decide in its bye-laws. It is obligatory for him to convene the Council for sessions, whenever one of its members so requests.

3. Calling the Supreme Council and the Council of Ministers into joint session whenever necessity demands.

4. Signing Union laws, decrees and decisions which the Supreme Council has sanctioned and promulgating them.

5. Appointing the Prime Minister, accepting his resignation and relieving him of

office with the consent of the Supreme Council. He shall also appoint the Deputy Prime Minister and the Ministers and shall receive their resignations and relieve them of office in accordance with a proposal from the Prime Minister of the Union.

6. Appointing the diplomatic representatives of the Union to foreign states and other senior Union officials both civil and military (with the exception of the President and Judges of the Supreme Court of the Union) and accepting their resignations and dismissing them with the consent of the Council of Ministers of the Union. Such appointments, acceptance of resignations and dismissals shall be accomplished by decrees and in accordance with Union laws.

7. Signing of letters of credence of diplomatic representatives of the Union to foreign states and organizations and accepting the credentials of diplomatic and consular representatives of foreign states to the Union and receiving their letters of credence. He shall similarly sign documents of appointment and credence of representatives.

8. Supervising the implementation of Union laws, decrees and decisions through the Council of Ministers of the Union and the competent Ministers.

9. Representing the Union internally, vis-a-vis other states and in all international relations.

10. Exercising the right of pardon and commutation of sentences and approving capital sentences according to the provisions of this Constitution and Union laws.

11. Conferring decorations and medals of honor, both civil and military, in accordance with the laws relating to such decorations and medals.

12. Any other power vested in him by the Supreme Council or vested in him in conformity with this Constitution or Union laws.

Chapter III. The Council of Ministers of the Union

Art. 55. The Council of Ministers of the Union shall consist of the Prime Minister, his Deputy and a number of Ministers.

Art. 56. Ministers shall be chosen from among citizens of the Union known for their competence and experience.

Art. 57. The Prime Minister, his Deputy and the Ministers shall, before assuming the responsibilities of their office, take the following oath before the President of the Union:

'I swear by Almighty God that I will be loyal to the United Arab Emirates; that I will respect its Constitution and laws; that I will discharge my duties faithfully; that I will completely observe the interests of the people of the Union and that I will completely safeguard the existence of the Union and its territorial integrity.'

Art. 58. The law shall define the jurisdiction of the Ministers and the powers of each Minister. The first Council of Ministers of the Union shall be composed of the following Ministers:

1. Foreign Affairs
2. Interior
3. Defence

4. Finance, Economy and Industry
5. Justice
6. Education
7. Public Health
8. Public Works and Agriculture
9. Communications, Post, Telegraph and Telephones
10. Labor and Social Affairs
11. Information
12. Planning

Art. 59. The Prime Minister shall preside over the meetings of the Council of Ministers. He shall call it into session, direct its debates, follow up the activities of Ministers and shall supervise the co-ordination of work between the various Ministries and in all executive organs of the Union.

The Deputy Prime Minister shall exercise all the powers of the Prime Minister in the event of his absence for any reason.

Art. 60. The Council of Ministers, in its capacity as the executive authority of the Union, and under the supreme control of the President of the Union and the Supreme Council, shall be responsible for dealing with all domestic and foreign affairs which are within the competence of the Union according to this Constitution and Union laws.

The Council of Ministers shall, in particular, assume the following powers:

1. Following up the implementation of the general policy of the Union Government, both domestic and foreign.

2. Initiating drafts of Federal Laws and submitting them to the Union National Assembly before they are raised to the President of the Union for presentation to the Supreme Council for sanction.

3. Drawing up the annual general budget of the Union, and the final accounts.

4. Preparing drafts of decrees and various decisions.

5. Issuing regulations necessary for the implementation of Union laws without amending or suspending such regulations or making any exemption from their execution. Issuing also police regulations and other regulations relating to the organization of public services and administrations, within the limits of this Constitution and Union laws. A special provision of the law or the Council of Ministers, may charge the competent Union Minister or any other administrative authority to promulgate some of such regulations.

6. Supervising the implementation of Union laws, decrees decisions and regulations by all the concerned authorities in the Union or in the Emirates.

7. Supervising the execution of judgments rendered by Union Law Courts and the implementation of international treaties and agreements concluded by the Union.

8. Appointment and dismissal of Union employees in accordance with the provisions of the law, provided that their appointment and dismissal do not require the issue of a decree.

9. Controlling the conduct of work in departments and public services of the Union and the conduct and discipline of Union employees in general.

10. Any other authority vested in it by law or by the Supreme Council within the limits of this Constitution.

Art. 61. Deliberations of the Council of Ministers shall be secret. Its resolutions shall be passed by a majority of its members. In the event that voting is evenly divided, the side on which the Prime Minister has voted shall prevail. The minority shall abide by the opinion of the majority.

Art. 62. While in office, the Prime Minister, his Deputy or any Union Minister, may not practice any profession, commercial or financial occupation or enter into any commercial transactions with the Government of the Union or the Governments of the Emirates, or combine with their office the membership of the board of directors of any financial or commercial company.

Furthermore, they may not combine with their office more than one official post in any of the Emirates and shall relinquish all other local official posts, if any.

Art. 63. The members of the Council of Ministers shall aim to serve in their conduct the interests of the Union, the promotion of public welfare and totally renounce personal benefits. They must not exploit their official capacities for their own interests or that of any person related to them.

Art. 64. The Prime Minister and the Ministers shall be politically responsible collectively before the President of the Union and the Supreme Council of the Union for the execution of the general policy of the Union both domestic and foreign. Each of them shall be personally responsible to the President of the Union and the Supreme Council for the activities of his Ministry or office.

The resignation of the Prime Minister, his removal from office, his death, or the vacating of his office for any reason whatsoever shall involve the resignation of the whole Cabinet. The President of the Union may require the Ministers to remain in office temporarily, to carry out immediate administration, until such time as a new Cabinet is formed.

Art. 65. At the beginning of every financial year, the Council of Ministers shall submit to the President of the Union for presentation to the Supreme Council, a detailed statement of internal achievements, on the Union's relations with other states and international organizations, together with the recommendations of the Cabinet on the best and most practical means of strengthening the foundations of the Union, consolidating its security and stability, achieving its goals and progress in all fields.

Art. 66. 1. The Council of Ministers shall draw up its own bye-laws including its rules of procedure.

2. The Council of Ministers shall establish a General Secretariat provided with a number of employees to assist it in the conduct of its business.

Art. 67. The Law shall prescribe the salaries of the Prime Minister, his Deputy and the other Ministers.

Chapter IV. General Provisions

SECTION I. GENERAL PROVISIONS

Art. 68. The National Assembly of the Union shall be composed of forty members. Seats shall be distributed to member Emirates as follows:

Abu Dhabi	–	8 seats
Dubai	–	8 seats
Sharjah	–	6 seats
Ras Al-Khaimah	–	6 seats
Ajman	–	4 seats
Umm Al-Qawain	–	4 seats
Fujairah	–	4 seats

Art. 69. Each Emirate shall be free to determine the method of selection of the citizens representing it in the Union Assembly.

Art. 70. A member of the Union National Assembly must satisfy the following conditions:

1. Must be a citizen of one of the Emirates of the Union, and permanently resident in the Emirate he represents in the Assembly.
2. Must be not less than twenty-five Gregorian years of age at the time of his selection.
3. Must enjoy civil status, good conduct, reputation and not previously convicted of a dishonorable offence unless he has been rehabilitated in accordance with the law.
4. Must have adequate knowledge of reading and writing.

Art. 71. Membership of the Union National Assembly shall be incompatible with any public office in the Union, including Ministerial portfolios.

Art. 72. The term of membership in the Union National Assembly shall be two Gregorian years commencing from the date of its first sitting. When this period expires, the Assembly shall be completely renewed for the time remaining until the end of the transitional period as laid down in Article 144 of this Constitution.

Any member who has completed his term may be re-elected.

Art. 73. Before assuming his duties in the Assembly or its Committees, a member of the Union National Assembly shall take the following oath before the Assembly in public session:

> 'I swear by Almighty God that I will be loyal to the United Arab Emirates; that I will respect the Constitution and the laws of the Union and that I will discharge my duties in the Assembly and its Committees honestly and truthfully.'

Art. 74. If, for any reason, a seat of any member of the Assembly becomes vacant before the end of the term of his membership, a replacement shall be selected within two months of the date on which the vacancy is announced by the Assembly, unless the vacancy occurs during the three months preceding the end of the term of the Assembly.

The new member shall complete the term of membership of his predecessor.

Art. 75. Sessions of the Union National Assembly shall be held in the Union capital. Exceptionally, sessions may be held in any other place within the Union on the basis of a decision taken by a majority vote of the members and with the approval of the Council of Ministers.

Art. 76. The Assembly shall decide upon the validity of the mandate of its members. It shall also decide upon disqualifying members, if they lose one of the required conditions, by a majority of all its members and on the proposal of five among them. The Assembly shall be competent to accept resignation from membership. The resignation shall be considered as final from the date of its acceptance by the Assembly.

Art. 77. A member of the National Assembly of the Union shall represent the whole people of the Union and not merely the Emirate which he represents in the Assembly.

SECTION 2. ORGANIZATION OF WORK IN THE ASSEMBLY

Art. 78. The Assembly shall hold an annual ordinary session lasting not less than six months, commencing in the third week of November each year. It may be called into extraordinary session whenever the need arises. The Assembly may not consider at an extraordinary session any matter other than those for which it has been called into session.

Notwithstanding the preceding paragraph, the President of the Union shall summon the Union National Assembly to convene its first ordinary session within a period not exceeding sixty days from the entry into force of this Constitution. This session shall end at the time appointed by the Supreme Council by decree.

Art. 79. The Assembly shall be summoned into session, and its session shall be terminated by decree issued by the President of the Union with the consent of the Council of Ministers of the Union. Any meeting held by the Council without a formal summons, or in a place other than that legally assigned for its meeting in accordance with this Constitution, shall be invalid and shall have no effect.

Nevertheless, if the Assembly is not called to hold its meeting for its annual ordinary session before the third week of November, the Assembly shall be *ipso facto* in session on the twenty-first of the said month.

Art. 80. The President of the Union shall inaugurate the ordinary annual session of the Assembly whereupon he shall deliver a speech reviewing the situation of the country and the important events and affairs which happened during the year and outlining the projects and reforms the Union Government plans to undertake during the new session. The President of the Union may depute his Vice-President or the Prime Minister to open the session or to deliver the speech.

The National Assembly shall select, from among its members, a committee to draft the reply to the Opening Speech, embodying the Assembly's observations and wishes, and shall submit the reply after approval by the Assembly to the President of the Union for submission to the Supreme Council.

Art. 81. Members of the Assembly shall not be censured for any opinions or views expressed in the course of carrying out their duties within the Assembly or its Committees.

Art. 82. Except in cases of 'flagrante delicto', no penal proceedings may be taken against any member while the Assembly is in session, without the authorization of the Assembly. The Assembly must be notified if such proceedings are taken while it is not is session.

Art. 83. The President of the Assembly and its other members shall be entitled, for the date of taking the oath before the Assembly, to a remuneration which shall be determined by law, and to travelling expenses from their place of residence to the place in which the Assembly is meeting.

Art. 84. The Assembly shall have a Bureau consisting of a President, a First and Second Vice-President and two controllers. The Assembly shall select them all from among its members.

The term of office of the controllers shall expire with the choice of new control-when the term of the Assembly expires or when it is dissolved in accordance with the provisions of the second paragraph of Article 88.

The term of office of the controllers shall expire with the choice of new controllers at the opening of the next ordinary session. If any post in the Bureau becomes vacant, the Assembly shall elect who shall fill it for the remaining period.

Art. 85. The Assembly shall have a Secretary General who shall be assisted by a number of staff who shall be directly responsible to the Assembly. The Assembly's standing orders shall lay down their conditions of service and their powers.

The Assembly shall lay down its standing orders, issued by decree promulgated by the President of the Union with the consent of the Council of Ministers.

The standing orders shall define the powers of the President of the Assembly, his two Vice-Presidents and the Controllers and shall define generally all matters pertaining to the Assembly, its committees, its members, its Secretariat, its employees, its rules and procedures of discussion and voting in the Assembly and the Committees and other matters within the limits of the provisions of this Constitution.

Art. 86. Sessions of the Assembly shall be public. Secret sessions may be held at the request of a representative of the Government, the President of the Assembly or one third of its members.

Art. 87. Deliberations of the Assembly shall not be valid unless a majority of its members at least are present. Resolutions shall be taken by an absolute majority of the votes of members present, except in cases where a special majority has been prescribed. If votes are equally divided, the side which the President of the session supports shall prevail.

Art. 88. Meetings of the Assembly may be adjourned by a decree promulgated by the President of the Union with the approval of the Council of Ministers of the Union for a period not exceeding one month, provided that such adjournment is not repeated in one session except with the approval of the Assembly and for once only. The period of adjournment shall not be deemed part of the term of the ordinary session.

The Assembly may also be dissolved by a decree promulgated by the President of the Union with the approval of the Supreme Council of the Union, provided that the decree of dissolution includes a summons to the new Assembly to come into session within sixty days of the date of the decree of dissolution. The Assembly may not be dissolved again for the same reason.

SECTION 3. POWERS OF THE NATIONAL ASSEMBLY

Art. 89. In so far as this does not conflict with the provisions of Article 110, Union Bills, including financial bills, shall be submitted to the National Assembly of the Union before their submission to the President of the Union for presentation to the Supreme Council for ratification. The National Assembly shall discuss these bills and may pass them, amend or reject them.

Art. 90. The Assembly shall examine during its ordinary session the Annual General Budget draft law of the Union and the draft law of the final accounts, in accordance with the provisions in Chapter Eight of this Constitution.

Art. 91. The Government shall inform the Union Assembly of international treaties and agreements concluded with other states and the various international organizations, together with appropriate explanations.

Art. 92. The Union National Assembly may discuss any general subject pertaining to the affairs of the Union unless the Council of Ministers informs the Union National Assembly that such discussion is contrary to the highest interests of the Union. The Prime Minister or the Minister concerned shall attend the debates. The Union National Assembly may express its recommendations and may define the subjects for debate. If the Council of Ministers does not approve of these recommendations, it shall notify the Union National Assembly of its reasons.

Art. 93. The Government of the Union shall be represented at sessions of the Union National Assembly by the Prime Minister or his deputy or one member of the Union Cabinet at least. The Prime Minister or his deputy or the competent Minister, shall answer questions put to them by any member of the Assembly requesting explanation of any matters within their jurisdication, in conformity with the procedures prescribed in the standing orders of the Assembly.

Chapter V. The Judiciary in the Union and the Emirates

Art. 94. Justice is on the basis of rule. In performing their duties, judges shall be independent and shall not be subject to any authority but the law and their own conscience.

Art. 95. The Union shall have a Union Supreme Court and Union Primary Tribunals as explained hereinafter.

Art. 96. The Union Supreme Court shall consist of a President and a number of judges, not exceeding five in all, who shall be appointed by decree, issued by the President of the Union after approval by the Supreme Council. The law shall prescribe the number of the chambers in the Court, their order and procedures, conditions of service and retirement for its members and the preconditions and qualifications required of them.

Art. 97. The President and the Judges of the Union Supreme Court shall not be removed while they administer justice. Their tenure of office shall not be terminated except for one of the following reasons:

1. Death.
2. Resignation.
3. Expiration of term of contract for those who are appointed by fixed term contract or completion of term of secondment.
4. Reaching retirement age.
5. Permanent incapacity to carry the burdens of their duties by reasons of ill health.
6. Disciplinary discharge on the basis of the reasons and proceedings stipulated in the law.
7. Appointment to other offices, with their consent.

Art. 98. The President and the Judges of the Union Supreme Court shall, before holding office, swear on oath before the President of the Union and in the presence of the Union Minister of Justice, that they will render justice without fear or favor and that they will be loyal to the Constitution and the laws of the Union.

Art. 99. The Union Supreme Court shall have jurisdiction in the following matters:

1. Various disputes between member Emirates in the Union, or between any one Emirate or more and the Union Government, whenever such disputes are submitted to the Court on the request of any of the interested parties.
2. Examination of the constitutionality of Union laws, if they are challenged by one or more of the Emirates on the grounds of violating the Constitution of the Union.

Examination of the constitutionality of legislations promulgated by one of the Emirates, if they are challenged by one of the Union authorities on the grounds of violation of the Constitution of the Union or of Union laws.

3. Examination of the constitutionality of laws, legislations and regulations in general, if such request is referred to it by any Court in the country during a pending case before it. The aforesaid Court shall be bound to accept the ruling of the Union Supreme Court rendered in this connection.
4. Interpretation of the provisions of the Constitution, when so requested by any Union authority or by the Government of any Emirate. Any such interpretation shall be considered binding on all.
5. Trial of Ministers and senior officials of the Union appointed by decree regarding their actions in carrying out their official duties on the demand of the Supreme Council and in accordance with the relevant law.
6. Crimes directly affecting the interests of the Union, such as crimes relating to its internal or external security, forgery of the official records or seals of any of the Union authorities and counterfeiting of currency.
7. Conflict of jurisdiction between the Union judicial authorities and the local judicial authorities in the Enirates.
8. Conflict of jurisdiction between the judicial authority in one Emirate and the

judicial authority in another Emirate. The rules relating thereof shall be regulated by a Union Law.

9. Any other jurisdiction stipulated in this Constitution, or which may be assigned to it by a Union law.

Art. 100. The Union Supreme Court shall hold its sittings in the capital of the Union. It may, exceptionally, assemble when necessary in the capital of one of the Emirates.

Art. 101. The judgments of the Union Supreme Court shall be final and binding upon all.

If the Court, in ruling on the constitutionality of laws, legislations and regulations, decides that a Union legislation is inconsistent with the Union Constitution, or that local legislations or regulations under consideration contain provisions which are inconsistent with the Union Constitution or with a Union law, the authority concerned in the Union or in the Emirate, accordingly, shall be obliged to hasten to take the necessary measures to remove or rectify the constitutional inconsistency.

Art. 102. The Union shall have one or more Union Primary Tribunals which shall sit in the permanent capital of the Union or in the capitals of some of the Emirates, in order to exercise the judicial powers within the sphere of their jurisdiction in the following cases:

1. Civil, commercial and administrative disputes between the Union and individuals whether the Union is the plaintiff or defendant.

2. Crimes committed within the boundaries of the permanent capital of the Union, with exception of such matters as are reserved for the Union Supreme Court under Article 99 of this Constitution.

3. Personal status cases, civil and commercial cases and other cases between individuals which shall arise in the permanent capital of the Union.

Art. 103. The law shall regulate all matters connnected with the Union Primary Tribunals in respect of their organization, formation, chambers, local jurisdiction, procedures to be followed before them, the oath to be sworn by their judges, conditions of service relating to them and the ways of appeal against their judgments.

The law may stipulate that appeals against the judgments of these Tribunals shall be heard before one of the chambers of the Union Supreme Court, in the cases and according to the procedures prescribed therein.

Art. 104. The local judicial authorities in each Emirate shall have jurisdiction in all judicial matters not assigned to the Union judicature in accordance with this Constitution.

Art. 105. All or part of the jurisdiction assigned to the local judicial authorities in accordance with the preceding Article may be transferred by a Union law issued at the request of the Emirate concerned, to the Primary Union Tribunals.

Circumstances in which appeals against judgments by the local judicial authorities in penal, civil, commercial and other litigations may be referred to the Union Tribunals, shall be defined by a Union law provided that its decision in such appeals shall be final.

Art. 106. The Union shall have a Public Prosecutor who shall be appointed by a Union decree issued with the approval of the Council of Ministers, assisted by a number of members of the Public Prosecutor's office.

The law shall regulate matters relating to the members of the Union Public Prosecutor's Office with respect to their method of appointment, ranks, promotion, retirement and the qualifications required of them.

Besides, the Union Law of Criminal Procedure and trials shall regulate the power of this body and its procedures and the competence of its assistants from the police and the public security officers.

Art. 107. The President of the Union may grant pardon from the execution of any sentence passed by a Union judicature before it is carried out or while it is being served or he may commute such sentence, on the basis of the recommendation of the Union Minister of Justice, after obtaining the approval of a committee formed under the chairmanship of the Minister and consisting of six members selected by the Union Council of Ministers for a term of three years which may be renewed. The members of the committee shall be chosen from citizens of good repute and capability.

Membership of the committee shall be gratis. Its deliberations shall be secret. Its decisions shall be issued by a majority vote.

Art. 108. No sentence of death imposed finally by a Union judicial authority shall be carried out until the President of the Union has confirmed the sentence. He may substitute it by an attenuate sentence in accordance with the procedure stipulated in the preceding Article.

Art. 109. There shall be no general amnesty for a crime or for specified crimes except by law.

The promulgation of the law of amnesty shall consider such crimes being deemed *non avenu*, and shall remit the execution of the sentence or the remaining part of it.

PART FIVE

UNION LEGISLATIONS AND DECREES AND THE AUTHORITIES HAVING JURISDICTION THEREIN

Chapter I. Union Laws

Art. 110. 1. Union Laws shall be promulgated in accordance with the provisions of this Article and other appropriate provisions of the Constitution.

2. A draft law shall become a law after the adoption of the following procedure:

(*a*) The Council of Ministers shall prepare a bill and submit it to the Union National Assembly.

(*b*) The Council of Ministers shall submit the bill to the president of the Union for his approval and presentation to the Supreme Council for ratification.

(*c*) The President of the Union shall sign the bill after ratification by the Supreme Council and shall promulgate it.

3. (*a*) If the Union National Assembly inserts any amendment to the bill and this amendment is not acceptable to the President of the Union or the Supreme Council, or if the Union National Assembly rejects the bill, the President of the Union or the Supreme Council may refer it back to the National Assembly. If the Union National Assembly introduces any amendment on that occasion which is not acceptable to the President of the Union or the Supreme Council, or of the Union National Assembly decides to reject the bill, the President of the Union may promulgate the law after ratification by the Supreme Council.

(*b*) The Term 'bill' in this clause shall means the draft which is submitted to the President of the Union by the Council of Ministers including the amendments, of any, made to it by the Union National Assembly.

4. Notwithstanding the foregoing, if the situation requires the promulgation of Union laws when the National Assembly is not in session, the Council of Ministers of the Union may issue them through the Supreme Council and the President of the Union, provided that the Union Assembly is notified at its next meeting.

Art. 111. Laws shall be published in the Official *Gazette* of the Union within a maximum of two weeks from the date of their signature and promulgation by the President of the Union after the Supreme Council has ratified them. Such laws shall become in force one month after the date of their publication in the said *Gazette,* unless another date is specified in the said law.

Art. 112. No laws may be applied except on what occurs as from the date they become in force and no retroactive effect shall result in such laws. The law may, however, stipulate the contrary in matters other than criminal, if necessity so requires.

Chapter II. Laws issued by Decrees

Art. 113. Should necessity arise for urgent promulgation of Union laws between sessions of the Supreme Council, the President of the Union together with the Council of Ministers may promulgate the necessary laws in the form of decree which shall have the force of law, provided that they are not inconsistent with the Constitution.

Such decree-laws must be referred to the Supreme Council within a week at the maximum for assent or rejection. If they are approved, they shall have the force of law and the Union National Assembly shall be notified at its next meeting.

However, if the Supreme Council does not approve them, they shall cease to have the force of law unless that it has decided to sanction their effectiveness during the preceding period, or to settle in some other way the effects arising therefrom.

Chapter III. Ordinary Decrees

Art. 114. No decree may be issued unless the Council of Ministers has confirmed it and the President of the Union or the Supreme Council, according to their powers, has ratified it. Decrees shall be published in the Official *Gazette* after signature by the President of the Union.

Art. 115. While the Supreme Council is out of session and if necessity arises, it may authorize the President of the Union and the Council of Ministers collectively to promulgate decrees whose ratification is within the power of the Supreme Council, provided that such authority shall not include ratification of international agreements and treaties or declaration or remission of martial law or declaration of a defensive war or appointment of the President or Judges of the Union Supreme Court.

PART SIX

THE EMIRATES

Art. 116. The Emirates shall exercise all powers not assigned to the Union by this Constitution. The Emirates shall all participate in the establishment of the Union and shall benefit from its existence, services and protection.

Art. 117. The exercise of rule in each Emirate shall aim in particular at the maintenance of security and order within its territories, the provision of public utilities for its inhabitants and the raising of social and economic standards.

Art. 118. The member Emirates of the Union shall all work for the coordination of their legislations in various fields with the intention of unifying such legislations as far as possible.

Two or more Emirates may, after obtaining the approval of the Supreme Council, agglomerate in a political or administrative unit, or unify all or part of their public services or establish a single or joint administration to run any such service.

Art. 119. Union law shall regulate with utmost ease matters pertaining to the execution of judgments, requests for commissions of rogation, serving legal documents and surrender of fugitives between member Emirates of the Union.

PART SEVEN

DISTRIBUTION OF LEGISLATIVE, EXECUTIVE AND INTERNATIONAL JURISDICTIONS BETWEEN THE UNION AND THE EMIRATES

Art. 120. The Union shall have exclusive legislative and executive jurisdiction in the following affairs:

1. Foreign affairs.
2. Defence and the Union Armed Forces.
3. Protection of the Union's security against internal or external threat.

4. Matters pertaining to security, order and rule in the permanent capital of the Union.

5. Matters relating to Union officials and Union judiciary.

6. Union finance and Union taxes, duties and fees.

7. Union public loans.

8. Postal, telegraph, telephone and wireless servies.

9. Construction, maintenance and improvement of Union roads which the Supreme Council has determined to be trunk roads. The organization of traffic on such roads.

10. Air Traffic Control and the issue of licences to aircrafts and pilots.

11. Education.

12. Public health and medical services.

13. Currency board and coinage.

14. Measures, standards and weights.

15. Electricity services.

16. Union nationality, passports, residence and immigration.

17. Union properties and all matter relating thereto.

18. Census affairs and statistics relevant to Union purposes.

19. Union Information.

Art. 121. Without prejudice to the provisions of this preceding Article, the Union shall have exclusive legislative jurisdiction in the following matters:

Labor relations and social security; real estate and expropriation in the public interest; extradition of criminals; banks; insurance of all kinds; protection of agricultural and animal wealth; major legislations relating to penal law, civil and commercial transactions and company law, procedures before the civil and criminal courts; protection of cultural, technical and industrial property and copyright; printing and publishing; import of arms and ammunitions except for use by the armed forces or the security forces belonging to any Emirate; other aviation affairs which are not within the executive jurisdiction of the Union; delimitation of territorial waters and regulation of navigation on the high seas.

Art. 122. The Emirates shall have jurisdiction in all matters not assigned to the exclusive jurisdiction of the Union in accordance with the provisions of the two preceding Articles.

Art. 123. As an exception to paragraph 1 of Article 120 concerning the exclusive jurisdiction of the Union in matters of foreign policy and international relations, the member Emirates of the Union may conclude limited agreements of a local and administrative nature with the neighbouring states or regions, save that such agreements are not inconsistent with the interests of the Union or with Union laws and provided that the Supreme Council of the Union is informed in advance. If the Council objects to the conclusion of such agreements, it shall be obligatory to suspend the matter until the Union Court has ruled on that objection as early as possible.

The Emirates may retain their membership in the OPEC organization and the Organization of Arab Petroleum Exporting Countries or may join them.

Art. 124. Before the conclusion of any treaty or international agreement which may affect the status of any one of the Emirates, the competent Union authorities shall consult that Emirate in advance. In the event of a dispute, the matter shall be submitted to the Union Supreme Court for ruling.

Art. 125. The Governments of the Emirates shall undertake the appropriate measures to implement the laws promulgated by the Union and the treaties and international agreements concluded by the Union, including the promulgation of the local laws, regulations, decisions and orders necessary for such implementation.

The Union authorities shall supervise the implementation by Emirate's Governments of the Union laws, decisions, treaties, agreements and Union judgments. The competent administrative and judicial authorities in the Emirates should forward to the Union authorities all possible assistance in this connection.

PART EIGHT

FINANCIAL AFFAIRS OF THE UNION

Art. 126. The general revenues of the Union shall consist of the income from the following resources:

1. Taxes, fees and duties imposed under a Union law in matters within the legislative and executive jurisdiction of the Union.
2. Fees and rates received by the Union in return for services provided.
3. Contribution made by member Emirates of the Union in the Annual Budget of the Union in accordance with the article herein coming after.
4. Union income from its own properties.

Art. 127. The member Emirates of the Union shall contribute a specified proportion of their annual revenues to cover the annual general budget expenditure of the Union, in the manner and on the scale to be prescribed in the Budget Law.

Art. 128. The law shall prescribe the method of preparing the general budget of the Union and the final accounts, The law shall also define the beginning of the financial year.

Art. 129. The draft annual budget of the Union, comprising estimates of revenues and expenditure, shall be referred to the Union National Assembly at least two months before the beginning of the financial year, for discussion and submission of comments thereon, before the draft budget is submitted to the Supreme Council of the Union, together with those comments, for assent.

Art. 130. The annual general budget shall be issued by a law. In all cases, where the budget law has not been promulgated before the beginning of the financial year, temporary monthly funds may be made by Union decree on the basis of one twelth of the funds of the previous financial year. Revenues shall be collected and expenditure disbursed in accordance with the laws in force at the end of the preceding financial year.

Art. 131. All expenditure not provided for in the budget, all expenditure in excess of the budget estimates and all transfers of sums from one part to another of the Budget must be covered by a law.

Notwithstanding the foregoing, in cases of extreme urgency, such expenditure or transfer may be arranged by decree-law in conformity with the provisions of Article 113 of this Constitution.

Art. 132. The Union shall allocate in its annual budget a sum from its revenue to be expended on building and construction projects, internal security and social affairs according to the urgent needs of some of the Emirates.

The execution of these projects and the disbursement thereon shall be drawn from these funds, accomplished by means of and under the supervision of the competent Union bodies with the agreement of the authorities of the Emirates concerned.

The Union may establish a special fund for this purpose.

Art. 133. No Union tax may be imposed, amended or abolished except by virtue of law. No person may be exempted from payment of such taxes except in the cases specified by law.

Union taxes, duties and fees may not be levied on any person except within the limits of the law and in accordance with its provisions.

Art. 134. No public loan may be contracted except by a Union law. No commitment involving the payment of sums from Union Exchequer in a future year or years may be concluded except by means of a Union law.

Art. 135. The final accounts of the financial administration of the Union for the completed financial year shall be referred to the Union National Assembly within the four months following the end of the said year, for its comments thereon, before their submission to the Supreme Council for approval, in the light of the Auditor General's report.

Art. 136. An independent Union department headed by an Auditor General who shall be appointed by decree, shall be established to audit the accounts of the Union and its organs and agencies, and to audit any other accounts assigned to the said department for that purpose in accordance with the law.

The law shall regulate this department and shall define its jurisdiction and the competence of those working therein, and the guarantees to be given to it, its head and the employees working in it in order that they may carry out their duties in the most efficient manner.

PART NINE

ARMED FORCES AND SECURITY FORCES

Art. 137. Every attack upon any member Emirates of the Union shall be considered an attack upon all the Emirates and upon the existence of the Union itself, which all Union and local forces will co-operate to repel by all means possible.

Art. 138. The Union shall have army, navy and air forces with unified training and command. The Commander in Chief of these forces and the Chief of the General Staff shall be appointed and dismissed by means of a Union decree.

The Union may have a Union Security Force.

The Union Council of Ministers shall be responsible directly to the President of the Union and the Supreme Council of the Union for the affairs of all these forces.

Art. 139. The law shall regulate military service, general or partial mobilization, the rights and duties of members of the Armed Forces, their disciplinary procedures and similarly the special regulations of the Union Security Forces.

Art. 140. The declaration of defensive war shall be declared by a Union decree issued by the President of the Union after its approval by the Supreme Council. Offensive war shall be prohibited in accordance with the provisions of international charters.

Art. 141. A Supreme Defence Council shall be set up under the chairmanship of the President of the Union. Among its members shall be the Vice-President of the Union, the Chairman of the Council of Ministers of the Union, the Ministers of Foreign Affairs, Defence, Finance, Interior, the Commander in Chief and the Chief of the General Staff. It shall advise and offer views on all matters pertaining to defence, maintenance of the peace and security of the Union, forming of the armed forces, their equipment and development and the determination of their posts and camps.

The Council may invite any military adviser or expert or other person it wishes to attend its meetings but they shall have no decisive say in its deliberations. All matters pertaining to this Council shall be regulated by means of a law.

Art. 142. The member Emirates shall have the right to set up local security forces ready and equipped to join the defensive machinery of the Union to defend, if need arises, the Union against any external agression.

Art. 143. Any Emirate shall have the right to request the assistance of the Armed Forces or the Security Forces of the Union in order to maintain security and order within its territories whenever it is exposed to danger. Such a request shall be submitted immediately to the Supreme Council of the Union for decision.

The Supreme Council may call upon the aid of the local armed forces belonging to any Emirate for this purpose provided that the Emirate requesting assistance and the Emirate to whom the forces belong agree.

The President of the Union and the Council of Ministers of the Union collectively, may, if the Supreme Council is not in session, take any immediate measure which cannot be delayed and considered necessary and may call the Supreme Council into immediate session.

PART TEN

FINAL AND TRANSITIONAL PROVISIONS

Art. 144. 1. Subject to the provisions of the following paragraphs, the provisions of this Constitution shall apply for a transitional period of five Gregorian years from the date of its entry into force in accordance with the provisions of Article 152.

2. (*a*) If the Supreme Council considers that the topmost interests of

the Union require the amendment of this Constitution, it shall submit a draft constitutional amendment to the Union National Assmebly.

(*b*) The procedure for approving the constitutional amendment shall be the same as the procedure for approving laws.

(*c*) The approval of the Union National Assembly for a draft constitutional amendment shall require the agreement of two thirds of the votes of members present.

The President of the Union shall sign the constitutional amendment in the name of the Supreme Council and as its representative and shall promulgate the amendment.

3. During the transitional period, the Supreme Council shall adopt the necessary measure to prepare a draft permanent Constitution to take the place of this temporary constitution. It shall submit the draft permanent Constitution to the Union National Assembly for debate before promulgating it.

4. The Supreme Council shall call the Union National Assembly into extraordinary session at a time not more tha six months before the end of the period of validity of this temporary Constitution. The permanent Constitution shall be presented at this session. It shall be promulgated according to the procedure laid down in paragraph 2 of this Article.

Art. 145. Under no circumstances, may any of the provisions of this Constitutoin be suspended, except when martial law is in force and within the limits specified by this law.

Notwithstanding the foregoing, sessions of the National Assembly of the Union may not be suspended during that period nor may the immunity of its members be violated.

Art. 146. In case of necessity defined by law, martial law shall be declared by a decree promulgated with the approval of the Supreme Council on the basis of a proposal made by the President of the Union with the consent of the Council of Ministers of the Union. Such decree shall be notified to the Union National Assembly at its next meeting.

Martial law shall be similarly lifted by decree issued with the approval of the Supreme Council when the need, for which it was imposed, no longer exists.

Art. 147. Nothing in the application of this Constitution shall affect treaties or agreements concluded by member Emirates with states or international organizations unless such treaties or agreements are amended or abrogated by agreement between the parties concerned.

Art. 148. All matters established by laws, regulations, decrees, orders and decisions in the various member Emirates of the Union in effect upon the coming into force of this Constitution, shall continue to be applicable unless amended or replaced in accordance with the provisions of this Constitution.

Similarly, the measures and organizations existing in the member Emirates shall continue to be effective until the promulgation of laws amending them in accordance with the provisions of the Constitution.

Art. 149. As an exception to the provisions of Article 121 of this Constitution, the Emirates may promulgate legislations necessary for the regulation of the matters set out in the said Article without violation of the provisions of Article 151 of this Constitution.

Art. 150. The Union authorities shall strive to issue the law referred to in this Constitution as quickly as possible so as to replace the existing legislations and systems, particularly those which are not consistent with the provisions of this Constitution.

Art. 151. The provisions of this Constitution shall prevail over the Constitutions of the member Emirates of the Union and the Union laws which are issued in accordance with the provisions of this Constitution shall have priority over the legislations, regulations and decisions issued by the authorities of the Emirates.

In case of conflict, that part of the inferior legislation which is inconsistent with the superior legislation shall be rendered null and void to the extent that removes the inconsistency. In case of dispute, the matter shall be referred to the Union Supreme Court for its ruling.

Art. 152. This Constitution shall take effect from the date to be fixed in a declaration to be issued by the Rulers signatories to this Constitution.

Signed in Dubai on this day the 18th July, 1971, corresponding to this day the 25th of the month of Jamad Awwal 1391.

(Signatures of the Rulers of Abu Dhabi, Dubai, Sharjah, Ajman, Umm Al Qawain, Fujairah).[1]

[1] Ras Al Khaimah joined the Union on the 10th February, 1972.

VANUATU

SUMMARY

INTERNATIONAL STATUS

Vanuatu is a member of the United Nations (September 15, 1981). It is a member of the Commonwealth of Nations and other international governmental organizations.

Vanuatu became independent on July 30, 1980. Formerly called the New Hebrides, the islands are 92% Melanesian in population. First known to Europe by Portuguese discovery in 1606, the first European settlers to come were Presbyterian and Catholic missionaries in 1848, followed by other colonists from Europe and Australia. In 1887, the islands were placed under a Franco-British naval commission; they became a condominium by a convention of 1906. Under a 1914 protocol, two resident commissioners, one British and one French, governed the islands. Melanesian nationalism began with United States' occupation of the islands during the Second World War and was accentuated with the decolonization of neighboring territories. Land claims against colonial tenure became active. In 1954, the first suggestion of local participation in administration was made and in 1957, by joint regulation of the resident commissioners, the Consultative Council of the New Hebrides was established. In 1975, a representative Assembly was decided upon but, the elections having been declared null because of fraud, the nationalist party, later the Vanuaaku Pati party (VAP, nationalist and Anglophone) refused to participate in the autonomous government established in 1977 with an elected representative Assembly to prepare the country for independence. The Anglo-French rivalries of the colonial period were reproduced in the period of local autonomy. Two months before independence, the island of Espiritu Santo (French speaking) rebelled and attempted secession. British and French military intervention put down the rebellion.

FORM OF NATIONAL GOVERNMENT

The Constitution of July 30, 1980, as amended in the same year, states that Vanuatu is a sovereign democratic republic.[1] Sovereignty belongs to the people.[2] A parliamentary system of government is provided.

RIGHTS OF THE PEOPLE

The Constitution guarantees the rights without discrimination to life, liberty, security of the person, protection of the law, freedom from inhuman treatment or forced labor, freedom of conscience and worship, of expression, assembly and association, of movement; equal treatment under the law, privacy of the home and protection of property; everyone is presumed innocent until proved guilty, no retroactive punishment, no double jeopardy are allowed; prompt and impartial trials are stipulated.[4] The franchise is universal, equal and secret from 18 years of age.[5] Political parties may be formed freely.[6]

LEGISLATIVE DEPARTMENT

The Constitution provides for a unicameral Parliament composed of members elected by a system that includes an element of proportional representation.[7] It meets twice a year.[8] Privileges and immunities are provided.[9] The term of office is 4 years subject to dissolution.[10]

There is provision for a National Council of Chiefs, composed of custom chiefs elected by their peers, holding one meeting a year with competence to discuss matters relating to custom and tradition.[11]

EXECUTIVE DEPARTMENT

The Constitution provides for a President as Head of State, elected by secret ballot by the Parliament and chairmen of the local government councils for a term of 5 years.[12] He has the power of pardon.[13]

The executive power is vested in the Prime Minister and Council of Ministers which must not exceed in number a quarter of the members of Parliament.[14] The Prime Minister is elected by Parliament and he appoints the other ministers who may or may not be members of Parliament.[15] The Council of Ministers is collectively responsible to Parliament.[16] There is provision for the public service,[17] an Ombudsman with a term of 5 years,[18] the ownership of land.[19] Local government and decentralization are stipulated.[20]

[1] Constitution, Art. 1.
[2] Id., Art. 4.
[3] Id., Art. 9–14.
[4] Id., Art. 5.
[5] Id., Art. 4.
[6] Id., Art. 4.
[7] Id., Art. 15–17.
[8] Id., Art. 19.
[9] Id., Art. 25.
[10] Id., Art. 26.
[11] Id., Art. 27–30.
[12] Id., Art. 31–34.
[13] Id., Art. 36.
[14] Id., Art. 37, 38.
[15] Id., Art. 39, 40, 42–44.
[16] Id., Art. 41.
[17] Id., Art. 55–58.
[18] Id., Art. 59–63.
[19] Id., Art. 71–79.
[20] Id., Art. 80, 81.

JUDICIAL DEPARTMENT

Administration of justice is vested in the judiciary.[21] The Supreme Court is composed of a Chief Justice appointed by the President and three other judges appointed by the President on the advice of the Judicial Services Commission who hold office until the age of retirement.[22] Parliament shall provide for appeals from the Supreme Court to a Court of Appeals composed of two or more judges of the Supreme Court.[23]

AREA, POPULATION, ETC.

The area of Vanuatu is 12,190 square kilometres, composed of 12 large and 60 smaller islands. The population is 123,000 (1981 estimate). The capital is Port Vila. The national language is Bislama and the official languages are Bislama, English and French; the local languages are to be protected.[24]

[21] Id., Art. 45.
[22] Id., Art. 45.
[23] Id., Art. 48.
[24] Id., Art. 3.

CONSTITUTION OF THE REPUBLIC OF VANUATU[1]

July 30, 1980, as amended in 1980

PREAMBLE

WE the people of Vanuatu,
PROUD of our struggle for freedom,
DETERMINED to safeguard the achievements of this struggle.
CHERISHING our ethnic, linguistic and cultural diversity.
MINDFUL at the same time of our common destiny.
HEREBY proclaim the establishment of the united and free Republic of Vanuatu founded on traditional Melanesian values, faith in God, and Christian principles,
AND for this purpose give ourselves this Constitution.

CHAPTER 1

THE STATE AND SOVEREIGNTY

1. The Republic of Vanuatu is a sovereign democratic state.

2. The Constitution is the supreme law of Vanuatu.

3. (1) The national language of the Republic is Bislama. The official languages are Bislama, English and French. The principal languages of education are English and French.

(2) The Republic shall protect the different local languages which are part of the national heritage and may declare one of them as a national language.

4. (1) National sovereignty belongs to the Vanuatu people which they exercise through their elected representatives.

(2) The franchise is universal, equal and secret. Subject to such conditions or restrictions as may be prescribed by Parliament, every citizen of Vanuatu who is at least 18 years of age shall be entitled to vote.

(3) Political parties may be formed freely and may contest elections. They shall respect the Constitution and the principles of democracy.

CHAPTER 2

FUNDAMENTAL RIGHTS AND DUTIES

Part 1. Fundamental Rights

5. (1) The Republic of Vanuatu recognises that, subject to any restrictions imposed by law on non-citizens, all persons are entitled to the following fundamental

[1] Supplied by the Attorney General's Chambers in June 1982. Ed.

rights and freedoms of the individual without discrimination on the grounds of race, place of origin, religious or traditional beliefs, political opinions, language or sex but subject to respect for the rights and freedoms of others and to the legitimate public interest in defence, safety, public order, welfare and health:

(*a*) life;
(*b*) liberty;
(*c*) security of person;
(*d*) protection of the law;
(*e*) freedom from inhuman treatment and forced labor;
(*f*) freedom of conscience and worship;
(*g*) freedome of expression;
(*h*) freedom of assembly and association;
(*i*) freedom of movement;
(*j*) protection for the privacy of the home and other property and from unjust deprivation of property;
(*k*) equal treatment under the law or administrative action, except that no law shall be inconsistent with this sub-paragraph insofar as it makes provision for the special benefit, welfare, protection or advancement of females, children and young persons, members of under-privileged groups or inhabitants of less developed areas.

(2) Protection of the law shall include the following:

(*a*) everyone charged with an offence shall have a fair hearing, within a reasonable time, by an independent and impartial court and be afforded a lawyer if it is a serious offence;
(*b*) everyone is presumed innocent until a court establishes his guilt according to law;
(*c*) everyone charged shall be informed promptly in a language he understands of the offence with which he is being charged;
(*d*) if an accused does not understand the language to be used in the proceedings he shall be provided with an interpreter throughout the proceedings;
(*e*) a person shall not be tried in his absence without his consent unless he makes it impossible for the court to proceed in his presence;
(*f*) no-one shall be convicted in respect of an act or omission which did did not constitute an offence known to written or custom law at the time it was committed;
(*g*) no-one shall be punished with a greater penalty than that which exists at the time of the commission of the offence;
(*h*) no person who has been pardoned, or tried and convicted or acquitted, shall be tried again for the same offence or any other offence of which he could have been convicted at his trial.

6. (1) Anyone who considers that any of the rights guaranteed to him by the Constitution has been, is being or is likely to be infringed may, independently of any other possible legal remedy, apply to the Supreme Court to enforce that right.

(2) The Supreme Court may make such orders, issue such writs and give such directions, including the payment of compensation, as it considers appropriate to enforce the right.

Part 2. Fundamental Duties

7. Every person has the following fundamental duties to himself and his descendants and to others:

(*a*) to respect and to act in the spirit of the Constitution;

(*b*) to recognise that he can fully develop his abilities and advance his true interests only by active participation in the development of the national community;

(*c*) to exercise the rights guaranteed or conferred by the Constitution and to use the opportunities made available to him under it to participate fully in the government of the Republic;

(*d*) to protect Vanuatu and to safeguard the national wealth, resources and environment in the interests of the present generation and of future generations;

(*e*) to work according to his talents in socially useful employment and, if necessary, to create for himself legitimate opportunities for such employment;

(*f*) to respect the rights and freedoms of others and to co-operate fully with others in the interests of interdependence and solidarity;

(*g*) to contribute, as required by law, according to his means, to the revenues required for the advancement of the Republic and the attainment of national objectives;

(*h*) in the case of a parent, to support, assist and educate all his children, legitimate and illegitimate, and in particular to give them a true understanding of their fundamental rights and duties and of the national objectives and of the culture and customs of the people of Vanuatu;

(*i*) in the case of a child, to respect his parents.

8. Except as provided by law, the fundamental duties are non-justiciable. Nevertheless it is the duty of all public authorities to encourage compliance with them so far as lies within their respective powers.

CHAPTER 3

CITIZENSHIP

9. On the day of Independence the following persons shall automatically become citizens of Vanuatu:

(*a*) a person who has or had 4 grandparents who belong to a tribe or community indigenous to Vanuatu; and

(*b*) a person of New Hebridean ancestry who has no citizenship, nationality or the status of an optant.

10. Every person who on the day of independence is a person of Ni-Vanuatu ancestry and has the nationality or citizenship of a foreign state or the status of an optant shall become a citizen of Vanuatu if he makes an application, or an application is made on his behalf by his parent or lawful guardian, within 3 months of the day of Independence or such longer period as Parliament may prescribe. The Vanuatu citizenship of such a person shall automatically lapse if he has not renounced his other citizenship or nationality within 3 months of the granting of Vanuatu citizenship or such longer period as Parliament may prescribe, except that in the case of a person under the age of 18 years the period of renunciation shall be 3 months after he has reached the age of 18 years.

11. Anyone born after the day of Independence, whether in Vanuatu or abroad, shall become a citizen of Vanuatu if at least one of his parents is a citizen of Vanuatu.

12. A national of a foreign state or a stateless person may apply to be naturalized as a citizen of Vanuatu if he has lived continuously in Vanuatu for at least 10 years immediately before the date of the application.

Parliament may prescribe further conditions of the eligibility to apply for naturalization and shall provide for the machinery to review and decide on applications for naturalization.

13. The Republic of Vanuatu does not recognise dual nationality. Any citizen of Vanuatu who is or becomes a citizen of another state shall cease to be a citizen of Vanuatu unless he renounces that other citizenship within 3 months of acquiring Vanuatu citizenship or that other citizenship, as the case may be, or such longer period as Parliament may prescribe, except that in the case of a person under the age of 18 years the period of renunciation shall be 3 months after he has reached the age of 18 years.

14. Parliament may make provision for the acquisition of citizenship of Vanuatu by persons not covered in the preceding Articles of this Chapter and may make provision for the deprivation and renunciation of citizenship of Vanuatu.

CHAPTER 4

PARLIAMENT

15. The Legislature shall consist of a single chamber which shall be known as Parliament.

16. (1) Parliament may make laws for the peace, order and good government of Vanuatu.

(2) Parliament may make laws by passing bills introduced either by one or more members or by the Prime Minister or a Minister.

(3) When a bill has been passed by Parliament it shall be presented to the President of the Republic who shall assent to it within 2 weeks.

(4) If the President considers that the bill is inconsistent with the provisions of the Constitution he shall refer it to the Supreme Court for its opinion.

The Bill shall not be promulgated if the Supreme Court considers it inconsistent with a provision of the Constitution.

17. (1) Parliament shall consist of members elected of the basis of universal franchise through an electoral system which includes an element of proportional representation so as to ensure fair representation of different political groups and opinions.

(2) Subject to such conditions or restrictions as may be prescribed by Parliament every citizen of Vanuatu who is at least 25 years of age shall be eligible to stand for election to Parliament.

18. (1) The general responsibility for the registration of voters and the conduct of elections to Parliament, the National Council of Chiefs and the local government shall vest in an Electoral Commission.

(2) A proposal for any law concerning the registration of voters or the election of members shall be referred to the Electoral Commission for advice before Parliament decides on it.

(3) The Electoral Commission shall consist of the Speaker of Parliament, as Chariman, and two members appointed by the President of the Republic on the advice of the Judicial Service Commission from among persons who are not members of or candidates for election to Parliament, the National Council of Chiefs or local government Councils.

(4) A person shall cease to be a member of the Electoral Commission if circumstances arise that, if he were not a member, would disqualify him for appointment as such.

(5) The Electoral Commission shall not be subject to the direction or control of any other person or body in the exercise of its functions.

19. (1) Parliament shall meet twice a year in ordinary session.

(2) Parliament may meet in extraordinary session at the request of the majority of its members, the Speaker or the Prime Minister.

(3) Unless otherwise provided in the Constitution, Parliament shall make its decisions by public vote by a simple majority of the members voting.

(4) Unless otherwise provided in the Constitution, the quorum shall be two thirds of the members of Parliament. If there is no such quorum at the first sitting in any session Parliament shall meet three days later, and a simple majority of members shall then constitute a quorum.

(5) Parliament shall make its own rules of procedure.

20. (1) At its first sitting after any general election Parliament shall elect a Speaker and one or more Deputy Speakers.

(2) The Speaker shall preside at sittings of Parliament and shall be responsible for maintaining order.

(3) The functions of Speaker may be exercised by a Deputy Speaker.

21. Parliament may establish committees and appoint members to them.

22. Unless otherwise provided proceedings of Parliament shall be held in public.

23. (1) Every year the Government shall present a bill for a budget to Parliament for its approval.

(2) No taxation shall be imposed or altered and no expenditure of public funds shall be incurred except by or under a law passed by Parliament.

(3) No motion for the levying or increase of taxation or for the expenditure of public funds shall be introduced unless it is supported by the Government.

(4) Parliament shall provide for the office of Auditor General, who shall be appointed by the Public Service Commission on its own initiative.

(5) The function of the Auditor General shall be to audit and report to Parliament and the Government on the public accounts of Vanuatu.

(6) The Auditor General shall not be subject to the direction or control of any other person or body in the exercise of his functions.

24. Treaties negotiated by the Government shall be presented to Parliament for ratification when they:

(*a*) concern international organizations, peace or trade;
(*b*) commit the expenditure of public funds;
(*c*) affect the status of people;
(*d*) require amendment of the laws of Vanuatu; or
(*e*) provide for the transfer, exchange or annexing of territory.

25. (1) No member of Parliament may be arrested, detained, prosecuted or proceeded against in respect of opinions given or votes cast by him in Parliament in the exercise of his office.

(2) No member may, during a session of Parliament or one of its Committees, be arrested or prosecuted for any offence, except with the authorization of Parliament in exceptional circumstances.

26. (1) Parliament, unless sooner dissolved under paragraph (2) or (3), shall continue for 4 years from the date of its election.

(2) Parliament may at any time decide, by resolution supported by votes of an absolute majority of the members at a special sitting when at least three fourths of the members are present, to dissolve Parliament. At least one week's notice of such a motion shall be given to the Speaker before the debate and the vote on it.

(3) The President of the Republic may, on the advice of the Council of Ministers, dissolve Parliament.

(4) General elections shall be held not earlier than 30 days and not later than 60 days after any dissolution.

(5) There shall be no dissolution of Parliament within 12 months of the general elections following a dissolution under paragraph (2) or (3).

CHAPTER 5

NATIONAL COUNCIL OF CHIEFS

27. (1) The National Council of Chief shall be composed of custom chiefs elected by their peers sitting in District Councils of Chiefs.

(2) The Council shall make its own rules of procedure.

(3) The Council shall hold at least one meeting a year. Further meetings may be held at the request of the Council, Parliament, or the Government.

(4) During the first sitting followng its election the Council shall elect its President.

28. (1) The National Council of Chiefs has a general competence to discuss all matters relating to custom and traditon and may make recommendations for the preservation and promotion of Ni-Vanuatu culture and languages.

(2) The Council may be consulted on any question, particularly any question relating to tradition and custom, in connnection with any bill before Parliament.

29. Parliament shall by law provide for the organization of the National Council of Chiefs and in particular for the role of chiefs at the village, island and district level.

30. (1) No member of the National Council of Chiefs may be arrested, detained, prosecuted or proceeded against in respect of opinions given or votes cast by him in the Council in the exercise of his office.

(2) No member may, during a session of the Council or of one of its committees, be arrested or prosecuted for any offence, except with the authorization of the Council in exceptional circumstances.

CHAPTER 6

HEAD OF STATE

31. The head of the Republic shall be known as the President and shall symbolise the unity of the nation.

32. The President of the Republic shall be elected in accordance with Schedule 1, by secret ballot by an electoral college consisting of Parliament and the Chairmen of the local government councils.

33. Any indigenous Vanuatu citizen qualified to be elected to Parliament shall be eligible for election as President of the Republic.

34. (1) The term of office of the President of the Republic shall be 5 years.

(2) The President of the Republic may be removed from office, only for gross misconduct or incapacity, by the electoral college provided for in Article 32 on a motion introduced by at least one third of the members of the college and passed by at least two thirds of its members, when at least three fourths of its members, including at least three fourths of the Chairmen of the local government councils, are present.

(3) At least two weeks notice of the motion provided for in paragraph (2) shall be given to the Speaker.

(4) If there is no quorum at the first sitting as provided in paragraph (2), the electoral college may meet and vote on the motion provided for in paragraph (2) a week later even if there is only a quorum of two thirds of the members of the college.

35. When there is a vacancy in the office of the President of the Republic or the President is overseas or incapacitated, the Speaker of Parliament shall perform the functions of the President. In the event of a vacancy in the office of the President of the Republic, elections to that office shall be held within 3 weeks of the vacancy arising.

36. The President of the Republic may pardon, commute or reduce a sentence imposed on a person convicted of an offence. Parliament may provide for a committee to advise the President in the exercise of this function.

CHAPTER 7

THE EXECUTIVE

37. (1) The executive power of the people of the Republic is vested in the Prime Minister and Council of Ministers and shall be exercised as provided by the Constitution or a law.

(2) the Prime Minister shall keep the President of the Republic fully informed concerning the general conduct of the government of the Republic.

(3) The President of the Republic may refer to the Supreme Court any regulation which he considers to be inconsistent with the Constitution.

38. (1) There shall be a Council of Ministers which shall consist of the Prime Minister and other Ministers.

(2) The number of Ministers, including the Prime Minister, shall not exceed a quarter of the number of members of Parliament.

39. The Prime Minister shall be elcted by Parliament from among its members be secret ballot in accordance with the rules in Schedule 2.

40. (1) The Prime Minister shall appoint the other Ministers from among the members of Parliament and may designate one of them as Deputy Prime Minister.

(2) The Prime Minister shall assign responsibilities for the conduct of government to the Ministers.

(3) The Prime Minister may remove the Ministers from office.

41. (1) The Council of Ministers shall be collectively responsible to Parliament.

(2) Parliament may pass a motion of no confidence in the Prime Minister. At least one week's notice of such a motion shall be given to the Speaker and the motion must be signed by one sixth of the members of Parliament. If it is supported by an absolute majority of the members of Parliament, the Prime Minister and other Ministers shall cease to hold office forthwith but shall continue to exercise their functions until a new Prime Minister is elected.

42. The Council of Ministers shall cease to hold office whenever the Prime Minister resigns or dies but shall continue to exercise their functions until a new Prime Minister is elected. In the case of the death of the Prime Minister, the Deputy Prime Minsiter, or if there is no Deputy Prime Minister a Minister appointed by the President of the Republic, shall act as Prime Minister until a new Prime Minister is elected.

43. A Minister, including the Prime Minister, shall also cease to hold office:

(*a*) when, after a general election, Parliament meets to elect a new Prime Minister;

(*b*) if he ceases to be a member of Parliament for any reason other than a dissolution of Parliament; or

(*c*) if he is elected as President of the Republic or as Speaker of Parliament.

44. Members of Parliament who are appointed Ministers shall retain their membership of Parliament.

CHAPTER 8

JUSTICE

45. (1) The administration of justice is vested in the judiciary, who are subject only to the Constitution and the law. The function of the judiciary is to resolve proceedings according to law. If there is no rule of law applicable to a matter before it, a court shall determine the matter according to substantial justice and whenever possible in conformity with custom.

(2) Except the Chief Justice the judiciary shall be appointed by the President acting on the advice of the Judicial Service Commission.

(3) All members of the judiciary shall hold office until they reach the age of retirement. They shall only be removed from office by the President of the Republic in the event of:

(*a*) conviction and sentence on a criminal charge; or

(*b*) a determination by the Judicial Service Commission of gross misconduct, incapacity or professional incompetence.

(4) The promotion and transfer of members of the judiciary may only be made by the President of the Republic on the advice of the Judicial Service Commission.

(5) Parliament may provide for the appointment by the President of the Republic, after consultation with the Judicial Service Commission, of acting judges for such periods as may be set out in their instruments of appointment.

(6) Paragraph (3) so far as it relates to removal from office shall apply to acting judges.

46. (1) The Judicial Service Commission shall consist of the Minister responsible for justice, as Chairman, the Chief Justice, the President of the Public Service Commission, and a representative of the National Council of Chiefs appointed by the Council.

(2) The Judicial Service Commission shall not be subject to the direction or control of any other person or body in the exercise of its functions.

47. (1) The Supreme Court has unlimited jurisdiction to hear and determine any civil or criminal proceedings, and such other jurisdiction and powers as may be conferred on it by the Constitution or by law.

(2) The Supreme Court shall consist of a Chief Justice and three other judges.

(3) The Chief Justice shall be apointed by the President of the Republic after consultation with the Prime Minister and the leader of the opposition.

(4) *Abrogated.*

(5) A person shall not be qualified for appointment as Chief Justice or other judge of the Supreme Court unless he is qualified to practise as a lawyer in Vanuatu.

48. Parliament shall provide for appeals from the original jurisdiction of the Supreme Court and may provide for appeals from such appellate jurisdiction as it may have to a Court of Appeal which shall be constituted by two or more judges of the Supreme Court sitting together.

49. Parliament may provide for the manner of the ascertainment of relevant rules of custom, and may in particular provide for persons knowledgeable in custom to sit with the judges of the Supreme Court or the Court of Appeal and take part in its proceedings.

50. Parliament shall provide for the establishement of village or island courts with jurisdiction over customary and other matters and shall provide for the role of chiefs in such courts.

51. (1) Anyone who considers that a provision of the Constitution has been infringed in relation to him may, without prejudice to any other legal remedy available to him, apply to the Supreme Court for redress.

(2) The Supreme Court has jurisdiction to determine the matter and to make such order as it considers appropriate to enforce the provisions of this Constitution.

(3) When a question concerning the interpretation of the Constitution arises before a subordinate court, and the court considers that the question concerns a fundamental point of law, the court shall submit the question to the Supreme Court for its determination.

52. The jurisdiction to hear and determine any question as to whether a person has been validly elected as a member of Parliament, the National Council of Chiefs, and a local government council or whether he has vacated his seat or has become disqualified to hold it shall vest in the Supreme Court.

53. The function of prosecution shall vest in the Public Prosecutor, who shall be appointed by the President of the Republic on the advice of the Judicial Service Commission. He shall not be subject to the direction or control of any other person or body in the exercise of his functions.

54. Parliament shall provide for the office of the Public Solicitor, appointed by the President of the Republic on the advice of the Judicial Service Commission, whose function shall be to provide legal assistance to needy persons.

CHAPTER 9

ADMINISTRATION

Part 1. The Public Service

55. (1) Public servants owe their allegiance to the Constitution and to the people of Vanuatu.

(2) Only citizens of Vanuatu shall be appointed to public office. The Public Service Commission shall determine other qualifications for appointment to the Public Service.

(3) No appointment shall be made to a post that has not been created in accordance with a law.

(4) The Prime Minister or the President of a Regional Council may, exceptionally, make provision for the recruitment of staff for a specified period to meet unforeseen needs.

In urgent cases, the Public Service Commission may, after consulting the Ministers responsible for finance and public administration, make such a decison instead of the Prime Minister.

(5) For as long as their posts exist, public servants shall not be removed from their posts except in accordance with the Constitution.

(6) Public servants shall be given increments in their salary in accordance with the law.

(7) Public servants shall leave the Public Service upon reaching retirement age or upon being dismissed by the Public Service Commission. They shall not be demoted without consultation with the Public Service Commission.

(8) The security of tenure of public servants provided for in paragraph (5) shall not prevent such compulsory early retirement as may be decided by law in order to ensure the renewal of holders of public offices.

56. (1) The rule of security of tenure provided for in Article 55(5) shall not apply to the personal political advisers of the Prime Minister and Ministers.

(2) Senior public servants in Ministries may be transferred by the Prime Minister to other posts of equivalent rank.

57. (1) The Public Service Commission shall be composed of five members appointed for three years by the President of the Republic after consultation with the Prime Minister.

(2) The President of the Republic shall appoint every year, from among the members of the Commission, a Chairman who shall be responsible for organizing its proceedings.

(3) A person shall be disqualified for appointment as a member of the Commission if he is a member of Parliament, the National Council of Chiefs or a local government council or if he exercises a position of responsibility within a political party.

(4) A person shall cease to be a member of the commission if circumstances arise that, if he were not a member, would disqualify him for appointment as such.

58. (1) The Public Service Commission shall be responsible for the appointment and promotion of public servants, and the selection of those to undergo training courses in Vanuatu or overseas. For such purposes it may organize competitive examinations.

(2) The Commission shall also be responsible for the discipline of public servants.

(3) The Commission shall have no authority over the members of the judiciary, the armed forces, the police and the teaching services.

(4) The Commission shall not be subject to the direction or control of any other person or body in the exercise of its functions.

Part 2. The Ombudsman

59. (1) The Ombudsman shal be appointed, for five years, by the President of the Republic after consultation with the Prime Minister, the Speaker of Parliament, the leaders of the political parties represented in Parliament, the President of the National Council of Chiefs, the Chairmen of the local government councils and the Chairmen of the Public Service Commission and the Judicial Service Commission.

(2) A person shall be disqualified for appointment as Ombudsman if he is a member of Parliament, the National Council of Chiefs or a local government council, if he holds any other public office, or if he exercises a position of responsibility within a political party.

(3) A person shall cease to be Ombudsman if circumstances arise that, if he were not the Ombudsman, would disqualify him for appointment as such.

60. (1) The Ombudsman may enquire into the conduct of any person or body to which this Article applies:

(*a*) upon receiving a complaint from a member of the public (or, if for reasons of incapacity, from his representative or a member of his family) who claims to have been the victim of an injustice as a result of particular conduct;

(*b*) at the request of a Minister, a member of Parliament, of the National Council of Chiefs or of a local government council;

(*c*) of his own initiative.

(2) This Article shall apply to all public servants, public authorities and ministerial departments, with the exception of the President of the Republic, the Judicial Service Commission, the Supreme Court and other judicial bodies.

(3) The Ombudsman may request any Minister, public servant, administrator, authority concerned or any person likely to assist him, to furnish him with information and documents needed for his enquiry.

(4) The Ombudsman shall grant the person or body complained of an opportunity to reply to the complaints made against them.

(5) The enquires of the Ombudsman shall be conducted in private.

61. (1) Wherever, after due enquiry, the Ombudsman concludes that a complaint is unjustified, he shall so inform the complainant and the Prime Minister and the head of the public department or authority concerned.

(2) Whenever, after due enquiry, the Ombudsman concludes that conduct was contrary to the law, based on error of law or of fact, delayed for unjustified reasons, or unjust or blatantly unreasonable and that, consequently, any decision taken should be annulled or changed or that any practice followed should be revised, he shall forward his finding to the Prime Minister and to the head of the public authority or department directly concerned.

(3) The report of the Ombudsman shall be public unless he decides to keep

the report, or parts of its, confidential to the Prime Minister and the person in charge of the relevant public service, on the grounds of public security or public interests. The complainant shall in any case to told of the findings of the Ombudsman.

(4) The Prime Minister or the person in charge of the relevant public service shall decide upon the findings of the Ombudsman within a reasonable time and the decision, with reasons, shall be given to the complainant forthwith. Any period limiting the time in which legal proceedings may be commenced shall not begin to run until the complainant has received the decision.

(5) The Ombudsman shall present a general report to Parliament each year and may make such additional reports as he considers necessary concerning the discharge of his functions and action taken on his findings. He may draw the attention of Parliament to any defects which appear to him to exist in the administration.

62. A citizen of Vanuatu may obtain, in the official language that he uses, the services which he may rightfully expect from the Republic's administration.

(2) Where a citizen considers that there has been a breach of paragraph (1) he may make a complaint to the Ombudsman who shall conduct an enquiry in accordance with Articles 60 and 61.

(3) The Ombudsman shall, each year, make a special report to Parliament concerning the observance of multilingualism and the measures likely to ensure its respect.

63. The Ombudsman shall not be subject to the direction or control of any other person or body in the exercise of his functions.

CHAPTER 10

LEADERSHIP CODE

64. (1) Any person defined as a leader in Article 65 has a duty to conduct himself in such a way, both in his public and private life, so as not to:

(*a*) place himself in a position in which he has or could have a conflict of interests or in which the fair exercise of his public or official duties might be compromised;
(*b*) demean his office or position;
(*c*) allow his integrity to be called into question; or
(*d*) endanger or diminish respect for and confidence in the integrity of the Government of Vanuatu.

(2) In particular, a leader shall not use his office for personal gain or enter into any transaction or engage in any enterprise or activity that might be expected to give rise to doubt in the public mind as to whether he is carrying out or has carried out the duty imposed by paragraph (1).

65. For the purposes of this Chapter, a leader means the President of the Republic, the Prime Minister and other Ministers, members of Parliament, and such public servants, officers of Government agencies and other officers as may be prescribed by law.

66. Parliament shall by law give effect to the principles of this Chapter.

CHAPTER 11

EMERGENCY POWERS

67. The Council of Ministers may make regulations for dealing with a public emergency whenever:

(*a*) the Republic is at war; or

(*b*) the President of the Republic acting on the advice of the Council of Ministers declares a state of emergency by reason of natural calamity or to prevent a threat to or to restore public order.

68. (1) When Parliament is in session a state of emergency declared under Article 67 shall cease to have effect at the end of one week unless approved by a resolution of Parliament supported by two thirds of its members.

(2) When Parliament is not in session a state of emergency shall cease to have effect at the end of 2 weeks.

(3) Where a resolution has been passed in accordance with paragraph (1) the state of emergency approved by it shall remain in force for the period authorized by the resolution except that no such resolution may authorize a state of emergency for more than 3 months at one time.

(4) Parliament may meet whenever it decides during a state of emergency.

(5) Parliament may not be dissolved under Article 26(2) or (3) during a state of emergency. If the life of a Parliament ends in accordance with Article 26(1) during a state of emergency the former members of that Parliament may meet for the purpose only of considering the state of emergency until the new Parliament first meets.

(6) Parliament may at any time terminate a state of emergency by a resolution supported by an absolute majority of its members.

69. (1) Subject to paragraph (2) regulations made by the Council of Ministers in accordance with Article 67 shall have effect notwithstanding the provisions of Chapter 2, Part 1 except that no regulation shall:

(*a*) derogate from the right to life and the freedom from inhuman treatment and forced labor; and

(*b*) make provision for the detention of a person without trial for more than one month unless such person is an enemy alien.

(2) Regulations made by the Council of Ministers in accordance with Article 67 shall be such as are reasonably necessary in the circumstances of the emergency to which they relate and as are justifiable in a democratic society.

70. Any citizen aggrieved by reason of regulations made by the Council of Ministers in accordance with Article 67 may complain to the Supreme Court which shall have jurisdiction to determine the validity of all or any of such regulations.

CHAPTER 12

LAND

71. All land in the Republic belongs to the indigenous custom owners and their desendants.

72. The rules of custom shall form the basis of ownership and use of land in the Republic.

73. Only indigenous citizens of the Republic who have acquired their land in accordance with a recognized system of land tenure shall have perpetual ownership of their land.

74. Parliament, after consultation with the National Council of Chiefs, shall provide for the implementation of Articles 71, 72 and 73 in a national land law and may make different provision for different categories of land, one of which shall be urban land.

75. Parliament shall prescribe such criteria for the assessment of compensation and the manner of its payment as it deems appropriate to persons whose interests are adversely affected by legislation under this Chapter.

76. (1) Where, consequent on the provisions of this Chapter, there is a dispute concerning the ownership of alienated land, the Government shall hold such land until the dispute is resolved.

(2) The Government shall arrange for the appropriate customary institutions or procedures to resolve disputes concerning the ownership of custom land.

77. (1) Notwithstanding Articles 71, 72 and 73 land transactions between an indigenous citizen and either a non-indigenous citizen or a non-citizen shall only be permitted with the consent of the Government.

(2) The consent required under paragraph (1) shall be given unless the transaction is prejudicial to the interests of:

(*a*) the custom owner or owners of the land:
(*b*) the indigenous citizen where he is not the custom owner;
(*c*) the community in whose locality the land is situated; or
(*d*) the Republic.

78. Notwithstanding Articles 71 and 72 the Government may own land acquired by it in the public interest.

79. (1) Notwithstanding Articles 71 and 72 the Government may buy land from custom owners for the purpose of transferring ownership of it to indigenous citizens or indigenous communities from over-populated islands.

(2) When redistributing land in accordance with paragraph (1), the Government shall give priority to ethnic, linguistic, customary and geographical ties.

CHAPTER 13

DECENTRALIZATION

80. The Republic of Vanuatu, conscious of the importance of decentralization to enable the people fully to participate in the government of their regions, shall enact legislation necessary to realize that ideal.

81. The legislation shall provide for the division of the Republic into Local Government Regions and for each region to be administered by a Local Government Council on which shall be representatives of custom chiefs.

CHAPTER 14

AMENDMENT TO THE CONSTITUTION

82. A bill for an amendment of the Constitution may be introduced either by the Prime Minister or any other member of Parliament.

83. A bill for an amendment of the Constitution shall not come into effect unless it is supported by the votes of no less than two thirds of all the members of Parliament at a special sitting of Parliament at which three quarters of the members are present. If there is no such quorum at the first sitting, Parliament may meet and make a decision by the same majority a week later even if only two thirds of the members are present.

84. A bill for an amendment of a provision of the Constitution regarding the status of Bislama, English and French, the electoral system or the parliamentary system. passed by Parliament under Article 83, shall not come into effect unless it has been supported in a national referendum.

CHAPTER 15

TRANSITIONAL PROVISIONS

85. Notwithstanding Chapter 6 the first President of the Republic shall:

(*a*) be such person as shall have been elected prior to the day of Independence by an electoral college constituted for that purpose by the Representative Assembly sitting with the Chairmen of the local government councils if then established;

(*b*) assume office on the day of Independence and hold office in accordance with the provisions of the Constitution.

86. The persons who immediately before the day of Independence hold office as Chief Minister or any other Minister shall as from that day hold office as Prime Minister or other Minister, as the case may be, as if they had been elected or appointed thereto under Chapter 7.

87. (1) The persons who immediately before the day of Independence are members of the Representative Assembly shall on that day become members of Parliament and shall hold their seats in Parliament in accordance with the Constitution.

(2) The person who immediately before the day of Independence holds the office of Chairman of the Representative Assembly shall as from that day act in the office of Speaker of Parliament until a person is elected to hold that office.

(3) The standing orders of the Representative Assembly in force immediately before the day of Independence shall have effect as from that day as the standing orders of Parliament until modified or replaced under Article 19(5) but shall be construed with such adaptations as may be necessary to bring them into conformity with the Constitution.

(4) Parliament shall, unless sooner dissolved, stand dissolved on the 14th November, 1983.

88. (1) Subject to the other provisions of the Constitution, a person who immediately before the day of Independence holds or acts in an office in the service of the Government of Vanuatu shall, as from that day, hold ar act in that office or the corresponding office estabished by or under the Constitution on the same terms and conditions as those on which he holds or acts in the office immediately before that day.

(2) Paragraph (1) is without prejudice to the power of Parliament to provide for the compulsory retirement of non-citizen officers to promote localization of offices.

(3) Notwithstanding Article 55(2), until a citizen of Vanuatu is qualified for appointment to a public office a non-citizen may be appointed to that office but, except in the case of a judge of the Supreme Court, shall be appointed for a limited period.

89. Notwithstanding Chapter 8, any person who immediately before the day of Independence holds office as a judge of th pre-Independence Supreme Court or of a District Court shall as from that day act in the office of judge of the Supreme Court until a substantive appointment is made to that office in accordance with Chapter 8. The President of the Republic may appoint one of them to act as Chief Justice until a substantive appointment is made to that office.

90. (1) All rights, liabilities and obligations of the Government of Vanuatu, whether arising out of contract or otherwise, shall, as from the day of Independence, be rights, liabilities and obligations of the Republic.

(2) Nothing in paragraph (1) shall prevent the Government of the Republic renegotiating rights, liabilities or obligations assumed under that paragraph.

91. After the general elections next following the Exchange of Notes providing for the entry into force of this Article, the Representative Assembly shall set up a Committee with equal representation of all political groups to make recommendations on an electoral system based on Article 17(1).

The recommendations of the Committee shall be included in a law enacted by Parliament by a two-thirds majority of its members at a special sitting of Parliament when at least three fourths of the members are present. If there is no such quorum at the first sitting, Parliament may meet and make a decision by the same majority a week later even if only two thirds of the members are present.

92. All legal proceedings, whether civil or criminal, pending immediately before the day of Independence before any court in Vanuatu shall be disposed of on and after that day in accordance with general or specific directions given by the Supreme Court subject to any law which may be enacted for that purpose.

93. (1) Until otherwise provided by Parliament, all Joint Regulations and subsidiary legislation made thereunder in force immediately before the day of independence shall continue in operation on and after that day as if they had been made in pursuance of the Constitution and shall be construed with such adaptations as may be necessary to bring them into conformity with the Constitution.

(2) Until otherwise provided by Parliament, the British and French laws in force or applied in Vanuatu immediately before the day of Independence shall on and after that day continue to apply to the extent that they are not expressly revoked or incompatible with the independent status of Vanuatu and wherever possible taking due account of custom.

(3) Customary law shall continue to have effect as part of the law of the Republic.

94. Abrogated.

SCHEDULES

(Not reproduced)

SOCIALIST REPUBLIC OF VIETNAM

SUMMARY

INTERNATIONAL STATUS

Vietnam is a member of the United Nations (September 20, 1977). It is a member of the Council for Mutual Economic Aid and other international organizations. Vietnam ratified the International Conventions on Social Economic and Cultural Rights and on Civil and Political Rights in 1982.

Vietnam, then the Empire of Annam, under the nominal suzerainty of China, contested Siam over control of the decadent neighboring Khmer and Laotian kingdoms until the conquest by France between 1858 and 1884, of all of Indochina. Cochin China in the south became a French colony in 1867, Annam (central) and Tonkin (northern) protectorates in 1884. Throughout the colonial period and especially from 1920 on, nationalist revolutionary groups operated. In 1920, Ho Chi Minh (under the name of Nguyen Van Thanh) became a member of the French Communist Party in Paris. In 1930, after time spent in Russia and China, he set up in Canton the Indochinese Communist Party. At the beginning of the second World War he fled to China and set up in 1941 the Viet Minh. In September 1940, Japanese troops moved into northern Vietnam and in 1941 into southern Vietnam, with the acquiescence of the French Vichy government. In March 1945, the Japanese took over the government and eliminated all French authority in Indochina. The Viet Minh, as the only organized Vietnamese military and political force, entered Hanoi on August 16, 1945, the day after the Japanese surrender, and proclaimed the country's independence as the Democratic Republic of Vietnam on September 2, 1945. Cambodia and Laos proclaimed their independence at the same time. The French returned to Indochina in early 1946, following a treaty with China providing for the withdrawal of Chinese troops (who had accepted the Japanese surrender). By agreement of March 1946, France recognized the Democratic Republic of Vietnam as a free state within the French Union, and agreed to withdraw gradually its troops. There was dissension between the French and the Viet Minh, the government of the latter consolidated its control of the north and of the independence movement in some other parts of the country, fighting broke out in Haiphong, and the Indochina War began in December 1946, with the Hanoi uprising. It lasted until the Geneva Conference of May 8, 1954.

The Geneva Conference consisted of 7 delegations from France, the United States, the Chinese People's Republic, Cambodia, Laos, the Vietnam Democratic Republic and the State of Vietnam (Saigon government led by Bao Daï), with the United Kingdom and the USSR as co-chairmen. The Geneva Agreement on the Cessation of Hostilities of July 20, 1954, comprised three cease-fire agreements covering Cambodia, Laos and Vietnam, and provided for the provisional division of the country at about the seventeenth parallel. The final Declaration of the Conference called for the establishment of democratic institutions through free general elections, to be held in July 1956. The United States and the State of Vietnam (Saigon) refused to subscribe to the final Declaration. The refusal of the Ngo Dinh Diem government in Saigon, supported by the United States, to permit elections lay at the root of the second Indochina War with the United States from 1961 to 1975.

In December 1960, the National Front for the Liberation of South Vietnam (FLN) was set up, directed and supplied by North Vietnam. In 1961, the United States began sending in troops and planes, in 1964 North Vietnam shifted from sending small units to sending regular regiments into the south, the United States began bombing North Vietnam, and in February 1965, the United States ordered an extensive build-up of its forces until, by 1967, it had an army of half a million men fighting with the South Vietnam government. After the Tet offensive by the North Vietnamese in 1968, the United States ordered a halt to bombing above the nineteenth parallel, and the Paris negotiations began on May 15, 1968. These negotiations continued through years of deadlock, of peace proposals on both sides, the 'Vietnamization' of the war, continued heavy fighting and bombing both of the north and of Cambodia. The Paris agreements of January 27, 1973, provided for a cease-fire in the south and the withdrawal of the United States forces, the peaceful reunification of the country and United States aid to North Vietnam for reconstruction. The South Vietnamese Army remained hostile and was defeated in the final 1975 offensive which ended with the taking of Saigon on April 30, 1975. Power was transferred to the Provisional Revolutionary Government of South Vietnam. On July 2, 1976, Vietnam was reunified and the Constitution of 1959 extended to the entire country, now named the Socialist Republic of Vietnam.

Frontier incidents with Cambodia under the Khmer Rouge régime led to virtual war between the two countries which terminated with the entry, on January 7, 1979, of Vietnamese troops into Phnom Penh, the eviction of the Pol Pot government and the installation of a Vietnamese backed government. Vietnam signed a treaty with the USSR in 1978, and joined the Council of Mutual Economic

Aid (COMECON) in July of that year. Chinese troops invaded Vietnam in February 1979 withdrawing after a month. The difficult economic situation of the country after the destruction of thirty years of war is intensified by natural disasters and problems of management, military expenditure against the menace of Chinese encirclement, the danger of United States imperialism together with Thailand supporting anti-government groups throughout Indochina. Vietnam has treaties of alliance and friendship with Cambodia and Laos under which it maintains troops in the two countries.

FORM OF NATIONAL GOVERNMENT

The Constitution of December 18, 1980, replaces the Constitution of December 31, 1959. It states that the Socialist Republic of Vietnam is an independent, sovereign and united country, a state of the proletarian dictatorship.[1] The collective masters of the country are the working people.[2] The Communist Party of Vietnam is the only force leading the State and society, and its organizations operate within the framework of the Constitution.[3] All power belongs to the People.[4] Vietnam continues to strengthen its friendship and co-operation with the Soviet Union, Laos, Kampuchea and other socialist countries on the basis of Marxist-Leninism and proletarian internationalism.[5] The economic system is described.[6] A chapter is devoted to culture, education, science and technology.[7]

RIGHTS OF THE PEOPLE

The rights and obligations of citizens are inseparable.[8] Citizens are equal before the law, have the right to participate in managing the affairs of state and society, have the right to vote and stand for elections.[9] Work is the right, obligation and privilege of citizens.[10] The rights to rest, social insurance, education, health care, housing are specified.[11] Women and men have equal rights, the state protects marriage, motherhood, the family and children.[12] Freedom of speech, press, assembly, demonstration, religion are provided; no one may misuse democratic freedoms to violate the interests of the state and people.[13] Citizens have the right to legal protection, arrests and detentions may not be made except by law, torture is forbidden, the inviolability of the home and correspondence is specified, as also freedom of movement and residence.[14] The right to scientific research and artistic activities, the rights of authors and inventors, the right to complain are listed.[15] The State grants privileges to disabled soldiers and families of fallen combatants, protects the rights of Vietnamese living abroad.[16] Citizens must be loyal and defend the

[1] Const., Art. 1, 2.
[2] Id., Art. 3.
[3] Id., Art. 4.
[4] Id., Art. 6.
[5] Id., Art. 14.
[6] Id., Art. 15–36.
[7] Id., Art. 37–49.
[8] Id., Art. 54.
[9] Id., Art. 55–67.
[10] Id., Art. 58.
[11] Id., Art. 59–62.
[12] Id., Art. 63–65.
[13] Id., Art. 67, 68.
[14] Id., Art. 69–71.
[15] Id.. Art. 72. 73.
[16] Id., Art. 74, 75.

homeland, protect and respect socialist property, pay taxes and participate in work on public projects.[17] All nationalities may use their own languages before the Courts.[18]

LEGISLATIVE DEPARTMENT

The National Assembly is vested with constitutional and legislative authority; it is the highest representative body of the people and the highest state authority.[19] It decides on its own organization.[20] Deputies are elected by universal direct, equal, secret suffrage for a term of 5 years.[21] The National Assembly meets in two sessions a year.[22] Immunities of deputies are provided.[23] The National Assembly elects the National Defense Council which is empowered to mobilize all forces needed to defend the homeland.[24] It elects the Council of Nationalities.[25]

EXECUTIVE DEPARTMENT

The Council of State is the highest continuously functioning body of the National Assembly and is the collective Presidency of Viet Nam.[26] It is elected from among National Assembly deputies and has the same term.[27] It promulgates the laws, issues decrees, interprets the Constitution, ratifies treaties, grants awards, declares war.[28] The Council of Ministers is the government of Viet Nam, the highest executive and administrative body; it is collectively and individually responsible and accountable to the National Assembly or the Council of State.[29] It is elected by the National Assembly.[30] Its executive and administrative functions are listed and include the suspension or repeal of inappropriate decisions or resolutions of ministries, People's Councils of the provinces and People's Communes.[31] The People's Councils and People's Committees which form the administrative units are described.[32]

JUDICIAL DEPARTMENT

The Supreme People's Court, the local courts and the Military Tribunals are the judicial bodies of Viet Nam; special tribunals may be set up by the National Assembly or Council of State in special circumstances.[33] The Supreme People's Court is the highest juridical body and supervises the proceedings of other courts.[34] Judges are elected: of the Supreme People's Court by the Council of State; of the local

[17] Id., Art. 76–81.
[18] Id., Art. 134.
[19] Id., Art. 82.
[20] Id., Art. 83.
[21] Id., Art. 7, 84.
[22] Id., Art. 85.
[23] Id., Art. 95.
[24] Id., Art. 90.
[25] Id., Art. 91.
[26] Id., Art. 98.
[27] Id., Art. 83, 99, 101.
[28] Id., Art. 100.
[29] Id., Art. 104, 112.
[30] Id., Art. 83.
[31] Id., Art. 107.
[32] Id., Art. 113.
[33] Id., Art. 128.
[34] Id., Art. 135.

courts by the councils of the provinces; in each case for the same term as that of the electing body (5 years and 4 years respectively).[35] During trials judges are independent and subject only to law.[36]

AREA, POPULATION, ETC.

The area of Viet Nam is 329,566 square kilometres, its population (1981 census) is 54,928,000. The capital is Hanoi.[37]

[35] Id., Art. 100, 101, 115, 116, 129.
[36] Id., Art. 131.
[37] Id., Art. 145.

CONSTITUTION OF THE SOCIALIST REPUBLIC OF VIETNAM[1]

December 18, 1980

PREAMBLE

Throughout their four-thousand-year-history, the Vietnamese people have worked hard and fought heroically to build and defend their country. This long and persistent struggle for independence and freedom has fostered the staunch and indomitable tradition of our nation.

Since 1930, under the leadership of the Communist Party of Viet Nam founded and forged by President Ho Chi Minh, and following the path of the great Russian October Revolution, our people successively defeated the Japanese, French and American imperialists and their henchmen. They have completed the people's national democratic revolution, and have embarked on a socialist revolution and are building socialism. Our country, formerly a colony and a semi-feudal country, has become an independent reunified, socialist state, a member of the world socialist community.

In 1945, following the defeat of fascism by the Soviet Army, our people successfully carried out the August Revolution. On September 2, 1945, President Ho Chi Minh proclaimed the Declaration of Independence. The Democratic Republic of Viet Nam, the first worker-peasant state in Southeast Asia, was born.

However, the French colonialists, with the assistance of U.S. imperialism, invaded our country once again. Our people, who 'would rather sacrifice all than lose our country and be enslaved', waged a long struggle against the invaders, and carried out a program of land reform. The great victory at Dien Bien Phu brought a glorious end to the war of resistance against the French colonialists. In 1954, the Geneva Agreements were signed on the basis of recognition of Viet Nam's independence, sovereignty, unity and territoritial integrity. The victory of the August Revolution and that of the anti-French resistance signalled the beginning of the collapse of colonialism throughout the world.

Stepping into the French colonialists shoes, the U.S. imperialists turned South Viet Nam into a neo-colony and military base of the United States, in an attempt to permanently partition our country, and to include South Viet Nam, Laos and Kampuchea into a counter-revolutionary front. Pursuing this scheme, they conducted an extremely barbarous war of aggression against Viet Nam. Imbued with the truth that 'Nothing is more precious than independence and freedom', our people fought heroically, detemined to liberate the South, defend the North and reunify the country. The successive victories of the peoples of Laos and Kampuchea, compelled the U.S. imperialists to sign the 1973 Paris Agreement on Viet Nam.

[1] Received from the Embassy of Vietnam in Paris in August 1981. Ed.

In the Spring of 1975, the Vietnamese people won total victory in a general offensive and uprising which culminated in the historic Ho Chi Minh Campaign. After 30 years of hard fighting, South Viet Nam – the 'Iron Fort of the Homeland' – was completely liberated.

While our entire people were struggling against the U.S. war of aggression, for national salvation, great achievements were recorded in the socialist revolution in the North: institution of socialist relations of production, abolition of the regime of human exploitation, building of the initial material and technical infrastructure of socialism, conduct of an ideological-cultural revolution, execution of the dual tasks of production and fighting, and fulfilment of the obligations of the great rear base towards the heroic South in the war of resistance to U.S. aggression.

The victories of the peoples of the three Indochina countries as a whole, and the Vietnamese people in particular, in the war against U.S. aggression, heralded the complete bankruptcy of neo-colonialism, contributed to the consolidation and extension of the world socialist system, encouraged the national liberation movements, and accelerated the offensive of the three revolutionary currents of the present era.

Following the complete liberation of the South, our people held free general elections throughout the country, and achieved national reunification. In July 1976, our country adopted the name of the *Socialist Republic of Viet Nam.*

No sooner had they emerged from thirty years of liberation war than our people, who were longing for peace to build their homeland, were confronted with the Chinese hegemonist aggressors and their henchmen in Kampuchea. Promoting our glorious national traditions, our army and people won resounding victories in both wars for national defence against the aggression by Kampuchean reactionaries on the south-western border and the Chinese hegemonists on the northern border, safeguarding our independence, sovereignty, unity and territorial integrity.

Credit for the great successive victories of the Vietnamese revolution goes to the Communist Party of Viet Nam which has creatively applied Marxism-Leninism, charted a correct line to lead the revolution in our country; upheld the two banners of national independence and socialism; consolidated the worker-peasant alliance led by the working class; closely united all social strata within the national united front; built and developed the people's armed forces; constantly strengthened the revolutionary administration; combined patriotism with proletarian internationalism, combined the strength of our people with the world revolutionary movement; and coordinated the struggles on the political, military and diplomatic planes.

These are victories of the ardent patriotism, the revolutionary heroism and the sublime spirit of sacrifice of our compatriots and combatants throughout the country who are of one mind in struggling for national liberation, construction and defence.

They are victories of the militant solidarity and the relations of cooperation and mutual assistance between the peoples of Viet Nam, Laos and Kampuchea; of the militant solidarity and great and effective aid of the Soviet Union and other fraternal socialist countries to the Vietnamese revolution; and of the forces of national independence, democracy and peace throughout the world which have actively supported the just cause of the Vietnamese people.

Our achievements have cost our people untold sacrifices and innumerable hardships. Our future is very bright, but our tasks are very difficult. Let our entire people strengthen unity and act upon the sacred testament of our great President Ho Chi Minh, and advance enthusiastically along the line charted by the Fourth Congress of the Communist Party of Viet Nam; 'To firmly enforce the proletarian dictatorship; promote the working people's right to collective mastery of society; to simultaneously implement the three revolutions, namely the revolution in the relations of production, the scientific and technological revolution, and the ideological and cultural revolution, with the scientific and technological revolution as the kingpin; step up socialist industrialisation, which is the central task of the period of transition to socialism; establish the system of socialist collective mastery and large-scale socialist production, develop the new culture and foster new socialist-oriented people; abolish the regime of human exploitation and eliminate poverty and backwardness; maintain constant vigilance and continuously strengthen national defence; maintain political security and social order; successfully build our homeland, Viet Nam, into a peaceful, independent, unified and socialist country; actively contribute to the struggle of the world's people for peace national independence, democracy and socialism.'

The Socialist Republic of Viet Nam needs a Constitution institutionalising the current line of the Communist Party of Viet Nam in the new stage. It is the Constitution of the period of transition to socialism on a national scale. Continuing and developing the Constitutions of 1946 and 1959, this Constitution sums up and affirms the gains of the revolutionary struggle of the Vietnamese people over the past half century, expresses the will and aspiration of the Vietnamese people, and guarantees the successful development of Vietnamese society in the coming period.

Being the fundamental law of the State, the present Constitution determines our political, economic, cultural and social system, the basic rights and obligations of citizens, the organizational structures and principles guiding the activities of State bodies. It specifies the relationships between the Party's leadership, the people's mastery, and State management in Vietnamese society.

Let the entire Vietnamese people unite closely under the invincible banner of the Communist Party of Viet Nam, and put this Constitution into effect in order to attain further great successes in the cause of building socialism and defending our socialist homeland.

CHAPTER I

THE SOCIALIST REPUBLIC OF VIET NAM POLITICAL SYSTEM

Art. 1. The Socialist Republic of Viet Nam is an independent sovereign and united country comprising its mainland, air space, territorial waters, and off-shore islands.

Art. 2. The Socialist Republic of Viet Nam is a State of proletarian dictatorship. Its historic mission is to establish the collective mastery of the working people; mobilize and organize the people to carry out simultaneuoulsy the three revolutions: in the relations of production, in science and technology, and in ideology and culture, with the scientific and technological revolution as the kingpin; abolish human exploitation; crush all acts of opposition by counter-revolutionary elements in the country and all acts of aggression and sabotage by external enemies; build socialism successfully and advance to communism; and contribute to consolidating peace and accelerate the revolutionary cause of the people throughout the world.

Art. 3. In the Socialist Republic of Viet Nam, the collective masters are the working people comprising the working class, the collective peasantry, the socialist intelligentsia and other laboring people, with the worker-peasant alliance, led by the working class, as the core. The State ensures the continuous perfection and consolidation of the working people's collective mastery in the political, economic, cultural and social fields; collective mastery in the whole country, and in each unit; collective mastery over society, over nature, and over oneself.

Art. 4. The Communist Party of Viet Nam, the vanguard and general staff of the Vietnamese working class, armed with Marxism-Leninism, is the only force leading the State and society, and the main factor determining all successes of the Vietnamese revolution.

The Party exists and struggles for the interests of the working class and the people of Viet Nam as a whole.

Its organizations operate within the framework of the Constitution.

Art. 5. The Socialist-Republic of Viet Nam is a unified State of all the nationalities living on Vietnamese territory, with equality in rights and obligations.

The State protects, strengthens and consolidates the great unity of all nationalities; it strictly prohibits any act of racial prejudice and any attempt to sow discord among nationalities.

All the nationalities have the right to use their own spoken languages and scripts, and to preserve and promote their fine customs, habits, traditions, and cultures.

The State accepts responsibility to take corrective measures to gradually eliminate inequalities in the levels of economic and cultural development between the different nationalities.

Art. 6. In the Socialist Republic of Viet Nam, all power belongs to the people.

The people exercise State power through the National Assembly and the Peoples's Councils at all levels which are elected by and accountable to the people.

The National Assembly and the People's Councils at all levels are the political bases of the system of State organizations.

The National Assembly, the People's Councils at all levels and other State bodies are organized and function according to the principle of democratic centralism.

Art. 7. National Assembly deputies and deputies to People's Councils at all levels are elected by universal suffrage. Voting is equal, direct and secret.

Electors have the right to recall National Assembly deputies and deputies to People's Councils at all levels who lose the confidence of the people.

Art. 8. All State bodies and all State employees must devotedly serve the people, maintain close relations with them, listen to them and accept their supervision, and promote socialist democracy. All manifestations of bureaucratism, arrogance and authoritarianism are strictly prohibited.

Art. 9. The Viet Nam Fatherland Front, which comprises the various political parties, the Viet Nam Confederation of Trade Unions, the Viet Nam Association of Collective Peasants, the Ho Chi Minh Communist Youth Union, the Viet Nam Women's Union, and other member organizations, is a firm prop of State.

The Front promotes the tradition of national unity, strengthens political and moral unity among the people, takes part in building and consolidating the people's power, educates and motivates the people to raise their sense of collective mastery, and to emulate one another in building socialism and defending the country.

Art. 10. The Viet Nam Confederation of Trade Unions is the largest mass organization of the Vietnamese working class, a school of communism, of economic management of the State.

Within the limits of thier competence, the trade unions take part in State affairs and supervise the work of State bodies, and participate in the management of factories. They educate workers and office employees; organize socialist emulation movements, and, together with State bodies, care for the lives of workers and office employees and protect their interests.

Art. 11. Collectives of working people at offices, factories, co-operatives, population centres and other basic units participate in State and social affairs including the planning of economic and cultural development, the protection of public property, the maintenance of political and social security and public order, and the organization of public life at the grassroots levels.

Art. 12. The State manages society according to law, and constantly strengthens the socialist legal system.

All State organs and social organizations, all State employees, all members of social organizations and all citizens must strictly abide by the Constitution and law, and must struggle resolutely to prevent and oppose crimes and violations of the Constitution and law.

Art. 13. Our socialist homeland, Viet Nam, is sacred and inviolable.

All schemes and actions prejudicial to the independence, sovereignty, unity and territorial integrity of the homeland, or the cause of socialist revolution and socialist construction shall be severely punished.

Art. 14. The Socialist Republic of Viet Nam continues to strengthen its fraternal friendship, militant solidarity and co-operation in all fields with the Soviet Union, Laos, Kampuchea and other socialist countries on the basis of Marxism - Leninism and proletarian internationalism; preserves and develops friendly relations with neighboring countries; unites with peoples struggling for national independence and social progress; pursues a policy of peaceful co-existence with countries of different political and social systems, on the basis of respect for each other's independence, sovereignty and territorial integrity, non-interference in each other's internal affairs, equality and mutual benefit; actively supports and contributes to the struggle of the world's people against imperialism, colonialism, neo-colonialism, hegemonism, and apartheid, for peace, national independence, democracy and socialism.

CHAPTER II

THE ECONOMIC SYSTEM

Art. 15. The Socialist Republic of Viet Nam is advancing directly from a society in which small-scale production predominates to socialism, bypassing the stage of capitalist development, to build a society with a modern industrial-agricultural economy, advanced culture, science and technology, a strong defence potential, and a civilized happy life.

The economic policies of the Socialist Republic of Viet Nam are aimed at progressively satisfying increasing material and cultural needs of the whole society by continuously developing production and raising social labor efficiency, on the basis of socialist collective mastery and modern science and technology.

Art. 16. The central task throughout the period of transition to socialism is the socialist industrialization of the country.

The State gives priority to a rational development of heavy industry on the basis of the development of agriculture and light industry, and the integration of industry and agriculture structure; it builds the centrally-run economy while developing the local economy, and combines the two into a unified national economic structure; combines the development of the productive forces with the institution and perfection of socialist relations of production; combines economic construction and national defence; and strengthens co-operation and mutual assistance with fraternal countries in the socialist community in the spirit of socialist internationalism and, at the same time, develops economic relations with other countries on the basis of respect for each other's independence and sovereignty, equality, and mutual benefit.

Art. 17. The State institutes regulations and takes necessary measures to ensure the working people's full exercise of their right to collective mastery of the means of production and the labor force, of production and distribution, of science and technology, in order to make economic development truly become the work of the entire people.

Art. 18. The State conducts a revolution in the relations of production, guides, utilizes and transforms non-socialist sectors of the economy, institutes and consolidates the system of socialist ownership of the means of production, with the aim of building a national economy with two essential components – the State sector under the ownership of the entire people, and the collective economic sector under the collective ownership of the working people.

The State sector plays the leading role in the national economy, and is given priority for development.

Art. 19. The lands, forests, rivers and lakes, mines, natural resources in the ground, in the territorial seas and on the continental shelf; industrial, agricultural, forestry, fishery and State commercial undertakings; banks and insurance organization; public utilities; the systems of transport by rail, road, river, sea and air; dykes and important irrigation works, defence installation; the systems of information and important irrigation works, defence installations; the systems of information nological research, and cultural and social establishments and other property defined by the law as belonging to the State – are under the ownership of the entire people.

Art. 20. Lands are put under State management according to general plans, to ensure their rational and economical use.

Collectives and individuals who have the use of land are allowed to continue to do so and to enjoy the fruits of their labor according to law.

Collectives and individuals who use the land have the responsibility to protect, replenish and exploit it in keeping with State policies and plans.

Lands reserved for agriculture and forestry may not be used for other purposes unless authorized by competent State organs.

Art. 21. The State holds a monopoly on foreign trade and all other economic relations with foreign countries.

Art. 22. State-run economic establishments operate according to the orientations and tasks laid down under the State plan; they implement a system of economic accounting and a system of managerial and individual responsibility; ensure the workers' and public employees' participation in management; raise the quality of products and services and economic efficiency; practise thrift; ensure accumulation for the State and the factories; scrupulously protect State property; and concern themselves with improving the working and living conditions of workers and public employees.

Art. 23. The State guides and assists in the development of the co-operative sector of the economy.

The property of co-operatives and other collective organizations of the working people is protected by the State in accordance with law.

Co-operatives operate in accordance with national and regional economic plans. They must ensure the constant development of production, increase the income and improve the living standards of their members, and fulfil all obligations to the State while accumulating capital for themselves.

The co-operative members' right to collective mastery in the management of co-operatives must be respected and promoted.

The family subsidiary small holdings of the co-operative members are recognized and protected by the State, in accordance with law.

Art. 24. The State encourages, guides and assists individual farmers, handicraft workers and other self-employed workers to advance towards the road of collective production, to form production co-operatives and other forms of mutual aid collectives on the principle of voluntariness.

Small trades people receive guidance and assistance to gradually switch to production or to other suitable occupations.

The law defines the limits for private economic activity in agriculture, small industry, handicrafts, applied arts and services.

Art. 25. In the Socialist Republic of Viet Nam, all economic bases of feudal landlords and comprador capitalists are nationalized without compensation.

Art. 26. The State conducts the socialist transformation of the private capitalist economy in both urban and rural areas by suitable forms.

Art. 27. The State protects the citizens' right of ownership of lawfully earned incomes, savings, housing, other personal possessions and the means of engaging in authorized private work.

The law protects the citizens' right of inheritance.

Art. 28. The State may, when it deems really necessary to the public interests, purchase or requisition with or without compensation, the property of individuals or of collectives.

The procedures for purchase or requisition are defined by law.

Art. 29. The State, proceeding from the requirements of economic and cultural development and of the strengthening of national development and of the strengthening of national defence, makes a rational distribution and utilization of the social labor force on a national scale as well as for each locality and unit.

Art. 30. The State educates and motivates the entire people to build socialism with industriousness and thrift; it defines and closely controls the use of the labor force, materials and capital in all economic activities and in the management of the State.

Art. 31. The State and collective economic organizations apply the principle: 'From each according to his ability, to each according to his work, 'while gradually increasing social benefits on the basis of development of the national economy.

Art. 32. The State, in coordination with the trade union and other people's organizations, combines political education and the enhancement of labor discipline with material incentives with the aim of promoting the socialist emulation movement.

Art. 33. The State guides the national economy according to unified plans; it promotes a sense of responsibility and the spririt of initiative and creativeness at all echelons, branches, basic units and individuals in elaborating and implementing State plans; it mobilizes all labor forces, natural resources, and material and technical resources of the country, so as to ensure a comprehensive balanced and steady development of the national economy at a rapid pace and with a high level of efficiency.

Art. 34. The State organizes social production along the lines of large scale socialist production; it builds and ceaselessly perfects the system of economic management; correctly applies the economic laws of socialism; applies the principles of democratic centralism and the principles of combining departmental management with regional and local management; combines the interests of the State with those of the collectives and the working people; elaborates and ensures respect for economic laws.

Art. 35. The law severely punishes all acts of speculation, hoarding and all other illegal undertakings that upset the market and undermine State plans, as well as all acts of corruption, theft, bribery, waste, or irresponsible actions that seriously damage the interests of the State and the people.

Art. 36. All State organs, factories, co-operatives, units of the people's armed forces and citizens have the duty to implement the policy of protecting, transforming and renewing natural resources, and of protecting and improving the environment.

CHAPTER III

CULTURE, EDUCATION, SCIENCE AND TECHNOLOGY

Art. 37. The Socialist Republic of Viet Nam promotes the ideological and cultural revolution, develops a new culture with a socialist content and a national, Party and people's character; moulds new generations of people motivated by a sense of collective mastery, the love of labor and respect for public property, possessing a certain cultural level, scientific and technical knowledge and good health, and animated by the love for the socialist homeland and proletarian internationalism.

Art. 38. Marxism-Leninism is the ideological system guiding the development of Vietnamese society.

The State broadly disseminates Marxism-Leninism, the line and policies of the Communist Party of Viet Nam, and the Constitution and laws of the Socialist Republic of Viet Nam. It preserves and develops the cultural and spiritual values of the nations, absorbs the best of world culture, combats feudal and bourgeois ideologies and the influences of imperialist and colonialist culture; criticizes petty-bourgeios ideology; builds a socialist way of life, and combats backward life-styles and superstitition.

Art. 39. The State pays attention to strengthening the material infrastructure, institutes regulations and takes necessary measures to ensure the working people's collective mastery over culture and education, and science and technology, and promotes the people's dynamism and creativeness – thereby involving the entire nation in the building of a new culture and a new society and making it possible for the entire people to enjoy the fine achievements of the national and world cultures.

Art. 40. Viet Nam's education must be constantly developed and improved by combining study and practice, and education and production labor and by developing close ties between the school and society, with a view to training qualified socialist workers and fostering revolutionary generations for the future.

Art. 41. The State has sole responsibility for education.

The State is responsible for ensuring a balanced development of the education system: infants' education, general education, vocational and higher education, job training schools, work-study schools, and in-service education. It continues the anti-illiteracy campaign, promotes complementary education and constantly raises the cultural and professional standards of the entire population.

The Ho Chi Minh Communist Youth Union, the family and society, together with the school, have the responsibility to educate youth and children.

Art. 42. The State promotes the scientific and technological revolution with the aim of developing the productive forces, increasing labor efficiency, speeding up socialist industrialization, improving living standards and strengthening national defence, and building an advanced science and technology for our country.

Art. 43. Social sciences, natural sciences, and technology are to be strongly developed. The State concerns itself with the dissemination and teaching of science and technology; combines teaching and research with production, everyday life, and national defence work; rationally develops and employs the contingent of managers, scientists, technicians and workers; encourages research, inventions and discoveries; pays attention to research and innovation; promotes the spirit of self-reliance, initiative and creativeness while applying results of advanced world science and technology; and promotes international co-operation in the fields of science and technology.

Art. 44. Vietnamese literature and art are developed on the basis of the perspective of Marxism-Leninism, and in keeping with the Communist Party of Viet Nam's line with regard to literature and art.

Encouragement in giving to the development of professional and amateur literary and artistic activities as a means of educating the people in the line and policies of the Party and the State, educating them in revolutionary ethics, thinking and sentiments, developing their aesthetic sense and raising and satisfying their cultural needs.

Art. 45. The work of the mass media, the press, publication, libraries, radio, television and cinema, will be developed and constantly improved with regard to political, ideological and artistic quality so as to guide public opinion, raise the political, cultural, scientific and technological levels of the entire population and mobilize them to participate in socialist emulation.

Art. 46. Historical and cultural relics, public works of art and sites of scenic or other significance shall be restored and protected.

Importance shall be attached to the work of preservation and to museums.

Art. 47. The State is responsible for the protection and improvement of the people's health; develops Vietnamese preventative medicine; combines modern and traditional medical and pharmaceutical practices; combines the techniques of prevention and cure with the emphasis on prevention; and combines State-run health services with people's health services at the grass-roots levels.

The State and society shall give protection to mothers and children and campaign for family planning.

Art. 48. Vietnamese sports and physical culture, with a national, scientific and popular character, shall be developed strongly and harmoniously in order to improve the health of the people and increase their physical fitness for socialist construction and national defence.

Art. 49. Tourism is encouraged and adequately organized.

CHAPTER IV

DEFENCE OF THE SOCIALIST HOMELAND

Art. 50. The Socialist Republic of Viet Nam maintains a national, comprehensive and modern defence system based on the integration of national construction and national defence, the combination of the strength of the people's Armed Forces with that of the entire people, and the combination of the strength of the tradition of struggle against foreign aggression with the strength of the socialist system.

Art. 51. The people's Armed Forces of the Socialist Republic of Viet Nam, absolutely loyal to the homeland and the people, have the duty to be prepared to defend the gains of the revolution, the independence, sovereignty, unity and territorial integrity of the nation, political security and social order and security, and the freedom, happiness and peaceful labor of the people, to join the entire people in building the country.

Art. 52. The State stimulates the people's patriotism and revolutionary heroism, enforces compulsory military service, operates the defence industry, and mobilizes the human and material resources necessary to build powerful people's Armed Forces and constantly augment the nation's defence potential.

All State bodies, social organizations and citizens must fulfil their obligations with regard to national defence and security as provided by law.

CHAPTER V

BASIC RIGHTS AND OBLIGATIONS OF CITIZENS

Art. 53. Citizens of the Socialist Republic of Viet Nam are persons granted Vietnamese citizenship by law.

Art. 54. The rights and obligations of citizens reflect the system of collective mastery of the working people, an harmonious combination of the requirements of social life and legitimate individual freedom, and a guarantee of the identity of interests between the State, the collective and the individual, on the principle: each for all, all for each.

The rights of citizens are inseparable from their obligations.

The State guarantees the rights of citizens; and citizens must fulfil their obligations towards the State and society.

Art. 55. All citizens are equal before the law.

Art. 56. Citizens have the right to take part in managing the affairs of the State and society.

Art. 57. All citizens, regardless of their ethnic origin, sex, social status, religion, cultural attainment, profession and term of residence, have the right to vote upon reaching the age of eighteen, and to stand for election to the National Assembly and the People's Councils at all levels upon attaining the age of twenty-one, with the exception of the insane or people deprived of such rights by law or People's Courts.

Art. 58. Work is the primary right, obligation and privilege of citizens. Citizens have the right to work. People fit for work must work as provided by law.

The State creates jobs on the basis of economic development plans, employs people according to both their personal aptitudes and desires, and social requirements. It fosters professional skills, preserves the health of the work-force, and constantly improves working conditions for both mental and physical labor.

The State institutes and enforces regulations aimed at preventing industrial accidents and occupational diseases.

Art. 59. Working people are entitled to rest.

The State regulates the conditions relating to work, rest and recreation for workers and office employees.

Working people are entitled to social insurance benefits in retirement, old age, sickness, or disability.

The State guides co-operatives in gradually making social insurance benefits available to their members.

Art. 60. Education is a right and obligation of citizens.

The State gradually enforces compulsory general education tuition-free, and grants scholarships to create favorable conditions for citizens to pursue their studies.

Art. 61. Citizens have the right to health care.

The State provides free medical examinations and treatment.

Art. 62. Citizens have the right to housing.

The State has a responsibility to directly improve the rate of housing construction while encouraging and assisting housing construction by collectives and individuals according to common plans, so as to gradually implement this right. The allotment of State housing space must be fair and equitable.

Art. 63. Women and men have equal rights in all respects – in political, economic, cultural, social and family life.

The State and society are responsible for raising the political, cultural, scientific, technical and professional standards of women, and constantly improving their role in society.

The State establishes work conditions suited to women's needs. Women and men receive equal pay for equal work. Women are entitled to pre- and postnatal paid leave if they are workers or office employees, or to maternity allowances if they are co-operative members.

The State and society ensure the development of maternity homes, crèches, kindergardens, community dining halls and other social amenities to create favorable conditions for women to produce, work, study and rest.

Art. 64. The family is the cell of society.

The State protects marriage and the family.

Marriage is based on the principles of voluntariness, progressiveness, monogamy, and equality between husband and wife.

Parents have an obligation to bring up and educate their children to become citizens useful to society. Children have an obligation to respect and care for their parents.

The State and society do not accept discrimination between children.

Art. 65. The State and society are responsible for the protection, care and education of children, and assume an increasing share of the responsibility to raise and educate children in order to improve their social life, study and development.

Art. 66. The State and society shall create conditions for the study, work and recreation of young people, assist them to develop their intellectual faculties, talents and physical fitness; the State and society shall foster the communist ideal and educate young people in revolutionary ethics.

Young people must fulfil their obligations as the shock-force in the emulation movement for socialist construction and national defence, in the three revolutions in the relations of production, science and technology, and ideology and culture.

Art. 67. Citizens enjoy freedom of speech, freedom of the press, freedom of assembly; freedom of association, and freedom to demonstrate in accordance with the interests of socialism and of the people.

The State shall create the necessary material conditions for the exercise of these rights.

No one may misuse democratic freedoms to violate the interests of the State and the people.

Art. 68. Citizens enjoy freedom of worhip, and may practise or not practise a religion.

No one may misuse religions to violate State laws or policies.

Art. 69. Citizens have the right to legal protection from physical violence.

No citizens may be arrested except on the authority of a People's court, or on the decision of the People's Organ of Control, or on a decision subject to ratification by the latter.

Arrests and detention of people must be made in accordance with law. All forms of coercion and torture are strictly prohibited.

Art. 70. Citizens have the right to protection by law with regard to their lives, property, honor and dignity.

Art. 71. Citizens have the right to inviolability with regard to their places of residence. No one is allowed to enter another person's home without the owner's consent, unless otherwise authorized by law. House searches may be made only by representatives of competent State bodies, in accordance with law.

Privacy of correspondence and telephone and telegraphic communications is guaranteed.

Freedom of movement and residence is respected, in accordance with law.

Art. 72. Citizens have the right to undertake scientific and technical research and to pursue literary, artistic and other cultural activities.

The State encourages and assists citizens in their scientific and technical, literary and artistic pursuits with a view to raising the quality of life, socialist construction and national defence. It fosters and promotes personal aptitudes and talents.

The rights of authors and inventors are guaranteed.

Art. 73. Citizens have the right to lodge with any State authority, a complaint or denunciation regarding transgressions of law by any State body, social organization, people's Armed Forces unit or individual, employed by those State bodies, organizations or units.

Complaints and denunciations must be examined and dealt with promptly.

Any violation of the legitimate rights of citizens must be promptly redressed and seriously dealt with. Victims are entitled to compensation.

Retaliation against persons who lodge complaints or denunciations is strictly prohibited.

Art. 74. The State enacts legislation granting privileges to disabled soldiers and families of fallen combatants, and creates conditions for disabled soldiers to recover their working ability, to find employment suited to their health conditions, and to lead a normal life.

Persons or families who have rendered meritorious services to the revolution are commended and rewarded, and receive proper care.

Old people and disabled persons with no family support receive assistance from the State and society.

Orphans are brought up and educated by the State and society.

Art. 75. The State protects the legitimate rights and interests of Vietnamese living abroad.

Art. 76. Citizens must be loyal to the homeland.

Treason against the homeland is the gravest crime against the nation.

Art. 77. To defend the socialist homeland is a sacred duty and noble right of citizens.

Citizens are obliged to do military service and take part in building a national defence force of the whole population.

Art. 78. Citizens are obliged to abide by the Constitution, law and labor discipline, to maintain political and social security and order, protect State secrets, and respect the regulations of the socialist society.

Art. 79. Socialist property is sacred and inviolable. Citizens are obliged to respect and protect it.

Art. 80. Citizens are obliged to pay taxes and take part in work on public projects in accordance with law.

Art. 81. Foreigners who are persecuted for struggling for freedom and national independence, for socialism, democracy and peace, or for engaging in scientific pursuits, are granted the right of asylum by the Socialist Republic of Viet Nam.

CHAPTER VI

THE NATIONAL ASSEMBLY

Art. 82. The National Assembly is the highest representative body of the people, the highest State authority in the Socialist Republic of Viet Nam.

The National Assembly is the only body vested with constitutional and legislative authority.

The National Assembly decides on fundamental domestic and foreign policies, objectives for economic and cultural development, the main principles governing the organization and functioning of the State apparatus and the social relations and activities of citizens.

The National Assembly exercises the right of supreme supervision of all activities of the State.

Art. 83. The National Assembly has the following duties and powers:

(1) To draw up, adopt and amend the Constitution;

(2) To make and amend laws;

(3) To exercise supreme supervision over the Constitution and laws;

(4) To pass State plans and ratify their implementation;

(5) To pass State budgets and ratify their implementation;

(6) To define the organization of the National Assembly, the Council of State, the Council of Ministers, the People's Council and People's Committee, the People's Court and the People's Organ of Control;

(7) To elect and remove the Chairman, Vice Chairmen and other members of the Council of State; the Chairman, Vice-Chairmen and other members of the Council of Ministers; the Chief Justice of the Supreme People's Court; and the Procurator-General of the Supreme People's Organ of Control;

(8) To decide on the institution or dissolution of ministries and State commissions;

(9) To examine reports by the Council of State, the Council of Ministers, the Supreme People's Court and the Procurator-General of the Supreme People's Organ of Control;

(10) To institute, revise, or repeal taxes;

(11) To delineate the boundaries of provinces and municipalities direcly under the central authority, and corresponding administrative units;

(12) To grant general amnesties;

(13) To decide on matters of war and peace;

(14) To delegate certain duties of State organs to social organizations for execution;

(15) To ratify or abrogate international treaties at the proposal of the Council of State.

The National Assembly may assume other duties and powers, when it deems it necessary;

Art. 84. The term of office of each legislature of the National Assembly is five years.

A new National Assembly must be elected two months before the term of office of the incumbent National Assembly expires. Electoral procedures and the number of deputies are defined by law.

Under special circumstances, the National Assembly may decide to prolong its term of office and take necessary measures to ensure its functioning.

Art. 85. The National Assembly shall meet regularly, twice a year, at the convocation of the Council of State.

The Council of State may convene extraordinary sessions of the National Assembly, by its own decision, or at the request of the Council of Ministers or of at least one third of the deputies.

A new legislature of the National Assembly must be convened not later than two months after its election.

The first session of each legislature of the National Assembly shall be opened by the Chairman of the Council of State. The Chairman of the Council of State shall preside over the sessions until the Chairman of the new National Assembly is elected.

Art. 86. The Council of State, the Council of Ministers, the chairman of the National Assembly, the National Defence Council, the Council of Nationalities, the various Commissions of the National Assembly, National Assembly deputies, the Supreme People's Court, the Procurator-General of the Supreme People's Organ of Control, the Viet Nam Fatherland Front, the political parties, the Viet Nam Confederation of Trade Unions, the Vietnamese Association of Collective Peasants, the Ho Chi Minh Communist Youth Union, and the Viet Nam Women's Union, have the right to submit draft laws to the National Assembly.

Art. 87. The adoption of bills and resolutions of the National Assembly requires a supporting vote by a majority of all its deputies, except for proposed constitutional amendments, as provided for in Article 147.

Laws must be promulgated not later than fifteen days after their adoption by the National Assembly.

Art. 88. The National Assembly shall elect a commission to verify the credentials of deputies of the National Assembly and, basing itself on the reports of that commission, decide whether to accept the credentials of deputies to the National Assembly.

Art. 89. The National Assembly shall elect its Chairman and Vice-Chairmen. The number of Vice-Chairmen shall be decided by the National Assembly.

The Chairman of the National Assembly shall preside over its meetings; ensure the observance of the National Assembly internal regulation; keep in touch with the deputies; regulate and coordinate activities of the National Assembly Commissions; certify the laws and resolutions adopted by the National Assembly; and conduct the National Assembly's external communications.

The Vice-Chairmen shall assist the Chairman in the discharge of these duties and powers.

The Chairman of the National Assembly is empowered to attend meetings of the Council of State.

Art. 90. The National Assembly shall elect the National Defence Council.

The National Defence Council is empowered to mobilize all forces and potentials of the country to defend the homeland.

In case of war, the National Assembly or the Council of State may vest the National Defence Council with special duties and powers.

Art. 91. The National Assembly shall elect the Council of Nationalities.

The Council of Nationalities shall study and make proposals on questions of nationalities to the National Assembly and the Council of State in supervising the implementation of policies on nationalities.

The Chairman of the Council of Nationalities may attend meetings of the Council of State.

Art. 92. The National Assembly shall elect its Standing Committees.

The Standing Committees study and examine the draft laws, draft decrees and other bills or reports entrusted to them by the National Assembly and the Council of State. They make proposals to the National Assembly and the Council of State on matters within their respective jurisdictions; and assist the National Assembly and the Council of State in exercising their supervisory power.

When necessary, the National Assembly and the Council of State may set up Interim Committees for specific purposes.

Art. 93. The National Defence Council, the Council of Nationalities, and National Assembly Committees have the right to request members of the Council of Ministers and other concerned officials to present or provide them with information. The persons to whom such requests are made have a responsibility to respond.

Art. 94. National Assembly deputies must maintain close contacts with voters, accept their supervision, report to them about their activities and those of the National Assembly, answer requests and petitions made by voters, examine and help to resolve complaints and denunciations made by voters.

National Assembly deputies shall publicize State laws and policies and motivate the people to take part in managing the State.

Art. 95. National Assembly deputies have the right to question the Council of Ministers and its members, the Chief Justice of the Supreme People's Court and the Procurator-General of the Supreme People's Organ of Control.

The organ or official so questioned must reply to the National Assembly during its meeting.

In case an investigation is deemed necessary, the national Assembly may decide to authorize the said organ or official to reply before the Council of State or at the next meeting of National Assembly.

National Assembly deputies have the right to make requests to State bodies. The persons in charge of these bodies shall receive the deputies, and examine and answer their requests.

Art. 96. National Assembly deputies may not be arrested or prosecuted without the consent of the National Assembly and, when the National Assembly is not in session, without the consent of the Council of State.

If a National Assembly deputy is held in custody for a flagrant offence, the authority responsible for the detention must immediately report the matter to the National Assembly or the Council of State for examination and decision.

Art. 97. State organs are obliged to create favorable conditions for National Assembly deputies to discharge their duties.

CHAPTER VII

THE COUNCIL OF STATE

The Council of State is the highest continuously functioning body of the National Assembly, and is the collective Presidency of the Socialist Republic of Viet Nam.

The Council of State discharges duties assigned and uses powers vested in it by the Constitution and the laws and resolutions of the National Assembly; it decides on important matters concerning the building of socialism and national defence; supervises the implementation of the laws, decrees and resolutions of the National Assembly and the Council of State; and supervises activities of the State apparatus.

The Council of State, through its Chairman, acts on behalf of the Socialist Republic of Viet Nam in domestic and foreign affairs.

The Council of State is responsible and accountable to the National Assembly.

Art. 99. The Council of State, elected from among National Assembly deputies, shall consist of

The Chairman of the Council of State,

The Vice-Chairmen of the Council of State,

The Secretary-General of the Council of State, and

The members of the Council of State.

The numbers of Vice-Chairmen and members of the Council of State are decided by the National Assembly.

Members of the Council of State cannot be concurrently members of the Council of Ministers.

Art. 100. The Council of State has the following duties and powers:

(1) To proclaim and preside over the election of deputies to the National Assembly;

(2) To convene meetings of the National Assembly;

(3) To promulgate laws;

(4) To issue decrees;

(5) To interpret the Constitution, laws and decrees;

(6) To decide to hold referenda;

(7) To supervise the work of the Council of Ministers, the Supreme People's Court and the Procurator-General of the Supreme People's Organ of Control;

(8) To suspend the implementation of, revise or rescind resolutions, decisions or orders of the Council of Ministers which contravene the Constitution, laws or decrees;

(9) To supervise and guide the activities of People's Councils at all levels, in order to promote their functions as representative organs of the people;

(10) To revise or rescind inappropriate resolutions of People's Councils of provinces, municipalities directly under the central authority and corresponding levels and to dissolve those councils where it is considered that they are acting in a manner seriously detrimental to the interests of the people;

(11) To decide, when the National Assembly is not in session, on the formation or dissolution of ministries or State Committees;

(12) To appoint or dismiss the Vice-Chairmen of the Council of Ministers, ministers and heads of State Committees when the National Assembly is not in session;

(13) To appoint or dismiss the deputy chief justices, judges and people's assessors of the Supreme People's Court; appoint and remove the deputy procurators-general and members of the Supreme People's Organ of Control;

(14) To appoint, remove or recall plenipotentiary diplomatic representatives of the Socialist Republic of Viet Nam to foreign countries and international organizations.

(15) To receive foreign plenipotentiary diplomatic representatives;

(16) To ratify or abrogate international treaties, except where it is deemed necessary to refer the matter to the National Assembly;

(17) To determine military, diplomatic and other grades and ranks;

(18) To institute and grant awards, orders, medals and honorific titles;

(19) To decide on granting special amnesties;

(20) To declare a state of war when the country is faced with foreign agression, when the National Assembly is not in session;

(21) To order general or local molilization or a state of siege in the whole country or parts of it;

Decisions of the Council of State as mentioned in Points 11, 12 and 20 must be submitted to the next session of the National Assembly for ratification;

When necessary, the National Assembly may vest the Council of State with other duties and powers.

Art. 101. The term of office of the Council of State corresponds to that of the National Assembly.

When the term of a National Assembly legislature expires, the Council of State shall continue its functions until the new legislature of the National Assembly elects a new Council of State.

Art. 102. The adoption of ordinances and resolutions of the Council of State requires a supporting vote by a majority of its membership.

Art. 103. The Chairman of the Council of State commands the people's armed forces of the whole country, and is concurrently the Chairman of the National Defence Council.

CHAPTER VIII

THE COUNCIL OF MINISTERS

Art. 104. The Council of Ministers is the Government of the Socialist Republic of Viet Nam, the highest executive and administrative State body of the highest body of State authority.

The Council of Ministers is entrusted with the unified management of the implementation of all political, economic, cultural, social, security, national defence and external activities of the State; it enhances the efficiency of the State apparatus from the centre down to the grassroots levels; it ensures respect for and observance of law; promotes the people's collective mastery; ensures the building of socialism, and the constant improvement of the material and cultural life of the people.

The Council of Ministers shall be responsible and accountable to the National Assembly; when the National Assembly is not in session, it shall be responsible and accountable to the Council of State.

Art. 105. The Council of Ministers consists of:

The Chairman of the Council of Ministers,

The Vice Chairmen of the Council of Ministers, and

The Ministers and the Heads of State Committees.

Art. 106. The President of the Viet Nam Confederation of Trade Unions has the right to attend meeting of the Council of Ministers.

The President of the Central Committee of the Viet Nam Fatherland Front, and leading representatives of mass organizations affiliated to the Front, may be invited to attend meetings of the Council of Ministers, when necessary.

Art. 107. The Council of Ministers has the following duties and powers:

(1) To ensure observance of the Constitution and law;

(2) To submit draft laws, draft decrees and other bills to the National Assembly and the Council of State;

(3) To draft the State plans and State budgets and submit them to the National Assembly, and organize the implementation of the State plans and State budgets;

(4) To undertake the unified management of the transformation and development of the national economy, the building and development of culture, education, science and technology;

(5) To improve the material and culture life of the people;

(6) To protect the legitimate rights of citizens and create conditions for them to enjoy their rights and fulfil their obligations;

(7) To organize national defence activities of the entire population, and build the people's armed forces;

(8) To ensure political security, and social order and security;

(9) To enforce moblization, a state of siege and other necessary measures to defend the homeland;

(10) To take measures to protect socialist property, and protect the interests of the State and society;

(11) To undertake unified management of finances, the currency and credits;

(12) To compile national inventories and statistics;

(13) To organize and administer the economic arbitration work of State;

(14) To organize and administer the insurance work of the State;

(15) To organize and administer the inspection and control work of the State;

(16) To organize and manage the State's foreign relations; to guide the implementation of treaties and agreements already signed;

(17) To build and perfect the State managerial apparatus from the centre to the grass roots levels; to train, foster, place and utilize the contingent of State cadres;

(18) To lead the work of the ministries and other organs under the authority of the Council of Ministers;

(19) To ensure that the People's Councils at all levels discharge the tasks and exercise the powers of organs of State authority in the localities.

(20) To lead the People's Councils at all levels.

(21) To create favorable conditions for the activities of the Viet Nam Fatherland Front and its member organizations;

(22) To ensure the dissemination of information and the education of the people with regard to the Constitution and law;

(23) To suspend the execution of, or revise or rescind inappropriate decisions, instructions and circulars of the Ministries and other bodies under the authority of the Council of Ministers;

(24) To suspend the execution of inappropriate resolutions of People's Councils of provinces, municipalities directly under the central authority and corresponding units, and request the Council of State to revise or annul such resolutions;

(25) To suspend the execution of or revise or rescind inappropriate decisions and instructions of People's Committees at all levels;

(26) To delineate the boundaries of administrative units below the level of the provinces and municipalities directly under the central authority and corresponding administrative units.

The National Assembly and the Council of State may, when necessary, assign other tasks to the Council of Ministers and vest it with other powers.

Art. 108. The term of office of the Council of Ministers coincides with that of the National Assembly.

At the end of the term of a legislature of the National Assembly, the Council of Ministers shall continue until the new legislature of the National Assembly elects a new Council of Ministers to perform its duties.

Art. 109. Proceeding from the Constitution, laws and ordinances, the Council of Ministers shall issue resolutions, decrees, decisions, instructions and circulars and supervise the implementation of these documents.

The adoption of resolutions, decrees and decisions of the Council of Ministers requires a supporting vote by a majority of its membership.

Art. 110. The Chairman of the Council of Ministers shall head the work of the Council, and supervise the implementation of decisions by the National Assembly, the Council of State, and the Council of Ministers itself and, on behalf of the Council of Ministers, shall guide the work of ministries and other bodies under the authority of the Council of Ministers and the People's Committee at all levels.

The Vice-Chairmen of the Council of Ministers shall assist the Chairman, and may be empowered to replace him in his absence.

Art. 111. Under the unified leadership of the Council of Ministers, the Ministers and the heads of other bodies under its authority shall organize and guide activities which fall within their respective spheres of responsibility on a national scale.

The ministers and heads of other bodies under the authority of the Council of Ministers, proceeding from laws enacted by the National Assembly, ordinances of the Council of State, and resolutions, decrees, decisions, instructions and circulars of the Council of Ministers, shall issue decisions, instructions and circulars and supervise the implementation of these documents.

Art. 112. Each member of the Council of Ministers shall be personally responsible for his work to the National Assembly, the Council of State and the Council of Ministers and, together with other members, shall bear collective responsibility for the activities of the Council of Ministers to the National Assembly and the Council of State.

CHAPTER IX

PEOPLE'S COUNCILS AND PEOPLE'S COMMITTEES

Art. 113. The administrative units of the Socialist Republic of Viet Nam are defined as follows:

The country is divided into provinces, municipalities directly under the central authority, and corresponding units;

Provinces are divided into districts, provincial towns and provincial capitals; municipalities directly under the central authority are divided into precincts or districts, and townships;

Districts are divided into villages and townships; provincial towns and provincial capitals are divided into wards and villages; precincts are divided into wards.

The above-mentioned administrative units form their own People's Councils and People's Committee.

Art. 114. The People's Councils are organs of State authority in their respective area; they shall be elected by the local population, and shall be responsible to it and to the higher authorities.

The People's Councils shall decide on, and take measures to build their localities in all fields, ensure the development of the economy and culture, the improvement of living standards of the local people and the fulfilment of the tasks assigned by the higher authorities.

In their activities, the People's Councils shall elicit the close cooperation of the Fatherland Front and mass organizations and the broad participation of citizens.

Art. 115. The People's Councils have the following duties and powers:

(1) To ensure respect for and strict observance of the Constitution and law in their localities, and decide on measures to carry out State policies and fulfil the tasks assigned by the higher authorities;

(2) To decide on local plans and budgets, and approve their execution;

(3) To take decisions on problems concerning production, circulation, distribution, cultural and social activities, and public catering in their localities;

(4) To ensure the building of national defence units embracing the entire population and of the people's armed forces in their localities;

(5) To ensure political and social security and public order;

(6) To protect socialist property;

(7) To ensure equality among ethnic groupings;

(8) To ensure the citizens' enjoyment of their rights and fulfilment of their obligations;

(9) To elect and remove members of People's Committees and members of People's Courts at corresponding levels;

(10) To revise or annul inappropriate decisions by the People's Committees at corresponding levels, or of People's Councils at the level immediately below them;

(11) To dissolve People's Councils at the level immediately below them when the latter do serious harm to the interests of the people.

Resolutions concerning such dissolution must be ratified by the People's Council at the level above them before they can take effect. The resolutions on dissolution by the People's Councils of provinces, municipalities directly under the central authority and corresponding levels must be ratified by the Council of State prior to their application;

(12) To supervise, within the limits of their responsibilities and powers, the observance of law by public offices, factories and other organizations at higher levels in their localities.

Art. 116. The term of office of the People's Councils of provinces, municipalities directly under the central authorities and corresponding levels shall be four years.

The term of office of the People's Council at other levels shall be two years.

Art. 117. The People's Councils, proceeding from State law and decisions of higher authorities, shall adopt appropriate resolutions and supervise their implementation.

The adoption of resolutions by a People's Council requires a supporting vote by a majority of its membership.

Art. 118. The People's Councils shall set up necessary commissions to assist them in making decisions regarding local undertakings and measures and in supervising the implementation of State laws and policies and resolutions of the councils.

Art. 119. Deputies to the People's Councils must maintain close relations with the electors, accept their supervision, regularly inform them of their activities and those of the People's Councils, respond to the requests and petitions made by the electors and examine and respond to complaints and denunciations by the people.

Deputies to the People's Councils shall publicise State laws and policies and resolutions of the People's Councils and motivate the local population to take part in the management of State affairs.

Art. 120. Deputies to the People's Councils have the right to question the People's Committees and other State organs in their localities. The organs so questioned must answer before the People's Councils within the time set by law.

Deputies to the People's Councils have the right to petition State organs in their localities. Leading officials of these organs have the responsibility to receive those deputies, and examine and deal with their petitions.

Art. 121. The People's Committees are the executive bodies of People's Councils, and are local administrative bodies of the State.

The People's Committees shall be responsible and accountable to the People's Councils at the same level, and to People's Committees at the level immediately above them; the People's Committee of provinces, municipalities directly under the central authority and corresponding levels shall be responsible and accountable to the People's Councils at the same level and to the Council of Ministers.

Each member of the People's Committees shall be personally responsible for his work to the People's Council and the People's Committee, and, together with other members, shall be collectively responsible for the activities of the People's Committee to the People's Council.

Art. 122. A People's Committee shall consist of the Chairman, one or more Vice-Chairmen, a Secretary and other members.

The presidents of local committees of the Viet Nam Fatherland Front and the leading officials of other mass organizations affiliated to the Front may be invited to attend meetings of People's Committees at the same level, when necessary.

Art. 123. The People's Committees shall convene meetings of People's Councils at the same levels; carry out their resolutions and decisions and the instruction of higher administrative bodies; manage local administrative work; and guide the organizations at all levels under their jurisdiction to fulfil State plans for economic and cultural development, for strengthening national defence, and for improving the people's living standards; and examine and deal with complaints, denunciations and petitions by the people.

Art. 124. The People's Committee at all levels, within the powers vested in them by law, shall take decisions and give instructions, and supervise their implementation.

The People's Committee have the right to suspend the execution of, or revise or rescind inappropriate decisions of organizations under their jurisdiction, and of People's Committees at lower levels, to suspend the execution of inappropriate decisions of People's Councils at the level below them, and at the same time to request People's Councils at the same level to revise or rescind such decisions.

Art. 125. The People's Committees shall create favorable conditions for activities of deputies to and committees of the People's Council. The Chairman of the People's Committee shall be responsible for regulating and coordinating the activities of the committees set up by the People's Council.

Art. 126. The term of office of the People's Committee corresponds to that of the People's Council.

When the term of office of the People's Council expires, the People's Committee shall continue to perform its duties until the new People's Council has elected a new People's Committee.

In the case of the People's Council being dissolved, the People's Committee at the level above it shall appoint an interim People's Committee to take charge until the new People's Council has elected a new People's Committee.

In the case of the dissolution of the People's Council of a province, a municipality directly under the central authority or a corresponding level, the Council of Ministers shall appoint an interim People's Committee.

CHAPTER X

PEOPLE'S COURTS AND PEOPLE'S ORGANS OF CONTROL

Art. 127. The People's Court and People's Organs of Control in the Socialist Republic of Viet Nam are, within their competence, obliged to protect the socialist legal system, the socialist system, the working people's right to collective mastery, and socialist property, and to ensure respect for the lives, property, freedom, honor and dignity of citizens.

Any act encroaching upon the interests of the State or the collective or the legitimate interests of citizens must be dealt with in accordance with law.

People's Courts

Art. 128. The Supreme People's Court, the local People's Courts, and the Military Tribunals are juridical bodies of the Socialist Republic of Viet Nam.

Under special circumstances, the National Assembly or the Council of State may decide to set up Special Tribunals.

Appropriate people's organizations shall be formed at the grass roots to deal with minor breaches of law or disputes, in accordance with law.

Art. 129. Judges of the People's Courts at all levels shall be elected.

The term of office of the Chief Justice, Deputy Chief Justice and judges of People's Courts at all levels corresponds to that of the bodies that elect them.

Art. 130. Trials at the People's Courts shall be held with the participation of people's assessors in keeping with law. In the administration of justice, the people's assessors have the same powers as judges.

People's assessors of People's Courts at all levels shall be elected. The term of office of people's assessors at the Supreme People's Court shall be two and a half years; that of people's assessors at local People's Court shall be two years.

Art. 131. During trials, judges and people's assessors are independent and subject only to law.

Art. 132. The People's Courts shall make judgments and pass sentence collectively by majority decision.

Art. 133. Proceedings in People's Courts shall be open to the public, unless otherwise stipulated by law.

The defendant's right to plead their cases is guaranteed.

A jurist organization may be formed to give legal assistance to the defendants and other persons concerned.

Art. 134. The People's Courts shall ensure to the citizens of all nationalities in the Socialist Republic of Viet Nam the right to use their own spoken languages and scripts before the Courts.

Art. 135. The Supreme People's Court is the highest juridical body of the Socialist Republic of Viet Nam.

The Supreme People's Court shall supervise the proceedings of local People's Courts and Military Courts.

The Supreme People's Court shall supervise the proceedings of the Special Courts, unless the National Assembly or the Council of State decides otherwise when setting up these Courts.

Art. 136. The Supreme People's Court shall be responsible and accountable to the National Assembly; when the National Assembly is not in session, it shall be responsible and accountable to the Council of State.

Local People's Courts shall be responsible and accountable to the People's Councils at the same levels.

Art. 137. The verdicts and decisions of the People's Courts, as soon as they take legal effect, must be respected by State organs, social organizations and all citizens; the persons and units concerned must strictly implement them.

The People's Organs of Control

Art. 138. The Supreme People's Organ of Control of the Socialist Republic of Viet Nam shall control the observance of law by the ministries and other bodies under the authority of the Council of Ministers, local organs of power, social organizations, State employees, and all citizens, exercise the right of public prosecution, and ensure the strict and uniform observance of law.

The local People's Organs of Control and the Military Organs of Control shall control the observance of law and exercise the right of public prosecution within their spheres of responsibility.

Art. 139. The term of office of the Procurator-General of the Supreme People's Organ of Control corresponds to that of the National Assembly.

Art. 140. A People's Organ of Control shall be led by its Chief Procurator.

The Chief Procurator of a lower People's Organ of Control shall be subordinate to his counterpart in the immediately senior People's Organ of Control; the chiefs of the local People's Organs of Control shall be under the unified leadership of the Procurator-General of the Supreme People's Organ of Control.

The Chief and Deputy Chief Procurators and members of People's Organs of Control shall be appointed and removed by the Procurator-General of the Supreme People's Organ of Control.

Art. 141. The Procurator-General of the Supreme People's Organ of Control shall be responsible and accountable to the National Assembly; when the National

Assembly is not in session, he shall be responsible and accountable to the Council of State.

CHAPTER XI

THE NATIONAL FLAG, NATIONAL EMBLEM, NATIONAL ANTHEM AND NATIONAL CAPITAL

Art. 142. The national flag of the Socialist Republic of Viet Nam consists of a rectangle of red cloth, with a five-pointed golden star in the middle; the ratio of the width of the flag to its length is 2–3.

Art. 143. The national emblem of the Socialist Republic of Viet Nam is round in form with a red background. In its centre is a five-pointed golden star framed by ears of rice. Its lower half is rimmed by a halved cogwheel with the inscription: The Socialist Republic of Viet Nam.

Art. 144. The national anthem of the Socialist Republic of Viet Nam shall be adopted by the National Assembly.

Art. 145. The Capital of the Socialist Republic of Viet Nam is Hanoi.

CHAPTER XII

LEGAL FORCE OF THE CONSTITUTION AND PROCEDURE FOR AMENDING THE CONSTITUTION

Art. 146. The Constitution of the Socialist Republic of Viet Nam is the fundamental law of the State and has supreme legal force.

All other legal documents must be consistent with the Constitution.

Art. 147. Only the National Assembly shall have power to amend the Constitution.

Amendments to the Constitution shall require for their adoption, a majority vote of not less than two thirds of the total number of deputies to the National Assembly.

The present Constitution was unanimously adopted by the National Assembly of the Socialist Republic of Viet Nam, Sixth Legislature, Seventh Session, at its meeting on 18th December, 1980, at 15:25 hours.

YEMEN ARAB REPUBLIC

SUMMARY

INTERNATIONAL STATUS

The Yemen Arab Republic (North Yemen) is a member of the United Nations (September 30, 1947). It is a member of the League of Arab States and of other international organizations. The Kingdom of Yemen was founded by a revolt against the Ottoman Empire in 1904. Yemen was under Ottoman rule from 1568 to 1630 and from 1849 to 1904, when it rose against the Turks. Ottoman rule was formally ended in 1918 when Turkey surrendered all its Arab territories. From 1958 to 1961 it federated with the United Arab Republic (Egypt) to form the United Arab States. On September 18, 1962, the Imam was deposed and a republic proclaimed, and on October 31, 1962, a provisional constitution was promulgated. From 1962 to 1970, there was civil war, Egypt supplying the troops to assist the republicans. The last Egyptian troops left in 1967. In 1977, President Hamidi was assassinated. In 1979, a ten day war between the Yemen Arab Republic and the Yemen People's Democratic Republic was ended by the Kuwait agreements. Negotiations between the two Yemens for a union based on proposals of a mixed constitutional committee formed at Kuwait went on through 1981 and 1982. Their progress was impeded by the serious fighting between government forces and guerrillas of the National Democratic Front near the South Yemen border and supplied by South Yemen. An agreement of January 1980 for the integration of the NDF into the political life of the country was never put into effect.

FORM OF NATIONAL GOVERNMENT

The provisional Constitution of June 19, 1974, replacing the Constitution of 1970, provides that Yemen is an Arab, Islamic and independent state, with a representative system, and that the Yemeni people form part of the Arab nation.[1] The people are the source of all authority.[2] The State religion is Islam and Islamic Sharia is the source of all laws.[3] Action is to be taken during the transitional period to restore constitutional and democratic life on a sound basis.[4]

RIGHTS OF THE PEOPLE

The Constitution states that Yemenis have equal rights and duties, personal freedoms is guaranteed, crimes and penalties may be only as laid down by law and there may be no retroactive penalties.[5] The home is inviolable; confiscation of funds and expropriation without compensation are prohibited.[6] Citizens have freedom of speech, writing and voting.[7] Places of worship and learning have immunity.[8]

LEGISLATIVE AND EXECUTIVE DEPARTMENTS

The Command Council assumes the legislative and executive authority of the State, and its chairman assumes the function of general sovereignty.[9] In February 1978, a 99 member Constitutional Peoples' Assembly was appointed by the Command Council which dissolved itself in April. The Peoples' Assembly was increased to 159 members in May 1979. A Committee for National Consultation composed of 52 members was set up in May 1980. The General People's Congress, 700 elected and 300 appointed members held its first meeting September 1982, and will meet every two years and be elected every four years.

JUDICIAL DEPARTMENT

The judiciary is independent and its verdicts are to be handed down and implemented in accordance with the principles of Sharia.[10]

AREA, POPULATION, ETC.

The area of Yemen is about 200,000 square kilometres, the population (1980 census) is 8,556,974. The capital is Sanaa. The official language is Arabic.[11]

[1] Prov. Const., Art. 1.
[2] Id., Art. 2.
[3] Id., Art. 3,4.
[4] Id., Art. 19.
[5] Id., Art. 6–8.
[6] Id., Art. 9–11.
[7] Id., Art. 12.
[8] Id., Art. 13.
[9] Id., Art. 14, 15.
[10] Id., Art. 17.
[11] Id., Art. 3.

PROVISIONAL CONSTITUTION[1]

(Published June 19th, 1974)

In the name of the people, the Chairman of the Command Council, having taken cognizance of Command Council Proclamation No. 1 for 1974, Command Council Proclamation No. 4 for 1974 suspending the Constitution, and Command Council Proclamation No. 5 for 1974 increasing the membership of the Command Council, and desiring to consolidate the bases of authority during the transitional period and to regulate the rights and duties of all employees in a manner conducive to fruitful production to raise the country to the level which we all hope it will attain, we announce in the name of the people that during the transitional period the country will be governed in accordance with the following rules:

CHAPTER ONE

GENERAL PRINCIPLES: THE STATE

Art. 1. Yemen is an Arab, Islamic, and independent state enjoying full sovereignty. Its system is republican. The Yemeni people are a part of the Arab nation.

Art. 2. The people are the source of all authority.

Art. 3. Islam is the state religion and Arabic the official state language.

Art. 4. The Islamic Sharia is the source of all laws.

Art. 5. Yemen is an indivisible whole and its defence is the sacred duty of all citizens.

CHAPTER TWO

RIGHTS AND DUTIES

Art. 6. Yemenis have equal rights and general duties.

Art. 7. Personal freedom is guaranteed in accordance with the provisions of the law.

Art. 8. There shall be no crime and no penalty except as laid down by law and there shall be no penalty for acts except those committed after the promulgation of the law (applying to them).

Art. 9. Homes are inviolate: it is therefore inadmisible to enter them except in such instances as prescribed by the law.

Art. 10. The confiscation of funds is prohibited, except within the confines of the law.

Art. 11. No person's property shall be expropriated except in the public interest, in the instances prescribed by the law, and with just compensation to the person.

[1] Europa Yearbook 1981

Art. 12. The citizens have the right to express their thoughts by means of speech, writing, or voting within the confines of the law.

Art. 13. Places of worship and learning have immunity which cannot be violated except in instances required by security needs and as prescribed by the law.

CHAPTER THREE

THE SYSTEM OF GOVERNMENT

Art. 14. The Chairman of the Command Council shall assume the function of general sovereignty, particularly in taking the measures he deems necessary to protect the revolution and the republican régime.

Art. 15. The Command Council shall assume the functions of the legislative and executive authorities of the state. It shall also have the power to lay down general policy and define its general framework.

Art. 16. The Government is the executive and administrative body responsible for carrying out the state's general policy as laid down by the Command Council.

Art. 17. The judiciary is independent, and there shall be no authority over it except for the law. Its verdicts shall be handed down and executed in accordance with the principles of the Sharia.

CHAPTER FOUR

CONCLUDING RULES

Art. 18. All the rules determined by the laws, bylaws and decisions prior to the issuance of this constitutional declaration shall remain in force unless they conflict with the rules of this declaration or unless they are amended or revoked.

Art. 19. During the transitional period action shall be taken to restore constitutional and democratic life on sound bases in view of the need to provide the Yemeni people with a dignified life and a bright future.

Art. 20. This constitutional declaration shall come into force from the date of its issuance and it shall be published in the Official *Gazette.*

YEMEN PEOPLE'S DEMOCRATIC REPUBLIC

SUMMARY

INTERNATIONAL STATUS

The People's Democratic Republic of Yemen (South Yemen) is a member of the United Nations (December 14, 1967). It is a member of the League of Arab States and of other

The Yemen P.D.R. became independent on November 30, 1967. Before independence its area was constituted by the colony of Aden and the Western and Eastern Aden protectorates composed of 23 protected states. By the ninth century, Islam had conquered the area and later the coastal part came under the control of Egyptians and of Turkey. In 1839, Aden was captured by Britain and its strategic and trading importance increased after the opening of the Suez Canal in 1869. After being ruled as part of British India it became in 1937 a Crown Colony. The British extended their authority eastward into the Hadramaut and northward by means of protection treaties with the local sheiks and by the 1950's, the Eastern and Western protectorates together with Aden Colony formed the Federation of South Arabia. A treaty of 1959 provided that it should become independent by 1968. The period preceding independence was characterised by increasing difficulties arising out of the differences between modern Aden and the poor traditional sheikdoms and sultanates of the Protectorates, rising Arab nationalism leading to violence and bitter fighting between two nationalist groups and the British. In 1967, the British began to pull out troops and federal rule collapsed. Following negotiations in Geneva between the British and the National Liberation Front, South Arabia was declared independent and renamed the People's Republic of Southern Yemen. In June 1969, the more radical wing of the NLF took power (it is now called the National Front), gave the country its present name, and committed it to the introduction of scientific socialism. During September–October 1972, there was war between the Yemen Arab Republic and the Yemen P.D.R. which was terminated by a cease fire. Skirmishes continue although the Yemenis consider themselves as one people and both countries advocate a united Yemen. An unsuccessful military rising in June 1978 against the National Front led by the then President led to the latter's execution and the refusal of various claims by the tribal chiefs. In October 1978 the Yemeni Socialist Party was established as the single party to lead and guide society and the state.

FORM OF NATIONAL GOVERNMENT

The Constitution of 1971, as amended on October 31, 1978, states that the Yemen P.D.R. is a sovereign democratic and people's republic, that aims toward the realisation of the United Democratic Yemen.[1] The Yemeni people is one and part of the Arab nation; the Yemeni Socialist Party is the leader and guide of the society and state.[2] All political power is exercised by the working people and the elected People's Councils are the basis of state power.[3] The State works in accordance with the Arab League Covenant, the principles of the United Nations, the United Nations Declaration of Human Rights and the principles of international law; it supports all struggles for national independence and condemns imperialism.[4] A section describes the economy.[5]

RIGHTS OF THE PEOPLE

The Constitution provides that all citizens are equal in their rights and duties with no discrimination and equal before the law; that the state must ensure equal rights for men and women in all fields and special protection for working women and their children.[6] Citizens have the rignt to work, workers the right to rest and social security.[7] Citizens have the right to education, medical care, accomodation, participation in designing the political, economic, social and cultural life, the right to assemble and demonstrate, freedom of expression, personal freedom; corporal punishment is prohibited.[8] Islam is the state religion but freedom of faith is guaranteed.[9] Retroactive punishments are forbidden, inviolability of dwellings and correspondence, freedom of scientific research and artistic creation, freedom of movement within the Republic are guaranteed.[10] A chapter describes the organizations and their rights and functions, in particular the General Confederation of Trade Unions, the Yemeni Socialist Youth Union, the General Union of Yemeni Women, the Democratic Yemeni Union of Peasants.[11]

[1] Const., Art. 1.
[2] Id., Art. 2.
[3] Id., Art. 6.
[4] Id., Art. 10.
[5] Id., Art. 12–22.
[6] Id., Art. 34–36.
[7] Id., Art. 37–39.
[8] Id., Art. 40–45.
[9] Id., Art. 47.
[10] Id., Art. 48–54.
[11] Art. 63–67.

LEGISLATIVE DEPARTMENT

The legislative organ, the People's Supreme Council, is the highest organ of state power and is composed of 111 members elected by free, universal, equal and direct elections by secret ballot, for a term of five years; it can be dissolved only by a two-thirds majority of its members.[12] It holds three yearly sessions.[13] Laws must be approved by two thirds of members present.[14] Members of the People's Supreme Council represent the people; they may not be blamed for opinions expressed in the course of their duties and criminal proceedings may not be taken against them except with the approval of the Council or its Presidium when the Council is not in session.[15]

EXECUTIVE DEPARTMENT

The highest executive and administrative organ is the Council of Ministers, elected by the People's Supreme Council at its first session, composed of the Prime Minister, his deputies and the ministers.[16] There is a chapter on the organs of the State's local authority and administration.[17]

JUDICIAL DEPARTMENT

Justice is administered by the Supreme Court and other courts whose functions and competence are regulated by law and whose activity should aim towards educating the citizens to respect the Constitution and the law, to love and be loyal to the revolution and the homeland.[18] Judges are elected by the People's Councils (which may withdraw their confidence) except in the military courts where they are appointed by the Presidium of the People's Supreme Council.[19] Judges are independent and the accused shall be guaranteed the right of defence.[20]

AREA, POPULATION, ETC.

The area is 336,869 square kilometres, the population (1981 estimate) 2,030,000. The official language is Arabic.[21] Aden is the capital.[22]

[12] Id., Art. 69–72.
[13] Id., Art. 75.
[14] Id., Art. 76.
[15] Id., Art. 85, 86.
[16] Id., Art. 99, 100.
[17] Id., Art. 112–118.
[18] Id., Art, 121.
[19] Id., Art, 122.
[20] Id., Art. 125, 127.
[21] Id., Art. 4.
[22] Id., Art. 135.

CONSTITUTION OF THE PEOPLE'S DEMOCRATIC REPUBLIC OF YEMEN[1]

1971 as amended October 31, 1978

PREAMBLE

Our Yemenic People in the two parts of the homeland had striven valiantly side by side to oust the invaders who were avaricious for its land and against the reactionary Imamite regime in the Northern part of the homeland and against colonialism, feudalism and rule of the Sultans in the Southern part of the homeland. Such is the living expression of the unity of the Yemeni people and Yemeni land.

The Yemeni people detonated the 26th September revolution and defended the republican regime in the Northern part of the homeland. It also detonated the 14th October revolution under the leadership of the National Front and achieved independence on the 30th of November.

All this affirms that despite the unnatural situations of the false division of the Yemeni land and people its struggle in the two parts is dialectically correlated in its unity not only against the imperialist and reactionary cabals against the Yemeni homeland but also for the purpose of finally getting rid of the division and restoring the natural situation for the democratic unity of Yemen.

Since the glorious corrective move on the 22nd of June 1969, a number of progressive achievements have been realized in all the fields, political, economical, social and cultural. Such were attained by arduous struggle for the purpose of fully realizing the noble aims for the materialization of which the toiling masses of our people-workers, peasants, intelligentsia, petty bourgeoisie and all honest groups of the people have been struggling. These aims are basically among the aims of the two revolutions of 26th September 1962 and 14th October 1963. The struggle of the Yemeni people shall continue until the realization of all the tasks of the national democratic revolution stage, the stategy of the Yemeni revolution including the construction of the United Democratic Yemen under the leadership of our Yemeni Socialist Party – the party of the Yemeni working class, its allies and the rest of the groups of the democratic and national movement – in our Yemeni homeland.

The struggle of our Yemeni people is dialectally correlated with the struggle of the Arab and other peoples on the way to freedom, democratic and social progress and peace. Our Yemeni people believe that their struggle is interconnected with the unity of the struggle of the Arab revolution movement for the purpose of realizing the democratic progressive Arab unity.

The Yemeni people regard all that they have achieved in their struggles as a revolutionary contribution to the international and Arab revolution movement.

Our Yemeni people consider this Constitution as the general basis for their national democratic regime and as organizing the political, economical, social and cultural life.

[1] Printed at 14 October Corporation, Aden. Supplied by Ministry of Foreign Affairs, April, 1981. Ed.

PART ONE

FOUNDATIONS OF THE NATIONAL DEMOCRATIC REGIME

Chapter One. The Political Foundations

Art. 1. The People's Democratic Republic of Yemen is a sovereign democratic and people's Republic. It is a state that expresses the interests of the workers, the peasants, the intelligentsia, the petty bourgeoisie and all the working populace and aims towards the realization of the United Democratic Yemen, and the absolute fulfilment of the basis of the national democratic revolution stage for the purpose of paving the way for the transition to the construction of socialism.

Art. 2. The Yemeni people is one people and it is part of the Arab nation and the Yemeni nationality is one. The Yemen constitutes a historical, economical and geographical unity.

The Yemeni Socialist Party, armed with the Scientific Socialism theory, is the leader and guide of the society and the state. It shall define the general horizon for the development of the society and the line of the state's internal and external policy.

The Yemeni Socialist Party shall lead the struggle of the people and their mass organizations towards the absolute victory of the Yemeni revolution's strategy and the achievement of the tasks of the national democratic revolution stage for the purpose of accomplishing the construction of socialism.

All organizations of the party shall work within the framework of the constitution.

Art. 4. Arabic shall be the official language.

Art. 5. The Law shall define the territory of the People's Democratic Republic of Yemen.

Art. 6. All the political power in the People's Democratic Republic of Yemen shall be exercised by the working people.

The elected People's Council are the basis of the state power. All other organs of the state are subject to their supervision and shall be called to account before them.

All the state organs shall function on the basis of democratic legality and they shall ensure the protection of the legal order and the workers' interests.

Art. 7. The People's Councils shall be formed on the basis of free, universal, equal and direct elections and by secret ballot in the constituencies in accordance with the provisions of the Electoral Law.

Every citizen, who has attained the age of eighteen by election day, shall have the right to vote.

Every citizen may be elected to the People's Local Councils if he has by election day attained the age of twenty one and he may be elected to the People's Supreme Council if he has by election day attained the age of twenty four.

Art. 8. The organization of the state power and its administration are subject to the principle of democratic centralization. Accordingly, all the state organs shall be elected by the people and be called to account before them. The elected people's representatives are obliged to submit periodic reports regarding their functions to their electorate.

The decisions of the high organs are binding upon the lower organs and the latter are responsible and accountable for their functions to the high organs.

The Executive organs and the organs of local government are subject in the exercise of their powers, to a two-fold subordination. Each of these organs is subject to the power of the people of its same level and is at the same time subjugated to the higher organ responsible for directing and implementing the administrative affairs and local government.

The democratic centralization combines the centralization of the state's planning and administration of the creative activities and initiatives of the state's local organs and the full responsibility of each of the state's organs and of every person for the work allocated to it.

Art. 9. The State shall direct the society's activity with the aim of achieving the tasks of the national democratic revolution as paving the way for the complete abolition of the exploitation of man by man and regarding work as the sole means to the enjoyment of the fruits of society.

Art. 10. (a) The State affirms working in accordance with the Covenant of the Arab League, the principles of the United Nations, the Universal Declaration of Human Rights and the generally recognized rules of international law. It resists the imperalist subjugation, condemns imperialism and its hostile disposition and supports and promotes all the people's struggle for national independence, social progress and the abolition of all forms of colonialism, zionism and racial discrimination.

(*b*) The State shall strengthen its relations with the Arab states and peoples in the manner that serves their social progress and emancipation and their democratic unity. It shall establish its relations with all states on the basis of equality, mutual respect, non-interference in internal affairs, mutual benefit and the peaceful coexistence between the states of various social regimes.

The People's Democratic Republic of Yemen shall not employ its armed forces against the liberty of any other people.

(*c*) The State shall strengthen its relations with the Socialist States.

(*d*) The State shall grant the right of political asylum to whoever is being persecuted because of this struggle for national liberation, social progress, peace and socialism.

Art. 11. The State shall patronize the Yemeni citizens residing abroad and strengthen their relations with the homeland. The State shall protect the legitimate rights of the Yemeni expatriates sanctioned by the international law.

Chapter Two. The Economic Foundations

Art. 12. The State shall develop the national economy on the basis of the substantive laws of scientific socialism and shall support and develop the branches of the national economy with the aim of satisfying the people's needs, the just distribution of the social wealth and the absolute application of the principle: 'from each according to his ability and for each according to his work'.

For this purpose the State shall lay the comprehensive plans for the development of the national economy, the rational investment of all the resources, the continuous increasing of work production, raising the standard of the workers's conscientiousness for the State and co-operative property, increasing and protecting the social wealth, enhancing discipline for work and developing the creation and initiatives of the workers.

Art. 13. The collective property: The property of the people represented by the State and that of the co-operatives and the mass organizations, is the basis of the national economy in the People's Democratic Republic of Yemen. It is sacrosanct and enjoys the protection of the State. The State shall develop it.

The collective property may not be employed for personal purposes.

Art. 14. The State is the sole owner of the land, the natural wealth and all its derivatives and the sources of energy existing underneath or above the land or within the limits of the territorial waters, the continental shelf and the exclusive economic zone.

The State shall also own the principal means of production in industry and agriculture. It shall further own and undertake, by itself, the services of the ports, banks, insurance, post, telecommunications and all the other basic services necessary for the development of the society.

The State shall sanction the currency, monetary and banking systems and shall encourage saving.

The State sector shall play the leading role in the national economy.

Art. 15. The State shall control foreign trade and direct it in the manner that serves the social and economic development plans.

The State shall direct home trade and support and develop the leading role of the state sector in it.

The State shall regulate and supervise the activity of the small merchants with the aim of protecting the consumers and shall lay and execute the prices policy to ensure the availability of the basic goods for the citizens.

Art. 16. The State shall work for the expansion of reforming the agricultural lands, the protection of the soil from erosion or disintergration, the development of the irrigation system and the exploitation of the subterranean waters in a scientific manner. It shall also work for the protection and increase of the livestock and the fish wealth sources.

The State shall work for the protection and improvement of the environment in the interest of the opulence of the citizens of the People's Democratic Republic of Yemen.

The protection of the environment is the duty of the society, the State and the citizen.

Art. 17. The co-operative property is the property of the co-operative societies of the peasants, the fishermen and the craftsmen, and the other co-operatives of the working people.

The co-operatives shall own the means of production and other properties deemed necessary to enable them to achieve the aims provided for by the law.

The State shall grant the co-operatives permanent and free usufruct over the lands.

The State shall support the co-operative property and the co-operative movement. It shall render special interest to the development of the productive agricultural co-operatives with the aim of increasing the agricultural production, improving the standard of living of the co-operative peasants and encouraging the voluntary affiliation of the peasants to the co-operatives.

Art. 18. The State shall protect the productive private property in so far as it does not, as far as its size and nature of its employment are concerned, contradict the social interests of the toiling masses during the national democratic revolution stage.

The State shall further support the productive activity of the private and combined enterprises with the aim of developing the national economy.

It shall protect the private property arising from the individual labor of the citizens and members of their families in all the socially beneficial sectors, and encourage the formation of co-operatives in these sectors in accordance with the Law.

Art. 19. The State shall protect the personal property arising from the personal income earned from their labor in accordance with the law. The employment of such property must not conflict with the public opulence.

The State shall regulate and protect the right of inheritance.

Art. 20. No foreigner may own any property in the People's Democratic Republic of Yemen except in accordance with conditions required by the law.

Further, no foreign capital may be invested except within limits required by the development of the national economy and in a manner that is consonant with the aims of the national democratic revolution and the laws. The State shall exercise control over the revenues and their use.

Art. 21. The State shall lead the national economy on the basis of the social and economic plans which shall have the force of law.

The plans shall be prepared and executed with the effective participation of the workers and the toiling masses and on basis of scientific studies and statistics.

The democratic centralization is the principle of the administration of the national economy in the People's Democratic Republic of Yemen. Such means the combination of the State's central leadership of the economic activity and the creative initiatives of the organs of the state's local authorities, the productive establishments, the mass organizations and all the workers.

The people's labor is reared in the People's Democratic Republic of Yemen, as a source for the development and growth of the national economy, the augmentation of the social wealth and the blooming of the personality of the new Yemeni materially and spiritually.

The State shall pursue making the useful social work the criterion for determining the status of the person in the society, and shall encourage the creative initiative of the citizens and their positive stand from the work.

Chapter Three. The Social and Cultural Foundations

Art. 23. All the State's measures shall serve the laborers, the peasants, the inteligentsia and all the workers with the aim of raising their standard in all the fields. They shall, further, prepare the circumstances necessary for enabling the working class to exercise its leading role in the society.

Art. 24. Public education shall serve the social progress, and every sector of the people has a right to it.

The State shall undertake public education in accordance with the requirements of the national democratic revolution. It shall execute, in this respect, a national, Yemeni and progressive curriculum that relies on the scientific socialism theory.

The State shall render every assistance for the progress of science and arts and shall, also, encourage the scientific and artistic inventions and the artistic creation and shall protect their results.

Art. 25. The State shall care for the Yemeni youth and their activities and shall work for the provision of the ideological and physical education necessary for them. It shall also take interest in their organizations and clubs in the manner that ensures their conscious and effective participation in the construction of the new Yemeni society.

Art. 26. The State shall work for the support of the family and shall protect mother and child. It shall take the political, economic, social and cultural measures necessary for the proper constitution of the family to enable it to perform its functions.

Art. 27. The State shall encourage marriage and the constitution of the family.

The law shall regulate the family relations on the basis of equality between man and woman in the rights and duties.

The State shall ensure, by means of the laws and measures, continuous improvement in realizing social stability for the family and extensive care for the children, and for this purpose, shall establish mother and child care centres throughout the Republic.

Art. 28. The State shall work for raising the standard of the under-developed areas with the aim of gradually obliterating the differences in the standard of living between the various parts of the Republic.

Art. 29. The State shall work for developing and encouraging the Yemeni national culture which serves the causes of freedom, progress and peace. It shall protect the progressive national heritage in the manner that serves the aims of the national democratic revolution stage.

The State shall work for the widest promulgation of the ideas of scientific socialism among the masses.

For this purpose, it shall establish the libraries, the institutions and the cultural and social centres and others.

Art. 30. The State shall preserve the Arabic and Islamic heritage.

It shall encourage the human culture and shall emancipate the society from the corrupt conceptions propagated by imperialism, colonialism and the foes of progress and from the reactionary tribal and clannish inclinations and thus render the national culture in the service of the national democratic revolution.

Chapter Four. Foundations of National Defence and Security

Art. 31. Defence of the homeland and of the revolutionary achievements of the people is the duty of every citizen.

The armed forces, the security forces and the public auxiliary shall protect the sanctity of the State of the People's Democratic Republic of Yemen including its air-space, territorial waters and its rights in the exclusive economic zone, the continental shelf and the national democratic achievements of the people against any attack.

Art. 32. The State shall regulate the defence of the homeland and the protection of the national democratic regime and the peaceful life of the citizens. It shall issue the laws that regulate the organs of defence and security and the compulsory national and military service.

Art. 33. The armed forces and the security forces shall participate with high effectiveness in the productive work and in the construction of the homeland. The State shall render great care to the development of these forces militarily and politically.

PART TWO

THE CITIZENS AND THEIR ORGANIZATIONS

Chapter One. The Fundamental Freedoms, the Basic Rights and Duties of the Citizens

Art. 34. The basic rights and duties of the citizens express the political, economical, social and cultural relations provided for in this Constitution and whose realization leads to the augmentation of the political activity of the working people, the development of their initiatives, the strengthening of the national democratic regime and the creation of the conditions necessary for the transition to the construction of socialism.

The State shall ensure the exercise of these rights and duties by all citizens in the way that accords with the people's interests and the aims of the national democratic revolution. It shall work for the expansion of these rights depending on the successes accomplished in the execution of the economic and social development plans.

Art. 35. All citizens are equal in their rights and duties irrespective of their sex, origin, religion, language, standard of education or social status.

All persons are equal before the law.

The State shall do whatever it can to realize this equality by means of providing equal political, economical, social and cultural opportunities.

Art. 36. The State shall ensure equal rights for men and women in all fields of life, the political, economical and social, and shall provide the necessary conditions for the realization of that equality.

The State shall also work for the creation of the circumstances that will enable the woman to combine between participation in the productive and social work and her role within the family sphere. It shall render special care to the vocational qualifying of the working woman.

The State shall, further, insure special protection for the working women and the children and shall establish kindergartens and nurseries for the children and all other such means of care as to be specified by the law.

Art. 37. Work is the right of every citizen and it is the duty of every able citizen in accordance with his ability, qualification and the the social interest.

Remuneration shall be determined according to the quantity and type of work.

The State shall ensure this right by developing the economy, augmenting the national income, providing democratic work conditions, the continuous increasing of the productive faculties, raising the standard of vocational qualification and expanding the scope of the vocational training and education.

The mass organizations shall participate in an effective manner in creating and developing work conditions, and shall provide full protection for the workers against abusive dismissal.

No citizen shall be hindered from practising his profession, job or work.

Art. 38. All workers have the right to rest, and the State shall ensure this right by means of regulating the working hours according to the law; the weekly and annual vacations are paid.

The State shall work for the preparation of the adequate circumstances to enable the workers to enjoy their right to rest by means of expanding and regulating the public recreation places and the workers' rest house and encouraging the mass organizations to play a greater role in this field.

Art. 39. Workers have the right to social security and to the vocational safety and health.

The State shall ensure full solicitude for every disabled and senile citizen.

The State shall, further, render special care to the families of the martyrs of the revolution and the homeland.

Art. 40. All citizens have the same right to education.

The State shall ensure this right through the extension of the education opportunities for all the people which has already been attained and through its plans that aim towards the expansion and development of the schools, institutes, universities and the educational and cultural institutions.

Education is free. The State shall render special care to the technical and vocational education and shall care for those who have previously been denied the right of education due to their social circumstances.

The State shall work for the complete abolition of illiteracy in the nearest possible time and shall encourage those who have been freed from illiteracy to continue their studies.

Art. 41. Medical care is the right of all citizens.

The State shall guarantee this right through the spreading of the free medical services throughout the Republic and through its plans which shall aim towards the protection and improvement of the environment, the care for preventive medicine and vocational health and safety and the development of all types of hospitals, health institutions and the people's clinics.

The State shall also care for the development of medicine and the propagation of medical consciousness among the citizens with the effective participation of the mass organizations.

Furthermore, the State and the mass organizations shall render extreme care to the health of the children.

Art. 42. Every citizen has the right to accommodation.

The State shall ensure this right through dependence on the execution of the economic and social plans, the construction and development of the dwellings owned by the state and the mass organizations, the gradual repairing of the old dwellings and encouraging the building of personal residences.

The State-owned dwellings shall be distributed among the citizens according to the law. The citizens shall care for the dwellings distributed to them.

Art. 43. Every citizen has the right to contribute in the designing of the political, economic, social and cultural life in accordance with principles specified in the Constitution.

The masses shall discuss the drafts of the social and economic plans and the basic laws before they are issued.

Every citizen has the right to lodge complaints and suggestions to the State organs and its institutions either directly or through his social organization.

Art. 44. All citizens have the right to assemble and demonstrate within the framework of the Constitution and its aims.

The State shall guarantee the freedom of expression by speech, writing, photographing or any other means of expression.

The law shall regulate the freedom of expression through the press and other means of propagation and information in the manner that strengthens the national democratic regime and preserves the public ethics and the State security without prejudice to the freedom and dignity of the citizens.

Art. 45. Personal freedom is guaranteed.

Arrests are not permissable except in connection with punishable deeds and they must be authorized by the law. No person shall be subjected to torture during investigations nor shall he be forced to admit or be treated in an inhuman manner.

Corporal punishment is prohibited.

Art. 46. Criminal responsibility is personal.

The law shall specify the cases in which persons are regarded materially responsible.

Art. 47. Islam is the State religion.

The freedom of faith in other religion is guaranteed.

The State shall protect the freedom of religious faith and of beliefs in accordance with the observed customs provided that it accords with the principles of the Constitution.

Art. 48. No punishment may be inflicted for acts committed before the enactment of the law incriminating such acts.

No punishment may be inflicted if not provided for by law.

No law may provide for a cruel or an unhuman penalty.

Punishment restricting liberty may not be inflicted except by the courts empowered with such competence by law.

Art. 49. Every citizen has the right to resort to the judicature for the protection of this legitimate rights and interests.

Self-defence is guaranteed.

The State shall facilitate resort to the judicature and the means of defence for the necessitous persons.

Every citizen has the right to be compensated for the damage suffered by him as a result of the illegal acts of the high-ranking officials.

The law shall regulate the basis and means of claiming such compensation.

Art. 50. No citizen may be deprived of his nationality except in the cases specified by the law.

Art. 51. Dwellings are inviolable and the law shall protect this inviolability. They may not be forcefully entered except in connection with punishable acts and in accordance with the law.

Art. 52. Privacy of correspondence and all means of communication is guaranteed.

This secrecy may not be disclosed except in the cases provided for by the law or which are necessitated by the protection of state security or the criminal trials.

Art. 53. The State shall guarantee freedom of scientific research and literary, artistic and cultural creativeness in accordance with the aims of the Constitution and shall provide the means for realizing that.

Art. 54. Movement within the Republic is guaranteed.

It may not be restricted except in the cases specified by the law or if such is necessiated by the protection of state security or public health.

The law shall regulate entry to and egress from the country and immigration.

Art. 55. No citizen of the People's Democratic Republic of Yemen may be extradited to a foreign power.

Art. 56. Defence of the Yemeni homeland, its sovereignty, unity, progress and national democratic regime is the duty of every citizen.

Art. 57. Every citizen must support, protect and develop the collective property as the material basis for the national democratic development.

Art. 58. Public service is a noble obligation and an honor.

Every person entrusted with it must perform it with honesty and with the most possible efficiency and with due consideration to the law and the public interest.

The law shall regulate the conditions for the performance of the public service, the responsibility of the public servants and the State's responsibibility towards the citizens.

Art. 59. Every person must contribute to the public revenue according to his ability. The State must observe, when imposing taxes, the citizen's incomes and their social status.

Art. 60. All citizens are obliged to strengthen the social and family relations. Parents are obliged to raise their children and to prepare them for the socially beneficial work, and it is the duty of the children to care for their parents and to render to them the necessary assistance whenever it is needed.

Art. 61. Every citizen must participate in the struggle for the achievement of the unity of the Yemeni people and land. He must protect and develop the new democratic relations and strive against the tribal, separatist, regional and clannish traditions, ideologies and customs which conflict with the aims of the national democratic revolution.

Art. 62. Every citizen must abide by the Constitution of the People's Democratic Republic of Yemen and its laws and must respect the principles of living in the national democratic society. The exercise of the rights and freedoms is not separable from the citizen's performance of his duties.

Chapter Two. The Organizations and their Rights

Art. 63. The State shall guarantee the right of congregation in the mass organizations which serve the aims of the Constitution and being at the forefront of which the General Confederation of Trade Unions of the Republic's Workers, The Yemeni Socialist Youth Union, The General Union of the Yemeni Women, the Democratic Yemeni Union of Peasants, the Organization of Committees for Popular Defence and other such organizations.

The State shall support the mass organizations with the aim of elevating their role and effectiveness in all the social activities, in developing democracy and organizing and mobilizing the workers, peasants, fishermen, women, youth and all the toiling masses for struggling for the continuous progress of the society and defending the achievements of the revolution.

Art. 64. The trade unions are class organizations. They organize the activity of the workers and officials and protect their interests. They shall participate in developing the national democratic revolution by mobilizing their members towards realizing the economic and social plans, raising the standard of the political, vocational and technical qualifying of the workers and officials and deepening the alliance between the working-class and the peasants.

The trade unions shall participate in regulating the participation of the toiling masses in the administration of the production affairs and its control and in planning work and production. They shall exercise mass control over the work and living conditions of the workers.

They shall, further, participate in the implementation of the labor and social security laws, in determining wages and developing the forms of material and spiritual incentives.

All trade unions shall unite in the General Confederation of Trade Unions of the Workers in the People's Democratic Republic of Yemen, and within its framework, the trade unions shall consolidate the workers' efforts towards exercising their rights as specified in the Constitution.

Art. 65. The Yemeni Socialist Youth Union is a mass organization which unites and organizes the efforts of the youth and their creative potentials. It shall prepare them for the socially beneficial work by means of raising the standard of their class and ideological awareness and rearing them with the sense of love, loyalty and fidelity for the cause of the Yemeni people and its social progress.

The Yemeni Socialist Youth Union shall participate effectively in organizing the Youth's efforts for the purpose of defending the homeland and the achievements of the artistic and sportive activities and in cherishing the Youth's connection with the workers' struggle along the way to accomplishing the tasks of the national democratic revolution.

Art. 66. The Democratic Yemeni Union of Peasants is a wide mass organization. It shall consolidate, mobilize and direct its members and all the peasants for the active contribution in executing the tasks connected with the accomplishment of the tasks of the national democratic revolution stage in the sphere of the economic, social and cultural transformations in the countryside.

The Democratic Yemeni Union of Peasants shall work for deepening the alliance between the peasants and the working class and creating brotherly relations between the co-operative peasants and the individual peasants.

It shall convince the peasants, by means of presenting the positive example, that the economy is best organized on the basis of co-operative collectivism. It shall also work for obliterating the illiteracy of the peasants and raising their educational, political and cultural standard.

The co-operative societies, which are formed on the basis of optional association, shall serve the cause of increasing productivety, developing the national economy, and raising the standard of living and of awareness of its members. The law shall regulate the types of co-operative societies, the means of their formation, their method of work and the manner of supervising and administering them.

Art. 67. The General Union of Yemeni women shall consolidate, regulate and direct the activity of the Yemeni women with the aim of augmenting their role in the struggle for resolving the joint causes with all the Yemeni mass organizations and for solving the special matters connected with the female movement.

The General Union of Yemeni Women shall work for the widest participation of the Yemeni women in the economic, social and political life, the structuring of the new life and the raising of their educational, cultural, vocational and technical standard. It shall struggle vigorously for the purpose of affirming and protecting the rights guaranteed for the women by the Constitution and the laws on the basis of parity with the man.

PART THREE

THE ORGANIZATION OF THE STATE POWER

Art. 68. There is one state power in the People's Democratic Republic of Yemen and it depends on the sovereignty of the working people.

The State power shall be exercised through the elected councils and the organizations formed by these councils in accordance with the aims and tasks of the Constitution.

Chapter One. The People's Supreme Council

Art. 69. The People's Supreme Council is the highest organ of the State power, and it is the legislative organ that sanctions the principles of the State policy and guarantees its coherent implementation through all the governmental and social organizations. On this basis, it approves the general fundamentals for the functions of the Presidium, the Council of Ministers and the other State organs and takes the necessary decisions in this matter.

The People's Supreme Council is the sole organ which has the right to enact laws.

Art. 70. The People's Supreme Council is exclusively empowered to deal with the following matters:

(1) Approving the Constitution and its amendments.

(2) Approving the economic and social plans.

(3) Approving the State Budget and its amendment and the reports connected with its implementation.

(4) Approving the international treaties connected with matters of defence, federation and adjustment of the borders.

(5) Forming the Presidium, the Council of Ministers and other organs subordinated to the People's Supreme Council.

Art. 71. The following matters shall be regulated by law enacted by the People's Supreme Council.

(1) Nationalization and the maximum limit of private property;

(2) The basis of regulating the public utilities and the public, co-operative and combined sectors;

(3) The basis of work relations and social securities;

(4) The general basis of property and the civil and commercial relations;

(5) The currency and monetary systems;

(6) Defining the governmental and public taxes;

(7) Defining the State's obligations;

(8) The basis connected with the exploitation of the natural wealth;

(9) The basis connected with the expenditure of the State properties;

(10) Declaring the general mobilization and organizing the obligations of the military service and the general principles for regulating national defence;

(11) Specifying the crimes, the penalties and the criminal and civil procedures;

(12) Nationality;

(13) The Electoral system;

(14) The Judicial system;

(15) The system of local government and its administration;

(16) The civil rights and the individual guarantees;

(17) The regulation connected with the mass organizations;

(18) The basis of foreign trade;

(19) The general principles of remunerations;

(20) The rules specially related to the payment of salaries, pensions, compensations, subsidies and rewards from the State Treasury.

(21) Specifying the salaries of the Chairman of the Presidium and its members, the Prime Minister. Members of the Council of Ministers, the Chief Justice of the Supreme Court, Judges of the Supreme Court and the Republic's Attorney General.

These matters may be regulated, in the intervals between the sessions of the People's Supreme Council, by means of decrees provided that such do not conflict with or lead to the amendment of a previous law. These decrees are subject to the ratification of the People's Supreme Council and they lose their legal force if the council does not ratify them during its following session.

Art. 72. The People's Supreme Council consists of a hundred and eleven (111) members elected by means of free, universal, equal and direct elections by secret ballot in the constituencies as specified in the Electoral law.

The term of office of the People's Supreme Council is five years commencing from the date of its first meeting.

Should the term of office of the People's Supreme Council terminate during a state of general mobilization, it shall be regarded as continuing till the termination of such state.

The People's Supreme Council may not be dissolved except by a resolution taken by a majority of two thirds of its members.

Art. 73. The People's Supreme Council shall determine in its first meeting, the legality of the membership of its members, and shall, for this purpose, elect a committee for contests of elections. The Committee shall review the propriety of the members, elections and shall decide on this matter. It shall also examine any contest regarding breach of the Electoral law. The Committee's decision shall not be regarded final unless it is ratified by the People's Supreme Council.

The oldest member assisted by the two youngest members shall chair the first meeting of the People's Supreme Council.

Art. 74. Members of the People's Supreme Council shall, during the council's first meeting, take the constitutional oath provided for in the By-Laws of the People's Supreme Council.

Art. 75. The People's Supreme Council shall hold three sessions per annum pursuant to an invitation from the Presidium. It may hold extraordinary sessions in pursuance of an invitation from the Presidium or on the request of the Council of Ministers or two thirds of the members of the People's Supreme Council.

The People's Supreme Council shall determine the agenda of its meetings pursuant to a suggestion from the Presidium.

The Council's meeting shall be regarded as lawful if attended by the majority of its members. Its resolutions shall be issued by a majority of its members present unless the Constitution provides otherwise.

The meetings of the People's Supreme Council shall be held in public, and it may convene meetings in camera pursuant to a suggestion from the Presidium, the Council of Ministers or a quarter of its members.

The meetings of the People's Supreme Council shall be chaired by the Presidium. The system of its meetings and its other internal activies shall be specified by the By-Laws approved by the People's Supreme Council.

Art. 76. The right to propose and proffer draft laws to the People's Supreme Council is enjoyed by the Presidium, the Council of Ministers, the Standing Committees of the People's Supreme Council, the Supreme Court, the Attorney General of the Republic and one third of the Council's members.

The right of legislative initiative is also enjoyed by the mass organizations mentioned in the Constitution. Their proposals must be proffered through their central bodies.

The approval of a draft law proffered to the People's Supreme Council requires the assent of a majority of two thirds of the members present.

Art. 77. The most important draft laws connected with the activity of the State and the society may be subjected to wide popular discussions pursuant to a decision of the People's Supreme Council or the Presidium.

Art. 78. All laws approved by the People's Supreme Council and signed by the Chairman of the Presidium must be published in the *Official Gazette* within fourteen days as from the date of their approval.

The laws shall come into force after fourteen days as from the date of publication unless the law provides otherwise.

Art. 79. The People's Supreme Council shall, in its first meeting elect from among its members the Chairman and members of the Presidium of the People's Supreme Council which shall consist of not less than eleven and not more than seventeen members.

The Presidium may elect from among its members a Vice-Chairman and appoint its Secretary.

The Presidium is responsible and accountable to the People's Supreme Council.

The People's Supreme Council may, pursuant to a request from at least one third of its members, reform the Presidium or relieve any of its members.

The adoption of such a decision requires a majority vote of the members of the People's Supreme Council.

Art. 80. The People's Supreme Council shall, during its first session, elect from among its members the Prime Minister pursuant to a proposal from the Presidium. It shall also elect, during the same session, the members of the Council of Ministers pursuant to a proposal from the Prime Minister. The majority of the members of the Council of Ministers must be members of the People's Supreme Council.

The People's Supreme Council shall supervise and control the functions of the Council of Ministers. The Council of Ministers and also every one of its members are responsible and accountable to the People's Supreme Council.

The People's Supreme Council may direct questions to the Prime Minister and members of the Council of Ministers concerning their functions. It may also request the attendance of the Minister concerned to reply to those questions.

Art. 81. The People's Supreme Council has the right to decide to withdraw confidence in the Prime Minister or in any member of the Council of Ministers. If confidence in the Prime Minister is withdrawn, the Council of Ministers must resign, and if confidence in a member of the Council of Ministers is withdrawn that member must resign. Matters of confidence may not, in any case, be propounded except in pursuance to a request from at least one third of the members of the People's Supreme Council.

The adoption of a decision to withdraw confidence requires a majority vote of the members of the People's Supreme Council.

Art. 82. The People's Supreme Council shall, during its first session, elect the Republic's Supreme Court which shall consist of the Chief Justice, one or more deputies and a number of judges.

The Supreme Court is the highest judicial organ. It exercises supervision over all the courts in the Republic. The Law shall define the functions, powers and system of functioning of the Republic's Supreme Court.

Art. 83. The People's Supreme Council shall appoint the Republic's Attorney-General. The Attorney-General shall exercise supreme supervision over the implementation of the laws by the ministries and other central departments, the organizations, corporations, foundations, the executive bureaus of the People's Local Councils, the social organizations, the co-operative societies, all the administrative officers and the citizens.

The Attorney-General shall be the head of the Attorney-General Chambers throughout the Republic.

Art. 84. The People's Supreme Council shall elect from among its members Standing Committees in the sphere of politics, economics, administration, law, science and culture. The Standing Committee shall discuss the draft laws and the resolutions of the People's Supreme Council prior to their discussion by the Council. They shall also supervise the application of the laws and all the resolutions of the People's Supreme Council and the Presidium, and the activity of the central and local organs of the State power and of all the organizations and corporations.

The Standing Committees have the right to invite the Ministers and officers in the ministries, organizations, corporations, co-operative societies and organizations and request them to submit elucidations and the necessary documents connected with their activities.

The By-Laws of the People's Supreme Council shall specify the number of the Standing Committees and the method of their work.

The People's Supreme Council may compose from among its members special ad hoc committees in accordance with its By-Laws.

Art. 85. Members of the People's Supreme Council are representatives of the People. Every member of the People's Supreme Council shall represent the public national interests of the people. It is his duty to strengthen his relations with the masses always and to refer back to his electorate, listen to their suggestions and comments and study them and reply to them with honesty. He shall explain to them the State policy and raise the standard of their understanding of the aims of the strategy of the national revolution at the Yemeni, Arabic and international level.

Art. 86. Members of the People's Supreme Council may not be blamed for the opinions which they express in the course of performing their duties in the Council or its committees.

The people's representatives enjoy immunity, and no criminal proceedings may be taken against them except with the approval of the People's Supreme Council or of the Presidium during the intervals between the Council's meetings provided that the Council approves such during its first subsequent meeting.

Art. 87. The People's representatives have the right to direct enquiries to the Council of Ministers, the ministers and the chairmen of the organs composed by the People's Supreme Council.

The Council of Ministers and the officer to whom the enquiries are directed are obliged to reply either orally or in writing at the same or next meeting.

Art. 88. All State organs are bound to proffer the necessary assistance to the members of the People's Supreme Council for the purpose of executing their functions.

Art. 89. The electorate in a constituency may request withdrawal of confidence in the member of the People's Supreme Council representing that constituency. Such a request ought to be submitted by one quarter of the electorate in that constituency. The People's Supreme Council shall take a decision on this matter by a majority vote of its members present.

Art. 90. No armed forces may enter the quarters of the People's Supreme Council except at the request of the Presidium.

Furthermore, entry with arms into the quarters of the People's Supreme Council may not be allowed except with the consent of the Presidium.

Chapter Two. The Presidium of the People's Supreme Council

Art. 91. The Presidium is the permanent organ of the People's Supreme Council. It is responsible and accountable to it for all its functions.

The Presidium shall perform the tasks of the highest organ of State power in the intervals between the sessions of the People's Supreme Council.

The Presidium shall issue the decrees and resolutions.

Art. 92. The Presidium shall consist of a chairman and no less than eleven and no more than seventeen members.

In the event of holding new elections for the People's Supreme Council, the Presidium shall be re-composed provided that the existing Presidium shall continue to perform its tasks until the election of a new Presidium.

Art. 93. Prior to assuming their functions, the chairman and members of the Presidium shall take the constitutional oath before the People's Supreme Council in accordance with the provisions of the By-Laws of the People's Supreme Council.

The Presidium shall undertake the following functions:

(1) Representing the Republic internally and externally;

(2) Supervising the implementation of the Constitution;

(3) Specifying the time for the elections of the People's Supreme Council and the People's Local Councils and supervising these elections.

(4) Convoking the People's Supreme Council;

(5) Proposing draft laws.

(6) Supervising the activity of the Standing Committees of the People's Supreme Council;

(7) Interpreting the Laws.

(8) The general direction of the People's Local Councils;

(9) Ratifying the international treaties and agreements which do not need ratification by the People's Supreme Council;

(10) Granting the medals and decorations provided for by law and permitting the bearing of medals and decorations granted by other states.

(11) Proposing the Prime Minister.

(12) Repealing the resolutions and orders of the Council of Ministers which contradict the laws.

(13) Designating the chairman and members of the Supreme Council for National Defence, the law shall regulate the functions and powers of this Council.

(14) Instituting the high military ranks.

(15) Designating and dismissing the officers assuming leading military posts in the State in accordance with the law.

(16) Declaring general mobilization in the event of a threat of an external aggression against the Republic in the intervals between meetings of the People's Supreme Council.

(17) Granting the right of political asylum.

(18) Establishing the diplomatic missions, designated and recalling the State's political representatives abroad.

(19) Accrediting the political representatives of the foreign countries.

(20) General amnesty and the remission or commuting of sentence.

(21) Any other task in accordance with the Constitution and the law.

Art. 94. The Presidium shall, in the intervals between the holding of sessions of the People's Supreme Council, perform the following tasks:

(1) Instituting and abolishing the ministries and the central organs subordinate to the Council of Ministers pursuant to a proposal from the Council of Ministers.

(2) Designating and relieving Ministers in pursuance to a proposal from the Prime Minister.

(3) Amending the annual plan and the State budget pursuant to a proposal from the Council of Ministers.

Art. 95. All the decrees and resolutions issued in connection with the matters mentioned in these articles shall be subject to the approval of the People's Supreme Council. Should the People's Supreme Council not approve them in its subsequent session they shall lose their legal force.

Art. 96. The Chairman of the Presidium shall administer its functions, chair its meetings and sign the decrees and resolutions taken by it.

Art. 97. The Chairman of the Presidium shall represent the Republic in its foreign relations.

Art. 98. The Presidium has the right to request from the Prime Minister reports connected with the realization of the tasks to be implemented by the Council of Ministers.

Chapter Three. The Council of Ministers

Art. 99. The Council of Ministers is the Government of the People's Democratic Republic of Yemen, and it is the highest executive and administrative organ of the State power.

The Council of Ministers shall consist of the Prime Minister, his deputies and the ministers. The law shall specify their tasks and powers.

The Council of Ministers shall issue the resolutions and orders in accordance with and in execution of the laws and the resolutions of the People's Supreme Council and its Presidium. It shall also ensure their application.

The resolutions and orders of the Council of Ministers shall be binding throughout the Republic.

Art. 100. The Council of Ministers shall be elected by the People's Supreme Council during its first session.

The Council of Ministers shall proffer, at that same session, the Government program for the entire period.

The Council of Ministers shall continue to perform its tasks and powers until the election of a new Council of Ministers.

Art. 101. The Council of Ministers is responsible and accountable for all its functions to the People's Supreme Council and also to the Presidium in the intervals between the sessions of the People's Supreme Council.

The Council of Ministers shall submit regular periodic reports regarding its functions to the People's Supreme Council.

Art. 102. The Prime Minister and members of the Council of Ministers shall take the same constitutional oath to be taken by members of the People's Supreme Council before the Council.

Art. 103. The Council of Ministers shall undertake the implementation of the State's public policy in the sphere of politics, economics, sociology, culture, defence and security as approved by the People's Supreme Council.

The Council of Ministers shall also be entrusted with the power of determining all the matters connected with the administration of the State which do not fall within the powers of the People's Supreme Council and the Presidium.

All members of the Council of Ministers are jointly responsible and every member is fully responsible for his particular sphere.

Art. 104. The Council of Ministers shall exercise the following powers:

(1) Proposing the broad outlines of the foreign and internal policy and profferring them to the People's Supreme Council;

(2) Proposing and profferring draft laws to the People's Supreme Council.

(3) Directing, co-ordinating and supervising the activity of the Ministries and the other central organs subordinated to it.

(4) Profferring the drafts of the social and economic plans and the annual budget to the People's Supreme Council, and regulating their implementation after they have been approved.

(5) Designating the members of the Supreme Council for National Planning. The law shall regulate the functions and powers of this Council.

(6) Preparing the State's final accounts, and profferring reports regarding them to the People's Supreme Council.

(7) Approving the international agreements and treaties prior to profferring them to the People's Supreme Council or the Presidium in accordance with the competence of each of them as specified in the Constitution.

(8) Taking the measures necessary for preserving the State's external and internal security and protecting the public order and the citizen's rights.

(9) Appointing, dismissing, transferring and disciplining the deputy ministers, heads of the central organs appurtenant to the Council of Ministers and the leading officers of their standard.

(10) Supervising the realization of the cadre's policy in the State organ.

(11) Directing the national economy and the social and cultural structure.

(12) Laying down and implementing the measures and procedures aiming towards raising the standard of living of the citizens.

(13) The general supervision of the structuring of the Armed Forces.

(14) The general supervision of the relations with the other states.

(15) Forming, whenever necessary, committees and department appurtenant to it and which shall work within the scope of its functions.

Art. 105. Resolutions of the Council of Ministers shall be binding on the executive bureaus of the People's Local Councils and must be implemented in all cases.

Chairmen of the executive bureaus of the People's Local Councils are accountable and responsible to the Council of Ministers.

Art. 106. The Council of Ministers has the right to revoke resolutions of the ministers and of the executive organs of the State's local authority including the executive bureaus of the People's Local Councils.

The Council of Ministers may suspend the implementation of the resolutions of the People's Local Council. The Presidium of the People's Supreme Council shall take the final decision in this matter.

Art. 107. The Prime Minister shall administer the functions of the Council of Ministers, chair its meetings and represent it in all matters connected with the implementation of the public policy.

The Prime Minister shall also supervise the implementation of the resolutions of the Council of Ministers and he has the right to request, from the Council's members reports of any of the ministries' affairs or on the functions they perform. They are obliged to submit them.

Art. 108. Should it become impossible for the Prime Minister to bear the Council of Ministers' responsibilities he must submit his resignation to the People's Supreme Council or to the Presidium and the latter ought, in this case, to submit this together with its written opinion to the People's Supreme Council to decide on the matter. A resolution accepting the resignation requires a majority vote of two thirds of the members of the People's Surpreme Council.

A member of the Council of Ministers shall submit his resignation to the Prime Minister. The People's Supreme Council shall take its decision by a majority vote of its members.

Should the resignation be submitted by the Prime Minister or by a majority of the members of the Council of Ministers and be accepted by a majority vote of two thirds of the members of the People's Supreme Council, the Council of Ministers must resign.

Art. 109. Should the Prime Minister find that his co-operation with a member of the Council of Ministers has become impossible he may proffer the matter to the Presidium to decide on whatever it deems adequate or he may submit adequate proposals to the People's Supreme Council to take any step it deems necessary.

Art. 110. Every Minister shall undertake to supervise his ministry's affairs and direct its departments throughout the Republic. He shall also implement the public policy of the Council of Ministers in his Ministry.

Every Minister is responsible to the Council of Ministers for the functions of his Ministry.

The law shall specify the cases in which the minister may issue the resolutions necessary for the implementation of the laws. The Council of Ministers has the right to revoke or amend the Ministers' resolutions that it deems inadequate.

Art. 111. The law shall specify the cases in which the employees may be appointed, dismissed, transferred or disciplined by a resolution of the Ministers concerned.

Chapter Four. Organs of the State's Local Authority and their administration

Art. 112. The organs of the State's local authority are the People's Local Councils in the provinces, districts and centres elected by the citizens for a period of two and a half years by means of free, universal, equal and direct elections and by secret ballot in the constituencies in accordance with the law.

The State's local authority and its organs is part of the sole power in the People's Democratic Republic of Yemen. The law shall regulate the organs of the State's local authority on the basis of democratic centralization.

The organs of the State's local authority shall issue, within the limits of their powers, resolutions binding on all the organizations, corporations, projects, co-operative societies, state farms, mass organizations, administrative officers and citizens within the area falling under their competence.

Art. 113. The People's Local Councils shall determine all local matters and issues taking as the basis of their work the entire interests of the State.

The People's Local Councils shall discuss the public issues and proffer proposals regarding them to the high State organs. They shall also exercise their activities with the firm co-operation of the mass organizations and the citizens.

Art. 114. The People's Local Councils shall undertake, within the scope of their area and inhabitants, the leadership of the economic, social and cultural structure. They shall approve the local plans and budget and ratify the reports related to their implementation.

The People's Local Councils shall supervise the functions of the organs subordinate to them and shall ensure the application of democratic legality and the protection of public property, public order and the citizens' rights.

The People's Local Councils are bound, when exercising their powers, by the necessities of development in and the public interest of their entire area.

Art. 115. The People's Local Councils shall elect their executive bureaus in accordance with the law.

The executive bureaus shall implement the tasks connected with the various activities of the People's Local Councils in the field of economic, social and cultural development.

The executive bureaus are responsible and accountable for all their functions to the People's Local Councils that elected them, and also to the higher executive organ responsible for directing the administrative matters and local government.

The executive bureaus shall submit regular periodic reports to the People's Local Councils and to the citizens in the places of their employment or residence.

Art. 116. The People's Local Council shall elect from among its members and the active citizens standing and ad hoc committees with the aims of strengthening the participation of the citizens and the mass organizations in the participation of the Councils' resolutions. The committees shall work for the implementation of the laws and the other legislations and the resolutions of the People's Local Council.

Art. 117. Members of the People's Local Councils are the representatives of the people in these councils, and every one of them is obliged to strengthen his relations with the masses, to accept his electorate's proposals and study them carefully and work for their implementation after they have been approved by the People's Local Council.

The member of the People's Local Council ought to explain the State's policy to his electorate and to develop the standard of their political awareness. He is obliged to submit regular periodic reports to them and to the mass organizations which proposed him.

Confidence may be withdrawn from a member of the People's Local Council if he misuses the confidence granted to him by the electorate and such shall be in accordance with the law.

Art. 118. The organs of the central State authority shall work for supporting People's Local Councils, developing their functions and extending their powers by means of the continuous transfer of their rights and duties to the organs of the state local authority in accordance with the development of the political, economical and social relations.

PART FOUR

THE DEMOCRATIC LEGALITY, THE JUDICIARY AND THE ATTORNEY GENERAL'S CHAMBERS

Art. 119. Democratic legality is regarded as one of the most important principles of the political and constitutional regime in the People's Democratic Republic of Yemen.

All the laws, decrees, resolutions and other legislations as well as the resolutions, regulations and measures taken by the State's organizations and the mass organizations must accord with the spirit and content of the Constitution.

The activity of the State organs, the mass organizations, all the superior officials and the citizens must accord with the laws and such shall be by means of their proper implementation.

The State shall guarantee democratic legality.

The laws, decrees and other legislations regulating the rights and duties of the citizens must be published in the manner that attains the widest scope of publicity.

All persons in charge in the State organs and the mass organizations must elucidate the laws to the masses throughout the Republic.

Art. 120. The democratic legality aims towards strengthening the national democratic regime and ensuring the protection of freedom and peaceful life of the citizens, their rights, interests and the human's dignity.

The enhancement of democratic legality is a joint task of the State organs, the mass organizations, the persons in charge and the citizens.

Art. 121. Justice in the People's Democratic Republic of Yemen shall be administered by the Supreme Court, the provisional courts, the divisional courts and the military courts. The law shall regulate their functions and competence.

The activity of all the courts shall aim towards educating the citizens to respect the Constitution and the law and to love and be loyal to the revolution and the homeland.

The constitution of extra-ordinary courts is not permissible.

Art. 122. The judges of the Supreme Court of the Republic and of the provisional and divisional courts shall be elected by the People's Councils concerned in accordance with the Constitution and the laws.

Judges of the military courts shall be appointed by the Presidium of the People's Supreme Council.

Confidence may be withdrawn from the judges by the councils that elected them if they infringe the confidence granted to them.

Art. 123. It is stipulated that judges must be chosen from among the citizens who are loyal to their homeland, revolution and national democratic regime. They must posses the necessary legal knowlege, life experiences and a high degree of ethical stability.

Art. 124. The State shall guarantee the steadily increasing participation of the citizens in the administration of justice.

The law shall regulate the details connected with the participation of the working people in the judiciary.

Art. 125. Judges are independent in their powers and are bound by the Constitution and the law in the realization of democratic legality.

The State shall provide the conditions that will aid the courts to solve the citizens' cases in a fast, just and democratic manner.

Art. 126. The courts shall adjudicate and pronounce their judgments in the name of the people.

Trials shall be held in public with some exceptional cases to be specified by law.

Art. 127. The accused shall be guaranteed the right of defence. No criminal punishment may be inflicted on any person except by a decision of the court and in accordance with the law.

Art. 128. The law shall regulate the legal profession with the aim of submitting legal aid to the citizens and the judicial persons.

The participation of the advocate in the criminal proceedings shall be compulsory in the cases provided for by law.

The law shall specify the cases in which legal aid shall be free of charge.

Art. 129. The statal arbitration panels shall, within the limits of their powers, determine the economic disputes between the ministries, organizations and corporations.

The law shall specify the functions, powers and system of work of the statal arbitration panels.

Art. 130. With the aim of realizing democratic legality, protecting the national democratic regime and defending the public property, the Republic's Attorney-General, his deputies, and representatives subordinate to him shall exercise supreme supervision over the precise and unified implementation of the laws by all the ministries, the other central departments, the organizations, corporations, the executive bureaus of the People's Local Councils, the social organizations, the co-operative societies, all the administrative superior officers and the citizens.

The Attorney-General shall appoint his civil and military deputies and they are responsible and accountable for their functions to him.

Art. 131. The People's Supreme Council shall appoint the Republic's Attorney-General.

The Attorney-General is responsible and accountable for his functions to the People's Supreme Council and to the Presidium in the intervals between the sessions of the People's Supreme Council.

The Attorney-General's Chambers shall be organized in a lineal manner throughout the Republic. They are independent of all the local organs and are subordinate only to the Republic's Attorney-General.

The law shall regulate the functions and powers of the Attorney-General's Chambers.

Art. 132. The Attorney-General shall direct the combating of crimes, and ensure that persons who commit crimes or any other breaches shall be called to account for their deeds before the courts. He shall also supervise the adherence to the law in the detention and prevention centres.

PART FIVE

THE REPUBLIC'S ENSIGN, ITS FLAG, CAPITAL AND NATIONAL ANTHEM

Art. 133. The People's Supreme Council shall sanction the Republic's ensign.

Art. 134. The national flag of the People's Democratic Republic of Yemen shall be composed of the horizontally arranged colors starting from the top as follows:

Red.

White.

Black.

There shall be a light blue triangle on the side near the staff with a Red pentacle at its centre.

The ratio of the flag's width to its length shall be 1 : 2.

Art. 135. The city of 'Aden' shall be the capital of the People's Democratic Republic of Yemen.

Art. 136. The People's Supreme Council shall sanction the national anthem of the People's Democratic Republic of Yemen.

PART SIX

OPERATION OF THE CONSTITUTION AND PRINCIPLES OF ITS AMENDMENTS

Art. 137. The Constitution is the organic law. It is binding and with immediate effect.

Art. 138. All laws and other legislations, of the State organs issued prior to amending this Constitution shall remain effective if they accord with the provisions of this present Constitution or if they have not been abolished or amended in accordance with its provisions.

Art. 139. The Constitution may be amended by a resolution of the People's Supreme Council pursuant to a proposal from a quarter of its members, the Presidium or the Council of Ministers. In order to be taken, such a resolution requires the assent of two thirds of the members of People's Supreme Council.

MIX
Papier aus verantwortungsvollen Quellen
Paper from responsible sources
FSC® C105338

If you have any concerns about our products,
you can contact us on
ProductSafety@springernature.com

In case Publisher is established outside the EU,
the EU authorized representative is:
Springer Nature Customer Service Center GmbH
Europaplatz 3, 69115 Heidelberg, Germany

Printed by Libri Plureos GmbH
in Hamburg, Germany